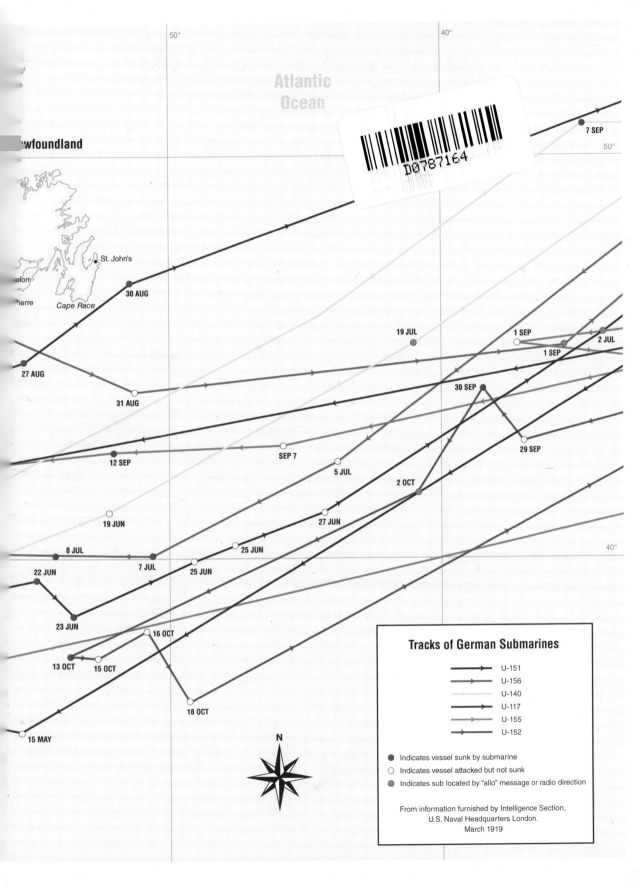

50°   40°

Atlantic
Ocean

wfoundland   7 SEP

                                                                                                              50°

St. John's

elon   30 AUG
Pierre   Cape Race

27 AUG   19 JUL   1 SEP   2 JUL
                                                                                                    1 SEP

                                        31 AUG   30 SEP

                                                    12 SEP   SEP 7   29 SEP

                                                                    5 JUL

                                                                              2 OCT

                                        19 JUN   27 JUN
                                                                                                              40°
                    8 JUL   25 JUN
        22 JUN   7 JUL   25 JUN

        23 JUN
                                        16 OCT

                13 OCT   15 OCT

                                18 OCT

    15 MAY   N

Tracks of German Submarines

→ U-151
→ U-156
→ U-140
→ U-117
→ U-155
→ U-152

● Indicates vessel sunk by submarine
○ Indicates vessel attacked but not sunk
● Indicates sub located by "allo" message or radio direction

From information furnished by Intelligence Section,
U.S. Naval Headquarters London.
March 1919

THE SEABOUND COAST

The Official History of the
Royal Canadian Navy, 1867–1939

■

VOLUME 1

THE SEABOUND COAST

The Official History of the
Royal Canadian Navy, 1867–1939

■

VOLUME 1

WILLIAM JOHNSTON

WILLIAM G.P. RAWLING

RICHARD H. GIMBLETT

JOHN MacFARLANE

DUNDURN PRESS
Toronto

Published by Dundurn Press Limited in co-operation with Department of National Defence and Public Works and Government Services Canada.

Project Editors: Michael Carroll and Allison Hirst
Copy Editor: Nigel Heseltine
Design: Heidy Lawrance, WeMakeBooks.ca
Printer: Friesens

Library and Archives Canada Cataloguing in Publication

The seabound coast / William Johnston ... [et al.].

Issued also in French under title: Du littoral à la mer.

"The official history of the Royal Canadian Navy, 1867-1939, volume 1".

Includes bibliographical references and index.

Issued also in electronic format.

ISBN 978-1-55488-907-5

1. Canada--History, Naval. 2. Canada. Royal Canadian Navy--History. I. Johnston, William Cameron, 1956-

FC231.S33 2010   359.00971   C2010-907290-1

1   2   3   4   5   14   13   12   11   10

 Canada Council for the Arts / Conseil des Arts du Canada    Canada   ONTARIO ARTS COUNCIL / CONSEIL DES ARTS DE L'ONTARIO

We acknowledge the support of the **Canada Council for the Arts** and the **Ontario Arts Council** for our publishing program. We also acknowledge the financial support of the **Government of Canada** through the **Canada Book Fund** and **Livres Canada Books**, and the **Government of Ontario** through the **Ontario Book Publishers Tax Credit** program, and the **Ontario Media Development Corporation**.

Care has been taken to trace the ownership of copyright material used in this book. The author and the publisher welcome any information enabling them to rectify any references or credits in subsequent editions.

J. Kirk Howard, President

Printed and bound in Canada
www.dundurn.com

Dundurn Press	Gazelle Book Services Limited	Dundurn Press
3 Church Street, Suite 500	White Cross Mills	2250 Military Road
Toronto, Ontario, Canada	High Town, Lancaster, England	Tonawanda, NY
M5E 1M2	LA1 4XS	U.S.A. 14150

Contents

Maps and Diagrams

Glossary of Acronyms

ADOT	Acting Director of Overseas Transport	ERA	Engine Room Artificer
AEF	American Expeditionary Force	FdU	Führer der Unterseeboote
APV	Auxiliary Patrol Vessel	FPS	Fisheries Protection Service
BC	British Columbia	GOC	General Officer Commanding
BEF	British Expeditionary Force	HB	US (convoys) to Bay of Biscay
CB	Cape Breton	HBM	His Britannic Majesty's
CDC	Colonial Defence Committee	HC	Homeward from Canada (replaced the HM convoy series designation)
CEF	Canadian Expeditionary Force		
CGS	Canadian Government Ship	HH	Homeward from Hampton Roads
C-in-C	Commander-in-Chief	HM	His/Her Majesty's
CID	Committee of Imperial Defence	HM	Homeward from Halifax (medium speed)
CNSO	Canadian Naval Staff Officer		
CO	Commanding Officer	HN	Homeward from New York
CPO	Chief Petty Officer	HMCS	His Majesty's Canadian Ship
CPR	Canadian Pacific Railway	HMS	His/Her Majesty's Ship
CXO	Chief Examination Officer	HS	Homeward from Sydney
DC	District of Columbia	HX	Homeward from Halifax
DMS	Director of Minesweeping	IMB	Imperial Munitions Board
DNS	Director of the Naval Service	jg	Junior Grade
DOD	Director of Operations Division	MIT	Massachusetts Institute of Technology
DOT	Director of Overseas Transport		
DTSD	Director of Training and Staff Duties	MP	Member Of Parliament
		NA&WI	North America and West Indies

NB	New Brunswick	RN	Royal Navy
NS	Nova Scotia	RNAS	Royal Naval Air Service
NSHQ	Naval Service Headquarters	RNCC	Royal Naval College of Canada
NWMP	North-West Mounted Police	RNCVR	Royal Naval Canadian Volunteer Reserve
PC	Privy Council		
PEI	Prince Edward Island	RNR	Royal Naval Reserve
PO	Petty Officer	RNVR	Royal Naval Volunteer Reserve
RAF	Royal Air Force	RP	Rendezvous Patrol
RAN	Royal Australian Navy	SNO	Senior Naval Officer
RCN	Royal Canadian Navy	TBD	Torpedo Boat Destroyer
RCNAS	Royal Canadian Naval Air Service	UK	United Kingdom
		US	United States
RCNR	Royal Canadian Naval Reserve	USN	United States Navy
RCNVR	Royal Canadian Naval Volunteer Reserve	USS	United States Ship
		VIP	Very Important Person
RFC	Royal Flying Corps	WT	Wireless Telegraphy
RMC	Royal Military College		

Acknowledgments

The authors would like to acknowledge the interest and support that successive defence ministers, chiefs of the defence staff, deputy ministers, admirals commanding Maritime Command, chiefs of the maritime staff, and other leaders of the Department of National Defence (DND) and the Canadian Armed Forces have provided to the Royal Canadian Navy history project. We also express our thanks to Director, History and Heritage, Dr. Serge Bernier, for the consistent support he has given us and to his predecessor, Dr. W.A.B. Douglas, under whom the navy's official history project was begun. The authors would also like to thank the chief historian at the Directorate of History and Heritage (DHH), Dr. Steve Harris, for his professional guidance and administrative management during the research and writing of this volume. In the same vein, we thank his predecessors as chief/senior historian, Dr. Roger Sarty and Dr. Norman Hillmer.

We are also appreciative of the assistance provided by the archivists at DHH, past and present, Owen Cooke, Dr. Isabel Campbell, Donna Porter, Warren Sinclair, and Valerie Casbourn, in organizing the naval records as well as the support of our other colleagues at the directorate, in particular, that of Dr. Yves Tremblay, Michael Whitby, and the late Brereton Greenhous.

We are also grateful for the help given to the authors by the numerous students from the University of Ottawa's archival co-operative program who have worked at DHH over the years. Administrative support for the publishing contract was provided by Shannon Klatt from DHH and by David Fortin, Janet Werk, and Tasia Papadatos from Public Works and Government Services Canada. We would also like to thank our good friend and colleague, the late Dr. Charles Rhéaume. He is greatly missed.

We must also acknowledge the assistance provided by the staffs at the United Kingdom National Archives in London, the Royal Archives in Windsor, the Public Archives of Nova Scotia, the Public Archives of Newfoundland, the British Columbia Archives, the Canadian War Museum, and, of course, Library and Archives Canada, the repository holding the bulk of the Canadian navy's records. Our thanks are due to John Armstrong, as well, who generously lent us many of the records he had collected for his book on the Halifax explosion and its aftermath, and to Peter Rindlisbacher for his kind permission to reproduce a number of his excellent naval paintings.

The immense task of translating the English manuscript for the French-language edition was expertly handled by Élisabeth Leboeuf, Stéphane Bédard, and their colleagues at the translation bureau. Similarly, production of the maps for this volume was performed by André-Christian Seguin and the staff at D2K Communications, while assistance with the cartography contract was provided by Maurice Desautels from DND's public affairs branch. We would also like to thank Thomas Johnston for suggesting the title of this volume. The song "Farewell to Nova Scotia," from which the title is taken, is, as far as we are aware, the only musical piece about a Canadian sailor during the First World War.

The authors would also like to thank the staff of Dundurn Press in Toronto for their courteous professionalism in producing this volume, in particular, Michael Carroll, the associate publisher and editorial director who oversaw the project, Nigel Heseltine, who edited the lengthy manuscript, and designer Jennifer Gallinger. Also, many thanks to the design team at WeMakeBooks.ca, Kim Monteforte, Beth Crane, and Heidy Lawrance, for adding their creative flair to the project.

In acknowledging the encouragement and support of our colleagues at the Directorate of History and Heritage and from within the Department of National Defence as a whole, the authors are solely responsible for any errors or omissions in this volume. Moreover, the inferences drawn and opinions expressed are ours alone, and the department is in no way responsible for their reading or the presentation of the facts as stated.

Canada and Sea Power

Sea power has been described as "the possession of that overbearing power on the sea which drives the enemy's flag from it, or allows it to appear only as a fugitive; and which, by controlling the great common [i.e., the world's oceans], closes the highways by which commerce moves to and from the enemy's shores."[1] In writing his 1890 study of *The Influence of Sea Power Upon History*, Captain Alfred Thayer Mahan, a United States Navy (USN) officer and thinker, was attempting to explain to the American public the benefits that a transoceanic naval policy held for an aspiring great power. Mahan's work laid out an historical argument in favour of "Blue Water" naval power by concentrating on the maritime development of a handful of European nations during the seventeenth and eighteenth centuries, paying particular attention to the rise of British naval power during that period. Although the author conveniently overlooked a number of important land-based empires in reaching his conclusions on the importance of sea power in international affairs,[2] his emphasis on the Royal Navy's (RN's) role in expanding the British Empire around the world is particularly relevant to a discussion of Canada and the sea. For much of its history, and certainly since the conclusion of the Seven Years' War in 1763, what is now Canada has been either a colony or close ally of the two dominant sea powers of the nineteenth and twentieth centuries. From confederation in 1867 until the Second World War, Canada could rely on the "naval mastery"[3] of the Royal Navy's battleships and cruisers to protect its commercial interests on "the great common" and keep enemy fleets—although not enemy submarines—far from its shores. Since 1945, the country's maritime commerce has received the same protection from the United States Navy's fleets of aircraft carriers and submarines. Any discussion of the role that naval power has played in Canadian history, therefore, practically begins and ends with that acknowledgement.

1. A.T. Mahan, *The Influence of Sea Power Upon History, 1660–1783* (Boston 1890; Dover ed. Toronto 1987), 138.

2. Paul M. Kennedy, *The Rise and Fall of British Naval Mastery* (London 1976), 7.

3. Recognizing that any maritime nation might possess some degree of sea power and a capability to achieve local command of the sea, Kennedy uses the term "naval mastery" to describe "a situation in which a country has so developed its maritime strength that it is superior to any rival power, and that its predominance is or could be exerted far outside its home waters, with the result that it is extremely difficult for other, lesser states to undertake maritime operations or trade without at least its tacit consent" and "suggesting a measure of maritime supremacy which only a few nations have ever achieved and which has marked them off from lesser rivals." Kennedy, *The Rise and Fall of British Naval Mastery*, 9.

The ever-presence of the Royal Navy on the world's oceans also explains, in large measure, why the new dominion did not feel the need to establish its own navy until after the country had celebrated its forty-third birthday. Canadian politicians had little motive to spend taxpayer dollars on warships or sailors when the country's maritime security was already guaranteed by the naval power and industrial might of the wealthiest nation on the planet. It was not until the early twentieth century that a growing requirement to protect national interests in coastal waters, together with the rise of a perceived German threat to Britain's naval mastery, gave domestic political impetus to the idea of forming a Canadian navy. Since the creation of the Royal Canadian Navy (RCN) in 1910, the nation's naval efforts have been divided between providing local defence in home waters and the desire to make some contribution to the collective defence of, initially, the British Empire and, in the post-Second World War era, the North Atlantic Treaty Organization.

Canada's delay in establishing a national navy also reflects the first three conditions, all related to geography, that Captain Mahan listed as being the elements most effecting the development of a nation's potential sea power: geographical position; physical conformation ("including as connected therewith, natural products and climate"); and extent of territory, "physical conditions which lead people to the sea or turn them from it."[4] While the new dominion's eastern coast flanked the great circle shipping route across the Atlantic Ocean, thus giving it a geographical position of strategic importance, the very extent of its coastline produced several of the disadvantages that Mahan believed were detrimental to the development of a nation's sea power. For one, Canada's Pacific and Atlantic coasts were separated by a huge continental land mass, with the agricultural and mineral wealth of its hinterland prompting the vast majority of Canadians to focus on inland expansion rather than pursuing a livelihood on the surrounding oceans. That reduced the proportion of the population that, as Mahan termed it, were "following the sea." In Canada's case, moreover, the presence of the economically and militarily more powerful United States (US) on its southern flank, a border thousands of kilometres long, convinced Ottawa to direct its limited defence resources into a national militia rather than any sort of naval force. Even so, Canadian naval development mirrored, in many ways, that of the United States, a country that Mahan characterized in 1890 as having had its potential sea power stunted by its geographic vastness, even though initial settlement had occurred along its Atlantic coast: "The [US] centre of power is no longer on the seaboard. Books and newspapers vie with one another in describing the wonderful growth, and the still undeveloped riches, of the interior. Capital there finds its best investments, labor its largest opportunities."[5] Following the settlement of their respective interiors, it is, perhaps, no coincidence that *The Influence of Sea Power Upon History* was published as Mahan's attempt to illustrate the importance of "Blue Water" naval power to an American audience just as Canadians were themselves beginning to contemplate the necessity of establishing their own local navy.

---

4. Mahan, *The Influence of Sea Power*, 28–29, 36. Elements to which this volume would add a fourth, namely, the important role the inland transportation network plays in determining a modern nation's shipping ports and patterns.

5. Ibid, 39.

Although the Royal Canadian Navy was not created until 1910, Canada's maritime history began centuries earlier with the arrival of Europeans to its shores, people who had, of necessity, to cross an ocean in order to sight its forested coastline for the first time. Such naval actions as occurred in Canadian waters before 1867, both off-shore and inland, were the result of the power struggles between France and Britain and, later, Britain and the United States. The role that European naval power played in the country's early history extends far beyond the occasional clash of wooden-walled warships in local waters, however. From the attempted settlements of the Vikings around 1000, to the exploitation of the cod fisheries off Newfoundland and the explorations of John Cabot and Jacques Cartier, Europeans found potentially profitable natural resources, particularly fish and furs, and a native population with which one could form trading partnerships for commercial gain.[6] They charted the many rivers and lakes near the coast, eventually seeking a Northwest Passage that would allow economic and political communication with Asia. After Samuel de Champlain established a trading post at Quebec in 1608, situated where the river narrows on cliffs that provided natural advantages for defence, French explorers voyaged north to Hudson Bay, south to the Mississippi, and west past Lake Erie, mapping out water routes and claiming territory in the name of the metropole throughout the seventeenth century. The result was an extensive—though thinly populated—area, defended by a series of forts and posts, all of which required trans-Atlantic resupply from France for weapons and trade goods.[7]

At the same time, the other northern European sea powers, England and the Netherlands, were establishing their own colonies in North America, attracted in part by the lucrative trade in furs. England's alliance with merchants of the Hudson's Bay Company, established in 1670, and, to an even greater extent, the mother country's support of its colonies along the Atlantic seaboard to the south, led to frequent skirmishes and raids, often with the aid of native allies, between the English, Dutch, and French colonists. The role that sea power could play in such battles was demonstrated in 1628 when English privateers under Captain David Kirke captured a French supply convoy bound for Quebec, forcing Champlain's garrison to endure a winter of severe privation. Returning the next year with an even stronger fleet, Kirke easily captured Quebec, taking Champlain and most of the French garrison to England and holding the outpost until it was restored to France in 1632. In a similar demonstration, a force of New Englanders under Major Robert Sedgwick sailed from Boston in 1654 and captured the French settlement of Port Royal, keeping Acadia under English rule until it was returned to France in 1667.[8]

---

6. Jan Glete, *Navies and Nations: Warships, Navies and State Building in Europe and America, 1500–1860* (Stockholm 1993), I, 22–64; Tryggvi J. Oleson, *Early Voyages and Northern Approaches, 1000–1632* (Toronto 1963), 202–03; Laurier Turgeon, "Pour redécouvrir notre 16e siècle: Les pêches à Terre-Neuve d'après les archives notariales de Bordeaux," *Revue d'histoire de l'Amérique française*, 39, no. 4, 1986, 523–49.

7. W.J. Eccles, *Canada Under Louis XIV: 1663–1701* (Toronto 1964), 43, 106; Jacques Mathieu, *La Nouvelle-France: Les Français en Amérique du Nord, XVIe-XVIIIe siècle* (Quebec 2001), 64–65.

8. Marcel Trudel, *The Beginnings of New France, 1524–1663* (Toronto 1973), 172–73; Gerald S. Graham, *Empire of the North Atlantic: The Maritime Struggle for North America* (Toronto 1950), 29–30; John B. Hattendorf, et al., eds., *British Naval Documents, 1204–1960* (Aldershot 1993), 270; Serge Bernier, et al., *Military History of Quebec City, 1608–2008* (Montreal 2008), 95–98; W.J. Eccles, *France in America* (New York 1972), 27–28; George F.G. Stanley, *Canada's Soldiers 1604–1954: The Military History of an Unmilitary People* (Toronto 1954), 4–5, 11.

Colonial rivalry was renewed when England and Holland clashed with France in the War of the League of Augsburg beginning in 1688. As in future Anglo-French wars, the degree of confrontation in the American colonies was influenced by the the strategy England adopted to exploit its seapower advantage over its land-based European rival. Although the superior numbers and seamanship of the Royal Navy allowed England to adopt a "Blue Water" strategy centred on fleet actions, naval blockade and colonial conquest—all designed to exert commercial pressure on France by interrupting its overseas trade—it also left the French free to concentrate their larger armies against their European opponents. To prevent France from completely dominating Europe—a situation that would have allowed Versailles to divert its considerable resources into a naval building program to overwhelm the Royal Navy—London had to complement its naval effort by sending English armies and money to the continent to aid their allies. As British Cabinet minister Lord Newcastle succinctly described it, England's strategy was to protect "our alliances on the continent, and so, by diverting the expense of France, enable us to maintain our superiority at sea."[9] London's thinking proved apt during the War of the League of Augsburg when the English and Dutch armies drained away French strength through a long, drawn-out stalemate on land that allowed the two sea powers time to overcome their enemy's initial naval success. After the decisive Anglo-Dutch victory in the English Channel off Barfleur in 1692, France lacked the maritime strength to rebuild a navy comparable to the one with which it began the conflict and for the remainder of the war was forced to concentrate its ocean efforts on prosecuting a commerce raiding campaign instead.

With the fighting between the Anglo-Dutch and French focused in Europe, the conflict in North America was restricted to small expeditions and raids. French expansion down the Mississippi valley as far south as Louisiana had been buttressed by a series of forts and trading posts that effectively hemmed in the English American colonies along the eastern seaboard. Prior to the war, France had moved to solidify its American position by encouraging immigration to increase the colony's population, by establishing a naval school at Quebec to train river pilots and chart-makers, and by sending a few Canadiens to develop their military and naval skills with more formal training in the French navy. Most notable among these was Pierre Le Moyne d'Iberville, who led four successful naval expeditions into Hudson Bay to capture the English forts along its shores during the war. During the winter of 1696–97, moreover, d'Iberville led 125 soldiers and Canadiens along the coast of Newfoundland, pillaging and burning the undefended English fishing settlements before eventually capturing St John's. Taking command of the forty-four gun *Pelican* later that spring, d'Iberville sailed to capture Fort Nelson on Hudson Bay with four consorts. After his small squadron was trapped by ice flows, however, only *Pelican* managed to extricate herself to press on toward the English fort where it engaged the ships *Hampshire* of fifty-two guns, *Dering* of thirty-six, and *Hudson's Bay* of thirty-two on 5 September 1697. In a four hour engagement, *Pelican* sank *Hampshire* and forced *Hudson's Bay* to strike her colours, while *Dering* was the lone English ship to escape. The heavily damaged *Pelican*, meanwhile, was driven ashore by storms and wrecked near Fort Nelson. The timely arrival

---

9. Newcastle quoted in Kennedy, *The Rise and Fall of British Naval Mastery*, 75.

of the remainder of the French squadron, which had since freed itself from the ice, then allowed d'Iberville to capture the fort. English colonists also enjoyed some success during the war, most notably when another New England force, this time under Sir William Phips, again captured Port Royal in 1690 before sailing up the St Lawrence in an unsuccessful attempt to take Quebec. With the fighting in Europe stalemated both on land and at sea, the War of the League of Augsburg was ended in September 1697 with the Treaty of Ryswick restoring both sides' conquests, including the return, for a second time, of Acadia to French control.[10]

During the Anglo-French wars of the first half of the eighteenth century, the use of seapower in support of colonial operations continued to be secondary to the fighting in Europe. With the success of her armies on land during the War of the Spanish Succession, 1702–1713, Britain (as England and Scotland became after the Act of Union in 1707) was finally able to exhaust French resources on land as well as at sea. Under the superb generalship of the Duke of Marlborough, the British-led coalition won a series of impressive victories on the continent, demonstrating that its troops and leaders were equal to the best in Europe and that London was willing to deploy them in strength to prevent French hegemony. Lacking any semblance of a real battle fleet, France once again resorted to an effective *guerre de course*, causing the Royal Navy to provide warships as escorts to convoyed British merchantmen. In North America the most notable achievement was the capture of Port Royal in 1710 by a force consisting largely of colonial troops. With the Treaty of Utrecht in 1713, a bankrupted France was forced to cede mainland Nova Scotia, Newfoundland, and its posts on Hudson Bay, concessions that increased the vulnerability of its remaining possessions in North America. French leaders subsequently encouraged the shipbuilding industry at Quebec and built several forts, most notably at Louisbourg on Cape Breton Island, hoping to protect both the fishery and the main entrance to the colony through the Gulf of St Lawrence.[11]

When war broke out between France and Britain in 1744—the War of the Austrian Succession—the fighting quickly spread to the colonies that had gained in importance to both economies in recent decades. For the first time, both sides despatched large naval fleets to North American waters to protect their interests. In the wake of attacks on New England vessels by French privateers from Louisbourg, American colonists mounted an expedition that captured the Cape Breton port in 1745 after a six-week siege, the New England effort being aided by British warships from Commodore Peter Warren's Atlantic squadron brought up from the Caribbean. A powerful French naval force under the Duc d'Anville set sail the following year to recapture the fortress but was devastated by Atlantic storms

---

10. Francis Parkman, *France and England in North America, II: Count Frontenac and New France under Louis XIV, A Half-Century of Conflict, Wolfe and Montcalm* (Library of America ed., New York 1983), 281–83; Richard Harding, *Seapower and Naval Warfare: 1650–1830* (Annapolis 1999), 157; Daniel Dessert, *La Royale: Vaisseaux et marins du Roi-Soleil* (Paris 1996), 277–86; G.N. Tucker, *The Naval Service of Canada, Its Official History, I: Origins and Early Years* (Ottawa 1952), 2.

11. Kennedy, *The Rise and Fall of British Naval Mastery*, 82–88; Dale Miquelon, *New France, 1701–1744: "A Supplement to Europe,"* (Toronto 1987), 217–20; Mathieu, *Nouvelle-France*, 171–72; Jacques Mathieu, *La Construction navale royale à Québec: 1739–1759* (Quebec 1971), 4–5, 49.

"A view of the Landing [of] the New England Forces in ye Expedition against Cape Breton, 1745. When after a siege of 40 days the Town and Fortress of Louisbourg and the important Territories there to belonging were recovered to the British Empire." (LAC C-001094)

during the crossing. Only a handful of French warships managed to reach safety in Chebucto Bay before returning home. In May 1747, a British squadron intercepted and defeated an escorted French convoy attempting to bring reinforcements and supplies to Quebec.[12] In the Treaty of Aix-la-Chapelle of 1748, however, Louisbourg was returned to France in exchange for relinquishing wartime gains made by French armies in Holland and India. The treaty—which turned out to be more of a temporary truce than a peace— reflected both French land and British sea power. Although the New England colonists were outraged that "the key to the Atlantic" had been returned to France so territory could be regained for Britain's Dutch allies, London was well aware that a continental commitment remained necessary to distract the French from concentrating their considerable resources on building a stronger navy, one that could ultimately threaten Britain's overseas colonies and trade. To further solidify its maritime position in North America, the Royal Navy established a naval and military base at Halifax in 1749, providing British warships with a large, accessible and well-protected harbour in the western North Atlantic.[13]

With the perceived economic and strategic importance of overseas colonies continuing to grow among the European powers, the elimination of French colonial trade became the focus of British strategy when the Anglo-French rivalry resumed open conflict in 1756. Indeed, the importance that Britain and France placed on their colonial campaigns during the Seven Years' War was in contrast to the secondary character of colonial operations in the earlier struggles and made the 1756–63 conflict, as some have termed it, the first true world war. By the early 1750s, both empires were seeking control of the Ohio River valley, where large areas lightly populated by the French were coveted by British colonists moving west through the Appalachians. With frontier skirmishes becoming more frequent, both Versailles and London despatched military reinforcements to North America. Although not yet formally at war, a French squadron narrowly escaped capture—losing only two transports—in the Strait of Belle Isle in June 1755 when it was surprised by a British fleet under Admiral Edward Boscawen. Anglo-French clashes in North America and the Mediterranean also coincided with growing European fears over the increased military strength of Frederick the Great's Prussia. Formal declarations of war in May 1756 pitted Britain and Prussia against France and her allies, Austria, Russia, Sweden, and Saxony.[14]

---

12. Julian Gwyn, ed., *The Royal Navy and North America: The Warren Papers, 1736–52* (London 1973), vii; George F. Stanley, *New France: The Last Phase, 1744–60* (Toronto 1968), introduction; Brian Tennyson and Roger Sarty, *Guardian of the Gulf: Sydney, Cape Breton, and the Atlantic Wars* (Toronto 2000), 14–15; Kennedy, *The Rise and Fall of British Naval Mastery*, 92–3.

13. Julian Gwyn, *Ashore and Afloat: The British Navy and the Halifax Naval Yard Before 1820* (Ottawa 2004), 3–26; Daniel A. Baugh, *British Naval Administration in the Age of Walpole* (Princeton 1965), 27.

14. James Pritchard, *Louis XV's Navy, 1748–1762: A Study of Organization and Administration* (Montreal and Kingston 1987), 126–27; Fred Anderson, *Crucible of War: The Seven Years' War and the Fate of Empire in British North America, 1754–1766* (New York 2000), xix; Kennedy, *The Rise and Fall of British Naval Mastery*, 98; Stanley, *New France*, 45–96; R. Ernest Dupuy and Trevor N. Dupuy, *The Encyclopedia of Military History from 3500 B.C. to the Present*, rev. ed. (New York 1986), 675–76, 705–06.

During the war's opening stages, a rebuilt French navy was able to elude the British naval blockade in Europe and escort reinforcements to both Canada and the West Indies, an increase in military strength that helped to repulse the initial attacks by British and colonial troops. By 1758, however, the Royal Navy's grip around coastal Europe had become more effective, making it difficult for the French to send further aid across the Atlantic. With French forces in North America largely cut off from Europe, the British government planned to take both Louisbourg and Quebec that summer, while making another thrust up the Lake Champlain valley. While the inland campaign was defeated by General Louis-Joseph Marquis de Montcalm at Fort Carillon, 12,000 troops under Major-General Jeffrey Amherst, supported by a fleet of twenty ships of the line, eighteen frigates, and 100 transports under Boscawen lay siege to Louisbourg in June. The French defenders, outnumbered three to one, put up a stiff resistance before surrendering on 27 July, delaying the British long enough to postpone the Quebec campaign until the following spring.[15]

In June 1759 Vice-Admiral Charles Saunders led a British armada of forty-nine warships—of which the largest was Saunders's flagship, the ninety-gun HMS *Neptune*—and some 120 transports up the St Lawrence to land a force of 8,500 British troops under the command of Major-General James Wolfe on the Isle of Orleans below Quebec. "The picture one gets is that of a steady stream of the elements of naval power moving up the river as the wind serves, until in due time Saunders has so much strength in the Quebec area that the French are no longer able to challenge him."[16] In fact, Saunders fleet was larger than the one Sir Edward Hawke had under his command when he decisively defeated the French navy at Quiberon Bay, off the mouth of the Loire River on the Biscay coast, later that year. Despite the powerful British armada controlling the river, however, Wolfe spent the entire summer trying to devise a means to attack the virtually impregnable fortress and its 14,000 defenders under Montcalm. Unable to breach the French defences on the Beauport shore below the town, Wolfe's brigade commanders recommended using the fleet to land the army above the fortress. As a prominent historian of the campaign has explained, "the brigadiers were in constant consultation with Saunders when making their plan, and the calculations in it concerning movements by water, embarkation and disembarkation are doubtless his. Naval officers are notoriously backward about giving advice on matters affecting land warfare; but this plan was as much a naval as an army one, and one cannot help wondering whether the silent, competent vice-admiral's association with it may not have been the factor that decided Wolfe to accept it."[17]

Passing above the town on the night of 12/13 September, Saunders landed Wolfe's men at the Anse au Foulon where they climbed the cliffs to the Plains of Abraham and cut French communications with Montreal and the French ships further up river. When Montcalm left the protection of his fortress walls to offer battle on the 13th, Wolfe's gamble paid off. In a short, sharp fight, the British won the day and the defeated French army retreated into

---

15. John B. Hattendorf, "The Struggle With France, 1690–1815," J.R. Hill, ed., *The Oxford Illustrated History of the Royal Navy* (Oxford 1995), 99; Julian S. Corbett, ed., *Fighting Instructions: 1530–1816* (London 1905), 219–24.

16. C.P. Stacey, *Quebec 1759: The Seige and the Battle* (Toronto 1959), 59.

17. Ibid, 100.

British sailors capture and burn the French ship *Prudent* of seventy-four guns, aground in Louisbourg Harbour, during the early morning hours of 26 July 1758. The fortress surrendered the next day. (LAC C-007111)

the city. After the bulk of the French forces abandoned the fortress to slip around the British army and move up river toward Montreal later that night, Quebec capitulated five days later.[18] As decisive as the battle on the open plain was, the course of the campaign has led another historian to suggest that "Wolfe's little army was really no more than a most efficient landing party from an overwhelming fleet."[19] The importance of naval power in the struggle for New France was demonstrated again in April 1760 when the 4,000-man British garrison that had wintered at Quebec was besieged by a 7,000-man French force, virtually the entire military strength left in the colony, that had been transported down river before the ice was out of the St Lawrence. Repeating Montcalm's mistake, the British moved out of the fortress only to be defeated in a battle that involved heavier casualties than the more famous (or infamous) September clash—the British losing 1,100 to the French 800 in the April contest versus some 600 to 700 on each side the year before. Although the besieging French were hopeful of recapturing Quebec, it was the arrival of a British squadron in the St Lawrence in mid-May—Saunders having left a strong detachment at Halifax with instructions to re-enter the river as early as possible in the spring—that forced the French to retreat on Montreal after their own supporting frigates were attacked and destroyed. Despite the French navy's crushing defeat at Quiberon Bay the previous November, a small squadron was sent from France with supplies and a few reinforcements but it was unable to pass the British ships blockading the river and was forced to take refuge in the Restigouche River where it was caught and destroyed in July 1760.[20]

With the tactical brilliance of Frederick the Great's Prussian armies (subsidized by the British treasury) confounding France's European allies and the Royal Navy effectively isolating France's overseas colonies, Britain completed the conquest of Canada in 1760. By war's end, British forces had also taken Guadaloupe, Dominica, and Martinique in the West Indies, eliminated French influence in India and even captured Manila in the Phillipines and Havana in Cuba (Spain having joined France in the war). The Royal Navy was also able to provide the 8,000 ships of Britain's merchant fleet with more effective protection against French privateers than in earlier conflicts, allowing a virtually untouched Britain to expand its trade and finance its dual naval/continental strategy. With the conclusion of peace in early 1763, Britain's naval mastery allowed it to emerge from the Seven Years' War as the only nation to have made major territorial gains, having been awarded all of France's North American empire except Louisiana and the islands of St Pierre and Miquelon off Newfoundland. Britain also received Florida in exchange for returning Havana to Spanish control.[21]

---

18. Ibid, 120–55; Julian S. Corbett, *England in the Seven Years' War: A Combined Strategy* (London 1907), I, 396–476; Vice-Admiral Sir Charles Saunders's despatch to John Clevland, Secretary of the Admiralty, 21 September 1759, Hattendorf, et al., eds., *British Naval Documents*, 393.

19. W.C.H. Wood quoted in Gerald S. Graham, *Sea Power and British North America, 1783–1820: A Study in British Colonial Policy* (New York 1968), 175.

20. Stacey, *Quebec 1759*, 161–66.

21. Kennedy, *The Rise and Fall of British Naval Mastery*, 105–07.

Inexplicably, the lessons of the war were soon forgotten in London as the Royal Navy's budget was slashed from £7 million in 1762 to £1.5 million seven years later, leaving its warships to rot in reserve. The effect of the neglect was demonstrated when the American colonists rebelled in 1775, and particularly so after France entered the conflict in 1778, and Spain the following year. Britain's inadequate naval forces meant, as historian Paul Kennedy has pointed out, that "she had insufficient strength to be superior everywhere and because she dared not withdraw from any of the four main theatres—the Channel, Gibraltar, the West Indies, the American seaboard—then she ended up being too weak in every one of them."[22] Moreover, London was unable to find a continental ally to distract French strength away from naval building. By the time General Charles Cornwallis was besieged and forced to capitulate at Yorktown in October 1781, the Royal Navy's North American fleet was contending with numerically superior French forces off Virginia, British warships in the Caribbean faced a sizable Spanish squadron, and the Channel fleet was preparing against attack by a combined French-Spanish fleet nearly twice its size.[23]

One area in which British naval power had remained in control during the American Revolution, however, was on the Great Lakes of Upper Canada. A British naval presence had been established on the lakes during the Seven Years' War when a dockyard was built at Fort Oswego on Lake Ontario to construct armed vessels for a planned attack on the French-held Fort Niagara. Although the venture failed when the fort and its vessels were captured by Montcalm in August 1756, RN officers returned to the lake in 1760 to build a small squadron to support the campaign against Montreal. With peace in 1763 the marine service, which had also built warships at Navy Island on the Niagara River for service on the upper lakes, was considerably reduced, being continued primarily as a transport and protection service for local trade. In 1776 the British expanded their freshwater squadrons, manning the vessels with both Admiralty-provided officers and men and colonial recruits. The British warships quickly gained control of the lakes with only an occasional skirmish with American rebels. In 1778 the fresh-water service—which soon came to be termed the "Provincial Marine"—was reorganized along more formal naval lines and divided into three divisions on Lake Champlain, Lake Ontario, and the upper lakes. Again reduced in size after the Revolutionary War, the Provincial Marine's remaining vessels continued in service but were "maintained by the quartermaster-general's department of the British Army to transport personnel and supplies for its several inland forts."[24]

---

22. Ibid, 109–10; Robert Gardiner, ed., *Navies and the American Revolution* (London 1996), 9–76; David Syrett, *The Royal Navy in American Waters, 1775–1783* (Aldershot 1989), 1.

23. Barry Gough, "Sea Power and British North America: The Maritime Foundations of the Canadian State," *British Journal of Canadian Studies*, I, (June 1986), 31–33; Daniel A. Baugh, "Why did Britain Lose Command of the Sea during the War for America?" Jeremy Black and Philip Woodfine, eds., *The British Navy and the Use of Naval Power in the 18th Century* (Leicester 1988), 150–63; David Syrett, *The Royal Navy in European Waters during the American Revolutionary War* (Columbia, SC 1998).

24. J. Mackay Hitsman, *The Incredible War of 1812: A Military History*, rev. ed. (Toronto 1999), 8; Robert Malcomson, "'Not Very Much Celebrated:' The Evolution and Nature of the Provincial Marine, 1755–1813," *The Northern Mariner*, XI, (January 2001), 26–31; W.H. Whitely, "The British Navy and the Siege of Quebec, 1775–6," *Canadian Historical Review*, LXI, no. 1, 1980, 3–27; Arthur B. Smith, *Legend of the Lake: The 22-Gun Brig-Sloop Ontario, 1780* (Kingston 1997), 95; Anderson, *Crucible of War*, 150–57.

British warships in Halifax Harbour during the American Revolution, as seen from Georges Island in 1777. (DND HS 35254)

The loss of the American colonies greatly altered the strategic situation in North America. Whereas the main threat to Britain's pre-1756 position had been a small number of French settlements and military outposts that relied on reinforcements from France, by 1784 what remained of British North America had to contend with a comparatively well-populated country on its southern borders. In Europe, meanwhile, the French Revolution and subsequent rise to power of Napoleon Bonaparte produced a twenty-five year period of near-continuous warfare. Throughout the struggle, the Royal Navy remained ubiquitously victorious even though it seldom outnumbered the enemy. From Admiral Lord Howe's victory of "The Glorious First of June" in 1794 to Horatio Nelson's at Trafalgar in 1805, superior British tactics and seamanship allowed the well-led Royal Navy to dominate its more numerous French, Spanish, and Dutch adversaries. Unable to compete with the professionalism of the British navy in open battle, the French once again resorted to a well-organized *guerre de course* to disrupt Britain's mercantile shipping. Between the Royal Navy's blockade of Europe and the prohibitory economic decrees of Napoleon's Continental System, the ongoing Anglo-French naval war led to increasing friction with the United States whose shipping and overseas trade had expanded greatly with the advantage of neutrality. By 1812, the effectiveness of the British blockade combined with the Royal Navy's insistence on searching American vessels for British deserters—the attack by HMS *Leopard* on the USS *Chesapeake* had already led the two countries to the brink of war in 1807—convinced the United States to declare war, a result that had an obvious impact on the British North American colonies.[25]

Britain's continuing naval superiority on the open ocean meant that the Royal Navy was not seriously challenged by the United States Navy's powerful frigates, except in actions between individual ships. As had been the case during the American Revolution, the value of British sea power was limited in a war against a continental opponent, particularly so when the British Army was already engaged in a long land campaign against the French on the Spanish peninsula and only a limited number of British regiments were available for North America. Nonetheless, the Royal Navy established an effective blockade of the American coast, to the extent that its divided naval resources permitted, which reduced US imports from $53 million in 1811 to $13 million in 1814 and exports from $61 million to $7 million over the same period. In sharp contrast to the difficulties the blockade caused for Americans, Haligonians enjoyed the wartime prosperity that results from having some 10,000 free-spending British sailors and soldiers based at their port. Nova Scotian's enthusiasm for the Royal Navy was evident in the warm welcome given to HMS *Shannon* when it escorted the captured frigate USS *Chesapeake* into Halifax on 6 June 1813. The experienced crew of the thirty-eight-gun British frigate boarded the larger American warship following an intense, fifteen minute engagement off Boston on 1 June.

In addition to running a blockade, the British were capable of launching amphibious operations against important coastal points along the US seaboard, however, the extent of the Royal Navy's reach into Canada was strictly limited by the rapids on the St Lawrence

25. Brian Lavery, *Nelson's Navy: The Ships, Men and Organisation, 1793–1815* (Annapolis 1989), 35; Kennedy, *The Rise and Fall of British Naval Mastery*, 123–37.

The British frigate HMS *Shannon*, part of the British squadron blockading the US eastern seaboard, decisively defeats the American frigate USS *Chesapeake* in a single-ship duel off Boston on 1 June 1813. (LAC C-041825)

River above Montreal. As a result, both sides had to build freshwater navies to contest control of the Great Lakes, including separate fleets for Lake Ontario and Lakes Erie and Huron, a circumstance that negated Britain's oceanic naval mastery. With Upper Canada's communications heavily tied to travel on the lakes, the inland naval balance exerted a tremendous influence over the entire campaign to control the province, with the victor being determined by which side won the shipbuilding—and hence the logistics—war.[26]

Upon the American declaration of war on 18 June 1812, the Provincial Marine had the sixteen-gun brig *Queen Charlotte* and the six-gun schooner *General Hunter* (shortly to be joined by the ten-gun schooner *Lady Prevost*) on Lake Erie, and the twenty-two-gun corvette *Royal George* and several older armed schooners on Lake Ontario. To oppose them the United States Navy had only the sixteen-gun brig *Oneida* at Sackets Harbor at the eastern end of Lake Ontario. It was a superiority that gave Canada initial control of the Great Lakes, an advantage the British were quick to exploit in the conflict's early months.[27] On 17 July a British amphibious expedition from nearby Fort St Joseph captured one of the most important forts on the far western frontier, Fort Mackinac, situated between Lakes Huron and Michigan, before its unsuspecting American garrison could be told they were at war. At Fort Detroit, meanwhile, Provincial Marine warships prevented American forces from transporting supplies, intercepted enemy despatches, and allowed a mixed force of British regulars and militia under Major-General Isaac Brock to travel unhindered along Lake Erie to reinforce the British naval base at Amherstburg. Crossing the Detroit River on 16 August under covering fire from *Queen Charlotte* and *General Hunter*, Brock's force of 700 regulars and militia, and 600 Natives moved on the American fort and convinced its commander to surrender his command of over 2,200 men, together with thirty-three artillery pieces, 2,500 muskets, and the unarmed brig *Adams*. Renamed *Detroit*, the second brig assured the Provincial Marine of unopposed control of Lake Erie for the remainder of the season.[28]

On Lake Ontario, Commodore Isaac Chauncey was appointed to command at Sackets Harbor in September 1812 and, after arming a group of converted merchant schooners to reinforce *Oneida*, was able to seize control of the lake. On 8 November, Chauncey's squadron chased *Royal George* into Kingston and forced her to take cover under the guns

---

26. Wade G. Dudley, *Splintering the Wooden Wall: The British Blockade of the United States, 1812–1815* (Annapolis 2003), 94–95, 144; Hitsman, *The Incredible War of 1812*, 158–59; Kennedy, *The Rise and Fall of British Naval Mastery*, 138–39. While Dudley argues that the reduction in trade was more the result of American imposed restrictions that kept US merchant ships safe in harbour and out of the Royal Navy's reach, he does acknowledge the blockade's consequences in that "the reduction in exports hindered the local economies of the United States, [while] the loss of trade to a government almost totally reliant on duties for income proved nearly devastating."

27. Hitsman, *The Incredible War of 1812*, 31; David Curtis Skaggs and Gerald T. Altoff, *A Signal Victory: The Lake Erie Campaign, 1812–1813* (Annapolis 1997), 13; Robert Malcomson, *Lords of the Lake: The Naval War on Lake Ontario, 1812–14* (Toronto 1998), 4–22.

28. Hitsman, *The Incredible War of 1812*, 78–82; C.P. Stacey, "Another Look at the Battle of Lake Erie," *Canadian Historical Review*, XXXIX, (March 1958), 43.

HMS *Shannon* leads the captured frigate *Chesapeake* into a wildly-cheering Halifax on 6 June 1813. (DND HS 35236)

of the harbour's fortifications.[29] With the opening of navigation in 1813, Chauncey used his naval superiority to launch a raid on the Upper Canada capital of York (now Toronto) on 27 April. Although the raid was primarily aimed at destroying the ships under construction there, it had the unintended effect of severely handicapping the buildup of the British squadron on Lake Erie. Among the items captured by the Americans were twenty cannon, while the British themselves destroyed large stores of cordage, canvas, and naval equipment before retreating on Kingston. The loss of these supplies was particularly devastating for the British efforts on Lake Erie because the naval base at Amherstburg already lay at the far end of a long, tenuous line of communication. With little in the way of naval ordnance or stores being manufactured in Canada, aside from a plentiful supply of timber (indeed, the Canadian colonies supplied the Royal Navy with most of its masts, sending 23,000 in 1811 alone), everything required to outfit a warship had to be imported from Britain and transported up the St Lawrence above Montreal to the Lake Ontario naval base at Kingston. Supplies for the squadron at Amherstburg either had to be shipped across the lake to Fort George at the mouth of the Niagara River and overland past the Falls (a route directly exposed to American attack) or to York and Burlington Heights before being sent overland to Long Point, and then down the length of Lake Erie to its western end. With the guns and stores needed by his squadron having been captured or destroyed at York, the Lake Erie commander, Lieutenant R.H. Barclay, RN, had to outfit his small fleet with whatever ordnance he could lay his hands on, with the result that his flagship, *Detroit*, had to be armed with a mixed-bag of ordnance—in Mahan's words "a more curiously composite battery probably never was mounted"—taken from the ramparts of Amherstburg's Fort Malden.[30]

Once the shipbuilding contest between the two sides began in earnest in 1813 with the establishment of a USN base at Erie, Pennsylvania on Lake Erie to complement the one at Sackets Harbor on Lake Ontario, Upper Canada's logistical difficulties gave the Americans a decided advantage. Naval supplies for Sackets Harbor were forwarded from the navy yard at New York and had a relatively easy journey up the Hudson and Mohawk Rivers to Oswego on Lake Ontario. The two brigs being built by the USN at Erie, meanwhile, were largely outfitted with supplies manufactured at Pittsburgh, which were forwarded to Lake Erie along the Allegheny River and French Creek. Ordnance for the American's Erie squadron came from the Washington navy yard (via the navy yard at Philadelphia, which also had good communications with Pittsburgh), as did drafts of naval ratings. Ironically, the effectiveness of the Royal Navy's blockade of US coastal ports increased the availability of American naval personnel and supplies being sent to the interior.[31] As a result of the American buildup on Lake Erie, the carronades of the US squadron's warships out-gunned Barclay's ill-equipped vessels when the two small fleets met at Put-in Bay on 10 September. Anxious to ensure that the much-needed supplies being stockpiled at Long Point were

29. C. Winton-Clare [R.C. Anderson], "A Shipbuilder's War," in Morris Zaslow, ed., *The Defended Border: Upper Canada and the War of 1812* (Toronto 1964), 167–68; Malcomson, *Lords of the Lake,* 37.

30. Mahan quoted in Stacey, "Another Look at the Battle of Lake Erie," 45; G.N. Tucker, *The Naval Service of Canada, Its Official History, I: Origins and Early Years* (Ottawa 1952), 39.

31. A.T. Mahan, *Sea Power in Its Relations to the War of 1812* (London 1905), I, 301–02.

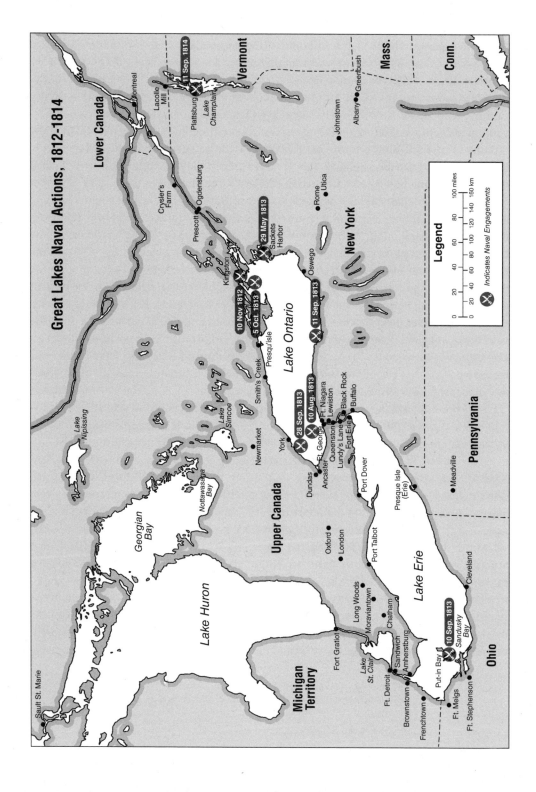

Great Lakes Naval Actions, 1812–1814

shipped to the British forces at Amherstburg without interference from the American squadron, a desperate Barclay sought out the action in which all six of his ships were defeated and captured. With the Unites States Navy in complete control of Lake Erie—a domination it would retain for the remainder of the war—the British Army had to abandon its position on the Detroit frontier and retreat east toward a better source of supply at Burlington Heights.[32]

On Lake Ontario, the shipbuilding race was more evenly contested. The fact that the British naval base at Kingston was much closer to Montreal meant that naval supplies from Britain were more readily available to outfit newly constructed warships. By the beginning of the 1813 navigation season, Chauncey had added the twenty-four-gun frigate *Madison* to his squadron to increase its superiority over the Provincial Marine. After attacking York at the end of April, the American fleet took part in the capture of Fort George, at the mouth of the Niagara River, on 27 May. Earlier that same month, however, the British squadron at Kingston had been reinforced with the launching of the twenty-three-gun corvette *Wolfe* and the arrival of Commodore Sir James Yeo and some 450 officers and seamen from the Royal Navy. After Yeo launched an unsuccessful attack on Sackets Harbor on 29 May, while the American squadron was engaged at the mouth of the Niagara, Chauncey decided the Provincial Marine squadron was too strong to be challenged until the latest American ship, the twenty-six-gun (all long-range cannons as opposed to the short-ranged carronades carried by most vessels on the lake) frigate *General Pike*, was ready for service in late July. Left in complete control of Lake Ontario for over a month, Yeo made a number of landings along the New York shore to destroy stores but his main accomplishment was appearing off Burlington Bay on 8 June, a move that helped convince the 3,000 American troops at Forty Mile Creek to pull back to Fort George following their defeat by 700 British soldiers in the Battle of Stoney Creek on the night of 5/6 June.[33]

With *General Pike*'s superiority in long-range cannon giving the US squadron the advantage, the Americans finally sailed from Sackets Harbor on 21 July, raiding York for a second time on the 30th. Neither fleet seemed particularly anxious to engage, however, when Yeo and Chauncey confronted each other off Niagara in early August (at which time the American schooners *Hamilton* and *Scourge* capsized and sank during a storm several miles off modern-day St Catharines). As one historian has described it, "for the next month Yeo and Chauncey, according to their own accounts, pursued one another around the lake; but, as one was only prepared to fight in calm weather at long range and the other in heavy weather at close quarters, it was not strange that no action took place."[34] Conditions favouring the American squadron did occur on 11 September off the Genesee River when a lack of wind left Yeo's ships becalmed and at the mercy of Chauncey's long-range guns. Fortunately for the British, the wind increased sufficiently for them to escape with only slight

---

32. Hitsman, *The Incredible War of 1812*, 168–73.

33. Malcomson, *Lords of the Lake*, 141–63; Winton-Clare, "A Shipbuilder's War," 168.

34. Winton-Clare, "A Shipbuilder's War," 169.

The Provincial Marine vessel *Royal George* engages Commodore Isaac Chauncey's flagship USS *Oneida* off Kingston on 8 November 1812. (LAC C-040593)

damage after a tense, ninety-minute bombardment. Whether reacting to the relative inaction on Lake Ontario or to Barclay's defeat on Lake Erie on the 10th, the governor-in-chief of British North America complained to London on 22 September that he "deplored the protracted contest on Lake Ontario for the naval ascendancy, Sir James Yeo having detained for this important object nearly the whole of the officers and seamen which were sent from England for himself, leaving Captain Barclay on Lake Erie to depend almost entirely on the exertions of soldiers" in manning his ships. In fact, the only serious naval engagement on Lake Ontario did not occur until 28 September when the American squadron found Yeo's ships off York and gave chase, with *General Pike* dismasting *Wolfe*'s main and mizzen-top-masts and forcing the British squadron to race west and seek cover on the lee shore of Burlington Bay in the face of a rising gale. One week after the action known as the "Burlington Races," Chauncey captured a convoy of schooners transporting supplies and troops off Prince Edward County and then spent the last few weeks of the navigation season blockading Yeo's squadron in Kingston.[35]

On 1 May 1814, the vessels of the Provincial Marine were officially taken on the establishment of the Royal Navy, the main result of which, aside from reorganizing the squadron's administration and officer seniority, was the renaming of Yeo's ships to avoid confusion with HM ships of the same name already on Admiralty strength. (In view of the importance attached to the superiority of the Royal Navy throughout the British Empire, the move was more than mere symbolism. It is interesting to note that, following Barclay's defeat on Lake Erie, one Halifax newspaper consoled its readers by suggesting that the loss was not as injurious to British naval prestige as it seemed because the defeated squadron was not Royal Navy "but was solely manned, equipped and managed by the public exertions of certain Canadians, who had formed themselves in a kind of lake fencibles. It was not the Royal Navy; but a local force; a kind of mercantile navy."[36]) That same day, 1 May, the Kingston squadron's newest warships, the sixty-gun frigate *Prince Regent* and the forty-four-gun frigate *Princess Charlotte*, completed outfitting and joined the "old" squadron for action, giving Yeo a temporary superiority to Chauncey's fleet. With the appearance of the new frigates, which together mounted fifty-four long 24-pounders on their gun decks, "the British on Lake Ontario possessed for the first time a proper armament of long guns as distinct from short-range carronades."[37] News that the Americans were building two new brigs and two large frigates of their own at Sackets Harbor, however, convinced Yeo that he needed a third new warship, one with "a description to look down all opposition." In late March, a keel was laid at the navy yard at Point Frederick, Kingston for a 104-gun ship-of-the-line that would be capable of destroying any USN warship being contemplated for the lake.[38]

---

35. Malcomson, *Lords of the Lake*, 188–93, 199–211.

36. Barry Gough, *Fighting Sail on Lake Huron and Georgian Bay: The War of 1812 and Its Aftermath* (St. Catharines 2002), 49; Skaggs and Altoff, *A Signal Victory*, 116–48.

37. C.P. Stacey, "The Ships of the British Squadron on Lake Ontario, 1812–1814," *Canadian Historical Review*, XXXIV, (December 1953), 321–22; Malcomson, *Lords of the Lake*, 263–5.

38. Yeo to Prevost, 13 April 1814, quoted in Malcomson, *Lords of the Lake*, 261.

Sir James Yeo, RN, arrived in Kingston in May 1813 to assume command of the Provincial Marine on the Great Lakes. (DND CN 6753)

With the American squadron unwilling to challenge Yeo until their own ships were completed, the British regained control of Lake Ontario for the first months of the 1814 navigation season but their only significant operation was a raid on the supply terminus of Oswego, New York, on 6 May. Although Yeo lifted his blockade of Sackets Harbor in early June, Chauncey refused to risk his squadron, thus allowing the British to continue transporting troops and supplies to Niagara where the British Army was resisting a 4,500-strong American force under Major-General Jacob Brown that had crossed the border and captured Fort Erie on 3 July. After defeating the British in the Battle of Chippawa on the 5th, Brown was at Queenston Heights overlooking Lake Ontario by the 10th to await the arrival of Chauncey's squadron and its support for the capture of Fort George and a further advance to Burlington. With no sign of the American ships needed to supply the intended campaign, Brown had no choice but to fall back to the south. On 25 July, the Americans were defeated at Lundy's Lane, directly above Niagara Falls, by a British force commanded by Lieutenant-General Sir Gordon Drummond. Retreating back down the peninsula, Brown's army was besieged for the remainder of the summer at Fort Erie. When Chauncey finally did sail out of Sackets Harbor on 31 July, the American squadron had the run of the lake for the next two months and, while only forcing one British transport aground during that time, made it difficult for the British to reinforce and resupply their forces surrounding Fort Erie.

Just as Chauncey's reticence infuriated Brown, Yeo's decision not to challenge the Americans until his 104-gun ship-of-the-line, HMS *St Lawrence* was ready for action in mid-October angered the British commander on the Niagara peninsula, Lieutenant-General Sir Gordon Drummond. It was, however, *St Lawrence*'s appearance on Lake Ontario and Chauncey's return to Sackets Harbor that finally convinced the Americans to abandon Fort Erie on 5 November and withdraw back to Buffalo. Earlier that autumn, a major British offensive down the Lake Champlain valley had been called off when its supporting naval force of four ships—barely completed and rushed into service—was defeated by a similar-sized USN squadron at the Battle of Plattsburgh on 11 September. On the eastern seaboard itself, a 4,000-man British amphibious expedition succeeded in capturing Washington, DC, during August, burning both the Capitol building and the White House before re-embarking on the warships of Vice-Admiral Sir Alexander Cochrane and undertaking a two-day bombardment of the defences around Baltimore, Maryland. Another example of the Royal Navy's superiority on the Atlantic occurred at the end of August when a 2,500-man British force with ten warships and a similar number of transports set out from Halifax and seized various points along the Penobscot River in Maine.[39]

With the signing of the Treaty of Ghent on 24 December 1814, both sides agreed to the *status quo ante bellum*, with all conquests being returned and without reference to the US grievances that had originally led to war. The Royal Navy's dominance on the ocean had not been seriously challenged by the small United States Navy, but sea power on the large inland lakes of Upper Canada had proven crucial to the conduct of land operations on the frontier. That its importance was understood in both London and Washington is evident

---

39. Winton-Clare, "A Shipbuilder's War," 169–71; Hitsman, *The Incredible War of 1812*, 240–48, 251–62; George
F.G. Stanley, *The War of 1812: Land Operations* (Ottawa 1983), 333–78.

from the fact that neither government censured either Yeo or Chauncey for their unwillingness to seek battle unless they had a clear superiority in strength. From Britain's perspective, with its military and naval resources overwhelmingly committed to the struggle against Napoleon, the conflict in North America appeared "to be more of a local quarrel, a strategical diversion." It had, however, reaffirmed the limitations of sea power in a conflict against a continental power like the United States and convinced many British statesmen of the military difficulties inherent in trying to defend British North America from attack by its southern neighbour. While unwilling to abandon Canada if faced with American aggression, whenever possible London sought to maintain good relations with Washington. As part of that effort, and in recognition of the importance naval superiority had played in the inland campaigns, Washington and London negotiated the Rush-Bagot Agreement in 1817 limiting naval armaments to one ship each on Lakes Champlain and Ontario and up to two ships each on the upper lakes. Military forces were unaffected by the agreement, however and fortifications continued to be built along the border. Between 1826 and 1832, the British also constructed a system of locks along the Rideau and Cataraqui rivers in eastern Upper Canada—the Rideau Canal—to by-pass the exposed water route along the St Lawrence and provide a more secure communication route between Kingston and Montreal.[40]

The end of the Napoleonic wars also ushered in an era of extended European peace, one that allowed British industry and commerce to expand at an unprecedented pace. The Royal Navy's "decisive victories in the eighteenth century had given its merchants the lion's share in maritime trade, which itself had stimulated the industrial revolution; yet this in turn was to provide the foundations for the country's continuing and increasing growth, making it into a new sort of state—the only real world power at that time."[41] With London as the centre of international finance, Britain's overseas investment and trade, both within and beyond the formal British Empire, expanded as well, carried abroad by its vast merchant fleet. The empire's actual land mass in 1815 was not particularly large, consisting primarily of British North America, parts of India, and the colony of New South Wales in Australia, but it did include a world-wide chain of strategically located islands and harbours, many of which had been acquired during the long struggle with France. With naval bases in such key places as Gibraltar, Malta, Cape Town, Sierra Leone, Ascension, Mauritius, and Ceylon (to which Singapore, the Falkland Islands, Aden and Hong Kong were added by 1841), the Royal Navy's role in Britain's commercial dominance was to control the important sea lanes along which its merchant ships traded with the world—and throughout the nineteenth century 60 percent of British exports and 80 percent of British investment went to regions outside the actual empire.[42]

---

40. Kennedy, *The Rise and Fall of British Naval Mastery*, 139; Hitsman, *The Incredible War of 1812*, 271–72, 279; Desmond Morton, *A Military History of Canada* (Edmonton 1985), 71–72.

41. Kennedy, *The Rise and Fall of British Naval Mastery*, 150.

42. Ibid, 154–5.

HM Ships *Confiance* (left) and *Linnet* (right) engage USS *Saratoga* off Plattsburg, New York on 11 September 1814. The defeat of the British warships convinced Sir George Prevost to call off his land offensive. (LAC C-10928)

The navy yard on Point Frederick, Kingston, circa 1815. The large, covered ship at left is the 104-gun HMS *St. Lawrence*. (LAC C-145243)

Within this world-wide system of naval bases, the only one located in British North America was Halifax. The Nova Scotian port had again proven its value to the Royal Navy during the War of 1812 when it served as a haven for British ships on blockade duty off the US eastern seaboard. In view of its strategic location in the western North Atlantic, the British government began work in 1828 to replace the fortifications overlooking the harbour and navy yard with a more modern citadel, a project that was not completed until 1856. The British Army also rebuilt similar fortifications to cover other important naval locations at Quebec (the Citadel) and Kingston (Fort Henry overlooking the navy yard on Point Frederick) during this period. Despite these building efforts, however, the Royal Navy's presence on the Great Lakes dissipated after 1815 and the naval station was officially closed in 1836.[43] When rebellions broke out in Upper and Lower Canada the following year, the most senior naval officer in the upper province was a retired RN officer, Captain Andrew Drew, of Woodstock. When a mob of Canadian rebels was defeated at Toronto in early December 1837, a mixed group of rebels and American sympathizers seized Navy Island in the Niagara River above the Falls, supplying their base from the New York shore using an American steamer. At the suggestion of the Canadian militia commander keeping watch on the captured island, Captain Drew led a small company of ex-sailors across the river to cut out the offending steamer, killing one American in the process, before sending the blazing vessel over the Falls.[44]

Indignation in the United States at the violation of their territory and a growing belief among some Americans along the border that the Canadian rebellions justified annexing British territory (American adventurers had, after all, seized Texas and declared their independence from Mexico a year earlier) resulted in further incursions by armed bands in early 1838 along the Detroit River, Pelee Island in Lake Erie, and on the Quebec–Vermont border. By February, the increased tensions had prompted the British government to suggest to Canadian authorities that they arm a small flotilla of steamboats to patrol the St Lawrence and Great Lakes. Two months later, Captain Williams Sandom, RN, arrived at Kingston and reactivated the naval station at Point Frederick as HMS *Niagara*. Sandom commanded a naval contingent of 267 officers and men transferred from the North America and West Indies (NA&WI) Squadron and purchased or chartered four gunboats, three paddle-wheel steam vessels, and a schooner. The schooner, commissioned as HMS *Bullfrog*, acted as a depot ship, while one of the armed steamers was commissioned as Her Majesty's Steam Vessel *Experiment*. London's foresight was evident in November 1838 when a force of 300 invaders, the vast majority of them Americans, crossed the St Lawrence and seized a group of stone buildings at Windmill Point, two kilometres downriver from Prescott, Upper Canada. In one of the stranger naval engagements in Canada, *Experiment* fired on the commandeered American steamer *United States* in mid-river, decapitating her pilot, knocking out her starboard engine, and preventing the vessel from being used to reinforce the intruders. Sandom's small fleet of steamers and gunboats, meanwhile, interdicted the

---

43. J. Mackay Hitsman, *Safeguarding Canada, 1763–1871*, rev. ed. (Toronto 1999); Donald E. Graves, *Guns Across the River, The Battle of the Windmill, 1838* (Toronto 2001), 212.

44. Tucker, *The Naval Service of Canada*, 39–42.

Captain Williams Sandom's small fleet of steamships provide supporting fire to British and Canadian forces on 13 November 1838 during the "Battle of the Windmill." (LAC C-041154)

river and gave supporting fire during the five-day Battle of the Windmill until the invaders surrendered to a besieging force of British regulars and Canadian militia.[45]

On the West Coast, Anglo-American tensions over Oregon during the 1840s, culminating with the 1846 Treaty of Washington that set the western border at the 49th parallel, revealed both the benefits and limitations in using the Royal Navy's sea power, and emphasized the fact that although warships could influence the US government, they could not control the growing numbers of Americans settling on the West Coast.[46] As the British Columbia region developed through the 1850s, the possibility of conflict increased not only with the Americans but, as a result of the Crimean War, with the Russians as well. From the time the Hudson's Bay Company established island trading posts in 1825 and British colonists began arriving at Victoria on Vancouver Island, war vessels from the Pacific squadron based at Callao and Valparaiso became increasingly frequent visitors. The harbour at Esquimalt was valued for its accessible deep water anchorage, with its sheer shore line allowing ships a sheltered mooring in all weather conditions and, after 1851, for its proximity to the British colonial government at Victoria. When gold seekers flocked to the Fraser River in 1858 and Anglo-American disagreement arose the following summer over Puget Sound's San Juan Island, Vancouver Island's governor called for further naval support. As a result, the number of ships on the Pacific Station increased to fifteen by 1860, after averaging eleven for the previous decade. With recurring threats encouraging the development of a more permanent establishment at Esquimalt, the naval base became Pacific Station Headquarters in 1862.[47]

The expansion of the Pacific Station reflected the increased dispersion of British naval strength around the world. Until the end of the Napoleonic wars, the Royal Navy had largely concentrated its warships in home waters and the Mediterranean. By 1848, however, Britain's growing interests and responsibilities meant that there were ninety-eight warships on foreign stations as opposed to thirty-one in the Mediterranean and thirty-five at home. With naval budgets restricted during long periods of peace, this dispersion of strength was achieved by reducing the number of ships of the line and redistributing sailors among an increasing number of frigates and gunboats. By the beginning of the 1860s, moreover, Britain's ability to maintain its sea mastery was complicated by the unprecedented rate of technological change in naval design. Although the motive power of their sails was augmented by steam-driven propellers, the 120-gun first-rates launched in 1859 were the last of the familiar three-decker wooden-walls to enter service. In contrast, HMS *Warrior*, launched in 1860 in response to the French ironclad *Gloire*, had a hull and armour

---

45. Graves, *Guns Across the River*, 88–92, 105–57.

46. Barry Gough, "Lieutenant William Peel, British Naval Intelligence, and the Oregon Crisis," *The Northern Mariner*, IV, (October 1994), 1–14; Donald Creighton, *The Story of Canada*, rev. ed. (Toronto 1975), 145.

47. Barry Gough, *Gunboat Frontier: British Maritime Authority and Northwest Coast Indians, 1846–1890* (Vancouver 1984), 26; Barry Gough, *The Royal Navy and the Northwest Coast of North America: 1810–1914* (Vancouver 1971), 152–66; Ronald Lovatt, *A History of the Defence of Victoria and Esquimalt, 1846–1893* (Ottawa 1980), 7, 15, 24; E.V. Longstaff, *Esquimalt Naval Base: A History of Its Work and Its Defences* (Victoria 1941), 10–12; Tucker, *Naval Service of Canada*, I, 55–59.

belt of iron and carried only forty guns but was designed to "be able to overtake and over-whelm any other warship in existence." Although the rise of "steam, steel and shellfire" led significant elements of the British public to fear that their battle fleet had become obsolete, the Royal Navy was able to maintain both the power of its line-of-battle and its presence on the world's shipping lanes. Indeed, "once the age of the steamship arrived, Britain's industrial strength enabled her to regain any temporary lead which [a rival] may have obtained in the design of individual vessels. The ability to build more and faster than anyone else, the virtual monopoly of the best stoking coals, and the immense financial resources of the nation—it was upon these very firm foundations that Britain's maritime mastery rested for the remainder of the century, together with the sheer experience and professionalism of the crews compared with those of less well-experienced navies."[48]

The security provided by the Royal Navy was never in question when the political leaders of the British American colonies met at Charlottetown and Quebec to discuss federation in 1864. Instead, with the American Civil War still raging south of the border, "it was the threat of American encroachment and the fear of American diplomatic or military aggression that had driven British North Americans to consider union as a measure of defence."[49] The impetus for union also came from Britain, where there was much concern of becoming embroiled in a war with the United States should the Americans decide to invade the northern colonies. With the cost of the 14,500 troops stationed in Canada and the maritimes in the spring of 1864 being borne by London, the British garrison was "the one great grievance of the British taxpayer against the colonies."[50] Fortunately for the future Canadian provinces (whose merchant marine, led by the Allan Line of steamships, would become the world's fourth largest by 1874[51]), no such resentment toward British North America attached itself to London's expenditure on the Royal Navy, where the naval bases at Halifax and Esquimalt were a positive contribution to imperial defence. The fact that the security provided by British naval superiority was largely taken for granted also left the United States as the only power that could directly interfere with the peace and prosperity of British North America. In concentrating on the land threat posed by their southern neighbour, however, Canada's "fathers of confederation" were minimizing the crucial role that sea power—from the long Anglo-French struggle for control of the continent to the successful defence against American invasion in 1812–14—had already played in determining the political configuration of the country they were about to create.

---

48. Kennedy, *The Rise and Fall of British Naval Mastery*, 172; Andrew Lambert, "Politics, Technology and Policy-Making, 1859–1865: Palmerston, Gladstone and the Management of the Ironclad Naval Race," *The Northern Mariner*, VIII (July 1998), 10; Robert Gardiner, ed., *Steam, Steel and Shellfire: The Steam Warship, 1815–1905* (London 1992), 50; Jan Glete, *Navies and Nations: Warships, Navies and State Building in Europe and America, 1500–1860* (Stockholm 1993), II, 446; Oscar Parkes, *British Battleships, Warrior 1860 to Vanguard 1950: A History of Design, Construction and Armament*, rev. ed. (London 1966), 1–17.

49. Creighton, *The Story of Canada*, 155.

50. C.P. Stacey, *Canada and the British Army, 1846–1871: A Study in the Practice of Responsible Government*, rev. ed. (Toronto 1963), ix, 155–97.

51. Trevor D. Heaver, "Shipping Industry," *The Canadian Encyclopedia* (Edmonton 1985), 1690.

SECTION 1

A National Navy

CHAPTER 1

The Naval Defence Question, 1867–1901

With the proclamation of the British North America (BNA) Act on 1 July 1867, Canada's federal parliament assumed responsibility for defence from the three colonial administrations that had been merged to create the new dominion. Although defence considerations had played an important role in the talks leading to confederation, conducted while the American Civil War was being fought by mass armies south of the border, Canadians were not particularly interested in building a large standing army or, indeed, a professional armed force of any sort. The fact that the relative defence responsibilities of the British and Canadian governments remained vague, with the mother country continuing to have sole responsibility for foreign policy, allowed Canadians to assume that British land and naval forces would arrive in the event of a crisis.[1] As such, the country's political leaders continued to think of the dominion's defence requirements solely in terms of establishing a citizen militia that could respond quickly to local foreign incursions or civil unrest. The militia bill introduced by Minister of Militia and Defence George-Étienne Cartier in March 1868 provided for an active militia of 40,000 men and a reserve militia of every able-bodied man between the ages of sixteen and sixty, a measure that would, in theory, mobilize 700,000 men for war.[2]

The need to create some sort of naval force to protect coastal waters was not even considered and no mention of Canadian naval forces was made in the initial defence debates. The establishment of separate federal ministries for militia and defence, and marine and fisheries suggested that Canadians were content to rely on the power of the Royal Navy to protect the country's coast.[3] For the next several decades, the predominant influence on the government's maritime policy was not the vastness of Canada's coastlines (the longest of any nation, even before the incorporation of Newfoundland and Labrador), nor its valuable

1. R.A. Preston, *The Defence of the Undefended Border: Planning for War in North America, 1867–1939* (Durham, NC 1967), 35; Roger Sarty, "The Origins of the Royal Canadian Navy—The Australian Connection," T.R. Frame, J.V.P. Goldrick, and P.D. Jones, eds., *Reflections on the Royal Australian Navy* (Kenthurst, New South Wales 1991), 75–76.

2. Desmond Morton, *Ministers and Generals: Politics and the Canadian Militia, 1868–1904* (Toronto 1970), 6–7.

3. Preston, *The Defence of the Undefended Border*, 35; and Sarty, "Origins of the RCN," 75–76.

maritime economy,[4] but the country's membership in the British Empire under the protection of the world's largest and strongest fleet. Located on the North Atlantic centre of British seapower, the original Canadian provinces were more secure against seaborne attack than any other part of the empire. Confidence bred of this fact underlay meagre Canadian defence expenditures and explained the priority given to transcontinental economic development over maritime affairs.[5]

The new government's decision to concentrate its defence budget on the militia meant that a number of local naval initiatives from the previous decade were allowed to wither. During the 1860s, as the British government became increasingly skeptical of the efficacy of sending British forces to North America, London wanted to see Canadians become more heavily involved in their own defence, including naval defence, and in particular defending the Great Lakes with improved fortifications and waterways. Locally supported armed services could not hope to win wars, but they might delay hostile forces and secure local bases until the Royal Navy arrived. In 1865, Westminster had passed legislation meant to encourage colonies to establish their own naval organizations. It specified that colonies, at their own expense, were authorized to provide, maintain, and use "a vessel or vessels of war," as well as raise and maintain seamen and a body of volunteers "entered on the terms of being bound to general service in the Royal Navy in [an] emergency."[6]

Such naval forces would have been built on the colonial naval militias that had been formed in the wake of strained Anglo-American relations during the US Civil War. The naval militias' role was to provide immediate reaction to any attack from south of the border and delay the enemy until British reinforcements arrived. The first such local naval groups were formed in Ontario, where the Militia Act of 1862 had authorized the establishment of seven "naval companies" at Dunnville and Port Stanley on Lake Erie, and at Hamilton, Kingston, Oakville, Garden Island, and Toronto on Lake Ontario. Each company was to be approximately sixty strong, recruited from among the lake-going public who would, it was expected, be more comfortable and effective in a naval militia than in the army. They were to be ready to outfit and man ships quickly, but clothing and equipment were never adequate, making winter drills difficult and unsatisfying. Nonetheless, when the Fenian group of Irish rebels threatened to launch raids against British North America from south of the border in 1866, defence preparations developed a certain urgency. Canada had

---

4. After Great Britain, the United States, and Norway. See Margaret R. Conrad and James K. Hiller, *Atlantic Canada: A Region in the Making* (Toronto 2001), 118.

5. Roger Sarty, "Canadian Naval Policy," nd, 1–2, unpublished Directorate of History and Heritage (hereafter DHH) narrative.

6. G.N. Tucker, *The Naval Service of Canada: Its Official History, I: Origins and Early Years* (Ottawa 1952), 374–76; Donald Creighton, *John A. Macdonald, I: The Young Politician* (Toronto 1998, first published 1952), 325, 410–14; Thomas Richard Melville, "Canada and Seapower: Canadian Naval Thought and Policy, 1860–1910" (PhD thesis, Duke University, 1981), 26–28, 38, 42, 46–48, 51–52, 54–55; C.P. Stacey, *Canada and the British Army, 1846–1871: A Study in the Practice of Responsible Government* (Toronto 1963, first published 1936), 136, 139, 145; Preston, *Undefended Border*, 26–43; J. Mackay Hitsman, *Safeguarding Canada, 1763–1871* (Toronto 1968), 177–86; Kenneth Bourne, *Britain and the Balance of Power in North America, 1815–1908* (London 1967), 279, 306; and Richard Preston, *Canada and "Imperial Defense:" A Study of the Origins of the British Commonwealth's Defense Organization, 1867–1919* (Toronto 1967), 47–51.

insisted that Britain should be responsible for what it considered to be an imperial problem, but London disagreed. The Royal Navy did help deter Fenians at Campobello, New Brunswick, in April, but the Canadian naval militias, using hired gunboats, were on their own when they helped to turn back the invaders at Fort Erie in June 1866.[7] The Toronto Naval Company prepared the steam vessels *Rescue* and *Magnet* for action, while the naval militia's brightest moment came when the Dunnville Naval Company, on the steamer *W.T. Robb*, chased retreating Fenians back across the Niagara River. The experience revealed, however, that if a naval militia was to avoid serious problems of poor training and inadequate armament, it would need a greater commitment of resources. After five years, when the danger of attack from the United States had diminished and after several local organizers ceased to be involved, the militia experiment on the lakes came to an end.[8]

Nova Scotia, meanwhile, had launched its own naval militia in April 1866 and within a year had signed up over 500 men in ten companies. The Royal Navy supported this initiative with equipment and training, but upon responsibility for defence being transferred to Ottawa the Department of Militia and Defence refused to consider a separate role for naval companies and allowed them to wither away. The last four of the Nova Scotia companies were converted to artillery in December 1870. Militia experiments with naval companies were also attempted at Bonaventure, New Carlisle, Carleton, and Gaspé, Quebec, under authority of the Militia Act of 1868. Referred to as "marine companies," they also were eventually disbanded because they lacked training and equipment.[9]

The possibility of a more permanent gunboat force on the Great Lakes remained a matter of some debate following confederation, with Britain and Canada each recommending that the other pay for the vessels. Canada had hired and manned the steamers that had served as gunboats during the Fenian raids, and when two of those, *Rescue* and *Michigan* (renamed *Prince Alfred*) were purchased outright, they became the first naval vessels armed by the Canadian government. The Royal Navy eventually supplied armament and fighting crews, and paid working expenses; it also sent three more gunboats, which remained on the lakes until late 1867. By then, although Canada argued that the Fenian threat remained, Britain believed it to be over. In April 1868 the British colonial secretary suggested that "the time has come when provision should be made for the manning and equipment of suitable vessels by the government of the dominion."[10] The following year, London once again stated that Canada should decide which armed naval forces it desired on the lakes,

7. Hereward Senior, *The Last Invasion: The Fenian Raids, 1866–1870* (Toronto 1991), 56; Greg Marquis, *In Armageddon's Shadow: The Civil War and Canada's Maritime Provinces* (Montreal and Kingston 1998), 278–81; and Brian Tennyson and Roger Sarty, *Guardian of the Gulf: Sydney, Cape Breton, and the Atlantic Wars* (Toronto 2000), 88–89.

8. Melville, "Canada and Sea Power," 2–107; C.P. Stacey, "The Fenian Troubles and Canadian Military Development, 1865–1871," *Canadian Defence Quarterly*, April 1936, 270–77; and Sarty, "Origins of the RCN," 75.

9. Melville, "Canada and Sea Power," 107–18; Canada, Parliament, *Report on the State of the Militia of the Dominion of Canada for the Year 1868* (Ottawa 1869), 68; and Canada, Parliament, *Report on the State of the Militia of the Dominion of Canada for the Year 1869* (Ottawa 1870), 10.

10. The Duke of Buckingham and Chandos to Viscount Monck, 14 April 1868, quoted in Melville, "Canada and Sea Power," 96, 101; and Stacey, *Canada and the British Army*, 190–93.

but reiterated that "this must now be done entirely at the expense of the dominion."[11] Unwilling to do so, Ottawa eventually laid up its two vessels, despite the assistance the gunboats had provided in transporting troops to the Red River in 1870. Since the naval militias had already disappeared from the lakes, Canada was once again entirely dependent on Britain for its naval defence.[12]

The negative implications of Canada's dependence on British naval power became evident whenever British and Canadian interests collided. Such had been the case in 1866 when Washington abrogated the 1854 treaty of reciprocity and American fishermen lost the legal right to fish the inshore waters of the Maritime provinces and in the Gulf of St Lawrence. With London focused on maintaining harmonious relations with the United States, British officials were unwilling to adopt measures (aside from a licensing system that was not adequately enforced) preventing Americans from fishing in Canadian waters despite Ottawa's requests. When the Royal Navy informed Canada in 1869 that it would be decreasing its presence in North American waters, Minister of Marine and Fisheries Peter Mitchell announced that he would commission six armed schooners manned by a "Marine Police" to protect the fisheries. He warned that "all national rights of fishery on our own coasts" were threatened and that "the time has arrived when we must either abandon this authoritative right, or assert and maintain it."[13] The Marine Police, whose authority was ultimately backed by British naval might, proved to be highly successful in limiting American access. After Canadian government schooners arrested twelve American vessels fishing illegally in Canadian waters in 1870, the United States was forced to settle the fisheries question by negotiating the Treaty of Washington in 1871. The treaty's ratification, accompanied by a substantial decrease in American naval and military strength in the post–Civil War period, allowed Canada's prime minister, Sir John A. Macdonald to declare that there was "not the slightest chance of a row between the United States and England" and that Canada "ought to take advantage of this to keep down our militia estimates." With economies in mind and having served its original purpose, the Marine Police was disbanded in 1873.[14]

---

11. Colonial Secretary to Sir John Young, 14 April 1869, quoted in Melville, "Canada and Sea Power," 103.

12. George H. Wyatt, "Report of Gunboat Agent," 3 February 1871, Canada, Parliament, *Report on the State of the Militia of the Dominion of Canada for the Year 1870* (Ottawa 1871), 132; Melville, "Canada and Sea Power," 56, 86–92, 104–05; Stacey, *Canada and the British Army*, 221; and Senior, *Last Invasion*, 104.

13. Peter Mitchell, "Annual Report of the Department of Marine and Fisheries, for the year ending 30th June 1869," 20 April 1870, 51, Canada, Parliament, *Sessional Papers 1870*, no. 11; Melville, "Canada and Sea Power," 16, 120–37; Ronald Duea Tallman, "Warships and Mackeral: The North Atlantic Fisheries in Canadian-American Relations, 1867–1877" (unpublished PhD thesis, University of Maine, 1971), 85–88, 92; and Ernest J. Chambers, *The Canadian Marine: A History of the Department of Marine and Fisheries* (Toronto 1905), 78–79.

14. Macdonald quoted in Preston, *The Defence of the Undefended Border*, 55; Bourne, *Balance of Power*, 307–09; Report by P.A. Scott, Marine and Fisheries Report, 315–16, Canada, Parliament, *Sessional Papers 1871*, no. 5; Tallman, "Warships and Mackeral," 281; T.E. Appleton, *Usque Ad Mare: Historique de la Garde côtière canadienne et de Services de la Marine* (Ottawa 1968), 40; Melville, "Canada and Sea Power," 130; and Michael L. Hadley and Roger Sarty, *Tin-pots and Pirate Ships: Canadian Naval Forces and German Sea Raiders, 1880–1918* (Montreal and Kingston 1991), 6.

The Royal Navy dockyard at Halifax circa 1870. (LAC PA-112191)

The Royal Navy's Pacific Squadron in Esquimalt Harbour circa 1870. One RN officer at that time stated that "it would be difficult to find a snugger harbour than Esquimalt; completely land-locked, surrounded on all sides by dense forests." (LAC PA-124071)

When Alexander Mackenzie's Liberal government replaced Macdonald's administration in late 1873, British officials urged it to upgrade artillery at Quebec, Montreal, and Kingston. British troops, meanwhile, continued to man the coast defences at Halifax, a port with continuing strategic and logistical value to the Royal Navy. Between 1861 and 1873 Britain spent considerable time and money keeping these defences up to date, including installing 9-inch rifled breech loaders, the standard coastal gun in British service at the time. Although Ottawa was willing to provide militia units to replace some of the British troops at the port in the event of war, they avoided any commitment that might lead the Admiralty to reduce further the size of the North American squadron. Other areas on the East Coast, such as the coal base at Sydney and another at Prince Edward Island (after it joined Confederation in 1873), were more clearly a Canadian responsibility. On the West Coast, meanwhile, ambitious plans for the base at Esquimalt were cancelled following budget cuts in 1869. Within another two years, however, the West Coast naval base assumed greater prominence in imperial thinking as the projected completion of the trans-continental Canadian railroad and its telegraphic connections would create a virtual northwest passage by rail. The Royal Navy's perceived importance to the region was made clear in 1871 when British Columbia insisted, as one of its conditions for joining Canada, that Ottawa promise to use its influence to ensure that Esquimalt would be maintained as a naval station. As on the East Coast, Canada was willing to provide some militia support for coastal defences, but nothing that could be considered naval in character.[15]

A deterioration of Anglo-Russian relations during the Russo-Turkish War of 1877–78 prompted fears among British Columbians that the West Coast was vulnerable to Russian naval attack. The reaction of the Mackenzie government to popular outbursts of imperial loyalty from English-speaking Canada was to propose some increased spending for coastal fortifications and to ask Britain to send some fast cruisers. Britain indicated that London, not Ottawa, would decide where and when cruisers would be stationed in an emergency. Although the signing of the Treaty of Berlin in July 1878 ended the immediate scare, Britain's Colonial Defence Committee (CDC) asked Canada to consider arming its merchant marine and requested that the dominion spend more on coastal artillery and underwater mines. Prime Minister Mackenzie had insisted during the crisis that Canada was "above shirking her duty in providing for the defence of her own coasts" but the costs involved meant that little was done.[16] Some improvements were made at Esquimalt as garri-

---

15. Roger Sarty, "Silent Sentry: A Military and Political History of Canadian Coast Defence, 1860–1945" (unpublished PhD thesis, University of Toronto, 1982), 5, 13, 43–48, 51, 72–74; Tennyson and Sarty, *Guardian of the Gulf*, 93; Clarence Stuart Mackinnon, "The Imperial Fortresses in Canada: Halifax and Esquimalt, 1871–1906," (unpublished PhD thesis, University of Toronto, 1965), 1–7, 45–100, 265–350; Barry Gough, *The Royal Navy and the Northwest Coast of North America: 1810–1914* (Vancouver 1971), 197, 218–19, 248; Thomas H. Raddall, *Halifax: Warden of the North* (Toronto 1948), 224–40; Barry Gough, *Gunboat Frontier: British Maritime Authority and Northwest Coast Indians, 1846–1890* (St Catharines 2002), 162, 170, 213; Ronald Lovatt, "A History of the Defence of Victoria and Esquimalt, 1846–1893" (unpublished manuscript, Environment Canada, 1980), 25; and Serge Bernier, *Le Patrimoine Militaire canadienne, d'hier à aujourd'hui*, III: *1872–2000* (Montreal 2000), 82.

16. Mackenzie to Dufferin, 11 June 1878 quoted in Preston, *Imperial Defense*, 122; Tennyson and Sarty, *Guardian of the Gulf*, 94–95; Glynn Barratt, *Russian Shadows on the British Northwest Coast of North America, 1810–1890: A Study of Rejection of Defence Responsibilities* (Vancouver 1983), 94–102; Sarty, "Silent Sentry," 53; Donald Schurman, *Imperial Defence, 1868–1887* (London 2000), 68; and Sarty, "Origins of the RCN," 78–79.

son troops were raised, batteries were built, and guns were borrowed from the Royal Navy, but such activity proved short lived when London once again raised doubts as to Esquimalt's importance as an imperial base.[17]

The return to power of the Conservative government of John A. Macdonald did little to alter Canada's approach to the naval defence question. In 1880, Macdonald repeated earlier expectations that Royal Navy protection, as promised to Canada in 1865, would arrive in time of need and emphasized that "the two points we think where the principal obligation rests upon England are Halifax and Esquimalt." The prime minister also suggested that Britain could recruit in Canada, if it paid the bills, for a naval reserve. Pointing to the promise that Canada was ready to help garrison Halifax if British troops were needed elsewhere, Macdonald reiterated that the dominion might also do more. "I have no doubt that, in case of war, that Canada, for her own protection, would fit out some of those vessels (swift ships of the commercial marine) at her own expense to protect her own shores."[18] He insisted, however, that Britain should not expect Canadian commitments during times of peace and that Ottawa's support required that any defence initiative had to address Canadian needs. Major-General Edward Selby-Smyth, the general officer commanding the Canadian militia, nonetheless persisted in warning that Canadian ports were "practically defenceless," and a seaborne component was essential to Canadian coast defence. He proposed a naval reserve for defending Canada only and "not for adding to the naval strength and supremacy of the empire beyond the purposes contemplated in the Colonial Naval Defence Act."[19] Although the Canadian Cabinet was not ready to establish another marine militia, it was willing to accept delivery of a training ship when one was offered but only after being assured that acceptance did not imply an obligation to form a naval reserve.[20]

Rather than encouraging the development of a Canadian navy, however, the experience with the training ship, HMS *Charybdis*, proved an embarrassment. Captain F.A. Scott, RN, was hired by the Department of Marine and Fisheries to bring the twenty-one year old screw corvette across the Atlantic from England. After she was officially accepted in December 1880, however, further examination revealed that her boilers were practically worn out and Scott recommended that repairs be made before departing for Canada the following June. Moreover, when the warship arrived in Saint John, New Brunswick, it soon became clear that further expensive repairs were needed to prepare her for training purposes. The public's attitude to the vessel was not improved when she broke loose in a storm and damaged other ships in the harbour. On another occasion two visitors drowned when the rotting gangplank collapsed. With the Canadian government receiving angry criticism at having

---

17. Sarty, "Silent Sentry," 54; Tennyson and Sarty, *Guardian of the Gulf*, 97; Gough, *The Royal Navy and the Northwest Coast*, 230; Lovatt, *Esquimalt*, 58–61, 77, 118; F.V. Longstaff, *Esquimalt Naval Base: A History of Its Work and Defences* (Vancouver 1942), 44; and Preston, *Imperial Defense*, 124.

18. Alice B. Stewart, "Sir John A. Macdonald and the Imperial Defence Commission of 1879," *Canadian Historical Review*, XXV, June 1954, 129–35.

19. 1879 militia report quoted in Preston, *Canada and "Imperial Defense,"* 120.

20. Sarty, "Origins of the RCN," 79–80; Melville, "Canada and Sea Power," 187–89; Lorne to Macdonald, 6 October 1880, Library and Archives Canada (hereafter LAC), Manuscript Group (MG) 27 IB4.

already spent $20–30,000 on repairs for a seemingly worthless vessel, it was decided to tow the ship to Halifax in August 1882 and return her to the Royal Navy. For many years afterward, the *Charybdis* farce was cited by critics as a warning against any effort to develop a Canadian navy.[21]

Within fifteen years of confederation the government of Canada had become responsible for a large geographical area with three long coasts. It had also made significant progress in implementing a national policy of encouraging east-west trade by increasing tariffs on imports from the United States (to force the development of manufacturing north of the border) and by completing a transcontinental railway. The latter played a central role in linking together parts of the new dominion, especially the Northwest Territories acquired from the Hudson's Bay Company in 1870. Britain also transferred jurisdiction over the Arctic islands to Canada in 1880, and from 1884 to 1886 the Department of Marine and Fisheries sent ships yearly to explore the region, seeking alternative routes for trade and navigation. By the 1880s Canada's waters were well charted, thanks in the main to the hydrographical work of both the Hudson's Bay Company and the Royal Navy. After the United States gave notice, in July 1884 (to take effect a year later), that it would abrogate the fisheries agreement in the 1871 Treaty of Washington, the Department of Marine and Fisheries once again organized a fisheries protection force, reconfirming that it would take steps, as it had with the Marine Police in 1870, to patrol its inshore waters.[22] Ottawa's attention to maritime matters, however, was soon diverted to the western plains when Louis Riel and his followers took up arms against the federal government.

Besides consolidating Ottawa's authority and bringing a more secure environment within which Macdonald's—and later Sir Wilfrid Laurier's—government could proceed with developing the nation's infrastructure, the 1880s were also characterized by a more formal approach to the previously ad hoc colonial–imperial defence relationship. The transformation of military relations between Britain and its self-governing colonies during the late nineteenth century was in no sense an orderly progression, but a groping amid uncertainties and constantly shifting circumstances. Revolutionary changes in naval technology profoundly unsettled maritime strategy, while the expanding fleets of competing naval powers eroded the Royal Navy's supremacy—at least in theory. Increasingly, the British government pressed the self-governing colonies for assistance in maintaining imperial naval strength with schemes that varied, often erratically from a colonial perspective, according

21. Melville, "Canada and Sea Power," 166–96, 236; Hadley, *Tin-pots and Pirate Ships*, 6; *Canadian Shipping and Marine Engineering News*, March 1960, 83, 122, copy in DHH, 81/520/8000, vol. 114, file 28; Sarty, "Silent Sentry," 53–82; Chambers, *The Canadian Marine*, 84; editorial, *Halifax Morning Chronicle*, 6 September 1881; editorial, *Halifax Morning Chronicle*, 2 August 1881; Melville, "Canada and Sea Power," 194–95; Desmond Morton, *A Military History of Canada: From Champlain to Kosovo* (Toronto 1999, first published 1985), 125.

22. J.L. Granatstein and Norman Hillmer, *For Better or For Worse: Canada and the United States to the 1990s* (Toronto 1991), 16–18; Appleton, *Usque Ad Mare*, 68, 91, 189, 302–42; Canada, Parliament, *Sessional Papers*, 1867–68, no. 19, 2, 19; Canada, Parliament, *Sessional Papers*, 1870, no. 12, 1–7; William Glover, "The Challenge of Navigation to Hydrography on the British Columbia Coast, 1850–1930," *The Northern Mariner*, VI, no. 4, 1996, 1–16; Hadley and Sarty, *Tin Pots*, 7–8; Melville, *Canada and Sea Power*, 196–99; Chambers, *The Canadian Marine*, 65, 71–85; and Sarty, "Origins of the RCN," 81.

HMS *Charybdis* undergoing repairs in the cofferdam at Esquimalt in 1870. Ten years later, the obsolete screw corvette would prove an embarrassment when it was acquired by the Canadian government. (LAC PA-124061)

to the state of international affairs and the dictates of new technology. Proposals for closer imperial co-operation, however, were extremely divisive within Canada because of polarization of attitudes toward Britain—largely on linguistic lines but also regionally. Although Canada's particular, local needs for maritime forces were modest, discussion of those requirements was invariably subsumed in the contentious imperial defence question.

As the largest of the self-governing dominions (and, for the period under consideration, the only one), Canada occupied a unique place in the structure of the British Empire. At once autonomous but not fully independent, the Canadian prime minister and his various government departments in Ottawa bore the weight of responsibility for internal matters, while London exercised it for external affairs, variously through the Foreign Office, the War Office, and the Admiralty, with the governor general and Colonial Office serving as conduits for the transmission of decisions and opinions between the two governments. The interaction of the various agencies set both the context for, and the specifics of, Canadian military and naval development. Perhaps not unnaturally, each came at the issue from a different perspective.

It is tempting to dismiss the lack of action by Canadian governments in matters of defence as evidence of their insularity and lack of confidence in the full potential of the nation. It is also easy to forget that, before the creation of mass bureaucracies, the problems of the day frequently enjoyed the personal attention of ministers and their highest officials. Set against the precarious state of the Canadian economy following the crash of 1873 and the structure of the British Empire itself, Ottawa's apparent inaction reflected the limited choices available to it. Economically, the last decades of the nineteenth century witnessed frequent cycles of depression interrupted by short spells of recovery and even "boom" times. Canadian governments attempted various stabilizing remedies, but a United States preoccupied with post–Civil War reconstruction could not be enticed to renegotiate reciprocity, while the general inclination of British governments for free trade precluded the establishment of preferential tariffs within the empire. As such, Macdonald settled upon a policy of tariff protection for central Canadian manufacturers—known as the National Policy—and then gradually broadened its scope to include western settlement, completion of the Canadian Pacific Railway, harbour development, and subsidies for fast steamship service to Europe and Asia to facilitate the export of Canadian products.[23] Since only the last of these elements had an outward dimension, concentration on internal development was a natural consequence. That little in the way of defence spending featured in this policy was of little or no concern to Ottawa.

The re-election of Conservative governments, even as these remained cautious in their approach to economic issues, speaks to the general success of the policy and underlying voter confidence. That confidence also explains in part the unique Canadian response to imperialism. The last "great age" of colonial expansion by European powers (soon to be joined by the United States and Japan) was only just beginning in the 1880s. Whereas the Great Powers sought colonies for a variety of commercial, military, and religious reasons,

---

23. Robert Craig Brown, "National Policy," *The Canadian Encyclopedia* (Toronto 1999), 1570.

in Canada, which had inherited a vast, undeveloped northwest territory, a mixture of "Christian idealism and anti-Americanism" found expression in calls for the nation to develop beyond colonial status by exercising a greater part in imperial decision-making.[24] The most active advocates were the members of the Imperial Federation League, founded in 1884 and centred mostly in Toronto. But their goal sprang from the fact that, beyond the symbolism of the British crown, there was no formal mechanism of government linking the British Empire together.

There was thus no one institution defining the nature of the military effort required to defend the British Empire. Although a profusion of naval technical developments allowed the War Office to argue that the Admiralty could no longer guarantee the insularity of the British Isles, the Royal Navy remained the predominant service, and, in the minds of their lordships, there was never any doubt as to their ability to guarantee that security. Indeed, between 1865 and 1890, there was no real threat to British naval supremacy from any combination of rivals; instead, the occasional alarmist Admiralty memorandum describing such threats was invariably a response to army attacks on the navy's role. British naval development through the 1860s and 1870s included short-range vessels with large-calibre turreted armament and requests for funding of these coastal monitors were presented in the annual estimates as a defensive measure. Home defence policy was founded upon the aggressive strategic assumption that any threat of invasion by continental powers could be overcome by reducing those navies in their fortified ports (known as the Cherbourg strategy, after the French port that was its principal geographic focus). In reaction, each of Britain's potential rivals—France, Russia, and the United States—implicitly acknowledged that they could not compete with the Royal Navy in building battle fleets of their own, and invested instead in strengthened systems of coastal fortifications for protection against British attack.[25]

Moreover, imperial defence was not a formal "system." Since there was no real threat to the empire after the conclusion of the Napoleonic wars, there never existed any overarching plan for its defence. British strategy in the event of war, such as it was, remained unchanged from that of the previous two centuries: the Royal Navy would ensure the security of the home islands and the protection of global trade, while the army mobilized and the navy expanded to go on the offensive.[26] The details of that strategy, however, were always in flux and open to interpretation. Indeed, it was one particular element of new technology that added an important complicating factor to the equation in the last half of the nineteenth century: the shift from wind to steam had necessitated the establishment of a worldwide chain of coal depots that in turn required defending. More than anything else, the British military planning process came to be driven by the need to bring some

---

24. D.R. Owram, "Imperialism," *The Canadian Encyclopedia*, 1144.

25. Andrew D. Lambert, "The Royal Navy, 1856–1914: Deterrence and the Strategy of World Power," Keith Neilson and Elizabeth Jane Errington, eds., *Navies and Global Defence: Theories and Strategy* (Westport, CT 1995), 73, 79–81; Sarty, "Silent Sentry," 3–5, 9–10; and E.R. Lewis, *Seacoast Fortifications of the United States: An Introductory History* (Washington, DC 1970), 37–89.

26. Lambert, "The Royal Navy, 1856–1914," 83–85.

coherence to the general protection of these overseas bases—and the increasing number of colonies that grew up around them. This ostensibly simple dictum was first described by Captain John Colomb of the Royal Marine Artillery in a pamphlet published in 1867, but its import was not fully appreciated until the Carnarvon Commission of 1879–82 collected evidence and deliberated upon "the condition and sufficiency of the means of the naval and military forces provided for the defence of the more important sea-ports within our colonial possessions and dependencies."[27] Its three reports mirrored Colomb's earlier theoretical work in describing progressive groupings of fortresses, stations, and other defence sites. In the case of Canada, these included Halifax in the fortress category as the main port (along with Bermuda) of the Royal Navy's North America and West Indies Squadron. Quebec City and Kingston already had citadel and fort status respectively, but there were conflicting views on Esquimalt. The majority of the commission held that the northeast Pacific backwater's distance from Britain, compounded by the proximity of the United States, made it indefensible against an American attack, and indeed that a more practical Pacific station headquarters would be Hong Kong. Allowance for a coast defence artillery battery was made only after Canadian insistence.[28] But British ministries remained philosophically disinclined to the whole notion of imperial defence and never allotted more than a fraction of the recommended funding. Moreover, although a Colonial Defence Committee was established in 1885, attempts at coordination proved to be little more than false starts until the establishment of the Committee of Imperial Defence (CID) in 1904.[29]

It should also be noted that imperial defence was not "imperial" until after 1885. Before that time, defence of the far-flung coaling stations was accepted as a local problem, well within the capacity of small army garrisons acting in combination with irregular colonial forces where appropriate. Local semi-autonomous forces were to the advantage of all parties: they put the financial and materiel burden of defence on the colonies, while providing an outlet for their growing self-sufficiency; they gave the War Office an opportunity to expand its role in colonial administration; and they allowed the Royal Navy to maintain its operational focus on Europe. Indeed, the Admiralty never took seriously earlier cruiser scares (usually Russian but sometimes French) because the purported threat was empty: the state of technology did not allow any nation—not even Britain—to combine sufficient effective armament in a single hull with the necessary operating range. That changed in the mid-1880s. The introduction of reliable propulsion (in the form of high-pressure water-tube boilers and triple-expansion engines) and nickel-steel armour (lighter weight for the material

---

27. Captain J.C.R. Colomb, "The Protection of our Commerce and the Distribution of our War Forces Considered," described in Schurman, *Imperial Defence*, 26–29, 83–125; Donald Schurman, *The Education of a Navy: The Development of British Naval Strategic Thought, 1867–1914* (Chicago 1965), 16–35; and John Beeler, "Steam, Strategy and Schurman: Imperial Defence in the Post-Crimean Era, 1856–1905," Greg Kennedy and Keith Neilson, eds., *Far Flung Lines: Studies in Imperial Defence in Honour of Donald Mackenzie Schurman* (London 1996), 36–38.

28. Schurman, *Imperial Defence*, 109–15, 159–68.

29. The standard text is Franklyn Arthur Johnson, *Defence by Committee: The British Committee of Imperial Defence, 1885–1959* (London 1960).

strength than previous alloys, allowing for higher freeboard and hence seaworthiness) finally made viable the creation of big-gun steam navies capable of operating on the high seas. Suddenly, the theoretical problem of enemy cruisers raiding isolated colonial outposts became the practical challenge of defending the sea lanes of the empire against hostile forces. But the same technology that enabled a credible threat to develop also increased the capacity of the Royal Navy to seek and destroy enemy battle fleets on the broad oceans—and the Admiralty concluded that the most efficient method to command such action on a global scale was to station powerful squadrons at strategic points abroad, organized as one imperial fleet with an increasing impetus toward central control by telegraph from London.[30]

The culmination of these developments came with Westminster's passage of the Naval Defence Act in March 1889. Famous for its declaration of the "Two Power Standard," in reality this was little more than public acknowledgement of a long-held British strategic principle: that the Royal Navy's establishment of first-class battleships "should be on such a scale that it should at least be equal to the naval strength of any two other countries ... it being understood that Britain required a substantial numerical superiority in cruisers for the defence of her extended lines of maritime supply." Where the 1889 legislation departed from precedent was in asserting that the standard be measured in terms of warships "of the newest type and most approved design."[31] Of the new vessels authorized for construction, the ten battleships—which included seven Royal Sovereign–class warships, the first of designer William White's high-freeboard battleships—would be allotted between the Home and Mediterranean Fleets, but a fair proportion of the forty-two cruisers of the new "protected" design would be dispersed among the formerly loose collection of foreign stations, which the Admiralty had already begun to consolidate with the establishment of the Australia and China squadrons in 1859 and 1864 respectively.[32]

The two Canadian stations offered interesting contrasts. The importance of the North America and West Indies Squadron, long based in Halifax, was reflected in its allocation of a force of modern types almost as soon as they became available. The Pacific station, on the other hand, lacked a credible threat (the Russian fleet was based primarily in European waters and Britain was always loath to include the United States in a list of potential enemies) and continued to warrant mostly hybrid sail-steam types well into the 1900s, with the exception only of the station commander's flagship.[33] Indeed, in many ways the British

---

30. Beeler, "Steam, Strategy and Schurman," 41–42; Jon Tetsuro Sumida, *In Defence of Naval Supremacy: Finance, Technology, and the British Naval Policy, 1889–1914* (Boston 1989), 12; Paul M. Kennedy, "Imperial Cable Communications and Strategy, 1870–1914," in Paul M. Kennedy, ed., *The War Plans of the Great Powers, 1880–1914* (London 1979).

31. Parliamentary debates quoted in Sumida, *In Defence of Naval Supremacy*, 14.

32. The largest single class of protected cruisers authorized under the 1889 plan was the twenty-one-ship Apollo class of 3,400 tons, armed with two 6-inch, six 4.7-inch, and eight 6-pounders. The class included HMS *Rainbow* commissioned 1893.

33. It is difficult to find information on the establishment of the various stations and fleet distribution in general, other than in *The Navy Lists* (promulgated semi-annually by the Admiralty). There is some good information in Barry Gough, *Northwest Coast of North America*, appx A. On the shifting boundaries of the RN's NA&WI and Pacific Stations, see the Admiralty Library holdings of RN station records.

Columbia coast more closely resembled other remote parts of the empire, where the irregular availability of coal saw the stationing of gunboats and iron-clad cruisers fitted with sails and masts long after these were relinquished elsewhere for battleships and protected cruisers.[34]

The authorized expenditure under the Naval Defence Act of 1889 was £21,500,000—a staggering amount, but not unreasonable considering the number of ships involved. As one observer has noted, the greater dimensions allowed by iron-steel construction and the coincident improvements in propulsion, protection and armament had led "to enormous growth in the cost of building a warship." The increasing technical complexity of the ships also placed an additional burden on the naval budget, in that they "could only be run efficiently with experienced crews that contained many technical specialists."[35] The need for increasingly complex training forced the Royal Navy to adopt a continuous-service professional body of seamen, with several significant consequences: not only did this give it a further qualitative advantage over the continental navies that continued to rely on conscription, but it also required peacetime manning levels to more closely reflect wartime requirements. This permanent regular force in turn required the establishment of a small naval reserve to make up the shortfall, little as it was, but this group too had to be well trained to be effective. The Royal Naval Reserve (RNR) was authorized in 1859 to a strength of 20,000, although the actual enrolment rarely approached that level in ensuing decades. However, as the shipbuilding programs detailed under the 1889 Naval Defence Act increased manning pressures on the Royal Navy, the need for an efficient naval reserve increased as well during the 1890s.[36]

Despite the overall increased costs of a modern navy, the result was not a severe financial problem for the British exchequer as innovative management and increasing prosperity in the last decades of the nineteenth century actually resulted in budgetary surpluses by the mid-1890s. From the British point of view, however, a sense of fairness suggested that the self-governing colonies, increasingly responsible for their own affairs, should contribute to the maintenance of the fleet from which all benefited. The growing public interest in naval matters was reflected in the establishment of such publications as Brassey's *Naval Annual* in 1886 and Jane's *All the World's Fighting Ships* in 1898 with the different options for the most efficient contribution figuring large in their discussions. While the Colonial Naval Defence Act of 1865 remained in effect, the rapid pace of technological change and the general sense that "the sea is one" increasingly argued against local naval forces, which were too costly for the colonies to maintain, and which should, were they to exist, be completely integrated with the regional RN station and available for general service where and as required. Suggestions for direct financial contributions seemed a more simple expedient, but raised grumbling of "no taxation without representation" reminiscent of the breakaway of the American colonies a century earlier. A more practical form of participation was

---

34. Richard Hill, *War at Sea in the Ironclad Age* (London 2000), 53.

35. Sumida, *In Defence of Naval Supremacy*, 8.

36. Ibiḍ, 12–18. See also Frank C. Bowen, *History of the Royal Naval Reserve* (London 1926).

the continued development of local defences and infrastructure at colonial expense. The raising of local branches of the RNR was frequently cited as something well within the budgetary and manpower capacity of many colonies.[37]

There was, therefore, a growing awareness by the latter 1880s—mostly in Britain, but also within colonial outposts—that imperial defence should be rationalized and the effort and expenditure (such as it was) somehow be better apportioned between Britain and the colonies. The emerging British view was that they no longer saw the colonies as burdens that should defend themselves, but as potential allies that could contribute to a central force. In most respects, the concept of greater planning and control from London, through the Admiralty and the War Office, was still understood to mean some undefined input from the colonies. Nowhere did these notions arouse great disagreement—most colonies welcomed the increased interest and participation of the home government—except in Canada, where the country was becoming accustomed to the exercise of its growing autonomy.

Indeed, if there was a "problem" in the overall concept of imperial defence, it was Canada's particular case—the only British overseas territory in direct proximity to a potentially hostile continental power. Not only did this immediate proximity increase the chances for war with another major power—the United States of America—but also the nature of the land frontier was such that the might of the Royal Navy could not be brought to bear over most of its length. That fact, plus the RN's greater concern with the restive European powers of France and Russia, led their lordships generally to agree with Canadian Prime Minister Macdonald's claim (made while providing evidence before the Carnarvon Commission in 1879) that "war with the United States was 'in the highest degree improbable,' and that, in any event the country was indefensible against a full-scale invasion from the south."[38] Still, the Admiralty and the War Office had no alternative but to continue to plan against the eventuality of an Anglo-American war, because Britain was ultimately responsible for the defence of Canada, and both agencies knew that defence rested upon the ability of the Royal Navy to deliver British regiments to reinforce the Canadian militia in the early stages of any conflict. But if there was general agreement between the British Army and the Royal Navy as to the ends, a number of factors reinforced their different perspectives as to means. The War Office, dealing with the concrete reality of territory to be defended and having direct contact through the British officer appointed the general officer commanding the Canadian militia, was largely preoccupied with the details of schemes for an active defence of the vital points of the Great Lakes, Montreal and Quebec. The focus of the British naval commanders of the North America and West Indies Station in Halifax and of the Pacific station in Esquimalt was directed outwards but this, together with their having no direct Canadian contacts, only reinforced the inclination of the Admiralty to view the problem in the abstract, best assured by general "command of

---

37. Sumida, *In Defence of Naval Supremacy*, 12ff.

38. Alice B. Stewart, "Sir John A. Macdonald and the Imperial Defence [*sic*—Carnarvon] Commission of 1879," *Canadian Historical Review*, XXV: 2 (June 1954), 122. (The commission was not identified as "imperial" at the time.) See also Sarty, "The RCN—The Australian Connection," 79–80; and Donald G. Creighton, *John A. Macdonald*, II: *The Old Chieftain, 1867–1891* (Toronto 1955), 295–96.

the seas," and to down-play concerns for local point defence as either army matters or parochial distractions.[39]

Canadians, having essentially been left to their own devices for the previous two decades following the withdrawal of the inland British garrisons in the 1860s and 1870s, might be excused for not grasping the changing circumstances of the 1880s. In this respect, British suggestions beginning in the latter half of the decade that the colonies should make monetary contributions to the establishment and upkeep of forces they might never see were especially difficult to fathom. At the same time, Macdonald's oft-repeated claim that there were few sources of tension between Canada and the US not of British origin—and therefore not requiring a large Canadian contribution to imperial defence—was true in many respects (and certainly so for those disagreements for which Britain might actually resort to armed conflict) but somewhat disingenuous in others. The fact that reciprocity could not be renegotiated indicated that there remained any number of unresolved bilateral trade issues across the North American border, and the large expanses of relatively unpopulated western prairie continued to excite expansionist American ambitions of Manifest Destiny. The National Policy offered mixed results to the resolution of those problems, in populating the west even while further isolating the Canadian economy. But two of the most contentious Canada–US issues were largely maritime in nature: the United States continued to lay claim to those arctic expanses not contiguous to the Hudson basin (especially the archipelago), and therefore technically outside of the Rupert's Land transfer to Canada; and the American decision to abrogate the fisheries convention of the Washington Treaty signalled the renewal of various off-shore resource issues on both coasts.[40]

The Macdonald government was aware of the consequences of the American decision to abrogate the convention, but had to add it to a list of priorities that became ever more intimidating. The country was in the midst of an economic depression that had begun over a decade before and showed signs of deepening rather than lifting. The Canadian Pacific Railway, which along with other such ventures had been front and centre in Canadian policy making since confederation, was once again on the verge of collapse as a company. The 1885 rebellion in the Northwest Territories also served to focus minds on military rather than naval matters during the decade. Combined with the ongoing tug of war between the federal government and the provinces, it was obviously not a propitious time for naval issues to figure prominently on the national agenda.[41]

Even as Ottawa's attention was directed to the West, the old marine economy of Atlantic Canada was gradually withering. Based as it was upon fishing, boat-building and the shipping trade, it declined as local merchants and industries put their faith on capturing a national market even though their enterprises tended to be smaller and less efficient than

39. Roger Sarty, "Canada and the Great Rapprochement, 1902–1914," B.J.C. McKercher and Lawrence Aronsen, eds., *The North Atlantic Triangle in a Changing World: Anglo-American-Canadian Relations, 1902–1956* (Toronto 1996), 13–15; and Morton, *A Military History of Canada*, 80–93.

40. See Morris Zaslow, *The Opening of the Canadian North, 1870–1914* (Toronto 1971) and Robert Craig Brown, *Canada's National Policy, 1883–1900: A Study in Canadian-American Relations* (Princeton 1964).

41. Donald Creighton, *John A. Macdonald*, II, 402, 405, 411.

those in central Canada. By the mid-1880s only one pillar remained—the fishery—and even it was coming under stress. If the Washington Treaty had ended an old set of fishery questions, a new set had now arisen. When the US government gave the required one-year notice to terminate the treaty's fisheries articles in July 1884, it was driven as much by New Englanders' continuing resentment of "unfair" Canadian competition under fisheries reciprocity, as by the fact that the saltwater fish stocks had dwindled to the point where "there were now fewer Canadian fish within the three-mile limit, and less American need of them for food or bait."[42] At the same time, Newfoundland's overtures toward reciprocity with the United States—instead of pursuing confederation with Canada—were devolving into a quasi-fish war.[43]

All these issues continued to fall under the purview of the Department of Marine and Fisheries, although its capacity to handle them had dwindled. The fisheries branch had declined in comparison to the marine branch following the supposed resolution of fisheries problems and the increasing number of departmental aids to marine navigation off both coasts and on the Great Lakes. Although the numbers of buoy tenders and ice-breakers had increased since 1871, due in part to the admission of the new provinces of British Columbia and Prince Edward Island, the Canadian fisheries patrol fleet had been reduced to a single sailing vessel, *La Canadienne*, for the entire Gulf and lower St Lawrence. She was replaced only in 1881 by a 154-foot iron-hulled, single-screw cruiser of the same name and, tellingly, had been built in a Scottish, rather than a Canadian, shipyard. If the actual requirement for patrol vessels had not increased, the need to demonstrate resolve in enforcement had and, as the department's 1886 annual report noted, "no other course was then left the Canadian government but to adopt measures for the protection of its rights."[44]

Accordingly, a formal Fisheries Protection Service (FPS) was established with the result that the departmental fleet "took on new life with modern armed vessels, and aggressive patrolling resumed."[45] Other reforms required to better manage the stressed Atlantic fish populations had already led the government to divide the Department of Marine and

---

42. Joseph Gough, *Fisheries Management in Canada, 1880–1910* (Ottawa 1991), 3–5; and Melville, "Canada and Sea Power," 198. The experience of one successful ship owner merchant, Sir Samuel Cunard, is pertinent. He had inaugurated regular transatlantic mail service by steamship for the British government in 1839, but was forced by stiff American competition to drop Halifax as a regular port of call in 1867, sending all Cunard liners thereafter direct to New York. Sir Samuel already had moved to England to supervise his shipping interests. See D.M.L. Farr, "Sir Samuel Cunard," *The Canadian Encyclopedia*, 609. For a general survey of the Maritime region economy, see Conrad and Hiller, *Atlantic Canada*, 135–60.

43. Kevin Major, *As Near to Heaven By Sea: A History of Newfoundland and Labrador* (Toronto 2001), 288.

44. Marine and Fisheries annual report quoted in Gough, *Fisheries Management in Canada*, 19; and Charles D. Maginley and Bernard Collin, *The Ships of Canada's Marine Services* (St Catharines 2001), 83–84. The sole vessel operated by the former colony of British Columbia, *Sir James Douglas*, was incorporated into the Marine fleet in 1871, but had not been concerned with fisheries duties, as there were no real issues beyond the capacity of the RN vessels on the Pacific station (at least initially). As for PEI, one of the articles of its joining Confederation in 1873 was the obligation of the dominion government to provide a winter communication service with the mainland, which could only be facilitated by icebreakers.

45. Joseph Gough, "Fisheries and Sovereignty in Canada: Some Historical Highlights," *Maritime Warfare Bulletin*, 2/92, 108.

Fisheries into two sections in 1884, each with its own deputy minister, and positioning it for a more rigorous application of the federal regulatory power. With the new fleet and organization came a new minister. George Eulas Foster was a New Brunswick lawyer recently recruited to federal politics by Macdonald for both his oratorical and organizational skills. It was an auspicious beginning for a man who would maintain a close interest in naval and military affairs —with more than one subsequent significant intervention—for the next four decades.

Although a civil institution with clearly limited responsibilities, the Fisheries Protection Service was given a quasi-naval organization and uniform, and invariably was commanded by retired Royal Navy officers.[46] By convention, all ships of the department flew the blue ensign with the Canadian coat of arms in the fly, but the fisheries cruisers were granted the additional distinction, under special warrant from the Admiralty, "of wearing the 'whiplash' [commissioning] pennant which is the distinguishing mark of a man-of-war." The visual similarity to an established naval force was further blurred by the types of vessels that came to comprise the fleet. The Canadian Government Ship (CGS) *Pelican*, for example, was a former Royal Navy composite sloop (that is, masted but with steam assist, built in 1877), while CG Ships *Petrel* and *Curlew*, employed respectively on the Great Lakes and the East Coast, and their sister, *Constance*, assigned to the Customs Preventive Service on the St Lawrence, were described as "screw ram-bowed gunboats,"[47] the ram having seen a resurgence in the late 19th century.

These latter vessels were acquired in 1892 by Foster's successor as minister, Charles Hibbert Tupper. A Nova Scotia lawyer, Tupper was anxious to make his name as a newly appointed Cabinet member and made enforcement of fishery regulations a high priority. A modus vivendi had already been reached in 1888, whereby American fishermen were granted commercial privileges in Canadian ports after purchasing a licence. At that time it seemed that the protection service—like the earlier Marine Police—might be disbanded, having served its immediate purpose, but the US Senate rejected the treaty. Tupper had little choice but to confirm the protection service as a permanent establishment and followed that decision up with the order for the cruisers *Petrel*, *Curlew*, and *Constance* after the Colonial Office refused, yet again, to sanction a Canadian request for assistance from Royal Navy ships on the Atlantic coast in redressing any lapses by the Americans.[48]

Generally, however, New Englanders lived within the spirit of the agreement, and the department's concerns were shifting to the freshwater fishery on the upper Great Lakes. In 1891, Tupper commissioned a special investigation into "the decline in the size and vigor

46. Little is known of the RN service of the three "captains" of the Canadian Marine (and later Fisheries) fleet, other than that it had varied considerably (as did, by anecdotal accounts, their competence): P.A. Scott, who commanded the fleet from its establishment in 1869 through 1887, had retired as a post captain; Andrew R. Gordon (1891 to 1893, "acting" since 1887) had retired as a lieutenant; and Osprey George Valentine Spain (1893 to 1908) as a sub-lieutenant. For fuller general biographical information see Melville, "Canada and Sea Power," *passim*.

47. Colin Campbell, "Fisheries Protection and Marine Service of Canada," *Canadian Almanac and Miscellaneous Directory, 1895* (Toronto 1894), 228.

48. Margaret Beattie Bogue, *Fishing the Great Lakes: an Environmental History, 1783–1933* (Madison, WI 2000), 216; Peter B. Waite, *Canada, 1874–1896: Arduous Destiny* (Toronto 1971), 205; and Brown, *The National Policy*, 34–36.

of the Great Lakes fish population," and its findings pointed to a number of factors, including "illegal fishing during spawning seasons [and] destruction of small fish in seines and in both pound and gill nets"—most of it at the hands of American fishermen on Lake Erie and lower Lake Huron. Those waters, then, became the patrol ground of CGS *Petrel* upon her commissioning in time for the 1894 season, with special orders to crack down on American poaching.[49]

The many years of service put in by *Petrel* and the other fisheries protection vessels on the lakes and both coasts were, for the most part, routine and uneventful even as they established a visible Canadian presence by making a number of seizures. But her inaugural season on the Great Lakes was to prove one of the most notorious of any fisheries patrol for another full century, indeed, until the dispute over turbot fishing with Spain in 1995. Already fitted with a 12-pounder gun as allowed under the terms of the Rush-Bagot Agreement, *Petrel*'s crew were also "furnished … with ten Spencer rifles, ten Colt revolvers, and ten cutlasses considered essential in the war on poachers." On 8 May 1894, the Canadian ship came upon a small fleet of American sportsmen fishing in the popular vicinity of Pelee Island. In what subsequently was sensationalized as the "Battle of Lake Erie," her captain, Edward Dunn, "an experienced Georgian Bay mariner and dedicated officer," quickly determined that they were fishing without licences, arrested some fifty of them and impounded their yachts. Although the image of a "cruiser armed with cannon sent to arrest sportfishermen in rowboats" was lampooned by the American press, the circumstances of the incident were indisputable. The US Department of State chose not to protest the incident and Tupper was satisfied that the seizure had made its point.[50] More important to this study, the Fisheries Protection Service had proven its worth.

The establishment of the protection service also provoked a discussion of the problem of defending Canada's coastline. Although the absence of comprehensive departmental files makes it difficult to distinguish cause and effect, the Department of Militia and Defence seems to have had almost as great an interest in the establishment and composition of the protection service as did its parent, the Department of Marine and Fisheries. The militia had always harboured an appreciation of the importance of naval control of the Great Lakes against American invasion (although this does not appear to have been formally recorded as a responsibility, at the time, of the Department of Militia and Defence). In the fall of 1884, however, a senior clerk in the militia minister's office was one of the first officials to recognize a connection between the continuing need for seaward Canadian naval defence and an opportunity for a practical solution to the American abrogation of the Fisheries Convention.[51]

Of course Minister of Militia and Defence Adolphe Caron remembered *Charybdis* only too well and the new British general officer commanding the militia, Sir Frederick Middleton, was not eager to repeat Selby-Smyth's misadventure either, but otherwise the

---

49. Bogue, *Fishing the Great Lakes*, 219–20.

50. Ibid, 230–33, 267–78; and Margaret Beattie Bogue, "The Canadian-American Contest for the Great Lakes Fish Harvest, 1872–1914," *The Northern Mariner*, XI: 3 (July 2001), 1–22.

51. Colin Campbell, "Armed Boat Service, and Torpedo Service, for Defence of the Coasts of Canada," 23 October 1884, LAC, Record Group (hereafter RG) 9, IIA1, vol. 605.

dynamics were very different. The clerk in question was Colin Campbell. A native Nova Scotian from an ardently pro-Conservative family, Campbell had served for nine years as a paymaster in the Royal Navy before joining the militia department in 1871 as a junior clerk and eventual promotion to the minister's office in 1882. Although not involved in the earlier fiasco, he was left to sort out its records. Unlike any of the protagonists, he understood Selby-Smyth's initial intentions and developed his own ideas as to where the scheme had gone wrong. An old shipmate of his was then serving as secretary to Vice-Admiral J.E. Commerell, the commander-in-chief (C-in-C) of the North America and West Indies Station, and upon being passed an unofficial outline of Campbell's plan, Commerell commended it to Governor General, the Marquess of Lansdowne, where it came to the attention of Lansdowne's military secretary, Lord Melgund (who later, as the Earl of Minto, himself a governor general, showed a continuing interest in naval projects). The ultimate result was the establishment in December 1884 of a "Commission on the Naval and Coast Defence of the Dominion," better known as the Defence Commission of 1885 (and occasionally as the Melgund Commission). Its members comprised Caron, Middleton, Deputy Minister C.E. Panet, and Lord Melgund, with Campbell as secretary.[52]

The commission met formally only once, where, as one study has remarked, the "enthusiasm [of Campbell and Melgund] compensat[ed] somewhat for the disinterest of their colleagues."[53] Campbell had sensed the opportunity to establish an effective naval reserve as "the nucleus of an efficient system of coast defence" virtually from the moment Washington signalled its intent in 1884 to abrogate the fisheries treaty, noting that "a force for patrolling the fisheries could readily be made more capable of more general naval duties." His plan was purposefully simple, and by extension inexpensive, both to avoid repetition of the *Charybdis* experience and to encourage the support of prudent Canadian politicians. Campbell seems to have appreciated that a permanent fisheries service was not really required for enforcement purposes. He considered it of secondary importance to the country's neglected coast defences. He proposed instead that "a marine militia ... trained to aid in the defence of Canada's coasts and fisheries" should be constituted under the aegis of the militia department. It would be manned by fishermen to whom the government already paid an annual bounty totaling $150,000. Under Campbell's scheme, in order to collect their bounty, the men would be required to enrol in the militia with some of their better boats being selected to mount small naval guns. Some of the naval militiamen would be trained to operate torpedo defences at Canadian ports.[54]

---

52. Melville, "Canada and Sea Power," 166–96, 236. Although the *Charybdis* had been acquired on the recommendation of Selby-Smyth, she was operated by Marine and Fisheries under the supervision of Captain Scott. Selby Smyth's intent had been for the ship to act as a training vessel for a Canadian naval reserve that in turn would man Canadian armed merchant cruisers. Luard, the incoming GOC, had not been directly involved with the ship, and according to Colin Campbell the lack of militia involvement had been part of the problem. See Melville, "Canada and Sea Power," 196–98, for a biographical sketch of Campbell.

53. Melville, "Canada and Sea Power," 218. The only other mention of the Defence Commission of 1885 is in Morton, *Ministers and Generals*, 72–73, which is generally dismissive of its efforts.

54. Colin Campbell, "Armed Boat Service, and Torpedo Service, for Defence of the Coasts of Canada," 23 October 1884, LAC, RG 9, IIA1, vol. 605.

Melgund, for his part, brought his broader military experience to bear.[55] He recommended that the commission should begin by setting out general guidelines, leaving the details to "professional experts." He envisioned initial investigations of seven specific areas. Not only did his list draw upon the earlier proposals by Selby-Smyth (from which it obviously was developed), but it also demonstrated both his grasp of the scope of the project and a sensitivity to the need to tie it all to the development of national infrastructure: utilization of the seafaring population; establishment of a torpedo force; possible conversion of steamers to cruisers; establishment of naval training vessels, perhaps on both coasts; formation of a railway corps for rapid deployment to danger points; establishment of complete telegraphic communications on the coasts; and, investigation and development of lateral communications and transportation along the coasts. Although somewhat expanded from Campbell's proposal, Melgund agreed that an important aspect of the investigations would be cost, with emphasis being placed on the Australian example.[56]

While Middleton remained uninterested, having come to North America seeking "a pleasant and undemanding means to a generalcy and because it would please his Canadian wife"[57]—Campbell described him as "obstructionist"—at least Caron did not attempt to dissuade the investigations. As a result, Campbell had to find additional support from some surprising quarters. An unexpected ally was Minister of Finance Sir Leonard Tilley. A father of Confederation and lieutenant-governor of New Brunswick at the time of the cruiser scare that had led to the acquisition of *Charybdis*, Tilley saw in Campbell's proposal a direct analogy to the New Brunswick Fencibles, a pre-Confederation marine militia. As one of the architects of the National Policy, he "was pessimistic about finding any additional funds for a substantial expansion of Canada's defence establishment," but admitted that "the expenses of improved defence would have to be met at some point," and was intrigued that the plan "was designed to make better use of existing expenditures than create a new one."[58] For very different reasons, Deputy Minister Panet came alive to other possibilities. Campbell's scheme suggested that the "creation of a naval militia with separate naval instructors might lead to a separate naval commander independent of the G[eneral] O[fficer] C[ommanding]."[59] Since assuming the position of deputy minister in 1875, Panet had regularly been at loggerheads with British officers over bureaucratic issues. Now he came to appreciate that the "division of the military branch of Militia and Defence under two rival commanders would enhance [his] position as head of the civilian branch."[60]

---

55. Melgund held a commission in the Scots Guards and had served in the Afghan campaign of 1879 and Egyptian campaign of 1882. After arriving in Canada in 1883, he had helped to organize the Nile Voyageurs expedition, in which the Department of Militia and Defence was not directly implicated.

56. Melgund to Campbell, 17 January 1885, quoted in Melville, "Canada and Sea Power," 207.

57. Ibid, 207.

58. Campbell to Melgund, 26 February 1885, quoted in ibid, 208.

59. Campbell to Melgund, 24 February 1885, Minto Papers, LAC, MG 27 IIB1.

60. Melville, "Canada and Sea Power," 208. On the relations between the deputy minister and the GOC, see Morton, *Ministers and Generals*, 20–21, 58.

When Campbell discovered a petition from a group of fishermen and seamen at Île Verte, Quebec, who wished to form a naval company, Panet supported his fellow Québécois.[61]

With the support of Melgund, Tilley, and Panet, by March 1885 Campbell seemed to have built a sufficiently broad base covering a range of government levels to overcome Middleton's indifference. Other events, however, conspired to scupper his naval militia plan. Louis Riel's proclamation of a provisional government in the Northwest Territories immediately diverted whatever interest there might have been for abstract issues of coast defence to the concrete problems of mobilizing the militia for an overland expedition. The Northwest Campaign was over by July, but by then the momentum for a naval militia had been lost, and not just because Melgund had returned to England. The government estimates published that March had included allowance for the Department of Marine and Fisheries to establish a protection force under its own authority, effectively destroying the underpinning of Campbell's plan. The militia clerk had already deduced that any future Canadian naval effort would be tied to a fisheries force, but where others saw the logic of placing the protection service under the Department of Marine and Fisheries, Campbell only saw the danger of breaking Militia and Defence's exclusive control of defence matters.[62] Indeed, the previous experience of *Charybdis* while under Marine and Fisheries control argued against that department's ability to manage a proper naval force.

The coincident timing of the Riel rebellion with the latest in a series of Russian naval scares—the most recent resulting from Russia's border incursions into Bulgaria and Afghanistan—drew attention to the British responsibility for the coast defence of Canada. The initial setbacks suffered by Middleton and the Northwest Field Force had led the governor general to observe that he "would have preferred a much smaller force of regulars if we could have had them." [63] But with the British Army concentrating its efforts on another northwest frontier—the one in India—and itself facing a manpower shortage, the Halifax garrison had been reduced to a single battalion, too thin to allow the despatch of regulars to the Canadian northwest as in 1870. On the opposite coast, where the Royal Navy had always questioned the value of Esquimalt as a naval base, the now-proven strategic value of the Canadian Pacific Railway (CPR) demanded an active defence of its western terminus. Indeed, this served to reinforce the status of Esquimalt as a naval base because of its forward location, instead of Burrard Inlet (as Vancouver was then still known). From the perspective of the War Office, "[t]he defence of the port of Esquimalt would to a great extent secure Burrard's [sic] Inlet and Nanaimo [site of an important colliery] against attack, thus rendering it unnecessary to fortify those places."[64] Additional coast artillery batteries were authorized for Esquimalt, with Canada finally committing a small permanent artillery garrison to supplement the British forces although, under the terms of the agreement, Ottawa paid no more than half the total cost. For Britain's part, recognizing that the ships on the

61. Campbell to Melgund, 20 March 1885, quoted in Melville, "Canada and Sea Power," 208.

62. Campbell to Panet, 2 April 1885, no. 15, 409–412, LAC, RG 9, IIA1, vol. 600.

63. Mackinnon, "Imperial Fortresses in Canada," 162–3.

64. War Office memorandum quoted in Sarty, "Silent Sentry," 60.

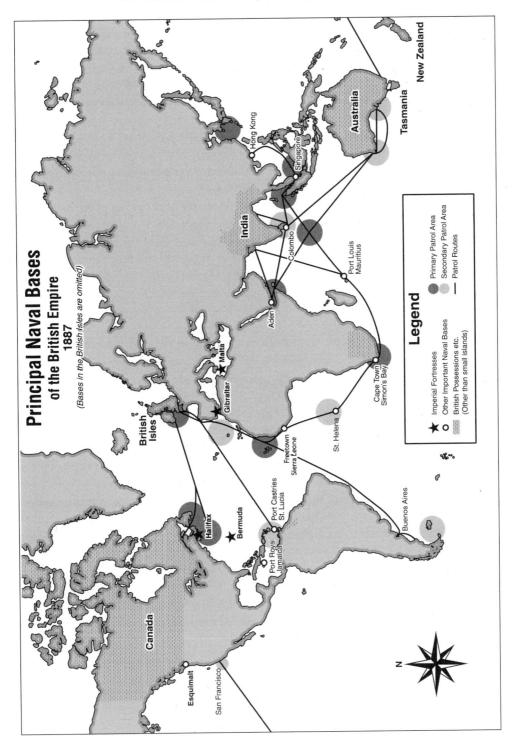

Principal Naval Bases
of the British Empire
1887
(Bases in the British Isles are omitted)

Legend

★ Imperial Fortresses
○ Other Important Naval Bases

British Possessions etc.
(Other than small islands)

● Primary Patrol Area
● Secondary Patrol Area
— Patrol Routes

New Zealand

Tasmania

Australia

Hong Kong

Singapore

India

Colombo

Port Louis
Mauritius

Aden

Malta

Gibraltar

British Isles

Cape Town
Simon's Bay

Freetown
Sierra Leone

St. Helena

Buenos Aires

Port Castries
St. Lucia

Halifax

Bermuda

Port Royal
Jamaica

Canada

Esquimalt

San Francisco

N

Pacific station were inadequate to meet a potential Russian hit-and-run attack—only a third-class cruiser was available at the time—the Admiralty purchased two Yarrow-built first-class torpedo boats, HM Ships *Swift* and *Sure*, from Chile. For their 6,000-mile journey, these were escorted from Valparaiso, where the RN still maintained a sub-station, to Esquimalt. Although little is recorded of their activities, they exercised from time to time until being placed in reserve in 1903.[65]

While the immediate effect of the Riel rebellion might have been to divert attention from Canadian naval development, the attending circumstances did bring some related issues into focus. The imminent completion of the transcontinental Canadian Pacific Railway was helping to meld the far-flung collection of British colonies into a coherent "empire," and the web of telegraph cables and steamship and rail lines that had spread across the globe from London created a growing sense of closeness, progress and confidence among all British subjects, whether they lived in Glasgow, Toronto, Bombay, or Hong Kong. Perversely, however, it also heightened the sense of isolation felt by colonists at the extremities of the empire who relied most upon those links. The Australasian colonies[66] and British Columbia—being the farthest removed from the home islands—were especially vulnerable in this respect, and it is no small point that the major centres in each were named "Victoria" as if to reinforce the connection. The Australian colony of Victoria had instigated the 1865 Colonial Naval Defence Act to enable it to operate a few naval vessels in co-operation with the Royal Navy, and Victoria, BC, had insisted upon the inclusion as an article of joining Canada in 1871 that Ottawa be required "to secure the continual maintenance of the naval station at Esquimalt."[67] Under this latter provision, the Admiralty had encouraged Canada to build a large graving dock in Esquimalt. Completed in 1887, HMS *Cormorant* was the first ship to enter for repairs on 20 July.

So it was that, as a further reaction to the Russian cruiser scare, the Admiralty commissioned a number of mercantile cruisers for the protection of trade in the Pacific.[68] This was the first instance of the Royal Navy actually taking up proper armed merchant cruisers and, although the success of peace negotiations with the Russians meant that none of these ships saw action, their potential utility should not be underestimated. The Admiralty's precautions were predicated upon the expected Russian employment of precisely this sort of merchant ship conversion. The plan to use British-flagged ships as a counter to them was more than credible, because the two sides would be fairly evenly matched, and any enemy operating in isolation and at extreme ranges would be wary of sustaining damage and easily scared off. To ensure that the ships to be so employed were immediately available, the Admiralty paid handsome subsidies to the steamship lines already engaged to carry mail.

---

65. Sarty, "Silent Sentry," 61–72; and Gough, *Northwest Coast of North America*, 230.

66. This was the contemporary term, used to encompass the disparate Australian colonies (they were not federated as the Commonwealth of Australia until 1901) and also New Zealand.

67. Preston, *Canada and "Imperial Defense,"* 132–33.

68. These comprised *Britannia* and *Coptic* on the Pacific station, *Lusitania* and *Massilia* on the Australia station, and *Pembroke Castle* on the China station. See Gough, *Northwest Coast of North America*, 230n.

The Cunard line, for example, had profited considerably in this respect, and such subsidies were a determining factor in the decision of the Canadian Pacific Railway in the fall of 1885 to propose "the establishment of a first-class line of steamships between the Pacific terminus of the railway and Japan and China…. The many advantages to imperial interests and the sense of security that would be created by a thoroughly efficient and purely British alternative route to the East," as opposed to that through the Mediterranean and Suez, which could be interrupted at several points, convinced the CPR's directors that the proposal would be accepted by the British government.[69] A tentative agreement was reached following the Colonial Conference held in London in 1887, although it was not concluded until July 1889. The initial contract, effective for ten years, was for an annual mail subsidy of £60,000, with the British government paying £45,000 and Canada £15,000. On this basis the CPR ordered three 6,000-ton vessels from the Naval Construction and Armaments Company of Barrow, Scotland (later to become Vickers Shipbuilding). The three "Empresses"— Empress of India, Empress of Japan and Empress of China—all made their maiden voyages in 1891. A condition in the contract called for gun platforms to be built on each ship, with Admiralty-supplied 4.7-inch guns being stored at Hong Kong and Vancouver for their quick conversion to armed merchant cruisers.[70]

This closely resembled the scheme proposed nearly a decade earlier by General Selby-Smyth, with certain important exceptions, most of which were developments intended to rectify the problems that had brought the earlier scheme to naught. The fact that the arrangement was between the British government and the CPR, and not directly involving Ottawa, removed one impediment. A problem remained, however, in obtaining trained supplementary crews for the armed merchant cruisers. This was a condition not unique to the Canadian vessels, and the additional seamen—mostly gunners—required to augment the regular merchant complements were intended primarily to come from the Royal Naval Reserve. Because the armed merchant cruisers were to be provided for the defence of the sea communications of the empire, many commentators saw the seafaring populations of the colonies as a possible source of manpower. This had been the basis of Selby-Smyth's plan and had recently been repeated by Lord Melgund in the development of Colin Campbell's scheme.

Melgund had also advised that Canada look to the Australian experience. Although the details of their situations were different, the Australian and Canadian naval experiences would inform each other throughout their subsequent histories, even without any coordinated intent to do so. In the first few years after the Colonial Naval Defence Act came into effect, the Australian colonies—like their Canadian cousins—did not take advantage of its provisions as quickly as might have been expected (only Victoria responded immediately, ordering the scaled-down monitor Cerberus). The Russian naval scares in the late 1870s that had inspired the Canadian acquisition of Charybdis also led New South Wales,

69. "CPR Directors' Report to the 1885 Annual General Meeting," quoted in George Musk, Canadian Pacific—The Story of a Famous Shipping Line (London 1989), 14.

70. Musk, Canadian Pacific, 17, 269.

Queensland, and South Australia to more resolute action. By the mid-1880s the disparate colonies were collectively operating some half-dozen warships, the largest being the screw-corvette *Wolverine* obtained by New South Wales in 1882. Otherwise, the vessels were small coastal craft of less than 1,000 tons displacement designed as mobile platforms for a comparatively large-bore breech-loading gun. New Zealand took a slightly different tack, having established a volunteer force for harbour patrol and ordering four spar torpedo boats that arrived in 1884. The 1865 act only allowed colonies to operate warships within the territorial three-mile limit, but that was precisely where they saw the need. *Cerberus*, for example, was intended to supplement the defence at the entrance to Port Phillip Bay (Melbourne), where the width of the strait was too wide to be covered by the existing coast artillery.[71] Indeed, in such "narrow seas" local defence problems were plausibly solved by this type of coastal craft.

For Canadian naval proponents, the circumstances were roughly similar to those extant in the approaches to Halifax and Saint John, or in the Gulf of St Lawrence and the Strait of Juan de Fuca. Moreover, such vessels were within the financial and manpower capacities of colonies to acquire, operate and maintain. They had to be built in Britain, however, and the need to sail them to their intended home brought the matter of their status into focus. When confronted with the need for a small flotilla of new Victorian warships to sail from England in 1884, the Admiralty decreed that colonial-owned vessels must fly the blue ensign with the colonial badge in the fly, as opposed to the naval white ensign preferred by the colony.[72]

The dynamic and respected Rear-Admiral George Tryon was despatched to take command of the Australia station specifically to negotiate "the organization of a special Australasian squadron that would be provided by the colonies and used for the defence of ports, but under Admiralty control."[73] The instruction included a provision that the concept, once proven, should be extended to other colonies, and especially to self-governing Canada.[74] Indeed, the reply of the Canadian governor general, the Marquess of Lansdowne, to Tryon's overture offered a distinct palliative to the earlier recommendation of Melgund: "It would ... be very inconvenient and dangerous to the stability of the empire, if progress [by the colonies] should lead to the creation of a number of independent colonial navies, under the control perhaps of hotheaded or ambitious colonial statesmen with a foreign policy of their own distinct from that of Downing St."[75]

Lansdowne followed the Australian negotiations closely, and "used every opportunity to

71. Richard Jackson, "New Zealand's Naval Defence," Bob Nicholls, "Colonial Naval Forces Before Federation," David Stevens and John Reeve, eds., *Southern Trident: Strategy, History and the Rise of Australian Naval Power* (Crows Nest, NSW 2000), 120–21, 128, 131–33.

72. Preston, *Canada and "Imperial Defense,"* 98.

73. Ibid, 98–99.

74. A. Cooper Key, "Naval Defence of Our Colonies," 28 October 1884, quoted in ibid, 98–99; and Admiral George Tryon, "Memorandum for the Governor-General of Canada," 27 August 1885, LAC, RG 7 G21, vol. 75, no. 165–4b.

75. Lansdowne to Tryon, 2 November 1885, LAC, MG 27 IB6, II, 296–300.

urge upon his own ministers action along a similar line."[76] Two years later the issue remained unresolved, prompting the colonial secretary to invite senior representatives from each of the self-governing colonies to attend "a conference for the discussion of certain mutual problems, especially that of defence."[77] Given the increasing anxiety over security in different quarters of the empire, it is likely that such a meeting would have been called eventually, but the immediate stimulus was agitation by the Imperial Federation League that the "happy occasion" of Queen Victoria's Golden Jubilee in April-May 1887 provided an ideal circumstance. Set against a backdrop of imperial fervour, it was the first opportunity extended to the self-governing colonies to shape the developing political structure of the empire.[78]

As such, the Canadian contribution was relatively inconsequential and reflected Ottawa's priorities. Neither Prime Minister Macdonald nor his most trusted representative, Minister of Finance Sir Charles Tupper, were able to attend when the conference's timing conflicted with the scheduled opening of a new session of parliament. Instead, Macdonald sent an old friend, Senator Sir Alexander Campbell, a former high commissioner to London, and Sandford Fleming, the surveyor of the Canadian Pacific Railway and a proponent of an intra-imperial system of cable communication who was still basking in his leading role in the adoption of world-wide standard time. Although each was distinguished, Macdonald was satisfied that "they were very unlikely to act with any great initiative or energy" on matters of substance, and indeed their contributions were little more than variations upon Macdonald's testimony to the Carnarvon Commission seven years earlier.[79] Campbell presented a "largely negative policy … in a speech longer than its content demanded,"[80] reminding the participants that Britain "maintains for imperial purposes, as for other purposes, the North American squadron, and so long as that squadron is at our doors, Canada does not need any other naval defence." For his part, Fleming described the strategic benefits of the Canadian Pacific Railway—built entirely at the expense of Canadian taxpayers and at no cost to Britain—that "practically brings what was once the most remote naval station [Esquimalt], in the most distant colony of the empire, within about two weeks of Portsmouth."[81] Emphasizing its usefulness as a postal, passenger, and telegraph route linking the United Kingdom (UK) and Australasia, he supported the CPR's bid for a mail subsidy by pointing out that any fast steamers operated across the Pacific by the company would be available for use as armed merchant cruisers in time of war.[82]

Dominating the conference was Alfred Deakin, head of the delegation from the Australian colony of Victoria, with nearly half the meetings being devoted to his particular concern—

76. Melville, "Canada and Sea Power," 261.

77. United Kingdom, Parliament, *Proceedings of the Colonial Conference, 1887* (London 1887), I, vii.

78. John Edward Kendle, *The Colonial and Imperial Conferences, 1887–1911: A Study in Imperial Organization* (London 1967), 7–8.

79. Creighton, *John A. Macdonald*, II, 475–76; and Sarty, "The RCN—The Australian Connection," 80.

80. Tucker, *The Naval Service of Canada*, I, 72.

81. United Kingdom, Parliament, *Proceedings of the Colonial Conference, 1887*, I, 192, 275.

82. Tucker, *The Naval Service of Canada*, I, 73.

naval defence. Whereas discussion of matters such as commercial treaties, imperial communications, and the powers of colonial governors resulted in little of concrete importance, the only real achievement of the conference was the Australian Naval Agreement. The terms of the deal were that, for an annual subsidy of £126,000 paid by the Australasian colonies for a ten-year period, Britain would build and provide a naval squadron of five third-class cruisers and two torpedo gunboats to supplement the existing establishment of the Australia station. The ships were to be commissioned in and manned by the Royal Navy, but could not be removed from Australian waters without the consent of the colonial authorities—a reasonable bargain, given the vessels' limited seakeeping abilities. The representative from the Cape Colony proposed that the arrangement be made more general, to be financed on the basis of a preferential tariff on goods entering the empire and proportioned to the value of imports from foreign sources as a rough indication of a colony's individual stake in the protection of the sea routes in time of war. This received some support, but began to unravel when the Canadian delegates observed that Canada would owe a relatively heavy contribution because of its very large imports overland from the United States. It died when the colonial secretary gave it "a reception so cold as to freeze it in its tracks," as a "damnable heresy … [to] the canon of free trade."[83] As Deakin observed, "until a very great change indeed comes over the manner of regarding fiscal questions in [Great Britain],… it is almost idle for us to raise the issue."[84] So the Australian Naval Agreement remained limited in focus. In the longer term, the Admiralty was to find that, in return for a modest step toward the goal of obtaining colonial contributions, a breech had been made in their more closely cherished tenet of centralized control, as the Australians would come to insist upon seeing the squadron as their own.

The results of the 1887 Colonial Conference, therefore, were mixed. From the contemporary imperialist's point of view, it was a major achievement. It established a precedent for similar meetings that were destined to become a permanent and notable imperial institution. Moreover, the whole question of general imperial defence as a joint responsibility was faced squarely for the first time since the eighteenth century. The conference also originated the practice of small colonial contributions toward the cost of the Royal Navy. On the other hand, the discussions revealed clearly the difficulties that were to beset every attempt to introduce the most effective measures of co-operation in time of peace. The colonies were eager to build an ambitious framework for economic collaboration, but Britain's predilection for free trade proved to be an insurmountable obstacle. The positive achievements of the conference were consequently limited, and in this respect all the later ones were destined to resemble it. In 1887, Canada showed that the problem of naval defence, local or imperial, had only a limited place in the minds of its people, and its representatives revealed their unwillingness to commit to a naval policy of any kind. Their successors were to take a similar stand at subsequent conferences over the course of the next twenty years.[85]

---

83. Ibid, 70–71; Kendle, *Colonial and Imperial Conferences*, 9; and Sarty, "The RCN—The Australian Connection," 79.

84. United Kingdom, Parliament, *Proceedings of the Colonial Conference, 1887*, I, 463.

85. Tucker, *The Naval Service of Canada*, I, 74.

Following the 1887 conference, the Canadian government allowed the CPR's bid for a mail subsidy to proceed knowing that it required that the Empresses be ready for conversion to armed merchant cruisers but no action was taken to investigate the naval initiatives of the Australian colonies. Whatever the military merits of the Australian plans, their connection to the concept of financial contribution presented constitutional challenges that no Canadian government would consider. As a result, while the British government "inundated Ottawa with papers urging Canadian cooperation in port and naval defence along the lines of the Australian effort" throughout the 1880s, "they were ignored."[86] Indeed, in the matter of defence generally, Canadian politicians were determined to do as they pleased, when they pleased—and then, only when absolutely required—without interference from what they perceived to be scheming imperial authorities.

Notwithstanding, the idea of a Canadian naval force persisted, kept alive by the independent analysis of Canadian officials interested in national defence issues. Practical schemes, such as that developed by Colin Campbell, were difficult for Canadian politicians to ignore completely, especially when they were sensitive to both fiscal and constitutional realities. Indeed, it is apparent that in the main they garnered higher level approval but failed to be implemented because of factors other than their intrinsic merit. The next such naval proposal was put forward in the fall of 1888 by the acting commander of the Fisheries Protection Service, Lieutenant Andrew R. Gordon.

The incumbent commander, Captain Scott, had been scheduled to retire late in 1888, but ill health forced him to turn over command to Lieutenant Gordon a year earlier than expected. Born in Britain in 1850, Gordon, like Scott and Colin Campbell, was a former Royal Navy officer who had first come to North America as a midshipman in the squadron at Halifax before seeing service with the British gunboat force on the Great Lakes during the Fenian raids of 1866. Although he retired from the British service in 1873 to settle west of Toronto as a farmer, he was aware of Selby-Smyth's naval militia plans through family connections and had offered his services as an instructor. When nothing came of that scheme, Gordon secured a position with the Department of Marine and Fisheries, commanding a series of expeditions overland into the northwest and then by sea into Hudson Bay to explore possible rail and port connections for shipping prairie grain to Europe. (His recommendation in favour of Churchill, Manitoba eventually would be implemented, but not until 1929.) His leadership skills led the Canadian government to offer him command of the fisheries cruiser CGS *Acadia* (which was little more than a converted steam-assisted yacht) when she was acquired in 1885, and subsequently of the entire protection service in 1887. The government was reluctant to make the command permanent until it was quite clear that there would be no settlement of the fisheries dispute (which would have rendered

---

86. Sarty, "The RCN—The Australian Connection," 80. This principle extended also to more general plans for the defence of Canada. Preston's *Canada and "Imperial Defense"* reads like a litany of ignored advice, as do Sarty's "Silent Sentry" and Mackinnon's "Imperial Fortresses." Again, whatever the hypothetical merit of the advice, the historical record has tended to prove its general worthlessness. Relegated as they were to collecting dust in the militia department archives, these documents are of no real value to the naval history of Canada, other than to acknowledge their existence and the fact that they were ignored. Readers interested in their individual details are invited to refer to the sources described above.

the entire Fisheries Protection Service unnecessary), and Gordon was not formally confirmed in the appointment until 1891. It is evident from departmental and personal correspondence, however, that he enjoyed the confidence and support not only of his minister, Sir Charles Tupper, but also of Prime Minister Macdonald.[87]

Gordon came to the post with a broad experience of Canadian naval issues as well as an appreciation of the infrastructure required. He was also aware of the difficulties of operating on the Great Lakes and in the Arctic and recognized the threat posed to Canada's coasts by auxiliary cruisers. Additionally, he assumed responsibility for fisheries matters at a time when Admiralty support for such efforts was waning, a fact that gave impetus to the line of thought Gordon had been developing for some time. In November 1886, while commanding *Acadia*, he had submitted a proposal to the minister that the protection service should acquire "two small naval vessels of [the torpedo-gunboat] class that would be particularly efficient for fisheries but which would also be of value for general naval defence." When in 1888 it was necessary to appropriate funds for a fisheries patrol vessel for the Pacific coast, Gordon exercised his authority as acting commander to propose that the department take the opportunity to purchase two torpedo-gunboats with the intent that they would "form the nucleus of a regular system of coast defence."[88]

Andrew Gordon's proposal was more than just a recommendation for the purchase of some ships. At thirty-five well-argued pages in length, it is an exception to Canadian bureaucratic paperwork of the period, and has been described as "certainly the most complete and probably the most valuable plan for Canadian naval defense presented to the dominion government in the nineteenth century." Beginning with a clear and full description of the dangers facing Canada from naval attack, Gordon (like Selby-Smyth before him) found the chief danger to lie in raids from converted merchant cruisers, particularly subsidized fast French mail steamers able to carry a heavy armament. Where he differed from Selby-Smyth and other contemporary analysts was in developing the remarkably prescient conclusion that the unsettled state of naval affairs would soon lead the Royal Navy to lose its quantitative and qualitative edge over its continental rivals, especially France. In 1879, the Admiralty had been unable to guarantee the despatch of additional forces to Canada and Gordon felt it extremely likely that in the event of war the Admiralty would be forced to recall ships from Canadian to British waters. Such a reduction of naval forces in North America would change the nature and seriousness of raids by enemy cruisers, and Canada would have to face them alone.[89]

To meet the increased threat (hypothetical as it was), Gordon proposed that the fixed defences of vulnerable ports such as Sydney should be improved by the addition of more artillery and of torpedo defences. His more important recommendation, however, was that

87. Melville, "Canada and Sea Power," 215–19, 222–23; and Maginley and Collin, *Ships of Canada's Marine Services*, 84.

88. Andrew Gordon to C.H. Tupper, 6 November 1888, LAC, RG 25, A-1, vol. 105; and Melville, "Canada and Sea Power," 226–28. The original 1886 letter (and the response to it) appear to have been among the records lost in the 1896 West Block fire. It is referred to in the 1888 correspondence, which only survived in the records of the Department of External Affairs because the then-minister of marine, C.H. Tupper, had to discuss the issue with the high commissioner in London.

89. Melville, "Canada and Sea Power," 229.

the Fisheries Protection Service be reorganized to serve as the nucleus of a naval force, through the acquisition of two torpedo-gunboats to serve in peacetime on the fisheries patrol and in wartime as a naval force to counter enemy cruisers. In this respect, Gordon was prescient in foreseeing the more general possibilities of the torpedo-gunboat type, as the forerunner of the torpedo-boat destroyer was called. The type was just entering service with the Royal Navy and was intended to screen ahead of the battlefleet, protecting the line of battle from enemy torpedo-boat flotillas and allowing the bigger ships to concentrate on the enemy's battleships. As such, torpedo-gunboats were designed to operate at sea with the fleet and to be faster and more heavily armed than the standard torpedo-boat, although initially not much larger so as to keep costs down.[90]

Gordon specifically recommended the acquisition of two vessels of the modified Rattlesnake class, the latest type in the Royal Navy. Their speed and range were their main advantage, while their armament of torpedoes and 4-inch guns was sufficient to make enemy cruisers seek their prey elsewhere rather than risk damage far from friendly ports. To be sure, they would be out-gunned by a merchant cruiser with 6-inch armament, and the early torpedoes were notoriously inaccurate and limited in range. But naval professionals everywhere were susceptible to the psychological possibilities of torpedo attack, and none more so than the French (in Gordon's mind the chief enemy) who had developed an entire theory of warfare in the *Jeune École* concept of massed torpedo-boat swarms to counter the British battlefleet. It was the strategy of a weaker naval power, precisely the position he believed the abandoned Canadian coasts would be in. In this respect, Gordon had made a radical departure from his Royal Navy brethren, and it allowed him to perceive a more general use of the torpedo-gunboat than the original purpose for which it had been adopted. He suggested certain modifications to the basic design, mostly to reduce costs, but emphasized the type's great advantages in meeting Canada's needs: their small size (550 tons, 200 feet in length and twenty-three feet in the beam); light draft (eleven feet); useful armament; relatively high speed (nineteen knots); long cruising range; and relatively low cost ($150,000). All of these were appropriate to the conditions of Canada's offshore areas, especially on the East Coast, where poaching fishermen could operate closer inshore than *Acadia*'s nineteen-foot draft allowed or could out run the twelve-knot *La Canadienne*. The torpedo-gunboat's range and speed would also make it unnecessary to hire additional vessels for a short period each year to cover for *Acadia* and *La Canadienne* as they slowly made their way between the various fishing grounds during overlapping seasons. An incidental, though not insignificant, advantage of their small size and draft was that it was possible for them to transit the St Lawrence and Welland canals into the upper Great Lakes. Finally, their acquisition would improve year-round employment of the protection service, which only operated on enforcement duties during the summer months. With the new warships, Gordon proposed conducting naval militia drills during winter, building up a trained manpower pool to man small steamers patrolling Canada's coasts and to operate fixed torpedo and artillery defences at important ports.[91]

---

90. Ibid, 230–32.

91. Andrew Gordon to C.H. Tupper, 6 November 1888, LAC, RG 25, A-1, vol. 105; and Melville, "Canada and Sea Power," 227–28.

Tupper was immediately enthusiastic about the scheme, and passed it directly to Macdonald. The prime minister saw through the argument for increasing the efficiency of the Fisheries Protection Service, however, and recognized that their true purpose was an attempt to establish the nucleus of a Canadian naval force. Nonetheless, he found the report "sensible" and began to consider the means to implement the proposals, while treading cautiously so as not to raise too much opposition. He accepted Tupper's recommendation to purchase the torpedo-gunboats under the guise of unarmed survey or fisheries vessels, with the actual armaments to be purchased and installed at a later date. Macdonald thought it wise to withhold information from the rest of Cabinet until Tupper could secure an informal opinion from the Admiralty on the suitability of torpedo-gunboats for Canadian service.[92]

Macdonald's support is not as surprising as might first appear. To be sure, his policy of naval dependence on Britain had been a cornerstone of confederation and he continued to reject proposals for imperial naval co-operation or contributions on the grounds that the Royal Navy maintained its Halifax and Esquimalt squadrons for British purposes. There was no Canadian rationale for a large cruiser force paid for by Ottawa but operated as part of the Royal Navy, one that could easily be called away from Canadian waters in an emergency. The prime minister was clearly aware of Canada's naval defence problems but tried to avoid taking action until there was a demonstrated need. Thus he had authorized Canadian naval action in 1866 to counter the Fenian raids and in 1885 when the fisheries were threatened. He had also allowed Selby-Smyth to proceed with the acquisition of *Charybdis* as part of a plan for Canadian merchant cruisers and had acquiesced to the formation of a top-level committee to study the coastal defence question in 1885. Three years later circumstances seemed to permit the investigation of Gordon's modest proposal, which could only buttress the developing national infrastructure, while assuring the defence of Canada's coasts against minor cruiser raids—and all under Canadian control.[93]

It was still necessary to seek Admiralty approval but there was no clear route for doing so. Gordon's status as acting commander of the protection service was not sufficient to overcome his substantive rank as a retired lieutenant in the eyes of their lordships. So when the Canadian high commissioner approached the Admiralty unofficially to ask about the Rattlesnake class, he did not include Gordon's overall proposal, but referred merely to fisheries duties. To this narrower purpose, the response was to recommend the Pheasant-class gunboat, the type the RN had previously employed on the North American fishing grounds, as the best fit for Canadian needs. The Pheasant-class were an older, deep-draft, high-masted, slow, and generally inferior design, and no great improvement on the vessels already in Canadian service (neither could they pass through the canal locks).

Even if Whitehall had been presented with Gordon's full proposal, it is unlikely they would have accepted so radical a departure from the accepted notions of sea power on which it was based. As much as the Admiralty was coming to appreciate the futility of a war with the United States, they maintained the idea that the navy would continue to per-

---

92. Tupper to Macdonald, 29 November 1888, LAC, MG 26A, vol. 286, 131226–228; and Macdonald to Tupper, 1 December 1888, LAC, MG 27, ID16, 95–96; and Melville, "Canada and Sea Power," 233–35.

93. Melville, "Canada and Sea Power," 236–38.

form its traditional function of imperial defence under all conditions. Should the Royal Navy be forced to abandon colonial waters temporarily, it would only be to concentrate the fleet for a decisive battle and any cruiser raids—however destructive locally—would be of little importance to the final outcome. Gordon's heresy was in proposing a non-traditional approach to ship roles: the torpedo-gunboat was designed for the specific function of screening the battle fleet from torpedo-boat attack and, in the Admiralty's view, there was little need to broaden its employment. Ordinary gunboats had been successful on miscellaneous duties in colonial waters for many years but it is unclear whether British officers appreciated the fact that this was due more to the absence of serious opposition than to their qualities as fighting vessels. Certainly, the specifics of Canadian requirements did not enter the Admiralty equation.[94] Neither, presumably, did they want to lend credibility to the *Jeune École* concept implicit in accepting Gordon's proposal.

Gordon, however, refused to accept London's dismissal of his scheme and continued to seek British approval by addressing their specific concerns. His subsequent submissions described the failings of the Pheasant-class and altered his suggestion of acquiring Rattlesnake torpedo-gunboats to a recommendation for the larger, faster, and more heavily armed Sharpshooter class, vessels that still retained the shallow draft and narrow beam needed to transit the locks to the Great Lakes. He also suggested that graduates of the Royal Military College (RMC) be offered commissions in the FPS after an additional year of training in naval subjects. But Gordon was being too comprehensive—or insufficiently focused—and in one of his later proposals the original plan for a "marine militia" was changed to an "imperial naval reserve." Although the latter might have gained some modest support from imperial federationists, it would surely have raised opposition in non-imperialist circles. Still, it is difficult to escape the conclusion that, however much Macdonald may have agreed with Gordon on the subject of Canada's defence needs, the lack of Admiralty support meant the practical end of the project.[95]

Gordon's belated appeal to enlist the support of Canadian imperialists in his naval militia scheme underscored the lack of interest from that quarter in naval matters. From one perspective, the limited influence of imperialist ideas on the various naval defence plans submitted to the government through the late 1880s probably accounts in large part for the essential "Canadian-ness" of those plans, and in consequence their acceptance by senior politicians. But from another perspective, those plans were developed by Canadian officials well-versed in the loosely defined economic and military structure of the British Empire. The link that Campbell and Gordon emphasized in their respective schemes, that a Canadian naval militia based upon the Fisheries Protection Service would serve to strengthen the national infrastructure, made it easy to recognize those plans as an adjunct to the National Policy. But a strong and increasingly autonomous Canada might also assume a greater role within the British Empire—a concept that could have been taken verbatim from the pamphlets of the Imperial Federation League. The late development of inter-

94. Ibid, 241–43.

95. Gordon to Tupper, 9 December 1889, LAC, MG 27, ID16, 163–65; Gordon to Tupper, 10 July 1891, LAC, RG 25, A-1, vol 107; and Melville, "Canada and Sea Power," 236–37.

Officers and ratings of the 1,770-ton torpedo cruiser HMS *Mohawk* in Halifax circa 1894. Halifax was one of the main naval bases for the warships of the North America and West Indies Station, giving the port a strong connection with the Royal Navy. (LAC PA-028543)

Pay parade onboard the second-class cruiser HMS *Indefatigable* at Halifax. The Royal Navy presence at the Canadian port had important economic as well as socio-cultural influences on Nova Scotia. (LAC PA-028433)

est in naval affairs on the part of Canadian imperialists also raises questions as to the nature of navalism in Canada and the relationship between them.

The premature deaths of Gordon and Campbell in 1893 and 1896 respectively left a void in Canadian naval thought, as there were no obvious successors in either the Department of Marine and Fisheries or Militia and Defence.[96] Such was not the case in the United States where, in 1889, an obscure American naval officer teaching at the recently established United States Naval War College, Captain Alfred Thayer Mahan, was preparing to publish a collection of his lectures on naval history in the age of sail. Hardly a captivating subject in an age obsessed with technical progress, his publisher urged Mahan to add an introductory chapter on "The Elements of Sea Power" so as to capitalize upon the controversy surrounding passage that year of Britain's Naval Defence Act. With its added focus on the importance of naval strength in national development, *The Influence of Sea Power Upon History* captured a general theory of war at sea in a popular format.[97] Although the belief that the "prophet of sea power" provoked a sudden interest in naval affairs is as mistaken as are most interpretations of his so-called dictums, Mahan's expression of geopolitical ideas on the relative strengths and weaknesses of maritime and land-locked states spoke to the social Darwinism of his age in a way that would influence the course of naval development throughout the world.

In general, Mahan's writings lent support to movements already in existence in the United States, Germany, and Japan that were advocating the construction of battleship and cruiser navies to emulate Britain's (although none were as yet contemplating parity as a realistic possibility). Indeed, even France was not immune to the influence, and the *Jeune École* found itself momentarily eclipsed by a return to the more traditional school of *la grande guerre*. But it was within the British Empire that Mahan's writings resonated most—his object of admiration, after all, was the Royal Navy in the age of sail—and they increased the impetus for a united imperial fleet under exclusive Admiralty control. As we have seen, where the Admiralty had previously taken a laissez-faire approach to colonial naval defence, encouraging the overseas governments to provide for their own local needs, their inclination to centralize now had a powerful supporting argument, namely, that Whitehall should "take a leading role in shaping the future of colonial naval forces."[98]

With a better-organized British exchequer by the late 1880s, economy was no longer the major consideration, although the Admiralty still believed in the principle of colonial contributions as the only reasonable exchange for dedicated regional squadrons. That those squadrons were subject to withdrawal in the event of an emergency elsewhere (a condition

96. Melville, "Canada and Sea Power," 213, 251–52.

97. Alfred Thayer Mahan, *The Influence of Sea Power Upon History, 1660–1783* (Boston 1890); Jon Tetsuro Sumida, *Inventing Grand Strategy and Teaching Naval Command: The Classic Works of Alfred Thayer Mahan Reconsidered* (Washington, DC 1997), 24–25.

98. Melville, "Canada and Sea Power," 256–57; Kenneth J. Hagan, "Apotheosis of Mahan: American Naval Strategy, 1889–1922," Neilson and Errington, *Navies and Global Defence*, 94–96; Holger H. Herwig, *"Luxury" Fleet: The Imperial German Navy, 1888–1918* (London 1987), 24–25; David C. Evans and Mark R. Peattie, *Kaigun: Strategy, Tactics, and Technology in the Imperial Japanese Navy, 1887–1941* (Annapolis, MD 1997), 12–15; and Hill, *War at Sea in the Ironclad Age*, 91–92.

applicable to the Australasian Squadron), or that they might not even be desired locally (as in the case of Canada), were issues never adequately taken into account. Nonetheless, it was through the notion of contributions that the Admiralty found it had a new ally, in the form of the Imperial Federation League, even though it came with a price and agenda of its own. With an updated appreciation of the principle of "no taxation without representation," this group—and its successor, the British Empire League—saw naval contributions as a powerful rationale for increased colonial participation in the policy-making apparatus of the empire— the exact antithesis of the Admiralty's goal. Still, despite disagreement as to details, there was a general commitment to the broader philosophy. When the Navy League was established in Britain in January 1895, "to spread information showing the vital importance to the British empire of the naval supremacy upon which depended its trade, empire, and national existence," many of the original members were also imperial federationists.[99] As their advocacy progressed, the league was aware of the inherent contradiction. For instance, the Navy League enlisted the new colonial secretary, Joseph Chamberlain (an avowed imperial federationist), in seeking the improvement of local port facilities and the establishment of colonial naval reserves as means to overcome the problems posed by "colonial opposition to cash contributions and Admiralty opposition to colonial fleets outside central control."[100] But try as they might to paper over the issue, the contradiction was not easily rationalized. The growing confidence of the colonial citizenry that fed the imperial federation movement was coming to be expressed in ways not previously envisioned. Although the contemporary language of the late nineteenth century was not so precise, there was an underlying appreciation of colonial warships as symbols of national pride. Australians, for example, quickly developed "a proprietorial attitude" by referring to the new special squadron as "our ships."[101]

This strange mix of nationalist and imperialist enthusiasm was also evident in Canada. When branches of the Navy League were established in Toronto in December 1895 (in fact, the first branch to be established outside Britain) and Victoria in March 1901, many of their founding members were imperial federationists. Publication of J. Hampden Burnham's *Canadians in the Imperial Naval and Military Service Abroad* was an undisguised attempt to inspire imperial sentiment with adventurous tales of native sons in far-off seas and lands. Mahan was also "a great favourite" with Canadian imperialists. As George Robert Parkin, one of the leading Canadian advocates of imperial federation, suggested: "By making England understand more fully than she ever understood before what sea power has meant in her history, [Mahan] has greatly stiffened English resolve not to surrender without a struggle the supremacy on the ocean which she has enjoyed so long."[102]

---

99. Navy League Constitution quoted in A.J. Marder, *The Anatomy of British Sea Power: A History of British Naval Policy in the Pre-Dreadnought Era, 1880–1905* (New York 1940), 49.

100. Navy League to Joseph Chamberlain, 16 April 1896, and enclosed pamphlet "The Colonies and the Navy," United Kingdom National Archives (hereafter UKNA), Colonial Office (hereafter CO) 323/410.

101. John Bach, *The Australia Station: A History of the Royal Navy in the South West Pacific, 1821–1913* (New South Wales 1986), 189.

102. Parkin quoted in Carl Berger, *The Sense of Power: Studies in the Ideas of Canadian Imperialism, 1873–1914* (Toronto 1970), 235.

The term "navalism," much like the notion of imperial federation, meant different things to different people and was far from being a monolithic concept. The impetus towards a Canadian naval service was rooted in the country's location in what has been termed the "North Atlantic Triangle,"[103] even as the nature of the imperial relationship—and the Royal Navy's place within it—was changing. It is not surprising, therefore, that attitudes toward both the British navy and its role in imperial defence developed differently in the four British North American cities—Halifax, Victoria, St John's, and Toronto—that had exhibited the greatest interest in naval matters.

Halifax, perhaps more than any of the others, defined itself most confidently in relation to the Royal Navy. A fine natural harbour, generally ice-free in winter and easily defended, it had become a mainstay of the North America and West Indies Station during the American Revolution. Although the commander-in-chief's headquarters were located in the more centrally positioned—and warmer—Bermuda, Halifax continued to act as the summer home port of the squadron with a guardship being maintained at the port during its winter sojourn. (The station also had a subsidiary base at Port Royal, Jamaica). Through the 1880s and 1890s, even as the squadron's primary rationale—war against the United States—was altered by circumstances, it maintained an active operational pace emblematic of the age of gunboat diplomacy. The station was allotted a variety of warships representative of those in service in the RN, but generally of the more modern types. With the US Navy still dedicated primarily to coast defence, the greater potential enemy was France, whose large number of Caribbean colonies made that area a likely sub-theatre of any general war. The squadron's strength was theoretically sufficient to allow its commander-in-chief to deal with any raiders operating either against his bases or the trans-Atlantic shipping lanes.[104]

Halifax, as one of those bases, enjoyed the frequent spectacle of the most powerful ships of the squadron concentrated in the harbour, for although a few of the smaller vessels were required to watch the Newfoundland fishery, in practice the majority of the station's gunboats were employed in the Caribbean. Along with the squadron's presence—and the associated imperial fortress established for its base protection—came a number of benefits to Halifax. The primary one was financial. The annual maintenance of the garrison and the squadron alone accrued hundreds of thousands of pounds sterling to local contractors. Added to that were the sums spent on the rebuilding of the fortress itself and construction of associated out-forts and batteries under the Carnarvon recommendations. As was the case at Esquimalt, a large naval dry dock was completed in 1889 with HMS *Canada*, a screw-corvette, being the first ship to enter the facility. These various projects coincided with the decline of older maritime industries so that the British military came to account for an important segment of the local economy.[105]

---

103. By John Bartlet Brebner in *North Atlantic Triangle: The Interplay of Canada, the United States and Great Britain* (New York 1945).

104. Roger Willock, "Gunboat Diplomacy: Operations of the North America and West Indies Squadron, 1875–1915, Part I: Canvas and Steam, 1875–1895," *American Neptune*, XXVIII:2 (April 1968), 26.

105. Mackinnon, "Imperial Fortresses," 147; Sarty, "Silent Sentry," 72–85; Raddall, *Warden of the North*, 237; and Conrad and Hiller, *Atlantic Canada*, 135–60.

The British squadron that accompanied the Royal Yacht HMS *Ophir* to Halifax in October 1901. Alongside the dockyard is the 2,135-ton third-class cruiser HMS *Psyche*. In the channel, from left to right, are the 11,000-ton first-class cruiser HMS *Diadem*, the 3,400-ton second-class cruiser HMS *Tribune*, the 7,700-ton first-class cruiser HMS *Crescent*, the 2,575-ton second-class cruiser HMS *Pallas*, *Diadem*'s sister ship HMS *Niobe*, *Psyche*'s sister ship HMS *Proserpine*, and, at the right edge of the photograph, the 3,600-ton second-class cruiser HMS *Indefatigable*. (DND Notman-9114)

A popular history of the city credits the transformation of the city's fortunes. "While the commercial life of Halifax sank into apathy after 1876, and while military life blazed up in a last display of imperial power, the spiritual life of the city experienced a cultural rebirth."[106] That renaissance also speaks to the social benefit to Haligonians of the imperial relationship. The officers of the garrison kept up a certain level of excitement and colour throughout the year, but "the arrival of the squadron, usually by the twenty-fourth of May, ushered in the season. There followed incessant dinners, dances and bonnet-hops, ashore and afloat. The admiral, general and Governor—that triangle of notables—would each receive formally at the garden parties. Regimental messes and private estates—Belmont, Oaklands, Rosebanks and the rest—were thrown open to the social swirl."[107] The height of excitement came in the fall of 1901, when the Duke and Duchess of York arrived in Halifax as the next-to-last stop on their "voyage around the British empire," on board the Royal Yacht *Ophir* and escorted by the powerful new first-class protected cruisers, HM Ships *Diadem* and *Niobe* (the same warship that would return to the port less than a decade later as the flagship of a fledging Royal Canadian Navy). So self-assured were Haligonians of their importance to the British navy, that the Navy League's efforts to establish a branch in the city were rejected as unnecessary. Nova Scotians had never been unconditional participants in confederation, and probably knew in their hearts that parsimonious central Canadian governments would never spend as much as London (as subsequent events would prove). The net effect was to be dismissive of any—necessarily more modest—Canadian naval initiatives as mere upstarts, usurping the proper place of the Royal Navy.[108]

At the other end of the country, Victoria nominally enjoyed a similar relationship with the British service, having the headquarters of the commander-in-chief of the Pacific Station in nearby Esquimalt, but in fact the link was much more tenuous. The naval harbour was good, although much smaller than Halifax, and physically separated from the commercial port and social centre of Victoria by a three-mile dirt road. If the climate was more pleasant than Halifax, that was more than offset by the port's isolation. While the presence of British gunboats allowed for occasional intervention against American encroachment in the Pacific Northwest, British trade in the region was slight and of little strategic value. Esquimalt was added as an after-thought on Colomb's list of coaling stations, and the Carnarvon Commission considered it only upon the insistence of Prime Minister Macdonald, who was upholding his end of the bargain that had brought British Columbia into confederation. Indeed, as one historian has pointed out, those articles of entry are note-

---

106. Raddall, *Warden of the North*, 238.

107. Mackinnon, "Imperial Fortresses," 151.

108. As late as the middle of the Second World War an article by a provincial archivist on the "Canadian Naval Tradition," written ostensibly "as a source of inspiration to us all" in the war effort, concentrated on the service of Canadians in the Royal Navy and the British service's importance to Halifax, while despairing that "a new generation has arisen that knew not Joseph [i.e., the Royal Navy]" and dismissing the RCN as a "tinpot navy." D.C. Harvey, "Nova Scotia and the Canadian Naval Tradition," *Canadian Historical Review*, XXIII: 3 (September 1942), 249. It is telling that Harvey's article does not mention the first director of the Canadian navy, Rear-Admiral Sir Charles Kingsmill, who was born and raised in Ontario, even though he had risen to the rank of rear-admiral in the British navy.

worthy for "their great attention to naval matters": "the dominion to assume the colonial debt, to begin a public works program, to guarantee a loan for a dry-dock at Esquimalt, to exert influence on the imperial government to maintain Esquimalt as a British naval station, and above all, to begin a railway to the Pacific."[109]

The British government of Ewart Gladstone and his Little Englanders was philosophically opposed to colonization and extension of empire. From London's perspective, the assignment of a few secondary vessels of the Royal Navy to a remote backwater was small price to pay to divest Britain of the colony. The Admiralty's indifference to Esquimalt is summarized in the terse observation "that an unfortunate base is better than no base at all."[110] Ironically, completion of both the dry dock and the CPR increased its value as an important link in what would come to be called the "All-Red Route" of imperial communications from Britain to Australia. Through the 1890s, as the strength of the US Pacific Fleet was being increased, a number of disputes with the United States—the Bering Sea pelagic sealing question, the influx of Americans during the Yukon gold rush, and the Alaska boundary dispute—convinced British Columbians that the naval presence of the Pacific Squadron should be maintained. In addition, contracts to maintain both the squadron and the garrisons of British regulars and Canadian militia, as well as the building of the dry dock and associated repair work, brought a certain amount of revenue into the local economy, though not in the same proportion as at Halifax, but more than Ottawa would have invested alone.[111]

In separate reports in 1896–97, the Admiralty and the War Office both determined that there was no naval or military rationale for retaining Esquimalt as an imperial base, but that it should still be supported for political reasons: Canada wanted the Pacific Squadron based there and "as Britain had pressed Canada for twenty years to strengthen the base any sudden decision to abandon it might harm imperial relations."[112] Victorians, however, were less certain of the long-term outcome and it is possible to detect a sensitivity to all of these impulses and an undercurrent of insecurity in their relationship with the Royal Navy that expressed itself in a constant effort to try to solidify it. They were generally successful although the frontline ships of the squadron were withdrawn during the South African (Boer) War in anticipation that hostilities might spill over into a general European conflict.[113]

---

109. Gough, *The Royal Navy and the Northwest Coast of North America*, 218.

110. Schurman, *Imperial Defence*, appx. 1, 59.

111. Mackinnon, "Imperial Fortresses," 262–366; Sarty, "Silent Sentry," 58–72. In 1887, the United States Pacific Fleet consisted of two coast defence ships and six small cruisers; by 1896 this had been increased by one first-class battleship, USS *Oregon*, and one other building. See Bourne, *Britain and the Balance of Power*, 373–74.

112. Esquimalt (Naval Intelligence), 11 December 1896, Esquimalt (War Office), 23 October 1897, UKNA, CAB 37/45; and see also Robert J.D. Page, "Canada and the Empire During Joseph Chamberlain's Tenure as Colonial Secretary" (unpublished D Phil thesis, Oxford 1971), 308–12.

113. During the early stages of the war, the Admiralty removed from the station two second-class protected cruisers—*Leander* and *Arethusa*, both launched 1882—replacing them with one similar cruiser, *Amphion*, only late in 1901. In the first half of 1901, therefore, the station strength was reduced to one armoured cruiser, *Warspite*, the one second-class protected cruiser, one torpedo boat, two torpedo boat destroyers, and two composite sloops. See Barry Gough, *The Royal Navy and the Northwest Coast of North America*, 256–66.

Feeling compelled to take direct action, Victorians established a local branch of the Navy League in June 1901, attracting a large membership and the backing of a number of prominent provincial figures. Most of these men were imperialists in the purest sense of the word—that is, with close links to the mother country, untempered by the strong nationalist element that was such a prominent fixture in the Toronto branch. Their aims being essentially the same as those of the parent league in Britain, it is not surprising that their propositions were directly influenced by it. Among the first orders of business was the passing of a motion for the joint maintenance through paid contributions of a local unit of the Royal Naval Reserve.[114]

The last years of the century also found Newfoundlanders experiencing a change in their imperial relationship. For decades, the Newfoundland fisheries, which employed some 85 percent of the workforce, had been regarded as a "nursery of fighting seamen" for the Royal Navy and by the 1890s it was a human resource that the Royal Navy was ready to exploit. The corollary was that Britain would ensure the colony's protection. Newfoundland's close connection to the Royal Navy—during the eighteenth and the first half of the nineteenth centuries both command of the Newfoundland station and its governorship had been a prime Admiralty appointment—came to be questioned when the local command became part of the North America and West Indies Station and the small imperial garrison was recalled in 1871, leaving the colony "effectively demilitarized."[115] Encouraged by Britain to progress beyond colonial status, Newfoundlanders found their political options limited, neither desiring to join Canadian federation nor permitted to pursue a policy of reciprocity with the United States that could have financed autonomous dominion status. Similarly pressed by the Colonial Office to attend to its self-defence, the government in St John's logically decided that "a naval defence force ... would enjoy greater success among a seafaring population than a military one."[116] Looking to the examples of the other colonial models, however, the cash-strapped Newfoundland exchequer—it had over-invested in a trans-island railway—was unable to finance either a local naval squadron or even a minimal fisheries protection flotilla of its own. Recognizing their dependence on the Royal Navy for regulation of the fishery, and perhaps being more comfortable with close ties to London, the hesitation of Newfoundlanders to pay a contribution was not based on the constitutional grounds put forward by Canada, but on the fact that such payment would, of necessity, be modest. When the broadening of the Royal Naval Reserve began to be addressed seriously in the late 1890s, therefore, it was quickly embraced as the obvious and practical solution.[117]

---

114. Victoria *Daily Times*, 26 June 1901. The reported membership included a former lieutenant-governor, several chief justices of the provincial supreme court, the Anglican bishop of British Columbia, all five local members of the provincial legislature, and Senator William Templeman, who later would serve as a minister in the Laurier Cabinet.

115. Bernard Ransom, "A Nursery of Fighting Seamen? The Newfoundland Royal Naval Reserve, 1901–1920," Michael L. Hadley, Rob Huebert and Fred W. Crickard, *A Nation's Navy: In Quest of Canadian Naval Identity* (Montreal 1996), 239.

116. Ransom, "A Nursery of Fighting Seamen?" 240.

117. "Ode to the Rock Is Still Rolling," Toronto *Globe and Mail*, 29 January 2002.

In the Ontario of the 1890s, there was evidence of much the same attachment to the Royal Navy as on the nation's coasts, although one with a distinctly Canadian flavour. Toronto already had its share of outspoken imperial federationists, led by the triumvirate of Colonel George T. Denison III, patriarch of a leading militia family, George M. Grant, principal of Queen's University but a frequent visitor to the provincial capital, and George R. Parkin, headmaster of Upper Canada College. All native-born Canadians—indeed, with deep United Empire Loyalist roots—they approached the notion as a logical development of Canadian nationalism and "regarded imperialism as a native product, embedded in the traditions of their country. Canadians possessed complete internal self-government and it remained only to assert their authority over the empire as a whole through some form of imperial federation.... What [these] imperialists defended, however, was not so much the imperial system as it then stood but rather the hope that as Canada grew in strength and population the empire would be transformed so as to accommodate her weight and influence."[118]

As noted previously, the imperial federationists had yet to exert any great influence on the various Canadian naval militia schemes. Naval matters did not figure prominently in their plans, other than general recognition of the principle that contribution should entail representation on imperial councils. Interestingly, Andrew Gordon began revising his original scheme (after its rejection by the Admiralty) to allow for an imperial naval reserve shortly after a Toronto speech by Denison in March 1890, arguing that the protection Canada's large merchant fleet derived from the Royal Navy "would be given as a right rather than as a privilege if Canada were to make a contribution to the Royal Navy."[119] With Gordon's death in 1891, nothing more came of either idea. It is odd that Denison never spoke more of naval matters, given that his younger brother John was then serving in the Royal Navy and would rise to the rank of admiral commanding the Devonport division of the Home Fleet in 1908–09.[120] Despite the militia's preoccupation with naval control of the lakes, Denison—and the Toronto group in general—rarely considered it in their proposals. But Mahan's writings sparked their interest and prepared the ground for the arrival of someone with the necessary experience and vision to focus their efforts.

That someone was Henry J. Wickham. A retired Royal Navy officer who "applied his specialized knowledge to Canadian conditions,"[121] Wickham first made his presence felt in 1894 with a paper delivered at the Royal Canadian Military Institute—a venerable Toronto institution, at which gathering Denison and the others were likely present—with recommendations for stimulating the Canadian merchant fleet's transition to steam and steel through government subsidies tied to their availability for conversion to fast auxiliary cruisers.[122] Although there is no evidence that Wickham collaborated with Colin Campbell and

118. Berger, *The Sense of Power*, 12–42, 259.

119. Melville, "Canada and Sea Power," 263–64.

120. "George T. Denison," W. Stewart Wallace, ed., *The Macmillan Dictionary of Canadian Biography* (Toronto 1963), 183.

121. Melville, "Canada and Sea Power," 290–91; and "Lt. Col. George Taylor Denison," Henry James Morgan, ed., *The Canadian Men and Women of the Time: A Handbook of Canadian Biography* (Toronto 1898), 261–63.

122. H.J. Wickham, "Canada's Maritime Position and Responsibilities," *Selected Papers from the Transactions of the Canadian Military Institute* (Welland and Toronto 1894–95).

Andrew Gordon, or had access to their reports, their underlying principles were strikingly similar. The core ideas, that the British fleet could not be everywhere and a Canadian squadron could fill the gap in a way that mere financial contributions to the Royal Navy could not, resonated with his audience. The Navy League was only just getting established in Britain, but within months Wickham had recruited the bulk of the Toronto lobby to join him in forming a Toronto branch in December 1895. A brilliant organizer as well as a superb communicator, he would serve as their honorary secretary and primary spokesman for the next decade and a half.[123]

Wickham's ideas continued to develop in the months that followed, and on lines that indicated some access to the plans of the deceased Campbell and Gordon. One of his papers, presented to the Toronto branch as a detailed scheme for the "Naval Defence of Canada," was printed in its entirety on the front page of the *Saturday Globe* on 20 June 1896. Beginning with the premises that there were strong constitutional objections to a policy of direct financial contributions without representation in the chambers determining naval policy, and that Canada's best contribution to imperial defence would be to put her own defences in an adequate state, the elements of the proposal were significant in a number of respects. Aiming at the formation of an efficient naval force to supplement the existing Canadian military organization, it called for the raising of a complete naval militia equivalent to the land forces, with permanent and reserve components to be based on a similar structure. Among the details envisioned were: the appointment of a naval officer to a position analogous to that of the general officer commanding the Canadian militia "to consult and co-operate with the latter"; the acquisition of torpedo boats for coast defence; the establishment of training schools on both coasts to serve as the naval equivalents of the schools of cavalry, infantry, and artillery of the Canadian permanent force; the formation of a naval reserve force similar to that of the militia; and adapting the existing Fisheries Protection Service to the requirements of defence. The article's publication in a prominent newspaper can be attributed to the fact that the president of the Toronto branch, W.B. McMurrich, an ex-mayor of the city, was also a director of the *Globe*. Since the latter was generally recognized as a Liberal organ, the publication of Wickham's article, three days before the general election that saw the end of the Conservative political dynasty, could not have been an accident. Wickham had chosen his allies well. The political landscape was evolving, and Canadian navalism along with it.[124]

When Wilfrid Laurier entered office in July 1896 as Canada's first French-Canadian prime minister, thoughts of naval or military matters were far from his mind. The campaign his Liberal party had waged to break nearly eighteen years of continuous Conservative rule was more an attack upon the Manitoba schools policy and various alleged scandals of Sir Charles Tupper's ministry than a re-evaluation of Canada's position in the imperial framework. But if he was content to inherit the assumption of his Conservative predecessors that

123. Melville, "Canada and Sea Power," 292.

124. "Naval Defence of Canada: A Paper Read by Mr [H.J.] Wickham Before the Toronto Branch of the Canadian Navy League," Toronto *Saturday Globe*, 20 June 1896.

the Royal Navy would see to enforcement of Canadian maritime concerns, it was not just because of the implied assurances of the Admiralty. The statement of Liberal Party policy adopted in 1893 had pointedly omitted any mention of military or naval affairs in deference to the strong French-Canadian wing of the caucus. From its perspective, any change in the scope of the existing Canadian military establishment threatened involvement in imperial wars—"far-away and bloody wars we can neither hinder nor halt," in the simple phrase of Honoré Mercier, the premier of Quebec from 1887 to 1891 and still a leading politician[125]—and would not be tolerated.

Unsurprisingly, the new government offered no response to the Navy League's proposals. Still, with the backing of the influential Toronto lobby, within six months, Wickham and his colleagues tried a different tack—that Canadians should be included in the Royal Naval Reserve a program already in existence by which merchant steamships were fitted for conversion to armed cruisers in return for an Admiralty subsidy. Obvious candidate ships were those of the recently inaugurated Canadian Pacific Line's mail and passenger service, and the league suggested that manning these vessels with crews belonging to a Canadian branch of the RNR would be an acceptable method of ensuring a supply of colonial manpower for the Royal Navy, while qualifying as a Canadian contribution to imperial naval defence. In pointing out that such a scheme would bring about the "consolidation of the empire by giving what would practically amount to preferential trade between the different parts thereof without touching the vexed question of tariffs," the proposal reflected the Toronto branch's sensitivity to Canadian political realities by suggesting a compromise that would satisfy both government objections to contribution and the manufacturing community's desire for a British preferential tariff.[126] Despite offering an alternate way forward on the naval issue, the Navy League's revised plan also went unanswered, and was forestalled by the introduction of a British preferential tariff in the government's April 1897 budget. That the Liberals were more focused on the "vexed question of tariffs" reflected its importance to the larger Canadian public and the fact that the Navy League was but one small voice among many.

The latter still had to be dealt with, however. In early 1897 a long memorandum from the Colonial Defence Committee arrived in Ottawa with the latest plan to set the defences of the empire in order.[127] Evidently motivated by the Franco-Russian alliance of 1894, the CDC accepted unequivocally the Royal Navy's position that it was impossible to protect every colonial port and coast from raiding cruisers, but that a strong, centrally directed fleet could assure the general security of the empire. It was an unabashed pitch for colonial contributions without any conditions on their use. In emphasizing Canada's lengthy land frontier while ignoring a possible naval role for the country, it appears that the Admiralty expected little from Ottawa. At about that time, the Admiralty also turned down a request from the Canadian government for assistance in conducting a survey of the ice conditions

---

125. "Des guerres lointaines et sanglantes que nous ne pourrions ni empêcher ni arrêter." Mercier quoted in Robert Rumilly, *Mercier* (Montreal 1936), 339.

126. Wickham to Laurier, 12 December 1896, LAC, MG 26 G, reel C-745, 9725–27.

127. "Colonial Defence," 31 December 1896, UKNA, CO 323/415.

in the Hudson Strait.[128] Laurier's thoughts on these coincident issues are not recorded, but the cumulative effect was to raise questions about the reliability of the Royal Navy to fulfill its commitment to Canadian maritime interests—and to bolster the prime minister's instincts against contribution payments.

If the CDC report offered no hint of direct naval support to Canadian defence, the Admiralty soon demonstrated a renewed interest in the problem. In April 1897, the Royal Navy finally decided to take action on an earlier report of the Joint Naval and Military Committee and sent an expert to survey the suitability of Canadian lake vessels for conversion to armed auxiliaries in time of war. At about the same time, consideration was also given to a submission by Sir William Van Horne, president of the CPR, for a special railway car designed to transport torpedo boats to the Great Lakes. Perhaps recognizing yet another ploy by the CPR to qualify for greater subsidies, their lordships demurred and said that although they might be "a valuable addition to the defence of Canada on her inland waters," torpedo boats alone would not ensure command of the lakes in a protracted contest. Instead, the British suggested a more effective defensive preparation—one less likely to arouse American suspicions—by improving the St Lawrence canal system so as to facilitate the navy's ability "to pass vessels of suitable size and armament to these waters at the outset of hostilities."[129]

Their lordships, however, were only hedging their bets. In mid-June 1897, shortly before the Colonial Conference, the CDC advised Colonial Secretary Joseph Chamberlain that contributions to the Royal Navy "were the most pressing need in imperial defence"[130]—a clear signal that the Admiralty intended to renew its efforts to seek colonial monetary assistance. Chamberlain had once warned the Imperial Federation (Defence) Committee that their demands for colonial contributions in return for a share in imperial policy-making should not be pushed to "extremities," as a rebuff could have disastrous effects.[131] Now, backed by the preliminary efforts of the Admiralty, the colonial secretary hoped to use the upcoming conference to press the premiers for greater naval efforts.

As for Canada's prime minister, Laurier's thoughts on naval defence were not yet well-defined. Although an adept domestic politician, he was still rather new to imperial and foreign affairs and went to London with only one objective—to arrange a general system of imperial preferential tariffs that would be beneficial to Canadian business. Perhaps because of his inexperience, he was swept up in the imperial fervour of the conference and accepted, among other things, a knighthood. Even before the conference started, Laurier made a number of clumsy pro-imperialist statements he would later come to regret.

---

128. Sir Donald Smith (Lord Strathcona) to Lord Goschen, 15 January 1897, Birmingham University Library (hereafter BUL), Joseph Chamberlain papers, JC 9/2/1Q/2; and Page, "Canada and the Empire," 304. The Canadians wished to investigate the possibility of using Hudson Bay and Hudson Strait as a commercial shipping route for Western grain. The survey was subsequently conducted, without assistance, by the marine department (although with a chartered vessel).

129. War Office to Under Secretary of State, Colonial Office, 25 March 1897, Chamberlain to Aberdeen, 5 April 1897, LAC, MG 26 G, reel C-748, 13713–714; and Admiralty to Colonial Office, 17 April 1897, UKNA, CO 547/114.

130. Nathan to Chamberlain, 12 June 1897, UKNA, CO 323/423.

131. Colonial Office memo, 12 November 1895, UKNA, CO 323/404.

Once formal proceedings began, his first venture into the naval discussion was a naïve proposal for a general fund for empire defence. It was immediately and pointedly rejected by the premier of New South Wales, whose colony had for some time been supporting the local Australasian naval squadron, while Canada contributed nothing at all to the Royal Navy. Faced with the challenge to make a concrete offer, "Laurier retreated into imprecise generalities."[132] He claimed that, for Canada, the question of naval defence remained an academic one that had yet to be discussed. Now, "no doubt Canada will consider it and give an answer." Although Chamberlain went on to outline some of the material advantages to colonial contributions, Laurier appeared not to notice as he attempted to impress upon the other delegates that Canada had not been negligent in her duty to the rest of the empire. In his eyes—and it was a gaze not unlike that of Macdonald—Canada had no need of naval protection, and therefore should not be called upon to pay a contribution since it was "an inaccessible country, the only accessible way being by the St Lawrence, and it is easily guarded." In fact, Laurier had arrived at the same conclusion as the Admiralty—that war with the United States was not a serious possibility—but had drawn an entirely different implication. Their lordships felt that Canada need not worry about her inland waters, would have no need for a naval force of her own and could therefore contribute freely to the Royal Navy, whereas Laurier took it to mean that Canada need do nothing.

Before naval defence came up again for discussion at the conference, Laurier evidently followed his own advice and finally considered the question. With his limited experience in imperial naval matters, two facts seemed abundantly clear: whenever asked for assistance, however infrequently, the Royal Navy had been unwilling to extend it; and, imperial commitments that might not meet the approval of Liberal supporters should not be made. Both ruled against contribution. When Chamberlain resurrected the naval defence question, this time flanked by Lord Goschen and Admiral Sir Frederick Richards, first lord and senior naval lord respectively, Laurier had his reply ready. After an exchange between the first lord and the premiers, during which the Canadian was noticeably silent, Chamberlain attempted to prod Laurier by suggesting he should have a private interview with Admiral Richards on the matter. To the astonishment of Goschen and the others in attendance, however, Laurier announced that he had nothing to say to him. The Canadian prime minister restated his previous stand more clearly: the naval question did not have the same importance for Canada as for some of the other colonies, because war was not a serious possibility in North America. Any Canadian differences with the United States were merely "family troubles which mean nothing very serious." That settled the issue for Canada. As the proceedings drew to a close, the Australian and New Zealand naval agreements were renewed and virtually all the other colonies extended offers of aid. In contrast, as Chamberlain coldly noted, "Canada has made no offer."[133]

Nonetheless, a threshold had been crossed. Although Laurier's statements can hardly be called a policy, the Canadian prime minister had been forced to address the issue. With

132. Page, "Canada and the Empire," 305.

133. United Kingdom, Parliament, *Proceedings of the Conference between Colonial Secretary and Premiers of Self-Governing Colonies, 1897* (London 1897), 140–50.

the realization that the assumption of British naval aid could not necessarily be depended upon, and that contributions were politically and constitutionally, unacceptable, went recognition that the broader problem of imperial naval defence was also a Canadian concern. Continued inaction would not make the other colonies and Britain any more amenable to the Canadian quest for an imperial preferential tariff. At the same time, adequate protection of Canadian maritime interests had somehow to be seen to be assured, in a manner compatible with the diverse elements of the Canadian political scene. For, although continuing to refute London's requests for financial contributions would meet any demands for no imperial entanglements, such a course would not be likely to satisfy for long the growing self-confidence of English-Canadian imperialists, who demanded greater Canadian autonomy while maintaining the image of imperial unity.

Ironically, the same imperial links that provided much of Canada's naval defence were also the most likely source of possible conflict with the United States. For direct Canada–US problems, such as sealing and fisheries questions and the emerging Alaska boundary dispute, the diplomatic assistance being provided by London was not making any measurable progress, at least none that promoted Canadian interests. Moreover, without sovereign status, Canada could not officially take a direct role in the negotiations. Although British control of the oceanic trade routes remained unquestioned, the Royal Navy could offer little aid to defend the Great Lakes in the event of a confrontation with the Americans. Laurier's electoral success in 1896, meanwhile, had been based in large part upon his breakthrough in Ontario, where the province's Loyalist origins and military steadfastness during the early nineteenth century remained a powerful motive—if largely mythic—force but one the prime minister could not afford to ignore. Out of the complex issues that surrounded the defence of the lakes during the first years of the Laurier government, there emerged a potent impetus for the creation of a Canadian naval force.

The Venezuela crisis of 1895 between Britain and the United States was the latest imperial problem to raise the spectre of invasion, with Ontario the most likely battleground. Although the crisis had long subsided when the Liberals took office, they inherited responsibility for dealing with its aftermath. Canadians had generally remained ambivalent as to the likelihood of actual war, and Laurier himself did not place much credence in the American threat, but the crisis served to emphasis the poor state of Canada's military readiness.[134] Not only did the topic prompt the expected discussion in militia circles, it also, for the first time in decades, drew attention to the problem of naval control of the Great Lakes. Ontarians' interest also induced Laurier to entertain some expression of the idea. Groups in Toronto and Guelph had their applications to form naval brigades approved by orders-in-council in August and October 1897 respectively.[135] The subject also convinced the Toronto Branch of the Canadian Navy League to put forward a naval militia scheme in June 1896, one that was as concerned for defensive needs on the lakes as on the seacoasts.

Of greater import was the militia department's renewed interest in developing a Canadian naval force. At the time of the crisis, the quartermaster-general, Colonel Percy Lake,

134. Preston, *Defence of the Undefended Border*, 125–48.

135. "RNR & RNVR," 27 June 1899, 25–1–1, LAC, RG 24, vol. 5597.

had rushed to England to acquire a variety of war supplies, including 40,000 Lee-Enfield rifles and quick-firing Maxim guns, the latter being suitable for mounting on smaller vessels. Indeed, while in England, Lake had impressed upon the War Office the general problems facing the defenders of Canada with a report that "concentrated wholly on the naval aspects."[136] His request to the Admiralty for "expert advice on such matters as the armament of the Canadian fisheries protection fleet and its employment in time of war" went unanswered, but a separate discussion of a recent report by the Colonial Defence Committee provided Lake with all the encouragement he needed. Returning to Canada, he made a special investigation of "Naval Control on the Great Lakes" and submitted a detailed memorandum on the subject to the general officer commanding the militia in February 1898.[137]

Concerned primarily with "the arming in time of war of vessels of the Fisheries Protection Fleet ... for service on the inland waters of Canada," the report not only bore obvious parallels to the Navy League paper, it was also sanctioned by Canadian authorities. Prepared "in communication with" Captain O.G.V. Spain (in command of the FPS since 1893) and "with the approval" of Minister of Marine and Fisheries Sir Louis Davies and Minister of Militia and Defence Sir Frederick Borden, it detailed plans for equipping *Petrel*, *Curlew*, and *Acadia* with both 12- and 6-pounder, quick-firing guns purchased in 1896 and stored in Quebec. Out of consideration for legitimate fears that their permanent installation might abrogate the Rush-Bagot Agreement and give the Americans cause to build up their own fleet on the lakes, the guns were not be mounted but simply held in readiness. To facilitate their rapid outfitting in a crisis, Lake recommended "the transfer of said guns and the attendant mountings and stores from the charge of the Department of Militia and Defence to that of the Department of Marine and Fisheries." The quartermaster-general also noted that the scheme "entirely met with the approval of the imperial authorities [i.e., the War Office] who considered it to be of great importance, and who also recommended that, so far as possible, a naval organization and training should be given to the men of the Fisheries Protection Fleet."[138] To this end, Lake said that provision for a naval militia was to be made in the upcoming Department of Marine and Fisheries estimates.

The timing of the report was opportune. On the day it was submitted, 24 February 1898, Borden also presented Cabinet with a recommendation by General Sir Alexander Montgomery-Moore, the British general commanding at Halifax (and hence the senior British military commander in North America), that "steps should be taken to prepare in time of peace a scheme of defence for the Dominion of Canada."[139] Two such steps had been recommended by the Colonial Defence Committee in the last days of the Tupper administration and then been passed to Laurier's ministry for consideration. One, stressing the importance of yearly training of the militia, had been met by the re-introduction of summer training camps by Borden soon after becoming militia minister. The other, calling for "the organization for naval defence for the Great Lakes," had been set aside in the expectation that the Royal Navy would

136. Gooch, "Great Britain and the Defence of Canada," 370.

137. Lake to Minister of Militia and Defence, 24 February 1898, 1005-3-1, LAC, RG 24, vol. 6197.

138. Ibid.

139. Borden to Aberdeen, 25 February 1898, LAC, MG 26 G, 219386.

meet the requirement. Since that had not happened, Lake's memorandum helped sway Cabinet opinion in favour of a closer examination of Canadian defence plans.[140]

For his part, Laurier was careful to keep the proposal within a strict framework by establishing a commission to investigate Canada's military needs. The governor general, Lord Aberdeen, through the Colonial Office, immediately requested that both the War Office and Admiralty extend the services of one naval and two military officers to assist in the investigation. Aberdeen already had agreed to Borden's suggestion that Colonel Lake be one of the military representatives, because of his "special knowledge of the country and of the conditions of the militia service," a clear and early recognition of Lake's sympathy for Canadian aspirations.[141] To minimize the danger that the imperial view would predominate, Borden insisted that he and Davies be included on the committee. The Admiralty made no secret of their displeasure at the additions, which their lordships "thought would bring no extra strength to the inquiry and which they therefore accepted with ill-concealed reluctance."[142] On the other hand, the new general officer commanding (GOC), Major-General Edward T.H. Hutton, thought that a defence commission independent of his membership and engaging politicians more directly "would have more influence and would strengthen his hand in reforming the militia."[143] Equally propitious for success was the arrival in May 1898 of a new governor general with his own thorough knowledge of the subject—the Earl of Minto, formerly Viscount Melgund.

When the commission convened in August 1898,[144] it was presided over by Major-General Edward Pemberton Leach, until recently the senior engineer officer at Halifax who had previously prepared reports on the defence of Montreal. The commission toured the country until November, hearing testimony from various military commanders as well as Captain Spain, and presented their conclusions in December. For the most part, their report dealt with the employment of British regulars augmented by Canadian militia, but they also incorporated several new elements. For one, a naval force was held to be critical to the overall scheme, as stressed in Hutton's public presentation of the committee's findings in his annual report on the militia:

> As a most important element in the defence of Canada, I cannot but impress the necessity of the naval defence of Lakes Erie and Ontario. The Militia Act of 1886 [sic, 1868] contemplated the formation of a naval brigade, and I

---

140. Colonial Defence Committee, "Canada. Defence of the Dominion," 27 March 1896, LAC, MG 26 G, 219374–381; and Morton, *Ministers and Generals*, 120.

141. Borden to Aberdeen, 26 February 1898, LAC, MG 26 G, 219387–388.

142. Admiralty to Colonial Office, 27 July 1898, UKNA, CO 42/859.

143. Preston, *Canada and "Imperial Defense,"* 245.

144. Known variously as the Canadian Defence Committee; Canadian Defence Commission; the Leach Commission (after its president); and "The Commission upon the Inter-Oceanic Communications of Canada for Imperial Purposes and their Defence," a title proposed by the new GOC (Major-General Hutton), probably to camouflage the true mission of the committee from the American and Canadian publics. See Preston, *Canada and "Imperial Defense,"* 245. Among themselves, the commissioners tended to refer to "the Joint Naval and Military Committee," possibly the first use of such term in a Canadian context.

strongly recommend that, steps should be taken with that intention. Training ships with an instructional staff might be obtained from the Admiralty. I feel sure that the formation of such a force would be productive of most valuable results, not only as a strong and most important element of defence, but as a means of educating the seafaring population, and of improving the shipping interests of the inland waters of Canada.[145]

The Leach Commission also broke new ground by identifying that there should be two principles governing the future organization of a Canadian army: not only the time-honoured defence of Canadian soil, but also the power to participate in the defence of the British Empire. In this regard, Hutton saw the naval force only in a local context and not as a participant defending the British Empire. In part, this was recognition that, whatever the Royal Navy's attitude to the defence of Canada, it was still the unquestioned master of the seas. A greater factor, however, was the very different views of the War Office and the Admiralty as to the probability of war with the United States.

Those differences were reflected most starkly in the commission's secret report.[146] It began with the strategic premise that "Canada's greatest danger is its proximity to the United States.... [which] in the event of war with England would, as in the past, attempt the invasion of Canada." The broad thrust of the plan was not new, other than for the fact of its being compiled under one cover, and included previous instructions for the employment of existing government vessels armed with the 12- and 6-pounder guns being stored at Quebec. This sprang from the "strategical consideration ... that the [coast] defence of the long water frontier of Canada would be impossible without active naval co-operation." The committee decreed that "an imperial officer must be appointed to take charge of naval action," his general objective being that "the ships that are available will perhaps be best employed in keeping open the canals in the St Lawrence system [i.e., including the Great Lakes], until the arrival of imperial vessels." The committee gave further detailed instructions toward achieving the necessary organization (including a list of suggested stations) in a lengthy twenty-one-page chapter on "the formation of a naval militia." These included the creation of a 2,000-strong naval militia, 1,500 of whom would be trained as gunners and seamen, and 500 as firemen. They also called for the establishment of two armed training ships for naval militia instruction, steam-driven vessels that were to be available as cruisers in the event of war. Furthermore, the fisheries protection fleet was to be prepared to receive heavier armament and fitted with modern magazines and shell rooms. The crews of the Fisheries Protection Service were also to be placed on a more permanent footing and trained to fire modern guns. Another of the commission's recommendations was to provide and store in Montreal and Toronto a stock of quick-firing guns and equipment ready for installation on lake steamers selected to act as armoured cruisers. Finally, the report sug-

---

145. Canada, Department of Militia and Defence, *Department of Militia and Defence for the Dominion of Canada, Report for the Year Ended 31st December 1898* (Ottawa 1899), 40.

146. Canada, Department of Militia and Defence, Committee on Canadian Defence, *Report No. 1: Defence Scheme* (Ottawa 1898).

gested that ammunition be provided for those vessels and that authority be given to expend practice ammunition to train seamen in firing at moving targets while underway.[147]

These plans, as contradictory as they might seem to the developing political environment of rapprochement with the United States, must be seen instead within the context of sound military contingency planning. Admittedly a concept that was still in its infancy in most militaries around the world, Canada's approach was less developed than its southern neighbour's, whose war plans anticipated a possible pre-emptive strike. Interestingly, Washington did not adhere to British assessments of their ability to mobilize overwhelming force in the long term, believing instead in the need for surprise so as to forestall a long war that the American public was unlikely to support. Military opinion in the United States, as in Britain and Canada, also focused on control of the Great Lakes as a paramount requirement and sought to circumvent the restrictions on military preparation in the area. In the immediate aftermath of the Venezuela crisis, for example, United States Navy Commander Charles Gridley was ordered on a secret reconnaissance by Secretary of the Navy H.A. Herbert "to seek out 130 ships which, armed with guns and torpedoes, could seize control of Lakes Erie, Ontario, and Champlain, and the upper St Lawrence River."[148]

Although there is no evidence of a link to Herbert's instructions, the United States also requested amendments to the Rush-Bagot agreement to allow "warships to be built on the lakes for use elsewhere and permitting other ships for naval training." Neither the British nor the Canadians saw any need for change, but the American position hardened early in the process with the outbreak of the Spanish–American War in April 1898. Wanting to take advantage of the industrial capacity of their builders on the lakes, the Americans put forward an essentially non-negotiable offer. In return for allowing production in Great Lakes yards (only one vessel could be built at a time, with delivery to the seaboard to be completed before the next ship was started) the United States would agree that no warships would be stationed on the lake, other than two unarmoured but armed vessels no greater than 1,000 tons "to be used solely for ... naval instruction and training." Six cutters would be allowed, but "for police and revenue service only." Fearing that the Americans would abrogate the treaty and "fill the lakes with warships" if he did not accept, Laurier went along, as did the British, who were consoled also by the CDC's opinion that "the revisions were allowable on strategical grounds."[149]

Further complicating the issue, Captain W.G. White, the Royal Navy officer on the Leach Commission, was proving to be an unexpected advocate of a Canadian naval militia. Pointing to the examples of a pair of old US steamers, *Yantic* and *Frolic* (each of about 900 tons and armed for the training use of the Michigan and Illinois militias, respectively), White recommended that "substantial training ships ... of such a class as to be able to give a good account of themselves" be established at both Montreal and Toronto, and that the fisheries vessels stationed below Montreal (and hence not subject to the Rush-Bagot limitations) be

---

147. Canada, Department of Militia and Defence, Committee on Canadian Defence, *Report No. II: Recommendations* (Ottawa 1898).

148. Preston, *Defence of the Undefended Border*, 133, 135.

149. Alvin C. Gluek, "The Invisible Revision of the Rush-Bagot Agreement, 1898–1914," *Canadian Historical Review*, LX (December 1979), 471–72.

prepared for "the reception of a more modern armament."[150] The fragmentary historical record makes it difficult to establish whether White was working upon his own intuition or upon direction from the Admiralty, but there are indications that the Admiralty wished to encourage greater colonial participation in the naval defence of the empire, especially in the cases of the two holdouts at the 1897 Colonial Conference, Canada and New-foundland. At the end of August 1898, the first lord, Viscount Goschen, addressed a long private letter to the commander-in-chief of the North America squadron. He wrote that "the question of the formation of a naval reserve in the colonies has been repeatedly under my consideration lately," and directed the C-in-C to start discussions with those governments regarding the establishment of local branches of such a force. "The Admiralty as you know have hitherto been cold on this subject…. Personally my view is that I would gladly—very gladly—welcome a colonial naval reserve, provided administrative difficulties can be over-come, and provided such a force be real and efficient."[151]

The recipient of Goschen's ruminations was Vice-Admiral Sir John Fisher, who had been third sea lord and comptroller of the navy when Goschen was appointed first lord in 1895. Better known for the revolutionary changes he would bring to the navy during his initial tenure as first sea lord, commencing in 1904, "Jacky" Fisher was already forming his con-ception of the future navy, and in the "backwater of naval activity" that was Halifax, he had ample opportunity to devote to thought. The dynamic Fisher had been appointed com-mander of the station in the fall of 1897 specifically with a mandate to reinforce the squadron "to strengthen diplomatic pressure at the conference table" over renewed Vene-zuela boundary issues. A year later, a confrontation between French and British forces in central Africa—the Fashoda incident—once again made France the object of Royal Navy attention with the result that Britain gave tacit support to the United States in its dispute with Spain. Even as Fisher, like most other British officers of the period, remained wary of the Americans, he was coming to appreciate that any moves taken by the colonies for their own local defence would lessen the burden on the Royal Navy. With the first lord's encouragement, over the winter of 1898–99 Fisher pressed upon Ottawa the urgency of tak-ing some action on the formation of a naval reserve as described by the Leach Commis-sion. In response to Fisher's first despatch, Laurier wrote to Minto from Washington—where he was a member of the Canada–UK joint high commission trying to resolve the Alaska boundary dispute, among other irritants—to state that the matter had been under con-sideration but that no conclusions had been reached. The prime minister suggested that Minto "write privately to Admiral Fisher to ask him not to press for an answer at this moment but to wait until we have concluded our labours here."[152]

150. White to Admiralty, 29 November 1898, UKNA, CO 42/859.

151. Goschen to Fisher, 31 August 1898, UKNA, Admiralty series (hereafter ADM) 128/112.

152. Minto to Fisher, 2 December 1898 and 13 January 1899, LAC, MG 27 II B1, Minto Letterbooks, vol. I; Fisher to Minto, 26 September 1898, UKNA, ADM 1/7573; Roger Willock, "Gunboat Diplomacy: Operations of the North America and West Indies Squadron, 1875–1915, Part II: Fuel Oil and Wireless," *American Neptune*, XXVIII:2 (April 1968), 87–92; and Admiral Sir R.H. Bacon, *The Life of Lord Fisher of Kilverstone, Admiral of the Fleet* (London 1929), 115–17.

In the event, the joint high commission talks collapsed in January 1899 over the question of the Alaska boundary, leaving the Rush-Bagot issue officially unresolved but with all sides believing there was a basic agreement. The rationale behind the Leach report's recommendations had largely evaporated. Indeed, initial Canadian action toward improving naval capability on the Great Lakes was muted by the militia's concentration on the land defences of southern Ontario. Nothing immediately tangible was realized on the naval side other than implementation of Colonel Lake's recommendation that the quick-firing artillery pieces and their mounts and stores be transferred to the marine department building at Quebec City. When the report was presented to Governor General Minto for forwarding to the Colonial Office, he noted that its strategical conditions pertained to "a considerably earlier period than the present," and doubted "if the Canadian public would be satisfied with any scheme which made no provision for the defence of Winnipeg and still more for the defence of Vancouver—a city which is growing from day to day in wealth and importance." Referring specifically to the proposed organization of a naval militia, he harkened back to his 1885 experience to observe that "there may be differences of opinion between the militia department and the Marine and Fisheries department—the latter at present having under its control the few government vessels the dominion possesses for protection of fisheries, etc., would probably wish to claim the development of the naval department together with the political patronage it would afford."[153]

Davies, still minister of marine and fisheries, maintained at least a personal interest in the project—he was the member for Queen's West in Prince Edward Island—and asserted privately to Captain White that "he is the proper head of any naval force that may be provided and he had already prepared a scheme for training the fishermen of the maritime provinces."[154] Sufficient attention had been drawn to the subject that rumours circulating around Ottawa drew the interest of opposition Conservatives such as Sam Hughes, a rising figure within the influential militia lobby. Even members of the Liberal caucus made pointed inquiries in parliament, asking if it was "the intention of the government to take any steps towards the formation of a naval reserve, or a naval brigade, or a marine militia of any kind in Canada, whether in connection with the present militia force or otherwise?"[155] Laurier and his ministers obfuscated, but it is evident that the naval project, far from having been dismissed, had been elevated to the level of serious government consideration. When Laurier sent Davies to London in September 1899 to meet with Colonial and Foreign Office officials in preparation for a renewed round of Alaska boundary talks in Washington, an important side trip was to speak with the first lord about the "proposed Canadian naval reserve."[156]

When the Royal Naval Reserve was established in 1859 to provide a body of trained men to assist the expansion of the regular navy in time of war, the reason for its establishment

153. Minto to Chamberlain, 5 April 1899, UKNA, CO 42/686; Gluek, "Invisible Revision of the Rush-Bagot Agreement," 472; and Militia and Defence, *Militia and Defence Report 1898*, 1–3.

154. White to Admiralty, 29 November 1898, UKNA, CO 42/859.

155. House of Commons, *Debates*, 4 April 1898, col. 3085, and 28 June 1899, col. 6048.

156. Davies to Joseph Chamberlain, 29 September 1899, Chamberlain Papers, BUL, JC 9/2/1G/2.

underscored what was to become a recurring problem of the RNR (and indeed, of most naval reserve forces to this day). The high degree of technical competence required of modern sailors, especially in the expanding specialty trades of engineering and gunnery, made it difficult for part-time sailors to obtain sufficient training to learn and maintain the necessary skills. When the 1889 Naval Defence Act was passed to address many of the shortfalls observed during the Russian war scare of 1885, the navy's increased numerical and technical needs placed further demands on trained manpower. As the writings of Brassey, Mahan and Jane led to a general expansion of naval awareness through the 1890s, one issue that received increasing attention was the need for a more effective reserve. The accessibility of this popular writing coincided with a surge in emigration from Britain to other parts of the empire. Many of these new colonists had previous naval or military experience, and the opportunity for continued application of those skills on a part-time basis, while seeing to the defence of their new homes, proved to be a popular outlet for a new form of patriotism.[157]

It was perhaps not unnatural that one of the first initiatives outside of Britain came from remote Vancouver, where many of these factors combined. Not only had the city been incorporated in 1886 after being selected as the western terminus of the Canadian Pacific Railway, the first CPR liners had also been financed in part by subsidies stipulating their availability for conversion as armed merchant cruisers. Although this arrangement may not have been widely known, Vancouverites were certainly aware of their relative isolation from the rest of the country, even if not as an outpost of the empire. For many years to come the city's population would lag behind that of Victoria, home to the provincial government and the locality in which the region's naval and military forces were concentrated. Rudyard Kipling was struck by the complete absence of defences around its "almost perfect harbour" when he passed through the city in 1889. "My interest was in the line—the real and accomplished railway which is to throw actual fighting troops into the East some day when our hold of the Suez Canal is temporarily loosened. All that Vancouver wants is a fat earthwork fort upon a hill—there are plenty of hills to choose from—a selection of big guns, a couple of regiments of infantry, and later on a big arsenal…. It is not seemly to leave unprotected the head-end of a big railway; for though Victoria and Esquimalt, our naval stations on Vancouver Island, are very near, so also is a place called Vladivostok, and though Vancouver Narrows [sic] are strait, they allow room enough for a man-of-war."[158]

A local businessman, C. Gardiner Johnson, of the New Westminster and Yale Pilotage Authority, felt much the same way. In March 1891 he submitted to the minister of militia and defence "some reasons why a naval reserve force would be a suitable one in Vancouver." Arguing that the local defences "must to a great extent if not entirely be dependent on marine defences and garrison artillery from its geographical location" and that "no other

---

157. Analytical literature on the RNR is sparse. The only full-length treatment devoted to the subject is Bowen's *History of the Royal Naval Reserve* published in 1926. See also Glenn J. Keough, "Imperial Defence and the Formation of the Newfoundland Royal Naval Reserve" (unpublished BA thesis, Memorial University of Newfoundland 1990) and Ransom, "A Nursery of Fighting Seamen?"

158. Kipling quoted in Peter N. Moogk, *Vancouver Defended: A History of the Men and Guns of the Lower Mainland Defences, 1859–1949* (Surrey, BC, 1978), 24.

branch of the service could possibly act owing to the dense brush and the nature of the country," he concluded that "a naval brigade would fulfill all requirements for defence as they would be trained to marine work and garrison gun drill. They would also be more effective if a sub-marine [*sic*] torpedo corps were attached to the brigade." He appended to the letter a list of eighty-three men from a variety of trades and occupations who "hereby apply to be enrolled as a corps of militia to be known as the 'VANCOUVER NAVAL BRIGADE.'"[159] While several of those applicants clearly made their living in the marine industries, a lesser number of them claimed military experience, making this very much a group of concerned citizens best fitting the later definition of untrained but enthusiastic volunteers.

On reviewing the proposal, the acting district adjutant general, Lieutenant-Colonel J.G. Holmes, recommended "the formation of two batteries of garrison artillery," not as a naval brigade, but as an expansion of the militia batteries at Esquimalt. With the establishment of a new battery also at Nanaimo, and incorporating an existing militia rifle company in Vancouver, that would make two brigades in the area—one each on the island and the mainland—able to concentrate within two hours, and large enough "to meet for drill which is now practically impossible."[160] As the distinction was a relatively minor one, Johnson agreed. For a while the matter threatened to be lost entirely in the complicated negotiations between the Canadian and British governments over the manning of the Esquimalt defences, but when the British Columbia Battalion of Garrison Artillery was reorganized in April 1893, it included a fifth company to be raised in Vancouver. Soon thereafter, the batteries at Victoria and Esquimalt were improved by the addition of modern breech-loading 6-inch guns and quick-firing 12-pounders, apparently a sufficient level of effort and firepower to quiet the local citizenry's anxieties.[161] Those guns might have been among the types to be fitted onto the armed merchant cruisers, but there would be no formal naval brigades in British Columbia just yet.

Within a few years, however, events on the far side of the Pacific returned the issue to the fore. On 1 May 1898, the Asiatic Squadron of the United States Navy under Commodore Dewey steamed into Manila Bay and destroyed the Spanish Pacific fleet before proceeding to reduce the port's shore batteries. All of Spain's Far East possessions were promptly taken over by the United States, and the Canadian public, along with the rest of the world, received a modern lesson on the importance of sea power in conquering an empire. In a personal letter to Laurier—the first of a long series that would span the next decade—H.J. Wickham of the Toronto Navy League was quick to use the example of "the present war between the US and Spain" to demonstrate "the urgent necessity ... to assist the Royal Navy locally in time of war." While underlining the value of coaling stations and docking facilities, Wickham's opinion was that such assistance should take the form of something a little more substantial, namely, "a Canadian naval reserve or militia [drilled] with the most modern weapons and under actual service conditions."[162]

---

159. Johnson to Sir Adolphe Caron, 21 March 1891, 25-1-1, LAC, RG 24, vol. 5597.

160. Holmes to Adjutant-general, 26 March 1892, 25-1-1, LAC, RG 24, vol. 5597.

161. Moogk, *Vancouver Defended*, 24, 31; and Sarty, "Silent Sentry," 58–72.

162. Wickham to Laurier, 7 May 1898, LAC, MG 26 G, 23127.

The league's concept of a "Canadian naval defence force" was the subject of a letter to the governor general, the contents of which were published in October 1898. Copies were widely circulated to politicians—including Laurier and Joseph Chamberlain—and to prominent businessmen. This proposal, with minor variations to keep it relevant to the times, was maintained as the platform of the Toronto branch for the next ten years. Elements of Wickham's 1896 schemes were highlighted, including the aim of the "establishment by the Dominion of Canada of a naval force to supplement our present militia system."[163] It also proposed, however, that modern reserve ships be obtained from the Royal Navy and stationed on both coasts where they could be counted in the strength of the respective Atlantic and Pacific squadrons. Since the vessels would be Canadian-manned and their expenses paid by Ottawa, the league felt its proposals avoided the constitutional objections to a direct cash contribution. It was estimated that a Canadian naval militia of some 5,000 men, constituting both an effective addition to the strength of the Royal Navy and a complement to the existing militia forces, could be maintained at an annual expenditure of only $250,000.

Laurier received the Navy League's proposal at about the same time as Minto forwarded the correspondence from Admiral Fisher on essentially the same subject. The commander of the North America squadron, acting upon Goschen's instructions and having learned of the Leach Commission recommendations for a Canadian naval militia from Captain White, wanted to add his support that "it be deemed desirable to establish a Canadian naval reserve." He was also anxious to receive further details so that he might incorporate "the [trained] men (fishermen and others) … available for embarkation in one of HM ships for six months service afloat."[164] Just as he had stalled in replying to Fisher's earlier inquiry, Laurier refused to acknowledge the Navy League's proposal, in part because he was immersed in the joint high commission discussions in Washington,[165] but also because he had not yet received the Leach Report with its analysis of Canadian requirements. Writing to the GOC, Major-General Hutton, in January 1899 on the general question of naval defences, Minto railed about Laurier's failure to address either Fisher's or the Navy League's recommendations. "I have repeatedly pressed the government here for an answer—and have at last got one, viz—that no doubt the matter has been reported on by the Defence Committee, and that an opinion can not be expressed till that report is out; also that as the minister of marine is at Washington, he has no time to consider the proposals—The delay is entirely on the part of Canada."[166]

The governor general's anger was perhaps misplaced since Laurier read the report soon thereafter and then permitted Minto to forward it for the consideration of the colonial secretary in London even though it was primarily concerned with the American threat on the Great Lakes. Its emphasis was part of the broader context for general militia reform, something

163. Navy League (Toronto branch) to Aberdeen, 14 October 1898, LAC, MG 26 G, 27513–518.

164. Fisher to Minto, 26 September 1898, UKNA, ADM 1/7573.

165. Minto to Fisher, 2 December 1898, LAC, MG 27 II B1, Minto Letterbooks, vol. I.

166. Minto to Hutton, 21 January 1899, LAC, MG 21, reel C-1218.

that the prime minister was already convinced needed to be addressed. He may have accepted the report's recommendation for a naval militia because it coincided with the views of the Navy League and, as was commented at the time, "the policy of [Laurier's] administration during its first term was peculiarly a Toronto and an Ontario policy."[167] His Toronto advisers saw nothing incompatible between Canadian constitutional evolution and the development of a local naval force. Laurier's natural caution would also have convinced him that this was not a sufficiently pressing issue to require immediate resolution. Nonetheless, when Davies travelled to London in September 1899, the prime minister felt there was little danger in permitting his minister to speak with Goschen about the "proposed Canadian naval reserve."

By then, Laurier had come to realize that interest in the proposition was spreading across the country. In much the same way that the Venezuela crisis had drawn the attention of Ontarians to their military and naval defences, the Spanish-American War and growing tensions in South Africa lent urgency to Vancouverites' belief that a local naval force needed to be established. Late in March (at the same time that Minto was despatching the Leach Commission Report to London and the issue was being raised in parliament), Minister of Militia and Defence Sir Frederick Borden received a petition from the president of the Vancouver Board of Trade (other signatories included the British Columbia minister of finance and the president of the Union Shipping Company) calling for "a corps of about 100 men to be organized for service afloat in war times in defence of the colony in imperial or dominion government vessels ... The title of the corps to be: The Vancouver Seamen Gunner Volunteers, Volunteer Marine Artillery, or Royal Naval Volunteers." Again, the latent power of the United States was both the catalyst and example. "Whereas for some time past a desire has been growing amongst a considerable section of the inhabitants to assist in a personal manner in maritime defence against attack by an enemy from oversea, to which this colony is particularly liable, from its growing trade and numerous open harbours open to casual raiding. And whereas this feeling was brought to a head during the late Spanish-American War, when volunteer naval corps were formed in all the coast towns of the United States, and at the large American towns on the Great Lakes, the volunteers thus raised being actually called to service and utilized in the United States Navy in various capacities."[168]

In forwarding the petition to the minister, Hutton minuted that he would consider this question during his forthcoming inspection tour of Vancouver. But when that had to be postponed until the autumn, he suggested the petition "be submitted to the Admiral commanding the north Pacific squadron, for any remarks he may wish to make," to which Hutton would add his own observations. It arrived back on the West Coast late in April, but with the planned departure in mid-May of the incumbent Pacific station commander, any further investigation was held over to await the arrival of his successor later that summer.[169]

167. John S. Willison to George Parkin, 2 June 1902, quoted in Guy Robertson MacLean, "The Imperial Federation Movement in Canada, 1844–1902," (unpublished PhD thesis, Duke University 1958), 197.

168. "RNR & RNVR," 27 June 1899, "Petition to the Commissioners for Executing the Office of Lord High Admiral of the United Kingdom of Great Britain and Ireland, Etc," 1 March 1899, 25–1-1, LAC, RG 24, vol. 5597.

169. Hutton to Borden, 20 March 1899 and 5 April 1899, Governor General's Secretary to Deputy Minister Militia and Defence, 10 November 1899, 25–1-1, LAC, RG 24, vol. 5597.

By that time Davies had departed for his own trip to England, but if the minister seemed ready to conduct his talks with the first lord without benefit of the Pacific commander's advice, he did have the unequivocal support of the Atlantic station commander.

Sir John Fisher had sent his inquiry to the governor of Newfoundland, where the promise of quick action was already becoming widely known. Indeed, the ground had been prepared by public discussion of the Toronto Navy League's May 1898 circular for a Canadian naval reserve. At the Colonial Conference of 1897, Newfoundland had been singled out as the only one of the ten self-governing colonies that had completely ignored British calls to shoulder some responsibility for imperial defence, however trifling the others' responses. The following summer the St John's press engaged in a lively discussion of the proposition that the Canadian naval reserve scheme seemed a reasonable avenue for Newfoundland to pursue. In the course of meetings in London that same summer between the governments of Newfoundland and Britain, Premier James A. Winter and Colonial Secretary Sir Joseph Chamberlain agreed upon "the desirability of establishing a [naval] reserve force in Newfoundland."[170]

With all this before it, the government of Newfoundland was able to respond more rapidly and positively to Admiral Fisher. Although they could not offer concrete answers to Fisher's specific questions as to number of men trained and location of drill sheds, if only because the scheme was not yet in place, the governor did reassure the admiral that recruiting posters were being distributed among the outports that winter. It was anticipated they would attract a large enrolment at that time since most fishermen were unemployed—the fishery normally lasting from June to October—making a reservist's RN pay an attractive supplement. (Although the Newfoundland wage rate was comparable to Britain's, Canadian wages were significantly higher and the Navy League had identified the pay differential as a potential disincentive to recruiting Canadian fishermen unless Ottawa augmented the low RN pay rate.) The Admiralty, it should be remembered, had only overcome its coolness to the naval reserve idea in 1897, when members were required to serve in a warship for six months' practical experience during their first five years in addition to twenty-eight days of initial training. The prospect of large numbers of committed recruits seemed an ideal opportunity to test the new system, and in the first lord's view, the experiment was all the more interesting for its colonial setting.[171]

Local politics however, conspired to stall any initial success. Despite the enthusiasm of the St John's newspapers, people in the outports appraised the scheme as being controlled by city politicians, whom they distrusted. This perception was only overcome when a new and more energetic governor, Sir Henry McCallum, undertook a personal tour of the outports at the end of the 1899 fishing season, in company with the local RN sub-station commander, Commodore G.A. Giffard, aboard HM Ships *Comus* and *Columbine*. That effort produced some 300 recruits, of whom fifty eventually embarked in the fall of 1900 on an

---

170. Quoted in Keough, "The Formation of the Newfoundland Royal Naval Reserve," 43; Minto to Hutton, 21 January 1899, LAC, MG 21, reel C-1218; St John's *Evening Herald*, 21 July 1898; and St John's *Evening Telegram*, 26 July, 3 August 1898.

171. Governor H. Murray to Fisher, 20 December 1898, PANL, GN 1/1/7; Goschen to Fisher, 31 August 1898, UKNA, ADM 128/112.

inaugural six-month training voyage aboard HMS *Charybdis* (not the old warship of unfortunate Canadian experience, but her next-of-name, a protected cruiser built under the 1889 scheme). Of these, forty-four were promoted to the rating of "qualified seaman," leading Commodore Giffard to note that "we all consider them to be now a useful and efficient body of men who would be a formidable addition to our personnel."[172] This was sufficient success to encourage the Newfoundland government to agree to the purchase of a training hulk and proceed with the formal establishment of a reserve division. Other difficulties would arise, especially when the impoverished Newfoundland government discovered that the full costs of the scheme threatened to exceed the £3,000 per annum allotted. However, a satisfactory arrangement was negotiated by Premier Robert Bond in the fall of 1901, permitting a second contingent of fifty reservists to embark in *Charybdis* for the winter cruise of 1901–02.[173] The final hurdle was cleared for the establishment of a local branch of the Royal Naval Reserve when London passed the Royal Naval Reserve Act in 1902 to provide financial assistance to colonial naval reserves and help cover the Newfoundland shortfall.

Despite the enthusiasm and interest in Toronto, which had helped move the naval reserve file in Newfoundland in the first place, such was not to be in Canada. Laurier's more cautious approach to creating a reserve force was overtaken by a series of events that began in the fall of 1899. When the new commander of the Pacific station, Rear-Admiral L.A. Beaumont, finally addressed "the general considerations of the value of Naval Auxiliary Corps in time of war, and the useful employment of such a corps in view of the local conditions which prevail at Vancouver," he arrived at a different conclusion than Fisher. Admitting that "the formation of local corps for defence purposes is of great value and should be encouraged," he assessed that the most practical force to be constituted should be ashore, based on static defences, and not afloat as proposed by the Vancouver petitioners:

> Directly it is sought to extend the training of a volunteer force—though it be at a large sea port—in the duties of seamen gunners afloat, the expense and difficulty of instruction are increased out of all proportion to the result, and the value of the individual for sea service, with all the training of the kind which can be given him as a volunteer, is but very slightly higher than the same man if disciplined and trained to arms ashore....
>
> Applying these general considerations to the special case of Vancouver, it would appear that such a force as is proposed ... could be fully employed dur-

---

172. Giffard to the Administrator, Newfoundland, 13 May 1901, PANL, GN 2/38. In a longer report to his C-in-C, NW&WI for forwarding to the Admiralty, Giffard reported, "My own opinion is that the experiment had turned out a decided success, and that there will be no difficulty in getting the number required by the Admiralty, viz., 300 Newfoundlanders, to enlist." Giffard to Bedford, 10 May 1901, UKNA, ADM 128/112; Keough, "The Formation of the Newfoundland Royal Naval Reserve," 43–44; and McCallum to Chamberlain, 9 September 1900, PANL, GN 1/1/7.

173. McCallum to Chamberlain, 3 May 1901, PANL, GN 1/2/0; Boyle to Chamberlain, 20 July 1901, McCallum to Deputy Colonial Secretary, 16 October 1901, UKNA, ADM 1/7573; and Ransom, "A Nursery of Fighting Seamen?," 242.

ing War in the protection and defence of the Port.... The geographical position of Vancouver is against the use of volunteer naval forces outside the limits of the port—there is no war service afloat which requires higher naval training on the part of officers and men than the patrol and protection of interior waters....

I am therefore of opinion that the proposals of the petitioners aim too high and contemplate a sphere of action which is unattainable, but, that based on the more moderate standard which I have indicated, a naval brigade—for that would appear to be a better name for such a corps—thoroughly disciplined and trained to the use of small arms, machine guns, and light quick firing guns, both from boats and from the shore, would be of value and could render great assistance in the defence of Vancouver.[174]

This was almost precisely what the 1891 proposal that had led to the establishment of the company of garrison artillery. Hutton echoed Beaumont's skepticism of the value of naval reservists, telling the militia minister that "the organization of a naval brigade is not of any important naval advantage unless the degree of training is of a very high order and of a practical character ... [that] is not possible under the local circumstances."[175] In March 1900, the militia department's deputy minister advised the Vancouver Naval Volunteer Committee that their proposal was "not found desirable at present," but "will not be lost sight of in case the defences of British Columbia come before the government at any time in the future."[176]

Ultimately, however, any plans that the Canadian government was considering for a naval reserve were pushed aside by the outbreak of war in South Africa. The Boer War diverted both the public's and military's attention from the naval issue. It quickly demonstrated, however, just how polarized Canada could become over military matters. For several days in mid-October 1899, Laurier's Cabinet appeared on the verge of disintegration as those ministers strongly opposed to sending Canadian troops to fight squared off against those who were just as committed to sending a contingent. With his ministers divided primarily on ethnic lines—French against English—Laurier faced the most serious crisis of his administration.[177]

In an atmosphere in which Quebec viewed all government actions with suspicion it was not long before even the cautious Laurier naval policy came in for criticism. The matter had been set aside the previous fall because of the Cabinet crisis, but in March 1900, Henri Bourassa, the independent member for Labelle, Quebec, took the government to task over the issue of a naval militia for Canada. The government had previously been questioned in the House of Commons about Canadian intentions, but not since the outbreak of war.

174. Beaumont to Minto, 20 November 1899, 25–1-1, LAC, RG 24, vol. 5597.

175. Hutton to Sir Frederick Borden, 13 December 1899, 25–1-1, LAC, RG 24, vol. 5597.

176. Pinnault to Max Macgowan (Honorary Secretary of Committee), 14 March 1900, 25–1-1, LAC, RG 24, vol. 5597.

177. C.P. Stacey, *Canada and the Age of Conflict: A History of Canadian External Policies*, I: *1867–1921* (Toronto 1977), 57–74.

Bourassa, a vocal opponent of Canada's role in South Africa, aimed his questions directly at Laurier with ominous undertones. At issue was an announcement made in the British house on 26 February by the new first lord, Lord Selborne, while introducing the naval estimates. Referencing Goschen's talks with Davies the previous September, Selborne suggested that negotiations with Ottawa for the establishment of a Canadian naval reserve were "very well advanced." Bourassa wanted to know why, "with a question of such importance, the British House of Commons should be seized with a knowledge of the project mentioned by the first lord of the Admiralty, and that negotiations should be 'very well advanced' without anybody in the Canadian House of Commons, which has been sitting for a month, being aware of anything going on."[178] Although Laurier managed temporarily to avoid answering on a point of order, he admitted under continued questioning the following week that, while no arrangements had been arrived at, there had been "informal communications between this government and the imperial authorities on the subject."[179] From that time onward, the prime minister was to have trouble on the naval issue from French-Canadian—specifically nationaliste—opposition members. Bourassa was soon joined by F.D. Monk, Conservative member for Jacques-Cartier, Quebec, in the role of watchdog over the government's actions on imperial matters. Whatever the strength of his Toronto base, Laurier could not go against the intelligentsia of his native Quebec. As a result, the distinction of establishing the first branch of the Royal Naval Reserve outside of England went to the colony of Newfoundland.

As the first "imperial" war in which Canada became directly involved, the South African conflict underscored the divisions that Laurier had to navigate in moving any naval plan forward. After the contingent crisis, any progress on the naval question was quickly interpreted as a mere concession to Canadian imperialists, with dangerous implications for the unity of the country. No matter how limited the government's intentions might be in respect of a local naval force, the nature of sea power—particularly given the popular "sea is one" philosophy demanding centralized Admiralty control—made it more easily construed as an imperial force. At the same time, such a philosophy also suggested that there would be limited support for any local initiative and interests likely to undermine the authority of the Royal Navy.

As it was, the question of forming a Canadian naval militia did not arise again that year. Indeed, the results of the general election of November 1900 clearly indicated that the economic recovery associated with the Liberals coming to power continued to hold sway. The loss of twelve seats in Ontario, while indicating some disquiet with the government's policy on the Boer War, was more than offset by consolidation of the Quebec and western vote, and by the maritimes' rejection of several leading Conservatives.[180] The personal defeat of Sir Charles Tupper as leader of the opposition party marked the end of an era, while the absence of George Eulas Foster from the commons as military and naval critic largely accounted for the lack of debate on imperial or defence issues in the 1901 session.

---

178. Canada, Parliament, House of Commons, *Debates*, 1 March 1900, cols. 1,123–24.

179. House of Commons, *Debates*, 7 March 1900, col. 1473.

180. Joseph Schull, *Laurier: The First Canadian* (Toronto 1965), 397.

As an interim leader, the Conservative Party turned to Robert Laird Borden, a Halifax lawyer and cousin of the Liberal minister of militia. Allowed by his physician to accept the position for only one year, Borden "conceived his primary task to be revitalization of the Conservative party and not the remolding of the empire."[181] Even though imperial federationists in Ontario formed a natural constituency for rebuilding his party, it seems odd that one of Borden's first public pronouncements as leader was on the naval issue, and on a line not far different from that of Laurier. At the annual meeting of the British Empire League in Ottawa in February 1901, Borden moved "a resolution in favour of the formation of a Royal Navy reserve amongst our seafaring men," based on his belief that the country's maritime population could be organized into "as effective a body of naval militia ... as Canada already possessed in its land forces." The motion was endorsed by Aulay Morrison, the Liberal MP for New Westminster, BC, who interjected that the time soon would come when Canada would have to maintain a large fleet of revenue-protecting vessels or warships to guard her fisheries, which were already being exploited on the Pacific coast by American fishermen.[182]

Also present at the meeting was H.J. Wickham, who spoke as well to the motion, clarifying that the resolution "did not aim at a joint maintenance of one naval force by the mother country and the colonies, for that would lead to all kinds of friction. The idea was to establish a naval force in Canada as the complement of our militia force and to manage it in accordance with the regulations of the Royal Naval Reserve, after being adapted to local conditions." The wording of Borden's resolution and the quickness of the Navy League secretary to amplify upon it suggests some co-operation between the two men (as well as its resemblance to Laurier's own developing policy). There was no further discussion and the resolution was adopted unanimously. In fact, the only other mention of the naval issue before the meeting was adjourned was a late rejoinder by F.D. Monk, who had been one of the more outspoken MPs opposed to Canadian troops in South Africa. At this juncture, however, he outlined the position of his province as being that French Canadians "would not stand aloof when great questions were being examined by the league, but would contribute their quota to the study of them." Monk gave a qualified endorsement of his leader's earlier resolution but stopped short of advocating a naval reserve, acknowledging simply that "doubtless, in the formation of a navy league, [Quebeckers] would give a good account of themselves."[183]

Although it would be some time before a Navy League branch was established in Quebec, a national consensus was emerging in favour of a Canadian naval force. Wickham was spreading the influence of the Toronto branch, while the branch in British Columbia would soon hold its first general meeting in Victoria. That these branches sometimes adopted conflicting stands was frequently lost on outside observers, including Laurier, who tended to view the league as one homogeneous organization rather than as a public forum to

---

181. Harold A. Wilson, *The Imperial Policy of Sir Robert Borden* (Gainsville, FA 1966), 5. Even Borden's official biography, Robert Craig Brown, *Robert Laird Borden: A Biography*, I: *1854–1914* (Toronto 1975) is unclear on his subject's attitudes to imperialism and nationalism at this period.

182. Toronto *Globe*, 14 February 1901.

183. Ibid.

"spread information, showing the vital importance to the British Empire of the naval supremacy upon which depended its trade, empire, and national existence."[184] Under this broad mandate, the prime minister can be excused for overlooking differences in detail to the general agreement that Canada should assume some measure of responsibility for her own naval defence. The "what" was not in question even if there was no consensus on the "how."

Quite unexpectedly—at least for those who adhered to the notion of "one sea, one navy"—a more flexible view began to emerge among imperial officials in London. In the spring of 1901, as the War Office once again prepared to urge the Canadian government to take action on the Leach Commission's recommendations, it asked the Admiralty "whether there has been any change in Canada's strategic situation in the last two years, and if the detailed recommendations [as to the establishment of a naval militia] still hold good." Whitehall replied with a curt "no change" to the strategic situation but did suggest that "as it is believed to be essential to the efficiency of a naval force that it should be administered by a separate department, my lords are of the opinion that any naval force which may be raised should be under the minister of Marine and Fisheries ... [and] should be closely affiliated to the Royal Navy."[185] The distinction was significant because Minto had inferred that any such new force should come under the control of the Department of Militia and Defence rather than Marine and Fisheries. By making that distinction, however, the Admiralty confirmed that it had no essential objection to a local Canadian force.

On 25 June 1901, barely a week later, the new Pacific Station commander, Rear-Admiral A.K. Bickford, lent support to the idea in his address to the inaugural meeting of the Victoria branch of the Navy League. Although unaware of what was being said in London, he was nevertheless in harmony with it in advocating the formation of a local naval reserve. Three months later, in September 1901, Bickford drew the attention of the Admiralty to "the dangerously weak state of the [Pacific] Squadron."[186] His intention was to argue the importance of having credible naval forces at hand to lend weight to the British negotiators in their talks with the Americans over the Alaska boundary and the proposed Panama canal. However, the response of the senior naval lord, Admiral Lord Walter Kerr, underscored the Admiralty's growing perception of the limitations on British naval power. "The very fact of the great naval superiority of the US squadron in the Pacific should show us how impossible it is for us in view of the requirements elsewhere to maintain a squadron in the Pacific capable of coping with it.... It is impossible for this country, in view of the greater development of foreign navies to be a superior force everywhere."[187]

In fact, the discussions between US Secretary of State John Hay and the British ambassador in Washington, Sir Julian Pauncefote, concerning construction of the Panama Canal,

---

184. Laurier quoted in Marder, *Anatomy of British Sea Power*, 49; and see also, Kenneth S. Mackenzie, "The Navy League of Canada, 1895–1995: A Century of Evolution," (unpublished manuscript, Navy League of Canada nd).

185. War Office to Admiralty, 29 May 1901, Admiralty to War Office, 17 June 1901, UKNA, ADM 1/7576.

186. Rear-Admiral Bickford to Admiralty, 17 September 1901, UKNA, ADM 1/7513; and Victoria *Daily Times*, 26 June 1901.

187. Kerr minute, 14 October 1901, UKNA, ADM 1/7513.

had been instrumental in revising Admiralty policy in American waters and began what has become known as the "Great Rapprochement."[188] London's position was already weakened by early reversals in the South African war (British forces sent to relieve the invested garrisons of Ladysmith and Mafeking suffered embarrassing defeats in the Battles of Magersfontein and Colenso in December 1899) and, as Pauncefote candidly suggested to the British prime minister, "America seems to be our only friend just now and it would be unfortunate to quarrel with her."[189] In January 1901, the foreign secretary had presented Cabinet with a memorandum stating that Britain's weakness in American waters as a result of the United States' victory over Spain provided an opportunity to gain American friendship by freely admitting the latter's local naval superiority. Two days later the first lord explicitly excluded the United States in telling Cabinet that the two-power standard should be determined only in terms of France and Russia. The British government's acceptance of the Hay-Pauncefote treaty in the spring of 1901, meanwhile, allowed the United States to proceed independently in building a canal across Panama, while ostensibly fostering warmer relations between the two countries.[190] Although Ottawa had no objection to greater Anglo-US friendship, its main concern remained to have fair and flexible discussions with the American administration on where the boundary between Alaska and Canada would be settled.[191]

The assassination of US President William McKinley on 14 September 1901 frustrated Ottawa's hopes of a fair settlement. McKinley's successor, the hard-bitten and expansionist vice-president, Theodore Roosevelt, was not one to bargain away American interests, and the prospects for a settlement even partially in Canada's favour diminished significantly. This Laurier more or less admitted in moving the minister who had had most to do with the Alaska discussions, Sir Louis Davies, from the Department of Marine and Fisheries to the Supreme Court of Canada on 24 September. That the other concerns of that ministry—including the establishment of a naval militia—were not particularly pressing was underlined by the delay in naming a successor. In selecting James Sutherland for the post in January 1902, Laurier chose a former minister without portfolio who had no real qualifications for Marine and Fisheries (or any other ministerial post) other than that he had held the Oxford North constituency since 1880 and had acted as party whip for Ontario. In his tenure as minister, Sutherland proved steady but not noteworthy, concerning himself mainly with minor patronage matters and improving the St Lawrence ship channel.

In that respect, Sutherland's appointment and the priorities he brought to his department probably reflected national sentiments writ large: aside from the flurry of activity in

---

188. Bourne, *Britain and the Balance of Power*, 346–51.

189. Pauncefote to Salisbury, 19 January 1900, quoted in Stacey, *Canada and the Age of Conflict*, I, 91.

190. Bourne, *Britain and the Balance of Power*, 350.

191. Stacey, *Canada and the Age of Conflict*, I, 92; and Senator Fairbanks to Laurier, 18 July 1901, Oscar Douglas Skelton, *Life and Letters of Sir Wilfrid Laurier*, I: *1841–1896* (Toronto 1965), 58.

Victoria, with the war in South Africa dominating discussion, the naval issue was dropping from public view. It was soldiers, not potential sailors, who mattered. Yet it was those soldiers who, in a way, gave a renewed voice to the campaign for a Canadian navy. Returning from their South African battlefields, they did not hide their doubts regarding the competence of many of the British commanders under whom they had served, and most were convinced that their units had been every bit as good—and perhaps even better—than the regiments of the British Army they had seen. As a result, not only was there a sense that the senior posts in the Canadian militia should now be filled by Canadians, but also that the militia itself need not slavishly adhere to the British model when it came to its organization and equipment. Although it is not possible to trace direct links, it was perhaps inevitable that the militia's new self-confidence would spill over into demands for a Canadian navy.

CHAPTER 2

Toward a National Navy, 1902–1909

The first decade of the twentieth century witnessed a sea change in the movement toward a Canadian navy. The Boer War closed out the Victorian age by shattering many of its long-held tenets. The success of Canadian soldiers on far-off veldts quickly led to demands for general militia reform—its professionalization and independence from British supervision. At sea, the Royal Navy remained uncontested, but increasingly affected by global strategic realignments. The German naval laws established by Admiral Tirpitz in 1898 would eventually develop into a serious challenge, but the "enemy" remained France or Russia or, more dangerously, a combination of the two. European hostility during the Boer War had been tempered by US neutrality (extended in return for an earlier free hand given the Americans in their war against Spain), paving the way for the "Great Rapprochement" with the United States. Coincident with the Anglo-Japanese alliance signed in 1902, all major threats to Britain were now to be found in European waters. For Canada, the withdrawal of British squadrons to concentrate in seas closer to home created a vacuum into which the tentative efforts of the previous decades proved a solid foundation for the establishment of a naval militia as part of general militia reform. Discussions with the Admiralty, toward that end, would take up most of the century's first decade.

When Queen Victoria died in January 1901 imperial forces were still bogged down in South Africa, and her son assumed the throne as Edward VII without great fanfare, but the prospect of peace by the spring of 1902 meant that his coronation could finally proceed. To put a more positive face on the delay, the colonial secretary, Joseph Chamberlain, seized the opportunity to combine the occasion with a conference of colonial ministers. In accepting the invitation, Prime Minister Wilfrid Laurier declined to offer any proposals for discussion, a position that received wide support at home. Still, imperial defence inevitably became a popular subject in Parliament and the press, and especially in terms of naval defence there was a marked change of Canadian attitudes from those of the 1890s. Although pro-imperial calls for direct contributions were rare (see, for example the Montreal *Herald*), most commentators repeated the now-familiar proposals for the formation of colonial branches of the Royal Naval Reserve, as proposed by the Navy League and also now endorsed by the British Empire League. There were also new voices in favour of a distinctly Canadian naval force, and these were non-partisan in nature. In the House of Commons, on 25 March 1902, A.E. Kemp, Conservative member for Toronto East, spoke in favour of the gradual build up of a Canadian navy, and Liberal newspapers, particularly the

Halifax Chronicle and the *London Advertiser*, advocated Canadian action toward improved defences by sea as well as by land.[1]

Laurier remained nonplussed by any of this pressure. In the important Commons debate of 12 May, in advance of his departure for the conference, he uttered his famous promise to decline to enter "the vortex of European militarism."[2] He went to London in June 1902 clearly willing to discuss trade and preferential tariffs, but determined to allow no concessions to imperial defence proposals, particularly naval schemes. To that end, Laurier was accompanied by ministers Frederick Borden (Militia and Defence), William Fielding (Finance), William Mulock (Postmaster-General), and William Paterson (Trade and Customs) while James Sutherland, minister of marine and fisheries, remained in Canada, out of the Admiralty's reach.

Anticipating hard-line colonial positions, in his opening remarks Chamberlain made reference to Laurier's well-known quip, "if you want our aid, call us to your council," and preempted its repetition with a statement of equal significance. "Gentlemen, we do want your aid. We do require your assistance in the administration of the vast empire which is yours as well as ours. The weary titan staggers under the too vast orb of its fate. We have borne the burden for many years. We think it is time that our children should assist us to support it, and whenever you make the request to us, be sure that we shall hasten gladly to call you to our councils. If you are prepared at any time to take any share, any proportionate share, in the burdens of the empire, we are prepared to meet you with any proposal for giving to you a corresponding voice in the policy of the empire."[3] Of the ten subsequent sessions of the conference, two full days were devoted to discussing naval defence, and these were flavoured by the Admiralty's own use of the "weary titan" theme to introduce a major shift in naval strategy. Although the Boer War was not a naval conflict, the general opposition of the continental powers had served to underscore British vulnerability to a potential Franco-Russo-German combination in European waters of a type not seen since the Napoleonic Wars a century before.

Mahanian concepts of climactic battle fleet engagements were also beginning to take hold of Admiralty planning, breathing new life into the traditional offensive spirit. In his own opening remarks on the second day of the conference, the first lord of the Admiralty, the Earl of Selborne, bluntly advised the colonial premiers that standard notions of defence of trade by dispersed squadrons were to be abandoned in favour of a more aggressive method of protecting the commerce and territory of the empire: "to find out where the ships of the enemy are, to concentrate the greatest possible force where those ships are, and

---

1. Montreal *Herald*, 4 April 1902; J. Castell Hopkins, *The Canadian Annual Review of Public Affairs, 1902* (Toronto 1903), 107–10, 141–45; Canada, Parliament, House of Commons, *Debates*, 25 March 1902, col. 1803; Halifax *Chronicle*, 26 March 1902; and London *Advertiser*, 6 June 1902. It should be noted that the political affiliation of the Montreal *Herald*, quoted above in support of contribution, also was Liberal.

2. Hopkins, *The Canadian Annual Review, 1902*, 141; and Canada, Parliament, House of Commons, *Debates*, 12 May 1902, col. 4726.

3. Canada, Parliament, House of Commons, *Debates*, 13 March 1900, col. 1846; and Maurice Ollivier, ed., *The Colonial and Imperial Conferences from 1887 to 1937*, I: *Colonial Conferences* (Ottawa 1954), 153–55.

to destroy those ships. It follows from this that there can be no localisation of naval forces in the strict sense of the word. There can be no local allocations of ships to protect the mouth of the Thames, to protect Liverpool, to protect Sydney [Australia], to protect Halifax."[4] Such a policy, however, "demanded a single fleet under Admiralty control which could be moved at will to meet any danger and precluded either the formation of colonial navies or the maintenance of Royal Navy squadrons solely for the protection of certain colonies."[5] This definite hardening of Admiralty policy—a complete reversal in just two to three years of the more open thinking of 1899—was made with little regard for colonial susceptibilities and completely set aside lessons learned about the importance of convoy.

In the Canadian case, if the Royal Navy were to concentrate in home waters, the worst fears of the Navy League in Victoria would be realized, and Canadian maritime interests generally would be left without the direct protection they had previously enjoyed. Laurier surely accepted Admiralty arguments that the new plan merely reflected reality, in that the Royal Navy presence of late already had been markedly decreased with no significant decline in the overall security afforded. So far as his thinking on things naval had developed, his greater worry focused on British hesitation to confront the Americans on such issues of Canadian maritime concern as the Alaska boundary and the Atlantic fisheries. But however marginally useful Laurier might have perceived the squadrons in Halifax and Esquimalt to be, a complete withdrawal of the British warships was sure to raise an outcry from the local citizenry; and that would serve only to reinforce demands for a local dominion force which, of necessity, would be inadequate unless enormous sums were devoted to its establishment. The Laurier government was no less dedicated to funding infrastructure development than its Conservative predecessors, and having added large-scale immigration to its list of objectives, there was little in the way of government money for naval defence. Canadian interests, therefore, were best served by maintaining the status quo, or at the very least a more gradual transition to alternative arrangements.

The other colonies felt much the same, if for different reasons. Prime Minister R.J. Seddon of New Zealand was the first to respond to the first lord's advisory, proclaiming that the Australasian colonies viewed a continuation of their existing contribution scheme as already meeting Chamberlain's criteria for representation, but nonetheless "they desire for many reasons that the ships of the squadrons should be kept in Australian and New Zealand waters." This line of argument allowed Laurier to focus the discussion on the familiar Canadian objections to direct contributions. His initial response as such was to emphasize that he considered expenditures on public works such as "canals, railways, harbours, improvements in rivers and so on" to be as important as and probably proportionately equitable

---

4. Britain, Colonial Office, *Minutes of Proceedings and Papers Laid Before the Conference* (London 1902), 18–37, 173–77; and Ollivier, ed., *The Colonial and Imperial Conferences*, 161–68, 201–05. Reference is made to both these sources because, although the Colonial Office document constitutes the official minutes of the proceedings whereas Ollivier is only a much-abbreviated digest, the latter is a more readily available source to researchers. A.J. Marder, *The Anatomy of British Sea Power: A History of British Naval Policy in the Pre-Dreadnought Era, 1880–1905* (New York 1940), 372–92.

5. J. Mackay Hitsman, "Canadian Naval Policy," (unpublished MA thesis, Queen's University 1940), 29.

Prime Minister Sir Wilfrid Laurier, front row third from left, at the 1902 Imperial Conference in London. Sir Robert Bond, the Newfoundland prime minister, and Sir R.J. Seddon, the New Zealand prime minister, are seated in the front row left and second from the left, respectively. To the right of Laurier are Sir Joseph Chamberlain, the British colonial secretary, Sir Edmund Barton, the Australian prime minister, Sir A. Hime, premier of Natal, and T.E. Fuller, representing the Cape Colony. Sir William Mulock, the Canadian postmaster general, is in the second row, fourth from the left, while the Canadian minister for customs and trade, William Paterson, is sixth from the left, followed by Rear-Admiral Custance, the director of naval intelligence, and Lord Selborne, the first lord of the Admiralty. William Fielding, the finance minister, is in the back row, third from the left. Sir Frederick Borden, the minister of militia and defence, who also accompanied the Canadian delegation to the conference, did not make it to the photo opportunity. (LAC C-001659)

Gun crew from the first-class cruiser HMS *Ariadne* demonstrating the loading drill on one of the ship's sixteen 6-inch guns at Halifax in 1903. (LAC PA-028473)

to Britain's own military expenditures (suggesting also that Britain did not have to invest in such public works).[6] Therefore, even with promises of representation, the contribution proposals were still unacceptable to the autonomous colonies.

Laurier therefore made an unusually blunt, although only slightly exaggerated, statement of his government's naval policy to that time. It appeared as part of a Canadian memorandum on general defence issues that refuted British calls for closer co-operation with imperial forces by committing to make the militia "an efficient force [through] ... a more liberal outlay for those necessary preparations of self-defence which every country has to assume and bear." The inclusion of naval defence among these considerations was a new factor, and on this the message was clear: although Canada was firmly against contribution, that was because the dominion also valued "highly the measure of local independence which has been granted it from time to time by the imperial authorities." To that extent, the memorandum continued, even though at present "Canadian expenditures for defence services are confined to the military side," if (it was implied) the naval defence of Canadian coasts could not be guaranteed by the Royal Navy, then the "Canadian government are prepared to consider the naval side of defence as well." A politician as shrewd as Laurier would not have offered such a commitment on rash impulse, and indeed the paper went on to express the intention to establish, at an early date, "a system whereby the maritime population would be trained into a naval reserve," the clear implication being a scheme containing elements of those described in the previous chapter. The memorandum concluded with the affirmation that the Canadian government had "the strongest desire to carry out their defence schemes in co-operation with the imperial authorities, and under the advice of experienced imperial officers, so far as this is consistent with the principle of local self-government, which has proved so great a factor in the promotion of imperial unity."[7]

The Admiralty did not want to convey the impression that it could not meet its responsibilities, nor did it wish to force unilateral action on a subject known to have been discussed in Canada, so in summarizing the naval discussions Selborne told the other delegates simply that "Sir Wilfrid Laurier informed me that [the Canadian government] are contemplating the establishment of a local naval force in the waters of Canada, but that they were not able to make any offer of assistance analogous to those enumerated" by the other colonial premiers. While the first lord heartily welcomed the contributions of the other colonies, he offered no support for the Canadian decision. He ended his remarks on the curt note that "the sea is all one, and the British navy must be all one.... If, on the contrary, the idea should unfortunately prevail that the problem is one of local defence, and that each part of the empire can be content to have its allotment of ships for the purpose of the separate protection of an individual spot, the only possible result would be that an enemy who had discarded this heresy, and combined his fleets, will attack in detail and destroy those separated British squadrons which could have defied defeat."[8]

---

6. Ollivier, ed., *The Colonial and Imperial Conferences*, 164–66.

7. Colonial Office, *Minutes of Proceedings and Papers Laid Before the [1902] Conference*, 261–62. This critical memorandum is presented in Ollivier, ed., *The Colonial and Imperial Conferences* only in précis form, and does not mention the naval aspects.

8. Colonial Office, *Minutes of Proceedings and Papers Laid Before the [1902] Conference*, 263–65.

His statement was aimed not just at the Canadian premier, however, as both Australia and New Zealand continued to insist that their increased donations (of £200,000 and £40,000 per annum respectively) go towards the improvement of the existing Australasian squadron, with the implication that otherwise they too might consider the local force option. (Prime Minister Sir Edmund Barton of Australia, a country that had recently been federated into a single commonwealth, was especially insistent on this point.) When the first lord met this further opposition to the concentration scheme, he realized that it was perhaps premature, and one result of the conference was that there would be no radical change in strategy for the time being. Royal Navy squadrons would remain on their stations until some other contingency could be worked out. As for the other participants at the conference, the precise agreement between the Admiralty and the governments of Australia and New Zealand called for the maintenance on the Australian station of a force consisting of a first-class armoured cruiser, two second-class and four third-class protected cruisers, four sloops, and a naval reserve of twenty-five officers and 700 seamen and stokers (from which one of the cruisers would be manned). The Cape Colony and Natal undertook to increase significantly their unconditional annual contributions, the former from £30,000 to £50,000, and Natal from £12,000 to £35,000.[9]

Premier Sir Robert Bond of Newfoundland obtained mixed results. Somewhat presciently, he painted St John's as the ideal location from which to secure the North Atlantic cables and grain traffic vital for British survival in time of war, but his bid to have that city established as a defended cruiser base failed. He was more successful in gaining acknowledgement that a local division of the Royal Naval Reserve be counted as a direct contribution by Newfoundland "according to its means" to imperial oceanic defence requirements. The arrangements finalized with Selborne were that, in return for £3,000 annually, the obsolescent screw corvette HMS *Calypso* (built in 1883) would be refitted locally and assigned to St John's as a reserve drillship. Commanded by a regular Royal Navy officer with long experience at British reserve training facilities, initially Commander R.M. Walker, and with a complement of twenty-eight regular RN instructors, the vessel was equipped with a modern quick-firing 5-inch and 6-inch main armament, together with two Maxims and two 14-inch torpedo tubes, and could accommodate up to 300 reservists. The training thus received would be consolidated through continuation of the annual training cruises, although *Calypso* arrived in port on 15 October 1902, too late to prepare any additional recruits for the late-November departure of HMS *Charybdis*.[10]

Still, the most significant development to come out of the conference was Canada's proposal. Some authors have claimed Laurier's statement at the conference as the origin of

9. G.N. Tucker, *The Naval Service of Canada: Its Official History, I: Origins and Early Years* (Ottawa 1952), 108; and Bob Nicholls, *Statesmen and Sailors: Australian Maritime Defence, 1870–1920* (Balmain, Australia 1995), 63–64.

10. Bernard Ransom, "A Nursery of Fighting Seamen? The Newfoundland Royal Naval Reserve, 1901–1920," in Michael Hadley, Rob Huebert, and Fred W. Crickard, eds., *A Nation's Navy, In Quest of Canadian Naval Identity* (Montreal 1996), 241, 243; Admiralty to Colonial Office, M.9881, 11 August 1902, Public Archives of Newfoundland (hereafter PANL), GN1/2/0; Colonial Office, *Minutes of Proceedings and Papers Laid Before the [1902] Conference*, 263–65; and Admiralty to C-in-C, NA&WI, 16 September 1902, United Kingdom National Archives (hereafter UKNA), Admiralty series (hereafter ADM) 128/112.

Canadian naval policy, while others have dismissed it as another tactic of the Canadian prime minister to avoid having to pay a contribution for the Royal Navy's upkeep.[11] These interpretations can be refuted, respectively, by the progress of Canadian thinking on naval matters to that point and by the firm stand of the Admiralty against colonial navies. In fact, though it seemed little more than a paper declaration, the Canadian ministers' memorandum on defence was a restatement of government intentions—as well known to Chamberlain and Selborne as they were to Laurier—that Canada would assume in due course a degree of responsibility for local naval defence. The important difference is that this time Laurier had been obliged to put the statement in writing.

The prime minister had other, immediate issues to deal with when he returned to Ottawa in October 1902, but resolution of these issues would be a critical development in the naval project to which he had just officially committed his government. Relations between Laurier and his Quebec lieutenant, Minister of Public Works Israël Tarte, had grown increasingly strained since Tarte's opposition to the formation of the South African contingents. Tarte had used the occasion of Laurier's absence from Canada to make a direct challenge for the leadership of the Liberal party. Dismissal of the rebellious minister necessitated a Cabinet shuffle that affected marine portfolios, with James Sutherland shifted to Public Works and Joseph-Raymond Fournier Préfontaine, until recently mayor of Montreal (1898–1902), elevated to the Department of Marine and Fisheries. Although not unexpected, the latter choice was somewhat controversial. Like his predecessor, Préfontaine carried no particular marine qualifications, other than his position on the Montreal Harbour Commission that went with the mayoralty. A powerful figure in municipal politics, however, Préfontaine had profited from an impressive political machine that in turn had inspired an ultimately successful local municipal reform movement, hastening his move to federal politics. But also as mayor he had supported Laurier in allowing volunteers to be sent to South Africa, for which Laurier remained grateful. Although it was not the prime minister's main consideration, having a man from Quebec with such favourable attitudes in charge of the marine department could prove useful in presenting a naval militia to that province. Thus began a feature of the Laurier Cabinet, naming a French Canadian to the Department of Marine and Fisheries, and later the Naval Service, portfolio.[12]

---

11. Hitsman, "Canadian Naval Policy," 31; and William Higham, "The Laurier-Borden Naval Controversy," (unpublished MA thesis, University of Toronto 1951), 27. This misleading impression was given credence by a subsequent Minister of Marine and Fisheries (L.P. Brodeur) in 1909, when he stated, "I must say that … as a consequence of the statements which were made at the Conference of 1902, we started immediately the nucleus of a navy." Britain, Colonial Office, *Proceedings of the 1909 Imperial Conference on Naval and Military Defence* (London 1909), 43. See also N.D. Brodeur, "L.P. Brodeur and the Origins of the Royal Canadian Navy," in James Boutilier, ed., *The RCN in Retrospect, 1910–1968* (Vancouver 1982), 14. The contrary view is most notably presented in John Edward Kendle, *The Colonial and Imperial Conferences, 1887–1911: A Study in Imperial Organization* (London 1967), 52. The previous official history, Tucker, *The Naval Service of Canada*, I, 109, concludes: "the evidence invalidates any statement that in 1902 the idea of forming a Canadian navy entered the field of practical politics." It is clear, however, that Tucker himself had not been privy to all the available evidence.

12. Richard Gimblett, "'The Incarnation of Energy': Raymond Préfontaine, the Hydrographic Survey of Canada and the Establishment of a Canadian Naval Militia," in William Glover, ed., *Charting Northern Waters: Essays in Commemoration of the Centenary of the Canadian Hydrographic Survey* (Montreal 2004), 74–92.

The prime minister's primary motive in Préfontaine's selection, however, was more practical. The battle with Tarte had unleashed a host of other problems revolving around preferential tariff, marine transportation, revival of the shipbuilding industry, and ministerial responsibility. At the same time, the priorities for developing national infrastructure were shifting to the marine sector; the new railroads opening the northern prairies required development of major ports at Prince Rupert and on Hudson Bay; a new shipping channel from Georgian Bay to the Ottawa River was planned to bypass potential American interference on the lower Great Lakes; a variety of business interests were pushing to revive the long-dormant issue of a fast Atlantic steamship service necessitating major redevelopment of the ports of Halifax, Quebec City, and Montreal; and the St Lawrence shipping channel required upgrading. Laurier took three full weeks to reorganize his Cabinet, using the time to usher in a major revision of the machinery of his government. A highlight of the exercise was the transfer of the majority of marine infrastructure responsibilities from the care of the Department of Public Works to that of Marine and Fisheries. Previously, the latter had been a sleepy backwater of buoys and fish, and the most recent minister, Sutherland, had been uninspired. For the task at hand, Laurier needed "a strong, aggressive man with many qualities of leadership ... [and being] the incarnation of energy"—and that is just how the Liberal party organ, the Toronto *Globe*, heralded Préfontaine's appointment on 11 November 1902.[13]

The new minister quickly turned his touted "genius for organizing" and "capacity for work" to the task of rationalizing inter-departmental responsibilities in marine matters. A broad thrust was sketched out in rough drafts of the appropriate legislation by the end of the 1902–03 fiscal year, but working out the bureaucratic administrative details to put it all into effect would take several more months. An order-in-council of 7 January 1904 officially transferred large segments of marine-oriented functions (such as all hydrographic work, public works projects in the St Lawrence Ship Channel, wharf repair, and jurisdiction over harbour commissioners, as well as all monies voted for the above listed projects) from the Departments of Public Works and of Railways and Canals to Marine and Fisheries. As well, the series of newly constructed Marconi wireless telegraphy (WT) stations on the East Coast were soon placed under the supervision of the marine department. Accompanying budgetary expenditures were so large that by April of that year claims were made that "these changes ... put Mr Préfontaine in control of the greatest spending department of the dominion government," and as events would demonstrate, the potential increase to his personal power and prestige was not lost upon the new minister.[14]

---

13. Hopkins, *The Canadian Annual Review, 1902*, 18; and Joseph Schull, *Laurier: The First Canadian* (Toronto 1965), 413–14.

14. J. Castell Hopkins, *The Canadian Annual Review of Public Affairs, 1904* (Toronto 1905), 27; Michele Brassard and Jean Hamelin, "Raymond Préfontaine," in Ramsay Cook and Jean Hamelin, eds., *Dictionary of Canadian Biography*, XIII: *1901–1910* (Toronto 1994), 843–44; Gourdeau to Préfontaine, 31 March 1903, rough draft of "An Act to Amend 'The Public Works Act,' nd, "Act Respecting the Department of Marine and Fisheries," nd, Préfontaine to Laurier, 6 July 1903, Préfontaine to Governor-General-in-Council, 7 January 1904, Library and Archives Canada (hereafter LAC), Manuscript Group (hereafter MG) 26 G, reel C-799, 71652–53, reel C-802, 74825–28, reel C-807, 80814–16; *Statutes of Canada*, 3 Edward VII, cap. 53; and T.E. Appleton, *Usque ad Mare: A History of the Canadian Coast Guard and Marine Services* (Ottawa 1968), 81–86.

Meanwhile, the Canadian public's naval awareness had received a measurable boost. As an immediate consequence of the 1902 Colonial Conference, the Navy League of Great Britain despatched an "Honorary Envoy to the Colonies," Harold Frazer Wyatt, on a speaking tour to organize branches of the league throughout the empire. His first stop was Canada, where from November 1902 to February 1903 he met his objective organizing branches in Montreal, Kingston, Ottawa, Saint John, Halifax, Sydney, Charlottetown, Quebec City, and Winnipeg, and speaking in other established centres such as Toronto, Victoria and Vancouver. Moreover, in each city he was able to attract important local personalities as branch officials.[15] In Ottawa, these included Sir Sanford Fleming as president, and three of Laurier's ministers in honorary positions: the newly appointed Préfontaine, along with Sir Frederick Borden and S.A. Fisher (Agriculture). Everywhere he went, Wyatt expressed his philosophy of a united fleet, but it seemed that Canadians had their own ideas about naval defence, and the Canadian ministers in particular were careful to state their alternate view.

The Montreal branch was organized about the same time as Préfontaine's appointment to Cabinet, and he used the occasion of a 19 November banquet in honour of Lord Dundonald, the GOC of the militia, to offer his first recorded thoughts on the naval issue. He "hoped the time would soon come when Canada would organize at least the nucleus of a navy, and believed that if parliament took such a step it would meet with the endorsation [sic] of all Canadians." Later, at the organizational meeting of the Ottawa branch on 24 November, militia minister Borden echoed this, being quoted as indicating that "the government fully recognize the duty of Canada to be in a position to bear its fair share of imperial defence. But the difficulty lay in the question of control. We are ready to do everything that will assist in forming the nucleus of a navy in this country." The net result of Wyatt's tour was the establishment of a number of peripheral Navy League branches in Canada, and although the distinguished Canadians attracted as members were willing enough to grant their blessings to the league's work, they proved to be not especially active on its behalf. To be certain, many resolutions were passed at the time, but once things settled after Wyatt's departure for Australasia, the centres of naval agitation in Canada remained in Toronto and Victoria.[16] Of more lasting significance were the public pronouncements by the ministers of marine and fisheries and of militia and defence. Almost certainly their use of the phrase "nucleus of a navy" had to have been authorized—if not initiated—by Laurier himself. Importantly, it had not attracted negative reaction, not even on the part of anti-imperialists such as Tarte and Bourassa.

At the organizing meeting of the Winnipeg branch of the Navy League on 20 January 1903, H.F. Wyatt quoted Sir Frederick Borden's use of the phrase "nucleus of a navy" as heralding "the government's recent announcement upon the subject of a new force."[17] He went on to allow that he had since learned "that this force was to consist of a Canadian

15. Hopkins, *The Canadian Annual Review, 1902*, 145–46; and J. Castell Hopkins, *The Canadian Annual Review of Public Affairs, 1903* (Toronto 1904), 267–68.

16. Hopkins, *The Canadian Annual Review, 1902*, 145–46; and Hopkins, *The Canadian Annual Review, 1903*, 267–68.

17. Hopkins, *The Canadian Annual Review, 1903*, 268.

naval militia, which was to receive its training in certain steamers to be provided by the dominion government.... Now a similar scheme had been formulated some three years ago by the Toronto branch of the Navy League [that would] ... ensure that the Canadian naval force should be used just exactly where it was most needed, namely, to strengthen the Royal Naval Reserve." Had he known the details of recent events in the Caribbean, he could have pointed to a practical application of such augmentation to a regular warship's crew. The now-annual Newfoundland contingent of naval reservists embarked in *Charybdis* for the winter of 1902–03 was finding its "training" to be especially eventful. Shortly after departing St John's, the cruiser was ordered to join the rest of the North America and West Indies Squadron as part of an Anglo-German-Italian force blockading Venezuela to press for the repayment of outstanding debts. Anxious not to risk its improving relations with the United States, and remaining somewhat suspicious of German intentions, Britain was determined to keep any intervention limited. In a quick sequence of actions on 13 December, the allied force shelled a chain of coastal forts. *Charybdis's* captain reported that the Newfoundlanders "performed creditably in action in the bombardment of the Puerto Cabello forts and the landings in Caracas ... as well as in the subsequent blockade of the Venezuelan coast," a rare occasion when colonial naval reservists saw action. The cruise was also noteworthy in that the reservists were under the supervision of Gunnery Lieutenant Walter Hose, who would become so enamoured of the colonial experience that he would marry a Newfoundland bride and eventually make Canada his home in 1911, as an early RN transfer to the fledgling RCN.[18]

It is not recorded whether Laurier knew of the employment of the Newfoundland contingent, but steps were already in place to assure a different employment of naval reservists in Canada. Following the transfer of Colonel Lake's quick-firing artillery pieces to the marine department stores at Quebec City in 1899, the new officer commanding the Fisheries Protection Service, Commander O.G.V. Spain, began to press the militia department to give his sailors training in their use. Spain had assumed command of the Fisheries Protection Service upon Gordon's untimely death in 1893, apparently by sole virtue of seniority, having joined the FPS several years earlier after retiring from the Royal Navy as a sub-lieutenant. As Gordon had discovered before him, his low substantive rank in the British service was an impediment in discussions with Admiralty officials and he was unable to compensate for their attitude by demonstrating any intellectual appreciation of sea power or administrative skill. Spain was canny enough, however, to recognize that his best chance for personal success lay in transforming the FPS into a naval militia along the lines previously advocated by Gordon. As we shall see, his period in command (until succeeded by Charles Kingsmill in 1908) was characterized by slow, if unsteady, progress toward that goal.

18. Ransom, "A Nursery of Fighting Seamen?" 242; HMS *Charybdis* log, 11–15 December 1902, UKNA, ADM 53/16950. For a fuller account of this Second Venezuelan Crisis see Henry J. Hendrix, "T.R. Averts Crisis," *USNI Proceedings*, December 2002, 66–69; and Roger Willock, "Gunboat Diplomacy: Operations of the North America and West Indies Squadron, 1875–1915, Part II: Fuel Oil and Wireless," *American Neptune*, XXVIII:2 (April 1968), 97–99. Walter Hose personnel records, 190, UKNA, ADM 196/44. Germany clearly was the instigator of the intervention, and even though US President Roosevelt had some sympathy for the European claims against the corrupt Venezuelan regime, the Monroe Doctrine needed to be upheld, so he despatched Admiral Dewey to take charge of the Atlantic fleet for "winter maneuvers." The allied attacks were completed the day before expiry of the American ultimatum to withdraw.

In Spain's view, the initial arrangement "of sending a sergeant to the ships as instructor was anything but satisfactory," so in January 1902 the deputy ministers of the two departments issued instructions for three officers and three men of the FPS to report to the Citadel for a six-week formal course during the fishing off-season. These results were "most satisfactory," and at precisely the same time that the Colonial Conference was winding down in August 1902 with the Canadian ministers' memorandum on defence, the minister responsible for fisheries, who had been left behind in Canada, was responding positively to a militia department invitation for the recent graduates to participate in the annual summer field and garrison artillery training at Saint John, New Brunswick. Spain was enthusiastic. "I am extremely anxious that a gun crew (ten men) should take part in the practice at S[ain]t John. All my officers and men who went to Quebec took First Class certificates in QF practice, and it is a great pity if this is not kept up." Building upon the additional success at the militia summer concentration, and with the approval of his new minister, later that fall Spain negotiated the detachment of an even larger ten-man contingent for the winter months of 1903. The officer in charge, Captain J. Pratt, commander of *Curlew*, provided a mid-course report on their activities: "all matters are progressing in a satisfactory manner, everybody is busy during the day at the several drills and during the evenings studying up for their written examinations in gunnery and ammunition.... There is a strong competitive feeling pervading all ranks in order to take the highest number of points.... Some of the men are not blessed with too much education and the examinations will be quite severe on them.... In my opinion a six week course, and the matters annually taken in hand, are about correct, and allows very little loafing." For his part, the commandant at Quebec commented approvingly on the final course report. "I cannot speak too highly of the conduct of all ranks while attached to the [School of Artillery] under my command. There was an entire absence of crime amongst the petty officers.... I consider these courses of much use to these officers and petty officers, and trust they may be continued next year."[19]

When these activities came to Bourassa's attention, he felt certain that something more was afoot. In March 1903 he proposed a motion calling for the provision of "copies of all correspondence exchanged between the Canadian ... and British [governments] on the subject of the organization of a naval school, training vessels, and of a naval reserve in Canada." When these were not forthcoming, he pressed an inquiry for return, to which no documents were tabled, probably because none of recent origin existed on that precise subject.[20] Rumours and speculation nonetheless persisted, while from the other political direction E.F. Clarke, the Conservative member for West Toronto, brought to the attention

19. Spain to Lieutenant-Colonel Wilson, 20 January 1901, Spain memos 27 October and 9 December 1902, Lieutenant-Colonel Pinnault to Lieutenant-Colonel Gourdeau, 17 January 1902, Spain minute to Wilson report on training, 14 March 1902, Pinnault to Gourdeau, 7 August 1902, Gourdeau to Pinnault, 14 August 1902, Spain minute (emphasis in original), nd [8 August 1902], Spain to Gourdeau, 31 December 1902, Spain to Wilson, 14 January 1903, Pratt to Spain, 21 February 1903, Wilson to Spain, 20 March 1903, LAC, Record Group (hereafter RG) 23, vol. 335, file 2914, mfm reel T-4020.

20. Canada, Parliament, House of Commons, *Debates*, 16 March 1903, col. 110, 24 July 1903, cols. 7297–8. There are no indications that the matter had been discussed with the Admiralty since the 1902 Conference, and certainly nothing of such a precise nature had transpired at that time.

of parliament an article appearing in the *Globe*'s 2 April edition speculating about "a scheme for establishing gunsheds on the sea coasts of Canada, where the fishermen may be trained in naval artillery." Pointing to the good results Newfoundland was having with *Calypso*, the paper claimed that "Raymond Préfontaine has before him a scheme which involves the appearance of three third-class cruisers in Canadian waters, one off the Atlantic coast, the second at Toronto, and the third on the British Columbia coast." It was presumed that the British government would supply the ships or that Ottawa would acquire "suitable vessels."[21]

As the *Globe* was still considered a Liberal organ, Clarke wanted to know if this was indeed the government's intention, but once again Laurier dismissed the press statements as "premature and unauthorized."[22] Clarke too pressed his questioning in the Commons, this time directed at Préfontaine. Before being rescued by the deputy speaker on a point of order, the minister of marine and fisheries was forced to concede that "the matter of the naval reserve is under consideration. It is being studied, just as the question of the militia reserve is being studied. I do not think that anything practical will be done in reference to this matter before next year. The two projects require a good deal of study as to the cost involved and as to how the whole scheme is to be carried out. So, we have not considered yet whether we shall buy old vessels or construct new ones. That is a question upon which information must be gathered, that we may establish the military service upon the best and most advantageous conditions."[23]

Importantly, Préfontaine did not deny the report. Indeed, if the details remained to be worked out, as a matter of policy the issue was already somewhat advanced. In March, the general officer commanding the Canadian militia, Lord Dundonald, reported to the War Office on recent conversations with his minister, Sir Frederick Borden, on the "Proposals for a Canadian Naval Force."

> The militia department cannot get even the money needed for bare military requirements, and there is no prospect of its being able to get any more for naval purposes. There is no means in the department for dealing adequately with the question.
>
> We both felt strongly that the authority which controlled the estuary of the St Lawrence (i.e., the Department of Marine and Fisheries) should also control the whole floating defence. The militia department has, therefore, given up the idea of attempting to organize a naval force.
>
> The new minister of Marine and Fisheries (who has charge of the Fisheries Protection fleet), M. Prefontaine [*sic*], is a powerful man, who is naturally bent on increasing the activity and influence of his department. He announced, immediately after his appointment, when he sketched his intended policy, that he proposed to take up the question of naval development. A small

21. Toronto *Globe*, 2 April 1903.

22. Canada, Parliament, House of Commons, *Debates*, 3 April 1903, cols. 944–5.

23. Ibid, *Debates*, 23 June 1903, col. 5296.

appropriation has already been made to this department for the purpose—about 25,000£....

I understand from Commander Spain, when he talked over the question of naval defence with me, that the marine department expects that the British Admiralty will be willing, when asked, to present them with a suitable training-ship as a free gift....

Should a naval school be started here, it is very important that the Admiralty should, if possible, have some voice in its control. Conditions can be laid down now while the naval force is in embryo and while money is an object which later on might never be agreed to. It must also be remembered in this connection that if any portion of the militia is taken from the control of the minister of militia, it is taken from the control of the imperial officer who commands the militia, and this imperial control should be reasserted in the person of a naval imperial officer.

Those in whose opinion I have confidence say that the only possible commander of the embryo navy is Commander Spain (late RN), the officer commanding the Fisheries Protection Fleet. He is a man with a certain following, and stands well with his minister, though his drink habits are not such as to commend him to many others. At the same time he is a capable officer, thoroughly British in sentiment, and keenly loyal to the British connection. His position is such that it would be difficult to pass him over; at the same time, in the interests of the empire, I strongly recommend that it be laid down that the officer commanding the Canadian naval force shall be an imperial officer appointed by the governor-general with the advice of the Admiralty.[24]

Within several months, Chamberlain referred the matter of "command and efficiency of militia" to the Colonial Defence Committee, with a specific request for an opinion on "the proposed modifications of the Militia Bill suggested by the dominion government." On the subject of "formation of a naval militia," the CDC repeated the recommendation of the Leach committee, that "Canada should take the same precautions" as the naval militias of the American Great Lakes states "and should raise and train a naval force and organize it to man the vessels at her disposal at the outbreak of war" and that "Canada should apply to the Admiralty for the services of a naval officer to organize this militia." The CDC observed simply that "no steps appear to have been yet taken to give effect to this important recommendation." The Admiralty response—a curt "their lordships concur in the terms of the memorandum"—did not address the issues raised, probably because of their presentation in the context of defending the Great Lakes, a prospect they had no desire to

24. "Remarks on the Inland Waters Naval Defence of Canada," 28 February 1903, enclosure (b) of Dundonald to Colonel Altham [WO Director of Intelligence], 6 March 1903, UKNA, ADM 1/7576; and "Canada: Command and Efficiency of Militia" nd, UKNA, Colonial Office (hereafter CO) 16448/03.

engage.[25] But neither did they object to the principles involved, and the CDC report to Chamberlain was therefore allowed to stand.

Back in Canada, in mid-June Minto had interviewed Préfontaine on the status of the investigation into the naval militia. A repetition of the minister's stock response, that the matter was under consideration and "would be further dealt with," led the governor general to despair at the glacial rate of progress:

> I cannot but think that the possibility of any definite action towards the formation of a naval reserve by my government is still somewhat remote; if any such idea genuinely exists, I am afraid it would seem to be in the direction of an enlargement or re-organization of the present small force of vessels and crews for coast-guard and other purposes, the officers and crews of which are appointed almost entirely for their political qualifications, the patronage for each vessel belonging to the member of parliament representing the district from which it is manned.
>
> I am much afraid that the commissioning by my government of any vessels for the training of naval reserves would in all probability be on the above lines.[26]

Of all people, Minto should have realized that even the act of thinking along those lines—being much what he, as Lord Melgund, had endorsed two decades previously—constituted progress by Canadian standards. The chief obstacle remained that Canadian ministers (for once in concert with the Admiralty) refused to take seriously the threat of American invasion across the lakes, and saw little to be gained from moving promptly on establishing a force to meet it. But it was the rise of the American bogeyman in somewhat different guise in the latter half of 1903 that pushed Laurier to take "definite action" on the measures he had dismissed as "premature and unauthorized."

By mid-summer that year, it was evident that the arbitration of the Alaska dispute was going distinctly against Canada on the undeniable legal grounds of not having allowable claims of occupancy of the territory. The prime minister realized that Canadian claims in other areas, particularly in the eastern Arctic islands, were comparably weak, as for years the only consistent non-native residents of these territories had been American sealers and fishermen. Laurier later told Minto that he was "really worried … about American expansion in Hudson Bay, in the Arctic, and in Newfoundland…. [T]hey could set up and occupy posts in the arctic for some years without anyone knowing it and that they could then claim possession by right of settlement."[27] To offset such an eventuality, in August 1903 he ordered the Department of Marine and Fisheries to mount an expedition to the eastern Arctic, leaving immediately. The department had undertaken Arctic voyages in the

25. Chamberlain to CDC, 11 May 1903, J.E. Clauson to Chamberlain, 28 July 1903, Admiralty to Colonial Office, 26 August 1903, UKNA, ADM 1/8904.

26. Minto to Chamberlain, 12 June 1903, UKNA, ADM 1/7576.

27. R.A. Preston, *The Defence of the Undefended Border: Planning for War in North America, 1867–1939* (Montreal 1977), 173–74.

past, but only occasionally and always of a purely scientific or exploratory nature; the explicit point this time was the enforcement of Canadian sovereignty. In this venture it is significant that no attempt was made to enlist the aid of the Royal Navy. Rather, not having a suitable vessel of its own, the marine department hired one, *Neptune*, a Newfoundland whaler that had been chartered in the past. Command of the expedition was vested, not in the ship's captain as usual, but in Major J.D. Moodie of the North-West Mounted Police (NWMP). Accompanied by a detachment of constables, over the winter of 1903–1904 he established the first permanent stations of the NWMP in the eastern Arctic for the "collection of customs, the administration of justice, and the enforcement of law and order."[28]

The impact of the Alaska arbitration did not end there. The final award, granting the United States full control of the Alaskan panhandle without any point of free Canadian access to the Yukon, was handed down on 21 October 1903. Although the Canadian delegation had been aware of the direction events were heading, the prime minister was still shocked at the final outcome. "Laurier did not regard the adverse decision as a consequence of Canada's military weakness," and he did not appeal to a British government determined not to let "subordinate [Canadian] interests ... stand in the way of Anglo-American accord." The prime minister realized that the dominion was on its own, and the only possible answer was greater autonomy; Canada had to tighten control in any area where the Americans could threaten it, and especially where British ambivalence might undermine it. Officially, reaction was expressed as renewed determination to seek greater independence in treaty-making rights, with both Laurier and Borden speaking strongly in support of the issue in parliament.[29] Behind the scenes, however, Laurier recognized that such power could only devolve in concert with an acceptance of increased responsibility in related matters, and to that end important developments were transpiring in the marine department.

Préfontaine was one of Laurier's strongest advocates of a treaty-making power. In part, his interest had much to do with the commonality of their basic attitudes on Canada's political status, but it also sprang from the opportunity to increase his prestige as minister. Since many of the remaining undefined areas in Canadian-American interaction were on the seas and the Great Lakes, much of the burden was sure to fall upon the Department of Marine and Fisheries, and Préfontaine's ministry, which was expanding, was primed to accept the challenge. For several years the commander of the Fisheries Protection Service had noted the need to up-grade the fleet's capability, particularly as American steam fishing tugs were proving their ability to out-run the aging Canadian fisheries cruisers. Now, on 10 October, shortly after Laurier first learned the thrust of the impending Alaska settlement, Préfontaine announced that a decision had been reached to proceed with the long-deferred purchase of new fisheries cruisers. *Petrel*, operating on Lake Erie, and *Acadia*, based on the East Coast, would be replaced with new vessels "constructed

---

28. Appleton, *Usque ad Mare*, 63–64.

29. R.A. Preston, *Canada and "Imperial Defense": A Study in the Origins of the British Commonwealth's Defense Organization, 1867–1919* (Durham, NC 1967), 332; Canada, Parliament, House of Commons, *Debates*, 23 October 1903, cols. 14773–843; and O.D. Skelton, *Life and Letters of Sir Wilfrid Laurier*, II: *1896–1919* (Toronto 1965), 62.

on plans prepared by the officers of the department." Later, in November, while in Toronto delivering a stump speech on the issue of the treaty-making power, Préfontaine explicitly linked the two issues by taking the opportunity to announce that the new cruiser for the Great Lakes would be constructed locally.[30]

Oddly, commentators at the time failed to recognize other overt links to military affairs. Earlier in the year, when the focus was still on the more general naval defence of the empire and the possible organization of a Canadian naval militia, only the *Toronto Star* drew the connection that "if Canadians desired Great Britain to stand by them to the point of war in such matters as that of Alaska they should aid in the organized defence of the empire." The *Globe* outlined a naval militia scheme by which the government would borrow or procure three third-class cruisers, but, under questioning in the Commons, the minister seemed to be at pains to dissociate the move from any military connection. No mention was made of a new vessel for the West Coast, perhaps because that would be too close to the scene of recent contention and draw attention to the new measures. Likewise, a request for funds to investigate the subject of a naval militia had been introduced as an addition to a previous estimate for the establishment of a school of navigation.[31] Presented in that context, neither move attracted more than cursory attention from the opposition.

Still, no one objected to the new vessels being described as "third class cruisers." If such terminology stemmed in part from their advertised employment in the traditional function of "fisheries cruiser," it borrowed just as much from the Royal Navy warship type designation, even if that suggested an embellishment of their actual size. By Canadian standards, the ships to be procured were visible demonstration that more than just a routine purchase had taken place. The Canadian Government Ships *Canada* (replacing *Acadia*) and *Vigilant* (replacing *Petrel*) were no ordinary fisheries cruisers. CGS *Canada*, 200 feet long and of 580 tons, was built in England by the veteran Vickers, Sons and Maxim, and clearly drew her lineage from the successful series of torpedo gunboats built by that yard for the Royal Navy in the late 1880s—precisely as advocated by Andrew Gordon, but less the torpedo armament. In turn, the slightly smaller 175-foot *Vigilant* was purchased from the Polson Iron Works in Toronto, and has been described as "the first modern warship to be built in Canada." Both ships were of steel construction with ram bows and quick-firing guns. Additionally, *Canada* was to be fitted with the Marconi wireless, a device only just then being installed on British battleships and larger cruisers. Even taking into account the need to modernize the fleet, the new vessels were easily the most technologically advanced—and expensive—fisheries cruisers procured in the pre-war years, and substantially increased the department's capabilities.[32]

---

30. Canada, Parliament, House of Commons, *Debates*, 10 October 1903, cols. 13659–60; Hopkins, *The Canadian Annual Review, 1903*, 118, 329; and Department of Marine and Fisheries, *Annual Report of Department of Marine and Fisheries, 1904—Marine* (Ottawa 1905), 95. While the aging *Acadia* was to be sold, the relatively newer *Petrel* was to be transferred to work on the East Coast where slower sailing schooners were still the vogue for fishing. The net gain to the department therefore was one ship.

31. Hopkins, *The Canadian Annual Review, 1903*, 269; and Canada, Parliament, House of Commons, *Debates*, 9 October 1903, col. 13545.

Other than the fact that they were acquired, and the circumstantial evidence described above there is little direct documentation exploring the timing of and reasons for the purchases. Certainly, the pieces of the puzzle all fit Minto's conclusion that Laurier was embarked—willingly, it should be added—upon a path that would see an upgraded Fisheries Protection Service leading to the establishment of a Canadian naval militia. Equally, there is nothing to suggest that Laurier's opinion as to its true military capacity differed from what he had told Dundonald regarding the militia upon his arrival in Canada: "You must not take the militia too seriously, for though it is useful for suppressing internal disturbances, it will not be required for the defences of the country, as the Monroe Doctrine protects us against enemy aggression." Contemporary observers who followed such matters closely, however, could be excused for taking seriously what seemed to be tentative moves towards the formation of a Canadian navy. Within days of the announcement of the new ship acquisitions, the British Submarine Boat Company offered to equip the Canadian fleet with submarines, then generally regarded as the best warships for port and coast defence.[33] Laurier's polite refusal must have been confusing, but it was as good an indication as any that he intended to emphasize the non-military role of the force.

A better idea of the direction Liberal policy was taking can be gleaned from the legislation that Préfontaine may already have been in the course of drafting, An Act Constituting the Naval Militia of Canada. Again, the documentary evidence regarding its development is slight, but the indications are that the government intended to present it in conjunction with Frederick Borden's revised militia bill early in the 1904 session. That the naval bill was patterned in the greater part after similar clauses in the revised Militia Act confirms that the proposed force was to be a complement to the militia, as recommended over the years by the Navy League and the militia itself. General expectations were also confirmed by the fact that no separate ministry was envisioned, the new organization falling under the control of the minister of marine and fisheries. What was new, but also in line with the revised Militia Act, was the establishment of a naval militia council, chaired by the minister and having "the power to deal with and administer matters relating to the naval militia." Similarly, with the position of a British-appointed GOC of the militia eliminated in favour of a chief of the general staff designated by the Canadian government, a "senior

---

32. Appleton, *Usque ad Mare*, 80. For photographs of *Canada* and *Vigilant* see pages 79 and 80 respectively. The classical definition of a cruiser is "any ship capable of undertaking scouting, commerce raiding and protection, and distant patrols," and as such it relates more to the notion of extended "cruising" capability than any particular size, and hence the further RN distinction as to 1st-class "armoured," and 2nd- and 3rd-class "protected" types. Still, the smallest such vessels in RN service were at least double the size of those envisioned for the Canadian FPS. On the idea of "cruiser" in the RCN, see Kenneth P. Hansen, "Kingsmill's Cruisers: The Cruiser Tradition in the Early Royal Canadian Navy," *The Northern Mariner*, XIII: 1 (January 2003), 37–52. The *Rattlesnake* and *Sharpshooter*, which classes *Canada* resembled, were barely a decade old and still in RN service, not yet supplanted by the revolutionary torpedo-boat destroyer *Turbine* then under development. See E.H.H. Archibald, *The Fighting Ship of the Royal Navy, A.D. 897–1984* (Poole, Dorsetshire 1984), 225, 228.

33. Lord Dundonald, *My Army Life* (London 1934), 191; Managing Director, British Submarine Boat Co. to Borden, 27 October 1903, Borden to Préfontaine, 14 November 1903, Préfontaine to Borden, 22 November 1903, 45-1-1, LAC, RG 24, vol. 3592; and Marder, *Anatomy of British Sea Power*, 363ff. Nicolas Lambert, *Sir John Fisher's Naval Revolution* (Columbia, SC 1999) expands upon the theme that submarines and torpedo-boat destroyers were the true basis of the first sea lord's fascination, and not dreadnought battleships.

officer commanding the marine service of Canada" was to be appointed in the rank of commodore. The military nature of the force allowed that "commissions of officers in the naval militia shall be granted by his majesty during pleasure," but continuity with Department of Marine and Fisheries fleets was assured, as "all commissions and appointments of officers in Canadian government vessels existing when this act comes into force shall be deemed to have been issued and made in the naval militia under this act."[34]

As was the case with the army, there were to be permanent, active and reserve components to the naval militia, but with an upper limit of 800 men, obviously to be drawn mostly from the Fisheries Protection Service. The permanent force was not planned to be more than a moderately expanded version of that former organization, which now employed slightly more than 500 officers and men. Service in the active naval militia was so far as possible to be voluntary, but could be raised by ballot if necessary. A major role for the force, like its militia counterpart, was indicated as being the domestic application of "aid of the civil power," a role further emphasized by the interpretation of the state of emergency under which the naval militia was liable to be called out for active service as "war, invasion, riot or insurrection, real or apprehended." As for the status of the force, it was allowed that the naval militia, when called out for the defence of Canada, could be liable to "active service anywhere in Canada, and also beyond Canada ... at any time when it appears advisable to do so." Moreover, in time of war the governor-in-council could place "any vessel of war belonging to Canada and the men and officers serving in such vessels" at the disposal of the Royal Navy. However unlikely it might be that a small fleet of fisheries cruisers could serve "beyond Canada" in company with the major fleets of the Royal Navy, the principle was important.[35]

A memorandum prepared by Spain a few years later to brief Préfontaine's successor provides a more general appreciation of the government's intentions: "The idea of formation of this proposed militia was as follows:—1st. It was never proposed to have a Canadian navy, out and out, but it was simply to improve, as far as possible, the existing organizations, rather than make direct contribution to the Royal Navy unaccompanied by constitutional representation.... 2ndly. It was proposed to create a colonial force, which would be, in all respects, equal, in point of efficiency to the Royal Naval Reserve, and would be put under the direct control of the Admiralty in time of war." Furthermore, "the naval militia was to be raised in Canada, and composed, exclusively, of sailors, whose usual occupation is upon any steam or sailing vessel in Canada." As well, "the regulations were to be the same as for the Royal Naval Reserve, as to age, physical, and other conditions, drill, pay, pensions, etc." Also, "For the purposes of drilling and training such a force, an arrangement was to be made between the Canadian and British governments, whereby some reserve ships were to be laid up at Canadian ports, and these ships were to be provided with officers and men, sufficient for the purpose of training the Canadian naval militia; and, also, that arrangements were to be made whereby officers and men of the Canadian force were to be

---

34. Spain to Gourdeau, 28 January 1907, and attachment: *An Act Constituting the Naval Militia of Canada* (Ottawa 1904), LAC, MG 27 II C4, vol. 2, file 14, reel H-1017.

35. Ibid.

received on board his majesty's vessels for certain periods." Finally, "all expense[s] in connection with this Canadian naval force were to be borne by the Canadian government."[36]

Among Spain's supporting memoranda was an especially long one on the subject of establishing a naval militia academy that spoke as much to the administrative details of the school as to the general philosophy of the service. Perhaps to underscore its distinction from the Royal Navy—or perhaps more accurately reflecting the personal interest of the minister through usage of the French term for "navy"—throughout this memo the term "marine" was used to describe the service. The minister was impressed that "the responsibility of commanding a ship, very often of considerable value, and the lives of officers and sailors, the armament of the ship, etc., can be given only to officers who have completed a scientical and technical naval course." He was equally convinced that "as our Canadian officers may be called to serve with those of the Royal Navy, they cannot be left in a state of inferiority as regards instruction." To those ends, he envisioned a naval equivalent of the Royal Military College of Canada in Kingston that "could be providentially located in Montreal." It was left unsaid that that city was the site of the minister's riding; rather "it would be possible to obtain professors who would give theoretical instruction in one or other language." It was to be a founding principle of the academy that instruction be given "alternately in English and French," technical and military subjects in the former language and the arts (including international marine law) in the latter, so that "the list of officers might be always mixed and [ships] commanded by [any] subject of his majesty, without distinction of origin."[37]

From all of this the basic tenets of Laurier's naval policy can be established: A Canadian naval force was to be a truly national institution, intended to enhance "dominion autonomy" by providing warships to safeguard Canadian territorial waters. At the same time, it was to be seen as a complement to the Royal Navy but its actual ability to perform such a role was strictly limited. In essence, then, what the prime minister had in mind was not a naval militia acting as a military force, but rather a more effective policing mechanism than existed at the time, which nevertheless had some military potential. Clearly, there was room for almost everyone to agree to such an initiative, and for his part Conservative leader Robert Borden admitted freely that "I took the stand … in 1900 [*sic*, 1901], when I was speaking only for myself, in favour of a Canadian naval militia. It seems to me that a proposal of this kind is likely to encounter less opposition in the province of Quebec than any other form of assistance to the naval defence of the empire." The response of Borden's Quebec lieutenant, F.D. Monk, was not unfavourable, a reaction that tended to confirm the soundness of the reasoning of both federal party leaders. Nonetheless, it remained a delicate form of logic, readily misinterpreted, and the danger continued to lie in the possibility that the nuances of the government's line of thought might be lost on the various segments of Canadian society, particularly as the idea challenged the traditional concepts

36. Spain to Gourdeau, "Memorandum for the Deputy Reference Canadian Naval Militia," 28 January 1907, LAC, MG 27 II C4, vol. 2, file 14, reel H-1017.

37. "Naval Militia Academy: Notes Relating to the Establishment of a Naval Academy for the Training of Boys to Serve Later as Naval Militia Officers of Canada," nd [1904], LAC, MG 27 II C4, vol. 2, file 14, reel H-1017.

of naval defence, and the extent of Canadian involvement in Anglo-American relations. Hence the caution the government showed in its progress toward its realization.[38]

In December 1903, Sir Frederick Borden travelled to London to discuss with the War Office the proposed changes to the Canadian Militia Act. One of the more decisive exchanges came during a meeting of the Committee of Imperial Defence on 11 December, to which Borden was invited, the first colonial minister so honoured. He was pleasantly surprised to discover that the British attitude to Canadian defence issues was changing. On practically every issue, including the contentious allowance for a Canadian officer to command the militia, Borden was well received and got much of what he wanted. To the need to amend the existing legislation to remove all references to "naval militia" so as to allow its establishment under the Department of Marine and Fisheries, there seems to have been no disagreement. If the Admiralty representatives otherwise projected an air of indifference to the whole prospect of colonial navies (for example, the minutes indicate no discussion as to the commander of the proposed service), they in turn must have been heartened by the appearance before them of a Canadian minister willing to address the matter seriously. This was indeed great progress since the acrimonious parting at the Colonial Conference the previous year.[39]

The idea of a Canadian naval force was developing some assurance. If ever one needed any proof, however, that history is not "a succession of inevitabilities," there stands the fitful progress toward the establishment of a Canadian naval militia over the years 1904–05. The necessary conditions seemed to come together several times over that period, but events got in the way. The first stumble came when Frederick Borden introduced his revised militia bill at the beginning of the new session in March 1904, noting that it omitted any reference to the naval militia because that would be provided for by a separate bill to be introduced by Préfontaine.[40] True, this was as agreed by all the necessary authorities, but the proposed naval militia bill, slated for first reading soon after in April, never made the order paper.

As with so much else concerning this issue throughout this period, the "why" remains unclear. Although the project gained the implicit approval of the requisite British officials while Borden was in England, in December 1903 another powerful member of Laurier's Cabinet, Minister of the Interior Clifford Sifton, publicly declared that he was not in favour of a navy. Claiming that "Canada needs no protection at sea," he maintained that the government's duty was to see to the country's development, especially the settling of the West. Expecting to go to the polls within the coming year, and not wanting to provoke a Cabinet split resulting from a public discussion of the naval question, Laurier decided that the

---

38. R.L. Borden to W. Evans, 16 December 1902, quoted in H.B. Neatby, *Laurier and a Liberal Quebec: A Study in Political Management* (Toronto 1972), 183–84.

39. Roger Flynn Sarty, "Silent Sentry: A Military and Political History of Canadian Coast Defence, 1860–1945," (unpublished PhD thesis, University of Toronto 1982), 114; Preston, *Canada and "Imperial Defense,"* 317; CID, minutes of the 26th meeting, 11 December 1903, UKNA, CAB 38/3; and Hopkins, *The Canadian Annual Review, 1903*, 277.

40. The phrase was used by Robert Tombs in his review of Dennis Showalter, *The Wars of German Unification* (London: Hopper Arnold, 2004) in the *Times Literary Supplement*, 5 November 2004, 12. Canada, Parliament, House of Commons, *Debates*, 22 March 1904, col. 260.

naval bill should not be introduced. Instead the naval militia would continue to be the subject of an inquiry initiated the previous October, and a sum to cover the expenses involved was reinstated in the marine department estimates.[41]

In the House of Commons, on the several occasions through the 1904 session that reference was made to the naval project, it created difficulties for the government. The opposition was supportive enough, but wanted more details, which Laurier was not yet prepared to disclose. For his part, Préfontaine tried to put off discussion, saying the Navy League had recommended the scheme and the government had then "thought [it] proper to put a certain amount in the estimates to enable us to study the question." That did not satisfy A.E. Kemp, who had spoken in favour of a Canadian navy in 1902 and now reminded Préfontaine that the minister had already admitted that "we should have a navy of some kind and not be dependent altogether on the navy of Great Britain." The matter had been under consideration long enough, he continued, and "the time has come when the government should spend some money on the nucleus of a Canadian navy." Préfontaine eventually relented and in August introduced a compromise measure intended to compensate for the non-introduction of the bill by allowing $50,000 in the departmental estimates "to provide for the organization of a naval militia for Canada."[42]

This failed to satisfy members of the opposition, who insisted the minister could not spend money in that fashion without a bill. Préfontaine was prepared to ignore them, but when Colonel Sam Hughes, the Conservative defence critic, threatened to launch a full inquiry into the proposed naval militia, Laurier ordered his minister to "let it drop." The dust was only beginning to settle after the Dundonald affair, which had seen the dismissal of the GOC after his public denouncement of government patronage interference in the militia. An election was imminent, and although the militia act presented by Borden to consolidate Canadian control over her own land forces was generally a popular move that had been anticipated for several years and served to deflect the damage done by Dundonald, reaction to a naval militia that could be construed as challenging the authority of the Royal Navy was as yet untested and potentially explosive. The opposition was on the attack, and Laurier sensed it was time to back off. The important thing for the moment was that funding for the department's new ships was allowed to pass without discussion.[43]

With that, the matter did indeed seem to drop. Defence was not an issue in the general election of 3 November 1904 that saw Laurier returned to power with his majority increased once again.[44] Even as it was being fought, however, Canada was very much on the minds of imperial authorities, who were precipitating a seismic realignment in the

41. Hopkins, *The Canadian Annual Review, 1903*, 274. Sifton was minister of the interior from 17 November 1896 until 28 February 1905, when he resigned from the Cabinet after a disagreement with Laurier over the western provinces schools issue. He remained a Liberal, but became increasingly dissatisfied with Laurier's policies.

42. Canada, Parliament, House of Commons, *Debates*, 21 June 1904, cols. 5267–70.

43. Ibid, cols. 8931, 8958; Desmond Morton, *Ministers and Generals: Politics and the Canadian Militia, 1868–1904* (Toronto 1970), 174ff; and John G. Armstrong, "The Dundonald Affair," *The Canadian Defence Quarterly*, XI: 2 (Autumn 1981), 39–45.

44. Schull, *Laurier*, 444.

The fisheries protection cruiser *Canada* being fitted out at the Vickers's shipyard in Barrow-in-Furness, England. An S-class light cruiser and the King Edward VII–class pre-dreadnought battleship *Dominion*, whose first commanding officer was Captain Charles Kingsmill, are being completed inboard of the Canadian vessel. (DND O-233)

defence structure of the empire. By the end of the process, within the short span of a year, Canada would finally have established a firm foundation for the assumption of greater control over her own military and naval defence.

At the December 1903 meeting of the Committee of Imperial Defence, which militia minister Frederick Borden attended, his primary concern had been to obtain British consent for the revisions to the militia act. Once those had been considered, however, the British authorities shifted the discussion to their primary concern, gauging the level of Canadian interest in taking over the defences at Halifax and Esquimalt. Laurier was always careful to despatch his ministers abroad with clear instructions, and although Borden had not been authorized to discuss this particular subject, it was not far removed from the general Canadian quest for greater military autonomy, and the militia minister did not feel he was out of place in offering a response. Perhaps because the response was unexpectedly positive, however, it was reflected in the minutes that Borden was committing his government to take over the Halifax and Esquimalt bases, when, in fact, he had merely stated that the Canadian government favoured the idea. Worse, the committee had admitted the Canadian militia minister to its membership, which severely upset Laurier (who accurately interpreted the move as an attempt at imperial centralization), with the result that the prime minister insisted that Borden ask Minto to have his remarks in reference to the imperial stations stricken from the record. Laurier probably also authorized Borden's accompanying note, however, which made it clear that Ottawa "was rejecting not the proposal as such but the impolitic way in which it had been pressed."[45]

The whole episode pointed to the development of views somewhat different from those normally expected in both Canada and Britain, but most of the rest of 1904 passed without either side fully appreciating the opportunity presented. From the British side, it was hardly a secret that the Royal Navy had long been a strong advocate of closing Esquimalt as a strategic liability in the event of war with the United States, and was prepared even to withdraw from Halifax if that would further diminish Anglo-American discord. The army, for its part, had previously been reluctant to dismiss the American threat, but a catalyst for new thinking came with the appointment in September 1903 of Hugh Arnold-Forster as secretary of state for war with a clear mandate to streamline the army's organization. He opted to do so by concentrating an expeditionary force in Britain, while ruling out the possibility of war with the United States. He therefore had considerable interest in completing the withdrawal of British garrisons from North America. Although it does not appear to have been explained to Borden as such, all those involved—the Canadian government, the War Office and the Admiralty—for once apparently shared the same thought. That was not always apparent, however, because the governor general was the official conduit of information between London and Ottawa and the incumbent, Lord Minto, was fixed in his belief that British garrisons were essential to maintaining imperial ties between colony and mother country. In his despatches to the Colonial Office concerning the request for revision of the CID minutes, therefore, Minto left the mistaken impression that Canada

---

45. Sarty, "Silent Sentry," 116; and CID minutes, 11 December 1903, UKNA, CAB 38/3.

would not consider taking over the bases.[46] In that light, even as other events through the course of 1904 confirmed Britain's strategic reorientation toward the continent, the CID remained pessimistic as to the chances for a mutually agreeable withdrawal from Canada. What eventually forced the issue was the appointment in October 1904 of Admiral Sir John Fisher to the position of first sea lord (the title was changed at his request), to undertake his long-planned reform of the Royal Navy, beginning with the withdrawal of the overseas battle fleets and their concentration in home waters.

Fisher's fleet redistribution typically has been credited to the need to meet the rising German naval threat, which he (somewhat later) claimed in his inimitable style to have first "divined" at the international disarmament conference at The Hague in 1899. The distinction might seem slight, but Fisher did not perceive the Imperial German Navy as a serious challenger to the Royal Navy until much later, and embarked on the concentration scheme only as one of several elements on a list of technological, personnel and organizational reforms aimed at effecting significant savings in the naval estimates by embracing a revolutionary concept in naval warfare. His ultimate vision was of a Royal Navy organized around a combination of "flotilla defence" and the "battle cruiser concept" to accomplish the RN's twin principal duties of preventing invasion of the United Kingdom and protecting sea communications with the rest of the empire. So-called "mosquito" fleets of torpedo-armed fast destroyers and submarines would infest the narrow waters of the English Channel and North Sea to deter invasion and raids against the British Isles, while "super-armoured cruisers"—later dubbed "battle cruisers"—would combat surface threats to oceanic communications with their speed and superior firepower.[47] Under that vision, traditional battle fleets were encumbrances, as they were vulnerable to torpedo attack while lacking the speed and endurance to catch commerce raiders. Their continued existence was required only as a stopgap until the other elements of the plan were in place.

Fisher was the first to admit that "naval experience is not sufficiently ripe to abolish totally the building of battleships," and his legacy will remain identified with the implementation of the next element in his reforms—the laying-down of HMS *Dreadnought* as the

---

46. Sarty, "Silent Sentry," 114–15, 117. He further concludes it was this false impression "that created the sense of drama on the British side of the subsequent transfer negotiations."

47. The standard account is Marder, *Anatomy of British Sea Power*, 456–67 but Lambert, *Fisher's Naval Revolution*, 89–94 demonstrates that as late as November 1903, when Balfour asked Fisher to address a report on "The Possibility of Serious Invasion," France was still considered the most probable potential enemy. Lambert's overall re-interpretation of British naval policy (one that is vigorously supported by Jon Sumida) effectively overturns Marder's appreciation of the period as set out in *From the Dreadnought to Scapa Flow: The Royal Navy in the Fisher Era*, I: *The Road to War, 1904–1914* (Oxford 1961). On the key point of Lambert's reassessment of Fisher's preference of the flotilla defence and battle cruiser concept over dreadnought development, the evidence examined for this volume supports the context of Lambert's reinterpretation and suggests that Marder over-stated the degree of Royal Navy concern for the German naval challenge, and also sets the date of its commencement too early (Marder ties it to the passing of Tirpitz's first German Naval Law in 1898, although it was probably not until at least the Dogger Bank crisis of October 1904, just after Fisher became first sea lord). Nonetheless, Marder remains the authority on many specifics of the chronology. See Daniel McNeil, "Technology, History and the Revolution in Military Affairs," *Canadian Military Journal* (Winter 2000–01), 7–17 for an explicit comparison of the early twentieth-century naval revolution to the early twenty-first century revolution in military affairs.

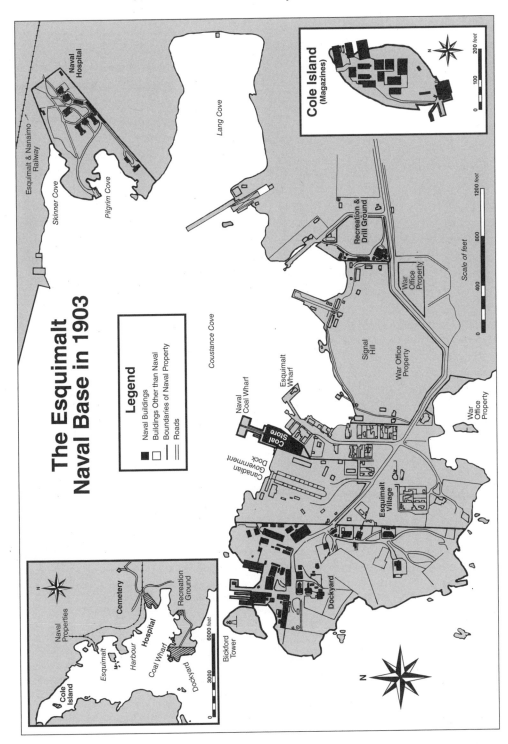

The Esquimalt Naval Base in 1903

Legend

- ■ Naval Buildings
- □ Buildings Other than Naval
- — Boundaries of Naval Property
- ═ Roads

Cole Island
(Magazines)

0   100   200 feet

Esquimalt & Nanaimo Railway

Naval Hospital

Skinner Cove

Pilgrim Cove

Lang Cove

Coustance Cove

Recreation & Drill Ground

War Office Property

Signal Hill

War Office Property

War Office Property

Scale of feet

0   400   800   1200 feet

Esquimalt Wharf

Naval Coal Wharf

Coal Store

Canadian Government Dock

Esquimalt Village

Dockyard

Bickford Tower

Cole Island

Naval Properties

Esquimalt Harbour

Cemetery

Hospital

Coal Wharf

Recreation Ground

Dockyard

0   3000   6000 feet

The crew of CGS *Canada* at "port arms" during a stop in Bermuda, circa 1905. (LAC PA-123950)

Intimidating American fishermen did not require particularly heavy weaponry. Crewmen demonstrate one of *Canada*'s 1¼-pounder guns, an example of which is preserved at the Canadian War Museum in Ottawa. (LAC PA-123952)

first all-big gun battleship in October 1905.[48] That this revolutionized naval warfare by pre-cipitating an unintended naval arms race with Germany should not obscure Fisher's con-tinued fascination at the time with the potential of flotilla defence and super-armoured cruisers. Certainly, on the matter of colonial naval development, the dreadnought con-struction race might have set the tone for debate, but that would have little direct impact on its actual form. Flotilla defence and the battle cruiser concept were other elements of Fisher's reforms that were more immediately critical to his views on dominion naval development.

In the complex interconnections of what Fisher styled his "naval necessities," his with-drawal of battle fleets from distant stations, and the scrapping of older gunboats and sloops deemed "too weak to fight and too slow to run away" did not decree the closing of those stations. In the first instance, his intent in doing away with obsolete vessels was to free their crews to address the continuing manpower shortages of the Royal Navy. In the second instance, overseas stations remained essential to the defence of imperial communica-tions, but could be rationalized to correspond to his five strategic keys that "lock up the world" for the empire: Singapore, the Cape of Good Hope, Alexandria/Suez, Gibraltar, and the Straits of Dover. To be sure, the signing of the Entente Cordiale in May 1904, follow-ing as it did the similar Anglo-Japanese Alliance of 1902 and the growing rapprochement with the Americans, meant that Britain had come to terms, either explicitly or implicitly, with three of its main naval challengers. Even so, Fisher always remained wary of the Americans, Japanese, and French, as potential adversaries, just as he did of the Germans. If his concen-tration scheme saw the closure of certain stations, the rationalized "strategic keys" would ensure continued British dominance by seeing the obsolete third-class trade protection cruisers at those stations replaced with the newer super-armoured cruisers, and they as well as other minor ports could rely on destroyer and submarine flotillas for their close defence.[49]

Fisher's reforms meant the dissolution of the Pacific Station and the reduction of the North America and West Indies Station to a new particular service squadron nominally home-ported in Plymouth. (Esquimalt in fact had already been downgraded in 1903, when Rear-Admiral Bickford was relieved by Commodore J.E.C. Goodrich.) The *Montreal Star* referred disparagingly to "the withdrawal of British naval protection from Canada as Gladstone withdrew military protection forty years ago." Faced with "the throwing of hun-dreds of men out of employment and the loss of considerable money spent yearly on sup-plies, etc.," reaction on the coasts was mixed. In Victoria, there were doubts "as to the terms of union with Canada under which it was pledged that the influence of the dominion gov-ernment will be used to secure the continued maintenance of the naval station at Esquimalt," while the *Halifax Chronicle* and the *Vancouver Province*, both of which were

---

48. Peter Kemp, ed., *The Papers of Sir John Fisher, Volume I* (London 1960), 40; and Robert Gardiner, ed., *Eclipse of the Big Gun: The Warship, 1906–1945* (Edison, NJ 2001) is a good general description of the genesis of the dreadnought battleship and battle cruiser. Fisher appointed a Committee of Designs in December 1904, *Dreadnought's* keel was laid on 2 October 1905 and she was completed on 3 October 1906.

49. Fisher quoted in Arthur Herman, *To Rule the Waves: How the British Navy Shaped the Modern World* (New York 2004), 480; Kemp, *The Papers of Sir John Fisher*, I, 160–61; and John H. Morrow, *The Great War: An Imperial History* (New York 2004), 13.

Liberal papers, called for the construction of a Canadian naval force for coast defence. When it was confirmed that Commodore Goodrich would be lowering his flag without replacement at the end of February 1905, even Victorians acquiesced to the inevitable, the Board of Trade urging the construction of a Canadian navy and the maintenance of the dry dock to meet the requirements of modern warships.[50]

It is not necessary to examine the whole process of the transfer of responsibility for the Halifax and Esquimalt garrisons. Once Fisher's fleet redistribution provided the impetus for the CID to decide at its 22 November 1904 meeting that the Colonial Office should begin negotiations with Canada, events transpired quickly. By February 1905 the two governments had agreed upon a general course of action, specific details were worked out in the ensuing months, and the transfer took effect on 1 July. When Canadian troops were raised faster than expected to replace the retiring British garrisons, Ottawa assumed formal control of the Halifax citadel on 16 January 1906, and of the fortifications at Esquimalt on 1 May of the same year.[51]

In the meantime, Canadian naval developments were also progressing. The marine department's annual report for 1904 made reference to the fact that a bill for the formation of a naval militia had been prepared for the recent session, but "owing to this matter requiring a great deal of discussion, it was laid over till the next session of parliament." Indeed, if Préfontaine did not have his bill, he at least had his ships: *Canada* had come off the slips at Barrow-in-Furness on 14 June 1904, and *Vigilant* had followed suit in Toronto on 11 September. Described as forming "the nucleus of the proposed Canadian naval militia," the former ship in particular seemed to be the focus of the minister's attention. He was on hand for her official arrival at Quebec City on 29 September (Spain had subjected her to an inspection routine at Gaspé for the previous two weeks), and under his authorization the vessel began preparations to "make a cruise to the West Indies during the winter, and ... to have her attached to the North American squadron."[52]

---

50. The Montreal *Star*, 30 November 1904; Hopkins, *The Canadian Annual Review, 1904*, 407, 461. Although Esquimalt was no longer a "station" port, the RN maintained a much-reduced presence there with the steam-assisted sloop *Shearwater* and the survey ship *Egeria* in order to continue hydrographic survey duties not yet assumed by the fledgling Canadian Hydrographic Service. See Barry Gough, *The Royal Navy and the Northwest Coast of North America, 1810–1914: A Study of British Maritime Ascendency* (Vancouver 1982), 238; and William Glover, "The Challenge of Navigation to Hydrography on the British Columbia Coast, 1850–1930," *The Northern Mariner*, VI:4 (October 1996), 8–10. The Australia, East Indies and China stations were absorbed into an Eastern Fleet based in Singapore; the Cape Squadron absorbed the West Indies, South Atlantic and West Coast of Africa stations; and the new Mediterranean Fleet was based at Gibraltar. The latter was considered part of the "home" concentration, and the initial redistribution saw it retain the greatest number of battleships (twelve, including all the most modern); the English Channel got the next best eight and the remaining eight earlier types went to the Home Fleet. See Marder, *From the Dreadnought*, I, 41, Willock, "Gunboat Diplomacy: II," 102–03.

51. CID, Minutes of the 58th Meeting, 22 November 1904, UKNA, CAB 38/6–1904; G.S. Clarke to Undersecretary of State for the Colonies, 23 November 1904, UKNA, C042/899; and Sarty, "Silent Sentry," 123–44. Sarty asserts that the general knowledge of Laurier's developing naval policy among "the politically literate public ... may account for the calm manner in which the news [of the fleet concentration and reduction of the overseas garrisons] was treated in all parts of the country except British Columbia."

52. *Annual Report of Marine and Fisheries, 1904—Marine*, 97–98; and Doug Maginley, "CGS Canada—The First Years," *Argonauta: The Newsletter of the Canadian Nautical Research Society*, XXI:1 (January 2004), 27.

After returning to Halifax for the installation of Marconi wireless telegraphy apparatus, more trials, and the embarkation of "naval militia recruits," by early January 1905 *Canada* was ready to fulfill the many expectations that had foreseen a Canadian government vessel engaging in naval manoeuvres in the Caribbean during the winter months. There was some concern that her cruise might have to be abandoned because of the "transitory state at present" of the North America and West Indies Squadron, but that was soon resolved, and on 1 February 1905 *Canada*—her officers dressed in "half-whites" naval summer uniform—proceeded to sea from Halifax toward Bermuda to join the Royal Navy squadron. The little Canadian ship did not actually integrate with the British vessels—her complement's low level of training made it dangerous for a ship "unfamiliar with fleet work" to participate in close manoeuvres, and British officers had no legal power of discipline over Canadians—but rather than deterring her captain, Commander Charles T. Knowlton, it gave him something to aspire to. His final report described how for three months the ship cruised the Caribbean, making ports of call and delivering salutes as would a warship, while her crew trained in "Maxim quick-firing gun, rifle and revolver drill, hand flag and semaphore signalling, pipe and bugle calls and Marconi wireless telegraphy." The automatic quick-firing gun practice, firing at a target while the ship was underway, was noted as being particularly successful. The ship had embarked "a large number of young fishermen as recruits," as Spain later recorded, and "this, according to the ... minister's idea, was proposed to be the beginning of the naval militia. On the return of this ship from her instructional cruise, the men who had already been trained were distributed amongst the other ships; fresh men taken on; and instruction continued. The material that we have in the Canadian naval militia is probably the best in the world."[53]

As a trial, *Canada*'s winter cruise was entirely successful. Once again, the conditions seemed ripe for the actual formation of a Canadian naval militia. There was, as we have seen, a broad consensus within the Canadian parliament that such an organization was appropriate for the country. In London, meanwhile, the first sea lord, Fisher, was in agreement, while the arrival of Earl Grey in Canada on 10 December 1904 signalled a far more amenable successor to Minto as governor general. Although also a keen imperialist, Grey's instincts as a former Liberal politician allowed him to develop "a more subtle understanding of colonial autonomy" than his Conservative soldier predecessor and to become "one of the most popular governors Canada has had."[54] As a final agreement on the garrison transfer was being reached in February 1905, Grey was evidently apprised of the country's interest in taking on greater naval responsibilities, and in a personal letter to First Lord Earl of Selborne, as "the private forecast of one who wishes to give you the earliest possible intimations of the demands that may be made upon you," he confided:

53. *Halifax Morning Chronicle*, 4 January 1905; Admiralty to C-in-C, NA&WI, 21 February 1905, UKNA, ADM 1/7474; Department of Marine and Fisheries, *Annual Report of Marine and Fisheries, 1906—Fisheries* (Ottawa 1906), 311–13; and Spain to Gourdeau, 28 January 1907, LAC, MG 27 II C4, vol. 2, file 14, reel H-1017.

54. Preston, *Canada and "Imperial Defense,"* 346; and W. Stewart Wallace, ed., *Macmillan Dictionary of Canadian Biography*, (Toronto 1963), 285–86.

My ministers have not yet definitely decided upon their naval programme, but I have reason to believe that their deliberations will shortly mature, and that I may be requested to approach HM's gov[ernmen]t for the loan of an officer on whose expert knowledge, judgement, and desire to help, they can implicitly rely. They are conscious of their limitations which, however, they are naturally not anxious to parade, and they will probably look for the assistance for a really able officer who understands the art of keeping in the background while the responsible minister, on his suggestion, carries out the policy which he thinks is the best the conditions of the country will allow. In short they will require a naval officer who will do for their naval establishments, schools, dockyards, etc. what General Lake is now doing with zeal and efficiency and absolutely no friction, for their army....

In considering the qualifications of the man likely to succeed in the position I have referred to, please remember the importance to be attached not only to the possession of a reasoned knowledge of the principles of his profession, and of a zealous, tactful and sympathetic temperament, but to the ability both to speak and write French fluently.

There is big work to be done in the province of Quebec if you can find the right man for it.... [French-Canadians] realise the advantages they enjoy from the protection of the British fleet, but argue that sentiment not self-interest is responsible for the suggestion that Canada should contribute to the naval defence of the empire—and that although an appeal to an Englishman's sentiment is natural, an appeal to a Frenchman can only be successful if it is made to his reason.[55]

There is no recorded response from Selborne, either supporting Grey's suggested candidate of Admiral Sir Edward Seymour, who had just retired after serving as commander-in-chief of the Home Fleet, or offering an alternative. Selborne must have taken the report of Canadian interest seriously, however, because soon afterward the Admiralty, in concert with the Colonial Defence Committee, set to work examining "the strategic conditions of Halifax and Esquimalt." At its seventy-third meeting on 28 June 1905, the Committee of Imperial Defence decided not to retain Esquimalt "as a fortified port" while stating that the current defences at Halifax "should be sufficient to deter a fleet, including battleships, which could not afford to incur serious losses, from attacking the sea defences, and to enable the attack of an organised expeditionary army, landed in the vicinity, to be resisted for a considerable period."[56]

When the CID met two weeks later for a more detailed discussion of the issue, the question of defence of the Great Lakes was the first to be broached. Any lingering doubt as to future British liability was finally settled, with all agreeing to Fisher's statement that "the Royal Navy cannot be held responsible for securing the command of Lake Ontario at the

55. Grey to Selborne (emphasis in original), 11 February 1905, LAC, MG 27 II B1, 003175–003178.

56. "Extract from the Minutes of the 73rd Meeting of the [CID]," 28 June 1905, UKNA, ADM 1/8904.

outbreak of a war with the United States," it being impossible to station small craft up the St Lawrence in peacetime without arousing American suspicion, and any despatched after the outbreak of war would arrive too late to act as an effective opposition. When the general staff representative suggested "Canada might be recommended to maintain submarines and torpedo craft at Halifax for this purpose," the chancellor of the exchequer cut him short. Austen Chamberlain had firmly entrenched views on the primacy of the Royal Navy, being the son of the former colonial secretary and having served as civil lord of the Admiralty from 1895 to 1900. He declared that he regarded "any scheme which tended to encourage the Canadians in the belief that their duties to the empire were limited to local defence as a retrograde and disastrous step," and proceeded to argue instead that "the colonies [should] be induced to spend money on building and maintaining a powerful vessel, such as a battle-ship or armoured-cruiser, [that being] the first step towards the establishment of colonial navies, which would … be as available for service with the British fleet in a great naval war as the land forces of these same colonies had proved to be in the South African struggle."[57]

Fisher is not recorded as having said anything, and Prime Minister Balfour ended the discussion by noting that he was "averse from suggesting to the Canadian government the desirability of their establishing a local navy; but if that government should ask advice, he was of the opinion that we should recommend to them to build torpedo craft and submarines, which would serve as the beginning of a future sea-going fleet." A follow-up letter from the Admiralty to the Colonial Office confirmed Fisher's view that, "in view of the strategic conditions at Halifax [we] consider that the establishment of a submarine boat flotilla at that port is worthy of consideration, as such a flotilla would probably do more to prevent a hostile fleet from closing in than several forts, and it could probably be maintained at less cost. It would also enable the minefields to be dispensed with.... At the same time of course it cannot be [overlooked] that of all kinds of naval activity, work in submarine boats demands the maximum skill and expert training to ensure efficient handling." An internal Admiralty memorandum on the subject added the further caveat that, "the crux is therefore, how Canadian seamen are to acquire this training."[58]

Canada's progress on winter manoeuvres must have seemed to be a positive first step. Colonial Secretary Lyttleton, however, concurred in Prime Minister Balfour's view that it was "undesirable" to approach the Canadians "unless that government should first ask his majesty's government for advice on the subject." As fate would have it once again, circumstances had now made that an unlikely event. The garrisoning of Halifax and Esquimalt had necessitated a large increase in the strength of the permanent force, and was proving to be one of the most costly operations ever undertaken by the militia. The 1905–1906 estimates prepared by the Militia Council were set at $5,496,090.00, an increase of one and a half million dollars, or almost 40 percent, over the previous year, mostly because of increases in allotments for pay, clothing, and provisions. (By comparison, the total militia expenditure for 1900–1901, at the height of the Boer War, had been only $3,000,000.) With the

---

57. "Extract from the Minutes of the 75th Meeting of the [CID]," 13 July 1905, ibid.

58. Ibid, Admiralty to Colonial Office, 11 August 1905, C.L. Ottley minute, 24 July 1905, ibid.

federal budget already pressed for continued funding of railways and western development, the militia estimates meant that sums that could have been allocated for a naval militia were unavailable. The *Canadian Military Gazette* expressed the military community's remorse, concluding that "unfortunately we cannot have everything, and that the assumption of these obligations will undoubtedly postpone the day when we may expect substantial government assistance towards a navy."[59]

Nonetheless, there still remained the question of what to do with the naval dockyards. Esquimalt, oddly enough, was less of a concern, because the continued presence of a small British squadron ensured its upkeep at British expense. Halifax was a different matter, for although the Royal Navy no longer required it for regular use, it was a valuable strategic resource—especially the dry dock—and the Admiralty naturally would desire it to be maintained and remain available for use when needed. It is unclear from the documentary evidence at whose initiative the subject was raised, but soon after the transfer of control of the fortifications, the focus turned to the waterfront. By the end of the summer, the Department of Marine and Fisheries fleet had occupied the "new" facilities, but were finding "the privilege of using the dockyard temporarily is so hedged about with conditions as to be of little service to the department." Préfontaine engaged the assistance of Lord Strathcona in seeking clarification from the Admiralty as to the "acquisition vs. placed at the disposal" status of the dockyard. By early November, the high commissioner in London was able to cable "Admiralty entirely favourable" to the idea of Canada formally occupying the facilities.[60] It merely remained to work out the details.

Préfontaine, meanwhile, was becoming enchanted with his little fleet. At one point in the previous year's debate over his department's budget, the opposition had questioned if the minister was pursuing the creation of a naval militia so as to increase his personal power. Whether or not that had been Préfontaine's intention at the time, his ego was stroked by the pomp surrounding his visit to Halifax to tour *Canada*, where "the minister was received on board by a guard of honour, and after leaving the ship's side was saluted with eleven guns." The Conservative *Halifax Herald* might refer disparagingly to "Préfontaine's navy," but the minister of marine and fisheries countered with a very active and effective public information campaign to advertise the steps taken toward building upon its nucleus. *Canada*'s winter cruise was both the highlight of the department's annual report for 1905 and the broad thrust of an "official" history commissioned by the department to promote the naval militia project, the latter claiming that "few, if any, of the works undertaken by the present administration of the dominion promise to be of greater national importance than the organization of a naval militia."[61]

---

59. Colonial Office to Admiralty, 17 August 1905, ibid; Department of Militia and Defence, *Militia and Defence Annual Report, 1904* (Ottawa 1905), 8; and *The Canadian Military Gazette*, 6 June 1905, 4.

60. Spain to Préfontaine, 31 August 1905, Préfontaine to Strathcona (emphasis in original),15 September 1905, Strathcona to Préfontaine, 9 November 1905, 51–4-2, pt 1, LAC, RG 24, vol. 5650; and Gough, *RN and NW Coast of North America*, 238.

61. *Marine and Fisheries Annual Report, 1905—Fisheries*, 311–12; *Halifax Herald*, 10 July 1905; and Ernest J.Chambers, *The Canadian Marine: A History of the Department of Marine and Fisheries* (Toronto 1905), 72, 85.

This propagandistic volume was published in November 1905, on the eve of a planned trip by Préfontaine to Britain to discuss various departmental matters with the appropriate imperial authorities. Cautious as ever when authorizing ministerial travel abroad, Laurier scrutinized the list of topics to be discussed, as the trip "will have such important and far-reaching effect in … the future policy and working of the department." The top priority was encouraging, but the list as finally approved, to Préfontaine's undoubted disappointment, had no specific reference to a naval militia or even the dockyard transfer, focusing instead on naval schools, pilotage matters, the management of large shipping ports, an enquiry regarding the establishment of lighthouse apparatus, and "most important of all," the question of providing a vessel for sweeping and ice-breaking along the St Lawrence ship channel between Montreal and Quebec.[62]

It was soon clear that the minister had a different idea of the purpose and priorities of his mission. On the eve of his departure, the *Canadian Military Gazette* reported that the goal of this "most active and progressive minister" was "to gather information to aid him in establishing the germ of a Canadian navy…. Those who know him intimately are authority for the statement that he is very much in earnest with his naval militia scheme."[63] Préfontaine himself, in a release to the press on 1 December 1905, stated that such was indeed the focus of his trip to Britain:

> The object of my visit is primarily to make a study of the best mode to be adopted for the organization of our marine department as a nucleus for a naval reserve. The dominion government to-day owns about forty vessels employed in the harbour and channel improvement service and in fishery protection duties. Two of these, the *Vigilant* and the *Canada*, might be described as third-class cruisers, and one of them, the *Canada*, carries a cannon. We are now face to face with a serious difficulty, the scarcity of proper officers and sailors. The dominion government employs about 1,000 officers and men. Some of the former have been in the British navy. We hope to adopt some system of naval training on the lines of the military school at Kingston. It might be possible to add to the college curriculum some courses on marine subjects, thus enabling the cadets there to make a choice between a naval and a military career.[64]

Besides the unexpected support from the voice-piece of the militia, other more influential newspapers also agreed with the actions of the minister of marine. The editor of the *Winnipeg Free Press* felt that the talks heralded a new stage in the constitutional development of the nation: "Canada in taking over the entire responsibility of her own defence; in modernizing her militia system; in making a start in the establishment of a Canadian navy, makes it very clear that she intends to be a factor in future in the world politics in

62. Gourdeau to Préfontaine, 13 November 1905, LAC, MG 26 G, reel C-828, 103354–356.

63. *The Canadian Military Gazette*, 28 November 1905, 7.

64. J. Castell Hopkins, *The Canadian Annual Review of Public Affairs, 1905* (Toronto 1906), 502.

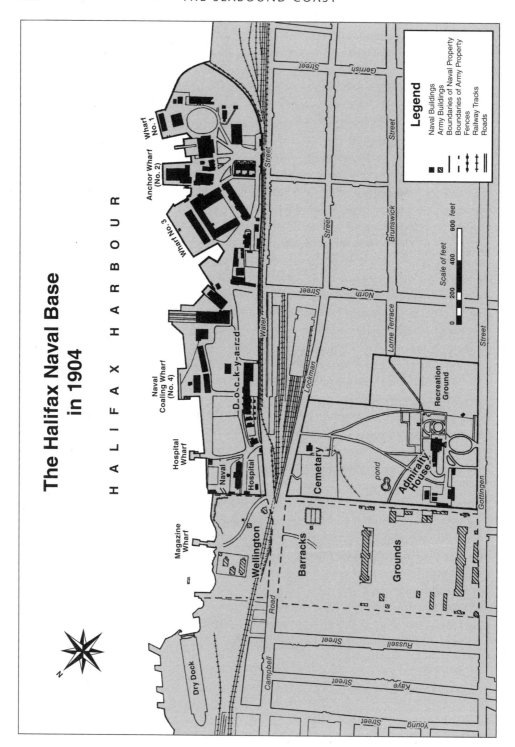

The Halifax Naval Base in 1904

HALIFAX HARBOUR

Legend

Naval Buildings
Army Buildings
Boundaries of Naval Property
Boundaries of Army Property
Fences
Railway Tracks
Roads

Scale of feet

0   200   400   600 feet

Wharf No. 1
Anchor Wharf (No. 2)
Wharf No. 3
Naval Coaling Wharf (No. 4)
D-o-c-k-y-a-r-d
Hospital Wharf
Magazine Wharf
Dry Dock
Wellington
Barracks
Grounds
Cemetary
Recreation Ground
pond
Admiralty House
Naval Hospital

Gerrish Street
Brunswick Street
North Street
Lorne Terrace
Lockman Street
Water Street
Gottingen Street
Campbell Road
Russell Street
Kaye Street
Young Street

alliance with the mother-land. But it will be an alliance, not a merger." When Grey asked Laurier to substantiate reports about a naval service, however, the prime minister replied that the suggestion "from the first to last line is a canard. I saw Préfontaine before he left, but he never mentioned any of those schemes. I understood that he was going to Europe on private business."[65]

Laurier knew that Préfontaine was in Europe on more than "private business," but did not expect anything to be done on the naval subject. Shortly after his arrival in England, Préfontaine officially broke the news to Laurier, cabling that he required the presence of Commander Spain to secure information relating to a "naval reserve organization." The prime minister returned the cable immediately, stating that Spain was engaged in his capacity as wreck commissioner and could not leave Canada; in the meantime "no arrangement should be undertaken with [the] Admiralty unless previous consultation with us here."[66] Undeterred, at a London dinner on 13 December, Préfontaine outlined the progress of his discussions with the Admiralty.

> As regards the navy we are as yet in our infancy—we are just beginning the task—and I happen to be in London as your guest tonight because my government has thought that we should establish in Canada a naval reserve or some kind of organization, that little by little will come to form a part of the great British navy, and be a power in defending the empire wherever and whenever the occasion may arise. It is very gratifying to me, as a Canadian, to be able to say that, when I am called upon in Canada, as minister of marine to present a report upon my mission in London, I shall be able to acknowledge how nicely, how loyally, and how splendidly, I have been received at the Admiralty by the authorities of the late government, and how well disposed are the representatives of the new government towards Canada. If the arrangements are carried out as they are proposed, there can be no question as to the result and I can tell my fellow-citizens of all the other colonies that, as regards a naval reserve and the organization of the navy, Canada will do its duty to the empire.[67]

Feeling it necessary to urge restraint upon Préfontaine, the prime minister cabled his "fear that nego[t]iations which are not to be concluded may lead to serious disappointment and trouble." Préfontaine, in a subsequent letter to his deputy minister, professed not to understand Laurier's attitude. The minister felt that he had extracted many useful concessions from the Admiralty, particularly "the English Admiralty's transfer of the wharfs, structures and buildings of Halifax and Esquimalt," and "information voluntarily provided

---

65. Winnipeg *Free Press*, 9 December 1905; and Laurier to Grey, 28 November 1905, LAC, MG 27 II B1, I-69, 213–14.

66. Préfontaine to Laurier, 5 December 1905, Laurier to Préfontaine (cable), 5 December 1905, LAC, MG 26 G, reel C-828, 103993, 103995.

67. Hopkins, *The Canadian Annual Review, 1905*, 503. Préfontaine's reference to "late and new governments" referred to the defeat of Balfour's Conservatives by Campbell-Bannerman's Liberals on 5 December 1905. Other than Lord Tweedmouth replacing the short-lived Earl of Cawdor (who had replaced Selborne on 22 March 1905), the senior naval officers in the Admiralty remained unchanged.

to me about what would need to be done to organize a naval militia." He cabled Laurier from Paris the next day: "There is no reason to fear complications through the good work that has been done by Strathcona and myself."[68] Laurier never did get the promised briefing on the unauthorized discussions from his minister of marine and fisheries. Préfontaine died in his sleep early Christmas morning, while staying with friends in Paris. As the chief proponent of the nucleus of Canada's navy, his death ended any immediate prospect of expansion beyond its embryonic state.

Préfontaine's unauthorized discussion of the naval project had threatened to disturb the fragile Canadian political balance on a number of fronts. Besides becoming an increasingly overt threat to Laurier's leadership, the minister had been attempting to accomplish too much, too soon. Yet Laurier had not objected to the naval militia scheme because of its potential results, that being an evolving government policy, but because of the method by which Préfontaine had been going about it. His death, therefore, did not signal the demise of Laurier's naval policy so much as a temporary halt to any overt moves. In fact, after an initial pause, the years 1906–09 would prove to be ones of fairly continuous—if slow and cautious—movement toward the formation of a Canadian naval service.

If the administration's objectives were to remain unchanged, the post of minister of marine and fisheries required someone not so politically ambitious. Laurier's choice to succeed Préfontaine was Louis-Philippe Brodeur who, although unable to claim any particular maritime experience, met the political qualifications handsomely. As a lawyer in Montreal, Brodeur had formed a partnership with Honoré Mercier, and in the House of Commons had represented Rouville, Quebec, since 1891. He was therefore one of the party's "old guard" and his reputation for integrity and wisdom inspired Laurier to nickname him "mon sage." His appointment was gazetted on 6 February 1906, and the *Canadian Annual Review* recorded both its general popularity and the personal prestige associated with it. "The promotion of Mr Brodeur was widely approved as being deserved and as indicating a steadily growing position in party popularity and government influence. With the new position went the Liberal leadership in Montreal and its district, and the new minister became, practically, Sir Wilfrid Laurier's first lieutenant in Quebec."[69] Brodeur's replacement as minister of inland revenue was William Templeman, who resigned his place in the senate to run for a Victoria seat. As a founding member of the Navy League in Victoria, his appointment meant one more ally for the Canadian naval cause at the Cabinet table.

The new minister of marine and fisheries had little time to settle into his office. On 23 January 1906, the American steamer *Valencia* drove aground in dense fog off the west coast of Vancouver Island with the loss of 126 lives. The wreck commissioner's report, published in April, concluded that the disaster could have been avoided had Marconi radio stations and other aids to navigation been in operation. This was easy fodder for opposition charges that, although such stations had been constructed on the East Coast, none existed

68. Laurier to Préfontaine, nd, Préfontaine to Gourdeau, 20 December 1905, Préfontaine to Laurier, 21 December 1905, LAC, MG 26 G, reel C-829, 104518–19, 104543–4.

69. J. Castell Hopkins, *The Canadian Annual Review of Public Affairs, 1906* (Toronto 1907), 537; and Brodeur, "L.P. Brodeur and the Origins of the RCN," 18.

as yet on the West, a condition attributed to Préfontaine's preference for Quebec patronage. Then in May came attacks upon the government's recently adopted northern expedition policy. In both 1904 and 1905, a department-owned ship, *Arctic*, captained by the distinguished Quebec sailor and explorer, Joseph Bernier, had effectively demonstrated Canadian sovereignty by steaming in the eastern Arctic region. This was quickly forgotten as parliamentary attention focused on "the quantities of victuals, rum, medicines, and stores carried" in the vessel and the alleged failure to secure them through competitive contract. It soon became apparent that Brodeur had inherited a patronage-ridden quagmire, and that Préfontaine had allowed questions of political influence centred in Quebec to dominate the department's logistical operations. The new minister found himself fully occupied for the rest of the year rectifying this state of affairs, while keeping it out of the public eye. In May an inquiry was launched into the outfitting of the Arctic expedition, and soon afterward Brodeur ordered both a thorough review of ship inspection procedures and the construction of five new Marconi wireless stations on the West Coast.[70]

While the new minister was getting settled, Laurier had occasion to meet the man who would eventually take charge of the Canadian naval service. After Préfontaine's death, the Admiralty had placed a battleship at the disposal of the Canadian government to return the minister's remains from France. The warship assigned, HMS *Dominion*, was commanded by a native Canadian, Captain Charles Edmund Kingsmill. Born in Guelph, Canada West, on 7 July 1855 and educated at Upper Canada College, Kingsmill had entered the Royal Navy in 1869. From 1890 onward he had commanded a number of vessels, including battleships, on virtually every station of the Royal Navy and had been given command of *Dominion* upon her launching in 1905. Conveying the remains of dead ministers was not a new duty for him, however, having transported the body of Prime Minister Sir John Thompson from Britain to Canada in 1894, duties that were obviously assigned to him because of his position as a Canadian of high rank in the Royal Navy. Despite his service overseas, Kingsmill still maintained close links with Canada and married Francis Beardmore of Toronto in October 1900.[71]

As a sign of gratitude for *Dominion*'s services, the Canadian chapters of the Imperial Order of the Daughters of the Empire prepared a gift of silver plate for the ship's wardroom, and invited the ship and her captain back to Quebec to accept it. An opportunity arose later that summer, but the voyage was marred when the battleship ran aground in Chaleur Bay on the evening of 19 August after the navigator misidentified a brush fire on shore for a lighthouse. In the consequent court-martial, Kingsmill received a severe reprimand for "grave neglect in duty" in not being on the bridge at the time of grounding. Still, the ship was able to proceed to Quebec for minor repairs, and the presentation was made as

---

70. Brodeur to Laurier, 7 April 1906, LAC, MG 26 G, reel C-834, 109324–330; Canada, Parliament, House of Commons, *Debates*, 10 April, 15 May 1906, cols. 1469–511, 3350–3399; and Toronto *Globe*, 24 and 25 January 1906. For an account of the expeditions see Yolande Dorion-Robitaille, *Captain J.E. Bernier's Contribution to Canadian Sovereignty in the Arctic* (Ottawa 1978).

71. Tweedmouth to Laurier, 27 December 1905, LAC, MG 26 G, reel C-829, 104701–21. For a more detailed study of Kingsmill's RN career, see Richard Gimblett, "Admiral Sir Charles E. Kingsmill: Forgotten Father," Michael Whitby, Richard Gimblett and Peter Haydon, eds., *The Admirals: Canada's Senior Naval Leadership in the Twentieth Century* (Toronto 2006), 31–53.

planned on 22 August, with both the governor general and Laurier in attendance. Publicly, the prime minister made a speech reiterating his views that "it was Canada's mission to develop her own resources and strength as an integral portion of the empire, instead of wasting them in unnecessary preparations for war; though should occasion call for it he was sure that Canada would do her duty to the empire."[72]

His actions in private, however, were far more nuanced. Although Laurier was usually cool to imperial military and naval officers, he seems to have developed a genuine liking for Kingsmill. Upon first meeting the captain and his wife in January, Laurier had loaned Mrs Kingsmill several books of photographs of the Northwest Mounted Police from his personal collection and he now accepted an invitation from Kingsmill to dine aboard his "fair vessel of war." Kingsmill was no ordinary Royal Navy officer, however. Not only was he a Canadian who had risen to senior command rank in the imperial service—the recent grounding incident was not an uncommon occurrence in those days of pre-modern aids to navigation, and his career was otherwise unblemished—he also had important family ties in Toronto, including his father's brother, Nicol, who was a lawyer with whom Laurier had had business dealings over the years and who was one of the members of the executive committee of the Navy League in that city. Possibly because of his Canadian background, Kingsmill also presented a less stuffy image than most imperial officers and probably exhibited a greater openness to sentiments of dominion autonomy.[73]

Meanwhile, Laurier took direct action to implement his government's naval policy by quietly concluding discussions with the Admiralty regarding the naval establishments at Halifax and Esquimalt. In early January 1906, even before Préfontaine's remains could begin their final return to Canada, the new colonial secretary, Lord Elgin, transmitted to Grey the Admiralty's willingness to complete the transfer of control of the dockyards. Certain conditions, intended to safeguard the Admiralty's future interests, were, however, presented in a broad form that left the details to be finalized later. So far as possible, the Canadian government was not to allow the naval facilities at the two ports to deteriorate beyond usefulness or employ them for non-government purposes and the Royal Navy was always to have access to them, particularly in time of war. For all his earlier admonitions to Préfontaine, Laurier concluded that these caveats were not inimical to the national interest and decided to act on his own in pursuing negotiations until a new minister of marine and fisheries could be appointed. The British proposal was accepted in principle in April and the Halifax dockyard was handed over to the Canadian government on 1 January 1907. Subsequent difficulties in actually meeting rigid British regulations for maintenance of the yards delayed Esquimalt's handover, leading the Admiralty to reconsider and substitute less exacting conditions. In March 1908, Ottawa finally announced that the revised terms were "quite satisfactory in every respect" and immediately authorized the take over. The transfers were not officially endorsed until the passage by Westminster of the Naval Establishments in British

---

72. Hopkins, *The Canadian Annual Review, 1906*, 532, 613; and "Report of Court-Martial," 7 March 1907, UKNA, ADM1/7954.

73. F. Constance Kingsmill to Laurier, 4 July 1906, LAC, MG 26 G, reel C-836, 111856A-111856C; and Kingsmill to Laurier, 7 August 1906, Laurier to Kingsmill, 10 August 1906, ibid, reel C-837, 112766–69.

Possessions Act in October 1909, but the final delay was due less to difficulties in the process than to the fact that both Canadian and imperial authorities were willing to be patient.[74]

Canada was now in possession of first-class docking and stores facilities capable of catering to warships of the most modern types. Since the "ownership of bases suggests the advisability of owning warships as well," the fact that Laurier had no hesitation in accepting responsibility for the Halifax and Esquimalt dockyards confirmed that progress toward the establishment of a Canadian naval force, of whatever size or shape, now had a firmer foundation. Moreover, the special status of the two bases as former imperial dockyards to be kept up to an agreed standard would have made it more difficult for Canada to remain neutral in any future conflict between Britain and a major naval power. Since the Department of Marine and Fisheries' own East Coast facilities were inadequate and in need of costly expansion, operations, including those of Canada, were immediately transferred to the former British bases. The only fly in the ointment was that *Canada*'s 1907 winter cruise to the Caribbean had to be cancelled because her commanding officer, Captain Knowlton, was also the Halifax superintendent, and he and his crew were required for employment "policeing [sic] and guarding the gates in the yard."[75]

The nature of the Canadian government's appreciation of its naval policy became evident when the minister of marine and fisheries was finally able to direct his full attention to the subject, about the same time as the transfer of the Halifax dockyard in January 1907. Brodeur inquired into the state of work on a naval militia, prompted not by concern as to how to use the newly acquired resources, but because political considerations were pressing. With the announcement of another colonial conference to be held in April, the minister was alerted from different quarters as to the urgency in developing an understanding of the issue. First, Henry Wickham offered the Navy League's opinion that the latest domestic and international developments provided great opportunities for "the colonies [to] proceed along the lines of their own national growth." In the specific area of naval defence this could best be achieved through the establishment of a subsidized fast steamship line in connection with a Canadian naval reserve force, with training vessels to be obtained from some of those "scrap heaped" by the Admiralty.[76] Soon after, A.C. Macdonnell, the Conservative member for Vancouver City, filed a parliamentary motion of inquiry "for a copy of all correspondence between the government of Canada and the government of Great Britain in reference to the establishment of a Canadian naval reserve."[77] The opposition's interest was nothing new, but Macdonnell's was, and in the previous session

---

74. Elgin to Grey, 6 January 1906, Strathcona to Brodeur, 16 March 1907, Colonial Office to Grey, 4 March 1908, 51–4-2, pt 1, LAC, RG 24, vol. 5650; PC 876M, 2 April 1906; PC 1697M, 11 March 1908; and Tucker, *The Naval Service of Canada*, I, 104–05, 376, app. III.

75. Knowlton to Spain, 13 April 1907, Knowlton to Spain, 29 January 1907, 51–4-2, pt 1, LAC, RG 24, vol. 5650; and Tucker, *The Naval Service of Canada*, I, 162.

76. Wickham to Laurier, 10 December 1906, "Summary of Memorial of 14 October 1898" [with new section added at the bottom referring to "Scrap Heaping"], nd, H.J. Wickham and C.F. Hamilton, "Proposals For FAST LINE in Connection with Canadian Naval Reserve Force: Imperial Co-operation—A Suggestion" (Reprinted from *The National Review*, May 1906), nd, LAC, MG 26 G, reel C-840, 116499–503.

77. House of Commons, *Debates*, 28 January 1907, col. 2147.

he had led the attack on the *Valencia* disaster. Anticipating another battle in parliament, Brodeur would need to have his facts straight on the naval issue.

Despite attempts to conduct a thorough investigation, Brodeur discovered that there was not much on file. The departmental submission from Captain Spain was a rather unimaginative recounting of *Canada*'s activities, "manned and armed in all respects the same as a man-of-war ... to be the beginning of the naval militia," with attached copies of the proposed Naval Militia Bill of 1904 and the memorandum on a Canadian naval militia academy. Spain confirmed that it had not been the government's intent in 1904 "to have a Canadian Navy, out and out," but "to create a colonial force, which would be, in all respects, equal, in point of efficiency to the Royal Naval Reserve, and would be put under the direct control of the Admiralty in time of war." The commander of the marine services concluded that "these ideas, of course, have never been carried out in any shape or form, and, as I have already endeavoured to explain, the only thing that has been done is the small item in connection with the cruiser *Canada*." Having learned that Préfontaine had had an interview with the executive of the British Navy League, Brodeur consulted their secretary in London as to the details. William C. Crutchley was less than helpful, doing no more than noting that the late minister had "appeared to be in complete sympathy and accord with the views put forward by my executive committee." Although Crutchley supported Wickham's proposal to take up obsolete RN vessels for training, the several enclosed copies of British Navy League publications, "in order that you may gather the line the Navy League has taken in connection with this very great and important matter," left the distinct impression that "one sea, one navy" remained the prevailing sentiment.[78]

In consequence, Brodeur was unable to form a good idea of the actual state of progress toward the establishment of a naval militia. When the issue did not arise in parliament as expected, the minister turned his energies to other preparations for the conference. The foremost concern of the Canadian delegation was still for an imperial preferential tariff, but the new Liberal administration in Westminster was if anything more set in maintaining laissez-faire free-trade principles than their Conservative predecessors, leaving Laurier to expect no better results than at past conferences. When queried by the colonial secretary as to suggestions for topics of discussion, Laurier refused to offer any, as he had in 1902, and repeated the suggestion that he was tempted not to go to London at all. When he did attend, he was accompanied only by Brodeur and Sir Frederick Borden. Greater defence cooperation promised to be a major topic of discussion, so the militia minister could not be left behind; he had, however, learned his brief by now and could be trusted not to entertain any new departures. To the extent that the prime minister discussed the issue of naval defence with the minister of marine and fisheries, Laurier seems to have overlooked the Admiralty's implicit message of goodwill in the smooth transfer of the Canadian dockyards. British officials had not been permitted to build upon that initiative, but they aroused Laurier's defensive instincts when the only documents sent as a basis for the forthcoming discussion comprised a list of direct colonial contributions, a tabulation on which Canada was noteworthy by its absence. With such signals pointing to yet another demand for a

---

78. Spain to Gourdeau, 28 January 1907, Crutchley to Brodeur, 31 January 1907, LAC, MG 27 II C4, vol. 2, file 14, reel H-1017.

Louis Philippe Brodeur in October 1903. Brodeur was appointed minister of marine and fisheries in the Laurier government in 1906 and served as the naval service's first cabinet minister in 1910–11. (LAC PA-027961)

monetary subsidy from the colonies, Laurier and his delegation entered the conference hall unprepared for the opportunity that indeed unfolded.[79]

The opportunity's genesis lay in Australian developments. The 1902 conference had been the occasion for renewal of the naval agreement by which the disparate Australasian colonies contributed to the maintenance of an auxiliary squadron in their waters; indeed, the renewal came at a higher rate of contribution, from £106,000 to £200,000, in return for the promise that more modern types would be sent to the station. While Fisher's fleet redistribution had changed those conditions, in advance of the 1907 conference New Zealand submitted a resolution that the contribution should be increased yet again. The equally simple Australian proposal, that provisions be reconsidered, belied a more complex situation. Agitation there for a separate local naval force had spawned a number of developments and those were to set the tone for the coming proceedings.[80]

As we have seen, several of the Australian colonies had established small local forces over the preceding couple of decades. The federation of the Commonwealth of Australia in 1901, not unlike Canadian confederation in 1867, was intended in part to simplify the defence burden. Although the original legislation to bring the colonial defence forces together under a central authority did not include naval forces (evidently because they were so small), it did provide the vehicle for Captain William Creswell, commandant of the Queensland Marine Defence Force, to emerge as the main lobbyist for the establishment of an independent Australian navy. His initial proposal, which paralleled remarkably the evolution of policy in Canada, met with the disapproval of the commander of the Australian station, Rear-Admiral Beaumont, the former commander of the Pacific station at Esquimalt. Not surprisingly, Beaumont pronounced his disapproved of the idea much as he had on the proposal to form a Vancouver naval brigade: "I put the case for Australian naval defence before the ministers so that they could appreciate how insufficient were the schemes involving either developing the state naval forces or the slow creation, ship by ship over many years and at great expense, of an inadequate form of naval defence."[81]

Creswell's suggestions went no further and were not a factor at the 1902 conference. Still, the subsequent renewal of the auxiliary squadron agreement was not universally popular in Australia. After the actual amalgamation of the state naval forces in January 1904, Creswell obtained the endorsement of Prime Minister J.C. Watson to start upgrading them through the loan of two or three torpedo boat destroyers. With destroyers already in short supply in the Royal Navy, London replied that such warships were unsuited to

---

79. Laurier would consult Fielding during the final days of the conference, but the finance minister was in England on private business.

80. The standard interpretation of the naval aspects of the 1907 conference is that little of substance was accomplished. Tucker, *The Naval Service of Canada*, I, 111–14, covers it almost dismissively, leaving the impression that Laurier remained opposed to the formation of a Canadian naval force. Preston, *Canada and "Imperial Defense,"* 369–72, is slightly more detailed, but has the Admiralty opposed to the creation of local forces. The revised interpretation presented here is due partly to the new understanding of the period from Lambert, *Fisher's Naval Revolution*, as well as to the recent discovery of substantial new material on local developments in both Canada and Australia; on Australia, there is the very thorough account in Nicholls, *Statesmen and Sailors*.

81. Beaumont to Admiralty, 14 November 1901, quoted in Nicholls, *Statesmen and Sailors*, 52, 24–26, 37–39, 42–43.

Australia's strategic situation and their provision would serve no useful purpose. The irrepressible Creswell had to await a change of Australian government before he could renew his lobbying. Incoming Prime Minister Alfred Deakin was so enthused that he despatched the Australian naval officer to London in the spring of 1906 to "acquaint himself with the latest developments in naval defence, especially in regard to torpedo boat destroyers, torpedo boats generally, and the latest organisation in the working of torpedo boat flotillas, including submarine vessels."[82] With Fisher, an enthusiast for flotilla defence, now in charge at the Admiralty, the Australian initiative received a favourable reception. In the wake of Creswell's visit, Whitehall responded that since "a considerable section of the Australian public are demanding the renunciation of the [auxiliary squadron] agreement and the institution of a local colonial navy, my lords feel … that as far as the immediate convenience of naval administration is concerned the abolition of the Australian naval contribution … would give them great satisfaction." On 26 September 1906, Deakin announced his government's decision to embark upon a six-year plan to develop an Australian naval force, commencing with the acquisition within the first three years of four torpedo boats and eight destroyers; during the second three years, "we should complete the whole scheme with any amendment experience might show to be necessary."[83]

It was with this understanding that Deakin arrived in London in April 1907 for the latest colonial conference anticipating Admiralty support for the establishment of an Australian naval force. Imperial naval defence, however, proved to be a less pressing issue than at previous gatherings. In part, the idea had lost much of its controversy, however, none of the parties involved expected that much of actual substance could be accomplished. Overwhelmingly, Fisher's reforms had served to re-establish confidence in the ability of the Royal Navy to defeat any potential foes. As we have seen, the Canadian delegation fully expected the status quo to prevail at the conference, while the Admiralty, having accepted the principle of separate colonial navies, proceeded in the belief that any such local establishments necessarily would be of limited immediate value. Even Deakin accepted it as fairly low on the list of priorities for discussion, which turned instead around preferential trade, commercial and legal relations, and immigration issues.[84] Nonetheless, the 1907

---

82. Governor-General to Colonial Secretary, 20 February 1906, quoted in Nicholls, *Statesmen and Sailors*, 102, 84; and Nicholls, "William Rook Creswell and an Australian Navy," T.R. Frame, J.V.P. Goldrick and P.D. Jones, eds., *Reflections on the Royal Australian Navy* (Kenthurst, NSW 1991), 44.

83. Admiralty to Commander-in-Chief Australian Station, 17 August 1906, and *Commonwealth Parliamentary Debates*, 26 September 1906, quoted Nicholls, *Statesmen and Sailors*, 111, 112–13. Nicholls demonstrates on page 120 that a subsequent analysis by the director of naval intelligence, Rear-Admiral Sir Charles Ottley, "Views on the Working of the Australian Naval Agreement," 27 February 1907 (UKNA, ADM 116/1241B), served as the basis for the opening remarks by the first lord at the impending colonial conference. In his memo, Ottley determined that "a dependent position in regard to naval power would be incompatible with a colony's autonomy and healthy development as a semi-independent state…. [The] Admiralty should do everything in its power to assist in the raising and development of local navies by providing officers and instructors, training seamen and generally help by giving advice in ordering and obtaining material. They should also discuss with colonial governments the employment and status of their naval forces."

84. Britain, Parliament, *Proceedings of the Colonial Conference, 1907* (London 1908); and see also a précis in Ollivier, ed., *The Colonial and Imperial Conferences*, I, 211–324.

conference marked an important turning point in imperial military relations, with the implicit rejection of previous notions of colonial commitment in favour of the "revolutionary departure" that "the basis of the military structure of the future commonwealth … henceforward [was to be] empire co-operation, rather than imperial organization."[85]

The new principle was most clearly demonstrated in the field of military defence. When the subject was raised on the fourth day of discussion, Borden quickly determined that the proposals for greater co-operation posed no immediate constitutional or political problems. In return for assurances of no direct War Office control over colonial forces, he felt safe in signalling Canadian acceptance of participation in an imperial general staff in a purely advisory capacity. The great irony, however, was that agreement upon standardization of weapons, training and organization would prove to be the biggest pre-war step toward "laying down a practical groundwork for the rapid mobilization of the empire's manpower into a roughly homogeneous force."[86]

Naval defence was not broached until the fifth day of the conference, 23 April, when the first lord, Lord Tweedmouth, quickly signalled that the same general principle applied: "I feel it a high privilege to sit at this table … with the prime ministers of the self-governing dominions of the king beyond the seas.… We welcome you, and we ask you to take some leading part in making more complete than it is at present the naval defence of the empire.… We want you to give us all the assistance you can, but we do not come to you as beggars; we gladly take all that you can give us, but at the same time, if you are not inclined to give us the help that we hope to have from you, we acknowledge our absolute obligation to defend the king's dominions across the seas to the best of our ability."[87] That over-arching responsibility, Tweedmouth maintained, would require the Admiralty to retain clear control of the distribution of the main battle fleets. However, after repeating the mantra that, "there is one sea, there is one empire, and there is one navy," he moved on to a new proposal.

> We are quite ready to enter into any arrangements with the colonies that may seem most suitable to them, and which may seem to bring advantage to the navy, and advantage to the colonies themselves.… His majesty's government recognize the natural desire of the self-governing colonies to have a more particular share in providing the naval defence force of the empire, and, so long as the condition of unity of command and direction of the fleet is maintained, they are ready to consider a modification of the existing arrangements to meet the views of the various colonies. In the opinion of the government, … it would be of great assistance if the colonial governments would undertake to provide for local service in the imperial squadrons the smaller vessels that are

85. Preston, *Canada and "Imperial Defense,"* 361; Britain, Parliament, *Proceedings of the Colonial Conference, 1907* (London 1908); and see also a précis in Ollivier, ed., *The Colonial and Imperial Conferences*, I, 211–324.

86. Nicholls, *Statesmen and Sailors*, 121.

87. Parliament, *Proceedings of the Colonial Conference, 1907*, 129; and Ollivier, ed., *The Colonial and Imperial Conferences*, I, 248.

useful for defence against possible raids or for co-operation with a squadron, and also to equip and maintain docks and fitting establishments which can be used by his majesty's ships.

The first lord emphasized the co-operative nature of such proposals, indicating that the Admiralty was willing "to make separate arrangements with each separate colony according to its own wishes," and that "probably the best way to start would be to allocate to local purposes certain portions of the subsidies already given." He continued:

> I understand that, in Australia particularly and in South Africa, it is desired to start some naval service of your own. Perhaps I might suggest that if the provision of the smaller craft which are necessarily incident to the work of a great fleet of modern battleships could be made locally, it would be a very great help to the general work of the navy. You cannot take the small craft such as torpedo boats and submarines across the ocean, and for warships to arrive in South Africa or in Australia or in New Zealand or in Canada, and find ready to their hand well-trained men in good vessels of this kind, would be an enormous advantage to them.... There is, I think, the further advantage in these small flotillas, that they will be an admirable means of coast defence; that you will be able by the use of them to avoid practically all danger from any sudden raid which might be made by a cruising squadron.... Above all things in this work [of flotilla defence] the submarine is probably the most important and the most effective weapon.... I am assured by my advisers at the Admiralty that it is a most important weapon; that it has already reached very considerable development; and is one upon which we may rely with great confidence.[88]

Having arrived in London anticipating a repeat of the Admiralty's pitch for colonial contributions to the maintenance of an increasingly concentrated Royal Navy, Laurier clearly was taken aback by the change in the British position. As the first lord ended his opening remarks, he turned to the Canadian prime minister as the senior of the colonial representatives to continue the discussion. Seeking to collect his thoughts, Laurier suggested Tweedmouth call first upon the premiers of Australia and New Zealand "as they have proposed resolutions." Deakin and Ward each found something of which to approve in Tweedmouth's presentation, the Australian not surprisingly pointing to the new allowance for local defence, and the New Zealander to the need to have confidence in the Admiralty's strategic direction. When it was again Laurier's turn to speak, he deferred to his marine minister. Instead of developing the line of thought suggested by Tweedmouth, however, Brodeur dismissed it with a simple "it will not be necessary for me ... to state the position which Canada intends to take in regard to this question of naval defence [because] our situation is a different one to that of the other colonies, and should be treated as such."

---

88. Parliament, *Proceedings of the Colonial Conference, 1907*, 130–31; and Ollivier, ed., *The Colonial and Imperial Conferences*, I, 249.

Turning quickly to his prepared text, Brodeur seized upon the implication in the pre-conference document prepared by the Admiralty that Canada was "supposed not to have spent any money at all upon naval defence."[89] After establishing from Tweedmouth that the costs of the British Fisheries Protection Service were included in the United Kingdom's naval expenditure, Brodeur made the claim that "the same thing should be done for Canada," namely that expenditure on the Fisheries Protection Service should be considered as naval expenditure. He proceeded to give a detailed account of other, similar examples, such as the establishment of wireless telegraphic stations on both coasts, taking over and enlarging the hydrographic survey, and the transfer of responsibility for the Halifax and Esquimalt dockyards. But the most important point he wished to make was that Canada, aside from these duties, was also making a more direct contribution "with regard to our naval militia." He drew attention to CGS *Canada*, upon which "men are now drilling every day ... and acquiring knowledge in connection with Naval matters." Especially in the combined fisheries protection and training functions, the minister felt that the nation was "carrying out in that way not only some local self-defence, but also imperial obligations."[90]

After this initial public exchange, the conference turned to other issues, and two weeks passed before naval defence again came to the fore. The adjournment provided an opportunity for the Admiralty to pursue private discussions with the various delegations, the most substantive being with the Australians, as recorded in a published memorandum. That exchange clearly demonstrated Deakin's intention to establish a viable local naval force, but formal agreement foundered upon the fact that he desired "a force which is imperial in character, if not for all intents and purposes an integral part of the Royal Navy." That would mean colonial political control over a portion of the Royal Navy, a condition to which the Admiralty could not consent. Recognizing that it was impossible to reconcile the two views, the memorandum concluded that "if the commonwealth still desires to establish a local force it should be clearly understood in the first place that it will be a purely colonial force."[91]

There is no similar record of talks between the Admiralty and the Canadian delegation, although it appears that informal discussions between the politicians were instrumental in each side gaining a better appreciation of the other's position. In open session on 8 May, the thirteenth day of the conference, the first lord announced the results of such private meetings. For one, he frankly admitted that "there has perhaps been some exaggeration in the idea that Canada does not do anything for the empire in this matter." The expansion of the Fisheries Protection Service and the takeover of the imperial dockyards were acknowledged to be "a very considerable contribution towards the general upkeep of our naval interests." He noted as well that the Canadian representatives had committed themselves "to do all that they can to expand the interest in the navy throughout the dominion." When it was his turn to speak, Brodeur simply restated his earlier position, while also agreeing

---

89. Ollivier, ed., *The Colonial and Imperial Conferences*, I, 251.

90. Parliament, *Proceedings of the Colonial Conference, 1907*, 139–42.

91. "Memorandum of Interview Between Mr Deakin (Premier of Australian Commonwealth) and Representatives of the Admiralty," 24 April 1907, quoted in Nicholls, *Statesmen and Sailors*, 122–23.

that the two sides had reconciled their misconceptions. He then took the opportunity to announce that Canada's parliament had already voted a large sum of money to purchase a new fisheries protection cruiser for the Pacific coast. The marine minister concluded with the declaration that since "Lord Tweedmouth has recognized that in this matter it should be left almost entirely to the colonies ... [Canada] will be very glad to work in co-operation with the imperial authorities, and under the advice of an imperial officer, so far as it is consistent with self-government."[92]

Later, outside the conference halls, in answer to persistent criticism by the British naval publicist Lord Brassey that Canada was not doing enough in the way of naval defence, Brodeur spelled out his plans more clearly. His government planned to build a new and larger fisheries protection cruiser on which a certain number of young men would be taught "seamanship and the handling of guns and warships." This "nucleus of a navy" would be developed in such a way that "in case of war, in which Canada would participate, [it] would be useful to the British Admiralty: in fact, I expect to be governed very largely in the organisation of that system by the experience of the British Admiralty and I am sure by what has been promised to us by Lord Tweedmouth, that we may rely entirely upon their good will in that respect."[93]

Brodeur's promise of future co-operation was not necessarily a firm naval policy, however. Laurier was quick to block a later resolution introduced by the premier of the Cape Colony summarizing the naval discussions that had taken place, but which he felt placed too much emphasis on the central role of the Admiralty. Laurier's failure to gain any ground in the preferential tariff discussions, however, led him to go against his earlier pledge and submit a resolution of his own at the final sitting of the conference, as a last-ditch attempt to breathe life into the idea. His proposal for an all-imperial "mail service to Australia and New Zealand," or the "All Red Route" as the project popularly became known, envisioned a fast steamship and rail service subsidized by Britain, Canada, Australia, and New Zealand "in equitable proportions." The route would link the empire by secure lines of communication, crossing only British Empire territories or dominions and those seas that were easily defended by the Royal Navy. Although the stated intent was to encourage intra-imperial trade and Laurier drew no defence-related arguments to support the scheme, the idea bore a close resemblance to the Toronto Navy League's proposals for a subsidized fast line and had many implications for imperial defence. A contemporary historian of the colonial and imperial conferences deduced that Laurier, like Canadian statesmen in the past, was reminding London that "works of public development—notably the Canadian Pacific Railway, which had opened an alternative line of communication with India—were equivalent to direct military and naval preparations as a contribution to imperial defence." But that analysis maintained also that, rather than advance the All Red Route, Laurier could have used the national development argument to make a case against Admiralty insistence on complete naval control, except that that would have committed him to creating a fleet unit.

92. Parliament, *Proceedings of the Colonial Conference, 1907*, 476, 488; and Canada, Parliament, House of Commons, *Debates*, 5 April 1907, col. 5906. The new vessel was to be 225 feet long, and have a displacement of 800 tons, and a speed of seventeen knots; a sum of $225,000 was set aside for the purchase.

93. Brodeur to Lord Brassey, 20 May 1907, LAC, MG 27 II C4, vol. 2, file 14, reel H-1017.

The resolution was adopted, but did not secure the other trade concessions the Canadian prime minister was seeking.[94]

Laurier would continue to invest significant political capital in promoting the All Red Route well into 1908, but with diminishing returns. The Navy League's Toronto branch complained in its annual report for 1907 that "had the scheme ... been accompanied by proposals for colonial naval reserves to man such steamers, as originally advocated by this branch, ... its chances of success would have been greatly increased." It is doubtful that the reserve scheme would have made any difference in view of the Admiralty's waning interest in the wartime conversion of steamships into armed cruisers. An exception was made to continue subsidizing two new Cunard liners capable of twenty-five knots, but only until the new Invincible class of dreadnought battle cruisers entered service later in 1908 to take up the task of protecting imperial trade routes. In any event, Laurier's promotion of the "All Red Route" did not result in any special recognition of Canadian rail or steamship lines by officials in London. It did, however, contribute to the laying of additional telegraph cables so as to create an "all-red" communications system. Eventually, the network would incorporate so many redundancies that even if an isolated cable station—such as the Cocos Islands, in the Pacific Ocean—was captured or destroyed, it could be bypassed. By 1911 British strategists calculated that an enemy would have to cut forty-nine telegraph cables to isolate Britain, fifteen to do the same to Canada and Newfoundland, and ten for each of Egypt and Malta.[95]

Also, even if the Colonial Conference of 1907 did not result in any concrete advances, it still must be counted as progress toward the realization of a Canadian naval service. Laurier's on-going concerns were alleviated by both the new spirit of co-operation exhibited by the Admiralty and its positive reception among Canadian public opinion makers. Interestingly, one of the earliest to pick up on it was the editor of *La Presse* in Montreal, who on 26 April urged the early construction of a purely Canadian fleet. One small sign of the prime minister's warming to naval affairs came midway through the conference, when Captain Kingsmill called upon Laurier's secretary for a brief interview with the prime minister and instead found himself and his wife invited to dine privately with the Lauriers. Kingsmill wanted to explain that reports of his having been found guilty of negligence for the grounding of *Dominion* "are absolutely false," clarifying the court-martial finding "because I know Sir Wilfrid wrote personally to thank the Admiralty and would not like him to think that I were unworthy of his consideration." There is no record of the table talk that evening, but it is a fair certainty that naval matters entered the conversation. A few days later Brodeur made his announcement of a new fisheries cruiser for British

---

94. Richard Jebb, *The Imperial Conference: A History and Study* (London 1911), II, 172, 174, 339–65; Preston, *Canada and "Imperial Defense,"* 371; Parliament, *Proceedings of the Colonial Conference, 1907,* 547–48. In reference to the "All Red Route," see Parliament, *Proceedings of the Colonial Conference, 1907,* 572–93; J. Castell Hopkins, *The Canadian Annual Review of Public Affairs, 1907* (Toronto 1908), 341–46; and J. Castell Hopkins, *The Canadian Annual Review of Public Affairs, 1908* (Toronto 1909), 597–99.

95. The Navy League (Toronto Branch), "Annual Report of the Executive Committee for 1907," 10 February 1908, LAC, MG 27 II C4, vol. 2, file 23, reel H-1017; and Paul M. Kennedy "Imperial Cable Communications and Strategy, 1870–1914," Paul M. Kennedy, ed., *The War Plans of the Great Powers, 1880–1914* (London 1979), 84, 86, 94.

Columbia and the implications for an expanded naval militia to cover that coast. Back in Ottawa, in the parliamentary debates over departmental estimates, Fielding explained away criticism of several expensive food items for *Canada* as necessary expenditures for the "flag-ship of the Canadian navy" without drawing undue notice of the statement.[96]

The fact remained, however, that naval matters were still not high on the list of Canadian political priorities. After the conference, the minister of marine and fisheries remained in England, not to hold further talks with the Admiralty officials, but to negotiate successfully with the Lloyd's insurance company for more favourable rates for vessels using the St Lawrence route, on the basis that the recent improvements to the channel made the sometimes prohibitive former rates no longer necessary. Then, Brodeur joined Fielding in Paris to start negotiations on trade and tariffs—the French Convention being signed on 19 September 1907—and it was not until 24 October that the two ministers arrived back in Canada. Nearly half a year had elapsed without the naval issue receiving Cabinet consideration.

Naval issues were once again thrust to the centre of public attention in December 1907 when President Roosevelt despatched the United States Navy's entire Atlantic battle fleet, comprising sixteen pre-dreadnought battleships, to circumnavigate the globe by way of the Pacific as a demonstration of American naval power. Popularly known as the "Great White Fleet" because of the ships' white paint scheme, the Atlantic fleet's world cruise signalled a dramatic shift of strategic focus, since traditionally the American navy had been concentrated in the Atlantic—"the only conceivable setting for a sea fight"—in reaction to previous Anglo-American tensions. The president had several reasons for ordering the cruise: a demonstration of the length of the trans-Cape Horn voyage so as to gain support for a speedy completion of the Panama Canal; an increase of American goodwill in Latin America; a stimulation of American pride in the navy and thereby increased sentiment for a large fleet; and, if nothing else, to provide the navy with some much needed ocean training. But as time went on, attention focused on what was presumed to be the Roosevelt's primary object: "to impress Japan with our power so that she would not be tempted to make trouble." The American president had earned a Nobel Peace Prize for his arbitration ending the Russo-Japanese War in 1905, and in the process had gained an appreciation for the capabilities and ambitions of the victorious Japanese. He saw the cruise as the best way to prevent any possibility of war with Japan by demonstrating, as he told German Admiral von Tirpitz, "that there were fleets of the white races which were totally different from the fleet of poor Rodjestvensky."[97] He hoped in turn to encourage among imperial Japanese authorities a better appreciation of American concerns in the Pacific.

Canadian politicians, meanwhile, watched the cruise with close interest since immigration from Japan was provoking alarm in British Columbia. Lacking the "big stick" the

96. Kingsmill to Lemaire, 29 April 1907, Laurier to Kingsmill, 29 April 1907, Kingsmill to Laurier, 1 May 1908, LAC, MG 26 G, reel C-848, 124682–684, 124686, reel C-862, 139926; Canada, Parliament, House of Commons, *Debates*, 5 April 1907, cols. 5964ff; and Hopkins, *The Canadian Annual Review, 1907*, 348. See also *Canadian Almanac and Miscellaneous Directory, 1908*, (Toronto 1908), 313, 475, 477 for press summaries concerning Kingsmill.

97. Roosevelt quoted in Walter Lord, *The Good Years: From 1900 to the First World War* (New York 1960), 206; and Howard K. Beale, *Theodore Roosevelt and the Rise of America to World Power* (Baltimore 1956), 328–29, 328n.

British, dominion, and colonial representatives at the April 1907 Colonial Conference in London. Front row, from left to right, are H.H. Asquith, British chancellor of the exchequer; Sir J.G. Ward, prime minister of New Zealand; Sir Wilfrid Laurier, prime minister of Canada; the Earl of Elgin, secretary of state for the colonies; A. Deakin, prime minister of Australia; F.R. Moor, prime minister of Natal; and David Lloyd George, president of the Board of Trade. From left to right in the second row are Winston Churchill, parliamentary under-secretary of state for the colonies; Sir Francis Hopwood, permanent under-secretary of state for the colonies; and Louis Botha, prime minister of the Transvaal. On the right of the second row are Louis Brodeur, Canadian minister of marine and fisheries, and Sir Robert Bond, prime minister of Newfoundland. Also in the photograph, standing in the back row right, is Sir Frederick Borden, Canadian minister of militia and defence. (LAC C-008013)

Americans could wield, Ottawa resorted to less brazen means of diplomacy to allay Caucasian concerns. When anti-oriental riots broke out in Vancouver in September 1907, Postmaster General Rodolphe Lemieux was sent to Japan to seek a firmer agreement from that government to uphold existing restrictions on emigration to Canada, and Deputy Minister of Labour William Lyon Mackenzie King was appointed a royal commissioner to investigate the incident. Nor did Laurier object when President Roosevelt invited King to Washington, on the basis of the deputy minister's study of Asian immigration, to discuss informally and unofficially "matters of common interest." With as yet no formal Canadian representation in Washington, the US president wanted King to operate as a channel of communication between the American and British Governments to facilitate a settlement of the question of Japanese immigration. He felt that the immediate Canadian interest in the problem would lead to more positive results, as the British ambassador to Washington, James Bryce, seemed "to view it more as an academic question."[98]

Despite efforts by Ottawa to downplay the Japanese immigration issue, the American cruise provoked a marked upsurge of Canadian interest in naval matters. While European governments and newspapers academically speculated on the chances of war between the United States and Japan, the Canadian public turned its eyes to their own country's coast defences. The governor general watched the progress of the USN's "Great White Fleet" with fascination and provided daily reports to Laurier and practically anyone else with whom he talked. Grey was quick to point out the weakness of Canadian defences and raised the spectre of a Japanese-American conflict in a December letter to the prime minister: "It would be mockery to ask whether you are prepared for this. I am not aware that your Cabinet have even considered the expediency, as have the gov[ernmen]t of Australia, of taking steps to defend their coasts against possible Japanese aggression. Your only security against the possibility of BC being occupied by the Japanese when it suits them to take possession lies in the Jap-Anglo [*sic*] alliance and in the present superior strength of the British navy."[99] Furthermore, although he regarded "the American navy as one of the reserves of the empire," he cautioned Laurier that "the US fleet and the Monroe Doctrine offer you no protection on which you can count." Neither did Grey discount the possibility that the Japanese might ambush the American fleet and deal it as humiliating a defeat as it had the Russian navy at Tsushima two years earlier. Furthermore, even if such a disaster did not befall the Americans, its fleet represented US interests, not Canadian.

---

98. R. MacGregor Dawson, *William Lyon Mackenzie King: A Political Biography*, I: *1874–1923* (Toronto 1958), 146, 151–53; Patricia Roy, *A White Man's Province* (Vancouver 1989), 202–05; and Mackenzie King private diary, 31 January 1908, LAC, MG 26 J13. The British were reluctant to arbitrate, even though the dominion was involved, because of the Anglo-Japanese Alliance, originally signed in 1902 and renewed in 1905, which called for non-intervention of the two island empires in the other's Far Eastern affairs. For a discussion of the terms and implications of the alliance, see Ian H. Nish, *Alliance in Decline: A Study in Anglo-Japanese Relations, 1908–23* (London 1972) and Robert Joseph Gowen, "British Legerdemain at the 1911 Conference: The Dominions, Defense Planning, and the Renewal of the Anglo-Japanese Alliance," *Journal of Modern History*, 52, (September 1980), 385–413.

99. Grey to Laurier (emphasis in original), 27 December 1907, LAC, MG 27, II B2, 2–216, 664–67; Beale, *Theodore Roosevelt*, 331; and Lord, *The Good Years*, 206–07.

Mackenzie King, from his vantage points in Ottawa and Washington, had come to a similar conclusion. Talks were progressing smoothly and the Japanese government was showing signs of co-operation, when, apparently prompted by a request from Prime Minister Deakin of Australia that the American fleet visit that country, Roosevelt asked King if Canada would like the American fleet to visit Vancouver and Victoria. Press editorials and public meetings in Vancouver had been "virtually requesting the American fleet to come to Canada," but the Canadian deputy minister could not reply without first consulting his own government. Back in Ottawa three days later, King discussed the matter at length with Grey.[100] The deputy minister felt that "it would be most unwise for the American fleet to be invited to come to Canadian waters. To begin with I did not think it is desirable that we should encourage a sentiment of dependence on the United States or to strengthen the annexationist feeling in the west ... if there was to be any fleet in our waters we would prefer to have the British fleet." Even that was not the most preferable course of action, however, and King pointed the way in which Liberal thinking on a naval policy was developing when he confided to his diary after a meeting with Laurier that:

> The situation reveals to me, too, so far as Canada is concerned, the necessity of our doing something in the way of our having a navy of our own. We must admit that in the present situation we are absolutely dependent upon the naval power of Great Britain for the protection of our own country against Asiatic invasion. We might as well face this squarely and meet the situation by contributions to the British government or by the beginning of a navy of our own, which, as a Canadian, would be the preferable course. In speaking of a navy of our own, I do not mean that we would act independently in any way of the British. An arrangement could be effected whereby a complete unity of action could be effected. I think, however, that it would be better for us in voting money to control expenditure and it is well to accompany any imperial sentiment by a healthy Canadian national spirit as well.[101]

The entire episode had highlighted the fact that the American—or, for that matter, any foreign—fleet could enter Canadian waters virtually unopposed and gave a fresh impetus to the sense of vulnerability felt by British Columbians. In the absence of a significant British naval presence, it was apparent that Ottawa would have to take action on its own. On 14 December 1907, even as the American fleet was setting off on its historic world circumnavigation, Laurier had set Brodeur once again to investigate the status of Canada's naval militia. The ostensible purpose was to bring down the returns that had been requested by A.C. Macdonnell nearly a year before (and which were still outstanding), but the marine minister judged the prime minister's fresh interest in the naval militia question important enough that he had a report prepared by early 1908. The Conservative member for Vancouver City, meanwhile, proceeded to lead an opposition attack through January

100. King private diary, 24 and 27 February 1908, LAC, MG 26 J13.

101. Ibid, 27 February 1908.

1908, with pointed questions on matters of familiar concern, such as the maintenance of the Esquimalt naval station, the future prospects of it and Halifax as "Canadian naval stations," Canadian contributions to imperial defence and whether the Fisheries Protection Service was to be counted toward it, and naval instruction in Canada.[102] Because of his recent handling of the material, Brodeur was able to answer the questions easily, but the persistence and detail of the questions showed that the opposition expected more affirmative action, and soon.

Shortly afterward, Brodeur was approached by C. Frederick Hamilton, an experienced member of both the House of Commons press gallery and, more recently, the executive committee of the Navy League in Toronto. Hamilton gave the minister a newspaper report of an address he had given to the Canadian Club in Orillia on "coastal defence" and a Canadian navy that had received extensive coverage in the *Orillia Packet*. The lengthy newspaper article summarized Canada's maritime interests, the country's vulnerability to attack on the seas and coasts, particularly if British cruisers were deployed to a contest in the North Sea, and the naval alternatives open to the Canadian government. He concluded by advocating "the establishment of a naval militia, whereby our sailors and fishermen could be trained to handle naval artillery, torpedoes, etc. This militia should be under our own control, as is our land militia. This should lead up to the establishment of flotillas of torpedo boats, destroyers, or submarines at suitable points on our coast-line. These should be manned by our own people, and under our own control."[103] Brodeur granted Hamilton an interview at the end of January to further discuss his proposal and the aims of the Toronto branch of the Navy League. In a subsequent letter to Wickham on 5 February 1908, Brodeur provided further details of the government's ideas for a naval militia built around CGS *Canada* and the forthcoming fisheries cruiser for the Pacific coast, noting that "our ideas are not dissimilar, and I believe that we are quite in accord upon the principle of the establishment of a naval reserve in Canada." He tempered his comments by reminding Wickham that "we are not, perhaps, going as fast as certain persons would like … to spend millions of dollars for the establishment of a naval militia, of which no immediate need seems to exist."[104]

The public's general approval for such a scheme, however, was difficult to resist. Barely a week after penning his letter to Wickham, Brodeur resurrected the prospect of a naval militia, while presenting his department's estimates to parliament. The opposition could not resist questioning the sincerity of the government's intentions, observing that the $10,000 sum requested would only cover the wages of *Canada*'s crew. When the Conservative member for Saint John City, J.W. Daniel, raised doubts as to the government's interpretation of a "naval militia," whether it should be a permanent force including *Canada*

---

102. Lemaire to Brodeur, 14 December 1907, Brodeur to Laurier, 31 December 1907, LAC, MG 26 G, reel C-857, 134422; and Canada, Parliament, House of Commons, *Debates*, 13 January 1908, cols. 1117–20.

103. C. Frederick Hamilton to Brodeur, 17 January 1908, LAC, MG 27 II C4, vol. 2, file 19, reel H-1017; and *Orillia Packet*, 9 January 1908. As well as publishing a series of articles on naval defence in the influential *University Magazine* during 1907, Hamilton had co-authored several articles with Wickham, notably the May 1906 "Proposals For Fast Line in Connection with Canadian Naval Reserve Force."

104. Wickham to Brodeur, 31 January 1908, Brodeur to Wickham, 5 February 1908, LAC, MG 27 II C4, vol. 2, file 23, reel H-1017.

and her sisters or, as he felt they intended, simply a body of trained men, Brodeur gave the familiar response that what was proposed was "merely the nucleus of the naval militia." His explanation repeated his determination to proceed slowly along the established lines of creating a force to better exert the dominion's growing autonomy: "the naval militia is based upon the fisheries protection service. Some day, instead of only having special boats for the fisheries protection service, I hope to have the naval militia take part in that work. At the time when the *Canada* was built, there was no organization except some boats like the *Curlew* and the *Vigilant* to patrol the coast. But it was thought we should have a boat on which a certain number of young men would be trained under the rules of the British Admiralty. That has been done for the last few years with satisfactory results. I should like our organization to be made in such a way."[105]

Before any new plans could be drawn up, however, the Department of Marine and Fisheries saw its normal operations disrupted in the early spring of 1908. Unlike previous delays, which had served generally to retard progress, this was to prove a real catalyst for change, as the root of the problem was the continuing misadministration of the department. It was generally recognized that Brodeur was working hard to correct the situation and that his prolonged absence in 1907 had limited his opportunities to do so. The governor general, for one, felt that after one and a half years "the public will be expecting to see some evidence of the change which you [Laurier] have encouraged them to anticipate from his [i.e., Brodeur's] administration." Grey further asserted that the greatest impediment lay in "the retention in positions of responsibility of men who are notoriously unfit for the positions they fill"—his prime target being the deputy minister, Colonel F.F.E. Gourdeau. Grey had "deplore[ed] the maladministration of the Public Works Dep[artmen]t and Marine and Fisheries" the previous August and reminded the prime minister that Laurier "had arranged with Brodeur in England that when he returned Gourdeau should be pensioned." Brodeur, however, was reluctant to retire the deputy minister since he "knows too much" about previous departmental patronage and that "in his superannuated independence [Gourdeau] might disclose revelations regarding the Préfontaine regime, which might be unpleasant!" The governor general also advised Laurier that Commander Spain, "who appears to me to be bright and clever," should be kept on, but in a subordinate position, and that Brodeur should consider "the idea of applying to the Admiralty for an officer who could take Spain's place. There must be many officers in HM navy who have the technical knowledge, which Spain who left the navy twenty years ago cannot have, who would be only too glad to place their services at the disposal of HM Canadian govt.... Mr Brodeur was unaware, until I informed him of the fact, that Mr Spain left HM navy about twenty years ago under a cloud which still makes it impossible for him to go on board a British man-of-war. This fact is sufficient to prove his unfitness for the position which he now holds." Grey concluded with the warning that, in his view, "the marine and fisheries department is the most vulnerable point in your administration."[106]

---

105. House of Commons, *Debates*, 14 February 1908, cols. 3222–5.

106. Grey to Laurier, 11 November 1907, "Memo of H.E. conversation with Sir W.L., 25 August 1907," nd, LAC, MG 27 II B2, 2–157, 471, 2–184, 580–583; and Hopkins, *The Canadian Annual Review, 1908*, 63.

This soon proved to be something of an understatement. While Brodeur continued to put off the decisive actions Grey was advocating, his department had become the object of an investigation by the Civil Service Commission into the efficiency of government bureaucracy. Its final report, brought down on 26 March 1908, subjected most ministries to only minor criticism. Marine and Fisheries, however, was singled out for a particularly long and scathing analysis, which focused, among other things, on the department's penchant for "constant blundering and confusion" with "no sign of ... an intelligent purpose, unless it be that of spending as much money as possible." The storm of opposition protest and demands for Brodeur's resignation were probably to be expected, but Grey was also unimpressed that his many warnings had gone unheeded by Laurier. The governor general strongly hinted that the prime minister should consider dissolution.[107]

Laurier, on the other hand, was certain that the government could ride out the storm. To ease some of the pressure, the prime minister announced on 1 April that the "very grave statements" in the recent report regarding marine officials warranted the formation of a royal commission to investigate the department, and he charged Walter Cassels, judge of the exchequer court of Canada, with the task. This was followed by notice the next day that several of the department's officers had been suspended and that the deputy minister's retirement was imminent. On 23 April, Georges J. Desbarats, since 1902 the director of the government shipyard at Sorel, was appointed in his place. Brodeur was not entirely happy with the new arrangement—the governor general informed Laurier that Desbarats was "a son-in-law of Mr Scott's [Sir Richard William Scott, Liberal leader in the Senate, 1902–1908], and is therefore not a persona grata to some of Mr Brodeur's friends"—but the new deputy minister was a conscientious and hard-working bureaucrat and soon set the department's administration on a more responsible footing.[108]

Shortly thereafter, the other half of Grey's recommendation, the replacement of the commander of the Marine Service, also came to fruition. Compounding the governor general's doubts as to Spain's professional suitability was increasing evidence of his administrative sloppiness, all confirming that he was not the best man to conduct detailed negotiations with the Admiralty concerning any change in the status of the Fisheries Protection Service.[109] Grey discussed with Brodeur in late April the problem of finding some qualified officer to replace Spain, and it seems that the minister had no doubt as to who that officer should be. As he informed Laurier at the beginning of May, "I understand from Mr Brodeur that he will be glad

107. *Royal Commission on the Civil Service* quoted in Michael Hadley and Roger Sarty, *Tin-pots and Pirate Ships: Canadian Naval Forces and German Sea Raiders, 1880–1918* (Montreal 1991), 18; Canada, Parliament, House of Commons, *Debates*, 26 March 1908, cols. 5620–49; and 30 March 1908, cols. 5826–44; Grey to Laurier, 25 March 1908, LAC, MG 26 G, reel C-1162, 205212–15.

108. Canada, Parliament, House of Commons, *Debates*, 1 April 1908, col. 6003, 2 April 1908, cols. 6060–1, 23 April 1908, col. 6982; and Grey to Laurier, 14 December 1908, LAC, MG 27 II B2, 3–348, 1026–27.

109. Spain had committed several indiscretions in claims for travelling expenses, at one point having to appeal to Laurier himself to put an end to calls for his resignation. Spain to Laurier, 12 January 1906, LAC, MG 26 G, reel C-830, 105919–27. The subject had most recently been raised in the House of Commons as another in the long string of marine department-related embarrassments. Canada, Parliament, House of Commons, *Debates*, 5 March 1908, col. 4405.

if he can secure Captain Kingsmill's services. I therefore assume that you will approve of my cabling to Lord Tweedmouth to say that you are prepared to appoint Capt. K as commander of your marine protection service and naval militia (perhaps you will be good enough to give me the exact title) if the Admiralty can recommend him as an officer fully competent to undertake the duties of that position." Within a fortnight the deal was completed, and with the concurrence of the Admiralty the transfer was made effective 15 May 1908. To facilitate it without provoking any constitutional problems, as had accompanied militia GOC appointments, Kingsmill was promoted to rear-admiral effective 12 May and not placed on the retired list until some months later—possibly to allow him to return to the British navy should the Canadian appointment not prove to his liking.[110]

Efforts to place a flag officer in charge of the Canadian marine service confirmed that a substantial increase in the status of the force was in the offing and that the appointment was made with the full concurrence of the Admiralty. The nearest equivalent command in the Royal Navy to that being assumed by Kingsmill was commander-in-chief of a station. The starting pay that the Canadians were offering was not nearly equivalent to Royal Navy rates—$3,000 per annum, as opposed to $8,000 plus allowances—but since his prospects within the RN now seemed diminished, perhaps the chance of an independent command and a return home appealed to him. That this was the direction in which Canada was heading was confirmed by the semi-official announcement of Kingsmill's appointment in the Toronto *Globe* under the front-page headline, "Canada To Have Naval Militia—A Canadian Admiral Has Already Been Appointed." The paper went on to report that "it is understood that his appointment presages an advance in the movement toward the development of a naval militia. This was ... begun some years ago under Commander Spain, and there are now seamen in training along British naval lines on the cruiser *Canada* and on some other vessels of the fleet of protective cruisers.... [However,] the development of the naval militia will be gradual, and will keep pace with the advance of public opinion in respect to assuming a large share in imperial defence."[111]

Public opinion was soon put to the test with the mid-July arrival at Quebec City of the Royal Navy's Channel Squadron and elements of American and French squadrons to join in the two-week celebration of the city's tercentenary. The newly launched *Indomitable*, the first of Fisher's dreadnought battle cruisers, was the centre of naval attention, but prominent alongside her on several occasions was CGS *Canada*. In a photographic review of the tercentenary, the Toronto *Globe* carried several pictures of the ship taking part in various activities, including a front-page image of *Canada* in full ceremonial flag dressing under the headline "Canada's Army and Navy At Quebec." At another point in the celebrations, the Toronto paper carried a photograph of Captain Charles T. Knowlton and Cadet John

---

110. Grey to Laurier, 1 May 1908, LAC, MG 27 II B2, 3-291, 866. Because of the lack of documentary evidence concerning Kingsmill's appointment, this letter raises the question of where the suggestion of Kingsmill's name originated: whether from Brodeur on Laurier's recommendation, or even on his own assumption that Laurier's acquaintance with the officer was more than casual for a reason; or from the Admiralty in response to some undocumented Canadian request. Kingsmill file, UKNA, ADM 196//19.

111. Toronto *Globe*, 18 May 1908.

Augustus Barron, both of *Canada*, proclaiming them "Canada's naval commander and her first cadet."[112]

Although the actual commander of the marine service did not attract the same public attention, Rear-Admiral Kingsmill was also on hand for the celebrations, the event providing a backdrop for a professional examination of the future of a Canadian naval service. Embarked aboard one of the British battleships was Julian Corbett, his presence arranged by the new director of naval intelligence, Rear-Admiral Edmund Slade, who, as a recent president of the Naval War College at Greenwich, had become acquainted with the naval historian. At the time of Kingsmill's appointment in May, the first sea lord—obviously recalling his experiences as North America station commander and at the recent colonial conference—had confided to Slade that he expected little to come of it. According to the intelligence director, Fisher said "he knows the Canadian [people] and that they are an unpatriotic grasping people who only stick to us for the good that they can get out of us, and that we ought to do nothing whatsoever for them." The tercentenary visit provided an opportunity to obtain an independent assessment, and Corbett was an ideal candidate for the task. His recently published *England in the Seven Years' War* had thoroughly described the siege and capture of the city in 1759, thereby acquainting him with Canadian strategic conditions. Fortuitously, that manuscript had formed the basis of his lecture notes to the course at the Naval War College in Greenwich over the winter of 1904–05, when Kingsmill was one of his students. Now Slade despatched Corbett "to discover whether there was any Canadian disposition to 'take the defence of her frontier in hand—and [towards] starting a naval militia.'" Undoubtedly, he shared with Corbett his own view, slightly more optimistic than Fisher's, that "it must be done very carefully and slowly without ostentation and parade, but if it is efficiently carried out she [Canada] will add enormously to the strength of the empire as a whole and assist the navy quite as much or more than if she went in for battleships and cruisers."[113]

When Corbett met his former student, he found Kingsmill immensely frustrated "at his own powerlessness to correct the very deficiencies that had plagued his predecessors"[114] in running the marine department:

> His pessimism was derived from two opinions. One was that the reservoir of, and facilities for, turning out competent officers were limited, and unhappily they were only available from the lower deck. There was a "total absence of any sense of discipline," and he supposed this impossible to inculcate without a fixed service system. The other discouraging feature was the prevalence of political patronage that was bound to frustrate the sound building of an officer corps. Concretely, he proposed introducing some permanence to the

112. Ibid, *Saturday Supplement*, 25 July, 8 August 1908.

113. Edmund Slade diary, 9 May and 1 July 1908 quoted in Donald M. Schurman, *Julian S. Corbett, 1854–1922: Historian of British Maritime Policy from Drake to Jellicoe* (London 1981), 99–101. The Fisher-Slade relationship is discussed in Lambert, *Fisher's Naval Revolution*, 173ff. The authors are indebted to Andrew Lambert for his insight regarding the Naval War College curriculum (conversation Gimblett-Lambert, London, October 2002).

114. Hadley and Sarty, *Tin-pots and Pirate Ships*, 19.

Charles Edmund Kingsmill, the first director of the naval service of Canada, photographed in December 1909. (LAC PA-042541)

service, employing personnel for at least a three year period, and taking the climate into consideration by employing the hands in the dockyard in the winter. But he was clearly not hopeful and "seemed to feel all this [was] only a poor substitute for money contributions to the Royal Navy."[115]

A subsequent interview with the governor general offered similarly low expectations. Queried as to "how Canadian opinion stood with regard to a navy," Grey responded that nothing was to be expected at that time as Canadians needed time to develop the resolve to make proper defence arrangements.[116]

In the end, Corbett's report to Slade proved generally positive, probably because his final conversation was with Major-General Sir Percy Lake, "a fine fellow with broad and clear views—[the] best authority by far on Canadian defence that I have met." The British officer had been serving since 1904 as chief of the general staff of the Canadian militia, and described to Corbett his experience of participating in the Leach Commission of 1898. He explained how he "wanted a torpedo flotilla, and he already had plans complete for moving it by rail to the Great Lakes when it was needed," a clear reference to the defence scheme produced as a result of the earlier commission. He also provided a candid assessment of the political circumstances surrounding the whole issue. "Lake stated that the local navy or naval militia was not nearly as hopeless as the governor general thought, but the ministers were corrupt. This, in his opinion, was sufficient reason for delaying a bill that had already existed in draft for three years, till after the next general election. He was also emphatic that any hint to Canadian ministers that the militia proposal would 'be satisfactory to England would do no good.'"[117]

Corbett's favourable impression of Lake was undoubtedly influenced by the fact that the general confirmed his own intellectual appreciation of the situation. One of the historian's purposes in writing *England in the Seven Years' War* was to supply "the required ingredients for the formulation of ... a maritime policy for Great Britain that would allow army and navy to work together." Lake had recognized for some time the important maritime dimensions of the defence of Canada, and since March 1908 had been actively pursuing the creation of an interdepartmental committee to coordinate a wide variety of measures that legally rested with the Department of Marine and Fisheries. They included restriction of trade with the enemy, examination of merchant vessels entering defended ports to ensure they were not disguised raiders, censorship of overseas communications, and gathering intelligence on American naval resources and activities on the Great Lakes. While the militia minister, Sir Frederick Borden, supported the proposal, Brodeur was steadfast in resisting any such efforts.[118]

---

115. Corbett diary, 15 July 1908, quoted in Schurman, *Corbett*, 109.

116. Ibid, 109.

117. Corbett diary, 28 July 1908, quoted in ibid, 110.

118. Donald M. Schurman, *The Education of a Navy: The Development of British Naval Strategic Thought, 1867–1914* (Chicago 1965), 164; Roger Sarty, *The Maritime Defence of Canada* (Toronto 1997), 16; and Deputy Minister of Marine and Fisheries to Deputy Minister of Militia and Defence, 10 December 1908, HQC 365–11, LAC, RG 24, mfm reel T-5052.

The battle-cruiser HMS *Indomitable* at the Quebec Tercentenary on 23 July 1908. As conceived by First Sea Lord "Jackie" Fisher, the battle cruiser's eight 12-inch guns and cruiser-like speed would allow it to sweep the world's shipping lanes of all enemy cruisers. (LAC PA-124708)

Still, the government was taking certain steps in that direction. A "flying start to an officer corps" was already underway, with six "naval cadets" having been embarked earlier that summer in CGS *Canada* for hands-on training in seamanship and navigation. "The minister had taken a personal hand ... Naval Cadet Victor G. Brodeur was his son; Barry German was the son of the Liberal MP for Welland–St Catharines; Percy Nelles's father was a retired senior army officer; Charles Beard's father was a senior government official; John Barron's was a judge; Trenwick [Henry] Bate was the son of a Liberal millionaire. All were insiders. They had written no entrance exams—the method of selection was informal to say the least." On another front, tenders for the long-awaited cruiser for the British Columbia coast were issued in June 1908. Then, in August, *Constance*, the aging sister ship to *Curlew* and *Petrel*, was transferred from the Department of Customs, further consolidating the position of the Fisheries Protection Service. Moreover, the general influence on the department of the appointments of Desbarats and Kingsmill should not be underrated, as the latent professionalism encouraged by the 1904 reforms was now given new purpose. On a related front, although the report of the Cassels commission clearing Brodeur of all charges against him, and even going so far as to praise the reforms he had inaugurated, was not released until 22 January 1909, the public at large seemed pleased with the operations of the department. Inertia might once again seem to be dogging any moves forward, but institutionally the marine department was better prepared than ever to initiate the naval project.[119]

It was against this setting that Kingsmill left Ottawa in August 1908 for Victoria and Vancouver on an inspection tour to assess the dominion's naval requirements.[120] His journey probably would not have amounted to much but for the breaking news early in September that the Admiralty had finally been able to craft a plan for the coast defence of Australia acceptable both to itself and to the Deakin government. As reported in the *Canadian Annual Review*, the so-called Australian scheme called for:

> responsibility for local naval defence and the provision of six torpedo-boat destroyers, nine submarines and two depot boats, at a cost of $6,387,500 together with the maintenance of seventy-nine officers and 1,125 men provided by the imperial government with as many as possible taken from amongst Australians. The administrative control of the flotilla was to rest with the commonwealth government, but the officers and men would form part of the imperial navy, and would be subject to the King's regulations. While in Australian waters they would be under commonwealth authority, but in other waters they would pass under the control of the senior imperial naval officer.

119. Tony German, *The Sea is at Our Gates: The History of the Canadian Navy* (Toronto 1990), 27; Canada, Parliament, House of Commons, *Debates*, 17 June 1908, col. 10732; and Canada, Department of Marine and Fisheries, *Annual Report of the Department of Marine and Fisheries—Marine* (Ottawa 1910), 32. See Charles D. Maginley and Bernard Collin, *The Ships of Canada's Marine Services* (St Catharines 2001), 86; and J. Castell Hopkins, *The Canadian Annual Review of Public Affairs, 1909* (Toronto 1910), 192.

120. Kingsmill to Laurier, 24 August 1908, LAC, MG 26 G, 143814–15.

The annual expense and maintenance would amount to $930,000 and the repairs be effected in local ship-building yards.[121]

The news served to propel the naval issue back onto the public stage in Canada, where it was widely discussed throughout the fall of 1908 and into the winter of 1909, with the positive exposure of the Quebec celebrations still relatively fresh to mind. While in scale it was somewhat different from the Canadian government's plans, the principle was basically the same—an autonomous colonial force responsible for naval matters in territorial waters. Although some elements of the conservative press from British Columbia and even central Canada continued to support contributions to the Royal Navy's upkeep, those calls were increasingly marginal. The point of departure for discussion was very much whether Canada should adopt a policy similar to Australia's. Dissent came from a somewhat surprising quarter, the *Canadian Military Gazette*, which contended that the project should not get out of hand and develop into a complete navy, as "a strong land force is better for imperial interests as a whole, than a baby fleet would be." Much study should be made "before any large expenditure will be sanctioned in this country for naval purposes, especially if such would come at the cost of a reduction of the militia vote." But perhaps most significant was that no voices of opposition were heard from Quebec, where Henri Bourassa was momentarily more concerned with provincial politics. Although the imperial relationship was still an important question to him, at the moment he was devoting his energies to the debate on the status of language rights and the Roman Catholic church in his native province. Since there were no fundamental differences on naval policy that might coalesce along party lines—Borden and Laurier were not that far apart on the matter, and neither wished to take precipitate action on an issue where there were few new votes to win—the naval question was not a factor in the 24 October 1908 federal general election, which returned Laurier to power with his substantial majority mostly intact.[122]

With the election out of the way, however, the dynamics within the Conservative party changed. They had not lost as badly in Ontario as in Quebec, but re-building the party was necessary and the better electoral prospects lay in Canada's largest province. Borden had the support of a number of prominent Torontonians unhappy with Liberal rule, among them journalist C.F. Hamilton, who argued that, with the Liberals continuing to prove impervious to criticism over various scandals—not the least of which was the misadministration of the marine department—perhaps it was time to pursue a more positive tack. Hamilton had been instrumental in turning the Toronto branch of the Navy League away from its pursuit of a Canadian offshoot of the Royal Naval Reserve and toward a return to its roots in seeking to establish a separate naval force and now convinced Borden to adopt the Australian model as a plank of the Conservative platform.[123]

---

121. Hopkins, *The Canadian Annual Review, 1908*, 589. See Nicholls, *Statesmen and Sailors*, 130–37.

122. Hopkins, *The Canadian Annual Review, 1908*, 229, 605–07; Hopkins, *The Canadian Annual Review, 1909*, 50; and *Canadian Military Gazette*, 22 September 1908, 5.

123. Robert Craig Brown, *Robert Laird Borden: A Biography*, I: *1854–1914* (Toronto 1975), 12–32, 137; and Hadley and Sarty, *Tin-pots and Pirate Ships*, 24–25.

The fact that support for this issue crossed party lines (many members of the Toronto Navy League were good Liberals, including Admiral Kingsmill's uncle), and that it seemed to be gaining public approval, argued strongly in favour of its likelihood for success in parliament. Early in 1909, George Foster, who as minister of marine and fisheries in 1885 had established the Fisheries Protection Service with a view to its evolution into a naval militia and was now the member for Toronto North, placed upon the House of Commons' order paper a Conservative notice of motion. It read: "in view of her great and varied resources, of her geographical position and national environment, and of that spirit of self-help and self-respect which alone befits a strong and growing people, Canada should no longer delay in assuming her proper share of the responsibility and financial burden incident to the suitable protection of her exposed coast line and great seaports." The 1909 *Canadian Annual Review* noted that "the situation at once became interesting and the ensuing discussion at Ottawa turned upon what action the government would take as to Mr Foster's motion; upon whether he and the Conservative leaders would change or expand it to meet the imperialistic wing of sentiment in their party; upon what the Quebec members of both parties would do in the premises."[124] Indeed, the concerns of the Conservative's Quebec wing, led by F.D. Monk, contributed to a delay of some two months before the motion would actually be introduced in the house.

On 1 February 1909 the imminence of the Foster resolution encouraged Kingsmill to submit a preliminary report to his minister on how "we should commence our work of assisting in the defence of our coasts."[125] A rough sketch with few supporting details, the report offered a methodical but realistic plan to implement existing government policy. Envisioning little more than upgrading the existing establishment, the major recommendations were the formation of a signal service connecting all important lighthouses, putting a dockyard at Quebec (in addition to those at Halifax and Esquimalt), and starting a training establishment at Halifax. From the latter, "the men trained in the first year would be available to man a destroyer or a scout [i.e., small cruiser] next year, and so on until we had sufficient officers and men well trained to man our proposed defence which should, in my opinion, be confined to destroyers and scouts for many a long day." That same day, in a separate, personal memorandum to Brodeur, Kingsmill continued to counsel moderation, demonstrating great understanding of his political masters' sensitivities. Noting the construction and upkeep costs of various classes of warships, he warned that it would be far better for the government to continue focusing, for the time being, on the country's development "as in that is our only hope of some day being in a position to defend our coasts as they should be." By embarking on too ambitious a project, "a young and partly developed country may, if not wreck itself, at any rate seriously injure its internal economy." At the same time, the admiral noted that "to spend money on partial defence or rather inadequate defence is to waste it."[126]

---

124. Hopkins, *The Canadian Annual Review, 1909*, 55. Foster's sponsorship of the resolution undoubtedly had much to do with the need to rehabilitate his own reputation in the Conservative party, where he was held largely responsible for the loss of Ontario in the 1908 election. See Brown, *Borden*, 137, 142.

125. "Memorandum on Coast Defence," 1 February 1909, LAC, MG 27 II C4, vol. 2, file 17, reel H-1017.

126. Kingsmill to Brodeur, 1 February 1909, ibid.

While policy makers digested Kingsmill's ideas, events transpired in Europe to add an international dimension to the Canadian naval issue. What was to become known as the dreadnought crisis was precipitated when, in introducing the estimates for the Royal Navy on 16 March 1909, Reginald McKenna, first lord of the Admiralty since April 1908, made public the British government's fear that it anticipated an acceleration in the German shipbuilding program that would leave the Royal Navy outnumbered in dreadnought battleships by 1912. McKenna, on the first sea lord's advice, requested that six British dreadnoughts be laid down in 1909–10 instead of the four that were planned at the time. In the ensuing debate, anti-German hysteria was whipped up to such a degree by both parliament and the press that the government was forced to accept an expanded building program of eight dreadnoughts for 1909–10 as the only means of ensuring Britain's command of the seas to the required degree. (The Royal Navy's ability to remain ahead of its German rival was never seriously doubted; disagreement centred on the degree to which the British lead should be maintained.)[127]

The crisis was reported in the Canadian press in much the same light as in Britain. The editor of the *Canadian Annual Review* summarized the Canadian response: "Distance from the scene and non-appreciation of what naval power and supremacy really meant to the individual as well as to the empire, was responsible to a certain extent for the somewhat critical attitude assumed by the [Canadian] press in regard to the British 'panic' and for the tendency to 'go slow' in speech and action." Whether Canadians in fact did not realize the full import of sea power, as Castell Hopkins claimed, is open to question, for the initial effect of the news from England was to draw attention to Foster's resolution on the parliamentary order paper. What was interpreted as a "tendency to 'go slow' in speech and action" was more accurately an affirmation of the Canadian belief in the ability of the Royal Navy to check the growth of the Reichsmarine, and that the time had arrived for Canada to assume more responsibility for her own naval defence. It was noted that, in accepting New Zealand's offer to contribute a dreadnought to meet the emergency, Prime Minister Asquith had declared that "so far as the coming official year is concerned [1909–10], the provision of the naval estimates afford ample security," but that the New Zealand offer would be included in the building program for 1910–11. Therefore, while some papers responded to the crisis in Britain by calling for the immediate construction by Canada of

127. Virtually every study—both general and specific—of the formation of the Canadian naval service has maintained a direct causal relationship between the dreadnought crisis in Britain and the formation of a Canadian navy. Even those few interpretations admitting the significance of Laurier's declaration of policy at the 1902 Colonial Conference have deferred to the popular interpretation when confronted with what appeared to be a massive and unprecedented up-surge in naval thinking in Canada in March 1909 as a result of events in Europe. It would be impossible and wrong to deny the importance of the German challenge to the Royal Navy in intensifying public opinion in Canada on naval matters but, given the state of Canadian thinking and the progress on the naval project to March 1909, it is possible to re-interpret the significance of the dreadnought crisis as having had a somewhat different effect upon Canadian naval development, and the subsequent formation of policy. The only studies besides this that maintain a continuous and unbroken path of development throughout the period irrespective of the dreadnought crisis are Brodeur, "The Origins of the RCN;" and Hadley and Sarty, *Tin-pots and Pirate Ships*. For a more complete examination of the development and course of the dreadnought crisis see Marder, *Dreadnought to Scapa Flow*, 151–85.

at least one or (more often) two dreadnoughts, where an opinion was stated as to the deployment of the ships it was generally along the lines of Sir Sandford Fleming's suggestion of "one for the Atlantic and one for the Pacific." The underlying assumption was that, of course, "such vessels would be under the control of the Canadian government, but that is only another way of saying that they would always be at the call of the empire in every worthy cause and in every time of danger."[128]

To be certain, there were dissenting views. Among these, the Ottawa *Citizen* declared itself firmly in favour of a direct cash contribution to the Royal Navy. "It must be apparent that the place for the colonies to defend their coasts is in the line of the British dreadnought fleet. The fate of that fleet will decide the fate of the colonies. If that fleet met with disaster, any trifling squadron, or warlike revenue cutters, or cheap warships, would be only so much more loot for the conquerors." In Montreal, *La Presse* was concerned that Canada should maintain the right to decide whether to abstain or to participate in a British war with some other power. Nevertheless, it too was in favour of naval development in Canada, but on the condition that "any ships built with the money of the Canadian taxpayer shall be under the absolute control of the Canadian government."[129]

Of all the wide variety of editorial comment being published, the two submissions that caught Laurier's interest were those of 27 March in the Montreal *Herald* and the Toronto *Globe*. The *Herald*, in commenting upon the "importance of the action taken by Cabinet in definitely preparing for a Canadian navy development," noted that it "has been evident for years that some such step as this would be taken." Moreover, Canadian military development had invariably come at times when Britain's burden "grew past bearing," as with the 1870 withdrawal of the garrisons and the 1905 take-over of the imperial fortresses. "Now that a hint is given of the possible inability of the British navy alone to keep the ocean free for shipping, Canada again avows her readiness to step in and take her share." At the same time, the *Globe* stated that the position laid down at the colonial conferences "should now be accepted as the settled Canadian policy.... What is done by Canada must be done deliberately along the line of Canadian policy, and in the light of consultation with the imperial government. The details must be settled, not by passing or panicky popular opinion, but, as Mr Asquith says, by the responsible authorities on the advice of experts. Whether it be dreadnoughts or fast cruisers or torpedo-boats, and where and when and how many, are questions not for the man in the street, but for the government."[130]

Against this broader public examination of the issue, the first naval debate in the Canadian parliament was something of an anti-climax. In supporting his motion, Foster discussed the two possible policies open to Canada: either a contribution of money or ships to the Admiralty, or the assumption by Canadians of the defence of their own ports and coasts in free co-operation with the forces of Britain. While accepting that a fixed sum contribution may be a "most willing gift," he admitted that there were serious objections to

---

128. Hopkins, *The Canadian Annual Review, 1909*, 50, 53; and Toronto *Globe*, 23, 24, and 25 March 1909.

129. Ottawa *Citizen*, 24 March 1909; Hopkins, *The Canadian Annual Review, 1909*, 52; and Toronto *Globe*, 26 March 1909.

130. The Montreal *Herald*, 27 March 1909; and Toronto *Globe*, 27 March 1909.

such a proposal. Instead, he was certain that the dominion would have its own naval force sooner or later, and the time was ripe "to see something grafted on the soil of Canada's nationhood." As the vessels of the Fisheries Protection Service were "simply children's toys" against even a third-class cruiser, a modest expansion of that service would not suffice; instead the government should consider urgent action along the lines of the Australian model. But Foster ended by advocating the contribution of a dreadnought to Britain. In response, Laurier insisted that "we are not to be carried away, we are not to be stampeded from what has been the settled policy and deliberate course which we have laid down, by any hasty, feverish action, however spectacular such action may be." He proceeded to trace the evolution of Canadian naval policy since it was first stated in 1902, showing that what the Conservatives were proposing was nothing new and that Canada had undertaken to develop her own defences by land and sea, and quoting Lord Tweedmouth's remarks at the most recent conference supporting this action.[131]

The leader of the opposition, Robert Borden, followed the prime minister, speaking also of the need for a Canadian naval force and stating his opposition to a policy of contributions. He, too, pointed specifically to the long gestation period of the naval project. "I do not think I am making any statement in breach of confidence when I say that I am thoroughly aware that the late Raymond Préfontaine thoroughly intended to establish a Canadian naval militia or naval force of some kind. He told me so about a year before his death. Mr Préfontaine was a man of large views and of great courage, and it may be … that a policy which would have been carried out otherwise has not been carried out owing to the present head of that department finding it necessary to devote his attention to other matters." As such, he recommended making contributions in an emergency, and that the government indicate an intention to act promptly. The rest of the debate consisted mostly of patriotic speeches, and although some were willing to consider a contribution should a serious emergency arise, the majority favoured the formal adoption of a naval policy and wanted a Canadian navy; no one suggested an immediate contribution of money or of dreadnoughts.[132]

While the debate was in progress, Laurier had a private discussion with Borden. When the two returned to the chamber, the prime minister made it clear he was willing to meet all the opposition leader's objections:

> This house fully recognizes the duty of the people of Canada, as they increase in numbers and wealth to assume in larger measure the responsibilities in national defence.
>
> The house is of opinion that under the present constitutional relations between the mother country and the self-governing dominions, the payment

---

131. Canada, Parliament, House of Commons, *Debates*, 29 March 1909, col. 3495, 3505. For discussions of the debate see Tucker, *The Naval Service of Canada*, I, 122–28; Hopkins, *The Canadian Annual Review, 1909*, 55–60; Hitsman, "Canadian Naval Policy," 45ff; and Hadley and Sarty, *Tin-pots and Pirate Ships*, 25.

132. Canada, Parliament, House of Commons, *Debates*, 29 March 1909, col. 3522; and Tucker, *The Naval Service of Canada*, I, 127.

of regular and periodical contributions to the imperial treasury for naval and military purposes would not, so far as Canada is concerned, be the most satisfactory solution of the question of defence.

The house will cordially approve of any necessary expenditure to promote the speedy organization of a Canadian naval service in co-operation with and in close relation to the imperial navy, along the lines suggested by the Admiralty at the last imperial conference, and in full sympathy with the view that the naval supremacy of Britain is essential to the security of commerce, the safety of the empire and the peace of the world.

The house expresses its firm conviction that whenever the need arises the Canadian people will be found ready and willing to make any sacrifice that is required to give to the imperial authorities the most loyal and hearty co-operation in every movement for the maintenance of the integrity and honour of the empire.[133]

The resolution was passed unanimously, by imperialist as well as nationalist, English-Canadian and French-Canadian, regardless of party, a clear indication of parliament's concern that some action must proceed along the lines of semi-autonomous naval development. But more specifically, it differed little in content or intent from the various statements made by Laurier and Brodeur, and Préfontaine before him—or for that matter Robert Borden—over the years. It was, therefore, above all, a victory for the Laurier naval policy; the logical conclusion of many years of slow and careful progress preparing the nation to look to the protection of her maritime sovereignty by her own means. Moreover, because of that same progress, the tools with which to give form to the Canadian naval force were already in place.

If the dreadnought crisis did not actually precipitate thinking on the establishment of a Canadian naval service, it certainly provided the incentive to turn talk into concrete action. Over the years, Laurier and Borden had been reluctant to force the issue, but there was little disagreement that Canada should assume, as had been declared at the 1902 Colonial Conference, full responsibility for the naval as well as the military defence of the dominion. By arousing a sense of controlled urgency, the dreadnought crisis created a climate of non-partisan support that made possible the unanimous acceptance of Laurier's amendment to the Foster resolution, in the process rewriting it to guide it onto the path of Canadian naval development already determined by the Laurier administration. The challenge for the government was to keep the projected naval force within the bounds of established policy. For the opposition, the challenge was to keep the government on a timetable to actually implement it. Therefore, when Foster rose in the house on 15 April to question the government as to its interpretation of the 29 March resolution and the steps proposed to carry it out, he was perhaps surprised at Laurier's unequivocal response. "The government have decided that, as shortly as possible after prorogation, the Minister of Marine and Fisheries (Mr Brodeur) and the Minister of Militia (Sir Frederick Borden) shall

---

133. Hopkins, *The Canadian Annual Review, 1909*, 60; and Tucker, *The Naval Service of Canada*, I, 126n.

proceed to London for the purpose of conferring with the Admiralty as to the best means to be adopted to give effect to the resolution of March 29."[134]

Reinforcing Laurier's desire to get the issue settled quickly was the realization that if it were allowed to drag it could disrupt Cabinet's internal harmony. In commenting on the debate on the Foster resolution, Grey for his part went somewhat beyond the bounds of his authority to express his concern that Laurier's policy "will not be regarded either in Canada or in England as a very effective contribution to the solution of the defence problem, unless it is followed up by a display of vigour in formulating a plan and in carrying that plan into effect such as past experience does not encourage us to hope from Mr Brodeur." He therefore submitted that "the necessity of taking prompt business action in this matter [makes] it desirable that the change of minister at the head of marine and fisheries department which you have more than once informed me was impending, should be hurried up.... I know you will have to face a little criticism from Quebec, but you are quite big enough and strong enough to disregard that criticism, if you share my view that the duty which Canada owes to the empire is to put the best business man she has got at the head of the marine dept., and Sifton is the best man." Clifford Sifton had left the Laurier Cabinet in early 1905, however, to protest the government's policy on the western schools issue and on occasion had positively declared himself against a Canadian navy. Although he remained a Liberal and a private member in the house, his attitude toward Quebec was hardening and the prime minister had no reason to consider Sifton an ally. Anxious to put off any suggestion that might resurrect old problems, Laurier quickly conferred with Brodeur, and on 6 April was able to write the governor general that the minister of marine and fisheries "has told me within the last twenty-four hours that he is coming to see me either this day or tomorrow, to expose me his plan for the re-organisation of his department. He has several appointments to make. I will deem it my duty to lay before your excellency the whole plan of Brodeur as soon as received from him."[135]

It actually took somewhat longer before Brodeur had something concrete to submit, for it was not until 19 April that Kingsmill completed a memorandum containing his professional advice as to how to set up a Canadian naval organization, based on his assessment of the previous autumn. It was essentially a more detailed submission of his earlier recommendations that Halifax and Esquimalt should have their defences and equipment put into good order and modernized, and that training be begun immediately on both coasts. Considering British Columbia, the Canadian admiral noted that "we have there a very important industry, and at present an imperfect protection." To correct this, Kingsmill recommended that two small cruisers, capable of training some 200 men, should be obtained from Britain. "These ships to be brought in, becoming in every way our property, sailing under our flag, but to be officered and partly manned by Royal Navy." Turning to the Atlantic, the admiral suggested much the same approach, except that the training goal should be 300 men. "We should procure on loan to start with one cruiser of 'Sirius' class and two torpedo boat destroyers. With these and the *Canada*, officered by Royal Naval offi-

---

134. Canada, Parliament, House of Commons, *Debates*, 15 April 1909, col. 4289.

135. Grey to Laurier, 30 March 1909 (two letters), Laurier to Grey, 6 April 1909, LAC, MG 27 II B2, 4–401, 1149, 4–402, mfm reel C-1358, 1152–55; and Schull, *Laurier*, 450–53, 518.

cers and instructors, we should train the crews of destroyers, and at the same time partly protect our fisheries on the Atlantic seaboard." Kingsmill recognized that the use of Royal Navy ships on loan was not a permanent solution and therefore also recommended a building program. "We should at once commence building destroyers and cruisers. What we should build, that is lay down, now as soon as possible, would be: two ocean going destroyers, vessels of 700 to 900 tons displacement, for the Atlantic; two coastal destroyers, vessels of 270 tons displacement, for the Pacific coast; four torpedo boats; the torpedo boats could be built, after a model has been obtained, in Canada, to save sending them round Cape Horn to British Columbia."[136]

In proposing such a program, Kingsmill showed that, like his counterpart in the militia, Major-General Sir Percy Lake, he was sympathetic to the government's political sensitivities as they applied to his service. The recommended classes of vessels were reasonably suited to the naval duties envisioned by Laurier, namely fisheries protection and close enforcement of sovereignty in coastal waters. In fact, Kingsmill had opened the memorandum with a statement of the plan on which Brodeur wished him to work, indicating his willingness to follow these directions.

> It is with a strong feeling of diffidence that I submit, single-handed, a scheme of naval defence for Canada, and wish to say that my views are given after due consideration of the fact that monetary contribution alone is out of the question, and that we must develop our naval assistance to the empire with this end always in view, that the Canadian navy is to be under the control of the dominion government, the question of its disposition in the event of war being a matter for those in authority at the time; also that at an early date we must use the newly started naval service for the protection of our fisheries, in fact, that fisheries protection and training go hand in hand, thus using the appropriation for the former in carrying out the latter, which, of course, will be a considerable assistance and in the end a better use will have been made of the money.[137]

Although the government was hesitant to adopt the scheme without Admiralty approval, it seemed to fit the sort of plan that Tweedmouth had expounded at the 1907 conference—and had proved acceptable for Australia—while at the same time meeting Canadian requirements. Canadian ministers therefore anticipated that upcoming discussions with the Admiralty would revolve around some closely related project.

However, a problem arose in the form of Sir Frederick Borden's worries as to the implications the new policy held for his department. In December 1908, as part of an overall drive to cut government expenditure, Borden had been told that "an effort is being made

136. Kingsmill to Brodeur, 19 April 1909, Kingsmill to Brodeur, 1 February 1909, 1017–1-1, pt 1, LAC, RG 24, vol. 3830.

137. Charles Panet [Private Secretary] to F.W. Borden, 16 December 1908, F.W. Borden Papers, Public Archives of Nova Scotia (hereafter PANS), MG 2, private letter books, vol. 15, 435–36.

to reduce your estimates by one million dollars." Although in the end his deputy minister was able to keep the vote for capital account as it was, militia expenditure in 1909–10 was decreased by over $540,000 from that of the previous year, largely at the expense of the politically important annual training. The dreadnought crisis had served to raise questions regarding the amount allotted to the militia department, the Montreal *Herald*, as part of its 27 March editorial, commenting that, in view of the militia's primary task as guarantor of internal security, "it is quite possible that the new condition [including naval expenditure] will warrant a recasting of the militia establishment, hitherto regarded as the sole object of our military concern, and at present, in the opinion of those who made the civil service investigation two years ago, maintained at an expense out of proportion to any contemplated emergency."[138]

During the debate on Foster's resolution, the leader of the opposition had suggested that Canadian naval expenditure should at least equal that of the militia, but partly at the expense of the latter department. Discussing aid of the civil power, Borden stated, "I would hardly think that an expenditure of $6,000,000 annually would be necessary for that purpose, and, while I am not prepared at the present to lay down any figure which would be a proper amount for the people of Canada to set apart for the purpose of defence, I do most unhesitatingly say that of the portion which the people of Canada should set aside for that purpose out of their public revenues, a very substantial portion, and, in my opinion, not less than one half of the amount appropriated for defence should be devoted for naval instead of to military defence." Later, Laurier chose to interpret this statement as inferring that Canadian naval expenditure should be about $3,000,000 annually. In a reply to a request from the prime minister to verify the feasibility of a scheme organized along such an appropriation, Kingsmill affirmed that "if we add to the services [Fisheries Protection Service and Hydrographic Surveys] … and building of barracks, battery and drill shed, bringing dockyards up to latest requirements of fleet—would certainly bring it up … to $3,000,000 for the first three years."[139]

The prime minister's decision in mid-April to send both Brodeur and Sir Frederick Borden to England for discussions with the Admiralty hardly reassured the militia minister. Shortly after the decision was announced, Borden wrote Laurier about his fears that the "additional burden of providing for our own local naval defence" would impair the budget of his own department, which was only just reaching an acceptable level and would need to be raised "if we are to develop the militia in the west up to the standard of development in the eastern provinces." The militia minister was seeking a commitment from his leader. "It seems to be the part of prudence to endeavour to reach some conclusion as to the total amount of money we shall be prepared to expend in providing for defence, as a whole, and I think this should be done before the mission to England is undertaken. No doubt one of the first questions we will be asked will be as to the amount of money available for

---

138. Ibid; Montreal *Herald*, 27 March 1909; and *Auditor General's Report, 1909–10: Summary of Expenditure, 1909–10* (Ottawa 1911), I, part C.

139. Canada, Parliament, House of Commons, *Debates*, 29 March 1909, cols. 3515–6; and "Note from Admiral Kingsmill's Office," nd, LAC, MG 26 G, 219420–421.

defence purposes as a whole, and how it is to be allotted." Knowing that imperial authorities preferred greater colonial military commitments, Borden took the precaution of suggesting that he and Brodeur should consult the Committee of Imperial Defence, "the most important body of the kind in the empire ... which invited me to its council in 1903," before consulting with the Admiralty.[140] Laurier's desires, however, were to keep the interference by British officials to a minimum. In the event, it appears that he was able to reassure his minister that the militia would not suffer for the navy's sake, as both would be performing necessary services to the country and Borden became firmly converted to the idea of a limited naval force.

Although Robert Borden had indicated what the opposition would consider to be an acceptable expenditure and Sir Frederick Borden had pressed Laurier for a fixed sum, the prime minister still refused to commit his government to a specific outlay. When Grey suggested to Laurier the advantages of having the two ministers announce at the outset of the 1909 London conference that Canada would spend $6,000,000 for naval purposes, he asked the governor general to reconsider his suggestion as the situation was already well in hand. Brodeur and Borden "have their general instructions which seem to me sufficiently precise. The first object of the conference is to lay down a plan of action, and towards that plan we will have to gravitate fast or slow, big or small, according to the development of our financial resources. The reasonable goal seems to me that we should do as much for the navy as for the militia, and this is well understood both by Borden and Brodeur. It is also well understood by them that we will not be able to reach that goal the first year."[141]

There remained competing government and opposition objectives, one seeking to keep the policy in check while the other aimed at its prompt implementation. In committee of supply on 15 May 1909, Brodeur maintained that the government's intention in obtaining warships was still "for the purpose of a training ship and to be used in the fishery protection service." The opposition member with whom the minister was debating, G.H. Barnard, did not dispute this, noting that in British Columbia, the "fisheries are almost the most valuable in the world, and yet they are absolutely without protection."[142] Barnard's exchange with the minister was underscored by the Conservative member's concern that something should be done immediately for protection of the fisheries. As far as Laurier was concerned, this was fine, so long as nothing was done precipitously that would interfere with the naval aspects of the government's policy. In fact, if both of these conditions could be met while the country was still united on the issue, the eventual success of the policy's implementation would be more than likely. But time and circumstances were working against the government's intentions. Although a success, Laurier's artful manipulation of the situation through the spring of 1909 was to prove to be the high-water mark of his naval policy, not a vindication of it.

---

140. Borden to Laurier, 17 April 1909, PANS, MG 2, M and D, vol. 54, 578–80.

141. Grey to Laurier, 26 July 1909, Laurier to Grey, 28 July 1909, LAC, MG 27 II B2, 4–428, 1811, 4–430, 1213–14.

142. Canada, Parliament, House of Commons, *Debates*, 14 May 1909, cols. 6683–5.

CHAPTER 3

The Naval Debates, 1909–1914

The first naval "debate" of March 1909 was anything but divisive, confirming instead the existence of a fairly broad non-partisan consensus among Canadian politicians supporting the "speedy establishment of a Canadian naval service." Since the 1902 Colonial Conference, Prime Minister Sir Wilfrid Laurier had carefully handled the issue to build a consensus across the population at large, including Quebec, and it had come to be accepted by both London and the Admiralty. All that changed over the summer of 1909, however. If the dreadnought crisis had been an affair manufactured at least initially for British domestic consumption, it had a galvanizing effect almost everywhere else. In its wake, the first sea lord, Admiral Sir John Fisher, recognized an unusual opportunity to put into practice his revolutionary theories of naval warfare. Colonial fleet units, comprising battle cruisers, destroyer flotillas, and submarines, were more evocative of a "navy" than the Canadian notion of a "naval militia." With the security of Britain and the empire apparently at risk, the rationale for a Canadian service had to be re-examined. For the next half decade, a national debate as to Canada's relationship to Britain was reflected in the birth and unsteady growth of a Canadian navy. A federal election would, in part, be lost on the issue and drastic new parliamentary procedures would be invoked even as the newly formed Royal Canadian Navy struggled to find its identity.

After having long deferred the decision to establish a Canadian navy, Laurier felt confident that the right combination of circumstances were aligned in the spring of 1909 to allow for the launch of the naval project. Little did he realize, however, that the strategic situation was shifting radically even as he prepared to move ahead. Although the popular perception has been to view the establishment of the Canadian navy within the context of an accelerating naval race between Britain and Germany, more recent scholarship is practically unanimous in concluding that at no time before the outbreak of the First World War did the Admiralty ever truly fear the German challenge. As we have seen, the so-called dreadnought crisis was a political manufacture aimed at circumventing the radical wing of Britain's Liberal Party in its quest for reduced naval expenditures.[1] Contemporary press

---

1. See, for example, A.J. Marder, *From Dreadnought to Scapa Flow, The Royal Navy in the Fisher Era: 1904–1919*, I: *The Road to War, 1904–1914* (Oxford 1961); Jon Tetsuro Sumida, *In Defence of Naval Supremacy: Finance, Technology, and British Naval Policy, 1889–1914* (Boston 1989); Nicolas Lambert, *Sir John Fisher's Naval Revolution* (Columbia, SC 1999); and Andrew D. Lambert, "The Royal Navy, 1856–1914: Deterrence and the Strategy of World Power," Keith Neilson and Elizabeth Jane Errington, eds., *Navies and Global Defense: Theories and Strategy* (Westport, CT 1995), 69–92, which argues that the offensive power of the Royal Navy increased throughout the period 1856–1914.

accounts suggest that Canadian editorial opinion generally believed that the Royal Navy remained predominant, and felt no real need for an emergency contribution to build and maintain warships other than as a demonstration of Canada's sentimental attachment to the mother country. General support did exist for the establishment of a Canadian navy that would take its place in assisting "the naval power and supremacy of the empire"—the word "defence" entering the discussion only for want of a better term.[2] Admiralty concerns about the uncertain status of its naval alliance with Japan provides a better explanation for the shift in London's attitude toward dominion naval forces that occurred in 1909.

At no time during Sir John Fisher's initial tenure as first sea lord (1904–1910) did the Board of Admiralty deviate from the position that "the formation of local navies was inevitable." Any reticence was at the political level, where mixed feelings existed as to the probability that greater dominion participation in the naval and military affairs of the empire would inevitably lead to calls for constitutional recognition of their autonomy. Although the Admiralty "consistently refused to have anything to do with what they termed 'sentimental navies,'" it concluded that the establishment of local forces should add to the overall security of the empire, and not detract from it.[3] Until the early summer of 1909, the Admiralty was generally satisfied with the Australian and, latterly, even the Canadian proposals to establish what amounted to torpedo boat flotillas for local harbour defence. Even in the wake of the dreadnought crisis, their lordships were happier with the earlier Australian proposal "to build twenty-odd destroyers, completely independent of the Royal Navy" than the prospect of having to man the additional pair of dreadnoughts recently offered by Australia and New Zealand.[4] If the battleships were indeed built in addition to existing plans, the gifts would only add to the British treasury's financial burden. It was the chancellor of the exchequer's view that "as there appears to be a general feeling in this country that ships presented by the colonies must not be treated as a grant-in-aid towards the reduction of the naval estimates ... [our] acceptance of such gifts not only does not relieve the naval estimates of expenditure, but throws on them the heavy annual cost of maintaining ships which they would not otherwise have to bear."[5]

To better coordinate the various offers from the dominions, the Admiralty proposed inviting representatives from each of them to a special conference in London during the summer of 1909 to discuss "the general question of naval and military defence of the empire"—the first such gathering to be designated "imperial" as opposed to "colonial." Laurier saw little point to it, however, stating that "my ministers have not sufficient infor-

---

2. J. Castell Hopkins, *The Canadian Annual Review of Public Affairs, 1909* (Toronto 1910), 50.

3. Nicholas Lambert, "Economy or Empire? The fleet unit concept and the quest of collective security in the Pacific, 1909–1914," Greg Kennedy and Keith Neilson, eds., *Far Flung Lines: Studies in Imperial Defence in Honour of Donald Mackenzie Schurman* (London 1996), 55–56.

4. Governor General of Australia to Crewe, 15 April 1909, Grey to Lewis Harcourt, April 1909, quoted in Lambert, "Economy or Empire?" 59.

5. Chancellor of the Exchequer, "Notes ... ," 20 May 1909, United Kingdom National Archives (hereafter UKNA), Colonial Office (hereafter CO) 537/571; and Michael Hadley and Roger Sarty, *Tin-pots & Pirate Ships: Canadian Naval Forces and German Sea Raiders, 1880–1918* (Montreal 1991), 27.

mation to warrant them in advising as to [the] necessity for such a formal conference." When the official invitations were issued on 30 April with the assurance of the colonial secretary, Lord Crewe, that "the conference would, of course, be of a purely consultative character," Laurier declined the invitation to participate personally, sending instead only Minister of Marine and Fisheries Louis-Philippe Brodeur and Minister of Militia Frederick Borden, accompanied by their principal advisers (Rear-Admiral Kingsmill and Major-General Percy Lake, respectively). The date was set for late-July.[6]

To this point, the Admiralty still had no plans to broaden the scope of the discussions. That changed at a meeting of the Committee of Imperial Defence on 29 June 1909, where "a complaint from Vice-Admiral Hedworth Lambton, commanding the China squadron, that the coastal defences protecting the naval base at Hong Kong were seriously inadequate" was discussed.[7] Fisher found Lambton's assessment "preposterous" since it seemed contingent on "the British navy being wiped out! It's really damnable!"[8] As the director of naval intelligence explained to the meeting, the Admiralty's position was that "so long as the government maintained the Two Power Standard ... the navy would guarantee the defence of all British defended ports around the world." In this specific case, "we could, even if we were engaged in a war with Germany, send out twenty battleships to Hong Kong, with a proper portion of armoured cruisers."[9] The ultimate guarantee for the security of British possessions in the Far East, however, rested upon maintaining the treaty with Japan. Despite its successful renegotiation in 1905, the region's sense of security was less certain after Britain elected a Liberal government whose platform included cutting naval expenditures to increase social reform spending. Fisher had been unable to follow through on the second part of his fleet redistribution scheme, namely, to replace obsolete battleships on distant stations with modern armoured cruisers. It was recognized that problems would arise if Japan, growing confident in the wake of its defeat of the Russian fleet at Tsushima, sensed British vulnerability and renounced the treaty, raising the possibility that Japan might not be friendly when the treaty expired in 1911. The Committee of Imperial Defence felt that waiting until relations were strained before sending reinforcements might have the opposite effect and precipitate hostilities, and instructed the Admiralty to maintain a significant naval presence in China by strengthening the squadron "before the termination of the alliance." Although largely an afterthought, the committee also recognized the reinforcement the Royal Navy would receive with the establishment of dominion naval forces in the Pacific.[10]

---

6. Grey to Crewe, 5 May 1909, Crewe to Grey, 30 April 1909, Canada, Parliament, House of Commons, *Imperial Conference on the Naval and Military Defence of the Empire, Correspondence Relating to the Summoning of the Conference* (*Sessional Paper No. 29a*; Ottawa 1910), 8–9. Since the sessional papers only include an edited transcription, a full transcript of the conference is in *Proceedings of the Imperial Conference on Naval and Military Defence at the Foreign Office, Whitehall*, copy in Library and Archives Canada (hereafter LAC), Manuscript Group (hereafter MG) 27 II C4, vol. 2, file 20, reel H-1017.

7. Lambton to Governor-General Hong Kong, 25 November 1908, UKNA, Admiralty (hereafter ADM) 1 /8890.

8. Fisher to J.A. Spender, editor of the *Westminster Gazette*, 2 July 1909, quoted in Lambert, "Economy or Empire?" 60.

9. Admiral Bethell, DNI, quoted in ibid, 60.

10. CID minutes, 29 June 1909, quoted in ibid, 60–61, 57; and Hadley and Sarty, *Tin-pots and Pirate Ships*, 27–28.

From there, it was only a short step to link Fisher's larger strategic plan to concentrate the navy's battleships in home waters—for purposes of economy rather than to counter any German threat—and his belief in the potential of the battle cruiser as the basis for defence of the empire's lines of communication. While the Admiralty staff worked to flesh out a formal proposal, the idea was circulated to the dominion conference participants. According to a contemporary report in the Canadian Annual Review, the Admiralty, apart from questions of making cash contributions or building up local forces, also suggested that consideration should be given to:

> "the gradual creation of an imperial flying squadron of eight battleships and cruisers of the same design, great speed and tremendous gun-power, as the *Indomitable* which took the Prince of Wales to Canada last year." It was suggested that Canada should provide one such battleship at an annual cost in interest and maintenance of £231,500; Australia another, New Zealand a third, India a fourth and the motherland the remaining four. The Canadian ship would remain Canadian in every sense of the word, would form a floating staff college for Canadian youths, and safeguard Canadian local interests. The ship would regularly visit Canadian ports with the rest of the fleet, and take a full share in British naval manouevres.[11]

The long-awaited Admiralty memorandum was unveiled by Reginald McKenna, the first lord since April 1908, when the naval defence question first came up for conference discussion on 3 August. McKenna began his presentation with the conciliatory recognition that, given the varying states of political development within the different colonies, the strategic ideal of all parts of the empire being asked to contribute to the maintenance of the British navy was not required. Instead, naval assistance might vary from a simple contribution of money to the provision of local naval forces, or—in deference to Canadian policy—to the "undertaking of certain local services not directly of a naval character, but which may relieve the imperial government from expenses which would otherwise fall on the British exchequer." Within that context, however, the Admiralty required the commitment of those dominions contemplating the second option (that is, a local naval force) that such forces be established on a secure foundation, so as to allow their contribution in time of need "immediately and materially to the requirements of imperial defence."

> In the opinion of the Admiralty, a dominion government desirous of creating a navy should aim at forming a distinct fleet unit; and the smallest unit is one which, while manageable in time of peace, is capable of being used in its component parts in time of war....
>
> The advantage of a unit of this kind is that ... it is capable of rapid combination with other similar fleet units. We have now, as you know, in the Far

---

11. Hopkins, *The Canadian Annual Review of Public Affairs, 1909*, 80.

East, the eastern fleet. There are three divisions—the Australian division, the China division, and the East Indies division....

In the case of Canada also we think that the fleet unit ... might in the future form an acceptable system, particularly with regard to the Pacific. If we had another fleet unit of this kind on the Pacific coast of Canada we should have, under circumstances under which they could be easily united, no less than four of these divisions, and they would together constitute a very powerful fleet.[12]

More than a squadron for the Pacific, the Admiralty was proposing to constitute a proper fleet that could act as a counter to Japanese ambitions. As such, local defence flotillas of torpedo craft and submarines would not be effective since their poor range and seakeeping capabilities preventing them from operating "on the high seas in the wider duties of protection of trade and preventing attacks from hostile cruisers and squadrons." Moreover, such a limited flotilla "would not in itself ... be a good means of gradually developing a self-contained fleet capable of both offence and defence. Unless a naval force—whatever its size—complies with this condition it can never take its proper place in the organization of an imperial navy distributed strategically over the whole area of British interests." What the Admiralty had in mind was a fleet unit consisting of a 12-inch-gunned armoured cruiser of the new Indomitable class, three unarmoured Bristol-class cruisers, six destroyers, and three submarines, along with the necessary auxiliaries, such as depot and store ships. Such a fleet unit would require at least 2,300 officers and men, would have an initial cost of £3,700,000, and would require an annual operating budget of £600,000.[13]

Laurier's concept of a Canadian fleet had studiously avoided anything even approaching that scale. During the conference discussions, Brodeur cautiously pointed out that McKenna had "spoken of the advisability of having a unit on the Pacific coast, but he did not mention anything with regard to the Atlantic coast. Would he have anything to suggest with regard to the Atlantic coast?" The first lord's reply clearly showed that the Admiralty and the Canadian government were not taking into account the same factors in their naval calculations:

I only referred to the Pacific squadron in its relation to the other squadrons we should have on the further side of the Pacific Ocean and the possible combination of them all into one fleet. With regard to the Atlantic side, it is so very much nearer to our own home waters, and we are so much freer consequently to send vessels of our own, that I do not think that there is quite the same urgency on the Atlantic side as on the Pacific side. While both oceans alike are open to you, the Atlantic coast is very much nearer to our own scene of operations.

---

12. *Proceedings of the Imperial Conference on Naval and Military Defence at the Foreign Office, Whitehall*, 3 August 1909, 34–35, 37, copy in LAC, MG 27 II C4, vol. 2, file 20, reel H-1017.

13. *Proceedings of the Imperial Conference on Naval and Military Defence at the Foreign Office, Whitehall*, 5 August 1909, 63–65, ibid. Under the prevailing exchange rate, £1.00 equalled about $5.00, making an initial outlay of $18,500,000 and annual expenditure of $3,000,000.

McKenna invited Brodeur to "tell us the lines upon which you would like to proceed, and then ask us whether we can offer any suggestions upon that. We do not want to appear to be pressing you." The Canadian minister preferred not to comment at the moment, and led the other representatives in a call for an adjournment for a few days so as to have time to examine the memorandum more closely.[14]

When the conference met again two days later, the Canadians opened the discussion. Sir Frederick Borden read into the record the revised Foster resolution of 29 March 1909, calling for the creation of a Canadian navy, as the Canadian delegation's mandate. Its three main principles were: that Canada wished to act on its own authority, in direct connection with the British authorities and under their guidance; that it wanted to act along the lines laid down by Lord Tweedmouth at the 1907 conference; and that, in an emergency, Canada might go beyond the "expenditure of her own money" to help Britain. Borden asked for a full discussion of the subject under the three headings the Admiralty proposed: the means of reconciling local control by the Canadian government over its naval forces with the principle of unity of command in time of war; the best means of interchanging ships and personnel between the British and the dominion navies; and plans for the transitional period during which the creation of complete dominion fleet units was under way.[15] He stressed, however, the political importance of a two-ocean fleet, even though the coasts were 6,500 kilometres apart and that Canada's national ambitions would not be satisfied by having a naval unit on only one ocean, relying on the Royal Navy for protection on the other, especially since the bulk of the Canadian population lived nearer the Atlantic than the Pacific coast. If "there is anything at all in the idea, as I believe there is, of allowing the people to see for themselves what they are doing in these matters of defence … I am inclined to think that we should start on both coasts at once, that that would be the only thing that would satisfy our people thoroughly."[16]

Brodeur spoke next, immediately seeking to temporize Borden's bold, if entirely pragmatic, stance. He began by expressing appreciation that the British authorities had recognized the principle of dominion autonomy in naval defence. Brodeur also pointed to the 29 March resolution as going beyond mere coastal defence to co-operation with imperial authorities but, with the militia minister having made clear Canadian concerns as to the distribution of the proposed fleet, he sought to refine its scope. As "a consequence of the statements which were made at the conference of 1902 we started immediately the nucleus of a navy. We bought a cruiser [CGS *Canada*] which we put on the Atlantic coast, which was not a very large one it is true, but which was a beginning tending to show our desire and our wish to carry out the idea which had been announced at the Conference of 1902." The existing Fisheries Protection Service was "not sufficient for the purpose which we have

---

14. *Proceedings of the Imperial Conference*, 3 August 1909, 37–38, copy in LAC, MG 27 II C4, vol. 2, file 20, reel H-1017.

15. G.N. Tucker, *The Naval Service of Canada: Its Official History, I: Origins and Early Years* (Ottawa 1952), 116–17.

16. *Proceedings of the Imperial Conference*, 5 August 1909, 41–42, copy in LAC, MG 27 II C4, vol. 2, file 20, reel H-1017.

in view. We would require certainly on the Pacific coast at least one if not two cruisers for the purpose of protecting our fisheries. On the Atlantic coast our protection is fairly good and probably sufficient." Ottawa was anxious to increase the service's strength, "and in connection with it we are anxious to establish a local naval force which would probably be useful in case of war." With that in mind, the Canadian government was willing "to establish some cruisers, not perhaps cruisers of the same importance as the one which has been suggested, but … at all events, we are willing to extend and to improve the existing service, and to increase it, in order that it should be not only a local service, but that it should be also a local force."[17]

With the Canadian delegates committed to gaining approval for a local naval force, but one within narrowly defined limits and with a manageable budget, the discussions were in danger of deteriorating into an impasse. The Admiralty's senior officers, meanwhile, remained committed to the position that local forces had to meet imperial standards of utility and efficiency. Quite apart from his personal belief in the strategic soundness of the fleet unit concept, Fisher was under great pressure to conclude a general imperial scheme. Although the dreadnought crisis had long since been resolved to the Admiralty's satisfaction, many of Fisher's critics continued to hold him personally responsible for having allowed Britain's naval forces to decay to the level where their lead might be questioned. Paradoxically, this worked to strengthen his bargaining position. The alternatives proposed for the dominions—a fleet unit or contributions—amounted to little choice at all. Those contemplating the establishment of a local force could not dispute the logic of efficiency, especially if it allowed suitable guarantees of autonomy, and Australia would take this road in adopting the fleet unit concept essentially as presented by the Admiralty. Otherwise, the option to provide contributions was not likely to be any more acceptable than in the past, and can only be seen as a push to embarrass wavering dominions, such as Canada, into abandoning their smaller projects and get on with concrete action. To a great extent, that is exactly what would transpire, but in the form of a compromise.[18]

The issue was eventually resolved by the fact that the political and military heads of the Admiralty had different priorities, although the conference's official proceedings give little indication of any divergence. It is evident, however, in the descriptions of the behind-the-scenes negotiations that Brodeur provided to Laurier, correspondence that presents a rare detailed account of the evolution of Canadian naval policy in this critical period. As the minister of marine pointed out to his prime minister, the imperatives for political harmony motivating the British civil authorities outweighed the purely naval concerns of the first sea lord. At dinner on 5 August, for instance, he and McKenna engaged in a long private discussion that concentrated entirely on the political considerations of the naval defence question. Brodeur left convinced that McKenna had gained a better understanding of the Canadian position:

---

17. Ibid, 43.

18. Marder, *From Dreadnought to Scapa Flow*, I, 171, 180ff; and Bob Nicholls, *Statesmen & Sailors: Australian Maritime Defence, 1870–1920* (Balmain, Australia 1995), 142–53.

It was pretty late when we parted, and on the way out he said to me "I understand the whole situation you find yourself in. We're going to get along just fine." He told me "I'm going to prepare another document for you that I'll sign once you've seen it and confirmed you're happy with it, and I'll make sure it's done in a way that will support the principles of your House resolution."[19]

McKenna's actions at the conference session the next day appear to confirm Brodeur's appraisal that a breakthrough had been reached. As the minister of marine reported to Laurier, not only had the first lord "made some remarks that were much more conciliatory," but in response to a critique made the previous day by the New Zealand prime minister, Sir Joseph Ward, on the ineffectiveness of local naval forces, "he [McKenna] repeated the arguments I had used with him in our conversation of the previous day & acknowledged that these local organizations might do valuable service." Moreover, McKenna acquiesced to the Canadian request that "the immediate nature that the local force should take" be a matter for a subcomittee formed of Brodeur, Borden, and Admiralty representatives, rather than a subject to be discussed by the conference as a whole.[20]

In anticipation of these private discussions, Brodeur informed Borden of his conversation with McKenna and suggested that the minister of militia have a similar private meeting with Fisher—on the grounds that Borden knew him personally—but also to minimize any misconception on the first sea lord's part that the Canadian position was based entirely on French-Canadian sentiment. The result, however, was hardly promising. According to Brodeur, Fisher was "absolutely unyielding: no Canadian navy unless you [Laurier] started with a dreadnought, and that unit had to be deployed in Pacific waters." But when the first sea lord adopted the same position at the first of the official delegation discussions, it was McKenna who intervened, saying that in Canada "the project wouldn't be feasible." In response to Fisher's pointed query as to what financial amount the Canadians were prepared to consider, Brodeur replied that "that issue had never been discussed." However, as the first sea lord would need an idea of the anticipated expenditure to prepare another memorandum specific to the Canadian resolution, "so I gave him two possible figures, namely, $2,000,000 a year and $3,000,000 a year."[21]

As Brodeur informed the prime minister, he was told by Sir Frederick Borden that "in a conversation that you [Laurier] had had with him [Borden], you had given him to understand that an annual expenditure of $3,000,000 might be acceptable." This was based in turn on Laurier's interpretation of Robert Borden's indication to parliament of what the opposition would consider an acceptable annual expenditure to assure their support. Brodeur's financial suggestion was made easier by the fact that "on the other hand,

19. Brodeur to Laurier, 10 August 1909, LAC, MG 26 G, reel C-879, 158796–813; and *Proceedings of the Imperial Conference,* 6 August 1909, 63–65, copy in LAC, MG 27 II C4, vol. 2, file 20, reel H-1017.

20. Brodeur to Laurier, 10 August 1909, LAC, MG 26 G, reel C-879.

21. Ibid.

[Finance Minister W.S.] Fielding told me the other day just before the conference started that we shouldn't be skimping on costs. So, supported by these statements, I thought I wouldn't be going too far in proposing two or three million dollars in expenditures." It appears, moreover, that Brodeur anticipated bargaining, explaining why he also included the lower sum: "The authorities at the Admiralty ... should give us an idea, if we decide to spend $2,000,000, the best way to go about it & they should also describe the sort of program we would have with annual expenditures of $3,000,000." It was hoped that the lower sum would divert the Admiralty's attention away from larger schemes, as originally suggested, and concentrate its thinking on ensuring that the $3,000,000 plan would be accepted. In summarizing the conference for Laurier on 10 August, Brodeur concluded with an enthusiastic note:

> The fact that the government, and the Admiralty in particular, has been persuaded of the uselessness of claiming a contribution so far as Canada is concerned is, I feel, a big step forward. We also note that your idea introduced at the 1902 conference has won some acceptance. You were alone at that time in seeking endorsement of our independence in the area of naval defence. Today, Australia is supporting your views and has even taken some effective measures towards this goal.[22]

True to their word, the Admiralty drew up two schemes, one for £400,000 and the other for £600,000, "omitting in both cases the cost of the present fishery service and hydrographic surveys but including the maintenance of Halifax and Esquimalt dockyards, and the wireless telegraph service, estimated at some £50,000 a year." The first plan called for "a force of cruisers and destroyers comprising four cruisers of improved Bristol class, one cruiser of the Boadicea class, and six destroyers of the improved River class. As regards submarines, it [was found] advisable to defer their construction because they required a highly trained and specialized complement. If it was decided to limit the plan to an expenditure of £400,000 a year, the Admiralty suggested that one Bristol, the Boadicea, and two destroyers should be omitted." Although neither side seriously considered adopting the lesser scheme, the agreed proposal was a definite compromise, reflecting the Admiralty's desire for a fleet unit, while at the same time taking into consideration Canadian wishes for cost and coastal distribution. The scheme was essentially a modified fleet unit, with the Indomitable-class battle cruiser replaced by the Boadicea and an extra Bristol, and the submarines and auxiliaries withdrawn. The minimal differences were underscored by the similar manning levels for the two schemes: 2,194 officers and men needed for the £600,000 plan, only slightly less than the 2,300 envisaged for the full fleet unit, but substantially more than the 1,408 sailors needed for the £400,000 plan. The bulk of the force, however, was to be located on the Atlantic, with the Admiralty suggesting that "the Boadicea and

22. Ibid.

destroyers might be placed on the Atlantic side, and the Bristol cruisers divided between the Atlantic and Pacific Ocean."[23]

Like most compromises, no one was completely satisfied although the Admiralty came closest to achieving its aims. The failure to include an Indomitable-class ship in the Canadian force must have been a personal blow to Fisher, since a Bristol and Boadicea combination in no way equalled the striking power of a battle cruiser. Still, the scheme closely reflected the Admiralty's intentions of having a unit capable of "working in concert" with the imperial navy, for the whole fleet would comprise ocean-going vessels that could be united if necessary without much delay. Fisher felt optimistic about the outcome: "It means eventually Canada, Australia, New Zealand, the Cape [i.e., South Africa], and India running a complete navy. We manage the job in Europe. They'll manage it against the Yankees, Japs [*sic*], and Chinese, as occasion requires it out there."[24]

To be sure, while accurately reflecting the $3,000,000 Canadian expenditure limit, the scheme went far beyond the intended scope of an "improved and extended" fisheries protection service. Sir Frederick Borden, usually not as sensitive to carefully defining Canada's place in the imperial defence equation as Laurier or Brodeur, flatly told the conference that:

> the resolution passed unanimously by the Canadian government referred to a certain specific statement made by the first lord of the Admiralty in 1907, from which it might, and I think does, appear that it might be possible—at any rate it led us to believe it would be possible—to begin the establishment of a navy in a smaller way than that indicated in the [Admiralty's first] memorandum. That is to say, I inferred, from the first lord's statement in 1907, that we could begin with smaller ships and build the larger ones later on. But the ideal of Canada is the construction of a navy as complete as possible, first for local defence, and secondly to co-operate with the imperial navy.[25]

The fact that Canada would be in possession of a sea-going fleet capable of actively participating in overseas wars radically altered the political significance of the whole scheme. While Brodeur's satisfaction with the Admiralty's proposal indicated he did not fully comprehend the politics, the prime minister immediately recognized the novelty of the fleet unit concept, referring to it as "this ideal programme?" Even so, Laurier underestimated the extent to which the British proposal would affect his plans for Canada's future naval development. The second paragraph of the Admiralty memorandum stated that "while, on naval

23. Admiralty memorandum, 20 July 1909, LAC, MG 27 II C4, vol. 2, file 20, reel H-1017; Tucker, *The Naval Service of Canada*, I, 119; and E.H.H. Archibald, *The Fighting Ship of the Royal Navy, A.D. 897–1984* (Poole, Dorset 1984), 207. If the £400,000 scheme had been adopted, "two *Bristols* would then be placed on the Pacific, and one *Bristol* and four destroyers on the Atlantic coast"—perhaps a further incentive for the Canadians to adopt the other, more visible, scheme.

24. Fisher to Esher, 13 September 1909, quoted in A.J. Marder, *Fear God and Dread Nought: The Correspondence of Admiral of the Fleet Lord Fisher of Kilverstone, II: Years of Power, 1904–1914* (London 1956), 264.

25. *Proceedings of the Imperial Conference*, 6 August 1909, 67, copy in LAC, MG 27 II C4, vol. 2, file 20, reel H-1017.

strategical considerations, it was thought that a fleet unit on the Pacific, as outlined by the Admiralty, might in future form an acceptable system of naval defence, it was recognized that Canada's double seaboard rendered the provision of a fleet unit unsuitable for the present." Laurier predicted that "paragraph II is going to cause us a few problems, namely, the Tories will be seizing on it to charge us with hamstringing the Admiralty. I should hasten to add, however, that the prospect of such attacks doesn't bother me in the least."[26]

Brodeur also believed that the Admiralty had failed to get its way, but concluded that McKenna could not say so publicly, as to do so would contradict the first sea lord's strategic evaluation. "Since he [McKenna] didn't want to appear to be abandoning his officers, he transferred to us, through this project, a large measure of the responsibility for rejecting the ideas put forward in the first Admiralty memorandum."[27] It has since been suggested that the exchange between the McKenna and Brodeur was something of a gentleman's agreement, which did not become public knowledge. McKenna was willing to abandon the concept of financial contributions, at least in so far as Canada was concerned, and was prepared to agree to the creation of a Canadian navy, but was not willing to let such decisions be known either within or outside the Admiralty.[28]

As he freely admitted, Laurier was quite willing to accept the public responsibility for opposing London's financial contribution request. His reservations with paragraph II of the final memorandum notwithstanding, Laurier was more than satisfied with the attitude that Brodeur and Borden had taken at the conference. He wrote Brodeur of the certainty that "during the next session we're going to have an ongoing battle 'on high jingo lines,'" but continued that "nothing could suit me better. I believe that on this point we're on solid ground and that the opinion of the country is solidly behind us." There was, he noted, in some of the major English Canadian centres—"Toronto, Halifax particularly, St John and maybe some others"—"there were some fairly pronounced and highly agitated jingoistic sentiments." Laurier nonetheless felt that there was no danger of this sentiment spreading among the rural population, "where we've always found our greatest support."[29] The conference had, after all, substantially altered his intended naval policy. A revamped Fisheries Protection Service was clearly an inadequate response to the unusual opportunity presented by London's support for a viable Canadian fleet to advance dominion autonomy. The prime minister was convinced that such a change could be taken in stride.

As their representatives returned from the conference, Canada and Australia found themselves committed to naval projects much larger in scope than either had previously envisioned. The similarities ended there, however, since each was effectively committed to proceeding in a different direction. While Australia had agreed to establish a fleet unit with significant direct input from the Royal Navy, Canada was still determined to build its more

---

26. Brodeur to Laurier, 19 August 1909, Laurier to Brodeur, 4 September 1909, LAC, MG 26 G, reel C-880, 159004–06, 159523–24.

27. Brodeur to Laurier, 26 August 1909, ibid, 159190–203.

28. N.D. Brodeur, "The Naval Service of Canada: The End of the Beginning" (unpublished paper presented to the "Royal Canadian Navy in Retrospect" conference, Royal Roads Military College, March 1980), 33–34.

29. Laurier to Brodeur, 26 August 1909, LAC, MG 26 G, reel C-880, 159190–203.

modest fleet on its own. Neither path would prove wholly successful, although the Australians would enjoy more initial success than the Canadians. Nonetheless, a more confident prime minister now authorized work on the Canadian naval service to proceed even though implementation of the scheme would have to measure up to the expectations of both parliament and the Admiralty. The fate of Laurier's naval policy now hung on the government's ability to meet these diverse criteria.

The immediate measures were straightforward enough. In his last letter from England on 26 August, Brodeur had informed Laurier of McKenna's willingness to loan Canada one or two cruisers, pending completion of the ships the Canadian government proposed building. Although accepting British warships on loan had not proven itself in the past, the Canadian minister recommended acceptance because a ship was needed immediately for fisheries protection off the BC coast and a warship could also serve as a training ship. The proposed vessels would each require a $20,000 refit to make them suitable for Canadian service, but since the fisheries department was already obliged to rent a ship on the West Coast for the fishing season at the rate of $4,500 a month, Brodeur felt that "we'll benefit from moving quickly on this issue."[30] Likewise, in his negotiations with the Admiralty, Rear-Admiral Kingsmill stressed the fact that the ships would be required by April 1910. To this end, the admiral pointed out, the Canadian government was quite willing to accept destroyers instead of the cruisers, as "it is most desirous to obtain at once some vessels to protect our fisheries there."[31]

Before Laurier could send a reply, Brodeur cabled news that in further negotiations the Admiralty had proven to be disposed to the sale of a cruiser for use in the Pacific for $250,000, and asked whether he should negotiate for a sale or a loan. An opportunity therefore presented itself of better asserting the "Canadian-ness" of the project, without having to borrow Royal Navy ships, while at the same time satisfying the opposition's demands for haste. Hoping to lend greater significance to the action, Laurier preferred to continue capitalizing on the broader political consensus. After consulting with the remainder of his Cabinet, Laurier advised Brodeur that "council prefers that you should not commit yourself. Arrange matters with Admiralty to be submitted to council and then approved by parliament."[32]

Before any of these arrangements could be made widely known, speculation began to develop among both the public and the military as to the government's actions. The *Canadian Military Gazette*, now reasonably confident that naval appropriations would not affect those of the militia, felt that "unless we have very badly misread public opinion this policy [i.e., the creation of a Canadian maritime force to co-operate with the British navy] will meet with very general acceptance," and was more concerned that the Canadian response should not take the route of a financial contribution, as it believed a "dominion navy man-

---

30. Ibid.

31. "Paper Laid Before Admiralty With Replies," August 1909, copy in LAC, MG 27 II C4, vol. 2, file 20, reel H-1017.

32. Brodeur to Laurier, 4 September 1909, Laurier to Brodeur, 11 September 1909, LAC, MG 26 G, reel C-880, 159203, 159523–24.

aged by the dominion government alone suffices to meet Canadian sentiment."[33] A press release on 8 October stated that the government would take steps leading to the speedy establishment of a Canadian navy in the coming session. It was contemplated that the building program would extend over several years and see "the construction of perhaps twelve war vessels, embracing two or three cruisers of the Bristol class, torpedo boats and destroyers. It was also stated that arrangements were being made for one of the older type of British cruisers to be brought to the Pacific coast to serve the dual purpose of a fisheries protection cruiser and a training ship. A similar cruiser, to serve the same purpose; might also be obtained for the Atlantic coast."[34]

Such a program was intended to provide the basis upon which a Canadian shipbuilding and repair industry could be established and in total was estimated to cost $15,000,000. But uncertainty soon spread as to the exact intention of the government in its naval policy. Rather than rallying support, the announcement inspired criticism from widely different sources, a reaction that manifested itself precisely along the pro-contribution lines feared by both the *Canadian Military Gazette* and the Liberals. It also came from another direction that Laurier had clearly not anticipated—the Quebec nationalistes.

The pro-contribution opposition had been expected because it had always openly existed. The dreadnought crisis earlier in the year had led its believers to press their case more vigorously. Calls for a cash gift to the Royal Navy were renewed in the latter part of October to bring their arguments to public attention before parliamentary debate commenced. The pro-contribution lobby had received encouragement from the visits of Admiral Lord Charles Beresford, a professional rival of Fisher's who had recently resigned from the Royal Navy, and of Lord Northcliffe, owner of the influential *London Times*. Although neither man spoke explicitly in favour of contributions (Beresford actually declared that the policy of a local or national navy was the best), by elaborating upon the danger the Royal Navy faced from a dreadnought-building Germany, both gave implicit support to the idea that Laurier's fleet would not be a sufficient addition to the defences of the empire. Because the visits of the two British lords were more obviously geared toward gathering colonial support for their individual causes at home, the Liberals paid little attention to arguments not likely to pass the test of Canada's parliament.[35]

The government did actively encourage the prime minister of New Zealand to come to Canada, even though Sir Joseph Ward had heartily declared himself in favour of contributions at the recently concluded imperial conference. When Ward announced his intention to return home by way of Canada, Brodeur wrote Laurier that "this would be wonderful from a political standpoint." Although there was the risk that any of the New Zealand prime minister's statements might encourage Canadian imperialists, there was also the advantage

---

33. *The Canadian Military Gazette,* 14 and 28 September 1909.

34. Hopkins, *The Canadian Annual Review, 1909,* 88–89.

35. Ibid, 112–23, 149–55; and see also Robert Craig Brown, *Robert Laird Borden: A Biography,* I: *1854–1914* (Toronto 1975), 157–58. Beresford had recently resigned from the Royal Navy in a bitter dispute with Fisher, and was now leading the drive to oust the first sea lord. Northcliffe, master of the "yellow press," knew that war hysteria sold papers and the Anglo-German "naval race" was too good an issue to be allowed to pass.

that Ward "would understand right away the nature of Canadian feelings and would certainly not make the mistake of attaching a lot of importance to the views of the jingoistic segment of society."[36] Nonetheless, with the safety of the British Isles being called into doubt by so many influential people, an increasing number of English-speaking Canadians began to lean toward the view expressed by Premier Palen Roblin of Manitoba in December 1909, namely, that contributions were the only effective way to show loyalty to the empire and that Laurier's "worthless proposals" would result in nothing more than a "tin pot" Canadian navy.[37]

More ominous was the rising opposition among some French Canadians. Although it was fear of nationaliste reaction that had delayed the implementation of the government's naval policy for so many years, Laurier had strangely discounted it once institution of the force became likely. His miscalculation that the nationalists would, at worst, reluctantly support the government is perhaps explained by the fact that F.D. Monk, leader of the Quebec Conservatives, had not participated in the March debate, even though present in the house, and had not subsequently commented on the issue. His silence ended with the opening of the new session of parliament in November. Protesting the secrecy of the recent imperial conference, Monk charged that the naval consolidation of the empire resulting from Laurier's "imperial drunkenness" would be "fatal to the principle of self-government" and demanded the question be submitted "to the judgment of the electorate."[38] For all Laurier's parliamentary assertions that "the Canadian fleet would not participate in imperial wars without the consent of the Canadian people," Monk's belief that the prime minister intended to build a "war navy [for] active participation in the defence of the empire" resonated deeply among some members of Quebec's political elite. Monk was soon joined in opposition to the navy by Laurier's old antagonist, Henri Bourassa, who would establish the paper Le Devoir in January 1910, mainly as a tool of opposition to the provincial government, and as a means of prominently opposing the navy bill as well. The prime minister sensed that this opposition was of a more personal nature, however, not specifically aimed at the government's naval policy. Perhaps because nationaliste arguments were based on a pessimistic interpretation of the policy—that Canada's navy would go to war on behalf of Britain regardless of the country's wishes—Laurier believed that this attack, as with that of the imperialists, could be easily defeated by a counter-appeal to reason.[39]

Although the naval debate had largely been non-partisan to this point, the new parliamentary session had a politically polarizing effect. Liberal opinion remained largely united behind Laurier and, even though English and French expressions of opposition were vastly different in appearance, they both sprang from politically conservative roots. Henri

---

36. Brodeur to Laurier, 10 August 1909, LAC, MG 26 G, reel C-879, 158796–813.

37. Winnipeg *Free Press*, 23 December 1909; and Hopkins, *The Canadian Annual Review, 1909*, 92–93.

38. Hopkins, *The Canadian Annual Review, 1909*, 98; and H.B. Neatby, *Laurier and a Liberal Quebec: A Study in Political Management* (Toronto 1972), 185. Brodeur similarly discounted any French Canadian opposition, and in fact felt that the greatest difficulty would be in gaining the acceptance of new Canadians on the prairies.

39. Mason Wade, *The French Canadians*, I: *1760–1911* (Toronto 1968), 565; and Hadley and Sarty, *Tin-pots and Pirate Ships*, 56.

Bourassa's addition to the critics' ranks served to obscure this political link, as did the initial argument between imperialists and nationalistes that a separate Canadian navy would involve too great an expenditure—a stand that would have found some sympathy among the "radical" elements of the British Liberal party. According to the spokesman for the pro-contribution Victoria branch of the Navy League, Clive Phillips-Wolley, there were three naval options open to Canada. The first, annexation by the United States, would result in paying proportionate tax dollars for defence on the order of $25,000,000 annually. The second, the building of a fleet unit as envisioned by the Admiralty, would cost $18,000,000 initially, with necessary annual upkeep cost of $3,000,000. The third option, direct cash contribution to the Royal Navy, was by his logic the cheapest, for, although he would give no sum, such a measure would certainly be somewhat less than $18,000,000. Along a slightly different line, the *Toronto Telegram* went so far as to claim that "a pledge of $50,000,000 at the recent juncture might have averted its actual expenditure by checking German ambitions."[40] For his part, F.D. Monk stressed the belief that the proposed navy would cost well over $20,000,000, money that could be put to better use than on munitions of war.[41]

These fiscal considerations were not the only elements in the debate and were, in fact, little more than initial posturing. With Brodeur incapacitated by illness, Laurier hoped to raise the tenor of discussion by overseeing passage of the naval bill himself. He drew up a series of notes during the fall of 1909 covering various aspects of the proposed naval policy and indicating his intention to appeal to both opposition factions on the grounds of Canadian nationalism. In one, entitled "Necessity for Naval Defence," the prime minister pointed to a navy's place in Canada's overall defence: "A police force is needed to protect our homes. Militia is required to defend our territory and suppress local riots. Navy required to protect our fisheries, protect our trade routes, and defend our coasts." Arguing that Canada's autonomy was almost complete in the political, military, fiscal, and commercial treaty-making fields, Laurier concluded that Canada must have its own navy as "obligation is a co-relative of power." Then, in anticipation of criticism on the costs involved, Laurier went through a careful reassessment of military and naval expenditure, reasoning that "with the $3,000,000 that we are going to add to our naval expenditure, our expenditure will be $1.64 per head." This was far above the $1.15 figure that the British had attributed to Canada at the 1909 conference, as well as being more than was spent by any other colony. The prime minister concluded that "Canada is the only self-governing dominion which has not been a charge upon the British exchequer for its defence in late years."[42]

Laurier's notes indicate that he hoped to use the proceedings of the 1909 conference to demonstrate that Canada had not in any way blocked the intentions of the imperial government, while at the same time reinforcing the "autonomy is nearly complete" theme for nationalists (both anglophone and francophone) by showing that the final decision was

---

40. Hopkins, *The Canadian Annual Review, 1909*, 95, 90–91; and Clive Phillips-Wolley, *The Canadian Naval Question* (Toronto 1910), 22.

41. *Ottawa Citizen*, 9 November 1909.

42. Laurier, "Notes re: Naval Debate," and "Necessity for Naval Defence," and "Canadian Military and Naval Expenditure," nd, LAC, MG 26 G, 219412, 219417.

exclusively Canadian. The Colonial Office disrupted his plans, however, by maintaining that the discussions were private, contained sensitive material, and should remain secret. Laurier protested on the grounds that it was "of the utmost importance that nothing in this subject be kept back, and that the people may have an opportunity of being acquainted with every think [*sic*—thing] that took place from the first to the last syllable."[43] Nonetheless, when the "Report of the Imperial Conference with Representatives of the Self-Governing Dominions on the Naval and Military Defence of the Empire, 1909," was presented to the House of Commons by Sir Frederick Borden on 17 November 1909, it was not the wished-for transcript, but a much-abridged summary of the proceedings approved by the Colonial Office.[44]

By the time Bill 95 (1909–10) respecting the Naval Service of Canada was introduced by Laurier on 12 January 1910, the prime minister had been forced to revise his arguments. The inability to secure full publication of the conference proceedings and the necessity to honour Brodeur's "gentlemen's agreement" with McKenna meant that the Liberals were deprived of some very powerful tools in the upcoming debate. But these difficulties did not really affect the problem of how to deal with those political elements opposed to the government policy. A simple appeal to Canadian nationalism would not be sufficient to gain wide parliamentary approval as both the imperialists and the nationalistes also claimed to be representing the dominion's interests. The Liberals, therefore, planned to argue that the introduction of the naval service would not jeopardize the aspirations of either camp. Despite these difficulties, the government entered the naval service debate confident of eventual success against the fragmented Conservative opposition. As a result, Robert Borden was faced with the difficult task of reconciling his personal approval of the policy with the imperialist and nationaliste elements in his ranks.[45]

Although the naval debate of 1910 was long and sometimes bitter, it exerted little influence on actual policy. The parliamentary discourse did, however, demonstrate the growing depth of opposition feelings. In contrast to the bipartisan accommodation Laurier and Borden had been able to engineer a year earlier, a true debate emerged in 1910. Both leaders drew on the experience gained with the Fisheries Protection Service to agree that there must be a Canadian navy tailored to local needs with aid to an imperial fleet being an additional question. It was in attempting to master the politics that swirled around conflicting views of Canada's destiny that their efforts diverged: Laurier's loose coalition of autonomous nations that would freely co-operate according to their own inclination in moments of crisis, or Borden's more closely united empire. With Canadian naval policy

---

43. Laurier to Grey, 6 November 1909, LAC, MG 26 II B2, reel C-1171.

44. Canada, Parliament, House of Commons, *Report of the Imperial Conference with Representatives of the Self-Governing Dominions on the Naval and Military Defence of the Empire, 1909* (Sess. Paper No. 29a; Ottawa 1910).

45. Canada, Parliament, House of Commons, *Debates*, 12 January 1910, cols. 1738–62. Borden finally would settle upon taking the route of opposing the government's policy primarily on the grounds that an immediate cash contribution should first be extended to cover the period until the Canadian navy became operational. See Brown, *Borden*, I, 159ff.

now involving the whole question of imperial relations, it is not surprising that debate ranged much more widely than the title of the bill implied. Members on both sides drew upon the views of eminent statesmen and admirals to argue that there was, or was not, an emergency; or that contributions by the dominion were, or were not, the best solution. The Monroe Doctrine was invoked upon occasion, usually to minimize its relevance, as it weighed against the need for any naval commitment. Conversely, the possibility of annexation by the United States was alternately used to support both the bill and an emergency contribution. Instinctively, both sides understood that the establishment of a naval service in the suggested form would seriously alter Ottawa's relations with London. But although the opposition remained divided on just what the effect would be, the government was convinced that their modest plan for improving the protection of Canada's sovereign interests would meet with the country's approval.[46]

Laurier introduced the Naval Service Act by announcing that the government planned to implement the larger of the two Admiralty proposals. Recent attacks on the naval policy had reaffirmed his earlier conviction of opting for the $3,000,000 scheme (out of a total government budget of $122 million that spent $272,000 for fisheries protection, $160,000 for hydrographic survey, and $150,000 for wireless stations), because it was more likely to impress a public that would consider it an adequate contribution and one capable of producing an autonomous naval force. The warships would all be built in Canada, with the assistance of British firms who would be encouraged to open yards in the country, regardless of the extra cost this might entail. As well, a naval college was to be established on the same principles as the Royal Military College in Kingston (except that all graduates would be commissioned), so that the new service's officers might eventually be exclusively Canadian. The only major change in the bill affected by the debate was administrative: an amendment providing for a separate Department of the Naval Service rather than keeping the navy under the Department of Marine and Fisheries. Also to be transferred to the new department were the Fisheries Protection Service, Tidal and Current Survey, Hydrographic Survey, and wireless telegraph branches, all responsibilities claimed in the past by Canadian representatives at colonial and imperial conferences as naval contributions. Both departments, however, would be responsible to the same minister.[47]

None of this swayed the opposition, however. Laurier's naval policy might have been acceptable as far as it went, but when the matter came down to the central issue of the imperial relationship, the contributionists did not believe the promise the prime minister had made in introducing the bill, namely, that "when Britain is at war Canada is at war; there is no distinction." Nor were the nationalists reassured by the fact that, unlike the Militia Act of 1904 (and the proposed naval militia act), which provided that "any male citizen of Canada from seventeen to sixty could be compelled to serve anywhere in the world so long as it could be shown to be in defence of the country," the naval bill specifically excluded compulsion of any kind.[48]

---

46. Tucker, *The Naval Service of Canada*, I, 132–9; and Roger Sarty, "Canadian Naval Policy, 1860–1939" (unpublished Directorate of History and Heritage (hereafter DHH) narrative, nd), 25–26.

47. House of Commons, *Debates*, 12 January 1910, cols. 1732–8.

Ultimately, the parliamentary debate exposed a serious flaw in the government's policy. Where Laurier usually preferred to follow public opinion on an issue, on the naval question there was now no easily defined consensus, and he and his ministers found themselves in the position of having to work against sizable minorities pushing in different directions. As a result, they were forced to defend the compromise scheme that had developed in the summer of 1909, a course that no one, not even the Liberals, really wanted. But the alternatives—contribution or nothing—were even more unpalatable. The government had taken up the task under the illusion that the original modest and non-partisan Canadian intentions would triumph. In the end, it was the government's substantial parliamentary majority that allowed the bill to pass easily, the act receiving royal assent on 4 May 1910. In the end, it was the Canadian public that would judge the government's naval policy in the next general election—one that was not expected before the fall of 1912—thereby granting the new Canadian navy time, presumably, to prove itself.[49]

Laurier remained convinced that his policy of semi-autonomous naval development was in the best interest of the country's development and hoped that once the scope of the navy's activities became known, the critics from both sides would be silenced or appeased. A great deal, therefore, hung upon getting the naval service into operation without delay. To that end, Rear-Admiral Kingsmill had remained in England after the 1909 defence conference to advance the government's naval initiative. Slated to become the new service's first director, Kingsmill explored the possibility of acquiring a pair of cruisers (one for each coast) from the Royal Navy as a temporary measure to get training underway in Canada before the navy's new-construction warships were delivered. The Admiralty's recommendations were in line with Kingsmill's own view that an Apollo-class cruiser from the 1890–91 building program—at twenty-one ships the largest class of protected cruisers in the Royal Navy—was an excellent initial type for the new navy. The Canadian admiral was also quite familiar with these vessels, having commanded one of the class, HMS *Scylla*, in the Channel squadron in 1903. Although nearly two decades old, the British navy had enjoyed great success with these sturdy ships: they were fast for their day, with a top speed of nearly nineteen knots; were well armed with a primary armament of single 6-inch guns forward and aft; and, at 3,400 tons, were superb long range cruisers. For Kingsmill they were ideal "with reference to the conditions of British Columbia … [where] it is necessary to have a ship away from the depot for weeks at a time, protecting the fisheries off the coast and in Hecate Strait."[50] The opposition's unexpected attacks through the late fall of 1909 shelved the government's intention to purchase the cruisers with parliamentary approval, so Brodeur arranged for the purchase of an Apollo under the outstanding 1907 Marine and Fisheries' vote of $225,000 to acquire a fisheries protection cruiser for the Pacific coast.[51]

---

48. Ibid, col. 1735; and Joseph Schull, *Laurier: The First Canadian* (Toronto 1965), 494.

49. For the text of the Naval Service Act, 1910 see Tucker, *The Naval Service of Canada,* I, appx. V, 377–85.

50. Kingsmill to Desbarats, 3 January 1910, "Brief History of HMCS *Rainbow*" DHH 81/520/8000, "HMCS *Rainbow.*" See Archibald, *The Fighting Ship in the Royal Navy,* 193 for class details.

Kingsmill felt that an Apollo-class cruiser "might not be sufficient" for the Atlantic coast, however, in view of the region's "much larger seafaring population to draw from." Instead, the prospective naval director informed Ottawa in early January 1910 that "their lordships would be equally as glad to part with one of the Spartiate class." A much larger vessel at 11,000 tons (and now more commonly referred to as the eight-ship Diadem class), she was slightly newer than the Apollos, having been built in 1896–98, and was armed with sixteen 6-inch guns. A larger cruiser would also offer the Canadian navy distinct training advantages, not only in increased crew capacity—a complement of 705 as compared to the 273 for an Apollo—but also because her secondary torpedo armament had submerged tubes, similar to what was expected in the new construction cruisers. Clinching Kingsmill's recommendation was the conclusion that "one great feature of [such] training ... will be that it will not be necessary to have so large a proportion of skilled ratings from England on the first manning of our new ships." As negotiations with the Admiralty progressed, specific vessels were identified, the Apollo-class HMS *Rainbow* and the Spartiate-class HMS *Niobe*, with payment for the latter being deferred until after commissioning so as to be included in the naval service vote.[52]

While in England, Kingsmill also secured the services of several Royal Navy officers to assist in the formidable task of establishing its bureaucratic framework. Those initially engaged were Commander J.D.D. Stewart as "Technical Adviser On All Naval Matters," Lieutenant R.M.T. Stephens as "Adviser On Gunnery Matters," and Staff Paymaster P.J. Ling as "Adviser on matters connected with Stores, Clothing, Victualling, etc." The three officers were loaned to the Department of Marine and Fisheries by the Royal Navy for a period of two years but transferred to the Naval Service upon its inception.[53] Stewart was given command of *Rainbow*, Stephens was appointed director of gunnery, and Ling was made secretary to the naval staff. As negotiations with the Admiralty progressed, three additional officers were loaned in the spring of 1910: Commander C.D. Roper to act as chief of staff to Kingsmill; Commander Edward H. Martin as superintendent of the Halifax dockyard; and Commander William Balfour Macdonald as captain of *Niobe*. Several of these (and

---

51. Canada, Parliament, "Auditor General's Report, 1909–10" (*Sessional Paper No.1*; Ottawa 1911), section O, 2, 172; and Kingsmill to Desbarats, 8 November 1909, "Correspondence Re: Purchase of *Rainbow*" (*Sessional Paper No. 146*; Ottawa 1910). The *Rainbow* in fact cost $218,585.60.

52. Kingsmill to Desbarats, 3 January 1910, DHH 81/520/8000, "HMCS *Rainbow*." The Admiralty initially tried to interest Kingsmill in an older vessel of the Edgar class (the correspondence specifically identifies *Hawke*, built in 1891), at 7,350 tons also large enough to accommodate an increased number of trainees, but Kingsmill refused because her 9.2-inch main armament was incompatible with the 6-inch guns of the Apollo class and the expected Bristol class. Again, see Archibald, *The Fighting Ship in the Royal Navy*, 195 and 199 for class details. It had been arranged with the Admiralty that *Niobe* would replace the Boadicea-class cruiser in the proposed naval establishment. See Fisher to Brodeur, 28 December 1909, (*Sessional Paper No. 146a*; Ottawa 1910), 4. Brodeur advised parliament on 5 December 1910 that the purchase price of *Niobe* was $1,046,333. J. Castell Hopkins, *The Canadian Annual Review of Public Affairs, 1910* (Toronto 1911), 211.

53. "Paper Laid Before Admiralty With Replies," August 1909, question 7, LAC, MG 27 II C4, vol. 2, file 20, reel H-1017; and Canada, Parliament, "Return to an Order of the House of Commons, dated the 15th December, 1909, calling for a List of all experts, technical advisers, etc., employed in connection with the Naval Defence programme" (*Sessional Paper No. 72*; Ottawa 1910).

other RN officers originally obtained on loan) eventually retired from the Royal Navy, like Kingsmill, to be commissioned into the Royal Canadian Navy, but it would be many years before Canadian-trained officers would be able to replace them. In order not to block the promotion opportunities of RCN officers, those on loan from the RN were almost always given temporary appointments, usually for four years, paid at Canadian rates, but with their period of employment counting as service in the RN.[54]

Their reasons for joining the new RCN varied from interest in different employment, to their personal selection by Kingsmill, or just as an opportunity to revive a lagging career. Commander Macdonald, for instance, fit at least the latter two of these categories. As he later recalled, "the British Admiralty asked me to go as captain of the *Niobe*, probably because I was born in Canada. Knowing what happens to naval officers who accept service in 'side shows,' I did not accept until I had a letter from their lordships stating that they would consider it excellent service, and verbally I was guaranteed my promotion when my turn came. I accepted, but was never promoted."[55] For much of the remaining non-specialist departmental work, an establishment was already in place under the direction of the deputy minister, G.J. Desbarats. Along with the transfer of several branches from Marine and Fisheries came a number of experienced bureaucrats: L.J. Beausoleil, chief accountant; J.A. Wilson, director of stores; C.P. Edwards, director of the radiotelegraph branch; W.J. Stewart, chief hydrographer; and Dr W.B. Dawson, director of the tidal and current survey. In November 1911, a civilian complement of sixty-six was authorized for the naval service, consisting of a deputy minister, sixty-one clerks, and four messengers.[56]

It would be difficult, and indeed wrong, to describe the resulting organization as anything but a very rudimentary "naval staff." To begin, there was the novelty of the term, with a general staff having only recently been introduced into the British Army (although the Germans had been operating one for nearly a century) and the Royal Navy itself being forced by the British government to address the concept of expanding the Admiralty from an administrative body to one with an ability to combine the new technology of radio with the existing worldwide network of telegraph cables to direct naval operations in the most distant seas. Such a level of activity was hardly required by a fledgling Naval Service Headquarters (NSHQ) concerned as it was, for the time being, with sorting out its own administration and overseeing a skeleton, two-cruiser navy. On the issue of establishing a naval service hospitable to French-Canadians, Kingsmill and his staff insisted on an English only policy, even on such simple measures as allowing entrance examinations to be conducted in either language, on the grounds that any attempt to combine the two languages would be "detrimental to the service."[57] The exclusion of French as a working language in the new

---

54. Tucker, *The Naval Service of Canada*, I, 150–51. Note that Tucker does not identify Roper in his listing.

55. Cdr. Macdonald quoted in S.W. Jackman, ed., *At Sea and By Land: The Reminiscences of William Balfour Macdonald, RN* (Victoria 1983), 17, 96.

56. Desbarats to Laurier, 2 April 1910, DHH 2001/13, file C-7; and Tucker, *The Naval Service of Canada*, I, 150–51.

navy was quietly accepted, probably because to have challenged it openly, but unsuccessfully, would have confirmed the worst fears of Bourassa and the Quebec nationalistes.[58]

According to the new department's organization chart, the director of the naval service (DNS) was not on a par with the deputy minister but was one step below, equal to the heads of the department's various civilian branches and reporting through Desbarats to a minister who was also responsible for the Department of Marine and Fisheries. As such, the experienced civil servant was, in theory at least, in a superior administrative position to the professional head of the Canadian navy. Nonetheless, the combination of Desbarats and Kingsmill, with their demonstrated professional competence and family ties to the governing Liberal party, provided the new Canadian navy with an effective administration. Before being appointed as deputy minister of marine and fisheries, Desbarats had risen by 1901 to be director of the government shipyard at Sorel. He remained deputy minister and comptroller of the Naval Service until its consolidation with the other armed services in 1922 when he became deputy minister of the newly formed Department of National Defence, a position he held until his retirement in 1932. Based solely on the department's organizational lines of authority, an earlier official historian of the RCN concluded that "Desbarats' authority and influence considerably exceeded those of most deputy ministers; and during the first two decades of its existence he probably had more to do with moulding the service than any other man."[59]

The designated lines of authority on an organization chart and the actual workings of a department, of course, can differ greatly depending on the personalities involved. In the case of the Department of the Naval Service, the conclusion of the earlier official history neither withstands an extensive examination of the navy's files nor accords with the professional interests of the deputy minister and director of the naval service. A career bureaucrat of the efficient, paper-pushing variety, Desbarats strictly confined himself to the civilian side of the department and the routine management of the minister's office. As such, he ensured that proper civil service procedures were followed in the administration of the department, particularly on matters of finance and government contracts, and provided a link with other civilian departments of government, at the deputy minister level, including forwarding formal naval correspondence to the deputy minister of external affairs for transmission to London. At no time during his tenure, however, did Desbarats ever offer an opinion on naval matters or attempt to influence naval policy in any way. Kingsmill's naval advice was always dutifully passed, entirely without comment or interference, to the minister. The only indication that Desbarats was involved in any way in the process was a cryptic "seen by minister" minuted in the margin. Similarly, drafts of formal naval

57. N.D. Brodeur, "L.P. Brodeur and the Origins of the Royal Canadian Navy," James A. Boutilier, ed., *The RCN in Retrospect, 1910–1968* (Vancouver 1982), 30–31.

58. Marc Milner, *Canada's Navy: The First Century* (Toronto 1999), 22–23.

59. Tucker, *The Naval Service of Canada*, I, 151. Tucker's suggestion of Desbarats' overarching influence is endorsed in both Hadley and Sarty, *Tin-pots and Pirate Ships*, 97; and J.G. Armstrong, *The Halifax Explosion and the Royal Canadian Navy: Inquiry and Intrigue* (Vancouver 2002), 83.

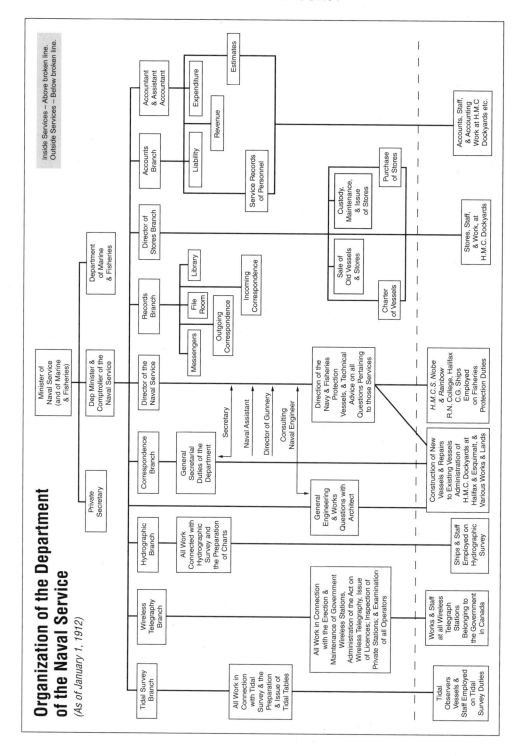

Organization of the Department of the Naval Service
(As of January 1, 1912)

Inside Services – Above broken line.
Outside Services – Below broken line.

correspondence with the Admiralty were always forwarded through government channels entirely without any attempt at alteration by the deputy minister. Indeed, a historian will search in vain through the department's files or the bureaucrat's personal diary[60] for a single thought on naval policy expressed by Desbarats (although comments on Ottawa's hot, humid summers and bitterly cold winters abound). Another of the department's civilian administrators, the director of stores, was far more likely to submit his views on departmental policy, but J.A. Wilson was also clearly a civil servant of greater intellectual depth than Desbarats.

Kingsmill, on the other hand, did not hesitate to give the minister his frank views on the needs of the Canadian navy. Aided for much of his tenure as naval director by his thoughtful and competent chief of staff, R.M.T. Stephens, the Canadian admiral had to fight for what little help the navy received against both the pro-British bias of the Borden government and the frustratingly erratic naval advice emanating from the Admiralty. He never, however, had to contend with any interference from his efficient, but mundane, deputy minister. If any individual in the Department of the Naval Service can lay claim to Tucker's assertion of having "more to do with moulding the service than any other man" that guiding hand, as we shall see, clearly belonged to Kingsmill. Nonetheless, Prime Minister Borden largely ignored the advice of his service chief in the critical formative years of the navy's existence in favour of the vacillating opinions coming from Whitehall, a situation the naval director seems largely to have resigned himself to and a reflection of his dedication to seeing the naval project eventually bear fruit.

Returning to the more immediate issues facing Kingsmill in 1909, CGS *Canada* was slated to continue operating as a training vessel to begin educating Canadian officer candidates as soon as possible. But, as the naval director had recommended in his earlier plan, the vessel's officers were replaced by volunteers from the Royal Naval Reserve to ensure a higher standard of training. Lieutenant Charles J. Stuart, RNR, took over as captain, and two other lieutenants were commissioned as first lieutenant and instructor respectively. They arrived in North America in early October 1909 so that changes could be made without disrupting *Canada*'s normal fisheries patrol duties.[61] A campaign was begun to find recruits to complement the first two naval cadets—one of whom, P.W. Nelles, would later rise to command the RCN—both of whom had joined *Canada* in 1908 for initial training as officers. It is perhaps symbolic of the political controversy surrounding the fledgling navy that all of the next batch of recruits had some connection to the government, which greatly facilitated their entry. As one historian has observed, "the minister had taken a personal hand in [the matter]. Naval Cadet Victor G. Brodeur was his son; Barry German was the son of the Liberal MP for Welland–St. Catharines ...; Charles Beard's father was a senior government official ... ; Trenwick Bate was the son of a Liberal millionaire. All were

---

60. Desbarats' personal diary, written almost exclusively in English, is in LAC, MG 30 E89 and provides proof that Ottawa's weather has changed little in the intervening ninety years but contains very little on naval policy.

61. Canada, Department of the Naval Service, *Report of the Department of the Naval Service for the Fiscal Year Ending March 31, 1911* (Ottawa 1912), 20–21.

insiders. They had written no entrance exams—the method of selection was informal to say the least."[62]

Eventually a more formal and rigorous process was established to obtain a larger number of qualified candidates. In the same spirit that envisioned a training academy for officers as a vital part of the earlier plans for a naval militia, the Naval Service Act included provision for the creation of a naval college "for the purpose of imparting a complete education in all branches of naval science, tactics and strategy," the expectation being that the college would eventually supply sufficient Canadian officers to reduce the need for British personnel.[63] Candidates for entry had to be British subjects between the ages of fourteen and sixteen years of age, be medically fit, successfully pass a competitive examination set and graded by the Civil Service Commission, and be able to pay for their own tuition, uniforms, and supplies. Patterned loosely on the Royal Naval College Britannia in Dartmouth, England, it also shared elements in common with the Royal Military College of Canada in Kingston, differing from the latter in offering only a two year program rather than three and requiring all graduates to serve a minimum length of time in the Canadian navy (at RMC it was the exception to be offered a militia commission upon graduation). There was some expectation that the two colleges would be co-located in Kingston, but Laurier preferred Halifax, "if only because better, cheaper, and more immediate facilities" were available there, with the old naval hospital in the dockyard identified as the temporary site for the naval college—where it remained until it was severely damaged in the explosion of December 1917.[64]

As with any newly established service, it would take time for the Canadian navy to develop its own professionals, and Canada initially had to rely on instructional staff loaned from the Royal Navy. Edward A.E. Nixon was nominally the first lieutenant of the college, but he effectively acted as commandant in place of the official head, the dockyard superintendent, Commander Martin. Promoted commander on the RCN list in August 1915, Nixon remained the actual administrator in charge of the college until its closure in 1922 and was considered by the cadets to have been "the very personification of the college—the driving force behind it, and the apostle of the standards by which all the boys lived."[65] The Royal Navy also supplied a director of studies, initially Naval Instructor Basil S. Hartley, who oversaw a combined British and Canadian civilian staff teaching mathematics, navigation, mechanics, physics, chemistry, engineering, seamanship, pilotage, geography, history (including naval history), English, French, and German. The cadets' two

---

62. Tony German, *The Sea is at Our Gates: The History of the Canadian Navy* (Toronto 1990), 27. Brodeur, the son of the minister, received his joining instructions almost immediately, the official letter of appointment from Kingsmill being dated 8 October 1909. German, the son of the member of parliament for Welland, Ontario, was signed on in February 1910, despite being slightly over-age, through the personal intervention of Laurier. For an account of German's early experiences, see Tony German, "The Last of the First," *Sentinel*, vol. 16, no. 2, (1980/2), 18–20.

63. Naval Service Act, 1910, sections 32–36; and G. William Hines, "The Royal Naval College of Canada, 1911–22," Adrian Preston and Peter Dennis, eds., *Swords and Covenants: Essays in Honour of the Centennial of the Royal Military College of Canada* (London 1976), 164.

64. Hines, "The Royal Naval College of Canada," 165.

65. Ibid, 167. For a personal recollection of the RNCC, see P. Willett Brock, "Commander E.A.E. Nixon and the Royal Naval College of Canada, 1910–22," Boutilier, ed., *The RCN in Retrospect*, 33–43.

The original group of Canadian naval cadets serving in CGS *Canada* photographed with the ship's fisheries officers. In the front row, left to right, are cadets Henry Bate, Percy Nelles and John Barron. Standing in the rear row, left to right, are cadets Charles Beard, Barry German, Victor Brodeur and W.G. Wright. (LAC Notman-19121)

years at the college were to be followed by another year training at sea in a cruiser in preparation for sitting the lieutenant's qualifying examination. In October 1910 royal permission was granted to add the prefix "Royal" to its title, a privilege the Royal Naval College of Canada (RNCC) enjoyed ten months before the navy itself. One month later, the civil service commission held an examination for thirty vacancies, with thirty-four boys taking part of which twenty-one passed. Entering on 19 January 1911, the RNCC's first class produced a large proportion of what would be the senior commanders of the Canadian navy in the Second World War, including L.W. Murray, G.C. Jones, C.R.H. Taylor, and F.L. Houghton.[66]

Recruiting for sailors did not begin in earnest until February 1911, after the training cruisers *Niobe* and *Rainbow* had arrived in Canada and were ready to accommodate them. Seamen were entered between the ages of fifteen and twenty-three, stokers from eighteen to twenty-three, and boys from fourteen to sixteen. All had to engage for seven years from the age of eighteen, with the option of re-engaging (if recommended) for one or two further periods of seven years each. In the early period, the Royal Navy was also relied on for a considerable proportion of the ratings required. This was not an uncommon practice, as the British navy had acted as mentor and exemplar to many navies around the world. Service in the RCN proved particularly attractive, at least initially, because sailors were paid by Ottawa at Canadian rates, which were more than twice the wages being paid to sailors in the Royal Navy. The Admiralty also allowed pensioners and fleet reserve men to enlist in the Canadian navy, with the time being counted as RN service. Many did enlist, entering for a period of five years under special service engagements that carried gratuities not payable to general service personnel. Additionally, living conditions in Canadian ships generally exceeded those in British warships, as the additional fittings required to handle the extremes of weather made them more comfortable.[67]

In acquiring *Rainbow* and *Niobe*, attention had been paid to the crew accommodations because no habitable naval depot or shore barracks had yet been built in either Halifax or Esquimalt. Although the Department of Marine and Fisheries had occupied portions of the facilities after the informal transfer of control of the dockyards some years earlier, legal technicalities had delayed formal Canadian ownership. As a result, the properties had not been properly maintained—other than a few areas in immediate use—since the British departure. The 1909 defence conference had cleared the way for London to pass the Naval Establishments in British Possessions Act in October 1909, but Ottawa requested that the transfer be postponed until the training cruisers had arrived at their respective ports. The legal transfers were made by British orders-in-council of 13 October 1910 for Halifax and 4 May 1911 for Esquimalt. The Canadian government was to maintain the facilities in operational condition, store fuel and supplies for the Royal Navy, allow the British to use the workshops and tools (they would pay for labour and materials), inform the Admiralty before converting the properties to any other use, and take responsibility for any existing liabilities while charging rent to tenants, but were otherwise free to use the facilities as it

66. Tucker, *The Naval Service of Canada*, I, 156; and Milner, *Canada's Navy*, 23.

67. Tucker, *The Naval Service of Canada*, I, 152–53.

saw fit. The decision of whether to invest in refurbishing the older properties or building new infrastructure was held in abeyance, with the result that up to the outbreak of the First World War, naval personnel not carried on the strength of the dockyard, or in the case of Halifax on the strength of the naval college, were entered onto the books of the training cruiser assigned to that particular coast.[68]

Before the two Canadian cruisers departed Britain for their new home ports, a number of alterations had to be carried out to make them more suitable as training ships. These involved the installation of new heating systems, up-to-date galley equipment, and "the latest design of Marconi wireless instruments," as well as the enlargement of the cadet gun-room, and principal messes, and the removal of obsolete secondary armament. In July 1910, Kingsmill returned to England to attend to the sea trials of the two cruisers and officially take them over from the Admiralty. *Rainbow* was commissioned "His Majesty's Canadian Ship" on 4 August 1910 and received her sailing orders four days later, the first such distinctions accorded a Canadian warship. She left Portsmouth on 20 August for Esquimalt, sailing around South America by way of the Strait of Magellan, a distance of 15,000 miles, because the Panama Canal was not yet completed. Near Callao, Peru, she signalled headquarters in Ottawa that the German cruiser *Bremen* had been spotted conducting firing practice at a moored target, but provided no greater detail.[69] The rest of the voyage was uneventful, and she arrived in Esquimalt on 7 November to a gala reception. The *Victoria Colonist* effused that "history was made at Esquimalt…. Canada's blue ensign [denoting a government, though not necessarily naval, vessel] flies for the first time on the dominion's own fighting ship in the Pacific—the ocean of the future where some of the world's greatest problems will have to be worked out." The *Victoria Times* added, "she is the first fruits on this coast of the Canadian naval policy, the necessary forerunner of the larger vessels which will add dignity to our name and prestige to our actions."[70]

HMCS *Niobe*, meanwhile, had commissioned in Devonport on 6 September and sailed for Canada a month later, sporting a silk white ensign presented by the Queen. Her arrival in Halifax was timed, somewhat presumptuously, for 21 October, the hundred-and-fifth anniversary of the Battle of Trafalgar. Kingsmill marked the occasion by embarking in Canada and transferring to *Niobe* at the harbour mouth, thus becoming the first RCN admiral to hoist his broad pennant in a warship in Canadian waters. Henri Bourassa's *Le Devoir* greeted her in true partisan fashion, observing "the cruiser *Niobe*, heart of the Canadian fleet (Canadian in peacetime, imperial in wartime), arrived yesterday in Halifax." Other reports were more positive. Even the *Halifax Herald*—no enthusiast of Laurier or his policies—allowed that "once more Halifax becomes a naval headquarters. The four letters look strange, but we may get accustomed to the change from the old fashioned HMS, which Halifax once knew." In his speech replying to *Niobe*'s twenty-one gun salute, the new minis-

68. Ibid, 161, 392–94; and LeBlanc, "Historical Synopsis of the Organization and Development of the RCN," nd, 17–22, DHH 87/93.

69. "Brief History of HMCS *Rainbow*," nd, DHH 81/520/8000, "HMCS *Rainbow*"; and "Brief History of HMCS *Niobe*," nd, DHH 81/520/8000, "HMCS *Niobe*."

70. Victoria *Colonist*, 8 November 1910; and Victoria *Times*, 7 November 1910.

ter of the naval service proclaimed that "this event tells the story of a dawning epoch of self-reliance" and increased responsibilities.[71]

As the acquisition of *Niobe* and *Rainbow* moved ahead, so too had the tendering process for their eventual replacements. The shipbuilding program was an essential element of the government's naval policy, both in acquiring modern warships and expanding shipyards in Canada. Its size had been determined at the 1909 conference where the agreed upon plan of four Bristol light cruisers, a slightly smaller Boadicea cruiser, and six improved River-class destroyers, although a compromise, was not far removed from what Kingsmill had described in his original assessments early that year. Whereas he had originally envisioned building an indigenous force through gradual expansion, eventually including modern cruisers, the agreed plan would acquire them simultaneously with the entire fleet in place within three years. This was not unmanageable with the full support of government and voters, but if either or both of those were to hesitate, progress would slow. Domestic ship-building had the distinct advantage of encouraging the development of a modern indus-try, but because Canada lacked a yard capable of constructing large and modern ships, the move had a number of drawbacks, in that the effort would result in additional costs and increase the time to completion. Laurier was willing to accept the disadvantages as he was sure the cost of building an all-Canadian fleet would garner the support of Canadian vot-ers. The advantages of developing a Canadian shipbuilding industry would outweigh such factors as the time required, increased cost and regional disaffection. What he failed to appreciate was that the additional time and the perceived slights to certain regions would prove fatal to his naval policy.[72]

It was evident from the start that British assistance would be essential, in providing both the necessary specifications and the engineering experience for such an advanced project. Accordingly, in March 1910 Kingsmill opened communications with the Admiralty, seek-ing advice on a list of approved shipbuilding firms and on the handling of sensitive detailed drawings. The Admiralty response was entirely positive, agreeing to provide access as nec-essary to approved firms as well as any Canadian companies wishing to develop a bid— subject to "special precautionary measures … to insure [*sic*] secrecy".—offering additionally to provide qualified Royal Navy overseers to monitor progress and quality of work, and to undertake the actual letting of any contracts as had been done for Australia.[73] In antici-pation of a positive response, Desbarats had published a "Notice Concerning Construction of Vessels for the Canadian Navy" on 8 July 1910. He subsequently directed Kingsmill to accept the offer of Admiralty overseers but emphasized that "it would be essential that these

---

71. Tucker, *The Naval Service of Canada*, I, 142–45; and *Le Devoir*, 22 October 1910; *Halifax Herald*, 22 October 1910; and Hopkins, *The Canadian Annual Review, 1910*, 214–15.

72. Kingsmill to Brodeur, 19 April 1909, 1017-1-1, pt. 1, LAC, Record Group (hereafter RG) 24, vol. 3830. The similarities between the two plans are remarkable: for instance, Kingsmill also advocated the immediate acquisition of training cruisers for each coast that could be given a second role, that of fisheries protection. See Archibald, *The Fighting Ship in the Royal Navy*, 207, 230 for class details.

73. Kingsmill to Admiralty Secretary, 4 March 1910, Kingsmill to Desbarats, 5 August 1910, 29–6-2, pt. 1, LAC, RG 24, vol. 5604.

The rather unimposing front entrance to the Royal Naval College of Canada in Halifax. (LAC e007140883)

Cadets in an electrical class at the college. (LAC PA-128513)

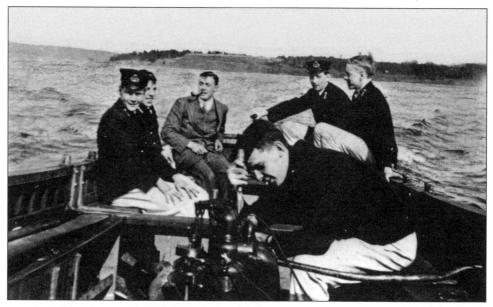

Cadets practising their boating skills. (LAC e007140884)

Staff and cadets of the first RNCC class of 1911 on the front steps of the college. (LAC PA-209545)

overseers should be for the time being, in the employ of the Canadian government." Although the department "would be very glad indeed" for their advice on the tenders received and "on the form of contract to be adopted," the "contract itself should be executed by the Canadian government and not the Admiralty.... The point which the Canadian government wishes to make perfectly clear is that the vessels are being built by them as a part of a distinct Canadian navy, and the various formal steps should be taken with that end in view."[74]

Despite that hopeful beginning, negotiations with the Admiralty soon became entangled in procedural difficulties that were not resolved until early 1911. By that time, over a dozen firms had indicated interest and a formal invitation to tender was finally issued on 4 February 1911. By May the requirement for the Boadicea-class cruiser had been dropped—her primary 4-inch gun armament being considered mismatched with the 6-inch guns of the other cruisers—the deletion being rationalized by the retention of *Niobe* in operational service. It had also been accepted that the intended timetable for construction was too ambitious. Firms were now asked to bid on the construction of four Bristol-class cruisers of the improved Weymouth type and six River-class destroyers of the improved Acorn type, all to be built in Canada within six years, with the first cruiser to be finished within three years of signing the contract, and another one each following year. Similarly, the first two destroyers were to be delivered within three years, and the additional ones at nine month intervals. Perhaps to simplify administration, it was intended that one firm would build all the ships of the program. While it was allowed that the vessels could be built on either coast, it was also pointed out that the terms of the Rush-Bagot Treaty prohibited the construction of warships on the Great Lakes. The reasoning behind the inclusion of that final stipulation is unclear, because Laurier had long since acquiesced to "the invisible revision" of Rush-Bagot by allowing the Americans to build warships on the lakes during the Spanish-American War (and then permitting the highly publicized passage into the Lakes of USS *Nashville*, a small third-class cruiser carrying eight 4-inch guns, in May 1909).[75]

To be sure, Bristol-class cruisers were too large to pass through the existing locks on the St Lawrence but, in recognizing the need to lure British builders to Canada, the government had recently passed legislation authorizing large subsidies to encourage the construction of dry docks and similar public works, monies that could have been directed to upgrading canals. The stipulation effectively precluded Ontario ship builders, and Laurier revealed where his own sympathies lay in allowing the Montreal Harbour Commission to provide the British firm of Vickers, Sons and Maxim deferred taxes and an

74. Desbarats to Kingsmill, 18 August 1910, 29–6-2, pt. 1, LAC, RG 24, vol. 5604.

75. Desbarats to Strathcona, 22 August 1910, 30 November 1910, 8 January 1911, and 12 September 1911, Admiralty to Strathcona, 9 September 1910, 29–6-2, pt. 1, LAC, RG 24, vol. 5604; Brodeur to Fisher, 24 December 1909, Fisher to Brodeur, 28 December 1909, "Correspondence Re: Purchase of *Niobe*" (*Sessional Paper No. 146a*; Ottawa 1910); and Alvin C. Gluek, "The Invisible Revision of the Rush-Bagot Agreement, 1898–1914," *Canadian Historical Review*, LX (December 1979), 466–84. Roger Sarty in "Canada and the Great Rapprochement, 1902–1914," B.J.C. McKercher and Lawrence Aronsen, eds., *The North Atlantic Triangle in a Changing World: Anglo-American-Canadian Relations, 1902–1956* (Toronto 1996), 35, notes that "perhaps the most striking thing about the furore over Rush-Bagot in 1909 was that it had no impact on the naval defence question."

extended lease on prime land to establish a shipyard in Montreal. With the added incentives of the Dry Dock Subsidies Act of 1910, construction on the new shipyard began in May 1910, eventually including a totally enclosed berth that could be heated to enable work through a typical Montreal winter when temperatures could dip to minus 30° Celsius. Canadian Vickers Limited was incorporated in June 1911 and proved to be "one of the more enduring legacies of Laurier's navalism," even as it diminished the prospects of naval support in Ontario.[76]

The government received seven tenders by the 1 May 1911 deadline, with six of the firms promising to establish shipyards in Canada. Other than Vickers, only one existing Canadian firm made a bid, the British and Canadian Shipbuilding and Dock Company, while one British firm mistakenly submitted a tender on the assumption that the ships could be built at its yard in England. The highest bid for ships to be built in Canada was $13,055,804, and the lowest was $11,280,000. The average of those six, at $12,421,4121, when compared to the $8,532,504 bid to build the vessels in Britain, shows that Laurier was not far off in his prediction of a 30-percent premium as the trade-off for building in Canada. While his departmental officials assessed the tenders, Brodeur used the occasion of an imperial conference in May and June 1911 to meet with representatives of the tendering firms and discuss the potential conditions of the contract. He returned to Ottawa to formally consider the bids, only to have parliament dissolved on 29 July before a decision could be made. As it was considered inappropriate for the government to award a contract during the course of an election campaign, a decision was postponed.[77]

Of the two warships the naval service had acquired, *Niobe* and *Rainbow*, the Admiralty began to raise the issue of their legal status even as the cruisers were being refitted in England. Although ostensibly a simple matter of scheduling, the British were unwilling to give a definite date for completion of the necessary work and it soon became apparent that the delays were tied to the larger issue of jurisdiction resulting from a shift of attitude within the Admiralty. The question of the Canadian ships' imperial status under the Naval Service Act arose at the same time that Australia was preparing its own naval legislation, the Naval Defence Act of 1910. Although both pieces of legislation allowed for exclusive control by the dominion government in time of peace, the circumstances under which control would revert to the Admiralty differed greatly. In the Canadian act, "emergency" was simply stated as "war, invasion or insurrection, real or apprehended," while the equivalent Australian interpretation defined "war" as "any invasion or apprehended invasion of, or attack or apprehended attack on the Commonwealth or any territory under the control of the Commonwealth by any enemy or armed force." Accordingly, on 5 February 1910, Kingsmill telegraphed his counterpart in Sydney to ask "whether, in the event of war, vessels of the Australian navy pass automatically without any action under control of Admiralty." The reply, received two days later, was that "transfer control to the Admiralty is not to be

76. Milner, *Canada's Navy*, 24–25; and J.D. Scott, *Vickers: A History* (London 1962), 58–59; and Eileen Reid Marcil, *Tall Ships and Tankers: The History of the Davie Shipbuilders* (Toronto 1997), 134–35.

77. Desbarats to Minister, 6 and 10 October 1911, DHH 2001/13; and Tucker, *The Naval Service of Canada*, I, 165.

automatic but subject to approval of Commonwealth government on declaration of war."[78] Laurier seemed satisfied that the differences in the acts were not great enough to necessitate amendments to the relevant sections concerning parliamentary control. The ambiguity of the Canadian "emergency" clause allowed for the use of naval forces, like the militia, in aid of the civil power, while sections 23 and 24 allowed the governor in council to place the naval service at the disposal of his majesty, subject to parliamentary approval within fifteen days.

The definition of jurisdiction had not been resolved to the Admiralty's satisfaction, although, initially at least, their lordships' preferences had been tempered by political expediency. Fisher had accepted McKenna's compromise with the assurance that the Canadians could eventually be brought around to participating in the proposed remodelling of naval dispositions in the Far East but the days of Fisher's influence were waning. The first sea lord fought a rearguard action against his increasingly numerous detractors throughout the fall of 1909 before agreeing to retirement in January 1910, the blow softened by his elevation to a peerage and the installment of Admiral Sir Arthur Wilson as the new first sea lord. Although a very capable officer afloat, as an administrator Wilson suffered from the dual handicaps of being "obstinate and full of idées fixes" and having an "inability to delegate work of any importance to others." As a result, according to historian Arthur Marder, "a new reform era could not be expected of Wilson. He did maintain the main lines of Fisher's policies; but he was not receptive to new ideas. His absorption in matériel policy, his neglect of personnel matters and the development of strategic thought, and his lack of vision made for a quiet though hardly progressive administration."[79]

Fisher's departure had been arranged on the understanding that his successor "must not reverse the reforms he had introduced over the previous five years." Lacking his predecessor's imagination, Wilson kept his part of the bargain even though he did not fully comprehend Fisher's naval revolution. "Universally regarded as the best fleet commander of his generation," the new first sea lord preferred building battleships for use in the North Sea. Over the course of his two years at the Admiralty, he greatly reduced the number of battle cruisers that Fisher had planned in favour of more dreadnoughts in the 1910–11 and 1911–12 estimates. Wilson's strategic concept, moreover, had little place for either viable local navies or dominion fleet units decentralized from Admiralty control. In Australia, where a battle cruiser had already been laid down as part of the 1909–10 program and the strategic situation provided some continued rationale for a regional squadron, Wilson was not strictly opposed to a fleet unit. In the Canadian case, where such a squadron would meet no strategic requirement either immediate or potential, the first sea lord was actively discouraging. There was no longer even an element of political incentive to temper the Admiralty's changed attitude, as McKenna found Wilson "very difficult" and preferred not to deal with him, instead focusing his energies on getting his estimates passed in the face

78. "Memorandum on Parliamentary Control of Navy," nd, LAC, MG 26 G, 219493–494; Strathcona to Brodeur, 7 February 1910, (*Sessional Paper No. 146*; Ottawa 1910), 6; and Tucker, *The Naval Service of Canada*, I, 385–92.

79. Marder, *From Dreadnought to Scapa Flow*, I, 213–14.

HMCS *Rainbow* entering Esquimalt Harbour on 7 November 1910 after completing her voyage from Portsmouth, England. (CWM 19790602-053)

Dignitaries are welcomed aboard *Rainbow* after her arrival at Esquimalt. Rear Admiral Kingsmill is in the centre of the photograph facing the camera. (CWM 19890167-005)

of renewed Cabinet opposition.[80] As a result, Canadian naval planning after January 1910 was influenced more by Admiralty policy than public debate. Although it is conjecture to tie the delays in refitting *Rainbow* and *Niobe* entirely to the change in attitude toward dominion navies, it is difficult to ignore the coincidence that the delay paralleled the duration of naval debate in Canada, suggesting that the Admiralty consciously postponed completion of work on the two cruisers.

There were certainly indications of British displeasure with the outcome of the debate in the Admiralty's implementation of Canadian policy. Their announcement in early June that *Rainbow* and *Niobe* were ready for commissioning was followed by notice that, pending resolution of questions as to whether the Naval Discipline Act binding sailors and officers to a code of discipline on the high seas would be applicable on Canadian ships, the Admiralty strongly recommended the adoption of "a provisional expedient ... that cruisers be commissioned by Admiralty under [the] white ensign and Naval Discipline Act, leaving of course full control of disposal of vessels to [the] Canadian Government."[81] Ottawa was understandably bewildered. Section 91 of the British North America Act gave authority for the Canadian parliament to legislate for a naval service; the Naval Service Act had included a clause providing for the crews of Canadian naval vessels to be held liable under the Naval Discipline Act; moreover, the King was commander-in-chief. The Admiralty remained adamant, however, that the Canadian government did not have the power "to legislate for discipline of ships of war outside Canadian waters," insisting instead that the scheme of having the ships under Admiralty commission but at Canada's disposal remained the best approach.[82] A standoff loomed as Ottawa remained equally determined that the ships be commissioned by Canada. While Paymaster P.J. Ling, in his newly appointed capacity as secretary to the Canadian naval staff, cabled the Admiralty that the "intention of [the] department is for the present vessels to be kept within territorial waters," Kingsmill was despatched to London to look into the matter personally, and A.B. Aylesworth, the Canadian minister of justice, in the Hague with regard to the fisheries treaty was asked to confer with the Admiralty on the legal question.[83]

Until a proper discussion of the legal question could be held, it was agreed that the "cruisers should sail as before proposed under instruction of Admiralty merely on voyage out, but that the formal transfer of vessels to Canadian government should take place in Canadian waters instead of here."[84] *Rainbow* sailed with the blue ensign at the stern, as was the custom for all other dominion government vessels that were understood to be non-military. *Niobe*'s captain, however, "short-circuited [the Canadian government] by asking

80. Nicolas Lambert, "Admiral Sir Arthur Knyvett-Wilson," Malcolm H. Murfett, ed., *The First Sea Lords: From Fisher to Mountbatten* (Westport, CT 1995), 35, 37–39. On the different strategic perspectives of Fisher and Wilson, see Lambert, *Fisher's Naval Revolution*, 201–06.

81. Greene, Assistant Secretary of the Admiralty, to Kingsmill, 16 June 1910, LAC, MG 27, II C4, docket 11.

82. Greene to Kingsmill, 27 June 1910, Private Secretary to First Lord (W.J. Evans) to Kingsmill, 30 June 1910, Kingsmill to Greene, 23 and 29 June 1910, LAC, MG 27 II C4, docket 11.

83. Ling to Admiralty, 4 July 1910, LAC, MG 27 II C4, docket 11.

84. Admiralty to Ottawa, 14 July 1910, LAC, MG 27 II C4, docket 11.

H.M. the Queen to present a white ensign to my ship ... [which] she very graciously did."[85] The formal transfer of *Niobe* did not occur until 12 November 1910, three weeks after her arrival in Halifax, and even then only after two messages from the government to the colonial secretary. Another suggestion by Lord Grey for a Canadianized white ensign, with a green maple leaf superimposed on the centre of the Cross of St George, seems to have been completely ignored by London, despite the governor general's admonition that "white ensign with no distinctive Canadian mark will not be agreed by ministers—they point out that it is the ensign at stern which denotes control."[86]

That more was at stake than the mere maintenance of discipline was revealed later that summer when the Admiralty forwarded a "Memorandum on Status of Dominion Ships of War" to Canada, Australia, and New Zealand. The document's opening quickly dispelled the subtleties that had guided the discussion at the 1909 Imperial Defence Conference, as it stipulated a very different set of governing principles for the new dominion navies: "while the administration and control of the Canadian and Australian naval forces should rest with the dominion governments, there should be the same standard of training and discipline in these forces as in the Royal Navy, and that they should all as far as possible develop as integral parts of one imperial navy." Accordingly, the remainder of the memorandum was concerned with setting the conditions for settlement of questions as to, first, "the measures requisite to give the naval forces of the dominions the international status of war-ships of a sovereign state," and second, "the means of employing the naval forces of the dominions on imperial services, so far as the governments of the dominions consent to such employment, in time of peace as well as during war."[87]

Paying such scant attention to colonial aspirations was also reflected in the Admiralty's suggestion that the simplest way of defining jurisdiction was to accord each dominion a particular "station" in which it would be responsible for the protection of the sovereign interests of the empire. In the Australian case, where there was the strategic imperative of filling the gap in naval defence left by the withdrawn Royal Navy squadrons and a greater chance of the dominion fleet unit coming into contact with hostile foreign powers, no difficulties were foreseen in the implementation of the scheme within the rough boundaries of the former Australasian station. At the same time it was felt that the "geographical situation of Canada does not permit of the assignment of any area outside of the territorial waters of the dominion similar to that which is possible in the case of Australia. How far the area of 'Canadian waters' should extend beyond the actual territorial waters of the dominion must be a matter for arrangement between the two [Canadian and imperial] governments."[88]

There were two obstacles to treating Canada the same as Australia. The first was the way the fleet unit question had been resolved at the 1909 conference: Australia had elected to build a full fleet unit, which could easily be incorporated into the imperial navy scheme;

85. Jackman, *At Sea and By Land*, 96.

86. Grey to Brodeur, 21 November 1910, Grey to Harcourt, 21 November 1910, Grey to Crewe, 7 November 1910, Grey to Harcourt, 16 November 1910, Harcourt to Grey, 16 November 1910, LAC, MG 27 II C4, docket 13.

87. Admiralty, "Memorandum on Status of Dominion Ships of War," August 1910, LAC, MG 26 G, 219575–584.

88. Ibid.

Canada had not. One year later, the Admiralty was simply adhering to the policy held in its original memorandum to the 1909 conference. In the simple calculations of the Wilson Admiralty, a fleet unit without a battle cruiser did not satisfy the basic criteria; hence, no fleet unit, no local control. The second obstacle was the Canadian requirement for a two-ocean navy: where a Pacific Station on the West Coast probably did not present an insurmountable problem, the Admiralty worldview did not allow for a Canadian station on the Atlantic. Indeed, Fisher's fleet reorganization of 1905 had included the abolition of the North America and West Indies Squadron, constituting in its place the Fourth Cruiser Squadron. Normally referred to as the "Particular Service Squadron," its wartime role was to be available to reinforce either the Channel or Atlantic fleets. In peacetime, "other than the fact that it was anticipated [it] would visit Canada, Bermuda, and the West Indies annually, it had no established itinerary nor an assigned base aside from its nominal home manning port at Plymouth."[89] If the limited missions the Royal Navy anticipated in the North Atlantic could be met by such a simple expedient, there was no need for a full station to be allocated to Canada.

The legal battle between the Canadian government and the Admiralty raged throughout the fall of 1910 and into the winter of 1911. Even when Lord Grey expressed his desire to cruise to the West Indies in *Niobe* in the spring of 1911 as a symbolic inauguration of the new navy and Kingsmill later insisted that such a cruise was essential to provide overdue training for the officers and men of the naval service, the Colonial Office and the Admiralty persisted in objecting to *Niobe* and *Rainbow* leaving territorial waters until the whole question of the status of dominion navies was resolved. This effectively limited *Niobe* to a berth in Halifax as an alongside training ship, while *Rainbow* conducted fisheries patrols in British Columbian territorial waters. Although both ships were performing duties pretty much in keeping with what had been anticipated when they were procured, their legal leash kept them from fulfilling the government's goal for a Canadian owned and controlled naval force. As Brodeur wrote to Grey in March 1911, "I am extremely sorry to learn that the Admiralty are opposed to the *Niobe* going to Bermuda. That is absolutely discouraging, because I do not know how it will be possible for us to carry out our project of the creation of a Canadian navy with such restrictions. I am sure that nobody here would have accepted the proposal of a local navy if we had been told that our vessels could not move outside of the three mile limit."[90]

If the Admiralty appears to have been overly doctrinaire in its attitude toward autonomous local naval forces, it was acting within the British government's own parameters. The root of the problem was not so much the status of dominion navies per se as it was the status of the dominions themselves. Although the exercise of Canadian control over its internal landmass and within immediate offshore waters had been evolving in the

---

89. Roger Willock, "Gunboat Diplomacy: Operations of the North America and West Indies Squadron, 1875–1915, Part II: Fuel Oil and Wireless," *American Neptune*, XXVIII:2 (April 1968), 102.

90. Brodeur to Grey, 13 March 1911, Grey to Harcourt, 22 November 1910, 4 March 1911, Harcourt to Grey, 25 November 1910, Grey to Brodeur, 10 and 14 March 1911, LAC, MG 27 II C4, docket 13; and Roger Sarty, *The Maritime Defence of Canada* (Toronto 1997), 63. Grey sympathized with the Canadian position, but he also tried to help them understand the Admiralty.

decades after confederation, the question of extending Ottawa's jurisdiction beyond the three-mile territorial limit had yet to be broached. The British government, through the power of the Royal Navy, believed themselves to be the de facto arbiter of international law around most of the globe. If an element of the imperial fleet was not under the direct control of London, it would challenge a wide variety of existing assumptions. For that reason, the status of dominion warships operating on the high seas was a matter of some import under international law. As one historian has observed, "the problems that had to be overcome while establishing an independent Canadian navy were ... inextricably interlinked with the development of Canada's independence in foreign affairs. Prior to the Statute of Westminster in 1931, Canada did not have the legal right to have a foreign policy separate from that of Britain."[91]

That does not mean that the jurisdiction issue was necessarily cast in stone. Political structures within the empire were evolving, especially in regard to the self-governing dominion in North America, which served to temper the Admiralty's reticence. The sheer isolation of Australia from any other significant power worked to diminish concerns in that quarter, just as Britain's rapprochement with the United States in the early twentieth century worked to reduce tensions between those two powers. Where disputes remained between Canada and the US, usually involving fish, treaty-making power was devolving from Britain to the dominion, though in a somewhat tenuous fashion. The 1908 commission of inquiry that had led to the reorganization of the Department of Marine and Fisheries had also pointed to the need for "an improvement in the administration of that class of public affairs which related to matters other than those of purely internal concern," and a bill for the creation of a Department of External Affairs had received Royal Assent on 19 May 1909.[92] Tellingly, Laurier declined to name a separate minister to the department in order to avoid confusion over jurisdiction and retained strict personal control of the portfolio—as, indeed, would prime ministers until 1946, when Mackenzie King appointed Louis St Laurent as the first secretary of state for external affairs.

The Asquith Liberals, meanwhile, had come to power in 1905 determined not to concede control over foreign policy to the dominions, even though they were less committed than their Conservative predecessors to imperial centralization. Over the years, defence had been seen as one of the stronger links binding the empire together, succeeding where efforts to arrange closer economic and political ties had failed. In the view of the British Liberals, the means to closer imperial defence efforts focused less upon overt centralization and more upon, as Asquith later termed it, "spontaneous cooperation." This interpretation had already paid dividends in Secretary of State for War Lord Haldane's efforts to form an

91. Dan McNeil, "The Development of Canadian Foreign Policy: A Naval Dimension," Peter T. Haydon and Ann L. Griffiths, eds., *Canada's Pacific Naval Presence: Purposeful or Peripheral* (Halifax 1999), 21.

92. Canada, Parliament, House of Commons, *Debates*, 2 March 1909, cols. 1978–2008.

93. CID minutes, 30 May 1911, quoted in Robert Joseph Gowen, "British Legerdemain at the 1911 Conference: The Dominions, Defense Planning, and the Renewal of the Anglo-Japanese Alliance," *Journal of Modern History*, VII: 3 (September 1980), 393–94; and see also Andrew Gordon, *The Rules of the Game: Jutland and British Naval Command* (London 1996), 274–77 and R.A. Preston, *Canada and "Imperial Defense": A Study of the Origins of the British Commonwealth's Defense Organization, 1867–1919* (Durham, NC 1967), 375–78.

imperial general staff and have colonial forces engage in common training so that they might gradually be prepared to fight on the European continent alongside the British Army.[93] The strategy had convinced Canada's minister of militia and defence, Sir Frederick Borden, to apply imperial standards to the militia's training and, to a degree, this was the argument McKenna had employed successfully on Brodeur in the summer of 1909. As it turned out, the first lord would soon have the chance to re-engage the Canadians on the issue.

The exasperation Brodeur had expressed in his letter to Lord Grey on 13 March 1911 over the status of the Canadian navy, however, soon abated. In the same letter, the minister of marine and fisheries informed the governor general that, after several delays, a Montreal lawyer, R.C. Smith, had been retained to go to London to discuss the legal question with the Admiralty in advance of the imperial conference that was scheduled for May. Without the benefit of private correspondence, it is difficult to glean the substance of Smith's negotiations beyond the technical details of his official reports.[94] What is noteworthy, however, is the surprising ease, after some initial lobbying, with which solutions were found for the four major areas of contention: the application of naval discipline; the limits of territorial jurisdiction; visiting foreign ports; and seniority when Canadian and British ships operated in company.

By the time Laurier, Brodeur and Borden arrived in London, much had been accomplished and it only remained for the naval minister and the Admiralty secretary to initial the document to be tabled at the conference. The combination of persistence and goodwill produced a solution that largely met the competing demands of dominion navies, imperial fleets acting as one, and those who protested that the dominions were doing little for their own or imperial defence.[95] The British prime minister set the tone in his opening remarks:

> There are ... proposals put forward from responsible quarters which aim at some closer form of political union as between the component members of the empire, and which, with that object, would develop existing, or devise new, machinery.... I pronounce no opinion on this class of proposals. I will only venture the observation that I am sure we shall not lose sight of the value of elasticity and flexibility in our imperial organisation, or of the importance of maintaining ... the principle of ministerial responsibility to parliament.... I will refer to one other topic of even greater moment—that of imperial defence. Two years ago, in pursuit of the first resolution of the conference of 1907, we summoned here in London a subsidiary conference to deal with the subject of defence, over which I had the honour to preside. The results achieved—particularly in the inauguration of the policy of dominion fleets adopted by Canada and Australia—are of a far-reaching character.... It is in the highest

---

94. Brodeur to Grey, 13 March 1911, LAC, MG 27 II C4, docket 13. There is considerable material in this respect in the Brodeur Papers' docket 14 as well. See also G.J. Desbarats biographical file, file B, DHH.

95. Brodeur, "L.P. Brodeur and the Origins of the Royal Canadian Navy," 30; and Tucker, *The Naval Service of Canada*, I, 168–69.

degree desirable that we should take advantage of your presence here to take stock of the possible risks and dangers to which we are or may be in common exposed; and to weigh carefully the adequacy, and the reciprocal adaptiveness, of the contributions we are respectively making to provide against them.[96]

As senior prime minister, Laurier led the dominions' response by remarking that it was his "happy privilege of representing here a country which has no grievances to set forth and very few suggestions to make," and "that if there is one principle upon which the British empire can live, it is imperial unity based upon local autonomy."[97] The actual conference discussion was anti-climatic, with the agreement requiring only the approval of the elected representatives attending the conference. As for Canada and Australia, the naval agreement included the following provisions:

1. The naval services and forces of both dominions were to be controlled exclusively by their respective governments.

2. Their training and discipline were to be generally the same as, and personnel interchangeable with, those of the Royal Navy.

3. The King's Regulations and Admiralty Instructions, and the Naval Discipline Act, as already adopted by the dominions were to be valid; but should the dominions desire any changes they would communicate with the British government.

4. The Admiralty agreed to lend to the younger services, during their infancy, whatever flag officers and other officers and men might be needed, such personnel to be, as far as possible, from or connected with the dominion concerned, and in any case volunteers.

5. The service of any officer of the Royal Navy in a dominion ship, or the converse, was to count for the purposes of retirement, pay, and promotion, as if it had been performed in that officer's own force.

6. Canadian and Australian naval stations were created and defined: the Canadian Atlantic station covered the waters north of 30°N and west of 40°W, except for certain waters off Newfoundland, and the Canadian Pacific station included the part of that ocean north of 30°N and east of the 180th meridian.

---

96. "Precis of the Proceedings," 23 May 1911, Maurice Ollivier, ed., *The Colonial and Imperial Conferences from 1887 to 1937*, II: *Imperial Conferences* (Ottawa 1954), 52–53.

97. Ibid, 54.

7. The Admiralty would be notified whenever it was intended to send dominion warships outside their own stations, and a dominion government, before sending one of its ships to a foreign port, would obtain the concurrence of the British government.

8. The commanding officer of a dominion warship in a foreign port would carry out the instructions of the British government in the event of any international question arising, in which case the government of the dominion concerned would be informed.

9. A dominion warship entering a foreign port without a previous arrangement, because of an emergency, would report her reasons for having put in to the commander in chief of that station or to the Admiralty.

10. In the case of a ship of the Royal Navy meeting a dominion warship, the senior officer should command in any ceremony of intercourse or where united action should have been decided upon; but not so as to interfere with the execution of any orders which the junior might have received from his own government.

11. In order to remove any uncertainty about seniority, dominion officers would be shown in the Navy List.

12. In the event of there being too few officers of the necessary rank belonging to a dominion service to complete a court martial ordered by that service, the Admiralty undertook to make the necessary arrangements if requested to do so.

13. In the interest of efficiency dominion warships were to take part from time to time in fleet exercises with ships of the Royal Navy, under command of the senior officer, who was not, however, to interfere further than necessary with the internal economy of the dominion ships concerned.

14. Australian and Canadian warships would fly the white ensign at the stern and the flag of the dominion at the jack-staff.

15. In time of war, when the naval service of a dominion, or any part thereof, were put at the disposal of the imperial government by the dominion authorities, the ships would form an integral part of the British fleet, and would remain under the control of the British Admiralty during the continuance of the war.[98]

---

98. Tucker, *The Naval Service of Canada*, I, 166–67.

The Canadian government, therefore, had prevailed on practically every issue other than having a distinctive dominion ensign. Presented with such a simple resolution, it is reasonable to ask why the Admiralty, after so much delay and obstructionism, was willing to forego its claims to virtually complete control of dominion navies. The answer lies in the fact that First Lord McKenna, with the backing of his prime minister, was able to use the conference forum to assert political control over the Admiralty. It was also apparent that the dominions were willing to concede standards of discipline and training to the Admiralty but would not accept surrendering ultimate control of their naval forces to London, no matter how anxious they were to get their navies operational. Taking a different tack, the War Office was finding that unity of discipline and training was assuring de facto integration of the empire's military forces even though the dominions would not agree to de jure unity of command. This does not appear to have gone unnoticed in the Admiralty's corridors. As one historian of the period has concluded:

> the most tempting explanation of why the British decided not to follow through with their initial design of squeezing the dominions for more binding commitments toward the defense of the empire was simply that, on second thought, none were really needed. [British] Liberal policy of relying on uniformity to integrate the armed forces of the empire was working too well by 1911 to risk changing it. All that the British had to do at the imperial conference was to make sure that the tempo of dominion defense activity did not slacken: imperial loyalty could be counted on in an emergency to do the rest.[99]

Indeed, the agreement's far greater territorial jurisdiction, in the form of a complete station off either coast, and higher standards of training meant that the Canadian government had been induced to greatly modify Laurier's original naval policy. Moreover, a fleet unit capable of effective integration with imperial naval forces in time of war had replaced what would have amounted to little more than an expanded fisheries protection service. Even if the Canadian navy did not include an Indomitable-class battle cruiser as its centrepiece, Laurier's pronouncement would remain definitive: "When Britain is at war, Canada is at war; there is no distinction."

The jurisdiction issue had not been resolved in time to allow the nascent Canadian fleet to participate in the naval review at Spithead on 24 June 1911 to celebrate the coronation of King George V. Canada was, however, represented by a marching contingent from *Niobe*, consisting of a lieutenant, two midshipmen—Percy Nelles and Victor Brodeur—and thirty-five ratings. Further official recognition came within a few weeks, when the Colonial Office responded to an outstanding request from the Canadian government with a notice that "his majesty having been graciously pleased to authorize that the Canadian naval forces shall be designated the 'Royal Canadian Navy,' this title is to be officially adopted, the abbreviation thereof being 'RCN.'"[100] With its status resolved and construction of a home-

---

99. Gowen, "British Legerdemain at the 1911 Conference," 411.

100. Desbarats to Undersecretary of State for External Affairs, 30 January 1911, Colonial Secretary to Governor-General, 16 August 1911, 15–1-4, LAC, RG 24, vol. 5591.

built fleet imminent, by the summer of 1911 the RCN's future seemed to have brightened. Unfortunately, it would quickly prove a false dawn.

Although the hurdle of Admiralty acceptance had finally been cleared, Laurier returned from London only to find that opposition to his government had grown and he was likely facing a general election a full year earlier than anticipated. In January, the prime minister had concluded negotiations for an expanded reciprocal trade agreement with the United States, which the two countries agreed specifically to implement through concurrent legislation rather than a formal treaty so that Canada would not have to seek British approval. In Laurier's absence, however, Robert Borden had stumped across the country building opposition to the reciprocity agreement and when parliament reconvened on 19 July he was sufficiently emboldened to mount a filibuster against the legislation. The tactic of invoking closure to cut off debate had not yet been conceived, so Laurier brought the filibuster to an end by asking the governor general to dissolve parliament on 29 July, fully confident he would win the general election set for 21 September. Most contemporary commentators agreed with the Montreal *Herald*'s evaluation that "each party will dwell on other subjects during the campaign, but the decision of the electorate will rest on Reciprocity."[101] That both parties planned to emphasize issues other than the navy is reflected in the fact that neither Liberal nor Conservative election manifestos made any mention of the navy. The only reference to the question at all was the claim by the Liberal press "that the reciprocity issue in Quebec would sidetrack the navy, eliminate the nationalists and leave the Laurier influence paramount."[102]

Neither party's leader doubted that the new naval service would be a crucial issue in Quebec, however. Anti-navy feeling had been evident in an Ottawa by-election in January 1910, where a traditionally Liberal seat was only narrowly won by Laurier's party after a campaign fought exclusively on the issue just as the naval bill was being introduced in parliament. An October 1910 byelection in Laurier's former constituency of Drummond-Arthabaska also featured the naval issue as its central theme. The resultant defeat of a well-known Liberal by an obscure nationaliste candidate jolted Laurier's confidence in his Quebec support. The implications of the October result were not lost on Robert Borden either. Although he did not agree with Monk's and Bourassa's opposition to a Canadian navy ever serving under Admiralty control, the Conservative leader preferred to overlook that discrepancy in the interests of party unity so as to keep alive the prospect of defeating Laurier in his home province. Fuelled by Conservative money from Ontario and with *Le Devoir* serving as its mouthpiece, the coalition of the Conservative Monk and the nationaliste Bourassa began to organize in earnest. The perceived threat to Liberal election chances in Quebec also convinced Laurier of the political wisdom of going to the polls a year early before Monk's claim that reciprocity was simply the prime minister's attempt "to dig a big ditch to hide the nefarious policy of his naval bill" could take root in the province.[103]

---

101. Montreal *Herald*, 31 July 1911; and Roger Riendeau, *A Brief History of Canada* (Markham 2000), 186.

102. J. Castell Hopkins, *The Canadian Annual Review of Public Affairs, 1911* (Toronto 1912), 158; and Schull, *Laurier*, 530.

103. Monk quoted in Norman Hillmer and J.L. Granatstein, *Empire to Umpire: Canada and the World to the 1990s* (Toronto 1994), 41; and Tucker, *The Naval Service of Canada*, I, 138–39.

The opposition's strategy of tying the navy personally to Laurier was not only good politics, it also recognized the way the prime minister had handled maritime affairs. Throughout his ministry, Laurier's predilection had always been to place his ministers of Marine and Fisheries nominally in charge of naval issues, while he actually managed their scope and timing. When Brodeur took ill in the fall of 1909, Laurier did away entirely with this façade, taking the lead in steering the passage of the Naval Service Act through parliament. Through the navy's first winter of 1910–11, in the wake of the Drummond-Arthabaska loss and while the jurisdiction question was being negotiated, he had proceeded cautiously. Now, secure in the knowledge that an acceptable Canadian naval policy was finally settled to British satisfaction, Laurier judged that the time had come to defend it vigorously to crush Bourassa's challenge to his power once and for all. In the lead up to the election call, he took two decisive actions to breathe life into the naval service. *Niobe*, which he had confined to the local Halifax area, was ordered to undertake a summer training cruise to Quebec City, Charlottetown, and Yarmouth—supposedly to show the flag but in truth for "electioneering ... by any other name."[104] At the same time, he named former Postmaster General Rodolphe Lemieux to be minister of the naval service, with the ailing Brodeur appointed to the Supreme Court. Lemieux also took over as Laurier's Quebec lieutenant to organize a formidable "résistance liberale" against the nationalistes.[105]

Even so, the Monk-Bourassa campaign had taken far too deep a hold for Québécois to be fully persuaded by Liberal claims that reciprocity was the real issue. It was in Ontario that free trade sidetracked naval policy—and then only at the expense of Liberal support. Borden, meanwhile, proved quite willing to play politics with Laurier's naval policy, characterizing it as being either too much or too little depending on the audience, letting nationalistes in Quebec denounce it as a tool of imperial machination, and implying in English Canada that the projected navy would uselessly lead to the dismemberment of the empire. His one major pronouncement on the issue was to label the Liberals' plan "an unfortunate blunder." He explained, "The question of Canada's permanent co-operation in imperial naval defence involves far-reaching consideration. The government proposals were clearly a political makeshift and not a serious attempt to deal with a difficult question. Responsibility for empire defence clearly involves some voice in empire policy. Canada's permanent and effective co-operation in naval defence can only be accomplished by proposals which take account of this consideration and any such proposals should be submitted to the people for their approval."[106]

The common thread within the Bourassa-Borden-Sifton-Monk coalition—described as "what a salad!" by Laurier[107]—was their distaste for both the Naval Service Act and Laurier personally. The group's widely differing opinions on a variety of other political questions made it inherently unstable, but it held together long enough to defeat the Laurier

104. German, *The Sea is at Our Gates*, 29.

105. Robert Rumilly, *Henri Bourassa* (Montreal 1953), 401–14.

106. Montreal *Gazette*, 15 and 16 August 1911.

107. Schull, *Laurier*, 531. See R.L. Borden, *Robert Laird Borden: His Memoirs* (Toronto 1938), I, 183–9 on the formation of the alliance.

government. In the end, while the naval issue was an important factor in the election result, it was hardly the decisive one. When the ballots were tallied on 21 September, Laurier still carried Quebec, although with a much-reduced majority of thirty-seven Liberals against twenty-seven Conservatives and nationalistes, suggesting that "his cautious policies still had considerable support there."[108] Most other provinces balanced off, but it was the Conservative sweep of Ontario on the issue of reciprocity that made the biggest difference with seventy-two seats against thirteen for the Liberals. Laurier's gamble that the implementation of his naval policy would prove to be its vindication was lost, but not decisively as an issue unto itself. With the Liberal defeat, however, the fate of the fledgling Royal Canadian Navy was placed in the hands of a coalition that had dedicated itself on the hustings to its demise.

Uncertainty about the navy's future during the ongoing debate meant that its development had already begun to stagnate under the Liberals, even before Robert Borden's Conservatives came to power. The failure to maintain essential facilities at either Halifax or Esquimalt in the half-dozen years since their transfer to Canadian control; Laurier's insistence that all ten warships be built in Canada whatever the delay; and caution in embarking upon an active recruiting and training program, combined to impede progress. To make matters worse, barely had *Niobe* commenced her 1911 summer training cruise than she ran aground in fog on the shoals off Cape Sable, Nova Scotia, on 30 July. Effective damage control by the crew saved the ship and Admiral Kingsmill rightly praised the efforts of the crew in the local press when he arrived in Halifax to assess the situation. "The discipline on the *Niobe* by the boys and young recruits was everything one could wish," the naval director informed the *Halifax Herald* in emphasizing the Canadian composition of the lower deck. "With the ship in the position she was, a gale of wind blowing and dense fog, the Canadian boys behaved fully up to the traditions of the British navy ... Of course, the ship's crew and officer displayed fine discipline, but I am speaking now of the Canadian boys and recruits."[109] Despite Kingsmill's public relations efforts, however, *Niobe*'s near-wrecking came to symbolize the new service. Repaired and refloated in the Halifax dry dock in January 1912, she was laid up pending the unveiling of the new government's naval policy.[110]

An important cause of the accident was faulty navigation, a court martial found that the course chosen by the navigator would have been a safe one, "provided no tide or current had been experienced," conditions seldom found in the area. The commander of Halifax dockyard, who was also the commander headquarter staff and senior lieutenant of the naval college, reported that the court martial "are of the opinion that the navigating officer, Lieutenant Charles White, should have been on the bridge himself between 10 pm and midnight to fix the ship's position and to take the only alternative of hauling out and running a line of soundings" when other navigation aids were obscured by fog. The waters *Niobe* was travelling through were simply too treacherous to leave the bridge to the officer

---

108. Hillmer and Granatstein, *Empire to Umpire*, 41.

109. *Halifax Herald*, 2 August 1911.

110. Canada, Department of the Naval Service, *Report of the Department of the Naval Service for the Fiscal Year Ending March 31, 1912* (Ottawa 1913), 18–19.

The 11,000-ton Diadem-class cruiser HMS *Niobe* carried sixteen 6-inch guns, twelve 12-pounders, five 3-pounders and two 18-inch torpedo tubes. (DND CN 6732)

Perhaps in reaction to the prohibition on *Niobe* leaving Canadian territorial waters, some of the cruiser's ratings demonstrate the lower deck's sense of humour. (CWM 20030174-033)

of the watch. The latter, Lieutenant Lord Alastair Graham, "should have realised that the shore lights were obscured and informed the Captain and Navigating Officer accordingly." As for the captain, Commander W.B. Macdonald, holding overall responsibility for the actions of his officers and ratings, an initial report found that he had been negligent in not ensuring that the navigating officer and the officer of the watch carried out their duties effectively. The ultimate finding on the matter, no doubt recognizing that the captain could not be disciplined every time someone under his command made a mistake, simply found that he had "left proper orders and had these been carried out he would have been informed of the shore lights not being sighted in time to have taken the necessary steps to avoid an accident."[111]

Having played partisan politics with the Canadian navy, using both ends of the naval debate to undermine Laurier in order to help win the election, Robert Borden arrived in office with no coherent naval policy of his own. On the other hand, it is easily overlooked that Borden, despite his opposition to Laurier's naval program, did recognize the need for a national naval force to meet Canadian requirements. Without fully understanding the degree to which shifting Admiralty policy had affected his predecessor's decisions, he believed Laurier had erred simply in attempting too ambitious a scheme. He would soon experience the vagaries of Admiralty policy for himself, but for the immediate future his previously firm stand against the Naval Service Act would make it difficult for him to carry out its provisions. Political necessity now dictated that any new policy would have to rationalize the disconnects between the opposing wings of his party. Hoping to rebuild the original consensus for expansion of the Fisheries Protection Service into a local defence force, Borden had only a vague notion of combining an "emergency contribution" with a "permanent policy."

The new prime minister planted the seeds for the two-track policy he had burdened himself with as far back as the debate over the Foster resolution, calling for the creation of a Canadian navy, in March 1909. Although his stand at that time clearly favoured creating a navy, he did allow that some sort of contribution might be necessary in the event of a serious emergency and slowly shifted the balance between these positions as the contributionist wing of his party increased its agitation. In a 1909 memorandum to Sir Richard McBride, the Conservative premier of British Columbia and an early vocal champion of financial contribution, Borden still argued for the development of a Canadian navy to "proceed cautiously and by slow beginnings."[112] During the opening debate on the Naval Service Act less than two months later he confirmed his previous position, describing Laurier's enlarged scheme as "too much for carrying experiments in the organization of a Canadian naval service," although also declaring that, with an emergency apparently "near at hand," he had come to feel the need for a cash contribution.[113] By the fall of 1910, against

---

111. Court Martial to DNS, 29 January 1912, Ling to Commander in Charge RNCC, 30 November 1911, "Conclusions," nd, Commander Halifax Dockyard to Secretary Naval Service, 14 August 1911, 1079-3-18, LAC, RG 24, vol. 4059.

112. Borden to McBride, 19 November 1909, British Columbia Archives (hereafter BCA), ADD MSS 347, series IV, vol, 1, file 1/5.

113. Canada, Parliament, House of Commons, *Debates*, 12 January 1910, col. 1749; Sarty, *Maritime Defence of Canada*, 20–21; and Tucker, *The Naval Service of Canada*, I, 175.

the backdrop of the Drummond-Arthabaska byelection, Borden's thinking on the issue had evolved to include a distinctly Canadian take on the principle of "no taxation without representation," stating that "when Canada, with the other great dominions within the empire, embarks upon a policy of permanent co-operation in the naval defence of the empire, it ought, from every constitutional standpoint, from every reasonable standpoint as well, to have some voice as to the issues of peace and war within the empire."[114]

When he became prime minister in September 1911, Borden was aware he was presiding over a divided federal party, one that had not exercised political power for more than a decade. His Cabinet selections reflected the need to include administrative experience, while downplaying policy differences on issues such as the naval question. As naval minister—which was still combined with responsibility for the Department of Marine and Fisheries—he appointed the former premier of New Brunswick, John Douglas Hazen, a contributionist. That side of the political equation was balanced by the appointment of Monk to Public Works, a move that left Lord Grey "a little uneasy and apprehensive ... that [this] does not mean a weak or retrogressive naval policy."[115] Whatever his views on the navy, Monk was the acknowledged leader of the Quebec Conservatives and therefore had to be in Cabinet, although his honesty suggested that the department would operate with less political patronage than previously.[116] Another change in the naval calculus was the replacement as governor general of the decidedly pro-navy Lord Grey with the Duke of Connaught, whose interest in things naval rarely exceeded indifference. Nonetheless, the administration of the naval service maintained some continuity, with Borden following the precedent set by Laurier in 1896 of not opting to dismiss, wholesale, dominion civil servants, even though, in this particular case, both Desbarats and Kingsmill had Liberal roots.

Although Borden was not anxious to revive the naval issue, his two-track policy was given some impetus in the fall of 1911. On 7 November, he had occasion to meet with Sir William White, a former director of naval construction at the Admiralty, who was visiting Canada in his capacity as a director of the Grand Trunk Railway. In the course of their conversation, Borden apparently asked the naval expert for his views on the question of Canadian naval policy. White responded with a memorandum to the prime minister describing ways that Canada could help in the naval defence of the empire. White's proposals included the old scheme of subsidizing mail steamships' conversion in wartime to auxiliary merchant cruisers, and a Canadian naval force with a number of protected cruisers, the construction of which might encourage the development of a modern shipbuilding industry in Canada, even though "it would take a considerable time before Canada could build warships both rapidly and cheaply." Finally, White suggested that even if dominion forces did not include dreadnought battleships, any assistance rendered by the dominions "will best take the form of financial contributions to [the] necessary expenditure on building and maintaining such a fleet."[117] Within only a couple of days of Borden's meeting with White,

114. Canada, Parliament, House of Commons, *Debates*, 21 November 1910, col. 35.

115. Grey to Borden, 29 September and 2 October 1911, LAC, MG 26 H, reel C-4199, 597–99, 601–02.

116. Brown, *Borden*, I, 207.

117. White to Borden, with enclosure, 28 December 1911, cited in Tucker, *The Naval Service of Canada*, I, 205–06.

Henri Bourassa wrote an editorial in *Le Devoir* on 9 November that "reviewed, almost sympathetically a recent argument … in favour of a naval contribution by Canada in return for imperial representation."[118]

Still, the government's inclination was to do nothing and its inaugural speech from the throne did not mention the naval issue. Laurier was quick to introduce the subject, however, seizing upon the inconsistencies in the Conservative camp to move an amendment to the speech and declaring the new government unconstitutional in having formed a Cabinet whose members held "diametrically opposite views on [such] a question of the highest importance to the dominion and to the empire."[119] Borden dismissed both the motion and the Laurier policy as ineffective, expensive and ill-considered. According to the prime minister, the Liberal alternative would have resulted in a disunited imperial navy and the construction of obsolete Canadian ships, despite an enormous expenditure of $55,000,000 over ten years. As to his own naval plans, "the whole policy must be reconsidered, and we shall reconsider it. In so grave and important a determination, affecting for all time to come the relations of this dominion to the rest of the empire, it is infinitely better to be right than to be in a hurry. The question of permanent co-operation between this dominion and the rest of the empire ought to be threshed out and debated before the people and they should be given an opportunity of pronouncing upon it. I say, further, that we shall take pains to ascertain in the meantime what are the conditions that confront the empire."[120] Later in the debate, Borden would go even further, downplaying the need for a monetary contribution by pointing to the British government's admission that earlier reports of accelerated German construction had been incorrect. Along with setting the stage for a return to the Admiralty for advice, and implicit support for Monk's demand for a plebiscite, the parameters of the ensuing debate had been established.

With nothing specific to put forward on his own policy, Borden returned the file to his naval minister. On 29 November 1911, Hazen notified parliament that "the government did not intend to accept any of the tenders for the projected warships, and that all the deposits which had been made in connection with them had been returned." The following March he announced that the Naval Service Act would be repealed, but not until the government had presented its alternative policy to parliament and the people. In the interim the act would remain on the statute books "for purposes in connection with the Fishery Protection Service and otherwise." Two weeks later, Borden confirmed his minister's position, stating that his government would not continue Laurier's naval program and adding that "as the government could not very well sink the ships and burn the buildings, the existing establishment would be continued until a new policy had been formulated." He declined, however, to present an alternative plan, or to suggest when one might be expected.[121]

---

118. Hopkins, The Canadian Annual Review, 1911, 311.

119. Canada, Parliament, House of Commons, *Debates*, 20 November 1911, col. 49–50.

120. Ibid, cols. 58–61.

121. Tucker, *The Naval Service of Canada*, I, 174.

Fatefully, the question of Canadian naval policy was immediately overtaken by events. Even as the Canadian prime minister was addressing the House of Commons, the first lord of the Admiralty presented the 1912–13 estimates for the Royal Navy to the British parliament. With a "brutally clear and frank" public abandonment of the "sham of the two power standard," McKenna stated that the new standard was for a 60 percent superiority in dreadnoughts over the German navy. This policy had, in fact, already been quietly adopted in April 1909 for internal consideration in affecting cost savings and in recognition of the unlikelihood of war with the United States, whose fleet ranked just after the German in numerical strength. The Agadir crisis in the summer of 1911, when the German gunboat *Panther* visited Morocco and frightened the British into thinking the Germans planned to build a base there, breathed substance into the perception of an Anglo-German naval rivalry. In Germany, Tirpitz argued that the crisis was the "first diplomatic reverse since Bismarck's day and that the only way to restore the nation's prestige was by strengthening the Navy," leading the Reichstag to authorize a supplementary naval bill aimed at achieving a 2:3 ratio in capital ships with the British, representing only a 50 percent British superiority.[122]

In Britain, the crisis exposed the enormous disparity between army and naval war planning. When called before the Committee of Imperial Defence to explain their plans during the crisis, the chief of the imperial general staff, General Sir Henry Wilson, presented a "coherent and comprehensive war plan" that had been drawn up by his army staff. In sharp contrast, the first sea lord, Admiral Sir Arthur K. Wilson—who had always maintained that the only war plans the Admiralty required were kept strictly in his head—gave a "rambling and almost unintelligible" presentation that exposed "his vaunted secret war plan … as a few silly platitudes, devoid of serious thought."[123] The first sea lord's sorry performance prompted Lord Haldane to threaten resignation from the War Office unless a proper naval staff was established, insisting that "the Fisher method, which [Admiral] Wilson appears to follow, that war plans should be locked in the brain of the first sea lord, is out of date and impracticable." Prime Minister Asquith's initial preference was to appoint Haldane as first lord to initiate reforms, but he settled instead upon his youthful home secretary, Winston Churchill, as much to have the first lord in the House of Commons to address the issue of expenditures as it was to silence Churchill's frequent criticisms of them.[124]

McKenna and Churchill exchanged offices on 25 October 1911, and the latter, a widely read student of military history, quickly set about learning his new trade, earning a reputation—for better or for worse—as an "amateur admiral." Within a short time, Admiral Wilson's emphatic rejection of the reorganization led directly to his dismissal and replacement as first sea lord by Admiral Sir Francis Bridgeman. The shake-up at the Admiralty had been watched carefully by Fisher, who hoped that his friendship with the new first lord would mean a return to the restructuring of the fleet around the twin concepts of fleet units and flotilla defence. Although Churchill was quite taken with Fisher's ideas, he was soon

122. J. Mackay, Hitsman, "Canadian Naval Policy," (unpublished MA thesis, Queen's University 1940), 95; and Marder, *From Dreadnought to Scapa Flow*, I, 183, 272.

123. N.A.M. Rodger, *The Admiralty* (Lavenham, Suffolk 1979), 127.

124. Haldane quoted in Marder, *From Dreadnought to Scapa Flow*, I, 246–47, 249.

persuaded by his official advisers to opt instead for a subtle but significant change to the battle cruiser–submarine combination. In May 1912 he announced development of the Queen Elizabeth–class of fast battleships—oil-fired warships capable of twenty-five knots with heavy armour, 15-inch main armament and a strong 6-inch secondary armament—and of high-speed submarines to work with the battle fleet as opposed to Fisher's preference for patrol submarines.[125]

The resulting emphasis upon the North Sea battle fleet was further affirmation of the Admiralty's move away from the Fisher reforms. The implicit return to an earlier age of tactical and strategic thought would eventually hold implications for the dominion fleets, but it was brought home sooner to Canada through the fateful intervention—and not for the last time—of British Columbia premier Sir Richard McBride. At the end of January 1912, McBride forwarded to naval minister Hazen an extract of a letter from Churchill, a McBride friend of many years, in which the first lord offered his fullest assistance to the Canadian government: "They can consult the Admiralty in perfect confidence that we will do all in our power to make their naval policy a brilliant success; and will not be hidebound or shrink from new departures provided that whatever moneys they think fit to employ shall be well spent according to the true principles by which sea power is maintained." Hazen in turn forwarded the extract to Borden with the observation that "we will·soon have to make up our minds as to what course we intend to pursue with regard to consulting the Admiralty, and I will not act upon Mr McBride's suggestion to drop a line to Mr Churchill until I have a talk with you with regard to the subject."[126]

There appears to have been no direct correspondence between the Canadian prime minister and the British first lord until the end of May 1912, when, prompted again by McBride (passing through Ottawa on return to British Columbia from London), Borden wrote to Churchill that he had "had the pleasure of conversing with [McBride] on some matters which he had discussed with you while in England.... It is practically arranged that Mr Hazen and I with one or two other members of the government will sail for England about the 26th or 28th of June, arriving in London early in July. There are several questions which I hope to take up with you immediately after our arrival."[127] The Canadian party comprised Borden, Hazen, Minister of Justice C.J. Doherty, and Postmaster General L.P. Pelletier, accompanied by their advisers Admiral Kingsmill and Sir Joseph Pope, the undersecretary of state for external affairs. Before their arrival in London in early July, Borden claimed that "there was no advance discussion on policy, as that was postponed until after my colleagues had been made acquainted with the results of our visit."[128]

On 11 July, Borden and his ministers were invited to attend a Committee of Imperial

---

125. Geoffrey Best, *Churchill and War* (London 2005), 41; Nicolas Lambert, "Admiral Sir Francis Bridgeman-Bridgeman," Murfett, ed., *The First Sea Lords*, 56; and Jon Tetsuro Sumida, "Churchill and British Sea Power," R.A.C. Parker, ed., *Winston Churchill: Studies in Statesmanship* (London 1995), 10.

126. Quoted in Gilbert Norman Tucker, "The Naval Policy of Sir Robert Borden," *Canadian Historical Review*, 2:1 (March 1947), 3, 4; and Tucker, *The Naval Service of Canada*, I, 176–77.

127. Borden quoted in Tucker, "The Naval Policy of Sir Robert Borden," 4.

128. Borden, *Memoirs*, I, 355.

Defence meeting, in keeping with the agreement that dominion representatives should be invited whenever questions affecting them were discussed. Borden clearly did not understand that the CID was a purely advisory committee but he and his colleagues were greatly impressed that Churchill brought them into their confidence with a detailed description of the German problem. Although confident of the Royal Navy's ability to meet the challenge, Churchill described how the threat had escalated since the passing of the spring estimates by the conclusion of a German alliance with Italy and Austro-Hungary, both of whom had embarked upon their own dreadnought building programs. The requirement to transfer at least three Royal Navy battleships back to the Mediterranean theatre meant, according to Churchill, "that we really ought to lay down now three more ships over and above the four we are building." The expense of laying down the extra ships could be absorbed, but the real difficulty was that the existing building program was already in proportion to that of the Germans. The sudden laying down by Britain of three extra dreadnoughts might stimulate naval competition and would cause the Germans to ask what new fact existed to justify the building of these additional ships: "If we could say that the new fact was that Canada had decided to take part in the defence of the British empire, that would be an answer which would involve no invidious comparisons, and which would absolve us from going into detailed calculations as to the number of Austrian and German vessels available at any particular moment." The first lord continued that the need was urgent, "and if it is the intention of Canada to render assistance to the naval forces of the British empire, now is the time when that aid would be most welcome and most timely." At the same time, he affirmed his hope of conducting consultations aimed at a permanent policy, and the meeting ended with an agreement to pursue such discussions while Asquith suggested that they should be followed by Canadian attendance at a second meeting of the defence committee.[129]

The subsequent meeting of the Canadian delegation with Churchill and other Admiralty officials, and Borden's private interview with the first lord on 13 July were, according to the prime minister, "very frank and intimate. Mr Churchill was fair and reasonable and was entirely disposed to give us assurance in writing as to the peril ... and as to the necessity for strong co-operation in naval defence by the dominions."[130] Although the possibility of an emergency contribution dominated the London discussions, Borden also pursued the question of Canadian naval development. His notes, although sketchy, reveal the government's priorities heading into the meeting with Churchill:

1. Shipbuilding in Canada. Swan, Vickers, Montreal, Halifax. Your ships or ours?

---

129. Churchill quoted in Tucker, *The Naval Service of Canada*, I, 179; Brown, *Borden*, I, 237; and Sumida contends in *In Defence of Naval Supremacy*, 189, and "Churchill and British Sea Power," 11–12, that, although the navy estimates of 1913 were some 50 percent above those of 1908, new taxes introduced in 1909 and an upturn in the British economy resulted in an expansion of the central government's revenue such that annual spending on social welfare over the same period nonetheless rose nearly tenfold.

130. Borden, *Memoirs*, I, 359.

Officers of *Niobe*'s gun room. Seated in the front row, from left to right, are Midshipmen Charles Beard, Victor Brodeur, John Barron, Percy Nelles, Henry Bate, and Hollingsworth. (LAC PA-126721)

2. Defences of our own coasts. Have you [a] scheme? Have you suggestions. Can you give report. Listen to our suggestions.

3. Dockyards....

4. Representation [on] Committee of Imperial Defence. Reconstitution of that Committee.

5. Semi official French utterance.

6. Your official statement as to necessity [for immediate contribution].

7. Attitude of British Liberal Press.

8. British preferences. German overtures. What do you propose.

9. Fast Atlantic Service—ships subsidized for Cruisers.[131]

Borden left Britain on 29 August with mixed success. Regarding attendance at imperial councils, Asquith's concession that the high commissioner should be a regular attendee, but still only "whenever questions concerning the dominions were discussed," did not go far enough as far as Borden was concerned, and the Canadian prime minister advised his British counterpart that in the near future it would be necessary that "the dominion should have a direct and immediate voice in foreign policy."[132] Between sessions with British ministers, Borden's desire to explore shipbuilding opportunities resulted in a series of informative tours of various yards, including Vickers at Barrow, the Elswick works at Newcastle, and John Brown's at Clydebank. Borden was disappointed by the Admiralty memorandum supporting the case for an immediate contribution, however. The draft was so inadequate that the prime minister returned it to Churchill with a note that "if this contribution was the best we could expect it would be idle for him to anticipate any results whatever from the government or the people of Canada."[133] The memorandum also failed to address the second, "permanent," track of Borden's haphazard naval policy:

> No doubt you will deal in subsequent memoranda with the other questions raised such as the importance and value of docks and harbour fortifications from the Admiralty standpoint, the best methods of harbour and coast defence, the arming of merchant steamships, the practicability of aiding the establishment of shipbuilding in Canada by the method suggested. These matters more

---

131. Borden handwritten notes, nd (July 1912), LAC, MG 26 H, reel C-4348.

132. CID minutes, 31 July 1912 quoted in Tucker, *The Naval Service of Canada*, I, 181–82.

133. Borden, *Memoirs*, I, 365.

particularly concern the question of a permanent policy which we hope to take up without much delay but which is not so pressing as the other.[134]

The Canadian prime minister's disquiet exposed a rift within the Admiralty. After writing the unsatisfactory paper himself without input from the sea lords, Churchill adopted a quite different tone after it was returned to him with Borden's comments:

> Winston then prepared another paper on different lines and sent it to the board, observing that they might criticize it, but that they should not alter it. The board were equally opposed to this new paper, and took it upon themselves to rewrite the whole thing on their own lines.... When the papers reached Asquith, Winston's paper was wholly disallowed: the sea lords' was adopted and that has gone to Canada. Winston is now denouncing Borden in the strongest language![135]

The revised memorandum gave a clear and detailed assessment of the apparent threat presented by the fleets of Germany and her new partners in the Triple Alliance, a point which Laurier appears not to have disputed when shown the memorandum under his status as a privy councillor. Even Monk was prepared to admit in Cabinet discussion that the situation was "grave and emergent."[136] For all that, the supposedly improved memorandum still fell far short of Borden's requirements, especially in its publishable version, which did not describe the need for assistance specifically in the construction of large capital ships, such as dreadnoughts, and therefore was insufficient argument to overcome either Laurier's opposition to the whole principle of contribution or Monk's demand for a plebiscite on naval policy. By that time, both positions were political risks Borden had decided to take. Confident in his government's majority, he accepted Monk's resignation from Cabinet in October 1912, with the assurance that he would not oppose the government except on the naval issue.

In Britain, the fallout from the memorandum ended with Bridgeman's dismissal as first sea lord and his replacement by Prince Louis of Battenberg in December 1912. Among Bridgeman's final acts, and one on which he seems not to have differed greatly from his political master, was the despatch of an in-depth analysis of a permanent Canadian naval policy. A clear statement of pre-war Admiralty strategy, the October memorandum on the "Best Method of Harbour and Coast Defence" and "Protection of Trade Routes in Atlantic and Pacific" began with an extended ten-page discourse on "the general principles [of command of the sea] upon which the naval defence of the empire has been hitherto based." After observing that "it is improbable that serious attacks will ever be made by ships upon … well-armed coast defences," the memorandum spent barely two pages discussing "Canadian requirements" in the categories of naval defended ports and defended commercial

---

134. Borden to Churchill, 28 August 1912, quoted in Tucker, *The Naval Service of Canada*, I, 183.

135. J.S. Sanders to A.J. Balfour, 10 October 1912 quoted in Randolph S. Churchill, *Winston S. Churchill, II: Young Statesman, 1901–1914* (Boston 1967), 610–11.

136. Tucker, *The Naval Service of Canada*, I, 184–86.

ports. The Admiralty recommended that Halifax on the East Coast and Vancouver ("Burrard Inlet") on the West be established as "important naval dockyards and bases for the fleet," with dry docks large enough to accommodate dreadnought battleships in each of those naval ports. It went on to contend that adequate fixed coast artillery and searchlight defences already existed at Halifax and could easily be installed at Vancouver. As for seaborne defences, "small local defence flotillas, consisting of torpedo-boats and submarines ... [and] An Examination Service, under naval responsibility, should also be established at each." Their lordships also felt that the existing defences at Esquimalt were adequate for it to be "maintained as a coaling station and subsidiary naval base."[137]

Turning to defended commercial ports, they recommended the inclusion in this category of Saint John, NB, Quebec City, and Prince Rupert, BC, at which "probably a few 6-inch guns and searchlights ... would answer all requirements," coupled with an examination service at each site. The existing fixed defences at Quebec were considered "fairly adequate," but the special circumstances of the St Lawrence estuary demanded the establishment of a local defence flotilla of torpedo-boats and submarines at Point de Monts on the North Shore, near Baie Comeau. Finally, as for trade on the open oceans, the "special arrangements ... for its protection" introduced the rationale for a monetary contribution, as "the construction and maintenance of the necessary cruisers add considerable sums to the British naval estimates, and any help from Canada would be most valuable in this direction." The latest Admiralty advice, therefore, called for small local flotillas of four to six torpedo-boats and three submarines at each of Halifax and Vancouver, as well as another in the Gulf of St Lawrence comprising twelve torpedo-boats and nine submarines led by a flotilla cruiser, and examination services at each of the several named ports. It envisioned no urgent need for even the modest ocean-going fleet units that had constituted the Laurier naval program three years earlier.[138] Even so, a Canadian navy that consisted of some twenty torpedo boats and a dozen submarines was vastly larger than the force of two obsolete submarines and one auxiliary torpedo boat. that was what Borden would actually allow the RCN during the First World War.

Along with the earlier memorandum on the need for contribution assistance, the Admiralty document was the perfect counterpoint for Borden's two-track naval policy. At the opening of parliament on 21 November 1912, the single most important item in the speech from the throne was the promise of a bill "to afford reasonable and necessary aid ... [to strengthen] the naval forces of the empire ... without delay."[139] Behind the scenes, Borden was also giving serious consideration to presenting a permanent policy to establish a Canadian naval force on both coasts in conjunction with the request for an emergency gift. In Cabinet discussions through November, the prime minister was able to dissuade the

---

137. Admiralty memorandum, October 1912, LAC, MG 26 H, reel C-4348.

138. This is contrary to the conclusion arrived at by Sarty, *Maritime Defence of Canada*, 21, 32–33, which rightly points to the new Admiralty concern with the defence of the North Atlantic trade route. What Sarty describes at this time as a British call for "assistance" is, in fact, a reversion to the monetary contribution to the imperial fleet and not, as he describes it, a validation of the Laurier fleet of Canadian-operated cruisers.

139. Canada, Parliament, House of Commons, *Debates*, 21 November 1912, cols. 2–3.

Rodolphe Lemieux, minister of marine and fisheries and the naval service in 1911. (LAC PA-162050)

members of his Quebec caucus from bolting by pointing to the modest plans for a small coastal flotilla and a substantial shipbuilding industry in their province. He remained unde-cided about the Canadian torpedo boat flotilla to the last moment, and in the end was talked out of it by the fateful advice of his Cabinet colleagues who considered it wiser to risk major initiatives one at a time.[140]

The Naval Aid Bill was a relatively uncomplicated measure of only five brief clauses, with no elaborate preamble justifying the principles behind the emergency contribution nor any stated intent to repeal the Naval Service Act, but rather a request for a sum not exceeding $35 million to be used "in the construction and equipment of battleships or armoured cruis-ers of the most modern and powerful type ... [to be placed] at the disposal of his majesty for the common defence of the empire."[141] The new governor general, the Duke of Con-naught, was back in the parliamentary gallery for its introduction on 5 December, and reported approvingly to his cousin, King George V, "how important and historical the occa-sion was. The house was crammed to its utmost capacity ... [and Borden's] words met with the approval of the house, many of the opposition applauding frequently." In recognizing "the loyalty and imperial spirit that has prompted the gov[ernmen]t to recommend the contribution," however, the governor general was sufficiently shrewd to realize that Bor-den's politicking on the naval question left Canada without a navy and with a government bereft of any policy to establish one beyond the two cruisers that were now tied up along-side at Halifax and Esquimalt:

> I am not quite sure exactly what the gov[ernmen]t are going to propose as the permanent naval organisation of Canada, something more practical and use-ful than the present [Laurier] naval bill I hope. This they want to repeal at once and I am urging them not to do this til they have an organisation to propose in its place. I think it would be a mistake for Canada, alone of all the great self governing dominions, to be without any system of naval defence.... I think you will agree with my view that for the moment an inferior and existing naval organisation is better than none.[142]

A week later he was reporting that, contrary to the initial non-partisan reception of the Borden bill, Laurier remained opposed, "condemning the gov[ernmen]t proposals for the navy and reasserting his belief in a Canadian separate navy.... His party have been much divided of late and his present notion is an attempt to bring them together again."[143]

The Naval Aid Bill precipitated one of the longest and fiercest political fights since con-federation, covering from beginning to end a period of twenty-three weeks of sustained

140. Borden diary, 4, 8, 13, 15, 20, and 27 November 1912, LAC, MG 26 H, reel C-1864; and Sarty, *Maritime Defence of Canada*, 21.

141. The text of the Naval Aid Bill (1912–13) is reproduced as appendix IX of Tucker, *The Naval Service of Canada*, I, 407–08.

142. Connaught to King George V, 6 December 1912, Connaught Papers, Royal Archives Windsor, GV/AA 41/24.

143. Connaught to King George V, 13 December 1912, ibid, GV/AA 41/25.

debate. In truth, neither party entered it entirely united, making their leaders' objective the assertion of personal control as much as the settling of policy. In consequence, the tenor was entirely partisan. According to the minister of the naval service, "the crux of the matter" was "whether or not an emergency existed." The government's contention was that a real and pressing emergency did exist, and that Canada had a duty to contribute in the most effective way possible to a united navy that could defend the empire more effectively and economically than several scattered autonomous fleets. The opposition took the stance that no serious emergency existed, and any cash contribution would be equivalent to payment of tribute, subverting the principle of dominion autonomy. For the first two readings of the bill, each party provided a succession of speakers with occasional votes on amendments and sub-amendments dividing generally along party lines, although several Quebec Conservatives did side with Laurier.

After passing second reading on 28 February, by 114 to eighty-four, the bill went to committee, and the opposition's tactics changed dramatically. For nearly two weeks in March 1913, the House of Commons sat in almost continuous session as the Liberals raised point after point of procedural obstruction. As one member put it, "we are going to sit until Christmas time, if necessary, to prevent the passage of this bill."[144] With the debate "descending into frivolity and license" and "obstruction reach[ing] the point of destroying parliamentary government" Borden wrote to the governor general on 8 March suggesting that "it must be arrested, condemned and banished."[145] Through a series of procedural tricks of their own, the Conservatives passed a motion at the end of April adopting a new set of rules to limit debate through closure. When debate on the Naval Aid Bill resumed on 6 May and again quickly descended into an impasse, the first use of closure in Canadian parliamentary history was invoked on the 9th. The bill went through committee the next day, and on 15 May passed its third reading, by a majority of 101 to sixty-eight.

Anticipating that the opposition filibuster in the House of Commons would be followed by the Liberals using their majority in the Senate to kill the legislation, Borden again began to seriously reconsider the introduction of a permanent policy to establish coastal flotillas. In private correspondence with Connaught at the height of the parliamentary debate, he described his general agreement with the original Laurier program of 1903–04 to slowly convert the Fisheries Protection Service into a fighting force, while underscoring that the Liberal leader's "error had been to do so little during the next five years and then to attempt too much too quickly in the wake of the Imperial Defence Conference."[146] Such an argument, however, conveniently overlooked the fact that the $35 million gift in the Naval Aid Bill exceeded the cost of Laurier's "too much, too quickly" naval proposals the Conservative prime minister had abandoned. While the additional money from Ottawa would barely be felt by the British taxpayer (who paid a mere 5 percent on incomes over 5,000 pounds, an income achieved only by the very wealthy), Borden's Naval Aid Bill did nothing to

144. Canada, Parliament, House of Commons, *Debates*, 14 March 1913, col. 5719.

145. Borden to Connaught, 8 March 1913, quoted in Brown, *Borden*, I, 241.

146. Sarty, *Maritime Defence of Canada*, 20.

provide Canadian taxpayers with a navy of their own and left the nation's valuable shipping lanes, within a few short years, unnecessarily vulnerable to enemy attack.[147]

The prime minister had already renewed correspondence with Churchill, who promised to help break the stalemate in Ottawa with an endorsement of Borden's permanent policy in his presentation of the Admiralty estimates to the British House of Commons at the end of March. To the first lord's plan to include the three proposed Canadian dreadnoughts in "an imperial cruising squadron based on Gibraltar" working in coordination with limited dominion naval organizations, Borden responded effusively that "we thoroughly approve … of [your] inspiring proposal." Emphasizing, however, that he did not wish to return to the conditions agreed to at the Colonial Conference of 1907, Borden recapitulated his priorities of the previous summer, providing, in effect, a précis of his policy.

> As Canada may eventually desire to establish and maintain one or more fleet units in co-operation with and close relation to the imperial navy, I would suggest that you should allude to their possible recall upon reasonable notice, as three ships might be required to form part of such unit or units. Later on this session we shall probably announce that, pending consideration of great and difficult problems attending the thorough co-operation of the dominions in matters affecting imperial defence and foreign policy, Canada proposes to undertake certain measures of defence which, while primarily designed for the protection of her own shores and her interests in contiguous waters, will nevertheless be of importance from an imperial standpoint. It is anticipated that this will be upon following lines:
>
> 1. Provision of dry docks, useful for commercial as well as Admiralty purposes.
>
> 2. Establishment of naval bases and fortification of ports and harbours, also defence of such ports and harbours by submarines, torpedo-boats, etc.
>
> 3. Training of officers in naval colleges and of men in training ships.
>
> 4. Subsidizing of fast and modern merchant vessels useful for scouting and other purposes, equipment of such ships with necessary guns and fittings, and manning by trained seamen.
>
> 5. Gradual extension of fishery protection service by addition of light cruisers manned by trained men and under naval discipline, which, while specifically useful for primary purpose of protecting fisheries, will also be effective and available in time of war.[148]

147. F.M.L Thompson, *The Cambridge Social History of Britain, 1750–1950, Volume 3, Social Agencies and Institutions* (Cambridge 1990), 54, 58.

These formed the core elements of the permanent policy Borden presented to parliament. He did not introduce his plans until his summary speech on the last day of debate on the Naval Aid Bill, probably to limit any unproductive exchange with Laurier, while planting the seeds for a potential division among Liberal senators. Many of the latter (like Sir George Ross, former premier of Ontario) were known to be favourably disposed to an emergency contribution. In many ways, although Borden still called for repeal of the Naval Service Act, his permanent policy harkened back to the scheme envisioned under the March 1909 Foster resolution, with a basic naval establishment for a coastal defence force, including retention of the two training cruisers, but as an integral part of the existing civil marine services. It differed from Laurier's naval policy, however, in several basic respects reflected in his willingness to subordinate Canadian interests to those of the Admiralty. Although Borden's much broader proposal for shipbuilding, like Laurier's, was intended to stimulate the redevelopment of a Canadian commercial industry, the government rejected the concept of separate navies, preferring the automatic passing of control of dominion fleets to the Admiralty in wartime. Moreover, Borden again made a clear linkage between the integration of imperial naval and foreign policies. In doing so, he could point to Churchill's recent statement to declare that, "unlike Laurier's unrealistically grand naval plan, this modest scheme had the Admiralty's full sanction,"[149] although the previous Liberal government had also managed to reach agreement with McKenna.

Borden's decision to link the two tracks of his naval policy came too late to find non-partisan acceptance. When the Naval Aid Bill was introduced in the Senate, where the Liberals held a clear majority after their long tenure in office, Laurier imposed party discipline to ensure its defeat. Instead of defeating the bill outright, however, Liberal senators played upon Borden's last-minute declaration in favour of a national naval service and put forward an amendment withholding their consent "until it is submitted to the judgment of the country." By a vote of fifty-one to twenty-seven, the Naval Aid Bill was returned to the House of Commons on 30 May 1913.[150]

Borden was not immediately deterred, but he clearly had no intention of dissolving parliament and taking the issue to voters. Instead, he secretly proposed to Churchill that the British government should lay down the three ships at once anyway, on the assurance that before their completion the Canadian government would introduce a bill to provide the means of paying for them. Churchill's cable responded that such an arrangement "would be open to criticism in both countries as seeming to go behind the formal decision of the

---

148. Churchill to Borden, 19 March 1913, Borden to Churchill, 23 March 1913, quoted in R.S. Churchill, *Winston S. Churchill*, Companion II, Part 3: *1911–1914* (Boston 1969), 1804–05, 1805–06. Tucker, *The Naval Service of Canada*, I, 197 notes that had the proposed Canadian dreadnoughts been authorized, they would have been completed as part of the Queen Elizabeth–class. Borden at one point had suggested to Churchill that any contributed ships should have Canadian names, and suggested *Acadia, Quebec*, and *Ontario*. Tucker, *The Naval Service of Canada*, I, 187.

149. Canada, Parliament, House of Commons, *Debates*, 15 May 1913, cols. 10036–38; Sarty, *Maritime Defence of Canada*, 22; and Brown, *Borden*, I, 244.

150. Canada, Parliament, Senate, *Debates*, 30 May 1913, col. 758; Tucker, *The Naval Service of Canada*, I, 197; and Brown, *Borden*, I, 243.

Canadian parliament and that we have no right at present to assume that Senate's vote could be reversed."[151] In the fall of 1913, Connaught reported to King George V that Borden "may put the 25,000,000 dollars into the estimates and it is hoped that the Senate will not be able to throw it out," and he would look for "some announcement of the proposed permanent naval policy of [the] gov[ernmen]t."[152] Borden also informed the first lord early in 1914 that "it is just possible that before end of session [scheduled for June] we may secure majority in Senate." The prime minister hoped to achieve that result by a redistribution of Senate seats (a separate bill was before parliament to amend the British North America Act by creating an additional twenty-four senators), appointing more Conservatives to replace aging Liberal senators as they died off, and invoking section 26 of the BNA Act to appoint six additional senators.[153]

As it happened, the political climate did not change sufficiently for Borden to reintroduce his naval policy to parliament before the outbreak of war in August. Even so, Canadian naval developments were being monitored in Berlin. Without diplomatic representation in Canada, official reports came by way of the German embassy in London, which provided a fairly accurate description of the shifting positions. In response to the introduction of the Naval Aid Bill, the German undersecretary of state for foreign affairs, Arthur Zimmermann, reasoned in December 1912, that "the granting of three dreadnoughts by Canada—a consequence of our latest naval law—seems to be excellent material for agitation." The defeat of the measure was naturally celebrated, and a year later, in October 1913, the German chargé d'affaires in London reported the fact that "in Canada the party warfare still rages over the question" as evidence that "it is difficult even for a Winston Churchill to persuade the colonies to believe in his fiction of a seriously threatened English world empire."[154] The German press generally took satisfaction with the defeat of the Naval Aid Bill as "a severe moral and material loss for [Britain's] imperial defence" and in the "unpleasant disruption in Britain's concept of world empire and in Churchill's idea of an imperial squadron." The most accurate and incisive observation of the state of affairs came from the captain of the German cruiser SMS *Hertha* in a report on his three-week visit to Halifax in the early fall of 1913:

> As in the previous year naval policy forms the principal point of contention of the two major parties in Canada. However, the businessmen and industrialists I met judge the naval question by no means according to its significance for Canada or England, but regard it merely as an election slogan.... The docks present a melancholy aspect.... The *Niobe*, with the breeches of all guns removed, is tied up alongside the dock as there are no maintenance person-

151. Tucker, *The Naval Service of Canada*, I, 200.

152. Connaught to King George V, 26 October and 29 November 1913, Connaught Papers, Royal Archives Windsor, GV/AA 41/36, 41/37.

153. Borden to Churchill, 10 January 1914, quoted in Tucker, *The Naval Service of Canada*, I, 202.

154. Zimmermann memorandum, 14 December 1912, Kühlmann to Bethmann-Hollweg, 21 October 1913, quoted in Tucker, *The Naval Service of Canada*, I, 199.

nel. English midshipmen from HMS *Cornwall* called the *Niobe* rotten, and a voyage aboard her as risky. [Older retired officers grumbled] bitterly that young people were listless and had lost the joy in work.... Nobody wanted to undertake tough demanding work of the service or in business any more.[155]

The well-maintained German cruiser, a potential enemy, contrasted starkly with the deteriorating *Niobe*, tied up alongside at Halifax dockyard. Nonetheless, the RCN remained, nominally at least, an operational service and provided its first report on operations during the 1911–12 season.[156] In its report the following year, however, the naval service made little attempt to conceal its cloudy future, noting that "owing to the uncertainty of the future naval policy, and the limited accommodation available, no special efforts have been made to obtain recruits for the navy." It is noteworthy that the large number of ratings on loan from the Royal Navy had raised the average age of *Niobe*'s complement to "well over thirty years—quite a number of ratings being between forty and forty-five years old." As for operations, "during the spring and summer the *Niobe* cruised around the coast of Nova Scotia and the Gulf of St Lawrence and also visited Quebec," before grounding off Cape Sable. *Rainbow*'s experiences were a better augury for the future, as she "made various cruises during the year on the Pacific coast for the training of recruits and to assist in fishery protection." Proving that she indeed had a role to play, *Rainbow* took the US fishing schooner *Edrie* into custody for illegal fishing in February 1913.[157]

Such minor naval triumphs proved ephemeral, however. In the department's 1913–14 report, Hazen noted that "owing to the decision of the government not to continue HMC Ships *Niobe* and *Rainbow* in full commission,... the course of exercises and training for these ships has been discontinued, and they are at present manned by nucleus crews." Sailors, on the other hand, had requirements that could not be ignored, such as health, nutrition, accommodation, and pay. Although health problems were mainly "of a minor character," a stoker of the Royal Fleet Reserve, George Cox, died of uremia, and Master-at-Arms William J. Harper, on pension from the Royal Navy, drowned in a boating accident. Tying up ships alongside neither ended the navy's activities nor prevented sailors from becoming casualties in the performance of their duties.[158]

At the prime minister's request, Kingsmill prepared a memorandum on the languishing state of the Canadian navy in December 1913. Working from the premise that "the question of a floating defence for the dominion is becoming more and more important," the admiral explained that "as this principle of policy ... on some sort of permanent naval service ... has not yet been definitely decided, I have found it very difficult, if not

155. Quoted in Hadley and Sarty, *Tin-pots and Pirate Ships*, 70.

156. Canada, Department of the Naval Service, *Report of the Department of the Naval Service for the Fiscal Year Ending 31st March, 1911* (Ottawa 1911), 15–19.

157. Ibid, *Report of the Department of the Naval Service for the Fiscal Year Ending 31st March, 1912* (Ottawa 1912), 8, 21.

158. Ibid, *Report of the Department of the Naval Service for the Fiscal Year Ending 31st March, 1914* (Ottawa 1914), 8, 24.

John Douglas Hazen served as naval minister in the Borden government from 1911 to 1917. (LAC C-4959)

impossible, to prepare a memorandum on the subject." Constrained by Borden's politically motivated opposition to an ocean-going national navy, Kingsmill pointed to "developments in the use of oil fuel now taking place in the imperial fleet" to argue the importance of Halifax as a defended naval base from which to protect the strategically important trade routes from Caribbean oil producers to Britain. The shortest ocean shipping lanes passed along the eastern seaboard of the United States and to the south of the Grand Banks before arcing across the North Atlantic. Whereas "for some years Halifax has been looked upon as rather remote from the sphere of operations in a war with a naval power other than the United States ... , [c]onsequently [it] is now becoming of greater importance as a base from which other ports in the dominion may be defended." Even though Kingsmill noted that the Admiralty had recently reconstituted the North America squadron, basing four armoured cruisers in Bermuda, he did not waste his time by suggesting to Borden the possibility of reviving the scheme envisioned under the Naval Service Act for a similar Canadian cruiser force. Rather, he sensibly argued for implementation of the more modest force recommended by the Admiralty a year earlier, namely, limited torpedo boat and submarine flotillas based at Halifax and in the Gulf of St Lawrence. Such a force, he believed, "could be maintained at Halifax at an early date if the Admiralty could render assistance by the loan of a certain number of officers and skilled ratings." The naval director refrained from pointing out that the original Royal Navy augmentees to *Niobe*'s crew had recently been returned to Britain for lack of employment.[159]

Two months passed before Borden forwarded the memorandum to Churchill, explaining that it was an initiative "prepared at my request and [on which] I would be glad to have in confidence the observations and criticisms of the Admiralty."[160] When Whitehall's comments arrived in early May 1914, they proved to be not at all what either Borden or Kingsmill expected. Far from simple encouragement to put the original analysis into effect, the Admiralty reply gave no indication that Whitehall was even aware that a naval debate had taken place in Canada and recommended very strongly the already-rejected Laurier plan "that a cruiser policy be adopted." Although agreeing with Kingsmill's analysis that "Halifax is a well situated and convenient harbour on which to base the naval forces used ... against enemy vessels in a war between Great Britain and any other European power with a strong navy," the Admiralty felt that the Canadian director's memorandum laid "undo stress on the oil fuel question." It pointed instead to the growing grain trade from Canada to the Britain as the "predominant factor" and "to the southward of Cape Race [as] the areas where enemy cruisers, if left alone, could operate with profit." Demonstrating its inability to recommend any kind of consistent policy, the Admiralty drew several conclusions that were at distinct odds from its earlier analysis. To begin, it stressed that, as "neither torpedo boats nor submarines in themselves are fitted for trade protection in such an area as the northwest Atlantic," the establishment of local flotillas was not "supported as being the best means of safeguarding either the local or the imperial interests of the region." Rather,

---

159. "Remarks on Naval Defence on the Atlantic Coast," December 1913, UKNA, ADM 1/8369.

160. Borden to Churchill, 18 February 1914, covering letter to Kingsmill memorandum, UKNA, ADM 1/8369.

"cruisers, being far more powerful and mobile than flotillas, are far better suited ... for the protection of commerce in areas removed from the main sphere of naval operations." Admitting to "the very limited number of cruisers the British Admiralty can allot to the North Atlantic in war," it was logical that the additional cruiser force would have to come from Canada.[161]

As a result, much of the British analysis was given over to extolling the virtues of cruisers as warships that were "self-contained, require a much smaller number of highly skilled ratings in proportion to the total, have a longer life, can be used in all waters and weather, and, as a first step towards creating a Canadian navy, are strongly recommended in preference to a policy of local flotillas, which are so much more limited in their action." The specific type recommended was a "modified and simplified" design of the Chatham-class light cruiser, capable of twenty-three knots with oil fuel, strengthened to allow operations near ice, with an "absence of complicated technical fittings and details," and "a uniform armament" of 6-inch guns. (The covering notes also contained a long debate, never resolved, among the members of the staff as to whether torpedoes were an unnecessary complication.) Additionally, the naval war staff strongly endorsed the integration of the Canadian naval service within the "efficient system of intelligence ... which other British dominions and colonies have already joined and which is now being perfected." Finally, it underscored the importance of tending both to basic infrastructure, as "the recent experience of [the battle cruiser] HMS *New Zealand* at Halifax shows the necessity of improving the coaling facilities at that place," and to organizing an "efficient system of recruiting ... [with] sufficient inducements ... to attract suitable men."[162]

In overturning the advice it had been offering for the past two years, the Admiralty had unwittingly turned the clock back, not to the situation of early 1909, as Borden desired, but to the one he had strenuously campaigned against in the general election of 1911. Far from repudiating Laurier's trimmed-down fleet unit as an unsatisfactory compromise, it now endorsed the light cruiser force as the scheme best suited to solving the Canadian naval dilemma. The ad hoc nature of the Admiralty's advice to Ottawa, in total disregard—or ignorance—of the Canadian naval debate, was a reflection of the immaturity of the naval staff system that had been imposed upon the Admiralty by Churchill in January 1912. Even then, not a single naval officer had any staff training. As one officer who served in the operations division later acknowledged, the Admiralty's naval staff was still in its infancy upon the outbreak of war in 1914:

> Neither the Chief of the War Staff nor the Director of Operations Division seemed to have any particular idea of what the War Staff was supposed to be doing, or how they should make use of it; they had been brought up in the tradition that the conduct of the operations of the fleet was a matter for the admiral alone, and that he needed no assistance in assimilating the whole sit-

161. "Admiralty Comments," 4 May 1914, under cover of Churchill to Borden, 6 May 1914, UKNA, ADM 1/8369.

162. Ibid; and Nicolas Lambert, "Strategic Command and Control for Maneuver Warfare: Creation of the Royal Navy's 'War Room' System, 1905–1915," *Journal of Military History*, LXIX (April 2005), 361–410.

uation in all its ramifications, and in reaching a decision, probably instanta-neously, upon what should be done and what orders should be issued in order to get it done.[163]

As we shall see, the delay in developing any sort of effective planning staff at the Admiralty, one that was capable of providing Ottawa with coherent and consistent policy advice, proved to be a serious impediment to the RCN's development and one that would continue to plague the Canadian navy throughout the First World War.

The latest British advice in favour of Laurier's cruiser policy was in part the result of a reorientation of the Admiralty's strategic thought. As explained in a recent re-interpretation of the Churchill-Fisher era, the battleship standard had secretly been abandoned by the first lord in December 1913. Looming British financial pressure on the Royal Navy's 1914 estimates, coupled with the strong performance of submarines in the 1913 fleet manoeuvres, forced a return to Fisher's concept of flotilla defence so as "to reduce navy estimates ... dependent upon the substitution of battleships for submarines."[164] Ironically, the failure of Ottawa to deliver funding for the three proposed dreadnoughts was ostensibly responsible at one level—minimal taxation on the British upper class being the main cause—for provoking the funding shortfall. Churchill was under intense pressure to reduce the naval estimates to below £50 million, which could be accomplished only by cutting two dreadnoughts from the construction program. He had originally proposed £52 million, an increase from £47 million the previous year, the difference being made up largely by the Canadian contribution.

The British estimates were finally approved on 11 February 1914, under a compromise formula that capped them at £51,580,000 for 1914–15, allowing for the accelerated construction of two dreadnoughts in 1914, but substantial reductions thereafter, and increased numbers of submarines. The revised calculations were based on the logic that "fourteen submarines would cost less to build than a battleship, they would absorb fewer than half the personnel, and they would be much less expensive to maintain." Critically, to make up the balance, details of the estimates in other areas saw comparatively minor adjustments, such as the new program allowing for the construction of only four light cruisers, where the Operations Division had calculated a requirement of twelve new light cruisers.[165]

Although the Admiralty itself seemed blissfully unaware of the Canadian naval debate, Churchill, at least, realized the inconsistency of Borden's position in view of the proposed reduction in the Royal Navy's estimates. Writing to Prime Minister Asquith in December 1913, the first lord explained:

---

163. H.G. Thursfield, *The Naval Staff of the Admiralty* (Naval Staff Monograph; London, 1939), 29.

164. Nicholas Lambert, "British Naval Policy, 1913–1914: Financial Limitation and Strategic Revolution," *Journal of Modern History*, 67 (September 1995), 618. The validity of this major reinterpretation of the work of Arthur Marder is explained by the fact that the radical strategic rethinking was put aside when overtaken by the events of 1914, with the Admiralty forced to conduct the Great War with the forces at hand, effectively demanding the battlefleet strategy favoured by Wilson.

165. Lambert, "British Naval Policy, 1913–1914," 616; and Marder, *From Dreadnought to Scapa Flow*, I, 325–26.

You must in [regards to my obligations towards Mr Borden] consider broad effects. How c[oul]d I argue in the H[ouse] of C[ommons] that the "emergency" was so far removed that our forecasted programme c[oul]d be halved, at the v[er]y time that the unfortunate Borden was arguing in Canada that it was so real and serious that three ships must be built at once ...? It w[oul]d destroy him.... The Medit[erranea]n decision was the foundation of the Canadian policy. All the argument for Borden stands on that.... The finance can be adjusted without fresh taxation. Borden will act. If he succeeds, the cabinet [battleship] policy in the Medit[erranea]n can be carried out. If he fails—then six months from now I can develop an argument ab[ou]t submarines in that sea wh[ich] will obviate a further constr[uctio]n of battleships for this [secon]dary theatre. Either way we can get through.[166]

While the naval staff was still working out the details of its response to the Canadian paper, Churchill sent a separate note to Borden on 6 March "suggesting that a naval officer of high rank should be sent to Canada to discuss with the government matters relating to [the] emergency and permanent naval policies," the idea being that such advice "would strengthen the government's hand for future action."[167] His nomination to undertake the mission was the second sea lord, Admiral Sir John Jellicoe, who was designated to take command of the Home Fleet at the end of 1914. Perhaps anticipating the appointment, Jellicoe argued that a good share of the increased submarine production should be directed to Canada, in the belief that "there was a far greater chance of extracting a Canadian contribution to imperial defense by suggesting that they should build submarines for the Royal Navy in their own yards than by demanding that they pay for battleships to be constructed in Britain."[168] Several months passed before Borden sent the formal request for the despatch of a naval officer "of adequate experience and capacity." On 11 July 1914, Churchill advised Battenberg that they should work out the details before the first sea lord proceeded on leave in August, so that Jellicoe could prepare for a September departure.[169] It would, in fact, be another five years before Jellicoe actually arrived to conduct his mission.

Borden acknowledged receipt of the Admiralty's paper on 8 June 1914, remarking only that parliamentary business had prevented him from studying it, but that he hoped to do so after parliament prorogued at the end of July.[170] By that time, of course, the implementation of a permanent naval policy had been overtaken by much larger events on the international stage. Nonetheless, the Borden government's first years had provided a somewhat ironic conclusion to Laurier's naval policy. In judging the "tin-pot navy," the Liberal leader's contemporary political opponents—and later historians—formed their

---

166. Churchill to Asquith, 18 December 1913, R.S. Churchill, *Winston S. Churchill*, Companion II, Part 3, 1834–35.

167. Tucker, *The Naval Service of Canada*, I, 208–09.

168. Lambert, "British Naval Policy, 1913–1914," 621.

169. Churchill to Battenberg, 11 July 1914, R.S. Churchill, *Winston S. Churchill*, Companion II, Part 3, 1986–87; and Tucker, *The Naval Service of Canada*, I, 208–09.

170. Borden to Churchill, 8 June 1914, Borden Papers, 68051.

Prime Minister Robert Borden and First Lord Winston Churchill outside the Admiralty building, Whitehall, London. (LAC C-002082)

verdict on the actual state of the Canadian fleet after 1913–14 rather than on what was intended for it up to the summer of 1911. In effect, however, the miscarriage of Borden's policy brought it closer to what Laurier had originally intended. With naval operations reduced in 1912 and curtailed in 1913, the most important operational concern of the Canadian navy was the Fisheries Protection Service. Ship types and defence requirements were secondary issues.[171] Laurier, in response to the Naval Aid Bill, had repeatedly declared that he would happily support the acquisition of dreadnoughts if they served as part of a Canadian navy under Ottawa's control. Borden, for his part, would not relent in his insistence that the naval act must be modified so that Canadian warships would automatically be available to the Admiralty. He was, in fact, pursuing a form of imperial naval union, urging the British government to give Canada a permanent voice in the formation of imperial foreign and defence policy in exchange for assistance to the Royal Navy. Constitutional issues were allowed to determine the outcome of the debate because there was no widespread sense in the country that naval defence was an urgent concern. As Borden explained to the governor general, "the greater part of Canada's population is inland and the sea sense of the people has not yet been developed."[172] Laurier, in urging his supporters not to press for a dissolution of parliament and an election on the naval issue in 1913, was more succinct in observing that "a campaign upon the high cost of living would be far more effective."[173]

As the European powers drifted toward war in the summer of 1914, the Canadian naval service was largely incapable of acting as an "integral part of an imperial navy." The whole RCN consisted of fewer than 350 officers and ratings, less than half of *Niobe*'s full complement. While the differing naval policies of Laurier and Borden pointed to the philosophical distinction between their views of Canadian national development—Laurier for increasing sovereignty as an independent nation, Borden for greater Canadian leadership within the empire—the basic question behind Canadian naval policy remained unanswered. Under Borden's leadership, Canada would enter the First World War having neither contributed dreadnoughts to an imperial fleet nor formed a proper naval service of her own.

---

171. Roger Sarty, "Canadian Naval Policy, 1860–1939" (unpublished DHH narrative nd), 34–35.

172. Borden to Connaught, 24 March 1913, Canada, Department of External Affairs, *Documents on Canadian External Relations*, I: *1909–1918* (Ottawa 1967), 279–81.

173. Laurier quoted in Roger Sarty, "Canadian Naval Policy, 1860–1939" (unpublished DHH narrative nd), 35.

A lower deck game of chess aboard *Niobe*. (CWM 19830056-022)

One of *Niobe*'s mess decks. (CWM 19820190-038)

SECTION 2

The First World War

CHAPTER 4

To War, 1914–1915

"Although at the present stage of naval defence it does not seem to be an important matter," Rear-Admiral Charles E. Kingsmill informed the deputy minister, while reviewing the Canadian government's war book plans in April 1914, "it would be as well to lay down now what would happen should we in the future inaugurate a naval service which would be able to carry out its responsibilities."[1] The naval director's statement was a reflection of his ongoing frustration with the naval policy—or lack of naval policy—of Prime Minister Robert Borden. Unfortunately, over the next four years Kingsmill would have little reason to alter his lament at the meagre resources with which the Royal Canadian Navy was being asked to undertake the nation's maritime defence. Despite Canada's willingness to recruit and maintain a four-division Canadian Corps on the battlefields of France and Belgium— one that would eventually gain a well-deserved reputation as one of the shock formations of the British Empire—the Borden government would never, in fact, provide the Canadian navy with the resources it needed "to carry out its responsibilities" to defend Canada's coastal waters during the First World War. With most of the government's wartime decisions on naval defence reflecting the inconsistent advice and empty promises Ottawa received from the British Admiralty in London, the remnants of Laurier's fledging naval service would have to safeguard Canada's maritime interests with essentially the same motley collection of seconded civilian vessels that a dubious Kingsmill was forced to contemplate when he drew up a Canadian naval war plan.

The Canadian admiral's skepticism about his government's naval intentions was not lessened by the fact that the only two warships the RCN possessed, the obsolescent cruisers *Niobe* and *Rainbow* (stationed at Halifax and Esquimalt respectively), were to be placed at the disposal of the Admiralty, under the terms of Section 23 of the Naval Service Act, "for general service in the Royal Navy" once war was declared and would, as a result, pass out of the operational control of Naval Service Headquarters.[2] For most of the duties assigned to the navy by the Canadian war book, the RCN would have to depend upon a handful of vessels transferred to its control from other government departments. As set out in the government's planning document, hostilities would begin once the war stage was "initiated by the receipt from the imperial government of the war telegram, with the

---

1. Kingsmill memo to Desbarats, 1 April 1914, 1019–2-2, pt. 1, Library and Archives Canada (hereafter LAC), Record Group (hereafter RG) 24, vol. 3855.

2. G.N. Tucker, *The Naval Service of Canada, Its Official History, I: Origins and Early Years* (Ottawa 1952), 215.

concurrence of the dominion government."[3] Once Ottawa declared the war stage, the naval service's immediate task was to carry out the naval portion of the defence schemes for the ports of Halifax and Esquimalt. It was also responsible for "enforcing the examination service at defended ports; closing certain wireless telegraph stations; enforcing censorship of wireless telegraph messages; [the] detention of enemy and neutral merchant vessels; [and the] collection and distribution of naval intelligence."[4] The examination service was to be "automatically enforced at the same time as the war stage of defence scheme[s] at Halifax and Esquimalt. The examination service at [the port of] Quebec is enforced by the militia department, the concurrence of the naval department being first obtained. An agreement with Marine and Fisheries department has been made by which the control of traffic in defended ports is transferred to [the] naval department."[5]

As the defence scheme for Halifax demonstrated, the duties assigned to Canada's navy were primarily supervisory, with most of the actual work being carried out by the civilian crews of federal government vessels. According to the war plan approved by Kingsmill on 7 July 1914 (nine days after the Austrian Archduke Franz Ferdinand and his wife were assassinated in Sarajevo, Bosnia) the navy was responsible for blocking the eastern passage into Halifax past McNab Island; placing net defences across the harbour entrance; making minesweeping arrangements and buoying the war channel; putting an examination service into force; assuming control of the wireless station at Camperdown; and transporting censorship staff and militia detachments to other coastal wireless stations; and controlling internal traffic in Halifax Harbour. While the designated chief minesweeping officer was the lieutenant (torpedoes) in *Niobe*—"if available"—the minesweeping force would consist of the Canadian Government Ships *Petrel*, *Constance*, and *Gulnare*, all with civilian crews. Similarly, the first lieutenant of the Royal Naval College of Canada was designated the chief officer of the examination service (CXO), although the actual examination officers were the three captains of the CG Ships *Canada*, *Curlew*, and *Vigilant*, of whom only the captain of *Canada* held a lieutenant's commission in the Royal Navy Reserve.[6] The examination service was not responsible for "the recognition and entry of HM Ships, for which purpose special arrangements are made." Rather, its primary duty was "to prevent the entry of hostile ships, other than ships of war, into the port." Even then, however, the examination service's role was one of identification, not strict control:

> In effecting this object [the examination service is] to avoid unnecessary restrictions on vessels using this port, such as would interfere with its full use, or would tend to deter shipping from using it. The passage through the defences of vessels which are recognised as friendly should therefore be expedited as far as possible....

---

3.   "War Book, Department of the Naval Service," January 1914, 1019–2-2, pt. 1, LAC, RG 24, vol. 3855.

4.   Ibid.

5.   Ibid.

6.   "Halifax Defence Scheme, Revised to 1st June 1914," nd, "Chapter VII, Local Naval Arrangements," 1001–1-7, pt. 1, LAC, RG 24, vol. 6196.

Incoming merchant vessels will be admitted to the examination anchorage at all times of the day and night, but when the port is closed no merchant vessels, except fleet auxiliaries and army transports, will be permitted to leave the anchorage for the purpose of entering the port. Incoming merchant vessels will, in the absence of the previous instructions from the examining steamer, proceed to the examination anchorage and there anchor.[7]

As the director of naval gunnery at Naval Service Headquarters, Lieutenant R.M.T. Stephens (a Royal Navy officer on loan to the RCN who would transfer to the RCN in the rank of commander on the outbreak of war), explained to the deputy minister, G.J. Desbarats, in February 1914, "the naval service is charged with the naval defence of Canada, but there are insufficient vessels under the authority of that department to carry out the various duties connected therewith." The vessels of the Department of Marine and Fisheries, including two ice-breakers, were needed to buoy a war channel leading into Halifax Harbour "for the purpose of ensuring that ships of all kinds have a safe entry into the harbour free from the enemy's mines" and to act as look-out vessels off that port. They would also be used to transport troops to guard the cable and wireless telegraph stations along the coast.[8]

Fortuitously, the naval sections of the government's war book were completed by the end of July 1914 and arrived in the deputy minister's office on the 29th, one day after Austria–Hungary declared war against Serbia. Just as Desbarats was preparing to sign the document, he was interrupted by a telephone call from Government House with word that the warning telegram, which set in motion the war book's precautionary stage, had been received from London. After Prime Minister Borden rushed back to Ottawa from a summer holiday in the Muskoka region of Ontario, a Cabinet meeting on 1 August confirmed to London "the firm assurance that if unhappily war should ensue, the Canadian people will be united in a common resolve to put forth every effort and to make every sacrifice necessary to ensure the integrity and maintain the honour of our empire." A second cable stated that Ottawa would "welcome any suggestions and advice which the imperial naval and military authorities may deem it expedient to offer" Canada on the most effective form of the nation's military contribution. Also on 1 August—the same day Germany declared war on Russia and mobilized to implement the Schlieffen Plan for invading France and Belgium—midshipmen from the Royal Naval College of Canada were recalled from leave, the naval authorities at Esquimalt were given the authority to enrol volunteers, and the crews of *Niobe* and *Rainbow* began to prepare their ships for active service. Order-in-Council PC 2049 of 4 August (the day Britain declared war on Germany) officially placed the two cruisers "at the disposal of his majesty for general service in the Royal Navy....

7. Halifax Defence Scheme, Revised to 1st June 1914, nd, "Examination Service," ibid.

8. Lt. R.M. Stephens, Director of Naval Gunnery and Cdr. Henry Thompson, RN, Officer Commanding Marine Service to Deputy Ministers of Naval Service and Marine and Fisheries, 5 February 1914, "Report on Cooperation between Department of Naval Service and Marine and Fisheries in Naval Defence of Canada," 1019-3-2, pt. 1, LAC, RG 24, vol. 3855.

together with the officers and seamen serving in such vessels" as part of Britain's trade protection cruiser force.[9]

Although the RN was the world's pre-eminent navy, the bulk of its strength was concentrated in home waters to defend the British Isles and prevent a breakout of the German High Seas Fleet. Its most powerful component, the Grand Fleet, had moved to its war station at Scapa Flow, off the northern tip of Scotland, on 28/29 July. On 2 August its aging commander, Admiral Sir George Callaghan, was replaced by fifty-two year-old Admiral Sir John Jellicoe. The Grand Fleet's incoming commander-in-chief had under him all twenty of Britain's commissioned dreadnought battleships as well as four of the nation's nine battle cruisers. In addition, Jellicoe's battle line was augmented by the pre-dreadnoughts *Agamemnon* and the eight King Edward VII–class battleships of the 3rd Battle Squadron, four cruiser squadrons (of which the 4th Cruiser Squadron was detached to the West Indies as part of the North American and West Indies Station), and four flotillas of destroyers. Attached to the Grand Fleet but based at Harwich, north of the Thames estuary, was a force of one submarine and two destroyer flotillas, which were to operate in the southern North Sea to counter any enemy destroyer or minelaying activities. The East Coast of Britain and the entrance to the English Channel was patrolled by four flotillas of destroyers, and local defence flotillas of older destroyers and torpedo boats were attached to the various naval ports. All these ships were kept in full commission ready for immediate action.[10]

Fourteen of the Royal Navy's remaining pre-dreadnought battleships, meanwhile, were deployed in the English Channel ports as the Second Fleet to cover the despatch of the British Expeditionary Force (BEF) to France. Nominally attached to the Second Fleet were four Home Defence patrol flotillas of destroyers and torpedo boats, and seven flotillas of submarines. Apart from the latter, which were kept on a war footing, these units were manned by all the specialist officers but only three-fifths of their full complement of men. They could be brought up to strength in a few hours by men undergoing training courses at various naval barracks but were otherwise ready to embark at short notice. The remainder of the Royal Navy's pre-dreadnought battleships and cruisers still on the active list were held as a reserve Third Fleet. These ships were manned on a "care and maintenance" basis by skeleton crews and could only be commissioned some time after mobilization once their crews had been brought up to strength by reservists. Although the Majestic- and Canopus-class battleships were "all on the brink of obsolescence" and "regarded as available for subsidiary services"—many would eventually see extensive service in the Mediterranean campaigns—the Third Fleet's five cruiser squadrons, despite being older, obsolescent ships themselves, were essential components of the Royal Navy's commerce protection force covering the vital Atlantic trade routes. With only the Grand Fleet's 4th Cruiser Squadron deployed in the Atlantic on the North America and West

---

9. Governor General to Colonial Secretary, 1 August 1914, in Canada, Department of External Affairs, *Documents on Canadian External Relations* [hereafter *DCER*]: I, *1909–1918* (Ottawa 1967), 37; Tucker, *The Naval Service of Canada*, I, 213; and PC 2049, 4 August 1914, *DCER*, I, 40.

10. Sir Julian Corbett, *Naval Operations*, I: *To The Battle of the Falklands, December 1914* (History of the Great War; London 1920), 11–16.

Indies Station, the Third Fleet cruisers were to provide covering patrols ranging from the northern exits of the North Sea to as far south as Cape Finisterre, Spain. The latter area was to be patrolled by the 9th Cruiser Squadron, which included three of HMCS *Niobe*'s sister ships, *Europa*, *Amphitrite*, and *Argonaut*.[11]

British naval strength in the world's other oceans and seas was more thinly spread. Of the remaining modern battle cruisers, three I-class ships formed the main fighting strength of the Mediterranean Fleet where, supplemented by four armoured cruisers and a light cruiser squadron, they joined with the French navy in keeping watch on the Italian and Austrian fleets, as well as the battle cruiser *Goeben* and the light cruiser *Breslau* of the German *Mittelmeerdivision*. The battle cruiser HMS *Invincible* was stationed at Queenstown, Ireland at the outbreak of war to guard the southwestern approaches to Britain, while HMS *Australia* remained in the southwest Pacific as the most powerful unit of the Australian squadron. As we have seen, both Australia and New Zealand had heeded the advice of the 1909 imperial naval conference and established naval squadrons of their own, with the Australian formation consisting of four light cruisers, three destroyers, and two submarines, in addition to *Australia*. While New Zealand's namesake battle cruiser was serving with the Grand Fleet at Scapa Flow, the island dominion maintained three older light cruisers and a sloop in its own waters. On the outbreak of war, the two dominion squadrons were to join forces with the Royal Navy's China and East Indies squadrons, each centred around one pre-dreadnought battleship, to form the Eastern Fleet under the commander-in-chief of the China station.[12]

From its base at Scapa Flow covering the northern exits from the North Sea, the Grand Fleet's main task was to keep the German High Seas Fleet and its thirteen dreadnought battleships, three battle cruisers, and, perhaps just as importantly, its cruisers from breaking into the North Atlantic shipping lanes and disrupting Britain's ocean lifelines.[13] As mentioned above, the Mediterranean Fleet, in co-operation with the French navy, had to keep an eye (a blind eye, as it turned out, since the enemy warships managed to reach safe harbour in Turkey), on the German battle cruiser *Goeben* and its possible interference in the transfer of French troops from North Africa to Europe. Aside from the *Mittelmeerdivision*, the greatest concentration of overseas German naval strength was the East Asiatic Cruiser Squadron based at Tsingtau, China. Under the command of Vice-Admiral Maximilian Graf von Spee, the German squadron boasted the newest of that country's armoured cruisers, *Scharnhorst* and *Gneisenau*, each armed with eight 8.2-inch and six 5.9-inch guns and capable of twenty knots. Spee's squadron also included the light cruisers *Emden*, *Leipzig*, and *Nurnberg*. The other significant German naval units operating abroad were the light cruisers *Konigsberg* in the Indian Ocean off the East Coast of Africa, and *Dresden* and *Karlsruhe* lurking in Caribbean waters with the capability to disrupt the important North Atlantic trade routes. A fourth German cruiser, *Strassburg*, had been steaming in the area of the Azores but was spotted returning to Germany by way of the English Channel on 31 July.[14]

---

11. Ibid, 12–13, 41.

12. Ibid, 14, 140.

13. Paul G. Halpern, *A Naval History of World War I* (Annapolis 1994), 8–9, 26–27.

HMCS *Niobe*, the RCN's most powerful warship, spent the first year of the war as part of the North America and West Indies Station cruiser force patrolling off the United States eastern seaboard. (CWM 20030174-045)

These warships were not the only German vessels that were of concern to the Royal Navy, however. With the second largest merchant marine in the world—although at 12 percent of the world's total, a distant second to Britain's—Germany possessed many fast liners that could easily be armed as auxiliary cruisers. Only a sixth of British merchant ships were capable of a speed greater than twelve knots, with most content to steam at eight to ten. An armed German liner capable of sixteen knots would, therefore, have little trouble running down any merchantman whose smoke was sighted on the horizon.[15] The greatest difficulty facing German commerce raiders, whether navy cruisers or armed liners, was Germany's lack of overseas bases. Before the war, the German navy attempted to overcome the supply problem by establishing a base or line of communication (*Etappe*) system with an *Etappenoffizier* appointed in each zone where operations might occur to coordinate the provision of coal, fuel oil, drinking water, and other supplies for the cruisers. As one naval historian of the First World War has pointed out, however, the *Etappe* system "was only partially successful":

> The German officials constantly skirmished with the various neutral authorities over neutrality regulations, and after the war broke out, there was a cat-and-mouse game between the Germans and the diplomatic and mercantile representatives of the Allies in numerous neutral harbors who constantly sought to uncover their activities and protest them to the authorities. Neutral powers curtailed the export of coal in some places. Moreover, some of the German supply ships and colliers were caught by Allied warships. German commanders often had to coal from prizes, and coal in fact became their constant preoccupation, limiting the amount of time they could spend on the sea lanes.[16]

Although almost all European countries were dependent on foreign imports for a portion of their food supply and industrial raw materials, Britain was particularly vulnerable to an interruption of its overseas traffic. The prewar British merchant marine, with more than 9,200 vessels totalling some 21,000,000 tons, represented 43 percent of the world's commercial shipping.[17] The British people were particularly dependent on imports for their food supply, with two-thirds of the food consumed being imported, including 70 to 80 percent of cereals, fruit and cheese, and 100 percent of their sugar. In terms of raw materials, cotton, silk, oil, and rubber were obtained exclusively from overseas, while 75 percent of wool was imported. Only 25 percent of iron ore came from abroad but the higher quality of the ores imported from Spain meant that 40 to 50 percent of the total production of pig iron was dependent on imports, while a large proportion of the raw

---

14. Ibid, 66; and C. Ernest Fayle, *Seaborne Trade,* I: *The Cruiser Period* (History of the Great War; London 1920), 104.

15. Fayle, *Seaborne Trade,* I, 13–21.

16. Halpern, *A Naval History of World War I,* 67.

17. Ibid, 65.

copper, tin, lead, and zinc used by British smelters was obtained from overseas. In addition, the United Kingdom annually imported some six to seven million tons of timber, a third of which was used as pit-props by the British coal industry, the nation's primary source of energy. As the British official history of seaborne trade has explained, "it is not too much to say that almost all the staple British industries were dependent for their prosperity upon the uninterrupted flow of commodities from oversea."

> Moreover, the vast expansion called for in military equipment and the enormous accumulation of munitions and war material necessitated by the conditions of modern warfare, strained the manufacturing resources of the country to their utmost at an early stage of the conflict, and involved large purchases abroad. In order to avert a collapse of the national strength it was essential that each of the three great branches of the import trade [which included imported manufactured goods such as optical instruments] should be maintained, and scarcely less important was the maintenance of the outward-bound traffic. For it was only by the uninterrupted flow of exports that imports could be paid for, and unemployment and distress amongst the industrial population avoided, without incurring crushing indebtedness to the producing countries. The task imposed upon the [Royal] Navy by the necessity of affording protection to this gigantic trade was a heavy one.[18]

Of the trade moving over the world's oceans, none was more important to Britain than that which came across the North Atlantic from the Americas. It was estimated that the traffic between Europe and the Atlantic ports of North America occupied a full one-sixth of the world's entire mercantile tonnage. In the two decades before the outbreak of war, Canada and the United States had, to a large extent, become the granaries of the world with imports of North American wheat alone accounting for 36 percent of total British consumption. Half of all bacon and hams, two-thirds of all cheese, and almost all the butter and lard imported by Britain, also came from North America. Although the British textile industry had attempted to develop other sources of supply for its raw cotton following the dislocation caused by the American Civil War—when the Union blockade led to widespread unemployment and British mills standing idle—when the First World War began, a full 75 percent of British cotton was still imported from the southern United States. American leather and tobacco, and Canadian lumber were also important items of the Atlantic trade before 1914, but it was the supply of North American petroleum and copper, needed by both the Royal Navy and Britain's munitions industries, that proved crucial following the outbreak of war.[19]

The United States merchant marine, at 4 percent of the world's total tonnage, was wholly inadequate to carry out that country's overseas trade, some 90 percent of which had

18. Fayle, *Seaborne Trade*, I, 4–5.

19. Ibid, 100–01.

to be shipped under foreign-flagged, predominately British, vessels. Up to half the sailings to and from Atlantic and Gulf ports, including those to South America and other European countries, were made by merchantmen flying the red ensign, and British ships were even more dominant on the North Atlantic routes. In 1913, for instance, 87 percent of the more than 4,000 ships that carried cargoes to and from Canada, Newfoundland, and the United States were British-flagged. The North Atlantic traffic was also distinguished by the large, fast passenger liners owned by the British, German, American, and French shipping companies. While they were the latest word in marine construction and engine power—not to mention in elegance of their accommodation and fittings—as they competed for the fastest crossing and the resulting public attention, the large liners had relatively little cargo capacity and normally restricted themselves to items of high value in proportion to bulk, routinely mail and bullion. Of greater importance to the conveying of trade were the more numerous cargo liners, some of which also carried passengers, that were each capable of shipping thousands of tons and ran "to a schedule as regular as those of the mail services." These were supplemented by tramp steamers carrying heavy or bulk goods of comparatively lower value, such as Canadian timber, with many of the tramps arriving in ballast (i.e., without cargo, but weighed down with rocks or water to maintain stability) to load North American grain.[20]

Most of this traffic followed the Great Circle route across the North Atlantic, the shortest track between New York City and the southern coast of Ireland. Traffic bound for Europe from the eastern seaboard of the United States, including ships originating in the Carolinas and the Gulf of Mexico, steamed northeast parallel to the coast of Nova Scotia to a focal point southeast of Cape Race, Newfoundland. In the summer months, they would be joined by ships exiting the Gulf of St Lawrence, vessels that had loaded at Montreal's extensive port facilities, which were served by four main rail lines that connected it to the continent's interior. When the St Lawrence closed to navigation during the winter, the Canadian traffic would originate from the ice-free port of St John, New Brunswick, and, to a lesser extent, Halifax, Nova Scotia.[21]

Though not heavily used for cargo, Halifax's proximity to the Cape Race focal point made it an important naval base for the British cruiser force that protected both the traffic exiting the Gulf of St Lawrence and the ships steaming northeast off the coast of Nova Scotia from the United States eastern seaboard. The Admiralty had warned Ottawa in May 1914 that the shipping lanes between New York and Cape Race offered an "excellent" area for German raiders and had stressed that more cruisers were needed to reinforce the "limited number" of warships the Royal Navy could "allot to the North Atlantic in war."[22] The only immediate contribution the RCN could provide, of course, was the obsolete *Niobe*, alongside at Halifax with only a skeleton crew. Nonetheless, as the inclusion of her

---

20. Ibid, 102.

21. Ibid, 103.

22. Admiralty, "Admiralty Comments on memorandum on 'Remarks on Naval Defence of the Atlantic Coast,'" 5 May 1914, Borden Papers, LAC, Manuscript Group (hereafter MG) 26H, vol. 126.

three sister ships in the 9th Cruiser Squadron demonstrated, the Canadian warship still represented a valuable reinforcement to Britain's thinly stretched trade protection force. With war appearing imminent, Naval Service Headquarters informed the captain in charge at Halifax dockyard on 1 August that "*Niobe* may commission. Telegraph earliest date probably available. Commence work immediately. Use fishery protection engine room staff as necessary under engineer officer *Niobe*."[23] By 12 August, Halifax was able to inform NSHQ that "everything has been completed in revised defence scheme except buoying the channel for war," a task that had been hindered by thick fog. The progress that had been made in preparing *Niobe* for sea, meanwhile, was reported as "satisfactory."[24]

While the Naval Service was directly responsible for the defensive arrangements at the designated naval ports of Halifax and Esquimalt, it also had to assist the army in organizing the defences at several other Canadian ports. Chief among these was Quebec, whose location near the mouth of the St Lawrence River made it the logical place to set up an examination service covering Montreal. As the chief examination officer at Quebec for most of the war, Commander G.O.R. Eliott later explained that the navy assumed an active role from the outset of hostilities.

> On hostilities being opened and war declared on August 4th, 1914, Commander Atwood, RN, was sent up from Halifax to assist and cooperate with military and civil authorities for the purpose of inaugurating a defence of the Port of Quebec. Barges were commandeered and filled with rock ballast for the purpose of being ready to block the channel north of Orleans Island. Water patrol of harbour and dry dock was put in force by commandeering tug boats and other available craft. Guards were placed at [the] bridge across Louise basin, also at the elevator and Immigration sheds and orders from minister of the naval service were issued that a company was to be raised composed of sailors and firemen and to be termed "Royal Naval Canadian Volunteer Reserve (RNCVR)."
>
> In conjunction with the foregoing an Examination Service was put into force. Boats were used belonging to the Canadian government marine service, and were stationed at Maheux Bay, Island of Orleans, in charge of Commander Atwood, RN, and three RCN midshipmen. The examination vessels were supported by a battery of 5-inch BL guns stations on Orleans Island at Maheux River.
>
> The examination service is for the purpose of stopping all ships, boarding them and examining papers, etc., which, if satisfactory the ship is given the secret signal for the day or night, as the case may be, same to be hoisted in a position where it could be best seen, to indicate to the batteries to let her pass the defences.

23. Naval Ottawa to Captain in Charge, HMC Dockyard, Halifax, 1 August 1914, 1047–19–2, LAC, RG 24, vol. 3969.

24. "Defensive Measures—1914. Reports on Situation. Copies for Chief of Staff," 12 August 1914, DHH 81/520/1440–05, vol. 4.

I was appointed to the Department of the Naval Service, Ottawa, as assistant examination officer, and on August 21st 1914 Commander Atwood was recalled to England, and I was appointed chief examination officer for the Port of Quebec, with office at the Custom House which was in touch by direct wire with militia headquarters, Citadel, and batteries at Martiniere and Beaumont, also to signal staff at St Jean Wharf, Island of Orleans, who were in touch with Examination Battery, and vessels at Maheaux Bay; also port war signal station situated on the highest point of the Island of Orleans and manned by militia; the object of Port war signal station was to keep a good lookout for all inward bound vessels, and if any man-of-war vessels of any kind approached, to challenge them, and if correct reply was made, to pass them through the defences by telephoning to the batteries, militia headquarters, and chief examination officer.

The above work was carried out until the close to navigation for River St Lawrence when ice conditions prohibited any more ships attempting to make the port of Quebec.[25]

The existence of naval and non-naval ports was not a distinction that the militia department easily grasped, however. Commander R.M.T. Stephens, Kingsmill's chief of staff and indispensable right hand, had to explain to the militia secretary in December 1914 that defensive arrangements at the naval ports of Halifax and Esquimalt "would be made by the senior naval officer who would consult the military officer in command on any details which concern the military. At other ports all arrangements would be made by the military officer in command who would consult the Department of the Naval Service, Ottawa, on any points which concern the navy. At these ports the Department of the Naval Service would provide examination vessels and their personnel, as far as possible, if requested to do so by the militia department. In the latter case, the vessels and their crews would be placed under the authority of the military officer in command."[26] The navy's willingness to take an active role in the defensive arrangements at Quebec was fully exploited by the general officer commanding the militia's 5th Division. Writing to the chief of the general staff, Major-General Willoughby Gwatkin, the following April, Stephens complained about the "distinct tendency at Quebec to foist all manner of services on to this department."

Since the outbreak of war we have paid (quite cheerfully) many thousands of dollars for work at Quebec with which this department has but an indirect concern. The accounts, however, have been forwarded, either by your department or the officer commanding 5th Division, and paid without demur.

These services include, for instance, the hire of barges for blocking the channel north of Orleans Island, and the charter of steamers with electric lights

---

25. Commander G.O.R. Eliott, RNR, "History of Work Carried Out at Quebec from Naval Transport Office," 1 December 1918, 1049–2-40, LAC, RG 24, vol. 3981.

26. Stephens to Military Secretary, Interdepartmental Committee, 6 December 1914, 1022–2-2, LAC, RG 24, vol. 3856.

for the benefit of martiniere batteries. The officer commanding 5th Division
now goes a step further and "presumes" the naval department will be responsible for the signalling arrangements at the examination battery, the port war
signal station and other shadowy spots.

Quebec is not a naval port, and consequently the navy has nothing to do
with it, properly speaking. In 1911, however, it was agreed that this department would provide the examination steamers and personnel, to work under
the officer commanding 5th Division. A few days after the outbreak of war this
arrangement was found unsatisfactory and we agreed to take over complete
responsibility for the examination service. This obviously did not include the
examination battery and still less the port war signal station, with which the
examination service has no connection.

I should be much obliged if it could be pointed out to the officer commanding 5th Division that the responsibility of the navy at Quebec ceases with
the examination steamers, and that the general floating defence of the port
is in his hands. I need not say that the chief examining officer will at all times
render every assistance possible to the militia authorities.[27]

At first glance, the situation on Canada's West Coast at the outbreak of war appeared
more promising. Not only were the Pacific shipping lanes less vital to Britain's economic
well-being, but the RCN's only warship at Esquimalt, the light cruiser *Rainbow*, had already
been prepared for duty at sea. Throughout the summer of 1914 the Royal Navy's only two
warships on the West Coast of North America, the aged sloops *Algerine* and *Shearwater*,
had been engaged off the West Coast of Mexico protecting British subjects from local civil
unrest. In their absence, NSHQ had agreed to prepare *Rainbow* to undertake a three-
months' patrol of the sealing grounds in the Bering Sea. Her crew had been brought up to
strength by drafts of sailors from both *Niobe* and Britain, and volunteers from the
Vancouver and Victoria naval companies.

The formation of volunteer companies in British Columbia was well in advance of the
rest of the country. Although there had been no official approval, an ad hoc naval
company was formed by a group of enthusiasts in Victoria in the summer of 1913 and
subsequently given permission by the naval minister, J.D. Hazen, to use the facilities at
Esquimalt for their parades. They also received encouragement from several of the
Rainbow's officers, including its commanding officer, Commander Walter Hose, who also
volunteered their time to provide some professional instruction. As a result, the Victoria
company was well positioned to provide sailors when PC 1313 of 18 May 1914
implemented the sections of the Naval Service Act providing for a reserve force. Called the
Royal Naval Canadian Volunteer Reserve (although the name would not be changed until
1923, many Canadian officers, including Admiral Kingsmill, occasionally referred to the
new organization as the more logical RCNVR by mistake), it comprised "persons who
volunteer ... when called out.... to serve in the vessels of the Naval Service of Canada or

---

27. Stephens to Major-General W. Gwatkin, 12 April 1915, ibid.

Built in 1895, the 1,050-ton HMS *Algerine* was one of two British sloops based at Esquimalt at the outbreak of war. (LAC PA-066841)

in those of the Royal Navy ... and in such ranks and ratings as are required for establishments on shore."[28]

At that time, the navy was authorized to enlist 400 volunteers in an Atlantic Division, 600 in a Lake Division, and 200 in a Pacific Division.[29] Despite the enthusiastic response across the country, the department did little to organize companies before war was declared; then, as Desbarats explained to the secretary of the Royal St Lawrence Yacht Club in Montreal at the end of August, more urgent wartime needs meant that "at the present moment it is not intended to proceed with the organization of the companies of naval volunteers as it is not possible to obtain instructional officers at a time like this when every available man is employed on the warships. The officers who had been retained for these duties have been obliged to leave for active service, and the department is therefore unable to undertake the organization or instruction of a volunteer corps."[30] Consequently, the only organized naval volunteers available were the men of the Vancouver and Victoria companies called out for service at Esquimalt, and together they would supply the RCN with most of the volunteer reservists enlisted during the first year and a half of the war. By November 1914, the two companies carried 313 volunteers on their nominal rolls, of whom 213 were actually serving.[31]

With only two warships, a few auxiliaries, and a small shore establishment to man, the RCN's manpower requirements were, at least for the first year of the war, relatively modest. Even so, the naval service was fortunate in being able to draw upon many retired British sailors living in Canada, particularly officers, to fill many of its positions both ashore and afloat. The Admiralty had agreed that the RCN could have first call on retired Royal Navy officers resident in Canada, while enlistment of Royal Naval Reserve ratings was greatly facilitated by the Canadian rates of pay, which, during the war, were up to three times rates received by the lower deck in the British service. Indeed, on the day following the declaration of war one of the RCN's strongest private supporters, Aemilius Jarvis, a wealthy Toronto stockbroker, avid yachtsman (having won the prestigious Canada's Cup Great Lakes yacht race in 1896 and 1901), and member of the Navy League of Canada, informed NSHQ that he had recruited fifty former RN ratings "who were likely-looking young men and willing to serve in *Niobe*."[32] By enlisting trained British naval reservists, the minuscule Canadian service was also relieved of the necessity of creating its own training establishment at the war's outset.

As part of their training, fifty of the Victoria reservists had already been assigned to

28. PC 1313, 18 May 1914.

29. Admiral Story to Secretary, Department of the Naval Service, 6 November 1914, 26–2-1, LAC, RG 24, vol. 5597.

30. Desbarats to R.G. Lyman, 31 August 1914, ibid See also Desbarats to W.S. Middleton, 25 July 1914, Kingsmill to Frank Pattinson, 6 July 1914, and Kingsmill to A.H.E. Fuller, 26 June 1914, ibid.

31. Stephens, "Memo to Director of the Naval Service," 18 November 1914, J.D. Hazen to Sir Robert Borden, 21 September 1914, ibid.

32. Tucker, *Naval Service of Canada*, I, 217, 220; and Fraser McKee, *The Armed Yachts of Canada* (Erin, Ontario, 1983), 28–29.

Personnel of the RNCVR outside the provincial legislature in Victoria, BC, in 1914. (LAC PA-115374)

Rainbow's company in preparation for the Bering Sea sealing patrol, but the cruiser was diverted to Vancouver in mid-July. A Japanese merchant ship, the *Komagata Maru*, had arrived at the port in May with 400 Indians hoping to enter Canada. When the authorities barred the Asians from leaving the ship, the would-be immigrants seized the vessel and refused to leave the harbour. They greeted a group of Vancouver police and local officials who attempted to board the merchantman on 18 July with a fusillade of coal, prompting the authorities to ask the Canadian cruiser for a show of naval force. According to Commander Hose, "as *Rainbow* steamed round the *Komagata Maru*, the latter's decks crowded with the recalcitrant Indians, one grizzled veteran, late of the Indian Army, put the relieving touch of humour on the otherwise serious outlook by standing on the upper bridge of the *Komagata* and semaphoring to the *Rainbow*—'our only ammunition is coal.'"[33]

Still the would-be immigrants, having lost their case in court—a previous though smaller group of Indians had managed to win admission—agreed to recross the Pacific but on condition that they be given the necessary victuals. Refusal led to a continuation of the standoff, and although Canadian naval lore would have it that *Rainbow*'s presence brought the incident to an end, evidence points to the federal minister of agriculture, Martin Bruell, as the *deus ex machina* on this occasion. His willingness to provide a few thousand dollars' worth of supplies convinced the protesters to leave Canadian waters, sailing for Hong Kong on the 23rd.[34] Perhaps the greatest irony in the exchange was the fact that the obsolete cruiser was little better armed than the *Komagata Maru*'s coal-throwing passengers, carrying only obsolete gunpowder shells for her main armament of two 6-inch guns. After returning to Esquimalt, Commander Hose was ordered by Ottawa on 1 August to prepare *Rainbow* "for active service trade protection grain ships going south. German cruiser *Nurnberg* or *Leipzig* is on west coast America. Obtain all information available as to merchant ships sailing from Canadian or United States ports. Telegraph demands for ordnance stores required to complete to fullest capacity."[35] Although *Rainbow* was alongside at Esquimalt she was only able to ammunition from the old Royal Navy stores available in the dockyard, a stockpile that did not include any high-explosive shells. A promised ammunition train from the East was delayed by the fact that the Canadian railways, as yet unorganized for war, were refusing to handle explosives. Besides the lack of suitable ammunition, the old cruiser had a wireless set that was capable of transmitting only two hundred miles and would have no collier, or dependable coaling station, available to her south of Vancouver Island.[36]

On the afternoon of 2 August, the Admiralty wired directly to Esquimalt with the news that the German cruiser *Leipzig* had been reported leaving the Mexican port of Mazatlan on the morning of 30 July and instructed *Rainbow* to "proceed south at once in order to get in touch with [the German cruiser] and generally guard [the] trade routes north of the equator." Uncertain whether or not his vessel had been placed under the Admiralty's direct

---

33. Quoted in Tucker, *Naval Service of Canada*, I, 149.

34. Hugh Johnston, *The Voyage of the Komagata Maru: The Sikh Challenge to Canada's Colour Bar* (Vancouver 1989), 84.

35. NSHQ to Hose, 1 August 1914, 1047–19–3, pt. 1, LAC, RG 24, vol. 5640.

36. Tucker, *The Naval Service of Canada*, I, 264–65.

orders, Hose repeated the message to NSHQ together with a request for further instructions. No doubt with his ship's considerable handicaps in mind, Hose also suggested a more cautious course of action than that proposed by London:

> With reference to Admiralty telegram submitted *Rainbow* may remain in the vicinity Cape Flattery until more accurate information is received *Leipzig*, observing that in [the] event of *Leipzig* appearing Cape Flattery with *Rainbow* twelve hundred miles distant and receiving no communications, [the] Pacific cable, Pachena WT station, and ships entering straits at mercy of *Leipzig* with opportunity to coal from prizes. Vessels working up the west coast of America could easily be warned to adhere closely to territorial waters as far as possible. Enquiry being made *Leipzig* through our consul.[37]

Despite the apparent wisdom of Hose's proposals, NSHQ was less disposed to interfere with the Admiralty's instructions and simply confirmed that he was "to proceed to sea forthwith to guard trade routes north of equator." They did, however, add that the cruiser was to keep "in touch with [the] Pachena [wireless station] until war has been declared." Given the limited range of *Rainbow*'s wireless set, NSHQ's ruling effectively meant that Hose would initially have to remain in the vicinity of the Juan de Fuca Strait.[38] Departing Esquimalt in the early hours of 3 August, the Canadian ship cruised off the Washington coast for the next two days between Cape Flattery at the entrance to the strait and Destruction Island seventy-five kilometres to the south. According to one of the witnesses at the Esquimalt dockyard, "few of those who saw her depart on that eventful occasion expect to see her return."[39]

Hose was able to take advantage of the extra time to address some of his ship's deficiencies by exercising action stations and conducting firing practices to calibrate the guns. At 2007 hours on 4 August, Hose finally received word from Ottawa that war had been declared and he immediately "shaped course for the south to protect trade." Within the hour, however, NSHQ ordered *Rainbow* to make for Vancouver to rendezvous with the important train carrying the ship's modern ammunition. According to his report of proceedings, Hose complied with the latest directive by "increasing speed so as to arrive at Esquimalt at daylight on the 5th, complete with coal there, proceed to Vancouver in the evening, and arrive at daylight on the 6th, the date on which the special train with ammunition for *Rainbow* was due."

> However at 6:00 pm on the 5th, when off Race Rocks Light, I received telegraphic instructions to proceed south to protect HM Ships *Algerine* and *Shearwater*, which, it was understood, had left San Diego in company on the

---

37. Hose to NSHQ, 2 August 1914, 1047–19–3, pt. 1, LAC, RG 24, vol. 5640; and Tucker, *The Naval Service of Canada*, I, 265.

38. NSHQ to Hose, 3 August 1914, 1047–19–3, pt. 1, LAC, RG 24, vol. 5640.

39. George Phillips quoted in Tucker, *The Naval Service of Canada*, I, 266.

Immigration inspector Malcolm Reid, member of parliament for Vancouver City Centre, H.H. Stevens, and Commander Walter Hose, left to right respectively, converse with a militia officer aboard HMCS *Rainbow* during the confrontation with the merchant ship *Komagata Maru* in English Bay, Vancouver, in July 1914. (LAC PA-034016)

4th, with the German cruisers off Magdalena Bay on the same day steaming north in chase. Course was altered and speed increased to 3/5th power, and I arrived off San Francisco at 6:00 am on the 7th. Calculating on information received it seemed that the *Algerine* and *Shearwater* must by that time either be in San Francisco or else, having stood well to seaward, be then to the northward of the port. I decided to go in and get the latest information on the situation from HBM consul-general and also complete with coal, as I had previously received telegraphic instruction from the [naval] department that the US government did not object to belligerents coaling in their ports.[40]

Indeed, Hose had been told by NSHQ on 3 August that "the United States does not prohibit belligerents from coaling in her ports" and that arrangements had been made to have 500 tons of coal waiting for *Rainbow* in California.[41] The coal had, in fact, been arranged by the British consul-general, but when the Canadian cruiser arrived in San Francisco on the morning of 7 August and prepared to take on the fuel, Hose "was informed by the naval and customs authorities that in accordance with the president's neutrality proclamation, I could only take in sufficient coal to enable me to reach the nearest British port. As I already had sufficient, it meant that I could not coal at all; however, on the plea that I had not a safe margin I was permitted to embark 50 ton." An hour and twenty minutes after *Rainbow* anchored in San Francisco harbour, the German freighter *Alexandria* was sighted off the Golden Gate entrance, a Hamburg-Amerika Line vessel that had reportedly been requisitioned by *Leipzig* to act as an auxiliary.

Although Hose was informed that *Leipzig* "had coaled at La Paz [Mexico] two days previously," he also received "various conflicting reports" as to the whereabouts of the two German cruisers. Unable to take on board the required coal, Hose "decided to leave San Francisco at midnight and proceed north partly in order to keep between the enemy and the two British sloops, and partly to meet the store ship which I expected would be on her way to the rendezvous two miles south of the Farralones Islands" that lay some twenty-five miles west of the Golden Gate.[42] At the very least, the Canadian cruiser's appearance on the American West Coast disrupted what little German trade was to be found. The enemy merchant ships that were caught on the Pacific coast on the outbreak of war "cut short their voyage at the nearest port, sending on their cargoes under the American flag, and numerous [German] sailing vessels of large size were held up in Californian and Mexican harbours."[43]

Of the two enemy cruisers suspected to be operating off the American coast only *Leipzig* was actually heading for San Francisco, a destination the warship would not reach until the

---

40. Hose to Senior Naval Officer (SNO), Esquimalt, Report of Proceedings, 17 August 1914, DHH 81/520/8000, "HMCS *Rainbow*," vol. 2.

41. NSHQ to Hose, 3 August 1914, 1047–19–3, pt. 1, LAC, RG 24, vol. 5640.

42. Hose to Senior Naval Officer, Esquimalt, Report of Proceedings, 17 August 1914, DHH 81/520/8000, "HMCS *Rainbow*," vol. 2; and Tucker, *The Naval Service of Canada*, I, 267.

43. Fayle, *Seaborne Trade*, I, 162–63.

11th. Unbeknownst to British naval intelligence, *Nurnberg* had left San Francisco on 21 July headed for the Far East to join Spee's two armoured cruisers, *Scharnhorst* and *Gneisenau*.[44] That *Leipzig* might be approaching his position was confirmed only an hour before the *Rainbow* was due to sail, when the British consul-general informed Hose that "he had received authentic news of a steam schooner which was to leave San Francisco the following morning (8th [August]) laden with lubricating oil and other stores for the German cruisers, and these stores were to be transhipped at sea. He deemed that either one or both of the cruisers were not far off the entrance to San Francisco Bay." According to Hose's report,

> It appeared to me that it was my duty, being apparently so close to the enemy, to try and get in touch with him at once, consequently I got under way at midnight and proceeded in misty weather to a point on the three mile limit fifteen miles to the southward of San Francisco, from there I steamed slowly to the southward all that forenoon, the weather being foggy and clear alternately. I did not, however, see anything of the schooner or the German cruisers.
>
> I did not deem it advisable to go far from the vicinity of my rendezvous with the [Canadian] store ship as I had no idea when she might arrive there, and with the amount of fog which was about, it was very likely that the store ship might be sighted by the enemy, without having come in contact with *Rainbow*.
>
> I continued to cruise off the Farralones Islands until 10am on the 10th; during this time wireless messages were continually being intercepted reporting *Rainbow's* position "en clair" and also code messages from a mail steamer which steamed around the ship. The vessel was the *Mongolia* and the president of the company she belongs to in San Francisco is a German. At 10am on the 10th I was forced to return north as my coal supply was reduced to the lowest safe margin.[45]

The decision to head north on 10 August proved to be a fortuitous one for *Rainbow's* makeshift crew as *Leipzig* appeared the following day in the waters the Canadian cruiser had been patrolling. There can be little doubt that Hose was anticipating an engagement when he left San Francisco harbour in the early hours of the 8th. One of the crew's first tasks after clearing the Golden Gate had been to tear out all the ship's flammable woodwork and toss it overboard. The appearance of *Rainbow's* woodwork washing ashore convinced skeptics that the obsolete warship had met her doom at the hands of the modern German cruiser. With the *Rainbow's* 6-inch main armament easily outranged by *Leipzig's* higher velocity 4-inch guns, such a scenario must have seemed as likely to the Canadian ship's crew as it did to the people on shore. Nonetheless, the fact that the

---

44. Corbett, *Naval Operations*, I, 145.

45. Hose to Senior Naval Officer, Esquimalt, Report of Proceedings, 17 August 1914, DHH 81/520/8000, "HMCS *Rainbow*," vol. 2.

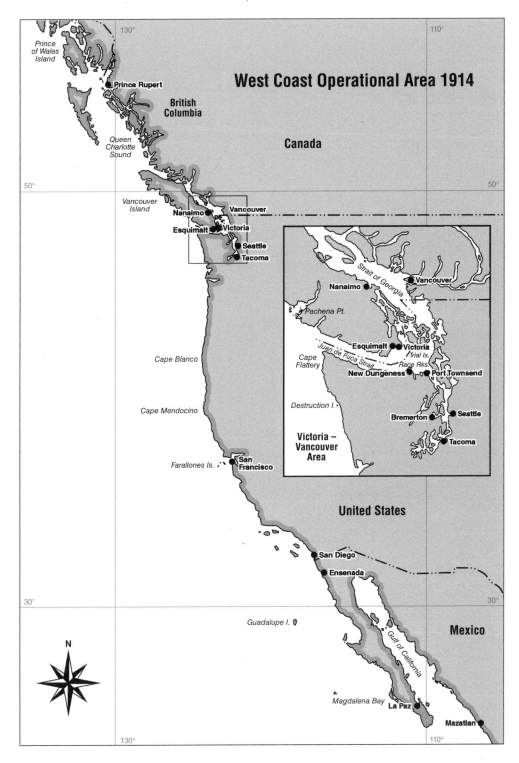

West Coast Operational Area 1914

Prince
of Wales
Island

● Prince Rupert

**British
Columbia**

Queen
Charlotte
Sound

Canada

130°

110°

50°

50°

Vancouver
Island

Nanaimo ●

Vancouver

Esquimalt ● ● Victoria

● Seattle

● Tacoma

Cape Blanco

Cape Mendocino

Farallones Is.

● San
Francisco

United States

San Diego ●

Ensenada ●

30°

30°

Guadalupe I. ●

N

Mexico

Gulf of California

Magdalena Bay   La Paz ●

Mazatlan ●

130°

110°

Inset:

Strait of Georgia

Vancouver ●

Nanaimo ●

Pachena Pt.

Juan de Fuca Strait

Esquimalt ● ● Victoria

Trial Is.

Cape
Flattery

Race Rks.

New Dungeness ● ● Port Townsend

Cape
Flattery

Destruction I.

Bremerton ● ● Seattle

● Tacoma

**Victoria –
Vancouver
Area**

The German cruiser SMS *Leipzig* coaling at San Francisco on 17 August 1914. (DND SMSLeipzig-03)

German cruiser was operating at a great distance from any possible repair facilities meant that her captain, *Fregattenkapitän* Haun, had to be wary of being damaged even if he sank his opponent. Hose could also have made use of the fog encountered off the Farallones to increase his chances of hitting the enemy even in the absence of high explosive shells.[46]

The prospect of *Rainbow* surviving a clash with a modern German cruiser was viewed by most people at Esquimalt as slight. Reflecting the long odds facing the Canadians, a Grand Trunk Pacific Railway coastal liner, the SS *Prince George*, had been hurriedly fitted as a hospital ship and sent south to accompany the RCN warship on her patrol— presumably to rescue and treat any survivors. As *Rainbow* was steaming back to Esquimalt on 12 August, the Grand Trunk liner was sighted shortly after 0800 hours. The ship's three funnels and cruiser stern (similar to those of *Leipzig* and *Nurnberg*) were immediately visible in the clear weather conditions so that, at a distance, *Prince George* presented an appearance that was not unlike that of the German raiders. Upon sighting "a vessel which appeared to be a warship," the RCN cruiser "immediately altered course about fourteen points to starboard and put on full speed while all hands went to action stations. A few minutes later the stranger was identified as a merchant ship which turned out to be *Prince George*. The latter carried an order that Commander Hose should return to Esquimalt and both vessels accordingly proceeded towards Cape Flattery."[47]

Investigating the incident in April 1961, RCN historian E.C. Russell was critical of Hose's actions upon sighting what he believed to be an enemy warship, suggesting that they called into question "the tactical intent of Commander Hose in altering ... nearly fourteen points ... away on sighting a supposed enemy. A smaller alteration of course would be expected if it was required in order to bring the after 6-inch gun to bear." Since the cruiser's "log clearly states that on *Rainbow*'s sighting of what turned out to be the *Prince George*, course was altered from N24W to S50E ... it is difficult to draw any conclusion other than the fact that *Rainbow* presented her stern to the supposed enemy and increased to full speed."[48] Tactfully questioned about the encounter in the summer of 1961, the long-retired admiral—"a very spry and well-preserved sailor" at age seventy-six—"had very clear recollections of that day."

> He himself was conning the ship when the ship that turned out to be the *Prince George* was sighted. He thought she was a German cruiser, *Leipzig* or *Nurnberg*. It was a clear day and he at once altered away onto almost a reciprocal course because:
> the *Rainbow* carried but half her war complement;
> about 25 percent of the ship's company were raw reservists of the month-old RNCVR;

46. Halpern, *A Naval History of World War I*, 80.

47. E.C. Russell, "*Rainbow*," 10 April 1961, DHH 81/520/8000, "HMCS *Rainbow*," vol. 2.

48. Ibid.

> it was known that the German Asiatic Squadron had only fast, new ships
> with heavier armament than the *Rainbow* and [were] manned by crack crews
> of the regular German navy; and
>
> he manoeuvred for time in order to clear away his stern 6-inch gun for the
> supposed stern chase that would surely follow.[49]

Far from demonstrating that he had merely been clearing the decks before moving in to engage the supposed German cruiser, Hose's interview simply explained the very good reasons as to why he had turned away from the enemy and made off at high speed. His statement did nothing to change Russell's mind about the intent behind *Rainbow*'s actions. "Although [Hose] believed that the German cruisers were on that coast," he commented soon after the 1961 interview, "he did not say why he was not cleared for action in advance, except to say that the ship had been so hurriedly and inadequately prepared for sea that she was in really no fit condition to fight. However, it is a fact that the Admiral [Hose] when captain of patrols at Sydney in 1918 court-martialled the captain of the *Hochelaga* [following the RCN's only First World War encounter with an enemy warship] for what amounted to turning away in the face of the enemy when that ship off St Pierre was faced with the superior fire-power of a German ocean-going submarine."[50]

While it may seem unfair to criticize *Rainbow*'s commander given his ship's obsolete armament, lack of high explosive ammunition, and the inadequate training of his scratch crew, the fact that Hose was anticipating a "supposed stern chase that would surely follow" indicates that he was ignoring the nature of commerce raiding operations in distant oceans (as well as the obvious, if natural, misperception that he was the one being hunted). With the raider's primary mission being the disruption and sinking of enemy commercial shipping, a German warship would only have engaged a British cruiser—even an obsolete one—in self-defence. The sight of *Rainbow*'s stern rapidly disappearing over the horizon was exactly what any German cruiser would have hoped to see. As the German official history has explained, *Leipzig*'s captain had to weigh "the advisability of winning an immediate military success by attacking the *Algerine* or *Shearwater* on their way to Esquimalt, by capturing one of the Canadian Pacific liners which could be fitted as an auxiliary cruiser, or by attacking the Canadian training ship *Rainbow*. Considering the importance of commerce raiding, however, these enterprises would scarcely have been justified; for even a successful action with the *Rainbow*, which was an older ship but which had mounted a heavier armament, might have resulted in such serious damage to the *Leipzig* as would have brought her career to a premature end."[51]

Whatever the inadequacies of his ship and crew, or the absence of fog to cover his approach, it was, nonetheless, Hose's clear duty to do his utmost to incapacitate any raider he was fortunate enough to intercept. As Russell was well aware, that objective could not

---

49. Russell, "HMCS *Rainbow* and Hospital Ship *Prince George*—encounter at sea 12 August, 1914," 15 June 1961, DHH 81/520/8000, "HMCS *Rainbow*," vol. 2.

50. Ibid.

51. Quoted in Tucker, *The Naval Service of Canada*, I, 274.

be accomplished by presenting one's stern to the enemy. It also did not escape Russell's attention that Hose had made no reference to his encounter with the hospital ship in his subsequent report of proceedings, even though *Prince George* had been specifically fitted out as a hospital ship and sent out to meet him. At the very least, Hose's actions on meeting *Prince George* call into question one historian's claim that "Hose and his men had never hesitated to push into danger when called upon" or that *Rainbow* was indeed prepared to meet "her end in a blaze of glory off San Francisco in August 1914."[52] It would appear from the evidence that the resulting cry of "Remember the *Rainbow*,"—which the historian in question suggests could have "become the stuff of legend" and "might well have become Canada's battle cry" during the First World War[53]—was unlikely to become reality on Commander Hose's watch.

Just how effectively a single enemy cruiser could disrupt merchant shipping was amply demonstrated by *Leipzig*'s appearance off San Francisco on 11 August. The German cruiser had been at Magdalena Bay on the Baja peninsula of Mexico when her captain received word of Britain's declaration of war. Making her way slowly north toward the shipping lanes near San Francisco, the ship rendezvoused with the city's German consul off the Farallones Islands on the 12th.

> When the German consul met the *Leipzig*, he was not even sure that the United States authorities would permit her to coal once, in spite of the fact that no objection [the consul clearly being misinformed] had been made to supplying the *Rainbow*. Such a refusal would have made it necessary to lay the *Leipzig* up before she had struck a single blow. As Captain Haun and his crew could not bear to think of such a thing, he determined to remain at sea for as long as he could, to try to hold up colliers and other merchant ships off the Golden Gate, and then [if there was still no coal available] to steam northward and engage the *Rainbow*. He therefore told the consul that he would return to San Francisco on the night of August 16–17 and enter the harbour, unless he should have been advised not to do so.
>
> The *Leipzig* cruised in territorial waters on August 12, proceeding as far northward as Cape Mendocino. She then made for the Farallones Islands, keeping from twenty to thirty miles from the coast. The *Rainbow* was not sighted, and all the merchant ships that came along were American. These the *Leipzig* did not interfere with in any way, so as not to wound American susceptibilities.[54]

The complete absence of British traffic along the California shipping lanes had been caused by the flood of rumours to the effect that two German cruisers were supposedly operating on the American West Coast. Such were the "frequent reports received as to the

---

52. Marc Milner, *Canada's Navy: The First Century* (Toronto 1999), 43.

53. Marc Milner, "The Original *Rainbow Warrior*," *Legion Magazine*, May/June 2004, 43–45.

54. German official history quoted in Tucker, *The Naval Service of Canada*, I, 274.

supposed movements of these ships" that "owners were generally unwilling to risk their vessels until the situation should be cleared up."[55] *Leipzig's* appearance off San Francisco on the 11th kept twenty-five British merchantmen confined to the harbour, resulting in the shipment of some 60,000 tons of barley being delayed. According to the British official history of seaborne trade, "the delay was serious; but it was at Seattle and the other ports of Puget Sound that the situation gave rise to the gravest concerns."

> At these ports the export season was in full swing, and large stocks of salmon, grain, flour and lumber were accumulating in the warehouses and on the quays. Many of the ships by which these should have been lifted were now detained in other ports, in some cases with their outward cargoes still on board, and there was no immediate prospect of their coming forward.... So uncertain was the situation, and so gravely was confidence shaken by the rumours which multiplied every day, that even steamers on the trans-Pacific tracks were mostly held in port, though in their case there was little to fear when an offing had been obtained. Sailings were suspended, not only on the American coast but at Yokohama and other Asiatic ports.... The results of the *Leipzig's* appearance off San Francisco thus illustrated in the most striking manner the powers of dislocation possessed by even a single cruiser when able to maintain herself off a focal point of trade.[56]

Fortunately for British shipping and the Canadian cruiser, *Leipzig* sailed south from San Francisco on the 18th for a rendezvous with Spee's Asiatic squadron off the South American coast. Captain Haun did not depart, however, until he had loudly advertised his ship's presence on the Pacific seaboard by personally landing and calling on the city's mayor, presenting the local zoo with a pair of Japanese bear cubs, and entertaining a group of journalists on board his ship with the pronouncement that *Leipzig* would "engage the enemy whenever and wherever we meet him. The number or size of our antagonists will make no difference to us. The traditions of the German navy shall be upheld."[57] His bold actions, as much as his rhetoric, undoubtedly added to the uncertainty of already nervous British ship owners.

While the German cruiser was paralyzing traffic along the Pacific seaboard, Commander Hose had returned to Esquimalt on the 13th after overtaking HMS *Shearwater* in the Straits of Juan de Fuca. After coaling and taking aboard high-explosive shells that had arrived for her guns—sadly the ammunition was still useless because it lacked the necessary fuses— *Rainbow* set out that same day to find *Algerine*. The missing sloop was discovered by *Prince George* shortly after dawn on the 14th near the Caroll Islands off the Washington coast, having run short of coal while struggling northward against headwinds. The Canadian cruiser escorted the two ships back to home waters, arriving at Esquimalt at 0700 hours on

---

55. Fayle, *Seaborne Trade*, I, 162.

56. Ibid, 163–64.

57. Quoted in Tucker, *The Naval Service of Canada*, I, 270.

15 August where she finally received the required fuses for her high-explosive shells.[58]

Properly ammunitioned for the first time since the outbreak of war, Hose asked for—and was granted—permission on the 18th to take *Rainbow* south to San Francisco in search of *Leipzig*. Whether or not he was feeling any qualms about the action he had taken upon sighting *Prince George*, there is no denying that the RCN commander was once again willing to run the risk of an uneven encounter with the modern enemy cruiser. Fortunately for all involved, the order was countermanded later that day and Hose returned to base to await the arrival of the modern Bristol-class light cruiser HMS *Newcastle* from the Royal Navy's China Station. As the RCN official historian pointedly commented in 1952, the British cruiser "came to protect waters which a former Canadian government had undertaken to defend, and there was irony in the fact that she was a Bristol. Of the four Bristol-class cruisers in the Canadian naval programme of 1910, two were to have been stationed on the Pacific coast."[59]

Newcastle was not the first reinforcement to arrive at the Canadian navy's Pacific base, however. Even as *Rainbow* had steamed out of Esquimalt in the early hours of 3 August—a seemingly forlorn hope against the pair of modern German cruisers presumed to be lurking off the American coast—the RCN's strength was being augmented in an unusual manner, one "that underscore[d] the informal nature of Canada's naval organization in 1914."[60] With the threat of war looming in Europe, many people in British Columbia perceived themselves to be acutely exposed to attack by *Leipzig* and *Nurnberg* if not by Spee's entire Pacific squadron. During a meeting of concerned citizens at the Union Club in Victoria on 29 July, the president of the Seattle Construction and Drydock Company, J.V. Paterson, revealed that his firm was willing to sell two submarines it had recently completed for the government of Chile. The boats had been ordered in 1911 from the Electric Boat Company of New Jersey and had been contracted to Paterson's Seattle firm for a price of $818,000. During their sea trials, however, the Chilean navy had refused to accept them on the grounds that they had failed to achieve the radius of action demanded in the contract in the overloaded state in which the Chileans insisted they be tested. As a result, the Seattle company was anxious to sell the completed submarines when Paterson (who would later insist he had travelled to British Columbia on other business) arrived in Victoria.[61]

The question of purchasing the two submarines to protect Canada's West Coast was soon brought to the attention of the British Columbia premier, Sir Richard McBride, a politician who was known to stand "in the forefront of proponents for maritime

---

58. Hose to Senior Naval Officer, Esquimalt, Report of Proceedings, 17 August 1914, DHH 81/520/8000, "HMCS *Rainbow*," vol. 2; and Tucker, *The Naval Service of Canada*, I, 269.

59. Tucker, *The Naval Service of Canada*, I, 270.

60. Michael Hadley and Roger Sarty, *Tin-pots and Pirate Ships: Canadian Naval Forces and German Sea Raiders, 1880–1918* (Montreal 1991), 98.

61. J.V. Paterson to Sir Richard McBride, 22 February 1915, quoted in Canada, Parliament, "Correspondence Relating to the Purchase of Two Submarines by the Canadian Government," 1915, copy in DHH 81/520/8000, "HMCS *CC-1* & *CC-2*."

defence."[62] The premier "took the matter of the submarines in charge, and conferences of leading men were held at McBride's office, at the dockyard, and elsewhere" including a meeting at the Esquimalt navy yard a mere two hours after *Rainbow* set out on 3 August. Later that day the commander in charge of the dockyard telegraphed NSHQ with the news that the RCN "could probably purchase" the boats for an "estimated cost [of] £115,000 [$575,000] each." Undoubtedly well-aware of the nervousness of Canada's West Coast citizens—and sensing an excellent business opportunity—Paterson insisted that the submarines' "price was not open to discussion at all" while promising that "the price included the cost of delivering the vessels at the border of Canadian territorial waters." Although those costs would be negligible, the statement at least reminded the Canadian authorities that a declaration of war with Germany would also undoubtedly bring into effect an American declaration of neutrality and a prohibition on the export of war materiel.[63]

NSHQ, meanwhile, was also interested in acquiring the submarines and on 4 August sent off two telegrams to the Admiralty asking for their advice. Aside from any questions concerning the suitability of the rejected Chilean submarines, the naval authorities in Ottawa also had to consider the availability of trained submariners to help crew the boats. While headquarters was scurrying to obtain information about the submarines, McBride, fearing that any postponement might jeopardize the sale, decided to act on his own responsibility and went ahead with the purchase using provincial funds. Captain W.H. Logan of the London Salvage Association, a leading force behind the British Columbia submarine meetings, was already in Seattle for that purpose together with an RNCVR sub-lieutenant. With McBride's assurance of payment, the two submarines cast off from the Seattle dockyard at 2200 hours on 4 August—seven hours after Britain's ultimatum to Germany had expired and four hours after Ottawa had received the war telegram from London. The two boats, with Paterson and Logan on board, secretly made their way out of harbour under cover of darkness and fog, running as quietly as possible on their electric motors since they had not obtained the necessary clearance papers from the American authorities. Once clear of the harbour entrance, the company-manned submarines switched to their diesel engines and quickly made for a rendezvous point five miles south of Trial Island where they were to meet the SS *Salvor* just outside Canadian territorial waters.[64]

On board the Canadian vessel was a retired RN submariner, Lieutenant-Commander Bertram Jones, who had been living in Victoria and had offered his services at the Esquimalt dockyard when war seemed imminent, and the chief engineer from the dockyard, Lieutenant R.H. Wood. Jones carried a cheque from the provincial government in the amount of $1,150,000 and was instructed to inspect the boats before handing over the money. After making a careful, four-hour examination of the submarines, Jones

---

62. Hadley and Sarty, *Tin-pots and Pirate Ships*, 89.

63. Esquimalt to NSHQ, 3 August 1914, quoted in Canada, Parliament, "Correspondence Relating to the Purchase of Two Submarines by the Canadian Government," 1915, copy in DHH 81/520/8000, "HMCS *CC-1* & *CC-2*," Tucker, *The Naval Service of Canada*, I, 284–85.

64. Tucker, *The Naval Service of Canada*, I, 285–86.

handed the cheque over to the impatient Paterson and the vessels proceeded to Esquimalt where they arrived safely on the morning of the 5th. It was not until the next day that the United States Navy despatched a cruiser to intercept the missing submarines in a belated effort to head them off before they violated the US president's neutrality proclamation. The USS *Milwaukee* left the Bremerton Navy Yard at 0800 hours on a futile search of American waters. Premier McBride, meanwhile, had informed the prime minister on 4 August of his intention to go ahead with the purchase, a move that received NSHQ's endorsement the following morning.[65] Borden telegraphed his own congratulations on McBride's initiative later that day.

> Yesterday morning we communicated with Admiralty as to advisability of securing two submarines mentioned, and as to feasibility of manning them, as without crew they would be useless. They advise purchase provided crews could be secured. As that has been accomplished we appreciate most warmly your action which will greatly tend to increase security on the Pacific coast, and send hearty thanks. Please advise us of their arrival.[66]

As the Admiralty later explained, their endorsement of the purchase had come after consulting with Sir Philip Watts, "for many years director of naval construction at the Admiralty and who is still called in from time to time to give the Admiralty the benefit of his great knowledge and experience. Sir Philip Watts is familiar with all the details of these boats and in his opinion they are well worth buying. He has explained that the only reason why the Chilian [*sic*] government did not wish to keep them was because their radius of action is not sufficiently wide for the purpose to which the Chilians intended to put them, but in his view, which is supported by the commodore of the British submarine service, they should prove useful vessels for coast defence."[67] Although McBride had gone ahead in purchasing the submarines without official approval from Ottawa—and, in so doing, allowing his administration to become the only Canadian provincial government to ever own warships—it is clear that his actions were completely in accord with NSHQ's and the government's wishes. The fact that Ottawa was able to approve the purchase within twenty-four hours indicates the urgency with which the federal authorities pursued the matter, even taking into account the relatively small government bureaucracy of 1914. By order in council on 7 August, the federal government assumed responsibility for the submarines, reimbursing British Columbia for their cost, while placing the boats at the operational disposal of the Admiralty. In keeping with earlier Australian practice that had christened two British E-class submarines *AE 1* and

---

65. NSHQ to Commander in Charge, Esquimalt, 5 August 1914, in "Correspondence Relating to the Purchase of Two Submarines by the Canadian Government," 1915, copy in DHH 81/520/8000, "HMCS *CC-1* & *CC-2*," Tucker, *The Naval Service of Canada*, I, 287.

66. Borden to McBride, 5 August 1914, in "Correspondence Relating to the Purchase of Two Submarines by the Canadian Government," 1915, copy in DHH 81/520/8000, "HMCS *CC-1* & *CC-2*."

67. E. March, Private Secretary, Admiralty to Sir George Perley, 21 August 1914, 1062-2-2, LAC, RG 24, vol. 4018.

HMC Submarine *CC 1* off Cape Flattery in April 1916. (DND CN 6378)

HMC Submarine *CC 2* in 1914. (DND E-60722)

AE 2, the Canadian boats, which were similar to the Royal Navy's C-class submarines, entered service as *CC 1* and *CC 2*.[68]

Nonetheless, the clandestine nature of the purchase of submarines already rejected by another government raised questions about the transaction. In February 1915, the former minister of public works in the Liberal Laurier administration, William Pugsley, questioned the propriety of buying submarines he claimed were overpriced, out of date, and not built according to their proper specifications. The fact that McBride had paid $332,000 more than the Chileans had contracted for and that Paterson had pocketed a $40,000 commission also helped to fuel Pugsley's House of Commons attack on the government. Although Hazen defended the purchase by noting that it had been recommended by Admiralty experts and that time was a factor because of American neutrality proclamations, the entire matter was eventually handed over to a royal commission later that summer. Chaired by Sir Charles Davidson, the commission had already been set up to look into other dubious war purchases made by the Borden government. Although the chief engineer at Esquimalt stated that "the workmanship put into the vessels does not approach the Admiralty standard of construction" and that their defects "indicate a lack of detailed inspection during the construction of the boats," the Davidson commission found that they were generally well-constructed and believed that they could not, under the circumstances, have been purchased for less.[69]

Such findings aside, it would appear that Paterson had earned his $40,000 commission. The design of the submarines had already been superseded by USN boats being built on adjoining slipways in the same Seattle shipyard and they both had defects. There is also no doubt that the shrewd Paterson had exploited the imminence of war—and the implications of United States neutrality—and played on British Columbians' fears to exact a premium price for the two obsolescent boats. The level of local insecurity was so high, in fact, that following reports that Japan had mobilized its forces—and ignoring Japan's treaty with the British Empire—British Columbia's Premier McBride sent Borden an anxious telegram asking him to contact the Admiralty immediately and stating his belief "that in the event [of a] British loss Japan would not hesitate co-operate with Germany. I know of treaties with Canada and England but in this time these [are] of little or no consequence."[70] Winston Churchill's immediate concern was that nothing be said that might insult a valuable ally. "Japan enters war of her own free choice," he reminded Borden; "she must be welcome[d]."[71] What Churchill did not mention was that of the two cruisers being despatched to reassure the people of British Columbia, the first to arrive, on 25 August, would be the Japanese armoured cruiser *Idzumo*.

Whether the submarine purchase actually calmed the nervous population of Canada's West Coast is open to argument, but whatever its impact, the Canadian navy had obtained

---

68. PC 2072, 7 August 1914; and Tucker, *The Naval Service of Canada*, I, 289.

69. Tucker, *The Naval Service of Canada*, I, 297–99.

70. Prime Minister to First Lord of the Admiralty, 13 August 1914, *DCER*, I, 43.

71. First Lord of the Admiralty to Prime Minister, 14 August 1914, *DCER*, I, 44.

two useful vessels for guarding the approaches to the Strait of Juan de Fuca. While hardly an overwhelming menace, their presence could have had a deterrent effect had a German raider ventured that far north. When operational control of the submarines was turned over to the Admiralty, the colonial secretary told the Canadians on 9 August that "their being on the coast cannot be too widely advertised but their actual position should be concealed. Plausible reports should be issued from time to time of their presence at different ports."[72] According to the German official history, *Leipzig*'s captain heard reports that Canada had purchased the two Chilean submarines as early as 6 August but the information does not appear to have influenced the German cruiser's movements.[73]

Although similar, the two submarines were not identical. *CC 1* was 144 feet in length and had five 18-inch torpedo tubes, four forward and one astern, while *CC 2* had only two tubes forward and one astern, allowing for a more tapered bow and a length of 152 feet. Since the Seattle company did not supply the vessels with torpedoes and *Rainbow* carried 14-inch tubes, ordnance for the submarines had to be shipped from *Niobe*'s supply in Halifax. Even then, the RCN's inexperience with torpedoes was evident in that the weapons "arrived from Halifax charged, some up to 1,500 pounds pressure. It is extremely fortunate that no accident occurred either on the railway or here."[74] The torpedoes were the boats' only weapons as neither vessel was equipped with a deck gun. Designed to make thirteen knots on the surface and ten knots submerged, *CC 1* actually managed a speed of over fifteen knots during a sea trial in early November.[75] The workmanship of their construction and obsolescent design aside, the boats were—as the Admiralty had recognized—suited to the coast defence role in which they were to be employed. Moreover, the submarines provided the RCN with some valuable practical experience with the type of vessel that was to have a large impact on the First World War at sea.

The crews for the two new boats exemplified the RCN's reliance on retired Royal Navy officers living in Canada at the outbreak of the war. Aside from Lieutenant Jones, who had inspected the submarines before their purchase, another former RN submariner, Adrian Keyes, younger brother of future British admiral Sir Roger Keyes, reported to Canadian authorities. In addition to the command of *CC 1*, Keyes was also given overall command of the submarine flotilla. It was, as Tucker's history recognized, "a real windfall for the Naval Service to obtain at this time a first-rate submarine commander of great ability and unusually wide training."[76] The first officer in *CC 1* was Lieutenant W.T. Walker, another retired RN officer who had originally been assigned to *Rainbow* for her sortie to San Francisco. The submarine's second officer was a graduate of the Royal Naval College of Canada, Midshipman W.M. Maitland-Dougall, while the rest of *CC 1*'s crew consisted of

---

72. Harcourt to Governor General, 9 August 1914, quoted in Tucker, *The Naval Service of Canada*, I, 290.

73. Tucker, *The Naval Service of Canada*, I, 300.

74. C.W. Trousdale, Commander in Charge Esquimalt Dockyard to Secretary, Dept. of the Naval Service, 22 August 1914, DHH 81/520/8000, "HMCS *CC-1* & *CC-2*."

75. Tucker, *The Naval Service of Canada*, I, 291–92; and Dave Perkins, *Canada's Submariners, 1914–1923* (Erin, Ontario, 1989), 33–37.

76. Tucker, *The Naval Service of Canada*, I, 291.

The crew of the submarine *CC 2* in 1914 with her navigation officer, Lieutenant Bernard L. Johnson, holding a bulldog. (DND CN 3034)

HMCS *Rainbow* cleared for action at Prince Rupert in 1914. (CWM 19890167-003)

three former British naval ratings and thirteen local RNCVR recruits. Aboard *CC 2*, Jones' navigation officer was Lieutenant B.L. Johnson, RNR, a merchant marine officer and experienced British Columbia coastal pilot, while his second officer, Midshipman J.G. Edwards, had attended the Royal Naval College at Osborne before being invalided out of the service short of graduation with rheumatic fever. The ratings for the second submarine were also a mix of RN seamen transferred from *Rainbow* and *Shearwater*, and RNCVR reservists.[77]

While the crews of the two Canadian submarines began the task of working up their boats, Hose put to sea in *Rainbow* on 20 August and shaped course for Prince Rupert, where the nervous citizens had reported spotting a three-funnelled cruiser similar to either *Leipzig* or *Nurnberg*. Arriving the next day, Hose made inquiries among the local population as to the supposed enemy sightings. The vehemence with which the citizens of Prince Rupert expressed their fears prompted him to telegraph NSHQ that there were "strong suspicions *Nurnberg* or *Leipzig* has coaled from US Steamship *Delhi* in vicinity of Prince of Wales Island on August 19th or August 20th." The carrying of coal to Prince Rupert in British ships was immediately suspended and *Rainbow* continued to patrol off the northern British Columbia coast until month's end, while the nearest German cruiser, *Leipzig*, spent the last days of August cruising slowly off the coast of Mexico in the Gulf of California, some 3,200 kilometres to the south.[78]

When *Rainbow* steamed back into Esquimalt harbour on 2 September, she was greeted by the recently arrived light cruiser HMS *Newcastle* and the Japanese armoured cruiser *Idzumo*. The armoured cruiser had arrived at Esquimalt two days after Japan's declaration of war on 23 August and five days before the arrival of *Newcastle*. As the senior naval officer present, *Newcastle*'s commander, Captain F.A. Powlett, automatically assumed command of all naval operations in Canadian West Coast waters, superseding the RCN's Commander Hose. Although his superior rank entitled Powlett to direct seaward operations, the British officer quickly assumed authority over the RCN dockyard at Esquimalt as well and throughout September issued instructions that drew on the resources of other Canadian government departments. Aided and abetted by a still anxious Premier McBride, Powlett had two guns mounted in a shore battery at Seymour Narrows, a treacherous stretch of water some 240 kilometres north of Victoria beyond the Strait of Georgia. The British captain then directed the local militia to man the battery and despatched CGS *Newington* to lay a makeshift minefield across the narrows along with obstructions that had been hastily assembled from local materials.[79]

For the cost-conscious naval department in Ottawa, the expense of preparing defences against the rather unlikely use of the the northern passage around Vancouver Island by

77. "Brief Biography of Captain B.L. Johnson," nd, "The First Royal Canadian Navy Officer to Command a Submarine," 24 December 1963, DHH 81/520/8000, "HMCS *CC-1* & *CC-2*," Tucker, *The Naval Service of Canada*, I, 297; and Perkins, *Canada's Submariners*, 40–45.

78. "Notes from Copy of Log, HMCS *Rainbow*, for month of August 1914," nd, DHH 81/520/8000, "HMCS *Rainbow*," vol. 2; and Tucker, *The Naval Service of Canada*, I, 271, 275.

79. For the details of these arrangements see the correspondence in file NSC 1047–7-5, LAC, RG 24, vol. 3967; and Hadley and Sarty, *Tin-pots and Pirate Ships*, 90–91.

Spee's Pacific squadron seemed excessive. The British captain's willingness to assume control ashore was facilitated by the fact that Esquimalt dockyard had recently seen a succession of naval officers in command. With Hose at sea aboard *Rainbow*, the dockyard's senior naval officer at the outbreak of war had been Lieutenant Henry Pilcher. Unfortunately, the stress of impending war and the clandestine purchase of *CC 1* and *CC 2*—Pilcher had wired NSHQ on 3 August with the recommendation that he "consider[ed] it most important to acquire [the boats] immediately"—proved too much for the RN lieutenant as symptoms of a nervous breakdown appeared shortly thereafter when "his actions showed that he roundly suspected the enemy of roaming at large in the streets of the town."[80] In the wake of Pilcher's collapse, the administration of the Esquimalt dockyard was handled by a succession of officers who managed to develop the defences of the naval base in spite of the constant turnover.

Before *Newcastle*'s arrival, the senior naval officer at the dockyard was Commander C.W. Trousdale, the captain of HMS *Shearwater*. Trousdale's report to Ottawa on 22 August indicated both the degree to which the defences had already been organized in Hose's absence and pointed out that a large number of retired naval officers were available on the West Coast to assume many of the required duties. A chart depot had been organized under the supervision of a retired lieutenant, C.C. Guy, who was "using chart sets and books of HMS *Algerine* and *Shearwater* for distribution to vessels requiring them. He is winding chronometers of both ships and generally supervising all navigational gear." Another retired British officer, Commander W.H. James, was in charge of the naval intelligence department and was "in touch with all agents connected with coal supply, suspected spies, foreign merchant ships, etc. and forwards weekly reports of work carried out." The administration of the naval depot, meanwhile, was handled by a serving RN officer, Assistant Paymaster H.A. Milman, who performed "all duties connected with victualling, pay, ledger, clothing, etc." Trousdale chose to employ "the only Active Service executive officer in the yard," Lieutenant W.S. Chalmers, as his secretary for administration and "staff officer for war purposes." As the senior naval officer explained, "I consider it essential to have someone who can deal with an emergency in event of my being away from the office night or day."[81]

The man in charge of the West Coast's examination service was retired RN Commander J.T. Shenton, who was also responsible for the port war signal station and had "been locally appointed" to command the two British sloops—*Algerine* and *Shearwater*, the latter employed as a depot ship for the two submarines to accommodate their crews in harbour—after most of their British crews had been transferred east to serve in HMCS *Niobe*. Shenton employed the Canadian Government Ships *Malaspina*, *Galiano*, and *Restless* for examination duties at Esquimalt. These vessels were joined by CGS *Newington* in patrolling the Johnstone Strait and CGS *Estevan* in providing relief guards for the wireless stations at Pachena and Cape Lazo and the telegraph cable station at Bamfield Creek. The harbour

80. Tucker, *The Naval Service of Canada*, I, 285, 291.

81. C.W. Trousdale, Commander in Charge Esquimalt Dockyard to Secretary, Dept. of the Naval Service, 22 August 1914, DHH 81/520/8000, "HMCS *CC-1* & *CC-2*."

itself was patrolled by five hired motor launches under the command of an RNCVR sub-lieutenant. The launches maintained an inshore patrol off the harbour's mouth and challenged unidentified craft entering Esquimalt by means of electric flash lamps. Although primarily manned by RNCVR sailors, "the owners of these boats have been extremely loyal and obliging in the matter of placing them at our disposal for transport purposes, etc. The crews are victualled and supplied by the dockyard."[82]

As much as the Canadian navy was dependent on retired RN officers to fill the most important posts, the largest single source of personnel at Esquimalt remained the recently raised RNCVR companies. Of the thirty-five RNCVR officers and 387 ratings on duty at the dockyard, ninety-five were serving in either *Rainbow*, or the auxiliaries *Prince George* and *Aid*. Most were under training in the naval barracks under the supervision of retired RN Commander Eustace Maude. As Commander Trousdale described in his August report, however, the volunteers were in dire need of further assistance from Ottawa. "As far as possible training has been carried out but there has been recently such a large demand for working parties that instruction has been somewhat retarded. Many men are almost destitute as regards clothing, as their *only* suit is the one they have used for coaling, etc. [Prior to the conversion to fuel oil, coaling was literally the dirtiest job a sailor had to carry out.] I wish to emphasize this point, as the men are very keen and proud of the uniform, and it is imperative that the latter be supplied at once. The 150 kits on the way here, but not yet arrived, will not be sufficient."[83]

Both Trousdale and Lieutenant Chalmers, British officers on loan to the Canadian service, were transferred to Halifax at the beginning of September to take charge of *Earl Grey*, a Canadian icebreaker that had been sold to the Russian government, for her voyage to Archangel.[84] Whenever *Rainbow* was at Esquimalt during September, Commander Hose resumed his duties as the dockyard's senior naval officer but it was evident to NSHQ that Hose could not adequately tend to his administrative duties while he was at sea. "Owing to frequent absences of *Rainbow* and as she is under Admiralty orders and her absences cannot always be foreseen," Ottawa informed the Canadian commander at the beginning of October, "it is necessary [to] appoint an independent officer for charge of naval [shore] establishments." As a result, Commander Shenton, the former head of the examination service and, most recently, Hose's second-in-command of the headquarters staff, was appointed by NSHQ to command the shore establishment at Esquimalt.[85]

Although the administration of the dockyard was being capably handled by the officers appointed by NSHQ, the problem of Captain Powlett's superior rank and his willingness to use it to interfere in British Columbia's coast defences still had to be addressed. The most obvious course of action for NSHQ to rein in Powlett and McBride—and their expenditures—and reassert Canadian control over shore activities on the West Coast was

---

82. Trousdale to Secretary, Naval Service, 22 August 1914, DHH 81/520/8000, "HMCS *CC-1* & *CC-2*."

83. Trousdale to Secretary, Naval Service, 22 August 1914, DHH 81/520/8000, "HMCS *CC-1* & *CC-2*."

84. Dept. of the Naval Service, *The Canadian Navy List for November 1914, corrected to 20th October 1914* (Ottawa 1914).

85. NSHQ to Hose, 2 October 1914, DHH 81/520/8000, "HMCS *CC-1* & *CC-2*."

to appoint an officer who was senior in rank to the British captain. Fortunately for naval headquarters, a retired RN admiral living in Guelph, Ontario, had offered his services to the Canadian navy at the outbreak of war. In recommending the appointment of Rear-Admiral W.O. Story as superintendent of Esquimalt dockyard, Kingsmill explained to the deputy minister that "he would act in a civil capacity and control the movements of vessels under the department and generally act as representative of the department in dealing with the imperial naval officers." Beyond that, Story's "greater experience" would be "useful in consultations with civil and military authorities in British Columbia and on all matters pertaining to defence" while his "maturer judgement" would "justify his appointment by avoiding reckless small expenditures such as have [recently] taken place in British Columbia."[86] Kingsmill's instructions to Story demonstrate both the uncertainty the RCN felt in matters of operational control in Canadian waters and the degree to which substantial naval expenditures continued to be frowned upon—even in wartime—by the Borden government:

> It is pointed out that this appointment does not permit of a flag being flown, nor does it give you any authority over the movements of HM or HMC ships. It is intended that this appointment should be purely an administrative one and you should act in an advisory capacity in questions arising as to the defence of the coast of British Columbia. Your dealings with the senior imperial service officer on the coast will require to be handled with great tact. The situation at present is somewhat curious: the captain of the *Newcastle* has considered it necessary to fit, with his own ratings, extempore electro contact mines which he proposes to place, in case of emergency, in the channel between Pulteney Point and Suquash in the vicinity of Alert Bay. The idea of mining channels used by commercial vessels does not commend itself to myself or to the technical officers of the department, but no definite decision has been arrived at as to the authority of the senior British naval officer and his action in the navigable waters of Canada, so that, beyond forwarding to the Admiralty copies of telegrams exchanged on the question of mining, nothing has been done, except that the officer-in-charge of Esquimalt dock-yard was informed that mines should not be laid except as a last resort.
>
> Another question that has not the concurrence of this department is the placing of 4-inch guns to command the channel at Seymour Narrows, but no obstruction has been placed in the way of this being carried out.
>
> The dominion government has placed at the disposal of the Admiralty the *Rainbow* and submarines *CC 1* and *CC 2*. The appointments to and distribution of personnel of these vessels still remain in the hands of the dominion government, but the movements of the ships are entirely at the disposal of the imperial service naval officers, except that attention is called to the fact that the

---

86. Kingsmill, "Memorandum for Deputy Minister," 8 October 1914, DHH 81/520/8000, "HMCS *Niobe*."

submarines should not be withdrawn from British Columbian waters without direct approval from the department.

Your attention is invited to the departmental methods in all questions entailing expenditure. Of late considerable expense has been incurred which it is considered might have been avoided.[87]

The retired admiral clearly understood the purpose of his appointment. Upon his arrival on the West Coast, Story quickly moved to establish the proper lines of communication with NSHQ, ensuring that the dockyard would request authority for its actions in place of the Powlett/McBride method of simply presenting Ottawa with *faits accomplis* and—just as important to the naval department—the bills.

Rear-Admiral Story also arrived at Esquimalt just as the strategic situation for British shipping in the Pacific seemed at its most perilous. Spee's Pacific Squadron, the most powerful and dangerous of the German naval forces at large at the outbreak of war, had spent the opening weeks of the conflict cruising slowly westward through the Marshall Islands to German Samoa, some 3,200 kilometres northeast of New Zealand. The Admiralty remained concerned at the possibility of Spee's squadron moving south to attack either Australia or New Zealand and kept its strongest forces, centred on the battle cruiser *Australia*, operating in the waters around New Guinea to cover troop movements. Japan's entry into the war on 23 August, however, forced the Germans further east to avoid a clash with the powerful Japanese squadrons that were patrolling the Caroline and Marshall island groups. On 22 September, Spee's squadron attacked the French port of Papeete on Tahiti, word of which indicated that he was indeed headed for the coast of South America. By 14 October, *Scharnhorst*, *Gneisenau*, and *Nurnberg* had rendezvoused with the light cruiser *Dresden*, recently arrived from the Atlantic, and *Leipzig* off Easter Island.[88]

Leaving the dangerous Japanese and Australian squadrons to search for him in the south-central Pacific, Spee was faced by only a small British squadron blocking his entry into the Atlantic Ocean through the Strait of Magellan. Based at the Falkland Islands and under the command of Rear-Admiral Sir Christopher Cradock, transferred south from the North America and West Indies Station, the "South East Coast of America" station comprised two older armoured cruisers, *Good Hope* and *Monmouth*, the light cruiser *Glasgow*, and the armed merchant cruiser *Otranto*. Cradock's two armoured cruisers were manned by coastguardsmen and reservists only recently called out, leaving the admiral with *Glasgow* as his only warship crewed by experienced regulars. The scratch crew of HMS *Good Hope* included four Canadian midshipmen, Malcolm Cann, William Palmer, Arthur Silver and John Hathaway, all graduates of the first class of the Royal Naval College of Canada. The Admiralty believed it had ensured the squadron's superiority over Spee by assigning to it the pre-dreadnought battleship *Canopus*. Unfortunately, a faulty report on the condition of the battleship's engines by her nervous engineer commander convinced

---

87. Kingsmill to Story, 12 October 1914, DHH 81/520/8000, "HMCS *Niobe.*"

88. Halpern, *A Naval History of World War I*, 88–91.

Cradock that the vessel could make only twelve knots and would be unable to keep up with the rest of his squadron.

Leaving the battleship to guard the colliers that were following in his wake, the British admiral passed through the Magellan Strait on 27 October and headed north up the west coast of Chile in search of the German squadron. Five days later, in the gathering dusk of 1 November, the British cruisers intercepted their quarry eighty kilometres off the Chilean port of Coronel. With his greater speed, gun range, and twice the weight of broadside—not to mention crack regular crews that had twice won the *Kriegsmarine*'s top gunnery award—Spee quickly despatched the two British armoured cruisers in an uneven fight that lasted little over an hour. Both ships were heavily hit and ablaze soon after the action commenced and sank with no survivors from the more than 1,600 sailors manning them. The four Canadian midshipmen, Cann, Palmer, Silver, and Hathaway, were thus the first RCN fatalities of the war. *Otranto*, which was wisely allowed to leave the line before the battle began, and *Glasgow* both managed to escape, with the latter signalling news of the disaster as she sped south. The most significant German loss was the expenditure of 42 percent of the squadron's 8.2-inch rounds, ammunition that could only be replenished if Spee's ships made it back to Germany.[89]

The Battle of Coronel was the first defeat the Royal Navy had suffered in over a century and was a cruel shock for both the Admiralty and British public, not to mention the already nervous citizens of British Columbia. Having badly misjudged the ability of Cradock's ships to defeat the German squadron, the Admiralty now despatched the battle cruisers *Invincible* and *Inflexible* from the Grand Fleet to reinforce the three armoured and two light cruisers being hurriedly concentrated off the East Coast of South America. They also assembled a new squadron of armoured cruisers off the coast of southern Africa and sent *Newcastle* and *Idzumo* south from Esquimalt to rendezvous with the battle cruiser *Australia* and the Japanese battleship *Hizen* off Manzanillo, Mexico. When *Newcastle* and *Idzumo* left Esquimalt, Commander Hose cabled Ottawa enquiring if the "Admiralty may be asked to arrange with senior officer of allied squadron … that Canadian ship *Rainbow* shall, if possible, be in company with squadron when engaged with enemy." In view of the heavy losses at Coronel, the request was refused on the sensible grounds that "if the *Rainbow* were lost, immediately there would be much criticism on account of her age in being sent to engage modern vessels." Too slow to keep up with the more powerful warships, *Rainbow* had to satisfy herself with putting to sea to serve as a wireless link between the British-Japanese squadron and Esquimalt.[90]

Aware that the British were likely to concentrate considerable force against him in the wake of Coronel, Spee remained off the Chilean coast until mid-November before loading his five warships with as much coal as they could carry and, accompanied by three supply ships, shaped course for the South Atlantic. Even then, the German squadron steamed south in a leisurely fashion, stopping for several days off Picton Island

89. Ibid, 92–93; and Richard Hough, *The Great War at Sea, 1914–1918* (Oxford 1983), 87–96; and Tucker, *The Naval Service of Canada*, I, 221; and Hadley and Sarty, *Tin-pots and Pirate Ships*, 85–86.

90. Halpern, *A Naval History of World War I*, 94–95; and Tucker, *The Naval Service of Canada*, I, 277–78.

The Royal Naval College of Canada class of 1914 on the college's front steps. The class included the four midshipmen killed at the Battle of Coronel on 1 November 1914. William A. Palmer stands in the back row, second from left and John V.W. Hathaway in the middle row, fourth from left, while Arthur W. Silver and Malcolm Cann are seated in the front row on the far right and centre respectively. (DND Notman-20003)

at the tip of South America to coal from a captured British vessel while the officers hunted ashore. Before departing, Spee called a conference of his senior officers, where it was decided to attack the British coaling base at Port Stanley in the Falkland Islands as they made their way north. It proved a fateful decision. The British battle cruisers *Invincible* and *Inflexible*, and the cruisers *Carnavon*, *Cornwall*, *Kent* and *Bristol*, under the command of Vice-Admiral Sir Doveton Sturdee, were also proceeding south at a less than rapid pace, having stopped to search merchant vessels en route before anchoring off the Abrolhos Rocks, fifty kilometres off the Brazilian coast (where they were joined by the Coronel survivor *Glasgow*), to coal and transfer stores. Sturdee, a rival of Fisher's for the position of first sea lord, had been assigned to command the powerful South Atlantic squadron by Churchill in order to remove him from the Admiralty after he had refused to resign his post as chief of staff.[91]

Although Sturdee did not display any urgency in steaming to the South Atlantic, he was blessed with more than his fair share of luck once he arrived. After finally reaching Port Stanley, in the Falkland Islands, on 7 December—Sturdee had been prodded by the capable captain of *Glasgow* to leave Abrolhos a day ahead of his planned schedule—the British ships were in the midst of coaling when the German squadron appeared on the horizon the following morning. Had Spee's ships simply avoided the Falklands and continued north out of sight of land, they could easily have escaped the stronger British force since it was Sturdee's intention to proceed south and enter the Pacific in search of his enemy. In the event, the German squadron fled southeast after sighting the British battle cruisers and being fired on by the battleship *Canopus*, now grounded in the harbour mud to act as a coastal battery. It took some two hours for *Invincible* and *Inflexible* to raise steam and clear the harbour but the unusually fine, clear weather allowed them to run down the two German armoured cruisers with their superior speed and sink them with their 12-inch armament. Despite rather poor gunnery, the battle cruisers sank *Scharnhorst* with all hands at 1617 hours before finishing off *Gneisenau* an hour and a half later. The accompanying British cruisers, meanwhile, sank *Leipzig* and *Nurnberg* as they tried to escape south. Of the 2,200 German sailors aboard the four warships, only 215 were rescued. The third German cruiser, *Dresden*, managed to make good her escape around Cape Horn but was caught by two British cruisers at the remote island of Mas a Tierra in the Pacific on 14 March 1915 and promptly scuttled by her crew.[92]

The successful outcome of the Battle of the Falklands, aside from demonstrating the validity of the battle cruiser concept in hunting down armoured cruisers, virtually eliminated the German surface raider threat from the world's oceans. During the four months that Spee's squadron was roaming the Pacific, its main impact was its potential threat to shipping since his cruisers actually sank few merchantmen. As *Leipzig* demonstrated during her brief foray to San Francisco, the greatest influence an enemy raider's presence had was the disruption of shipping schedules and routines. For the apprehensive citizens of British Columbia, the victory in the South Atlantic freed them

91. Halpern, *A Naval History of World War I*, 97–98; and Hough, *The Great War at Sea*, 104–05.

92. Halpern, *A Naval History of World War I*, 99–100; and Hough, *The Great War at Sea*, 111–20.

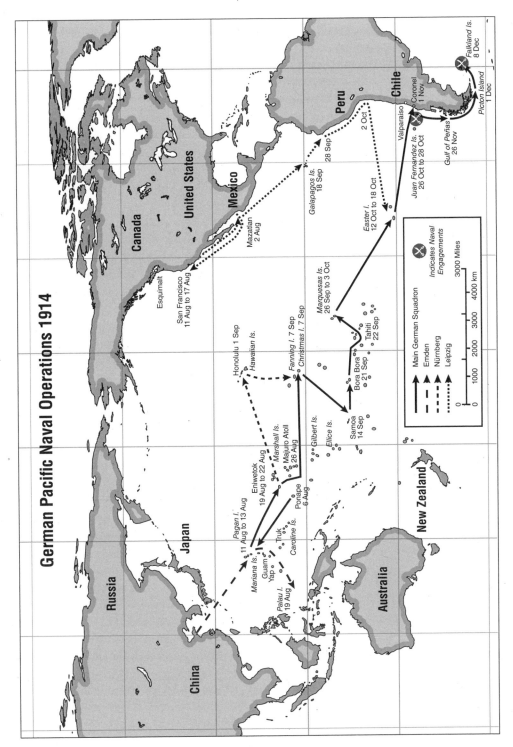

German Pacific Naval Operations 1914

from the fear of a sudden enemy descent upon their coast. Thereafter, the only real concern lay in the potential danger posed by German merchantmen in ports along the American West Coast being fitted out as armed commerce raiders. In that case, although she was over twenty years old, HMCS *Rainbow* was still faster than all but a few commercial vessels and adequately armed to subdue them.

The potential threat of German merchantmen lying in America's eastern ports was the RCN's chief concern on the Atlantic coast as well. As we have seen, the outbreak of war found HMCS *Niobe* alongside at Halifax being fitted for sea duty. The obsolescent warship was scheduled to join Sir Christopher Cradock's Fourth Cruiser Squadron (Cradock not having as yet been sent by the Admiralty to meet his fate at Coronel) on the North America and West Indies Station to keep watch over the western North Atlantic shipping lanes generally, and New York in particular. When the Admiralty's warning telegram was issued on 27 July, 1914, a week before war began, Admiral Cradock was at Vera Cruz, Mexico, with four of his five cruisers, the fifth, *Lancaster* being under repair at Bermuda. The British admiral's immediate concern was the reported presence of German cruisers, *Karlsruhe* and *Dresden* (the latter another of the South Atlantic actors), in the Caribbean. Uncertain of the enemy's exact location or intentions, Cradock assigned *Essex* to join *Lancaster* in patrolling the North Atlantic shipping lanes from both New York and the Gulf of St Lawrence, while the flagship *Suffolk*, together with *Berwick* and *Bristol*, shadowed the German warships.[93]

On 3 August Cradock was instructed by the Admiralty "to operate only to west of 40 degrees W longitude for protection of trade in North America and West Indies, [with] primary bases [at] Halifax and Jamaica."[94] The threat of war also produced its share of false reports, not least from Canadian and Newfoundland waters, information that the Admiralty quickly passed on to its cruiser squadrons with little apparent effort to analyze its credibility. On the evening of the 3rd, for instance, Cradock was informed that "from reliable information, two German cruisers are reported in the neighbourhood of Heart's Content, Newfoundland." Since Heart's Content was the terminus of one of the trans-Atlantic telegraph cables as well as home to a wireless station, the admiral was instructed to despatch one of his cruisers immediately. Cradock detailed *Essex* to investigate the Newfoundland report, while *Lancaster* was assigned to patrol the Cabot Strait. By the following day, London's emphasis had shifted to American waters where "German cruisers [were] reported off New York to escort two German liners *Kronprinz Wilhelm* and *Vaterland* painted grey probably armed with 10,000 reservists on board. They are to be searched for and shadowed."[95]

Clearly the two German cruisers in the Caribbean could not have been everywhere at once. Later, on the 4th, the Admiralty was at least able to provide some judgment in informing Cradock that "on appreciation of situation it appears that the danger point to

---

93. Admiralty, Naval Staff, Training and Staff Duties Division, *Naval Staff Monographs*, IX: *The Atlantic Ocean, 1914–1915, Including the Battles of Coronel and the Falkland Islands* (London 1923), 8–9.

94. Admiralty to Rear-Admiral Commanding, 4th CS, 3 August 1914, quoted in *Naval Staff Monographs*, IX, 264.

95. Admiralty to SNO, Bermuda, 3 August 1914, Admiralty to RAC, 4th CS, 4 August 1914, quoted in ibid, 10–11, 25, 265.

The cruiser HMS *Cornwall* at Esquimalt repairing some of the eighteen hits she received at the Battle of the Falkland Islands on 8 December 1914 where she sank the German cruiser *Leipzig*. *Cornwall* was a sister ship to HMS *Monmouth,* sunk at the Battle of Coronel. (DND E-38800)

trade in your allotted area appears to be in the neighbourhood of New York. British trade is being advised not to sail until some of your cruisers arrive." The vulnerability of the important North Atlantic trade quickly brought reinforcements. Two French cruisers homeward bound from the Caribbean, *Conde* and *Descartes*, were ordered back to the region to operate under Cradock's command, while the armoured cruiser HMS *Good Hope* and the pre-dreadnought battleship HMS *Glory* were ordered to Halifax to help cover the entrance to the Gulf of St Lawrence, which the Admiralty was reporting as "being threatened by one German cruiser and some armed merchantmen." As its naval staff history acknowledges, these rumours "served to deepen the Admiralty's anxiety. When Admiral Cradock reported that the disposition of his cruisers would be such that homeward bound merchant vessels should be able to leave New York on August 7, they ordered him to arrange to protect the southern entrance of the Gulf of St Lawrence as well as the approach to New York."[96]

In fact, the two German cruisers were still well south of New York. On the outbreak of war *Dresden* had been ordered to work her way down the coast of South America to attack trade in the area of the River Plate, a task in which she would have little luck before being ordered to the Pacific to rendezvous with Spee's squadron. *Karlsruhe*, on the other hand, would have greater success after an initial close encounter with Cradock's cruisers. On 6 August she rendezvoused with the large North German Lloyd liner *Kronprinz Wilhelm* in the open sea some 190 kilometres northeast of the Bahamas. The German liner had slipped out of New York on the 3rd in order for the light cruiser to equip her as an armed merchant cruiser. *Karlsruhe* had just finished transferring two 3.4-inch guns and was in the process of shifting the ammunition for them when Cradock appeared on the horizon in the armoured cruiser *Suffolk*, having been guided to the spot by wireless intercepts of messages passed between the German ships. The enemy vessels quickly made off in different directions with *Suffolk* in pursuit of *Karlsruhe*, but the superior speed of the light cruiser put her over the northern horizon by sunset. In moonlight later that night, the German cruiser was again intercepted, by the light cruiser *Bristol*, and was only able to escape for a second time, after an exchange of gunfire, because the poor quality of coal in the British ship eventually reduced her speed to eighteen knots. For the next three months *Karlsruhe* operated off the less-patrolled coast of northeast Brazil where she accounted for one Dutch and fifteen British merchant ships totalling 72,805 tons. All British efforts to locate the raider proved futile and it was only when an unexplained internal explosion sank *Karlsruhe* on 4 November 480 kilometres from the Barbados that the threat was finally removed.[97]

Although the only German cruisers loose in the Atlantic were operating south of the Caribbean, the escape of the large liner *Kronprinz Wilhelm* demonstrated that the threat posed by German merchant ships lying in American harbours had to be taken seriously. Before the declaration of war, the vessels of the Central Powers had sought refuge in neutral ports around the world. Ninety-one enemy ships had taken safety in the Atlantic ports of North

---

96. Admiralty to RAC, 4th CS, 4 and 6 August 1914, Admiralty to *Good Hope* and *Drake*, 5 August 1914, quoted in ibid, 16, 265–66.

97. Ibid, 18–19; and Halpern, *A Naval History of World War I*, 78–9.

America, with the heaviest concentration, thirty-two merchantmen, in New York. Together with the liners sheltering at Boston, these vessels were particularly dangerous because of their proximity to the North Atlantic shipping lanes.[98] Smaller German ships could be used as colliers to supply the merchant raiders with coal, the shortage of which would prove to be the auxiliary cruiser's greatest handicap. The 14,900 ton *Kronprinz Wilhelm* was one of the more successful of the armed liners and accounted for fifteen merchantmen (totalling 60,522 tons) while operating off the coast of Brazil over the winter of 1914–15. Although her captain was able to coal from captured vessels, the damage inflicted on his own ship from doing so while underway, as the two ships bumped together, as well as a general shortage of fresh food, eventually forced him to intern his ship at Hampton Roads, Virginia in April 1915. A second auxiliary cruiser, the *Prinz Eitel Friedrich*, began her wartime career at Spee's base at Tsingtau, China and managed to capture or sink eleven ships totalling 33,342 tons as she made her way around the world before she, too, was forced by a lack of coal and food to accept internment at Hampton Roads in March 1915.[99]

While Cradock was establishing a cruiser patrol scheme for the western North Atlantic during August, the refitting of HMCS *Niobe* was making rapid progress at Halifax. When word came on 1 August to prepare the warship for operations, her crew consisted only of an engineer lieutenant-commander, an artificer engineer, five engine room artificers (ERAs), four stoker petty officers, and three stokers. The remainder of her skeleton crew had been sent west for duty in *Rainbow*. A request to the Admiralty for assistance in providing experienced British personnel for *Niobe*'s complement was turned down. Fortunately the return of *Algerine* and *Shearwater* to Esquimalt, and the decision to pay them off freed their crews for service in the Canadian cruiser, including Captain Robert Corbett. Corbett who had commanded *Algerine*, took command of *Niobe*. Altogether some sixteen RN officers and 194 ratings joined the cruiser's crew. These were supplemented by twenty-eight RCN and RNCVR officers and some 360 RCN and RNCVR ratings. The crew was finally brought up to full strength when the government of Newfoundland agreed to assign one officer and 106 ratings from the Royal Newfoundland Naval Reserve to the ship. Any disappointment the Newfoundlanders may have felt at serving in the old Canadian cruiser would have been dispelled by the subsequent news that they would be paid at RCN rates—roughly twice the amount they would have received in a British ship.[100]

After emerging from dry dock, *Niobe* was ready for a full power trial on 1 September, the results of which her captain reported to NSHQ as being "most satisfactory. Worked up to 104 revolutions, ammunition completed to full stowage. Coaling tonight; have reported myself to Fourth Cruiser Squadron; leave here tomorrow for St John's in accordance with orders,"[101] to pick up the Newfoundland reservists that would complete the ship's crew.

---

98. Tucker, *The Naval Service of Canada*, I, 240–41.

99. Halpern, *A Naval History of World War I*, 81–82.

100. Naval Ottawa to *Niobe*, 21 September 1914, 1047–19–2, LAC, RG 24, vol. 3969; "Brief History of HMCS *Niobe*," 26 October 1961, 45–47, DHH 81/520/8000, "HMCS *Niobe*," vol. 1; and Tucker, *The Naval Service of Canada*, I, 242.

101. *Niobe* to Naval Ottawa, 1 September 1914, 1047–19–2, LAC, RG 24, vol. 3969.

The ship had managed a respectable nineteen knots during the trial, not that much slower than her design speed of 20.5 knots of twenty years before. The Halifax *Morning Chronicle* reported the spectacle of the large Canadian cruiser heading out to sea the next morning.

> HMCS *Niobe* put to sea at 7:30 yesterday morning for the first time in several years. Since she came out of the dry dock where her bottom was overhauled and cleaned, the *Niobe* has been anchored in the stream, having the final touches put to her before sailing for sea. All day Monday the cruiser was busily coaling from the collier *Louisburg* and this operation was maintained until a late hour that night. At seven yesterday morning the cruiser's anchors were hoisted and she steamed rapidly down the harbour, passing Chebucto Head before eight o'clock. The *Niobe* will assist in the protection of the transatlantic trade routes. It is suggested that the Canadian cruiser will be ordered to the Gulf of St Lawrence as a guard for British shipping in those waters.[102]

Although it had been intended that *Niobe* would join HMS *Lancaster* in patrolling the Gulf of St Lawrence, the cruiser was handed a new assignment as she was returning to Halifax from St John's with her full crew. On 19 August, the British government cabled Ottawa asking if it could supply an infantry battalion to replace the British unit garrisoning Bermuda. The country's only permanent force battalion, the Royal Canadian Regiment, was selected and proceeded to Halifax aboard the transport *Canada*. At noon on 11 September, the transport sailed for Bermuda under escort from *Niobe*, arriving safely at Hamilton two days later.[103] By the time the two ships returned to Halifax on the 17th, the cruiser's condenser had developed a defect and the ship required a week alongside to remedy the problem. The fact that the aging Canadian warship required repair so soon after beginning operations undoubtedly influenced the Admiralty's decision not to include *Niobe* as part of the escort for the troopship convoy that was about to sail for England carrying the 1st Canadian Infantry Division. Only ten days after the ship had returned to Halifax with *Canada*, NSHQ was informed by the new commander-in-chief, North America and West Indies Station, Rear-Admiral R.S. Phipps-Hornby (Cradock having been assigned to command the ill-fated cruiser force in the South Atlantic), that *"Niobe* is not now proceeding to England."[104]

To escort the Canadian troop convoy from Quebec City, the Admiralty initially assigned only four light cruisers from the Twelfth Cruiser Squadron that had been maintaining a patrol in the western English Channel. When the militia minister, Sir Sam Hughes, questioned the strength of the escort on the 16th, however, his inquiry "determined the Admiralty to increase it."

102. Halifax *Morning Chronicle*, 2 September 1914.

103. Dockyard, Halifax to Naval Ottawa, 13 September 1914, NSC 1047–19–2, LAC, RG 24, vol. 3969; and A. Fortescue Duguid, *Official History of the Canadian Forces in the Great War, 1914–1919, I: From the Outbreak of War to the Formation of the Canadian Corps, August 1914–September 1915* (Ottawa 1938), 70–71.

104. C-in-C to Naval Ottawa, 27 September 1914, NSC 1047–19–2, LAC, RG 24, vol. 3969.

They were thus able to reply that the escort would be four cruisers besides the [battleship] *Glory* and *Niobe*, reinforced midway by a second battleship, while the Grand Fleet covered the escort from attack by any large force of the enemy. An additional factor of safety was provided in that the route chosen was that used in winter by shipping between the St Lawrence and England; at the period when the convoy would cross the Atlantic, Canadian traffic would be using the Belle Isle route, far to the northward, and there was therefore little chance of the convoy being sighted by ordinary merchant ships till it was nearing home [i.e., England]....

The removal of the *Glory* and *Niobe* from his command for escort duties left Admiral Hornby very weak. He pointed out that a cruiser in the St Lawrence and two off New York were all he could maintain, so that Philadelphia, whence so many suspicious vessels came, had to go unwatched. The Admiralty met his wishes by giving him back the *Niobe*, as the escort would be sufficient without her, and, moreover, she would most probably develop defects on the long voyage.[105]

The sight of only the four light cruisers actually at Quebec City on the eve of departure— *Glory* was to sail from Halifax and join the convoy at sea, an arrangement about which the Admiralty failed to inform NSHQ[106]—once again prompted Hughes, in Quebec to see the first contingent off, to wire Prime Minister Borden that "escort is altogether inadequate: its strength should be increased." A hasty inquiry to London on 3 October, the convoy's scheduled departure date, brought the Admiralty's assurance "that every reasonable precaution has been taken and the escort is considered safe. They do not, therefore, intend to increase the number of ships accompanying the expedition across the Atlantic, being satisfied as to the adequacy of the arrangements made to protect it. The cancelling of their sailing on the grounds of inadequate escort will rest, therefore, with the Canadian government."[107] His bluster called, Hughes relented and the thirty-one ship convoy weighed anchor later that afternoon. As described by an army officer aboard one of the transports, "cruiser *Eclipse*, steaming slowly, passed SS *Bermudian* (3rd ship in column Z) at exactly 3pm."

Cruiser *Eclipse* reached leading cruiser position at head of column Z when all ships in the column hove up anchors and proceeded, following cruiser *Eclipse* at speed of nine knots, keeping in column formation. The other leading cruisers steamed to their respective positions at head of columns Y and X at same time....

It was six o'clock when the last ship in column X steamed out past the entrance of the bay to sea, followed by HM Cruiser *Talbot*. The weather

---

105. Admiralty, *Naval Staff Monographs*, IX, 92.

106. R.M. Stephens, "Memo: For the Director of the Naval Service," 10 November 1914, 1023-7-3, pt. 1, LAC, RG 24, vol. 3857.

107. Admiralty, *Naval Staff Monographs*, IX, 94.

The Canopus-class pre-dreadnought battleship HMS *Glory*, left, and the Devonshire-class cruiser HMS *Carnarvon*, right, in Halifax Harbour in 1914. *Glory* was in Canadian waters to provide an initial escort for the sailing of the Canadian Expeditionary Force's First Division when it departed for Britain in October 1914. (LAC PA-112339)

conditions were perfect, a clear setting sun with a full bright moon, a light breeze from NNE making one of nature's most perfect Canadian autumn evenings.... It can truly be said that one has seldom seen such a perfect sight before, and, may be, will never see such a perfect sight again....

As soon as column Z was out at sea, speed was reduced in order to let the other two columns as they came out get up abeam of column Z, making three columns abreast in fleet formation. Then the course for all ships to steer was signalled by flagship cruiser *Charybdis* to leading cruisers, the cruisers signalling same to all transport ships in their respective columns; and the convoy proceeded on the first leg of the course of 2,450 miles to its final destination.[108]

Two days after departing Quebec, the convoy was joined by the pre-dreadnought battle-ship *Glory*, which escorted them to mid-Atlantic before turning back for Halifax. One day after the battleship parted company, the Canadian convoy's escort was reinforced by another pre-dreadnought, *Majestic*, and one of the Grand Fleet's newest battle cruisers, the 13.5-inch gunned *Princess Royal*. With the powerful battle cruiser's capability to defeat any enemy surface raider the convoy could possibly have encountered, the first Canadian contingent reached Plymouth undisturbed on 14 October. As has been pointed out by one naval historian of the war, however, "the real protection of the convoy [from the ships of the German High Seas Fleet] came from the occupation by close to three cruiser squadrons of the cruiser [patrol] areas in the North Sea. These zones between Peterhead and Norway had been established in September. The light cruisers and battle squadrons of the Grand Fleet were out in support, and there was a second line of protection with the two battle cruiser squadrons to sight any ship that might have passed through the main line at night. Jellicoe kept his screening operation at full force from the 2nd to the 10th."[109]

Her condenser repaired, *Niobe* sailed from Halifax on 6 October to take station off New York as part of Phipps-Hornby's blockading cruiser force. News that the RCN warship was part of the British patrol forces soon leaked to the Canadian public. "If officers of an incoming merchantman that reached port [in New York] tonight are not mistaken in their identification," the *Ottawa Citizen* proudly reported on the 12th, "one of the British warships now on guard off New York harbor is the Canadian cruiser *Niobe*. The arriving steamer was the *Vauban*, from South American ports. When she was outside the Ambrose Channel lightship at seven o'clock tonight a warship suddenly threw her powerful searchlight across the *Vauban*'s bow. Then with a Morse-light the warship ordered the merchantman to stop. A cutter in charge of a British naval officer promptly put off and pulled alongside the *Vauban*. The officer boarded her and after a conversation with Captain Byrne allowed him to proceed into port."[110] The warship's routine challenge of the

---

108. "The Log of the SS *Bermudian*, Quebec to Plymouth, 1914," nd, DHH, AHS unit file LdSH (RC).

109. Halpern, *A Naval History of World War I*, 87.

110. The *Ottawa Citizen*, 12 October 1914.

merchantman was typical of the duties Hornby's cruisers performed during their two- to three-week patrols on station. After returning to Halifax in mid-October, however, *Niobe*'s next assignment took her north for a search of the Gulf of St Lawrence where a German cruiser had been reported. Departing on the 22nd, the cruiser "searched Newfoundland coast to Pistolet Bay and north coast of Anticosti" Island but "saw no hostile craft" before returning on the 31st.[111]

Thereafter, the Canadian cruiser took her place in the regular rotation of warships patrolling the American coast. Writing in 1944, her executive officer, Commander C.E. Aglionby, RCN, recalled that *Niobe* was part of "the blockading squadron of the Royal Navy off New York harbour, inside which there were thirty-eight German ships including some fast liners, which could act as commerce destroyers if they could escape."

> We boarded and searched all vessels leaving the harbour, and in the early days took off many German reservists who were trying to get back to Germany in neutral ships.... We had to pass many things in neutral ships which we knew were destined for Germany, to be used against our men. One particular example I remember was a large sailing ship carrying a cargo of cotton bound for Hamburg, but this was not contraband at that time and we had to allow it to go on. It was very monotonous work, especially after the first few weeks when, owing to reports of possible submarine attacks, we had to keep steaming up and down, zig-zagging the whole time. After the first few weeks, owing to complaints in the American press by German sympathizers to the effect that we were sitting on Uncle Sam's doorstep preventing people coming in and out, we had to keep our patrol almost out of sight of land. The American Navy were very friendly to us, and when their ships passed us they used to cheer ship and play British tunes. One day when we had news that [the large German liner] *Vaterland* had raised steam and would probably bolt out at night, we overheard a signal made by wireless *en clair* from one American ship to another "it is the Dutch *Vaderland* not the German *Vaterland* which is going out tonight."
>
> We used to spend sixteen days at sea, return to Halifax for coal and provision, and then resume our beat. This was done in all weathers, and sometimes the temperature off Nova Scotia would fall to twenty degrees below zero, and then the spray would freeze into a solid coating all over the ship, making it almost impossible to work the guns. Our most exciting moment perhaps was when the *Niobe* was ordered down to Newport News in Virginia, for which port a German armed raider was making. We were unlucky enough to meet a 100 mile an hour gale, and the ship had to turn head to sea and go slow till the weather moderated. During this time we had many SOS messages, but were unable to render any assistance. When the weather moderated and

---

111. Dockyard, Halifax to Naval Ottawa, 22 October 1914, Radio via Fame Point to Naval Ottawa, 28 October 1914, Dockyard, Halifax to Naval Ottawa, 1047–19–2, LAC, RG 24, vol. 3969.

HMCS *Niobe* in the Halifax dry dock. As was the case with her sister-ships on the other side of the Atlantic, the obsolescent cruiser was counted on by the Admiralty to augment the Royal Navy's cruiser patrol force upon the outbreak of war. (DND CN 6593)

Gunnery training on *Niobe's* 6-inch main armament. (CWM 200301174-006)

we arrived off the harbour, the German raider had passed in. She was given twenty-four hours to put to sea again and declared her intention of doing so, so we waited just outside the three mile limit for her. When the twenty-four hours expired, however, she decided not to risk it.[112]

The armed raider in Commander Aglionby's account was *Prinz Eitel Friedrich*, which turned up off the Virginia coast unexpectedly on 10 March 1915. *Niobe* was on patrol off New York at the time and she had returned to Halifax to coal before proceeding south to join three other British cruisers and the battleship *Glory* in keeping watch to prevent the German raider's escape. Although the patrolling squadron received reports in early April that the liner was making preparations to get underway, they proved false and *Prinz Eitel Friedrich* was interned on the 6th.[113]

As for the German merchant ships in New York harbour, by early November 1914 the British consul general reached an arrangement with the American authorities to provide some warning of any enemy attempt to leave United States waters.[114] The presence of the Anglo-Canadian cruiser force off the harbour entrance was sufficient to convince the German ships to remain in port throughout *Niobe*'s nine months of operations.[115] Even so, not all of the cruiser operations off New York were "routine," a fact that was made evident to NSHQ in late January 1915 when they received a letter, by way of the governor general, from a New York legal firm enquiring about a merchant ship that was rammed by one of the cruisers on station off the harbour entrance.

> We have the honour to inform you that about 7.45 pm on January 9th 1915, fifteen miles to the eastward of Ambrose Channel Lightship, which is situated at the entrance to New York Harbour, the steamship *Bayamo* belonging to our client, the New York and Cuba Steamship Company, was struck and seriously damaged by a vessel which, so far as we can learn, was a man-of-war. The colliding vessel sometime prior to the collision had been using a searchlight; later she was signalling with what appeared to be a Morse winker light; and her manoeuvres, 'closing in towards our client's vessel, indicated that she wished to speak or examine the *Bayamo*.
>
> The weather was clear with an overcast sky, making the night so dark that it was impossible for the officers of the *Bayamo* to distinguish the details of hull, or rig of the other vessel; and after the accident, they were unable to ascertain her name.
>
> In view of all the information we have obtained, it seems probable to us that the colliding vessel may have been one of the British men-of-war which

---

112. Aglionby's account is quoted in Tucker, *The Naval Service of Canada*, I, 243–44.

113. "Brief History of HMCS *Niobe*," 26 October 1961, 55–56, DHH 81/520/8000, "HMCS *Niobe*," vol. 1.

114. St John's, Nfld, to Naval Ottawa, 7 November 1914, 1048-3-1, LAC, RG 24, vol. 3592.

115. Tucker, *The Naval Service of Canada*, I, 244.

have been cruising off the entrance to this harbour, and we are anxious to obtain information as to which, if any, of those vessels was in collision at the time above mentioned.

We are advised that the British embassy at Washington, has no information upon the subject, but suggests the desirability of addressing a communication to the Canadian admiralty office and suggesting that if a British or Canadian vessel were in collision with the *Bayamo* there would be no disposition to hold back any of the facts. We should therefore greatly appreciate information as to whether that office has received any information as to this collision.[116]

After being asked by the Department of External Affairs "to cause a suitable reply to be made," NSHQ inquired of Admiral Hornby "if he has any information which can be forwarded to enquirers."[117] The commander-in-chief immediately identified the offending cruiser as HMS *Charybdis* but asked that "as the matter has been reported to Admiralty direct, I do not wish that information be divulged without their sanction." Bowing to the admiral's wishes (but contrary to the Washington embassy's assertion that "there would be no disposition to hold back any of the facts"), NSHQ falsely informed External Affairs that "the department has no information of any warship having been in collision with the *Bayamo*. It is recommended that [the American lawyers] should apply through their agent in Great Britain to the Admiralty, who will undoubtedly supply any information in their possession."[118]

While Phipps-Hornby's cruiser force was securing the western North Atlantic against the surface raider threat, the naval service still had to provide for the defence of Canada's Atlantic coast. The navy was relying principally on the civilian government vessels and crews that had been pressed into service on the outbreak of war but were fortunate to receive a welcomed reinforcement from one of its wealthy, and most colourful, private benefactors. J.K.L. Ross was the son of one of the men who had made a substantial sum building the Canadian Pacific Railway. Having inherited his father's fortune in 1913, Ross was the epitome of the millionaire sportsman, routinely travelling to Britain before the war to participate in the races held by the Royal Yacht Squadron. He also gained a reputation as a profligate spender (he would eventually declare bankruptcy in 1928), buying many yachts, automobiles, and race horses (one of which would win the prestigious Triple Crown in 1919). Ross was also an ardent supporter of Borden's bill to give Britain $35 million for the construction of three battleships and, upon the bill's defeat in the senate, he suggested that the money could be raised by private subscription and offered to contribute $500,000 to get the fund started. In August 1914, Ross was reputed to have handed the prime minister a cheque for the half-million "to be used by the government in any manner that

---

116. Burlingham, Montgomery and Beecher to Governor General of Canada, 21 January 1915, 1048-1-2, LAC, RG 24, vol. 3620.

117. Acting Under Secretary of State for External Affairs to Desbarats, 28 January 1915, Naval Ottawa to Dockyard, Halifax, 28 January 1915, ibid.

118. Rear-Admiral Commanding to Naval Ottawa, 29 January 1915, Desbarats to External Affairs, 29 January 1915, ibid.

might seem best for the defence of Canada and the empire, without reservation or accounting."[119]

A patriot as well as a philanthropist, Ross was a captain in the militia, but his desire to see active service in the army on the outbreak of war was derailed when he was judged medically unfit. Ross then turned his attention to the navy and quickly donated his most recently purchased yacht, *Albacore*, to the RCN as a training vessel. After he "offered himself for service in the Royal Naval Canadian Volunteer Reserve," Ross "proceeded to the United States on a private mission."[120] The thirty-eight year old millionaire arrived in New York in early August 1914 determined to buy the steam turbine yacht *Tarantula* from the American railroad magnate W.K. Vanderbilt. *Tarantula* was one of the first high-speed turbine-engined ships ever built. She was patterned after the smaller *Turbinia* in which Sir Charles Parsons had conducted his turbine trials for the Royal Navy. Launched in 1902 by Yarrow and Company in Britain, Vanderbilt had taken advantage of *Tarantula*'s twenty-five knot speed to make high-speed commutes down the East River in New York to his lower Manhattan railway offices even though the ship's heavy wake caused damage to moored vessels and shore facilities.[121]

With her hull modelled along the same lines as the torpedo-boats Yarrow had built for the Royal Navy, the yacht was suitable for conversion into a coastal torpedo-boat. "The purchase of this vessel," Admiral Kingsmill later explained to the naval minister, "and bringing it from the United States was attended by a great deal of worry on account of the United States having prohibited the sale of any vessels which were likely to be used for belligerent purposes. However, the vessel was obtained and ... fitted out more or less secretly at a great deal of expense [by Ross]. Later on she was brought to Halifax where she was armed and fitted with a torpedo tube."[122] Ross arrived at Halifax with *Tarantula* and her civilian crew on 10 September where the captain-in-charge of the dockyard, Captain E.H. Martin, RCN, recommended further work needed to convert her into a warship. In order to maintain the pretence that the ship had not been brought to Canada with the intention of employing her as a naval vessel, however, the deputy minister addressed a letter to Ross on the 24th in an apparent ruse to provide a suitable explanation should the purchase be questioned by the American authorities.

> It has been reported to me that the appearance of your yacht, the *Tarantula*, now lying in Halifax Harbour, is so much that of a torpedo boat and so unlike an ordinary yacht that her appearance on the coast might cause anxiety to shipping if she were allowed to cruise, and also it is quite possible that this vessel, if she approached a man-of-war at night, would be fired upon. Taking the above circumstances into consideration, it appears to be necessary to

---

119. McKee, *The Armed Yachts of Canada*, 20; and J. Bannerman, "How J.K.L. Ross Spent Sixteen Millions," April 1955, DHH, J.K.L. Ross biographical file.

120. Kingsmill to C.C. Ballantyne, 4 December 1917, DHH, J.K.L. Ross biographical file.

121. McKee, *The Armed Yachts of Canada*, 22.

122. Kingsmill to C.C. Ballantyne, 4 December 1917, DHH, J.K.L. Ross biographical file.

instruct the naval officer in charge at Halifax to intern this ship for the present. It would further appear that this vessel, from her high speed, would be of service to the government and the department would be glad to hear from you on what terms you would dispose of her.[123]

In an effort to make it more difficult for the Americans to trace the ship, the navy quickly changed the name of the vessel from the warlike *Tarantula* to the decidedly less-aggressive sounding *Tuna*. On the same day that Desbarats was writing to Ross to ask "on what terms you would dispose of her," both Ross and Kingsmill were already referring to the vessel by her new name. Ross sold the yacht to the naval service for the nominal sum of one dollar, his only stipulation being "that at the end of this war, if the *Tuna* is still fit for sea, your department offer to return her to me in whatever condition she may be in at that time."[124] As for the ship's crew, the director of the naval service was keen to have them entered on the RNCVR rolls, particularly given the engine room staff's knowledge of the vessel's turbines. "Mr Ross has had thirteen years experience yachting," Kingsmill explained, also on the 24th, "and has practical knowledge of the sea."

> He volunteers for service in the RCNVR [*sic*] and submits his request to be appointed to the *Tuna*. Mr Ross is the very man for this; he would, of course, not be in command when the vessel is armed.
>
> Mr Ross' sailing master, a Nova Scotian by birth, knows every inch of the Nova Scotian and New Brunswick coasts and is a seaman pure and simply, not the class of man to make an officer in the RCNVR [*sic*] but it is essential to retain him; he is necessary as a pilot and in Mr Ross' interests we should keep him. He could be appointed a supernumerary officer of F[isheries] P[rotection] Service and lent to *Tuna*.
>
> The other persons serving in the *Tuna* volunteer for service in the RCN for "temporary service during war." The engineer can be made an acting artificer engineer and his assistants acting engine room artificers. Mr Ross is desirous of retaining the engineer who has been in the vessel five years and will make up to him the difference between the pay he will receive as chief artificer engineer and what he is receiving now.[125]

Contrary to the director's assertion to Desbarats, Ross received a lieutenant's commission in the RNCVR and was given command of *Tuna* once her conversion, which included the fitting of a 3-pounder gun and two 14-inch torpedo tubes, was completed in early December. His training consisted of "a course of gunnery and instruction in torpedo," preparation that was probably sufficient to command a volunteer crew he had brought

123. Desbarats to J.K.L. Ross, 24 September 1914, 86–3-6, LAC, RG 24, vol. 5673.

124. Ross to Desbarats, 24 September 1914, ibid.

125. Kingsmill to Desbarats, 24 September 1914, ibid.

Niobe's bridge and forward 6-inch guns. (CWM 19830056-012)

into the service himself and whose pay he was topping up from his own pocket. Canada's newest warship was commissioned as a tender to HMCS *Diana*, the Royal Naval College of Canada's training schooner, that had been pressed into service as Halifax's shore establishment when *Niobe* had been readied for sea duty. As NSHQ explained to Captain Martin, "the officers and ship's company are to be borne on the books of *Diana* for pay and all are to take the oath of allegiance before being placed on the ship's books.... Mr C. Mitchell is to be rated chief petty officer, RCNVR [*sic*]. Mr J.S. Paterson is appointed chief artificer engineer, RCN, for temporary service, on highest scale of pay."[126]

Tuna spent the winter patrolling off the entrance to Halifax and provided the RCN with its only offensive weapon for the port's defences aside from whichever of Admiral Hornby's cruisers might be alongside.[127] In his own report on the harbour's defences on 22 September, the C-in-C, North America and West Indies Station, had recommended that "in view of [the] amount of fog, etc., which may be expected [and would restrict the vision of the coastal batteries], some mobile defence is also much needed. Two vessels carrying whiteheads [torpedoes] and two submarines would greatly facilitate safety of port. Latter would also practically prevent destruction of Camperdown W/T station by shell fire— which is now an easy matter.... In making these proposals I am guided by consideration that in present war, attack in force by torpedo craft improbable, but that rush by cruisers or armed merchant cruisers or even a boat attack may be attempted, especially in later stages of war."[128] The arrival of HMCS *Tuna* to bolster the Halifax defences "was much appreciated by the then commander-in-chief, as Canada had no vessels whatever for patrol work" on the East Coast.[129]

Elsewhere along the Nova Scotia coast the RCN relied on the government vessels that had been pressed into naval service. Even then, some of the larger ports were provided with little in the way of harbour patrols. At the end of October 1914, for instance, a concerned resident of Sydney wrote to the naval minister, J.D. Hazen, to report that "considerable anxiety is felt in our city owing to the absolute lack of facilities for naval defence. The very fact that Halifax Harbour is being dragged for mines adds to the apprehension in this community. Some of the British fleet have been back and forward to this port since the outbreak of war, and with the very large number of Austrians and Germans (some six or seven hundred) in our midst, a great many people apprehend that some of these might mine our harbour."[130] With his greater appreciation of the naval situation, Kingsmill showed little sympathy for the many letters the minister received from jittery citizens expecting a sudden German descent upon their coast. In responding to the letter, the naval director cynically pointed out "that the port of Sydney is one that it is not

---

126. Kingsmill to Captain in Charge, HMC Dockyard, Halifax, 25 September 1914, ibid; and "RCN Shore Establishments on the Canadian East Coast, 1910—1919," nd, DHH 81/520/8000, "HMCS *Niobe*," vol. 1.

127. Kingsmill to C.C. Ballantyne, 4 December 1917, DHH, J.K.L. Ross biographical file.

128. Hornby to Kingsmill, 22 September 1914, 1001–5-3, LAC, RG 24, vol. 6194.

129. Kingsmill to C.C. Ballantyne, 4 December 1917, DHH, J.K.L. Ross biographical file.

130. J.W. Madden, Sydney, NS to J.D. Hazen, 29 October 1914, 1047–22–1, LAC, RG 24, vol. 3970.

likely the enemy would take the trouble to mine. If the large number of Austrians and Germans in the place mine the harbour one might almost say that the people of Sydney would deserve it…. I would suggest that the harbour authorities of Sydney should employ a couple of boats and organize a police patrol and then they would be at rest with regard to the large number of Austrians and Germans in the place."[131]

With scant resources, the RCN had to concentrate on those waters that seemed most exposed, the most important being Halifax, which was serving as the main base for Hornby's cruisers patrolling off New York. During the winter, the navy did maintain a Bay of Fundy patrol consisting of five vessels, with the captain of *Acadia*, Lieutenant Eliott, who during the summer shipping season served as the chief examination officer at Quebec, as the senior officer in charge. As NSHQ explained in its orders to Eliott, he was to employ two of his ships, *Acadia* and *Sable I*, on a patrol between Yarmouth and Grand Manan Island off the New Brunswick shore.

> This patrol is to be based on Yarmouth and one ship is to be continually at sea on the lookout. Details as to communication will be sent from Ottawa. Whenever it is impossible to keep the sea, a full report is to be forwarded and after such occurrence both ships should proceed and search the bay. The *Sable I* is to be fitted out as A Boat for minesweeping, *Acadia* as B Boat. Practice at minesweeping is to take place when weather permits in order to accustom the crew to the work. All reports, etc. to be made to captain in charge, Halifax, NS.
>
> The *Curlew*, *Constance*, *Petrel*, will patrol the Grand Manan Channel, working between the Grand Manan Islands and Etang Harbour, or other suitable harbour in the vicinity. No vessels should pass through this channel without being seen, and their movements watched. Ships that are known to the captain as ordinary traders need not be interfered with, but a stranger should be followed and watched and any suspicious actions at once reported. One of these ships will be taken in hand at a time and defects made good. The commanding officers of *Curlew*, *Constance*, *Petrel*, will continue to report their movements to Ottawa. When on patrol at Yarmouth; should anything prevent them [from] proceeding or any suspicious vessel be seen, also report [to] s[enior] o[fficer] patrols at Halifax.[132]

On other occasions the navy's patrol vessels might be despatched to investigate reports of suspicious activity along the coast. During a visit to Halifax in April 1915, for instance, Admiral Kingsmill detailed *Tuna* to Tor Bay, Nova Scotia, to follow up a report that the Germans had secretly established a submarine base in the vicinity. As he explained to NSHQ, the "locality has [an] unsavoury reputation; consider it very desirable secret service officer should operate on coast of Nova Scotia, East Halifax. Am recalling *Petrel* to patrol

---

131. Kingsmill, "Memorandum for Deputy Minister," 2 November 1914, ibid.

132. Kingsmill, "General Orders for Captain in Charge, Bay of Fundy Patrol," 14 December 1914, 1065–3-1, LAC, RG 24, vol. 4030.

eastward shore."[133] *Tuna*'s patrol made clear, however, that it was unlikely that any activity—enemy or otherwise—could take place along the coast without the local populace being instantly aware. "On your instructions, I left Halifax with HMCS *Tuna* at daylight of April 16th for Tor Bay," Lieutenant Ross explained in his report to Kingsmill, "in order to find out, if possible, whether there was anything in the report of a German submarine base being established in the vicinity of Tor Bay."

> For the Germans to establish a submarine base that would be of any service to them it would be necessary, in my opinion, to place it in some out of the way harbour or on the sheltered side of some island, so that a submarine could approach this base in any weather.
>
> Along the Nova Scotia coast between Halifax and Canso I do not believe there is any harbour or cove that they could send a ship to establish such a base without attracting the attention of the local fishermen, who know every ship that usually sails this coast.
>
> If any strange ship approached these shores and did anything out of the usual, these fishermen would investigate her, if for no other reason than curiosity. Working on this theory I went into Country Harbour, Isaac Harbour, Tor Bay, Cole Harbour, and made inquiries from residents of Whitehead. In fact my inquiries covered a longer line than this, because anything unusual that happens in the shipping line along this coast, travels for miles with almost the speed of telegraph, for example:—I went into Country Harbour in a thick fog and it was known in the neighboring harbours in a very short time. I had not been anchored one hour in Cole Harbour when the Customs House officer, "Mr Wells," from Whitehead was alongside. I only give these instances to show how the local fishermen watch what goes on along this coast, and to prove that if a ship of any kind attempted to establish a base anywhere along this coast it would be impossible for her to do so without the local fishermen knowing something about it....
>
> I passed quite close to two islands both named Goose Island, I also made inquiries as to whether any strangers had been on these islands lately, or if any material had been shipped to these islands in any way; from these inquiries I gathered that no strangers have landed on these islands, and I do not believe that there is a wireless plant on them, or anywhere along the coast that I patrolled during the past five days. As we steamed by these islands, I looked them over carefully with my glasses and saw no suspicious signs. Neither of these islands are more than eighty feet high and both of them are in a fairly populous vicinity where fishermen are round them all the time. I left instructions with their customs officer, Wells, to wire men at the dockyard, Halifax, if he saw or heard of any suspicious ship in any way round the coast.[134]

---

133. Kingsmill to Naval Ottawa, 13 April 1915, 1047–30–2, LAC, RG 24, vol. 3970.

134. Ross to Kingsmill, 22 April 1915, ibid.

Apparently the only vessel that the customs officer, Clarence V. Wells, found suspicious was HMCS *Tuna* herself. As soon as he returned to shore from his visit with Ross, Wells wired the naval service's deputy minister in Ottawa to report that "there is now lying off Cole Harbour, Guysboro County [Nova Scotia], a ship of strange appearance. I have just come from on board. Her commander gives his name as Lieutenant J.K.L. Ross, RNCVR, and says his vessel is the torpedo boat HMCS *Tuna*, but refuses to show his ship's papers. Ship has no name or number. Showing is a steel ship, painted grey. Has two smoke stacks and more than one hundred fifty feet in length. Very narrow, sitting low to the water." Aside from demonstrating a keen ability to describe naval vessels, Wells's report on *Tuna* prompted NSHQ to ask Halifax "if there is any reason for her not having her name on her stern and [the deputy minister] asks, if there is no reason, that you will put it on."[135]

At the same time that Ross was arousing the suspicions of the local populace with his turbine-powered yacht, NSHQ had also followed up Kingsmill's suggestion and asked Canada's chief commissioner of police, Lieutenant-Colonel A.P. Sherwood, to send an agent to the area. On the outbreak of war, Sherwood had assembled an intelligence network to combat enemy subversion and his agents' reports did much to deflate the wild gossip that quickly grew about German spy rings and saboteurs operating just across the country's border with the United States. As the head of the navy's small intelligence branch at NSHQ, in addition to his duties as chief of staff, Commander Stephens worked closely with both Sherwood and the militia's chief of the general staff, Major-General Sir Willoughby Gwatkin, in dealing with intelligence matters.[136] Two weeks after *Tuna*'s return to Halifax, Sherwood was able to report to Stephens that Ross's experience "confirms the investigation which I am having made, so far as it has gone. A special officer of mine is working along the coast from Halifax to Tor Bay, by land, and has found nothing out of the way."[137]

Although the intelligence section (with Stephens at its head) had been created only in December 1913, the department had been interested in developing an intelligence organization from the moment the Naval Service Act was passed into law in 1910. At that time, however, the Admiralty had advised Ottawa that "it has not been considered that [British] naval administration requires the formation of a department and general staff on the lines of the army organization and this should be borne in mind in dealing with proposals for the establishment of an intelligence department at the ministry of naval service." As a result, London advised that the Canadian navy would require only a small staff, whose duties would be no more than "to superintend the collection of information likely to be of use in the special circumstances of the dominion." Indeed, since the Canadian militia department was already passing both military and naval intelligence to the War Office in a monthly diary, the Admiralty maintained that there was no require-

135. C.V. Wells to Desbarats, 18 April 1915, Stephens to Martin, 19 April 1915, 86–3-6, LAC, RG 24, vol. 5673.

136. Stephens, Director of Gunnery, "Memorandum for Deputy Minister," 13 December 1913, 1023–4-1, LAC, RG 24, vol. 3856.

137. Stephens to Sherwood, 14 April 1915, Sherwood to Stephens, 5 May 1915, 1047–30–2, LAC, RG 24, vol. 3970; and Hadley and Sarty, *Tin-pots and Pirate Ships*, 108.

ment for the new naval service to duplicate that effort. Instead, "for the present" it should confine its activity "to reproducing and circulating" information for its own use, but any naval information received from the militia department was to be combined with their own intelligence and forwarded to London. In return, the Admiralty would "send periodically to the Department of Naval Service such intelligence as they consider will be of use to the Canadian naval forces."[138] Accordingly, when Stephens took up his intelligence duties, his primary task was "to improve the existing practice regarding confidential correspondence" as well as the custody and distribution of confidential books and documents. With his four-man staff (one officer and three civilian clerks), he would also continue to contribute to the government war book.[139]

If the Admiralty considered Canadian intelligence-gathering to be of little consequence, Canada itself was of considerable importance to the Royal Navy for the transmission of naval intelligence, because no fewer than eighteen undersea cables made landfall in Nova Scotia, where they could connect to the North American land network. Given this excellent access to the world-wide telegraph system the Admiralty used to control naval operations across the globe,[140] Halifax was an obvious choice for the intelligence centre that would serve the western North Atlantic area. Stephens saw that too. Until 1913, the Halifax defence scheme had the paymaster of the Royal Naval College of Canada assume the role of naval intelligence officer in time of war in addition to his duties as secretary to the senior naval officer of the port. While working on the department's war book planning in the summer of 1913, Stephens (still only a lieutenant and before his appointment to head the intelligence section) made arrangements for the establishment of a separate intelligence office at Halifax with *Niobe*'s navigator, Lieutenant Charles White, serving as naval intelligence officer.[141] Subsequently, the war book confirmed that, beginning in the precautionary stage, naval intelligence was to be "collected by the wireless telegraph stations and despatched to naval intelligence officers at Halifax and Esquimalt."[142]

That raised issues regarding the imperial relationship. Although Canada was not yet an independent, sovereign political entity, and although the naval service understood full well the importance of imperial co-operation, there was no good reason why Canada's naval service should not maintain control of naval establishments on Canadian soil. Indeed, the fact that Canada's first obligation to imperial defence was home defence had been acknowledged years before. While the British Army had learned to tread lightly when it came to trying to steer Canada in any particular direction as its militia organization matured, the Admiralty continued to have difficulty with anything that threatened complete

---

138. Graham Greene, Admiralty Secretary, to Desbarats, 14 December 1910, and enclosed Admiralty memorandum, nd, 1023-4-1, LAC, RG 24, vol. 3856.

139. Lieutenant R.M. Stephens, Director of Naval Gunnery, "Memo for Deputy Minister," 13 December 1913, ibid.

140. Nicholas A. Lambert, "Strategic Command and Control for Maneuver Warfare: Creation of the Royal Navy's 'War Room' System, 1905–1915," *The Journal of Military History*, 96, (April 2005), 361–410.

141. "Naval Intelligence Centre Halifax, History," nd, 1023–7-3, pt. 1, LAC, RG 24, vol. 3857.

142. "War Book, Department of the Naval Service," January 1914, 1019–2-2, pt. 1, LAC, RG 24, vol. 3855.

imperial control. When, for example, NSHQ proposed in 1911 that Canadian officers reporting on the arrivals and sailings of foreign naval and merchant ships in North American ports should do so through Ottawa, the British government interpreted such involvement as indicating that Canada "would prefer to make separate arrangements for the transmission of naval intelligence rather than join in with the scheme proposed by the Admiralty, the basis of which is direct communication between reporting officers on the one hand and the Admiralty and intelligence officers on the other, in order that the two latter may obtain all information with the least possible delay." With the Borden government exhibiting little urgency regarding naval questions, it was not until the spring of 1914 that a compromise was proposed so that Canada could take "part in a scheme which will now be world-wide" provided Ottawa did not "have any objection to the Canadian reporting officers, in order to avoid delay and assimilate the arrangements to the Admiralty scheme, reporting direct to the Admiralty in addition to the Department of the Naval Service at Ottawa."[143]

As mentioned above, the department established local naval intelligence centres at both Halifax and Esquimalt "whose duty it was to keep the senior naval officers at those places and the department at Ottawa informed of all intelligence. Reporting stations made their reports direct to the naval intelligence officers for this purpose." In keeping with the war book arrangements, the staffs of the intelligence offices at Ottawa, Halifax and Esquimalt were expanded when the warning telegram was received in August, and when Rear-Admiral Sir Christopher Cradock, commanding the Fourth Cruiser Squadron, arrived in Halifax shortly after the outbreak of war, he adopted the RCN's local intelligence office as the centre for distribution of intelligence to the fleet, "thus utilising it," in NSHQ's view, "for the purpose for which it was intended."[144] At the same time, Lieutenant White was instructed to review all the information he received and forward all intelligence considered of sufficient interest or importance to Ottawa. "Not wishing to hamper operations in the slightest" when Cradock designated Halifax as a naval intelligence centre on 19 August, NSHQ took no action other than to remind the RCN officer in charge of the Halifax dockyard, Captain E.H. Martin, that "imperial officers had no jurisdiction over Halifax."[145]

On Canada's West Coast, the Esquimalt intelligence centre was the only such imperial organization in the eastern Pacific. As arranged with the Admiralty, the centre's "area of observation" was from the United States-Mexico border west to Honolulu, northwest to a point north of the Midway Islands and then due north to the Bering Sea along the 180th degree of longitude. All British consuls and agents on the US West Coast, Alaska, and Hawaii were instructed to report to Admiral Story, while also submitting reports to London and Hong Kong. The consular officers on the Mexican and Central American Pacific coast reported to the intelligence centre at Kingston, Jamaica, which was "instructed to keep

143. Harcourt, Colonial Secretary, to Governor General of Canada, 24 April 1914, 1023–4-3, pt. 1, LAC, RG 24, vol. 3856.

144. Kingsmill to Admiralty, 11 January 1915, ibid.

145. R.M. Stephens, "Memo: For the Director of the Naval Service," 10 November 1914, 1023–7-3, pt. 1, LAC, RG 24, vol. 3857.

Esquimalt informed of all enemy ship movements in the Pacific portion of its area of observation."[146] NSHQ, meanwhile, instructed the Esquimalt centre to repeat all intelligence it received directly to Ottawa.[147] Typical of the messages being passed to NSHQ from the RCN's West Coast centre were reports on German naval reservists in Mexico and the United States that were trying to make their way back to Germany and the movements of the German merchant cruiser *Prinz Eitel Frederick*. The Japanese consul in Lima informed Esquimalt that the merchant steamer *Coluso* was chased by the German auxiliary cruiser after leaving Valparaiso, Chile, on 1 November and only managed to escape when a Chilean destroyer intervened. Four days later, NSHQ received a report that the *Prinz Eitel Frederick* had left Valparaiso in consort with the German merchant ship *Negada*, with the German auxiliary warship taking "on board between one hundred and two hundred men from sailing vessels in port."[148]

Although the Esquimalt centre does not appear to have had any difficulty performing the functions that Ottawa had envisaged in establishing it, such was not the case with Halifax. Not long after the East Coast organization had been declared the "centre for the distribution of naval intelligence" by Cradock, NSHQ noticed that the flow of information to Ottawa "became less and eventually died away altogether."[149] For some reason, not altogether clear, Lieutenant White was either failing in his duty or, more likely, had been instructed by Cradock's successor in command of the North America station, Rear-Admiral R.S. Phipps-Hornby, not to pass Admiralty messages addressed to the C-in-C (and almost all intelligence from London would have been so addressed) on to Ottawa. Worse was to follow. On 1 October the Admiralty abruptly ordered Phipps-Hornby to supplant the Canadian office at Halifax. All diplomatic consuls and reporting officers along the United States eastern seaboard had been instructed to report to a new naval intelligence centre at St John's, Newfoundland, rather than to Halifax, while arrangements were still "being made for exchange of intelligence between new intelligence officer and director of naval service Ottawa."[150] Phipps-Hornby, who had not been consulted despite being the commander-in-chief of the station concerned, immediately recognized the foolishness of the Admiralty's decision and strongly protested to London that the "arrangements indicated will result in serious delay in information reaching ships as to position which it is now most necessary for them to occupy. Submit that Halifax continues to act as intelligence centre as heretofore observing that Halifax has performed duty well and arrangements for transmission to ships, which it is undesirable to upset, have been made.

146. Admiralty to Kingsmill, and enclosed memorandum, 20 November 1914, 1023-4-3, pt. 1, LAC, RG 24, vol. 3856.

147. Naval Ottawa to Admiral Superintendent, Dockyard, Esquimalt, 20 November 1914, ibid.

148. Montevideo, Uruguay, to Director Naval Service, Ottawa, 7 November 1914, Naval Ottawa to Admiralty, 28 October 1914, Naval Ottawa to Captain in Charge, HMC Dockyard Halifax, 28 October 1914, Esquimalt to Naval Ottawa, 3 November 1914, 1023-7-1, pt. 1, LAC, RG 24, vol. 3857.

149. R.M. Stephens, "Memo: For the Director of the Naval Service," 10 November 1914, 1023-7-3, pt. 1, ibid.

150. Admiralty to Rear-Admiral Cruiser Force H, 1 October 1914, United Kingdom National Archives (hereafter UKNA), Admiralty series (hereafter ADM) 137/37.

If the officer at St John's be retained, he should be regarded as subsidiary and not super-seding Halifax."[151]

The Admiralty, however, was in no mood to have its decisions questioned. Unable or unwilling to offer a reasonable explanation for the shift to St John's, the Admiralty fell back on the specious argument that its decisions, once made, were unalterable:

> Complete arrangements having been made with Foreign Office and other departments regarding St John's intelligence centre, it has now been definitely established and instructions have been issued to all concerned. As St John's centre forms part of world wide scheme, no change can now be made. Intelligence officer St John's will receive and circulate to ships all information respecting movements etc. received from reporting officers which reports hitherto passed through Ottawa. All information will be sent as before to ships stationed at Halifax and to all other ships whose positions are reported. Delay should therefore not occur.[152]

Within days of establishing the St John's intelligence centre, the Admiralty demonstrated the impracticality of its own decision by informing the intelligence officer at Jamaica to "send intelligence direct to Ad[miral] Hornby, [and] not through St John's."[153] There was little Ottawa could do about the decision, at least insofar as imperial distribution was concerned, but the continued lack of information being sent from Halifax to Ottawa remained a problem. Eventually, in early November, NSHQ found it necessary to remind Halifax that the intelligence centre had been established "for purpose of keeping department informed of news coming under his observation. Information so far received has been exceedingly meagre. All information obtained through wireless telegraph stations should be communicated and generally speaking all code and cipher messages passing through or intercepted by wireless telegraph stations should be repeated to headquarters, except those which can clearly be classed as not being intelligence."[154] While the necessity of keeping Ottawa informed was largely lost on British officers, the RCN's chief of staff clearly explained its importance in a memorandum to Kingsmill:

> The commander in chief says he thinks this is unnecessary as many of them only contain reports of ships boarded, suspected embarkation of reservists, etc. These are just matters, however, which are of interest to the dominion government as it is constantly receiving information from the British ambassador at Washington and consuls in the United States as to contraband being shipped and reservists concentrating or departing from United States

---

151. Rear-Admiral Cruiser Force H to Admiralty, 2 October 1914, ibid.

152. Admiralty to Rear-Admiral Cruiser Force H, 2 October 1914, ibid.

153. Admiralty to IO Jamaica, 4 October 1914, ibid.

154. Naval Ottawa to Captain in Charge, HMC Dockyard, Halifax, 5 November 1914, 1023–7-3, pt. 1, LAC, RG 24, vol. 3857.

ports. If these wireless telegraph messages referred to are repeated to Ottawa, the department is then in a better position to reply intelligently to questions asked them by the governor-general, prime minister and other high officers.

As an instance of what an intelligence centre should not be, Halifax was conspicuous in the case of the *Brindilla:*

This ship was a prize, captured and brought into Halifax, adjudicated upon by a Prize Court in Halifax, released by order of the court, coaled and departed Halifax and from first to last not a single word regarding her was received from the naval intelligence officer at Halifax.

With regard to naval intelligence officer at St John's, the Admiralty telegraphed on October 1st that he was instructed to keep Ottawa informed. He occasionally reports intelligence to Ottawa, but there is good reason to believe he generally omits to do so. In any case the department has no authority over him.

With regard to the movements of ships, it would appear also of some importance that the dominion government should be in possession of information as to what steps are being taken for the protection of Canadian trade and coasts and the least that can be done in return for the hospitality gladly accorded of Canadian resources, whether of wireless telegraph stations, dockyards or other things. It appears quite indefensible, as actually occurred, that a squadron should concentrate in the Gulf of St Lawrence as a convoy to the Canadian contingent without the dominion government being informed of their presence and movements.

Giving discretion to the naval intelligence officer at Halifax to report such matters as he considers of interest to the dominion government has been tried and found wanting. This is not altogether his fault as he is not in a position to know exactly what is of interest to the government. If, however, he reports everything, the department will soon be able to point out what things are unnecessary. Finally, it is observed that the whole idea of officers in the Canadian service being in possession of information which they do not communicate to their government is wrong in principle.[155]

Despite Kingsmill's November instructions to Halifax that it was to keep Ottawa fully informed of all intelligence, the East Coast centre continued to provide only intermittent reports. The naval director therefore ordered Captain Martin "to remedy this state of affairs" by giving "strict instructions … to the naval intelligence officer at Halifax that headquarters is to be kept informed of all intelligence received from the various intelligence centres."[156] Lieutenant White's failure to forward the information required by NSHQ until strict orders were issued by Kingsmill illustrates the problems the fledgling RCN encountered when all of its professional officers had been trained by, and spent the

---

155. R.M. Stephens, "Memo: For the Director of the Naval Service," 10 November 1914, ibid.

156. Kingsmill to Captain in Charge, HMC Dockyard, Halifax, 3 December 1914, ibid.

bulk of their naval careers with, the Royal Navy. When the Canadian navy's complete subordination to the RN was taken for granted by British officers, it was easy for some officers on the RCN list to blur the distinction between the two services and revert to the mindset of their recent service in the British navy. Although they were now being paid by Ottawa rather than London, their sense of obligation to the new Canadian service could be overwhelmed under the pressure of wartime operations by long-established loyalties to the Royal Navy.

Kingsmill and Stephens, on the other hand, never forgot their primary loyalty. Using the Esquimalt intelligence arrangement as his example, the former approached London in January 1915 to restore the Halifax centre as the focus of "naval intelligence arrangements for the North Atlantic." The naval director's purpose—aside from seeking to keep the Canadian naval department informed of vital North American intelligence on matters such as German merchant ship movements and the possible arming of enemy raiders in US ports—was to try and avoid the unnecessary confusion and delay that the Admiralty's initiatives were creating. As Kingsmill pointed out, the establishment of the centre at St John's meant that all intelligence intended for Admiral Phipps-Hornby, whether it came from consular offices in the United States, other naval intelligence centres or from NSHQ in Ottawa, now had to be forwarded to the intelligence officer in Newfoundland with the result "that it probably passes through (or close to) Halifax, and has to return again, thus causing considerable loss of time." The intelligence department at NSHQ, meanwhile, was also "in continual communication with the consular officers in different parts of the American continent. It does not seem possible to avoid this as the department has employed a number of agents in the United States and Mexico for the purpose of obtaining information, and it is often convenient to communicate with them through the consuls. Besides this, the department has a large number of communications with consuls regarding exports, contraband and other matters." The communication difficulties were compounded by the fact that the Admiralty had not provided NSHQ "with the same ciphers and documents as are supplied to naval intelligence officers," forcing the Canadian department to use either a government or public code when contacting consuls in the United States.

> The department is the more impelled to put forward these suggestions as there is undoubtedly at present some slight confusion and overlapping. This is exemplified at the times when instructions telegraphed from the Admiralty are forwarded on to the naval ports and it is then found that similar instructions have been sent direct to one place but not to the other; whilst at other times instructions have been sent to a naval port but not to the department. It would be convenient, if it could be found possible, either to send all instructions, orders, etc. through the department for distribution or to send a copy of all such instructions to the department for information.[157]

---

157. Kingsmill to Admiralty, 11 January 1915, 1023–4-3, pt. 1, LAC, RG 24, vol. 3856.

The Admiralty simply repeated its argument—and one that ran counter to the stated opinions of both Phipps-Hornby and Kingsmill, the two commanders directly involved— that "from the point of view of the Admiralty, St John's is the most convenient position for an intelligence centre in the North Atlantic, and as all arrangements have now been made for it to act as such it is considered inadvisable to abolish it and replace it by Halifax whilst the war is in progress." All that the Admiralty allowed was a vaguely worded assurance that Halifax and St John's would exchange intelligence "as necessary" and a willingness to supply Ottawa and Halifax with "the various Admiralty publications supplied to intelligence officers."[158]

For its part, the Foreign Office proved even more officious at the news that the Canadian naval department had its own agents in the United States and was communicating directly with British consular offices south of the border. Asserting their surprise that NSHQ "had any communications with consuls regarding exports and contraband," the Foreign Office insisted that proper method for contact with British consuls was for the "governor general to inform his majesty's ambassador at Washington of any business, other than of a purely routine nature, which is being transacted between the Canadian government and his majesty's consular officers in the United States." Professing that the foreign secretary, Sir Edward Grey, "fully agrees as to the necessity for co-ordination between the Canadian authorities and the authorities of his majesty's government," they also insisted that "the exchange of information should be mutual and the proper agent of co-ordination is the governor general."[159]

The confusion that NSHQ had been seeking to avoid was amply demonstrated just a few weeks later when the president of the Canadian Pacific Railway Company, Sir Thomas Shaughnessy, reported some intelligence information he had received from his transportation sources in the United States. In addition to its Pacific shipping service, the CPR had acquired two Atlantic shipping lines in 1903 and 1909, and was one of the world's largest shipowners at the outbreak of war. Shaughnessy, an ardent supporter of the imperial war effort who was providing loans and senior transportation staff to assist in its prosecution, did not hesitate to pass on to the Canadian government any information he heard from his extensive shipping contacts.[160] At the end of March, Shaughnessy told the governor general, the Duke of Connaught, of a report that a "concerted move is about to be made involving dash of German [war]ships from Baltic into Atlantic in conjunction with sailing of German [merchant]ships in New York, Boston, and Newport. It is desired to get British cruisers away from New York to allow as many Germans to escape as possible, expected half their number will be sunk, but remainder to act as supply ships to men of war from Baltic. Bermuda is said to be objective of Baltic ships and raids on Canadian coast

---

158. Graham Greene, Secretary, Admiralty to Foreign Office, 5 February 1915, enclosed in Colonial Office to Duke of Connaught, Governor General, 23 February 1915, 1023-7-3, pt. 1, LAC, RG 24, vol. 3857.

159. W. Langley, Foreign Office to Admiralty, 18 February 1915, enclosed in Colonial Office to Duke of Connaught, Governor General, 23 February 1915, ibid.

160. Theodore D. Regehr, "Shaughnessy, Thomas George, 1st Baron Shaughnessy," *Dictionary of Canadian Biography*, XV: *1921 to 1930* (Toronto 2005), 923–27.

are included in scheme.... Admiralty has been informed. Ends. Inform [intelligence centre at] St John's."[161]

Having been largely cut out of the Admiralty's intelligence network by Whitehall's unwillingness to accept a Canadian intelligence centre at Halifax, NSHQ was not well-positioned to assess the validity of the information Shaughnessy had provided. Since the president of the CPR had already indicated to Ottawa that he had communicated the information to the British government and NSHQ had passed the intelligence to Halifax, with orders to inform St John's of the matter, no further action was taken by headquarters. In the event, however, the information was delayed in reaching London, either because the British officials Shaughnessy informed did not pass the message on or there was a breakdown somewhere between Halifax, St John's, and London. Although the confusion was essentially of the Admiralty's own making, Kingsmill was rebuked for not passing the information directly to London: "Although the information given may not have been of very great value, still it is an advantage that anything which professes to be circumstantial and to have a certain weight behind it should be communicated fully to the Board."[162]

Recognizing the futility of further protest, the department accepted both the Admiralty's implied criticism and the argument "that it is undesirable to change the existing arrangements at St John's during the war, and further proposals will be deferred until after the close of the war. Halifax will, therefore, as proposed by the Admiralty, act as intelligence centre for the Atlantic coast of Canada, and will exchange information with the Naval Intelligence Centre at St John's."[163] Only ten days later, however, Stephens was once again reminding Kingsmill that it was still necessary clearly to delineate a proper line of communication between London and Canada. "Some confusion is evident at the present time in Admiralty communications, especially telegrams. Telegrams are sometimes sent direct to Halifax and Esquimalt and sometimes through Ottawa. The result is that neither place is quite sure whether the other has received the information or not, and much unnecessary telegraphing ensues."[164] The Canadian naval director quickly sought the clarification his chief of staff believed was necessary, proposing to London "that all communications from the Admiralty intended for Canadian establishments or Canadian ships in home waters should pass through the department at Ottawa. Of course I do not mean that while the *Rainbow* or any ship is acting under the direct orders of a senior naval officer it is 'necessary' to inform the department, but the procedure would be to inform the senior officer direct and he would give his orders and, in ordinary courtesy, inform the department."[165] The Admiralty largely assented to the Canadian request, agreeing that

161. Naval Ottawa to Captain in Charge, HMC Dockyard, Halifax, 31 March 1915, 1048–13–6, LAC, RG 24, vol. 3704.

162. Admiralty to Kingsmill, 26 April 1915, ibid.

163. Desbarats to Undersecretary of State for External Affairs, 26 April 1915, 1023–4-3, pt. 1, LAC, RG 24, vol. 3856.

164. Stephens memorandum, 6 May 1915, ibid.

165. Kingsmill to Admiralty, 12 May 1915, ibid.

orders for Canadian shore establishments and depot ships would be sent through NSHQ, while orders for *Niobe* or *Rainbow* "if sent from Admiralty direct should be repeated to Naval Ottawa [NSHQ's telegraph address], if they are in Canadian waters."[166]

Once again, there was at least an agreement, but the procedures it laid down for the distribution of information were far more cumbersome—and segregated—than those set down in August 1914 (and which were working perfectly well on the West Coast, where the function of the Esquimalt intelligence centre was never subject to debate). The reason, it turns out, had everything to do with geography—and nothing to do with efficiency. There was no alternative to Esquimalt because there was no separate British colony on the West Coast. On the East Coast, however, there was Newfoundland, and as the director of the intelligence division at the Admiralty admitted candidly in an internal study produced in October 1917, "the intelligence centre at St John's was originally established there rather than at Halifax in order that Admiralty might retain control over it and avoid friction with Canadian naval authorities, though it has always been recognized that Halifax was the more suitable port for an intelligence centre in this part of the world."[167] And, it should be added, despite the testimony of the RN station commander-in-chief that the Canadian centre had performed well before the change was made.[168] In any event, the source of whatever friction there was in the RCN's relationship with the Royal Navy over the nonsensical supplanting of Halifax by St John's cannot be laid at the feet of Kingsmill and Stephens. And, as the chief of staff's November memorandum had made clear,[169] NSHQ had a very real operational requirement to obtain intelligence relevant to Canadian territorial waters, even if the Admiralty could not be convinced to provide it.

As frustrating and annoying as the British attitude to the Canadian intelligence centre at Halifax may have been to NSHQ, the creation of a Royal Navy centre at St John's to manage the flow of information at an "empire" level had little practical impact on wider Canadian government concerns. Even the sub-text—that Ottawa need not worry about and did not have a role to play in events occurring beyond the country's territorial waters—seems not to have registered with the prime minister or his Cabinet. Perhaps this reflected the Borden government's on-going indifference to matters naval, its understanding of the meaning of "imperial co-operation," or its preoccupation with militia minister Sam Hughes's fight to establish a distinct identity for the Canadian Expeditionary Force (CEF). While Kingsmill had no desire to be a mere cipher for the Admiralty, both he and Stephens understood that to allow British naval officers to assume unfettered control of whatever Canadian naval establishments they coveted would quickly render the very idea of a Royal Canadian Navy meaningless.

Nevertheless, the intelligence centre issue did raise a broader question: when was it right to have supposedly broader imperial interests trump Canadian initiatives? Over the winter

---

166. Graham Greene, Admiralty Secretary to Kingsmill, 7 June 1915, ibid.

167. Director of Intelligence Division memoranda, 2 and 10 October 1917, "Historical Section Summary ... Intelligence Centre in North Atlantic," UKNA, ADM 137/1026.

168. Rear-Admiral Cruiser Force H to Admiralty, 2 October 1914, ibid.

169. R.M. Stephens, "Memo: For the Director of the Naval Service," 10 November 1914, 1023–7-3, pt. 1, LAC, RG 24, vol. 3857.

of 1914–15, one Canadian initiative involved shipbuilding and, more generally, the ultimate role the RCN would play in the conflict. Before the outbreak of war, the British first lord, Winston Churchill, had considered the possibility of building "cruisers or other craft" in Canada as a means of making Borden's proposed financial contribution for Royal Navy battleships more palatable to a majority of the Canadian public. The second sea lord at the time, Vice-Admiral Sir John Jellicoe, had amended the British proposal with the suggestion that Canadian yards could be used to build submarines for the Royal Navy as the Canadian contribution to imperial naval defence.[170] Although the Admiralty's submarine proposal did not lead directly to a reworking of Borden's moribund contribution policy, in August 1914 Vickers in Montreal approached the Canadian naval department with a proposal to build three of the American Holland-type submarines that the Electric Boat Company of New London, Connecticut, was then supplying to the United States Navy. Vickers proposed to build the three boats at a cost of $572,000 each—$3,000 less than Canada paid for *CC 1* and *CC 2*—and have them ready for commissioning by early 1915, provided a contract was let by the end of August. NSHQ urgently sought the Admiralty's advice as to whether London would recommend their procurement, only to be told that the "purchase of three submarines offered [by] Canada Vickers Company are not recommended. Apart from objections and other difficulties, date given for delivery is considered impossible."[171]

Despite having told NSHQ not to order submarines from Vickers, the Admiralty soon changed its mind about the speed with which submarines could be built in North America. While in England seeking contracts from the War Office, Charles Schwabb, the president of the Bethlehem Steel Corporation, an American steel-making conglomerate that included shipbuilding firms in both California and Massachusetts, was put in contact with the first sea lord. Admiral "Jackie" Fisher was impressed by Schwabb's assurance that his company could deliver twenty Holland-type submarines within ten months, half the time it was taking British yards to build similar boats for the Royal Navy. Although the $500,000 price per boat was twice what the Admiralty paid for similar British-built submarines, Fisher quickly struck a contract and the keels were laid for all twenty hulls in American shipyards by mid-November. The United States government was concerned that building submarines for the Royal Navy would violate American neutrality and contested the legality of the contract in the courts. After visiting the Vickers's shipyard in Montreal in early December, Schwabb returned to England to conclude a new contract for ten of the twenty submarines to be built at the Canadian yard, allowing the Bethlehem president to announce publicly that the contract for the submarines to be built in America had been cancelled. In the meantime, the Vickers's yard in Montreal was leased to the Admiralty by her British parent company for the use of the Bethlehem Steel Corporation.[172]

---

170. Nicholas A. Lambert, *Sir John Fisher's Naval Revolution* (Columbia, South Carolina 1999), 302.

171. Naval Ottawa to Admiralty, 26 August 1914, Admiralty to Naval Ottawa, 28 August 1914, 1062–4-2, LAC, RG 24, vol. 4018.

172. Gaddis Smith, *Britain's Clandestine Submarines, 1914–1915* (Hamden, Connecticut 1975), 29–39; and Tucker, *The Naval Service of Canada*, I, 235–36; and Perkins, *Canada's Submariners*, 59–63; and Hadley and Sarty, *Tinpots and Pirate Ships*, 120.

Since neither the Admiralty nor Bethlehem Steel were anxious to have their circumvention of US neutrality publicized, the British government unwisely decided not to inform Ottawa of the decision to build the submarines at Vickers. Coming only four months after forcefully telling NSHQ that submarines should not be built at Montreal for the RCN, Whitehall's failure to take the Canadian government into its confidence provoked understandable resentment in Ottawa. When Ottawa had approached the Admiralty in early October for advice regarding possible Canadian naval co-operation in the war, London had replied that they did not "think anything effectual can now be done as ships take too long to build and advise Canadian assistance be concentrated on Army."[173] Compounding apparent British deceit, Prime Minister Borden had approached London in late November with yet another suggestion that Vickers's Montreal facilities should be used by the Canadian government to order either destroyers or submarines for the defence of Halifax, stating that the company believed it would be able to complete construction of a warship contract "in about eighteen months."[174] Although the Admiralty and Bethlehem were already investigating the use of the Canadian Vickers's shipyard, the first lord gave no intimation of that fact to Borden in replying that there was "no immediate need for submarines at Halifax" and "no reason for your undertaking any special new construction at present for purpose mentioned and says you should reassure your people on subject."[175]

The British government's blatant disregard of Canadian politicians and officials could not be concealed, however, once construction of the ten submarines, employing more than 2,000 shipyard workers in Montreal, was begun in January. The first official word came in mid-month when the British colonial secretary, Lewis Harcourt, informed the governor general that the Admiralty had found it "necessary to undertake construction of submarines for his majesty's government in Vickers Canadian Company's yard at Montreal. The contract is with Bethlehem Steel Corporation of New York, who originally contemplated construction at port on east coast of United States." The colonial secretary also warned Ottawa that the matter "should be kept absolutely secret"[176] although the secrecy was meant to keep Washington in the dark rather than Berlin. For its part the Canadian government assured London "that they will gladly co-operate" with British shipbuilding contracts, with the proviso that in future they would "be grateful if a somewhat earlier intimation could be given to them."[177] The sense of outrage Canadian officials felt at the manner in which the Admiralty had ignored Ottawa is evident in the memorandum the normally staid Desbarats addressed to the naval minister in mid-February:

---

173. Acting High Commissioner to Prime Minister, 10 October 1914, *DCER*, I, 52; and Smith, *Britain's Clandestine Submarines*, 74.

174. Borden to Acting High Commissioner in United Kingdom, 25 November 1914, *DCER*, I, 59.

175. Acting High Commissioner to Prime Minister, 4 December 1914, ibid, 61.

176. Colonial Secretary to Governor General, 16 January 1915, ibid, 63–64.

177. Governor General to Colonial Secretary, 21 January 1915, ibid, 64.

In August 1914 a proposal was submitted to the department by Canadian Vickers Limited to build submarines at their yard in Montreal for the Canadian Government. This proposal was submitted to the Admiralty, who recommended that it be refused. The reasons for refusal were chiefly general—objections were made to the design submitted and to the time of delivery, which was considered too short to be possible.

In the first days of January verbal inquiries were made at the department as to the truth of rumours which were being circulated to the effect that submarines were being built at the shipyard of Canadian Vickers at Montreal, but, as no information had been received by the Canadian government on this subject, and bearing in mind the fact that the Admiralty had advised against the construction of submarines in this yard, denials were given to these rumours. The rumours grew, and became so insistent, that unofficial inquiries were made, and it was ascertained that vessels of this description were being constructed at Montreal.

It was not, however, until January 13th that the department received indirect information in the shape of a despatch from the British ambassador at Washington, which stated that fifteen submarines would be completed at Montreal from imported materials. The date of this despatch was January 6th but it only reached the department on January 13th.

On January 16th Sir George Perley cabled to the prime minister, stating that ten or more submarines would be built at Montreal, and that the Colonial Office was advising the dominion government of this fact. (Such telegram was sent by the Colonial Office on that same date but only reached the department on February 8th).

Official information as to the construction of these submarines was, therefore, given to the department one month after it was known around the streets in Montreal, at which time it was known in various circles that a contract for submarines was being executed in the yards of Canadian Vickers.[178]

As objectionable as London's duplicity had been, Kingsmill realized that there was still an opportunity to increase Canada's East Coast defences. By the time the first three submarine hulls were launched in April, four RN submarine crews had arrived in Montreal in anticipation of their completion. Aware of a shortage of British submarine crews in the rapidly expanding Royal Navy, the Canadian naval director suggested at the end of April that the RCN could use the crews from *CC 1* and *CC 2* in Esquimalt to "give the Admiralty effective assistance in navigating the boats to England."[179] The RCN had six officers and forty-two trained submarine ratings available at Esquimalt, the vast majority of whom had transferred to the Canadian navy from the British submarine service. Aside from the fact that "it would be a gracious act to offer these men before an official request comes" from

178. Desbarats, "Memorandum to the Minister," 17 February 1915, 1062–6-1, pt. 1, LAC, RG 24, vol. 4019.

179. Kingsmill to The Military Secretary to the Governor General, 30 April 1915, 1062–6-5, ibid.

the Admiralty, Kingsmill also believed that "it would be of benefit to our service to send as many men as possible to gain experience and to relieve them of the monotony of serving in submarines on the Pacific coast, where there are no enemy ships."[180]

By demonstrating the RCN's ability to assist the Royal Navy in getting the H-boats to Britain, the Canadian admiral was hoping to persuade the Admiralty to divert two of them to Halifax. Although the RCN had the small patrol boats *Tuna* and *Albacore* at the Nova Scotia port and had "fitted them with improvised torpedo armament," Kingsmill explained to the governor general's military secretary that "they cannot be considered an adequate defence."

> The attention of the Naval Department has again been drawn to this matter owing to the frequent rumours of an attempt on the part of the German fleet to escape from the North Sea and scatter over the trade routes. That sooner or later something of this sort will be done is the opinion of most naval officers. You will not have forgotten that the information forwarded by Sir Thomas Shaughnessy a short time ago, definitely stated that included in such scheme would be raids on Canadian coasts.
>
> The most effective method of keeping the enemies' [*sic*] cruisers a respectable distance from the Canadian coast is the menace of attack by torpedo craft, and especially by submarines. The foregoing considerations seem to me sufficiently strong to make it desirable to enquire of the Admiralty if they would be willing for two of the submarines now building at Montreal to be stationed at Halifax for the defence of that port. I should not put forward this proposal did I not understand that the Admiralty now have a very large number of submarines available for service.[181]

Prime Minister Borden had difficulty comprehending Kingsmill's scheme and was not in the mood to offer the Admiralty assistance in any event. After asking the Admiralty in early April why they had originally placed the contract for submarines in the United States rather than Montreal, the prime minister had tersely informed London that the "explanation of Admiralty officials is very unsatisfactory and unconvincing as they made no effort whatever to obtain information as to what could be accomplished in Canada." Faced with Kingsmill's proposal to assist those same Admiralty officials, Borden said Canada was in no position to have submarine crews sail the H-boats to Britain, while having "to provide crews for Esquimalt and Halifax." Beyond that, he added the curt request "that the British government should hand over two of the [Montreal-built] submarines to the Canadian Navy."[182] Kingsmill now had to intervene, and in the process

---

180. Kingsmill, "Memorandum for the Information of the Minister," 6 May 1915, ibid.

181. Kingsmill to The Military Secretary to the Governor General, 30 April 1915, 1017–11–2, pt. 1, LAC, RG 24, vol. 3846.

182. Lt. Col. Stanton, Military Secretary to Governor General to Kingsmill, 3 May 1915, 1062–6–5, LAC, RG 24, vol. 4019.

proved that his reaction to the intelligence centre issue had more to do with the operational requirements of NSHQ than with dogmatic nationalism. Borden's approach, he told the military secretary to the governor general, indicated that "the prime minister does not understand the matter at all. We do not propose at the same time to provide crews for Esquimalt and Halifax and send men to England. At Esquimalt, we have the crews, without officers, for three submarines, and what I propose is that we should lend two of these crews to the Admiralty to take the submarines building in Montreal, to England, the crews returning to Canada. If the Admiralty do not agree to leave at Halifax one or two submarines, these crews would go back to their duties at Esquimalt. The situation as I should like to arrange it, would then be that we should have two submarines at Esquimalt and one crew, and two submarines at Halifax and two crews."[183]

When Kingsmill's offer was finally presented to the British government, however, they responded "that Canadian ratings for navigating submarines will not be required by Admiralty unless their services can be spared for duration of war."[184] Although the naval director believed that Canada should lend the submariners to Britain for the duration—not least because they had been trained in the Royal Navy, had volunteered for overseas service, and the Admiralty had a prior right to them—a piqued Borden and Hazen decided otherwise. Ignoring Kingsmill's advice to the contrary, the politicians tersely (and dishonestly) informed London that they had "decided that owing to the exigencies of the service, it will not be possible to spare the crews of the Canadian submarines for the duration of the war."[185] The first four Montreal-built submarines, H1 to H4, departed for Quebec before 29 May to complete their trials with all-British crews before proceeding on to St John's, Newfoundland, on 7 June with HMCS *Canada* as escort. After a stormy transit of the Gulf of St Lawrence, the four boats left the Newfoundland capital on 20 June bound for Gibraltar and service in the Mediterranean. Two of the Esquimalt submariners did manage to make it overseas with the H-boats. Lieutenant B.L. Johnson had been a pilot in the British Columbia pilotage service for many years before joining the RNCVR in 1914 and being assigned as first lieutenant of *CC 2*. His extensive sea experience and service in the Esquimalt submarines led to his appointment as commanding officer of *H8*. The other Canadian officer assigned to the H-boats was Midshipman W.M. Maitland-Dougall, a young RCN officer who had graduated second in the first class of the Royal Naval College of Canada. After serving in the Canadian submarines at Esquimalt and then NSHQ, Kingsmill recommended Maitland-Dougall as a young officer capable of serving as navigator in *H10*. The two Canadian officers sailed with the last six H-boats when they departed Canadian waters for England on 22 July.[186]

At the same time that the Canadian government was turning down Kingsmill's proposal to lend entire RCN submarine crews to the RN for the duration, Ottawa continued to press

---

183. Kingsmill to Stanton, 5 May 1915, ibid.

184. Colonial Office to Governor General, 25 May 1915, ibid.

185. Desbarats to Undersecretary of State for External Affairs, 2 June 1915, Stephens, "Memorandum: For Deputy Minister," 26 May 1915, Stephens to Commander A.H. Quicke, 2 June 1915, ibid.

186. Perkins, *Canada's Submariners*, 42–43, 71–86.

the Admiralty to assign two of the H-boats for the defence of Halifax. In mid-May London had informed the governor general that improving the naval defence of Halifax was "not in the opinion of Admiralty urgent," and that they could not spare any of the ten submarines building at Montreal for Canada's East Coast but did suggest that the Canadian government could order two additional H-boats from Canadian Vickers for themselves.[187] The Duke of Connaught nevertheless wired Winston Churchill once again on 21 May "to impress on you the importance of some submarines being kept at Halifax as I hardly think the danger to which this and other eastern Canadian ports are exposed from raiding cruisers is realized by the Admiralty."[188] Borden also pressed the case for submarines a few days later, pointedly reminding London that it was at the British government's request that Canada had concentrated on raising an expeditionary force rather than devoting its resources to naval defence: "Early in war Admiralty informed us that Canada's energies should be devoted to military forces for purposes of this war. Therefore we have done nothing for naval purposes except purchase of two submarines.... Assume Admiralty still hold view that our resources should be devoted to raising and equipping military forces.'[189] The prime minister evidently believed that Canada's recent sacrifices on the Western Front during the Second Battle of Ypres in April placed a greater obligation on the Royal Navy to provide for Canada's maritime defence.

By the end of May 1915 NSHQ began to explore the Admiralty's suggestion that Canada should build its own submarines at Montreal and asked London for "their opinion as to the best general type of boat" for the RCN.[190] In pursuing a possible contract with Canadian Vickers, the naval department was quoted a price of $650,000 per submarine, a sum in line with the amount paid by the Admiralty for the first eight H-boats and only $75,000 more than Ottawa had paid for the much inferior *CC 1* and *CC 2*. As much as Borden may have felt that Britain should provide two of the Vickers's submarines for the defence of Halifax, he was not prepared to meet the Canadian firm's price. Informing the department that Vicker's asking price was "high," the prime minister rejected the possibility of building submarines for the Canadian navy at Montreal.[191] Surprisingly, Borden's decision did not entirely disappoint naval headquarters. Stephens, for one, was willing to see a silver lining in the prime minister's attitude and believed that it might be premature to commit the department to a particular type of warship, while the RCN's role in the war had yet to be determined:

> As has been stated on previous occasions the defence of Halifax must be considered incomplete whilst there is little or no form of torpedo defence. The Colonial Defence Committee have recommended both destroyers and submarines as necessary.

187. Harcourt to Governor General, 14 May 1915, 1017–11–2, pt. 1, LAC, RG 24, vol. 3846.

188. Governor General to Colonial Secretary, 21 May 1915, *DCER*, I, 73.

189. Prime Minister to Acting High Commissioner in United Kingdom, 26 May 1915, ibid, 73.

190. Naval Ottawa to Admiralty, 29 May 1915, 1017–11–2, pt. 1, LAC, RG 24, vol. 3846.

191. Desbarats to Borden, 14 June 1915, Borden to Desbarats, 15 June 1915, LAC, MG 26 H, vol. 54, 26470–74.

Before, however, adopting any particular type of submarine, it seems highly desirable that the strategical policy of the department should be fixed beforehand, in order that the Department may not incur censure later on or cause disappointment through inability to perform expected feats. If the department intends these submarines to be exclusively used for coast defence purposes, a certain (comparatively inferior) type will possibly meet requirements. If, however, the department desires that these submarines should take an active part in offensive operations against an enemy's coast, then the very latest and most superior type would probably be required.... Whilst considering the type of submarine best suited to conform to Canadian policy, it would also appear wise to review the immediate general policy to be adopted in naval defence.

Naval affairs are in such a state of flux at the present time, that the policy of yesterday is by no means necessarily suitable for today. A few months ago it was at least considered improbable that German submarines would appear off Nova Scotia; today it is freely anticipated. An important point for decision then is whether recent changes in naval affairs should modify former decisions as to immediate Canadian naval policy.[192]

Stephens's calm acceptance of Borden's decision was not entirely shared by the naval director, however, who acidly commented that there was no point in discussing warship types unless the prime minister showed "any serious indication of formulating a naval policy."[193] As the officer who had been brought back to Canada to take command of the proposed Canadian navy, Kingsmill was understandably frustrated by the government's continuing reluctance to build any sort of naval force with which Canada could defend its own maritime interests. Having been elected on a naval platform that opposed the creation of a functioning Canadian navy, the prime minister seemed determined to trust in the British government's implied promise of naval protection contained in Churchill's recommendation—as Borden had recently reminded London—"that Canada's energies should be devoted to military forces for purposes of this war."[194] It must have seemed remarkable to Kingsmill that the outbreak of war had done nothing to change the Canadian government's attitude to naval defence and, just as he had bemoaned in peacetime the previous April, Borden was still unwilling to "inaugurate a Naval Service which would be able to carry out its responsibilities."[195] Although the prime minister had clearly been annoyed by the British approach on the submarine question, that annoyance had not resulted in any practical benefit to the navy.

---

192. Stephens, "Memorandum: For Director of Naval Service," 17 June 1915, 1017–11–2, pt. 1, LAC, RG 24, vol. 3846.

193. Kingsmill to Stephens, 3 July 1915, ibid.

194. Prime Minister to Acting High Commissioner in United Kingdom, 26 May 1915, *DCER*, I, 73.

195. Kingsmill to Desbarats, 1 April 1914, 1019–2–2, pt. 1, LAC, RG 24, vol. 3855.

Meanwhile, one of the two ocean-going holdovers from the Laurier naval policy, HMCS *Niobe*, had continued to operate throughout the spring and early summer as part of Admiral Hornby's cruiser squadron on patrol off New York. By July, however, the old cruiser was rapidly wearing out. Like her three sister ships operating with the Ninth Cruiser Squadron in the Bay of Biscay, her days of commissioned service were at an end. *Niobe* left Halifax for a final patrol off New York on 4 July 1915, where "more ships were stopped, signalled, sometimes chased. She continued to make her 250 miles odd per day and sometimes exceeded 300." After returning to port on 17 July, it was found that her funnels were "rapidly deteriorating and collapsing," her boilers were worn out and her bulkheads were in equally bad shape. The Canadian government discussed the possibility of exchanging *Niobe* for a British cruiser, but the warship proposed by the Admiralty, HMS *Sutlej*, was in such poor condition herself that it was possible that neither vessel would be capable of an ocean crossing. At the time of her last patrol, *Niobe*'s lower deck consisted of 192 RN ratings, 106 Newfoundland RNR ratings, and 333 Canadian ratings and it was suggested that they could be more "usefully employed" manning local patrol vessels. As well, the Canadian cruiser was still valuable as a depot ship, helping overcome the shortage of naval accommodation in Halifax, a task for which she was "considered suitable as discomforts and conditions in existing barracks last winter undesirable to repeat."[196]

The decision was made, and from 6 September *Niobe* ceased to be at the disposal of the Admiralty for operations and was recommissioned as a depot ship for the ratings previously in barracks ashore, as well as for drafts of sailors passing through Halifax. She would also serve as a parent ship for vessels employed on patrol work and provide office space for the various naval staff officers employed in the Halifax area.[197] With the threat of German surface raiders breaking out from American ports on the Eastern seaboard adequately contained by Hornby's existing cruiser force, *Niobe*'s new employment reflected the changing nature of the RCN's duties off the East Coast. For the future, the navy's main operational concern would centre on the possibility of enemy submarines entering Canadian waters and operating from supply bases established in remote coves or bays along the coast.

---

196. *Niobe* to Kingsmill, 18 July 1915, 047–19–2, LAC, RG 24, vol. 3969; and "Brief History of HMCS *Niobe*," 26 October 1961, 58–59, DHH 81/520/8000, "HMCS *Niobe*," vol. 1.

197. "Brief History of HMCS *Niobe*," 26 October 1961, 60, DHH 81/520/8000, "HMCS *Niobe*," vol. 1.

Three of the H-class submarines built at Canadian Vickers alongside HMCS *Diana*, formerly *Arthur W*, at No. 4 Jetty in Halifax prior to departing for Devonport, England on 22 July 1915. (CWM 19830056-019)

CHAPTER 5

Watching for U-Boats
Off Canada's East Coast, 1915–1916

With the rusting-out cruiser Niobe serving as a floating barracks and naval office in the Halifax dockyard, the East Coast strength of the Royal Canadian Navy was reduced to the few ex-government vessels, converted civilian yachts, and hired trawlers that had been brought together in the opening months of the war. Six small vessels, *Baleine*, *Deliverance*, *Gopher*, *Musquash*, *Sable*, and *Premier*, had been fitted out for duty as minesweepers, four of which were employed each morning or during foggy days to sweep the channel that had been marked with buoys from the entrance to Halifax Harbour to several miles out to sea. The remaining two minesweepers would be available to act as patrol vessels joining HMC Ships *Tuna*, *Canada*, and *Margaret* (the latter an ex-Customs ship) in watching the Halifax approaches. The two vessels that had patrolled the Bay of Fundy throughout the winter of 1914–15, the government ships *Sable* and *Acadia*, were also available "to watch for suspicious vessels ... which might be engaged in minelaying, for enemy submarines and floating bases for the latter, and also to investigate rumours concerning them." While the RCN also maintained its examination services at Halifax and Quebec, the Canadian service lacked the means, and had taken no steps to institute, a naval force to protect transports leaving Canadian waters. The only notable addition that had been made to Halifax's naval defences was the placing of anti-submarine nets across the entrance to the harbour in June 1915.[1]

Laying-up the worn-out *Niobe* was also an indication that the nature of Germany's *guerre de course* against merchant shipping was changing. From their early forays with naval surface forces and auxiliary raiders against more distant sea lanes, the Germans shifted the emphasis of their naval campaign to better use the stealth of their U-boat fleet. At the outbreak of war, the *Reichsmarine* had viewed submarines primarily as units of the main battle fleet, to be employed in advanced patrol lines to attack enemy dreadnoughts as they manoeuvred to engage the German fleet or as they emerged from the sanctuary of their harbours. That role seemed to be confirmed in early September 1914 when *U 21* sank the British flotilla leader *Pathfinder* with a torpedo fired from a distance of one mile. On 22 September, the Royal Navy witnessed a more graphic demonstration of the striking power of the submarine when the three 10,000 ton cruisers *Aboukir*, *Hogue*, and *Cressy* were

---

1. Kingsmill, "Memo for Information of Minister," 11 August 1915, 1062–13–4, Library and Archives Canada (hereafter LAC), Record Group (hereafter RG) 24, vol. 4022.

torpedoed and sunk in less than one hour by a single German U-boat off the Belgian coast with the loss of 1,400 sailors. For much of the remainder of the war, fear of attack by submerged submarines—"periscopitis"—would afflict Britain's Grand Fleet whenever it sortied into the North Sea.[2]

Less noticed, but equally important, was an attack made by *U 17* the following month off the coast of Norway. On 22 October the German submarine stopped the British steamer *Glitra* fourteen miles off shore. After allowing the crew time to abandon ship, the submariners opened the 866-ton vessel's sea cocks and sent her to the bottom. The entire operation was carried out according to the accepted international rules for commerce warfare as the *Glitra* became the first merchant ship ever sunk by submarine action.[3] The attack was not, however, part of an organized German campaign against Allied shipping; although a French liner was damaged—and some thirty civilians killed—in the English Channel four days later by a torpedo fired by *U 24*, the submariners believed that the vessel was a troopship carrying combatants to France. It was not until 23 November that another U-boat, *U 21*, actually sank two merchant ships off the coast of Normandy, the submarine's captain appearing "almost apologetic in his new role of commerce destroyer, explaining he could not accommodate the crews in the submarine, but that war was war."[4]

Although the *Führer der Unterseeboote*, or *FdU*, *Korvettenkapitän* Hermann Bauer, had recommended to the commander of the German High Seas Fleet that Germany should begin commerce raiding with submarines off the British coast, the suggestion was turned down by the chief of *Admiralstab*, Admiral Hugo von Pohl, on the grounds that British naval actions did not yet justify the severe violations of international law necessary to conduct a successful submarine offensive against merchant shipping. The annihilation of von Spee's Pacific squadron at the Falkland Islands and the general ineffectiveness of other surface raiders in disrupting Allied trade during the war's opening months increased the desire within German official circles to launch an unrestricted submarine campaign. Bauer submitted a second memorandum at the end of December 1914 suggesting that the relatively small number of U-boats available were nonetheless sufficient to justify the commencement of a submarine offensive off the British coast at the end of January 1915. With the endorsement of the senior officers of the High Seas Fleet, the proposal to launch unrestricted submarine warfare against British merchant shipping was approved by the *Admiralstab* on 1 February and proclaimed three days later.[5]

The 4 February proclamation of an unrestricted war zone in which every merchant ship was liable to be targeted made it a virtual certainty that neutral ships plying British waters would eventually be attacked. U-boat commanders were instructed not to risk their submarines by surfacing to examine and identify vessels but to attack any ship within the declared zone surrounding Britain, Ireland, and the entire length of the English Channel.

---

2. Richard Hough, *The Great War at Sea, 1914–1918* (Oxford 1983), 62, 171–72.

3. Hough, *The Great War at Sea,* 169; and Paul G. Halpern, *A Naval History of World War I* (Annapolis 1994), 292.

4. Halpern, *A Naval History,* 292.

5. Ibid, 293.

The British misuse of neutral flags on some of its merchant ships also meant that any vessel was liable to attack without notice whether it was from a neutral nation or not. Even so, a strong protest from the United States government prompted Berlin to modify its instructions to U-boat commanders to preclude attacks on neutral shipping. With only a few operational boats available to prosecute the campaign, Germany's naval leaders realized that such a restriction would render the submarine blockade impotent if neutral vessels—responsible for carrying one quarter of all British trade—were allowed free passage. The *Admiralstab*'s threat to discontinue the offensive before it had even begun prompted a compromise with the German foreign office that exempted neutral ships but allowed U-boat commanders to prosecute the submarine campaign with the utmost vigour and assured them "they would not be held responsible if, despite the exercise of great care, mistakes were made."[6]

Despite the small number of U-boats actually operating in British waters at any one time—an average of four in early 1915, only two of which were likely to be on station to the west of the British Isles—the results achieved by the German submariners more than made up for their small numbers. During the first three months of the campaign, U-boats sank 115 ships totalling 255,000 tons, while losing five submarines, an exchange ratio of more than twenty steamers sunk for each U-boat lost. The number of sinkings inflicted by a relatively small force was a clear indication of the inadequacy of the Royal Navy's initial anti-submarine measures. During March 1915, for instance, the RN's most successful countermeasure proved to be ramming. *U 12* was sunk in that fashion by a British destroyer in the approaches to the Firth of Forth on 10 March, while the battleship HMS *Dreadnought* ran down *U 29* as she manoeuvred to attack HMS *Neptune* on the 18th. The commander of *U 29*, *Korvettenkapitän* Weddigen, had been responsible for the sinkings of the *Aboukir*, *Hogue*, and *Cressy* earlier in the war. The British also established mine barriers in the Dover Strait and the North Channel to the Irish Sea but the barriers were relatively ineffective in sinking submarines and usually provided only a hindrance to their passage. Nonetheless, in mid-April the *FdU* ordered submarines to proceed to their West Coast operational areas by the northern route around the British Isles after several incidents in the Dover nets, including the sinking of *U 8*, even though the change added 2,240 kilometres to the voyage and reduced the amount of time each U-boat could remain on patrol. The Royal Navy's other experiments—lines of drifters towing either indicator nets with flares that were supposed to be triggered if fouled or "explosive sweeps" (wires fitted with explosives)—proved ineffective.[7]

Rather than any countermeasures by the British navy, the greatest threat to the German submarine campaign came from the diplomatic front in response to attacks made on neutral ships, several of which were torpedoed and sunk without warning even though they were trading between neutral ports. While the Germans agreed to pay compensation to neutral nations for their shipping losses—the Dutch being particularly irate that steamers trading between Amsterdam and neutral ports were being torpedoed without warning—the most serious incident was *U 20*'s sinking of the large British passenger liner *Lusitania* on 7 May. Although the Cunard liner was hit by only one torpedo, it happened

---

6. Ibid, 295.

7. Ibid, 296–98.

to strike a hold carrying illicit ammunition and explosives that had been loaded in New York. The force of the secondary explosion quickly sent the ship to the bottom with the loss of 1,201 lives. With 128 Americans among the dead, the government of the United States was indignant and strongly protested the attack's brutality to Berlin. In reaction, the German chancellor, Theobald von Bethmann-Hollweg, convinced the Kaiser to order a suspension of attacks on passenger liners over the strong objections of the *Admiralstab*. Despite the new restrictions, which American President Woodrow Wilson seemed willing to accept, a greater number of operational U-boats allowed the Germans to increase their sinkings over the summer of 1915 as compared to the March-May period. From June to September 1915, German submarines accounted for 355 ships totalling 532,116 tons.[8]

It was against this background of sinkings by German submarines in British waters, the gravity of the threat being emphasized by the heavy loss of life when the *Lusitania* went down, that Naval Service Headquarters received intelligence from the British consul-general in New York—as British naval intelligence arrangements in the North Atlantic now dictated, the warning came by way of the Colonial Office—of possible enemy naval operations being mounted against Canadian shipping from south of the border. London warned the Canadian naval authorities to take seriously any rumours emanating from the United States that German agents might attempt to establish supply bases for submarines along remote stretches of Newfoundland, Labrador or St Pierre.[9] Similar fears had prompted the RCN to undertake a limited number of coastal patrols off Nova Scotia and the Bay of Fundy in the autumn of 1914. Over the course of the winter, the "many rumours of ships leaving the United States with mines to be dropped in the St Lawrence" prompted the department to consider the question of establishing a patrol in the Gulf of St Lawrence on the opening of navigation. Once the ice had cleared in the spring of 1915, Vice-Admiral Kingsmill despatched the unarmed charter steamer *Sable I* as the first vessel intended for a patrol force in the Gulf. He also suggested to the deputy minister, G.J. Desbarats, that a letter should be written to the Newfoundland government "informing them of our intention and requesting the use of their harbours and that they give instructions to the harbour authorities to render all assistance."[10] As it would be throughout the war—resources permitting—St John's was most co-operative and immediately issued instructions "to the harbour authorities to render all possible assistance to the ships engaged in the patrol work."[11]

NSHQ's efforts to establish a patrol force in the Gulf were given added impetus in early June when the secretary of state for the colonies, Bonar Law[12] informed Ottawa that the

---

8. Ibid, 298–99.

9. Michael Hadley and Roger Sarty, *Tin-pots and Pirate Ships: Canadian Naval Forces and German Sea Raiders, 1880– 1918* (Montreal 1991), 113.

10. Kingsmill to deputy minister, 10 March 1915, 1062–13–4, LAC, RG 24, vol. 4022; and Brian Tennyson and Roger Sarty, *Guardian of the Gulf: Sydney, Cape Breton, and the Atlantic Wars* (Toronto 2000), 131.

11. Governor of Nfld. to Governor General of Canada, 7 April 1915, 1062–13–4, LAC, RG 24, vol. 4022.

12. The New Brunswick-born Law, as Conservative Party leader, had pressured Liberal Prime Minister Herbert Asquith to form a coalition government which Law, closely advised by fellow New Brunswicker Max Aitken, joined as its colonial secretary in May 1915.

British consul-general in New York had received information "that Germany intends to send to the Atlantic coast one or two submarines. Admiralty states latest type of submarine has radius of 3,000 miles and it is to be expected that full advantage of their possibilities will be taken by the enemy." London also recommended the steps Canadian authorities should take to prevent U-boats from operating from isolated locales:

> Difficulties of supply and communication in neutral countries and on uninhabited coasts probably not insuperable. Activities of these submarine boats will be hampered by early notification to proper naval authorities of their presence and by carefully watching and reporting where necessary of sale of fuel. It is suggested by Admiralty that your government should exercise vigilance over all embarkations of lubricating and fuel oils suitable for submarine boats, for example any oil with flash point over 100 degrees Fahrenheit ... and not too viscous. Admiralty also suggests system of obtaining information should be extended to any outlying ports in which submarine boats may meet supply ships and information so obtained together with information respecting suspicious shipments of oil should be forwarded to Naval Intelligence centres through reporting officers. Government of Newfoundland has been sent similar telegram.[13]

The Admiralty's warning accorded with NSHQ's own view regarding the necessity of establishing a naval patrol in the Gulf of St Lawrence to guard against incursions by enemy submarines. Canadian planning received further motivation when Vice-Admiral Sir George Patey, who had recently replaced Phipps-Hornby as the commander-in-chief, North America and West Indies Station, wrote the governor general on the subject the following week. The Duke of Connaught, who took his position as the nominal commander-in-chief of Canadian forces seriously, had visited Patey aboard his flagship HMS *Leviathan* in Halifax, prompting the British admiral to submit a general outline of the precautions he considered necessary against possible attacks by German submarines operating in Canadian or Newfoundland waters: "(a) An organized system of coast watching from the shore and arranging for the reports in connection therewith. (b) The patrol of Belle Isle and Cabot Straits and the Gulf of St Lawrence by suitable vessels of good speed, armed with guns sufficient to destroy a submarine. (c) Arrangements for patrol vessels to visit periodically the uninhabited portions of the coast, especially Labrador, where it is possible that Germans might establish a submarine supply base in one of the numerous inlets (the inhabited portions would come under (a) above). (d) Supervision of the banking fleet of fishing vessels."[14]

London gave further encouragement to the creation of a Canadian naval patrol on 25 June, though it suggested using smaller, more lightly armed vessels than the commander-in-chief had proposed. In the Admiralty's opinion, the "possibility of German submarines operating in Canadian waters" made it "desirable that steps should be taken to patrol coast

---

13. Law to Governor-General of Canada, 9 June 1915, 1062–13–4, LAC, RG 24, vol. 4022.

14. Patey to Governor-General, 16 June 1915, ibid.

HMCS *Canada* in her wartime configuration with 12-pounders fore and aft. (DND CN 3793)

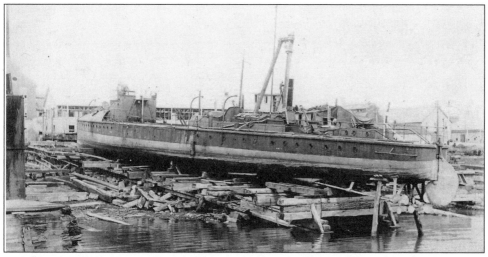

The torpedo boat HMCS *Tuna* undergoing a general overhaul at the Sorel, Quebec, shipyard in July 1916. J.K.L. Ross purchased the turbine-powered yacht, then called *Tarantula*, from American railway magnate W.K. Vanderbilt and brought her to Halifax in September 1914, selling her to the Canadian navy for a dollar. (DND CN 215)

HMCS *Margaret* was built by Thorneycrofts in England for the customs service but was immediately assigned to naval duties upon arrival in Canada in August 1914. *Margaret* had a handy top speed of fifteen knots but was only armed with two 6-pounders forward, both guns being of unique design with a limited ammunition supply. (DND CN 3226)

by small craft obtained locally to prevent unfrequented harbours being used as a base of operation, also that arrangements should be made for rapidly increasing this patrol service so as to deal with any submarines which may reach Canadian waters."[15] Having already anticipated such a step, Kingsmill was able to provide his government with a response within twenty-four hours. The director's reliable chief of staff, Commander R.M. Stephens, had already put together a scheme for ten patrol vessels to keep a watch on the waters of the Gulf and the coast of Nova Scotia between Halifax, Cape Race, and the Strait of Belle Isle. Five already being available—HMC Ships *Canada*, *Margaret*, *Sable I*, *Premier*, and *Tuna*— there was a requirement for five more.[16] The naval director pointed to London's concerns in recommending to the deputy minister that the RCN organize a coast watch reserve of hired fishing boats.

> The Admiralty points to the fact that the possibility of a German raid by sub-marines is not considered unworthy of attention by them. There is only one thing that would prevent one or several of the latest German under sea craft from operating in the Gulf of St Lawrence, that is the uncertainty of obtaining supplies on this side of the Atlantic.
>
> There are several ways of overcoming this and which a determined enemy might try, namely:
>
> To be accompanied by a supply vessel, which would be left somewhere out of the ordinary trade route. The patrolling in this case devolves upon the Admiralty.
>
> The sending of supplies by neutral vessel to a rendezvous, as for instance, the fishing banks where it would not be difficult to remain unobserved and apparently fishing. There are several methods to combat this: (a) to see our own bankers' captains and promise them a substantial reward for giving information that would lead to capture of any neutral fishing vessel having supplies other than for purpose of fishing. (b) By patrol. This would, if undertaken by Canada, need at least two armed vessels of good seakeeping qualities.
>
> By sending supplies to and sinking same in one of the unfrequented harbours of Newfoundland and Canada, Atlantic coast. The only method of combating this would be by an organized system of coast watching in connection with a coast patrol by small but numerous vessels.
>
> The Admiralty also consider it necessary to advise us to arrange so that patrol can be strengthened at any time. This would necessitate our taking over extra vessels and preparing them so that we could immediately make use of them. Although it will not be necessary to arm all patrols with more than rifles, we should have as many armed vessels as possible.
>
> It will be necessary for military reasons to place the officers and men under the Discipline Act, so it is proposed to enroll them temporarily in the

---

15. Admiralty to NSHQ, telegram no. 326, 25 June 1915, ibid.

16. [Stephens], "Memorandum," nd, ibid.

RNCVR. This will not involve a great increase in expenditure, pay of RNCVR being somewhat similar to Fisheries Protection Service and coast wages. This must be taken into consideration when chartering vessels.

The empire being at war the power of the government to commandeer the necessary number of vessels should be considered in dealing with the owners of those offered for charter. I would respectfully submit to the minister that we shall be failing in our share if we do not now put our best efforts forward. From the attached it will be seen the numbers of vessels required and the scheme for enrolling the RNCVR (Motor Craft Reserve).[17]

Stephens's attached memoranda outlined the terms for organizing a motor craft reserve to "provide a trained force to patrol the coasts, quickly capable of a large increase if enemy's vessels are known to be on the coast." Under the scheme, the naval service would "enrol a large number of motor fishing vessels, say 250 to start with, whose owners volunteer their services when called upon. The crew to join the Royal Navy [sic] Canadian Volunteer (Motor Craft Reserve), which would have slightly different regulations to the Royal Navy [sic] Canadian Volunteer Reserve." The department would compensate the owner of each motor boat an agreed sum to cover maintenance and crew pay, while offering individual crewmen a victualling allowance and limited form of naval uniform. Once called out, the motor boat crews—who would be armed only with rifles—would "be under naval discipline and fly the White Ensign.... The boats to be grouped in sections, each section under a naval officer. When called out in war, this officer to be on board an armed patrol vessel stationed in that section.... Under existing conditions, a few boats would be required in each section for patrol work; these could be, if considered desirable, changed every month. In the event of enemy vessels appearing off the coast, all would be called out."[18]

A more dire Admiralty warning two days later, although not specifically stating that German submarines were actually on their way, was sufficiently ominous to prompt a concerned NSHQ to take immediate action to protect Canada's undefended East Coast. "It is not considered necessary to close Belle Isle Strait at present," Whitehall warned on 28 June, "but it is desirable that fishing vessels should be warned to keep a good look out for any strange vessels using unfrequented creeks or harbours and report their presence or movements as such vessels might be supply ships for submarines. Local authorities should be also warned to have any Germans or foreigners coming to the coast settlements kept under observation."[19] Kingsmill assured the British authorities that the "danger of submarines is fully recognised," while emphasizing that it was "impossible" for the RCN "to provide efficient protection for transports on this side. Am endeavouring to establish armed patrol in Gulf of St Lawrence. Eastern limits being line from Scatari Island, C[ape] B[reton Island] to St Pierre and Belle Isle, but much difficulty in providing suitable craft."[20]

---

17. Kingsmill to Desbarats, 26 June 1915, ibid.

18. Stephens, "Royal Navy Canadian Volunteer (Motor Craft Reserve)," 26 June 1915, ibid.

19. Admiralty to Naval Ottawa, 28 June 1915, ibid.

20. Kingsmill to Admiralty, 7 July 1915, ibid.

Naval Service Headquarters responded with a more detailed plan for establishing a naval patrol in short order. The ten armed vessels previously recommended by Stephens would, the chief of staff explained at the end of June, "patrol and watch the coast for small craft acting as bases for enemy submarines. In this work they will be assisted by a certain number of motor boats that will visit all the small bays and creeks along the coast. The armed patrol [vessels] will act as a parent ship to these boats" but would also be required "to attack a submarine if one is sighted or to rapidly proceed to a spot if one is reported elsewhere." Acting as a parent vessel for the motor patrol boats would require little other than "good sea keeping qualities" but the requirement to attack German submarines would demand faster ships than the RCN had previously taken into service. Stephens reminded his director that:

> the speed of a large modern submarine may be taken as eighteen knots, which will no doubt be reduced somewhat on service, but it would not be safe to estimate it at less than fifteen knots. The greater speed of the [defensive] patrol the more likely she is to get within range before the submarine dives, in my opinion fifteen knots should be the minimum speed of the patrol. It will probably be diff[icult] to obtain offers of such vessels in Canada, voluntarily. I am of the opinion that, if necessary, ships should be requisitioned or obtained in the United States. The vessels hitherto offered the department, with one or two exceptions have been unsuitable for this work, but this is partly due to minesweeping having been the principal object in view. Size and speed within limits was not object, and the advertisements called for a smaller class of vessel than is now required. It is considered that the requirements of the situation now call for ships of 175 feet to 225 feet and fifteen knots speed.[21]

Based on his chief of staff's assessment, Kingsmill sent a memorandum to the deputy minister outlining the proposed Gulf of St Lawrence patrol. Besides the ten armed patrol ships, the naval director envisaged that the St Lawrence force would "require ten small gasoline motor craft in order to organize a system of coast watching."

> The idea is that one armed patrol from Sydney will always be moving along the coast from Cape Ray to the Straits of Belle Isle, two will be operating in Cabot Strait, and one will be continually on the move between Cape Ray and Cape Race. These vessels will arrange to obtain information from the patrol boats at frequent intervals. The patrol boats will also have the land wires to communicate with the officer in charge of the whole patrol, whom we propose stationing at Sydney.
>
> From Gaspé, with two vessels operating and four motor boats along the north shores of the St Lawrence, we should be able to arrange that three of these boats and one of the armed patrol are always patrolling the coast, while one goes back, fills up with stores, etc. for the smaller boats and then takes her

---

21. Stephens to Kingsmill, 30 June 1915, ibid.

turn patrolling. It may not be possible to get small motor boats for this and may be necessary to take over some of the fishing schooners with auxiliary power. Until we advertise and get some offers it seems to me impossible to give any estimate of the probable cost of this patrol.

The vessels we require for armed patrol should, as Commander Stephens's states, have as much speed as is possible and I consider that no vessels of under 150 feet should be accepted and no speed of less than 12 knots, and if it is possible to get ships of 15 knots it would be much better. Each of these vessels should have wireless or should be able to instal wireless.

One condition of the charter must be that the officers and crew place themselves under the Department of the Naval Service and are enrolled as members of the Royal Naval Canadian Volunteer Reserve. This is only a matter of discipline and they should be paid and ship[s] found by the owners. It will be necessary to provide a small quantity of uniform.[22]

The naval director's proposals were eagerly accepted by nervous federal politicians after they read the Admiralty's warnings of an imminent German submarine threat to Canada's maritime traffic. In a diary entry for 29 June, Desbarats recorded that the acting naval minister, T.W. Crothers, was "anxious to have action taken immediately and gave instructions to have [additional patrol] vessels obtained immediately." The naval minister, J.D. Hazen, expressed a similar opinion when he returned to Ottawa two days later, complaining that the naval service was "not going fast enough in obtaining patrol vessels though [we] have telegraphed advertisements to the papers" for suitable private yachts. Called to attend a Cabinet meeting on 14 July, Desbarats found the politicians "alarmed at rumoured submarine operations in St Lawrence" and was forced to try and "allay their fears without much success."[23] Two weeks later the Conservative government's most senior member, minister for trade and commerce Sir George Foster, confided to his diary that "we are defenceless [and] can only watch and wait."[24] Even though Prime Minister Borden had clearly stated to London at the end of May that the Canadian government had "done nothing for naval purposes except purchase of two submarines,"[25] the frightened Cabinet wanted to believe that a suitable navy could be assembled on a few weeks' notice. Despite having turned down the navy's proposal to build two H-class submarines at Canadian Vickers in mid-June as being too expensive,[26] the government still received better value from the RCN than they seemed willing to pay for when NSHQ assigned the first patrol vessels to Sydney, Nova Scotia, in mid-July to establish a Canadian naval presence in the Gulf of St Lawrence.

---

22. Kingsmill to Desbarats, 30 June 1915, ibid.

23. G. Desbarats diary, 29 June, 1 and 14 July 1915, LAC, Manuscript Group (hereafter MG) 30 E89, pt. 1.

24. G. Foster diary, 3 August 1915, LAC, MG 27 II D7, pt. 4.

25. Prime Minister to Acting High Commissioner in United Kingdom, 26 May 1915, in Canada, Department of External Affairs, *Documents on Canadian External Relations* (hereafter *DCER*) (Ottawa 1967), I, 73.

26. Desbarats to Borden, 14 June 1915, Borden to Desbarats, 15 June 1915, LAC, MG 26 H, vol. 54, 26470–74.

In organizing the Gulf patrol, Kingsmill wisely decided to set it up as a command separate from Halifax. Undoubtedly concerned that the British commander-in-chief might try to exercise *de facto* control of Gulf operations with little reference to Canadian needs or priorities, the director wanted to ensure that the patrol remained exclusively in NSHQ's hands by placing it beyond the immediate scrutiny of the influential Vice-Admiral Patey in Halifax. As he explained to the captain superintendent at Halifax, Captain Edward Martin, on 6 July, the patrol was to be commanded by an officer acting under the direct orders of NSHQ with his headquarters at Sydney.[27] The strictly Canadian purpose of the patrol was emphasized in explaining its duties to Martin: "(a) To keep a lookout for enemy craft. (b) To search the coast for small craft, which might be used as oil depots and floating bases for enemy submarines. (c) To constantly visit the signal stations, lighthouses and places difficult of access to ascertain that the local officials are alive to the necessity of keeping a sharp look-out for suspicious craft and persons, and reporting them in accordance with their instructions. (d) To board all suspicious craft."[28] Keeping a watchful eye on the Canadian coast, in other words, was not to be compromised in order to provide anti-submarine protection for Patey's cruisers as they entered or exited Halifax.

The local nature of the Sydney patrols was also evident in the arrangements Canada made with Newfoundland to coordinate their joint maritime defence. In an 8 July telegram, the governor of Newfoundland asked Ottawa to keep the colony's authorities informed "of the number, duties and position of their patrol ships expecially in vicinity of Cabot Straits. It would be useful if Canadian patrol ships could be informed [by St John's] of any suspicious vessels reported to the Newfoundland authorities which may be in the same vicinity as the patrol ships so that the latter could investigate. Such information could be communicated in cypher to them by wireless by the Admiralty intelligence officer [in St John's] if the Admiralty approves."[29] The coordination of patrol plans was fully endorsed by NSHQ along with arrangements to ensure that the responsible authorities were kept informed of each other's activities. Any information about suspicious vessels provided by Newfoundland authorities was to be telegraphed to Captain Martin in Halifax and to the senior officer at Sydney. Martin was in direct communication with both Ottawa and Admiral Patey, while the headquarters at Sydney controlled the patrol vessels in the St Lawrence. Both Halifax and Sydney were also in direct communication with the naval intelligence centre at St John's.[30]

Despite establishing an effective communications network in the Gulf region, NSHQ was careful to safeguard its control of the St Lawrence patrols. On 19 July, for instance, the British officer in charge of the St John's intelligence centre, Captain G.H.F. Abraham, Royal Marines, tried to gain surreptitious control of the Canadian patrol by establishing a direct communications link between himself and the individual patrol vessels. "With a view to

27. NSHQ to Captain in Charge, HMC Dockyard, Halifax, 6 July 1915, 1062–13–4, LAC, RG 24, vol. 4022.

28. NSHQ to Captain in Charge, HMC Dockyard, Halifax, 6 July 1915, ibid.

29. Governor of Newfoundland to Governor-General of Canada, ibid.

30. Stephens to Undersecretary of State for External Affairs, 14 July 1915, ibid.

investigation of reports reaching me concerning enemy's submarines and their supply ships in that part of Newfoundland patrolled by HMC S[hips]," Abraham suggested to Ottawa "that ships be instructed to receive messages from me by wireless as to such reports which would be accompanied by a request to investigate; and that they should inform me of result of investigations.... Can you keep me informed by telegraph of movements of Canadian patrol vessels so that I may know what ships to call up?"[31] NSHQ refused to be drawn in, however, and promptly informed Abraham that he was to "telegraph all intelligence to Naval Intelligence Office, Halifax, who is always in communication with senior officer St Lawrence patrol. Latter officer will take any steps he considers necessary to investigate rumours and will communicate result to Halifax, who will keep you informed. If you consider the matter urgent, communicate with St Lawrence patrol informing Halifax of action taken."[32] The Royal Navy, in other words, was to be kept at arm's length from the new St Lawrence patrol. The command relationship and organization of the Gulf patrol flotilla was also clearly explained in the standing orders NSHQ issued to Sydney on 22 July:

> The senior officer of the patrol will act under the direct orders of the department. The headquarters of the patrol will be at Sydney, C[ape] B[reton]. The senior officer will arrange the patrols so that each vessel returns to her base periodically to coal, refit and give leave. The patrol is to ascertain if any small craft which may be used by the enemy as submarine bases are frequenting the harbours and inlets in the patrol area. A constant examination of such places must consequently be made by means of the patrol vessels and motor boats. All signal stations, lighthouse keepers, customs officials and postmasters in the patrol area have been warned to keep a lookout for suspicious vessels and persons in their localities, and to report any such by telegraph to the department. The senior officer of the patrol should make arrangements to be kept informed by them in the same way, but this is not to counteract their previous instructions to report to the department. The patrol will also keep a constant lookout for the enemy's submarines. No persons are to be allowed on board the patrol vessels as passengers without previous sanction of the director of the naval service. Officers and men are to be cautioned not to speak to representatives of the press or other persons regarding the duties on which they are employed.
>
> The patrol vessels will be commissioned under the White Ensign and the discipline will be in accordance with the King's Regulations and Admiralty Instructions. Officers must remember that the men with whom they have to deal are totally unaccustomed to discipline, and that great tact will be necessary in their dealings with the men. The usual routine of a man-of-war, in so far as is possible, is to be maintained.

---

31. Intelligence Officer, St John's to Naval Ottawa, 19 July 1915, ibid.

32. Naval Ottawa to Intelligence Officer, St John's, 23 July 1915, ibid.

Ships' companies are to be regularly exercised at fire and collision quarters, abandon ship, rifle exercises, and the other usual drills. Opportunity should occasionally be taken to exercise at target practice, but economy of ammunition is necessary.

The senior officer will direct the movements of all patrol vessels in accordance with general instructions received from the director of the naval service. Ships arriving or leaving harbour will telegraph their arrival or departure to the department. The senior officer will make his own arrangements for keeping himself informed of the movements of the vessels under his command. The senior officer will always keep the department informed of his proposed movements well in advance.

Stores for patrol vessels will be obtained through Halifax dockyard, except such minor articles as must be obtained locally to meet urgent requirements....

Large repairs will, as a general rule, be carried out at Halifax, but in the event of small repairs being required, local tenders may be obtained and reported to headquarters for decision.[33]

On 15 July, the first two vessels of the St Lawrence patrol entered Sydney Harbour. HMC Ships *Margaret* and *Sinmac* typified the wide assortment of warships the RCN had gathered to watch the country's coastline. *Margaret* had been built by Thorneycroft's in England as a Customs cruiser and had barely arrived in Canada in August 1914 when she was assigned to patrol work in the St Lawrence River and Gulf of St Lawrence. When it was decided in January 1915 to recommission the vessel under the white ensign, the fisheries officers and crew "were asked if they would volunteer" for the naval service. A somewhat disgusted Kingsmill informed the commissioner of customs on the 25th that "the reply to this was in the negative, with the exception of the steward and two firemen. I am not aware of how you would wish to deal with these people or whether any of the crew are kept on full or half pay during the winter months. The naval authorities at Halifax have been instructed to send them to their homes."[34] To help fill out her complement, ten able seamen were loaned to the RCN from HMS *Charybdis* "temporarily for the period of hostilities" along with ten stokers from HMS *Suffolk*. The remainder of her crew, and most of her officers, came from the RCN itself after the vessel was formally commissioned into the Canadian naval service on 3 February 1915.[35]

A twin-funnelled vessel, 182 feet in length, with twin screws to propel her at fifteen knots, the ship was comparable in size and speed to a Second World War corvette. One of the first RCN officers assigned to her, Midshipman Leonard W. Murray, recalled that her

---

33. "Standing Orders for St. Lawrence Patrol," 22 July 1915, 1065-2-2, LAC, RG 24, vol. 4030.

34. Kingsmill to the Commissioner of Customs, 25 January 1915, 58-16-6, LAC, RG 24, vol. 5659.

35. C-in-C, NA&WI to Kingsmill, 25 January 1915, ibid; and Rear-Admiral L.W. Murray to E.C. Russell, 6 September 1964, Department of National Defence, Directorate of History and Heritage, (hereafter DHH) 81/520/8000, HMCS *Margaret*; and see also Ken MacPherson and John Burgess, *The Ships of Canada's Naval Forces: A Complete Pictorial History of Canadian Warships* (Toronto 1985), 19.

"twin screws out-turning ... made her very handy to handle but very difficult for the engine room staff." Although built in a pre-war British shipyard, the design and workmanship appear to have been barely adequate since, as Murray remembered, the engines gave "trouble as not being man enough [i.e., powerful enough] for the job. The cylinders also gave trouble and wore into a barrel shape."[36] After being employed until June "on rather fruitless patrols of Halifax Harbour," the ship was laid up in the navy yard to retube a boiler that had run out of water during a full power trial. *Margaret* was armed with two small 6-pounder guns that, according to Murray, were "the only ones of their kind ... to have been made." As a result, the ship was "limited to the amount of ammunition we could use. I was given to understand that the 100 rounds we had on board were the lot. Apparently the customs service had had no target practice and I could find no record of proper gun trials. In my time we fired six rounds from each gun at an iceberg in the Strait of Belle Isle. We chose a large one so that we could not very well miss. It gave the gun's crew a bit of confidence to know both that it would go off and that it would not explode."[37]

The second ship to arrive in Sydney in July, the *Sinmac*, was little more than a tug and not particularly suited to naval work. After inspecting the vessel in October, Kingsmill informed the deputy minister that he could "not understand how she was ever accepted" by the RCN's consulting naval engineer, Engineer Commander P.C.W. Howe. As the disappointed naval director explained in rejecting the ship for further naval service: "With the gun in the bow and steaming in smooth water with any wind at all she throws the spray so high over her bow that the gun cannot be worked. Her decks are all iron and she has not heating arrangements. I instructed the senior officer of the St Lawrence Patrol to dismount the gun and mounting and send it to Halifax at the first opportunity in a man of war. And the *Sinmac* to proceed to Montreal" for disposal.[38]

Reinforcements were already on the way after the wealthy Lieutenant J.K.L. Ross, whose purchase of the turbine-powered yacht *Tarantula* the previous year gave the RCN its only twenty-five-knot vessel, departed for New York City in June to purchase another turbine yacht, *Winchester*, owned by Charles Rouss. Built along the lines of a torpedo-boat destroyer—a style popular among New York millionaires commuting to and from work in the city along the Hudson River—the twin-funnelled vessel had a low hull with a raised forecastle extended back to form a compass platform over the saloon and a tall mast amidships. *Winchester* was 202 feet long and 18 feet in the beam which made her comparable in size to the Royal Navy's small E-class destroyers of the 1901–04 programs. The British ships, however, had reciprocating engines and could make only twenty-five knots whereas the yacht's turbines developed 6,000 horsepower on twin shafts and drove the vessel through the water at thirty-two knots, reputedly the highest speed of any yacht in North America.[39]

36. Rear-Admiral L.W. Murray to E.C. Russell, 6 September 1964, DHH 81/520/8000, HMCS *Margaret*.

37. Murray to Russell, 6 September 1964, DHH 81/520/8000, HMCS *Margaret*; and see also MacPherson and Burgess, *The Ships of Canada's Naval Forces*, 206.

38. Kingsmill to Desbarats, 26 October 1915, 58–15–1, LAC, RG 24, vol. 5659.

39. Edgar J. March, *British Destroyers: A History of Development, 1892–1953* (London 1966), 70; and Naval Historical Section, "Brief History of HMCS *Grilse* (I) and (II)," 6 March 1961, DHH 81/520/8000, HMCS *Grilse* (I).

After paying $100,000 for the vessel, Ross telegraphed NSHQ on 29 June advising that "everything satisfactorily arranged, will proceed tonight to Yarmouth" in a hurried effort to put to sea before the American authorities were alerted of the purchase and moved to prevent her sailing.[40] Ross arrived in Halifax on 2 July despite Kingsmill's later admission that "getting the *Winchester* out [of the United States in disregard of neutrality laws] was a still more difficult job than that of the *Tuna*."[41]

Whereas Ross had previously made a gift of *Tuna* to the Canadian government, the Montreal playboy's shortage of funds in the spring of 1915 prompted Ottawa to purchase *Winchester* from him for the same price he had paid in New York, a transaction that was made official by the Privy Council (PC) on 12 August. In the meantime, *Winchester* was commissioned into the Canadian navy as HMCS *Grilse* on 15 July and departed for the Vickers's yard in Montreal carrying the 12-pounder gun and 14-inch torpedo tube that were to be mounted on her decks. The gun was mounted on her forecastle—a second 12-pounder was later placed on her quarter-deck—while the after deck-house was removed to make room for the torpedo tube and the three torpedoes she carried on deck. The mast was also moved forward to directly behind the bridge, while a second mast was added "to give her a high, horizontal antenna to improve the performance of her radio equipment."[42] Alterations were also made to her living quarters to accommodate a crew of forty. The inclining experiments conducted at that time indicated that she had a metacentric height of one foot, giving her a "stability greater than many vessels of a similar class in the British navy."[43] Indeed, except the two obsolescent cruisers with which the RCN had begun the conflict, the vessel's speed and torpedo tube made the modest *Grilse* the most powerful surface ship Canada possessed during the First World War.

NSHQ recognized *Grilse*'s operational possibilities from the outset and the vessel was intended for employment near the Gulf's shipping lanes as the RCN's primary offensive unit. As Kingsmill explained to the deputy minister soon after the ship was purchased, the navy did not consider "that she would do ordinary patrol work. This vessel being of high power and capable of being armed with one or two 12 pounders and torpedo tubes would be absolutely lost in performing the ordinary duties of patrol in the Gulf of St Lawrence." While *Grilse* could "from time to time," relieve one of the Gulf patrol vessels, it was Kingsmill's intention that she "be kept as near the trade route passing Cape Breton Island and the Cabot Straits as is possible, so that she can immediately proceed in search of any enemy vessel reported in the vicinity or to any of our ships in distress from an enemy act."[44]

The turbine-powered yacht's offensive potential contrasted with the more mundane capabilities of the final two American yachts acquired by the RCN during the war, vessels that were purchased for the St Lawrence patrol in the wake of the Admiralty's late-June

---

40. Telegram quoted in Naval Historical Section, "Brief History of HMCS *Grilse* (I) and (II)," 6 March 1961, ibid.

41. Kingsmill quoted in "Brief History of HMCS *Grilse* (I) and (II)," 6 March 1961, ibid.

42. Ibid; and for correspondence on the purchase of *Winchester* from Ross see file 58–52–1, LAC, RG 24, vol. 5661.

43. Quoted "Brief History of HMCS *Grilse* (I) and (II)," 6 March 1961, DHH 81/520/8000, HMCS *Grilse* (I).

44. Kingsmill, "Memorandum for the Deputy Minister," 23 July 1915, 1062–13–4, LAC, RG 24, vol. 4022.

warnings of an imminent submarine threat to Canadian waters. Anxious to avoid conflicting with American neutrality laws, the RCN used a wealthy Toronto banker and naval enthusiast, Aemilius Jarvis, to "act as intermediary between the Canadian government and the owners, in order to avoid any question which may arise with the American government in selling ships to be used subsequently for belligerent purposes."[45] Upon war being declared the previous August, Jarvis had turned his Bay Street offices into an informal recruiting office for both the Royal and Canadian navies, an act that led him to be referred to in the local newspapers as the RN's chief recruiting officer. Naval Service Headquarters entered negotiations in July 1915 with the New York shipbrokers Cox and Stevens for the purchase of the yachts *Columbia* and *Waterus*. Although the RCN had originally contemplated buying three American yachts for a sum of $250,000, an examination of the ships' plans by Canadian technical officers limited the purchase to the two New York vessels for the sum of $155,000, an amount that included $15,000 for Cox and Stevens. The ships were given British registration before departing New York with *Columbia* being renamed *Stadacona* and *Waterus* becoming *Hochelaga*. Despite complaints by naval minister Hazen that the navy was not moving quickly enough for Canada's frightened Cabinet ministers, both ships arrived in Halifax by mid-August where they were quickly commissioned into the RCN before being sent on to Vickers in Montreal for refit as naval vessels. Since the civilians that brought them to Halifax were unwilling to serve in the Canadian naval service, crews were assigned from the naval personnel at the dockyard for the passage to Montreal.[46]

Although built on opposite sides of the Atlantic, both vessels were remarkably similar in size, speed, and appearance. The New Jersey-built *Stadacona* was just over 200 feet in length overall, and was designed more for comfort than speed. The vessel's steam reciprocating engine generated only ninety-nine horsepower but could still drive her 682 tons at a speed of thirteen knots. Her generous accommodations even allowed the ship's midshipmen to share double cabins with bunks and mahogany chests of drawers for their kit. Fitted with a 4-inch gun forward (a 12 pounder was added aft later in the war) and an 18-inch searchlight on the foremast, *Stadacona*'s high freeboard meant that the ship tended to roll badly in a sea. *Hochelaga*, on the other hand, being slightly shorter at just under 200 feet in length and somewhat lighter at 571 registered tons, was reputed to have "kept the sea well" while making an identical top speed of thirteen knots. After completing their fitting out at Montreal—*Hochelaga* received a single 12-pounder forward—both patrol vessels arrived at Sydney to take up their Gulf patrols in September.[47]

In the meantime, the work of the RCN's Gulf flotilla had begun with HMC Ships *Margaret* and *Sable* keeping watch on the main entrance to the Gulf of St Lawrence, while

---

45. Desbarats to Aemilius Jarvis, 29 July 1915, 58–57–2, LAC, RG 24, vol. 5663.

46. Desbarats diary, 29 June, 1 and 14 July 1915, LAC, MG 30 E89, pt. 1; and Fraser McKee, *The Armed Yachts of Canada* (Erin, Ontario, 1983), 29–32.

47. Naval Historical Section, "A Brief History of the Name 'Hochelaga' in the Royal Canadian Navy," 26 July 1955, DHH 81/520/8000, HMCS *Hochelaga*; Naval Historical Section, "Brief History of HMCS *Stadacona* (steam yacht)," nd, DHH 81/520/8000, HMCS *Stadacona*; and McKee, *The Armed Yachts of Canada*, 32.

the navy's hired civilian motorboats patrolled the shoreline.[48] As related by Leonard Murray, one of *Margaret*'s midshipmen, the initial deployment of the Gulf force to Sydney remained an *ad hoc* arrangement:

> When we went to Sydney our CO [Commander Burrard A. Smith] was recognized as the senior officer of the Gulf of St Lawrence Patrols and I found myself as the gunnery officer (patrols). This entailed taking care of the new arrivals, tugs, yachts, and all sorts of craft to which a 12 pdr. or 3 pdr. gun had been fitted in Montreal and sent to Sydney. We had to find out what they were fitted with, (no one took the trouble to write ahead. The first we knew was a ship of sorts turning up and asking where they could find someone connected with the navy), and make out the usual demands on the ordnance stores officer in Halifax. With the greatest efficiency the stuff would appear within a week and we put it onboard. If the ship had, in the meantime, gone off on patrol we had to keep the ammunition in a box-car in the station yard. But things were very peaceful and it never occurred to anyone to put a guard on it. One of the ships, a tug of the Sincennes-MacNaughton Line came down with a gun platform cocked up at the same angle as the rising flare of the fore deck. It was at about 20 to 25 degrees and the gun pivot was at the same angle from the vertical. That ship never did very well at target practice until we had it put straight.[49]

Such was the perceived threat of U-boats operating off North American coasts that the vessel in question, the tug *Sinmac*, had not even reached Sydney when NSHQ was already directing her "to patrol the Belle Isle Strait immediately on her arrival" to investigate a "report from Washington regarding submarines."[50] Newfoundland was also in the process of establishing a patrol of small vessels and motorboats to search for "suspicious craft and for supplies for such which may be hidden in unfrequented places. All ships on the coast have been instructed to watch suspicious craft or any remarkable occurrence and report to home defence committee" in St John's.[51] A message passed to NSHQ from the dockyard in Halifax covering the activities of the British colony's patrols gives some indication of the reports that were reaching naval authorities.

> Following message received from St John's begins: Patrol at Grosis Island. Report seeing periscope of submarine 5.30 pm 1st August off North coast of Grosis Island coming from North Pyrgos Bight and moving south half west. Submarine was immediately followed by large black steamer. *Petrel* also reports

48. Tennyson and Sarty, *Guardian of the Gulf,* 133.

49. Rear-Admiral L.W. Murray to E.C. Russell, 6 September 1964, DHH 81/520/8000, HMCS *Margaret.*

50. Naval Ottawa to Patrols Sydney, 26 July 1915, 1065–2-1, LAC, RG 24, vol. 4030.

51. Colonial Secretary, St John's to Naval Ottawa, 30 June 1915, 1065–4-1, ibid.

seeing unknown steamer, two masts, one funnel 4.00 am 31st July one mile east of Bell Island. *Petrel* fired 6 inch gun but steamer took no notice and sailed on. Speed of *Petrel* seven knots, so pursuit impossible. *Petrel*'s WT has broken down. She is telegraphing from St Anthony. Suspicious ship at Horse Island reported by magistrate at La Soie who is also investigating rumoured depot of oil. German American tourists reported at various stations on coast; they are being arrested. Newfoundland government are sending SS *Fogata* from Saint John's to this area. She will have one 12 pdr. gun 3 cwt. and one 3 pdr. gun and wireless installation, wireless call sign VYC. She cannot sail before Wednesday. Newfoundland government enquire whether Canadian patrol ship can be sent forthwith to investigate matter. Ends. Patrol Sydney being informed.[52]

With a steady stream of correspondence and telegrams arriving from Halifax and Ottawa, the flotilla's senior officer was handicapped by having to perform the diverse duties of the patrol's administration in harbour while also commanding a sea-going warship, HMCS *Margaret*, as it followed up the many reports of submarines operating in the Gulf. Commander Burrard Smith had volunteered for the naval service soon after the outbreak of war and initially been given a temporary commission at his former RN rank of lieutenant (his seniority dating from 1 April 1897). As Murray recalled, Smith had been "passed over for promotion [in the RN] and received the promotion on retirement. He was growing fruit in the Okanaghan [*sic*] Valley" when he offered his services to the RCN.[53] Writing to NSHQ at the end of July to complain about the burden of paperwork ashore at Sydney, Smith explained that the organization of administration "greatly increases the clerical work and I find it difficult to keep that close touch with affairs for which I am personally responsible, and which I feel to be necessary at the present time."

> The difficulty is increased when I am at sea and by remaining much in harbour I feel that the services of the *Margaret* are to a certain extent being wasted especially as we are short of armed patrol vessels. I would submit that efficiency would be increased if I were stationed at the office and if Lieutenant [H.G.] Jarvis were given command of the *Margaret* at any rate while the St Lawrence Patrol is in existence. Under this arrangement I hardly think there should be any difficulty at sea as each patrol vessel will be working independently on her own area and would rarely meet one another.
>
> My idea would be to keep Lieutenant Jarvis sufficiently informed and endeavour that at each period at sea the *Margaret* would be stationed on a

---

52. Navyard Halifax to Naval Ottawa, 2 August 1915, 1065–2-1, ibid.

53. Colonial Secretary, St John's to Naval Ottawa, 30 June 1915, 1065–4-1, ibid; and Department of the Naval Service, *The Canadian Navy List for January 1915* (Ottawa 1915), 15.

The crew of HMCS *Margaret* in July 1915. Seated in the middle of the front row, fifth from the left, is her commanding officer, Commander Burrard A. Smith. Midshipman (and future admiral) L.W. Murray is seated in the front row, third from the left. (LAC e010752874)

different patrol relieving one of the other vessels for coal, etc. By this plan Lieutenant Jarvis would be enabled to give me reports as to conditions on all the various patrol areas. He would also be sufficiently in touch with affairs to be able to relieve me at the office for a short period if I considered it necessary to make a personal inspection.[54]

Naval headquarters had already anticipated Smith's concerns, however, and the Admiralty had been approached concerning the possibility of lending the services of a suitable RN officer to the Canadian navy to act as senior officer at Sydney. Kingsmill informed *Margaret*'s commanding officer (CO) on 10 August that "Captain F.C. Pasco, RN, ret, has been appointed by the Admiralty for this purpose. He sailed from Melbourne, Australia on the 5th instant and should be here at the end of this month. In the meantime, as very few vessels of the patrol are ready and the patrol will not be in working order, I do not think it necessary to change the commanding officer of the *Margaret*."[55] Fred Pasco had been serving with the Royal Navy in Australia but retired from the service on the outbreak of war with the hope of obtaining a commission with the Australian expeditionary force. After being rejected by the Australians for frontline service because of age, Pasco readily accepted Canada's offer to command the Gulf patrol flotilla and arrived at Sydney on 5 September 1915.[56] According to a junior RCN officer who served under him, Pasco "was a gruff old fellow who's [*sic*] specialty was 'finding fault.' ... For us this meant having every button on duty with no deviation from rules contained in the so-called naval bible, 'Kings Rules and Regulations' [*sic*]." Nevertheless, the flotilla commander also "had a humane side in his make up" that was appreciated by the sailors under him. An example of this side of Pasco's character was in evidence one winter after Sydney had been closed for the season and the flotilla's vessels were in Halifax:

> During this period prohibition was in force in Halifax and deliveries of evil spirits came via the underground route, the beer in bottles from the Dartmouth Brewery being packed in barrels stenciled on the outside SUGAR. One of those barrels was waiting until Captain Pasco went ashore before being unpacked. The following morning there was a sigh of relief when Captain Pasco walked down the gangway. Immediately Lieutenant T. Dutton and the chief steward went into action. Apparently the old man had forgot something and backtracked and caught them redhanded. In a loud voice he said, "What is this?" Tommy Dutton was equal to the occasion and answered, "Sugar, sir." Then the old man whispered, "Don't forget to send some sugar to my cabin." Some time later he said to Lieutenant Dutton, "Don't you think it is time to get some more sugar?"[57]

---

54. Smith to Kingsmill, 30 July 1915, 1065-2-1, LAC, RG 24, vol. 4030.

55. Kingsmill to Smith, 10 August 1915, ibid.

56. Hadley and Sarty, *Tin-pots and Pirate Ships*, 122.

57. W. McLaurin to E.C. Russell, 11 February 1963, DHH 81/520/8000, HMCS *Protector* (Base).

The small force that Pasco found waiting for him in Sydney could not have inspired much confidence. By month's end, the Gulf flotilla's patrol vessels consisted of the former government vessels *Canada* and *Margaret*, the patrol vessel *Sable I*, the tug *Sinmac* and the yacht *Florence*. Ross's turbine-yacht *Grilse*, which was normally stationed at Halifax, was temporarily placed under the orders of the senior officer at Sydney "to act as escort to transport in St Lawrence."[58] Of the Sydney vessels, *Sinmac* and *Florence* proved unseaworthy in anything but a calm sea, while the living conditions aboard *Sable I* during longer patrols eventually prompted nine ratings to jump ship rather than proceed to sea on 10 November. As was typical with many of the vessels the RCN had taken up since the outbreak of war, the ocean-going steamer *Sable I* had been chartered, with her civilian crew, from the Halifax firm of Farquhar and Company for $160 a day. In August, however, NSHQ decided to commission the ship under the white ensign with fourteen of her fifteen crewmen volunteering to enrol in the RNCVR.[59] (Her civilian captain was replaced by an RNR officer serving in the RCN, Lieutenant-Commander B.L. Vinden.) In fact, upon hearing *Sable I* was to be commissioned in the RCN, the former civilian crew refused to go to sea until they received the higher pay rates of the Canadian navy. Nonetheless, as the patrol season was winding down in mid-November, nine of her crew "broke out of the ship for various reasons, principally because they wanted drink. There was no concerted action. They had no complaint of their treatment on board, but stated that the lower deck was very uncomfortable, the deck being bare iron and water came down in a seaway, and it was very cold." Vinden imposed ninety days detention on all nine of them.[60]

The addition of *Stadacona* and *Hochelaga* in September and the hiring of civilian motorboats to keep an eye on the many bays and inlets along the Gulf of St Lawrence coast at least allowed the RCN to maintain a presence in the area and investigate the many rumours and false sightings being reported by the anxious civilian population. The mix of RN and RNR officers and senior ratings gave their largely RNCVR crews a measure of naval experience, while providing some on the job training during actual patrols.[61] It was obvious, however, that more systematic training for the RNCVR sailors would require the Royal Navy's assistance, as Kingsmill acknowledged to the Admiralty later that summer:

> The crews are composed of the only seamen obtainable. They are only partially trained and further systematic training is essential to make the armament useful. Now that *Niobe* is paid off and officers and men are returning to England, I am unable to carry this out. As this search and patrol is of some value to HM ships operating in western Atlantic, I most respectfully submit for the

---

58. Naval Ottawa to Navyard Halifax, 23 August 1915, 1065–2-1, LAC, RG 24, vol. 4030.

59. PC 3099, 14 December 1914, Farquhar and Company to Hazen, 4 August 1915, Director of Stores to Captain Farquhar, 3 August 1915, Lieutenant-Commander B.L. Vinden to Kingsmill, nd, DHH 81/520/8000, *Sable I*.

60. Naval Ottawa to Captain Superintendent Halifax, 12 November 1915, Senior Officer, St Lawrence Patrol to Captain Superintendent Halifax, 17 November 1915, Captain Superintendent to Senior Officer Patrols, Halifax, 20 November 1915, "Notes on HQ 58–33–6," DHH 81/520/8000, *Sable I*.

61. Hadley and Sarty, *Tin-pots and Pirate Ships*, 123.

HMCS *Grilse*'s destroyer lines and 6,000-horsepower turbine engines made her the fastest warship in the RCN's First World War arsenal. Armed with 12-pounder guns forward and aft and a single torpedo tube amidships, *Grilse*'s thirty-two-knot top speed made her the only Canadian warship (aside from the much smaller *Tuna*) that was capable of overtaking a surfaced U-boat. (DND HS 9807)

favourable consideration of their lordships, my request that some assistance may be given, and would suggest the minimum numbers required would be an instructional warrant officer and two gunners mates. The instructional staff might be obtained from pensioners. The duty of the warrant officer would merely be superintendence and maintenance of discipline, so that age and gunnery qualifications need not essentially be considered in this case.[62]

In the meantime, two chief petty officers (CPOs) were assigned as instructors to *Canada* and *Florence* "not as part of complement but to give crew instruction until course in *Niobe* commences."[63] It was not until the following March, however, that a retired RN lieutenant and a gunnery petty officer were lent to the Naval Ordnance Depot at Halifax as instructors.[64]

Clearly the standard of naval professionalism to be expected of the ships of the Gulf flotilla was not as high as NSHQ would have liked. At the end of August, for instance, Ottawa had to remind Sydney of the proper procedures to be used in stopping merchant ships in the St Lawrence after headquarters received *Sinmac*'s weekly report for the week ending 14 August. "It appears that the signal DV not being obeyed, *Sinmac* fired two rounds from her gun. The firing of a gun is a well understood signal to heave to, consequently if it is only intended that a ship should show her Ensign, firing should not be resorted to. The proper procedure in this case after the vessel did not obey the signal DV, was to have hoisted the signal to heave to and then if necessary to have fired a gun. The attention of all commanding officers of patrol vessels is to be called to this memorandum."[65] One month later, Pasco had to call upon the commanding officers of *Margaret* and *Sable I* for reports on the four week period they had spent in Sydney repairing mechanical breakdowns. As Pasco reported to Ottawa: "The commanding officer HMCS *Margaret*'s reason for his own vessel being in port appears to me to be satisfactory. With regard to *Sable I*, I find between 17th and 27th August she went out for gun trials [once] on 22nd, returning the same day. I can see no reason she should have remained in Sydney so long, and consider it would have been better if Commander Smith had sent her on patrol duty on completion of gun trials. HMCS *Sinmac* also would have been better employed on patrol duty, than being in Sydney Harbour between August 10th and 16th. Since taking over the command on 5th September, I have endeavoured to keep the patrol ships on the move as much as possible."[66]

A further idea of the difficulties facing the Sydney force's operations is provided by the sighting report that *Grilse* was detailed to investigate in mid-October. On 24 September, the Sydney headquarters received a report from a miner at Little Bras d'Or Bridge that he had

---

62. Kingsmill to Admiralty, 2 September 1915, 53–6-1, pt 2, LAC, RG 24, vol. 5651.

63. Naval Ottawa to Captain Superintendent, Halifax, 27 October 1915, ibid.

64. Admiralty to Kingsmill, 14 March 1916, ibid.

65. Naval Ottawa to Senior Officer, St Lawrence Patrol, 28 August 1915, 1065–2-1, LAC, RG 24, vol. 4030.

66. Captain Pasco to The Secretary, Department of the Naval Service, 4 October 1915, ibid.

spotted a submarine off Cape Breton on the 5th. With Captain Pasco away on an inspection of Prince Edward Island, no action was taken on the report until 13 October when the flotilla's senior officer returned. Pasco immediately despatched Lieutenant Ross and the *Grilse* to follow up on the, by now, five-week old sighting. When Ross reached Little Bras d'Or, however, the miner was at work and the RNCVR officer contented himself with interviewing the local customs officer. That official had talked with the miner and confirmed his impression that he had definitely sighted a submarine. Ross also asked about a "suspicious stranger" who was reported to be working on a local farm and doing some fishing. The stranger was said to be of Danish descent who spoke German fluently. Unable to meet with either the miner or the Danish stranger, Ross returned to Sydney on the 13th to report his findings—or lack thereof—to Pasco.[67]

Determining the German-speaking Dane to be of more interest than the submarine sighting report, Pasco sent *Grilse* back to Little Bras d'Or Bridge on 15 October to dig up more information on the stranger. This time, however, the turbine-yacht was accompanied by the naval motor launch *Two Brothers*, with the intention of discovering if the Danish interloper was acting on behalf of the enemy.

> Midshipman R.F. Lawson, RCN, was in charge of the small vessel which was painted black for the occasion while he and his crew were dressed as fishermen. He was to pretend to fish off Cape Dauphin, keeping a lookout for the submarine and for any suspicious activities ashore. Unfortunately, *Two Brothers* was unable that day to weather Cranberry Point, just outside Sydney, so could not reach her station until the 16th. Meanwhile *Grilse* sailed direct for Ingonish, where the customs officer informed Ross that no fishing vessel from that port had been sold that year. It was blowing hard, so the reconnoitring of Cape Dauphin was impossible and *Grilse* anchored in St Ann's Bay.
>
> During the night *Grilse* was ordered by radio to St Peter's Inlet, in the Bras d'Or Lakes, to meet Admiral Kingsmill, director of the naval service. She weighed [anchor] at 0500 and passed through the Bras d'Or as day was breaking. That afternoon at 1300, *Two Brothers* reached Cape Dauphin and began fishing. With his telescope, Mr Lawson kept the suspected house under observation. On at least one occasion he saw that a man was standing by the door returning his gaze with binoculars. During the night he landed on Cape Dauphin to investigate a cave and the next day, the 17th, he passed through the Bras d'Or and investigated all the bays and inlets along the north shore for traces of fuel dumps. He found nothing.
>
> Coming back from St Peter's Inlet on 18 October, *Grilse* fell in with *Two Brothers*, and Midshipman Lawson came on board to report. Going on, *Grilse* called at Kelly's Cove where she landed a party under Lieutenant C.O. Julian, RNCVR, to make enquiries at Big Bras d'Or. There he found that the bird had flown; the stranger had got up early on the 16th, in time to see *Grilse* steaming

---

67. "Brief History of HMCS *Grilse*," 6 March 1961, 6–7, DHH 81/520/8000, HMCS *Grilse* (I).

through the Bras d'Or, had asked his landlady what warships might be doing around there, and had packed his bag and left the same day. Jessome [the customs officer] also found this out on the 18th and telephoned the news to Sydney where Captain Pasco had a search made for the man. It was found, however, that he had signed on the British SS *Dunelm* as donkeyman on the 16th, and sailed for Manchester in her. Lieutenant Julian was told also that the suspect had been working for his landlord for his keep only, that he received remittance from Denmark and that, though a Dane, he spoke German well. The British authorities were asked to keep a watch for him when *Dunelm* should arrive, but before she did, a police report came in showing that there was no grounds for the suspicions. The man was simply an unemployed miner. He had signed on the ship in order to make enough money to buy a boat and go fishing on his own account. The investigation was dropped.

HMC Ships *Canada*, *Grilse*, and *Hochelaga* spent 2 and 3 November on another wild goose chase—this time after a submarine reported off Pictou Island by a farmer. When Lieutenant Ross interviewed the man on the second day of the search, he concluded that the object sighted had been a small boat in heavy seas, so the search was called off.[68]

The armed yacht HMCS *Stadacona*, formerly the American-registered *Columbia*, fitted with a single 4-inch gun forward, a 12-pounder aft, and an 18-inch searchlight on the foremast. Built more for comfort than speed, the 682-ton yacht had a top speed of thirteen knots. (DND CN 3275)

The former yacht *Waterus*, HMCS *Hochelaga* was less heavily armed than *Stadacona*, mounting only a single 12-pounder forward, but had a similar top speed of thirteen knots and was considered to be the better sea boat of the two. (DND CN 3399)

Although such incidents may seem more comic opera than serious naval patrol, they were entirely in keeping with the suspicious mood of the country—among both the general public and the authorities in equal measure—toward anyone with apparent ties to Germany or the Central Powers.[69]

Even then, the small force of converted yachts, fisheries vessels, and hired motor boats that Kingsmill had assembled at Sydney eventually drew critical comment from the ever cost-conscious Canadian prime minister. Despite the strong warnings the Admiralty had issued in late June that led NSHQ, urged on by nervous Cabinet ministers, to establish the Gulf flotilla in the first place, London quickly backtracked on its earlier forecasts when Prime Minister Borden visited the British capital in July. In the meantime, NSHQ had appealed to the Royal Navy to lend it any anti-submarine vessels it might have available, particularly destroyers. When the naval department's request for assistance was promptly rejected by the Admiralty, Borden did not hide his embarrassment—completely unwarranted in view of London's dire warnings and the reaction of his own Cabinet—that the RCN was bothering the British with its troubles. On 14 July, the Canadian prime minister telegraphed Ottawa that the British "have no light craft available and leave matter to best arrangements you can make. While they think every precaution should be taken, they do not regard the situation as serious. They think one or two of your vessels should be furnished with light guns capable of sinking submarine craft. Swift type used by Jack Ross would be specially suitable."[70] Three days later, NSHQ was informed that:

---

69. For a full description of the many reports about German spies and agents thought to be operating in the United States and Canada during this period see Hadley and Sarty, *Tin-pots and Pirate Ships*, 105–16.

70. Borden to PMO, Ottawa, 14 July 1915, 1062–13–4, LAC, RG 24, vol. 4022.

The Admiralty are not of the opinion that the probability of German submarines operating in Canadian waters in the near future is great. As it is possible for submarines to cross the Atlantic, the Admiralty recently called the attention of the naval authorities at Ottawa to the desirability of taking steps to patrol the coast with small craft in order to have an organization ready to prevent unfrequented harbours being used as bases of operations, and to enable any submarines to be dealt with which might reach Canadian waters. This precautionary measure appears to have been interpreted in Canada as an expression of opinion by the Admiralty, that submarine operations are to be expected in the immediate future, which was not the intention.[71]

As it was, the naval service had already committed its two most warlike vessels, *Canada* and *Grilse*, to the escort of more valuable transports in the Gulf of St Lawrence. On 19 July, for instance, the two warships had escorted the transports *Herschel* and *Hesperian* down the St Lawrence from Quebec City but the inadequacy of such protection was demonstrated at the end of the month when the troopship *Caledonia*, carrying the 38th Battalion, CEF, overseas from Montreal had to be left undefended, while her escort proceeded to Newfoundland to investigate reports of periscope sightings off the colony's coast. The unprotected *Caledonia* then had to disembark her troops at Quebec City and sail for Halifax in ballast, while the Canadian battalion made its way to the Nova Scotia port by train to rendezvous with the ship for the voyage overseas.[72]

The Admiralty's seeming indifference to the defence of Canada's shipping lanes prompted NSHQ to respond by pointing out the inconsistent nature of British exhortations. In a 5 August memorandum for the director, Stephens reiterated that the need for fast warships "for anti-submarine purposes is urgent. They are needed to accompany transports out some considerable distance to sea and to chase submarines. They should be good sea-keeping boats of twenty knots speed, armed with one gun.... If transports sail from one port only, say Halifax, it is considered that four boats are necessary. As, however, there can be no guarantee that only one port will be used, it is considered that six boats should be provided. This in no way takes into consideration the general protection of trade routes. It is desirable that a definite policy should be laid down as to what the department is required to do in this matter; the department will then be in a better position to state what is required in the way of ships and other material." Endorsing Stephens's usual clear thinking, Kingsmill minuted that "to delay in these matters now is next to criminal."[73]

Knowing that an effective anti-submarine defence could not simply be thrown together at the last minute in response to the latest intelligence warning, the naval director was equally blunt in his assessment of the Admiralty's attitude in a memorandum to the

---

71. Admiralty to NSHQ, 17 July 1915, ibid.

72. "Notes on 47–5-11 (1047–5-11) Defensive Measures, Reports on Situation," nd, DHH 81/520/1440–11, file 1; and Hadley and Sarty, *Tin-pots and Pirate Ships,* 124–25.

73. Stephens, "Memorandum for Director of Naval Service," 5 August 1915, 1062–13–4, LAC, RG 24, vol. 4022; and "Notes on 1062–13–4," nd, 3, DHH 81/520/1440–11, file 1.

minister the following week:

> I venture to suggest that the question of convoying vessels with troops, and vessels with cargo valuable to the war operations, to a safe offing, should be taken up with the Admiralty or home [i.e., British] government. Once the enemy submarines commence operations in the west Atlantic it is not reasonable to suppose that the Admiralty, well aware of the difficulties attendant upon the raising of an efficient naval force in this country, propose to trust to luck in getting overseas our troops and munitions from here and the United States. A plain statement to the home government of what we propose to do and length of time it is going to take to do it might draw something from the Admiralty. It appears to me that as we are all working to the same end it would be better to let the Admiralty send, if they can and will, destroyers or fast armed patrol [vessels] and let Canada pay the bill than to purchase vessels not altogether suitable. If it is proposed to build, I would also suggest that Admiralty be asked advice as to best class of vessel to build.[74]

Ironically, in view of his opposition to Laurier's naval plans, the prime minister had now come to believe that Canada required a powerful cruiser on the East Coast as a symbol of the country's naval power. While in London, Borden made arrangements with the Admiralty to exchange *Niobe*, about to be laid up in Halifax, for the somewhat more modern Bacchanti-class cruiser *Sutlej*. To Borden's surprise and disappointment, NSHQ quickly rejected the British offer, as it was, rightly, more concerned about the submarine threat to Canada's shipping lanes than that posed by German merchant cruisers. Kingsmill preferred to use the 333 Canadian sailors released from *Niobe*'s crew to man the patrol ships of the St Lawrence flotilla, while converting the worn-out cruiser to floating accommodation at Halifax, where barrack space was desperately needed. Borden's resentment of Kingsmill's rejection of the British offer was made clear in his 13 August telegram to Hazen. "Admiralty see no objection to your proposal [to use *Niobe*'s sailors for the Gulf flotilla] if all imperial ranks and ratings are set free from *Niobe*. It seems to me, however, most unfortunate that in the midst of this war the only Canadian cruiser in Atlantic should be out of commission. The Admiralty [cruiser] proposal, if feasible, is in my judgment greatly preferable. Their memorandum to me states that you may not clearly recognise that the submarine danger on the Canadian coast is potential not actual. They deprecate exaggerated measures of precaution."[75]

Borden's naive preference for the acquisition of large cruisers over small patrol vessels foundered when Kingsmill's proposal to lay up *Niobe* was endorsed by Admiral Patey who looked forward to the release of the old cruiser's 400 British and Newfoundland seamen for service on other Royal Navy vessels. The Admiralty's acceptance of the RCN proposal, however, prompted London to give the Canadian prime minister a memorandum from the

74. Kingsmill, "Memorandum," 10 August 1915, 1062–13–4, LAC, RG 24, vol. 4022.

75. Borden to Hazen, 13 August 1915, copy in "Notes on 1062–13–4," nd, DHH 81/520/1440–11.

Admiralty secretary, Sir William Graham-Greene, outlining its concerns that NSHQ may have been focusing to too great an extent on the submarine threat to North America.

> It is understood that the numbers of Canadian naval ranks and ratings now in *Niobe* are approximately what will be required to run the patrol of small craft on the Canadian coast which it has recently been decided to institute. Moreover, in her present state the *Niobe* is not fit for service as a fighting unit and therefore the suggestion that she should be paid off and retained as a hulk at Halifax would be very appropriate.
>
> If all imperial ranks and ratings (and also if possible all Newfoundland reservists) are set free from *Niobe*, the Admiralty see no objection to the proposed arrangement. At the same time, the Admiralty have to be prepared for the probability of being called upon to find the crew for another large cruiser for service in American waters. It is not contemplated to commission such a vessel immediately nor, if commissioned, would there probably be any occasion to accept the generous suggestion that the cost of maintenance should be met by the Canadian government. The point which the Admiralty desire to emphasize is the need for making the fullest and most economical use of the available trained personnel, both imperial and dominion and they would value an assurance that any surplus of dominion personnel will at once be notified, so that it may be employed wherever it can most advantageously be used.
>
> As regards the Canadian local patrol, while the Admiralty are anxious to see it set on foot on lines which will admit of its expansion as may be necessary, they think it may not be clearly enough recognized that the submarine danger on the Canadian coast is potential, not actual. Exaggerated measures of precaution are to be deprecated. It is out of the question at the present moment to detach destroyers from Home and Mediterranean waters, where they are employed to meet urgent and pressing needs (and are in fact too few for the work required of them). The Admiralty do not think it would be right to consider seriously the despatch of destroyers to Canada until enemy submarines actually appear in Canadian waters.[76]

Realizing the inadequacy of the small fleet of converted yachts and former fisheries vessels that the RCN had hastily assembled to counter a potential submarine threat, Kingsmill was not amused by the latest Admiralty advice when he finally received Graham-Greene's memorandum in September. It was particularly galling since the director of the naval service would inevitably have to shoulder the blame if and when German submarines began sinking valuable merchant ships in Canadian waters—whether their Lordships had advised against the RCN taking reasonable precautionary measures or not. Responding on 28 September, Kingsmill reminded his political superiors of the many warnings that had come from London throughout the spring and summer of 1915, as well

76. Graham-Greene, "Memorandum for Sir R. Borden," August 1915, 1062–13–4, LAC, RG 24, vol. 4022.

as information Ottawa had received from its own agents in the United States, that had drawn NSHQ's attention to the potential threat of submarine attack. Without raising the matter of the Canadian Cabinet's own frightened reaction to the Admiralty's June warnings, the irked naval director demonstrated both foresight and common sense in defending the relatively small measures his department had instituted to meet the presumed threat.

> With reference to the action taken by this department, I submit that, after due consideration of the following, it will be admitted that the officers of the department have not asked for an unnecessary number of vessels, nor have they taken "exaggerated measures of precaution" which their lordships deprecate.
>
> The commander in chief of the North American and West Indies Station received last November a letter from the Admiralty referring to precautions against enemy minelayers, and on 8th January 1915 he addressed a letter to the Director of Naval Service on the subject…. In sections (C) and (D) of paragraph 4 of this letter he asks for a lookout and patrol service of armed vessels. In reply to this we armed the *Canada* and *Margaret*, and later the *Tuna*, and commissioned them under the White Ensign.
>
> Other correspondence passed between the director of the naval service and commander in chief and the question of patrolling the Gulf of St Lawrence was taken up, and the *Sable I* and *Premier* were armed, every effort being made so that it would not be necessary to incur too much expense. This patrol was for the purpose of preventing attempts of enemy vessels to lay mines.
>
> During June efforts were made to obtain vessels to increase the patrol but these were not obtainable in Canada or Great Britain. Five vessels were asked for. Sir John Eaton of Toronto lent his steam yacht the *Florence;* she was armed and commissioned.
>
> The *Sinmac*, a sea-going tug, was chartered and armed.
>
> Lieut. J.K.L. Ross, RNCVR, purchased a vessel in the United States and presented her to the government for service during the war; she was re-named the *Grilse*, was armed and commissioned. This vessel was subsequently purchased by the government.
>
> Two vessels, re-named the *Hochelaga* and *Stadacona*, were purchased in the United States, refitted at Canadian Vickers, Montreal, armed and commissioned. Twelve small motor boats were also chartered….
>
> With reference to the part of Sir William Graham Greene's memo in which he says that the Admiralty "would value an assurance that any surplus of dominion personnel will at once be notified, so that it may be employed wherever it can most advantageously be used"; our personnel consists almost

entirely of untrained officers and men. Were we given any assistance in the way of instructors we would be able to send to the mother country some ratings whom we could train in our patrol vessels, taken from the seafaring class. They would not be numerous but would help to fill gaps when seamen are required without extensive naval training and would justify the sending of one or two instructors.

With regard to the Canadian local patrol, the memorandum states "while the Admiralty are anxious to see it set on foot on lines which will admit of its expansion as may be necessary," etc., etc.; I must draw attention to the fact that to expand the patrol is not feasible without building. We have now exhausted all available vessels in this country; moreover the speed of the vessels we now have makes them useless for running down submarines. If the Admiralty are unable to detach destroyers now it does not seem likely that they will be able to later on.

As the pressure on the enemy submarines in the war zone increases so does the likelihood of their appearing in Canadian waters; if they do we are not in a position to defend our transports from attack. There is no likelihood of submarines appearing in Canadian waters until next spring but if the war goes on and the Admiralty continue their successful campaign against them, I feel sure that the enemy will attempt a serious attack in the western Atlantic.[77]

Kingsmill's resentment of the Admiralty's admonitions was reinforced when his political masters decided that even the small efforts the RCN had undertaken in the Gulf of St Lawrence were more than either the situation required or the department's budget would allow. The extent of the government's pecuniary thinking was made clear to the naval director on 9 October when he received a message from Desbarats that "the minister, having considered the statement in your memorandum … of September 28th that 'there is no likelihood of submarines appearing in Canadian waters until next spring,' wishes that you would immediately review the present situation of the patrol service with a view to cancelling charters of any vessels that are not required and thus reducing the expenditure on this service. Kindly look into this matter and report as soon as possible."[78] Such gratuitously worded instructions—particularly in view of Hazen's own fearful reaction to the submarine threat in June that had prompted the navy to form the Gulf of St Lawrence patrol in the first place—would have tested the calm of the most faithful government servant. Kingsmill, however, managed to confine himself to the facts when he replied at month's end:

With reference to your memorandum of 9th October, the following action had been taken with regard to cancelling charters of vessels not required during the winter. The *Sinmac* has been directed to return to Canadian Vickers with a view

77. Kingsmill, "Memorandum for the Deputy Minister," 28 September 1915, ibid.

78. Desbarats to Kingsmill, 9 October 1915, ibid.

The crew of HMCS *Canada* in September 1916. The ship's commanding officer, Lieutenant-Commander Charles J. Stuart, is seated in the middle of the second row with the ship's mascot at his feet. Immediately to the right of Stuart is the captain of patrols, Captain F.C.C. Pasco. (DND BN 4277)

to having the gun mounting placed in her by them removed. I do not consider it would be advisable, at any time, to re-charter this vessel for patrol service. Arrangements have been made for laying up the *Premier* at Halifax, when her time of service expires, that is 5th November. A memorandum has been placed before you stating that if the *Acadia* is available during the winter, the services of *Sable I* can be dispensed with. The senior officer of the St Lawrence patrol is endeavouring to recall all the small patrol vessels from the coast of Newfoundland. As soon as their charters expire they will be dispensed with.[79]

Borden's unfair reproach of Kingsmill for having acted on London's warnings—and the naval minister's own spinelessness in not informing the prime minister of his role in urging the navy to take action—marked a disappointing conclusion to the RCN's first patrol season, one in which the naval service had managed to organize a coastal patrol with only minimal resources. No less frustrating was the often contradictory information and advice the Admiralty expected NSHQ to act upon. Some of the apparent confusion was legitimate in that the Royal Navy was responding to German initiatives, but much was not so easily justified. At times Whitehall appeared to view enemy capabilities as intentions and were trying to come up with a response to everything the Germans might do; at other times, it seems that the answers Canada received had more to do with whose desk in the Admiralty its questions crossed than with a considered, collective view.

For his part, however, Kingsmill had no doubts about what his duty to Canada was and did not allow Borden's reproach to deflect him from making arrangements for the 1916 season. Specifically, the naval director sought to establish a scheme to coordinate the patrol activities of the RCN with those of Newfoundland. The Newfoundland Division of the Royal Naval Reserve trained some 1,400 sailors between 1902 and 1914; of the 400 who immediately answered the call to arms in August 1914, 106 were drafted to fill out *Niobe*'s crew for her patrols off New York, while another 600 Newfoundlanders had enlisted in the reserve division by October 1914. The self-governing colony also recruited an infantry battalion, the Newfoundland Regiment, primarily for service overseas, the first 500 of whom had sailed in the convoy carrying the first Canadian contingent to Britain in October.[80] Acting on the same urgent warnings that had prompted NSHQ to set up the Gulf patrol force, St John's had also instituted a coastal patrol to keep a watch for any suspicious activity of vessels during the summer of 1915. As established by the administration's Home Defence Committee, Newfoundland's defensive preparations were meant to cover the colony's coastline outside the Gulf of St Lawrence and consisted of the small patrol vessels *Fogata*, operating off the northeast coast of Newfoundland, *Petrel* patrolling off southeastern Labrador, and *Hump* off northeastern Labrador. Detachments of the Newfoundland Regiment were also posted at selected points along the island's coast, while the Newfoundland Constabulary provided officers to cover the coast of Labrador. A motor

79. Kingsmill to Desbarats, 29 October 1915, ibid.

80. W. David Parsons, "Newfoundland and the Great War," in Briton C. Busch, ed., *Canada and the Great War: Western Front Association Papers* (Montreal and Kingston 2003), 147–48.

boat service similar to Canada's had also been established to make night patrols along the various coasts. The Newfoundland government informed Ottawa in mid-September that it would be discontinuing such defence measures at the conclusion of the navigation season, except for a constabulary detachment that was "to be quartered throughout the winter at the Moravian settlements in which missionaries of German nationality have been permitted to remain at their mission stations, provisionally, until next summer." St John's insisted, however, that "it is intended by the Home Defence Committee to profit from the experiences of this season and to elaborate during the winter so effective a system of control for the next open season that it will be highly perilous for any enemy submarine or supply ship to attempt to utilize a base on shore."[81]

At the end of September, Kingsmill wrote to the commander-in-chief, North America and West Indies Station in Halifax, Vice-Admiral Patey, for his views on the defence arrangements that should be made between Canada and Newfoundland. As the naval director explained, it was "desirable" to reach a suitable patrol arrangement between Newfoundland, the Canadian navy, and the C-in-C "in order to prevent confusion." The principal points Kingsmill believed needed to be addressed were responsibility for joint patrols, which the director felt should be under one officer's control, the lines of communication between the main authorities, and the allotment of defined patrol areas, all of which were matters that could "be most quickly and effectively solved by a conference of representatives of the three parties interested."[82] Although the deputy minister reminded Kingsmill that questions involving government-to-government relations should be submitted to the naval minister first, the naval director waited until he received Patey's response before approaching Hazen with his own views.

Not surprisingly, the British admiral endorsed Kingsmill's suggestions for naval co-operation, including holding a conference of all interested parties. Unable to attend himself, Patey offered to provide advice and suggested that Captain Pasco of the RCN and Commander A. MacDermott, the RN officer in command of the Newfoundland patrols, work out the details for co-operation assisted by "such other departmental members [as] the governments interested may consider desirable." The commander-in-chief also recommended that Pasco "should be in general charge" with MacDermott as his assistant, responsible for the Newfoundland area. Specific patrol areas would best be defined by the two officers involved with all reports from the Canadian area being sent directly to Sydney, while those from Newfoundland would be sent to Pasco via St John's. In the British admiral's view, MacDermott should "deal at once with situations requiring immediate action in his areas, informing senior officer at Sydney of action taken," while Pasco would keep the commander-in-chief informed of all patrol reports through the naval staff at Halifax.[83]

81. Governor of Newfoundland to Governor General of Canada, 16 September 1915, 1065–4-1, LAC, RG 24, vol. 4030.

82. Kingsmill to C-in-C, NA&WI, 29 September 1915, ibid.

83. Patey to Kingsmill, 23 October 1915, ibid.

Armed with the advice of the senior British naval officer in the Western Atlantic, Kingsmill approached Hazen on 11 November, explaining that the existence of three different naval authorities exercising control over patrol operations on the Canadian and Newfoundland coasts had "led to a certain amount of uncertainty, overlapping and confusion, and it is considered most desirable that during the winter an organised scheme of operations should be laid down before next spring." Noting the commander-in-chief's agreement, Kingsmill suggested that the Newfoundland government "be invited to send representatives to a conference to be held in Ottawa at a later date."[84] The proposal was quickly endorsed by the naval minister who also suggested Halifax as an equally suitable location for the conference.[85] As is often the case in negotiations, both sides were anxious to have the discussions held on their own territory, where they would have the advantage of immediate consultation and were more likely to be able to influence delegates. At the suggestion of the Newfoundland prime minister, the island's governor, W.E. Davidson, wrote Canada's governor general to propose that Pasco be authorized "to visit St John's for the purpose of an informal conference. Some such informal exchange of views would be useful as a preliminary measure, to clear the issues and settle the general scope of the precautions to be adopted in 1916 for the defence of the shipping and the coast from the possible depredations of hostile submarines."[86] Writing confidentially to the Duke of Connaught that same day, Davidson agreed that there should be "close cooperation between the Dominion of Canada and the Colony of Newfoundland" although Newfoundland's contribution was "necessarily limited to its means." The governor also agreed that command of the patrols should be "under one central control" but felt that the colony would be able to handle the land defence of its own coastline against enemy landings "provided that such hostile acts are not carried out with forces exceeding those carried on submarines or supply ships." Davidson believed, however, that the extent of the area to be patrolled should not exceed 320 kilometres from the Atlantic steamship routes that passed through the Cabot Straits. The governor envisaged the colony's contribution to the patrol as being four to six "suitably armed vessels" of the 100-ton whaling steamer type, two or three of which were available in Newfoundland, crewed by members of the Newfoundland RNR "in the pay of the Admiralty."[87]

Although both sides were in basic agreement as to the intended patrol arrangements, the government-to-government nature of the negotiations inevitably slowed what should have been a straightforward conference, as correspondence was passed up and down diplomatic channels between governor and governor general. Becoming worried at the lack of progress, the naval director finally wrote to Desbarats in early January to express his frustration at the navy's inability to settle strictly naval questions, pointing out "that the winter is rapidly advancing and this is a matter which should be taken up without

---

84. Kingsmill, "Memorandum for the Information of the Minister," 11 November 1915, ibid.

85. Desbarats minute, 15 November 1915, ibid.

86. W.E. Davidson (Governor of Newfoundland) to Governor General, 15 December 1915, ibid.

87. Davidson to Governor General, personal and confidential,15 December 1915, ibid.

The ice-encrusted forward gun of HMCS *Stadacona* in early 1916. Although the RCN's patrol vessels normally operated in the approaches to Halifax during the winter months, that did not mean they escaped rough seas and bitter cold. The pre-dreadnought battleship HMS *Caesar* can be seen in the distance. (DND CN 4065)

delay. I am not aware in what way the attendance of Captain Pasco, the officer I would suggest should represent the naval service, should commit the Canadian government to any action, but if we can find out what they propose over there, we may be able to draw up some scheme on which we can get the opinion of the officer in charge of this station, namely the commander in chief of HM ships and vessels."[88] One week later the naval minister agreed that Pasco should proceed to St John's to begin informal discussions with the Newfoundland government.[89] Demonstrating the urgency with which he regarded the conference, Kingsmill immediately provided the senior officer of patrols with instructions to guide him in the negotiations:

> On arrival report yourself to his excellency the governor, as the representative of the Department of the Naval Service of Canada, and that you have come with a view to consulting with his officers as to the best means of preventing the enemy forming bases etc. on the Atlantic coast for submarines or other purposes. You are to have it understood that you are not empowered to commit the dominion government to any action whatever, but you may state for the information of his excellency and officers that you will have for patrol purposes, the following armed vessels: *Grilse, Canada, Margaret, Stadacona* and *Hochelaga;* also *Gulnare, Petrel* and *Florence,* unarmed and available for coast patrol; that it is proposed at present to patrol with these latter, or others, the north shore of the Gulf of St Lawrence from Belle Isle. It must be borne in mind that the armed patrol are not of sufficient tonnage to undertake long cruises at sea.
>
> The question of patrolling the banks of Newfoundland will crop up. I am of opinion that the enemy may find it more difficult to establish a base on our territory than to obtain supplies from a supply ship cruising with the fishing fleet. Vessels similar to the fishing vessels might be obtained and loaded with oil and stores and rendezvous off the banks and I consider the best means, after considering fast cruisers, would be to employ the same class of vessel to meet this contingency.
>
> Another thing to be considered is the fact that it is almost impossible to obtain any steam vessels in Canada suitable for patrol. The Newfoundland authorities state there are several useful vessels to be had; you should inspect each and report, and obtain if possible, an offer for charter, crew to be provided excepting engineers.[90]

Pasco visited Newfoundland in early February, where he met with the Defence Committee of the Executive Council of Newfoundland on the 12th for a general discussion

---

88. Kingsmill to Desbarats, 5 January 1916, ibid.

89. Desbarats to Undersecretary of State for External Affairs, 12 January 1916, ibid.

90. Kingsmill to Senior Officer of Patrols, 12 January 1916, Kingsmill to Pasco, 13 January 1916, ibid.

of the patrol question. The Newfoundland government stated at the outset that it did not believe that the length of patrolled coastline needed to be extended—and that St John's was unable to undertake an expansion in any case—and that it planned to have only two armed vessels, both equipped with wireless, detailed to the coastal patrol. It also did not believe that any patrol was necessary until ice had cleared from the many bays and inlets in mid-June and that the most likely place for an enemy supply vessel to operate was on the outer edge of the Grand Banks fishery rather than from a shore base. As a result, the Newfoundland government planned to have four additional armed vessels to patrol the outer edge of the Grand Banks, two of which would be on patrol with the other two in relief. It was hoped that the four vessels would be steam trawlers outfitted with screened guns so that they would retain their commercial fishing appearance, but the St John's negotiators made it clear that they expected "these vessels to be chartered by Canada; Newfoundland government providing and paying the crews." As partial recompense, the cash-strapped St John's administration was willing to loan the RCN up to fifty of its trained Newfoundland RNR sailors to help man Canadian patrol vessels, although they would be paid by Ottawa. Pasco was also made aware of the difficulties involved in either warning or protecting the fishing fleets: "The question arose as to the method to be adopted to receive information from the large fishing fleets. These vessels all act independently and return to land for bait, etc., at odd intervals, and without reference to each other in any way, therefore, the idea, originally entertained by me, of fitting wireless in the craft captained by the Admiral of the fishing fleet, and from whom the patrol vessels could receive reports of anything suspicious, fell through, as no such organisation exists."[91]

The Newfoundland delegation also agreed that the sea patrol would be "under the sole control of Captain Pasco" at Sydney. It was stipulated, however, that the "three or four" vessels of the Grand Banks patrol would be based in St John's and controlled by MacDermott as Pasco's deputy. Canada was also to arm and equip a schooner with wireless for the Grand Banks, her duty being "to board all unknown and foreign fishing vessels and to collect and communicate to the patrol any information picked up amongst the fishing fleet. The crew to be men with a knowledge of the types of craft usually visiting the banks. The vessel to be manned in Newfoundland and based on a Newfoundland port." St John's would control the two vessels, one of which would be the Newfoundland customs vessel *Fiona*, detailed to patrol the coast of the main island from St Pierre east to Belle Isle "but with the distinct understanding that her patrol duties take precedence, and that the senior naval officer, Sydney, can order her to visit any point should he need to." All the Newfoundland patrol arrangements were in addition to the RCN's own Gulf patrol.[92]

Even as Kingsmill was concurring in the proposed patrol arrangements for the 1916 season, the question of the Canadian navy's ability to defend the nation's coasts was raised in the House of Commons in Ottawa. Upon returning from a visit to the Halifax dockyard in March 1916, the Liberal member for Pictou, Nova Scotia, E.M MacDonald, presented a

91. Pasco to Kingsmill, 18 February 1916, ibid.

92. Davidson to Morris, "Memorandum," 12 February 1916, enclosed in Governor of Newfoundland to Governor General of Canada, 14 February 1916, ibid.

Although HMCS *Acadia*, seen here in September 1918, was not formally commissioned until 1917, the hydrographic vessel had performed naval duties since 1914. She carried a 4-inch gun forward but her usefulness as a patrol vessel was hampered by her eight-knot top speed. (LAC e007140896)

motion for the government to provide "a return showing a list of vessels, belonging to the Canadian government which are on service under the provision of the Canadian Naval Act, and of all vessels not now in service and their present condition."[93] Specifically, the Pictou MP complained that "while we have heard a great deal about what Canada is doing upon the land, we have heard nothing about what Canada is doing on the sea, or about what she ought to do on the sea." MacDonald then proceeded to ask a series of pointed questions about the government's conduct of naval affairs since the outbreak of war, questions that cast serious doubt on the seriousness with which Prime Minister Borden viewed Canadian naval affairs. The MP's comments were particularly telling given the obvious absence of any purpose-built warships, such as destroyers or submarines, other than *Niobe*, from the RCN's East Coast order of battle. Why, the member wanted to know, was Canada in the "humiliating position that apparently we have no vessels of any kind, and that, if any German ships made their escape from a conflict in the North Sea, and came across the Atlantic, we would be absolutely defenceless," whereas "Australia has not only her own defence provided for, but she is able to send the [cruisers] *Sydney* and *Melbourne* on service, both of these warships having, during the past six or seven months, formed part of the British squadron which is at present in the southern Atlantic"? Why had the Admiralty ordered submarines from the Vickers's plant in Montreal, while the Canadian government had not placed any orders for either destroyers or submarines? Why had Newfoundland sent a thousand sailors to serve in the Royal Navy, while Canada had sent only a handful? Why had the government recruited naval volunteers in British Columbia but had "not ask[ed] the men in the fishing counties of eastern Canada to serve in the navy?" Why had the Canadian navy purchased yachts, such as *Stadacona*, in the United States when "any one who visited the Halifax dockyard last January could see that she was not in condition to go to sea" or relied on gifts of vessels being made by wealthy Canadians such as Sir John Eaton?

> Then there was the *Tuna*, which was being repaired, and is still undergoing repairs. Then there was the *Margaret*, a small boat; I don't know where she was, but any one who has seen her would realize that she was not fit for Atlantic service. With the exception of the *Niobe*, these were the only vessels that the Canadian Naval Service had at Halifax in January 1916. The *Niobe* was tied up at the wharf, with her guns dismantled, and she was being stripped. A house had been built over her for winter, and there was a large number of men going up and down her decks, apparently doing nothing. I think about seven hundred men were on board, and apparently they were there without any purpose whatever. So the only vessel we had on the Atlantic coast in January 1916 was this small vessel the *Canada*. Is that a proper position for a self-respecting country like Canada to be in?.... I would like to know from the Minister of the Naval Service why Canada has not determined to do her part with men on the sea, as she has done with the men on the land.[94]

---

93. Canada, Parliament, House of Commons, *Debates*, 13 March 1916, 1667.

94. Ibid, 1671–72.

The naval minister largely deflected the Pictou MP's questioning of the government's anaemic naval policy by returning to an earlier debate where MacDonald had raised questions about the Halifax dockyard appearing to be idle during a visit he had made on 2 January. Hazen tried to belittle the MP's concerns by pointing out that he "naturally finds the dockyard a quiet spot on Sunday, especially on a Sunday succeeding a holiday so generally observed as New Year's Day. It is hardly fair for the hon. gentleman to represent the condition he found on Sunday as being the ordinary conditions prevailing in this dockyard. As a matter of fact, since the war broke out, the dockyard has been an extremely busy place. A large number of warships have been based upon Halifax, and the work of repairing these ships and keeping up their supplies, filling vacancies in their crews, providing for their sick and finding accommodation for the crews sent out to recommission them has proved quite a tax on the small staff maintained at the yard.... It has, not only in our opinion, but in the opinion of the lords of the Admiralty as well, been doing extremely good work."[95]

The naval minister also took some political satisfaction in suggesting that the failure to provide the Royal Navy with major warships, as the Australians had done, was because the Liberals in the senate had voted down the Borden government's bill to pay the cost of three dreadnoughts. "While we have not been able to do very much in the way of actual defensive operations ... we could have done a great deal in the way of defensive and offensive operations if we had had those three capital ships of war; and more than that, my hon. friends opposite, when they were in power, might have done something if they had not held up their tenders for six months in order, in the elections of 1911, to get the votes of people in certain localities by making them believe that each of those localities would be the place where the ships would be built when the contracts were finally entered into. My hon. friend opposite says that we are doing nothing; that we have only had vessels for patrol work and minesweeping purposes. All that work has been entered upon by the naval department after careful consultation with the authorities of the Admiralty, with their full approval and in some cases at their request."[96]

Hazen countered Macdonald's criticism that Ottawa was failing to provide the Royal Navy with personnel by producing the British government's own requests that Canada concentrate her recruiting efforts in expanding and keeping up to strength the Canadian Expeditionary Force on the Western Front. Nonetheless, the naval department had assisted in forwarding a number of retired or reserve naval officers and ratings who were resident in Canada at the outbreak of war. Hazen estimated their number to be several hundred "and may possibly have exceeded 1,000." He also announced that 200 officers had entered the Royal Naval Air Service (RNAS) from Canada, of which 176 had already been sent overseas. In addition, the Admiralty had asked the naval department "to have lists made of the men willing to serve in the Royal Naval Reserve Motor Boat Patrol. We called for applications, and several hundred applications have been received up to the present time. We are informed by the Admiralty, who asked us to prepare a list of these men, that an

---

95. Ibid, 1671–72.

96. Ibid, 1679.

officer is coming to Canada to look over the men who have applied, to examine them for their fitness and make selections from their number."[97]

In his remarks on the navy's role in the war effort to date, the naval minister also raised the important (and often overlooked) part the RCN was playing in overseeing the shipment of vital war supplies across the Atlantic through an organization being run by the acting director of overseas transport, A.H. Harris.[98] Indeed, with the threat of German submarine attack still confined to European waters some 3,000 kilometres from Canada's shores, the navy's greatest contribution to the war effort in the first two years of the conflict may well have been the assistance the department rendered in forwarding the country's agricultural produce and growing war production to the fighting front. At the same time, the navy's close involvement with A.H. Harris gave NSHQ a deeper appreciation of the Canadian transportation network's organization and problems, an understanding of which was to inform the department's decisions for defending the nation's East Coast shipping lanes throughout the war.

Nonetheless, the ad hoc nature of the administrative arrangements between the Canadian naval department and the acting director of overseas transport also resulted in a relationship that was, at times, uneasy. The rationale for a government-controlled transportation service to organize the shipment of war supplies to Europe had arisen soon after the declaration of war. On 24 August, the Colonial Office had telegraphed the Canadian government asking Ottawa if it could find homeward freights for the Admiralty-chartered colliers that were stockpiling coal in North America for the Royal Navy warships operating in the northwest Atlantic. The Naval Service complied by finding ordinary commercial cargoes for the ships' return voyages but at the end of September 1914 the Admiralty made the additional request that NSHQ also arrange for the transportation of army service wagons bound for the United Kingdom. The appeal quickly resulted in the naval department being asked to provide ocean transport for large quantities of war office stores, which were subsequently shipped overseas using both private freighters and Admiralty colliers. The growing volume of war-related shipping convinced the Canadian government of the importance of securing the services of an expert overseas transportation officer to coordinate traffic, and after approaching the president of the Canadian Pacific Railway Company concerning the appointment of an acting director of overseas transport, Sir Thomas Shaughnessy readily agreed to place the services of one of his senior employees, A.H. Harris, at the government's disposal, together with a number of CP staff and their Montreal offices, the company continuing to pay all their salaries. As Harris later explained, "immediately on my appointment, I entered into negotiations for the chartering of suitable vessels, and by anticipating charter conditions and securing ships in many instances months in advance of requirements, the government was enabled to move war materiel, munitions, supplies, etc., at ocean freights approximating those prevailing in normal times."[99]

---

97. Ibid, 1680.

98. Ibid, 1681.

99. A.H. Harris, "Memorandum," 3 January 1916, 1048–18–2, LAC, RG 24, vol. 3714.

Even with these measures in place, however, the volume of war-related traffic across the Atlantic quickly led to a shortage of available tonnage and a rapid rise in freight rates. Writing to the British government at the end of January 1915, the Canadian acting high commissioner in London, Sir George Perley, inquired into the steps London proposed to alleviate the great increases that were occurring in the cost of shipping war supplies:

> I am glad to see that a special committee of the cabinet is at present considering the increasing prices of food, as they are no doubt in large measure due to the freight rates, for which it is very necessary that some remedy should be found. I am just in receipt of a cable from my prime minister showing that the Canadian government is greatly exercised over the situation in this regard. He tells me that freights have enormously increased during the past two weeks, and that the cost of transport will become entirely excessive on supplies ordered in Canada by the British and Allied governments unless some remedy is found. He suggests that the British government might arrange so that some of the ships now held under charter by the Admiralty might be assigned for the purpose of carrying supplies and war material from Canada to Great Britain in order to save the situation ... In this connection I may say that, during the past few days, we have received from the War Office an order to furnish from Canada four thousand tons a week each of hay and oats during the next five months. This is in addition to many orders for other kinds of supplies and munitions of war, and it will be impossible to fill them all unless the necessary tonnage can be obtained at reasonable rates. Canada is of course much interested in this question because we want to provide as much work as possible for our people at this period, and at the same time I take it that it is imperative for you to make all arrangements necessary to enable this country to obtain the requisite food and war supplies.[100]

The Canadian government soon despatched the acting director of overseas shipping to London to secure more reasonably priced transport. Meeting with War Office officials on 9 February, Harris pointed out that, even at this early stage of the war, the scarcity of ocean tonnage combined with excessive freight rates had led to congestion on the nation's railways as some 600 fully loaded freight cars of war materiel were sitting idle at Canadian ports:

> A statement was submitted showing that during the next five months the shipments of forage from Canada to Havre [France] will amount to 10,000 tons a week (5,000 tons of hay and 5,000 tons of oats). Transport must also be found for large quantities of clothing, saddlery, ammunition, oleum and other supplies for the War Office. It is estimated that for these purposes shipping of the capacity of over 1,200,000 cubic feet will be required each week. In addition the dominion government have undertaken to transport blankets and

---

100. Sir George Perley to Walter Runciman, 27 January 1915, 1048–18–5, ibid.

artillery harness and saddlery for the French government and also 8,000 horses (to be shipped in the next 60 days) as well as remounts at 1,500 a month, for the Canadian contingent.[101]

As a result of Harris's plea, the Admiralty agreed to allocate eighteen of its previously chartered merchant ships to Canada for the shipment of war supplies, six of which were suitable for transporting remounts for the army. The British also promised to assign further ships to the Canadian service as the volume of war supplies increased. In view of such arrangements, Perley was able to report to Borden that "the time happened to be exactly right for getting something done. The question of high freight rates and lack of shipping has been under considerable discussion here for two or three months, and we have made several efforts to try and get the departments here to find some remedy. However, during the last three or four weeks the question has become very acute.... Under these circumstances, Mr Harris' arrival here was well-timed, and the work which we have been able to do in a fortnight would ordinarily have taken three or four times as long. I want you to know that I think Mr Harris has been very tactful and successful in his discussions with the officials here."[102]

Having secured a small portion of the Admiralty's chartered merchant ships, Harris set about organizing the overseas transport service from his Canadian Pacific offices at the port of Montreal. The fact that Sir Thomas Shaughnessy had made his experienced staff available to the government greatly simplified what would otherwise have been a monumental task had the tiny naval department been assigned complete responsibility. The importance of having the CPR's transport professionals on hand was certainly appreciated by NSHQ in explaining their relationship with Harris a few months later:

> The Canadian Pacific Railway Company have handled, free of all charges, except the usual nominal agency fee of $100, all the clerical work and supervision involved in loading these steamers. Accounts for pilotage, stevedoring, port charges, etc., have been defrayed by them and collected from the department.... Arrangements have been completed so that all munitions of War handled by this department, the Department of Agriculture, the Canadian Shell Committee and the British Army Supply Office in Montreal are forwarded for shipment to the acting DOT [Director of Overseas Transport] at Shed 16, Montreal. This shed was rented by the various departments concerned from the Board of Harbour Commissioners for storage of these supplies and loading of transports....
>
> This department works in conjunction with the Admiralty as regards the movement of these ships, their sailing orders and cargoes—the organization of the latter being specially entrusted to the acting DOT. Full details of the cargo are cabled to the Admiralty, giving the date of sailing, port of discharge and probable date of arrival, in the case of each transport so that the necessary

101. "Note of Conference at War Office, 9th February 1915," nd, 1048–17–4, pt. 1, LAC, RG 24, vol. 3707.

102. Sir George Perley to Sir Robert Borden, 17 February 1915, 1048–18–5, LAC, RG 24, vol. 3714.

arrangements may be made in advance for speedy dispatch on arrival and distribution of cargo. This concentration of the export of supplies has undoubtedly facilitated the movement of stores from this country and has also resulted in economies amounting to hundreds of thousands of dollars if not into millions.

In order to meet more completely the wishes of the Admiralty in respect of sailing directions and advance advice of sailings and with a view of obtaining still further economies of valuable time and space the Department of Militia and Defence have been approached with a view to making this consolidation of export traffic more complete. They have expressed themselves ready to avail themselves of these facilities if the necessity arises.

With regard to the transportation of troops—the Admiralty in cases where they have supplied ships have made the necessary arrangements as to requisition, sailing orders and escort through this department. With regard to transportation, the Admiralty considers this department responsible that all ships leaving Canada with government stores or troops, receive proper sailing directions. The necessity, therefore, from this point of view, of all shipments from Canada being handled by one person such as the acting DOT is apparent.

The tonnage handled up to date by this transport service exceeds 300,000 tons, and includes shipments of hay, oats, shells, waggons, motor trucks, sleighs, clothing, harness, oleum, acetone, and many miscellaneous items. The A[cting]DOT has reported direct on this work to the prime minister.[103]

An important part of Harris's—and NSHQ's—task was to convince the various government agencies and departments forwarding war supplies to Europe that they could do so more economically by making use of the newly created overseas transport organization. A hard-driving, confident businessman whose friendship with Borden afforded him direct access to the prime minister, the CP manager was never afraid to take on greater responsibilities as the war progressed. By May 1915, Harris was already attempting to extend his transportation organization to cover the entire area of northeastern North America—the rationale for which he explained to the naval department's director of stores, J.A. Wilson, as a reasonable cost-cutting measure.

Purchasing agents of the imperial government in Canada, including the Canada Shell Committee, could with advantage be instructed to advise manufacturers to consign all material to director overseas transport, Montreal. The supplies would be forwarded on transports and prompt movement ensured. In cases where transports or colliers were not available and time [was] an element, freight engagements would be made by the director overseas transport with ordinary liners.

---

103. Naval Service memorandum, "Transportation," [June 1915], 1048–17–1, pt. 1, LAC, RG 24, vol. 3706.

War Office supplies purchased in the United States at points north of the Ohio River could with advantage to the imperial government be routed inland to Montreal consigned to director overseas transport and thence forwarded on Admiralty ships to destination. If additional transports were found necessary they could be supplied on time charter by the Admiralty, thereby effecting saving in freights and commissions. Common prudence would dictate due consideration being given to this suggestion in view of the recent decision of the American Line not to carry further consignments of war material, and the possibility that similar action may be taken by English companies operating passenger vessels between US north Atlantic ports and Liverpool. In case of War Office material which of necessity must be exported through New York, Philadelphia or Baltimore, supervision could also be exercised by the director of overseas transport. The New York export organization of the Canadian Pacific is effective and could be utilized as an adjunct to the Office....

I was told in confidence that the naval service had recently received cable instructions from the Admiralty advising that arrangements had been made with Messrs Lunham & Moore, Freight Brokers, New York, to supervise the freighting, inland and ocean, of all war material and supplies purchased on account of the British government in the United States and Canada for [financial] consideration ... Freight brokers are paid a commission by ship owners to secure cargoes for vessels or vessels for cargoes, the cargoes and vessels in the case of Canada are furnished by the British government, hence the uneconomic spectacle is presented of foreign freight brokers being paid a commission by the British government to supervise the forwarding of supplies which in so far as Canada is concerned can be carried on Admiralty time chartered transports, the general supervision of which is being conducted by a staff of trained CP officials as a labor of love.[104]

Harris was, of course, correct to point out the savings available to the government by centralizing the shipment of war supplies under his control. He did not mention, however, that the shipment of a greater volume of freight through Montreal, much of which was brought to the port over his company's rail lines, was also good business for both Canadian Pacific and the port of Montreal. Doing his part in helping to rationalize the movement of Canadian war supplies, J.A. Wilson informed both the chairman of the Canadian Shell Committee and the British Army supply depot in Montreal of the financial savings to be had by shipping materiel by way of the Admiralty chartered vessels being provided solely for the movement of government stores free of ocean freight charges. Since the Shell Committee already had to provide the naval department with the particulars of any ships it was using to transport shells to Britain, it was a relatively easy task to convince them to make use of Harris's organization.[105]

104. A.H. Harris to J.A. Wilson, 14 May 1915, ibid.

105. J. A. Wilson to Col. Bartram, Chairman, Canadian Shell Committee and to Lt. J.A. Johnston, British Army Supply Depot, Montreal, 21 May 1915, ibid.

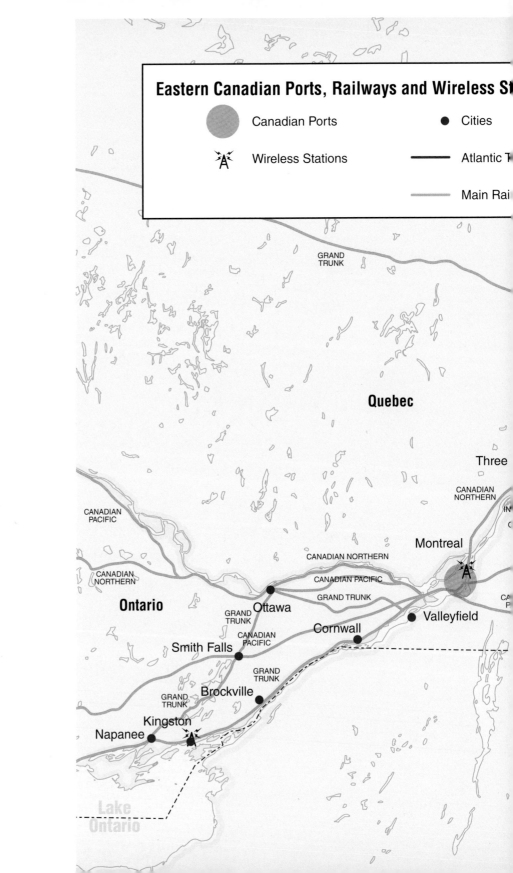

Eastern Canadian Ports, Railways and Wireless S[tations]

Canadian Ports   ● Cities

Wireless Stations   —— Atlantic T[...]

—— Main Rai[l...]

GRAND
TRUNK

Quebec

Three

CANADIAN
NORTHERN

CANADIAN
PACIFIC

CANADIAN
NORTHERN

CANADIAN NORTHERN

Montreal

CANADIAN PACIFIC

Ontario   GRAND TRUNK

GRAND
TRUNK   **Ottawa**   ● **Valleyfield**

CANADIAN
PACIFIC   **Cornwall**

Smith Falls

GRAND
TRUNK

GRAND
TRUNK   **Brockville**

Kingston

Napanee

Lake
Ontario

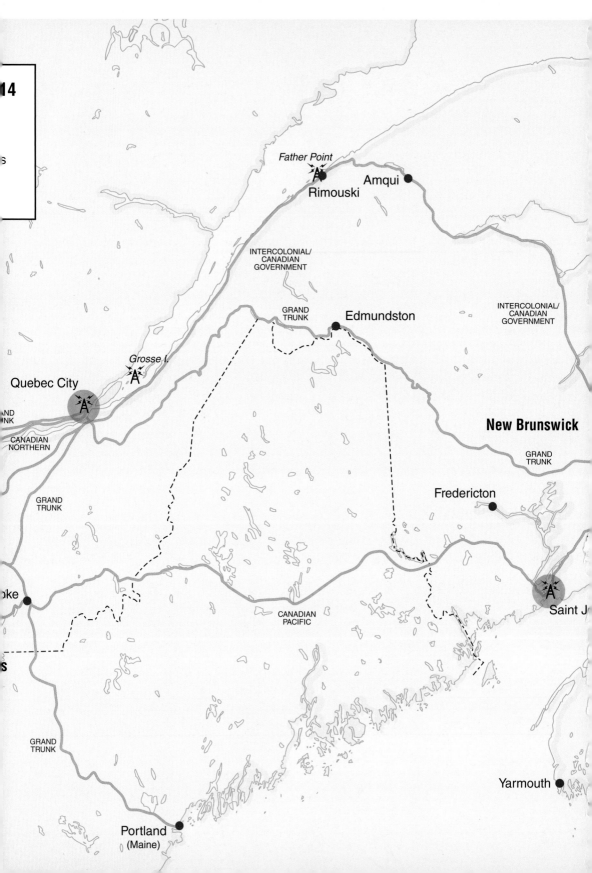

14

Father Point
Rimouski
Amqui

INTERCOLONIAL/
CANADIAN
GOVERNMENT

GRAND
TRUNK
Edmundston

INTERCOLONIAL/
CANADIAN
GOVERNMENT

Grosse I.

Quebec City

ND
NK

CANADIAN
NORTHERN

New Brunswick

GRAND
TRUNK

GRAND
TRUNK

Fredericton

oke

CANADIAN
PACIFIC

Saint J

s

GRAND
TRUNK

Yarmouth

Portland
(Maine)

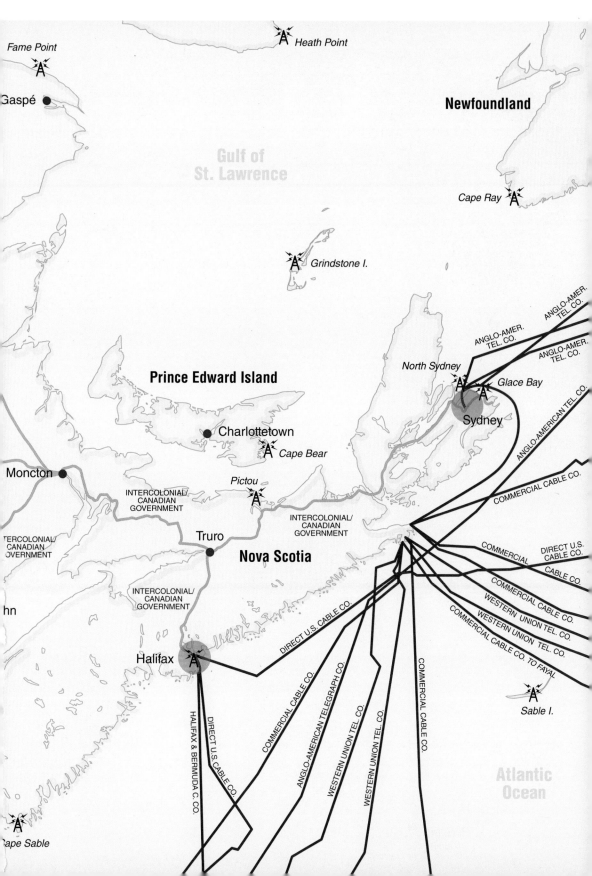

Fame Point

Gaspé

Heath Point

Newfoundland

Gulf of
St. Lawrence

Cape Ray

Grindstone I.

Prince Edward Island

North Sydney

Glace Bay

ANGLO-AMER.
TEL. CO.

ANGLO-AMER.
TEL. CO.

ANGLO-AMER.
TEL. CO.

Sydney

ANGLO-AMERICAN TEL. CO.

Charlottetown

Cape Bear

Moncton

Pictou

INTERCOLONIAL/
CANADIAN
GOVERNMENT

INTERCOLONIAL/
CANADIAN
GOVERNMENT

COMMERCIAL CABLE CO.

TERCOLONIAL/
OVERNMENT

Truro

Nova Scotia

COMMERCIAL
CABLE CO.

DIRECT U.S.
CABLE CO.

INTERCOLONIAL/
CANADIAN
GOVERNMENT

COMMERCIAL CABLE CO.

WESTERN UNION TEL. CO.

hn

WESTERN UNION TEL. CO.

COMMERCIAL CABLE CO. TO FAVAL

DIRECT U.S. CABLE CO.

Halifax

Sable I.

HALIFAX & BERMUDA C. CO.

DIRECT U.S. CABLE CO.

COMMERCIAL CABLE CO.

ANGLO-AMERICAN TELEGRAPH CO.

WESTERN UNION TEL. CO.

WESTERN UNION TEL. CO.

COMMERCIAL CABLE CO.

Atlantic
Ocean

Cape Sable

The Canadian militia department was initially reluctant to make use of the new transport organization and stubbornly preferred to continue making its own transport arrangements with little regard for either Harris's expertise or the Canadian navy's role in the process. The dangers and inefficiencies created by the army's deliberate lack of co-operation were well-illustrated during May and June, when the militia department despatched a series of vessels overseas without informing NSHQ of their departure. Lacking that information, NSHQ was unable to notify the Admiralty of their expected arrival in British home waters, leaving the British service unable to ensure either the availability of local escort or the necessary arrangements for the ships' prompt unloading once in port. The navy's thoughtful chief of staff realized that the "difficulty is primarily caused by the creation of the naval department. [Other] departments and officials have been slow to realize that a new department has been brought into being, which of necessity must take away from other departments certain portions of their previous work. In the past, all [military] transport arrangements have been in the hands of the militia department because there was no other department to handle them."[106]

Although sensitive to the likely cause of the problem, NSHQ was not about to abrogate its responsibility to ensure that all transports received the latest Admiralty orders and submarine reports—something that was not happening with independent sailings organized by the militia department—and that information on their departure was quickly communicated to London.[107] But all attempts to persuade the army to change its procedures failed. Worse still, it turned out that four of the eighteen transports allocated to Canada were actually handed over to the militia department—to continue in its independent, and careless, ways.[108] Harris (and the navy) complained, to no effect, until a conference was called in August to resolve the matter. Writing to the acting prime minister, Sir George Foster, on 4 August, Desbarats outlined the naval department's position.

> The difficulties which have arisen between the naval and militia departments are due primarily to the question of the safety of the transports at sea. The Admiralty, and the naval department acting in cooperation with them, are responsible for their safety, and cannot divest themselves of this responsibility if they would. It is therefore, necessary that the provision of ships, their movements, sailing instructions and general control should be in naval hands....
>
> The government appointed Mr A.H. Harris as acting director of overseas

106. Stephens, "Memorandum: For the Director of the Naval Service," 27 June 1915, 1048–17–12, LAC, RG 24, vol. 3711.

107. Stephens to Desbarats, 1 July 1915, ibid; and Stephens to Military Secretary, Interdepartmental Committee, 9 June 1915, Stephens, "Memorandum Regarding the Transportation of Stores," 9 June 1915, 1048–18–2, LAC, RG 24, vol. 3714.

108. Stephens to Desbarats, 1 July 1915, 1048–17–12, LAC, RG 24, vol. 3711; R.S. White, Collector of Customs, Montreal to Commander Stephens, 14 June 1915, Major-General W. Gwatkin to Stephens, 19 June 1915, Harris to Stephens, 15, 17 and 19 June 1915, Harris to Desbarats, 23 June 1915, Desbarats to deputy minister, Dept. of Militia and Defence, 28 July 1915, 1048–17–1, pt. 1, LAC, RG 24, vol. 3706; and Harris to Borden, 25 June 1915, 1048–18–2, LAC, RG 24, vol. 3714.

transport and his organization has been utilized to consolidate all shipments from Canada. This arrangement may now be considered in good working order except that certain branches in the militia do not take advantage of it. The result again is that information necessary for the safety of the ship may be overlooked. This has frequently happened and has been the source of a great deal of trouble and also of danger to transports.

The aim of the naval department is therefore to consolidate all government freight with a view to both economy and efficiency. At this forthcoming conference it is desired only to settle the main question of responsibility, the details being left for discussion between departmental officials. It is not the desire of the naval department to interfere in any way with existing methods and requirements of the militia department.[109]

The results of the 5 August meeting completely vindicated the RCN's position in regard to control of ocean transports. Despite sending an impressive militia delegation to the meeting, including the acting minister, the deputy minister, the chief of the general staff, the quartermaster general, and the director of supplies and transport, to meet with the navy's two representatives, Desbarats and Stephens, the force of the navy's argument for sole control of transport was obvious. The meeting agreed "that relations should be readjusted between the Department of the Naval Service and the Department of Militia and Defence, for otherwise it would be impossible to avoid the mischievous results of dual control and divided responsibility; and that, in connection with oversea transport, there were duties, hitherto performed by the militia department which should be assumed forthwith by the Department of the Naval Service."[110] As a face saving measure, the militia department was allowed to continue to charter other vessels, as required, for troops and cargo provided that arrangements for the shipping of war supplies was left in the hands of the acting director of overseas transport. The RCN's overall responsibility was underscored by the fact that, for all transports, whether chartered by the Admiralty or the militia, the navy was "to take sole charge directly embarkation has been carried out; to issue all orders to masters; and to be the medium of correspondence with the Admiralty. The militia department is relieved of all responsibility for the protection of transports while at sea."[111]

As the government department responsible for the despatch of all merchant ships overseas from Canadian ports, including those transporting troops, horses, and stores for the militia, the expansion of the naval service's administrative duties ashore should not be overlooked—as the Liberal member for Pictou had done in the House of Commons—when assessing the importance of the RCN's wartime role. The progress that Harris's transport organization was able to make in forwarding supplies to Britain and France, even before the Admiralty-chartered transports were made available, was impressive. From 28 August

---

109. Desbarats to Sir George Foster, 4 August 1915, 1048–17–12, LAC, RG 24, vol. 3711.

110. "Memorandum, Oversea Transport," [5 August 1915], ibid.

111. Ibid.

1914 to the close of navigation that year, Harris shipped 119,701 tons of supplies on imperial and Canadian account from the port of Montreal, Canada's main shipping terminal. Over the winter of 1914–15, when shipments were made from the all-season ports of Halifax, Nova Scotia, and West St John, New Brunswick, Harris's organization sent a further 125,212 tons of supplies overseas. Writing directly to Sir Robert Borden on 20 May 1915—one of a series of regular updates Harris routinely provided the prime minister—the acting director of overseas transport estimated that savings to the British government from August 1914 to the end of April 1915 amounted to $1,000,000 compared with the freight rates of the Canada-Havre Line and $1,800,000 on the New York ocean lines.[112]

Numbers increased markedly once Montreal reopened to navigation in 1915. From an average of 42,000 tons of supplies shipped each month from May to July 1915, 58,544 tons cleared from Canadian ports in August, 69,891 tons in September, 70,037 tons in October, and a new high of 107,370 tons in November 1915.[113] Once ice closed the St Lawrence to navigation, the shipment of supplies naturally shifted to Halifax and St John. Of the two East Coast ports, the greatest volume of supplies passed through St John, where the naval department had expanded facilities at Harris's urging. The president of Canadian Pacific Railways also handed control of virtually all movement on the CP rail line between Montreal and St John over to the acting DOT, enabling Harris to ensure a steady flow of supplies to the New Brunswick port. From December 1915 to the end of March 1916, 322,033 tons of war materiel were shipped from St John, while Halifax handled an additional 181,187 tons. The numbers for the previous winter had been 63,993 and 14,516 tons, respectively.[114]

The war supplies shipped in the first months of the war consisted mainly of oats and hay to feed the enormous number of horses used by First World War armies, as well as preserved meat, cheese, timber, clothing and equipment, saddlery and harness, oleum (overproof sulphuric acid), wagons, and remounts. At this stage of the war, the production of artillery shells and ammunition in Canada had not yet reached significant levels. By June 1915 there were sufficient munitions being produced in Canada to ship 1,000 tons of shell each week. As Harris informed his counterpart at the Admiralty, the Director of Transports, Sir Graeme Thomson, the shells would "be distributed in the various holds to facilitate prompt discharge at UK port and forwarded in 1,000 ton lots. The balance of the cargo—hay and oats—will be loaded on top and vessel cleared for Havre in the usual way, the divisional naval transport officer at that port being notified by cable of the nature of the cargo, will arrange prompt discharge."[115] The efficiency of Harris's transport organization was a reflection of his drive and personality. With his ready access to the

112. Harris to Sir Robert Borden, 20 May 1915, 1048-18-1, pt. 1, LAC, RG 24, vol. 3713.

113. Harris to Desbarats, 9 June, 6 July, 9 August, 13 November, and 12 December 1916, ibid.

114. Harris to Desbarats, 1 May 1916, Harris to J.D. Hazen, 11 April 1916, ibid.

115. Harris to Thompson, 27 May 1915, 1048-17-1, pt. 1, LAC, RG 24, vol. 3706. Such was the volume of ship-ping space being taken up with the hay and oats needed to feed the vast number of horses being used by the Allied armies in France that in May 1916 the British Cabinet War Committee raised the possibility of dis-banding the BEF's cavalry units as a means of freeing up shipping space for more vital war supplies. Robin Prior and Trevor Wilson, *The Somme* (New Haven 2005), 12–13.

prime minister, however, it was not always clear whether the CP businessman believed he was working for the naval department or whether the naval department was working for him. When Harris determined in the fall of 1915 that even greater efficiencies would result from government control of the movement of war materiel on inland rail lines, he did not hesitate to approach the railways to make the necessary arrangements and then presented his results directly to the prime minister to relay them to the naval minister. Writing to J.D. Hazen on 11 November, Borden unquestioningly accepted Harris's arrangements and instructed the naval minister to carry them out.

> Mr Harris has had discussions with the officials of the Grand Trunk, Canadian Pacific and Intercolonial Railways with respect to the routing of such supplies. It is considered that in view of the probable serious congestion at Halifax and St John during the coming winter and in view of the fact that the Admiralty transports in stress of weather and otherwise are likely to arrive with irregularity, the inland routing in order to be effectively dealt with must be left to some central control. This seems very necessary in order to insure proper connection at the seaboard and to prevent large quantities of freight being shipped to any particular port before vessels will be available to load the same which would result in blocking the railway terminals. It is pointed out that transports ought not to be waiting at St John for cargo with traffic moving to Halifax or vice versa. May I ask therefore that the arrangements for routing shall be made through Mr A.H. Harris as acting DOT and that you will be good enough to carry out such routing arrangements as may be made in his office from time to time.[116]

The naval minister could only point out that munitions firms under contract to the Admiralty or War Office had previously been free to choose their own method of shipping war materiel to the port of embarkation and had not come under naval department authority, while the government's own Shell Committee, Department of Agriculture, and Department of Militia and Defence also made their own arrangements for inland transportation but would presumably now be advised of the government's new policy.[117] When Harris wrote to the navy's director of stores, J.A. Wilson, the following week, he left little doubt who was in charge: "you will see that the routing of our transport inland is taken out of the hands of the shipper and placed in the hands of the government as represented by this office. I would ask you therefore to be kind enough to advise me of such contracts as you may have in order that I may notify shippers accordingly, and when entering into further contracts I shall be obliged if you will notify them to take their routing instructions from this office."[118]

---

116. R.L. Borden to J.D. Hazen, 11 November 1915, ibid.

117. Hazen to Borden, 12 November 1915, ibid.

118. Harris to J.A. Wilson, 18 November 1915, ibid.

For all the success that Harris's organization had achieved by the end of 1915, the naval department was becoming increasingly concerned about the *ad hoc* nature of its relationship with, and responsibility for, the acting DOT. The problem of having financial responsibility but no actual control was brought to the minister's attention in December 1915 by the epitome of the government bureaucrat, G.J. Desbarats. As the deputy minister expressed his concerns, "the department has already assumed considerable responsibilities, by a process of gradual growth, and these are still continuing to grow. The Admiralty now look to this department to represent them in Canada, as all correspondence passes through the department. Mr Harris has handled the service most successfully. Ships arrive, are loaded and sail again with a minimum of delay and confusion, and it is believed economically also. It will be noticed however, that although the department is apparently held responsible by the Admiralty for all that is done, the department has no real control."[119] In presenting the matter to his minister, Desbarats left little doubt that he wanted the lines of authority to be clearly defined.

> Since the opening of the war this department has acted as agent in Canada for the British Admiralty and as such is now paying out large sums of money for various services. One of the services which entails a very heavy expenditure is that of the transport ships carrying munitions, stores, provisions and other supplies for the use of the army in the field. Vessels are chartered by the Admiralty and while the charters are handled in England a number of accounts have to be paid on this side. The disbursements are made by this department and charged against the Admiralty for future adjustment....
>
> A number of accounts are received in this department certified by Mr Harris, or by one of the accountant officers of the CPR. This department has never been advised as to Mr Harris' authority and has no information as to the departments to which he reports and to which he is responsible. This department has no direct authority over Mr. Harris and while it advises him freely it has no power to enforce any instructions or to direct any of the expenditure made by Mr Harris, or to supervise the contracts in regard to supplying the ships, although it is paying the accounts on Mr Harris' certificates. The amounts paid on this account during the season of navigation on the East Coast amount to $726,000.00 and have been increasing during the fall and will likely be higher during the winter months on account of the increasing number of transports.
>
> It would seem advisable to have the situation perfectly clear and it would be well if this department could be advised as to the limits of Mr Harris' authority, and should be properly authorized to accept Mr Harris' certificates as to expenditures if the Government has authorized him to disburse monies for their account.

---

119. "Development of the Transport Service," nd, copy attached to Desbarats, "Memo to the Minister," 8 December 1915, 1048–18–2, LAC, RG 24, vol. 3714.

The system so far has worked quite well and, while the department has not always seen eye to eye with Mr Harris, there has been no serious friction. The Canadian Pacific Railway have placed at the disposal of the government an expert staff which handles the shipping end of the transports in an expeditious manner and as far as can be seen with due economy, and my desire is to have the matter placed in proper shape and to have our own authority in the matter defined so as to avoid any future trouble.[120]

When the naval minister brought the matter to Borden's attention the next day, he too emphasized the need to delineate the limits of Harris's authority, particularly where it concerned the expenditure of government money. Hazen explained to the prime minister that on those occasions when there had been differences of opinion between the businessman and the naval department, Harris had used his relationship with Borden to tell NSHQ "that he would go to you, suggesting that you were the only one who he considered had authority in connection with matters with which he is concerned." With the shipment of war supplies and the department's expenditures on overseas transport increasing monthly, the naval minister fully supported his subordinates in stressing the importance of having the government set out clear lines of authority: "The naval department is not at all anxious to exercise authority over Mr Harris and has no fault to find with the way he is doing his work, but there should be some understanding with regard to his authority in respect to matters for which the naval department, in the end, has to take the responsibility. As the matter stands at present, we have no information that Mr Harris is authorized by the Admiralty, by the Canadian government or by anybody else to incur the expenditures which we are called upon to meet."[121]

The CP businessman was not particularly interested in becoming a civil servant, however, or in having his authority curtailed in any way by the naval department. Responding to the concerns raised by its officials, Harris emphasized the efficiency of the overseas transport service as it was originally constituted and reminded them of the fact that a civilian had been "selected as its director in order to ensure the best possible commercial results. We have worked in this closest harmony with the naval service, accepting and carrying out their instructions to the letter on all matters affecting naval policy. We also furnish them, for the information of the Admiralty, with regular statements as to the character and quantity of cargoes cleared."[122] More important than any of his arguments, however, were the acting DOT's close ties to the prime minister. Bending to Harris's strong desire to remain independent of direct departmental control, Borden opted to have him report directly to a Cabinet subcommittee consisting of himself, the minister of trade and commerce, the minister of the naval service, the minister of militia, and A.E. Kemp, the head of the War Purchasing Commission. Order-in-Council PC 34 of 12 January 1916 established the Cabinet subcommittee to provide some political oversight of the work

120. Desbarats, "Memo to the Minister," 8 December 1915, ibid.

121. Hazen to Borden, 9 December 1915, ibid.

122. Harris, "Memorandum," 3 January 1916, ibid.

of the overseas transport service.[123] From the outset, it was apparent to naval officials that little of substance had been altered by simply introducing a subcommittee into the relationship. Within a week, Hazen was once again objecting that the new arrangement did not provide any authority "under which the Department of the Naval Service could defray expenses incurred by Mr Harris on behalf of the transport service."[124] As the naval department anticipated, the Cabinet subcommittee met very seldom and quickly became a nonentity.[125] In fact, the department's concerns over its vaguely defined relationship with the director of overseas transport would continue to linger for some time and it would take two more busy shipping seasons before the navy was able to prompt the government into action.

123. "Report of the Committee of the Privy Council," 12 January 1916, ibid.

124. Hazen to Borden, 18 January 1916, ibid.

125. Kingsmill to Graeme Thomson, Director of Transports, Admiralty, 28 November 1917, ibid.

The port of Montreal and the Grand Trunk Railway grain elevator, circa 1890. With four main rail lines connecting it to the interior of the continent, Montreal was Canada's most important east coast shipping port. (LAC PA-149196)

CHAPTER 6

From Destroyers to Trawlers, 1916–1917

"The expense involved in strengthening the [Gulf of St Lawrence] Patrol is nothing," the commander-in-chief, North America and West Indies Station warned the Canadian government in January 1916, "compared to the loss that would be incurred and dislocation of traffic that would ensue if the enemy submarines got the upper hand, even for a short time, in Canadian and Newfoundland waters."[1] Vice-Admiral Sir George Patey was writing the Duke of Connaught in response to concerns the governor general had expressed about the limited strength of the Canadian anti-submarine patrol force for the 1916 navigation season. The British admiral was eager to encourage Ottawa to increase both the number and quality of the vessels employed in the Gulf patrol that the Royal Canadian Navy had established at Sydney, Nova Scotia, the previous summer because he was convinced that U-boats would eventually be forced to seek easier targets in the relatively unguarded shipping lanes off North America. It was Patey's (rather too optimistic) belief that German submarines had already been "practically cleared out of the waters surrounding the British Isles" and driven into the Mediterranean. Once the Royal Navy succeeded "in making the Mediterranean too hot for them," Patey felt it was reasonable to assume that the U-boats would transfer their operations to North American waters. "Under these circumstances I would most respectfully point out, as I did last summer, that, although the vessels at present available are most useful as a watch and for communicating intelligence, they do not include enough vessels of sufficient speed and power to successfully cope with the German submarines should they appear off the coasts of Canada and Newfoundland." In fact, Patey observed, only HMC Ships *Canada* and *Grilse* "would appear to have any chance of overhauling a submarine on the surface—the others are very lightly armed and of slow speed." As to the governor general's suggestion that the Canadian submarines *CC 1* and *CC 2* be brought around to the East Coast from Esquimalt, the British admiral was skeptical, pointing out that the "two submarines, having no guns, would be no match for the German submarines, although they are useful for defence of harbours or [torpedo] attacks on enemy vessels."[2]

---

1. Patey to Governor General of Canada, 11 January 1916, United Kingdom National Archives (hereafter UKNA), Admiralty series (hereafter ADM) 116/1400.

2. Patey to Governor General of Canada, 11 January 1916, ibid.

As much as Patey's advice was a fair reflection of the meagre strength and capabilities of the RCN's patrol forces, the Admiralty (where attention was focused on the waters surrounding the United Kingdom) was far more circumspect in its analysis of the submarine threat to North America and not at all enamoured of the advice the C-in-C was giving to the Canadians. In a February internal Admiralty minute, the director of the operations division (DOD), Captain Thomas Jackson, stated that "the control of the patrol arrangements" had already been discussed with Vice-Admiral Kingsmill and that "these proposals seem to be all that are necessary." The DOD did not believe that Patey, in "trying to induce the Canadian government to provide better armed and faster vessels," had fully "considered operating against the submarines' base. If a submarine ever succeeded in opening operations against shipping off the Canadian and Newfoundland coasts, she would be dependent on a floating base whose destruction would finish her."[3] The chief of the war staff, Rear-Admiral Sir Henry Oliver, on the other hand, felt it was "satisfactory that he [Patey] is trying to induce the gov't to provide more and better patrol vessels" but also added that "a floating base would possibly be a steamer which could be searched for by vessels of the NA&WI Squadron."[4] The British naval staff's views, however, ignored both the possibility that long-range submarines might operate off North America without replenishment and the fact that the C-in-C's cruisers were vulnerable to attack by U-boats and would have to take refuge behind the Halifax anti-submarine net defences—a steel net suspended from floats across the entrance to harbours—whenever a German submarine was thought to be present. Just how willing Patey's cruisers would have been to seek out an enemy depot ship, the presence of which would presumably indicate that submarines were also lurking in the vicinity, is open to speculation.

Not surprisingly, the C-in-C's view that the RCN required more powerful warships than the collection of armed yachts, fisheries vessels and motor boats that had made up the 1915 Gulf patrol was in complete accord with the opinions held by most of Canada's senior naval officers. In planning for the upcoming season, the commander of the 1915 Gulf patrol, Captain F. Pasco, had pointed out in a February memorandum that only the turbine-powered *Grilse* had the speed needed to overhaul a U-boat trying to escape on the surface.[5] Pasco, however, suggested that if twelve additional motor launches were added to the auxiliary patrol vessels (APVs) of the previous summer then "we might count ourselves as ready to ward off any submarine attacks."[6] Kingsmill, on the other hand, believed that more powerful warships were required, even after being forced to digest the criticisms the prime minister had made to belittle the navy's 1915 efforts as unnecessary. As we have seen, one of Kingsmill's chief concerns at the conclusion of the 1915 shipping season had been to establish a firm basis for co-operation between the naval forces of the RCN, Newfoundland, and the Royal Navy, a task that Captain Pasco's meetings in St John's

---

3. DOD minute, 3 February 1916, ibid.

4. Rear-Admiral H. Oliver minute, 4 February 1916, ibid.

5. Pasco to Kingsmill, 19 February 1916, 1065–4-2, Library and Archives Canada (hereafter LAC), Record Group (hereafter RG) 24, vol. 4030.

6. Pasco to Kingsmill, 19 February 1916, ibid.

Grilse's bridge and forecastle with its 12-pounder gun. (LAC e007140903)

in February had successfully achieved. In assessing the new patrol arrangements with the island colony, however, the importance of strengthening the Canadian patrol was never far from the naval director's mind. As he explained to his chief of staff, Commander R.M. Stephens, two weeks after receiving Pasco's report on the St John's conference, the greatest handicap facing the RCN was its inability to acquire the type of vessels needed to make its patrol force effective. Having already scoured the United States and Canada to find *Grilse*, *Hochelaga*, and *Stadacona*, Kingsmill believed it was "impossible to procure" in North America even the small number of vessels the Newfoundland authorities had recommended be added to the patrol to prevent a disguised enemy supply ship from taking station amid the Grand Banks fishing fleet.[7]

The only realistic possibility of immediate assistance rested in whatever aid could be provided by the British navy and Naval Service Headquarters took the opportunity presented in forwarding the Canada-Newfoundland defence arrangements in early March to lay the situation before the Admiralty: "The growth in the transport of munitions and troops from Canada has been so enormous during the past nine months that it appears to the department that the enemy is more likely to attempt attack by submarines on this side of the Atlantic this year than was the case last year. The decisions of the conference at St John's are concurred in generally by the department, but it is not possible to obtain in Canada suitable vessels for patrol work even on such a limited scale as is proposed. It is particularly difficult to obtain those suitable for work in the vicinity of the Great Banks, which position it is considered important should be adequately patrolled. The department therefore desires to enquire of the Lords Commissioners of the Admiralty as to what measures they recommend should be undertaken by Canada with regard to naval patrols during the coming season and to enquire what, if any, assistance the Admiralty could provide."[8]

If NSHQ was hoping the Admiralty would supply them with either useful advice or additional patrol vessels, they were undoubtedly disappointed with the reply they received from London on 13 April. Whitehall's response was seemingly indifferent to both the small size of the Canadian navy and the immense extent of coastline and shipping lanes it was expected to patrol. The Admiralty's recommendations were also inconsistent in suggesting both that "all armed available vessels" should be concentrated in "the approaches to St John's, Halifax and Cabot Strait" where enemy submarines were most likely to operate, while at the same time, stating that the destruction of enemy supply ships, most likely to be found in unfrequented harbours well away from the shipping lanes, would "prove most profitable plan as this would cripple submarines." The Admiralty simply repeated their earlier advice that supply ships were to "be dealt with by continual coast watching and sea-going patrol service," but did so without any acknowledgement that the RCN had only a handful of inadequate patrol vessels in service and that no other civilian yachts were available in North America for purchase and conversion. Their lordships also discounted

7. Kingsmill to Stephens, 29 February 1916, 1065-4-1, ibid.

8. Desbarats to Undersecretary of State for External Affairs, 2 March 1916, (letter prepared by Stephens to be forwarded to Colonial Office for Admiralty), ibid.

the possibility of enemy supply ships blending in with the fishing vessels on the Grand Banks and told Ottawa that a patrol of the fishing grounds was "not considered essential." Ignoring the fact that Canada had sent all of its available naval guns to Britain early in the war, NSHQ was also instructed to equip its patrol vessels with "12-pounder or heavier guns" but the Admiralty, in accordance with the stipulation recommended by its chief of the war staff, Rear-Admiral Oliver, "regretted … that they cannot supply any additional vessels" for Canada's defence.[9]

With only dubious advice to offer the RCN, it seemed that London was content to leave NSHQ to improvise its coastal patrols for the fast-approaching 1916 season with the few resources it already had at hand. The British response did at least include a memorandum by the director of the operations division, Captain Jackson, outlining the Admiralty's assessment of the submarine threat in North American waters:

> In the event of submarines operating off the Newfoundland and Canadian coasts, they are likely to be well armed vessels of the latest types, and it is improbable that any lighter guns than a 12 pdr will be able, unless at very short range, to damage them sufficiently to put them out of action. Patrol vessels with a smaller armament than 12 pdrs may cause them to shift their cruising ground but are unlikely to inflict any injury of consequence. It is desirable, therefore, that so far as possible all patrol vessels should carry 12 pdr or heavier guns.
>
> The supply vessels are also likely to be armed, and it cannot be foreseen what guns they may carry. Such vessels may select anchorages in unfrequented harbours in which to meet, supply and refit their submarines, and it is in such harbours that they should be sought. A combination of a coast-watching and a sea-going patrol service should enable these vessels to be found and attacked. It must be borne in mind that the destruction of the base ship will cripple the submarines.
>
> As the submarines would desire to do as much damage as possible before they are driven away, it is probable that they would operate in waters in which traffic is comparatively congested, such as the approaches to Halifax, St John's and the Cabot Straits. Should they be driven to operate further east, the present arrangements for the disposal of trade would have to be still further emphasized. Owing to the vast area in which any submarines which cross the Atlantic will be able to operate, there will be difficulty in hunting them with patrol vessels owing to the large number which would be required, and it may prove more profitable to search for and destroy their bases, afloat and ashore.
>
> For these reasons, it does not appear that patrol vessels on the Great Banks are essential. It would seem better to concentrate all available armed vessels in the nearer waters in which the trade cannot be sufficiently dispersed. This

9. Bonar Law to Governor General of Canada, 13 April 1916, ibid; and Oliver minute, 7 April 1916, UKNA, ADM 116/1400.

is more particularly the case as there will apparently be difficulty in obtaining a sufficient number of vessels to maintain a satisfactory patrol, and it will be better to concentrate all efforts on protecting the main shipping rather than to dissipate the available forces in trying to do too much.

The fitting of W/T to patrol vessels, even if of low power and small radius, adds greatly to their utility. I am to express their lordships' regret that they are unable to supply any additional vessels beyond those available locally for the Canadian and Newfoundland coast patrol.[10]

In Kingsmill's opinion, the British reply contained "nothing new to what we are arranging to carry out, except that the Admiralty do not consider patrol vessels on the Grand Banks essential." The naval director interpreted London's response to mean that they did "not consider that there is much danger of a determined attack on our trade routes at this side of the Atlantic for the present." As he went on to explain to the deputy minister, G.J. Desbarats, "if they are unable to supply any additional vessels at present it is very unlikely that they will ever be able to do so, and it makes it desirable that we should consider the future as far as our Canadian trade routes are concerned, contiguous to our coasts."[11] In view of the latest British claim that they were unable to supply the RCN with patrol vessels, Kingsmill returned to his earlier conviction that Canada would only be able to acquire the warships it needed to defend the East Coast shipping lanes if the navy had the vessels built in a Canadian shipyard. The admiral was thinking along those lines the previous month when, through naval minister Hazen, he had asked the British government if it was advisable for the RCN to construct two destroyers and two submarines in Canada. London replied to that proposal on 5 April by advising "that destroyers being valuable for local protection against submarines, such money as may be available should be devoted to construction of destroyers rather than submarines."[12] Left out of the official British response was Oliver's suggestion that "if both types of vessels were wanted [in an emergency by Canada], the Admiralty would not be in a position to lend destroyers but they could send a few submarines at a pinch."[13]

With London unwilling to provide any reinforcements for the RCN's patrol, Kingsmill quickly turned to the Admiralty's advice that building destroyers in Canada was preferable to constructing submarines and suggested to the Canadian government that the possibility of building destroyers for the RCN at Canadian Vickers be pursued. Both politicians and bureaucrats in Ottawa were, of course, well aware that the Montreal shipyard had assembled H-class submarines for the British government in 1915 and was now construc-

10. W.F. Nicholson, Secretary, Admiralty to Undersecretary of State, Colonial Office, 8 April 1916, 1065–4-1, LAC, RG 24, vol. 4030; and T. Jackson minute, 7 April 1916, UKNA, ADM 116/1400.

11. Kingsmill, "Memorandum for the Deputy Minister," 17 April 1916, 1062–12–1, LAC, RG 24, vol. 4020.

12. Governor General to Colonial Secretary, 5 April 1916, UKNA, ADM 137/1202. In September, Kingsmill had told Desbarats "that to expand the patrol is not feasible without building." Kingsmill, "Memorandum for the Deputy Minister," 28 September 1915, 1062–13–4, LAC, RG 24, vol. 4022.

13. Oliver minute, 28 March 1918, UKNA, ADM 137/1202.

ting motor launches for the Royal Navy. As he explained to Desbarats, letting contracts in the spring of 1916 would allow Vickers to complete the destroyers in time to protect the important North American shipping lanes by the fall of 1917:

> Sometime ago I was informed by the management of the Canadian Vickers Limited in conversation, that it was quite possible to build torpedo boat destroyers in Canada; in fact they made light of any difficulty. I am not aware whether there are any other firms in Canada capable of undertaking such work, but the question of time is a great factor in this matter and it would be of the greatest value to have the torpedo boat destroyers ready for the campaign of 1917, when the greatest pressure will be felt by the Allies' need for munitions and the transport of food to the United Kingdom and France. If such vessels could not be got ready by then, however, it must not be concluded that they will be valueless afterwards; but as it is too late to do anything this year I consider every effort should be made to get some defences as it is generally considered the prelude to the end of the war will be naval actions and attacks by the German fleet, which will never be content to remain under the shelter of the guns of Heligoland and finally be towed out.
>
> In view of the fact that it might not be possible to get these vessels for the campaign of 1917 until the autumn, the following telegram has been sent, which leaves the situation, as far as the Admiralty go, that we are still waiting for their advice. "It has been suggested to the minister that it would be well for the Canadian government to give a contract for the construction of two or three destroyers at Montreal. The minister wishes to be advised whether under existing conditions you think Canada should undertake the construction of these vessels."
>
> It appeared to me that in the meantime the matter might be taken up and if the Admiralty do not advise it, it could be easily dropped but information might be obtained as to what firms could build the vessels and plans of the vessels they advise asked for from the Admiralty. In the 1913–14 programme they had a number of vessels of the L Class, averaging about 960 to 970 tons, with a speed of twenty-nine knots and a range of 1,460 miles. These vessels had oil bunkers and were to carry 235 tons of oil fuel on a war footing, armed with three 4-inch guns, one machine gun and two double revolving torpedo tubes, carried a complement of seventy-three officers and men.
>
> It would take all our resources to man two such vessels and we would have to recall from the Admiralty two of our engineer lieutenants and all our [executive branch] lieutenants and commence training at once stokers in oil fuel burning ships. We would have to arrange to have instructed torpedomen and seamen gunners.[14]

---

14. Kingsmill, "Memorandum for the Deputy Minister," 17 April 1916, 1062–12–1, LAC, RG 24, vol. 4020.

While the establishment of even a small force of two or three destroyers would have stretched the RCN's immediate reserve of trained manpower, Kingsmill knew that only a fast, 4-inch gunned destroyer would be able to take on an enemy submarine. He was also clearly skeptical of the Admiralty's assurances that North America was unlikely to face a serious submarine threat at some point in the future. Not only was the Canadian admiral able to foresee that leaving supply transports unprotected as they departed North American ports would make them an increasingly promising target for U-boats as the war progressed, he also wanted Canada to acquire a few genuine warships in the event of more aggressive action by the German High Seas Fleet. Writing, as he was, six weeks before the Battle of Jutland, the possibility of a breakout into the Atlantic by a major German naval unit was certainly not far-fetched and, in fact, precautions against a raid being attempted by an enemy battle cruiser would continue to be taken by both the Royal Navy and United States Navy until the end of the war.[15] The greatest weakness in Kingsmill's thinking, one that was shared by his political masters, was his willingness to accept the Admiralty's verdict on matters of North American defence even when their lordships' opinion ran counter to his own, better informed judgment of Canadian conditions.

Ottawa's willingness to accept London's advice on naval matters was made all the more unfortunate by the Admiralty staff's difficulty in providing a consistent strategy for North American waters. As we have seen, Whitehall's naval staff system was only established in the years immediately preceding the First World War and many senior Royal Navy officers had difficulty understanding its function or delegating responsibility to it. According to one British naval historian, under the chief of the war staff "all administration was concentrated in the war staff, and actual staff work was scarcely undertaken. Planning was largely abandoned under the pressure of war, but control of operations was scarcely improved thereby. The operations division lacked any creative thought, and in practice had little to do with operations.... Those unwise enough to offer unpalatable advice to their seniors ran some risk of disciplinary action. The staff officers were the weaker members of a generation whose training had been exclusively concerned with materiel and administration, and whose general education was gravely deficient.... As late as 1916, after two years of war, [the Admiralty] was still sending forces to operate together without telling them that other British ships were at sea. Its incompetence at cyphering and decyphering caused confusion and delay, while many signals to the Admiralty went completely unanswered."[16]

Under Oliver and the first sea lord, Admiral Sir Henry Jackson, "the fetish of centralization was carried to extraordinary lengths" as both officers had difficulty delegating authority—a trait common within the Admiralty. Oliver, an "untiring and efficient" administrator, "had no interest in strategy, and could not delegate even his typing" while the first sea lord, even at the height of the war, "was concerning himself with the excessive wine-bills of junior officers on remote stations."[17] According to one of the more thoughtful officers

---

15. C-in-C, NA&WI to Senior Naval Officer, New York, Halifax, et cetera, Kingsmill for information, 15 October 1918, 1048–48–18, LAC, RG 24, vol. 3775.

16. N.A.M. Rodger, *The Admiralty* (Lavenham, Suffolk 1979), 130.

17. Rodger, *The Admiralty*, 131.

who served in the Admiralty's operations division the following year, the DOD had "quite an imposing staff on paper, but few of those officers had much to do with actual operations and not one had received any staff training. I should say that at least half of them were employed on routine tasks, compiling reports, returns, etc., which could have been done equally well by civilian clerks supervised by an officer."[18] As the Canadian authorities were to discover throughout the course of the war, the British naval staff's inability to generate or maintain a war plan (beyond the fluctuating thoughts of the first sea lord of the moment) meant that the advice offered up by the Admiralty was often contradictory so that, as had occurred in 1915, Ottawa might be told to build up a patrol force to meet an urgent submarine threat one month and then Prime Minister Borden would be informed a few weeks later that precautions were unnecessary since no danger existed.

The Admiralty staff's lack of cohesive thought was again on display in its handling of Kingsmill's proposal to construct Canadian destroyers at Vickers's Montreal shipyard. As the proposal made its way through the corridors of Whitehall on 22 April, Sir Henry Oliver quickly gave it his endorsement, suggesting that London "reply in the affirmative, unless Montreal is doing work for Admiralty which would be delayed by building these destroyers."[19] Two days later the director of naval construction, Sir Eustace H.T. d'Eyncourt, "recommended that the latest Admiralty 'M' designs be adopted as we could supply complete detailed drawings to be worked to" should the decision be made to proceed with construction at Montreal. The DNC was more skeptical of Vickers's suggested date of delivery, stating that "it would be a very good performance if they can deliver before the close of navigation 1917, and it is hardly thought that this will be achieved."[20] (As had been the case with the faster build times of the Vickers-built H-class submarines in 1915, the slower pace of construction in UK shipyards usually prompted pessimism from British officials when assessing contracts with North American firms.)

Other Admiralty officers also went on record offering assistance to the RCN's warship plans. On the 25th, one official minuted that "to give the Canadian authorities the best possible chance of completing these vessels by the time named it should be arranged to send, as soon as possible after a definite decision is reached, the whole of the available information" as to drawings, specifications, structural sketches, models, and lists of required materials. Two weeks later, another was willing to offer full assistance, suggesting that "the Canadian government be requested to communicate by cable as soon as possible their wishes as to the supply of machinery designs and drawings and the requirements in outline as to the supply from this country of any auxiliary machinery and materials including turbines, turbine gearing, boilers or parts of boilers or tubes, shafting, condensers or condenser tubes etc. It may be desirable on receipt of this reply for Canadian officers to visit this country to discuss these matters in further detail, and probably for Admiralty officers to give assistance or advice in Canada."[21]

---

18. Vice-Admiral K.G.B. Dewar, *The Navy From Within* (London 1939), 217.

19. Oliver minute, 22 April 1916, UKNA, ADM 137/1202.

20. DNC minute, 24 April 1916, ibid.

21. G.G. Goodwin minute, 10 May 1916, ibid.

Despite this apparent willingness to assist the RCN with its destroyer proposal, as the file reached the higher levels of the Admiralty support for Canadian warship construction was inadvertently transformed into discouragement. While the first sea lord minuted that he had "no objection" to Canada building destroyers at Montreal, he added the qualification that "at the same time it might be mentioned that mercantile tonnage is an equal necessity and may be better within their capabilities."[22] Jackson's view that Canadian shipbuilding capacity might be better employed in constructing merchant ships rather than destroyers was then endorsed by the first lord, Sir Arthur Balfour.[23] As a result of Jackson's and Balfour's qualified approval of Canadian-built destroyers, the reply that Whitehall eventually drafted placed far greater emphasis on the problems Vickers would face in completing the destroyers within a useful time frame and the importance the Admiralty placed on building merchant ship tonnage instead. Writing to the governor general on 26 May, Bonar Law, the colonial secretary, observed that it was "with much pleasure that Admiralty note offer of your government to construct two or three destroyers and they will gladly afford every assistance desired," before seemingly pulling the rug out from under Kingsmill's destroyer scheme by suggesting that it seemed "doubtful whether delivery of any [of] these vessels would be effected before close of navigation in 1917." The reply also made a point of emphasizing "that it deserves consideration whether arrangements such as those indicated, which may not result in addition of any actual naval units to forces of empire for summer of 1918, is under the circumstances really most economical utilization of Canadian and imperial resources and whether, as at present additional mercantile tonnage is of equal imperial necessity to naval tonnage, the energies of Canadian yards could not perhaps be better employed on construction of merchant ships."[24]

Whether it was the Admiralty's specific intention to have the Vickers's shipyard concentrate on building merchant tonnage rather than a few extremely valuable destroyers—the answering telegram did, after all, state that the Admiralty noted the Canadian offer "with much pleasure"—the overall effect of the wording was, at best, highly ambiguous as to its intent. Given the language with which the Admiralty qualified its decidedly lukewarm endorsement, it is not surprising that the Canadian government interpreted the British response as discouraging their destroyer proposal—an interpretation that Whitehall readily acknowledged to be correct the following November.[25] The British government was already employing the Vickers yard in Montreal to build 550 anti-submarine motor launches for the Royal Navy and, as Oliver's minute of 22 April had pointed out, the Admiralty wanted to maintain the Canadian yard's capacity for its own future use and did not want contracts for RCN warships to interfere with it.[26] In view of

---

22. Jackson minute, 16 May 1916, ibid.

23. Balfour minute, 20 May 1916, ibid.

24. Bonar Law to Governor-General of Canada, 26 May 1916, 1062–12–1, LAC, RG 24, vol. 4020; and telegram drafts, 23 May 1916, UKNA, ADM 137/1202.

25. Captain T. Jackson memorandum, 26 November 1916, UKNA, ADM 116/1400.

26. Oliver minute, 22 April 1916, UKNA, ADM 137/1202; and Archibald Hurd, *The Merchant Navy* (London 1924), II, 266–67; and G.N. Tucker, *The Naval Service of Canada, Its Official History, I: Origins and Early Years* (Ottawa 1952), 234.

the obvious inference to be drawn from London's response that the Admiralty would prefer Canada not to undertake the construction of destroyers at Montreal, Kingsmill enquired of the deputy minister whether "anything further is to be done in this department" in regard to the destroyer scheme. After consulting the naval minister, Desbarats minuted the naval director with Hazen's instruction that no action was to be taken at present.[27]

After having received an apparent Admiralty endorsement for the idea of Canadian destroyer construction in early April, Whitehall's apparent reversal a few weeks later must have come as a rude surprise—not to mention a major disappointment—to the Canadian naval director. With the Vickers's shipyard expressing easy confidence in its ability to construct warships and London stating that naval money was better spent building destroyers than submarines, Kingsmill had to have been confident that his mid-April destroyer proposal would receive the Admiralty's blessing. The setback to RCN expansion is all the more inexplicable in view of the three destroyers the Royal Australian Navy (RAN) was completing at its Cockatoo Island dockyard outside Sydney. The RAN had purchased three I-class destroyers from Britain in 1910, of which one was disassembled and shipped to the dominion to be re-erected at Cockatoo Island. With that experience in reassembly, the Australian dockyard began construction of an I-class ship—at 250 feet in length and 700 tons, the vessels could make twenty-eight knots carrying one 4-inch gun, three 12-pounder guns, and three 18-inch torpedo tubes—in the spring of 1914, commissioning the destroyer in December 1915. Two other I-class destroyers were laid down in February 1915 and were commissioned in July and August 1916.[28] Whitehall's lack of support for a Canadian proposal that was very similar to the one the Australians had already undertaken is all the more puzzling in view of the importance to the Allied war effort of the vast supplies being shipped from Canada, and particularly so when the Royal Navy was short of destroyers itself.

Without the Admiralty's endorsement, Kingsmill's destroyer building plans were dead in the water. Having been elected with a naval policy that called for the scrapping of Laurier's plans for a Canadian navy and replacing it with financial support for the Royal Navy, the Borden government would have needed a strong directive from Whitehall for it to have considered building the sizable warships, such as destroyers, that it had belittled the Laurier administration for proposing. Short of merchant ships being sunk in Canadian waters or full Admiralty support—which their lordships clearly did not provide in April 1916—Kingsmill had little hope of convincing the prime minister to proceed with a large Canadian shipbuilding project. Given Canadian Vickers's demonstrated expertise in building submarines and motor launches for the Admiralty and the proximity of American shipyards and technical expertise, there is ample reason to believe that Vickers would have been able to build destroyers for the RCN—a result that would have given Canada a far more effective naval force with which to combat the U-boat campaign that developed in Canadian waters in the summer of 1918.

---

27. Kingsmill to Desbarats, 21 June 1916, Desbarats minute, nd, 1062–12–1, LAC, RG 24, vol. 4020; and Desbarats to Under Secretary of State for External Affairs, 17 November 1916, 1065–7-2, pt 1, LAC, RG 24, vol. 4031.

28. Ross Gillett, *Australian and New Zealand Warships, 1914–1945* (Sydney 1983), 12, 40–41; and *Jane's Fighting Ships 1919* (London 1919), 153.

With or without a destroyer contract in place at Canadian Vickers, NSHQ had to base its plans for the 1916 shipping season on the same collection of auxiliary patrol vessels it had deployed the previous summer. According to the plan Kingsmill forwarded to Captain Pasco in early May, the RCN's seaward patrols were once again to be supplemented inshore by motor boats manned by RNCVR sailors armed with rifles. The combined RCN/Newfoundland patrol was to operate in three main areas: Area A, the Cabot Straits with headquarters at Sydney; Area B, the southern and western shores of Newfoundland from Cape Ray to Belle Isle with headquarters at Bonne Bay; and Area C, the Labrador coast from Belle Isle north to Natashkwan, headquartered at Mutton Bay. Seven of the RCN's patrol vessels were allotted to these areas, with the five most effective ships, *Canada*, *Grilse*, *Hochelaga*, *Stadacona*, and *Margaret*, stationed at Sydney for patrol work in the high-traffic sea lanes of the Cabot Straits. As Canada's best escort, indeed the only vessel the RCN possessed that was capable of providing troopships with reasonable protection from surfaced submarines, it was expected that *Grilse* would periodically be detached for special duties escorting those troopships that sailed from Quebec.[29]

The vessels provided by the Newfoundland government, meanwhile, would be supplemented by the *Florence* and *Gulnare*, with the former operating in Area B off the West Coast of Newfoundland and the latter in Area C along the Labrador coast. After the end of May, the Area B and C patrols would be reinforced by six rifle-armed motor boats inshore and supplied by the RCN vessels operating with them. These arrangements left the *Premier* available to patrol as an armed lookout vessel in the vicinity of the outer automatic buoy in the approaches to Halifax. The four vessels that had been fitted out as minesweepers, *Deliverance*, *Baleine*, *Gopher*, and *Musquash*, could be employed in keeping a lookout off Halifax in addition to fulfilling their main duties sweeping the shipping channel to the port. The torpedo boat *Tuna*, meanwhile, remained at Halifax where her speed made her a useful vessel for scouting purposes in the immediate approaches or along the coast. The Halifax-based ships were not part of Captain Pasco's command, however, as they fell under the direction of the captain superintendent of the Halifax dockyard, Captain E.H. Martin, the minesweepers being under the immediate supervision of the port's naval transport officer, Commander G. Holloway.[30]

In making these dispositions, Kingsmill could not forget the rebuke he had received from the government at the end of the 1915 season over the expenses the navy had incurred in hiring a few motorboats to supplement the small number of auxiliary patrol vessels being used to keep a watch for enemy supply bases or ships along the eastern coastline. As a result, he could not ignore even the smallest expenses the following summer. In early May, for instance, the admiral instructed Captain Pasco that "strict orders will be given" to the rifle-armed sailors aboard the motor boats "that ammunition is not to be wasted." (He presumably had potshots at seagulls or whales in mind, and was not insisting that the riflemen were to close to within "whites of their eyes" range before

29. Kingsmill to Pasco, 2 May 1916, 1065–4-2, Confidential circular letters Nos. 155/16, 156/16, and 157/16, all 5 May 1916, 1065–2-1, pt 1, LAC, RG 24, vol. 4030.

30. Kingsmill, "Memorandum for Commodore Coke," 22 March 1917, 1065–7-3, LAC, RG 24, vol. 4031.

engaging German submariners.) He also warned Pasco "that the *Grilse* is an exceedingly expensive vessel to run and she is not to be allowed to fly around the place just as Lieutenant Ross wishes."[31] While J.K.L. Ross may have had money, the RCN clearly did not. Such parsimonious instructions merely underline the degree to which the government was demanding that Kingsmill operate the navy on a shoestring budget. Perhaps the most sympathetic ear the naval director had outside of NSHQ itself was the British commander-in-chief of the North America and West Indies Station, an officer who clearly understood the weakness of the Canadian naval position. After a spring in which the Admiralty had refused either to transfer any of its own auxiliary patrol vessels to the RCN or to sanction the construction of destroyers in Canada, Vice-Admiral Patey told Kingsmill in late May that "the arrangements seem to be as good as can be made with the resources at present available, but I consider the patrol should be strengthened when possible. It should be clearly understood that, should enemy submarines appear off the Canadian coasts, my cruisers are not protection to transports against submarine attack."[32]

Newfoundland's contribution to the 1916 joint patrol, meanwhile, consisted of the vessels *Fogata*, *Cabot*, and *Petrel* under the supervision of the Royal Navy's Commander A. MacDermott in St John's. The largest of the three, *Fogata*, was commanded by Lieutenant-Commander C.E. Carter, RN, retired, and "equipped with a 12 pounder gun and a 3 pounder gun with trained gun crews." The whaler *Cabot*, meanwhile, was commanded by "Mr O'Neill, a member of the Newfoundland Constabulary who will carry a temporary commission as 2nd lieutenant in the Newfoundland Regiment."[33] Such appointments indicate the difficulty both Newfoundland and Canada experienced in obtaining suitable naval officers to command their patrol vessels. Carter's appointment, in particular, drew the attention of NSHQ. In early July, Desbarats wrote to St John's to inform the Newfoundland authorities "that Lieutenant-Commander Cornelius E. Carter, RN, retired, who is stated to be in command of the *Fogata*, was employed under the naval service department shortly after the war broke out, and tendered his resignation on the 4th January, 1915, giving as his reason the fact that he found it difficult to contend with his duties through occasional loss of memory, consequent on sunstroke whilst on active service in the Persian Gulf."[34]

Questions concerning the abilities of some of the officers pressed into service were not confined to Newfoundland alone. On 12 July, Kingsmill received an anonymous letter from "a conservative member [of parliament] interested in the Canadian navy" that outlined some of the gossip that was making the rounds of Sydney, Nova Scotia:

> Pardon me for taking the liberty of writing you in reference to HMCS *Margaret* now lying at Sydney NS, but, being very much interested in the welfare of the Canadian navy it has been submitted to me, that owing to the treatment of

31. Kingsmill to Pasco, 2 May 1916, 1065–4-2, LAC, RG 24, vol. 4030.

32. Patey to Kingsmill, 22 May 1916, 1065–4-1, ibid.

33. Governor Davidson to Governor-General of Canada, 12 June 1916, ibid.

34. Desbarats to Undersecretary of State for External Affairs for transmission to Davidson, 5 July 1916, ibid.

the crew by the captain and engineer it is causing a great deal of discontent in regards to the allowance of money for victualling. The officers are allowed sixty cents per day and the crew fifty cents per day. It is very peculiar that the officers and CPO's should get the best food, while the crew who get the work, get all the bad food, and when taken in front of the captain to make a complaint, they are told that it is as good as theirs and fit to eat. If that were the case where would the complaint of the men come in. Also they are told that they would be severely punished if they complained again.

It is a shocking state of affairs and ought to be seen to at once so as to prevent unnecessary trouble and sickness which is prevalent. No doubt if inquiry is made the officer will deny it, but I believe it is only too true. The last three or four days of their last patrol, the food wasn't fit for consumption, and not enough of it. What is the chief steward doing with the money allowed for the crew's maintenance which is somewhere near $1,200 per month? He seems to afford a few dollars per month to all his staff, but not out of his own money. There is only one answer to that. No, for the way the crew are fed it would cost about $700 per month, and the other is shared between the officers, especially the captain. Is it fair to all concerned that the rate payers moneys should be grafted in this scandalous manner? Inquiries must be made concerning this. Also on the Yarmouth, St John patrol the amount of coal for this said ship is far from being correct, as it did not go on board the ship. The government paid for a certain amount supplied by a private contractor, who drew the money and shared it with the officers. It is time some of those people were put out and gentlemen replace them. So leaving this for you to deal with.[35]

Given that the letter was submitted anonymously, Kingsmill would have nothing to do with it, tersely minuting across the top: "The Coward's Weapon. *No* Action."[36] For his part the CO of *Margaret*, Lieutenant A.J. May, RNCVR, was making his own complaint to the naval director about the amount of alcohol his men were consuming at Sydney. Although nominally a prohibition town, May stated that there was plenty of illicit booze available, most of which was "absolutely poisonous."[37] It is, moreover, questionable whether the living conditions aboard one of the RCN's auxiliaries would have been considered substandard by the RN ratings who made up much of the crew, particularly given the fact that RCN pay was twice that received in the British service.

However, as Lieutenant May indicated to Captain Pasco in requesting one to two months' leave for members of his crew in December 1916, many of his men were long-service British sailors who had not been home in several years: "Not been home since 1912. Married and not seen wife since 1912"; "Not been home since 1910. Mother in bad health. Wishes to see parents. Had no leave at all"; "Not been home since 1914. Married.

35. Anonymous to Kingsmill, 12 July 1916, 58–16–6, LAC, RG 24, vol. 5659.

36. Kingsmill minute, nd, ibid.

37. May to Kingsmill, 14 August 1916, notes from HQ 58–16–1, note 6, DHH 81/520/8000, HMCS *Margaret*.

Wishes to see wife. Lost two children since leaving England"; "Not been home since 1912. Mother in very bad health. Wishes to see her son"; "Three children and one born October 3rd 1914, since leaving August 2nd 1914"; "Not been home since 1909. To see grandfather 76 years"; "Not been home since 1907. Father died 1916. Mother alive, 75 years. Wishes to see her. Other brothers at front."[38] When combined with the sheer boredom of conducting routine patrols thousands of kilometres away from the nearest submarine, it is understandable that there was some discontent among sailors on the East Coast and a desire by some to see action overseas in RN ships.[39] And for whatever reason, RCN officers seem to have taken a relaxed, even sympathetic attitude toward their crews. By September, Captain Martin in Halifax had written to NSHQ "complaining bitterly about [the] failure of officers of patrol vessels to discipline their men. Instead of charging offenders and punishing them, the CO's merely turn the troublemakers back to *Niobe*, saying they are unsuitable, and demand replacements. Most of the trouble is with engine room staffs." Ottawa felt that Martin's suggestion to only replace sailors in cases of death, desertion, or promotion was too drastic but did rule that all future exchanges of personnel would have to be sanctioned by NSHQ.[40]

Another sign of the Gulf patrol's inactivity over the summer of 1916 was the fact that during an inspection tour of Sydney in September, Kingsmill ordered HMCS *Grilse* to Halifax because "she was too extravagant in fuel for this work," while also giving "instructions that she was only to be used [at Halifax] on special patrols when important ships were to enter or leave harbour and that her cruising speed was not to exceed thirteen knots."[41] Another of the patrol's main vessels, HMCS *Stadacona*, was occasionally employed as a yacht for visiting VIPs during the summer months in addition to her other duties.[42] As one of the midshipmen serving aboard her at that time, H.W.S. Soulsby, later recalled, the ship was well-suited to the role of official yacht:

> She was an interesting ship. Built as a private yacht she must have been "tops" when she was new, in the Gay Nineties. When I was in her, in 1916, there were two photograph albums still on board which recorded a cruise in the Mediterranean in the early 1900s I think it was, showing places on the Riviera, Venice, etc. The owner's sleeping cabin was still as the owners' used it—a mahoghany-panelled room with a large brass double bed in it. This room was kept locked and no one was allowed in it.

---

38. May to Pasco, 7 December 1916, 58–16–6, LAC, RG 24, vol. 5659.

39. Pasco to Kingsmill, 9 October 1916, 26–16–2, pt. 1, LAC, RG 24, vol. 5597.

40. "Notes on: HQ 58–53–6, Patrols & Auxs., St Lawrence Patrol, Personnel," nd, vol. 2, note 1, Martin to Kingsmill, 2 September 1916, NSHQ memorandum, 11 September 1916, DHH 81/520/1440–11, "East Coast Patrols," file 4.

41. Naval Historical Section, "Brief History of HMCS *Grilse*," 6 March 1961, 11, DHH 81/520/8000, "HMCS *Grilse*."

42. "Survey of file 58–58–1: Patrol Boats & Auxiliaries—HMCS *Stadacona*—General Data & Correspondence," nd, notes 10 and 11, DHH 81/520/8000, "HMCS *Stadacona*."

The dining saloon was forward under the bridge, and there was a passage-way from the after living quarters to it. This passage was completely glassed in where it went through the engine-room and one could watch the engines as one walked along it. As midshipmen entitled only to a hammock and chest, [Midshipman D.St.G.] Lindsay and I felt very comfortable in a double cabin with a bunk to sleep in and lockers and chests-of-drawers to keep our gear in.... She was very lively in any kind of a lop—high freeboard, a diamond-shaped waterline plan and not much dead weight for her size, contributed to this characteristic—and I was often very sea-sick on board her.[43]

Despite the absence of an immediate enemy threat, the East Coast navy did have some useful purpose during 1916. In relinquishing his post as commander-in-chief of the North American station in early September, Vice-Admiral Patey—whose experience with dominion navies allowed him to take a more sympathetic view of their problems—provided the Admiralty with his assessment of the RCN. In the British admiral's opinion, "the Canadian patrol vessels are not sufficiently powerful or numerous to deal with enemy submarines should they appear on these coasts, but I consider that the establishment of the [Gulf] patrol, and the placing of the [anti-submarine] net across the entrance of Halifax Harbour (both of course being perfectly well known to the German Admiralty) have had the effect of keeping enemy submarines away from Canadian waters." Although such a view of the enemy's motivation was too optimistic, Patey acknowledged that "the intrusion of political interests into Canadian naval policy has practically strangled the naval service." Nonetheless, the British C-in-C was complimentary of the fact that Kingsmill "has always been ready to give any assistance in his power" and that Captain Martin, "the captain superintendent of Halifax dockyard, and Engineer Captain [W.S.] Frowd, have been indefatigable in their efforts to assist the fleet in every way."[44] Although, as Kingsmill had long been aware,[45] the dockyard was in need of modernization, it was still able to provide sufficient repair facilities to meet the immediate repair needs of the North America and West Indies Station's cruisers that were keeping watch on the United States' eastern seaboard. Annual refits, however, required a return to British shipyards.[46]

Two RCN warships were also sent to operate outside of Canadian waters in 1916. On 11 December HMCS *Grilse* left Halifax for an intended four-month assignment to the Caribbean to act under the orders of the new C-in-C, North America and West Indies Station, Vice-Admiral Sir Montague Browning. Unsuited to winter operations off Halifax, the turbine yacht turned torpedo boat destroyer had been sent to Jamaica the previous winter for a similar tour of duty, earning the C-in-C's praise as having "rendered several

---

43. H.W.S. Soulsby to The Editor, The "Crowsnest," 8 October 1955, ibid.

44. Patey to Admiralty, 5 September 1916, UKNA, ADM 137/1263.

45. Kingsmill, "Memorandum for the Minister," 5 November 1918, Gibbs, "Memorandum for the Director of the Naval Service," 28 October 1918, 1065–1-1, pt. 1, LAC, RG 24, vol. 4029.

46. Browning to Admiralty, 22 September and 5 October 1916, UKNA, ADM 137/504.

useful services."[47] On both the outward and homeward voyages, however, *Grilse* had run out of fuel and had to be taken under tow to reach port. The cause on the 1915 southern trip had been a strong four-day long gale that slowed her progress on the initial leg to Bermuda, while the fuel shortage on the return voyage that spring was the result of "miscalculation of her consumption."[48] Shaping course for Bermuda in 1916 for the first leg of the voyage to the Caribbean, the torpedo boat destroyer was better prepared for the long passage after having an extra fuel tank fitted and another 2,000 gallons of fuel oil stored in barrels lashed on deck. Despite setting out with a favourable weather forecast, the ship once again ran into heavy weather only one day out of Halifax. By the afternoon of the 12th the seas were too high for the small warship to make any headway and at 1400 hours her CO, Lieutenant Walter Wingate, an RNCVR officer who had replaced Lieutenant Ross in July, ordered her to run for shelter at Shelburne, Nova Scotia. With seas breaking inboard and the ship rolling violently, a party of seamen went on deck to throw the extra fuel barrels over the side and reduce the top weight. By the time the task was completed at 1710 hours, one seaman had broken his leg when he was thrown against the torpedo tube, and two other sailors were missing overboard. An hour-and-a-half later, a large wave carried away the aerial trunk for the wireless:

> Up to that time the ship had been in regular contact with the shore stations, but now she could not transmit or receive. The wireless operators, Simon McLean and Ernest Clements, went on deck and, lashing themselves to the mainmast, rigged a jury lead through the hatch since water pouring through the broken insulator [grounded] any lead they rigged that way. Soon after that the captain sent down instructions to make a distress message and at 2000 the senior operator began sending: "In distress Lat 4340 N Long 6450 W. Require immediate assistance." He heard no reply. After adjustments to his gear he continued transmitting. Still he received no reply, but at 2030 he did hear the station at Sable Island "send something about *Grilse* in distress with position, saying we required assistance." The antenna lead was then found to be [grounding] on the mast, so the operators again went on deck, put on life-lines and tried to get their gear working again. The senior operator returned to the office to try to send a signal but his assistant [McLean] remained on deck. He took off his life-line and was probably preparing to follow down the hatchway. He was not seen again.[49]

A short time later another party of sailors went on deck to deal with the water-filled lifeboats that were reducing the ship's stability in the mountainous seas. As the work was proceeding, Lieutenant Wingate spotted a huge wave bearing down on the ship. "He shouted

47. Patey to Kingsmill, 28 April 1916, 58–52–1, LAC, RG 24, vol. 5661.

48. Naval Historical Section, "Brief History of HMCS *Grilse*," 6 March 1961, 10, DHH 81/520/8000, "HMCS *Grilse*."

49. Ibid, 15.

an order for all hands to hold fast for their lives, but nowhere is it mentioned that the order was heard above the gale. *Grilse* was in the best possible attitude to ride the sea but even so she broached to. The sea beat her down and threw her over to starboard on her beam ends—the pendulum in the engine-room showed a roll of 89 degrees. The bridge wing supports buckled, the after funnel was crushed, the engine-room skylight was stove in and the mainmast went by the board."[50] By the time the ship righted herself, four more sailors from the deck party, including wireless operator Clements, had vanished over the side. With water flooding the engine room to a depth of four feet and the ship listing 20° to starboard Sub-Lieutenant Cyril Fry led a working party to improvise a cover over the engine room, while a bucket brigade tried to assist the pumps in gaining on the water forward.

By morning on the 13th, NSHQ had been informed by Halifax that "signal reported 11.40 pm from Cape Sable, *Grilse* says 'now sinking.' Barrington calling at intervals, nothing heard from *Grilse* after 1.00 am."[51] Halifax also instructed *Margaret*, then on the port's outer patrol, and *Stadacona* at Shelburne to search for *Grilse* at her last reported position, while Barrington wireless station broadcast a message en clair to all ships in the area to render assistance. Once the public was alerted that the warship was missing, headquarters began to receive enquiries from anxious relatives and with no further word from the vessel, finally sent out telegrams to the next of kin on the 14th informing them that *Grilse* "was lost at sea with all hands." Only shortly before midnight that same day did Ottawa receive a message from Shelburne that *Grilse* had limped into harbour. After surviving a gale wind of Force 7 or 8 for over thirty-six hours, a moderation in the weather had allowed the damaged Canadian torpedo boat destroyer to restart her engines and enter the Nova Scotia port at 2145 hours.[52]

One week later, HMCS *Margaret* towed the battered warship back to Halifax where she was paid off and placed in dockyard hands for refit. The subsequent court of inquiry found "that the ship was properly navigated. That the primary cause of the loss of life and damage to the ship was the extreme violence of the weather encountered. Reviewing the circumstances, and having considered the evidence, we are of the opinion that no blame is attributable to the commanding officer, officers, or ship's company of the *Grilse*." Nonetheless, the court did feel that the incorrect position *Grilse* had radioed to shore authorities on the evening of the 12th was "a regrettable feature" of the incident, since it meant that the subsequent search for the vessel was conducted over the wrong area, and pointed out that it "could hardly have occurred had Lieutenant Wingate checked it." When *Grilse* was recommissioned for service on 10 May 1917, she did so with a new captain, Commander J.T. Shenton, new officers, and a new crew.[53]

Although the Canadian navy was primarily occupied with protecting the important East Coast shipping lanes, the RCN continued to maintain a naval presence in the Pacific

---

50. Ibid, 16–17.

51. Navyard Halifax to Naval Ottawa, 13 December 1916, quoted in ibid, 11.

52. Ibid, 12, 18–20.

53. Ibid, 20–21.

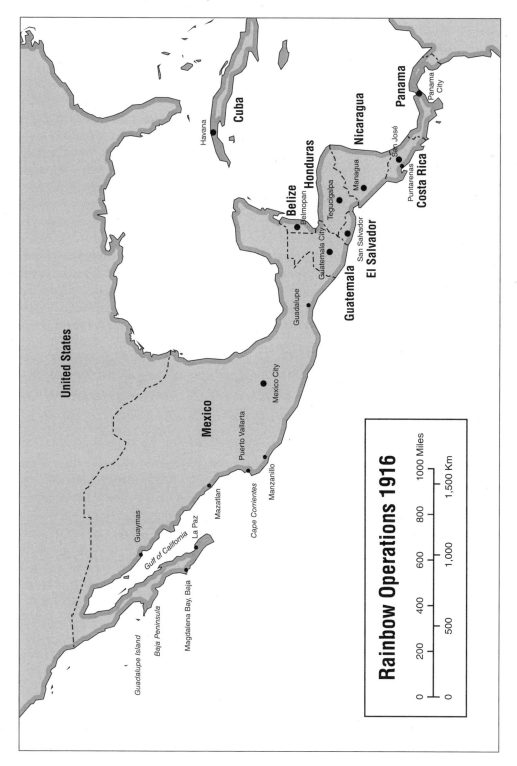

Rainbow Operations 1916

where HMCS *Rainbow*, despite her obsolescence, performed useful reconnaissance work during 1916 on German shipping activity along the coast of Mexico and Central America. The need for such a mission resulted from a request by the British chargé d'affaires in Mexico to have a warship present in the area during the spring. The Canadian cruiser, still under the command of Walter Hose, was earmarked for the operation because "no other ship was available" and the Admiralty completed the necessary arrangements with NSHQ on 4 February 1916.[54] *Rainbow* had undertaken a similar patrol in the spring of 1915 but had been limited in its movements by the lack of an accompanying collier. That handicap was remedied the following summer with the despatch of *South Pacific* to the Mexican coast in advance of *Rainbow*'s departure from Esquimalt on 24 February. Proceeding south to a coaling rendezvous with *South Pacific* at Magdalena Bay near the tip of the Baja California peninsula on 2 March, *Rainbow* spent the next two months patrolling the West Coast of Mexico and Central America.

By month's end, the Canadian cruiser had ranged as far south as Punta Arenas, Costa Rica, in company with her collier, making frequent calls at neutral ports to ascertain, with the aid of British consular officials, if there was any enemy activity in support of possible German surface raiders. Returning to Manzanillo, Mexico, in early April, Hose found the chief concern of the British consul was the safety of foreign nationals, particularly United States citizens, in view of the "serious condition of the Mexico–American situation" after a US Army punitive expedition under Brigadier-General John J. Pershing crossed into Mexico in mid-March in a vain attempt to capture the bandit-revolutionist leader Francisco "Pancho" Villa. Although *Rainbow* continued to patrol off the coast, Hose "arranged to leave the *South Pacific* in Manzanillo to be available to remove refugees if necessary, this arrangement fitted with my own programme and relieved the anxiety of the British consul as regards the safety of foreigners."[55]

It was not until the later half of April that *Rainbow* made her first seizure of a vessel believed to be working on behalf of the enemy. Shortly before departing Mazatlan, Mexico, on 16 April, Hose spotted an auxiliary power schooner "approaching the port under power, but sighted too late to enable me to weigh and close her before she got into territorial waters. The schooner proved to be the *Oregon* flying the US flag." Suspicious of the vessel, the Canadian cruiser spent the next week patrolling off Guaymas in the Gulf of California, the schooner's next destination. On the 23rd, the Canadian cruiser intercepted and stopped the American-flagged but German-owned vessel. "On receiving the report of the boarding officer, [Hose] decided to send her to Esquimalt for adjudication."[56] Taking the schooner in tow, *Rainbow* proceeded to La Paz, where most of the Mexican crew was landed, before taking up the hunt for her next quarry, the German-owned schooner *Leonor*. As Hose explained in his subsequent report of proceedings, the Canadian cruiser steamed to Cape Corrientes off Puerto Vallarta "to lie in wait." Hose received regular wireless updates on the movements of the *Leonor* "by means of a code and system I had arranged

---

54. T. Jackson minute, 8 July 1916, UKNA, ADM 137/762.

55. Hose to NSHQ, 25 April 1916, ibid.

56. Ibid.

with the [British] vice-consuls at La Paz, Mazatlan and Manzanillo" thereby allowing *Rainbow* to remain out of sight over the horizon. "It had been my intention to meet HBM vice-consul at Mazatlan outside the three mile limit off that port and give him telegrams for dispatch to Ottawa, but since the capture of the *Oregon* was likely very soon to be generally known, I considered it desirable to give the impression that *Rainbow* had gone away from the coast with the *Oregon* and consequently decided not to appear off Mazatlan."[57]

Although concerned that a shortage of provisions would force him to abandon the attempt to capture the German-owned schooner, Hose stayed on patrol until the Mexican-flagged vessel was finally sighted on the morning of 2 May. *Rainbow* discharged the schooner's passengers and crew at Mazatlan before taking the ship in tow for a rendezvous with *South Pacific* and *Oregon* at Guadalupe Island off the northern Baja peninsula.[58] The captures prompted the German representative of the Hamburg-Amerika Line at Manzanillo, Adolfo Stoll, to write the US vice-consul at the port on 8 May with complaints from his "clients" about the "risk in shipping in American bottoms as they heard about the capture of the American schooner *Oregon* by an English cruiser in the Gulf of California a few weeks ago. As the same raider has also captured recently the Mexican schooner *Leonor* they presume that no cargo will be safe hereafter and desire to be informed about the matter."[59] Even though *Oregon* had carried a US flag when captured by *Rainbow*, American officials did not share Stoll's outrage, informing the German shipping agent that "vessels wholly owned by American citizens are American vessels, such vessel loses her privileges as a registered vessel in being sold to a foreigner."[60]

Unfortunately, gale-force winds were encountered after the Canadian cruiser and her prize rounded the tip of Baja California and it was not until 12 May that *Rainbow* and *South Pacific*, with *Leonor* and *Oregon* in tow respectively, shaped course for Esquimalt. Heavy weather continued to dog their northern progress for the next several days, with the ships' speed often reduced to only three or four knots. With the Canadian vessels only provisioned until 22 May, Hose radioed HMS *Newcastle* on the 16th to ask the British cruiser to provide *South Pacific* and *Oregon* with supplies, while *Rainbow* and *Leonor* set a faster pace for Esquimalt. The British warship had been operating in South American waters during *Rainbow*'s cruise and finally overtook the *South Pacific* and her prize on 21 May "in a gale of wind off San Francisco," but it was not until the following morning that the weather abated sufficiently to allow *Newcastle* to pass provisions to them.[61] Despite the continuing storm, *Rainbow* arrived at Esquimalt with her prize in tow on the morning of the 21st.

In reporting on the cruise to Ottawa, Hose made a point of praising the work of one of his RNCVR officers, Lieutenant Walter Wingate (who was soon transferred east

57. Hose to NSHQ, 21 May 1916, ibid.

58. Ibid.

59. Adolfo Stoll, Hamburg-Amerika Line to Richard Stadden, American vice consul in charge, Manzanillo, 8 May 1916, ibid.

60. Richard Stadden, American vice consul in charge, Manzanillo to Adolfo Stoll, 8 May 1916, ibid.

61. Captain F.A. Powlett, HMS *Newcastle* to Admiralty, 1 June 1916, Hose to NSHQ, 21 May 1916, ibid.

HMCS *Rainbow* arrives back in Esquimalt on 21 May 1916 with the captured German schooner *Leonor* in tow. (DND CN 6366)

to command *Grilse*), in boarding the captured vessels and searching their papers.[62] As he recalled soon after the war, *Rainbow*'s CO was also proud of the conduct of his crew, a majority of whom were RNCVR sailors:

> Owing to the fact that these captures were made at the end of [a] three months cruise and that during the 3,000 miles of towing done by *Rainbow* extraordinary adverse weather conditions were experienced, very short rations had to be resorted to for some weeks before Esquimalt was reached, but in this, as in all other discomforts experienced by the men, nothing but good humour prevailed.
>
> An amusing cartoon appeared on the mess deck the day before reaching Esquimalt, depicting an elongated and emaciated squad fallen in on the quarterdeck and underneath written: "Physical drill—All hands through the ring-bolt."
>
> But there was other value than that of keeping on the lookout in those years of patrolling the Pacific from 1914 to 1917—there was the training work. After each cruise a new batch of "amateur sailors" was embarked from the depot at Esquimalt and a large percentage of the RNCVR ranks and ratings who afterwards were employed in anti-submarine work on both sides of the Atlantic had their first insight into man-of-war routine on board HMCS *Rainbow*.[63]

The Admiralty's assessment of the three-month cruise was restrained by concerns that the Canadian warship had not kept the senior naval officer in the Pacific, Captain F.A. Powlett of *Newcastle*, sufficiently informed of her movements and that copies of Hose's reports of proceedings had not been forwarded to him. The director of the operations division in Whitehall observed that "the Department of the Naval Service seems to have run things very fine and to have had no scheme thought out for re-provisioning the *Rainbow* if her cruise lasted longer than anticipated. The necessity for supplying fuel was recognized and colliers were arranged for; that for supplying food was not seen."[64] Hose had, of course, decided to remain on patrol off Mexico for as long as he felt prudent in order to capture *Leonor* only to have the misfortune of making his way north in the face of two weeks of extremely adverse weather conditions. Rather than congratulate the Canadian cruiser for an otherwise successful operation, however, the Admiralty drew attention to the mistakes made, addressing a letter to Kingsmill in mid-July "to point out that no arrangements were evidently made for reprovisioning HMCS *Rainbow* if her cruise lasted longer than anticipated, and that consequently a serious shortage was narrowly averted. Her commanding officer did not apparently allow enough margin for delay, bad weather or accident. I am to suggest that in future, on a cruise of this sort, HMCS *Rainbow* should take a reserve supply of provisions in her collier."[65]

---

62. Hose to NSHQ, 21 May 1916, ibid.

63. Hose to Mr S. Brent, 19 February 1919, DHH 81/520/1000–5-5.

64. Captain T. Jackson minutes, 8 July and 21 June 1916, Rear-Admiral H. Oliver minute, 21 June 1916, UKNA, ADM 137/762.

65. Admiralty to Kingsmill, 13 July 1916, ibid.

Something the Admiralty could not find fault with, however, was the continuing efficiency of the overseas transport organization being directed by the CPR's Arthur Harris. The volume of war supplies shipped overseas continued to grow in 1916 with some thirty to thirty-five Admiralty-chartered transports being cleared from Canadian ports each month that the St Lawrence was open to navigation. The 1,368,455 tons of war supplies that Harris's organization handled from May to November 1916 was a three-fold increase over the 431,763 tons moved over the same period in 1915, while the average number of transports in Canadian service increased to eighty-two from a mere twenty the year before.[66] During the calendar year as a whole, the transport service shipped 1,464,625 tons of war supplies with over half, 772,149 tons, being shipped from Montreal. The ice-free ports of St John, New Brunswick, and Halifax, Nova Scotia, on the other hand, shipped 401,525 and 337,980 tons, respectively, almost all of it loaded between early December and the middle of May.[67] As the Admiralty informed Harris at the end of July, "the importance of the Canadian store service has throughout been recognized here, and the fleet on this service has in the past been increased to, and maintained at, as high a figure as possible." London was also appreciative "of the manner in which the increased quantities of stores have been handled and shipped. The many difficulties, railway and otherwise, attendant on the service are fully recognized on this side, and transports appear to have been handled with the best possible despatch."[68]

As successful as the 1916 shipping season had been, however, the naval service remained concerned that it was required to authorize the finances of an organization over which it had no real control. The Cabinet subcommittee that Borden had set up by order-in-council in January 1916 to oversee Harris's work seldom convened and quickly came to be regarded at NSHQ as a nonentity.[69] As a result, the question of the overseas director's relationship with the naval department was taken up once again by the director of stores, J.A. Wilson, at the end of the 1916 season. Pointing out that under the terms of PC 34, Harris was to have become a civil servant, paid by the Canadian government, Wilson "found that the transference has never fully been completed as Mr Harris is still paid by the [Canadian Pacific] company.... While no objection could be taken to this course as a temporary measure, the organization has grown so large and the work promises to continue for such a lengthy period, it is submitted that the question of whether it would not be better to defray this expense out of the War Vote, rather than allowing it to continue to be met from the funds of an outside corporation, which is also largely concerned in transportation work should be reconsidered." Although the director of stores did not say it explicitly, Harris's

---

66. Harris to Desbarats, 12 December 1916, 1048–18–1, pt. 1, LAC, RG 24, vol. 3713.

67. Harris to Desbarats, 8 May, 9 June, 6 July, 9 August, and 13 November 1916, 22 January, 8 February, 10 March, and 11 April 1917, ibid; and Harris to Desbarats, 12 October, 13 November, and 20 December 1917, 1048–18–1, pt. 3, LAC, RG 24, vol. 3714.

68. Graeme Thomson, Transport Department, Admiralty to A.H. Harris, Acting Director of Overseas Transport, 31 July 1916, 1048–18–1, pt. 1, LAC, RG 24, vol. 3713.

69. Kingsmill to Graeme Thomson, Director of Transports, Admiralty, 28 November 1917, 1048–18–2, LAC, RG 24 vol. 3714.

continuing status as a Canadian Pacific employee placed him in a conflict of interest since his complete power over the inland transportation network would allow him to direct war shipments to maximize his company's rail lines and profits. It was also Wilson's contention "that the present is an opportune time to raise the question as Mr Harris, it is understood, has received notification from the premier that he is now to be styled the 'director of overseas transport' instead of as formerly acting director of overseas transport."[70] While Wilson's suggestions received the support of the navy's chief of staff, Commander Stephens, Harris's political connections with the prime minister, as demonstrated by the removal of the "acting" part of his title, were more than naval minister Hazen was willing to challenge. Desbarats's only reply to his subordinate was to minute that the paper had been "seen by minister who is not prepared to act as suggested."[71]

Coordinating the naval aspects of forwarding Canadian war supplies was not the only direct assistance NSHQ was able to offer the British war effort, however. Although the British government had advised Ottawa in October 1914 that it would be better to concentrate Canada's war effort on an expeditionary force rather than diverting resources into its naval service, there were a number of young Canadians who preferred to serve in the navy rather than the army. Early in the war, NSHQ had arranged transportation for any RNR officers and men resident in Canada at the outbreak of war who wished to return to Britain and provided assistance to the Admiralty in enrolling men directly into the Royal Naval Air Service, the Yacht Patrol Service, and the Royal Naval Auxiliary Patrol (Motor Boat Service). Ottawa was less willing to let members of the RNCVR leave for Britain during the conflict's initial stages, however. When nine officers and 120 sailors of the RNCVR volunteered to go to Britain to join the recently formed Royal Naval Brigade, raised for service ashore, the men were advised to join the Canadian Expeditionary Force if they wished to fight on land.[72]

With the RCN preoccupied during 1915 with keeping the crews of its two cruisers up to strength, and with organizing and manning a patrol service in the Gulf of St Lawrence, it was not until early 1916 that the question of sending RNCVR sailors overseas was raised again. On 10 February, the naval service minister asked London if authorities there would be interested in recruiting Canadians for service in the Royal Navy. Hazen's main stipulation was that the British would have to train the recruits themselves since the RCN had not instructors nor facilities to spare for the task.[73] The Admiralty responded favourably, suggesting that the men should be enrolled in the Royal Navy at British rates of pay for service in the RN's auxiliary patrol. Despatching Captain Rupert Guinness and a small naval party to Canada in May, the Royal Navy recruiters quickly discovered that would-be Canadian sailors were uninterested in joining the British service when the RN rate of pay for an able-bodied seaman was only forty cents a day when the regular RCN was

70. J.A. Wilson, "Memo to Deputy Minister," 23 January 1917, ibid.

71. Stephens minute, 23 January 1917, Desbarats minute, 26 January 1917, ibid.

72. Tucker, *Naval Service of Canada*, I, 220–22.

73. Desbarats to Canadian High Commissioner, 10 February 1916, cited in Tucker, *Naval Service of Canada*, I, 220. Unfortunately the pertinent file with the correspondence, NS 62–16–1, has since disappeared.

paying seventy cents and the CEF $1.10 for similarly qualified men.[74] With Guinness unable to recruit Canadians under the terms being offered, Ottawa intervened the following month with an offer "to recruit men into the Canadian Naval Volunteer Reserve [*sic*] and place them at the disposal of the Admiralty for service in the imperial navy." The Admiralty agreed to the Canadian proposal at the end of July and promptly informed Ottawa that they would "be glad to secure the services of 2,000 men in the various ratings in the current calendar year. Any further men that the Canadian government may be disposed to offer over and above these numbers could be utilised to meet the requirements of the fleet during the calendar year 1917."[75]

Kingsmill still had some concerns that the RCN would need "the most concise information from the Admiralty as to how it is proposed to utilize the men sent over, and a clear statement as to period of service and what are the prospects of advancement," and insisted that the naval recruits would have to be paid the same $1.10 per day that CEF soldiers received. Even then, the naval director realized that recruiting 2,000 men over the next nine months "would mean a very considerable amount of extra work" for the RCN's "limited staff."[76] For one thing, the RNCVR was not organized to conduct a national recruiting campaign. The volunteer sailors, as Commander Stephens pointed out, had joined "local detachments, each with their own officers and headquarters," while the overseas proposal did "not contemplate any officers, or any local instruction." The chief of staff suggested that the need for a new pay scale could be avoided if the recruits joined the RCN for the duration of the war since a regular sailor's pay of seventy cents a day (as opposed to the eighty cents paid to RNCVR sailors), when added to the RN pay of forty cents a day, would equal the $1.10 being paid by the CEF.[77] When the terms of enlistment were finalized on 9 September 1916 by order-in-council PC 2130, it was decided to enlist up to 5,000 sailors into the RNCVR for service overseas, rather than into the RCN, but pay them the CEF rate of $1.10 per day as opposed to the eighty cents that volunteers remaining in Canada received.[78]

The naval department organized naval recruiting committees in each province to begin the enlistment campaign. The provincial committees, composed of "gentlemen who are willing to help in this recruiting," were to "meet together and elect an executive committee to organize and carry out a recruiting campaign in their province." Subcommittees were formed "to organize a local campaign in their own towns" under the guidance of the provincial committee. Although local physicians were to give each prospective recruit a medical examination, the men were not sworn into the service until they had been examined by a naval doctor in either Halifax or Esquimalt. The provincial committees were also encouraged to enlist "suitable men who have had some sea experience" as

---

74. Tucker, *Naval Service of Canada*, I, 220; and Stephens, "Proposed Scheme for Entry and Pay," 8 August 1916, "Table of Pay," 26–16–2, pt. 1, LAC, RG 24, vol. 5597.

75. W. Graham Greene, Admiralty Secretary to Undersecretary of State, Colonial Office, 31 July 1916, ibid.

76. Kingsmill, "Memorandum for Deputy Minister," 9 August 1916, ibid.

77. Stephens, "Proposed Scheme for Entry and Pay," 8 August 1916, "Table of Pay," ibid.

78. PC 2130, 9 September 1916.

RNCVR recruiting petty officers because they could provide a "naval face" in the recruiting offices. These petty officers were not part of the Overseas Division but were carried on the books of NSHQ, the number required in each province being left to the discretion of the individual committees.[79] Assistance in the recruiting campaign was also provided by militia district recruiters who were instructed to display navy recruiting posters in their offices and provide medical examinations if a naval doctor was unavailable. It was stipulated, however, that naval recruiting officers were "not allowed to enlist in the RNCVR men serving in the Canadian Expeditionary Force."[80]

At the end of September, Desbarats provided the Admiralty with the enlistment details for the proposed Overseas Division including the assurance that the Canadians would be borne on NSHQ's books "for *full pay* [by the Canadian government] for the entire period of their service." As a means of ensuring their continued identification as Canadian sailors, it was explained that "men proceeding overseas will be supplied with RNCVR cap ribbons, and it is requested that they may be permitted to continue to wear these cap ribbons throughout the entire period of their service."[81] While London was "anxious that full advantage should be taken of the generous offer of the Canadian government" to recruit 5,000 men for the Royal Navy over the next twelve months, it asked for further details regarding the higher rates of pay being given the RNCVR sailors.[82] On 7 November, NSHQ reiterated that RNCVR sailors would only receive RN rates of pay while overseas, with the remainder of their wages being held on account in Canada. It was also suggested that RNCVR drafts be distributed equally between the RN depots at Devonport, Portsmouth and Chatham where it was "presumed that men will undergo a course of training in the depots before being drafted to sea-going ships and vessels. All men when arriving in the depots in England will hold the rating of ordinary seaman, and it is left to the discretion of the Admiralty to utilize recruits, who have volunteered for stokers' duties, in that capacity, and to promote men to higher ratings as they see fit." Rather than requesting to have its sailors be allowed to wear cap ribbons identifying them as RNCVR, however, Ottawa used more forceful language in its November reply, insisting that "they will be permitted to wear [RNCVR cap ribbons] throughout their entire period of service."[83]

One of the first Canadians to enlist in the navy's Overseas Division was H.C. Manuel, who was working in Saskatchewan in 1916 as an employee of the Grand Trunk Pacific Railway. Since RNCVR sailors served overseas as individuals rather than as an identified unit, Manuel's account of his experiences—besides being one of a very few first person accounts left by an RCN sailor—provides a valuable illustration of a typical Canadian's service in the Overseas Division. As Manuel explained to the naval historical section in 1951, there was "pressure for all young men to enlist" but when he broached the subject

---

79. "Organization for the Obtaining of Recruits for the RNCVR Overseas Division By Establishment of Provincial Committees," nd, 26–16–2, pt. 1, LAC, RG 24, vol. 5597.

80. Adjutant General to Officers Commanding Districts, 19 September 1916, ibid.

81. Desbarats to Admiralty, 28 September 1916, ibid.

82. Admiralty to Colonial Office, 10 October 1916, ibid.

83. Desbarats to Admiralty, 7 November 1916, ibid.

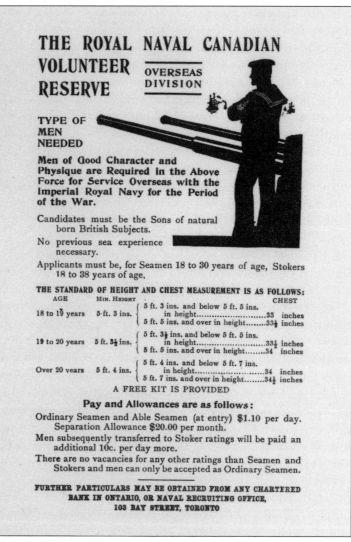

A 1916 recruiting poster for the RNCVR Overseas Division. The advertised pay of $1.10 per day was the same rate that Canadian Expeditionary Force recruits received and well in excess of a Royal Navy rating's pay of forty cents per day. (LAC e007140888)

with his boss "he commended me for my feelings but [in view of the shortage of railway staff] asked me to wait for a while until things were better adjusted. There was always the argument that the railway was an important link in the country's defence and must be manned."

The situation drifted along in this way until the spring of 1916 when I succeeded in getting away for a long postponed vacation. I knew in my mind then that I would be enlisting before long, although of course we all thought the war might be over [at] any time. In the fall of 1916, when in Winnipeg, I saw that recruiting had started for the RNCVR. Presumably England was having trouble finding sufficient suitable men for her navy and, as Canada's navy had already practically folded up, owing to the *Niobe* and *Rainbow* having finally accepted their inevitable role of becoming depot ships permanently moored to the docks, they were recruiting in Canada.

By this time much of the glamour of life in the trenches had worn off. I was always fond of the water from having been brought up on a lake in Ontario, where I had done considerable boating. I went in to enquire about joining and came out after signing the necessary papers and with the understanding that I would have time to give notice to the railway and wind up my affairs.... I reported back to Winnipeg on December 5th and, in company with another recruit, travelled east....

My first ship was the aforementioned *Niobe*—she was packed with the Canadian naval Halifax depot staff and recruits. After a few days there, the issue of additional kit and some instructions on how to wear our uniforms, etc. they started drafting for England. Fifty were selected and sent aboard the *Olympic* which apparently sailed that night. The next day one hundred more, including me, were drafted aboard HMS *Calgarian*, an auxiliary cruiser. When we sailed much to our surprise the *Olympic* sailed out of Bedford Basin and we escorted her for two or three days, after which she ran away and left us having much superior speed. We were at sea for Christmas [1916] and had rather an eventful voyage for a bunch of raw recruits....

The one hundred and fifty ratings included in this first draft were sent, fifty each, to the three naval training stations in England, viz., Portsmouth, Devonport and Chatham. I was sent to Chatham.... We were given a course of basic training which was strenuous but effective and by March [1917] we were ready for draft, but for three weeks were assigned to an old wooden ship tied up in the dockyard and used as a stokers' training ship, as a maintenance crew.

I might say at this point that the arrangement under which we were paid was rather unique—we were paid $1.10 per day by Canada, the same as was paid in the Canadian Army. While in the Royal Navy we were at all times paid on the same basis as Royal Naval ratings. It is my understanding our pay as ordinary seamen or special allowances was paid by the Royal Navy. The rest of our Canadian money was held in Canada for us. We were permitted to have most of it paid to someone in Canada who could send it on to us if desired.

Under this arrangement there was no dissatisfaction among the English ratings on account of our drawing higher pay. Generally speaking this worked alright, although some of the older Royal Naval ratings always resented us, mainly on account of the fact that they knew we were getting much higher pay and subsequently much more rapid promotion.

The first draft for sea duty from the RNCVR was to [the cruiser] HMS *Bacchante*, but I was not included in it. By the time recruiting had started for the RNCVR, men were drifting in from the more remote parts of Canada [to volunteer], much the way I had done, consequently it was rather surprising the number of men from lumber camps, ranches, etc., that were included in our first draft of one hundred and fifty, in other words, lumber-jacks and cowboys. The *Bacchante* turned out to be quite the pusser ship and the Canadians did not take kindly to the rigid British discipline, in fact they proved quite a headache to the officers as they acted as ringleaders for the British ratings and, according to rumours that reached us, the crew was almost constantly under special discipline. The ship was stationed on the West African coast and on one occasion some of the Canadians decided to leave and stole the steam pinnace, starting off up the coast. They were, of course, soon overtaken and returned to the ship.

It was rumoured that the Canadians had proven so poorly adapted to strict naval discipline on the *Bacchante* that it was decided they would serve to better advantage on smaller ships and divided into smaller groups. Whether this was so or not, the fact remains that the whole set up was later changed with this in view. Typical of the Royal Navy, however, they did not give up on the men sent to the *Bacchante*. Although the rest of us finally all ended up on small craft, these men were kept on regular naval ships throughout the war. The only time I saw any of them again, they were on one of the destroyers in the crack flotilla out of Harwich, assigned to the channel meat run, just after the Germans had trapped them off the Dutch coast and really battered them.[84]

After completing his training at Chatham at the end of March 1917, Manuel was drafted to an auxiliary cruiser, HMS *Mantua*, serving as a convoy escort between Britain and South Africa. After only one convoy trip, however, the RNCVR sailor was recalled ashore for gunnery training before being sent to Milford Haven, Wales, for two-months duty on an anti-submarine drifter patrolling the St George's channel. In November 1917, Manuel and another Canadian rating were transferred to a base near Grimsby on the English East Coast

---

84. H.C. Manuel, "Memories of the Royal Naval Canadian Volunteer Reserve," 1951, DHH 81/520/1440–5, vol. 4, file 2.

His Majesty's Transport *Olympic* at Halifax in 1916. The White Star liner, a sister ship of the ill-fated *Titanic*, was chartered by the Canadian government during 1916–17 to carry Canadian troops overseas. Affectionately referred to as "Old Reliable," *Olympic* safely transported some 66,000 troops and 41,000 civilians during the war. (DND CN 4066)

for service on a trawler escorting ships between the Firth of Forth and Bergen, Norway. After "a rather eventful winter in the North Sea," Manuel was sent to Devonport in February 1918 where "all the Canadian ratings were being assembled."

> Some had already been returned to Canada for duty on Canada's east coast in Canadian ships. After some delay, we were drafted to Gibraltar where we were assigned to Canadian-built drifters which, we understood, had been brought across the Atlantic by Newfoundland crews. They could certainly not be classed as outstanding examples of the shipbuilders' craft. They were ninety-three feet long, twenty foot beam, all wooden construction with a top speed of six knots. We could not chase anything but neither could we run away. They mounted a three-pounder [gun]. They were manned with all-Canadian crews and I had more sea experience than any man aboard. Some of the later drafts from Canada had been rushed through schools and given commissions as warrant officers for the purpose of obtaining captains for the ships.
>
> Our crew consisted of the following—Captain, a Welshman who had been farming in Canada; P.[etty] O.[fficer]—mate, from Vancouver where he had had some experience with small boating; P.O.—chief engineer, had run a small lighting plant in southern Alberta; P.O.—second engineer was a railway fireman; one stoker had come from college in southwestern Ontario and the other from a railway shop in northwestern Ontario. The three other deck hands were one farmer from Saskatchewan, one young chap from a fishing village in Prince Edward Island and one from some coast city in Nova Scotia. The cook was a homesteader from northern Alberta who apparently never had lived very well, based on our experience with his ability in the galley. I was the gunner on the ship and for a while had to double as signalman as the man trained for that duty had a limited education and was not interested in signalling. I had picked it up during my spare time on other ships.
>
> Some of the ships were sent to the Azores but we were ordered, along with three other ships, to Freetown, Sierra Leone, West Africa, where we arrived in April after an eventful voyage in our semi-submarines. The motley crew soon shook down and the ship ran smoothly so far as operation was concerned. We found on arrival at Freetown that our duty was to sweep for mines.[85]

Manuel's and the other three Canadian-manned drifters spent the remainder of the war in west Africa where the 1918 influenza epidemic proved to be more dangerous than enemy mines, claiming the life of the mate in Manuel's crew. Following the armistice in November, the Canadians at Freetown returned to England in early 1919, where they turned over their drifters, and did not finally reach Halifax until May.[86]

While the Overseas Division recruiting campaign was being established in the fall of

---

85. Ibid.

86. Ibid.

1916, the navy also recognized that at least a portion of the sailors who were already serving in its patrol forces wanted to see service in RN ships overseas. In October, for instance, Pasco reported having "received numerous applications from RNCVR ratings in patrol flotilla requesting transfer to RNCVR for overseas service."[87] Not wanting to see its patrol forces denuded of experienced sailors, NSHQ insisted that RNCVR applications for transfer to the Overseas Division "will in no case be entertained unless the applicants can provide substitutes acceptable to the commanding officers of the ships in which they serve."[88] By December 1916, however, provisions had been made to allow Overseas Division recruits to "volunteer for duty in home waters" with each case being "referred to the department for decision." "Men in the RNCVR desirous of transferring to the RNCVR Overseas Division are to be placed on a roster as they apply and may exchange with RNCVR Overseas Division recruits volunteering for duty in home waters, provided fit and useful men are retained in their place."[89] During the last two years of the conflict, the need to retain sailors in Canada to fill the crews of the RCN's rapidly expanding patrol forces meant that a far greater proportion of RNCVR recruits remained in Canada rather than being sent overseas. As a result, while Ottawa's original recruiting proposal had been to send up to 5,000 Canadian sailors to the Royal Navy as part of the Overseas Division, only some 1,700 RNCVRs were eventually sent across the Atlantic, while the majority, 6,300 volunteer sailors, served in Canadian waters during the war.[90]

Even as NSHQ was moving to assist the Royal Navy by establishing an Overseas Division for service in European waters, the battlefields in France were witnessing two of the bloodiest slogging offensives of the war. Striking before the Allies could launch their own planned offensive, the Fifth German Army attacked the well-fortified, but lightly garrisoned, French salient around Verdun on 21 February 1916. Determined to hold the salient at all cost, French reinforcements were rushed into the area, and their commander's instruction—"*Ils ne passeront pas!*" ("They shall not pass!")—became France's motto for the remainder of the war. Repeated German attacks through the end of August succeeded in capturing Fort Vaux and reduced French communications into the salient to a single secondary road but were unable to capture Verdun. A French counter-offensive in the fall managed to retake most of the ground lost since February and brought the ten-month battle to a close. The desperate fighting cost some 542,000 French and 434,000 German casualties. In the meantime, a joint Anglo-French offensive had been opened astride the Somme River on 1 July to divert German strength away from Verdun. With the British Fourth Army taking the leading role, the straight-ahead assault on the German frontline on the first day proved disastrous, incurring nearly 60,000 British casualties for little gain. Undaunted, British commander-in-chief Sir Douglas Haig continued the offensive until mid-November, even though he was only able to push the frontline forward some ten

87. Pasco to Kingsmill, 9 October 1916, 26–16–2, pt. 1, LAC, RG 24, vol. 5597.

88. NSHQ to Senior Officer Patrols, 13 October 1916, ibid.

89. NSHQ to Superintendent, HMC Dockyard, Esquimalt, 4 December 1916, ibid.

90. Tucker, *The Naval Service of Canada*, I, 221.

kilometres. The Canadian Corps entered the battle at the beginning of September and in the next few months suffered 24,000 casualties in a series of attacks to the left of the Albert-Bapaume Road. Altogether, the Battle of the Somme cost the British 420,000, the French 204,000, and the Germans 650,000 casualties, staggering losses that, when added to the dead and wounded of Verdun, underscored the fact that by 1916 the fighting had deteriorated into a campaign of attrition.[91]

At sea, 1916 also saw the long-anticipated clash between the German High Seas Fleet and the British Grand Fleet off the coast of Jutland. Aided by the Admiralty's radio intelligence organization, Room 40, of enemy naval movements, the British Grand Fleet had maintained a distant blockade of the German fleet from its base at Scapa Flow in northern Scotland.[92] Although their respective battle cruisers had engaged in several limited North Sea actions since the outbreak of war, most notably a running gun battle across the Dogger Bank in January 1915, the fleets' battleship squadrons had yet to come within sight of each other. That inaction ended when the High Seas Fleet, with sixteen modern dreadnoughts, left Wilhelmshaven in the early morning hours of 31 May and shaped course north for the Skagerrak, hoping to ambush a portion of the British fleet. Warned by Room 40 that the enemy battlefleet was about to put to sea, Sir John Jellicoe led the entire Grand Fleet of 151 warships, twenty-eight of which were dreadnoughts, across the North Sea to intercept three hours before the German fleet sailed.[93]

On the afternoon of the 31st, the German battle cruiser squadron was sighted by its counterpart and a running gun battle ensued as the German ships turned south to draw the British battle cruisers onto the High Seas Fleet's main battleline. Turret hits by the accurate German gunfire blew apart the battle cruisers *Indefatigable* and *Queen Mary* within twenty minutes of each other, prompting the battle cruiser commander, Vice-Admiral David Beatty, to remark that "there seems to be something wrong with our bloody ships today."[94] Turning north upon sighting the High Seas Fleet, Beatty then led the Germans back toward the

---

91. John Keegan, *The First World War* (New York 1999), 278–99; and G.W.L. Nicholson, *Canadian Expeditionary Force, 1914–1919* (Ottawa 1964), 130–31, 160–200, 250.

92. Jason Hines, "Sins of Omission and Commission: A Reassessment of the Role of Intelligence in the Battle of Jutland," *The Journal of Military History,* LXXII (October 2008), 1121–22.

93. Ibid, 1126.

94. W.S. Chalmers, *The Life and Letters of David, Earl Beatty* (London 1951), 234; and Nicholas A. Lambert, "'Our Bloody Ships' or 'Our Bloody System'? Jutland and the Loss of the Battle Cruisers, 1916," *The Journal of Military History,* LXII (January 1998), 29–55. Lambert points out that in the aftermath of the battle the Admiralty "swiftly agreed that the explosions were due to the gun crews having ignored cordite safety regulations in an effort to speed their rate of gunfire. They found ample evidence to indicate that in addition to the charges normally in transit from the magazines to the guns there were large numbers of unprotected cartridges inside the turrets stacked for 'ready use.' Under these conditions, they concluded, each turret became its own magazine in which case a single hit on any turret would have produced an enormous explosion and consequently the loss of the ship. In effect, the officers and men of the lost battle cruisers were largely responsible for their own deaths. The senior officers who had condoned the dangerous practices, moreover, were guilty of complicity." Lambert, "Our Bloody Ships," 31. See also Arthur J. Marder, *From the Dreadnought to Scapa Flow, The Royal Navy in the Fisher Era,* III: *Jutland and After (May 1916-December 1916)* (London 1966), 208–14.

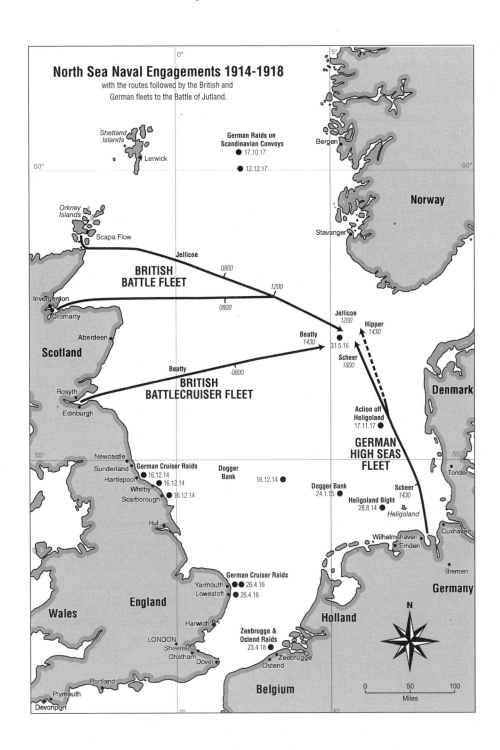

North Sea Naval Engagements 1914-1918
with the routes followed by the British and
German fleets to the Battle of Jutland.

Shetland
Islands

Lerwick

**German Raids on
Scandinavian Convoys**
● 17.10.17

● 12.12.17

Bergen

60°   60°

Norway

Orkney
Islands

Scapa Flow

Stavanger

Jellicoe

**BRITISH
BATTLE FLEET**

0800

1200

0800

Invergordon

Cromarty

Jellicoe
1200

Hipper
1430

Aberdeen

Beatty
1430

31.5.16

Scheer
1800

Scotland

Beatty

0800

**BRITISH
BATTLECRUISER FLEET**

Denmark

Rosyth

Edinburgh

Action off
Heligoland
17.11.17 ●

**GERMAN
HIGH SEAS
FLEET**

55°   55°

Newcastle

Tonder

Sunderland

German Cruiser Raids
● 16.12.14

Hartlepool ●

● 16.12.14

Whitby

Scarborough ● 16.12.14

Dogger
Bank

16.12.14 ●

Dogger Bank
24.1.15 ●

Scheer
1430

Heligoland Bight
28.8.14 ●

Heligoland

Hull

Wilhelmshaven ●
● Emden

Cuxhaven

● Bremen

German Cruiser Raids

Yarmouth ● ● 26.4.16

Lowestoft ● 26.4.16

England

Germany

Wales

Harwich ●

Holland

N

LONDON

Sheerness ●

Chatham

Dover ●

**Zeebrugge &
Ostend Raids**
23.4.18 ●

Zeebrugge

Ostend

Portland

Belgium

0   50   100

Plymouth

Devonport

Miles

Grand Fleet's battleships. Jellicoe was successful in crossing the enemy battleline's "T" but a quick German turn away allowed them to escape the superior firepower of the British dreadnoughts. Although the British scored many hits on the German battleships in the exchange, it was the battle cruiser HMS *Invincible* that disappeared in yet another catastrophic magazine explosion. After escaping from the first encounter, the Germans once again stumbled into the Grand Fleet shortly after 1900 hours before making another hasty retreat. Despite Jellicoe's efforts to keep his forces between the High Seas Fleet and the entrances to its base, mist and darkness prevented him from doing so. By the morning of 1 June, the Germans had passed astern of the British battleline and reached the safety of the Horn Reefs swept channel.[95]

In terms of casualties and ship losses, the material results of the Battle of Jutland heavily favoured the Germans. The loss of virtually the entire ships' companies in the three destroyed battle cruisers meant that the Grand Fleet's casualties stood at 6,097 for the battle as opposed to the High Seas Fleet's loss of 2,551 sailors. Besides the three battle cruisers, the British fleet lost three armoured cruisers and eight destroyers, a total of fourteen warships. The Germans lost eleven ships, including the battle cruiser *Lützow*, which succumbed to battle damage on the homeward voyage, and the pre-dreadnought battleship *Pommern*, which disintegrated after being hit by a torpedo.[96] The fact that the High Seas Fleet managed to escape relatively unscathed was especially disappointing to a British public that had expected the Grand Fleet to inflict a Trafalgar-like battle of annihilation on the enemy. Nonetheless, the battle had not altered the strategic situation since the Royal Navy still controlled the world's trade routes and was in position to continue the blockade of Germany. Although the High Seas Fleet sortied once again in August 1916, it quickly returned to Wilhelmshaven at the first reported sighting of an enemy force (as, indeed, did the Grand Fleet itself).[97] With her surface forces effectively confined to the southern North Sea, Germany's future naval effort would concentrate almost exclusively on the submarine campaign against Allied merchant shipping.

One month after the Battle of Jutland North America's vulnerability to submarine attack was dramatically brought home to both British and Canadian naval authorities by the sudden arrival of a German submarine off the coast of the United States. On 8 July the unarmed submarine freighter *U-Deutschland* entered Chesapeake Bay bound for Baltimore, Maryland, carrying a cargo of dye-stuffs, chemicals and pharmaceuticals. Built by Krupp's Germania Werft in Kiel, the *U-Deutschland* was the largest U-freighter ever built, measuring sixty-five metres long, 8.9 metres wide, and displacing 1,558 tons surfaced and 1,860 tons submerged. At a surface speed of ten knots, Krupp's submarine freighter had a range of

95. Marder, *Dreadnought to Scapa Flow,* III, 36–162; Andrew Gordon, *The Rules of the Game: Jutland and British Naval Command* (London 1996), 81–154, 403–502; Paul G. Halpern, *A Naval History of World War I* (Annapolis 1994), 310–29; Geoffrey Bennett, *Naval Battles of the First World War,* rev. ed. (London 1983), 141–223; and Richard Hough, *The Great War At Sea* (Oxford 1983), 211–66.

96. Marder, *Dreadnought to Scapa Flow,* III, 166–87; Bennett, *Naval Battles,* 223; and Hough, *The Great War At Sea,* 256–57, 260–61.

97. Gordon, *The Rules of the Game,* 562–601; Keegan, *The First World War,* 269–74; and Hough, *The Great War At Sea,* 299–300.

The unarmed U-freighter *Deutschland* at Baltimore, Maryland, in July 1916.
The stern view emphasizes the submarine's nine-metre width. (DND
Deutschland-011)

U-Deutschland received a warm greeting from many Americans with German sympathies during its stay at the Maryland port. (DND Deutschland-001)

The German combat submarine *U 53* during her visit to Newport, Rhode Island, 7 October 1916. (DND CN 5054)

14,000 nautical miles carrying 740 tons of cargo, more than sufficient range to operate in North American waters and return to Germany without need of refuelling. Although the London *Daily News*, reacting to rumours of the building of a German submarine freighter, had already suggested that such a vessel could enter American ports as legally as the surface merchant ships of any other nation could, the British government protested to Washington that the *U-Deutschland* should be interned immediately upon entering Baltimore. After examination by a team of three US naval officers, however, the unarmed U-freighter was judged a merchant vessel and the American government granted her the normal privileges associated with a merchant ship visiting a neutral port. Loaded with cargo for the return voyage, the *U-Deutschland* left Baltimore on 2 August, avoided the British cruiser patrols off the American coast, and reached Bremerhaven, Germany on the 23rd.[98]

Questions of the belligerent status of enemy merchant U-boats were not at issue on 7 October 1916 when the combat submarine *U 53* sailed into Newport, Rhode Island. She had departed Wilhelmshaven on 15 September in anticipation of escorting a second U-freighter, *U-Bremen*, in her departure from New London, Connecticut. In the event, the *U-Bremen* was lost at sea without a trace. That left *U 53* free to interdict Allied shipping off the American coast after putting into Newport. By converting half the capacity of the U-boat's buoyancy tanks into fuel storage to extend her range, a 750-ton submarine designed for service in European waters was converted into a trans-Atlantic raider capable of operating, for a short time at least, off the coast of the northeastern United States or Canada. After cruising off the entrance to New London on the night of 6–7 October, *U 53* and her commander, *Kapitänleutnant* Hans Rose, rounded Block Island and made a triumphant entry into Newport's harbour that afternoon escorted by the American submarine *D 2*. Word of the U-boat's arrival at Newport was passed from Naval Service Headquarters to Captain Pasco in Sydney that evening.[99]

A more detailed account of *U 53*'s visit to Newport, made by an anonymous Pinkerton agent, was forwarded to Kingsmill on 12 October by the chief commissioner of the Dominion Police, A.P. Sherwood.

> On arriving at Newport, RI, I learned that the German submarine *U 53* was equipped with two guns and eight or nine torpedoes. This boat arrived in the harbour at about 2 p.m. and left again at 5:20 p.m.
>
> I talked with Captain Thomas Shea, the harbour master. He boarded this submarine immediately after her arrival in the inner harbour, and he told me that this boat was about 240 feet long and carried a crew of about thirty men and three officers. The first officer of the submarine had a good command of the English language. Captain Shea further advised me that the reason for the

---

98. Navyard Halifax to Naval Ottawa, 9 July 1916, 1062–13-2, LAC, RG 24, vol. 4021; and M. Hadley and R. Sarty, *Tin-pots and Pirate Ships: Canadian Naval Forces and German Sea Raiders, 1880–1918* (Montreal and Kingston 1991), 136–43.

99. Naval Ottawa to Patrols Sydney, 7 October 1916, 1062–13–13, pt. 1, LAC, RG 24, vol. 4026; and Hadley and Sarty, *Tin-pots and Pirate Ships*, 145–54.

submarine coming into the harbour was to send a message to the German consul and nothing was taken on board before the boat sailed. Captain Shea instructed the first officer of the submarine not to permit anybody to leave or board the boat until the crew was examined by the proper state officials, but there were many society people and US naval officers who boarded this submarine nevertheless.

I talked with Captain Driscoll, a pilot at Newport, and he told me that the German submarine *U 53* was a fighting boat and was going to get after some of the Allied ships, probably leaving New York today; and he also stated to me that it had been rumoured that the *U 53* was going to get after some of the troop ships leaving Halifax and other Canadian ports for France and England.

As for what particular purpose the *U 53* came to the United States waters nobody seemed to know, yet it is the general opinion of the naval men here that the *U 53* probably came over in search of the *Bremen* or else to destroy some of the British ships, especially the troop ships leaving Canada.

When the *U 53* left harbour at 5:20 p.m. today she proceeded about three miles from the inner harbour and then submerged, and was out of sight in about twenty-five minutes.[100]

The Pinkerton agent would not, in any event, have had difficulty in speaking to the many Americans, both civilian and naval, who had visited the U-boat. According to the commander of the Newport Naval District "the freedom with which [*U 53*'s] officers and crew conversed with [their American] visitors, and their willingness to show all parts of the ship were very surprising. They stated that they were willing to tell all they knew and to show all they had—this to officers and civilians alike."[101] For his part, the U-boat's CO, *Kapitänleutnant* Rose, was surprised to find that the Germans' reception was "quite warm. Younger [USN] officers frequently took our watch-officers aside to encourage them to sink British cruisers; many expressed the sincere wish for our success.... The U-boat was always surrounded by a swarm of rowboats and motorboats; the nautical and technical achievement of the ocean passage received full praise."[102] After only two and a half hours in port, *U 53* weighed anchor and shaped course to the east for the Nantucket light-ship.

Beginning at dawn on 8 October, the U-boat proceeded to sink four merchant ships, totalling 16,926 tons, and the British-registered passenger ship *Stephano* bound from Halifax to New York with 146 passengers. In each case, Rose stopped the ship, examined her papers, and allowed the crew and passengers to take to lifeboats before sinking the vessel either with artillery fire, scuttling charges or torpedoes. As news of the attacks was radioed ashore by the victims, the US Navy deployed sixteen destroyers from Newport to

---

100. A.P. Sherwood to Kingsmill, 12 October 1916, 1062–13–13, pt. 1, LAC, RG 24, vol. 4026; and Hadley and Sarty, *Tin-pots and Pirate Ships,* 159.

101. Commandant, Naval Station, Narragansett Bay, RI to Navy Department (Operations), "Arrival of German Submarine U-53," 7 October 1916, quoted in Hadley and Sarty, *Tin-pots and Pirate Ships,* 154.

102. *Kapitänleutnant* Hans Rose quoted in Hadley and Sarty, *Tin-pots and Pirate Ships,* 155.

investigate but, as one of the American warships informed another by megaphone: "Do not interfere with German submarine and her legitimate prey or send out any message regarding location or movement of submarine. There are thirty survivors still on the lightship, who can come to you in their own boats. We have sixty-eight on board."[103] With USN destroyers unable to intervene, aside from rescuing survivors, U 53 was free to conduct her attacks throughout 8 October before shaping course for Germany late that night. The actions of the USN were tinged with irony, the US government having recently complained about the belligerent actions of Browning's cruisers off the American coast. Indeed, only three days earlier, the Admiralty had warned its officers that since "the US government are exaggerating and exploiting for political purposes in view of forthcoming election even the most trifling incidents in which HM ships can be represented as having offended American susceptibilities," they were to "exercise greatest discretion and forbearance in order to avoid giving excuses for complaints of this nature however unjustified."[104] Before departing Newport on the 7th, however, Rose had apparently informed the American naval authorities there that he planned to raid shipping and had suggested that USN vessels should be present to rescue survivors. In a secret American message to their London embassy that was intercepted by the Admiralty on 11 October, the US authorities privately acknowledged that under the circumstances, "we actively assisted [German] submarine operations" and "it is not surprising to learn Allies inclined to protest against it as grave breach of neutrality."[105]

Despite repeated Admiralty assurances that Canada faced a minimal maritime threat and that the Royal Navy could defend the approaches to North America, the appearance of a German U-boat on the coast of the United States prompted the Commander-in-Chief, North America and West Indies Station, Vice-Admiral Sir Montague Browning, to beat a quick retreat with his naval forces. After being told by the Admiralty that "it is of greater importance to prevent German submarine sinking our cruisers and getting a cheap success than that a continuous watch should be maintained off United States ports," the British C-in-C was granted "perfect freedom to move patrolling vessels away or do whatever you consider best in the circumstances."[106] With "no suitable vessel at my disposal to operate against submarines," Browning decided to withdraw his cruisers from the US coast and seek shelter in the relative security of Bedford Basin, despite the possibility that U 53 might have been operating in the approaches to Halifax by the evening of 8 October.[107] In informing NSHQ of his decision, the British admiral asked the Canadian naval authorities

---

103. Commanding Officer, USS *Drayton* to Commander, Destroyer Force, Atlantic Fleet, 8 October 1916, "Report of Movements," quoted in Hadley and Sarty, *Tin-pots and Pirate Ships*, 169; and US Navy Department, Office of Naval Records and Library, Historical Section, *German Submarine Activities on the Atlantic Coast of the United States and Canada* (Washington 1920), 22–3.

104. Admiralty to SNO, Gibraltar, et al., 5 October 1918, UKNA, ADM 137/324.

105. "From Chief Censor, Admiralty, Intercepted Message," 10 October 1916, ibid.

106. Admiralty to C-in-C, NA&WI, 8 October 1916, ibid.

107. Browning to Admiralty, 16 October 1916, UKNA, ADM 137/504; and Browning to Admiralty, 8 October 1916, UKNA, ADM 137/324.

in Halifax to have the inner leading lights on Georges Island and the Dartmouth shore extinguished as well as any lights in houses facing either seaward or toward Halifax Harbour. Browning went on to recommend that "the question of extinguishing the coast lights in approaches to harbour should be considered as soon as possible on the same lines as at British Defended Ports."[108]

After confirming that the rather alarmist telegram was indeed from the British commander-in-chief,[109] it was left to Admiral Kingsmill to provide a voice of calm in the face of a possible German submarine attack in Canadian waters. In a memorandum to the minister of the naval service, the Canadian admiral rationally explained the problems involved in complying completely with Browning's recommendations. Although Kingsmill had "no great objection" to extinguishing the leading lights on Georges Island and the Dartmouth shore, this should only be done if "we can keep our Examination Service going with an extra small patrol boat on duty." As the Canadian naval director went on to point out, however, complying with the commander-in-chief's request to extinguish all coastal lights could not be considered "on the same lines as the British defended ports. Halifax is not merely a defended port as are those spoken of as defended ports in the United Kingdom, Halifax being one of our important shipping ports and harbours of refuge, and it seems to me that by a short notice extinguishing [of] coast lights leading to the approaches to Halifax, we might lose more shipping and tonnage than submarines could account for even taking into consideration the possibility and probability of there being several of them on this side of the Atlantic. In the United Kingdom, defended ports are absolutely closed and all aid to navigation extinguished at night."[110] Although Halifax was not used as a shipping port for Canadian war supplies during the summer months—indeed, the last shipment of 1,258 tons had departed the Nova Scotia port in July and no war supplies were shipped from there at all from August to November—it remained, as Kingsmill alluded, a busy harbour, not only as a port of call for Canadian coastal shipping but also for neutral vessels directed there to have their cargoes examined for contraband items.

Although agreeing to extinguish the leading lights in Halifax Harbour itself, as Browning had requested, Kingsmill informed Halifax that it was "not considered advisable to interfere at this juncture with coast lights."[111] At the same time, the naval director instructed Captain Pasco in Sydney to "accede to any request" Browning might make in regard to the RCN's Gulf patrol vessels but also that he was immediately to report any action taken to NSHQ.[112] Naval headquarters also reminded the captain superintendent at Halifax that he should telephone the fishing villages along the Nova Scotia coast to warn "them of the submarine and instructing them to keep

---

108. [C-in-C, NA&WI] to Naval Ottawa, 230, 8 October 1916, 1062–13–13, pt. 1, LAC, RG 24, vol. 4026.

109. Naval Ottawa to Navyard Halifax, 8 October 1916, 611, Navyard Halifax to Naval Ottawa, 231, 8 October 1916, ibid.

110. Kingsmill, "Memo for Information of the Minister," 8 October 1916, ibid.

111. Naval Ottawa to Navyard Halifax, 8 October 1916, ibid.

112. Kingsmill to Patrols, Sydney, 479, 9 October 1916, Naval Ottawa to Navyard Halifax, 628, for C-in-C, 9 October 1916, ibid.

a lookout."[113] The Canadian public's co-operation was also sought in regard to warning of the threat. Ottawa's chief press censor, Ernest J. Chambers, reminded both the Canadian Press and Western Associated Press organizations on 8 October that it was "of the utmost importance that censorship rules as to naval and shipping news be rigidly adhered to ... Particular care should be taken to prevent any leakage of news from Canada referring to precautions taken to meet the present situation."[114] This was reinforced the following day by the chief censor's insightful assertion "that the submarine activity off the Atlantic Coast is designed more for the moral effect upon ship owners and shippers than for the actual naval object accomplished by the destruction of ships. The press can assist to defeat the object of the enemy by exerting its powerful steadying influence at the present moment."[115]

The other measures adopted were instigated upon instructions from both London and the C-in-C. The Admiralty advised Ottawa on 8 October to have all reporting officers in Canadian ports instruct merchant ship masters to sail "shortly after dark so as to obtain as good an offing as possible before daylight next morning. All lights are to be extinguished as soon as they are clear of harbour."[116] Elaborating on his request several days later, Browning asked the Canadian naval authorities to supply all merchant vessels with the exact courses they were to follow upon departure from Canadian ports out to 200 miles. Such courses were to be varied as much as possible to scatter the trans-Atlantic traffic and avoid the normal trade routes and departure points. The British C-in-C also recommended that vessels bound for neutral ports should try to make land some distance from their destination and then keep within the neutral's territorial waters. It was to be impressed upon ship's captains, however, "that submarines may be met anywhere in Atlantic Ocean and not only near coasts."[117]

With the RCN's patrol vessels at his disposal, Browning asked NSHQ that "until the end of month at any rate every effort should be made to protect his majesty's ships and transports in approaches to the port of Halifax and that all patrol vessels armed with 12-pounder guns and above should concentrate here accordingly." The British continued to assume that German submarines required the assistance of a supply base in order to operate in North American waters and Browning wanted all those patrol vessels that were unsuitable for the Halifax patrol to proceed to the Grand Banks off Newfoundland to search for the "enemy's submarine supply ship."[118] The British admiral's proposed dispositions for Canada's patrol vessels, however, failed to appreciate the actual shipping situation. While concentrating the RCN's most effective patrol vessels at Halifax, a port of

---

113. Naval Ottawa to Navyard Halifax, 624, 9 October 1916, ibid.

114. Chambers to Canadian Press Limited, Toronto and Westher Associated Press, Winnipeg, 8 October 1916, ibid.

115. Chambers to Press Censors, Toronto and Winnipeg, 9 October 1916, ibid.

116. Admiralty to Naval Ottawa, 949, 8 October 1916, ibid; and Admiralty to C-in-C, NA&WI, et al., 8 October 1916, UKNA, ADM 137/324.

117. C-in-C, NA&WI to Naval Ottawa, 272, 12 October 1916, 1062–13–13, pt. 1, LAC, RG 24, vol. 4026.

118. C-in-C, NA&WI to Naval Ottawa, 244, 9 October 1916, ibid.

relatively minor significance from the overseas transport perspective, would cover Browning's cruisers as they scurried into Bedford Basin, it would leave unprotected the important merchant ships carrying war supplies to Europe through the Gulf of St Lawrence. In the moment of perceived crisis, it was clearly the C-in-C's judgment to place the immediate safety of his own warships ahead of the task of protecting Allied merchant ships from North Atlantic raiders.

Diverting patrol vessels to protect Browning's cruisers was not the only assistance the Canadian navy provided British authorities. As the department in charge of the government's radiotelegraph service, NSHQ controlled both government and commercial stations throughout the nation. Following word from the British ambassador in Washington that the German government had reserved the use of a wireless station at Tuckerton, New Jersey to broadcast messages on the night of 10 October, NSHQ notified radiotelegraph stations on the East Coast to "keep look out for suspicious signals transmitted about four hundred metres.... Any signals intercepted should be telegraphed immediately to Navyard Halifax and Naval Ottawa stating wave length, time, date, and character of spark."[119] According to Ambassador Spring Rice, "if messages of interest not in cypher are intercepted, you should be informed and I should be glad of summary by telegraph here. Messages may relate to submarine warfare, or to peace, or may be addressed to submarines."[120] Foreshadowing the role the RCN would later play in radio intelligence and direction finding in coming decades, the department's general superintendent of the Radiotelegraph Branch explained which of the East Coast stations could best meet the situation's requirements.

> The following can be spared for interception without seriously interfering with the commercial or naval service: Cape Sable, Sable Island, Cape Ray, Father Point, Grosse Isle, Three Rivers, HMCS *Niobe*.
>
> Sable Island cannot be used as that station cannot report interception, except by wireless. Belle Isle is an important commercial station. It is, however, the only one available in that locality and must accordingly be included in any scheme of interception.
>
> As the wavelength of 400 metres is very near the commercial wavelength, the coast stations by adjusting their receiver to about 500 metres would be able to hear signals made on 400 metres from ships not too far away. With this in view, it is recommended that the following stations be instructed to stand by exclusively on 400 metres and the balance instructed to carry on with their commercial work, but keep a sharp lookout for suspicious signals on a shorter wavelength: Cape Sable, HMCS *Niobe*, Cape Ray, Belle Isle, Grindstone Island, Father Point.[121]

---

119. Naval Ottawa to Officers-in-Charge, Government Radiotelegraph Stations, Cape Race, Nfld, Partridge Island and St John, NB, and Fame Point, Que., 10 October 1916, ibid.

120. Spring Rice to Governor General of Canada, 10 October 1916, ibid.

121. General Superintendent, Radiotelegraph Branch, "Memo to the Director Naval Service: Interception of Signals on the East Coast and Gulf," nd, ibid.

In the event, however, the added precautions proved unnecessary since the German submarine departed North American waters immediately after sinking the five ships on 8 October. Nonetheless, *U 53*'s exposure of the vulnerability of the North American shipping lanes was reinforced three weeks later when the *U-Deutschland* submarine freighter visited the United States on her second commercial voyage. Arriving at New London, Connecticut on 1 November, the third successful trans-Atlantic voyage by a German submarine finally convinced the Admiralty of the need to revise its advice regarding the Royal Canadian Navy's defence arrangements. On 11 November 1916, the British colonial secretary, Andrew Bonar Law, informed the Canadian government of Whitehall's reversal of policy: "Admiralty urge importance of increasing number of armed patrol vessels in view of activity of German submarines in North Atlantic. Present twelve vessels insufficient to provide reasonable means of defence against serious attack on trade in Newfoundland and Canadian waters. In the opinion of the Admiralty suitable patrol for these waters should comprise about thirty-six steam vessels and if desired Admiralty would be prepared to lend an officer experienced in patrol work to advise the Newfoundland and Canadian governments as regards procuring and organizing vessels."[122]

Three days later, Bonar Law provided a further explanation of the Admiralty's new thinking. Ostensibly the British sea lords were responding to a telegram received from the governor of Newfoundland on 25 October proclaiming the colony's complete satisfaction "that there is no part of the coast of Labrador or Newfoundland which can be used with any degree of security as a base for German submarine operations." Since the colony had dutifully followed London's advice in implementing all the anti-submarine precautions the Admiralty had said were necessary, Governor Davidson's attitude was understandable. In view of the few small patrol vessels Newfoundland could actually muster, however, the governor was dreadfully optimistic in suggesting that the mere knowledge of the colony's defence arrangements "should suffice to forbid submarine commanders from venturing into the traps set for them. It would have been useless to keep our measures secret, nor would it have been desirable, for it is better to prevent a raid than to crush it. As it is, we have three well-found patrol vessels supported by a chain of local observers and the officers and crew of those patrol vessels desire nothing better than to engage a hostile vessel armed or unarmed."[123] Coming as it did only two weeks after *U 53*'s successful foray into North American waters, an operation the U-boat had completed without benefit of refuelling, Davidson's assurances seem little more than bravado even if they were entirely in keeping, as far as the colony knew, with the Admiralty's expressed views on the subject of North American defence.

In addressing themselves to the question of expanding the naval defence of Canada and Newfoundland, the Admiralty was at least willing to acknowledge that as recently as April

---

122. Colonial Secretary to Governor-General of Canada, 11 November 1916, 1065–7-2, pt. 1, LAC, RG 24, vol. 4031.

123. "Extract from a report by the Governor of Newfoundland," 25 October 1916, in Colonial Secretary to Governor-General of Canada, 14 November 1916, ibid; and Kingsmill to Secretary of the Admiralty, 22 November 1917, 1017–10–1, pt. 1, LAC, RG 24, vol. 3831.

1916 they had told both the Newfoundland and Canadian governments that "a combination of coast-watching and a sea-going patrol service should enable these [U-boat supply] vessels to be found and attacked. It must be borne in mind that the destruction of the base ship will cripple the submarines."[124] Far from admitting any misjudgment, however, the Admiralty merely spoke to recent anti-submarine lessons:

> From experience gained in the United Kingdom, my lords are unable to share the governor's conclusion that knowledge of the preparations which have been made will deter enemy submarines from operating on the Newfoundland and Canadian coast. In their lordships' opinion no competent submarine officer would be deterred by existing preparations, however full his knowledge of them.
>
> I am accordingly to request that action may be taken to impress upon the Newfoundland and Canadian governments the importance of increasing the number of armed patrol vessels, as, should Germany decide to make a serious submarine attack on trade in these waters, the present twelve vessels would be insufficient to provide a reasonable measure of defence. A suitable patrol for Newfoundland and Canadian waters should comprise about thirty-six steam vessels, and, if desired, the Admiralty would be prepared to lend an officer experienced in patrol work to advise the Newfoundland and dominion governments as regards procuring and organising the vessels.[125]

For the officers who had repeatedly been denied Admiralty support for increasing the Canadian navy's meagre anti-submarine forces, the latest series of directives from London landed in Ottawa with a loud thud. In replying to Whitehall's initial telegram of 11 November, NSHQ displayed its annoyance with the Admiralty's changing assessments of the submarine threat in North American waters. In language that was blunt by normal diplomatic standards, the Canadian government flatly rejected the notion that the inadequate anti-submarine measures now being decried by Whitehall were in any way Ottawa's fault.

> Canadian government notes that Admiralty consider that present twelve vessels are insufficient measure against serious attack on trade in these waters and that thirty-six vessels are considered necessary. It is desired to point out, however, that in accordance with wishes of Admiralty every possible trained seaman has been sent over to England, while active recruiting is now being carried on for men to serve overseas in the Royal Navy. Further, when Canadian government was disposed to build destroyers early this year, Admiralty did not encourage idea. Representative of War Office has recently been allowed to purchase or charter in Canada a number of vessels which might have been useful for patrol work although number of such in Canada is strictly limited.

124. Admiralty letter, 8 April 1916, quoted in Colonial Secretary to Governor-General of Canada, 14 November 1916, 1065–7-2, pt. 1, LAC, RG 24, vol. 4031.

125. Colonial Secretary to Governor-General of Canada, 14 November 1916, ibid.

As danger to Admiralty store transports and Canadian trade in near future from enemy submarines appears to be growing serious, Canadian government considers adequate protection should be accorded by Admiralty.[126]

Although the government had rejected London's call for a domestic expansion of the East Coast patrol fleet, insisting instead that it was the Royal Navy's responsibility, the RCN's senior officer knew that Ottawa's position was more an expression of irritation with the Admiralty's fickle war direction. Whatever his own frustration with the inconsistency of British naval advice, Kingsmill realized there was now a genuine opportunity to augment the nation's maritime defences and immediately took action to increase the number of auxiliary patrol vessels. In a 4 December memorandum to Desbarats he pointed to three steam vessels that could be converted for the anti-submarine patrol and suggested that HMCS *Rainbow* be laid up, so her experienced ratings could be used as crewmen for another twenty patrol vessels. His attitude extended to including the RCN's responsibility for the maritime defence of the Newfoundland colony since "enemy vessels taking refuge in ports off the coast of Labrador or Newfoundland for the purpose of supplying submarines are acting against Canadian trade, compared to which the trade from Newfoundland is negligible.... To enable us to increase our patrol and have ships ready by the time the ice is off the Labrador coast we should commence immediately obtaining ships and endeavouring to get men. With regard to the men, it is submitted that the men being recruited for Overseas Division cannot be spared; we should keep them and train them."[127]

As much as the Canadian admiral was able to move on to practical solutions, his political superiors were not yet willing to ignore such a complete reversal of policy—and its implied criticism of Canadian inaction—so easily. As an angry Prime Minister Borden noted in his diary on the 13th, the Royal Navy had "always said they could take care of everything on [the] ocean."[128] Two days after Kingsmill's memorandum tacitly acknowledged that the RCN would eventually have to assemble a thirty-six vessel patrol fleet on its own, the government reiterated its position that, as the Admiralty had proclaimed since the outbreak of war, Canada's maritime defence was a Royal Navy responsibility. In asking the undersecretary of state for external affairs to respond to the Admiralty's telegram of 14 November, Desbarats informed Joseph Pope that "the Department has nothing further to add to my letter ... of the 17th ultimo in reply to the Colonial Office telegram of the 11th ultimo," and added, rather caustically, "I beg to observe, however, that no reply has been received to the above mentioned letter." In asking Pope "to request that a reply may be hastened from the Colonial Office" the naval deputy minister explained that "my minister desires to emphasize the necessity of the Admiralty providing adequate protection for vessels frequenting Canadian ports."[129]

---

126. Desbarats to Under Secretary of State for External Affairs, for transmission to British Secretary of State for Colonies, 17 November 1916, ibid.

127. Kingsmill, Memorandum for the Deputy Minister, "Atlantic Coast Patrol," 4 December 1916, ibid.

128. Borden diary, 13 November 1916, LAC, Manuscript Group (hereafter MG) 26 H, reel C-1864.

129. Desbarats to Undersecretary of State for External Affairs, 6 December 1916, 1065–7-2, pt. 1, LAC, RG 24, vol. 4031.

Ottawa certainly had every right to be upset by the Admiralty's obvious inference that the lack of a larger patrol fleet was a Canadian failing. As described in their initial response to Whitehall, the RCN had repeatedly sought the Admiralty's support for expanding the anti-submarine force on Canada's East Coast. In each instance, the sea lords had rejected the necessity of making any expansion beyond a mere coast-watch service and, in so doing, had often undermined the credibility of the fledging RCN in the eyes of the Borden government. The reproachful tone of the Admiralty's reversal of policy was all the more galling to Canadian naval officers given Whitehall's tepid reaction to NSHQ's proposal the previous spring—pointedly referred to in Ottawa's 17 November response—to build three destroyers at Vickers in Montreal for use as an escort force on the East Coast shipping lanes. As we have seen, it was the Admiralty's assertion that Canadian yards would be better employed building merchant ships that convinced the government to abandon Kingsmill's destroyer scheme.

That rejection had not, however, altered NSHQ's conviction that only naval vessels with the size, speed, and armament of a destroyer were capable of effectively dealing with a genuine submarine threat. In the wake of *U 53*'s attack on shipping off the American coast, that conviction had already prompted the Canadian naval minister to cable the Admiralty on 3 November strongly urging "that torpedo boat destroyers should be sent to Canada to protect trade routes from Halifax and St John." As Hazen's request explained, the latest desire to have at least a small force of destroyers stemmed directly from the "late presence of German submarine in North American waters and frequent reports of submarines sighted near Canadian coasts."[130] In its own telegram on the 14th asking for an immediate expansion of the RCN's patrol forces, however, Whitehall studiously avoided any mention of the naval minister's earlier telegram and claimed that they were merely responding to the Newfoundland governor's overly optimistic assessment of the naval situation. In ignoring Ottawa's plea for destroyers, the Admiralty also took its time answering the Canadian telegram of 17 November. After urging London to respond throughout December, the Canadian government finally sent a rather terse summary of the situation (via the governor general) at month's end:

> My advisers desire to call attention to the telegram from Admiralty of 11th November last and through colonial secretary to their reply to colonial secretary of 18th November as well as their further cables of 7th and 15th December to none of which any reply has been received. In May last minister of naval service suggested to Admiralty advisability of his department constructing three torpedo boat destroyers at Canadian Vickers's yards but Admiralty's reply was regarded as discouraging the proposal. In early months of the war my advisers requested advice from Admiralty as to advisability of Canada undertaking to supplement naval defence of empire and reply received indicated Admiralty view that such action was unnecessary and that Canada's efforts should be concentrated on provision of military forces. Under these circumstances the Admiralty's intimation that we must provide against danger

---

130. Hazen to Admiralty, 3 November 1916, 1062–13–13, pt 2, LAC, RG 24, vol. 4026.

of submarines on our coast is very serious especially as many boats suitable for patrol work were acquired by War Office in Canada in September last and the recruiting for overseas forces in Canada has denuded this country of most suitable men for such purpose and every available gun has been sent to the British government. My advisers would be grateful for immediate reply to unanswered telegrams above mentioned and for a precise statement of the Admiralty's ability to provide against the danger of submarines on our coast. If responsibility for protection of our coast against submarines must be undertaken by Canadian government immediate action is imperative and it is absolutely essential that the officer asked for in despatch of 15 December should be sent immediately.... If Admiralty is unable to afford protection against danger of submarines on our coast Canadian government may find it necessary to take over all available ship yards for the purpose of making necessary provision against that peril. In conclusion, my advisers hope that having regard to all the considerations above set forth the Admiralty will make a clear and precise statement of the situation as they regard it accompanied with such recommendations to my government as will permit of necessary action being taken without a moment's unnecessary delay.[131]

The Admiralty did not seem to share Ottawa's concern that time was of the essence if Canada was to build the necessary patrol vessels for the 1917 shipping season. Despite repeated statements from the RCN that suitable patrol vessels were not available for purchase in North America, British officials continued to insist that "it should be not very difficult to acquire steam vessels in Canadian waters or on the lakes or, failing this, to purchase them in the USA."[132] The RN's senior officers, meanwhile, were equally dismissive of the Canadian government's protests against the latest Admiralty policy directive. They acknowledged that the RCN was recruiting sailors for service in British waters but glibly commented that the subtraction of the 400 sailors that Canada would require to man the twenty-four additional vessels "would not appreciably affect the manning of the [Royal] Navy." They restated their reservations about Kingsmill's destroyer scheme by pointing out that the warships "would probably not be ready before the summer of 1918," and their construction would not have affected "the total number of patrol vessels available now." The Admiralty also claimed ignorance of the War Office's recent purchase of steam vessels in Canada and could only conclude that "it may have been" the Colonial Office that had given permission. Deciding to wait until they found out more about the War Office purchases, Whitehall's response to Ottawa's demands for an answer was delayed until mid-January.[133] At least one official in the Admiralty, however,

---

131. Draft cable from the Governor General to the Colonial Secretary, 28 December 1916, 1065–7-2, pt 1, LAC, RG 24, vol. 4031.

132. Rear-Admiral H. Oliver minute, 3 November 1916, UKNA, ADM 116/1400.

133. Captain T. Jackson minute, 26 November 1916, Oliver minute, 27 November 1916, ibid; and Long to Governor General, 10 January 1917, 1065–7-2, pt 1, LAC, RG 24, vol 4031.

was willing to recognize that the rejection of Ottawa's proposal for "building destroyers evidently rankles," and that it would be "necessary to show sympathy to the Canadian government in this matter," since it did "not appear that the question has been very adroitly handled."[134]

In light of London's December silence on the issue, it was not until the last day of 1916 that NSHQ was approached by a British officer about the patrol situation. At Whitehall's direction, Vice-Admiral Browning wrote Ottawa on the question of employing the three Newfoundland summer patrol vessels in Canadian waters during the winter months.[135] Kingsmill's reply, that only the *Fogata* could be employed to advantage off Halifax, indicated the degree to which suitable patrol vessels were scarce indeed.[136] British officials also seemed to be grasping at straws when they telegraphed Ottawa on New Year's Day 1917 to ask about the "present position regarding the whaler *Grib*. It is understood by the Admiralty that she is still for sale and they suggest she might be used in North American waters for patrol work."[137] Once again, Kingsmill's reply indicated the dearth of proper vessels even as he acceded to the British suggestion by agreeing to employ *Grib* on minesweeping duties: "This vessel would require considerable alterations before we could use her as a minesweeper; she would be no use as a patrol vessel. There is plenty of time to prepare her for use in the spring and I would suggest that the Admiralty be informed that we propose chartering her for use as a minesweeper."[138]

London's recommendation that the RCN acquire *Grib* as a patrol vessel (a clear demonstration that the Admiralty, despite their denials, was intimately aware of the steam vessels for sale in North America, even though the War Office had not thought *Grib* suitable for purchase themselves) was an indication of the gulf that existed between what the Admiralty viewed as required for patrol work in North American waters and what NSHQ knew was needed. That gulf was further emphasized on 10 January when their lordships finally communicated their advice for the expansion of the RCN's patrol forces. While stating that "it is recognised by the Admiralty that situation is one of considerable difficulty for your ministers," they refused to acknowledge that their previous advice was at all responsible for the vulnerable state of Canada's naval defences. Moreover, they informed Ottawa that "they greatly regret that dearth of small craft at home makes it impossible to provide any patrol vessels from United Kingdom for service in Canadian waters."

> Need for such craft however is very urgent and although it is desirable to build some at once it is still more necessary to make use of any which are or could be made available immediately. Patrols in home waters are composed mainly of trawlers [of] low speed and general type of vessel required is one of good sea-

---

134. INS minute, 2 January 1917, UKNA, ADM 116/1400.

135. C-in-C, NA&WI to Naval Ottawa, 31 December 1916, 1065–7-2, pt 1, LAC, RG 24, vol 4031.

136. Naval Ottawa to Britannia, 2 January 1917, Navyard to Naval Ottawa, 2 January 1917, ibid.

137. Long to Governor-General, 1 January 1917, ibid.

138. Kingsmill, Memorandum for the Deputy Minister, 8 January 1917, ibid.

going qualities capable of carrying twelve-pounder quick-firing gun and wireless telegraph installation smaller guns being unsuitable. It is suggested by Admiralty that your ministers should consider whether suitable vessels of similar type could be obtained from whalers and sea-going fishing vessels with auxiliary motive power. Officer with practical experience of auxiliary patrol at home will be sent to Canada immediately and will render all possible assistance to your ministers in organization of service generally.[139]

Although the Admiralty were not wrong in asserting that their patrols were composed mainly of trawlers of low speed, such a statement did not give an accurate picture of the true nature of the anti-submarine defences in British home waters. From the beginning of the war, troopships had been convoyed and escorted, primarily by cruisers or battleships, to guard against German surface raiders, but they were also met by destroyers as they approached British waters to guard against submarine attack. Since 1915, moreover, ships with specially valuable cargoes were met by destroyers in the approaches to Britain and escorted into port. (Indeed in July 1915, Canada's minister of militia and defence, Sir Sam Hughes, had requested that the liner he was travelling on from New York to England should be given a destroyer escort when she neared British waters. Not sharing the Canadian minister's evaluation of his importance to the war effort, however, the request was turned down by the Admiralty stating that "the available destroyers are already detailed to escort other vessels."[140]) By the end of 1916 there was a flotilla of fourteen destroyers based at Devonport dedicated solely to anti-submarine work where they escorted an average of some 4.4 ships per day into harbour. Those numbers would grow to thirty-eight by June 1917, with another thirty-two destroyers based at Queenstown, Ireland, twenty-eight of them American.[141]

The British destroyers were supplemented by 107 naval sloops and patrol boats that were all available for anti-submarine work in January 1917. The seventy-eight Flower-class sloops available had originally been designed as fleet minesweepers but their 16.5-knot speed made them valuable in the anti-submarine role. Two hundred and sixty-two feet in length and displacing 1,200 tons, they carried two 12-pounders and two 3-pounders. The twenty-nine patrol boats or "P-boats" were turbine-powered, low-silhouette warships that could make twenty knots. Armed with one 4-inch and one or two 12-pounder guns and two 14-inch torpedo tubes, P-boats were 245 feet in length and 613 tons. Both types were used in the destroyer role, giving the Royal Navy's anti-submarine forces an escort/hunting force of 121 fast warships.[142] In Canadian waters, meanwhile, only HMCS *Grilse* could match the speed

139. Long to Governor General, 10 January 1917, ibid.

140. Gwatkin to R.M. Stephens, Naval Sec., Interdepartmental Committee, 7 July 1915, Admiralty to Naval Ottawa, 8 July 1915, 1048–1-8, LAC, RG 24, vol. 3621.

141. John Jellicoe, *The Submarine Peril: The Admiralty Policy in 1917* (London 1934), 16–18, 114–15.

142. F.J. Dittmar and J.J. Colledge, *British Warships, 1914–1919* (London 1972), 93–95, 98; D.R. Messimer, *Find and Destroy: Antisubmarine Warfare in World War I* (Annapolis 2001), 126–27; and Jellicoe, *The Submarine Peril*, 113–15.

of the Royal Navy's sloops and P-boats, which were larger and better-armed than any other RCN anti-submarine vessel. The force of fast anti-submarine vessels that escorted troopships and those with valuable cargoes or patrolled the shipping lanes were further supplemented by vessels outfitted as Q-ships, or decoy merchant vessels, intended to lure U-boats toward them before opening fire from hidden gun positions. The number of Q-ships operating in the western approaches continued to grow in 1917—reaching a high of seventy-eight by July—despite their decreasing effectiveness as wary U-boat commanders became more proficient at recognizing them through their periscopes.[143]

Close inshore, the Royal Navy had assembled a vast armada of slow trawlers, drifters, and motor launches to patrol coastal shipping routes around the home islands. By the beginning of 1917, the auxiliary patrol numbered some 2,700 vessels in home waters. Another 550 auxiliary vessels were deployed in the Mediterranean, White Sea, and West Indies.[144] Admiral Sir John Jellicoe, commander-in-chief of Britain's Grand Fleet, pointed out in a memorandum to the Admiralty in late October 1916 that "the patrol trawler is rapidly becoming ineffective, owing to her low speed and poor armament. If these vessels are retained, re-armament is essential."[145] By far the greatest problem Jellicoe would have to confront upon taking over as first sea lord in early December 1916 was the U-boat menace, and as he later candidly admitted, "it was with the greatest possible reluctance that I gave up my command [of the Grand Fleet] to take on what I realized would be most difficult work, particularly on account of our shortage of destroyers, the vessels most needed for action against submarines."[146] The British official naval history, published in 1931, stated the need just as succinctly: "in the danger zone, at any rate, real security could only be guaranteed by destroyers."[147]

Kingsmill, of course, had reached the same conclusions on both the need for destroyers and the inadequacy of slow auxiliaries armed with single 12-pounder guns. The Admiralty's latest assertion that all Canada required was an auxiliary patrol force of thirty-six slow steam vessels, rather than destroyers, did little to convince the Canadian naval director otherwise. Although the submarine threat to North American waters in January 1917 was more potential than actual, it is difficult to see how the Admiralty could honestly have believed that a force of thirty-six patrol auxiliaries would protect Canada's extended shipping lanes when 2,700 such vessels were having only a minimal impact along Britain's coastline. Moreover, aside from *Grilse*, the RCN would have had no fast patrol ships to match the Royal Navy's 121 destroyers, sloops, and P-boats that formed the backbone of Britain's escort and patrol forces.

The auxiliary patrol being advocated by Whitehall would have provided some protection to merchant ships in the immediate approaches to St John or Halifax during the

---

143. Halpern, *A Naval History of World War I*, 343; and Jellicoe, *The Submarine Peril*, 11.

144. Dittmar and Colledge, *British Warships, 1914–1919*, 147–48.

145. Jellicoe to Admiralty, 29 October 1916, quoted in Jellicoe, *The Submarine Peril*, 3.

146. Jellicoe, *The Submarine Peril*, 9.

147. Henry Newbolt, *Naval Operations* (London 1931), V, 18.

winter shipping season but would offer only a limited screen along the heavily travelled Gulf of St Lawrence route during the remainder of the year when Montreal resumed its place as Canada's main Atlantic port. With the cruisers of the North America and West Indies Station likely to make for port at the first sign of a U-boat and American neutrality making it impossible to base escort forces off the United States coast, the problem that would be created for the Allies by a German offensive in American waters—such as the October operations *U 53* had indicated were clearly possible—must have appeared virtually unsolvable. It would seem that the Admiralty's latest call for the RCN to expand its trawler patrol forces, vessels that were too slow and under-gunned to provide effective protection, was made with the hope that a U-boat offensive on the western side of the Atlantic would never, in fact, materialize.

At the same time, London's claim that it could not spare any of the 2,700 auxiliaries patrolling Britain's coastline to bolster North America's defences in the event of a submarine offensive was peculiarly short-sighted. After all, a merchant ship sunk in undefended North American waters was just as lost to the war effort as one sunk in more well-patrolled British waters. Given the Admiralty's insistence since the outbreak of war that the Royal Navy would take care of Canada's maritime defence, it was, as Canadian officials were aware, rather duplicitous of Britain not to contemplate giving an assurance to Ottawa that in the event of a submarine offensive off North America the country would be willing to detach at least a handful of its P-boats or sloops and several flotillas of auxiliary trawlers to meet the situation. It also clearly rankled Canadian officials that when they had offered to build destroyers in the spring of 1916, the Admiralty had responded by suggesting that Canadian yards would be better employed building merchant ships instead of the sloops or patrol boats that were required to mount an effective anti-submarine defence.

The accompanying British proposal to provide the Canadian auxiliary patrol service with an experienced British officer to command was interpreted by NSHQ as something of an affront. As was further explained to Ottawa on 12 January, the Admiralty proposed sending a "flag officer on retired list with war experience who would be given the rank of Commodore Royal Naval Reserve. This officer would advise ministers of naval service as to information and organization of patrol service and if your ministers so desire would be in executive command of same when formed with freedom to dispose of it as he might consider most advantageous."[148] Given that such a force already existed and was commanded by Captain Pasco, the Canadian navy's reaction to the suggestion was made clear in a memorandum Kingsmill addressed to the deputy minister on 16 January:

> I would suggest the following reply: "My ministers will be pleased to accept the services of the officer proposed for the purpose mentioned, on the understanding that he is appointed to *Niobe* and becomes an officer of the Department of the Naval Service by whom his advice will be appreciated."
>
> In suggesting the above reply I wish to point out that it would seem from Mr Long's telegram almost as if there were an intention to create a separate

---

148. Long to Governor-General of Canada, 12 January 1917, 1065–7-2, pt 1, LAC, RG 24, vol 4031.

command out here under the Admiralty, which, if their lordships consider necessary, shows an utter want of appreciation of the work done by this department since the outbreak of war. Knowing full well we have not a proper organization we have most warmly appreciated and acted on the advice of the Admiralty on every occasion. Our patrol vessels, such as they have been, have hitherto been disposed with the concurrence of the commander in chief on the station and any alteration in that disposition by his expressed wish, has been immediately attended to.

If the Admiralty send an officer here in whom they have faith and consider competent to take charge of the patrols it is unlikely that his wishes will not be at all times concurred in. At the same time, any other arrangement than that proposed in the reply telegram will put this department entirely on a wrong footing in the country generally and would be a slight which I do not think deserving.[149]

In accepting the British offer of an RN officer to organize the auxiliary patrol, the Canadian government followed Kingsmill's advice and insisted that the officer be appointed to *Niobe* as an officer of the Canadian naval service and—as was clearly Ottawa's plan—subject to NSHQ's direction.[150]

On the matter of acquiring more auxiliary patrol vessels, however, only limited progress could be made. Although the Admiralty had dismissed Ottawa's claim that suitable steam vessels were not readily available in North America, the number of vessels that could be added at short notice to the Gulf patrol's forces indicates the validity of the assertion. Two vessels, *Acadia* and *Cartier*, were commissioned into the RCN from the department's hydrographic survey. At 170 feet in length and 1,050 tons, *Acadia* was the larger, but also slower, of the two vessels. *Cartier*'s 556 tons on 164 feet could manage a useful twelve knots, while *Acadia* could make only eight. In a practical sense, *Acadia*'s slow speed made her little more than an armed buoy in terms of hunting German submarines. A third hydrographic survey ship, CGS *Bayfield*, although never commissioned, was employed as a depot ship for motor launches patrolling the coast of Newfoundland. To these the navy was only able to add the 355-ton, eleven-knot steamer *Laurentian* purchased from Canada Steamship Lines and the 483-ton, nine-knot *Lady Evelyn* transferred from the postmaster general's department later that spring. Looking to the United States, the only other vessels the RCN was able to purchase were seven New England-built fishing trawlers ranging in size from 205 to 390 tons. Commissioned as *PV I* to *PV VII*, they did increase the number of auxiliaries available even though their eight-knot speed left them best suited to minesweeping duties.[151]

---

149. Kingsmill to Desbarats, 16 January 1917, ibid.

150. Desbarats to Undersecretary of State for External Affairs, 16 January 1917, ibid.

151. Ken MacPherson and Ron Barrie, *The Ships of Canada's Naval Forces, 1910–2002* (St. Catharines 2002), 17–18, 22, 24; and Kingsmill, "Memorandum for the Information of the Minister," 26 January 1917, 1065–7-2, pt 1, LAC, RG 24, vol. 4031; and Notes on *Bayfield*, nd, DHH 81/520/8000, CGS *Bayfield*.

The auxiliary patrol vessel HMCS *Cartier*, seen here in September 1918, was transferred from the hydrographic department in the spring of 1917. It had a useful top speed of twelve knots. (LAC e007140900)

Also commissioned in the spring of 1917, the 355-ton HMCS *Laurentian* was purchased from Canada Steamship Lines. (DND CN 3269)

HMCS *Lady Evelyn* was another of the RCN's 1917 additions. Transferred from the postmaster general's department, its usefulness as a patrol vessel was limited by its nine-knot top speed. (LAC e007140905)

PV II, one of the seven New England fishing trawlers the RCN purchased in the United States to augment their minesweeping fleet. (DND PV2)

Since the eleven additional vessels still left the RCN twelve short of the thirty-six suggested by the Admiralty, the naval department also approached Canadian shipyards to see if they could build auxiliary vessels required for the patrol service. As Kingsmill explained to the minister at the end of January, "Polson Iron Works and Canadian Vickers Limited are taking up the question of a class of vessel, which, while one would not recommend it as an ideal patrol vessel, seems to be the best we can get built in the time. They would also appear to be vessels which could be used afterwards for protection of our fisheries and perhaps on the Pacific Coast in the fishing industry. The representative of the Canadian Vickers the other day pointed out that he could not deliver before the end of July but could deliver twelve by the end of November. After consideration of this I should think it useless having any vessels which could not be delivered and put in commission after the end of September."[152]

Even when the required number of patrol auxiliaries were built or purchased, the navy still had to arm them and provide enough trained gunners. In mid-January NSHQ informed Whitehall that there was no reserve of either trained seamen or guns in Canada since all surplus naval ordnance in the country had already been sent to Britain. Ottawa needed to know if the Admiralty could provide the "requisite number of guns and sufficient trained men for each, with instructional petty officers and armourer ratings? *Rainbow* is approaching time when extensive refit absolutely necessary. If she were paid off number of trained men would be available and four 12-pdr guns, also six 4.7 [inch] guns would be liberated for defence of merchantmen."[153] After making enquiries in the United States regarding the possibility of purchasing naval guns there, however, NSHQ had to inform London that none were available from south of the border.[154] Finally, on 27 January, Prime Minister Borden wrote directly to the first lord, Sir Edward Carson, to explain the situation—and Canada's requirements—at a higher level.

Minister naval service informs me that we have now in commission thirteen vessels which require thirteen 12 pounder guns to complete their armament. Arrangements have been made to purchase ten and build twelve vessels to carry two 12 pounders each. For these vessels forty-four 12 pounders will be required, bringing our total requirements up to fifty-six guns. All such guns formerly available in Canada have been sent to Great Britain and we find it impossible to purchase on this continent. It is also urgently necessary that a sufficient number of trained gunnery ratings to man these fifty-six guns should be sent here as soon as possible. I should be most grateful for your personal consideration to this matter as the responsibilities placed upon the Canadian government in this respect were quite unexpected and the provision of ships which we are making by most strenuous efforts will be useless unless we can be assisted with guns and gun ratings as above indicated.[155]

152. Kingsmill, "Memorandum for the Information of the Minister," 26 January 1917, 1065–7-2, pt 1, LAC, RG 24, vol 4031.

153. Desbarats to Undersecretary of State for External Affairs, 16 January 1917, ibid.

154. Desbarats to Undersecretary of State for External Affairs, 24 January 1917, ibid.

155. Governor General of Canada to Colonial Secretary, 27 January 1917, ibid.

Canadian Battle-class trawlers under construction at Polson Iron Works in Toronto on 31 March 1917. (LAC PA-125824)

The launch of the Battle-class trawler *St. Eloi* at Polson Iron Works in Toronto on 2 August 1917. (LAC e007140889)

The first of the thirty-six Imperial trawlers ordered by the Admiralty, *TR 1*, under construction at Port Arthur, Ontario, in 1917. (LAC B-002994)

Officials in Whitehall were unmoved by Borden's oblique reminder that it was the Admiralty's failure to provide for the nation's maritime defence that had left Canada in the lurch. In a telegram of 30 January, it concurred in the decision to pay off *Rainbow* and use the men "set free" for service with the Atlantic coast patrol. The Admiralty made it clear, however, that the guns needed by the patrol service would not be available from Britain. Instead, their lordships suggested that Ottawa might consult the representatives of the British Ministry of Munitions in Washington concerning the possibility of purchasing 12-pounders from the United States, and listed several American firms that might be able to produce the required ordnance. Failing that, the Admiralty was willing to part with some of the 12-pounder guns it had on order with the American manufacturer Driggs, Seabury Company. The mountings and ammunition for the guns would be sent from England.[156] Such an arrangement was agreeable to Ottawa, and after exchanging the six 4.7-inch guns from *Rainbow* for six 12-pounder pieces taken off defensively armed merchant ships, NSHQ calculated that it would require forty-seven guns from the Admiralty's order with Driggs, Seabury to provide the auxiliaries with two each.[157]

The question of guns and mountings was addressed by the first lord in his response to Borden's January letter. Sir Edward Carson began by reducing Canada's requirements for 12-pounders in half by recommending that only one gun be fitted on each auxiliary "which is heavier armament than that carried by the majority of our patrol vessels." Insisting that the British government was "most anxious to do all in our power to assist you" the first lord assured Borden that he would "endeavour to meet your requirements from guns and mountings at present under manufacture." Fifteen of the Driggs, Seabury 12-pounders that were "ready and nearly ready for shipment from New York" would immediately be transferred to the Canadian government with their mountings and ammunition being sent from England. "Further 12-pounder guns from the same firm will be similarly transferred as they become available to complete the twenty-three required for vessels commissioned or purchased. Please let me know approximate date when the additional twelve guns will be required for the twelve further vessels about to be built. Question of lending you trained gunnery ratings is not easy but is engaging our earnest attention."[158]

These arrangements were satisfactory to Ottawa and it was requested that the guns, mountings, and ammunition be delivered to the Halifax dockyard. Borden acknowledged the "difficulty of providing skilled gunnery ratings but consider, for efficiency, efforts should be made to supply them."[159] Realizing that it was unlikely to be able to count on the Royal Navy, however, NSHQ also informed Admiral Story in Esquimalt of the intention to pay off *Rainbow* in early April and use her crew to man the expanded Atlantic patrol. In the meantime, Story was to make every effort "to train as gunlayers and seaman gunners

---

156. Long to Governor General, 30 January 1917, ibid.

157. Desbarats to Undersecretary of State for External Affairs, 2 February 1917, ibid.

158. Long to Governor-General, 8 February 1917, ibid.

159. Desbarats to Governor-General's secretary, Prime Minister for First Lord, 11 February 1917, ibid.

every available man of ship's company and RNCVR. *Shearwater* also to be utilized for this purpose."[160]

The naval department also moved quickly to arrange for the construction of twelve steel trawlers in Canadian yards. On 2 February the minister, J.D. Hazen, asked for authorization to construct twelve trawlers and disclosed that negotiations had already begun with the Polson Iron Works in Toronto and Vickers in Montreal. Both firms had forecast that they could complete the contract within seven months of the specifications and plans being delivered at a cost of between $155,000 and $160,000 per vessel. Hazen's recommendation that the contract be split between the two shipyards was approved and order-in-council PC 339 of 8 February authorized the construction of six 130-foot, 350-ton steam trawlers at each yard.[161] Even as the naval department was arranging the construction of its own patrol trawlers, however, the Admiralty had decided to greatly expand the scheme:

> View of Admiralty is that Canadian resources should immediately be utilized for output of patrol boats, that is steel vessels of trawler type with as good speed as can be obtained on the dimensions and wooden steam drifters, say, thirty-six of the former and one hundred of the latter. Admiralty would be glad if Canadian government could undertake this programme and if so could state as early as possible by what date vessels could be constructed. These vessels are additional not only to the thirteen already in commission but also to the twenty-two others for the building or purchase of which your ministers are understood to be arranging. Designs are being prepared of vessels considered most suitable and will be sent for the guidance of your ministers if they decide to undertake work. It is understood that information in Canada as to designs and costs of drifters which might be built has already been collected by the Imperial Munitions Board.[162]

The Borden government quickly embraced the latest British proposal, responding three days later that it would "proceed immediately with orders" for the thirty-six trawlers and 100 wooden drifters.[163] The trawlers were to be steam-driven steel vessels of the Castle class, 125 feet between perpendiculars, with a width of twenty-three feet six inches, and power from 480 horsepower triple expansion engines. As an indication of their commercial fishing design, the Admiralty pointed out the obvious in explaining that "arrangements shown on the drawing for fish ponds on upper deck and plan of hold for ice and fish stowage are not required." The 84-foot wooden drifters were powered by a 200 horsepower engine. Both trawlers and drifters would be capable of nine or ten knots with the former being armed with single 12-pounders

160. Naval Ottawa to Navyard, Esquimalt, 13 February 1917, ibid.

161. Dan G. Harris, "Canadian Warship Construction on the Great Lakes and Upper St. Lawrence," *Inland Seas*, vol. 2, Summer 1986, 115.

162. Long to Governor General, 5 February 1917, 1065–7-2, pt 1, LAC, RG 24, vol 4031.

163. Governor General to Colonial Secretary, 8 February 1917, ibid.

and the later with a 6-pounder each.[164] Besides the drawings and specifications, the Admiralty also agreed to send "two officers specially experienced in construction of craft ... to assist in supervision and fitting out of 36 trawlers and 100 wooden drifters."[165]

Although the Canadian naval department was capable of overseeing the construction of its own twelve trawlers, the expanded scheme suggested the need for a new branch within the department to undertake the construction program's administration, particularly in view of the extreme difficulty of obtaining the necessary wood, steel, and machinery in an expanding war economy. When, on 10 February, the vice-president and managing director of Canada Steamship Lines, J.W. Norcross, offered, free of charge to the government, to organize a central office to supervise the project, Hazen readily accepted. At the deputy minister's suggestion, Norcross and his CSL staff would oversee the purchase of steel and wood required for construction, place orders for the main engines, boilers, and equipment, and draw up contracts with the shipyards for the construction of hulls and the installation of machinery. The total cost of the program was expected to be in the vicinity of $11,000,000 and would be under the general supervision of the naval service.[166]

As had been the case with Arthur Harris's energetic organization of the Overseas Transport branch in the offices of Canadian Pacific in Montreal, the new director of ship construction demonstrated no little zeal in quickly putting together his staff on the sixth floor of the Canada Steamship Lines building in Montreal. One day after his meeting with Hazen, Norcross had assembled his staff and sorted out his purchasing, clerical, and accounting departments. He also quickly secured the 5,000 tons of steel required for construction before convening a meeting of the main Canadian shipbuilding firms on the 15th.[167] In contracting out the construction, Norcross "utilized the entire capacity of the Dominion of Canada," and spread the work among some two dozen firms.[168] By the end of March, the Royal Navy officer loaned to Canada to provide technical advice, Commander J.W. Skentelbery, RNVR (Royal Naval Volunteer Reserve), was able to report that "the work is well in hand and all materials ordered, particularly the timber which was wisely ordered in good time as it is difficult to obtain, but it is now coming to hand and the keels will be laid shortly.... Several modifications will be necessary to suit the material available in this country but this will not affect the vessels in any way." Among the alterations to the Admiralty's plans were the fitting of electric lights in place of the British acetylene gas installation, electric fittings being "easily obtained in the country," moving the gun forward "in a similar manner to the new Canadian trawlers" being built for the RCN and fitting a steam windlass in the drifters in place of the capstan.[169] Although

---

164. Long to Governor General, 14 February 1917, ibid.

165. Admiralty to Naval Ottawa, 21 February 1917, ibid.

166. Desbarats memorandum, 10 February 1917, PC 516, 27 February 1917, 29–16–1, pt. 1, LAC, RG 24, vol. 5604.

167. "Memorandum of what has been done by Mr J.W. Norcross up to date," 12 February 1917, ibid.

168. Norcross to Desbarats, 6 March 1917, ibid.

169. Report of Commander J.W. Skentelbery, RNVR, quoted in Commodore Coke to the Secretary, Department of the Naval Service, 26 March 1917, ibid.

Desbarats had problems with the profit margins of the contracts and their compliance with government contracting requirements, Norcross assured him that "with the amount of material which the government is supplying to builders, they would get no profit whatever if they did not receive this 10 percent" margin.[170]

Although the Borden government had agreed to purchase additional patrol auxiliaries to bring the RCN's East Coast forces up to the thirty-six vessels now being demanded by the Admiralty, it was as yet unable completely to set aside its long-standing aversion to naval expenditures for home defence. Seeking whatever means possible to strengthen its defence of the East Coast shipping lanes in early 1917, the naval department began to explore the possibility of establishing aerial patrols to augment the work of its surface vessels. On 10 February, Hazen referred a proposal to form a Canadian naval air service to the Interdepartmental Committee of the navy and militia departments.[171] At the same time, NSHQ referred its seaplane proposal to the Admiralty with a request for help in organizing an air service if it was considered feasible.[172] The Interdepartmental Committee was "of the opinion that an air service is necessary for the adequate defence of the Atlantic coast," and decided to solicit the views of the officer commanding the Royal Flying Corps (RFC) in Canada, Lieutenant-Colonel C.G. Hoare. Meeting again on the 12th, the interdepartmental representatives:

> considered that if an Air Service was organised, the minimum requirements would be a seaplane station at Halifax and another at Sydney.
> The Committee in coming to this decision was guided by the following facts:
> (1) Halifax is the principal naval base on the Atlantic Coast, to and from which men-of-war are all proceeding. It is most likely, therefore, that enemy submarines would carry on their activities in its vicinity.
> (2) Through Cabot Strait passes in the summer, the great majority of the overseas trade of the dominion; and, therefore, this vicinity is a probable theatre of operations for enemy submarines. Sydney being already the base of the naval patrols is a convenient spot for an air station. It may be necessary to have a small advanced station on North Point later.
> (3) In the winter the Atlantic overseas trade is concentrated at Halifax and St John. A station at [Halifax] is considered sufficient to deal with this at present.[173]

Lieutenant-Colonel Hoare, meanwhile, informed Kingsmill that he did not believe that a Canadian air service was a practical proposition, citing repair and supply difficulties.[174]

---

170. Desbarats to Norcross, 2 April 1917, Norcross to Desbarats, 9 April 1917, ibid.

171. J.D.F. Kealey, "Naval Aviation in Canada During the First World War," nd, 4, DHH 74/25.

172. Desbarats to Undersecretary of State for External Affairs, 10 February 1917, 1034–3-3, pt. 1, LAC, RG 24, vol. 3894.

173. Stephens, "Memorandum for: Director of Naval Service," 21 March 1917, DHH 77/58, vol. 20, file 2.

174. Hoare to Kingsmill, 14 February 1917, 1034–3-3, pt. 1, LAC, RG 24, vol. 3894.

Hoare's job, however, was to oversee the RFC Canada training scheme and he would always remain leery of supporting any plan for a Canadian version of the rival Royal Naval Air Service, one that might later encroach on his own training program.[175] Despite the army officer's discouragement, the naval minister took up the question of a Canadian air service with the Admiralty when he accompanied Prime Minister Borden to London in mid-February. British officials agreed to the Canadian proposal "provided scheme can be carried out without affecting more urgent services," and on 28 February Hazen wired NSHQ that RNAS officers were being sent to Canada to help establish it.[176] The head of the RNAS advisory group, Wing Commander J.W. Seddon, arrived in Ottawa in mid-March and immediately set about making enquiries. He submitted his recommendations to Kingsmill one week later with a plan for an air service of fourteen seaplanes based at Halifax, another twenty seaplanes at Sydney, with a combined complement of twenty-three officers and 277 men.[177] The navy's representative on the interdepartmental committee, Commander Stephens, estimated the cost of the two air stations, with thirty-four aircraft and some 300 personnel, to be $1,500,000. The Imperial Munitions Board (IMB) had already been contacted and was "prepared to undertake the building of the necessary establishments and the construction of the seaplanes," although it would probably be necessary "to obtain a few machines from the Admiralty to start with whilst the Canadian machines are being built." In asking Kingsmill to obtain governmental approval for the expenditure, the chief of staff also emphasized the urgency of the proposal, stating that "if the scheme is to be of any use during the coming summer, it is imperative to start the construction of the buildings and the seaplanes immediately."[178]

With both Borden and Hazen away in London, the remainder of the Cabinet met at the end of March to discuss the plan. The acting prime minister, Sir George Foster, cabled Borden later that day with the government's decision: "Council unanimously of opinion establishment inadvisable. Cost entailed will exceed two and a half millions for first year, abstract skilled men for construction badly needed in other works, utility limited by our seasonal changes. Money better used in providing [more sea] patrols."[179] In view of the Cabinet rejection, primarily on the grounds of cost, Stephens asked Seddon to compose an alternative scheme for a more limited—and cheaper—air patrol service in the vicinity of Sydney only. Unfortunately, even the more modest air service proposal could not interest Cabinet as ministers stood by their original decision. With no prospect of fulfilling the

175. S.F. Wise, *Canadian Airmen and the First World War* (Official History of the Royal Canadian Air Force, I: Toronto 1980), 603, 605n.

176. Admiralty to Browning, 7 March 1917, UKNA, ADM 137/654; Hazen to Naval Ottawa, 28 February 1917, 1034-3-3, pt. 1, LAC, RG 24, vol. 3894; and Kealey, "Naval Aviation in Canada During the First World War," nd, 4–5, DHH 74/25.

177. Wing Commander J.W. Seddon, "Memo: For Director of the Naval Service," 21 March 1917, DHH 77/58, vol. 20, file 2.

178. Stephens, "Memorandum for: Director of Naval Service," 21 March 1917, ibid.

179. Foster to Borden, 30 March 1917, 1034–3-3, pt. 1, LAC, RG 24, vol. 3894; and Wise, *Canadian Airmen and the First World War*, I, 603.

job they had arrived in Canada to carry out, the RNAS advisory group remained in the country for a few more weeks to forward the aircraft and supplies already sent by the Admiralty to Halifax on to the United States, the Allies' new "associate power" following its declaration of war against the central powers on 6 April. Four of the crated seaplanes that arrived in Nova Scotia after Seddon's party had left were subsequently discovered by Kingsmill during a September inspection tour of Halifax dockyard. With the government unwilling to pay for a Canadian air patrol, the forgotten aircraft were donated to the US Naval Flying Corps for their flying training schools in Florida.[180]

The Cabinet's refusal to fund the relatively modest cost of a small air service to protect the East Coast shipping lanes—even a reduced scheme limited to one air station at Sydney—marked the end of a disappointing twelve months for the RCN, a period in which the navy had seen its hopes of building destroyers in Canada transformed into a scheme to construct slow, under-gunned trawlers in their place. Despite NSHQ's clear understanding that only destroyers and air patrols could offer any hope of adequately protecting Canada's shipping lanes from marauding U-boats, it was hamstrung in its ability to implement an effective defence by both its own politicians and the Admiralty's often contradictory staff work and preoccupation with British waters. The fact that Borden was willing to finance the construction of twelve trawlers for the RCN once the Admiralty recommended it, demonstrated the extent to which the prime minister was willing to follow whatever advice emanated from Whitehall, no matter how inconsistent it might be. It also illustrates the next to impossible task the naval director faced in convincing his own government of the necessity of reinforcing the navy when his plans had not received London's stamp of approval. It would appear that if the Admiralty had managed to express its approval for Kingsmill's destroyer scheme in April, rather than advocating the construction of merchant tonnage instead, Borden would most likely have agreed to building destroyers at Canadian Vickers. Unfortunately, the constraints placed upon NSHQ's plans now meant that the RCN would have to face the 1917 shipping season with only its expanded collection of patrol auxiliaries, and the promise of equally inadequate trawler reinforcements later in the summer, rather than the destroyers and aircraft it would need if the warning provided by *U 53*'s initial foray into North American waters was ever followed by a more concerted German submarine campaign.

---

180. Kealey, "Naval Aviation in Canada During the First World War," nd, 7, DHH 74/25.

CHAPTER 7

British Commodores
and the Convoy System, 1917

With its hopes for a small destroyer force covered by air patrols having been dashed by the Admiralty on the one hand and the Borden government on the other, the Canadian navy had to plan for the 1917 shipping season with only a modestly augmented auxiliary patrol fleet to meet London's recommended force, including minesweepers, of thirty-six vessels. The first of the twelve Battle-class trawlers ordered from Canadian shipyards would not be available, however, until the late autumn. The first six, HMC Ships *Festubert*, *Messines*, *St Eloi*, *St Julien*, *Vimy*, and *Ypres*—all named for battles fought by the Canadian Corps in France—were not commissioned until 13 November 1917, just at the end of the St Lawrence shipping season. The seven New England fishing trawlers the navy had purchased in the United States, meanwhile, were to be employed primarily as minesweepers. Only the newly acquired auxiliaries *Acadia*, *Cartier*, *Lady Evelyn*, and *Laurentian*, once they were armed and commissioned, would be available to reinforce the navy's seaward patrols in 1917. The naval department was also overseeing the work of the director of ship construction, J.W. Norcross, in building 136 trawlers and drifters for the British government in Canadian shipyards. These small vessels belonged to the Admiralty, however, and all indications were that they would be sent overseas for Royal Navy employment, as had been the case with the 550 motor launches built by Canadian Vickers in 1915–16.

While the navy struggled over the winter of 1916–17 to find the auxiliaries it needed to meet the Admiralty's thirty-six vessel requirement (as, indeed, it had warned London would be the case), the question of who would command the expanded Canadian patrol remained unsettled. As we have seen, the British telegram of 11 November informing Ottawa of the Admiralty's change of attitude toward Canada's maritime defence also contained an offer to lend the RCN "an officer experienced in patrol work to advise the Newfoundland and Canadian governments."[1] Although the Canadian naval director was wary that the offer was a British attempt to take over control of the RCN's patrol forces, Ottawa had "gladly" accepted with the provision—insisted upon by Kingsmill—that the officer be "appointed to *Niobe* and becomes an officer of the Department of the Naval Service by whom his advice will be appreciated." Although it was the Canadian admiral's

---

1. Colonial Secretary to Governor-General of Canada, 11 November 1916, 1065–7-2, pt. 1, Library and Archives Canada (hereafter LAC), Record Group (hereafter RG) 24, vol. 4031.

intention that the loaned British officer be subject to NSHQ's direction, he was obviously concerned that if a more senior naval officer were selected the appointee might well arrive in Canada convinced that he understood naval matters better than any colonial officials and would assert his senior rank to assume control. As Kingsmill confided to deputy minister Desbarats in mid-January, "it would seem ... as if there were an intention to create a separate command out here under the Admiralty."[2] It did not bode well, therefore, when the Admiralty informed Ottawa in late February that it had selected retired Vice-Admiral Sir Charles Coke to fill the Canadian patrol appointment.

Despite London's assurance that Coke would "drop his naval rank and be appointed to *Niobe* from 18th February as Commodore Royal Naval Reserve second class becoming temporarily officer of Department of the Naval Service," the appointment of a Royal Navy vice-admiral meant that he was of equal rank to the officer under whom he would supposedly be serving. It also would not be lost on either officer that Kingsmill's highest RN rank had been captain and that he had risen to rear-admiral only on the retired list.[3] Moreover, the British vice-admiral was not explicitly told by the Admiralty that he would be directly subordinate to NSHQ. Instead, London merely instructed him that it had "placed your services at the disposal of the dominion and Newfoundland governments for carrying out the joint patrol of the coast ... While holding this appointment you will give all possible assistance in your power to the dominion and Newfoundland governments for the purpose of organizing the patrol vessels and rendering them as efficient as possible for their duty of combatting the operations of enemy submarines."[4] Such ambiguous and misleading wording—that he would be working for both the Canadian and Newfoundland governments in organizing a joint patrol with no mention of his status as an officer of the Canadian naval department—could be construed as indicating that Coke was simply to keep both Ottawa and St John's informed of his decisions. Whether he would defer to NSHQ's direction as one of its officers, as Ottawa had insisted upon, or whether Whitehall was indeed trying "to create a separate command out here under the Admiralty," as Kingsmill feared and the less-than-forthcoming instructions to Coke suggested, remained to be determined.

Before being sent to Canada, the British vice-admiral had served as commander-in-chief, Irish coast, in charge of the anti-submarine patrols at Queenstown at the time the *Lusitania* was torpedoed and sunk in May 1915. The subsequent public enquiry scapegoated the *Lusitania*'s master, Captain William Turner, for the disaster but the failure to warn the passenger liner of a U-boat operating off the Irish coast was yet another example of the Admiralty staff's frequent inability to disseminate important information. Although he had received "contradictory and often very dubious information" from London and there was more than enough blame to go around, Coke was the only naval officer to receive any

2. Kingsmill to Desbarats, 16 January 1917, Colonial Secretary to Governor-General of Canada, 11 November 1916, Desbarats to Undersecretary of State for External Affairs, 15 December 1916, ibid.

3. Long to Governor-General, 20 February 1917, ibid; and M. Hadley and R. Sarty, *Tin-pots and Pirate Ships: Canadian Naval Forces and German Sea Raiders, 1880–1918* (Montreal and Kingston 1991), 190.

4. Graham Greene to Vice-Admiral Sir Chas. H. Coke, 21 February 1917, 1065–7-2, pt. 1, LAC, RG 24, vol. 4031.

penalty as a result of the liner's sinking, being relieved of his command at the end of the month.[5] It says something of the Admiralty's view of the relative importance of the RCN and its auxiliary patrol that they deemed a shelved admiral to be suitable for the same task in Canada from which he had been relieved of command in Ireland.

Soon after Coke arrived in Canada, Kingsmill prepared a memorandum for the British admiral's information that outlined the disposition of the RCN's available patrol auxiliaries and the nature of the organization that NSHQ had employed to date. As the naval director explained, the auxiliary patrol effectively comprised only the five vessels—*Canada*, *Grilse*, *Margaret*, *Stadacona*, and *Hochelaga*—that Captain Pasco had based at Sydney to cover the main shipping lane through the Cabot Strait. The four minesweepers and *Premier*, meanwhile, had kept a lookout in the approaches to Halifax along with the "useful fast vessel" *Tuna*. Apart from these ships, Coke would have the department's two former hydrographic survey ships, *Acadia* and *Cartier*, which had been commissioned in January 1917. The naval director also informed the British officer that the navy would, in all probability, be acquiring the vessels *Bayfield* and *Laurentian*. (In the event the *Bayfield* remained a government ship, while *Laurentian* and *Lady Evelyn* were commissioned into the RCN as patrol vessels in May and June 1917 respectively).[6]

As to the navy's manpower, Kingsmill assured Coke that *Rainbow* at Esquimalt was busy training ratings as gunlayers for the eastern patrol force, seamen who would be joined by another "forty-six ratings RNCVR, trained as efficient, which means that they will still have to be taught a good deal." Paying off the West-Coast cruiser at the end of April would also release several lieutenants who could easily serve as commanding officers of the new patrol auxiliaries and two warrant officer gunners who would be used to train gunners in the East Coast fleet. The gunnery warrant officers would be additional to the lieutenant and two chief petty officers on loan from the Royal Navy to visit the various patrol vessels and provide further gunnery instruction to their crews. Furthermore, *Niobe* was "busily engaged training boys for signal and general duties of a vessel, so that they may, later on, relieve other ratings and be distributed among the patrols."[7]

More important, from NSHQ's perspective, was the issue of the command and control of Canada's patrol forces. In broaching the subject with Coke, Kingsmill carefully explained the arrangements that had been put in place and the role that NSHQ had played in coordinating harbour defences with the St Lawrence patrols and the movement of transports:

> Taking into consideration that the commander-in-chief [North America and West Indies Station] has always been in close touch with Halifax, I have hitherto left the five vessels and any extra one[s] detailed for the time being

5. Patrick Beesly, *Room 40: British Naval Intelligence, 1914–18* (London 1982), 84–120.

6. Kingsmill, "Memorandum for Commodore Coke, RNR," 22 March 1917, 1065–7-3, LAC, RG 24, vol. 4031; and Ken MacPherson and John Burgess, *The Ships of Canada's Naval Forces: A Complete Pictorial History of Canadian Warships* (Toronto 1985), 15–18.

7. Kingsmill, "Memorandum for Commodore Coke, RNR," 22 March 1917, 1065–7-3, LAC, RG 24, vol. 4031.

The Imperial trawlers *TR 2* and *TR 37* shortly after their launch at Port Arthur, Ontario, on 12 September 1917. (LAC B-020162)

Imperial drifters being completed at the Davie Shipbuilding and Repair Company in August 1917. (LAC PA-171102)

entirely in the charge of the senior Canadian naval officer at Halifax, Captain E.H. Martin, and having always considered that it would be better for the commander-in-chief to inform him direct as to any requests he might wish to make as to the disposal of the other patrol vessels. On several occasions the commander-in-chief has asked for more patrols at Halifax to assist transports leaving or to look out for incoming treasure ships. The captain-in-charge has communicated direct with Ottawa and Ottawa being entirely in touch with the movements of the patrols has been able to direct the senior officer patrols accordingly.

As you have expressed a distinct wish that you should be in charge of all vessels that we call patrols, I am quite willing to recede from my position. I wish to take this opportunity of placing my views on record, that is, that the vessels employed in the immediate defence of the harbour limits of Halifax should be immediately under the direction of the captain and senior Canadian officer at that port.[8]

As for the question of where Coke should locate his headquarters, the naval director once again assured him that "in this matter I wish you not to be influenced by my views" even as he carefully explained them. While conceding that Halifax was "the centre of all things naval on the Atlantic coast" Kingsmill clearly indicated that he believed the commodore of patrols should be based at Sydney during the summer shipping season, as had been the case in 1915 and 1916, since "the majority of the patrol vessels will be operating from Sydney and Gaspé protecting the long lane from Quebec to the open sea through the Cabot Straits." The naval director tried to ease Coke into accepting Sydney as his base by informing him that in future the crews of all patrol vessels would be borne on the books of *Stadacona*, based in Sydney, as opposed to the previous practice of placing them on *Niobe*'s books in Halifax. Kingsmill also made the point that *Stadacona* "has been fitted out and is convenient for a senior officer's ship, that is there is cabin accommodation and possibilities of enlarging in order to have office room." In addition, he proposed bringing Walter Hose, *Rainbow*'s commanding officer, east to have charge of the Gaspé patrol forces when the cruiser was paid off, informing Coke "that I do not think you will find a more energetic or useful officer."[9]

Already in Ottawa to sort out his command arrangements, Coke responded to Kingsmill's memorandum the next day. He assured the naval director that he planned to carry out his duties "as far as possible without disturbing or disarranging any organization at present in force" but otherwise indicated that he was not about to be unduly influenced by Kingsmill's views. In the strongest terms, Coke refused to contemplate having NSHQ act as a coordinating authority between the overseas transports organization, the commander-in-chief North America and West Indies, and the patrol service and rejected the use of Sydney as the patrol's main base:

8. Ibid.

9. Ibid.

I consider it to be of paramount importance that I should be given complete executive command of the whole of the patrol service, and be able to organize and dispose of the vessels as I may consider expedient. All matters and correspondence with reference to patrols would therefore come through me as commodore of patrols. I would, in my turn, be responsible to the department for the anti-submarine defence of the Atlantic coasts and harbours....

As regards my headquarters, I regard it as essential that this should be Halifax, as this port is the naval centre in the east and is in touch with the imperial Atlantic squadron: it is furthermore available as a base during the whole year, which is not the case with other bases such as Sydney, CB.[10]

It was clear that in Coke's view, his command of the patrols would require NSHQ, in Kingsmill's words, to "recede" from its coordinating role in East Coast defence. Despite the British officer's assurance that he would be responsible to Ottawa, there was a disquieting tone to his correspondence that suggested the commodore of patrols did not want, and would not seek, Ottawa's advice in exercising his command but would merely inform NSHQ of his decisions. In discussing Coke's response with his chief of staff, Commander Stephens, Kingsmill found several aspects disturbing. The commodore's suggestion that the RCN should appoint an officer to oversee the Newfoundland patrols, for instance, demonstrated the common misunderstanding of many British officers that the British Empire was a single political entity controlled from London. As Kingsmill commented to Stephens, "it would not be possible for us, even if we had one, to appoint an officer to act at St John's, nor is it seen exactly how an officer appointed by the Admiralty would have control over our fleets except by some mutual agreement." The naval director was also leery of having the commodore of patrols headquartered in Halifax where Royal Navy seniority might make a commodore RNR subordinate to an RN captain who happened to be visiting the port. In a crisis, the possibility existed that naval protocol would take command of the Canadian patrols out of Coke's hands and place it in those of a visiting RN captain, completely removing NSHQ from the chain of command. Kingsmill was also uneasy regarding the British officer's desire to control all patrol vessels and emphasized to Stephens that "in the commodore's absence, however, the defensive arrangements for the port must be in the hands of the senior Canadian naval officer present."[11] With ice still blocking the St Lawrence River and the commodore about to depart on a tour of Newfoundland, resolving these important questions would have to await Coke's return.

Kingsmill was also troubled by the fact that, upon his arrival, Coke revealed that he had been told by the Admiralty that the thirty-six trawlers and 100 drifters being built in Canada on British account were, in fact, meant to serve with the Canadian patrol rather than being sent overseas. It was the first intimation Ottawa had had that such was the case, and Sir George Foster, the acting prime minister, immediately telegraphed Sir Robert

---

10. C.H. Coke, "Memorandum for the Director of Naval Service," 23 March 1917, ibid.

11. Kingsmill, "Memorandum for Chief of Staff," 24 March 1917, ibid.

Borden in London: "No intimation has been given to us that it was intended to use latter ships in Canadian waters or that Canadian crews would be needed. Men responding to naval recruiting appeal [i.e., the RNCVR Overseas Division] have been sent to England and it will be most difficult if not impossible to provide crews for these additional ships. The imperial government has promised to provide guns for the thirty-six Canadian vessels but no mention has been made of guns for the one hundred and thirty-six ships. Please discuss matter fully with Admiralty and advise promptly in reference to the additional ships being constructed for Admiralty as instructions to Admiral Coke are entirely at variance with information furnished by Colonial Office."[12]

Commodore Coke, meanwhile, had returned to Halifax in mid-April, and submitted a report on his tour of Newfoundland and its defences. NSHQ did not have any serious dispute with the commodore's patrol arrangements for the colony other than to remind him that all patrol vessels under his command were available to serve in any waters where they might be required and that the additional 12-pounder guns he had promised to St John's would have to be supplied by the Admiralty since Canada had none to spare.[13] The question of where he should locate his headquarters and main base, however, remained a contentious issue. Immediately upon the commodore's return, Kingsmill telegraphed Halifax asking Coke to forward his objections in writing as to the use of Sydney as the main patrol base. As the naval director explained: "It is feared that you are considering that the defences of Halifax approaches [are] your first and paramount duty. It is realized that the provision of vessels and precautions to be taken are most important and your advice is most acceptable, but having organized the mobile defences of Halifax, the department considers the operation of same can be safely left in hands of captain superintendent, Halifax and your attention given to protection of trade route from Halifax, St John and Montreal to Europe. There can be no possible doubt that Sydney is the central position."[14]

Before Coke replied to Ottawa's latest instruction, he met with the British commander-in-chief, Vice-Admiral Browning, who had arrived at Halifax during the early morning hours of the 18th.[15] After conferring with the British admiral, Coke reiterated his position to Ottawa that, although he may have been responsible to NSHQ for the East Coast patrols, he was not about to accept its advice. As far as transferring his headquarters to Sydney, as Kingsmill was pressing him to do, the commodore insisted once again "that Halifax is in all respects suited for this purpose."

> It is the most central port on the coast. It is strongly defended against attack from the sea. It is the strategic centre where one is in touch with the centre

12. Foster to Borden, 21 March 1917, 1065–7-2, pt. 1, ibid.

13. Coke to Director of the Naval Service, 16 April 1917, Kingsmill to Commodore of Patrols, 21 April 1917, Naval Ottawa to Navyard Halifax, 21 April 1917, 426, 1065–7-3, ibid.

14. Naval Ottawa to Navyard Halifax, 16 April 1917, ibid.

15. Browning to Naval Ottawa, 24 April 1917, 1001–5-3, pt. 1, LAC, RG 24, vol. 6194. It is the opinion of Hadley and Sarty, *Tin-pots and Pirate Ships,* 191 that Coke "helped foment the [subsequent] imbroglio between Kingsmill and the commander-in-chief, North America and West Indies Station."

of naval intelligence and the commander-in-chief; it has a dockyard where principal repairs will be carried out, the depot ship, *Niobe*, is admirably adapted for carrying out the necessary training of officers and men; it is moreover open to the sea all the year around, which is regarded as being a very important point. The advent of the United States to our cause should be borne in mind, and in cooperating with their patrols Halifax is the most convenient port. Halifax is, in fact, the place of all things naval in dominion waters.

At Sydney these advantages do not obtain; it is an undefended port and moreover it is closed by ice for about four months in the year, which important fact alone makes it quite unsuitable as a main base for the Canadian patrols. It is, of course, most valuable as a sub-base for the St Lawrence patrol, but only minor repairs could be carried out there....

I have strongly in my mind the great importance of the St Lawrence, but at the same time I realize the importance of Halifax. At present there are five large armoured cruisers in the port, and the harbour is full of merchant ships. In addition, the great importance of Halifax as the departure port for Canadian troopships and treasure ships should not, I consider, be lost sight of. Approaches must be kept clear and arrangements made for escort, and later on I hope to have nets and hydrophones available here, as well as for the approaches to the St Lawrence. I propose practically to divide my time between the two areas.

I consider that it is absolutely necessary [that] the commodore of patrols should, under the naval department, be in entire charge of the patrols, and I consider that to place the Halifax minesweepers, etc., under the orders of the captain superintendent would be absolutely fatal to efficiency. I consider that the dual authority proposed would create an impossible situation, and I came out on the distinct understanding that the commodore of patrols would have complete executive control of the patrol service, and I was informed by the Admiralty that this provision had been agreed to between the imperial and Canadian governments.[16]

Not surprisingly, there were a number of points in Coke's memorandum with which the Canadian naval director took issue, not least the commodore's contention that Halifax was "the most central port on the coast," and the main dockyard for repairs. As Kingsmill minuted before passing the document on to his chief of staff, the fact that the navy yard at Halifax was already overworked meant that every ship patrolling to the eastward of the port should be sent to repair slips at Sydney and Pictou. Acknowledging that the difference between a sub-base and a main base was largely one of semantics, the director's chief concern centred on Coke's continuing insistence that he should have "complete executive control," and that "this provision had been agreed to between the imperial and Canadian governments."[17]

---

16. Coke to Director of Department of Naval Service, 18 April 1917, 1065–7-3, LAC, RG 24, vol. 4031.

17. Kingsmill's undated minutes on Coke to Director of Department of Naval Service, 18 April 1917, ibid.

Kingsmill passed the commodore's memorandum to Stephens asking for his views on the question. When the chief of staff's response confined itself to the narrower question of who should control a port's immediate defences, Kingsmill asked that a further memorandum be prepared to clearly present "the views of this department" to Coke, and emphasize the point that the Halifax and Sydney defences were in the hands of the captain superintendent and the senior naval officer appointed to Sydney. Cutting to the heart of the matter, the director wanted the issue of Coke's "complete executive control" dealt with and asked that Stephens quote the pertinent correspondence between London and Ottawa as to the British admiral's status. "The memorandum will be laid before the minister and should be quite clear. The question of main base need not be considered—a statement that there will be a base at Sydney as well as at Halifax and that Halifax is to be relieved [of repair work] as much as possible will do."[18]

The memorandum prepared by the department was authorized "by command" and sent to Coke on 30 April. As Kingsmill had directed, it clearly laid out the command arrangements and restrictions that were to govern the commodore in his command of the East Coast patrols:

> On due reflection the department has decided that one officer cannot efficiently control both the seagoing patrols in all parts of the Canada—Newfoundland area, and the defensive arrangements at such widely scattered ports as St John, NB, Halifax, Sydney, St John's, Nfld., etc.
>
> It has also been decided that the senior naval officers at the various ports should have allotted to them a certain number of minesweepers and, if necessary, patrol vessels for the defence of the ports.
>
> The commodore will be responsible for the general patrol of the coast, including minesweeping, but the senior officer of ports where one is stationed, should be responsible for the defence of the approaches to the ports.
>
> It is pointed out that there is a great difference in the two forms of minesweeping; the commodore's ships would sweep only in localities and at times when it is believed mines have been laid; the local port minesweepers, on the contrary, would sweep daily. It seems therefore additionally reasonable that they should be under the orders of an officer permanently stationed on the spot.
>
> This organization also appears necessary as the defence of a port is a joint one with the militia; the senior naval officer, being a permanent officer, is, and always has been in touch with the militia and is fully cognizant of the defensive arrangements of the port, whilst the commodore, being frequently away, is out of touch with them.
>
> It does not appear desirable that, in the commodore's absence, his representative and junior officer should handle this important matter, but that it should be handled by the permanent senior naval officer....
>
> With regard to the question of bases, it is immaterial which is called the

---

18. R.M. Stephens, "Memo: For Director of the Naval Service," 24 April 1917, Kingsmill minute, nd, ibid.

"main" base. Arrangements are being made by which repairs can be executed at Sydney and Pictou, where there is a slip which will take most of the patrol vessels we at present have. Halifax is naturally also a base and taking into consideration the establishment of a base at Sydney no more storage accommodation should be asked for at Halifax than is necessary....

Regarding the statement made that there was a "distinct understanding that the commodore of patrols would have complete executive control of the patrol service," nothing on the departmental files bears out this statement....

It will be noted that the services of the officer in question were accepted on condition that he became an officer of the department. It is not considered possible that at any moment there was an idea prevalent that the whole question of our defence should be in the hands of an officer acting on his own responsibility.

The views of the department having been clearly expressed, they await the scheme of action proposed by you on these lines.[19]

From NSHQ's perspective, Coke's insistence on having complete control of all RCN East Coast vessels only deepened Kingsmill's concern that the appointment of a senior RN officer to Canada's East Coast would result in an effort "to create a separate command out here under the Admiralty."[20] At a minimum, the fact that the British commodore had been accurately stating the Admiralty's instructions that he was to "have complete executive control of the patrol service," and that such a provision, as far as he knew, "had been agreed to between the imperial and Canadian governments,"[21] indicates the degree to which London was insensitive to issues of Canadian autonomy on the dominion's East Coast. Although Coke's status as an officer of the Canadian naval department allowed NSHQ to order the commodore to follow their instructions, a simultaneous attempt by the British commander-in-chief to sideline Ottawa from the East Coast's chain of command represented a greater threat to Canada's navy and was more problematic to resolve.

In contrast to Patey's command of the North America and West Indies Station—or, indeed, that of his later successor at the station, Vice-Admiral W.L. Grant—Sir Montague Browning proved to be the prickliest and least sympathetic to Canadian concerns of any of the naval officers holding the North American command during the war. Known as "Hooky" after an 1889 accident severed his left hand, the British admiral was, according to Walter Hose, the "hardest nut in the Royal Navy."[22] As we have seen, Browning had been alarmed by the sudden appearance of *U 53* off the American coast the previous October. Among his recommendations for improving Halifax's defences at that time—aside from the unwise advice that Canadian authorities turn off all navigation lights to the port—was

19. NSHQ to Commodore of Patrols, 30 April 1917, ibid.

20. Kingsmill to Desbarats, 16 January 1917, 1065-7-2, pt. 1, ibid.

21. Coke to Director of Department of Naval Service, 18 April 1917, 1065-7-3, ibid.

22. Michael Simpson, ed., *Anglo-American Naval Relations, 1917–1919* (Aldershot, UK 1991), 18n; and Hadley and Sarty, *Tin-pots and Pirate Ships*, 196–97.

a demand that the harbour should be protected by a second anti-submarine net across the entry channel between McNab Island and the mainland. In response, NSHQ had directed the captain superintendent at the dockyard, Captain E.H. Martin, to proceed with its construction over the course of the winter. Although the new net was primarily needed to cover the new ocean terminals that were being built at the south end of the harbour outside the existing net that extended to either side of George Island, Ottawa informed Martin that the "matter is considered most important and to take precedence over all other work." The only change that Kingsmill made to Browning's request was to move the second net closer to the harbour entrance than the admiral had proposed, to a point at "the end of the new [ocean terminal] pier near Reid Rock to head of shoal off Ives Point" on the northwest tip of McNab Island. The change would allow the many local ships that frequented Halifax to have access to the Northwest Arm as an anchorage in the event of heavy weather without having to pass them through a gate in the anti-submarine net.[23]

In the event, construction of the second net was held up throughout the winter by a combination of delays in delivering the materials to Halifax and the amount of ice drifting out from Bedford Basin.[24] In the meantime, Browning demonstrated his disregard for Canadian autonomy by arbitrarily designating the highest ranking RN officer at the port as "senior naval officer, Halifax." As the C-in-C explained to the Admiralty in February, "considerable telegraphic correspondence between myself and the senior naval officer, Halifax, and the director of naval service, Ottawa, respectively has been necessary in order to fix responsibility between the imperial and Canadian officers. While laying stress upon the necessity for mutual cooperation between the Canadian and naval authorities, I informed the director of naval service that I considered that it was most desirable that the senior naval officer (Captain [Boyle] Somerville of [the cruiser HMS] *Devonshire*—an officer of tact and experience) should give decisions on questions requiring settlement 'on the spot.' To this there was some demur on the part of the Canadian government."[25] Since it was well beyond the admiral's powers to appoint a "senior naval officer, Halifax"—the British C-in-C was not responsible to the Canadian government and had no authority over the RCN[26]—it is hardly surprising that Ottawa objected to his desire to place one of his cruiser captains in charge of the port. For his part, Browning simply ignored the Canadian position and informed the Admiralty the following month that "Captain Somerville has shown much tact and judgment as senior naval officer, Halifax." Treating Somerville as the *de facto* commander of the Canadian port, Browning had him report on all naval aspects at Halifax, from the examination of neutral vessels to questions regarding its defences. In mid-March, for instance, Somerville informed his chief that the second anti-submarine net was "being put together by degrees but weather conditions" had "delayed matters considerably." For his part, Browning did not express any concern when the British captain

---

23. Kingsmill to Captain Superintendent, Halifax, 30 May 1917, 1001–5-3, pt 1, LAC, RG 24, vol. 6194.

24. Browning to Admiralty, 5 January and 14 March 1917, United Kingdom National Archives (hereafter UKNA), Admiralty (hereafter ADM) 137/504.

25. Browning to Admiralty, 24 February 1917, ibid.

26. Hadley and Sarty, *Tin-pots and Pirate Ships*, 97.

could only promise that he "hoped ... to have it in place in April," even though that left open the possibility that the net would not finally be in place until the following month.[27]

Whatever Browning may have been trying to accomplish by arbitrarily anointing Somerville as the "senior naval officer, Halifax," Coke's arrival in Canada the following week—with his RN vice-admiral rank—ended any mention of the C-in-C's pseudo-appointment in his correspondence with the Admiralty. As we have seen, Browning conferred with Coke upon his arrival at Halifax on 18 April when they discussed the commodore's 4 April letter regarding the "importance of organising a proper defence for the port of Halifax."[28] Although Coke immediately wrote to Ottawa insisting, once again, on his being granted "complete executive control" of all RCN East Coast forces, Browning waited several more days before firing his own broadside in Ottawa's direction. The C-in-C was in Halifax to meet the members of a British naval mission led by Sir Arthur Balfour, the British foreign secretary, on 20 April. The Balfour mission was on its way to Washington to discuss naval co-operation and Browning briefed its officials on the talks he had held the previous week with the US navy department.[29] Although the British naval mission departed for Washington the following day, it was Browning's understanding that the foreign secretary and his naval adviser, Rear-Admiral Sir Dudley R. de Chair, would "proceed to Ottawa before returning to England."[30]

After conferring with both Coke and the Balfour mission in Halifax on the 18th and 20th, the C-in-C sent a long telegraph to NSHQ on 22 April stating that he was "much concerned to find on arrival at Halifax from Washington backward state of completion of outer net defences and mine sweepers.... The importance of preserving safety of port and free movements of allied and neutral shipping into and out of Halifax cannot be overestimated and the urgency of the measures recommended by me requires every effort to be made to complete them at earliest possible date. I find that the net itself is ready but only sixty-two out of the 182 floats, and gate vessel and moorings are not in place. Four of the six additional mine sweepers are in hand [of the seven New England trawlers, *PV I* to *PV VII*, the RCN had purchased in the United States early in 1917], but progressing slowly, a fifth has arrived but has no winch." The British admiral went on to assert that completion of the minesweepers had been delayed by a decision to have them fitted out with bathrooms. Having "consulted with commodore patrols and with his entire concurrence," Browning demanded that Kingsmill undertake "immediate measures" to loosen Ottawa's oversight of the navy's East Coast operations. The "immediate measures" Browning proposed included supplying the Halifax dockyard "forthwith with additional skilled labour, unobtainable locally, to hasten work," and authorizing Captain Martin "to employ any outside firm on any work without waiting for contract to be taken." The C-

---

27. Browning to Admiralty, 14 March 1917, UKNA, ADM 137/504.

28. Commodore of Patrols to Commander-in-Chief, North America and West Indies, 4 April 1917, Browning to Naval Ottawa, No. 678, 24 April 1917, 1001–5-3, pt 1, LAC, RG 24, vol. 6194.

29. "General Report on the Progress of Negotiations with United States Navy Department, &c, in Connection with Mr Balfour's Mission," 15 May 1917, UKNA, ADM 137/1436.

30. Browning to Admiralty, 30 April 1917, ibid.

in-C also wanted the work on the minesweepers "to be completed forthwith," the wood required to complete the net floats "to be given priority of rail transport," and for "ordinary procedures in regard to defect [i.e., repair] lists and store orders to be suspended."

"What is required," Browning asserted in laying the blame firmly at the feet of NSHQ, "is greater elasticity and decentralization primarily at Halifax; secondly, at other ports. No reflection is intended upon captain superintendent Halifax or the dockyard who do splendid work, but just as Admiralty give free hand to British yards, so it is strongly recommended that navy department, Ottawa, should do the same."[31]

In making his demands for immediate reform of the Halifax command arrangements, Browning referred to an Admiralty telegram on 13 April, disseminated to both NSHQ and the North American station, that London had "reason to suspect that one or two minelaying submarines are crossing Atlantic."[32] Although such intelligence undoubtedly suggested the need to improve the minesweeping forces at Halifax, the C-in-C's emphasis on the urgent necessity of immediately completing the second anti-submarine net seems somewhat contrived. The entrance to the harbour along the mainland and McNab Island was already well-lined with coast artillery and searchlight batteries, while the primary anti-submarine net across George Island was in place to prevent any penetration of the main harbour. Only seven months earlier, the previous C-in-C had expressed his satisfaction with "the placing of the [first] net across the entrance of Halifax Harbour," German knowledge of which he believed "had the effect of keeping enemy submarines away from Canadian waters."[33] The second anti-submarine net being insisted upon by Browning was mainly designed to cover the new ocean terminals, still under construction along the harbour's south end, which lay outside the first net. Halifax did serve as a naval base for British warships—and a sanctuary for Browning's cruisers whenever U-boats threatened North American waters—but the entry of the United States into the war had diminished the importance of that role, while the loading of trans-Atlantic ships was already in the process of shifting from St John and Halifax to Montreal in anticipation of the opening of the St Lawrence to summer traffic.

Nonetheless, Browning ensured that his complaints received the widest political audience possible by sending a copy of his telegram to the Admiralty. He also requested NSHQ to forward a copy of his criticisms and suggestions to the Canadian governor general, a man who took his nominal position as commander-in-chief of Canadian forces seriously and had always been critical of the Borden government's "failure to prepare more thoroughly for coastal defence."[34] Kingsmill's initial reaction was to tell Browning to forward his telegram to the governor general himself but the department reconsidered and submitted the C-in-C's

---

31. Commander-in-Chief to Naval Ottawa, 658, 22 April 1917, 1001–5-3, pt 1, LAC, RG 24, vol. 6194.

32. Admiralty to Naval Ottawa, 13 April 1917, 1062–13-2, pt 2, LAC, RG 24, vol. 4021; and Hadley and Sarty, *Tin-pots and Pirate Ships,* 189.

33. Vice-Admiral Patey to Admiralty, 5 September 1916, UKNA, ADM 137/1263.

34. Hadley and Sarty, *Tin-pots and Pirate Ships,* 97, 116; Commander-in-Chief to Naval Ottawa, 658, 22 April 1917, 1001–5-3, pt 1, LAC, RG 24, vol. 6194; and Browning to Admiralty, 23 April 1917, UKNA, ADM 137/655.

suggestions to Connaught on the 24th.[35] While Browning's attempt to draw the governor general into the fray had little impact on the discussions, the Admiralty quickly involved itself in the issue. Only a day after receiving a copy of the C-in-C's curtly worded telegram to Ottawa, the first sea lord took advantage of Borden's and Hazen's presence in London to lend support to Browning's position. Cabling Ottawa on the 24th, Borden referred to the C-in-C's telegram to Kingsmill and commented, "regarding net defence and minesweepers, Halifax, Admiral Jellicoe has asked me to state he considers matters therein of great importance and requests immediate consideration be given and work proceeded with as quickly as possible."[36] NSHQ responded to the prime minister's involvement by cabling that the "nets are being proceeded with [as] rapidly as possible," and would "be in place April 30th or shortly after." In the meantime, headquarters hoped to take advantage of the first sea lord's sudden interest in Canada's naval defence to get some action on their previously ignored requests for badly needed equipment, informing Borden that the "minesweepers are being fitted out ... but trawler winches are urgently required for them from Admiralty. See telegrams 14, 203, 259 and 392 from naval department to Admiralty. Please ask them to supply immediately."[37]

The long delays that routinely accompanied Canadian requests for naval equipment—and the Admiralty's seeming indifference to Ottawa's repeated entreaties to reinforce their patrol fleet—could not have made Browning's implied criticism any easier for NSHQ to accept even if Jellicoe had not been pressing Borden directly. One of naval headquarter's first actions upon receiving the C-in-C's telegram was to cable Sir George Foster, the minister of trade and commerce who was already in Washington on other government business, to have him urge the Americans to release the last two of the seven New England trawlers the RCN had purchased but whose registry US authorities had previously refused to transfer for neutrality reasons. Ottawa was also hoping that the Balfour naval mission might be able to convince the Americans to provide some badly needed reinforcement: "It has been suggested that United States might assist in the protection of Halifax and the Gulf [of] St Lawrence. Admiral De Chair [accompanying Balfour as his naval advisor] could advise you as to possibilities. Department has been urging outside protection at Halifax and Gulf by destroyers [but] Admiralty so far unable to carry out our wishes. Would you take up these matters with view co-operation United States and advise prospects of action being taken. Urgent."[38] In the event, however, NSHQ's hopes that the Balfour mission might ask the USN for naval assistance proved fruitless. Despite Browning's apparently pressing concern for the defence of Halifax, the British mission did not even raise the question of assisting the RCN in any of their Washington discussions.[39]

35. Kingsmill to Browning, 23 April 1917, Desbarats to Governor General's Secretary, 24 April 1917, 1001–5-3, pt 1, LAC, RG 24, vol. 6194.

36. Borden to Prime Minister's Office, Hazen for Desbarats, 24 April 1917, ibid.

37. Naval Ottawa to Hazen, 26 April 1917, ibid.

38. Naval Ottawa to British Ambassador, Washington, Reid for Foster, 23 April 1917, ibid.

39. Rear-Admiral de Chair to Admiralty, "General Report on the Progress of Negotiations with United States Navy Department, &c, in Connection with Mr Balfour's Mission," 15 May 1917, de Chair to Admiralty, "Continuation of General Report on the Progress of Negotiations with United States Navy Department, &c, in Connection with Mr Balfour's Mission, from the 15th May 1917," 7 June 1917, UKNA, ADM 137/1436.

Whether Browning's telegram was the result of the C-in-C's reaction to the possibility that minelaying U-boats were heading for North American waters or, as Kingsmill feared, was part of an effort to place Coke in unfettered command of Canada's maritime defences under the C-in-C's direct control,[40] the Canadian naval director now had to fend off a serious British attempt to sideline Naval Service Headquarters from the East Coast. Although Commodore Coke came under NSHQ's authority and could be ordered to focus on Sydney, Browning had to be handled more delicately. Writing to the C-in-C on 24 April, Kingsmill assured the British admiral that "in this matter the dockyard authorities in Halifax have not, in any way, been hampered as to purchase or provision of vessels, moorings, etc."[41] The naval director went on to explain that in its own strategic assessment of the precedence that should be assigned to traffic on the overcrowded East Coast rail line during the winter months, NSHQ had considered the shipment of war supplies to Halifax to have a higher priority than the provision of timber for a second anti-submarine net at the port. "In view of the ice conditions on the Atlantic coast, Halifax was considered safe from submarine attack and no special effort was made to obtain transport of this material as that would have meant delay to provisions and munitions [for transport overseas] anxiously asked for daily. Now that the St Lawrence is open for navigation the material may be very shortly expected at Halifax, the congestion on the railways having eased" once Montreal had reopened.[42]

As for the additional minesweepers, the naval director explained that of the seven fishing trawlers the RCN had purchased in the United States, commissioned as *PV I* to *PV VII*, only five had been procured before Washington had slapped an embargo on the transfer of the remaining two vessels. Of the five vessels in Canadian hands, the naval director must have taken some satisfaction in being able to inform Browning that NSHQ's orders "to proceed with all haste to fit these vessels out as armed minesweepers" had been delayed by Coke's insistence "that they were not suitable as such, and he proposed fitting them out as drifters." The drifter nets routinely used by British fishermen had been adapted by the Royal Navy's auxiliaries for passive anti-submarine defence in the approach channels to ports by—it was hoped—snagging U-boats attempting a submerged entry. Canadian fishermen, on the other hand, did not use drifter nets for fishing and had no experience with them. With no nets available for drifters and with the RCN "being sadly in need of patrol vessels," Kingsmill had countermanded Coke's directive and ordered Halifax "to proceed with the changes originally decided upon and fit them out as patrol vessels."[43]

Turning to the "immediate measures" Browning had demanded be made to Halifax's administration, Kingsmill assured the C-in-C that his concerns would "receive the consideration of the department." The naval director pointed out, however, the necessary differences between British and Canadian procedures, most of which were because of the vast

---

40. Hadley and Sarty, *Tin-pots and Pirate Ships*, 190.

41. Kingsmill to Commander in Chief, North America and West Indian Station, 24 April 1917, 1001–5-3, pt 1, LAC, RG 24, vol. 6194.

42. Ibid.

43. Ibid.

discrepancy in the scale of operations and supply between the world's biggest navy and one of the world's smallest. Since many of the naval stores were unavailable in North America and had to be obtained from Britain—where the Admiralty was often slow, if not altogether remiss, in satisfying the RCN's calls for particular items—the dockyard in Halifax could hardly be expected to furnish British warships with the array of spares and equipment that were readily available in British home bases. The naval director also told Browning that "Halifax dockyard has always been authorized to employ any outside firm on any important work," and that Captain Martin "can rest assured that any time he considers it necessary to work overtime, he will not find anyone finding fault." As for the minesweepers being delayed "for the purpose of fitting baths," the Canadian naval director dismissed the C-in-C's assertion by stating that "it would appear that you have been misinformed." Kingsmill did not, however, hide the fact that he rejected almost all of Browning's criticisms and ended his letter by insisting that "it is not considered [that] the Yard and methods in vogue are so much in need of reform as the [C-in-C's] telegram would suggest."[44]

Despite the validity of Kingsmill's explanation, his letter failed to deflect Admiral Browning from his quest to place Halifax beyond Ottawa's immediate purview. Responding on 2 May, the British C-in-C ignored NSHQ's justification that war supplies going to Halifax for shipment overseas should have a higher priority than placing a second anti-submarine net during the winter months.

> As commander-in-chief, my effort is directed to giving such advice as I can to the director of naval service towards ensuring the safety of the principal Canadian ports against oversea attack by the enemy. If a long interval elapses between the acceptance of the advice and the execution of the measures recommended, I have to consider firstly, whether the urgency is fully realized, and secondly, whether I can make any further suggestions based on procedure which the Admiralty has been obliged to adopt since the war in regard to giving local authorities a relatively free hand in regard to details of expenditure, etc.
>
> It cannot be regarded as satisfactory that with every desire to press matters forward the existing system does not, in fact, do so, and this admits of no doubt, as the object lessons are before us....
>
> I do not know the exact procedure at Ottawa, but I believe that the director of naval service has to refer matters entailing expenditure to the minister of Marine and Fisheries, the deputy minister dealing with matters of stores. Under this system local war measures of urgency cannot be expeditiously carried out, and my advice therefore is that it should be reconsidered.[45]

Although some historians have accepted Browning's allegations regarding "Canada's byzantine administrative procedures" at face value and are skeptical of Kingsmill's

44. Ibid.

45. Browning to Director of the Naval Service, 2 May 1917, 1001–5-3, pt 1, LAC, RG 24, vol. 6194.

"assurances that Ottawa's close and direct control had not stifled initiative at Halifax,"[46] such an interpretation is not supported by the facts. The British admiral's assertions were certainly rejected by Canadian naval officials in both Halifax and Ottawa. The deputy minister minuted Browning's letter that "a reply should be drawn up stating the position of the department. The C-in-C is under a wrong impression and should be given full information."[47] Kingsmill, too, dismissed the British admiral's continued insistence that because the work was not yet completed, the fault lay with headquarters in Ottawa. In response to the C-in-C's claim of urgency, the naval director noted the amount of ice that was still in the Gulf of St Lawrence in May and the often treacherous winter conditions in the approaches to Halifax, minuting that "there was no value in placing the nets in winter." As for the problem being the result of NSHQ's administrative procedures, Kingsmill stated that he was "not aware of any local war measure of urgency that has been delayed. The C-in-C must have his information from Halifax and the head of departments there are being called upon to give instances." It was clear to the naval director that any lack of initiative most likely lay with the man in charge of the dockyard. "Halifax has had a free hand—but the market is not there and apparently because they have not themselves given the purchase orders for stores, have sat down and waited" for requested items to arrive from Britain.[48]

NSHQ was correct in asserting that the delayed delivery of the lumber needed to complete the submarine net floats had been a deliberate decision based on its own risk assessment of the situation rather than oversight. During the winter months the rail lines to the east and south of Montreal had to carry all the war supplies being shipped overseas to the open ports of St John and Halifax. The congested transportation situation had already been explained to the Admiralty the previous February in response to a British inquiry as to the feasibility of carrying American-made munitions to Montreal for shipment and the practicality of sending Canadian-produced munitions to the eastern ports entirely by Canadian rail lines. NSHQ's response had indicated the extent to which a port's usefulness was a function of its rail connections to the interior rather than the extent of its harbour. Montreal, with its many rail lines, was well connected to both Canadian and American industrial centres and Kingsmill had assured the Admiralty that Canada's main eastern port could be used to ship munitions produced in the American Midwest. The rail connections to Halifax and St John, however, were more problematic. Halifax was poorly served by a single rail line, one that suffered from steep grades and was frequently rendered impassable by winter snowstorms. St John, on the other hand, had a direct rail connection to Montreal as well as a branch line running down from Moncton. More important, the New Brunswick port also had connections to the United States railway network. The Canadian naval director informed London, therefore, that with only one rail line to the maritimes running

46. Hadley and Sarty, *Tin-pots and Pirate Ships,* 189.

47. Desbarats minute, 8 May 1917, on Browning to Director of the Naval Service, 2 May 1917, 1001–5-3, pt 1, LAC, RG 24, vol. 6194.

48. Kingsmill minutes, nd, on Browning to Director of the Naval Service, 2 May 1917, ibid.

entirely through Canadian territory it was not possible to ship Canadian-manufactured munitions to the East Coast by an all-Canadian railway route. Even after sending some 35,000 tons of munitions to St John using US rail lines, "the congestion on the railways and adverse weather conditions render it impossible to haul sufficient munitions to either Halifax or St John to fill the ships at present on the Canadian transport service."[49] No Canadian munitions had been shipped through (still-neutral) American ports but quantities of floor, oats, and hay had been sent overseas from Portland, Maine.

Kingsmill's assessment of the rail situation was fully supported by a memorandum from the director of overseas transport, the most knowledgeable man anywhere on the movement of Canadian war supplies. A.H. Harris believed that shipping American-made munitions from the Chicago-Duluth area overseas through Montreal was "the most natural route" but also explained the difficulties associated with Halifax and St John in the winter months: "The quantity of Canadian munitions which can be exported from Halifax and St John during the winter season is governed solely by railway facilities and the weather. As a matter of fact the railways are not at the moment in a position—through climatic conditions—to haul sufficient munitions to either St John or Halifax to fill our own transports, therefore space requisitioned on commercial liners for munitions in February and March is not likely to be availed of.... The government railway is finding difficulty even in hauling its proportion of imperial supplies to Halifax. If during the winter season commercial vessels now using the ports of Halifax and St John were diverted to American ports the facilities for handling overseas traffic would be almost doubled at West St John but not materially increased at Halifax."[50]

Since Browning's 2 May letter indicated that he planned to continue pressing the case for Halifax's autonomy from Ottawa, Kingsmill asked his chief of staff to provide the C-in-C with a concise summary of both the strategic and administrative situation in Canada:

> The department is aware that much apparent delay has taken place in the placing of the outer net at Halifax. It has been necessary, however, during the winter to consider very carefully what measures were most essential for immediate adoption in view of the congested state of the railways, the lack of rolling stock, and the urgent need for munitions in Europe. In view of the fact that the appearance of submarines off Halifax during the winter was improbable, it was decided that it was more necessary to utilise all existing railway cars for the carriage of munitions, with the expectation that on the opening of navigation the situation would be less strained and the material for the nets could be hurried to Halifax. It is understood that the outer net is now about ready to be placed....
>
> The method of authorizing expenditure in Canada differs considerably from that in use in England. At Halifax, the captain superintendent has authority to incur minor expenses. Matters which entail a greater expenditure

49. Kingsmill to Admiralty, 16 February 1917, 1048–17–23, LAC, RG 24, vol. 3713.

50. Harris to Deputy Minister Naval Service, 15 February 1917, Harris to J.W. Flavelle, 1 March 1917, 1048–17–23, LAC, RG 24, vol. 3713.

are referred to the department. During the war this has been almost invariably done by telegraph, and always so if there was any urgency. The matter is then considered by the department, and the expenditure is authorized or not by the minister. If the amount concerned is of some magnitude, it is necessary to obtain authority for the expenditure by order in council. The placing of contracts involving any considerable sum of money in the purchase of stores is in the hands of the War Purchasing Commission. Whilst the foregoing procedure may appear slow, authorisation for completion of defects and ordinary expenditures have always been expeditiously granted.[51]

The assertion that the department's administration was handled "expeditiously" and did not impede work being carried out at the dockyard in Halifax was borne out when Captain Martin's subordinate officers made their reports as part of an internal review of procedures. Although the officers were, indeed, responding to a direct question from Ottawa, there does not appear to be anything contrived in their answers. The carpenter lieutenant at the dockyard, J.H. Davey, stated "that no delay is caused by the ordinary procedure regarding defect list, the work is often completed before the arrival of its approval, and taken in hand [as] soon as men are available. The greatest delay is caused by the non-delivery of material. Overtime to expedite work which is considered absolutely necessary for war essentials has been employed."[52] The naval store officer also assured Ottawa that as far as his department was concerned, "there is no known instance where delay has been caused by carrying out store orders as affecting war measures. Were all store orders carried out invariably to the letter there is no doubt that a certain amount of delay would have been involved. However, a wide view of such orders has been taken and varied to meet war conditions."[53] The chief engineer at the dockyard, Engineer Captain W.S. Frowd, asserted that there was, in fact, a great deal of elasticity in the RCN's day-to-day administration:

> No delay has ever been caused in carrying out war measures by the ordinary procedure as regards defect lists and store orders, other than that there is difficulty occasionally in getting delivery from the contractors of certain stores.
>
> Repairs to imperial ships are not carried out on the defect list system as this would involve delay in preparing estimates, etc. The routine in vogue is for ships requiring repairs to submit a list of the same to the captain superintendent, and the work is taken in hand immediately without further action by the dockyard officers.
>
> In accordance with instructions received ... the maintenance and repair of armed patrol vessels has been recognized as the most important work to be carried out by Halifax dockyard.

51. R.M. Stephens, for Director of the Naval Service, to Commander in Chief, North America and West Indies Station, 9 May 1917, 1001-5-3, pt 1, LAC, RG 24, vol. 6194.

52. Carpenter Lieutenant J. H. Davey to Captain Superintendent, Halifax, 11 May 1917, ibid.

53. Artificer Engineer W. Laurie to Captain Superintendent, 11 May 1917, ibid.

Overtime has been freely resorted to, but on occasions it has been disturbed by strikes, and also by the fact that when any of Messrs Brookfields' men are employed on ships, the boilermakers have refused to work alongside them.[54]

Despite Stephens's assurances, Vice-Admiral Browning was not deflected from his effort to sideline Kingsmill from the chain of command. Aware that Sir Arthur Balfour and the British naval mission were to make a stop over in Ottawa on their homeward trip from Washington, the C-in-C used the opportunity of the foreign secretary's presence to press his case. In anticipation of the Ottawa meeting scheduled for the end of May, NSHQ had its director of stores, J.A. Wilson, prepare a further memorandum illuminating some of the unique aspects of the Canadian situation of which British officials might not be fully aware. Wilson was a public servant of some capacity who would go on to become the naval department's assistant deputy minister before his interest in aviation—developed during the formation of the Canadian Naval Air Service during the war's final months—led him to become an assistant director of the Royal Canadian Air Force and then the controller of civil aviation with the Department of Transport.[55] Among the unavoidable differences in Canadian and British practice, Wilson's memorandum pointed out the disparity between the Royal Navy's huge supply chain and the stores available to the minuscule RCN. As a concise synopsis by a well-placed official of the problems faced by the Canadian naval service, and one that effectively challenged Browning's charges, it deserves to be quoted at length:

> With reference to delays in providing material and stores at Halifax dockyard. This is due solely to difficulties in obtaining supplies and transportation difficulties and not in any case, so far as I am aware, to time lost through following routine procedure or red tape methods. As the naval store officer observes, a wide view is invariably taken and in cases of urgency the routine procedure of dealing with demands, purchases and issues, is carried out to complete and regularize our systems only after action is taken to meet the emergency. The naval store officer purchases locally if possible or demands by wire on headquarters. Tenders are obtained by wire or long distance phone and orders placed in the same way. Stores are shipped by express rather than freight if necessary. Issues are made at night or on Sundays from the dockyard continually and demands to cover put through the regular system later.
>
> The purchasing work has on no occasion been delayed by our relations with the War Purchasing Commission and this opportunity is taken of stating that the peculiar conditions under which much of our work is carried on have been most fully recognized by that body and their regulations have been most liberally construed in order that no inconvenience or delays may be

---

54. Engineer Captain W.S. Frowd to Captain Superintendent, 11 May 1917, ibid.

55. W.A.B. Douglas, *The Creation of a National Air Force* (The Official History of the Royal Canadian Air Force, II; Toronto 1986), 41, 62, 220.

experienced. All urgent orders are placed without reference to them and full details submitted later for their approval of our action. In no case has any question been raised as to the reasonableness of the action taken....

The greatest attention to hastening action cannot overcome the physical conditions of the country, the great distances stores must be shipped, the present congestion of the railways in eastern Canada and the United States and the snowbound conditions during winter. The most difficult state of the market for all supplies must also be taken into account. It is not too much to say that ordinary methods must be entirely suspended in buying much of the material required. This has been done in the case of the order for chain and anchors for Sydney. Only the greatest luck enabled us to fill the order without recourse to the Admiralty. Had instant advantage not been taken of a remarkable chance and exceptional measures not been used this could not have been obtained at any price in Canada or the United States. Wire rope orders are most difficult to fill owing to the difficulty of obtaining supplies of wire and so on in almost every case.

Imperial officers are used to dealing with home dockyards which supply hundreds of ships and therefore can carry a very great quantity of stores. Halifax dockyard, with only the *Niobe*, now not in full commission, and a few small ships permanently attached cannot do so to the same extent. To meet imperial requirements and unforeseen demands the stock held has been more than doubled since 1914, and now totals $650,000. Even with this large reserve available it is impossible to provide for all requirements so that issues may be made from stock. In the exceptional circumstances now obtaining special orders take time to fill and this should be borne in mind. Every effort is being made to give satisfaction, however, and if delays occur it is not for want of effort or endeavour on the part of the naval store officer's or Ottawa['s] staff.[56]

Armed with the department's evidence collected from both Halifax dockyard officers and J.A. Wilson, Kingsmill entered the meeting in the naval minister's office on 29 May well supported by the facts. In addition to Browning and the foreign secretary, the British delegation at the meeting included Rear-Admiral Sir Dudley R. de Chair, Balfour's naval adviser, and the British ambassador to Washington, Sir Cecil Spring Rice. Although it has been suggested that Balfour and Browning "confronted Kingsmill ... in a scene that did little to improve already strained relations between the military and civilian authorities within the [Canadian] department,"[57] such a claim does not fit the circumstances of the meeting. The naval director completely understood the Canadian situation, both as to the RCN's procedures and Halifax's relative insignificance to Canada's overseas shipping, and had the backing of all the department's senior officials, both naval and civilian. With

---

56. J.A. Wilson, "Memo," 23 May 1917, 1001–5-3, pt 1, LAC, RG 24, vol. 6194.

57. Hadley and Sarty, *Tin-pots and Pirate Ships,* 189.

Browning over-estimating the port's importance, and having already admitted the he did "not know the exact procedure at Ottawa,"[58] the meeting did not transpire in the manner, or produce the intended result, that the British officials thought it would. In reporting to the Admiralty on his visit to Ottawa, Browning chose to downplay its significance, merely stating that he had "conferred with his excellency the governor general, Mr Balfour and officials of the Canadian government on the various questions referred to in my telegram to Admiralty [of 23 April] ... regarding the speeding up of the various work in hand in connection with the sea and harbour defence of Canada."[59] Admiral de Chair, on the other hand, was far more candid in his report on the meeting, informing London that "it was not considered advisable for political reasons to press for Admiral Kingsmill's supersession at present, but as a result of Mr Balfour's action it is hoped the situation will be improved."[60] With Hazen joining the rest of his department in backing the naval director, Browning's efforts to sideline Kingsmill (de Chair's original draft had used the word "suppression") and remove Ottawa from the naval chain of command on the East Coast had clearly failed.

As for the "strained relations" within the Canadian naval department itself, Desbarats not only agreed with Kingsmill that Browning was "under a wrong impression,"[61] but the meeting did not result in any revision of Ottawa's administrative procedures. The claim that Kingsmill "had been subject to Desbarats' close control"[62] is similarly disputed by the director's own minute that he was "not aware of any local war measure of urgency that has been delayed" by Ottawa's administration.[63] (It also does not reflect the fact that there is no record of the deputy minister ever expressing a single thought on naval policy. Indeed, an examination of the naval files shows that Kingsmill generally treated Desbarats as the minister's office administrator.) Moreover, since the outbreak of war NSHQ's attempts to expand the naval service by building warships in Canada had been frustrated more by the Admiralty's inconsistent advice as by penny-pinching politicians in Ottawa—although the Cabinet's frugality had indeed cost the navy its scheme for air patrols in 1917. Although the Canadian naval director had been needlessly—and uncharitably—rebuked by his political masters at the end of the 1915 shipping season for hiring motor boats to supplement Canada's coastal patrols, the unquestioning acceptance with which the prime minister routinely greeted the Admiralty's views early in the war—an awe inspired by the Royal Navy's century-long maritime supremacy, and, perhaps, his own Nova Scotia roots—had begun to dissipate by 1917. The Admiralty's sudden flip-flop on the need to expand

58. Browning to Director of the Naval Service, 2 May 1917, 1001–5-3, pt 1, LAC, RG 24, vol. 6194.

59. Browning to Admiralty, 10 June 1917, UKNA, ADM 137/504.

60. de Chair to Admiralty, "Continuation of General Report on the Progress of Negotiations with United States Navy Department, &c, in Connection with Mr Balfour's Mission, from the 15th May 1917," 7 June 1917, UKNA, ADM 137/1436.

61. Desbarats minute, 8 May 1917, 1001–5-3, pt 1, LAC, RG 24, vol. 6194.

62. Hadley and Sarty, *Tin-pots and Pirate Ships,* 189.

63. Kingsmill minute, nd, on Browning to Director of the Naval Service, 2 May 1917, 1001–5-3, pt 1, LAC, RG 24, vol. 6194.

the RCN's East Coast flotilla in late 1916 in particular, had made Borden slightly more skeptical of their lordships' vacillating opinions.

Rather than Kingsmill being embarrassed by the meeting in Hazen's office, the only Canadian officer to be taken to task for his role in the affair was the captain superintendent at Halifax, Edward Martin. As the naval director had indicated in a minute on Browning's 2 May telegram, Kingsmill strongly suspected that the British admiral's misinformation had been supplied by someone in the Nova Scotia capital, namely, Captain Martin. The Canadian admiral had also shared his suspicions of the captain superintendent with Hazen by the time they met with the British delegation on the 29th. In a tersely worded telegram to Martin the next day, Kingsmill explained that "the meeting was called because the commander-in-chief of the North American Station had expressed his views as to the unsatisfactory situation in Halifax, particularly as regards the second net defence.... During the discussion the commander-in-chief stated that he considered that things would be in a better shape if the captain superintendent had a freer hand at Halifax. On the expression of this view, Mr Hazen asked him if he had heard that from the captain superintendent himself and the commander in chief replied, 'Yes.'" The naval director made no effort to hide his growing disapproval of Martin's performance at Halifax. Angered at the captain's perceived disloyalty in trying to shift responsibility for his own lack of initiative onto naval headquarters, Kingsmill told his subordinate that "it cannot be looked upon as a correct method simply because the stores" for the second anti-submarine net were ordered in Ottawa, "that no effort should be made to hasten them." Moreover, Martin had "frequently been told (and occasionally acted on the understanding) that a personal letter or wire to the director of naval service would receive the latter's immediate attention." As a result, "the minister of the naval service has instructed me to ask the captain superintendent for any explanation he may see fit to offer."[64]

The fact that Martin had a hand in fomenting Browning's charges of administrative incompetence within the Canadian department was not the only reason for Ottawa's displeasure. Three days before the meeting in Hazen's office, Kingsmill had rebuked the captain superintendent for not keeping NSHQ properly informed of proceedings in Halifax. Examples of Martin's failure to keep Ottawa abreast of events included communications breakdowns related to the recent arrival of the liner *Olympic* in Halifax with the prime minister of New Zealand aboard, the seizure of a Dutch steamer at the port, and the arrival of an Italian mission bound for the United States for which NSHQ was to arrange a special train from Halifax. Since the outbreak of war Martin had been required to make a daily report to Ottawa "for the purpose of keeping the department informed of what was happening at the various ports" but that report had since deteriorated "into a monotonous 'situation unchanged.'" The captain was instructed to provide the naval director with a "full and carefully considered" explanation for his unsatisfactory performance.[65] Kingsmill's growing unease with Martin during the spring

---

64. Kingsmill to Captain Superintendent, 30 May 1917, ibid.

65. Kingsmill to Captain Superintendent, 26 May 1917, and enclosed memorandum by chief of staff, 1023–7-3, pt 1, LAC, RG 24, vol. 3857.

of 1917 resulted in the captain's removal from the Halifax command six months later.

In finally disposing of Browning's attempt to isolate the Canadian naval director from the East Coast navy, Kingsmill had managed to maintain the RCN's authority over both its shore establishments and its patrol forces. As we have seen, NSHQ had given Commodore Coke his orders "by command" at the end of April. The Canadian admiral's insistence that it was "not considered possible that at any moment there was an idea prevalent that the whole question of our defence should be in the hands of an officer acting on his own responsibility" could not be ignored by the commodore of patrols even though Browning continued to campaign against NSHQ for another month. As instructed by Ottawa's 30 April telegram, Coke submitted his plans for the allocation of vessels for both local port defence and the patrol service. Even then, however, the British commodore was not willing to bend to NSHQ entirely and indicated in his response that he would maintain his headquarters at Halifax and fly his pennant from the auxiliary patrol vessel HMCS *Stadacona*. When not in use as the senior officer's ship, Coke informed Kingsmill on 4 May, *Stadacona* would be employed on the Nova Scotia coast patrol. With the commodore also indicating that *Grilse* would be based at Halifax as well, his immediate dispositions left only *Acadia*, *Margaret*, and *Canada* for assignment to Sydney and the important St Lawrence patrol. As other auxiliaries—*Hochelaga*, *Cartier*, and *Laurentian*—became available, they would also be sent to Sydney to reinforce and extend the lines of patrol. Coke agreed to NSHQ's demand that local defence vessels would be under the immediate command of the senior Canadian naval officer at each port and listed the minesweeping and local patrol vessels he was allocating to Captain Martin in Halifax, although the vessels to be assigned to other ports, particularly Sydney, were to be decided upon only after the commodore had a chance to inspect the ports. Despite Coke's continuing predisposition toward Halifax, the commodore's proposed assignments for the auxiliary patrol vessels immediately available satisfied NSHQ for the time being and the naval director initialled the memo "approved."[66]

While Coke's relief as C-in-C Irish Coast following the sinking of the *Lusitania* in May 1915 might have raised some concern as to his competence, the performance of two of the staff officers he brought with him to North America left little doubt as to their abilities. The officer Coke selected to act as his secretary was, according to NSHQ, "very inexperienced"[67] and Ottawa even had to remind him to type file numbers on the commodore's correspondence so that it could be referred to more easily. Coke's chief of staff, meanwhile, was an RNR officer who had been appointed to the rank of commander shortly before coming to Canada. It quickly became evident that Commander Walter Stafford had been promoted simply for the purpose of seniority as Coke's chief of staff. As Kingsmill subsequently explained, "this officer was junior to many of our own RNR officers and a deal of discontent has ensued. It should be submitted that it is not necessary to promote officers coming out for the reasons stated; if officers are promoted for meritorious service and then sent out the situation is different."[68]

66. Coke to NSHQ, 4 May 1917, 1065–7-2, pt. 1, LAC, RG 24, vol. 4031.

67. Kingsmill memorandum, 24 June 1917, ibid.

68. Kingsmill to Coke, 5 May 1917, ibid.

Before becoming aware of Stafford's lack of ability, Kingsmill had asked Coke if he would appoint one of his staff officers to relieve Commander G.C. Holloway of his extra duties commanding the Halifax minesweeping flotilla so he could concentrate on overseeing the transport traffic at the port.[69] At the time, the commodore of patrols had insisted that his staff was too small to release any officer but changed his mind the following month and proposed placing Commander Stafford in charge of the Halifax minesweepers in addition to his staff work.[70] Kingsmill quickly reversed himself in a telegram that contained more than a hint of sarcasm.

> It was understood that Commander Stafford was the expert in drifters and gen-
> erally in the little ships on mine-sweeping. Still, you propose to leave him in
> charge of the minesweepers at Halifax; I hope you will reconsider your sug-
> gestion. It is much better in my opinion that Stafford should remain with you
> on your staff so that you may send him at any moment to any part of the coast
> where the sweepers or drifters or patrols are in difficulty. I am getting a rather
> decent class of seamen coming in for skippers and there will be no difficulty
> in releasing Commander Holloway from some of his transport duties at Hal-
> ifax and letting him, as hitherto, act under the captain superintendent in
> charge of the minesweepers instead of Stafford.[71]

Although Coke pointed out that he was simply complying with Kingsmill's earlier request, the naval director had evidently heard enough complaints about Stafford to instruct the commodore that "it would be as well if you took with you, wherever you went, Commander Stafford, and with this in view I have been seeking to obtain an officer who has had some experience in transport work to relieve Holloway of some of his duties." After finding a suitable officer, Kingsmill told Coke that he could "let you have Stafford free; I am sure you should have him with you."[72]

The other two officers who accompanied the commodore to Canada had also become a point of contention between Coke and Kingsmill, although for quite different reasons. Both were technical officers sent by the Admiralty to assist the naval department with the trawler and drifter building program. Since NSHQ had let the contracts and was overseeing the project on behalf of the Admiralty, Ottawa assumed that the technical officers were being seconded to the Canadian navy. When NSHQ attempted to appoint one of the officers, Commander J.W. Skentelbery, RNVR, to headquarters, however, Coke vetoed the move. According to the commodore: "I personally selected him from the officers available for appointment to my staff at the time. He was therefore to remain on my staff and be responsible to me alone as intended by his appointment, but that in order to assist the

---

69. Kingsmill, "Memorandum for Commodore Coke, RNR," 22 March 1917, ibid.

70. Coke, "Memorandum for the Director of Naval Service," 23 March 1917, Coke to Director of the Naval Service, 24 April 1917, ibid.

71. Kingsmill to Coke, 5 May 1917, ibid.

72. Kingsmill to Coke, 18 May 1917, Coke to Kingsmill, 9 May 1917, ibid.

department the following arrangements should come into force: (a) His headquarters to be at Montreal as being the best centre for supervising the construction of the vessels. (b) He may communicate direct with the department and receive orders direct from the department, but is to hold himself available to assist me when I require his services."[73] In outlining the situation to the deputy minister, Kingsmill indicated that the real cause of the mix-up lay with Whitehall: "At present moment one of the officers sent out by Admiralty is retained by Commodore Coke—the other [Skentelbery] has an office at Montreal and is continually travelling and the department gets very little assistance. This is all due to a mistake in [the Admiralty] instructing the Commodore that he was in charge of shipbuilding—a proposition never mentioned to the department."[74]

As the ice cleared from the St Lawrence and shipping resumed from the port of Montreal for the 1917 season, NSHQ continued to have difficulty in convincing the British commodore that he should keep Ottawa fully informed of his patrol plans and dispositions. On 13 June, Kingsmill despatched a report from Commander Skentelbery in Montreal on the progress being made with the trawler program and repeated his request that Coke "forward me as soon as possible a scheme, drawn up on the supposition that the vessels will be finished according to the programme, as to how you propose placing them." The naval director was also anxious to have the commodore keep NSHQ informed as to "the disposition of the vessels you now have, what their cruising areas is [*sic*], etc." Recalling the arrangement he had established with Captain Pasco during the 1916 season, Kingsmill explained to Coke that "the department should be in a position at any moment to take action in an emergency, and know exactly what vessels are in certain neighbour-hoods from day to day. Last year we received reports from Sydney so that at any moment if anything happened we could place our hands on a vessel if required."[75]

The naval director's desire to have NSHQ serve as a co-ordinating authority for East Coast operations has led some historians to support the commodore's position on the need for autonomous operational command. According to this view, "Kingsmill was wrong in insisting that he could co-ordinate seagoing operations more effectively than either of the commands at Sydney or Halifax; Coke had been right about the need for a senior naval officer to exercise broad command of the increasingly complex operations on the east coast."[76] Such a contention, however, overlooks the central role that NSHQ was already playing in coordinating the RCN's operational functions, including the Overseas Transport organization based in Montreal, the work of the naval transport and routing offices located at the main Canadian ports, and the despatch of operational intelligence to both London and the East Coast on such matters as merchant sailings from Canada. In view of the rather small size of the RCN's officer corps, it would have been difficult for the naval service to find sufficient qualified officers to staff a second headquarters organization on the East Coast, one that would, in any event, largely be duplicating the functions already being performed

---

73. Commodore of Patrols to Kingsmill, 23 April 1917, ibid.

74. Kingsmill, "Memorandum," 24 June 1917, ibid.

75. Kingsmill to Commodore of Patrols, 13 June 1917, ibid.

76. Hadley and Sarty, *Tin-pots and Pirate Ships,* 191.

by NSHQ. Such an East Coast headquarters would also have required a commanding officer who clearly understood the domestic shipping situation as regards the country's railway network and the seasonal shifts in Canada's shipping lanes and traffic patterns. Furthermore, it would have required an officer sensitive to the local concerns of coastal ship traffic and the fishing fleet (as, for example, in placing the second anti-submarine net at Halifax so as to allow small vessels access to the Northwest Arm in the event of sudden bad weather). With their over-emphasis on the importance of Halifax, the only Canadian port the Royal Navy's warships still used, both Browning and Coke had demonstrated that the knowledge and qualities required "to exercise broad command" on the East Coast were not necessarily to be found in British officers with little prior knowledge of North America.

The development of the telegraph and wireless telegraphy had already transformed the Admiralty's role in the strategic command and control of the Royal Navy. Although the sea lords had begun the twentieth century believing that their role in war was one of administration and fleet support, the communications revolution convinced Admiral Sir John Fisher, while first sea lord from 1905 to 1910, that "the marvelous development of wireless telegraphy" had given the Royal Navy "an immense accession of strength."[77] It led the director of naval intelligence to write in 1908 that "the advance of wireless telegraphy has been so great and so rapid that an entirely new development of strategic organization becomes imperative. With the present installation it is possible to receive information and to transmit orders over a large area from the Admiralty with certainty…. The result of this enormous advance is that the Admiralty are compelled to assume the responsibility for the strategic movements of the fleet in a far more complete manner than was ever formerly practicable."[78] With the development of its War Room intelligence centre, the Admiralty began to consider directly controlling the movements of warships at sea rather than merely ordering squadrons to a given area. Fisher believed that in future, "the Admiralty alone (and no Admiral under it) must conduct the war."[79]

Experience during the early stages of the First World War had only reinforced that view. In particular, the escape of the German battle cruiser squadron from a superior British force after it bombarded Scarborough and Hartlepool on 16 December 1914 had "convinced strategists at the Admiralty that the advantages of relying on the War Room system outweighed the anticipated problems. Besides, the only alternative, leaving full control in the hands of tactical commanders, had been tried and failed." As British naval historian Nicholas Lambert has astutely observed: "The War Room system was intended to provide the naval leadership in London with, to use modern parlance, 'strategic situation awareness' by interpreting data to predict an enemy's deployments and intentions…. Instead of being limited in time of war to providing mere administrative support, the Admiralty became the navy's strategic and operational command center."[80]

---

77. Fisher to unknown [King Edward VII], 16 September 1908, quoted in Nicholas A. Lambert, "Strategic Command and Control for Maneuver Warfare: Creation of the Royal Navy's 'War Room' System, 1905–1915," *The Journal of Military History*, 69 (April 2005), 384.

78. "Wireless Telegraphy in War," 4 July 1908, quoted in ibid, 385.

79. Fisher to Grey, 23 January 1908, quoted in ibid, 388.

80. Ibid, 407–08.

For its part, Ottawa also had reliable, direct telegraph and telephone communications with Halifax, Sydney, and Montreal and could easily communicate by telegraph with the Admiralty and its worldwide system of intelligence centres. While communication lines between Halifax and Sydney were good, communications within the maritime provinces themselves were often limited. A commander of patrols with "broad command" of all East Coast operations would have been entirely reliant on *Stadacona*'s wireless set whenever he ventured to sea and could easily find himself isolated by bad weather, and out of communication, along any stretch of the Nova Scotian or Newfoundland coast. Reducing NSHQ's status to that of an administrative headquarters would have negated the "situation awareness" that already existed in Ottawa, particularly as regards merchant ship departures and arrivals and the routing instructions RCN officers had given them at various ports. Of course, Kingsmill's objectives in demanding that he be kept fully informed of patrol dispositions were more limited than what the Admiralty was trying to achieve. Whereas the War Room system "enabled the Admiralty to vector centrally located forces towards specific threats and with economy of force,"[81] the Canadian admiral simply wanted to be able "to take action in an emergency ... so that at any moment if anything happened we could place our hands on a vessel if required."[82] That need was all the more acute if, in the event a genuine U-boat threat materialized, the officer commanding Canada's patrol forces was more concerned with protecting the C-in-C's cruisers sheltering in Halifax than defending Canada's merchant ship traffic as it proceeded through the Gulf of St Lawrence.

Kingsmill's repeated efforts to have Coke submit a plan for the East Coast patrol organization were finally rewarded on 19 June. It was the British commodore's recommendation that the trawlers and drifters being built to Admiralty order be organized into units of five drifters and one trawler, the latter acting as leader. The trawler would have a commissioned officer to command the unit whose primary duty was "to constantly exercise his vessels." Patrolling would be done in line abreast at visual distance with the trawler in the centre of the formation. Since each unit would require a trawler at all times, Coke recommended having one spare trawler for every two patrol units to allow for reliefs for coaling. If the construction program proceeded on schedule, and eight trawlers and twenty-two drifters were completed by August, the commodore proposed forming four units with two trawlers as spares and leaving two drifters that Coke would "be very glad indeed of for special work." The commodore planned to station two of the four patrol units at Sydney for the Cabot Strait patrol, one at Gaspé for the inner St Lawrence, and one at Halifax to operate on the Nova Scotia coast.[83]

The auxiliary patrol vessels, meanwhile, would principally be used to patrol the Cabot Strait from the base at Sydney. Coke also planned to keep *Grilse*—"which is simply invaluable being the only ship of sufficient speed to overhaul a modern German submarine"—on the Nova Scotia coast for the time being because, he claimed, there was no oil fuel available at Sydney. The commodore also asserted that he had "made no disposition for the Bay of Fundy

81. Ibid, 408.

82. Kingsmill to Commodore of Patrols, 13 June 1917, 1065-7-2, pt. 1, LAC, RG 24, vol. 4031.

83. Commodore of Patrols to NSHQ, 19 June 1917, ibid.

for, as at present arranged, the US patrol [the United States having entered the war as an associate power on 6 April 1917] accept responsibility for it."[84] In a follow-up memorandum the next day, Coke gave a more detailed picture of the position of his auxiliaries. *Stadacona* (flying the commodore's broad pendant), *Margaret*, *Canada*, and *Cartier* were based at Sydney to cover the Cabot Straits, while *Acadia* was at Gaspé for the inner St Lawrence patrol. *Hochelaga* was proceeding to Quebec in compliance with NSHQ's instructions, *Grilse* had just returned to Halifax after a patrol to Guysboro, Nova Scotia, at the commander-in-chief's request, and *Laurentian* was also at Halifax fitting out. Information as to the position of the various patrols, Coke assured Ottawa, would be forwarded weekly.[85]

Although more helpful than the commodore's earlier attitude, Kingsmill was still not satisfied, minuting to Stephens that "this information is useful but what is wanted is an arrangement with commodore by which we can place our hands on any vessel that is nearest the position in which a vessel is required."[86] The naval director also pointed out that Coke's understanding of the US Navy's responsibilities in the Bay of Fundy was incorrect. A subsequent message was sent to Halifax explaining that the Americans only provided a cruiser patrol in the general area, while the RCN remained responsible for patrolling "our own coasts."[87] In a separate telegram, Ottawa pointed out that "the Imperial Oil Co. for two previous seasons made arrangements to complete *Grilse* with fuel at Sydney. The matter should be taken up with them and see if it would not be possible at small cost to have a [rail] car at Sydney refilled from time to time. At the same time it is not desirable until submarines do appear that the *Grilse* should be taken from the Nova Scotian patrol, on account of the extra cost of fuel."[88]

NSHQ's ongoing turmoil with Coke was suddenly resolved on 22 June when Ottawa received a cable from London asking if the Canadian government would agree to his removal: "Admiralty consider that it would be desirable in imperial interests for Commodore Coke to be relieved by some younger officer more familiar with patrol work. At the time Commodore Coke's name was proposed for this work it was considered by Admiralty that his experience on the Irish coast during the war qualified him for the post but evidence has reached them that his advancing age has seriously told on him. Name of another officer will be put forward as Coke's successor if this change is concurred in."[89]

In the absence of any documentation clarifying who specifically suggested Coke's recall, it has been speculated that the action was taken by the Admiralty at Kingsmill's instigation.[90] That there is no record of any discussion, or even a minute on any

84. Ibid.

85. Commodore of Patrols to NSHQ, 20 June 1917, ibid.

86. Kingsmill minute, nd, on Commodore of Patrols to NSHQ, 20 June 1917, ibid.

87. NSHQ to Coke, 30 June 1917, Kingsmill minute, nd, on Commodore of Patrols to NSHQ, 19 June 1917, ibid.

88. NSHQ to Coke, 30 June 1917, ibid.

89. Long to Governor General, 22 June 1917, ibid.

90. Brian Tennyson and Roger Sarty, *Guardian of the Gulf: Sydney, Cape Breton, and the Atlantic Wars* (Toronto 2000), 147.

memorandum, in NSHQ's files about the possibility of asking for the commodore's removal, as one would expect before such a move, as well as the tone of the director's comments about working with Coke in the days leading up to receipt of the 22 June telegram from London, suggests that the Admiralty may have been acting on information received from a different quarter. As much as Kingsmill must have rejoiced at the Admiralty's decision to recall the commodore, a more likely candidate as the source of the "evidence" reaching Whitehall about Coke's declining abilities was, perhaps, the commander-in-chief, North America and West Indies Station.

At the end of May, the British embassy in Washington had informed Ottawa that the US Navy wanted to discuss the naval situation on the East Coast with the "officer commanding Halifax and St Lawrence patrol."[91] Kingsmill subsequently informed Coke that both he and Commander Stephens were to travel to Washington to take part in the proposed patrol conference. Those instructions were soon altered, however, on the suggestion of Admiral Browning. The C-in-C informed NSHQ on 3 June that he had had a brief meeting with Coke in Halifax the previous day. As Browning explained, Coke's "orders for disposition of patrol vessels under construction are not yet prepared nor, as I understand, commenced. I think it extremely inadvisable, therefore, that he should proceed to Washington at present."[92] Acting on the C-in-C's recommendation, only Stephens was sent to Washington to confer with American naval authorities (see Chapter 8). Coming only days after the 29 May meeting in Hazen's office in Ottawa, the British admiral may have been smarting from Kingsmill's refutation of his allegations of mismanagement. Browning's decision to raise a fuss over the Halifax defences had, in part, been instigated by the commodore of patrols' own desire to have complete autonomy from Ottawa and the C-in-C may simply have decided to cut Coke lose in the wake of the Ottawa meeting.[93] In view of his involvement in the attempt to relegate NSHQ to a mere administrative headquarters, the C-in-C was certainly aware of the difficulties the Canadian naval director was having in getting the commodore to commit to a plan of operations centered on the Gulf of St Lawrence. Since there is no evidence that Kingsmill communicated his dissatisfaction to London, while NSHQ memoranda written well into June continued to assume Coke would remain in charge of the patrols for some time,[94] it is not unreasonable to suggest that Browning's impression of the commodore's inadequate performance may well have been the "evidence" the Admiralty acted upon in relieving Coke of his duties.

There is no doubt, however, that news of the commodore's removal was greeted enthusiastically by Ottawa. Kingsmill quickly went on record that "the change should be made without delay."[95] Nor was Coke the only British officer on the East Coast of whom

91. British Embassy Washington to Governor General, 26 May 1917, 1065–7-3, LAC, RG 24, vol. 4031.

92. C-in-C to Naval Ottawa, 3 June 1917, ibid.

93. Hadley and Sarty, *Tin-pots and Pirate Ships,* 191.

94. See, for example, Commander Stephens, "Memorandum for Commodore Gaunt," 13 June 1917, Kingsmill minute, nd, on Commodore of Patrols to NSHQ, 20 June 1917, 1065–7-3, LAC, RG 24, vol. 4031.

95. Kingsmill, "Memorandum," 24 June 1917, ibid.

NSHQ wished to see the last. In the Canadian reply to Whitehall's telegram, the governor general made it clear that "my government hope that Commander Stafford will also return to United Kingdom with Commodore Coke."[96] What is somewhat surprising, in view of the many difficulties the RCN had just experienced with Coke and Browning, is that Kingsmill did not immediately question the Admiralty's stated intention of naming another British officer to take charge of the Canadian patrols. Instead, the Canadian naval director merely sought to clarify the main points of contention before the commodore's replacement was sent to Canada. Two days after receiving the British telegram recalling Coke, Kingsmill clarified the errors that had been made—many of them by the Admiralty in its initial instructions—in the commodore's appointment so that they could be avoided in instructing his replacement.

> The officer relieving Commodore Coke should not have anything to do with the officers appointed to assist the department in carrying out the ship building programme proposed by the Admiralty, viz., of 100 drifters and thirty-six trawlers. The senior officer of patrols will have his hands full looking after the present vessels and others as they come forward for commissioning....
>
> It is not desirable that we should have an officer of such high rank as Commodore Coke, for though he only ranked as commodore RNR, the fact that he was an admiral could not be overlooked.
>
> The relieving officer should have it more clearly pointed out to him that he is an officer of the department. If the Admiralty have any suggestions or instructions to give the officer before leaving [England], copies of same should be sent to the department; in the present case Commodore Coke was told all sorts of things apparently, as for instance when he was told that his base would be Sydney, he made many objections and told me he came out on the understanding that he was to have entire charge of organisation of the patrol. We accepted the services of an officer to assist in the organisation and to take executive command if so desired....
>
> The present commodore wished, even after the views of the department were expressed, to take the matter into his hands. Only by direct order did he desist. All these misunderstandings could be avoided if it is understood that what is done in England need not necessarily be suitable here.[97]

Kingsmill's memorandum tacitly indicated that the real problem had been less one of Commodore Coke's attitude and more one of the Admiralty's ongoing indifference to Canadian autonomy in instructing its officers. Just as the Borden government and Canadian army officers had occasionally to remind London that the Canadian Corps, as a dominion formation, could not simply be treated as an integral part of the British Army without reference to Ottawa, the RCN had to contend with a similar imperial mindset. As Kingsmill

---

96. Governor General to Colonial Secretary, 30 June 1917, ibid.

97. Kingsmill, "Memorandum," 24 June 1917, ibid.

had hoped, the Canadian government faithfully followed his advice in replying to the British telegram recalling Coke, particularly in regard to the relationship that any future British officer sent to Canada would have with NSHQ: "he should clearly understand he is under orders of Department of Naval Service. Copy of any instructions given to him by Admiralty should be sent to department named above. It is considered by my government that duties of this officer should be to assist in organization of patrol and if so desired [by Ottawa] to take executive command, but he should not interfere with existing organization at ports."[98]

As clearly as NSHQ expressed itself on the issue, however, it quickly became apparent that Whitehall's approach had not changed significantly. The Admiralty did, at least, agree to appoint an officer of lesser rank than Coke and recommended Commander J.O. Hatcher, DSO, RN "who has good experience in patrol work."[99] Despite the clear wording of the Canadian government that Coke's replacement would only "take executive command if so desired,"[100] the Admiralty's own terms for Hatcher's appointment were that he was appointed to "*Niobe*, additional for charge of Patrols with acting rank of Captain."[101] From the wording of London's telegram—that Hatcher was being appointed to *Niobe* "for charge of patrols"—it was immediately evident to Kingsmill that nothing had changed in the way the Admiralty proposed to deal with NSHQ. Indeed, the only indication that anyone in Whitehall had actually read Ottawa's telegram was their lordships' willingness to appoint a commander as acting captain rather than an admiral as acting commodore even though, in fact, an RN captain was considered equivalent to a commodore RNR.

The Admiralty telegram announcing the terms of Hatcher's appointment proved to be the last straw as far as Kingsmill was concerned. The Canadian naval director promptly decided that it was time to stand up to their lordships and assert the RCN's authority to appoint its own officers to command in Canadian waters. He placed his views before the minister on 1 August in a memorandum that recommended solving the problem once and for all. After quoting from the Canadian government's telegram to London that Coke's replacement would only "take executive command if so desired" by NSHQ—and under-lining the words "if so desired"—Kingsmill pointed out the discrepancy in the Admiralty's terms of Hatcher's appointment. Phrasing it as diplomatically as he could, the naval director suggested to the minister that "I am quite certain that it is merely through carelessness that the telegram was sent to us that he was appointed *Niobe* additional for charge of patrols, as the Admiralty cannot appoint anyone to *Niobe* in any capacity; we have to do that." Kingsmill's solution was to appoint acting Captain Walter Hose, the former commanding officer of HMCS *Rainbow*, to command the East Coast patrols, explaining that Hose was well acquainted with the Newfoundland coast and Gulf of St Lawrence operational areas from his previous service in those waters.[102] Unstated, of course, was the fact that Hose was

98. "Paraphrase of cypher telegram from Governor General to Mr Long," 30 June 1917, ibid.

99. Long to Governor General, 11 July 1917, ibid.

100. "Paraphrase of cypher telegram from Governor General to Mr Long," 30 June 1917, ibid.

101. Long to Governor General, 28 July 1917, ibid.

102. Kingsmill, "Memorandum for the Minister," 1 August 1917, ibid.

Commander Walter Hose on the deck of HMCS *Rainbow* in 1914. (LAC PA-141880)

also an RCN officer and would fully understand, and was part of, the Canadian chain of command.

As for Captain Hatcher, Kingsmill suggested that he "would be more useful to the department in an advisory capacity without having any actual command." Nonetheless, the naval director displayed a hint of caution in confronting Whitehall so blatantly. Since Hatcher had sailed from England on 28 July and was not due in Halifax for another week, Kingsmill proposed that he wait until the British officer arrived in Canada before telling him "the ideas of the department;"[103] actually informing the Admiralty would be delayed even longer. The minister raised no objections to Kingsmill's suggested course of action provided "our correspondence with the Admiralty has not given some other impression."[104] It was not until 15 August, therefore, that the naval director wrote the Admiralty with the news that the Canadian patrol was to be commanded by "Commander Walter Hose, acting captain RCN" and that Hatcher "is taking up his duties in connection with the patrol as advisory officer. The situation at present is that none of the drifters or trawlers ordered by the Admiralty are in commission or likely to be for some time. Consequently it is thought desirable that an officer conversant with the customs and manning of the Canadian naval service should take charge of the patrol as it is, leaving Captain Hatcher free for any operations of minesweepers or drifters which may hereafter be necessary. Owing to the wide area over which our patrol is extended, it is considered that an officer with technical knowledge would be much more useful to the department if he is not tied down by the ordinary work, etc, in dealing with the personnel."[105]

Hose, meanwhile, proceeded to Sydney on 14 August to relieve Commodore Coke. Whether as a courtesy or to make sure the commodore and his staff had actually left the country, Hose accompanied Coke to Quebec City aboard *Stadacona*. The Newfoundland government was told that an RCN officer would be replacing the British commodore at the same time that the Admiralty was so informed, but the reply from St John's concurring in the appointment reached Ottawa a full month before Whitehall responded.[106] It was not until 25 September that London passed on its concern that "as the duties assigned to Captain Hatcher are not those which he was informed by Admiralty he would take up on arrival they think in justice to him he should be given the opportunity—if he so desires—of withdrawing from post which is of different nature to one to which he supposed he was being appointed. Admiralty ask that Hatcher may be directed to state explicitly whether he is content to continue in present appointment as now defined. If not minister would doubtless agree that he should be released to return to United Kingdom."[107]

As demanded by the Admiralty, Hatcher had to state in writing that he had no objection to his new appointment. To his credit, the British captain not only explained that he had

---

103. Ibid.

104. Desbarats minute, nd, on ibid.

105. Kingsmill to Admiralty, 15 August 1917, ibid.

106. Governor of Newfoundland to Governor General, 21 August 1917, ibid.

107. Long to Governor General, 25 September 1917, ibid.

received a "full explanation of the situation" from Kingsmill, but that "providing my services are entirely satisfactory, I feel it my duty and am therefore willing to remain with the Canadian government as advisory officer to the patrols." In finally bringing the matter of command to a close, Kingsmill reiterated to London that it was the RCN's prerogative to appoint its own officers in Canadian waters:

> I hope in reply it may be pointed out that all the communications from this department referred to the fact that we would be pleased to have an officer to assist us, and who might, if considered necessary by ourselves, be appointed to the command of the patrols, and that at no time was it accepted that the Admiralty should appoint an officer to command. As will be seen by Captain Hatcher's submission, he received a full explanation of the situation: he has not at any time raised any objection.
>
> Taking up the question of the command of patrols, I do not consider that the appointment of Captain Hatcher to such a charge would be beneficial, notwithstanding his technical knowledge of the requirements. When we get the material that is necessary for the patrol for minesweeping, etc, Captain Hatcher can be very usefully employed supervising the fitting out and construction, etc, of the vessels.[108]

The decision that Hose was best suited to command the Canadian patrol forces was an acknowledgement by Kingsmill that the root cause of the problem was not Coke but the Admiralty itself. It had, by any measure, been a frustrating year and a half for the RCN in its relations with their lordships. From the rejection of Kingsmill's destroyer construction scheme in the spring of 1916 to the appointment of Commodore Coke and his replacement by Captain Hatcher, Whitehall had demonstrated indifference to both the defence requirements of North American waters and the need to foster the development of a fledging dominion navy. As the naval director realized, the appointment of the younger, more capable Hatcher would not alter Whitehall's attitude to Canada's maritime defence and would perpetuate London's apparent belief that it, and not Ottawa, should control the patrol forces in Canadian waters. Just as Rear-Admiral Story had been appointed superintendent of Esquimalt dockyard in 1914 to ensure that Canada retained control of its shore facilities in the presence of higher ranking Royal Navy officers, Kingsmill's refusal to accept the Admiralty's terms for Hatcher's appointment asserted that the Canadian navy was an autonomous force afloat as well as ashore.

While Coke's removal finally convinced Kingsmill to appoint a Canadian officer to command the RCN's East Coast forces, the navy was able to organize its 1917 patrols in the knowledge that the U-boat threat to North American shipping lanes remained, for the moment at least, only a potential one. Such was not the case in the waters surrounding the United Kingdom where the German navy had unleashed an unrestricted submarine campaign in February 1917. With merchant ship losses rising to catastrophic levels

---

108. Kingsmill, "Memorandum to the Deputy Minister," 12 October 1917, ibid.

through the spring, the Admiralty's direction of the larger anti-submarine war was increasingly being called into question in British government circles. Some officials in London were critical of the Admiralty's delay in implementing what they believed was the most effective weapon available to deal with the U-boat threat—the adoption of a general system of convoy for merchant shipping.

In October 1916, the German chief of the *Admiralstab*, Admiral Henning von Holtzendorff, had launched a new restricted submarine campaign following internationally recognized prize rules. The decision to renew the offensive was prompted by the entry into service of the newly constructed UB.II boats with the Flanders flotilla. They were larger, more heavily armed and with a greater range than earlier submarines and the Germans were able to increase the number of operational boats from 119 in October 1916 to 148 by January 1917. The influx of new U-boats allowed the Germans to sink an average of 189 ships and 326,072 tons per month over the four-month period. About 20 percent of these ships were sunk by torpedo and three-quarters were despatched by gunfire.[109]

Even though the Germans were largely complying with the rules for a restricted campaign, as the predominate use of gunfire attests, the Royal Navy was little more successful in sinking German submarines than it had been at the start of the war—despite the destroyers, patrol boats, and sloops that had reinforced the several thousand trawlers and drifters of Britain's anti-submarine fleet and the introduction of improved hydrophones and depth charges. The Royal Navy continued to base its strategy on conducting "offensive patrols" along the main shipping routes with special "hunting patrols" being formed to sweep the lanes of the western approaches. The surface forces were also reinforced by aircraft of the Royal Naval Air Service, particularly by the Short Type 184 seaplane that was the mainstay of air patrols in 1916–17, and by non-rigid airships that could remain stationary over a given area and had the weight-lifting capacity to carry wireless sets. Still, with more U-boats to hunt and stronger anti-submarine forces, the British were able to sink only two submarines in January 1917.[110]

The substantial results being achieved by their restricted campaign were still considered insufficient by those in Germany who favoured conducting unrestricted submarine warfare to force Britain out of the war—most notably High Seas Fleet officers Reinhard Scheer, Adolf von Trotha, and Magnus von Levetzow. In a 22 December memorandum, Holtzendorff argued in favour of breaking Britain's shipping backbone in an effort to win the war by the end of 1917, before Germany was herself exhausted and forced to sue for peace. He based his advice, as did most of his fellow proponents of an unrestricted campaign, on the fact that British imports of wheat were particularly vulnerable to interruption. A poor world harvest in 1916 was expected to reduce the amount of wheat Britain could receive from her traditional sources in Canada and the United States, forcing her to seek further supplies from more distant Argentina and Australia. The chief of the *Admiralstab* suggested that an unrestricted submarine offensive would sink some 600,000 tons a month, a total that would, after five months, reduce shipping to and from Britain by as much as 40

---

109. Paul G. Halpern, *A Naval History of World War I* (Annapolis 1994), 335–36.

110. John Terraine, *The U-Boat Wars, 1916–1945* (New York 1989), 35–38.

percent. A continuation of the restricted campaign, on the other hand, would sink only half that amount and fail to produce the desired capitulation. Although Chancellor Bethmann-Hollweg remained opposed, fearful that "the help which America could give to our enemies was higher than the High Command imagined it to be,"[111] Kaiser Wilhelm II's shift of support in favour of an unrestricted campaign meant that the German politician could no longer prevent it. Holtzendorff's argument carried the day at a conference of senior army and navy officers on 9 January 1917—presided over by the Kaiser and attended by Hollweg—where it was decided that unrestricted submarine warfare would commence on 1 February.[112] On 31 January, the German ambassador to the United States informed Washington that all pledges as to restrictions on submarine warfare were withdrawn as of the next day. "Germany will start a blockade on allied countries including whole of United Kingdom, France and Italy, using over 300 submarines. Neutrals are warned that every neutral ship with cargo bound for Allied countries will be sunk.... United States government having failed to stop illegal blockade, all former promises are repudiated."[113]

In terms of merchant tonnage sunk, the first three months of the unrestricted campaign suggested that the Germans' all-out strategy was the correct one. A total of 540,006 tons were sunk in February and another 593,841 tons in March, representing 500 ships sent to the bottom. In April 1917, the Allies lost 395 ships totalling 881,027 tons, the highest shipping losses sustained in a single month during the war, with Britain's merchant fleet suffering 62 percent of the April total. That loss rate simply could not be sustained. Moreover, there was no lasting good news from the land battles in France. Although the four divisions of the Canadian Corps had achieved a remarkable, but unexpected, success at Vimy Ridge from 9–12 April, the larger British Battle of Arras (of which Vimy was a part) soon degenerated into a tough slugging match that achieved few territorial gains. And that failure meant that the Germans' attention was not diverted away from General Henri Nivelle's French offensive in the Champagne. Losses there, for little gain, broke the morale of the French Army, and led to wide-spread mutiny in many of its formations. In the air, meanwhile, the Royal Flying Corps lost 316 aircraft during "Bloody April," largely because the German air force received the latest versions of its fighters ahead of British squadrons.[114]

In short, April 1917 could very well have been one of the bleakest months of the First World War but for one development—the entry of the United States into the war as an "associate" power on the Allied side. Although the Germans had recognized that an unrestricted campaign might draw the Americans into the conflict, Holtzendorff had argued that "fear of a break [with the United States] must not hinder us from using this

---

111. Bethmann-Hollweg quoted in Henry Newbolt, *Naval Operations* (London 1928), IV, 269.

112. Halpern, *A Naval History of World War I*, 337–38; Newbolt, *Naval Operations*, IV, 263–71; and Terraine, *The U-Boat Wars*, 14–16.

113. Ambassador Spring Rice to Governor General of Canada, 31 January 1917, HQS 1686, pt 2, LAC, RG 24, vol. 2532; and Department of the Naval Service, "Naval Intelligence Report No. 6," 5 February 1917, DHH.

114. Terraine, *The U-Boat Wars*, 40, 46.

weapon which promises success."[115] Two days after Germany commenced unrestricted submarine warfare, Washington broke off diplomatic relations. Although American entry into the war was still not a foregone conclusion, British intelligence revealed to President Woodrow Wilson the contents of an intercepted telegram from the German foreign secretary, Arthur Zimmermann, to the Mexican government proposing an alliance against the United States. Together with the deaths of a handful of American citizens in ships torpedoed by the Germans, Wilson finally asked congress for a declaration of war on 2 April. Four days later, the United States was formally at war with Germany.[116] It remained to be seen, however, whether the German high command was correct to gamble on knocking Britain out of the war before the Americans mobilized sufficient strength to affect the fighting.

It was not until it entered the war that the United States government was informed of just how dire a situation the Allies faced. Since the British had stopped releasing figures for shipping losses (so as not to alarm neutral ship owners whose vessels still carried a significant proportion of Britain's overseas trade), the general public was unaware of the amount of tonnage being sunk in the unrestricted campaign. When American Rear-Admiral W.S. Sims, in England to take command of US naval forces in Europe, met with the first sea lord on 9 April, he "was fairly astounded" at the actual figures, having "never imagined anything so terrible."

> I expressed my consternation to Admiral Jellicoe. "Yes," he said, as quietly as though he was discussing the weather and not the future of the British empire, "it is impossible for us to go on with the war, if losses like this continue."
>
> "What are you doing about it?" I asked.
>
> "Everything that we can. We are increasing our anti-submarine forces in every possible way…. But the situation is very serious, and we shall need all the assistance we can get."
>
> "It looks as though the Germans are winning the war," I remarked.
>
> "They will win, unless we can stop these losses—and stop them soon," the admiral replied.
>
> "Is there no solution for the problem?" I asked.
>
> "Absolutely none that we can see now." Jellicoe announced.[117]

Born in Port Hope, Ontario, to a Canadian mother, Sims had never concealed his admiration for either Britain or the Royal Navy, a disposition that had factored into his selection for the overseas post. It also, however, led to the United States Navy's chief of naval operations, Rear-Admiral W.S. Benson, being suspicious of his ultimate loyalty to the American navy. According to Sims, Benson's parting instructions had been, "Don't let the British pull the wool over your eyes. It is none of our business pulling their chestnuts

115. Holtzendorff memorandum, 22 December 1916, quoted in Halpern, *A Naval History of World War I*, 338.

116. Halpern, *A Naval History of World War I*, 340–41.

117. W.S. Sims and B. J. Hendrick, *The Victory at Sea* (Garden City, NY 1921), 6–7.

out of the fire. We would as soon fight the British as the Germans."[118] Despite his chief's attitude, Sims was determined to have the USN send all the destroyers it could to reinforce the escort forces in British waters from the moment he learned the true extent of Allied shipping losses.[119] Although it was in Britain's interest to portray the situation in the direst of terms to ensure receiving as much American naval aid—and particularly destroyers—as possible, the first sea lord was hardly overstating the peril Britain was facing or the impotence of the Royal Navy's existing methods of submarine detection and attack. During the first three months of the unrestricted campaign, the Germans had lost a mere nine U-boats, two of them to their own minefields, for an exchange rate of one U-boat lost for every fifty-three merchant ships sunk in February and one boat for every 167 ships sunk in April.[120]

Nonetheless, the prevailing opinion in Britain remained in favour of offensive hunting patrols using sloops or destroyers to track down submarines rather than the more passive method of escorting either individual ships or those in convoy. The arguments against convoy had been voiced by senior naval officers on 2 November 1916 when called before the Cabinet War Committee in response to a letter from Jellicoe—at the time still commanding the Grand Fleet at Scapa Flow—to the prime minister expressing concern about the growing threat posed by submarine attacks on merchant ships. The official view of the Admiralty was firmly set out in a January 1917 pamphlet critical of adopting a convoy system:

> Whenever possible, vessels should sail singly, escorted as considered necessary. The system of several ships sailing together in a convoy is not recommended in any area where submarine attack is a possibility. It is evident that the larger the number of ships forming the convoy, the greater is the chance of a submarine being enabled to attack successfully, the greater the difficulty of the escort in preventing such an attack. In the case of defensively armed merchant vessels, it is preferable that they should sail singly rather than that they should be formed into a convoy with several other vessels. A submarine could remain at a distance and fire her torpedo into the middle of a convoy with every chance of success. A defensively armed merchant vessel of good speed should rarely, if ever, be captured. If the submarine comes to the surface to overtake and attack with her gun, the merchant vessel's gun will nearly always make the submarine dive, in which case the preponderance of speed will allow of the merchant ship escaping.[121]

---

118. Sims's 1920 testimony before the congressional committee investigating the naval conduct of the war, quoted in Halpern, *A Naval History of World War I*, 358.

119. Hadley and Sarty, *Tin-pots and Pirate Ships*, 196.

120. Halpern, *A Naval History of World War I*, 341.

121. Henry Newbolt, *Naval Operations* (London 1931), V, 5.

One reform that Jellicoe did institute upon being appointed first sea lord at the beginning of December 1916 was to create an Anti-Submarine Division at the Admiralty under Rear-Admiral A.L. Duff.[122] Like most Admiralty officers (and, indeed, most officers in the French and American navies as well[123]), Duff was skeptical of the practicality of convoy, believing that "differences of speed, loss of the safety afforded by zig-zagging, and the inevitable tendency of merchant ships to straggle at night are some of the reasons against an organised system of convoy."[124] Whether Jellicoe himself was fully convinced that convoy was operationally wrong-headed has been a matter of debate. He was not quick to embrace the idea, but (unlike many others) he also did not reject it out of hand. Soon after his appointment as first sea lord he had minuted the chief of staff, Vice-Admiral Sir H.F. Oliver, that some form of convoy for the North Atlantic trade routes might become necessary, and, according to the British official historian, "even after Admiral Jellicoe had read Admiral Oliver's catalogue of difficulties, he minuted the paper with the remark that the whole question must be borne in mind and brought up again later if needs be. That is, he still withheld judgment."[125] The critical factor, Jellicoe wrote after the war (when the effectiveness of convoy had been clearly demonstrated) was that "we could not possibly produce the necessary escort vessels; and that until this difficulty was overcome we should have to postpone the introduction of convoy."[126]

One of the strongest advocates for the adoption of a general system of merchant convoys was the Cabinet's influential secretary, Sir Maurice Hankey. Recognizing that "unquestionably the bulk of the best naval opinion has up to now been against it," on 11 February 1917 the Cabinet secretary nevertheless suggested to Prime Minister Lloyd George that "circumstances ... have changed, and the question arises for serious consideration whether some of the objections have not lost a good deal of force, while others are outweighed by the comparative failure of the present system." The weaknesses of that system were, in Hankey's view, "obvious." The U-boat commander, by "placing himself on the trade route ... has merely to await his prey.... If he confines himself to the use of the torpedo the risks he runs are infinitesimal. He attacks in most cases without having to fight at all.... The attack of trade routes is a 'soft thing' for the submarine with a constant stream of isolated merchant ships, almost devoid of offensive power, to choose from." Hankey concluded his memorandum by pointing out that "perhaps the best commentary on the convoy system is that it is invariably adopted by our main fleet, and for our transports."[127]

Still, even Hankey failed to appreciate the true advantage that the convoy system offered as a means of defence. The basic fallacy in the Admiralty's argument that a convoy of merchant ships was more susceptible to attack than ships proceeding singly was that it

---

122. Halpern, *A Naval History of World War I*, 343; and Terraine, *The U-Boat Wars*, 24.

123. Terraine, *The U-Boat Wars*, 55.

124. Admiral Duff quoted in Newbolt, *Naval Operations*, V, 7.

125. Ibid, 6.

126. Jellicoe, *The Submarine Peril*, 111.

127. Hankey memorandum, 11 February 1917, quoted in Newbolt, *Naval Operations*, V, 10–14.

ignored the very vastness of the ocean itself. Whether on the trade routes or not, convoys were as difficult to find as individual ships and, as the former (and future) first lord, Winston Churchill, explained in 1927: "Here then was the key to the success of the convoy system against U-boats. The concentration of ships greatly reduced the number of targets in a given area and thus made it more difficult for the submarines to locate their prey. Moreover, the convoys were easily controlled and could be quickly deflected by wireless from areas known to be dangerous at any given moment. Finally the destroyers, instead of being dissipated on patrol over wide areas, were concentrated at the point of hostile attack and opportunities of offensive action frequently arose."[128] Rather than counting on a steady stream of merchant vessels from which to choose targets, the adoption of convoy would mean that U-boat commanders would suddenly find large portions of the ocean virtually empty of shipping altogether. In the spring of 1917, however, senior admirals unaccustomed to a naval staff system continued to rely on their professional intuition rather than any statistical or operational analysis before coming to a decision. In those circumstances, it must be said that Hankey's "outsider" intuition proved more accurate than that of most naval officers, a not unsurprising result perhaps, given that the advantages of convoy were, in many ways, counterintuitive.

The Cabinet secretary's memorandum served as a basis for discussion of the submarine problem at a meeting held two days later between Prime Minister David Lloyd George, the first lord, Sir Edward Carson, Jellicoe and Duff. The principles underlying the Cabinet secretary's arguments were acknowledged by Jellicoe and Duff as sound but they remained unconvinced that a general convoy system was as yet practical, particularly in view of the shortage of destroyers that would be needed as escorts. As a result, Lloyd George did not press the Admiralty for a firm decision at the meeting and for the next month the question of convoy was not raised in Cabinet even though the first sea lord was in regular attendance to brief the politicians on the anti-submarine campaign. Whenever the Cabinet questioned the Admiralty about convoy, Jellicoe simply replied that the matter was under consideration and the first sea lord was never under any great political pressure to do otherwise.[129]

While the Admiralty remained unconvinced about the practicality of a general system of convoy, there were certain shipping routes where high losses had already necessitated action. Sinkings of ships carrying coal from Britain to France across the dangerous waters of the English Channel had prompted the Admiralty to adopt convoy sailings in February 1917. Although the coal ships were only organized by tentative, modestly protected "controlled sailings," results were dramatic. According to the British official history, "the reduction of losses in a trade which had hitherto been particularly afflicted was decidedly impressive, and it contributed in a marked degree to decisions made later on."[130] To counter heavy losses being incurred by ships engaged in trade with the Scandinavian countries, an early April conference of naval officers recommended that that traffic should

---

128. Winston Churchill, *The World Crisis: 1916–1918, Part II* (London 1927), 364–65.

129. Newbolt, *Naval Operations*, V, 14–15.

130. Ibid, 15.

also be placed in convoy. Although a number of the local senior officers disagreed with the recommendation when it was forwarded to the Admiralty, Jellicoe decided that the "system was to be tried, and a report sent fortnightly on its working."[131]

Since there was no habit or tradition within the Admiralty that called for the naval staff to undertake research and provide reasoned analysis of specific problems, most new ideas had to be put forward as personal initiatives in the hope that they would find an institutional champion. In preparing his February memorandum for the prime minister, for instance, Hankey had been assisted by Commander R.G.H. Henderson, the officer who controlled the sailings of ships in the cross-Channel coal trade with France. One of the arguments raised by the Admiralty against a general system of convoy was the large number of vessels that would have to be organized and escorted, and the belief that this was beyond the navy's capacity to manage. The figures provided by the Ministry of Shipping, which showed that over 2,400 ships arrived in British ports each week, requiring, on average, the convoying of some 350 ships per day, could be read in that light; but as Henderson pointed out, these statistics included the large number of smaller merchant vessels that moved along the coast from port to port. The more important figure was the number of large ocean-going merchant ships that were actually involved in trans-Atlantic trade. That amounted to only 120 to 140 per week, he maintained, so a more reasonable twenty large ships per day was the likely number requiring convoy.[132] In view of these calculations, the shortage of destroyer escorts would be less acute if a system of convoy was initially instituted for the vital trans-Atlantic traffic only.

As April shipping losses climbed to a staggering total of 881,027 tons, Jellicoe and Duff still hoped that the U-boat menace could be overcome—or at least held in check—by the simple expedient of increasing the number of vessels and weapons being employed in the Royal Navy's existing anti-submarine force. In a memorandum prepared for the Cabinet on 23 April, Jellicoe's immediate demand was for more destroyers, the type of warship most needed for anti-submarine warfare, and asked that the United States Navy send a large force of such vessels to the United Kingdom. He also urged the construction of more merchant ships to offset the sinkings, particularly those with very large hulls that could survive a normal torpedo attack. Increased mining off German submarine ports was also viable, but the first sea lord recognized that such a campaign would be ineffective until an improved British mine was produced. Perhaps succumbing to desperation, Jellicoe also suggested that Britain should import the largest possible reserve of foodstuffs while the shipping to do so still existed.[133]

What the first sea lord did not mention in his memorandum was a growing resignation within the Admiralty that the introduction of a system of convoy was likely the only means not yet tried that might stem the shipping losses. Their lordships were also under growing political dissatisfaction with their handling of the problem. On 25 April Cabinet met to discuss the grave situation, believing that the time had arrived "when a closer

---

131. Jellicoe quoted in ibid, 16.

132. Ibid, 18; and Halpern, *A Naval History of World War I*, 355, 360.

133. Henry Newbolt, *Naval Operations* (London 1928), IV, 380.

examination of all possible methods was necessary, even if it involved a critical survey of the naval administration itself." The politicians concluded that the prime minister should visit the Admiralty "to investigate all the means at present used in anti-submarine warfare, on the ground that recent inquiries had made it clear that there was not sufficient co-ordination in the present efforts to deal with the [unrestricted] campaign."[134] One day after the Cabinet meeting, Admiral Duff forwarded to Jellicoe a paper on the volume of trade to be protected and the number of escorts it required with the suggestion "that the time has arrived when we must be ready to introduce a comprehensive scheme of convoy at any moment. The sudden and large increases of our daily losses in merchant ships, together with the experience we have gained in the case of the French coal trade, afford sufficient reason for believing that we can accept the many disadvantages of large convoys with the certainty of a great reduction in our present losses."[135] As Duff's minute pointed out, such a decision was made easier by the entry of the United States into the war, which would allow for convoys to be organized directly in American ports and the reinforcement of the escort forces by USN destroyers.

Jellicoe approved Duff's recommendation on 27 April, much to the relief of the prime minister. Visiting the Admiralty on the 30th in accordance with the Cabinet decision of the 25th, Lloyd George was able to report that the first sea lord had reconsidered the question of convoy.

> I was gratified to learn from Admiral Duff that he had completely altered his view in regard to the adoption of a system of convoy, and I gather that the first sea lord shares his views, at any rate to the extent of an experiment....
>
> I much regret that some time must elapse before convoy can be in full working order, and I consider that the Admiralty ought to press on with the matter as rapidly as possible.
>
> As the views of the Admiralty are now in complete accord with the views of the war cabinet on this question, and as convoys have just come into operations on some routes [the coal trade with France and the Scandinavian trade route] and are being organised on others, further comment is unnecessary.[136]

According to Jellicoe's post-war recollection, his motivation in agreeing to introduce general convoy was the large increase in the number of sinkings in the weeks leading up to 27 April.

> In the first half of April 1917, there had been a reduction in the number of vessels sunk by submarine attack, but in the latter part of that month the figures ran up at such a rate that it became obvious that some change of system was essential if it could conceivably be introduced....

---

134. Newbolt, *Naval Operations*, V, 19.

135. Duff minute, 26 April 1917 quoted in ibid, 19.

136. Lloyd George minute quoted in ibid, 19.

It has frequently been erroneously stated that the Admiralty decision in this matter was the result of pressure brought to bear on the Admiralty from the war cabinet and civilian quarters. Possibly this idea has arisen from the proceedings at the war cabinet on April 25, previously mentioned, but it is quite incorrect. The views of experienced naval officers on a technical question involving the gravest responsibility could not possibly be affected by outside opinion, however high the quarter from which that opinion emanated.[137]

While Jellicoe was in all probability understating the influence the Cabinet meeting of the 25th had played in his decision, it is true that he had not faced great political pressure to adopt convoy before that time. Perhaps more than any other factor, it was the success of the Germans' unrestricted campaign during its first three months that left the Admiralty with no other option but to adopt a new system of defence as quickly as it did. The amount of tonnage sent to the bottom by the Germans from February to April, an average of 671,625 tons per month, exceeded the 600,000 ton average (over a five month period) that Holtzendorff had projected would be needed to defeat the British. With disaster looming as the rate of sinkings climbed in the second half of April, Jellicoe really had little other choice than the one he made on the 27th.

Although the Admiralty had committed itself to implementing a system of convoy, it would inevitably take some months to organize Allied shipping on a large-scale basis. Ships for a trial convoy were quickly assembled at Gibraltar and the necessary instructions issued for its departure on the evening of 10 May. Until the 18th, the sixteen-ship convoy was escorted north by two "special service" converted merchantmen and three armed yachts, then it was met by six destroyers sent out from Devonport for its passage through the dangerous submarine zone. All ships arrived safely in Britain on the 20th having, to the navy's surprise, kept station satisfactorily while maintaining a speed of 6.5 knots.[138] The successful arrival of the Gibraltar convoy was followed by the departure, four days later, of another experimental convoy, this time twelve ships from Hampton Roads, Virginia. Washington was informed of the Admiralty's decision to adopt a system of convoy on 1 May and asked if the USN could provide fourteen cruisers to act as an ocean escort force. Although Sims had become a strong advocate for convoy, Benson and the navy department remained highly skeptical, expressing "the opinion that it was not advisable to adopt a general system."[139] The Americans denied London's request to have the Hampton Roads convoy escorted by one of the groups of USN destroyers sailing for Queenstown and recommended that convoys should consist of no more than four merchant ships. Despite the navy department's misgivings, a twelve-ship convoy departed Hampton Roads escorted by a single British cruiser on 24 May and arrived safely in Britain on 7 June after being met by eight destroyers on the other side of the ocean and escorted

137. Jellicoe, *The Submarine Peril*, 122, 130–31.

138. Terraine, *The U-Boat Wars*, 60.

139. Jellicoe, *The Submarine Peril*, 129.

through the danger zone.[140] There was a sharp drop in sinkings during May, to 596,629 gross tons, but the decrease was primarily because of a reduction in the number of U-boats operating that month, from an average of fifty in April to forty boats in May. As ships continued to sail individually in June, while the Admiralty organized its transoceanic convoys, sinkings rose to 687,507 gross tons, the second highest monthly total of the war after April 1917. There was some improvement in the figures over the summer but the total tonnage sunk remained large as 557,988 tons were sent to the bottom in July and 511,730 tons in August.[141]

Soon after the decision was made to organize the first, experimental convoys, the Admiralty appointed a committee of staff officers, chaired by a captain, to study establishing a complete system. The convoy committee's report in early June laid out the arrangements needed for setting up administrative staffs to assist the port convoy officers at all the assembly ports, both in Britain and overseas, the additional signalling equipment required for all convoyed merchant ships, and the standard instructions that would be supplied to all escorts, convoy commodores and merchant ship masters. The committee also proposed a program of eight outward and eight homeward bound convoys every eight days with each convoy having a cruiser escort on the open ocean before being met by a flotilla of six destroyers to escort it through the danger zone in home waters, making for a requirement of fourteen flotillas. The success of the two experimental convoys convinced Jellicoe to implement the committee's proposals as the necessary escorts became available to do so.[142]

As a result, a system of convoy was put in place for the vital trans-Atlantic traffic during July. The first of the regular North American convoys, the "HH" series (homeward from Hampton Roads) were started at four-day intervals on 2 July. "HN" convoys (homeward from New York) began sailing at eight-day intervals on 14 July. The Admiralty also organized convoys from the west African port of Dakar for ships in the South Atlantic coming from Australia and the East and group sailings from Gibraltar for the Mediterranean traffic. It was originally intended that ships from Montreal would rendezvous at sea with convoys from New York but the prevalence of fog off the Canadian East Coast forced the Admiralty's convoy committee to reconsider that option. On 22 June the commander-in-chief, North America and West Indies Station was informed that the committee had decided to extend the convoy system to Canadian ports as well. The first of the Sydney HS convoys (homeward from Sydney), HS 1, a total of seventeen merchant ships, sailed from the Cape Breton port on 10 July commencing a regular eight-day cycle. The first of the troopship "HX" convoys (homeward from Halifax) sailed for the first time on 21 August and included any merchant ships from New York or Montreal capable of maintaining 12.5 knots or more. The importance of the North American routes is demonstrated by the increasing share of imports these vessels brought to Britain. From a quarter of British imports at the start of the war, North American goods had risen to form 37 percent of

140. Halpern, *A Naval History of World War I*, 361; and Jellicoe, *The Submarine Peril*, 130.

141. Terraine, *The U-Boat Wars*, 63–65, 80.

142. Newbolt, *Naval Operations*, V, 48–50.

imports by 1916 and to nearly 50 percent during 1917–18. Canada, despite the much smaller size of its economy compared to that of the United States, supplied a quarter of the North American total.[143]

The trans-Atlantic convoys were provided with either a pre-dreadnought battleship or cruiser throughout their passage—HS 1 was accompanied by the cruiser HMS *Highflyer* from the North America and West Indies Station—to guard against the threat from German surface raiders. Each convoy was met outside the submarine danger zone by a destroyer force and escorted into coastal waters for dispersion. Underestimating the degree of protection afforded by a given number of escorts, the Admiralty preferred smaller convoys, stipulating that they should average just twenty ships, with six escorts required when fewer than sixteen ships sailed, and eight in convoys of twenty-two or more. As the convoy system took shape during July 1917, the Royal Navy had sixty-four destroyers, eleven sloops, and sixteen P-boats available for escort duties in the western approaches to Britain, a figure that rose to a peak of 195 escorts, of which 115 were destroyers, by April 1918.[144]

Perhaps understandably, the implementation of convoy did not immediately instil great confidence among the merchant sailors themselves, all of whom had spent their entire careers steaming independently over the world's oceans. In one such example from September 1917, the masters of the steamers *Lake Manitoba* and *Corinthian* reported their concerns to the RCN's naval intelligence officer in Montreal, including their belief that the addition of slower vessels exposed a convoy to greater danger than they felt was prudent.

> We left Lamlash [in the United Kingdom] on the 12th of September in a convoy of fourteen ships including an armed cruiser *Wyncote* also a leader yacht *Albion* which led the convoy as far as the Mull of Kintyre, where a further additional convoy formed up, six columns abreast and also the escorts—three T[orpedo] B[oat] D[estroyer]s, three sloops and two armed cruisers.
>
> During the whole of the time the above named vessels w[ere] in the convoy, we steamed at half-speed and slow, this was necessary to enable me to keep station with the admiral's ship *Wyncote*. Some of the ships were bad station keepers owing to the lack of speed.
>
> The zig-zagging courses … w[ere] in my estimation of very mild nature and the fact of the convoy proceeding at such slow speed rendered the whole thing futile. I sincerely protest against these conditions, having to sail in a convoy of mixed speeds from three knots to eight; furthermore no zig-zagging was done at night time and we were well into the daylight before we commenced, and would cease to zig-zag at least two hours before dark, and the fact of steaming at such erratic slow speed, and keeping stations with ships of slow speed is nothing more or less than suicide. I am of the firm opinion had we

143. Ibid, 52; Hadley and Sarty, *Tin-pots and Pirate Ships*, 200–01; and Tennyson and Sarty, *Guardian of the Gulf*, 144.

144. Newbolt, *Naval Operations*, V, 48–49; and Terraine, *The U-Boat Wars*, 62–64.

been observed by enemy submarines we certainly would have fared badly. Armed cruisers and sloops offer no protection in a large convoy whilst having to steam at such slow speed.

On one particular occasion part of the convoy left apparently for another destination towards the north from about 14 [degrees] West. The signal was hoisted on the admiral's ship of all ships to rejoin convoy and for them to take up their alloted positions in the convoy, and whilse [sic] this evolution was taking place the rest of the convoy had to reduce speed. These conditions, I maintain, are serious, as I consider that it is absolutely necessary for all ships to steam at top speed and zig-zag vigorously the whole time in the war zone without exception.

I am also convinced that destroyers are the only type of vessels that offer any protection to merchant ships, furthermore I do not agree with large convoys of mixed speeds. It is also necessary when selecting ships for convoy for ten knots, to select ships that are capable of maintaining that speed or at least a knot or so less, and for the leading ship to adjust the distance in the zig-zagging. Having to slow down is absolutely suicide, as we had to do on several occasions in this particular convoy; and to do this selecting it will be necessary to have a person who is acquainted with conditions on board the various types of vessels in the mercantile marine.

We consider that four ships of equal speed zig-zagging at top speed in a convoy would answer the purpose much better from about 18 degrees west to the [British] coast and vice-versa. Several masters in this particular convoy agree with me that we were fortunate that no enemy submarines were about, otherwise we would have fared very badly.[145]

Although the convoy had a strong escort of three destroyers and three sloops, the merchant captains were clearly uncomfortable with both the lack of zig-zagging at night and the need to steam at slow speed to maintain formation. Their suggestion that merchantmen would be safer proceeding through submarine-infested waters in four-ship groups, however, failed to appreciate that one of the most important factors contributing to convoy's success was that by passing a large number of vessels through the danger zone at one time it effectively emptied the shipping lanes of traffic. Aware that establishing the new shipping system was bound to have some growing pains, Kingsmill simply forwarded the merchant captains' concerns to the Admiralty in early October without comment.[146]

Until the British port convoy officer appointed by the Admiralty arrived in Canada on 1 August, the organization and despatch of the first Sydney convoys was undertaken by the port's naval transport officer, the senior RCN officer at Sydney, Captain Pasco. It was not until after HS 4 had sailed that Rear-Admiral Bertram M. Chambers, a retired Royal

---

145. C. Griffiths, Master of *Lake Manitoba, and* D.G. Gammock, Master of *Corinthian,* to Naval Intelligence
     Officer, Montreal, 24 September 1917, 1048–48–1, pt. 2, LAC, RG 24, vol. 3772.

146. Kingsmill to Admiralty, 2 October 1917, ibid.

Navy officer who had returned to the service earlier in the war to help manage shipping in British ports, arrived at Sydney to take up his new duties. He was pleasantly surprised to find "that the convoy duties at Sydney had been efficiently carried out previous to my arrival" by the RCN's existing organization headed by Pasco.[147] The RCN officer had already rented offices in the new *Sydney Daily Post* building near the waterfront, that Chambers felt were "very convenient," and after viewing the facilities and the extent of the assistance the RCN was able to offer, the British admiral was more than satisfied with the Canadian arrangements.

> The harbour is a magnificent one and I consider that the southwest arm will probably prove ample for our needs, berthing accommodations being available for some thirty vessels without any crowding.
>
> As regards the staff ... no difficulty should be experienced in getting suitable assistance locally. I am asking Ottawa that Lieutenant [James] Murray may be retained until the arrival of Lieutenant Peugh, my second assistant.
>
> The only exception to the foregoing statement is with regard to the two chief engineers, but I do not think that these will be required, at least for the present. Such assistance as is needed in this direction can be afforded by Engineer Lieutenant C.G. Parkyn, RCN, who is the officer at present employed on transport work under Captain Pasco. This last officer informs me that he will have no difficulty in sparing Lieutenant Parkyn when required....
>
> A coding office already exists at this port for the needs of transports Sydney—(Captain Pasco)—and it will, I consider, be able to give me all the assistance I require for the present, thus avoiding the duplication of staffs.[148]

Given the well-developed shore organization the RCN already had in place for the control of shipping, it is hardly surprising that Admiral Chambers was pleased. Since the earliest stages of the war, Naval Service Headquarters had served as a channel of communication between the Admiralty and the director of overseas transport in the task of co-ordinating and despatching all government store ships from Canadian ports. Although storeships were chartered by the Admiralty, the director of overseas transport and his staff had the enormous responsibility of organizing the movement of war goods over the inland railways to the various ports and overseeing the efficient loading of each vessel so that her cargo could be discharged promptly at the correct European destination. With merchant ships often unloading at two different ports—Portsmouth and Cherbourg, for instance—Harris's officials had to ensure that supplies to be unloaded first in Britain were loaded last in Canada. The details of each vessel's cargo were then passed to the naval transport officer at each port before the ship sailed and that information, together with the date and time of departure and expected date of arrival at her destination was sent to Ottawa so that NSHQ could telegraph the relevant details to the Admiralty. The naval

---

147. B.M. Chambers to Admiralty, 7 August 1917, UKNA, ADM 137/1435.

148. Ibid.

transport officer was also responsible for issuing all orders regarding the route and desti-nation of all transports carrying government stores. Canadian troopships were under the control of the Department of Militia and Defence, but once the troops were embarked the vessels took their orders from the naval authorities. Unless proceeding singly, most troopships sailed in convoy escorted by RN cruisers, usually from the North America and West Indies Station. Coordination of sailing arrangements between the Admiralty and the militia department was carried out by NSHQ.[149]

During the 1916 shipping season, Canada had begun the special routing of all overseas merchant ships based on information provided by the Admiralty concerning enemy submarine concentrations and activity. The issuing of routing instructions was made by the RCN's routing office located at each port, and ship's masters had to produce a slip signed by the routing officer showing that they had received their routing instructions and necessary intelligence reports as well as updated code books before the collector of customs would clear the vessel to sail. Before the commencement of convoys from Sydney, the Cape Breton port had served principally as the main base for the RCN's Gulf of St Lawrence patrol and most merchant ships stopping there did so only to take on coal, with just a few vessels calling in to load steel products destined for France. As the port's naval transport officer, Captain Pasco was assisted by an RNCVR lieutenant, A.S. Woods, first lieutenant of the *Lansdowne* shore establishment, who served as the officer in charge of code books as well as the port's routing officer. Pasco's staff occupied offices near the waterfront at 145 Esplanade, which included a large chart table on which all shipping routes were laid off on a chart of the North Atlantic before they were handed to ship's masters. During the 1916 season the port routing office routed 141 ships, primarily to British and French ports. The pace of work increased the following year with 131 ships being given route instructions prior to the introduction of convoy in July. As a result, another room was added in early 1917 "to accommodate masters who were waiting for their routes, as at times, as many as seven or eight were in the office at once, talking and asking questions, while the routes were being made out." The institution of the convoy system in Canadian waters did not eliminate the work of the routing office since all ships in convoy still had to receive instructions in case they became separated from the group. Such was the volume of work in Sydney that a second RNCVR lieutenant, J.C. Caine, was posted to relieve Woods of some of his workload and serve exclusively as the port's routing officer.[150]

At Halifax, routing instructions were handled by an RNCVR lieutenant under the supervision of the Canadian naval staff officer (CNSO). The latter's position had evolved from that of the naval intelligence officer at Halifax and incorporated the latter's duties with a number of additional ones. The intelligence office set up by the RCN's Commander Charles White at Halifax on the outbreak of war was moved aboard HMCS *Niobe* in the summer of 1915 when the cruiser was laid up alongside the dockyard. In October 1916 a retired RN officer serving in the RCN, Commander G.B. Eldridge, assumed the appointment with the title naval intelligence officer being changed to that of naval staff officer the following

---

149. "Instructions for Transport Service at Headquarters," 18 April 1917, 1048–17–20, LAC, RG 24, vol. 3712.

150. A.S. Woods to NSHQ, 10 January 1919, 1049–2–40, LAC, RG 24, vol. 3981.

Niobe alongside the Halifax dockyard where it served as a floating barracks and naval office. The cruiser's quarter-deck was covered over to provide additional office space for the Canadian Naval Staff Officer and his staff. (DND CN 3310)

month and the prefix "Canadian" being added in December.[151] The change in title reflected the additional duties assigned to the position. Soon after arriving aboard *Niobe*, Eldridge took over responsibility for routing overseas ships from Customs House, as well as the routing of local coastal traffic. Those RNCVR lieutenants who were selected to serve as routing officers at other Canadian ports were sent first to Halifax for instruction in their duties. Although troop convoys sailing from Halifax were the responsibility of the commander-in-chief, North America and West Indies Station, under Eldridge the system evolved so that route orders were provided by the CNSO on the basis of Admiralty telegrams. The routing instructions were then delivered to the commander-in-chief or to the officer commanding the escorting cruiser for distribution to the individual troopships of the convoy.[152]

The greater part of the Halifax naval staff office's work, however, was related to its intelligence and communications functions. The office's communications centre was equipped with both telephone and telegraph lines connecting it to all the necessary authorities in Halifax, including the war signal station, the military, the examination service, and shipping agents, as well as to NSHQ in Ottawa and other RCN shore establishments on the East Coast. It also controlled wireless communications from the main wireless stations at St John's and Cape Race, Newfoundland, as well as the Sable Island, Camperdown, Barrington and other smaller Canadian wireless stations. The results of radio direction-finding work on the Canadian coast also passed through the naval staff office; since the outbreak of war, four direction finding stations had been built at Cape Sable, Chebucto Head, and Canso in Nova Scotia, and Cape Race in Newfoundland. Although these stations could fix the position of enemy warships based on their radio transmissions, their main importance in Canadian waters was to act as an aid to navigation for vessels in fog or making landfall by enabling them to check their calculated position against that provided by the D/F station.[153]

In addition, Eldridge was responsible for issuing war warnings and notices to ships at sea and for dealing with distress signals received from ships along the Canadian coast or adjacent waters. The naval staff office—whose personnel numbered twenty-five by war's end—received all reports of hostile activity that had been transmitted to the various coastal wireless stations. It also broadcast daily North Atlantic ice reports to ships at sea; detailed knowledge of the changing ice conditions in the North Atlantic being an important consideration in the Canadian routing instructions given to merchant vessels.[154] During the course of the war, RCN officers found that "routing officers in [the] United Kingdom routing ships to Canadian and northern United States ports have not had the requisite knowledge of North Atlantic ice conditions and have routed ships, whose masters were also

151. "Naval Intelligence Centre Halifax, History," nd, 1023–7-3, pt 1, LAC, RG 24, vol. 3857.

152. Kingsmill to Admiralty, 2 April 1919, "Routing Office Halifax," 1049–2-40, LAC, RG 24, vol. 3981.

153. Department of the Naval Service, *Report of the Department of the Naval Service for the Fiscal Year Ending March 31, 1919* (Ottawa 1920), 48.

154. Canadian Naval Staff Officer to Admiral Superintendent, Halifax, 13 December 1918, 1049–2-40, LAC, RG 24, vol. 3981.

strangers to ice conditions, right into where heavy ice fields were to be encountered. Consequently, in many cases, ships suffered very considerable damage, which in itself was bad—but in view of the serious delays and scarcity of dry docks, and the ever decreasing available tonnage—was worse."[155]

Such problems were compounded by a failure to provide empty transports with sufficient ballast for a winter crossing of the Atlantic back to North America. Over the winter of 1916–17 the naval transport officer at Halifax, Commander G. Holloway, had kept statistics on the damage sustained by merchant ships from the pounding they had received steaming west. Since many of the transports pressed into North Atlantic service had originally been designed for service in the calmer waters of the Far East, they were particularly susceptible to damage from heavy seas. British officials believed that ships would require only water ballast, while RCN officers insisted that a heavier ballast of well-distributed sand was needed to keep transports riding sufficiently low in the water for an Atlantic winter crossing.[156] In early January 1917, NSHQ complained to the Admiralty about the increasing number "of transports arriving in Canada with leaky rivets and other damage due to heavy pounding in sea," and the fact that damaged merchant ships were not being repaired during their stopovers in the United Kingdom. Ottawa made a point of reminding Whitehall that "ballast can easily be discharged this side without serious delay."[157] Two days later, NSHQ informed the Admiralty that the director of overseas transport was reporting that the growing shortage of transports was causing "insuperable difficulties inland" as war supplies were backed up along the rail network, a situation that finally prompted Ottawa to complain about "conflicting orders urging movement [of] specific stores. One cable instructs preference flour, another preference forestry material, another munitions. [Harris] respectfully suggests that these instructions should come from one central authority familiar with current transport difficulties."[158]

Even as Ottawa was pointing out these problems to London, the control of shipping was in the process of being reorganized by the British government. In February 1917 the Admiralty's transport department was transferred to a newly created Ministry of Shipping, with Graeme Thomson retaining his position as director of transports and shipping but reporting to both the Admiralty for naval and military matters and to the controller of shipping.[159] At Halifax, meanwhile, Commander Holloway reported that the situation of damaged transports had improved briefly following the Canadian complaints in January 1917 as merchant ship masters reported "that for a short time afterwards they had no difficulty in getting ballast to put their ships in the best sea-going trim. But it again appears from information ... that there is difficulty in obtaining ballast; also ships are being routed

---

155. Commander G.O.R. Eliott, "History of Work Carried out at Quebec from Naval Transport Office …," 1 December 1918, ibid.

156. "Notes on Delays and Damage to Transports During This Winter's Season," nd, 1048–17–1, pt 4, LAC, RG 24, vol. 3707.

157. Naval Ottawa to Admiralty, 7 January 1917, ibid.

158. Naval Ottawa to Admiralty, 9 January 1917, ibid.

159. C. Ernest Fayle, *Seaborne Trade, III: The Period of Unrestricted Submarine Warfare* (London 1924), 5–13.

too far north." Although some vessels could be repaired by "tipping," others were tied up waiting for precious dry dock space to become available in Halifax.[160]

With the introduction of convoy, the Halifax naval staff office handled all coding and decoding for the port convoy officer and continued to issue confidential books and documents to all merchant ships. It also provided ships' masters with information concerning obstructions on the sea routes, ice reports, and the latest intelligence on navigation lights and the entrances to various ports of destination. The fleet distributing station at Halifax was responsible for supplying code books, classified documents and British and Canadian naval publications to the warships and bases of the North America and West Indies Station until March 1918, when responsibility for the distribution of written material for ships employed on home water convoy duties was transferred to the senior naval officer in Liverpool. The Halifax station, meanwhile, continued to distribute Canadian naval documents to East Coast HMC ships. In addition, the naval staff office incorporated the fleet mail office for the receipt and despatch of all imperial and Canadian naval mails including those for HM transports.[161]

Similar duties, although on a smaller scale, were handled by RCN officers at other Canadian ports. Besides his intelligence duties, the district intelligence officer at Esquimalt, Commander F. James, with a staff of nine, acted as chief naval censor for the district and the port's routing officer.[162] When the St Lawrence was open to navigation, Commander G.O.R. Eliott, a Royal Naval Reserve officer serving in the RCN, performed the duties of chief examination officer, naval transport officer, routing officer, and naval recruiting officer at the port of Quebec, with offices in the Customs House. His staff of four, including two RNCVR lieutenants for the examination service, was expanded in May 1917 as the navy took over responsibility from the militia for the port war signal station, located on the highest point of land on the Island of Orleans. Manned by an RNCVR lieutenant and five signalmen, the war signal station kept a lookout for all incoming vessels, challenging any approaching warships for the correct reply before allowing them to pass through the defences. Although the examination service was "a mere matter of routine work and no untoward event occurred to cause one to stop any suspicious ships," Eliott's naval transport duties became "much more onerous" during the 1916 and 1917 seasons. Although in 1916 troopships were generally being despatched from Halifax rather than Quebec, RNCVR "drafts of various numbers were arriving monthly to proceed to Bermuda to qualify as gunlayers, and others were returning after one month's practice and qualifying. Freight transports were loading cargoes in Quebec, and others were calling to take on board large motor launches built by the Davie Shipbuilding Company, Quebec, and Canadian Vickers,

160. Naval Transport Officer Halifax to The Captain Superintendent, Halifax Dockyard, 20 March 1917, 1048–17–1, pt 4, LAC, RG 24, vol. 3707.

161. Canadian Naval Staff Officer to Admiral Superintendent, Halifax, 13 December 1918, 1049–2-40, LAC, RG 24, vol. 3981.

162. Lieutenant J.D. Laurie, "Esquimalt Intelligence Centre. Short History of," 9 October 1921, 1023-7-4, pt 1, LAC, RG 24, vol. 3857.

Montreal. In all, 264 of these motor launches were shipped during the season of navigation of 1916 from Quebec, on the decks of store transports."[163]

The institution of convoys from Sydney the following summer meant that Eliott only had to route overseas transports as far as Cape Breton, although all coastal traffic continued to be routed through to its final destination. As we shall see, Quebec also served as the point at which the trawlers and drifters being built by inland yards were completed and commissioned. As these vessels began arriving in the fall of 1917, crews were sent from Halifax "consisting of recruited skippers, mates, and men of the RNCVR and RCN." A total of twenty-two trawlers and twenty-nine drifters were commissioned at Quebec and sent on to the East Coast patrol at Sydney and Halifax before the early onset of ice in the St Lawrence forced the remaining vessels to be laid up for the winter.[164] With the closing of the St Lawrence to navigation each December, Commander Eliott moved to St John, New Brunswick, to take up the duties of naval transport officer at that port as, from December to April each year, the New Brunswick harbour facilities replaced Montreal as the main outlet for war supplies being shipped overseas from Canada. The increased winter activity resulted in an influx of personnel from Sydney and Quebec as those ports closed to shipping. From a 1917 summertime staff of one RNCVR lieutenant and a chief writer to handle code work, the naval transport offices in the Stockton Building on Prince William Street in St John expanded that winter to include Captain Pasco, transferred from Sydney as senior naval officer, Commander Eliott from Quebec, two lieutenants and a staff of fourteen. During the winter months St John normally handled more than twice the tonnage of supplies shipped through Halifax, a disparity that the Halifax Explosion in December 1917 (see Chapter 8) increased (898,287 tons of supplies from St John compared to a mere 125,887 from Halifax from December 1917 to April 1918). The naval staff at St John handled the control of shipping duties in routing merchant ships to their destinations. The vast majority of these were sent to Halifax for convoy although other routes included coastal traffic and merchantmen departing for the Mediterranean or South Atlantic.[165]

With other naval transport and routing offices in Montreal, Louisbourg in Cape Breton, and Vancouver and Esquimalt in British Columbia, all in direct communication with NSHQ in Ottawa, the RCN already had an effective control of shipping organization in place long before Rear-Admiral Chambers arrived at Sydney. Naval Service Headquarters was in close touch with, and fully conversant in, the operations of the director of overseas transport and his organization in a way that British naval officers new to Canada— Admirals Browning and Coke, for instance—often seemed to ignore. It is not surprising, therefore, that Chambers had a relatively easy time establishing himself as the port convoy officer since the most difficult work, matching the movement of war supplies over the heavily taxed rail network to the available transports as they arrived, was being handled

163. Commander G.O.R. Eliott, "History of Work Carried out at Quebec from Naval Transport Office …," 1 December 1918, 1049–2–40, LAC, RG 24, vol. 3981.

164. Ibid.

165. Naval Transport Officer, St John to NSHQ, 13 January 1919, ibid; and Director Overseas Transport to Desbarats, 15 May, 15 April, 10 March, and 13 February 1918, 1048–18–1, pt 4, Director Overseas Transport to Desbarats, 9 January 1919, 1048–18–1, pt 5, LAC, RG 24, vol. 3714.

by the overseas transport organization in Montreal and coordinated on the naval side by NSHQ in Ottawa. Canadian naval officers understood that it was the country's rail network carrying war supplies to the eastern ports that determined (together with winter weather conditions) the pattern and routines of Canada's overseas shipping far more than did the availability of a small naval dockyard at Halifax to repair and victual British warships. The establishment of the convoy system in the North Atlantic increased Halifax's importance as a convoy assembly port for shipping from New York and Boston but it continued, as it had throughout the war, to play second fiddle to St John as an ice-free shipping port.

Admiral Chambers's task of despatching groups of loaded merchant ships was a relatively straightforward one once he had fitted his small British staff—heavily augmented by RNCVR officers already working at Sydney—within the larger, existing Canadian organizations that were already handling the shipment of overseas supplies, coding, and confidential book duties, and the arrangements for local anti-submarine escort and minesweeping. One of the most important duties was routing all departing ships and the British admiral quickly came to appreciate the fact that he was able to rely on an experienced officer in Lieutenant Caine, RNCVR, of Captain Pasco's staff. As Chambers explained to the Admiralty in mid-October: "The work of routing requires very great care for efficient performance, to say nothing of some seafaring knowledge, a natural aptitude for the work and a good memory. It should be performed by an officer who is not liable to be called upon to perform other work whilst drafting routes, since undivided attention is necessary unless blunders are to creep in involving perhaps disastrous results. It has undoubtedly been a great convenience to have had the assistance of a careful and experienced routing officer like Lieutenant Caine during the first months of our work here, when my staff and myself have been acquiring a knowledge of the system and learning where pitfalls lie and how to avoid them. Upon transfer to Halifax [for the winter], I shall lose Lieutenant Caine's assistance and the additional work involved will be considerable.... Routing with my present staff may present considerable difficulties."[166]

Whether as a result of his appreciation of the assistance he received from the RCN's shore organization or his natural common-sense, Chambers made no effort to isolate NSHQ from East Coast operations as Coke and Browning had attempted. In part the ease with which Chambers was able to establish himself as port convoy officer was because his position was entirely new and not one that was replacing or superseding a role the Canadian navy was already performing. By concentrating on his convoy duties and readily accepting the expertise RCN officers had to offer, the British officer did not provoke the same concern in Ottawa as Coke. NSHQ's experience in parrying British efforts to, in Kingsmill's words, "create a separate command out here under the Admiralty,"[167] made Ottawa wary of any future attempt by RN officers to assert unwarranted authority over the Canadian navy. The introduction of the convoy system was not the only war development during 1917 that would impact the RCN, however. Over the war's last 18

---

166. Rear-Admiral, Sydney to Admiralty, 19 October 1917, UKNA, ADM 137/1435.

167. Kingsmill to Desbarats, 16 January 1917, 1065–7-3, LAC, RG 24, vol. 4031.

months, Kingsmill's ongoing efforts to strengthen the navy's patrol forces for the protection of the convoy assembly ports and the shipping lanes through the Gulf of St Lawrence would receive a boost from the entry of the United States into the war. As NSHQ would discover, the neighbour to the south often proved a more willing source of material assistance to the RCN than the Royal Navy.

CHAPTER 8

Pilot Error, 1917–1918

Just as the Royal Canadian Navy would look to its southern neighbour for material assistance after April 1917, the entry of the United States of America into the war was one of the considerations the Admiralty had taken into account in adopting the convoy system. Whitehall was hoping the US Navy could be persuaded to send the bulk of its destroyer forces to United Kingdom waters to help overcome the shortage of convoy escorts. An initial division of six US destroyers was despatched to Queenstown, Ireland by May 1917 but the Admiralty soon realized it had underestimated the degree to which the American navy was unprepared for the type of naval war that had developed since 1914. One USN officer has described his service in April 1917 as consisting "principally of a strong force of [thirty-three] battleships, about fifty sea-going destroyers, forty-four submarines, and a few old cruisers." The American navy's imbalance toward the traditional battleline reflected a lack of appreciation among many of its senior officers of the extent to which Germany's employment of its U-boat fleet in a *guerre de course* against Allied shipping—rather than in direct support of its battleships—had altered the nature of submarine warfare. By the spring of 1917, modern destroyers and cruisers were more badly needed to protect the Allies' extensive sea lanes than the USN's "strong force of battleships."[1]

In terms of manpower, the US Navy was 35,000 sailors short of its 87,000 establishment, only 10 percent of its warships were fully manned, and only one-third of the remainder were ready for service. Compared to the number of destroyers in commission in the Royal Navy, 139 in the Grand Fleet to screen its forty-four capital ships and over a hundred additional destroyers of varying ages for use in trade protection in the approaches to the United Kingdom, the USN barely had sufficient modern destroyers to protect its own battle line let alone provide convoy escorts. In order to provide a small immediate reinforcement to the United Kingdom, the Americans reduced the number of destroyers assigned to screen their battle fleet to eighteen ships. Its remaining destroyers, including some forty older destroyers and torpedo boats, were assigned to the Atlantic and Gulf of Mexico coasts as an anti-submarine force but there was little else available to counter a U-boat offensive off the eastern seaboard.[2]

---

1. Captain G.S. Knox, "The United States Navy," Earl Brassey, ed., *The Naval Annual, 1919* (London 1919), 68–69.

2. Michael Simpson, ed., Anglo-American Naval Relations, 1917–1919 (Aldershot, UK 1991), 10–11; and M. Hadley and R. Sarty, Tin-pots and Pirate Ships: Canadian Naval Forces and German Sea Raiders, 1880–1918 (Montreal and Kingston 1991), 193–94.

Within days of the United States' declaration of war, the Admiralty ordered Vice-Admiral Browning to Washington to discuss Anglo-American naval co-operation. In the same telegram, Whitehall also directed the Canadian naval staff officer at Halifax, Commander G.B. Eldridge, to be ready to proceed to the United States and advise the Americans on port boom defences (and without reference to Ottawa despite his position in the RCN).[3] After meeting with US naval authorities, the British C-in-C reported to the Admiralty on the 13th that the Americans had agreed to have one cruiser squadron ready on the northeastern seaboard should a German raider escape the British blockade and reach the North Atlantic. The USN cruisers would coordinate their operations with Browning's warships, the American area of responsibility being the waters from the latitude of Cape Sable at the southern tip of Nova Scotia "to the longitude of 50 degrees west, thence south to parallel of 20 degrees north" running through the Gulf of Mexico. The only direct mention of Canadian waters was an agreement that "if and when" enemy submarines appeared off North America, the USN would "attempt to send several submarines to the Canadian coast but this only possible if a parent ship or accommodation of men on shore provided."[4] Although the Americans felt their submarine service was as yet "inefficient" for operations, they were willing "to send submarines to Halifax if and when required." In view of their misgivings the British admiral assured them "that the moral effect of the presence of such craft at Canadian ports would be useful."[5] It was a rather dubious contention on Browning's part, however, since the Admiralty had already acknowledged that submarines operating against other submarines was "not a method that produces any great material effect."[6]

Browning's arguments in favour of an immediate USN reinforcement for British waters were strengthened when the Balfour naval mission arrived in Washington on 24 April. Although an initial division of six American destroyers would arrive at Queenstown, Ireland in early May, the British delegation convinced the American naval secretary, Josephus Daniels, of the need for even greater assistance with the result that by 5 July the number of USN destroyers in British waters had grown to thirty-five. Aside from the fifty modern fleet destroyers, any other modern anti-submarine escorts would have to be built from scratch. During the course of the war the United States ordered over 250 new destroyers and 350 small, 80-ton "submarine chaser" motor launches. The latter vessels were not well suited to work as escorts, however, and were normally "employed in offensive work only. They were equipped with listening devices, the efficient use of which necessitated isolation from other types of vessels in order to avoid sound interferences. Their light battery, one 3-inch gun, required them to operate in groups for mutual support

---

3. Admiralty to Browning, 29 March 1917, quoted in Simpson, ed., *Anglo-American Naval Relations, 1917–1919*, 18–19.

4. Browning to Admiralty, 13 April 1917, quoted in ibid, 33–34; and "Notes on NSC 1065-7-4," nd, Directorate of History and Heritage (hereafter DHH) 81/520/1550–157/1.

5. Browning to Admiralty, "Report of Proceedings since arrival in the United States," 13 April 1917, quoted in Simpson, ed., *Anglo-American Naval Relations, 1917–1919*, 36.

6. Memorandum by Jellicoe, 9 April 1917, quoted in ibid, 32.

in the event of enemy submarines engaging with guns. If proper tactics were employed, operations by small groups facilitated hunting by sound, and the final attack with depth charges."[7]

Although Browning was routinely in contact with NSHQ on a number of matters both before and after his April talks with the Americans, he made no effort to keep Ottawa informed of the discussions or even to let them know they had taken place, despite the fact that several points of the talks touched directly on areas of Canadian concern. It was not until the following month that the C-in-C mentioned to Captain Martin in Halifax that the USN had agreed to assume "sea patrol duty" as far north and east as Cape Sable, although he cautioned Martin that the agreement "will not materially reduce the need to protect shipping and the city itself from submarine attack." This was the first intimation any Canadian naval officer had received of Browning's Washington conversations and the existence of a patrol agreement with the United States Navy. When word of Martin's conversation was passed to Ottawa, a puzzled NSHQ began seeking information from the C-in-C concerning the arrangements he had made with the Americans for sea patrols off southern Nova Scotia. On 13 May, the Admiralty finally provided Ottawa with the text of the agreement, and, four days later, Browning informed Commodore Coke (who, it will be recalled, was not relieved of his command until August) that the USN would also be providing patrols for the Bay of Fundy.[8] As it turned out, however, the British C-in-C was himself misinformed and did not fully understand the nature of the agreement he had made with the Americans.

In the absence of any reinforcement being offered by the Royal Navy, the encouraging news about American patrol intentions led NSHQ to look to the United States as a possible source of assistance for Canada's anti-submarine efforts. Two weeks after Browning's belated disclosures, the British embassy in Washington finally informed the Canadian government of American interest in the RCN's patrols: "it is suggested by [US] navy department that the officer commanding Halifax and St Lawrence patrol should come to Washington to discuss whole question of patrol with them as it is felt that there must be mutual understanding and cooperation in whole operation of west Atlantic patrol."[9] In a memorandum to the naval director at the end of May, Stephens pointed out that the area of USN patrols reported by Browning on the 14th did not include the Bay of Fundy, while the latter's letter to Coke on the 17th clearly stated that the bay would be an American responsibility and suggested that "definite arrangements" should be made to sort out the confusion.[10] Under the circumstances Ottawa believed that the US naval authorities were "prepared to take over certain patrol of our coasts and wished for a consultation with the

7. Knox, "The United States Navy," 71, 73; Henry Newbolt, *Naval Operations* (London 1931), V, 34–35; and Hadley and Sarty, *Tin-pots and Pirate Ships,* 193–94.

8. "Notes on NSC 1065-7-4," nd, DHH 81/520/1550–157/1; and Hadley and Sarty, *Tin-pots and Pirate Ships,* 197–98.

9. Barclay, British Embassy Washington to Governor General, 26 May 1917, 1065–7-3, Library and Archives Canada (hereafter LAC), Record Group (hereafter RG) 24, vol. 4031.

10. "Notes on NSC 1065–7-4," nd, DHH 81/520/1550–157/1.

11. Kingsmill, "Memorandum for the Chief of Staff," 8 June 1917, 1065–7-3, LAC, RG 24, vol. 4,031.

officer commanding our patrols."[11] As we have seen, Browning and Kingsmill agreed that in view of Coke's delay in drawing up a comprehensive patrol plan for the East Coast, it was unwise to send the British commodore to Washington.

Minister Hazen, however, still wanted NSHQ to contact American naval authorities "with respect to the Bay of Fundy patrol and other matters of communication between this department and the United States authorities" and the Canadian naval director elected to send his dependable chief of staff to Washington to hold preliminary discussions.[12] While Kingsmill believed that Coke's presence at such talks "would be of little value," he wanted Stephens to open Ottawa's lines of communication to Washington since "the US naval authorities may, for the sake of their own defence, feel inclined to take over a certain part of the patrol at once." He also wanted to ensure that both Browning's cruisers and Canadian patrol vessels could communicate with and know the locations of US warships, but stipulated that Stephens not make any firm commitments on the means of communication. Still, Kingsmill suggested that American vessels could patrol the waters of the Gulf of Maine to the west of a north-south line through Cape Sable at the southern tip of Nova Scotia: "The waters immediately to the eastward of this, being exceedingly dangerous, require local knowledge and the fact that so many fishing boats are operating around the [Frenchman's] Point make it desirable that our own people should patrol this neighbourhood. Of course the ports to the eastward as far as Shelbourne will be at all times open to them when they want to take shelter from bad weather."[13]

Shortly before departing Ottawa for the American capital, Stephens asked Kingsmill for further clarification of the RCN's intentions for the Bay of Fundy patrols. Specifically, the chief of staff wanted to know the extent to that Canada wished to patrol her own territorial waters in the bay or if she was willing to have the USN undertake that responsibility and, irrespective of the outer patrol arrangements, whether Canada wanted to patrol the approaches to her own ports.[14] Kingsmill's response, received by Stephens in Washington, concurred in having the Americans patrol the Bay of Fundy generally but stipulated that the RCN would continue to patrol both Canadian territorial waters and the approaches to her ports. The naval director did not object, however, to US warships being free to take action within Canada's territorial waters should the situation require it. He also wanted Stephens to assure the Americans that Canada would render "every assistance" to US vessels employed off the Canadian coast.[15]

Once in Washington, Stephens quickly discovered Browning's misinterpretation of his agreement, which covered only the "sea patrol" by USN cruisers operating on the North Atlantic shipping lanes and did not include the patrol of any coastal waters.[16] After meeting with Secretary of the Navy Daniels, "who greeted me cordially and said he

---

12. Kingsmill to Commander-in-Chief, 8 June 1917, ibid.

13. Kingsmill, "Memorandum for the Chief of Staff," 8 June 1917, ibid.

14. Stephens, "Memo: For Director of the Naval Service," 8 June 1917, ibid.

15. Naval Ottawa to British Embassy, Washington, 11 June 1917, ibid.

16. Stephens, "Memorandum for Commodore Gaunt," 13 June 1917, ibid.

considered it most necessary that there should be co-operation between the two patrol services," the Canadian chief of staff was informed "that the navy department distinguished between the sea patrol and the coast patrol," and directed him to see Captain G.R. Marvell, the officer in charge of the local coast patrol. As Stephens subsequently reported to Kingsmill, it did not appear that the United States Navy was in a position to assist Canada any time soon:

> Captain Marvell informed me that the sea patrol was carried out by the regular ships of the United States Navy within the area agreed upon with the commander in chief, North America and West Indies. The coast patrol was carried out by the naval reserves and their area was generally recognized as extending out to the fifty fathom line. In the northern area (which most concerns Canada) the fifty fathom line approaches so close to the coast that the limit of the coast patrol is extended to twenty miles from the coast.
>
> No arrangements had been made for the assumption of any coast patrol beyond the United States-Canada frontier. Captain Marvell explained that as regards the sea patrol of the Bay of Fundy, United States ships might occasionally be found there, say once in three months, and I gathered that he did not consider that the appearance of enemy raiders or other surface vessels in the Bay was a likely contingency.
>
> I enquired as to the attitude of the navy department towards the coast patrol of the Bay of Fundy and southern coast of Nova Scotia, explaining that I was not authorized to make definite proposals. Captain Marvell at once stated he could not give any opinion without further consideration of the question. He subsequently stated that logically the patrol of the Bay of Fundy was a matter for Canada to carry out; that that part of the coast should in his opinion be patrolled by men with intimate local knowledge. With regard to the Nova Scotia coast he was less decided, but I gathered that that matter could probably be arranged, if necessary, in the future *when ships were available* [Stephens's emphasis]. The question of providing ships is evidently a difficulty. A number of those available have been sent to Europe. There appears to be plenty of vessels in the country, but the navy department has not power to requisition them. The mercantile interests seemingly are reluctant to release them for naval purposes.[17]

The USN had organized its eastern seaboard into patrol divisions with each commanded by a flag officer or captain with a staff of regular naval officers. The northern division, with headquarters in Boston, extended from the Canadian boundary to Cape Cod. The patrol vessels themselves, none of which were fitted for minesweeping, were manned by naval reservists. There was a six-ship flotilla of minesweepers based at Boston and a similar minesweeping force at New York. American naval officials also proved most co-operative

---

17. Stephens, "Memo: For Director of the Naval Service," 15 June 1917, ibid.

when it came to the regular exchange of intelligence between Ottawa and Washington, with the Department of Naval Intelligence asking only "that a list of subjects concerning which intelligence was particularly required [by NSHQ] might be furnished." The US director of naval communications was similarly receptive and suggested that the most suitable code for joint use by US and Canadian patrol vessels was the United States radio code with supplementary cipher, copies of which were to be supplied to NSHQ "as soon as the number required is notified."[18] The helpful American attitude toward exchanging information, despite their own lack of coastal patrol resources, was a refreshing change from the Royal Navy's frequent neglect in disseminating intelligence to the RCN, even on matters of direct importance to Canada. The United States, in contradistinction, soon posted a liaison officer to Halifax, Captain J.F. Hines, whom Browning found to be "a real help.... I send all my messages to [the US] navy department through him; he is always most prompt and business-like; and he keeps his mouth very firmly closed in this land [USA] of indiscreet talk!"[19]

Had NSHQ been aware of it, Canada's senior naval officers could at least have taken some consolation from the fact that the Admiralty's treatment of the United States Navy was little better than its customary disregard of the RCN. In a letter to Browning in July, the US chief of naval operations complained that "I sometimes wonder if your service realizes how much in earnest we are and fully and heartily we want to cooperate with you; we get very little [information about the naval war], in fact nothing about what your policy is except to have us send over as many tugs, anti-submarine craft as we can."[20] In an attempt to get some sense of British naval policy, Admiral Benson sent the commander-in-chief, Atlantic Fleet, Admiral H.T. Mayo, to the Admiralty in August 1917 to try to learn the Royal Navy's plans for the future prosecution of the naval war.[21] Once in London, the American admiral was astounded to discover the lack of systemic rigour with which the British Empire's maritime defence was being directed by the naval staff in Whitehall. In an insightful report to Washington, Mayo explained the somewhat haphazard management style of senior RN officers.

> There is little doubt that the British Admiralty is at a loss when asked for the history of the war to date. Reports of operations are so isolated and scattered and without system that there is not available any comprehensive record of original plans, the governing reasons therefore, and the degree of success or failure in each case. The inevitable inference is that the war has been carried on from day to day and not according to any comprehensive policy to serve as a guide to plans looking to the effective coordination and cooperation of effort against the enemy.
>
> It is apparent that, despite the so-called war-staff arrangements put into

18. Ibid.

19. Browning to Benson, 26 July 1917, quoted in Simpson, ed., *Anglo-American Naval Relations, 1917–1919*, 92.

20. Browning to Jellicoe, 20 July 1917, quoted in ibid, 90.

21. Sims to Daniels, 31 July 1917, Browning to Jellicoe, 10 August 1917, quoted in ibid, 93.

effect in the Admiralty during the past three years, until very recently there has been no planning section, nor was there any definite body of men charged with the function of looking ahead, or even looking back to see where in lay the causes of success or failure, nor any means of furnishing the heads of the Admiralty with analyses and summaries of past operations in order that decisions as to continuing old operations or undertaking new ones, might be reached with a due sense of "perspective" both as to past operations, and as to the coordination of new operations in a general plan.

The statement of present Admiralty policy, originally dated July 1917, ... is not really a statement of policy but rather a summary of current activities.[22]

The American admiral had learned, in short, what Canadians had already experienced: that the Admiralty's approach to running the naval war, essentially from day to day, largely explained the contradictory instructions Ottawa had received over the past three years. Never having had time to develop an effective naval staff before 1914, it was proving difficult under the pressure of war for the Admiralty to look beyond current operations and plan future ones. Until an actual submarine threat had appeared off North America, therefore, Whitehall had only instructed Canada to organize a small coast-watching service and not to build any naval vessels of their own. When *U 53* began sinking ships in the approaches to New York, the Admiralty then demanded that the RCN's patrol forces be expanded immediately. London's lack of forward planning was especially frustrating for an NSHQ that was acutely aware that the RCN had no purpose-built naval vessels with which to counter a U-boat offensive. Believing that enemy submarines would eventually operate in Canadian waters, the RCN's senior officers had the time to contemplate the steps that needed to be taken to meet possible developments a year or two down the road. Kingsmill's desire to have Vickers start building a few destroyers in the spring of 1916, even though they were not expected to be completed until the fall of 1917, was a case in point. But as Admiral Mayo had found, three years into the war, the Admiralty still did not have an organization in place to analyze its own operations, let alone one that could properly identify Canada's requirements and recommend action in advance of events. As a result, Kingsmill's destroyer scheme had been rejected primarily on the strength of a spur-of-the-moment decision by the first sea lord.

Admittedly, such ability as NSHQ had to plan ahead was largely a function of the Canadian navy's small size and the fact that Kingsmill had been in charge of the service since its formation and could personally recall each issue (not to mention that an East Coast practically without anti-submarine forces also tended to concentrate the mind). What the RCN's leadership lacked, not least in the eyes of Canadian politicians, was the Admiralty's credibility and stature that came from centuries of experience and the power and prestige that resulted from countless naval battles won. As a result, it was virtually impossible for a handful of RCN officers crowded on the top floors of an Ottawa business

---

22. "Admiral Mayo's general impressions regarding conditions in the Admiralty," September 1917, quoted in ibid, 97.

establishment—the Rhea, later known as the Daly, building at the corner of Rideau Street and Sussex Drive that housed NSHQ—to ignore Admiralty pronouncements and persuade the Borden government to adopt an alternate course of action to the one London proposed. It meant, as well, that the local knowledge Kingsmill and Stephens brought to the question of Canadian naval defence resonated little with the navy department in Washington, which was itself under great pressure from London to send all available anti-submarine forces overseas, if their suggestions did not have Whitehall's endorsement.

As a result, the American entry into the war had little immediate impact on the size of the RCN's anti-submarine force. As we have seen, the navy purchased or transferred from other government departments a limited number of vessels to expand its small fleet over the spring and summer of 1917, but the additional craft did not significantly alter the defensive arrangements from those that Captain Pasco had put in place during the 1916 shipping season. With the seven New England fishing trawlers the naval service purchased in the United States, *PV I* to *PV VII*, employed on minesweeping duties, thirteen auxiliary patrol vessels, including the newly commissioned ships *Acadia*, *Cartier*, *Laurentian*, and *Lady Evelyn*, were available to Captain Walter Hose when he arrived in Sydney to take over the Canadian patrol from Commodore Coke in mid-August.[23] Hose had no sooner reached the Cape Breton port than he temporarily turned over command to Pasco in order, at Kingsmill's request, to accompany the departing British admiral to Quebec City aboard HMCS *Stadacona*.[24]

As it was, Hose's performance upon resuming his duties at Sydney did not immediately instil great confidence at NSHQ. The visits of *U 53* and *Deutschland* to the US East Coast the previous year had demonstrated the feasibility of U-boats operating in North American waters and gave added credence to the continuing stream of civilians reporting submarines off Canada's coast. The Admiralty's message in April 1917 that it had "reason to suspect that one or two minelaying submarines are crossing the Atlantic," for instance, meant that sighting reports could not simply be ignored, no matter how dubious they might otherwise have seemed.[25] Shortly after Hose took up his duties at Sydney, a report was received from the administrator at Saint Pierre that a submarine had been sighted by fishermen in the early morning hours of 22 August, twenty-five miles west of the French island. A skeptical Hose simply passed the information on to all of his patrols vessels, but did not send a ship to Saint Pierre to investigate and took no further action himself. It was not until the following day that Ottawa, firmly convinced that such "action should have been taken on hearing report," ordered Hose to "send someone in at once to investigate" and he despatched HMCS *Acadia* to the French island.[26] Although *Acadia*'s commanding officer was "convinced that fisherman saw [a] submarine," Hose continued to discount the

23. Hatcher, Memo for the Director of the Naval Service, 24 October 1917, 1065–7-3, LAC, RG 24, vol. 4031.

24. Kingsmill to Transports Sydney, 8 August 1917, ibid.

25. Admiralty to Naval Ottawa, 13 April 1917, 1062–13–2, pt 2, LAC, RG 24, vol. 4021.

26. Naval Ottawa to Transports, Sydney, 22 August 1917, Patrols Sydney to Naval Ottawa, 22 August 1917, Naval Ottawa to Transports Sydney, 23 August 1917, ibid.

possibility since no other sighting was subsequently made, even when a convoy sailed from Sydney a few days later. As he informed Ottawa, the captain of patrols could do no more than escort "convoys clear of Sydney with as many armed vessels as I can muster, until they are formed up."[27] Belatedly checking on submarine sighting reports (no matter how dubious Hose might believe them to be) and providing limited protection to merchant ships as they formed into convoy in the Sydney approaches were, in reality, the only defensive measures that the auxiliary patrol force was capable of providing during the fall of 1917.

As Hose had suspected, there were no German submarines in Canadian waters and, indeed, no U-boats crossed the Atlantic during 1917. That was fortunate since none of the twelve Battle-class trawlers the RCN had ordered in February, nor any of the trawlers and drifters being built in Canadian yards for the Admiralty, were delivered to Sydney in time to take part in the 1917 shipping season. Although the demands of building such small vessels were not beyond the ability of Canadian shipyards, growing shortages of labour and material, the result of North America's rapidly expanding war economy following the United States' entry into the conflict, forced increasing delay. Whereas the absence of new warship contracts in 1916 had confined work at Canada's most advanced shipyard, Vickers in Montreal, primarily to ship repairs and refits once the 1915 Admiralty contracts for submarines and motor launches had been completed, such was not the case by the second half of 1917.[28] As American war industry expanded over the summer, keeping skilled labour from seeking higher wages south of the border proved difficult, even for well-established firms like Vickers. In July, for instance, work on the hulls of the wooden drifters in Montreal had to be stopped after a New York firm that was also building wooden ships for the Imperial Munitions Board made "extravagant offers of from sixty-two cents to sixty-five cents per hour for plankers and have taken the entire force from Canadian Vickers Yard." As the Canadian director of ship construction overseeing the British contract in Canada explained to Desbarats, "this is very poor business, as I understand that the British government is paying for both drifters and ships, and builders are bidding against each other for men." Planking required ship's carpenters that were "almost impossible to get," and J.W. Norcross wished "to point out emphatically that it will be impossible to deliver the one hundred drifters this year unless this practice is stopped at once."[29] The deputy minister, for his part, assured Norcross that he had taken the matter up with a representative of the IMB but suggested that ship's carpenters were readily available in the maritime provinces and said that he still expected the director of ship construction "to complete these ships according to your programme."[30]

The twelve Battle-class trawlers the RCN had contracted for in February 1917 were

---

27. Patrols Sydney to Naval Ottawa, 30 August 1917, ibid.

28. G.N. Tucker, *The Naval Service of Canada: Its Official History,* I: *Origins and Early Years* (Ottawa 1952), 235; and Graham D. Taylor, "A Merchant of Death in a Peaceable Kingdom: Canadian Vickers, 1911–1927," in *Canadian Papers in Business History* (Victoria 1989), I, 220–1, copy in DHH 91/409.

29. Norcross to Desbarats, 18 July 1917, 29–16–1, pt 2, LAC, RG 24, vol. 5604.

30. Desbarats to Norcross, 21 July 1917, ibid.

The Imperial trawler *TR 20* being fitted out at Kingston Shipyard with *TR 53* under construction. (LAC PA-192044)

The Battle-class trawlers *Festubert, St. Eloi, St. Julien, Vimy, Ypres,* and *Messines* being completed at Polson's in the fall of 1917. (DND CN 3949)

originally scheduled to be delivered by August, but, in view of the delays, only the six vessels built at the Polson Iron Works in Toronto were delivered before December 1917. The six Toronto trawlers—HMC Ships *Vimy, Ypres, St Julien, St Eloi, Messines,* and *Festubert,* all named for battles of the Canadian Corps in France—were commissioned on 13 November and sailed to Halifax for the winter.[31] The six trawlers being built by Canadian Vickers in Montreal, of which the hulls of two, HMC Ships *Thiepval* and *Loos,* were built by the Kingston Shipbuilding Company, suffered greater delays because of difficulties in procuring engines. Although the hulls for the Vickers's trawlers were finished in the summer, the firm did not receive the engines and boilers, parts of which had to come from Britain, until later in the fall. Writing in early December, Desbarats showed little sympathy for the Montreal firm's problems and pointed out that delivery had been "promised to begin last August" whereas "the first two were delivered this week." Instead, the deputy minister instructed Vickers to send the four completed trawlers to Halifax immediately, while keeping the other two in Montreal over the winter to complete their fitting out.[32] In the event, the first two Vickers's trawlers, *Arleux* and *Armentieres,* were not commissioned until 5 June 1918, the remaining four being commissioned by 1 August.[33]

In anticipation of receiving both the twelve Battle-class trawlers the RCN had ordered and the thirty-six trawlers and 100 wooden drifters being built in Canada on Admiralty account, NSHQ had begun drawing up plans for their use before the summer 1917 shipping season had concluded. With Captain Hose in Sydney, Kingsmill gave the job of drafting an East Coast defence scheme to the officer the Admiralty had originally sent out to replace Commodore Coke. Captain J.O. Hatcher's design "for an effective defence of the Atlantic coast" was meant to defend against enemy submarines "who would probably lay minefields or attack convoys leaving [port] by torpedo." He based his plan on the assumption that all the Admiralty trawlers and drifters building in Canada would be available to the RCN. The trawlers were to be used primarily as minesweepers to keep clear a "war channel" extending beyond the entrance channel already being cleared by those minesweepers that were attached to each port. Those minesweepers assigned to the defence of Halifax would remain under the command of the captain superintendent, E.H. Martin, but the war channel sweepers would be under the command of the captain of patrols, "who would receive his instructions directly from the director of naval service."[34]

Hatcher also proposed using thirty-six of the imperial wooden drifters to set up a drift net defence on the approaches to Halifax. The wooden drifters were to have a single 6-pounder gun and depth charges to attack submarines that might run afoul of the net barrage. With their drift nets submerged as far as 120 feet below the surface, the line of drifters would still allow large merchant ships to steam safely over the barricade. The thirty-six drifters were to be organized into three groups of twelve with two groups always at sea

---

31. Ken MacPherson and Ron Barrie, *The Ships of Canada's Naval Forces, 1910–2002* (St. Catharines 2002), 28–31.

32. Desbarats to Canadian Vickers, 6 December 1917, Vickers to Desbarats, 3 and 11 December 1917, NSS 29–16–1, pt 2, LAC, RG 24, vol. 5604.

33. MacPherson and Barrie, *The Ships of Canada's Naval Forces,* 27–31.

34. Hatcher to Kingsmill, "Submitted," 3 October 1917, 1017–10–3, pt 1, LAC, RG 24, vol. 3832.

and the third in port resting, overhauling, and repairing. Each group would also have a trawler assigned to it as an officer's ship. Aware that the handling of wire drift nets was unknown to most Canadian fishermen and would require "men of experience," Hatcher suggested "that a proportion of skippers, second hands, and deck hands be obtained from the imperial service to instruct and show how the work is to be done." The British officer also recommended that "the disposition of the drifters is to be altered at intervals by the captain in charge of patrols, always bearing in mind that the main object is the protection of the approach to the port."[35]

Hatcher called for a similar system of trawler/drifter defence for Sydney. While a thirty-seven mile long channel from the Cape Breton port was currently being swept by a single pair of trawlers, the British officer strongly recommended that the pair be expanded to twelve trawlers organized into two groups as at Halifax. He also recommended a similar force of thirty-six drifters and three trawlers to work in the approaches to the Cabot Straits. All the trawlers and drifters, as at Halifax, would come under the command of the captain of patrols. As the main port for assembling Canadian merchant ships into convoys during the summer months, Hatcher agreed with previous RCN policy that Sydney was "a most suitable port as a base of patrol vessels" but sensibly recommended concentrating the patrols across the mouth of the Gulf:

> I would strongly recommend all patrol vessels now being used inside the Straits of Cabot to be withdrawn and organized to the eastward of Cape North, Cape Breton Island, and Cape Ray, Newfoundland. This would guard the approach and entrance to the Gulf of St Lawrence, the great object being to keep the enemy's vessels out of the Gulf.
>
> Patrol vessels allocated for the Straits of Cabot should be solely and entirely for the duties of patrol and should consist of at least twelve vessels based on Sydney. Patrol vessels should be divided into three groups of which two groups should be constantly on patrol, and one group resting. The two groups on patrol should be organized to patrol in opposite directions, and allocated to certain areas, and so arranged that vessels in each group should meet at an appointed crossing for the purpose of communicating news. Patrols should be so arranged that the maximum of steaming time would be the period vessels should remain at sea.[36]

Hatcher did not consider the other two entrances to the Gulf, the Straits of Belle Isle around northern Newfoundland and the narrow Cut of Canso between Cape Breton Island and the mainland, to be of practical use for submarines because of ice and bad weather in the former's case and the powerful tides in the latter's. Even in the Cabot Strait, the defence would be aided by the "difficulty of navigation through fogs, weather, etc." that "would

---

35. Ibid.

36. Ibid.

necessitate the approach to the Straits by submarine being taken on the surface." During the winter months, the patrol vessels at Sydney could be transferred to St John, New Brunswick, for similar work in the Bay of Fundy.[37]

The additional auxiliary vessels at both Halifax and Sydney would also require some expansion of the port facilities on the East Coast, whether at the Halifax dockyard itself or at some other point. Once in commission, the imperial drifters would require a wharf at least 120 yards long by twenty yards deep "to allow the whole length of a drift net to be laid out for fitting, overhauling, and or repairing." Warehouse accommodation would also have to be built or rented near the wharf "for storage of nets, wires, and general fittings, stores issued by trawlers, drifters, and patrol vessels. There should also be the means of erecting a workshop for the general running repairs to engines and machinery generally, carpenter shop for repairs to wooden vessels, and for the making and repairing of kites." Although Sydney already had "sufficient facilities for the general upkeep of all vessels," including the recent purchase of a floating dry dock, the British officer recommended that the naval service take over the sheds and wharf of Rhodes, Curry & Co. Ltd. for storage and, if necessary, additional accommodation for extra personnel and shore staffs.[38]

By the time Hatcher submitted his report to NSHQ at the beginning of October 1917, however, some of the assumptions on which it was based had already been overtaken by events. For one, London had changed its mind on the allocation of the thirty-six imperial trawlers and 100 drifters. Rather than handing all the vessels over to the RCN as Coke had so confidently asserted based on what the Admiralty had told him, Ottawa was now informed that the plan was to transfer the first twenty trawlers and fifty drifters to be completed in Canada to European waters to reinforce the Royal Navy's own patrols. Since the Admiralty had never definitely stated where the Canadian–built vessels were to be assigned, NSHQ had accepted at face value the assumption that they would be used to help fill Canadian defence needs. Nonetheless, as Hatcher asserted in a memorandum he attached to his defence proposals before submitting them to Kingsmill on 3 October, the reduction did not alter "the question of what is considered necessary for an efficient anti-submarine defence for the Atlantic ports and coast of Canada."[39] As other historians have pointed out, however, the Admiralty's "decision turned Hatcher's plan into a paper exercise" that can best be described as "incongruous."[40]

The Canadian naval director promptly sent a copy of Hatcher's revised proposals to Admiral Browning for his views on the subject, particularly on the question of swept channels out to the 100 fathom line. Kingsmill also solicited the views of his chief of staff and the captain of patrols. The Canadian captain was less sanguine than Hatcher about the effects of the reduction in the number of imperial trawlers and drifters available, pointing out that "a complete anti-submarine defence ... would require at least all the vessels originally proposed by the Admiralty for use in Canadian waters." Since that possibility had been negated by London's decision to appropriate the first twenty trawlers and fifty

37. Ibid.

38. Ibid.

39. Hatcher, "Memo: For Director of the Naval Service," 3 October 1917, ibid.

40. Hadley and Sarty, *Tin-pots and Pirate Ships*, 208.

drifters for itself, Hose questioned whether it would be better to let the British navy have all 100 drifters, if the RCN was allowed to keep twenty-four imperial trawlers instead of sixteen. Hose was unconvinced of the effectiveness of drifters in the first place, and was especially doubtful of their utility when their limited numbers were divided between Halifax and Sydney, arguing that "to split them up would give inadequate protection to both."[41] Although the captain of patrols' skepticism about the use of drifters was based primarily on his assessment of their utility in Canadian waters, his intuition was fully borne out by the vessels' wartime record. Although the Royal Navy remained a firm believer in the value of drifters towing nets to entangle submarines throughout the war, the technique was demonstrably unsuccessful with only three U-boats, two German and one Austrian, ever being sunk after becoming ensnared in drifter nets, even though the RN deployed hundreds of such vessels in both British and Mediterranean waters.[42] As much as Hatcher might take issue with Hose's knowledge of the proper tactical deployment of drifters, the entire technical debate was largely meaningless in a Canadian context. In fact, the captain of patrols demonstrated greater insight by contending that the RCN should exchange all 100 Canadian-built drifters for some additional trawlers, a measure that he believed would provide sufficient vessels to sweep in front of convoys as they transited the Grand Banks.

> As regards the scheme of patrolling with paravanes ahead of convoys leaving Sydney. If these convoys did, after reaching the 100 fathom line off Sydney, shape course over 200 miles south of Cape Race to skirt the Newfoundland Banks, undoubtedly it would be unnecessary to utilize our patrol vessels for paravane sweeping in front of them, but the fact at present is that these "slow convoys" of thirty vessels do invariably cross the Newfoundland banks at pretty regular intervals of eight days, and so long as that is the case, I do think that paravane sweeping ahead of them is important....
>
> As I say, the whole question seems to me, since the number of drifters has been reduced so greatly, to be as follows: Whether you get, on the whole, a greater measure of defence for the shipping on this coast from fifty drifters and sixteen Admiralty trawlers plus the Canadian vessels, or from twenty-four Admiralty trawlers plus the Canadian vessels. Also, if the former is decided upon, whether it is advisable to split the drifters by detailing twenty-five to each port, or to utilize them all off Sydney.[43]

For the most part, Admiral Browning shared the prevailing British view about the value of drifters and endorsed Hatcher's scheme although he wanted to see the drifters deployed some three to four miles further out to sea than the British captain had suggested. The

---

41. Hose to Kingsmill, 8 October 1917, 1017–10–3, pt 1, LAC, RG 24, vol. 3832.

42. Paul G. Halpern, *A Naval History of World War I* (Annapolis 1994),160; and Dwight R. Messimer, *Find and Destroy: Antisubmarine Warfare in World War I* (Annapolis, Maryland 2001), 42–43, 82–85.

43. Hose to Kingsmill, 8 October 1917, 1017–10–3, pt 1, LAC, RG 24, vol. 3832.

commander-in-chief also expressed a preference for the swept channels he had recommended the previous March, and believed that the long, narrow channels that Hatcher wanted "entirely overlooked" the difficulty incoming ships would experience in finding them, arguing that it was "too much to expect that incoming vessels will be able to arrive at arbitrarily fixed points on the 100-fathom line." Browning also preferred his own minesweeping plan for Sydney, a scheme that Commodore Coke had put into effect in June, and "recommended that additional vessels as they become available should be employed on an extension of this scheme."[44]

In his memorandum to Kingsmill at the end of October, Commander Stephens—who had evidently also been influenced by the Royal Navy's general regard for the employment of drifters—was more supportive of Hatcher's proposals than either Browning or Hose. While the chief of staff recognized that the reduction of drifters from 100 to fifty "reduces the completeness of the defence," he still believed that twenty-five drifters at both Halifax and Sydney was "a defence not to be despised." He also recognized that incoming merchant ships might have difficulty locating the start of the swept war channel into each port "but at least outgoing ships could pass through it; whilst incoming merchant ships could communicate with the patrol vessel on the 100 fathom line and be directed to the channel." Stephens's only alteration to Hatcher's scheme was to fix the division of authority between the captain of patrols and the senior naval officer at Sydney "at extreme gun range from the outer ... battery, so that the naval and militia officers responsible for the safety of the port may be in a state of complete certainty as to the identity and occupation of all vessels within range."[45]

Having received responses from the main officers concerned, Admiral Kingsmill passed Hatcher's report to the deputy minister on 30 October. The naval director, who shared Hose's skepticism of the relative effectiveness of drifters, explained that the captain of patrols had suggested "that the protection might be more efficiently carried out if, instead of using the drifters at all, the Admiralty would leave an extra number of trawlers that are building." In endorsing Hose's view that additional trawlers would offer better protection against submarines than any number of drifters, particularly in Canadian waters where fishermen had no experience in the use of drift nets, Kingsmill acidly observed that "any submarine approaching our coasts and suddenly seeing some ten or more small vessels not very far apart, knowing full well that fishing is not done by the drifter trawler on this coast, would give them a very wide berth." Moreover, while the Royal Navy could easily recruit British fishermen with drift net experience, the RCN would have to train the Canadian drifter crews from scratch since "we have not even got the men skilled in the drifter trawler work to recruit from." As futile as it seemed to Kingsmill to deploy drifters in Canadian waters, he wanted the entire question placed before the Admiralty "that they should be asked to give an opinion on the two schemes. I may say that we have not received any advice from the Admiralty on the questions of defence.... When it comes to spending a large sum of money,

44. Browning to Kingsmill, 13 October 1917, ibid.

45. Stephens to Kingsmill, 29 October 1917, ibid.

46. Kingsmill, "Memorandum to the Deputy Minister," 30 October 1917, ibid.

which this defence will mean, I consider that we should have proper advice."[46]

As the department's chief administrator, Desbarats asked if Kingsmill would, in the meantime, prepare an "approximate estimate" of the cost of the defence scheme for the minister's information.[47] The naval director was willing to make "a rough estimate" but insisted that a final defence scheme could only be drawn up after the Admiralty's views on the subject were obtained:

> I desire to point out, however, that the naval policy of Canada has never yet been clearly defined. The Admiralty, some two years ago [in fact, twelve months previously], said they considered thirty-six patrol vessels on the Atlantic coast were necessary, but gave no reasons for their opinion or remarks as to their disposition or use. Later they asked if Canada could build 100 drifters and thirty-six trawlers, not saying for what purpose and it has been assumed by the officers the Admiralty have sent out that they were to be used for defence of these coasts, but the department has never had any information as to their views. At any rate it now seems that they consider a less number necessary for they have withdrawn fifty drifters and sixteen [in fact, twenty] trawlers.
>
> I do not think any satisfactory decision can be come to until the department and the Admiralty work in real co-operation. The department desires to know:
> What are the probable chances of an attack on the Canadian coasts?
> What is the probable scale of this attack?
> What scale of defence does the Admiralty recommend the department to adopt?
> What is the Admiralty prepared to do in the case of such attack?
> Until answers are given to these questions no scheme with a sound basis can be undertaken by the department.
> I therefore recommend that immediate steps be taken to ascertain from the Admiralty their views on these matters, as the department is not in a position to obtain it otherwise.[48]

In emphasizing the vacilliting—or nonexistent—nature of the Admiralty's advice on Canadian naval defence, Kingsmill was again reflecting NSHQ's exasperation with Whitehall's inability to provide firm answers to what were, after all, reasonable questions for a dominion navy to ask. To make proper preparations, Canada's naval service clearly needed something more concrete and consistent than the Admiralty had provided to date.

Although Desbarats had offhandedly suggested earlier in October that Hatcher might be sent to England "to influence the Board [of Admiralty] to agree with his scheme," Kingsmill did not trust the British officer's opinions and insisted that Captain E.H. Martin

---

47. Desbarats minute, 31 October 1917, on ibid.

48. Kingsmill, "Memorandum for the Minister," 12 November 1917, ibid.

also be sent to London as the RCN's main spokesman. As the director described, the captain superintendent was "well aware of the difficulties of obtaining stores" from Britain and would, therefore, be better suited to take "this matter up on our behalf with the Admiralty."[49] As was normally the case on questions of naval policy within the department, the deputy minister deferred to Kingsmill, and it was Martin who represented the RCN "in order that the Admiralty officials will have someone at hand who is in touch with local conditions, difficulties of purchases, etc."[50] The naval director communicated his instructions for the London trip to Martin on 17 November, explaining that the question of Canada's East Coast defence had been referred to the Admiralty "with a request that we may be given some advice." After reporting to the first sea lord, the captain superintendent was to hold himself "in readiness to attend such committee as may enquire into the subject." The naval director also made it clear that although Hatcher would be accompanying Martin to London before returning to duty with the Royal Navy, "it is most distinctly pointed out that he is there to explain his plans and does not represent the department in any way, and should not be brought to any meeting by you as an expert or as one who is in any way cognizant of local conditions in Canada." At the same time, Kingsmill cautioned Martin not to "express your opinion unless asked, but explain that you are there to be able to give information as to local conditions, and also to explain that what is wished for by the department is advice as to the best means of defence, taking into consideration the material with which we have to work, the difficulty of obtaining certain stores etc., and, not the least important, the necessity of economy."[51]

Since Whitehall had discouraged every proposal to have Canadian Vickers build either submarines or destroyers for the RCN, Ottawa was now pointedly asking the Admiralty "what steps they propose to take should there be an attack by submarines on the shipping sailing to and from Atlantic ports." The Canadian government wanted the Royal Navy to live up to its 1914 pledge to, in Sir Robert Borden's words, "take care of everything on [the] ocean,"[52] and Kingsmill undoubtedly hoped the Admiralty would send a few anti-submarine destroyers to Halifax or Sydney in the event U-boats began operating in Canadian waters. To that end, Martin was instructed that "it will be of advantage if you are able to state exactly what would be required at Halifax should they base destroyer divisions on that port. As we have already discussed this question, it is only necessary to state that the waters inside McNabb [sic] Island to the Eastern Passage seem well suited for establishing a base, but that time is necessary. Captain Pasco, with whom you will consult at Halifax before embarking, should furnish you with his views of Sydney as a suitable base. In both bases the facilities or otherwise for oiling [needed by destroyers] should be

49. Kingsmill, "Memorandum to the Deputy Minister," 30 October 1917, ibid.

50. Director of the Naval Service of Canada to Secretary of the Admiralty, 22 November 1917, 1017–10–1, pt. 1, LAC, RG 24, vol. 3831.

51. Kingsmill to Martin, 17 November 1917, ibid.

52. Borden diary, 13 November 1916, LAC, Manuscript Group (hereafter MG) 26 H, reel C-1864.

53. Kingsmill to Martin, 17 November 1917, 1017–10–1, pt. 1, LAC, RG 24, vol. 3831.

pointed out."[53]

At the same time that the Canadian government despatched its telegram looking for London's advice—or, more accurately, seeking a firm commitment from the Royal Navy to send destroyers to Canada in the event of attack—Kingsmill sent his own letter to the Admiralty to explain the situation in which it had placed the RCN. Just as the Canadian government had done one year earlier in venting its frustration with London's fickle advice,[54] and only four months after the British had tried to have Kingsmill removed from his post, the naval director's annoyance spilled over as he placed the complete litany on the table. Observing that the imperial government had never "clearly advised the dominion government as to what the Admiralty expected of the Department of the Naval Service of Canada in the way of offensive or defensive measures," Kingsmill proceeded to update their lordships on the correspondence regarding Canadian defensive measures that had passed between NSHQ and the Admiralty during the previous twelve months.[55] Specifically, the naval director pointed to the lack of information provided by Whitehall concerning the intended deployment of the trawlers and drifters being built in Canada on imperial account. Although "several telegrams were sent," the Admiralty had never given "any hint" to Ottawa that "these vessels were for use in the western Atlantic, or were to form part of the Newfoundland and Canadian patrol." Kingsmill reminded their lordships that when he had arrived in the spring of 1917, Commodore Coke had stated that the trawlers and drifters were meant for the RCN but "his statement to that effect was the first that was known here that these vessels were to be utilized on these coasts, nor have the department yet heard from the Admiralty direct that this was ever their intention. There were certain arrangements made as to manning these drifters and trawlers which led the department to suppose they were intended for other waters, and several questions as to the disposal of the drifters asked by telegram still remain unanswered." Accordingly, when Captain Hatcher—whom Kingsmill criticized as being "evidently … not very well up in the use of paravanes for small ships"—drew up his proposed defence scheme, he assumed that the Canadian patrol force would incorporate the 100 drifters and thirty-six trawlers in addition to the RCN's auxiliary patrol vessels only to have London withdraw the first fifty drifters and twenty trawlers for overseas employment. It was "this last action, taken into consideration with all that had gone before" that had now convinced the Canadian government to seek a definite answer from London.[56]

In urging a reply to Ottawa's questions, Kingsmill stressed that Whitehall not forget the inexperienced manpower pool upon which the RCN would have to draw in any further expansion:

> The officers in command of the vessels of the Canadian patrol have had, with two exceptions, no knowledge of naval matters prior to the outbreak of

54. Desbarats to Under Secretary of State for External Affairs, for transmission to British Secretary of State for Colonies, 17 November 1916, NSC 1065–7-2, pt. 1, LAC, RG 24, vol. 4031.

55. DNS to Admiralty, 22 November 1917, 1017–10–1, pt. 1, LAC, RG 24, vol. 3831.

56. Ibid.

hostilities, while there is no exception in the case of the other officers.

With regard to the ratings, the majority of petty officers are ex-RN, while the remainder are in most cases volunteers from all ranks of life—from sea life very few.

With this material, unless it is possible to lend more persons competent to instruct them in the methods in vogue as to the use of nets, depth charges, paravanes, etc., not very much can be expected.

It is also requested that the department may be kept informed as to the developments in the use of hydrophones. It is regretted that we have no spare officer to send to England to obtain this information.[57]

As Kingsmill went on to explain, the RCN officer that he was willing to spare for the London trip, Captain Martin, was being sent "in order that the Admiralty officials will have someone at hand who is in touch with local conditions, difficulties of purchase, etc."[58]

In the event, however, Martin did not resume his duties at Halifax after returning from Britain. The decision to replace Martin as captain superintendent was effectively made in mid-November when the British convoy officer at Sydney, Rear-Admiral Chambers, was preparing to transfer his offices to Halifax as the HS convoy assembly port during the winter shipping season. Before the shift of offices, London sent a message to Ottawa proposing that the rear-admiral be "described as 'senior naval officer afloat, Halifax.'" The Admiralty claimed that the change in title was being made "in order that his position may not conflict with that of officers of the Canadian naval establishments at Halifax and at the same time to provide necessary authority and continuity of control in regard to convoy work," and insisted that Chambers's "relations with Canadian naval authorities and commander-in-chief, North America and West Indies station will remain as before."[59] Well-aware that port convoy officers came directly under Admiralty orders and conscious as ever of the importance of maintaining the RCN's control over Canadian shore establishments, Kingsmill believed that Whitehall's choice of title could only disrupt the proper chain of command at the port:

I cannot see how such action can lead to anything but unutterable confusion at Halifax, nor is it possible to see what advantage can be arrived at by altering the title of Rear Admiral Chambers from "convoy officer" to "senior naval officer afloat."

The senior naval officer afloat has charge of everything that is afloat in Halifax, including minesweepers and patrol vessels outside the port, or the title

57. Ibid.

58. Ibid.

59. Secretary of State for the Colonies to Governor General, 19 November 1917, 1048–48–1, pt. 3, LAC, RG 24, vol. 3772.

means nothing. It is most undesireable to have an officer coming from England to take charge over the heads of our officers who have been in Halifax and on the coast since the war and are cognizant of all local conditions. The statement that his relations with the Canadian naval authorities will remain as before cannot be understood.

Submit that the following reply be sent to Mr Long: "Reference to your telegram nineteenth November 1917 my ministers request that this matter may receive due reconsideration. It is not understood what advantage can be gained by the description of Rear Admiral Chambers as suggested as senior naval officer afloat at Halifax. As convoy officer at Sydney he has had the close cooperation of the Canadian naval officers and he will receive the same at Halifax."[60]

The Admiralty responded by assuring Ottawa that they had proposed the title change "not at all with the object of interfering with the Canadian naval authorities, but in order that he should have control of any imperial vessels visiting the port in connection with escort work." In its place, the Admiralty now suggested that Chambers be described as "port convoy officer and senior officer of escorts Halifax" a title that received NSHQ's approval.[61] Nonetheless, the British proposals made Kingsmill wary of London's motivation in seeking an unnecessary alteration to Chambers's title in the first place. In the naval director's view, further action by the naval department was required if it was to ensure that the RCN's authority in Halifax would not be arbitrarily ignored by higher-ranking British officers "coming out from England to take charge over the heads of our officers."[62] Kingsmill's solution was to have the dockyard superintendents at Halifax and Esquimalt switch posts so that Vice-Admiral W.O. Story, promoted on the Royal Navy's retired list, would outrank every British officer on the Canadian East Coast, including Chambers. (Kingsmill, it will be recalled, had used Story's superior rank for a similar purpose at Esquimalt in 1914).[63] Besides placing an RCN vice-admiral on the East Coast, the move would also have the effect of relegating Captain Martin to the war's northeastern Pacific backwater. Kingsmill could not have forgotten the superintendent's duplicity the previous spring in suggesting to Vice-Admiral Browning that any problems at Halifax were the result of NSHQ's faulty administration, a perceived disloyalty that had contributed to the British effort to have him replaced as naval director.[64] In the event, however, the intended move had to be delayed for several months because Story's seniority on the Admiralty list meant that he would also outrank the current commander-in-chief, North America and West Indies Station. It was not until Browning was replaced in February 1918

60. Kingsmill to Desbarats, "Memorandum for the Deputy Minister," 21 November 1917, ibid.

61. Long to Governor General, 8 December 1917, Desbarats to Undersecretary of State for External Affairs, 12 December 1917, ibid.

62. Kingsmill to Desbarats, "Memorandum for the Deputy Minister," 21 November 1917, ibid.

63. Hadley and Sarty, *Tin-pots and Pirate Ships*, 91, 202.

64. Kingsmill to Captain Superintendent, 30 May 1917, 1001–5-3, pt 1, LAC, RG 24, vol. 6194.

that Story could be sent to Halifax in a junior capacity to the incoming C-in-C.

The Canadian department's sensitivity to Admiralty encroachment had already been heightened at the end of August when London belatedly decided to close down the intelligence centre at St John's, and shift its responsibilities to both Halifax and Bermuda. The decision was prompted by Chambers's winter move to Halifax and the port's importance to the North Atlantic convoy system. As will be recalled, the Canadian naval director had objected to the St John's centre when it was initially established in October 1914 and suggested that it would be far more efficient to retain Halifax as the intelligence centre for the western North Atlantic. Whitehall had responded at that time by informing Kingsmill that "from the point of view of the Admiralty, St John's is the most convenient position for intelligence centre in North Atlantic and it is considered inadvisable to abolish it and replace it by Halifax whilst the war is in progress." As we have seen, that reply was less than truthful, the main objective having actually been to "retain" Admiralty control and "avoid friction with Canadian naval authorities."[65] Now, however, an internal Admiralty memorandum by the director of the intelligence division admitted that Halifax was "more conveniently situated," and, in addition to receiving the same information from US ports as St John's, was also provided with information "from Canadian reporting officers."[66]

For Kingsmill, at least, the background to this *volte-face* was deliciously ironic since it had been prompted by late-August complaints from the Admiralty that the Canadian naval staff officer at Halifax had failed to forward an important message on ships' routing to Admiral Browning.[67] Having argued against the decision to establish the main intelligence centre at St John's in the first place, the Canadian naval director exhibited palpable delight when he explained that it was by Admiralty decree that St John's, and not Halifax, was responsible for forwarding London's correspondence to Browning:

> In this connection I beg to draw attention to the correspondence between the Admiralty, the Foreign Office and the department in January to April 1915 regarding the proposed establishment of a naval intelligence centre at Halifax.
>
> In that correspondence it was finally agreed that as from the point of view of the Admiralty, St John's is the most convenient position for an intelligence centre in the North Atlantic, further proposals would be deferred until after the close of the war.
>
> It will therefore be realized that the Canadian naval staff officer, Halifax, is not responsible for communicating Admiralty instructions for reporting officers to the commander-in-chief, as this duty devolves upon the general staff officer, St John's.
>
> I need not add, however, that at all times the services of the Canadian naval

---

65. Director of Intelligence Division, 3 February 1915, Admiralty to Director of Naval Service of Canada, 4 March 1915, quoted in "Historical Section Summary, Papers Titled Treasury 19.9.14," nd, United Kingdom National Archives (hereafter UKNA), Admiralty (hereafter ADM) 137/1026.

66. Director of Intelligence Division, 2 and 10 October 1917, quoted in "Historical Section Summary, Papers Titled Treasury 19.9.14," nd, ibid.

67. Admiralty to Naval Ottawa, 29 August 1917, 1023–4-3, pt. 1, LAC, RG 24, vol. 3856.

staff officer, Halifax, are at the command of the commander-in-chief, and the desired information would have been furnished to the commander-in-chief had it been in the power of the Canadian naval staff officer to do so.[68]

Kingsmill's message to London quickly resulted in the general staff officer for the St John's centre, Major G.H.F. Abraham, Royal Marines, being despatched to Ottawa for a liaison visit. Furthermore, a telegram from Browning insisting that "the wording of Admiralty telegram ... of 29th August appears to have been misleading, in that it implied that I had made a complaint to their lordships that I had been 'unable to obtain' from the Canadian naval staff officer a copy of the Admiralty message in question."[69] On 5 October London asked NSHQ if it would have any objection to the St John's intelligence centre being abolished and "Halifax being recognized as naval intelligence centre for North America and communicating direct with Admiralty on all matters connected with naval intelligence. Any instructions sent direct from Admiralty to Halifax being repeated to naval department, Ottawa. If you concur, formal proposal will be made through Colonial Office."[70] Since the latest British offer appeared to correct the mistake made in 1914, Kingsmill immediately responded with his approval. Commander Eldridge in Halifax, meanwhile, was informed that the St John's centre was to be replaced by the naval staff officer's intelligence organization at Halifax and asked "what additional staff, if any, you will require" to carry out his new duties.[71]

When the Colonial Office proposal reached Ottawa in mid-October, however, it was instantly obvious that the Admiralty's views regarding control had not changed since their original objections to using a Canadian intelligence centre had arisen in 1914. According to the Colonial Office telegram, it was essential "for Admiralty to communicate direct with Halifax respecting all questions connected with naval intelligence as to which they would propose following arrangements. (1) Centre at Halifax with staff should be transferred from Department of Naval Service and placed under Admiralty as greater part of work done by the centre would be for the Admiralty and HM ships on the station. (2) Centre should keep Ottawa informed of all naval intelligence received by it which had not been already sent to Ottawa from other sources. (3) All instructions and intelligence sent by Admiralty to Halifax should be repeated to Ottawa. (4) All route instructions for merchant vessels should be sent by Admiralty to both Halifax and Ottawa latter undertake responsibility of distributing instructions route-giving officers in Canada (except Halifax) as at present."[72] In other words, as the Admiralty Intelligence Division admitted in its own internal documents, while Halifax would be "recognized as centre for North Atlantic," it

---

68. Kingsmill to Admiralty, 29 August 1917, ibid.

69. Browning to Kingsmill, 8 and 10 September 1917, ibid.

70. Admiralty to Naval Ottawa, 5 October 1917, ibid.

71. Naval Ottawa to Admiralty, 5 October 1917, Stephens to Navinet Halifax, 5 October 1917, ibid.

72. Colonial Secretary to Governor General of Canada, 16 October 1917, ibid.

73. Director of Intelligence Division, 2 and 10 October 1917, quoted in "Historical Section Summary, Papers Titled Treasury 19.9.14," nd, UKNA, ADM 137/1026.

would cease to be a Canadian organization.[73]

Kingsmill perceived immediately what was afoot and, soon after receiving the latest British proposal, cabled the Royal Australian Navy to enquire "if Australian naval intelligence centres are under Admiralty control or under that of [the Australian] Navy Board?"[74] Informed that the Australian centres were controlled by the Navy Board in Melbourne and not by the Admiralty,[75] Commander Stephens immediately set out the reasons why the issue was of such importance to the fledging RCN's future.

> On October 5th the Admiralty telegraphed the department asking if, in the event of the naval intelligence centre at St John's being abolished, there would be any objection to Halifax being recognized as the naval intelligence centre for the North Atlantic and communicating direct with Admiralty on all matters connected with naval intelligence.
>
> It has been the desire of the department ever since the outbreak of war that Halifax should be the naval intelligence centre for the North Atlantic as that is the logical place for it, whilst direct communication with the Admiralty and Halifax on naval intelligence matters has been the practice since outbreak of war. In consequence the department concurred in the Admiralty proposal [of 5 October].
>
> The proposal now put forward through the Colonial Office suggests, however, that control of the centre should pass from the department to the Admiralty, and is open to serious objection from the Canadian point of view.
>
> The department must have a naval intelligence officer at Halifax. The duties of this officer are inextricably mixed with those of Canadian officers, and it is therefore necessary that he should be under the department. The only solution than the present appears to be the establishment of two naval intelligence officers, one Canadian and one Admiralty, which is highly undesirable.
>
> I would also point out that the naval intelligence centre for the North Pacific is situated at Esquimalt and is under control of the department and not under the Admiralty.
>
> In reply to a telegraphic enquiry the Australian Navy Board states that Australian naval intelligence centres are under control of the Navy Board.
>
> The present proposals bring to the front an aspect of Admiralty policy, viz. Admiralty control in Canada, which is of some importance to the present and future welfare of the Canadian service. Little was heard of it whilst the war and its effects were more distant from Canada than now, but as operations extend so does the Admiralty move. The first important point in this connection was the establishing at Halifax of the naval control officer solely under Admiralty authority; the next was the establishing of the port convoy officer at Sydney

---

74. Naval Ottawa to Navy Board, Melbourne, 19 October 1917, 1023–4-3, pt. 1, LAC, RG 24, vol. 3856.

75. Dowsa [Melbourne] to Naval Ottawa, 21 October 1917, ibid.

also solely under the Admiralty. The present proposal is the third and is open to more objection than the other two inasmuch as it dislocates existing organization whereas there was no previous organization in the two other cases.

I am of opinion that this continuous process is very derogatory to the department and is the cause of difficulty and dissatisfaction amongst officers.

It is true that the department lacks experienced officers for these duties and must needs depend upon the Admiralty for their supply, but once officers are loaned it appears to me that the department should be fully trusted to see that they carry out their necessary duties, if there is to be any sort of cooperation between the two services.

The Admiralty has, of course, full command on the high seas, but in Canadian waters, it is necessary that the department should be supreme in all circumstances if the department is to be anything but a name only.

It is therefore recommended that whilst the department concurs in the other proposals, the Admiralty should be asked to reconsider their proposal to place the naval intelligence centre at Halifax under Admiralty control.[76]

In submitting the navy's views to the minister on 25 October, Kingsmill "entirely concur[ed]" with his chief of staff's comments while adding a few further objections of his own. The Admiralty's "plea that the greater part of the work done by the centre would be for the Admiralty and his majesty's ships on the station" had "come rather late," in the naval director's view, since that had been the case ever since the Canadian intelligence centre had been organized. He also did not like the British suggestion that Halifax "keep Ottawa informed of all naval intelligence received by it which had not been already sent to Ottawa," believing that such a vague arrangement "would only lead to mistake and uncertainty" as to which messages needed to be passed on to NSHQ. Kingsmill also reminded the minister that the intelligence centre at Halifax was entirely an RCN organization:

With the exception of the naval staff officer himself, all the officers of the staff are Canadians, trained by ourselves since the outbreak of war. They are all on Canadian pay and have their wives and families in Canada. If they were transferred to the Admiralty there would be a great deal of dissatisfaction on account of lesser pay, and we would be unable to train another staff.

Considering the amount of care and attention that has been given to form this intelligence centre and getting things in working order, by Commander Stephens and the staff, the proposal is hardly understood. My view of it is that this is a reply from the Intelligence Branch at the Admiralty to the fact that we have returned to England two officers whom they sent out as assistants, who turned out absolutely useless. The third sent out, a soldier, not at all conversant with naval terms and consequently of little use in a naval

---

76. Stephens, "Memo: For Director of the Naval Service," 22 October 1917, ibid.

centre, has applied to return to England.

I have lately been in Halifax, and the commander-in-chief of the North American and West Indian Station expressed his high opinion of Captain Eldridge and the staff operating the naval intelligence centre at Halifax. Had he desired any change, I am quite certain he would have expressed his views to me.

I would submit that the Admiralty be asked to reconsider the proposal expressed in the cypher telegram of the 16th October.[77]

Ottawa duly informed the Admiralty that Canada was prepared to undertake the naval intelligence work at Halifax in place of the St John's centre, assuring their lordships that the "naval department will be glad to continue to afford every assistance to Admiralty as in the past," but insisted that the organization would remain under RCN control.[78] With intelligence work having been efficiently carried out by the Canadian naval staff in Halifax since the outbreak of war, the actual "shift" of responsibility was simply a question of London's asserting its presumed authority. As the British themselves recognized, the Halifax centre already received the "same information as St John's from US ports and in addition receives reports from Canadian reporting officers and as Halifax is more conveniently situated than St John's the C-in-C makes use of former rather than latter."[79]

Despite the efficiency of the RCN staff and the obvious trust the C-in-C had in the Halifax centre, Whitehall was not prepared to accept the proven Canadian organization aboard *Niobe* unless it was directly controlled by the Admiralty. As though to confirm Stephens's astute observation about the Royal Navy's desire to control any Canadian establishments of importance, the Intelligence Division promptly rejected Ottawa's response: "Canadian authorities evidently do not intend to transfer control of intelligence centre at Halifax to Admiralty and reply is therefore not satisfactory. It is proposed to abolish St John's and transfer its duties to Bermuda, returning Halifax as an additional Canadian centre in this area."[80] The St John's intelligence centre was closed down on 29 December 1917.[81]

Given the trust Admiral Browning had placed in the Halifax centre and the breadth of information available there—the CNSO's organization also controlled the Canadian wireless stations along the coast (as it would the radio direction finding stations erected in 1918[82]),

---

77. Kingsmill, "Memorandum to the Minister," 25 October 1917, ibid.

78. Governor General to Colonial Office, 5 November 1917, quoted in "Historical Section Summary, Papers Titled Treasury 19.9.14," nd, UKNA, ADM 137/1026.

79. Director of Intelligence Division, 2 and 10 October 1917, quoted in "Historical Section Summary, Papers Titled Treasury 19.9.14," nd, UKNA, ADM 137/1026.

80. Director of Intelligence Division, 13 November 1917, quoted in "Historical Section Summary, Papers Titled Treasury 19.9.14," nd, ibid.

81. Admiralty to Foreign Office, 4 December 1917, [UK] to Governor of Newfoundland, 31 December 1917, quoted in "Historical Section Summary, Papers Titled Treasury 19.9.14," nd, ibid.

82. Department of the Naval Service, "Naval Intelligence Report No. 49, 3 December 1917, 552, DHH.

was fully aware of North Atlantic ice conditions, and was in routine communication with both NSHQ and port reporting officers throughout North America—this was a strict issue of control, and not of the competence of the Canadian intelligence staff. That important Admiralty messages might be transmitted only to out-of-the-way Bermuda with no guarantee that they would be repeated to the convoy hub at Halifax seems not to have entered the Admiralty's calculations. But in the end, it was that isolation that counted. In October 1918 the C-in-C, North America and West Indies Station observed that "Bermuda is singularly isolated and the naval intelligence officer, when there, has little else to do." By then, however, Halifax was not the obvious alternative; rather, the C-in-C asked whether the centre could be transferred to the US East Coast, because of "the great use made of New York ... by Allied men of war, and its facilities as a distributing centre."[83]

As valuable as local knowledge was to the intelligence files produced at Halifax, Naval Service Headquarter's relationship with the Canadian overseas transport organization gave it experience of North American transportation networks that was, perhaps, even more important in co-ordinating protection for the flow of Canadian war supplies to Europe. In 1916, the transport service had despatched some 2,145,000 tons with such efficiency that, as A.H. Harris proudly reported to Ottawa, "not one cent has been paid the railway companies for demurrage [reimbursement for delays in unloading freight cars] nor have vessels been detained waiting for cargoes."[84] Despite delays along the inadequate eastern Canadian rail network over the winter of 1916–17, the volume of imperial war supplies continued to increase as 1,169,644 tons were shipped from December 1916 to April 1917, 493,090 tons more than had been sent overseas during the same period in 1915–16. Most of the supplies, 700,353 tons, were loaded at St John, New Brunswick, while Halifax passed 340,180 tons of Canadian-produced war goods through its terminals. Congestion on the eastern railways, however, prompted the transport department to ship 84,887 tons through the American ports of Boston and Portland, Maine, and a further 44,224 tons from other Canadian ports, principally Vancouver.[85]

An important feature of the winter shipping was a decrease in the number of Admiralty-chartered transports assigned to the Canadian service, and the increased use of requisitioned space on commercial liners to carry war supplies. This was a partial response to the growing shortage of merchant tonnage in the wake of the Germans' unrestricted submarine campaign and reflected Admiralty attempts to reorganize shipping and place it on a more efficient footing world-wide. Whereas Canadian transports had previously been loaded with supplies bound for both Britain and France and off-loaded in both countries, much of the tonnage destined for British ports was now to be transported in commercial liners so that the vessels would only have to stop at one port. At the same time, the Admiralty also asked to have the liners coal at Sydney, Nova Scotia, rather than in Wales, where delays had proven endemic. Of the 101 ships loaded by the Canadian transport

83. Admiral W.L. Grant, General Letter No. 8, 1 October 1918, UKNA, ADM 137/504.

84. A.H. Harris, "Memorandum for Hon. J.D. Hazen," 18 January 1917, 1048-18-1, pt 1, LAC, RG 24, vol. 3713.

85. Harris to Desbarats, 12 December 1916, and 22 January, 8 February, 10 March, 11 April, and 14 May 1917, ibid.

department in March and April 1917, thirty-seven were liners, all but three of which were loaded at St John.[86] As Harris informed Desbarats in mid-April, "I should not be at all surprised if on the opening of navigation [to] Montreal, all transports were withdrawn except those destined to French and Mediterranean ports, that is the programme the War Office and Admiralty are now working on. The arrangement, I regret to say, adds considerably to our embarrassments and anxieties, but there is no help for it."[87] To be fair, the anticipated embarrassment and complications resulting from shipping companies' reluctance to carry some commodities in their liners was recognized by the British transport department, which assured Ottawa that the Admiralty would inform the liner companies that "they must carry in free space any particular consignments recommended by us through you."[88]

With the reopening of the St Lawrence in May, Montreal resumed its place as the dominant port in Canada. Over the seven-month summer shipping season, 2,447,096 tons of war supplies were loaded at Montreal for overseas shipment, including oats and hay, some 87.5 percent of the Canadian total of 2,798,369 tons shipped from May to December. St John and Halifax, in contrast, ranked a distant second and third with a mere 140,169 and 99,110 tons being shipped from each port, respectively, over half of which was loaded in May as the eastern railways cleared the winter backlog of supplies from their lines. The amount shipped was a 1,429,904 ton increase over the totals for the same period in 1916, an indication of the extent to which the Canadian economy had expanded to supply the war needs of the Allied powers. As Harris had predicted, a growing proportion of those shipments were sent on ocean liners—238 transports and 177 passenger liners clearing Montreal by the end of November. In all, 287 transports and 221 liners were loaded during the summer season, including several auxiliary cruisers loaded at Halifax before proceeding as part of a convoy's escort.[89] Such had been the expansion of the war effort that by the summer of 1917 fully 89 percent of all space in ships leaving Canadian ports was being requisitioned for government service.[90]

Despite the overall increase in war supplies shipped over the whole calendar year, there was a noticeable decline in shipments throughout the fall of 1917 from 457,487 in August to 264,979 in October. Queried by NSHQ in early December, Harris explained that "the diminution in tonnage is consequent on the transference of British purchasing power from Canada to the United States.... As an instance, I might say, that last year we were moving 40,000 tons of Canadian grown oats to France. This year no Canadian oats have been purchased. It was only by protesting to the [British] minister of shipping that I secured a

---

86. Harris to Desbarats, 11 April and 14 May 1917, ibid.

87. Harris to Desbarats, 19 April 1917, ibid.

88. Admiralty to Naval Ottawa, 619, 27 April 1917, 1048–17–1, pt 4, LAC, RG 24, vol. 3707.

89. Harris to Desbarats, 8 June, 11 July, 8 August, and 10 September 1917, 1048–18–1, pt 2, LAC, RG 24, vol. 3713; and Harris to Desbarats, 12 October, 13 November, and 20 December 1917, and 18 January 1918, 1048–18–1, pt 3, LAC, RG 24, vol. 3714.

90. Stephens, "Memo: For Director of the Naval Service and Deputy Minister," 18 July 1917, 1048–18–1, pt 2, LAC, RG 24, vol. 3713.

monthly movement of 18,500 tons of American oats through Canada on my agreeing to furnish cars for inland transportation. I mention this as one of many instances of which I had to deal with recently." The director of overseas transport pointed out that with the American oats shipped through Montreal, the November tonnage had increased significantly over the October totals to 417,862 tons.[91] He also proudly reported to NSHQ that since the beginning of the war there had "been no delay to vessels waiting cargo— excepting in two or three isolated cases at Halifax wholly beyond our control—nor has any demurrage been paid to railway or inland navigation companies."[92]

While NSHQ never questioned the efficiency with which Harris's organization moved the impressive totals of war supplies, both on the nation's railways and in loading ocean transports, it remained uneasy about its lack of administrative oversight of the CPR manager's operations even though the naval department was responsible for approving, both on its own account and that of the British government, all overseas transport expenses. With his friendship with Prime Minister Borden guaranteeing him powerful political support, moreover, A.H. Harris was not a man to shy away from increasing his own responsibilities, moves that usually meant an increase in the naval department's financial liability. Although the director of overseas transport had always kept Ottawa informed of the movement of supplies as a matter of routine, it was apparent that he consider this to be more of a courtesy than an operational requirement. For example, after discussions at the Admiralty in October 1916, Harris and his British counterpart had agreed that information about munitions contracts placed in Canada would be communicated directly between them, without the need to inform NSHQ.[93] While the Canadian naval department concurred in most of the arrangements Harris had made in London, Ottawa objected to any efforts at removing it from the information loop. Writing to the Admiralty in mid-December, NSHQ explained its belief that all Admiralty messages to and from Harris "should continue to be issued through the department as in the past," a measure "considered necessary in order that we may be fully informed at all times as to all particulars concerning the service."[94] The Admiralty's secretary, Graham Greene, agreed to pass all communications to Harris through NSHQ, provided that telegrams dealing solely with transport arrangements would be passed verbatim to the director of overseas transport, and assured Kingsmill that he would remain fully responsible for issuing all sailing orders and "for all matters relating to the safety and protection of the vessels."[95]

Considering the Admiralty's poor record of keeping the RCN informed of important issues affecting Canada, emphasizing such a stipulation was wise. Even as Whitehall passed

---

91. Stephens to Harris, 3 December 1917, Harris to Stephens, 5 December 1917, 1048–18–1, pt 3, LAC, RG 24, vol. 3714.

92. Harris to Desbarats, 5 December 1917, ibid.

93. "Memorandum of Proceedings of a Conference Held at the Admiralty on 3rd October, to Discuss the Arrangements During the Ensuing Winter for the Shipment of Munitions, Forage, etc. From Canada," nd, 1048–18–10, LAC, RG 24, vol. 3715.

94. Desbarats to The Secretary of the Admiralty, 15 December 1916, ibid.

95. Greene to Director of Naval Service, 20 December 1916, ibid.

on its assurances, it came to NSHQ's attention that the Admiralty was sending telegrams directly to Harris without any information being sent to the Canadian naval department. On 24 January 1917, the deputy minister once again wrote to Graham Greene complaining that although London had agreed that NSHQ would serve "as the sole medium of communication between Mr Harris and the Admiralty,… there has been a distinct departure from this course, the extent of which is not fully known." While assuring London that the RCN's relations with Harris "have always been most friendly and we fully recognize the excellent work he performed," NSHQ explained the reasons why "it is not considered advisable that the department should be wholly ignored" when it came to matters concerning the transport of war supplies overseas:

> Instructions regarding some matters continue to pass through the department as formerly, while on others the information is evidently forwarded direct to Mr Harris.
>
> A recent communication from him gives some particulars of expected movements of traffic, forecasting new features of the work and large increases of the [overseas transport] service of which the department has received no notification whatever. You will readily understand that this state of matters cannot continue without resulting in confusion, friction and loss of efficiency.
>
> The acting director of overseas transport has been under a very great strain for many months and should his health be effected as has happened in the past, the department would be called on to exercise a much greater supervision during his absence. Outside parties and other departments of the government look to me for information and settlement of questions which arise from time to time regarding conduct of the service. The department is also responsible for the payment of all claims on account of the service incurred on this side of the Atlantic. For these reasons, which appear good and sufficient, it is necessary that we should be fully informed of all Admiralty instructions in the matter. The most suitable way to obtain this information appears to be that we should remain the sole medium of communication on all questions regarding the service as in the past.
>
> Another action which I would deprecate is the practice of sending copies to Mr Harris of Admiralty letters to this department concerning matters of policy.[96]

The Admiralty, however, had evidently changed its view on its preferred method of communication with the Canadian transport organization. While acknowledging "that certain telegrams dealing with the requisitioning of space in liners for the conveyance of munitions were inadvertently sent direct to Mr Harris without repetition to your department," London asserted that communicating directly with the director of overseas transport and simply repeating such telegrams to Ottawa "frequently results in the saving of time and my lords hesitate to discontinue this practice." Although Greene assured

---

96. Desbarats to The Secretary of the Admiralty, 24 January 1917, ibid.

Pierre Le Moyne d'Iberville's ship *Pelican* exchanges broadsides with HMS *Hampshire* during their engagement in Hudson Bay on 5 September 1697. (Peter Rindlisbacher)

"A most efficient landing party from an overwhelming fleet." Francis Swayne's depiction of Vice-Admiral Saunders's warships landing Wolfe's men at Anse au Foulon above Quebec on the night of 12/13 September 1759. (LAC C-002736k)

The Provincial Marine vessels *Queen Charlotte* and *General Hunter* bombard Fort Detroit in support of Major-General Isaac Brock's crossing of the Detroit River on 16 August 1812 in the campaign that captured the American fort. (Peter Rindlisbacher)

The Provincial Marine vessel *Royal George*, sheltering under the guns of the Kingston shore batteries, exchanges shots with Commodore Isaac Chauncey's flagship USS *Oneida* (right) and the rest of the American squadron on 8 November 1812. It was the only naval engagement of the war fought within sight of Kingston. (Peter Rindlisbacher)

The climax of the Battle of Lake Erie on 10 September 1813 as the brig USS *Niagara* cut across the bows of the two entangled Provincial Marine ships, *Queen Charlotte* and *Detroit*. The American formation's broadsides, double-shotted at close range, finished Barclay's squadron as a fighting force. (Peter Rindlisbacher)

US Ships *Sylph* (left) and *General Pike* of Chauncey's squadron take advantage of their longer-range cannon to fire on the becalmed warships of Sir James Yeo's squadron (from left to right) *Melville*, *Royal George*, and *Sir Sydney Smith*, off the Genesee River on 11 September 1813. (Peter Rindlisbacher)

The climactic moment of the 28 September 1813 "Burlington Races" engagement west of York, when Chauncey's USS *General Pike*, having partially dismasted Yeo's *Wolfe*, is prevented from inflicting further damage by *Royal George* cutting between the two flagships and firing broadsides in the rising gale. (Peter Rindlisbacher)

Sir James Yeo's 1814 squadron close hauled in line ahead formation with HMS *St Lawrence* leading, followed by HM Ships *Princess Charlotte, Earl of Moira, Montreal, Niagara, Lord Melville, Star,* and *Sir Sydney Smith.* (Peter Rindlisbacher)

HMCS Niobe, by D. Landry, from the Canadian War Museum's Beaverbrook Collection of War Art. (CWM 19860286-001)

Rainbow *at Esquimalt* by Peter Rindlisbacher, courtesy of the artist.

Convoy in Bedford Basin by Arthur Lismer, from the Canadian War Museum's Beaverbrook Collection of War Art. (CWM 19710261-0344)

Protecting Our Commerce by William Birchall, from the Canadian War Museum's Beaverbrook Collection of War Art. (CWM 19870087-002)

Desbarats "that any important letters involving discussions on matters of policy will, as before, be sent to the department only,"[97] that was little consolation to NSHQ.

There was, of course, never any question of the tremendously difficult job the director of overseas transport had taken on in 1914 or the effectiveness with which he and his staff in Montreal had handled the task. With the transport service continuing to expand over the summer 1917 shipping season, the navy's chief of staff once again set out the problem inherent in the RCN's relationship with the transport director in a memorandum to Kingsmill. Stephens emphasized that Harris had created "a thoroughly well-organized concern and any considerable disturbance in it would probably be disastrous to efficiency" but nonetheless felt that the time had come to make the director of overseas transport and his staff, all of whom were still employees of the Canadian Pacific Railway, civil servants within the naval department. Harris's position with the CPR placed him in a serious conflict of interest since he determined how much government business each railway company received, including CP's competitors. By severing Harris and his organization's direct tie to the CPR, the navy's chief of staff believed it would eliminate the "great source of friction between the department, the director overseas transport and the shipping companies, and is the more anomalous now that practically all freight space in ships of all lines is requisitioned."[98] Harris's personal friendship with the prime minister, together with the undeniable efficiency of his organization, made it unlikely that such recommendations would be acted upon at the ministerial level. Indeed, Kingsmill acknowledged as much—and reflected his own jaded experience of Ottawa politics—when he passed on Stephens's views to the deputy minister, adding that it was "better the transport should be handled by the CPR board than by political appointees."[99]

If Harris was aware of the naval department's concerns about its responsibility for an organization over which it had no real control, he did not allow it to bother him or to keep him from further expanding his own responsibilities. As the increasing movement of US Army troops to France began to overwhelm the available liners departing American ports in the fall of 1917, the British Ministry of Shipping representative in New York, Captain Connop Guthrie, suggested that the overseas transport offices in Montreal should keep them informed of any liner accommodation in British liners sailing from Canadian ports that could be made available to the United States. If the Americans wished to make use of the space, Guthrie would then make the arrangements through the CPR offices in Montreal. Harris immediately suggested that he also be made responsible for arranging all Canadian troop reservations on liners, a proposal he insisted was needed in the interests of efficiency but one that would also supplant the procedure that had been in place since the outbreak of war whereby the militia department in Ottawa made its own arrangements with the steamship companies and then informed NSHQ. Without consulting either the naval or militia departments, Harris asked

---

97. Greene to Desbarats, 5 March 1917, ibid.

98. Stephens, "Memo: For the Director of the Naval Service and Deputy Minister," 18 July 1917, 1048–18–1, pt 2, LAC, RG 24, vol. 3713.

99. Kingsmill minute, nd, on Stephens, "Memo: For the Director of the Naval Service and Deputy Minister," 18 July 1917, ibid.

Guthrie to contact the Admiralty so that "instructions should be issued through the proper channels to the militia department, Ottawa, making it necessary for space for Canadian troop reservations on liners to go through his [i.e., Harris's] office." The Canadian transport director then issued his own instructions to the shipping companies for all troop movements "and advised the naval and militia departments at Ottawa of the arrangement." Even though his proposal had been made without reference to Ottawa, Harris was clearly unhappy when he informed Guthrie in early December that "the arrangement ... is not being carried out by the naval department." Asserting that he did "not propose to take on any additional responsibility which is not clearly defined," the transport director asked Guthrie to "discontinue referring any questions on this subject to my office," and deal "only with the naval service."[100] In keeping with the militia department's long-standing insistence on handling its own troop movements, NSHQ continued to coordinate reservations for CEF drafts overseas, while "working in close touch" with Guthrie in New York whenever accommodation became available for US troops.[101]

Harris's willingness to act unilaterally prompted Desbarats to inform the transport director that, "when desirous of approaching the Admiralty with regard to this department's actions, I should be glad if in future you will be good enough to approach the department first, in order to ensure that your proposals are in harmony wth the policy of the department, rather than subsequently as in the present instance."[102] Commenting within the department on the latest Harris attempt at by-passing government channels, or even keeping the departments concerned informed of his proposals, J.A. Wilson expressed his support for the idea of finally placing the overseas transport organization officially within the federal government:

> Mr Harris is more or less of a free lance. Neither he nor his staff are paid by the government. His arrangements with other governments are made independently of the Canadian government and without their knowledge or consent in advance, so far as is known, and at times conflict with proposals made on behalf of our authorities. He takes the initiative continually in regard to proposals for the extension of his activities and limitation of ours and other Canadian government authorities and corresponds direct with the authorities of other governments on matters of policy affecting the Canadian government.
>
> Any shadowy authority which they may have exercised at one time over the director of transport's organization has vanished long ago except as regards the financial responsibility for all expenses he may incur, for which, needless to say, the imperial government requires our certificate and approval. We remain, in effect, financially responsible for transactions over which we have no control.[103]

---

100. Harris to Guthrie, 4 December 1917, 1048–17–29, ibid.

101. Naval Ottawa to Admiralty, 17 December 1917, ibid.

102. Desbarats to Harris, 30 November 1917, ibid.

103. J.A. Wilson, "Memo: To Chief of Staff," 23 November 1917, ibid.

The director of stores emphasized that "criticism of Mr Harris or his organization is very far from my mind" but argued that "the only solution so far as can be seen is to bring Mr Harris with his staff into government service and appoint him regularly as head of a new department, or branch of this one, with clearly defined duties. This need not conflict with his present activities nor lessen his authority or the efficiency of his organization in any way, rather the reverse as added force would be given to his decisions."[104] Even as Wilson's memorandum was being circulated in Ottawa, a catastrophic explosion in Halifax would finally lead to a resolution of the director of transport's relationship with NSHQ— while also dealing the navy's reputation with the Canadian public a serious blow.

Although the first of the Halifax convoys had only been organized on 21 August 1917, the Royal Navy had shifted the examination port for all neutral vessels loaded in American ports, and bound for either Holland or Scandinavia, to the Nova Scotian capital in February of that year.[105] Besides the Scandinavian traffic, merchant vessels chartered by the Belgian Relief Committee had, since April 1917, been given safe conduct passes by the German government, through the Swiss consul general in Montreal, before clearing Canadian ports.[106] One such vessel, the Norwegian-registered *Imo*, arrived in Halifax in early December 1917 to coal before proceeding to New York. Delays in loading the coal, however, prevented the former Cunard liner from departing on schedule on the 5th, and it was not until the examination officer opened the port's boom defences the next morning that the ship would be able to sail. Also on the afternoon of the 5th, a French freighter, the 3,121-ton *Mont Blanc*, arrived at the examination anchorage after proceeding singly along the eastern seaboard from New York. Boarded by one of the RCN's examination officers, an RNCVR mate, *Mont Blanc* had been loaded in the American port with 3,000 tons of wet and dry picric acid, TNT, and gun cotton. In addition, drums of flammable benzol were stacked three or four high on her fore and after decks. With insufficient light remaining to navigate the Halifax Harbour channel safely into Bedford Basin that day, *Mont Blanc* was instructed to remain in the examination harbour until the next morning.[107]

At 0730 hours on the bright, clear morning of 6 December, *Mont Blanc* was given permission by the examination service to proceed through the Halifax channel, the second vessel to make the transit into Bedford Basin that morning. With Francis Mackey of the Halifax pilotage service on the bridge to assist her captain, Aimé Le Médec, the French freighter proceeded at a cautious four knots—one knot below the channel's speed limit— through the two anti-submarine booms and into Halifax Harbour. As *Mont Blanc* was progressing along the city's waterfront, the Belgian relief ship *Imo* weighed anchor at 0810 hours and began to manoeuvre her way past the many merchant ships in Bedford Basin

---

104. Ibid.

105. Admiralty to Naval Ottawa, 16 February 1917, Naval Ottawa to Admiralty, 16 February 1917, Admiralty to Browning, 17 February 1917, UKNA, ADM 137/583; and Department of the Naval Service, "Naval Intelligence Report No. 9," 26 February 1917, 95, DHH.

106. Department of the Naval Service, "Naval Intelligence Report No. 14," 2 April 1917, 148.

107. J.G. Armstrong, *The Halifax Explosion and the Royal Canadian Navy: Inquiry and Intrigue* (Vancouver 2002), 29–30.

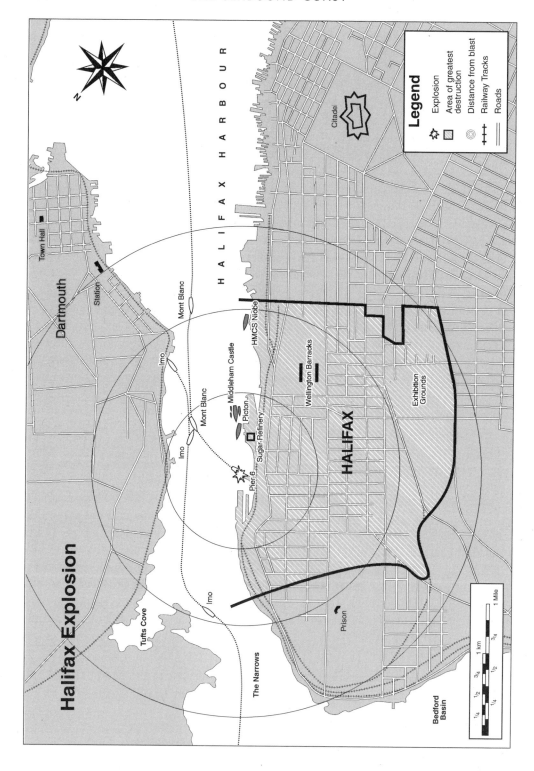

Halifax Explosion

Legend

✩ Explosion

▨ Area of greatest destruction

◎ Distance from blast

┼┼┼ Railway Tracks

══ Roads

Dartmouth

Town Hall

Station

HALIFAX HARBOUR

Mont Blanc

HMCS Niobe

Citadel

Imo

Middleham Castle

Mont Blanc

Picton

Sugar Refinery

Pier 6

Wellington Barracks

HALIFAX

Exhibition Grounds

Imo

Imo

Tufts Cove

The Narrows

Prison

Bedford Basin

¼ ½ ¾ 1 km

¼ ½ ¾ 1 Mile

under the guidance of another Halifax pilot, William Hayes. After being delayed in coaling the previous day, *Imo* appeared anxious to make up for lost time and increased speed to seven knots as she cleared the basin's anchored vessels and headed for the Halifax channel. Picking up even more speed—according to one sailor who witnessed the event "going as fast as any ship he ever saw" in the channel—the Belgian vessel inexplicably proceeded south into the Narrows along its eastern, or Dartmouth, side, the same side along which *Mont Blanc* was now slowly steaming north. Although the internationally recognized convention is for ships to keep to starboard and pass each other along their respective port sides, *Imo's* reckless action brought the Belgian vessel onto a high-speed course directly toward the French ship. As *Mont Blanc* was abreast of the dry dock just north of the naval dockyard, the two vessels sighted each other and the French ship reduced her speed even further to "dead slow," whistling her intention to pass *Imo* to starboard in proper accordance with the rules of the road. For reasons that will forever be unknown, the Belgian ship whistled her intention to pass to the east of *Mont Blanc*—contrary to the widely accepted rules for navigation in channels or harbours—and continued at excessive speed on a collision course with the explosives-laden ship. Even after *Mont Blanc* again whistled that she would keep to starboard and steered even closer to the Dartmouth shore, *Imo* gave two more blasts to indicate that she wanted to pass the French ship on the wrong side. At the last minute both vessels took simultaneous avoiding action by swerving toward mid-channel and collided at 0845 hours abreast of Pier 6, half a mile north of the naval dockyard. *Imo's* bow cut into *Mont Blanc's* starboard side near her fore hatch, a relatively minor collision had it not ignited some of the ship's cargo, either the dry picric acid in the hold or, more likely, the contents of the benzol drums stowed on her upper deck.[108]

From the cautious manner in which *Mont Blanc's* captain had guided his ship toward Bedford Basin before the collision, Le Médec was obviously sensitive to the explosive cargo he was carrying. Hugging the Dartmouth shore and steaming at four knots, later reduced to "dead slow," the only other action he could have taken to avoid *Imo*, given the course and speed adopted by the Belgian ship, would have been to stop his vessel completely and reverse his engines. Once his ship was on fire, however, *Mont Blanc's* captain and crew demonstrated a cowardly disregard for the safety of anyone but themselves. Rather than calling to the engine room for full speed so that he could run his otherwise lightly damaged ship away from heavily populated Halifax—perhaps driving her aground in Tuft's Cove to the northeast—Le Médec and his crew quickly abandoned *Mont Blanc*, leaving the burning vessel to drift west onto Pier 6 and the city of Halifax. The crew took to their boats and rowed for the more distant Dartmouth shore in a successful effort to save themselves, but made no attempt to warn other vessels in the area or the people ashore of the

---

108. Armstrong, *The Halifax Explosion*, 32–35. During the inquiry into the explosion, an American explosives expert testified that it was more likely to have been the dry picric acid that initially caught fire since the benzol had been treated and was much less volatile. The explosives expert may, however, have underestimated the amount of heat that would have been generated by the grinding of steel hull against steel hull in a collision and, hence, the likelihood of the treated benzol igniting, which it certainly did, even if not providing the initial spark. Henry summation, 31 January 1918, 2120, "Investigation Mont Blanc and Imo Collision at Halifax December 1917," 1043, LAC, RG 42, vol. 597.

The shattered north end of Halifax in December 1917. Pier 6, against which the *Mont Blanc* came to rest before exploding, was located in the devastated area just above the first passenger car on the Intercolonial rail line. Pier 8 is still in use, with Tuft's Cove visible on the opposite shore. (LAC C-019945)

The wrecked Acadia Sugar Refinery with the Belgian relief ship *Imo* lying beached on the Dartmouth shore. (LAC C-019944)

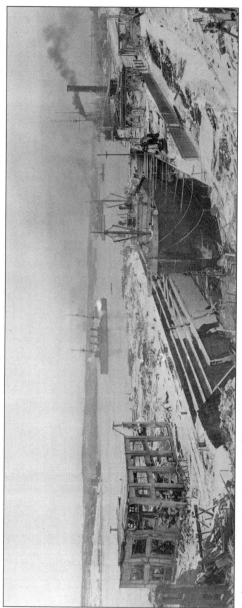

Looking south toward the dockyard with *Niobe* making smoke from one of its two remaining funnels and the cruiser HMS *Highflyer* lying in the channel. The merchant ship SS *Hovland* was in the dry dock at the time of the explosion. (LAC C-019953)

Imo remained beached on the Dartmouth shore throughout the winter of 1917–18. (LAC PA-138907)

imminent danger of the ship's cargo exploding despite passing within twenty feet of the RCN drifter *CD 73* on her way to assist the burning ship. Unaware of the immediate peril, other vessels and sailors made for the French ship in an effort to assist in putting out the fire. The RCN's Acting Boatswain Albert Mattison led a six-man crew to the stricken vessel in the *Niobe*'s steam pinnace and several of the Canadian sailors were seen climbing aboard *Mont Blanc* as she lay aground and ablaze next to Pier 6. The British cruiser HMS *Highflyer* sent the ship's whaler and a seven-man crew to assist. Understandably, the burning merchantman also drew many North-end Haligonians to their windows or directly to the waterfront to observe the firefighting efforts. Despite the heroic efforts of the RCN sailors, however, the French freighter exploded at 0904 hours in the largest detonation of manufactured explosives to that time.[109]

The massive explosion of *Mont Blanc*'s cargo killed some 1,600 people, most of them instantaneously, and injured another 9,000, many of whom were cut by flying glass as they stood at windows looking out at the burning ship. It also left some 6,000 Haligonians homeless in the heavily damaged northeastern section of the city. Given its proximity to the explosion, some 700 metres south of Pier 6, the naval dockyard suffered extensively. Although the *Niobe*'s upper works were severely impacted by blast, and the ship lost two of her four funnels, the static cruiser suffered no major structural damage. With many of the crew protected within the confines of the old cruiser's armour plating, only twenty-two Canadian naval personnel were killed or later died of their injuries, a number that included those attending to the burning freighter.[110] Captain Fred Pasco, the acting captain superintendent of the dockyard, was one of the sailors injured in the explosion and was temporarily replaced by Walter Hose as the senior Canadian officer in the port. The captain of patrols cabled NSHQ with a damage assessment later that evening: "Regret to report French munition ship *Mont Blanc* blew up at 9 am after collision with Belgian Relief ship in Narrows leading to Basin. Most yard buildings practically wrecked, certain number of service casualties and deaths but unable at present to report numbers or names. Understand Rear-Admiral Chambers has already reported that no convoy work or other operations can be carried out from Halifax at present. I concur in this. Damage to city very extensive and it appears that the town to the north [of the] dockyard is destroyed."[111]

The greatest destruction and heaviest casualties were among the unfortunate citizens of north Halifax. Their plight was made even worse by a strong snow storm that blew into the devastated city on the 7th, collapsing damaged roofs and hampering the massive relief effort that began almost immediately. Prime Minister Sir Robert Borden, in the midst of a federal election campaign, quickly hastened to the Nova Scotia capital remarking that "one cannot realize the force of the explosion or the extent of the destruction without visiting the scene. At least one square mile of the city is absolutely wiped out. Many of the houses which remain standing are so shattered as to be utterly useless without extensive

---

109. Armstrong, *The Halifax Explosion,* 37–40.

110. G.N. Tucker, *The Naval Service of Canada: Its Official History, I: Origins and Early Years* (Ottawa 1952), 231.

111. Navyard Halifax to Naval Ottawa, 6 December 1917, 37–25–3, LAC, RG 24, vol. 5634.

repairs."[112] Medical aid from other provinces arrived in the city by the evening of the 7th, while a hospital ship and medical teams were quickly despatched from the United States. The British government contributed £1,000,000 to the relief effort, while Ottawa eventually appropriated $15,000,000 and set up a commission to administer the funds.[113]

Once initial shock had worn off and senior naval officers had a chance to survey the damage—Admiral Kingsmill departed Ottawa for the Nova Scotia capital on the evening of the 7th—it was apparent that Halifax's main role as a convoy assembly port had not been greatly disturbed despite the city's devastation. Although Rear-Admiral Chambers had asked Ottawa on the 6th to "notify all centres that convoy work Halifax suspended,"[114] the situation was reassessed following a meeting of naval and transport officials two days later. On 9 December the British convoy officer cabled NSHQ that he considered "that convoy work can be carried on immediately" with the first convoy departing on the 10th.[115] NSHQ promptly agreed and notified all ports "to send ships to Halifax for convoy as usual."[116] The naval dockyard, which prior to the explosion had been barely capable of maintaining the RCN's own auxiliary vessels while assisting Browning's cruisers, had had most of its buildings either destroyed or rendered unsafe. The RCN's director of stores, J.A. Wilson, departed Ottawa for Halifax on the evening of the explosion to see for himself the damage that had been inflicted on the dockyard facilities. A week later Wilson was able to report that men and materials were arriving in the dockyard and that the "work would be rushed to completion."[117] By the 18th, the director of stores informed Ottawa that the "store office now open, routine business can be handled. Do not rush too much down all at once but let it come gradually, staff still short.... Main machine shop now running, other work progressing satisfactorily."[118]

As bad as the devastation had been in the area north of the naval dockyard, Wilson reported in mid-January that "the recent disaster at Halifax will not greatly effect" the port's operation. While the three piers located north of the dockyard, numbers 7, 8, and 9, had been destroyed and two piers south of the naval base, 2 and 3, were damaged in the explosion, the later two "were put in use again immediately. To replace 7, 8, and 9, facilities are being provided on the inner end of Pier A at the new terminals" along the harbour's southern end "which should take care of as much traffic as could be handled at the destroyed sheds at Richmond." Even with the new terminal, however, Wilson emphasized that the most important factor limiting Halifax's use as a shipping port remained the "inadequate single-track railway with heavy grades" that connected the port to the

112. Borden quoted in Tucker, *The Naval Service of Canada*, 230; and Robert Craig Brown, *Robert Laird Borden, A Biography*, II: *1914–1937* (Toronto 1980), 121–22.

113. Tucker, *The Naval Service of Canada*, 231.

114. R.A. [Chambers] to Naval Ottawa, 6 December 1917, 1048–48–1, pt. 3, LAC, RG 24, vol. 3772.

115. Halifax [Chambers] to Naval Ottawa, 9 December 1917, ibid.

116. Naval Ottawa to Navyard Halifax, 10 December 1917, ibid.

117. J.A. Wilson to Desbarats, 15 December 1917, 37–25–3, LAC, RG 24, vol. 5635.

118. Wilson to Naval Ottawa, 18 December 1917, ibid.

The victualling stores shed in the Halifax Dockyard following the 6 December 1917 explosion. (DND CN 3321)

Even those homes left standing in the north end of Halifax were heavily damaged by the blast. (LAC C-017501)

Canadian interior. Added to the inadequate rail connection was the fact that, even before the explosion, the port's facilities could not "be compared with those at other ports.... Arrangements could probably be made for the embarkation of as many troops as could be carried there by the railways," although "the other facilities of the port such as coaling, watering, etc., leave much to be desired. These factors, together with the inadequate railway connections limit the use of the port."[119]

For the Royal Canadian Navy, the Halifax explosion's greatest impact resulted from public reaction, both in terms of local fears of a repetition of the catastrophe and a more general desire to assign blame to someone in authority. With their city shattered, Haligonians were understandably apprehensive about any munitions that now passed through their port. On the morning of the explosion, rumours that a military magazine in the devastated area was on fire and about to explode prompted a mass stampede of terrified civilians (as well as some soldiers and sailors) to the open areas near the Citadel and to Point Pleasant Park further south. It was symptomatic of an understandable nervousness that would linger for several months. On 20 December the British port convoy officer, Rear-Admiral Chambers, notified the Admiralty that "in view of unrest amongst civil population [of] Halifax owing to passage of munitions ships through crowded harbour in close proximity of town, I submit that where possible vessels with large cargoes of high explosives from United States should always be despatched in Norfolk convoys."[120] In a subsequent report two weeks later, Chambers explained that there was still "much nervousness displayed" by Haligonians. "The nervous state of the community is evidenced by the report which came to me last Sunday night that a ship was on fire in the Bedford Basin, and that the people in the neighbourhood were leaving their houses and going into the woods, though the night was [a] bitter one, below zero and a blizzard blowing. A vessel sent to the Basin was unable to get through the Narrows in the blinding snow and went ashore. I have since been quite unable to discover that any fire actually existed whatever."[121]

To ease the public's anxiety, in early January NSHQ directed the captain superintendent, the recovered Captain Pasco, to implement a number of new regulations for the arrival and departure of munitions ships in Halifax Harbour. Upon arrival, ships carrying explosives were now anchored in the examination harbour until the chief examining officer was ready to escort them into Bedford Basin with his own tug. All other shipping was to be halted during this movement. On sailing, Rear-Admiral Chambers assigned munition ships their order in the convoy, and while the merchant ships made their way out of the basin, no other movement of ships was permitted. If a munitions ship had to change berth, the chief examining officer was to inform the captain superintendent who would not give his approval for a move until he was certain all other traffic had been stopped. As Pasco explained, the "duties assigned to harbour master in [the] old traffic regulations [have] not been carried out as he has no boat. These duties have devolved on chief examining officer."[122]

119. Wilson, "Memorandum," 24 January 1918, 1048–18–15, LAC, RG 24, vol. 3715.

120. Chambers to Admiralty (repeated to NSHQ), 20 December 1917, 1048–48–1, pt. 3, LAC, RG 24, vol. 3772.

121. Chambers to Admiralty, Report No. 105/18, 5 January 1918, UKNA, Adm 137/1620.

122. Kingsmill to Pasco, 18 January 1918, Pasco to Kingsmill, 18 January 1918, 1048–17–30, LAC, RG 24, vol. 3713.

The acting captain superintendent also informed Kingsmill of the precautions he had instituted for the loading of explosives onto merchant vessels, namely, that all hatches were securely battened down, that there was no smoking allowed on board and that all hoses were connected. Munitions ships were also required to have an officer of the ship and one quartermaster always on watch with a special watchman on duty at all times to see that the regulation prohibiting smoking was strictly carried out. It was the naval transport officer's responsibility to see that the regulations were complied with and the individual ship's captains were "to immediately report any untoward happening to the naval transport officer."[123] In asking Pasco to keep NSHQ informed of even the smallest events at Halifax that might cause public concern, Kingsmill outlined the political function of the captain superintendent's information, namely, that it "put the department in a position to relieve the minister of a great deal of worry and anxiety. Times are not normal with regard to Halifax. You must keep us informed of any untoward happenings."[124]

The "worry and anxiety" the naval director alluded to was a reference to the clamouring of the Halifax public and press to have someone held directly responsible for the 6 December catastrophe. As is always the case in a politically charged atmosphere, the new naval minister—Liberal C.C. Ballantyne had replaced J.D. Hazen as minister of the naval service in mid-October upon joining Borden's Union government—wanted the department's officials to ensure that none of the accusations being flung about Halifax were aimed at him. Ballantyne was not the only official anxious to avoid the public's wrath, however. In early January, Rear-Admiral Chambers confided to London that "the aftermath of the Halifax explosion still continues, and there is much nervousness displayed. The local papers are seeking for a victim to sacrifice, but so far they have kept (at least directly) from imputing blame to the Admiralty or the convoy system."[125] The British port convoy officer's concern that responsibility for the catastrophe might be attached to the Royal Navy was not without foundation. The loading of *Mont Blanc* with the dangerous combination of benzol and high explosives at New York had been done under the supervision of the shipping agents at that port. The explosives-laden ship had then been directed to Halifax for escort to Europe, by the Royal Navy's convoy officers. As the port convoy officer, Chambers had been as well-informed of *Mont Blanc*'s volatile cargo as anyone in the RCN, but the British officer had not issued any warning that special precautions should be taken in regard to the vessel. Both NSHQ and Chambers also knew that it was the dangerous loading of the French ship with her mixture of flammable benzol on deck and high explosives in the cargo spaces that had resulted in the fire following her collision with *Imo* and, hence, the explosion.[126]

The main forum available for Haligonians to concentrate their search for a "victim to sacrifice" was the public inquiry into the collision set up by the Department of Marine

123. Pasco to NSHQ, 24 January 1918, ibid.

124. Naval Ottawa to Navyard, 22 January 1918, ibid.

125. Chambers to Admiralty, 5 January 1918, UKNA, ADM 137/1620.

126. (Rear-Admiral Chambers), "The Halifax Explosion," *The Naval Review*, February 1920, VIII, No. 1, 445.

Liberal C.C. Ballantyne joined Borden's Union Government in mid-October 1917, replacing J.D. Hazen as naval minister. (LAC PA-005730)

immediately after the catastrophe. Although inquiries into maritime accidents involving loss or damage to ships or marine facilities were routinely held by the Marine department's wreck commissioner, under the authority of the Canada Shipping Act, public distress at the extent of the devastation and loss of life resulted in fervent press coverage of the Halifax inquiry's entire proceedings. The inquiry had the full support of Prime Minister Borden who, after touring the devastated city on 8 December, had instructed Ballantyne, the minister of marine as well as the naval service, to have the inquiry "instituted without delay."[127] It was chaired by Judge Arthur Drysdale, the local judicial representative of the Admiralty Division of the Exchequer Court of Canada. In view of the gravity of the situation and the intense public focus on it, Drysdale was assisted by the appointment of two nautical assessors: the dominion wreck commissioner, Louis Demers, and an experienced naval officer, the captain of patrols, Walter Hose. The marine department also appointed a prominent Halifax lawyer, William A. Henry, to serve as crown counsel to the inquiry. He was responsible for organizing the proceedings and conducting the initial examination of witnesses. Also represented by counsel in the proceedings were the shipping companies that owned *Mont Blanc* and *Imo*, the City of Halifax, and the Halifax Pilotage Commission, whose pilots had been in charge of the two vessels at the time of the collision.[128]

Once the inquiry began on 13 December, the lawyer representing *Imo*'s owners, Charles Burchell, proved to be particularly zealous in his efforts to divert responsibility away from the actions of the Belgian Relief ship. Despite the fact that the two men most directly responsible for the collision were the captain and pilot of *Imo*, Burchell skilfully used the fact that both had been killed when the *Mont Blanc* exploded—it was the lawyer's contention that it was against the tenets of British fair play to speak ill of the dead, a rather specious argument that was inexplicably accepted by the inquiry—to shift the focus away from the reckless actions of his client's ship and onto the conduct of others. The main cause of the explosion, the dangerous loading of *Mont Blanc* with benzol and high explosives by the New York shipping agents and her routing to Halifax by the Admiralty for convoy, was also quickly excluded from the inquiry's purview. It was the crown counsel's opinion that "no court of inquiry authorized by the Canadian government would have jurisdiction to investigate proceedings of the Admiralty."[129] As a result, it was decided that the Drysdale inquiry would be unable to look into the circumstances of the French ship until after her arrival in the Halifax examination anchorage. Henry's opinion meant that the investigation of witnesses would be confined to "the circumstances relating to the *Mont Blanc* from that time on, including the system governing the movement of ships in and out of the harbour, with a view to ascertaining whether that system adequately protected life and property in the areas surrounding the harbour."[130]

With the parties most responsible for the disaster, the captain and pilot of *Imo* and the

---

127. Borden to Ballantyne, 8 December 1917, LAC, MG 26 H, reel C-4325.

128. Armstrong, *The Halifax Explosion*, 117–22.

129. Henry to Alexander Johnston, Deputy Minister of Marine and Fisheries, 22 December 1917, 9704–244, pt. 1, LAC, RG 12, vol. 2827.

130. Henry to Johnston, 2 January 1918, ibid.

Admiralty, excluded from the inquiry's examination, the search for scapegoats quickly turned to the possibilities that remained: the captain and pilot of the French ship and any officer of the Royal Canadian Navy who could be connected to the disaster. In his examination of *Mont Blanc's* captain, Le Médec, Burchell effectively emphasized the uncontested fact that his only concern following the collision had been to save himself and his crew rather than steer his vessel away from the city's heavily populated North end or even provide a warning to those around him.[131] The line of questioning employed by *Imo's* lawyer played upon the public's anger at the French crew's spineless behaviour in hastily abandoning their ship and allowing her to drift against the Halifax shore.

Although the Drysdale inquiry was limited to examining only the events that had occurred within the confines of Halifax Harbour, it was apparent to NSHQ that the cause of the explosion was the decision to load *Mont Blanc* in New York with both flammable benzol and high explosives. Commenting on the nervous situation in Halifax in early January, and the excessive traffic precautions that had been adopted in an effort to calm the public's hysteria, A.H. Harris assured NSHQ that such a perilous cargo mix as *Mont Blanc* had carried was not permitted in Canadian ports. The director of overseas transport explained that "practically all liners carry a small quantity of explosives, but in no instance do we permit loading of inflammable material, such as petrol, and explosives on the same ship."[132] While such a dangerous practice was never allowed in Canada, Kingsmill sought assurances from the Admiralty that its representatives in the United States would never again send a ship as dangerously loaded as *Mont Blanc* into Canadian waters. A week before the Halifax inquiry resumed in late January, NSHQ telegraphed the Admiralty to request "that the authority who directs ships to assemble at Canadian ports for convoy may be instructed not to send any vessels whose loading has not been carried out under supervision that satisfies them."[133] On the same day, Kingsmill also telegraphed the British shipping representative in New York, Captain Sir Connop Guthrie, to demand that he be informed "who is responsible in US ports for the proper stowage of cargo in British and foreign merchant vessels."[134]

Captain Guthrie's response on 19 January indicated the degree to which everyone involved wanted to distance themselves from the catastrophe and pass responsibility onto others. The British officer admitted that "in case of liners, line agents, and in case of transports [such as *Mont Blanc*], my sub-agents render assistance [in] this matter but captains [of the individual ships] in all cases must bear the final responsibility."[135] While it is a truism that captains are ultimately responsible for their vessel's condition, Guthrie's response neatly ignored the wartime pressures on ships' captains to carry desperately needed supplies to Europe. It also did not absolve Guthrie from his role in allowing his

---

131. Armstrong, *The Halifax Explosion*, 124.

132. A.H. Harris, "Memo: For Chief of Staff, Dept. of the Naval Service," 3 January 1918, 1048–17–30, LAC, RG 24, vol. 3713.

133. Naval Ottawa to Admiralty, 17 January 1918, 1048–48–1, pt. 3, LAC, RG 24, vol. 3772.

134. Naval Ottawa to Amphibious, New York, 17 January 1918, ibid.

135. Guthrie [Amphibious] New York to Naval Ottawa, 19 January 1918, ibid.

agents to load merchant ships that would have to enter populated ports for both convoy and unloading with the dangerous mix of inflammables and high explosives. For its part, the Admiralty was more circumspect in its assurances to Kingsmill, merely stating that "attention to loading is being given."[136] To the naval director's credit, he kept his silence throughout the public furor that followed and refused to point the finger of blame in the Admiralty's direction.

Although NSHQ plainly understood the actual cause of the Halifax explosion and had instituted measures—indeed, an exaggerated degree of precaution for traffic within the harbour—both to restore public confidence and ensure that the disaster would not be repeated, the marine department inquiry was more interested in the responsibility of Canadian officials. By the time the first RCN officers were called to the witness stand in late January, the Canadian navy's likely or possible culpability for the disaster was being advanced by the Halifax newspapers. On 21 December, the more strident and sensationalist of these, the *Halifax Herald*, published a letter to the editor demanding that the Drysdale inquiry find out "where lays the ultimate responsibility for permitting such ships to come into our midst ... So far the naval department have preserved a judicious silence ... We now want the answers."[137] Even the more circumspect Halifax *Morning Chronicle* shared the public's belief that the RCN must have been negligent in controlling ship movements within the harbour: "The naval authorities have a large number of boats of various sorts at their command in this harbour, but so far as we have learned, none of them were employed in escorting the *Mont Blanc* on her way to Bedford Basin. Why? The public has a right to know, why these and other precautions which we might mention were not taken and, above all, why the risk of allowing these two steamers to meet ... was taken."[138]

The first naval officer to take the stand at the inquiry, the acting captain superintendent at the time of the explosion, Captain Fred Pasco, proved to be a composed witness who gave an unruffled performance under questioning and one of the few people who came to the heart of the matter in their testimony. Pasco derided the suggestion that munitions ships should carry red flags when approaching or leaving ports, stating that "it would be suicidal—giving information to enemy agents." He also pointed to *Mont Blanc*'s dangerous loading as the main cause of the explosion. Conceding that ship collisions were possible in any port, the naval captain insisted that such a happening should not present a grave danger, commenting that "I don't expect a ship to blow up because she has had a collision." Moreover, in preparing the regulations for the port of Sydney, Pasco pointed out that he had not felt it necessary to take special precautions for munitions ships, stating that "it certainly did not occur to me that a ship would be coming up a harbour like a piece of fireworks ready to be exploded."[139]

In retrospect, the captain superintendent's insightful comments largely explain why

136. Admiralty to Naval Ottawa, 19 January 1918, ibid.

137. *Halifax Herald*, 21 December 1917, quoted in Armstrong, *The Halifax Explosion*, 127.

138. Halifax *Morning Chronicle*, 20 December 1917, quoted in Armstrong, *The Halifax Explosion*, 127.

139. "Deposition of Frederick C.C. Pasco," 23 January 1918, "Investigation Mont Blanc and Imo Collision at Halifax December 1917," 1043, LAC, RG 42, vol. 597.

no special precautions were taken for *Mont Blanc* by either the Admiralty, Admiral Chambers, or the RCN's examination officers at the harbour entrance—there was no reason for any of them to suspect that the ship was in any danger of blowing up, even if she was involved in a collision, simply because she was carrying high explosives. After all, of the millions of tons of high explosives that were shipped overseas during the two world wars of the 20th century, only *Mont Blanc* exploded as a result of a collision. Unfortunately, Pasco's illuminating testimony was largely ignored by the inquiry's various lawyers as they searched for someone who could be held accountable for the disaster.

Pasco's calm demeanour and insight was not shared by the port's chief examination officer, however, when he followed the acting captain superintendent onto the witness stand. An increasingly nervous Commander F.E. Wyatt quickly proved to be his own worst enemy. Rather than sticking to the basic facts—there were no special regulations for the movement of munitions or explosives ships in British Empire ports, no one had told him that *Mont Blanc* required special treatment upon her arrival, there was no reason to contemplate a collision on such a clear, fine morning as 6 December—Wyatt fell into the trap of tacitly agreeing with opposing counsel that, in hindsight, he should have been sufficiently clairvoyant to recognize the danger posed by *Mont Blanc*'s dangerous loading and stopped all traffic while escorting the French ship to her berth in order to preclude any possibility of a collision. His weakness as a witness eventually allowed Burchell to badger him into giving contradictory answers that suggested that by allowing the French vessel to pass the anti-submarine nets and proceed into the harbour he had directly contributed to the explosion.[140] Wyatt's testimony ignored the fact that the extraordinary procedures the RCN had put in place for munitions ships following the explosion were not used in any other port in the British Empire and had been introduced primarily as a public relations exercise to calm jittery Haligonians. The examination officer also failed to explain that the main reason he received reports from the harbour's pilots about the movement of ships was for the opening and closing of the anti-submarine gates and to report to the Admiralty that merchant ships were at sea. Wyatt's uncanny ability to falsely incriminate himself on the witness stand included his own ludicrous suggestion that, had he known *Imo* was leaving Bedford Basin, he would have prevented her departure. In the end, the examination officer surrendered to the thinking behind most of the inquiry's proceedings, namely, that the magnitude of the disaster should, in itself, have made it possible for officials to see into the future so as to prevent the collision from taking place.

Although there was no evidence that anyone in Halifax—including Chambers, Pasco, and Wyatt—had thought that the arrival of *Mont Blanc* was sufficiently unusual to necessitate halting all traffic while the French freighter steamed up to the Basin, the examination officer's claim opened himself, and the RCN, to the charge that they had been lax in controlling harbour traffic. Wyatt's testimony that he would have stopped *Imo* on the morning of 6 December ignored Pasco's point that harbour collisions, while possible, should not result in ships exploding "like a piece of fireworks."[141] Sensing the

---

140. Testimony of Commander F. Wyatt, 23, 24 and 28 January 1918, ibid, 1091–98, 1197–1267, 1676–98.

141. "Deposition of Frederick C.C. Pasco," 23 January 1918, ibid, 1043.

public noose tightening around him as his testimony drew to a close on 28 January, however, the desperate naval officer felt driven to claim even greater clairvoyant powers by stating that "I had an idea or knew that something would happen, and I did not want to be the man to be made to suffer for it."[142] With so many of the inquiry's lawyers anxious to fulfill the public's desire to blame someone in authority, Wyatt's panic on the witness stand made him the obvious choice to meet Haligonians' demand for a Canadian scapegoat.

Wyatt's naval position, however, had already been dealt a fatal blow by a shipping incident that occurred during his first day in court. As examination officer, Wyatt was responsible for overseeing the navy's newly instituted regulations governing the movement of shipping within the harbour, specifically, the halting of all traffic whenever munitions ships were transiting to or from Bedford Basin. Before leaving for the courthouse on 23 January, Wyatt had supervised the departure of a large convoy from Halifax. One of the vessels due to sail with the convoy, the steamer *Galileo* with a cargo of shrapnel shells, had been delayed in coaling after an earlier fire in one of her bunkers. Following the passage of the last of the convoy vessels, except *Galileo*, out of the anti-submarine gates, Wyatt had raised the signal to allow those ships waiting outside the harbour to enter but neglected to hoist a signal to prevent *Galileo* from departing Bedford Basin. With Chamber's deputy, Captain James Turnbull, urging *Galileo* to sail as quickly as possible to join her convoy—the RN officer had already told Wyatt "something about taking a chance," an option which the examination officer refused to accept—the munitions ship subsequently entered the Narrows and passed an upward-bound oiler. Although Wyatt's assistant attempted to intercept *Galileo* and telephoned the harbour gates to prevent the entrance of any more vessels, the passing of a munitions ship with another vessel, as completely harmless as the incident had been, did not go unnoticed by the nervous citizens of Halifax.[143]

The yellow journalism of the *Halifax Herald*, meanwhile, was leading the public outcry against the navy's perceived ineptitude. In its 25 January edition, the newspaper vilified Wyatt as a bungling incompetent, demanding in its headline "That Commander Wyatt Shall Not Continue Another Hour in Charge of Halifax Harbour."[144] The *Herald* also renewed its call for Hose to retire as one of the inquiry's nautical assessors and ridiculed the "new regulations" that "had been framed and were being enforced by the Canadian naval authorities.... There is sufficient reason, yes imperative reason, for the suspension of Commander Wyatt before the sun sets today. But that was not all—the detailed evidence [at the inquiry] ... shows a rankness of inefficiency and an abundance of bungling which gives cause for wonderment that a disaster like that of December 6th, had not occurred before and has not since been repeated."[145] Contrary to the view of the *Herald*, *Galileo*'s cargo of shrapnel shells posed no danger of explosion, even in the unlikely event that she

142. Testimony of Commander F. Wyatt, 28 January 1918, ibid, 1688.

143. Armstrong, *The Halifax Explosion*, 144, 147.

144. *Halifax Herald,* 25 January 1918, quoted in Armstrong, *The Halifax Explosion,*154.

145. *Halifax Herald,* 25 January 1918, copy in 37–25–1, pt. 1, LAC, RG 24, vol. 5634.

had collided with the oiler. Nonetheless, it was clear that the RCN's own regulations had been violated as a result of Wyatt's inefficiency. When the rattled chief examination officer dissembled about the circumstances of the violation when questioned by Pasco, the captain superintendent, with Kingsmill's permission, promptly suspended Wyatt from further duty.[146]

The third senior RCN officer to testify at the inquiry was the former captain superintendent of the dockyard, Captain E.H. Martin. Having returned to Canada from his mission to the United Kingdom, Martin was despatched from Ottawa to account for the naval regulations and procedures in effect in Halifax before the explosion. Just as Wyatt had been led to do under questioning, the former captain superintendent also claimed remarkable foresight by agreeing that he would have recognized *Mont Blanc*'s arrival at Halifax as "an exceptional occurrence," and would have given the ship "a clear passage here, or else anchored her between the nets until there was a clear passage."[147] Martin's assertions blatantly ignored the fact that *Mont Blanc* was not considered exceptional by any other naval authority—including Wyatt—until *after* she blew up. By attempting to suggest that, had he been present, he would have prevented the accident by halting all other shipping, Martin foolishly played into the public's belief that naval mismanagement of harbour traffic was a key factor in the disaster. On the other hand, when specifically asked by crown counsel, W.A. Henry, whether he considered the newly instituted regulations prohibiting the simultaneous passage of two ships through the Narrows to be necessary, Martin replied: "I cannot see any difficulty in taking two ships up this harbour—there is plenty of room.... I have just come from Portsmouth where it is narrower than here, and there are ships of all descriptions passing in and out, and observing the rules of the road." In response to Henry's pointed question that "there is no such regulation there [in Portsmouth] as is proposed for here," in regard to ships carrying explosives or munitions, Martin simply stated, "the rules of the road governs it."[148]

In view of Wyatt's weak performance on the witness stand and, to a lesser extent, Martin's, it was left to the crown counsel to present the actual facts of the disaster in his summation. Given the public hysteria in Halifax, Henry showed remarkable impartiality—and courage—in addressing each of the main issues before the inquiry. He did not believe that *Imo*'s presence on the Dartmouth side of the Narrows could be justified. While the Admiralty's role in the disaster had been excluded from the proceedings, Henry also made a point of alluding to it in his summation. In response to those who had argued that the munitions ship should not have been sent to Halifax, he said that "if so, it was not the fault of the Canadian naval service. Perhaps this court cannot deal with the fault; that they got information this ship has been ordered here and it is their duty to receive her. They cannot say to the British empire or the Republic of France or the United States, we won't allow her to come here. She is ordered to Halifax to join the convoy; ordered by people who have

---

146. Pasco to Kingsmill, 25 January 1918, 521, 26 January 1918, 536, 1048–17–30, LAC, RG 24, vol. 3713.

147. Testimony of Captain E.H. Martin, 26 January 1918, 1590, Investigation Mont Blanc and Imo Collision at Halifax December 1917, 1688, LAC, RG 42, vol. 597.

148. Ibid.

the right to give orders to the Canadian naval service." Henry also directly attacked the underlying assumption of many of the lawyers' questions, most of the press' venom and, indeed, much of Wyatt's and Martin's own testimony, namely, that those in authority should somehow have had the foresight to prevent a freak accident from occurring:

> Commander Wyatt tells us that if he had happened to know that the *Imo* was coming out the next morning he believes he would have so arranged matters so that they should not have met in the harbour. But it is quite possible he would not. He is speaking after the event. He might very well have said to himself there is no reason to apprehend danger to this vessel, the harbour is wide, she is not going up until daylight in the morning, I will keep her there tonight and when we open the gates in the morning it will be broad daylight: there was no reason to anticipate any particular danger: let her go up. I say the concurrence of the naval opinion we have had before this court on the subject is if he had done that, even with the knowledge there were other ships likely to come down, he would not have to be censured, it was [a] perfectly proper thing for a naval officer to do nothing—the harbour is guarded by regulations—rules of the road which would make it absolutely impossible if they were observed as he had every right to suppose they would be....
>
> Any provision in the regulations for stoppage of traffic in Halifax harbour under certain conditions would be a regulation made on the assumption that a law was going to be violated, such a regulation was not needed so long as the law was observed—I mean the rule of the road. I do not think it was incumbent on anybody either in making the rules and regulations for Halifax harbour or in carrying them out to go on the assumption the law of the land was going to be violated. I think that is exoneration of the naval service department and its officers....
>
> While I have the utmost sympathy for the people of Halifax in the irreparable losses they have sustained ... I have no sympathy with the attempt to find a scapegoat for the explosion which took place on the 6th of December and to find that scapegoat among the officers of the Canadian naval service. I do not think that is where the blame belongs....
>
> There is an extraordinary coincidence the only ship which came here which might be termed ... a floating arsenal, that was the one picked out by hazard to be collided with and exploded. The *Imo* could have run into 999 out of 1,000 and fire would not have been caused and even if it had been caused there would be no explosives on board to explode.[149]

Unfortunately, integrity and common sense were in short supply at the inquiry and the crown counsel was virtually alone in demonstrating the honesty needed to make such statements in the face of Haligonians' understandably intense anger over the disaster. A

---

149. Henry summation, 31 January 1918, ibid, 2124–25.

lack of judicial backbone was certainly evident when the Drysdale inquiry released its findings on 4 February 1918. The conclusions arrived at by the nautical assessors were largely those demanded by the Halifax press and public and bore little relation to the evidence presented in court. To the astonishment of everyone familiar with its circumstances, the inquiry placed the full blame for the collision on the pilot and captain of the *Mont Blanc*. Correctly stating that the "collision was caused by violation of the rules of navigation," Drysdale, Demers, and Hose incredulously found that Mackey and Le Médec "were wholly responsible for violating the rules of the road."[150]

Just how such a conclusion could be sustained given that *Mont Blanc* had been proceeding very slowly down the proper side of the channel while *Imo* was speeding down the wrong side, was not revealed in the nautical assessors' findings. The conclusion did not persuade Rear-Admiral Chambers who, in his April report to the Admiralty, identified *Imo* as "the prime cause of the disaster."[151] (The British admiral chose to ignore that *Mont Blanc*'s incredibly dangerous loading was, in fact, "the prime cause of the disaster," while *Imo* was simply the prime cause of the collision). To compound the injustice of their conclusions—and as a further demonstration of the degree to which they had completely surrendered to the intense public feeling in Halifax—the assessors spinelessly suggested that "in view of the gross neglect of the rules of navigation by Pilot Mackey, the attention of the law officers of the crown should be called to the evidence taken on this investigation with a view to a criminal prosecution of such pilot," and recommended that similar action be taken by the French authorities in regard to Le Médec. The only conclusion the inquiry reached that was actually sustained by the evidence was its finding that "the master and pilot of the *Mont Blanc* are guilty of neglect of the public safety in not taking proper steps to warn the inhabitants of the city of a probable explosion."[152]

The thinking behind the false conclusion as to who was at fault in the collision was laid out in two memoranda the dominion wreck commissioner, Demers, submitted to Drysdale before counsel summations at the end of January. Taking his cue from Burchell's spurious claim that British fair play precluded casting blame on the dead pilot and captain of *Imo*, Demers argued that it was *Mont Blanc*'s responsibility alone to ensure that she avoided a collision at all costs and should, therefore, have steered to port and reversed engines upon hearing *Imo*'s original two-whistle blast that she intended, by local convention, to violate the rules of the road and pass to starboard of the French ship.[153] While failing to state why he believed that the ship ignoring the rules of the road had the right of way, Demers's assertion disregarded the possibility that turning *Mont Blanc* to port might simply have placed itself in the path of the speeding *Imo* if the relief ship had then steered to starboard to avoid the slow-moving French vessel, the situation that actually occurred when the ships closed on one another. Demers's rationalization for finding *Mont Blanc* at fault was

---

150. Drysdale, Demers and Hose to Minister of Marine, 4 February 1918, 80–5-13, LAC, RG 24, vol. 5671.

151. Chambers to Admiralty, 22 April 1918, 105/28, UKNA, ADM 137/1620. See also L.E. Ouimet to Chief Press Censor, 14 December 1917, file 350, LAC, RG 6E, vol. 621.

152. Drysdale, Demers and Hose to Minister of Marine, 4 February 1918, 80–5-13, LAC, RG 24, vol. 5671.

153. Armstrong, *The Halifax Explosion*, 190–92.

all the more illogical given the inquiry's censure of the pilot of an American steamer that had earlier passed *Imo* starboard side to starboard side at the entrance to the Narrows in clear violation of the rules of the road while condemning Mackey for not doing so.[154] The wreck commissioner's reasoning was also flatly contradicted by the testimony of Mate John Makiny who witnessed the collision from the deck of the tug *Nereid* but had been too injured to testify at the inquiry (he subsequently did so at the manslaughter preliminary hearing against Mackey, Le Médec, and Wyatt). The experienced RNCVR sailor clearly stated that the collision had resulted from *Imo*'s last-minute change of course to starboard following the French ship's change to port.[155]

Unfortunately for the RCN, the nautical assessors' willingness to capitulate to local public hysteria extended to the conclusions they reached about Commander Wyatt's culpability for the disaster. The inquiry's three members chose to ignore W.A. Henry's rational summation of the evidence and found the chief examination officer to be "guilty of neglect in performing his duty as CXO in not taking proper steps to ensure the regulations being carried out and especially in not keeping himself fully acquainted with the movements and intended movements of vessels in the harbour."[156] Once again, the moving force in reaching such a finding appears to have been Demers. In one of the memoranda he submitted to Drysdale at the end of January, the wreck commissioner argued that it was Wyatt's duty to ensure "that when ordering traffic movement, nothing could intervene to prevent or cause interruption or come in conflict with a prearranged and determined programme of seeing that the way was absolutely clear for the *Mont Blanc*'s passage from the harbour to Bedford Basin."[157] Once again, however, Demers's assertion that it had been the chief examination officer's duty to halt all other traffic when *Mont Blanc* proceeded toward Bedford Basin was completely false. As Henry had pointed out in his summation, no such regulation existed on 6 December and, logically, none was needed if, as the naval authorities had every right to believe, the rules of the road were properly followed.

The assessors also concluded that it was Wyatt's job to ensure "the efficient carrying out of traffic regulations by the pilots." While the RCN, through its various examination services, did have authority over the movement of vessels in and out of Canadian ports (based on the same "Regulations for the Control of Internal Traffic at Defended Ports in Time of War" that were in force throughout the British Empire[158]), in practice the pilots primarily reported the movement of ships to the navy as a further check on which ships had proceeded to sea and as a needed notification for the opening and closing of the anti-submarine nets, control of which rested with the examination service. The assessors'

---

154. Drysdale, Demers, and Hose to Minister of Marine, 4 February 1918, 80–5-13, LAC, RG 24, vol. 5671.

155. Armstrong, *The Halifax Explosion*, 197.

156. Drysdale, Demers, and Hose to Minister of Marine, 4 February 1918, 80–5-13, LAC, RG 24, vol. 5671.

157. Demers to Drysdale, 28 January 1918, Demers to Drysdale, "Addenda to Report," 29 January 1918, LAC, MG 26 H, vol. 90, reel C-4325.

158. "Memorandum for G.J. Desbarats, Re: Control of Navigation, Halifax Harbour, during Period of the War," 10 January 1918, 37–25–8, LAC, RG 24, vol. 5635.

censure of the Halifax pilotage authority for not immediately suspending Mackey's licence was a clear admission that it was the pilotage authority's responsibility, not Wyatt's, to ensure that Halifax pilots were competent to follow the internationally recognized rules of the road and the authority's duty to take the necessary disciplinary action if they were not.[159] Having already been relieved of his examination duties over the *Galileo* incident, Wyatt was the only naval officer the assessors were willing to censure, claiming "that the evidence is far from satisfactory that he ever took any efficient steps to bring to the notice of the captain superintendent neglect on the part of the pilots."[160]

Writing to the deputy minister of Marine, A. Johnston, on the day the inquiry's findings were released, the crown counsel, W.A. Henry, made it clear that he found the assessors' conclusions puzzling and at variance with the evidence. Henry believed that the unfounded conclusions of Drysdale, Demers, and Hose would, in all likelihood, be overturned by a higher court:

> Of the judgement delivered by the court, it would not be proper, perhaps, for me to say all I feel. I am and have been throughout satisfied that the Department of the Naval Service and its officers were entirely free from blame and should not be held responsible in any way for the disaster. The harbour regulations were sufficient, in my opinion, to safeguard the port, in view of the existence of rules of the road designed to prevent collisions, and I cannot see why regulations should have been framed based upon the assumption that the rules of the road would be infringed.
>
> The officials charged with the carrying out of the regulations were not, I consider, to blame for not taking precautions not required by the regulations. The evidence was all to the effect that Commander Wyatt would not have been to blame even if he had known that the *Imo* was to sail on the morning of December 6th, in permitting the *Mont Blanc* to enter the harbour. The court has disregarded that evidence, apparently, and placed some of the blame upon him….
>
> The decision that the whole responsibility for the collision falls upon the *Mont Blanc* has come as a great surprise to most people. It was expected that the *Imo* would have been found to be primarily at fault for being and remaining on the wrong side of the channel, and that the *Mont Blanc* might also be found to blame for a manoeuvre performed just before the collision. I hardly think that the higher courts will take the same view of the facts when an appeal is asserted from the Admiralty decision which will undoubtedly follow the judgement just delivered.[161]

---

159. Drysdale, Demers, and Hose to Minister of Marine, 4 February 1918, 80–5-13, LAC, RG 24, vol. 5671.

160. Ibid.

161. Henry to A. Johnston, Deputy Minister of Marine, 4 February 1918, LAC, MG 26 H, vol. 90, reel C-4325.

As Henry guessed, the appeal by the French ship's owners to the Supreme Court of Canada, while not completely reversing Drysdale's ruling, resulted in a split finding against both *Imo* and *Mont Blanc*. The decision of the Canadian court was upheld in March 1920 by the Judicial Committee of the Privy Council in London, whose sober reflection on the facts of the accident was not distorted by an angry public or press. Although the London court clearly believed that *Imo* had been travelling at excessive speed down the wrong side of the Narrows and could "have crossed into and remained in her own water, as she was bound to do, but never did," it ruled "that both ships are to blame for their reciprocal neglect" in allowing themselves "to approach within 400 feet of each other on practically opposite courses, thus incurring risk of collision, and indeed practically bringing about the collision, instead of reversing their engines and going astern, ... [which] they, as a matter of good seamanship, could and should have done, long before the ships came so close together." Even then, the judicial committee found that the French ship "must at the time of the collision have had little, if any, way on her," whereas the Belgian ship "in order to inflict the injury to the *Mont Blanc*, which it is proved she did inflict, must have struck that ship with more force and at a higher rate of speed than her witnesses admit."[162] Unlike the Halifax inquiry, the judicial committee viewed the collision as entirely the result of navigating errors by the pilots and did not attribute any blame to the naval authorities, pointing out that even in "the Narrows, the stretch of water between mid-channel and each of the bounding shores would be 250 yards, i.e., 750 feet, so that each incoming and outgoing ship would, in the absence of obstructions, have ample room to steam to her destination exclusively through her own water."[163]

To compound the injustice of the Drysdale inquiry's findings, Mackey, Le Médec, and Wyatt were immediately arrested by the Halifax police and charged with manslaughter. (In yet another example of the surreal atmosphere prevailing in the Nova Scotia capital, the sole victim named in the manslaughter charge was the man most culpable for causing the collision, *Imo*'s pilot, William Hayes.) Even the fair-minded W.A. Henry did not like the men's chances in a courtroom, informing Ottawa that "in the present state of feeling in this community, a jury is likely to convict anyone charged with negligence in connection with the explosion."[164] Fortunately for the trio, their cases were presided over by one of the few judges in Nova Scotia with the integrity to allow common sense and the law to outweigh the public's demand for revenge. Justice Benjamin Russell dismissed the cases against Le Médec and Hayes on the grounds of *habeas corpus*, but added "that there is not a single fact proved or even stated in the evidence [at the inquiry] that is not consistent with the exercise of the highest degree of care and thought on the part of the pilot in charge of the *Mont Blanc*."[165] Only the case against Wyatt went to trial in mid-April, the former examination officer's lawyer being provided, at Kingsmill's insistence, by the federal

---

162. "Judgement of the Lords of the Judicial Committee of the Privy Council, delivered the 22nd March 1920," nd, 18–19, 7704–244, pt. 3, LAC, RG 12, vol. 2827.

163. Ibid, 3.

164. Henry to A. Johnston, Deputy Minister of Marine, 4 February 1918, LAC, MG 26 H, vol. 90, reel C-4325.

165. Justice Russell quoted in Armstrong, *Halifax Explosion*, 198.

Justice Department. Also appearing before Justice Russell, Wyatt was acquitted in a trial lasting less than a day as the jury accepted Russell's instructions to them "that there is nothing in the eyes of the law to justify the charge of manslaughter."[166] Having already been relieved of his duties over the *Galileo* incident, Wyatt was discharged from the navy on 3 May 1918, his "services no longer required."[167]

From a strictly RCN perspective, the most disappointing aspect of the findings was that Captain Walter Hose had completely concurred with the inquiry's conclusions. The fact that those findings falsely accused a fellow RCN officer of neglect of duty and unnecessarily tarnished the reputation of his own service made his complicity in the result all the more disturbing, regardless of the degree to which such a conclusion may have accorded with Halifax opinion. The Royal Canadian Navy, the naval department and Admiral Kingsmill had all been pilloried in the press, particularly by the Halifax newspapers. For his part, Kingsmill remained completely unperturbed by the press's demands that he be replaced as naval director and, just as impressive, stood four-square behind Captain Hose when he became the object of attack. When the Halifax newspapers called for Hose's resignation from the inquiry in mid-January, an increasingly annoyed Pasco informed NSHQ that the "*Herald* continues to abuse Captain Hose daily."[168] The naval director's common sense advice was to assure the captain superintendent that "there can be no personal attack on Hose. No harm will result from *Herald* abuse. Better treat it with contempt. Let *Herald* continue to bark up the wrong tree."[169] An agitated Pasco was not so easily persuaded, however. The day after receiving Kingsmill's telegram, he submitted "cuttings from the *Halifax Herald*, which is an example of what appears in that paper and the Halifax *Evening Mail* daily. These articles are entirely ridiculous, the statements made untrue and indirectly slanderous, and naturally, appearing day after day, they have become a source of annoyance to Captain Hose and difficult to altogether treat with contempt."[170] In view of Pasco's anxiety, Kingsmill's next instruction was sent "By Command": "The *Herald* would be only too glad to enter into a controversy and no correspondence with that paper is to take place."[171] At the same time, Kingsmill followed the more appropriate course of having the minister of the naval service write to Judge Drysdale in support of Hose. He also arranged for Ballantyne to ask the prime minister to write the owner of the *Halifax Herald* calling attention to his paper's unjust attacks on the captain of patrols.[172]

The owner of the *Halifax Herald*, Conservative Senator William Dennis, was an influential Nova Scotian and a key figure in the system of political patronage in the province. As such, Dennis had little time for federal officials, such as Kingsmill, who tried

---

166. Justice Russell quoted in ibid, 201.

167. Ibid, 202.

168. Navyard to Naval Ottawa, 12 January 1918, 37–25–2, pt. 3, LAC, RG 24, vol. 5634.

169. Naval Ottawa to Navyard Halifax, 13 January 1918, ibid.

170. Captain Superintendent to DNS, 14 January 1918, ibid.

171. NSHQ to Captain Superintendent, 21 January 1918, ibid.

172. Kingsmill minute, nd, on Captain Superintendent to DNS, 14 January 1918, ibid.

to avoid political favouritism when making naval appointments or awarding contracts, and he freely used his paper to attack both the Canadian navy and its director. The fact that Kingsmill had been awarded a knighthood on London's New Year's honours list just as the RCN was coming under fire for its alleged role in the Halifax explosion also made the admiral a ripe target. In a particularly vicious 31 January editorial, the *Herald* claimed "that Ottawa does not take Admiral Kingsmill any too seriously. He is jokingly referred to as the man who was created an admiral for losing a ship [Kingsmill had been captain of HMS *Dominion* in 1906 when the warship was damaged after running aground in the Bay de Chaleur], is more famous in the capital for his social than for his naval exploits, and the knighthood recently conferred upon him is mostly regarded as one of those insoluble mysteries which every now and again baffle the ingenuity of the public mind."[173] The day after the Drysdale inquiry's conclusions were released, the Ottawa *Evening Journal* adopted a similar tone in attacking the RCN as a whole: "the controlling of traffic in Halifax harbour was a policeman's job.... Yet upon this simple policeman's job the Canadian naval service, with all its frills and feathers, its admirals and commanders, captains and lieutenants, fine uniforms and gold lace fell down.... The minister of this department, and the dominion government, must see that the confidence of the people of Canada in the whole administration of the Canadian naval service is shattered.... The Canadian naval service has received a black eye. If for no other reason than that of providing the British Admiralty with assurances for the future, drastic action by the dominion government is imperative."[174]

As much as Canadian naval officers realized that newspaper depictions of RCN ineptitude were, in Kingsmill's words, "entirely ridiculous" and "untrue," a continuous press assault on the navy's reputation would eventually damage morale. In mid-February, the chief press censor for Canada, Colonel E.J. Chambers, offered to write "a few friendly letters to the editors of Halifax newspapers" to explain "that some of the criticisms directed against naval officers have tended to create an undesirable condition in the discipline of the naval service."[175] While the Canadian naval director was "not hopeful" that such letters would "accomplish some useful purpose," he did explain to the press censor what he believed was behind the Halifax attitude. "The fact of the matter is that in and about Halifax, which is a hotbed of patronage, the navy is not very popular as, from the first organization we have had to fight this very undesirable form of making appointments, that is patronage, and consequently gentlemen like the mayor and the proprietor of the *Halifax Herald* do not love us. Personally, I do not care a snap of the fingers what they say in the press as to my conduct of my office, but when they abuse generally every officer in Halifax, it is very bad for discipline and I am afraid will be a boomerang to some of the young men there who do think that the opinions expressed by the *Halifax Herald* are of any weight."[176] Although Kingsmill's assertion that he was unconcerned about press

---

173. *Halifax Herald,* 31 January 1918.

174. Ottawa *Evening Journal,* 5 February 1918.

175. Chambers to Kingsmill, 12 February 1918, and enclosures, file 350, LAC, RG 6E, vol. 621.

176. Kingsmill to Chambers, 14 February 1918, ibid.

aspersions directed at himself was unlikely to have been mere bravado, asking for the chief press censor's aid on behalf of the navy in Halifax demonstrates the director's genuine concern for the slings and arrows being directed at the officers and sailors under his command.

One other issue flowed from the release of the inquiry's findings. As Wyatt succumbed to duress on the Halifax inquiry witness stand, he had sought to shift the inquiry's attention away from himself by referring to several complaints he had brought to the attention of Captain Martin the previous year about the berthing of vessels by the pilots. Although the complaints involved pilots taking vessels to more convenient berths than those assigned by the naval authorities, the dominion wreck commissioner took up the CXO's mention of pilotage complaints in his 29 January memorandum to Drysdale and extended them to suggest that the federal authorities should have "recommended drastic measures to prevent such infringement of regulations."[177] When Ballantyne forwarded the inquiry's findings to the prime minister on 12 February, Borden insisted that Demers's accusations "receive very grave consideration."[178] Although the navy was perplexed as to how the wreck commissioner—whose judgment of the evidence was already demonstrably suspect—could have placed such an illogical interpretation on minor complaints about the berthing of vessels, complaints that clearly had no bearing on the *Imo–Mont Blanc* collision, it quickly produced its correspondence on the matter. As explained to the minister, the complaints involved "minor cases of disobedience on the part of individual pilots, chiefly in anchoring vessels in their wrong berth. It is considered that these cases were due more to want of practice than anything else."[179] The infringements of the berthing regulations had been handled by the usual "Notice to Mariners."[180] In forwarding the correspondence to the prime minister, Ballantyne added that he "really cannot find any justification for Captain Demers' remarks."[181] Borden, too, seemed satisfied and the explosion inquiry received scant attention when the House of Commons resumed sitting in March 1918.[182]

In fact, as anyone who was not caught up in the public's fears of another explosion was aware, the risk of collision in Halifax Harbour following the introduction of convoy

---

177. Demers to Drysdale, "Addenda to Report," 29 January 1918, LAC, MG 26 H, vol. 90, reel C-4325.

178. Ballantyne to Borden, 12 February 1918, Borden to Ballantyne, 18 February 1918, ibid.

179. "Responsibility of the Navy at Halifax in Time of War," nd, 1001–13–1, LAC, RG 24, vol. 6197.

180. NSHQ to Martin, 30 September 1918, LAC, MG 26 H, vol. 90, reel C-4325.

181. Ballantyne to Borden, 1 March 1918, ibid.

182. Armstrong, *The Halifax Explosion,* 203. Although Armstrong suggests that Borden's questioning of Ballantyne and the naval department's response represented an "apparent intrigue and cover-up" of a potential scandal resulting from NSHQ ignoring serious problems in the management of Halifax Harbour, the evidence does not support such a contention. In view of the fact that Demers's memoranda to Drysdale are full of questionable reasoning and misconstrued evidence, it would seem that the wreck commissioner may have had his own agenda. It is not surprising, therefore, that Demers's strange view of events were as easily dismissed by NSHQ as they were by W.A. Henry. Far from being the departmental crisis that Armstrong claims, the inquiry's findings merited only the briefest of mentions in the deputy minister's diary. Armstrong, *The Halifax Explosion,* 192–96; and Desbarats Diary, 4 February 1918, LAC, MG 30 E89, vol. 5.

remained, as it had been throughout the war, extremely slight. Haligonians might well have characterized the perfectly safe passing of *Galileo* and an oiler in the Narrows—with hundreds of feet to spare between them—as a "near collision" but more objective observers understood, as Kingsmill explained to Pasco, that "times are not normal with regard to Halifax."[183] The same incident demonstrated that naval officers understood that the precautions introduced after the explosion were excessive, as when Captain Turnbull dismissed Mate Iceton's concerns and directed *Galileo* to depart as quickly as possible to catch up to its convoy. The British officer knew that the danger to the munitions ship was negligible inside the harbour defences, while a solo Atlantic crossing would expose the vessel to the real threat of attack by U-boats. Certainly the minor complaints the navy had made about the berthing of ships, and possible financial responsibility for damaged piers, do not demonstrate, as one historian has claimed, that "the federal government had long been aware of the dangers of a collision in Halifax harbour but had done nothing."[184]

Nonetheless, there was no denying that the RCN's tenuous reputation with the Canadian public, and the citizens of Nova Scotia in particular, had suffered as a result of the explosion. The views expressed by the Ottawa *Evening Journal*'s editorial writers that "the Canadian naval service ... fell down," and had "received a black eye"[185] for its administration of Halifax Harbour were typical of the attitude held by many Canadians toward the fledgling RCN, particularly when compared to the prestige and power of the Royal Navy. This was especially true in Halifax, where the upstart RCN was often viewed as a contemptible usurper of the British navy's long-established role in the port. Such opinions were easily sustained when Nova Scotians could see the sleek grey cruisers of the North America and West Indies Station arriving regularly in Halifax Harbour, while the RCN warships protecting its approaches were a motley collection of converted yachts and fishing trawlers.[186] The public, of course, was entirely unaware that NSHQ was equally dissatisfied with the navy's lack of a destroyer force, one that was needed to deal effectively with a U-boat threat in Canadian waters, or that it was the Admiralty that had repeatedly discouraged Ottawa's suggestions that it should procure better warships. As we shall see, NSHQ's frustration with the Admiralty's dissembling would continue throughout the war's final year even as the RCN's reputation with the Canadian public received a further setback when a German submarine offensive finally materialized off the East Coast of North America.

183. Naval Ottawa to Navyard Halifax, 22 January 1918, 1048–17–30, LAC, RG 24, vol. 3713.

184. J.L. Granatstein, *Hell's Corner: An Illustrated History of Canada's Great War, 1914–1918* (Toronto 2004), 125.

185. Ottawa *Evening Journal*, 5 February 1918.

186. Stephen Kimber, *Sailors, Slackers and Blind Pigs: Halifax at War* (np 2003), 21; T.H. Raddall, *Halifax: Warden of the North* (Toronto 1948), 255; Armstrong, *The Halifax Explosion*, 23; and Hadley and Sarty, *Tin-pots and Pirate Ships*, 204.

CHAPTER 9

Preparations and Frustrations, January to May 1918

Even as the Drysdale inquiry was playing itself out in Nova Scotia, Naval Service Headquarters had already turned its attention to the more urgent matter of anti-submarine measures that would have to be put in place for the coming shipping season. As we have seen, Ottawa cabled London on 24 November 1917 asking the Admiralty for its views on the nature of the threat Canada would face and, in particular, on the probable chances of a submarine offensive being launched off the Canadian Atlantic coast as well as the scale of attack that might be expected. NSHQ also wanted to know what advice the Admiralty could offer in drawing up a defence scheme, and what material assistance Canada could anticipate should an attack develop "to such an extent as would point to continuance of enemy attempts to carry on submarine war on this side of the Atlantic."[1]

With considerable alacrity (in view of the complexity of the Canadian request), the Admiralty had its answer prepared by 3 January, transmitting it to Ottawa the following week. Perhaps even more surprising was the degree of honesty with which British naval officers addressed Canada's questions. Given the Admiralty's great desire to have all available destroyers, both RN and USN, concentrated in United Kingdom waters to counter the main German U-boat campaign, there was a natural impulse to downplay the submarine threat to North America so as not to alarm Washington into keeping a significant portion of its destroyer force on the eastern seaboard. Rather than disparage a possible U-boat threat, however, the Admiralty considered it to be "very probable that an attack by one of the new submarine cruisers may be expected at any time after March, but prevalence of drift ice may act to a certain extent as a deterrent; but where the convoys can go, there the submarine can also go, and an attack on shipping issuing from Halifax or other ports on the Atlantic seaboard is to be contemplated. It is more likely that the Germans would send one submarine on an experimental cruise of this sort, and depending on its success would then consider whether submarine attack in force was a policy to be seriously and continuously followed." Even if more than one submarine were operating off the Canadian coast at one time, "the measures necessary to protect shipping will be the same, based on the assumption that at any moment one submarine will be in a position to attack every outgoing convoy."[2]

---

1. Director of the Naval Service of Canada to Secretary of the Admiralty, 22 November 1917, 1017–10–1, pt. 1, Library and Archives Canada, (hereafter LAC), Record Group (hereafter RG) 24, vol. 3831.

2. Admiralty to Under Secretary of State, Colonial Office, for transmission to Ottawa, and enclosure, 3 January 1918, ibid.

The tactics London anticipated the submarine cruisers would employ also affected the type of convoy escorts the Admiralty believed were required. Although it was assumed that long-range U-boats would "doubtless carry a large supply of torpedoes," the Admiralty believed that the time and distance required for a trans-Atlantic war patrol and the extended absence from port would mean that the enemy would have to rely primarily on her deck guns to attack merchant ships. In that event, London recommended "that each outward convoy, in addition to the escort cruiser, should take with it for, say 200 miles, two vessels, which in concert could beat off a submarine cruiser. This could be done by two destroyers of course, or two sloops, or a combination of destroyer or sloop with a fast trawler."[3] As everyone at NSHQ knew, of course, the RCN had neither destroyers, nor sloops, nor fast trawlers, and, aside from HMCS *Grilse*, no vessel with the required speed to overtake—let alone successfully engage—a surfaced submarine cruiser.

On the question of available minesweeping forces, the Canadian navy was in far better shape, having maintained a swept channel in the Halifax approaches since the outbreak of war. The Admiralty did not consider "that there is much danger of mines being laid in the entrance to Canadian harbours by submarines" as it was not "a paying concern" for U-boats to transport mines 3,000 miles. They did expect, however, that German raiders disguised as neutral merchant ships would likely be able to lay mines off the Canadian coast "since it has already happened in other parts of the world." The fact that mines could be laid "at any time and without warning" meant that exploratory searches with sweep gear would be necessary daily. "For this purpose, the force now in Canadian waters together with those that will be shortly available, is sufficient; and with regard to this, therefore, the question resolves itself into a matter of the best apparatus to use" for conducting the sweeps.[4]

Perhaps in order to give Ottawa a complete defensive plan—Admiral Kingsmill's November letter to the Admiralty had stated that London had never "clearly advised the dominion government as to what the Admiralty expected of the Department of the Naval Service of Canada"[5]—the memorandum also gave a detailed accounting of the mine-sweeping force it believed was needed for the approaches to the convoy assembly ports of Halifax and Sydney. It recommended that ten minesweeping trawlers at Halifax and six at Sydney be equipped with the "A" sweep for clearing mines. (In use since the outbreak of war, the "A" sweep was a single wire sweep kept at the required depth by waterkites, and towed between two minesweepers steaming in line abreast some 500 metres apart.) They also mapped out five entrance channels for Halifax and two entrance channels for Sydney. In laying these out, the memorandum explained that "the shortest route to the deepest water is always advisable, as mines need not be expected in water over sixty fathoms." The entrance channels were to be "varied from time to time and as much as possible, [with] sweeping adapted to take place shortly before the convoy leaves or enters, and along its line of entrance." The British did not feel it necessary to do a completely thorough sweep of the channels, however, until mines were suspected of having been laid. In addition to

3. Ibid.

4. Ibid.

5. Director of the Naval Service to Admiralty, 22 November 1917, ibid.

the regular minesweepers, it was suggested that a secondary force of trawlers be deployed with Actaeon sweeps to patrol to seaward of the swept channels in case "a large number of mines be laid at some distance from the port by a raider." (The Actaeon, named for the parent ship of the torpedo school at Sheerness, had been developed in 1915 as a single-ship sweep. It consisted of a lighter wire towed from each quarter of a minesweeper with a small kite, a depth float, and an explosive grapnel to cut the mine's mooring cable. Its single-ship design made it particularly useful in locating new minefields. In view of the great tidal variations in the Bay of Fundy, the Admiralty did not consider it necessary to provide a minesweeping force in the approaches to St John. London also wanted the RCN to assign an additional twelve drifters to augment the trawler minesweepers "should the enemy scatter mines away from the assembly ports, and thus cause minesweeping trawlers to be diverted."[6]

Turning to the question of anti-submarine requirements, the Admiralty memorandum stated: "as it is expected that only one or two submarines would be operating at the same time, traffic should be spread on the coastal route when not in convoy. A comprehensive system of patrols is not recommended, nor is it necessary if traffic is spread." The memorandum then laid out the forces the RCN required to support the convoys:

> The convoy assembly ports should have adequate forces for:
> (a) Provision of convoy escort for first 200–300 miles.
> (b) Additional escort until dark hours of first day out or until formed up.
> (c) Patrol of the approaches to the port at all times.
> For these services at Halifax and Sydney, the numbers required are:
> For (a) –
> Escort of fast convoy) 1 sloop or TBD [torpedo boat destroyer]
>) 1 fast trawler
> Escort of slow convoy) 2 sloops or TBDs
>) 2 fast trawlers
>) 4 trawlers
> Spare for above) 1 sloop or TBD
>) 1 fast trawler
>) 1 trawler
> For (b) and (c) – 12 trawlers
> 24 drifters
> For patrol of Gulf and River St Lawrence, and to provide a striking force available to be sent anywhere without disorganising the system of patrols and escorting, the following numbers should be sufficient:
> 2 sloops
> 2 fast trawlers
> 9 trawlers
> 18 miscellaneous patrol vessels.[7]

---

6. Admiralty to Under Secretary of State, Colonial Office, for transmission to Ottawa, and enclosure, 3 January 1918, ibid.

Implementing the entire defence scheme required thirty-six trawlers, thirty-six drifters, six destroyers or sloops, and six fast trawlers, in addition to the vessels already available in the RCN patrol force. The additional vessels would be provided by assigning the first thirty Admiralty trawlers completed in Canada to the RCN, including the remaining six Battle-class trawlers that were still under construction, as well as the first thirty-six Admiralty drifters that became available, not counting those drifters that had already departed Halifax for Europe. The most important warships in the scheme, the six destroyers or sloops and the six fast trawlers, were, according to the telegram, to be supplied "from England or USA." Armed with modern 4-inch guns, these twelve fast escorts would be the backbone of the Admiralty's proposed patrol scheme, supplemented by the three Canadian auxiliary patrol vessels—HMC Ships *Stadacona*, *Acadia*, and *Lady Evelyn*—that also carried 4-inch guns, though of an obsolete pattern. Of the Canadian patrol ships, only the 12-pounder-armed *Grilse* had the required speed to catch a U-boat, although NSHQ questioned her seaworthiness if operating at any distance from harbour. While the memorandum did not specifically say so, it was implied that the 12-pounder and 6-pounder guns on the trawlers and drifters were considered inadequate to take on the 5.9-inch guns of German submarine cruisers. In answer to the last question NSHQ had posed in November—"what does Admiralty propose to do in event of such attack developing"—London's response was "that the above proposals are adequate to any submarine activity that may occur."[8]

Perhaps the most remarkable aspect of the Admiralty memorandum was the candidness with which the British assessed the Canadian situation. As it admitted, the key to the proposed scheme were the twelve destroyers and fast trawlers needed to escort the convoys out to a maximum of 300 miles. It was a stunning reversal of opinion that the Admiralty now acknowledged that destroyers and fast trawlers were necessary for North American convoy protection, even if only one German submarine cruiser were operating off the Canadian coast.[9] Moreover, the Admiralty had finally committed itself to supplying the twelve fast escorts that were essential to the scheme's success. In view of the Royal Navy's preoccupation with concentrating all possible destroyers, including those of the United States Navy, in British home waters, it was somewhat ominous, however, that the Admiralty stated that the destroyers and fast escorts would be assigned to Canadian waters from either its own forces or those of the USN. As it was explained to the naval minister at the beginning of March, "the Admiralty proposed to supply the six TBDs, or possibly to obtain them from the American navy," and "will also supply the six fast trawlers. It is presumed that these twelve vessels will be manned and maintained by the Admiralty."[10] Nevertheless, a pleased NSHQ could only assume that the Admiralty, having for the first time in the war compiled a comprehensive defence plan for Canadian waters, would make good on its word.

---

7. Ibid.

8. Ibid.

9. Ibid.

10. Desbarats to Minister, 2 March 1918, ibid.

Even as the Admiralty memorandum was being communicated to Ottawa on 11 January, the captain of patrols—in Halifax as one of the Drysdale inquiry's nautical assessors—was forwarding his own thoughts on the weakness of the East Coast patrol force for the coming shipping season. During the inquiry's Christmas adjournment, acting Captain Walter Hose put to paper his concerns about the problems the Atlantic coast patrol was facing in 1918, particularly the inadequate armament of its vessels in view "of the latest development in submarine design and construction by Germany."[11] Submitting his views to NSHQ on 15 January, that is to say before he was aware of the Admiralty's latest proposal, the captain of patrols came to remarkably similar conclusions. The main threat, he observed, was "the large ocean cruising submarine ... armed with either the 4.1[-inch] or the 5.9[-inch] gun and ... a surface speed of from fifteen to eighteen knots," and it was clear to him that RCN "vessels with an armament insufficient to cope with submarines armed as above would be practically at their mercy, more particularly when the deficiency in speed of the vessels composing the Canadian coast patrol is considered." The fact that 4-inch guns were now being mounted on the larger anti-submarine trawlers being used in British waters was evidence enough that the Royal Navy considered a larger gun armament to be "vital" to combating U-boats. While he conceded that 12-pounder guns could still be "very effective against the smaller submarines" that were operating in British waters, "for patrol purposes in particular I would submit that 4-inch guns are indispensable, particularly in these waters, where submarines with smaller weapons than 4.1 guns are hardly likely to appear."[12]

Unless his auxiliary patrol vessels were equipped with modern 4-inch guns, Hose argued, he could "not but consider them at the mercy of the present day ocean-going submarine." Three of his patrol vessels did carry 4-inch weapons, but they were "not of modern enough type to be of any value." It was the breach-loading Mark VII gun that was required, and in Hose's view five of the auxiliaries—*Stadacona*, *Hochelaga*, *Acadia*, *Cartier*, and *Lady Evelyn*—were capable of mounting that gun forward. Two of the ex-fisheries cruisers, *Margaret* and *Canada*, "could each carry a 4-inch gun aft," and although "this is not an ideal position," it was, in his view, "very much better than no 4-inch gun at all. I would submit that arrangements be made, if possible to ensure this work being carried out by April, even at the cost of losing the services of these vessels to a certain extent during the winter months." Indeed, such was Hose's belief in the need for 4-inch gunned vessels

---

11. Captain of Patrols to NSHQ, 15 January 1918, 1017–10–4, pt. 1, LAC, RG 24, vol. 3832. Although Michael Hadley and Roger Sarty claim on page 212 of *Tin-pots and Pirate Ships: Canadian Naval Forces and German Sea Raiders, 1880–1918* (Montreal and Kingston 1991) that Hose's 15 January memorandum was in response to the Admiralty scheme laid out in its 3 January memorandum to Ottawa, that would not appear to be the case. If Hose's memorandum was a reply to the Admiralty's latest scheme, the captain of patrols would most certainly have made some reference to it, particularly its stunning promise of six destroyers and six fast trawlers. The fact that Hose did not mention the British proposals would indicate that his 15 January memorandum resulted from his own concerns as he reflected on the coming shipping season while the Drysdale inquiry was adjourned for Christmas. Moreover, since the Admiralty memo was not communicated by the Colonial Office to the Canadian capital until 11 January, it is unlikely that it could have made its way through the consecutive in-baskets of the Governor General, the Department of External Affairs, Desbarats, and Kingsmill to have reached Hose in Halifax in time for him to write a response by the 15th.

12. Captain of Patrols to NSHQ, 15 January 1918, 1017–10–4, pt. 1, LAC, RG 24, vol. 3832.

to take on the German U-cruisers that he recommended that all the trawlers on order or not yet completed in Canada for the Admiralty be cancelled and twenty-four larger trawlers be ordered in their place. These were to be armed with the Mark VII gun and would be similar to those the Admiralty had recently tested in British waters. Hose also urged that the construction of the large trawlers "be hastened by all means possible, and that, as they are completed, they should take the place of the smaller Admiralty trawlers allocated to Canadian waters; the smaller trawlers being despatched to England on relief, as they are of undoubted value there against the smaller submarines."[13]

As further reinforcement to his deficient forces, the captain of patrols also wanted NSHQ to reactivate HMCS *Rainbow* and arm her with eight 4-inch guns before sending her around to the Atlantic coast. Having spent the first three years of the war in command of the old cruiser, Hose was fully aware of the warship's mechanical condition and operating capabilities and believed she was still an effective vessel. As recently as two years earlier, he explained, the *Rainbow*'s engines had done "the revolutions for eighteen knots without exceeding horsepower," and, with her boilers recently repaired, he was "confident that in case of necessity she could now steam fifteen knots as long as her coal lasts." As well as being "a most valuable addition to the defence of convoys and shipping generally" on Canada's East Coast, Hose felt that the cruiser "would fill a very much needed want of a vessel for carrying out modern gunnery training," a requirement that would only grow in 1918 as more vessels were commissioned into the East Coast patrol flotillas. Even if the East Coast ships were up-gunned and reinforced by *Rainbow*, Hose knew that more would be required. With an eye on the increasing importance of air patrols in combating the U-boat menace in British waters, the Canadian captain asked that five seaplanes and a coastal airship be stationed in the Halifax vicinity "for patrol and anti-submarine work, and that the necessary station be built at once." Hose's most urgent demand—and one that showed he had not yet been informed of the Admiralty's 3 January proposals—he saved for the memorandum's last sentence: "Get seven modern torpedo boat destroyers out here."[14]

Hose was undoubtedly relieved, therefore, when he was informed of London's response. While suggesting a lesser number of escorts and patrol vessels—six destroyers or sloops and six fast trawlers as opposed to Hose's seven destroyers and twenty-four large trawlers—the British proposals would result in considerable improvement. Most significantly there was a general recognition that faster, better-armed vessels were required to deal with the cruiser submarine threat than the small, slow trawlers, and drifters the Admiralty had ordered in 1917, vessels that were armed with inadequate 12- and 6-pounder guns. In the Admiralty scheme, the six destroyers or sloops and six fast trawlers would all be armed with the modern 4-inch guns that Hose had called for. Perhaps the greatest difference between the Admiralty and Hose plans was the British willingness to make greater use of the imperial trawlers and drifters being built in Canada for minesweeping duties. In order to receive the needed reinforcements, Hose was quite prepared to hand the entire order of 136 imperial trawlers and drifters over to the Royal Navy for employment in United

---

13. Ibid.

14. Ibid.

Kingdom waters, vessels the captain of patrols viewed as useless in an anti-U-cruiser role, leaving the minesweeping task to the force of small vessels already deployed at Halifax, supplemented by the RCN's twelve Battle-class trawlers. However, preoccupied by his Halifax duties when the Drysdale inquiry resumed in mid-January—and undoubtedly distracted by the vilification he was subjected to in the local press—Hose was unable to turn his full attention to drafting a patrol plan that was based on the Admiralty's latest recommendations until later the following month.

Changes in the Admiralty's appointments in the western Atlantic, meanwhile, finally allowed Kingsmill to implement his plan to place Vice-Admiral Story in command at Halifax. It will be recalled that the naval director had been unable to make the appointment the previous November because Story was senior, by virtue of time in rank, to Vice-Admiral Browning. At the end of January 1918, however, Browning's replacement as C-in-C by an officer of greater seniority, Vice-Admiral W.L. Grant, finally allowed the Canadian naval director to make the desired move.[15] Not only did the arrival of Story in Halifax as admiral superintendent preclude the possible encroachment of British officers over the Canadian East Coast shore establishment, it also provided Kingsmill with a position for E.H. Martin as captain superintendent at Esquimalt.[16]

With Story installed at Halifax and Hose busy with his inquiry duties, Kingsmill gave the minister his own preliminary views on the Admiralty's defence proposals in early February. In particular, the naval director wanted to prepare the minister for the expenditure the government would incur in developing the repair facilities and proper bases that the proposed anti-submarine force would require. He also wanted to reduce unnecessary departmental red tape involved in the "many small matters requiring early attention," and sought the minister's approval to delegate authority for local stores purchases to the responsible East Coast officers, asking that "the admiral superintendent at Halifax and the captain of patrols at Sydney, may be directed to do their best to obtain necessary stores and to proceed with the work without being hampered by referring all details to headquarters for approval." Kingsmill took considerable satisfaction in pointing out that the British authorities had finally accepted NSHQ's long-stated insistence that the RCN's main concentration of force should be at Sydney, rather than Halifax, to cover the busy St Lawrence shipping lanes. As the director explained, the proposed British "organization is one in which I personally concur thoroughly and is on the lines of that which we proposed in opposition to that laid down by Captain Hatcher and by Commodore Coke."[17]

Kingsmill also believed that the Admiralty was committed to providing the destroyers/sloops and fast trawlers their scheme of defence called for as well as thirty of the trawlers and thirty-six of the drifters being built in Canadian shipyards on British order. With the Admiralty seemingly committed to supplying seventy-eight of the 108 vessels

15. "Naval Intelligence Report No. 57," 28 January 1918, DHH.

16. Hadley and Sarty, *Tin-pots and Pirate Ships*, 202; and J.G. Armstrong, *The Halifax Explosion and the Royal Canadian Navy: Inquiry and Intrigue* (Vancouver 2002), 172.

17. Kingsmill, "Memorandum for the Minister," nd [February 1918], 1017–10–4, pt. 1, LAC, RG 24, vol. 3832.

required for East Coast convoy defence, the number of RCN patrol and minesweeping vessels Canada would have to provide amounted to only thirty. The total would be made up by using nine of the navy's auxiliary patrol vessels already in service, the twelve Canadian-built Battle-class trawlers, and nine Canadian minesweepers, particularly the *PV*-numbered series of seven New England fishing trawlers. Even here, however, Kingsmill admitted that there were "some lame ducks." The boilers in HMCS *Canada* were worn out, *Lady Evelyn* and *Laurentian* were unfit for heavy weather, *Grilse* was "suitable for escort duty only near a harbour of refuge," and six of the twelve Battle-class trawlers had "not yet been proved as fit for seagoing work." On the plus side, the RCN did have the two submarines (albeit unarmed) that had been brought around to Halifax the previous fall together with their parent ship, HMCS *Shearwater*. Once the latter was armed and ready for sea, Kingsmill proposed to have the flotilla "operate with a wandering lead [i.e., a roving patrol] sometimes off Sydney and at another [time] off Halifax or elsewhere."[18]

Expecting the Admiralty to supply most of the vessels in the East Coast force, Kingsmill wanted the minister to understand that the greatest requirement for the RCN would be "to provide proper bases for the number of vessels proposed and [that] great improvements in facilities will have to be made at Halifax before the dockyard can look after them." Repair facilities for the larger Sydney force would also be a priority. These had previously been carried out by the Sydney Foundry Company, "but not very satisfactorily. We have also Pictou to fall back upon." Officering and manning the vessels would require some assistance from the British since the RCN had "for the past year endeavoured to obtain personnel to man a force of the dimensions proposed by the Admiralty, but we have not met with the success hoped for. We shall have to ask the Admiralty's assistance in the matter of skippers, mates and engineers, as well as in trained hands for certain duties on deck and in the engine room." The RCN already had sufficient signalmen and wireless operators for the vessels and Kingsmill believed the remainder of the untrained RNCVR sailors required could be obtained from the navy's Overseas Division.[19]

Once the Drysdale inquiry had run its course in early February, Kingsmill and Hose were able to turn their attention to preparing a comprehensive defence plan that incorporated the destroyers and fast trawlers promised by the Admiralty. At mid-month Desbarats recorded in his diary that the naval director and captain of patrols had "been busy all week working out defence scheme for east coast" to submit to the minister.[20] With the twelve 4-inch gunned destroyers and fast trawlers forming the backbone of the East Coast force, Hose was able to dispense with his plan to bring *Rainbow* east and arm her with eight modern 4-inch guns. The detailed scheme worked out by Hose and approved by Kingsmill divided the Admiralty-supplied fast escorts between the patrol forces stationed at Halifax, Sydney, and the mobile patrol flotilla that covered the Gulf of St Lawrence, and acted as a strategic reserve. For planning purposes, Hose assumed that the six primary escorts supplied by the Admiralty would consist of four destroyers and two sloops. At both

18. Ibid.

19. Ibid.

20. Desbarats Diary, 22 February 1918, LAC, Manuscript Group (hereafter MG) 30 E89, vol. 5.

Halifax and Sydney, the escorts were divided between convoy escorts and "forming up" or "outer" patrols, and "inner" patrols.[21]

The fast convoy escort force at Halifax was to consist of two destroyers and one fast trawler, all three vessels escorting each convoy out to sea for a distance of 300 miles, sufficient to take the merchant ships one hundred miles to the east of Sable Island and out beyond the 100 fathom line. While accompanying convoys, the fast escorts would be under the orders of the commanding officer of its cruiser escort. In harbour, the three warships would alternate laying up for boiler cleaning and machinery examinations, while the two vessels that were not laid up would alternate days as "ready" and "standby" boats. All three fast escorts were to be berthed in Bedford Basin. Hose assigned four imperial trawlers and eight drifters to the "forming up" escort, the vessels being divided (in an unspecified manner) into three divisions. All three would escort the Halifax convoys out of the harbour until they had formed into their convoy columns and were proceeding to sea. In the seven day period between convoy sailings, one of the divisions would lay up for boiler cleaning and machinery repairs, while the other two would conduct "outer" patrols in the Halifax approaches with each of the patrolling divisions alternately returning to harbour one day out of seven for coaling and provisioning. The captain of patrols also allocated HMC Ships *Grilse* and *PV VII* to an "inner" patrol on alternate five-day periods in the vicinity of the whistling buoy and to act as an escort for inbound Allied warships. The Halifax minesweeping division consisted of ten trawlers divided into pairs and was berthed in the Northwest Arm outside the anti-submarine nets. The trawlers were to sweep the prescribed entry channels daily with at least three pairs of sweepers operating each day. While one pair of minesweepers would have one week in five off for repairs and boiler maintenance, the other two pairs would spend one day each week coaling. The total of thirty-three vessels assigned by Hose to Halifax had a sea-going complement of 650 ranks and ratings, 150 of whom Hose presumed would be British sailors serving in the three RN fast escorts, the others being, primarily, RNCVR ratings. All personnel of the patrol squadron at Halifax were to be borne on the books of HMCS *Stadacona* (Halifax).[22]

Given the St Lawrence's greater volume of traffic during the summer shipping season, Hose allocated the largest number of escorts to Sydney. The escorts for the slow convoys were divided into three divisions as well, with two destroyers forming the first division, three fast trawlers the second, and five imperial trawlers the third. Every convoy escort would be equipped with hydrophones to listen for submerged U-boats. All three divisions were to escort each of the Sydney convoys out to sea for a distance of 300 miles, sufficient to take the convoy to the south of Cape Race, Newfoundland. As was the case with the Halifax convoy escorts, the Sydney-based vessels would operate under the orders of the commanding officer of the ocean escorts while with the convoy itself. The "forming up" and "outer patrol" forces at Sydney were also more numerous than at Halifax, Hose proposing to form two divisions of three trawlers and five drifters each, and a third division with two trawlers and six drifters. All three divisions would proceed to sea with each

21. Walter Hose, "Memorandum for DNS," nd [February 1918], 1017–10–1, pt. 1, LAC, RG 24, vol. 3831.

22. Ibid.

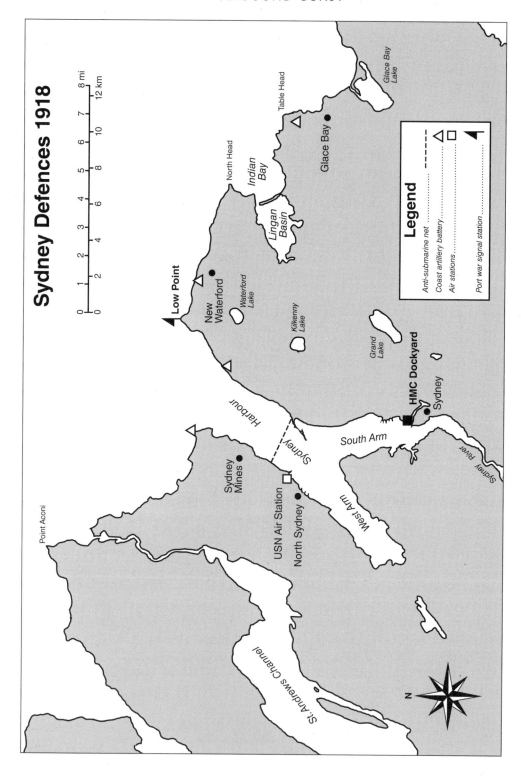

Sydney Defences 1918

Legend

Anti-submarine net ....
Coast artillery battery ....
Air stations ....
Port war signal station ....

Point Aconi

St. Andrew's Channel

North Sydney

USN Air Station

Sydney Mines

West Arm

South Arm

Sydney River

Sydney

HMC Dockyard

Grand Lake

Harbour

Kilkenny Lake

Waterford Lake

New Waterford

Low Point

Lingan Basin

Indian Bay

North Head

Table Head

Glace Bay

Glace Bay Lake

N

convoy until it was formed up and heading for the Cabot Straits. Three trawlers and five drifters of the twenty-four "forming up" escorts were to be equipped with hydrophones for submarine detection.[23] Under Hose's plan, each slow Sydney convoy would have a considerable degree of anti-submarine protection, with two destroyers and three fast trawlers carrying 4-inch guns acting as escorts, along with the five imperial trawlers of the third division and the convoy's normal British cruiser ocean escort. A total of eight trawlers and sixteen drifters would provide additional protection while the convoy left Sydney Harbour and formed into columns.

Between convoy cycles, one of the two destroyers would be kept ready to proceed to sea at short notice, while one fast trawler would be off duty for maintenance. The other two would alternate days as "ready" and "standby" boats. The three trawler and drifter divisions would alternate between layup in harbour and conducting outer patrols in the Sydney approaches. Two additional drifters, both equipped with hydrophones and wireless telegraphy, were designated to conduct a continuous "inner patrol" off the entrance to the harbour. The minesweeping force at the Cape Breton port consisted of six of the seven New England fishing trawlers, *PV I* to *PV VI*, operating in pairs in five-day rotations so that four trawlers would be sweeping the approach channels each day. Another four drifters were allocated as a minesweeping reserve, primarily to be deployed if mines were discovered further away from the assembly port so as not to divert the trawler minesweeper effort from Sydney's swept channels.[24]

The forces available for convoy escort at Sydney and Halifax were supported by the captain of patrols' strategic reserve, the mobile patrol flotilla, a redesignated version of various Gulf patrol flotillas from previous shipping seasons. In the 1918 plan, however, the flotilla would be strongly reinforced by two sloops (or two destroyers depending on which the Admiralty supplied) and two fast trawlers. Armed with the modern 4-inch guns Hose knew were essential against ocean-going U-boats, the four British warships were the heart of the RCN's mobile reserve. The sloops and fast trawlers were to be augmented by the best of the Canadian navy's tinpot fleet: eight auxiliary patrol vessels that had previously been the core of the RCN's patrol forces, the twelve Battle-class trawlers the RCN had ordered in 1917, and six of the Canadian-built imperial trawlers. Based primarily on Sydney, the mobile flotilla was to be divided into four divisions with six of the auxiliary patrol vessels distributed in the divisions and two, *Stadacona* and *Laurentian*, being held for "special duties" at the captain of patrols' discretion. The 1st Division consisted of one RN sloop, the APVs *Acadia*, and *Margaret*, and the Battle-class trawlers *Festubert*, *St Eloi*, and *Armentieres*. The 2nd Division was to consists of the second RN sloop, the APVs *Cartier* and *Lady Evelyn*, and the Battle-class trawlers *Ypres*, *Messines*, and *Givenchy*. Both divisions included a hydrophone-equipped imperial trawler. The 3rd and 4th Divisions had only one APV each, *Canada* and *Hochelaga*, respectively, one RN fast trawler and three Battle-class trawlers each (*Vimy*, *Thiepval*, and *Arras* in the 3rd, and *St Julien*, *Arleux*, and *Loos* in the 4th). The 3rd and 4th Divisions also included two hydrophone-equipped imperial

23. Ibid.

24. Ibid.

trawlers. The seventy-six minesweepers and escorts Hose planned to assign to Sydney would have a total complement of some 1,700 sailors all of whom would be borne on the books of HMCS *Stadacona* (Sydney). The 250 ratings of the Sydney shore establishment were to be borne on the books of the port's depot, HMCS *Lansdowne*.[25]

The mobile patrol flotilla was organized to fulfill the Admiralty recommendation to have "a striking force available to be sent anywhere without disorganizing the system of patrols and escort," one that could cover both the St Lawrence River and Gulf.[26] It was Hose's desire to operate the flotilla's four divisions on an eight-day cycle, with one division on "layup" at the main base at Sydney, while the others shifted every eight days in rotation between three "cruising bases." One of the bases would be established at Gaspé to cover the entrance to the St Lawrence River; a second at Bonne Bay, Newfoundland, for patrols in either the Straits of Belle Isle or the Cabot Straits; and a third base at St John's, Newfoundland, where the vessels could operate "as an advance force in the event of a submarine being reported south of Cape Race or on the Grand Banks." The captain of patrols wanted the flotilla's vessels to coal at their various cruising bases rather than at Sydney because the facilities there were already working to capacity to meet the needs of the large number of merchant ships and escorts at the port. Hose also believed it was better that "the flotilla should coal frequently, partly in order to be always ready for a distant call, and partly because large coalings are undesirable with small ships' companies."[27] It was the captain of patrols' intention "that the division which has just completed its 'layup' at the main base (Sydney) should proceed to one of the cruising bases, the division at that base moving on to the next, and so on, the fourth of the divisions, moving into the main base for 'layup.' While not desirable to expend coal more than is necessary when not proceeding to meet some call or emergency, some nine days of sea time each month is considered necessary for maintaining the efficiency of the flotilla, and this would be attained by the change of base to base as arranged." Hose was also willing to consider Louisbourg, Cape Breton as an alternative base to St John's with the additional suggestion "that the division on leaving Sydney does a sweep across the Cabot Straits and then to St Pierre and back to Louisbourg."[28]

The 109 vessels that comprised Hose's proposed East Coast patrol force would require a monthly total of some 7,600 tons of coal for their routine operations. As the captain of patrols pointed out, however, "the absolutely inadequate coaling facilities now existing has hampered the work of the few vessels operating in the patrol squadron, and considerable outlay in providing proper coaling facilities is immediately necessary if efficient and organized work is to be carried out by the squadron in order to give the measure of protection to convoys, etc., which is considered necessary by the Admiralty."[29]

---

25. Ibid.

26. Admiralty to Under Secretary of State, Colonial Office, for transmission to Ottawa, and enclosure, 3 January 1918, ibid.

27. Walter Hose, "Memorandum for DNS," nd [February 1918], ibid.

28. Ibid.

29. Ibid.

Oil supply for the expected destroyers was more readily available through the Imperial Oil Company wharves at Dartmouth and Africville in Bedford Basin. With one of the wharves at Sydney having a rail line to it, Hose did not foresee any difficulty in arranging for tank cars to make a regular delivery of the required fuel oil at that port either. General naval stores were to be issued on a divisional basis at both Sydney and Halifax, *Laurentian* being utilized as a storeship operating between the two East Coast ports. More specialized naval stores would have to be supplied by Britain. The Admiralty had sent the RCN fifteen sets of Actaeon sweeps for training purposes but an additional 100 sets were required for the initial outfitting of minesweepers. Canada also had only 140 D- and G-type depth charges on hand, all of which were being fitted to patrol vessels other than drifters and a further 500 D-type and 200 G-type had "been demanded from the Admiralty." The RCN also had twenty-seven general service hydrophones in stock but considered the "portable directional" hydrophone to be "the most generally useful and ninety of these with proper proportion of spare parts have been demanded."[30]

In submitting Hose's patrol scheme to the naval minister on 22 February, Kingsmill took issue only with the captain's desire to provide coaling facilities at the Newfoundland ports of St John's and Bonne Bay, preferring to coal the mobile flotilla at Gaspé and Louisbourg instead. Otherwise, the naval director "concur[red] entirely" with Hose's plan "and consider his scheme as worked out shows that great care has been taken in the matter." Kingsmill reminded naval minister Ballantyne that the navy was "exceedingly short" of trained staff officers to work at the bases in Sydney and Halifax, but felt that "the immediate necessity is to obtain an accountant officer from the Admiralty for the purpose of victualling etc., the officers and crews of the torpedo boat destroyers, sloops and fast trawlers they propose sending over."[31] In his financial statement to the minister outlining the estimated costs of the defence scheme, deputy minister Desbarats once again explained that NSHQ was operating on the assumption that the twelve RN warships would be manned and maintained by the Admiralty. The remaining ninety-six patrol vessels, trawlers, and drifters, however, would "be manned by men from the Canadian Navy. It is probable that there will be difficulty in obtaining some of the ratings needed for these ships and in that case it will be necessary to borrow them from the Admiralty, but most of the officers and men needed can be drawn from the men who have been enlisted for this purpose and are now under training in the RNCVR."[32] Desbarats's estimated expenditure of $4 million per annum had been calculated by J.A. Wilson based on the estimated annual cost of operating each ship, the six destroyers, at $100,000 per year, being the most expensive. Wilson's estimates included "a fair proportion of the cost of running the patrol base workshops, as the cost of repairs of the vessels within reasonable limits, is provided for."[33]

Ballantyne submitted the navy's defence scheme to the Cabinet War Committee on 5 March. Despite the increased naval expenditures entailed, the politicians—as was the case

---

30. Ibid.

31. Kingsmill, "Memorandum for the Minister," 21 February, 1918, ibid.

32. Desbarats, "Memo to the Minister," 2 March 1918, ibid.

33. J.A. Wilson, "Memorandum to the Deputy Minister," 27 February 1918, ibid.

with virtually every action recommended by the Admiralty—promptly agreed "that the Canadian government would undertake the responsibility of handling the patrol along the lines suggested in Captain Hose's report." The naval minister's only instructions to Kingsmill were to "take the proper steps to see that the recommendations made by the Admiralty are carried out," and to inform Whitehall of the Canadian measures.[34] With its government's approval of the proposed scheme, the Canadian navy at last had in place a comprehensive and realistic plan that provided the nation's eastern shipping lanes with an effective defence. It was also a vindication of Kingsmill's objection to previous British attempts to concentrate the RCN's patrol forces at Halifax. As the telegram NSHQ sent to the Admiralty stated, only thirty-three vessels would be based at the Nova Scotia capital, while seventy-five would be assigned to Sydney, of which thirty-one would form the navy's strategic reserve represented by the St. Lawrence patrol. Kingsmill explained to their lordships that all Canadian patrol vessels would be under the command of the captain of patrols but those vessels allocated to Halifax would also be under the local control of the admiral superintendent. Escorts for specific convoys would be assigned as necessary and would then come under the orders of the convoy's senior officer of escorts "until no longer required by him."[35]

Once the twelve fast escorts were in place, the RCN would, for the first time in the war, have a true anti-submarine capability, as opposed to the collection of inadequate armed yachts and ex-fishery patrol vessels it had been forced to employ during the first three shipping seasons. While the total of 108 East Coast escorts might sound impressive, it was the Admiralty's offer to provide Canada with twelve well-armed destroyers and fast trawlers that gave the navy's plan both its offensive punch and its credibility. The RCN scheme did make use of the trawlers and drifters that were being built in significant numbers in Canada, but these were to be employed in the secondary role of screening convoys as they formed up in the immediate approaches to Sydney and Halifax. As we have seen, Hose had already dismissed the value of the small imperial trawlers in his January submission to NSHQ, stating that with their slow speed and 12-pounder guns they would "be practically at [the] mercy" of the U-cruisers and recommending that they be exchanged for a smaller number of large, 4-inch-gunned trawlers.[36] The value of the hundred 6-pounder-armed drifters was even more dubious. It was the availability of the Admiralty-ordered trawlers and drifters that had resulted in their incorporation into the plan rather than any actual utility they might represent. As Hose and Kingsmill were well aware, without the twelve destroyers and fast trawlers from the Royal Navy, the RCN's East Coast defence plan would be an empty shell of trawlers, drifters and auxiliary patrol vessels of only limited value.

Even though Hose and Kingsmill were only deploying the available trawlers and drifters to augment the dozen warships promised by the Admiralty, the need to complete, maintain, and man a sizable fleet of small escorts still required a considerable training and logistics effort on the part of the Canadian navy. The problem of completing these vessels and making them seaworthy was exacerbated by the speed with which the thirty-six

---

34. Ballantyne, "Memo to the Deputy Minister of the Naval Service," 6 March 1918, ibid.

35. Naval Ottawa to Admiralty, 8 March 1918, ibid.

36. Captain of Patrols to NSHQ, 15 January 1918, 1017–10–4, pt. 1, LAC, RG 24, vol. 3832.

trawlers and 100 drifters had, at the urging of the British government, been contracted for and constructed in a wartime market that was already short of skilled labour and raw materials. As we have seen, the government asked J.W. Norcross of Canada Steamship Lines in Montreal to undertake the supervision of all shipyard work in the country. Shortages of steel and marine fittings meant that the Canadian government had to supply these materials, many of them purchased in the United States, if the shipyards were to have any chance of completing their contracts by the end of 1917. The inability of some of the yards to build boilers and engines also necessitated contracting American firms to build forty-seven of the engines and forty-two of the boilers. Although all the engines and boilers contracted for in Canada were delivered on schedule, deliveries of these items from the United States were delayed several months by work stoppages at American companies. As a result, only ninety of the 136 vessels were delivered to the navy in 1917 before the onset of winter closed the St Lawrence to navigation.[37]

Of the trawlers and drifters that had been accepted by the RCN in 1917, most were laid up in the Quebec City basin for the winter. In nearly all cases they still required work—in some instances considerable work—to correct defects and render them serviceable. The task was made more difficult by the wartime conditions under which the vessels were constructed, with non-specialist firms being forced to improvise the manufacture of winches, wireless sets, anchors, chains, sails, and compasses that were not part of their regular business. The amount of scrambling that Norcross had to do to scrounge the necessary equipment from across North America also meant that items were not always ideally suited to the tasks for which they were intended and might not mesh smoothly with the vessel's other machinery. Such wartime difficulties aside, by mid-February the naval officer overseeing the trawler and drifter programme, Commander J.W. Skentelbery, RNVR, reported to Kingsmill that three of the Admiralty trawlers had been delivered to Halifax together with the six Canadian Battle-class vessels that had been built by the Polson Iron Works of Toronto.[38]

There still remained six Canadian trawlers to be completed, of which *Armentieres* and *Arleux* were at Quebec City awaiting the installation of winches, *Givenchy* and *Arras* were at the Vickers's basin in Montreal also awaiting their winches, while *Thiepval* and *Loos* were at the government yard at Sorel where they required "a considerable amount of work completing." The thirty-two imperial trawlers that remained from the initial Admiralty order were evenly divided between those vessels that were still building and those that had been laid up for the winter along the St Lawrence, at Montreal, Sorel, Trois Rivières, and Quebec City. Skentelbery warned the naval director that twenty-six trawler crews would be needed to take over the vessels once the ice had cleared the river. The RNVR officer suggested that the crews should arrive on board their trawler two weeks before the vessel was ready to depart for the East Coast so that they could "be employed closing up machinery and boilers and getting their vessel ready for sea. I suggest full crews be sent as their services can be fully utilised and they can live on their own vessels."[39]

---

37. J.W. Norcross to C.C. Ballantyne, 12 January 1918, 29–16–1, pt. 3, LAC, RG 24, vol. 5605.

38. Skentelbery to Kingsmill, 13 February 1918, ibid.

39. Ibid.

Finding the skilled personnel to man the patrol fleet was another problem and Hose expected to have difficulty finding the sixty-one experienced skippers that were needed to command the individual trawlers and drifters. Although the patrol service had a enough RNCVR ratings to supply the bulk of the navy's personnel needs, there was a shortage of skilled ratings such as carpenters and engineers—100 of the latter being required—as well as some 120 cooks and stewards. The captain of patrols asked NSHQ to approach the militia department in regard to the navy's personnel requirements so that "the necessary numbers of engineers, carpenters, etc., may be requisitioned under the Military Service Act."[40] Hose was particularly anxious to have three experienced naval skippers, who had been seconded during the winter months to serve as pilots guiding merchant ships, returned to the patrol service and asked Kingsmill to ensure "that they may be recalled immediately we need skippers to bring down the vessels now up river."[41]

Although ice would not allow the trawlers and drifters to clear the St Lawrence until May, the captain of patrols was also making arrangements to expedite commissioning the vessels. As he explained to Ottawa in early March, Hose had shipped the available 6-pounder guns and mountings to the Davies shipyard for installation in the sixteen wireless-equipped drifters tied up at Quebec and was in communication with Skentelbery to see that the necessary work was in hand to ensure that the needed trawlers and drifters were "absolutely ready to start on their programme work immediately on leaving the river." Hose also sent NSHQ his requirements for Actaeon minesweeping gear to be supplied by the Admiralty and explained that his crews were "rapidly getting all the depth charges we have in stock fitted to our existing vessels and all the skippers and mates are getting one day's instruction each in them."[42] The captain of patrols had also briefed the new commander-in-chief, North America and West Indies Station, Vice-Admiral W.L. Grant, on the Canadian plan, only to find that the British officer had his own doubts about the Admiralty trawlers and drifters assigned to the Canadians.

> I have had a couple of conferences with the commander-in-chief over the proposed organization of the patrols, and so far as it goes to meet the Admiralty's views as expressed in their memorandum, he concurs in it, but I rather gather that he, personally, does not think the scheme, more particularly as regards the classes of vessels selected by the Admiralty, altogether the best to meet the particular enemy craft which we may expect to come on the scene. However, these are the vessels which the Admiralty have given us to perform certain duties and he concurs in our arrangement of them.[43]

At the same time that Hose was informing Kingsmill of Grant's reservations about the inadequacy of the Admiralty's choice of patrol vessels, the British admiral despatched his

---

40. Hose, "Memorandum for the Director of the Naval Service," 18 February 1918, 1065–7-6, LAC, RG 24, vol. 4031.

41. Hose to Kingsmill, 2 March 1918, 1017–10-4, pt. 1, LAC, RG 24, vol. 3832.

42. Ibid.

43. Ibid.

own memorandum to the Canadian naval director explaining that he had conferred "with the officers of the Royal Canadian Navy responsible for the organization and equipment of the patrol and minesweeping vessels for the protection of shipping." As he explained to Kingsmill, the C-in-C was sufficiently concerned about the inadequacy of the naval forces available to Hose that he had telegraphed the Admiralty to "urge immediate steps to hasten" the arrival of the six destroyers and six fast trawlers "to place the organization on the best possible basis."[44] Grant also emphasized his belief that the situation facing the North American shipping lanes during the 1918 season was one of great potential danger:

> In view of the vital interests at stake and the natural geographical features which offer so strong an inducement to the enemy to undertake a submarine and mine offensive in the area mentioned against Allied troop and cargo vessels and convoys as soon as weather and ice conditions admit, I cannot but regard the position as involving grave risks and feel it my duty to urge that every effort be made to have the whole flotilla completely equipped and organised and at work in their assigned positions at as early a date as possible.
>
> Pending the equipment and organisation of the full flotilla I would suggest that such vessels as are, or become, available be organised to the best immediate advantage and be prepared to undertake their duties as soon as weather conditions render it advisable.[45]

As much as Grant may have had concerns about the inadequacy of the trawlers and drifters the Admiralty had decreed should constitute the bulk of the RCN's patrol forces, the C-in-C understood as fully as NSHQ that it was the fast, 4-inch-gunned vessels the British had promised to supply that were the key to an effective defence of Canada's Atlantic coast. The British admiral was unpleasantly surprised to discover soon after taking up his appointment, therefore, that the Admiralty had not taken any steps toward providing the twelve vital escorts. In one of his first communications with Whitehall after assuming command, the vice-admiral asked if "any co-ordinated scheme [had] been drawn up with United States for protection against powerful submarine cruisers and raiders" in the North American shipping lanes. As he explained, the only plan he could find was a copy of the 3 January letter from the Admiralty to Ottawa "which [I] consider quite inadequate and show no definite provision of necessary forces. I cannot urge too strongly the immediate importance of a full and careful consideration and organization of all our forces to meet this very positive danger."[46]

Shortly thereafter Grant again telegraphed London to ask that "immediate steps" be taken to hasten the arrival of the six destroyers and six fast trawlers from Britain "in order

44. Vice-Admiral W.L. Grant to NSHQ, 2 March 1918, 1065–7-6, LAC, RG 24, vol. 4031.

45. Ibid.

46. C-in-C to Admiralty, 25 February 1918, 863, United Kingdom National Archives (hereafter UKNA), Admiralty (hereafter ADM) 116/1400; and Telegram 863 also quoted in Grant to Admiralty, General Letter No. 1, 1 March 1918, UKNA, ADM 137/504.

to place [the Canadian] organization on best basis possible."[47] The British C-in-C also urged NSHQ to speed the delivery of the Canadian-built trawlers and drifters by "pointing out the vital interests at stake in the hope that the Canadian officers responsible, who are loyally doing their best, may be given the best possible assistance by the Canadian government and that the opening of the St Lawrence may see prompt delivery of all the vessels fully equipped." In his 1 March report to Whitehall, the British admiral reminded his superiors of Canada's geography, and that "the coast and the gulf and estuary of the St Lawrence afford such assistance to submarines and minelayers that the delay in the provision and organization of the necessary patrol and minesweeping services to such a late and critical period of the war may involve very serious consequences."[48]

Clearly Grant, like Kingsmill, had taken Admiralty promises at face value and, again like Kingsmill, believed the modern vessels would soon arrive. The situation, however, was not that simple. Admiral Sir John Jellicoe was replaced as first sea lord on 27 December 1917 by Admiral Sir Rosslyn Wemyss, and there was a period of administrative confusion during which the new head of the navy, as he told the American Sims, was "a little busy just now getting this new organisation into working order, but it won't be very long before I will have very little to do personally."[49] Jellicoe, apparently, had tried to do "most of the work himself," something Wemyss sought to avoid.[50] Perhaps because of the change at the top— or perhaps because of sloppy staff work—the 3 January promise by the Admiralty to supply twelve fast escorts to Canada was allowed to be despatched just a few days after London had finally persuaded the United States Navy that all anti-submarine vessels, British and American, should be concentrated in United Kingdom waters.

That policy had not been the thinking in the US Navy, which preferred to maintain considerable strength off the American coast for much of 1917. It was not until the US chief of naval operations, Rear-Admiral W.S. Benson, visited the Admiralty in December that he was convinced otherwise, declaring that he would "send over every destroyer that can get across the ocean under her own power or by being towed."[51] Benson made good on his commitment almost immediately in the US Navy's February 1918 war plan for the defence of the eastern seaboard against U-cruiser operations. Accepting the British analysis that the threat to shipping posed by a trans-Atlantic submarine offensive was slight compared to the unrestricted campaign in European waters, the American naval staff reduced home defence requirements to a minimum, retaining only nine modern destroyers on the East Coast.[52] Moreover, as soon became clear, that number was not likely to be increased any time soon as the American destroyer-construction program fell short of expectations.[53]

---

47. Telegram 872 quoted in Grant to Admiralty, General Letter No. 1, 1 March 1918, UKNA, ADM 137/504.

48. Grant to Admiralty, General Letter No. 1, 1 March 1918, ibid.

49. Sims to Benson, 15 January 1918, quoted in Michael Simpson, ed., *Anglo-American Naval Relations, 1917–1919* (Aldershot, UK 1991), 148.

50. Bayly to Sims, 16 January 1918, quoted in ibid, 149.

51. Sims to Bayly, 10 December 1917, quoted in ibid, 260.

52. Hadley and Sarty, *Tin-pots and Pirate Ships*, 214.

53. Sims to Bayly, 31 January 1918, quoted in Simpson, ed., *Anglo-American Naval Relations,* 271; and Hadley and Sarty, *Tin-pots and Pirate Ships,* 214.

In short, the Admiralty's promise to send destroyers to Canada could only have been justified if the Royal Navy was prepared to break faith with the US Navy, something it was not about to do. But neither Grant, who took up his appointment as C-in-C in February, nor Naval Service Headquarters, had been informed of the Anglo-American anti-submarine policy, so that when Whitehall finally responded to the Canadian patrol proposals in mid-March, the substance of its reply was shattering. In a telegram so brief as to be almost insulting, the Admiralty accepted the Canadian defence scheme only in so far as it concerned the RCN's auxiliary patrol vessels and the trawlers and drifters being built in Canada. As for the "six fast trawlers mentioned in Admiralty letter [of] 3rd January," London dumped the entire problem of finding suitable vessels in the lap of Vice-Admiral Grant, informing Ottawa that the "C-in-C NA&WI has been directed to communicate with the Canadian government." The Admiralty was even more vague in regard to the six destroyers mentioned in its 3 January letter, merely informing NSHQ that "the question of the provision of additional fast craft should the necessity for them arise is being discussed by C-in-C with United States naval authorities."[54]

Although the Admiralty's January letter had unequivocally stated that Canadian convoys required fast escorts, "which in concert could beat off a submarine cruiser," this was the first indication either Ottawa or Grant had received since then that Whitehall was unwilling to supply the RCN with the destroyers or sloops it had said were needed. The extent to which the Admiralty was reneging on its January assessment was more fully revealed on 18 March when Vice-Admiral Grant—no doubt with much chagrin, given his own view that the 3 January Admiralty memorandum was "quite inadequate" to meet the "positive danger" of submarine attack in Canadian waters—fulfilled his orders "to communicate with the Canadian government" in regard to the fast trawlers. But, ill-informed of the Admiralty's plans himself, the British admiral simply relayed the contents of the telegram he had received from London on the 16th, bluntly informing Ottawa that "it will not be possible to send six fast trawlers from England for some months." Grant had also been directed by London to "consult with US naval authorities as to provision of additional destroyers and fast fleet auxiliaries" to Canada even though the USN's policy of maintaining minimal destroyer forces on its own coast precluded that possibility as well. Even if the C-in-C was able to pry six destroyers from the USN, the Admiralty cautioned him that "until there is evidence that submarines are likely to operate on Canadian Atlantic coast it does not appear necessary for these craft to be sent to Halifax or Sydney before the emergency arises."[55] In passing on the information London had given him, a frustrated Grant admitted to Ottawa that "no definite arrangement has yet been made with United States as regards additional fast craft."[56]

London's latest reversal completely eviscerated NSHQ's carefully laid defence plans for the 1918 season. The Admiralty also appeared to have been less than honest in telling the RCN in January that it would supply the six destroyers and six fast trawlers either "from

---

54. Admiralty to Naval Ottawa, 105, 16 March 1918, 1065–7-6, LAC, RG 24, vol. 4031.

55. Admiralty to Britannia, Halifax [Grant], 16 March 1918, 1017–10–4, pt. 1, LAC, RG 24, vol. 3832; and C-in-C to Admiralty, 25 February 1918, 863, UKNA, ADM 116/1400.

56. Grant to Naval Ottawa, 18 March 1918, 1065–7-6, LAC, RG 24, vol. 4031.

England or USA"[57] when, in fact, the warships had been promised before the British had even consulted the USN as to the possibility of their providing the vessels. All that Whitehall was now willing to say on the matter was that the US naval representative in London, Admiral Sims, "may have communicated with US naval authorities in view of letter sent to him 10th Jan[uary] ... asking whether it would be possible for six US destroyers to be provided for Canadian patrol by 1st April."[58] In holding out the apparent possibility that Canada might still receive destroyers from the Americans, however, the Admiralty was merely compounding the confusion it had already created by not informing either Grant or the Canadians of the firm Anglo-American policy of concentrating all destroyers and fast escorts in British waters.

As accustomed as NSHQ had become to sudden reversals in Admiralty thinking, it was easier for the USN's chief of naval operations to concur with the British desire to deploy all destroyers in the waters surrounding the United Kingdom than it was for Kingsmill. With large numbers of destroyers being built in American shipyards, vessels the USN could retain in home waters should the cruiser submarine menace require it—as indeed was the case by September 1918 when the USN was employing thirty ocean-going destroyers as convoy escorts in western Atlantic waters[59]—Benson was in a much better position to accede to the British view. Kingsmill, on the other hand, did not have any warships capable of combating the U-boats expected in Canadian waters and was entirely reliant on either the Royal Navy or the USN to supply them. In a crisis, the RCN suspected that it was unlikely to receive priority attention, no matter how important Canadian shipping might be to the Allied war effort. The RCN was at least fortunate that the new C-in-C was truly sympathetic to Canada's exposed position. At the beginning of April, Grant informed London that he was planning to meet with Ballantyne and Kingsmill soon "for the purpose of discussing ... the whole question of coast patrols, coastal escorts, air service, etc., for which co-ordination between Newfoundland, Canada and United States is essential."[60]

As the man directly responsible for the RCN's East Coast patrols, Captain Hose was understandably disturbed when Grant showed him the Admiralty telegrams advising that the twelve 4-inch-gunned escorts upon which his plans depended would not be available. The captain of patrols quickly expressed his disappointment to Ottawa, pointing out that the Admiralty had withdrawn the required fast warships without having altered their original assessment that the new submarine cruisers could be expected off North America any time after March. As Hose reminded NSHQ, "there is nothing to show that this probability of U Cruisers operating on this side has in any way lessened, and all that can be gathered from the attached telegram is the inability of the Admiralty to provide at

---

57. Admiralty to Under Secretary of State, Colonial Office, for transmission to Ottawa, and enclosure, 3 January 1918, 1017–10–1, pt. 1, LAC, RG 24, vol. 3831.

58. Admiralty to Britannia, Halifax [Grant], 16 March 1918, 1017–10–4, pt. 1, LAC, RG 24, vol. 3832.

59. US Navy Department to Admiralty, "Distribution of United States Naval Forces Employed against Enemy Submarines in Western Atlantic Waters," 1 September 1918, 5 September 1918, quoted in Simpson, ed., *Anglo-American Naval Relations, 1917–1919*, 469.

60. Grant to Admiralty, General Letter No. 2, 1 April 1918, UKNA, ADM 137/504.

present, or for some months, the defence which they deemed necessary."[61] In view of the reported heavy armament of two 5.9-inch and two 4-inch guns mounted on the long-range U-boats, their prolonged cruising capability of up to five months and their high surface speed, Hose "urgently" submitted to NSHQ "that the safety of the large, slow convoys leaving Canadian ports and of the great number of ships proceeding along the coasts to the ports of assembly, is very greatly jeopardized" by the Admiralty's decision not to supply 4-inch-gunned warships. It was likely, therefore, that "a U-Cruiser could operate on these coasts for a very considerable time before any vessels fit to cope with her could be brought on the scene." Moreover, the presence of much stronger USN patrol forces off the American coast, together with the need to use the cruisers of the North America and West Indies Squadron as ocean escorts for convoys, provided "additional reason for the U-Cruiser to operate off the Canadian coast so long as the [RCN's] patrol remains, as at present, totally inadequate to cope with it."[62]

In the absence of any other warships, Hose revived his January proposal to rearm the mothballed *Rainbow* with 4-inch guns and bring her to the East Coast.

> HMCS *Rainbow* could be got ready for service with eight modern 4-inch guns in a short time. Sixteen seaplanes could be built in Canada and sufficient volunteers from the Canadian patrol squadron trained at Toronto and in a few weeks aerodromes for ten planes at Sydney and six at Shelburne could be erected.
>
> I would submit that their lordships be asked by telegram, in view of their inability to provide fast vessels with 4-inch guns, to supply the necessary guns for *Rainbow*, observing that this vessel can now steam eighteen knots.
>
> It is quite realized that one vessel is insufficient to maintain the necessary patrol, but one efficient vessel together with available aircraft would reduce very considerably the amount of time that a U-cruiser could operate with impunity in any one area.
>
> Since the Admiralty are unable to send 4-inch gun vessels there is not one gun in the whole force of ninety-seven vessels employed or to be employed in the Canadian coast patrol which would be able to get within range of a U-cruiser before the patrol vessel would, in all probability, be sunk.
>
> It is most respectfully and at the same time most strongly urged that if shipping is attacked this summer off the Canadian coast and the full measure of defence of which the dominion is capable is not provided that it will reflect seriously on the patrol service, which is responsible for the protection of the immensely valuable shipping on Canadian coasts.[63]

---

61. Captain of Patrols to NSHQ, 25 March 1918, 1017–10–4, pt. 1, LAC, RG 24, vol. 3832.

62. Ibid.

63. Ibid.

The urgency with which the captain of patrols put forward his proposals was not lost on NSHQ. Ottawa, however, could not escape the reality that the RCN's capabilities were dependent on what the British were willing to supply. A week before Hose prepared his memorandum, Kingsmill had made his own recommendation to recommission HMCS *Rainbow* and bring her to the Atlantic coast. While on a west coast tour of Esquimalt in mid-March, the naval director had telegraphed Stephens that in his opinion both the Canadian cruiser and the sloop *Algerine* would be fit to perform patrol duties guarding the fishing fleet on the Grand Banks "after comparatively small refit. Inform Admiralty and state that if they wish us to commission them they would have to arm vessels and lend a few artificers and stokers. My proposal would be to commission these vessels with reduced complement outside engineering and stoke hold ratings."[64] The Admiralty, however, quickly turned down Kingsmill's proposal to arm and despatch *Rainbow* to the Atlantic and were equally unwilling to supply the RCN with modern 4-inch guns.[65] The sense of futility that existed at NSHQ when it came to acquiring the needed weapons and equipment from the Admiralty is evident in the message Stephens attached in passing Hose's memorandum to Kingsmill: "Captain of patrols ... points out the inferiority of the armament of patrol vessels to that of German submarines. I concur generally in his view but it seems useless to belabour the point as the Admiralty so persistently state a 12-pounder gun is sufficient."[66] In replying directly to Hose, however, headquarters did not communicate its own concerns about the inadequacy of the gun armament and simply informed the captain of patrols that the Admiralty "considered a 12-pounder gun is sufficient for auxiliary patrol vessels." The chief of staff was more hopeful about the provision of air patrols and noted that "the question of air defences on the Atlantic coast has frequently engaged the attention of the department and is again being made the subject of enquiry."[67]

Although yet another Canadian effort to strengthen the country's naval defences had been turned down, the fact that NSHQ had approached London with its *Rainbow* proposal demonstrates the degree to which Kingsmill, faced with a desperate situation, was willing to embrace any idea that might increase "the full measure of defence of which the dominion is capable." As captain of the Canadian cruiser until 1916, Hose was well-placed to know the condition of the vessel's aging machinery, an opinion that was concurred in by the naval director during his visit to Esquimalt. While Kingsmill was sufficiently convinced to seek the Admiralty's concurrence in rearming *Rainbow* and bringing her around to the Atlantic, the Canadian admiral also realized that the plan would require that Britain supply the cruiser with modern 4-inch guns. A warship of *Rainbow*'s size armed with small 12-pounders would have been a liability for the East Coast patrols, requiring a large crew for a vessel that would have been as completely at a submarine's mercy as any

---

64. Kingsmill to Stephens, 18 March 1918, 559, 1065-7-6, LAC, RG 24, vol. 4031.

65. R.M. Stephens minute, nd, on Captain of Patrols to NS.HQ, 25 March 1918, 1017–10–4, pt. 1, LAC, RG 24, vol. 3832.

66. Stephens to Kingsmill, 28 March 1918, ibid.

67. NSHQ to Captain of Patrols, 28 March 1918, ibid.

of the RCN's other auxiliary patrol vessels. Kingsmill, Stephens, and Hose all realized, as the captain of patrols had repeatedly stated, that Canada's collection of trawlers and armed yachts could easily be sunk by a U-cruiser's superior artillery before the German submarine came within range of a 12-pounder gun.

While NSHQ may have seemed overly anxious to be reinforced by destroyers and fast trawlers before enemy submarines appeared on the North American side of the Atlantic, there were sound reasons for the RCN to seek the fast escorts it needed before U-cruisers actually began sinking merchant ships off the Canadian coast. Without knowing in advance what warships might be sent to Canadian waters, NSHQ could not integrate them into a coherent plan of operations or provide for any special logistical needs, such as fuel oil or turbine parts, that the reinforcements might require. Moreover, waiting until a crisis was at hand would not allow the RCN to gain any experience employing fast escorts in convoy defence or to train its own personnel if the Canadian navy was required to man or maintain the vessels itself. (Although, aside from a small handful of RN engineering officers, chief ERAs, and chief stokers, NSHQ believed Canada could man six destroyers with RCN personnel after a short training period.)[68] There was also no guarantee that the American naval authorities would ever be willing to despatch destroyers to Canada if their own shipping lanes were under attack and, unlike the USN, the RCN had no fast escorts of its own to divert from elsewhere.

No matter how carefully he perceived the RCN's requirements—and as early as the spring of 1916 NSHQ had clearly determined that the navy required at least a handful of destroyers if it was adequately to protect the East Coast shipping lanes—Kingsmill was never in a position to oppose London's opinion and convince his political masters to accept his naval advice over that of the Admiralty. It was an issue of credibility, deserved or not. The underdeveloped state of Canadian industry was a further constraint on the naval director's actions. Any RCN equipment decision that ran counter to the Admiralty's opinion would still have required British technical or material assistance in order to be implemented. Vickers, for example, would have had difficulty building destroyers without some technical support and turbine engines from either Britain or the United States. Similarly, Hose's *Rainbow* proposal made little sense if Whitehall was unwilling to supply the RCN with the modern 4-inch guns the aging cruiser needed to make her effective against a surfaced U-cruiser, weapons which Canadian industry was still incapable of producing. Forced to operate within the constraints imposed by the Admiralty and

---

68. Commenting in October 1918 on a proposal to man six RCN destroyers, the director of operations at NSHQ, Acting Commander John P. Gibbs, a Royal Navy officer with three years' destroyer experience, believed that "practically no personnel would be required [on loan] from the imperial service to man the destroyers," aside from three engineering lieutenants and a dozen chief ERAs and stokers, given that there were "sufficient lieutenants in the RCN" who were serving in RN warships, "several of them having had a large amount of destroyer experience," to provide the needed commanding and watchkeeping officers. Gibbs also did not feel that any RN ratings would be needed since "the standard of education is so high in Canada that the [RCN] men should be able to be trained with comparative ease and quickness." Gibbs, "Memorandum for the Director of the Naval Service," 28 October 1918, 1065-1-1, pt. 1, LAC, RG 24, vol. 4029. In March 1918 there were fifty-six RCN lieutenants, sub-lieutenants and midshipmen on loan to the Royal Navy serving in British warships. Department of the Naval Service, *The Canadian Navy List for April 1918* (Ottawa 1918), 17–27.

Canada's own politicians, the RCN's freedom of action throughout the First World War was severely limited.

The consequences for the Canadian navy of being so closely bound by Admiralty advice were exacerbated by the haphazard nature of Whitehall's strategic planning. As we have seen, the commander-in-chief of the US Atlantic fleet, Admiral H.T. Mayo, had been appalled by the absence of a systematic planning process when he visited the Admiralty in the summer of 1917.[69] Largely as a result of American insistence on a comprehensive war plan,[70] an Allied Naval Council, consisting of the ministers of marine of the main allied nations, was set up in December 1917. (Canada, as an appendage of the British government, was not represented by her minister). As the first lord, Sir Eric Geddes, informed his war Cabinet colleagues, the council had been established "to ensure the closest touch and complete co-operation between the Allied fleets," and "to watch over the general conduct of the naval war and to ensure the co-ordination of effort at sea."[71]

Among the naval threats discussed by the Allied Council when it met in January 1918 were "the probable theatres of operation of the new German submarine cruisers," and "the best methods of dealing with them and of protecting shipping from attack."[72] Since the cruiser submarine was the only warship the Germans had that could realistically threaten the North American coast, the views of senior Allied naval leaders regarding its capabilities and probable deployment areas had a considerable impact on the RCN's operations during the summer of 1918. Much of the council's discussion of the threat was based on intelligence assessments supplied by the Admiralty. The first sea lord, Admiral Sir Rosslyn Wemyss, set the tone of deliberations by asserting that "the submarine cruiser cannot be looked upon as being quite in the same category as the present submarine.... It seems unlikely that a craft of this description with a large radius of action will take up the available space in such an uneconomical way as by carrying mines. The probability is that it will be used for torpedoes and guns. The submarine cruiser should therefore be considered as a raider which is able as a means of defence to submerge and hide."[73]

The USN's representative, Vice-Admiral Sims, pointed to the estimated length of time it took for the large submarines to dive and emphasized that "it is unlikely that they will operate where they are exposed to attack by the more nimble of their enemies, such as destroyers; and probably they will always operate where they are reasonably safe, since a submarine which takes three minutes to dive is in great danger if sighted within a reasonable distance by a destroyer."

> If ... the characteristics of these big submarines are properly understood, they
> have all the radius of action necessary to maintain themselves at sea until they

---

69. "Admiral Mayo's general impressions regarding conditions in the Admiralty," September 1917, quoted in Simpson, ed., *Anglo-American Naval Relations*, 97.

70. Ibid, 60.

71. Geddes memorandum for War Cabinet, 11 December 1917, quoted in ibid, 142–43.

72. Allied Naval Council minutes, January 1918, 8, UKNA, ADM 137/836.

73. Ibid, 25.

can use up all their ammunition, both for guns and torpedoes, and they will need no fuel or stores, the real limitation of their work being the amount of ammunition they can carry, and the endurance of their crews. It is improbable that they will lay mines on the American coast, since it is a long way to go for a doubtful result, and any mines laid could be discovered and swept up in a week. The later submarine cruisers appear much more dangerous than those of the converted Deutschland class, since they have a surface speed of sixteen knots, and one of these boats can be imagined sighting a convoy in the day time, following it up at a distance on the surface, and then closing at night and picking off the ships one by one during the darkness, both by gun and torpedo attack. Such a submarine should be able to get one merchant ship out of the convoy with every torpedo fired, since it is very difficult at night to do anything against her. The question is what is to be done against the submarine in case of such an attack. There appears to be no definite solution in sight, but the fact is clearly brought out that if we are to oppose the submarine we must fight him and hunt him wherever he may be, and neutralise him to the greatest extent possible by the use of vessels with the necessary speed and fitted with the necessary apparatus for listening under the water. In other words, hunting squadrons must be organised, composed not only of destroyers, but also of cruisers.[74]

Despite the American admiral's rather chilling analysis of what a long-range submarine in contact with a convoy might be capable of, the Naval Council's decision on the actions required to counter the U-cruiser threat had already been determined by the Anglo-American agreement to concentrate their anti-submarine forces in British home waters. The deliberations contained more than a small element of hope that the Germans would attack shipping in those areas the Allies most wanted them to, rather than in areas where the defences were weakest and where U-boats would have the greatest effect. The French representative, Vice-Admiral F. de Bon, for instance, believed that the shipping lanes "especially threatened" by the U-cruisers lay off the Azores and Canary Islands and that the allied navies should concentrate on strengthening convoy escorts in those zones. The possibility that long-range U-boats might operate more profitably against the vitally important—but virtually undefended—shipping lanes of northeastern North America was largely ignored by the allied admirals. The anglophile Sims went so far as to belittle the idea that it was possible to escort a large number of convoys with destroyers, claiming that although the USN had initially provided two destroyers and a cruiser as escorts to US troop convoys, experience had shown the system unworkable in bad weather and that a two destroyer escort for all American troop convoys would require at least forty-five destroyers. "To apply that system to all the convoys that come across the Atlantic would require all the destroyers that the Allies possess."[75] With Sims's support, the British argued—rather

74. Ibid.

75. Ibid, 27.

incongruously given the acknowledged capabilities of the vessels—that U-cruisers should be treated as surface raiders rather than as submarines.[76]

The methods the Allied navies were to use to defend against long-range submarines were more clearly laid out when the Naval Council met in Rome the following month:

> The question of the cruiser-submarine is one very difficult of solution, because of the extensive field of operations. Tactically it is less efficient than the small submarine, except for the increased range of its guns. The tendency of our answer to the cruiser-submarine attack will be towards a further diversion of forces to defensive arrangements, and a further slowing up of shipping through extension of the convoy system. Even if it were sound policy, it is impossible to guard shipping in distant waters against the torpedo attack of cruiser-submarines. Greater zig-zag areas, increased armament of merchant ships, increased numbers and skill of armed guards [i.e., lookouts], increased vigilance regarding lights, radio signals, smoke, etc., all palliative measures, is the best reply available at present to the cruiser-submarine.... As the convoy system becomes more fully organised, it will then be possible to place one specially armed ship in each convoy and thus be sure that in the absence of an ocean escort, we will still have sufficient gun power with each convoy to reply to the gunfire of a cruiser-submarine.[77]

The Naval Council's decision to adopt only "palliative measures" to combat the U-cruiser threat contained more than a little wishful thinking. Despite having clearly stated that any long-range U-boat that contacted a convoy was capable of "picking off the ships one by one during the darkness, both by gun and torpedo attack,"[78] the council was not prepared to interfere with the policy of concentrating all destroyer escorts in British home waters. Just how council members believed that a single merchant ship armed with a 4-inch or 6-inch gun was going to drive off a U-cruiser and prevent her from closing with a convoy was never realistically addressed. It did not require much imagination to see that a surfaced submarine with a speed of sixteen knots could easily follow a slower-moving, unescorted convoy from beyond gun range in daylight and then close in to sink merchant ships at will during the hours of darkness, a fate that no amount of zig-zagging or vigilance was going to prevent. Although the Halifax and Sydney convoys were routinely escorted by a British cruiser, the warship would still be theoretically vulnerable to the torpedoes of an aggressively handled U-cruiser, leaving the German submarine free to pick off merchant ships by gunfire.

Convinced there were no Allied resources to spare to provide an anti-submarine defence off the coast of North America, the Admiralty was content to leave the protection of these vital shipping lanes in the hands of the United States Navy. Even then, however, the

---

76. Ibid, 28.

77. Allied Naval Council minutes, February 1918, 86, ibid.

78. Allied Naval Council minutes, January 1918, 25, ibid.

Americans wanted to ensure that there was proper coordination with their British associates. In particular, the US chief of naval operations was concerned that the "lack of a central controlling British authority on shore in Washington DC, lead[s] sometimes to a confusion of requests and a certain lack of thorough cooperation in any plan which affects our joint forces operating on this side [of the] Atlantic. This is especially true of [the] convoy situation now and would immediately [be]come acute involving all joint plans and operations of any sort [the] instant a single cruising submarine were to appear on our coast." Benson asked Sims to approach the Admiralty with a view to appointing a British convoy representative to the American capital "because were a submarine to operate off our coast undoubtedly [US navy] department would take some form of action into its hands, especially as regards routing for incoming vessels and it is desired that we not only have full information on this subject but also take no separate action where present lack of centralization would force us to go."[79] The American proposal quickly met with London's approval, the first sea lord explaining that Vice-Admiral Grant was the "ultimate convoy authority as well as commander British naval forces in America." As a result, the British C-in-C was invited to establish his headquarters in Washington, while an officer from the Admiralty's Trade Division was also attached to the convoy section of the American navy department.[80]

Grant reluctantly berthed his flagship, HMS *Warrior* (a yacht loaned to the Royal Navy by her American owner), at the American capital in recognition of "the increasing weight of the United States" in the Allied war effort. Although he had initially hoped to use "Halifax as my headquarters with frequent visits and intimate touch with Washington," he had little choice but to yield to both London's and the US naval department's insistent views. Despite now being closely tied to the American capital, Grant was nonetheless anxious to reassure Ottawa "that my location at Washington for the time being will not in any way affect my duties as C-in-C as they affect Canada."[81] There were also advantages for Canada in having the British admiral establish his offices in Washington. After Britain chose not to supply the RCN with the twelve destroyers and fast trawlers, NSHQ had to follow the Admiralty's suggestion and look to Grant for assistance in obtaining additional anti-submarine vessels from the United States.

Nonetheless, the British admiral's position in Washington was initially made more difficult by the fact that he still was unclear of the intention of British policy for the defence of North American waters. As the C-in-C explained in his report to the Admiralty for the month of March, his complaints that "nothing was known of the six destroyers and six fast sloops to come from England or the United States" for Canadian service had only resulted in being told "that it would not be possible to send from England—at any rate for some months—any fast trawlers and that I would discuss with the US naval authorities the question of the provision of the additional fast craft should the necessity arise."[82] Such an

79. Benson to Sims, 20 February 1918, quoted in Simpson, ed., *Anglo-American Naval Relations*, 456–57.

80. Sims to Benson, 25 February, Sims to Benson, 1 March, Benson to Sims, 3 March, and Sims to Admiralty, 16 March 1918, quoted in ibid, 457–58.

81. Grant to Admiralty, General Letter No. 2, 1 April 1918, UKNA, ADM 137/504.

82. Ibid.

indifferent response was not one the British admiral was prepared to accept in view of the stern warnings the Admiralty had previously sent of the serious threat posed by long-range U-cruisers. "I cannot but concur in the view generally expressed [on] this side that we are very open to a sudden attack and sinkings possibly of large troop transports and am afraid that this would probably cause great popular commotion in Canada and the United States. At the same time the US are fully prepared to accept the home [i.e., Admiralty] ruling as to the relative degree of menace and the consequent most expedient appropriation of the destroyers and small craft at our disposal." Grant went on to point out that the instructions the Admiralty had been sending across the Atlantic "are somewhat conflicting but I read them as meaning that the policy of getting all possible destroyers into European waters with as little delay as possible will not be waived in any degree." Although Grant had been told that the Admiralty had "no intention to propose any alteration in policy of US authorities" to send America's destroyers to Britain, he made it clear to London "that if US, Canada and myself concur in the necessity of keeping a minimum [of anti-submarine forces in North American waters], we will keep them; this reading I propose to act upon so far as I myself am concerned."[83]

As good as his word, Grant telegraphed NSHQ on 3 April asking them to provide him with "the minimum number of fast craft you consider necessary to your organization with which I can approach United States."[84] Replying the next day, Kingsmill quickly cut the two destroyers and two fast trawlers from the navy's strategic reserve, the mobile patrol flotilla, thereby reducing the RCN's minimum requirements for its East Coast defence plan to eight fast escorts. Moreover, if the Admiralty decided that convoys were no longer going to be assembled at Halifax as it had recently proposed, the Canadian navy's requirements could be reduced by three additional fast escorts, the number that Hose had assigned to convoy duties at that port, thus allowing the naval director to inform Grant that the "minimum requirements would be five fast craft, with armament not less than 4-inch guns" to operate with the Sydney convoys.[85] Although the proposed reductions were passed to the British admiral without comment, the ease with which NSHQ was able to eliminate the Halifax escorts is yet another indication of the port's relative insignificance as either a shipping port or a naval base for RCN operations despite its magnificent anchorage and the naval dockyard inherited from the North America and West Indies Station.

With the British C-in-C now pressing the Americans to provide the fast escorts the Admiralty had indicated Canada needed, it is not surprising that the US chief of naval operations found Grant's representations to be in conflict with the agreed Anglo-American policy. Having acceded to Admiralty pressure in December 1917 to send almost the entire US destroyer force to Britain, Benson was soon complaining to Sims about the British admiral's lobbying efforts to obtain the minimum requirement of five destroyers for the RCN.

---

83. Ibid.

84. C-in-C to Naval Ottawa, 3 April 1918, 1065–7-6, LAC, RG 24, vol. 4031.

85. Naval Ottawa to C-in-C, 4 April 1918, ibid.

The question of allocating some of our new destroyers to the port of Halifax, Nova Scotia [i.e., to Canada], for protection of that area and of convoys sailing from there is one that is being pushed by Canadian authority and British commander-in-chief [in] these waters. Minimum number of destroyers wanted for this duty five. We are sending our destroyers abroad as fast as they can be made available; reserves only twelve, speed ten knots, on entire coast, most of which are either crippled, under repair or engaged on important experimental work. To allocate five additional destroyers to Halifax, Nova Scotia, will cripple our efforts abroad and in our opinion that is not justified now. The [US navy] department desires a definite statement from you, backed up by the Admiralty, as to correctness of our present policy or whether they advise yielding to the Canadian desires. It is further considered desirable to increase the reserve on our own coast due to the prospect of submarine operations here. This information requested not from any desire on our part to hold back destroyers but is dictated by the necessity which would naturally arise from protecting adequately the numerous convoys sailing from our ports. In case of attack on Canadian coast, we naturally would go [to their] assistance with such force as could be spared from [US forces needed to combat an] imminent attack on our own coast.[86]

Although Benson's telegram confirmed that he was still committed to the policy of concentration in British waters, the fact that he had also indicated a belief that it was now "desirable to increase the reserve on our own coast due to the prospect of submarine operations here" suggested that the CNO had been listening to Grant's warnings about the U-cruiser threat. Such heresy provoked an unequivocal response from Sims in London:

After consultation with Admiralty, I can say unreservedly that they are in entire agreement with me in regarding as correct the department's present policy and in recommending against yielding to the Canadian desires. This same subject was broached some months ago before Vice-Admiral Browning came home and it was decided at that time that there was no necessity for allocating destroyers to the port of Halifax, Nova Scotia, and furthermore that if such allocation were made there would be an immediate demand for similar allocation to United States ports such as New York and Hampton Roads. Such dispersion of force would be contrary to sound military principles and should be avoided at all costs.

The department will be kept supplied with all information obtainable here as to probability of hostile operations on home coasts.[87]

86. Benson to Sims, 4640, 7 April 1918, KD 1911–1927, United States National Archives (hereafter USNA), RG 45, box 221; and Simpson, ed., *Anglo-American Naval Relations*, 462–63.

87. Sims to Benson, 6352, 11 April 1918, ibid.

Armed with the "definite statement" he had sought from Sims, Admiral Benson was able to confront Grant in mid-April concerning the discrepancy between the Admiralty's stated policy and the C-in-C's own actions. Showing Grant the contents of Sims's telegram urging the USN to resist "yielding to the Canadian desires," Benson asked pointed questions about the discrepancy between the Admiralty's stated policy of concentration in British waters and the C-in-C's attempts to acquire resources for Canada. Sims's telegram was also the first indication the British admiral had received that London had decided against providing destroyers—either RN or USN—to protect the Canadian coast. As the British naval representative in Washington, Grant was understandably livid that the Americans were being kept better informed of Admiralty policy than he was. After giving himself several days to let his anger subside, he fired off a telegram to the Admiralty on 18 April vigorously protesting at having been kept in the dark about British policy. Insisting that neither he nor the Canadians had been badgering the US naval department, he stated that he had merely been carrying out the Admiralty's own advice contained in its 3 January assessment, one which he had every reason to believe was still current. Most importantly, the Admiralty's repeated failure to keep him informed of Allied naval policy, aside from his own personal embarrassment, undermined his credibility with American naval officials in Washington. The annoyed C-in-C could only plead with London to "please prevent communications which might lead the United States to suppose [that] I misrepresent facts or act contrary to Admiralty wishes."[88]

In fact, it was an amazing failure of communications that had placed Grant in such an embarrassing position; but how the Admiralty could fail to notice that the C-in-C North America was not kept abreast of Anglo-American agreements is beyond understanding other than as an instance of supremely lax staff procedures. (The failure to inform Canada is easier to understand, if still inexcusable.) Yet the fast escort question was not an isolated incident. Although naval aviation had not been mentioned in the Admiralty's 3 January assessment of Canadian naval defence requirements, it had evidently been given further consideration within the corridors of Whitehall during the winter of 1917–1918. It will be recalled (see Chapter 6) that an earlier proposal by NSHQ to form a Canadian naval air squadron on the East Coast had been endorsed by both the Admiralty and Prime Minister Borden in the spring of 1917 only to be turned down, for financial reasons, by Cabinet during the PM's absence in London. Despite the rejection by Ottawa, the advantages of forming a Canadian air patrol continued to receive the attention of the Admiralty's air department. Early in 1918, the air department considered diverting three seaplane tenders, HM Ships *Engadine*, *Riviera*, and *Vindex*, to Canada's East Coast, but the idea was rejected by the Admiralty's operations committee. Ruling that the tenders could more usefully be employed in the Mediterranean, the committee recommended that any air patrols operating over Canadian waters should be shore based.[89]

88. Grant to Admiralty, 18 April 1918, UKNA, ADM 116/1400; and Hadley and Sarty, *Tin-pots and Pirate Ships*, 215.

89. S.F. Wise, *Canadian Airmen and the First World War* (The Official History of the Royal Canadian Air Force, I; Toronto 1980), 604.

Although the latest Admiralty discussions had taken place without consulting the Canadian government, the idea of forming an East Coast air service was an agreeable concept given the navy's support for the 1917 proposal. Nonetheless, Ottawa was taken by surprise when the Admiralty sent a telegram to NSHQ on 26 February 1918 to suggest that Flight-Commander John Barron, a Canadian from Stratford, Ontario who was serving as an airship pilot in the Royal Naval Air Service and was currently in Washington, might come to Ottawa "in the event of your government contemplating any submarine measures involving the use of airships."[90] The Admiralty's initial suggestion was followed by a more detailed scheme of air patrols forwarded from London on 11 March. Based on a report prepared by Captain F.R. Scarlett for the operations committee, and taking the submarine threat to North America seriously, it recommended the establishment of a Canadian air service, together with the seaplane, airship, and kite balloon factories needed to support it. Until the Canadian service could be established, it was suggested that the United States be approached to extend its own coastal seaplane organization to cover Nova Scotia and Newfoundland.[91]

After repeating the earlier warning "that enemy submarines may be expected to operate off the Canadian coast in the near future," officials in Whitehall pointed out to Ottawa "the desirability of establishing an airship construction works and kite balloon factory."

> Aircraft will, my lords anticipate, be required on the Canadian coast for anti-submarine purposes and also for the protection of convoys and shipping from enemy submarines.... The American authorities are carrying out an experiment for taking kite balloons across the Atlantic with convoys, and if this proves feasible, it is considered that the same arrangements should be adopted for vessels sailing from Canadian ports. If not, convoys should be met by suitable craft flying kite balloons at different positions up to two days out from the base. This method is only recommended provided that hunting craft and kite balloons are also used for offensive purposes against submarines and not purely for escort duties.... It is also recommended the same procedure should be adopted in regard to seaplanes, and that as soon as possible the manufacture of seaplanes should be commenced in Canada, and seaplane stations established for anti-submarine work.[92]

It was made clear, however, "that it would be impossible to give any considerable assistance from this country as the available aircraft personnel and seaplane carriers are required for duty in home waters and the Mediterranean.... Also there is no material or labour in this

---

90. Colonial Secretary to Governor General, 26 February 1918, 1034–3-4, pt. 1, LAC, RG 24, vol. 3894; and Dave Kealey, "Naval Aviation in Canada during the First World War," nd, DHH 74/25.

91. Wise, *Canadian Airmen and the First World War*, 604.

92. Alex Flint for Secretary, Admiralty to Under Secretary of State, Colonial Office, 7 March 1918, 1017–10–7, pt. 1, LAC, RG 24, vol. 3833; and Secretary of State for the Colonies to Governor General, 11 March 1918, 1034–3-4, pt. 1, ibid, vol. 3894.

country available for the production of the aircraft which may be required for Canada." Having shut the door on any meaningful assistance from Britain, the Admiralty followed Scarlett's recommendation and suggested that Canada look south of the border for the initial supply of seaplanes, kite balloons, and equipment, while the country was establishing its own sources of manufacture. The British government also wanted Canada to extend its air patrols to provide coverage for the coasts of Newfoundland as well, asking that Ottawa approach the governor of the British colony "to cooperate in devising air defences for the coasts of Nova Scotia and Newfoundland, and in approaching the United States authorities, should the assistance of the latter in extending their seaplane organization be required."[93]

Given that the establishment of a Canadian air patrol had been rejected on financial grounds by his Cabinet the previous year, Prime Minister Borden was less than enthusiastic about the latest British suggestion. On 15 March, the Canadian government gave London a cautious reply to its air proposal by pointing out that "it is of course impossible to organize the manufacture of seaplanes and kite balloons in time for service during the approaching season of navigation. Minister of naval service is sending officers to the United States to arrange for such assistance as may be available there."[94] Ballantyne, meanwhile, had already despatched his deputy minister to Washington to see what assistance the Americans might have to offer in the way of aircraft or kite balloons. The choice of a civilian representative may not have been the wisest course, however, as Desbarats was given a far more negative message than British naval officers were receiving. In his Washington meetings, the Canadian deputy minister was told that the USN was itself deficient of air assets because of shortfalls in production, and could not offer Canada any immediate assistance for its air service.[95]

Fortunately, the British air proposals were not as summarily dismissed by Kingsmill. Despite the prime minister's reluctance, the naval director cabled London on the 19th to ask for detailed plans and specifications for any airships, kite balloons, and seaplanes the Admiralty considered suitable, with a view to constructing them in Canada.[96] Flight Commander Barron also began making inquiries in Washington on Canada's behalf and, in sharp contrast to the cool response to Desbarats's inquiries, was promised every assistance in the production and supply of kite balloons and airships for the RCN. By the end of March NSHQ was informed by the Imperial Munitions Board that Canadian Aeroplanes Ltd. of Toronto was capable of constructing airships and seaplanes and was awaiting plans from London before beginning production, an opinion confirmed by Barron during a visit to Toronto in mid-April.[97] The possibility of even greater American co-operation was suggested

93. Alex Flint for Secretary, Admiralty to Under Secretary of State, Colonial Office, 7 March 1918, 1017–10–7, pt. 1, LAC, RG 24, vol. 3833.

94. Governor General to Colonial Secretary, 15 March 1918, 1034–3-4, pt. 1, LAC, RG 24, vol. 3894.

95. Desbarats Diary, 14, 18, and 19 March 1918, LAC, MG 30 E89, vol. 5; and Hadley and Sarty, *Tin-pots and Pirate Ships*, 216.

96. Naval Ottawa to Admiralty, 19 March 1918, 1034–3-4, pt. 1, LAC, RG 24, vol. 3894.

97. Flight Commander Barron to Kingsmill, 21 March 1918, Barron to Kingsmill, 16 April 1918, ibid; and Dave Kealey, "Naval Aviation in Canada during the First World War," nd, 10, DHH 74/25.

when the USN sent a lieutenant from its naval aviation service to Halifax to discuss "the possibility of establishing an aerial patrol across the entrance to the Bay of Fundy." The US naval authorities envisaged a joint patrol by both USN and RCN aircraft with a base in the United States and another at Louisbourg on Cape Breton Island.[98]

Convinced of the importance of fully co-operating with the Americans, Vice-Admiral Grant cabled NSHQ in early April that "the necessary coordination of adjacent escort and patrol services of United States and Canadian and Newfoundland vessels can only be secured by meeting and exchange of arrangements between representatives." The C-in-C also revealed that the commander of the US First Naval District headquartered in Boston, Rear-Admiral Spencer S. Wood, was anxious to co-operate with RCN patrols in the Bay of Fundy and to undertake "escort when necessary of ships through that area."[99] As eager as he was to pursue discussions with the USN, Grant apparently shared Wood's ignorance that the Bay of Fundy was only used by Canadian merchant shipping during the winter season, which, in the absence of an enemy threat during those months, was unescorted as it made its way from St John to Halifax. The British admiral also did not know that the RCN had sent Stephens to Boston in 1917 to follow up on what had appeared to be a promising American proposal to provide patrols in the Bay of Fundy to discover that it only referred to cruiser patrols to seaward of Canadian waters. Not being terribly concerned about the Fundy backwater, Kingsmill provided only a tepid response to Grant's enthusiasm. Pointing out that the Admiralty had not advised the RCN to organize a patrol in the Bay but that it could use its mobile flotilla in the area "when necessary," the naval director suggested that the British admiral confer with Wood himself. Already desperately short of patrol vessels, NSHQ was not terribly worried about a relative backwater that was only important during the winter months when U-boats would not be operating in the western Atlantic. Kingsmill simply promised the British admiral that he would "endeavour to meet your views" for the coordination of patrols in the Fundy area, while pointing out that it was "understood Admiralty was dealing with [the] matter."[100]

By the beginning of April, Ottawa was harbouring few illusions about the extent to which the Admiralty had washed its hands of virtually any matter that dealt with Canada's maritime defence. Not only had London abandoned its January assessment of Canadian requirements but the latest British suggestion that NSHQ should seek air resources from the Americans had proven equally fruitless. It is not surprising, therefore, that when Grant visited Ottawa in the second week of April, he "found the Canadian authorities, having placed all their resources at the disposal of the Admiralty, perturbed at the failure to supply the destroyers and fast craft said to be needed." As much as he sympathized with the legitimacy of Canadian complaints about the to-ing and fro-ing of Admiralty policy, however, the British admiral (who had not as yet been enlightened by Admiral Benson about the Admiralty's destroyer policy) reiterated that it "was necessary to turn to the

---

98. Admiral Superintendent, Halifax to Kingsmill, 23 March 1918, 1034–3-4, pt. 1, LAC, RG 24, vol. 3894; and Dave Kealey, "Naval Aviation in Canada during the First World War," nd, 11, DHH 74/25.

99. C-in-C, NA&WI to Naval Ottawa, 1 April 1918, 1065–7-6, LAC, RG 24, vol. 4031.

100. Naval Ottawa to C-in-C, 2 April 1918, ibid.

United States" for help and "promised to obtain what was possible [in the way of escorts] on my return to Washington, DC, and to raise the matter of air patrol for Canadian coasts in which Canada was able of herself to do but little." Commenting on the Ottawa meetings to the Admiralty, the C-in-C said that he had "every reason to hope that my visit may have had useful results in clearing the air and promoting a closer understanding and co-ordination of effort" with the Americans in regard to both convoy organization and naval defence.[101]

Grant's message emphasizing the importance of co-operation with the United States Navy was one that Kingsmill had already accepted. Even as Grant was visiting Ottawa, the naval director sent instructions to Captain Hose to proceed to Boston to meet with the American naval district commander. Although the captain of patrols was fully occupied with the administrative arrangements for the expanded East Coast trawler and drifter force, Kingsmill ordered him to "get in touch with Admiral Wood, USN commander First Naval District Headquarters, Boston. Visit him and report any proposals he has for cooperation. Enquire particularly his views re: patrol [of] fishing banks."[102] The amount of work involved in organizing the East Coast fleet, however, was already beginning to take a physical toll on Hose and his proposed trip to Boston was postponed while he was temporarily placed on the sick list.[103]

It was upon his return to the American capital from Ottawa that the British commander-in-chief was confronted by the US chief of naval operations about the discrepancy between the Admiralty's policy of concentrating all destroyers in home waters and Grant's attempts to acquire American reinforcements for the RCN. Overcoming his anger at being informed of British policy second-hand by the American navy, Grant immediately incorporated his new appreciation of Anglo-American strategic policy in his correspondence with Ottawa. He still believed, however, that significant American assistance was possible and remained committed to Canada/US co-operation. Cabling NSHQ on 13 April, the British admiral asked that Hose come to Washington for discussions before meeting with Admiral Wood in Boston: "Every possible destroyer required in Home waters. US Navy Department anxious to give utmost help possible both patrol and air services. Suggest Hose and our best air representative come immediately to Washington to discuss with navy department and put whole matter on working basis estimates. Suggest they visit Admiral Wood, Boston, on return journey to coordinate patrol and air services which US navy department and myself consider essential."[104] Kingsmill quickly complied, informing Grant that he, too, would travel to Boston to join the Wood/Hose meeting following the captain of patrols' trip to Washington to explore the possibilities of establishing air bases in Nova Scotia.[105] Whatever personal embarrassment the Admiralty's poor staff work may have caused him in the

---

101. Grant to Admiralty, General Letter No. 3, 3 May 1918, UKNA, ADM 137/504.

102. Naval Ottawa to Navyard Halifax, 11 April 1918, 1065–7-6, LAC, RG 24, vol. 4031.

103. Naval Ottawa to Navyard Halifax, 12 April 1918, Naval Ottawa to Britannia, Washington, 14 April 1918, ibid.

104. C-in-C to Naval Ottawa, 13 April 1918, 1065–7-6, LAC, RG 24, vol. 4031.

105. Naval Ottawa to C-in-C, 14 April 1918, ibid.

American capital, the British C-in-C's response indicated that he was not about to let the lack of support from London influence his commitment to assist the RCN in acquiring some semblance of an effective anti-submarine force.

In accordance with the naval director's instructions, Hose departed Halifax by train for Washington on 18 April where he attended a meeting at the Navy Board offices to discuss the question of air patrols off the Canadian coast. Grant's chief of staff, Captain V.H. Haggard, accompanied the Canadian officer to the meetings for "a careful discussion" of the air units that were required, the possible location of air bases and "what assistance could be rendered by the United States in meeting the various requirements which might prove difficult to fill in Canada, both as regards personnel and material." The meeting with the Americans was primarily, however, an exchange of information "in a general sense" about possible air station locations "from the point of view of local conditions of weather, terrain, communications, supply, etc." The Washington discussions were framed by the fact that the RCN's surface patrol would no longer include the twelve fast escorts upon which Hose's February patrol plan had been based or indeed—as Benson had made clear to Grant—the five USN destroyers Kingsmill had said were the minimum number necessary, and that the Admiralty had suggested to Ottawa as replacements for the withdrawn British vessels. As Hose explained in his report to NSHQ, the weakness of the patrol vessels available to him "had an important bearing on the air patrols." "Since the Canadian coast patrol contains no units or combination of vessels which are sufficiently fast or powerful in armament to operate offensively against a U-cruiser, it will be to the air service that we must look for any chance of rendering such an enemy hors-de-combat, though the floating [i.e., surface] patrol squadron may stave off an attack." As a result, the captain of patrols outlined to his American hosts both "the full measure of air patrol which it is considered the situation as regards shipping and its liability to attack from U-cruisers calls for" as well as "the minimum force that is required" to give some measure of air protection to Canadian shipping lanes.[106] The Canadian need was large, and the Americans had clearly shown that they considered their own interests first, but Hose was optimistic: indeed, foreseeing no serious impediments to establishing an air service, he recommended that NSHQ go ahead and issue contracts for the work that was needed to build the air bases.[107]

Following the meeting, Hose and Haggard drew up a memorandum outlining how best to employ the RCN's available patrol craft and determine the consequent Canadian air requirement. The minesweeping arrangements of Hose's earlier patrol plan remained unchanged in the absence of the twelve fast escorts from Britain, but the escort forces would now largely be confined to operating in the immediate approaches to both Halifax and Sydney. Without a fast escort force at Halifax, the defence would consist only of the four imperial trawlers originally assigned to the forming up and approaches patrol and HMCS *Grilse* of the inner port patrol. Although Sydney would retain an escort force for its slow convoys, this was now reduced to a marginally useful five imperial trawlers as opposed to the two destroyers and three fast trawlers Hose had previously assigned to that

---

106. Hose, "Memorandum for Director of Naval Service, 20 April 1918, 1017–10–7, pt. 1, LAC, RG 24, vol. 3833.

107. Ibid.

role. The mobile patrol flotilla, also based at Sydney, was similarly enfeebled by the absence of two destroyers or sloops and two fast trawlers that were to have given the RCN's strategic reserve its offensive capability. Thus reduced, the Canadian navy's "offensive" force would consist largely of the same handful of armed yachts and ex-fisheries vessels with which it had been patrolling the Gulf of St Lawrence since 1915.[108]

In view of such weakness, Hose and Haggard fully embraced the possibility of using a combination of dirigibles, seaplanes, and kite balloons to supplement each convoy's defences. They envisaged a typical convoy air escort as consisting of "two kite balloons towed by patrol vessels and stationed on each bow, two dirigibles scouting ahead of and around the convoy. Seaplanes should be used to scout ahead of the course of the convoy immediately proceeding its departure." The captive kite balloons extended the range of visibility of the convoy's surface escorts and could direct them in the event of a submarine sighting or, by providing an early warning, allow a convoy to alter course and avoid immediate danger altogether. Dirigibles had the advantage of being able to keep in close touch with a slow moving convoy and could provide reconnaissance in good weather conditions, while seaplanes were very good for offensive work and could patrol larger areas of ocean in a shorter time. But the relatively short endurance of the latter made their use in bad weather "dangerous if not impossible." Dirigibles offered a greater advantage in foggy weather since their greater endurance made them "capable of surer navigation than seaplanes and can select time and place of landing with greater ease."[109]

The convoy assembly ports of Sydney and Halifax were to have the larger air stations, each consisting of a flight of six seaplanes, four kite balloons and three dirigibles, with the Sydney station providing general air patrols for the Cabot Straits as well as for individual convoys. In addition, Hose and Haggard recommended smaller stations at both Cape Race, Newfoundland, and Cape Sable at the southern tip of Nova Scotia. With the "probability it will be necessary to route both convoys and west-bound traffic close to Cape Race," a Newfoundland air base for two dirigibles and four kite balloons would cover the vulnerable point that, being 270 miles from Sydney, was beyond the range of seaplanes based on Cape Breton Island. They recognized that "the difficulty of establishing an air station in the Cape Race district may prove insuperable but the matter should be fully considered before being abandoned." A unit of two dirigibles or three seaplanes was suggested for the Cape Sable station, a location that would also provide for American defence by covering the northern part of the Gulf of Maine. The maintenance of air patrols along the entire Canadian East Coast was not just for convoy protection, however, since air coverage "off these places is rendered necessary by the continuous stream of west-bound [coastal] traffic not in convoy and shipping proceeding to the assembling ports."[110]

---

108. [Haggard and Hose] to Commander-in-Chief, NA&WI, 20 April 1918, ibid; and Kingsmill, "Memorandum for the Minister," 21 February 1918, Hose, "Memorandum for DNS," nd, 1017–10–1, pt. 1, LAC, RG 24, vol. 3831.

109. [Haggard and Hose] to Commander-in-Chief, NA&WI, 20 April 1918, 1017–10–7, pt. 1, LAC, RG 24, vol. 3833.

110. Ibid.

Stating requirements was one thing; providing machines and trained airmen was entirely more difficult. Fortunately for the Canadians, Vice-Admiral Grant's lobbying efforts on their behalf—despite Admiral Benson's stricture against basing any USN destroyers at Canadian convoy ports—had convinced their American neighbours to provide much of what was required for the air patrols. Hose was thus able to leave the Washington meetings with a Naval Department promise to supply twelve Curtiss HS-1 flying boats (the HS designating H model, single engine—a traditional pusher flying boat with a 200-horsepower engine driving a three-blade propellor[111]) by the end of June, together with the loan of American aircrew until Canadian pilots were trained. It was Hose's recommendation to Ottawa that the navy place orders with the Canadian Aeroplane Company for the construction of additional aircraft and place tenders for the construction of the aerodromes, runways and barracks. He also suggested that an arrangement could be made with the Royal Flying Corps Canada training organization in Toronto to provide initial training for Canadian aircrew who would then "complete their training in seaplane work in [the] United States," while commanding officers for the air stations might be provided by applying "to imperial air force for services of injured officers."[112]

As far as dirigibles and kite balloons were concerned, the US navy department had told Hose that the the Goodyear Rubber Company in Akron, Ohio would be able to construct two envelopes for the airships by 1 July at the latest and would probably be able to construct the entire airship. Hydrogen plants could also be procured in the United States or from their Canadian branch companies, and US authorities estimated that training of the necessary personnel would take about three months. The Americans also offered to make places available in their training organization to instruct Canadian ratings in handling dirigibles. Furthermore, the United States was able immediately to supply the RCN with kite balloons, their winches and generators, and train Canadian personnel, a course that would take some two months, "including one month free ballooning." The captain of patrols recommended that NSHQ act quickly in taking up the USN's offers of equipment and training assistance by selecting Canadian personnel for training in the United States, while at the same time placing airship orders both in Akron and Toronto and commencing construction of sheds, barracks, and workshops for the airship stations. Hose urged NSHQ to decide on the composition of units and the sites of the air stations "without delay."[113]

The aircraft proposals were not the only aid the Americans were able to offer. The captain of patrols also reported how Captain W.V. Pratt, the USN's assistant chief of naval operations (identified by Hose as the chief of staff) had raised "another matter which was mentioned prior to the conference," one that would reinforce the RCN's surface patrols. Pratt told Hose that the US navy department was prepared to send six of its submarine-chasers, two torpedo boats, and a submarine to Canadian waters "to be utilized by the

---

111. Peter M. Bowers, *Curtiss Aircraft, 1907–1947* (Annapolis, Maryland 1979), 100–02.

112. [Haggard and Hose] to Commander-in-Chief, NA&WI, 20 April 1918, 1017–10–7, pt. 1, LAC, RG 24, vol. 3833.

113. Ibid.

Department of the Naval Service as considered desirable." The Americans agreed to make the torpedo boats and submarine immediately available, while the six American-manned subchasers would be despatched "in about one month." The captain of patrols had little difficulty in allocating the USN reinforcements to his rather thin order of battle, submitting that "one TB should be attached to the air section at Halifax and one to that at Sydney, that the submarine should be stationed at Halifax in readiness to proceed to attack a U-cruiser if called upon, and that the six chasers should be allocated three to Halifax and three to Sydney as convoy escorts to proceed with convoys as far as fuel will admit."[114]

As Hose's anticipation for employing the US reinforcements suggests, they would be among the fastest escorts available to him once the six subchasers and their USN crews arrived at Halifax in mid-May. One-hundred-and-ten feet long and fifteen feet in the beam, the wooden subchasers were powered by three 220-horsepower gasoline engines, one to each propellor shaft. Designed for a top speed of 17.5 knots, the Admiralty was aware that "when loaded with full equipment and stores, sixteen knots may be considered the highest speed available," slower than standard motor launches and little better than a surfaced U-boat. The motorboat mounted a 3-inch short-barrel 23-calibre gun forward, but was also fitted with depth charge chutes at the stern, and often carried a "Y" gun amidships to project the charges off either side. Her submarine detection devices consisted of hydrophones of the K- and C- types. The C-tube hydrophone was a simple mechanical device, an inverted "T" of brass tubing with rubber balls at the ends of the cross piece held in the water that transmitted sound to the operator wearing a medical stethoscope. The more advanced K-tube was actually an electrical device dropped in the water for use when the patrol vessel was stopped. It had the advantage of eliminating water noises and allowed the operator to determine a bearing on an underwater noise.[115] As originally envisaged by the USN, groups of three subchasers would each work in conjunction with a destroyer, proceeding ahead of the warship to listen for a submarine and then calling up the destroyer to make the actual attack.[116]

Hose's enthusiasm for the submarine chasers was somewhat misplaced, however, as both the Royal and United States navies had already determined that the vessels were less than ideal for the role the captain of patrols was planning for them, information that was never shared with the RCN. As early as September 1917, the Admiralty's anti-submarine division had decided that "it is not considered that the proposed submarine chasers are worth getting over here [i.e., in Britain]."[117] As the division's director explained at that time, his views were "largely influenced by un-official remarks of US officers over here who think little of these craft. They were built, I understand, as an answer to any popular demand that might arise as the result of enemy submarines operating on American coasts,

---

114. Hose, "Memorandum for Director of Naval Service, 20 April 1918, NSC 1017–10–7, pt. 1, LAC, RG 24, vol. 3833; and Simpson, ed., *Anglo-American Naval Relations, 1917–1919,* 68n.

115. "Description of 110 ft Submarine Chasers," nd, UKNA, ADM 137/1437; and Dwight R. Messimer, *Find and Destroy: Antisubmarine Warfare in World War I* (Annapolis, Maryland 2001), 117–19.

116. Washington to 3rd Sea Lord, Admiralty, 357, 2 September 1917, UKNA, ADM 137/1437.

117. Captain W.W. Fisher minute, Director Anti-Submarine Division, 4 September 1917, ibid.

in the event of most of their craft being [on] our side of the Atlantic. Now they can point to a large number of chasers ready to deal with the U-boat when he appears, though they are not sanguine as regards the actual effectiveness of the measure…. Anti-submarine craft fall under one of three categories: (1) Escorting; (2) Patrolling; (3) Hunting. These chasers cannot carry out (1), can only do (2) near the coast and in good weather, and as regards (3), a successful hunt may be protracted and the issue may call for a good gun, and in these respects the 110-feet chaser does not meet requirements."[118]

The low regard in which subchasers were held had not altered when the Allied Naval Council reviewed the deployment of US subchasers to Europe in February 1918. At those meetings, Vice-Admiral Sims candidly informed his colleagues "that the utility of the chasers is quite small, except under very favourable circumstances, unless they are accompanied by a vessel having sufficient speed in a seaway to render effective assistance, and they generally worked with a destroyer. In any moderate sea the chasers lose their speed." The first sea lord agreed with that view as Admiral Wemyss insisted "that the chasers should only be employed in hunting submarines and not for escort purposes."[119] None of this was explained to Hose, while he was in Washington, with the result that neither the captain of patrols nor NSHQ understood that their proposed employment of the subchasers—as convoy escorts, in turbulent northern seas, without destroyer backing—would actually violate three of the limitations on their use agreed upon at the February Naval Council meeting. While their mere presence on the Canadian East Coast would address the same public relations problem as existed in the United States (where officials could "point to a large number of chasers ready to deal with the U-boat when he appears"[120]) in the absence of anything else, the arrival of the six US motorboats in mid-May simply added to the collection of inadequate escorts the RCN already had available to monitor the approaches to the convoy assembly ports. Although NSHQ was not thinking in those terms, the greatest value that any of the navy's escorts might have was in their potential "scarecrow" effect in dissuading less-aggressive U-boat commanders from attacking an escorted convoy. Canada's surface ship weakness also placed an added premium on the importance of the naval aircraft the RCN hoped to have operating out of both Halifax and Sydney.

Nor could the importance of strengthening co-operation with the United States Navy, particularly with the First Naval District that bordered Canadian waters, be overlooked. Following his meetings with American naval officials in Washington, Captain Hose travelled to Boston for his meeting at naval district headquarters on 22 April accompanied by Captain Haggard, the C-in-C's chief of staff, and Major Cheeseman, the North American station's fleet wireless officer. The most significant possibility discussed was to have the commandant of the First Naval District, Rear-Admiral Spencer Wood, take over responsibility for "coastal patrols, sea patrols, protection of traffic and offensive action taken against submarines, as far east as the 65th meridian (Lock[e]port, NS) including the outer

118. Captain W.W. Fisher minute, Director Anti-Submarine Division, 8 September 1917, ibid.

119. Allied Naval Council minutes, February 1918, 27–29, UKNA, ADM 137/836.

120. DASD minute, 8 September 1917, UKNA, ADM 137/1437.

part of the Bay of Fundy."[121] Although the patrol area to be taken over by the Americans was well-removed from the Canadian shipping lanes in the Gulf of St Lawrence, it did relieve the RCN of some responsibility for defending the local coastal traffic and fishing vessels that frequented those waters during the summer months. It also made the USN responsible for protecting any merchantmen who might be routed independently from New York to Halifax for convoy until they were within 200 kilometres of Chebucto Head.

Other points raised related primarily to establishing an accepted means of communication between the admiral superintendent at Halifax and Admiral Wood in Boston. These included use of the current edition of the allied code for messages between the dockyard and First Naval District headquarters, agreed upon recognition signals between US and Canadian warships, common squared charts prepared for adjacent sea areas, the procedures to be followed in each country for entering defended ports, and an exchange of detailed information about each navy's organization. The two navies were also to use the current edition of the auxiliary code "for directing operations of patrol in the United States and Canadian adjacent areas, to insure each knowing what is going on by interception [of radio messages]. All important movements to be communicated by land wire in addition."[122]

The conference's conclusions were discussed in a further meeting on 24 April between Kingsmill and Wood following the Canadian naval director's arrival in Boston. Both admirals approved the arrangements already agreed to without change.[123] The shift of American responsibility to the northeast to cover the waters west of Lockeport, Nova Scotia, also required the government's approval to give the USN patrol ships the legal authority to visit and search all vessels within Canadian territorial waters, power that was granted to the American warships by order-in-council on 22 June.[124] In the meantime, the USN's auxiliary patrol force commander made arrangements with Hose in early May to take over the government wharf at Shelburne, Nova Scotia, for use as a base, including fencing off the area and erecting a number of temporary buildings for offices and storerooms.[125]

The United States was not, of course, the only East Coast ally with whom the Canadian navy had to make arrangements. In late 1917, Newfoundland had provided the RCN with some 300 ratings from the Newfoundland division of the Royal Naval Reserve for service on the trawlers and drifters being built in Canada.[126] When Ottawa asked if the Newfoundland government proposed to commission any patrol vessels for the summer

---

121. Hose to NSHQ, 26 April 1918, and attached "Recommendations of conference held at Boston April 22nd, 1918 discussing measures for obtaining cooperation between United States and Canadian Patrol Forces," nd, 1017–10–7, pt. 1, LAC, RG 24, vol. 3833.

122. Ibid.

123. Rear-Admiral S.S. Wood to Secretary of the Navy (Operations), Navy Department, Washington, 25 April 1918, ibid.

124. PC 1543, 18 June 1918, copy in ibid.

125. Hose to NSHQ, 7 May 1918, ibid.

126. W. David Parsons, "Newfoundland and the Great War," in Briton C. Busch, ed., *Canada and the Great War: Western Front Association Papers* (Montreal and Kingston 2003), 156.

1918 shipping season and operate them jointly with the RCN's auxiliary patrol along the same lines as the previous summer,[127] the Newfoundland governor indicated that St John's had decided to abandon any meaningful effort at naval defence, not least because of the reported capability and armament of the new German long-range submarines. "After full consideration my ministers doubt [the] wisdom of commissioning patrol vessels this summer. They have no vessels faster than ten knots or capable of out-ranging [by gunfire] a submarine. Money spent on vessels seems to us useless. We propose, however, to retain local police character through the medium of coastguard steamers."[128] With no significant merchant fleet of its own, the Newfoundland government did not have the same obligation as Ottawa to secure the St Lawrence shipping lanes.

As revealed from the tone of a letter from Newfoundland Governor C. Alexander Harris to the governor general of Canada, the authorities in St John's were as uninformed of current Allied naval policy as Ottawa and had not even received an updated assessment of the threat posed by long-range German submarines. Given the Admiralty's inability to keep even the commander-in-chief of British naval forces in the western Atlantic informed of shifts in policy, it is not terribly surprising that the Newfoundland government was operating on the basis of two-year old threat assessments. Governor Harris explained that the proposed "police" patrol was to be "a system whereby motor boats in the various outports can be used for intelligence purposes. Their mission would be to examine the coast and isolated bays within the limit of their range and to keep the authorities informed of anything that might point to the presence of enemy submarines using any points on this coast as bases." Although that had indeed been the rationale for the coast patrols organized in 1915 and 1916, it was well-known—outside of Newfoundland at any rate—that long-range U-cruisers did not require any resupply to operate in North American waters. The Newfoundland governor did take some satisfaction in pointing out that Captain Hose had confided to the senior naval officer at St John's, Commander A. MacDermott, that he agreed with the decision "that the system of Newfoundland patrol vessels as carried out last year is not justified by the expense involved."[129]

In his confidential letter to St John's, Hose had also informed MacDermott that the RCN was to be supplied with six destroyers and six fast trawlers from Britain, and that he was preparing a patrol scheme that incorporated the needed reinforcements. (Grant, of course, only told NSHQ that it would not be receiving the twelve fast escorts on 13 April, immediately after he found out himself, and two days before the Newfoundland governor wrote to Ottawa.[130]) Under the mistaken impression that destroyers were readily available, Harris "strongly" urged the governor general "that a destroyer or fast sloop should be based on the port of St John's and so be available also for the protection of the capital in a way which could not be effected by slow-moving patrol vessels.... It would if possible be

127. Desbarats to Under Secretary of State for External Affairs, 7 March 1918, 1065-4-3, LAC, RG 24, vol. 4030.

128. Governor of Newfoundland to Governor General of Canada, 4 April 1918, ibid.

129. Governor C.A. Harris to Governor General of Canada, 15 April 1918, 1017–10–1, pt. 1, LAC, RG 24, vol. 3832.

130. C-in-C, NA&WI to Naval Ottawa, 13 April 1918, 1065–7-6, LAC, RG 24, vol. 4031.

desirable that two such warships as indicated should be based on St John's as this would enable one at least to be always at sea: and I would beg that in your scheme of the naval defence of Canada and in your arrangements with the commander-in-chief, NA&WIS, your excellency should endeavour to include such an allocation as I have indicated independently of any steps that may be taken for the protection of the trade routes and more vulnerable ports on the mainland."[131] Under the circumstances, Kingsmill could only minute on the Harris letter that Canada did not have "any such vessels unless Admiralty provide."[132] More useful for the East Coast's defence, the Newfoundland government was "willing to pay for a flight of seaplanes" based at St John's "and recognize the great advantage that the presence of a flight would confer both as a protection and with a view to obtaining information of the movements of ships in the neighbourhood of the Avalon Peninsula."[133] As we have seen, the establishment of a small air base at Cape Race capable of handling two dirigibles and four kite balloons was raised the following week during Hose's discussions with American naval officials in Washington.

Newfoundland's inability to contribute to naval defence was confirmed by Commander MacDermott in a letter to Hose at the beginning of May. Not only would the colony not be commissioning any patrol vessels in 1918 but the government had also been unable to obtain any motorboats that were suitable for patrolling the bays and inlets along the coast. The best that St John's could offer was to have fishermen "frequenting the coast immediately report any suspicious circumstances to the nearest telegraph station," supported by four coastal steamers that would be available to investigate any reports received. The steamers would only be armed, however, if Canada could supply its neighbour with 12-pounder guns, weapons that were already in short supply in the RCN.[134] Even the earlier offer of financing a seaplane station on the Avalon peninsula was soon withdrawn by St John's. As Governor Harris explained to the Canadian governor general in early June, his ministers had "unfortunately ... advised me that in their opinion the fog prevalent on this coast during the summer makes the use of aeroplanes practically impossible. They regard any expenditure upon these machines as next to useless.... The point of the argument is this—during the greater part of the summer a thick bank of fog lies a little way out all the way from Cape Race to north of St John's; and a submarine, by sounding, can find her way under cover of this fog to a charted position, even immediately outside the Narrows [at the entrance to St John's harbour], without giving an airplane a single opportunity of spotting her or making any effective attack. I trust that no inconvenience will have been caused to you by the sudden strong expression of view by my ministers contrary to that which they first indicated in conference with me."[135]

---

131. Governor C.A. Harris to Governor General of Canada, 15 April 1918, 1017–10–1, pt. 1, LAC, RG 24, vol. 3832.

132. Kingsmill minute, nd, on ibid.

133. Governor C.A. Harris to Governor General of Canada, 15 April 1918, ibid.

134. Commander A. MacDermott to Captain of Patrols, 1 May 1918, attached to Hose to NSHQ, 7 May 1918, ibid.

135. Governor Harris to Governor General of Canada, 1 June 1918, ibid.

St John's lack of naval resources placed a greater burden on the RCN to provide for the defence of another maritime interest shared by Newfoundland and Canada: the protection of their two fishing fleets should the Germans choose to operate against commercial vessels on the Grand Banks. Such a requirement had first been raised by the French government at the Allied Naval Council in January. France had its own considerable fishing fleet and proposed arming each of its fishing vessels with two guns of either 65mm, 57mm, or 47mm (corresponding to 9-, 6-, and 3-pounder guns). After convoying the fishing vessels through the submarine danger zone around France, Paris proposed protecting their fishing fleet on the Banks with eight "well-armed" schooners manned by French naval crews.[136] Although the United States, which also had considerable fishing interests operating out of New England ports, offered to assist in the protection effort, London was largely indifferent to the fate of non-British fishing fleets working in North American waters. The Admiralty cabled NSHQ in early March to inform the Canadians that the Royal Navy was unable to provide any protecting vessels and to enquire if the RCN would "assist with France and US in protecting fishing vessels on the banks."[137]

As usual, the one resource that London was able to supply in relative abundance was advice. For the fleets fishing off the Grand Banks, Nova Scotian banks, and in the Gulf of Maine, the Admiralty

> recommended that the vessels should keep in groups and that protecting vessels should be furnished; four to the Newfoundland banks, four off Nova Scotia, and four off the United States of America banks should be ample. It was thought best that, if possible, there should be a patrol vessel of each nationality [i.e., French, Newfoundland, Canadian, and American] in each area.
>
> It was not considered that the fisheries were liable to continual attack, but that owing to the extension of danger zones, and the increase of size and radius of action of submarines, the menace existed especially where the routes of steamers crossed the fishing grounds that some protection, moral more than actual, was advisable.[138]

By drawing on the auxiliary patrol vessels of the St Lawrence patrol, NSHQ expected to be able to provide from two to six ships for the Banks, although the larger number would represent a considerable drain on the RCN's already limited patrol resources. Maintaining six vessels on patrol near the fishing fleets would mean assigning eighteen patrol vessels to the task, given that "one third of them would be in patrol, one third going or returning, and one third in harbour."[139] After consulting with fisheries department officials,[140]

136. Allied Naval Council minutes, January 1918, 57–58, UKNA, ADM 137/836.

137. Naval Ottawa to Navyard Esquimalt, Stephens for Kingsmill, 11 March 1918, 1065–7-6, LAC, RG 24, vol. 4031.

138. Alex Flint for Admiralty Secretary to Under Secretary of State, Colonial Office, 1 March 1918, 1017–10–6, pt, 1, LAC, RG 24, vol. 3832.

139. Commander R.M. Stephens, "Memo: For the Minister," 13 March 1918, 1017–10–1, pt. 1, LAC, RG 24, vol. 3832.

Kingsmill was able to brief Grant, explaining that the salt fish fleet was based on Lunenburg, Nova Scotia, and fished on the Grand Banks from mid-March until sometime in November. Since the Lunenburg ships "generally go together ... there would probably not be much difficulty in arranging for these vessels to fish together in groups," thereby allowing for the proposed multinational patrol vessels to provide them with some protection. The number of Canadian fishing vessels operating on the Grand Banks normally numbered some 125, while the number of Newfoundland vessels fishing in those waters was somewhere between eighty and 100. However, protecting the Canadian fishing vessels engaged in the fresh fish business, primarily based at Digby, Yarmouth, Shelburne, and Queens, Nova Scotia, was more problematic. They fished all year round on the Brown Banks south and southeast of Nova Scotia and proceeded to their fishing grounds independently of one another. Kingsmill informed the commander-in-chief that "the fishing interests state it would be impossible to collect these vessels in groups either going to or returning from the Banks or when fishing." The only suggestion he could offer was to have the fishing vessels report to a patrol ship on arriving or leaving the Brown Banks.[141]

Even NSHQ's willingness to provide a few patrol vessels and organize the Canadian fishing fleet into groups seemed largely irrelevant when it received Grant's reply in mid-May:

> The US navy department is taking no steps to arm or protect American fishing vessels. A small measure of protection will, however, be given by the two gunboats of the ice patrol now being instituted, one of which will always be at sea: these should be made acquainted with and included as a factor in the measures taken.
>
> The arrangements made by the French government have been delayed owing to the loss of the ship carrying the guns intended for arming the schooners and to the delay in delivery of the schooners themselves: the first schooner will be on the banks about 1st June, and the remainder before the end of August. The fishing boats themselves will be armed as previously arranged....
>
> In the absence of warships, an effective defence of a widely scattered fishing fleet cannot be ensured, but even a light gun will act as a deterrent to a submarine which is hardly likely to incur risk in attacking such craft after having come so far afield.
>
> It is suggested, as regards the Canadian fishing vessels, that these should be made self-defensive so far as is feasible by arming a proportion with a light gun. The guns' crews formed, if no objection is seen, from among the fishermen themselves [who] would require a short course of instruction, and it is sugges-

---

140. Stephens, "Memo: For Superintendent of Fisheries," 15 March 1918, NSHQ to Captain of Patrols, 19 March 1918, Superintendent of Fisheries to R. Hockin and H.H. Marshall, 22 March 1918, R. Hockin to Deputy Minister of the Naval Service, 30 March 1918, H.H. Marshall to Superintendent of Fisheries, 15 April 1918, 1017–10–6, pt, 1, LAC, RG 24, vol. 3832 .

141. Kingsmill to Grant, 29 April 1918, ibid.

ted this could be done on board an armed patrol vessel at Halifax, a few rounds being fired at a target.[142]

It apparently did not occur to Grant that civilian fishermen might object to being asked to engage powerful German long-range submarines (armed with 5.9-inch guns) with any sort of weapon, let alone the "light guns" being proposed by the commander-in-chief. It was one thing for the British admiral to trust in the deterrent effect of such defensive fire on the naval crew of a U-cruiser, it was quite another to expect civilians to put it to the test. Sweeping aside the surreal, NSHQ neatly sidestepped the issue by simply reminding Grant that there were "no guns available for arming fishing vessels."[143] Kingsmill was still prepared to allocate three patrol vessels to the Grand Banks "if such a course should be considered necessary" but pointed out that "they would only be small trawlers and only one would be on the Banks at a time."[144] Although arrangements were made in mid-June between Hose, the American patrol vessels at Shelburne and the commander of the French schooners for a common means of communication,[145] it was not until early July that Grant responded to Kingsmill's more limited proposal. It was the commander-in-chief's view that three armed trawlers were "inadequate to fill any useful purpose" and "would be more profitably employed on coastal patrol and escort duties, whence they could be diverted for patrol of the banks when the need arises," a course of action that the hard-pressed Canadian naval director approved.[146] The US decision not to defend the American fishing fleet, despite having greater naval resources to deploy, undoubtedly contributed to Kingsmill's decision not to allocate scarce patrol trawlers specifically to the banks. Moreover, it must have seemed improbable to naval planners—as Grant's May reply had indicated—that the German navy would send long-range submarines to North American waters simply to attack fishing trawlers on the Grand Banks when the freighters and ocean liners carrying the increasing flow of vital war supplies and troop reinforcements to Europe were strategically more important targets.

Although the convoy system introduced in 1917 had drastically reduced the amount of trans-Atlantic traffic being sunk by the U-boat campaign—up to the end of May 1918 only 1.06 percent of 5,156 homeward and 0.57 percent of 4,357 outward-bound ships had been sunk in Atlantic convoys[147]—the Allies were still faced with a worrisome shortfall of available ocean tonnage by the beginning of 1918. After twelve months of unrestricted submarine warfare, worldwide shipping had been reduced by over six million tons, of which 3,750,000 tons had been registered in the United Kingdom. Britain's ocean-going

---

142. Grant to Kingsmill, 14 May 1918, ibid; and Grant to Secretary of the Admiralty, 1 June 1918, UKNA, ADM 137/504.

143. Kingsmill minute, nd, on Grant to Kingsmill, 14 May 1918, 1017–10–6, pt, 1, LAC, RG 24, vol. 3832.

144. Kingsmill to Grant, 22 May 1918, ibid.

145. Hose to NSHQ, 11 June 1918, ibid.

146. Grant to Kingsmill, 3 July 1918, Kingsmill minute, 13 July 1918, ibid.

147. "Extract from Confidential Naval Orders, dated 24th July 1918," nd, ibid.

merchant ships had been hardest hit with 3.5 million tons sunk, a figure that represented 20 percent of the total tonnage available at the start of 1917. An additional 925,000 tons of British shipping had been damaged by enemy action, with most of the damaged ships being put out of service for a period of from four to six months. Overwhelmed by the sheer volume of repair work needed, there were some 1.5 million tons of merchant shipping under or awaiting repair in British dockyards by the end of January 1918. Such losses could not be offset by the 1,250,000 tons of new merchant construction that emerged from British yards during the year or the requisitioning of neutral vessels. As a result, the January 1917 total of 3,731 ocean-going steamers totalling 16,591,000 tons had been reduced to 3,153 steamers and 14,547,000 tons by the following January. At the same time, the failure of the French and Italian harvests in 1917 forced the Allies to import an extra two million tons of cereals to Europe in 1918. This was in addition to transporting the bulk of the American Expeditionary Force (AEF) to France, estimated to involve the movement of 400,000 US troops by 30 April and 800,000 by the end of September 1918.[148]

If the Allies were to maintain the flow of food and war supplies across the world's oceans, therefore, a further rationalization of shipping was necessary. By shifting liners from the Australasian and South Atlantic trade routes to the North Atlantic, the Allies managed to increase the total tonnage, including tramp steamers and chartered neutral vessels, plying the vital shipping lanes between North America and Europe from 2,300,000 tons on 1 January to 2,775,000 tons on 1 April.[149] The need to transport American troops to the battlefields of France was also given a renewed urgency on 21 March when the German Army launched its spring offensive on the Western Front. Rupturing the lines of the British Fifth Army in Picardy and driving toward the important rail centre of Amiens, the success of the German offensive prompted the British commander-in-chief, Field Marshal Sir Douglas Haig, to issue his famous "backs to the wall" order of the day on 11 April. By the 10th, the German offensive toward Amiens ended at a cost of 163,500 British, 77,000 French, and 239,000 German casualties. A second German offensive in Flanders was opened on 9 April and had soon recaptured much of the ground won by the BEF, including the gains made by the Canadian Corps, in the bloody battle of Passchendaele the previous autumn. The crisis finally convinced Allied leaders of the necessity of unity of command and in early April French general Ferdinand Foch was appointed commander-in-chief on the Western Front. In late March, meanwhile, the first two American Army divisions sent to the front, the 26th and 42nd, took over quiet sectors of the French line. By the end of April, as Allied casualties grew to 330,000 and the German total to 348,300, three American divisions had entered the line in the French sector.[150]

By that time the Allies had already undertaken a reorganization of North Atlantic convoys. The new scheme shifted the port of assembly for the fast ocean liners of the HX

148. C. Ernest Fayle, *Seaborne Trade*, III: *The Period of Unrestricted Submarine Warfare* (History of the Great War; London 1924), 243, 247, 255–57.

149. Ibid, 287.

150. G.W.L. Nicholson, *Canadian Expeditionary Force, 1914–1919* (Official History of the Canadian Army in the First World War; Ottawa 1962), 364–74.

convoys from Halifax to New York, the main port of embarkation for American troops proceeding to Europe. The HX convoys would continue to run in eight-day cycles with all ships capable of maintaining a speed of at least thirteen knots in fair seas and able to run at fourteen knots through the danger zone around the British Isles. New York was also the port of assembly for 9.5-knot convoys running every eight days to East Coast ports in Britain. By assigning up to sixty thirteen-knot liners to the New York to Liverpool run, it was estimated that HX convoys could transport up to 140,000 American troops each month to the British port. Halifax, in the meantime, was to become the port of assembly for a mixed troopship and cargo vessel convoy for ships that were not quite fast enough for the HX convoys but could maintain a speed of eleven and a half knots. The medium-speed Halifax convoys were also to run on an eight-day cycle with destinations alternating between East and West Coast British ports. It was expected that up to half the ships in the Halifax convoys would load in New York, the remainder loading at Boston, Portland, St John, and Halifax. Once the ice had cleared from the St Lawrence, the traffic loaded at Montreal would replace the shipping from the latter two Canadian ports. The slow convoys assembled at Sydney, Nova Scotia, were unaffected by such changes although it was expected that some cargo would be diverted to the faster liners so as to reduce the number of tramp steamers sailing in the HS convoys.[151]

Another gain in trans-Atlantic carrying capacity was achieved by increasing the efficiency of the shore organizations in both Liverpool and New York. By reducing the turnaround time in port to ten days, round trip voyages were reduced from fifty-two days in 1917 to forty days in 1918. Over the winter of 1917–18, there had been a noticeable congestion along the US eastern seaboard as the amount of war supplies arriving from inland overwhelmed American port facilities—much to the chagrin of Canadian authorities as their port elevators and terminals were being underused.[152] A New York Convoy Committee was established under the chairmanship of Captain Connop Guthrie of the Ministry of Shipping "to effect a very considerable speed-up in the turn-around of steamers, by obtaining preference in cargo delivery and loading arrangements for such vessels as needed the greatest effort to enable them to make a sailing date."[153] At the same time, the shipping control organization in the United States was overhauled and an American Shipping Control Committee formed with considerable input from the British Ministry of Shipping and the director of transports, Graeme Thomson. The United States authorities, however, confined their attention primarily to arranging the US Army's troopship convoys and willingly left the question of organizing cargo convoys in the hands of British officers. It was not until September 1918 that the navy department decided to exert a greater say in convoy matters, particularly the HB convoys (US to Bay of Biscay ports) that were chiefly American in character.[154] With the more efficient grouping of

151. Fayle, *Seaborne Trade*, III, 313–16; and Hadley and Sarty, *Tin-pots and Pirate Ships*, 215–16.

152. Harris to Guthrie, 1 April 1918, Harris to Guthrie, 2 April 1918, 1048–18–17, LAC, RG 24, vol. 3715.

153. Fayle, *Seaborne Trade*, III, 317.

154. Vice-Admiral W.L. Grant to Admiralty, 28 December 1918, "United States Convoys," UKNA, ADM 137/2658.

vessels of the same speed in convoys and the reduced time spent in port, the effect was a net gain in tonnage. Even so, the improvement "was badly needed" and "the available tonnage was only just equal to the fulfilment of essential requirements."[155]

Typically, the reorganization of the trans-Atlantic convoy system had been undertaken without consulting Canadian authorities, despite the fact that the changes had a considerable impact on the movement of Canada's war supplies. There had, however, been rumours around Ottawa since early March that a change was pending. When A.H. Harris was called to London in late February by the British director of transports to discuss redefining his functions in relation to the Canadian government,[156] NSHQ received the following candid telegram on 1 March from one of the CPR vice-presidents: "Warn you movement now on foot to send all our passenger steamers to New York instead of Canadian ports, loading all Canadian troops in future at New York, putting management in the hands of four officials connected with Harris's department [of Overseas Transport] in place of the [steamship] companies. Will keep you advised."[157] Understandably wary of Harris's penchant for bypassing the Department of the Naval Service in an effort to gather greater powers in his own office, NSHQ incorrectly assumed that the diversion of traffic to New York was his doing. Commander Stephens quickly passed the information on to the militia department with the expected result. As the chief of staff informed Kingsmill, "there are the strongest objections on the part of that department to his [i.e., Harris's] proposal. I am of opinion that it would be one most inadvisable to adopt from the Canadian point of view, especially as it would lengthen the sea journey of Canadian troops, that being the reason which the Admiralty has advanced as making the embarkation port for troops Halifax instead of Montreal. It would be advisable to inform the Admiralty of the Canadian government's view before definite proposals are put forward."[158] With Kingsmill's agreement that the "matter should be taken up with the minister without delay," and that the "naval service and militia dep[artmen]t should take matter up concurrently,"[159] NSHQ informed the Admiralty the next day that they had heard the rumour that a "proposal is being considered for fast convoys to sail from New York. If this would mean suspension of fast convoy from Halifax involving embarkation of Canadian troops New York, strongest objections are likely to be raised by Canadian government."[160]

Such rumours were confirmed when the Admiralty cable informing Grant that "fast Halifax convoys will in future sail from New York" was eventually passed to Ottawa on 20 March by naval authorities in Halifax.[161] The British admiral had been told of the revised

155. Fayle, *Seaborne Trade*, III, 169, 318–19.

156. Graeme Thomson, Director of Transports, Admiralty to Director of the Naval Service, 3 January 1918, 1048–18–2, LAC, RG 24, vol. 3714.

157. Quoted in Stephens, "Memo: For Director of the Naval Service," 1 March 1918, 1048–48–12, LAC, RG 24, vol. 3775.

158. Stephens, "Memo: For Director of the Naval Service," 1 March 1918, ibid.

159. Kingsmill minute, nd, on ibid.

160. Naval Ottawa to Admiralty, 2 March 1918, ibid.

161. Halifax to Naval Ottawa, 20 March 1918, ibid.

scheme by the Admiralty on 9 March, prompting Grant to send his own "protest against new convoy arrangements having been made without consultation of C-in-C."[162] When NSHQ complained that the 9 March telegram to Grant about the shift of fast liners to the United States "had not been repeated here and it was only in the course of conversation with Guthrie [in New York] that department was made aware of any proposed changes," the Admiralty simply expressed its "regret that this was not done on this occasion," and claimed it had all been "an oversight."[163] Nonetheless, the lack of both information and consultation left Canadian officials skeptical of British assurances. It was not until a week later that the British dominions secretary cabled Prime Minister Borden that he had been "privately informed question [of] diversion Canadian liners to United States ports is under consideration and decision imminent in connection convoy arrangements," even though the decision had actually been made some three weeks earlier. "It is essential that greatest possible number American troops should be carried and this the only way," London explained. "If this arrangement decided upon an equivalent of non-passenger tonnage would be sent to counter-balance diversion of liners."[164]

While NSHQ may have been disappointed at not being informed of matters with direct consequences for the RCN, the diversion of Canadian liners to New York carried with it a significant economic impact for the country, which prompted a political response that went beyond simple military or naval considerations. Since the financial implications of a shift of HX convoys to New York would be most directly felt by his own employer, Canadian Pacific Railways, it is not surprising that the director of overseas transport was strongly opposed to the change. Harris was not convinced by the Admiralty's assurances that the new convoy arrangements merely meant the substitution of ten or eleven knot transports for the fourteen knot liners transferred to New York. The Canadian transport director insisted that the perishable food cargo normally loaded at Montreal could not be carried in slower convoys without spoiling "unless the vessels substituted be furnished with refrigeration," and threatened that the "matter will undoubtedly come up in parliament."[165] To ensure that his concerns would indeed be taken up by Canadian politicians, Harris sent copies of his protests to the Admiralty directly to C.C. Ballantyne, despite the businessman's less than cordial relations with the new naval minister.[166]

Ottawa's complaints centered on the dislocation to Canadian trade of those items that were normally shipped by fast liners. Not only would Canada's overseas mail now be forwarded through American ports, but 36,000 tons of imports per month (based on the 1916–17 season totals) would now have to pass through the United States with a consequent loss of income for both Canadian railway companies and the port of Montreal.

---

162. Admiralty to C-in-C, NA&WI, 9 March 1918, C-in-C, NA&WI to Admiralty, 14 March 1918, UKNA, ADM 137/767.

163. Naval Ottawa to Admiralty, 20 March 1918, Admiralty to Naval Ottawa, 21 March 1918, 1048–48–12, LAC, RG 24, vol. 3775.

164. Dominion [Secretary] to Prime Minister, Ottawa, 27 March 1918, ibid.

165. Harris to Transports Admiralty, 29 March 1918, ibid.

166. Harris to Ballantyne, 28 March and 5 April 1918, ibid.

Furthermore, the scheme would cause "inconvenience, delay, and unnecessary expense to importers." Since Canada's exports of war supplies far outweighed its imports, however, the greatest impact would be on the export of perishable foods that were normally shipped in refrigerated holds or in the "cool air space" of fast liners, colder Canadian waters and the quicker voyage allowing perishables to reach Britain without refrigeration even during the summer months. As for the transport of freight and service personnel via the US eastern seaboard, that would involve "an unnecessary rail haul of 840 miles at a time when conservation of fuel and railway equipment necessary [for the added distance], is not considered provident." With the British proposals continuing to designate Halifax as the assembly port for the new HM convoy series (later redesignated as HC—homeward from Canada), even though most of the medium-speed transports were loaded at Montreal, the Canadian navy was compelled to point out once again that "Sydney and not Halifax is the natural rendezvous for slow vessels sailing from the St Lawrence."[167]

The altered convoy system also increased the possibility that Montreal's excellent port facilities would be further underemployed. Although served by two double-track and two single-track railways, and with twenty-one modern steamship loading sheds capable of berthing thirty ocean-going vessels at one time, the port's terminals had not been used at more than 50 percent of capacity since the outbreak of war. As the director of overseas transport was quick to remind the British Ministry of Shipping's representative in New York, Sir Connop Guthrie, "Montreal has the finest grain facilities of any port on the continent of America.... and in the seven months of the year the port is open has handled in pre-war times almost as much grain as the ports of Boston and New York put together in the whole twelve months."[168]

The shift of fast liners to New York would also create serious financial losses for Canadian transportation companies, including Canadian Pacific Railways. As Harris, the railway businessman, explained: "Montreal owing to its terminal facilities, short rail haul, and cooler ocean route, has always been the favourite port of US perishables, and these cannot be carried in the class of vessel which will probably be allotted the St Lawrence route. The proposition would leave Montreal with rough freight only, munitions, grain, flour, etc. All profitable high-class export traffic on which the railways mainly depend for revenue would be diverted to United States ports."[169] At the same time, Harris believed that American business interests were at play in the decision to shift so much of the traffic that normally passed through Montreal down to the US eastern seaboard. In his letter to Guthrie, the director of overseas transport expressed a concern that he "sometimes felt that the overshadowing influence of US interests has influenced you apparently to accept the advice of men naturally prejudiced in favor of American ports and routes, and whose knowledge of Canadian railway transportation and dock facilities is not based on experience."[170] Of course, Ottawa's politicians hardly needed a reminder that revenue

---

167. "Memorandum," 27 March 1918, ibid.

168. Harris to Guthrie, 1 April 1918, 1048–18–17, LAC, RG 24, vol. 3715.

169. "Memorandum," 27 March 1918, 1048–48–12, LAC, RG 24, vol. 3775.

170. Harris to Guthrie, 1 April 1918, 1048–18–17, LAC, RG 24, vol. 3715.

would also be diverted from tax-paying Canadian companies to railways and port authorities in the United States and Harris did not shy away from warning Guthrie that "the Dominion government is pressing me as to quantity and character of tonnage the Canadian ports may expect during the next eight months."[171]

Harris's arguments in favour of Montreal were supported by statistics demonstrating "that vessels have been turned around more expeditiously at Montreal than at any port in the United States." He also noted the amount of congestion that had occurred in American ports during the previous winter. Had Montreal's elevator capacity been used during 1917–18 instead of shipping grain down to New York, for example, it "could have been railed either to Portland or West St John providing cargoes for continuous sailings, throughout the winter season, and the serious delays to transports held at the US seaboard—to that extent—would have been minimized."[172] Although the Ministry of Shipping was attempting to improve the turnaround time for ocean liners at both Liverpool and New York in conjunction with their decision to shift HX convoys to the US port, Harris's contention was that existing port facilities (to handle the cargo) and rail lines (that connected a port to the interior) were as important a consideration as actual sailing times.

The transport director's resistance to the new British convoy scheme was bolstered by the Department of Militia and Defence's equally firm opposition "to any proposal" to have CEF reinforcements embarked at New York rather than Halifax. The militia department noted that if the British proposal to use large passenger liners like the *Olympic* were implemented, the army could not guarantee that it would always be able to fill the spaces available.[173] In the meantime, the British Ministry of Shipping tried to assure Harris that sufficient refrigerator tonnage would be sent to transport any meat products being shipped from Montreal—a total of 50,000 tons per month as agreed upon with the US Food Administration—and insisted that the fast Canadian liners being shifted to New York "will be replaced by slower but still suitable vessels."[174]

In making its views known to London in mid-April, the Canadian government chose to focus its complaints—just as Grant had done—on the lack of consultation involved in the decision-making process. Even the polite language used by the governor general in his telegram to the colonial secretary could not obscure Ottawa's extreme displeasure:

> Your telegram April 8th respecting diversion of shipping has been carefully considered by my advisers. They regret the necessity of recording their opinion that the failure to consult them respecting the proposed arrangements is not satisfactorily explained and indeed is not explained at all. In view of this they hope they may have an explicit assurance that in respect of matters so vitally

171. Harris to Guthrie, 2 April 1918, ibid.

172. Harris to Guthrie, 1 April 1918, ibid.

173. "Extract from Report of Proceedings of the 60th meeting of the Interdepartmental Committee," 2 April 1918, 1048–48–12, LAC, RG 24, vol. 3775.

174. Harris to Ministry of Shipping, 2088, and Ministry of Shipping to Harris, 428, quoted in Harris to Ballantyne, 5 April 1918, ibid.

concerning this country his majesty's government will not proceed upon the principle of deciding first and consulting the Canadian government afterwards. Unless a definite understanding to this effect is reached without undue delay my advisers will consider it their duty to make a frank disclosure to the Canadian parliament and have the whole situation reviewed.[175]

In its reply, London chose to ignore the Canadian complaint about Whitehall's methods, emphasizing instead that the "War Cabinet have directed that the conveyance of troops to France is a matter of utmost urgency, and must be expedited in every way possible."[176] It was left to Grant to explain that the 11.5-knot HM convoys departing Halifax every eight days were expected to transport some 51,000 troops in May alone. According to the British admiral, they would average eight or nine troopships with half of the troops loading at Montreal or Halifax and the remaining 50 percent embarking from American ports before sailing to Halifax.[177] Montreal was designated by the British as the Canadian port of embarkation because the single-line railway to Halifax rendered it impossible to transport 50,000 American troops per month into Nova Scotia without tying up an unwarranted amount of rolling stock. Ottawa much preferred embarking Canadian troops at Halifax (with its shorter ocean passage) but was willing to have American soldiers depart from Montreal "if the United States authorities consider it necessary."[178] In communicating his government's grudging approval of the proposed transport of Canadian and US troops from Montreal instead of Halifax, Ballantyne pointed out to Grant that the Admiralty had advised Ottawa in 1915 "that by reason of submarine peril St Lawrence route should not be used for this purpose and that all troops should embark at Halifax or St John." Nonetheless, "having regard to the urgency of the situation" the Canadian government was willing to relent "upon the distinct understanding that Admiralty takes full and complete responsibility for use of St Lawrence route."[179] Of course the naval minister did not attempt to explain why an outraged Canadian public would hold the Admiralty "fully and completely" responsible should a Canadian troopship be sunk in St Lawrence waters that were—at least in theory—being patrolled by the RCN.

The animosity created in Ottawa by Whitehall's dismissive treatment of Canada's transport concerns prompted the government to ask Grant to come to the capital for another face-to-face meeting in mid-May. Accompanied by Sir Thomas Royden, the chairman of the United Kingdom Chamber of Shipping, the C-in-C travelled to Ottawa on 19 May "at the urgent request of the Canadian authorities." The two British representatives met with Prime Minister Borden, minister of militia and defence, S.C. Mewburn, as well

---

175. Governor General of Canada to Colonial Secretary, 16 April 1918, ibid.

176. Secretary of State for Colonies to Governor General of Canada, 16 April 1918, ibid.

177. C-in-C to Canadian Naval Minister, 26 April 1918, ibid.

178. Kingsmill, "Memorandum: For the Minister," 29 April 1918, C-in-C, NA&WI to Naval Ottawa, 28 April 1918, ibid.

179. Ballantyne to Grant, 29 April 1918, ibid.

as Ballantyne and Kingsmill, in the naval minister's office on the 21st, and explained London's decisions in an effort to placate hard feelings. As Grant indicated in his monthly report to the Admiralty, he was not without some sympathy for Canadian complaints, while patently avoiding any direct criticism of officials in London:

> As will be known, the Canadian government were very sore at what they considered [to be] the want of consideration shown them from home, more especially with regard to diversion of Canadian ships without reference to them, and the type of ship chosen and the little notice given for the transport of their troops: it has, of course, to be recognised both with regard to departures and arrivals by transport that the amplest notice possible is required when the connecting railway journey may be anything up to a week.
>
> The diversion of Canadian ships and the class of ship allotted for Canadian troops merely required explanation of the reasons and have been, I think, readily accepted: other points such as the return of convalescents and women and children on suitable ships with due notice are, I think, in a fair way to full agreement and the difficulty of unforeseen delay of ships after troops are entrained for them will be met by better organisation and the use of concentration camps at suitable points on the railways.
>
> Lack of proper touch between shipping ministry, convoy officers and Canadian military and naval services was at the root of the failure to co-ordinate arrivals of troops with readiness of transports; but the refusal of the Canadian ministers to have anything to do with Sir Arthur Harris [A.H. having received a knighthood in early 1918] so far as troops are concerned, coupled with their objection to the shipping ministry, rendered it necessary specially to adjust the machinery to meet the want.[180]

As we have seen, the friction between the director of overseas transport and officials in the naval department over the former's relationship to NSHQ had arisen almost from the time A.H. Harris had assumed his appointment with no clearly defined lines of authority or responsibility. At the 21 May meeting in Ballantyne's office, Grant could not help but notice the animosity of both the naval minister and Kingsmill toward the CPR businessman. "It has been suggested to me that Sir Arthur Harris should be removed to some other sphere," the British admiral told London, "but this I believe to be unnecessary as, though the Canadian government have, from what I was told, real grounds for complaint against him, he has, I understand, done his work admirably.... I may say that in spite of my expressed anxiety to meet Sir Arthur Harris, he has never been allowed by the Minister of Naval Service to come to Ottawa when I was there."[181] Grant believed that the appointment of an RN officer, Captain J.D. Greenshields, to act as shipping manager in Canada, would alleviate many of the government's concerns. Headquartered primarily in

---

180. Grant to Admiralty, 1 June 1918, UKNA, ADM 137/504.

181. Ibid.

Montreal and communicating directly with both Chambers in Halifax and Kingsmill in Ottawa, Greenshields was to "act thoroughly in concert with the Canadian authorities and they should always be informed of any proposals for changes, et cetera, before making them."[182]

Contrary to the C-in-C's hope, however, it would take an actual alteration in the organization chart before the problem of Harris's stormy relations with the naval department was finally solved. After yet another acerbic exchange between the director of overseas transport and NSHQ,[183] Kingsmill had written directly to the British director of transports, Graeme Thomson, in November 1917 in an effort to finally resolve the "somewhat mixed" relationship resulting from Harris's "status of independence." Stating that "the department has supported him consistently in all his work, which has been of a high order"—an accurate assessment of both parties—the naval director asserted that "Mr Harris has always appeared to resent any control that the department might exercise or appear to exercise over him." Particularly problematic was the fact that both NSHQ and the Admiralty had agreed that questions of policy would be dealt with through Ottawa, an arrangement that Harris continued to ignore by insisting on dealing directly with London on all matters. "The situation has, therefore, become very embarrassing to the department and has become more so now that the Admiralty has supplied Mr Harris with the general cypher. He would not unnaturally assume that it is the desire of the imperial authorities to develop communications between him and them." Although Kingsmill insisted that the Canadian navy "would gladly withdraw from the transport service altogether," and that the department only wished "to act in such a manner as will be an aid to efficiency," he wanted answers from Thomson as to the degree to which NSHQ should continue to be responsible for financial control over the director of overseas transport, for communicating coded messages between London and Ottawa regarding ships and cargo, and the navy's role in repairing, docking, and salvaging damaged merchant ships.[184]

The British director of transports eventually responded to Kingsmill's letter early in the new year by promising to summon Harris to London "as soon as possible" to work out "a closer definition" of his responsibilities.[185] In the meantime, however, the Halifax explosion and the public's perception that an inept RCN was somehow to blame for the disaster fuelled the navy's frustration at being held responsible for matters over which it had no actual control—whether it was the dangerous loading of merchant ships with explosives in foreign ports, the assembly of convoys, or a non-existent authority over the actions of Harris's transport organization in Montreal. In a memorandum to the naval minister in the weeks following the release of the Drysdale Inquiry's findings in February 1918, Kingsmill expressed his concern that "the recent explosion at Halifax has called

---

182. Ibid.

183. Harris to Stephens, 25 October 1917, Stephens to Harris, 27 October 1917, Harris to Stephens, 1 November 1917, Stephens, "Memo to Director of Overseas Transport," 7 November 1917, 1048–48–3, pt. 1, LAC, RG 24, vol 3772.

184. Kingsmill to Graeme Thomson, 28 November 1917, 1048–18–2, LAC, RG 24, vol. 3714.

185. Thomson to Kingsmill, 3 January 1918, ibid.

attention generally to the question of loading munitions at our different ports." In particular, the naval director referred Ballantyne to an April 1916 memorandum from Commander Stephens

> calling attention to the fact that there were on the date of his memo awaiting shipment in or close to the sheds at Montreal, which are in the centre of the city, over five thousand tons of explosive, and the amount was being rapidly increased. A letter was written on the 29th April 1916 to the director of overseas transport to which no reply has been received.... I am afraid, as things stand at present, if there were an accident in the City of Montreal, the Department of the Naval Service would receive the blame, although I cannot, myself, see the responsibility of the naval officers of the department in the matter. Certainly as the director of the naval service, I have no control over the director of overseas transport whatever.[186]

The degree of frustration evident in the naval director's summation accurately reflected NSHQ's sense of helplessness in meeting the many responsibilities it had been assigned. In the wake of the Halifax explosion, the RCN had received a large proportion of public scorn for the catastrophe when the navy's only real shortcoming was a lack of clairvoyance in foreseeing a freak accident. At the same time as the Drysdale inquiry was casting its own aspersions on the navy, the Admiralty's recommendation that the defence of Canada's East Coast shipping lanes required a minimum of six destroyers and six fast trawlers had been completely undercut by the Royal Navy's unwillingness to provide them. The RCN was left to face the prospect of combating long-range U-boats without benefit of the very warships it would need to do so. It did not take much imagination for Kingsmill to foresee the day when the navy would once again have to bear the brunt of blame for a catastrophic mishap in Montreal for which it was in no way responsible.

It must have come as some relief, therefore, when the naval director was informed that the British government was now in a position to transfer Harris's Montreal organization to its own Ministry of Shipping. The expansion of the British ministry's organization in the United States, including a financial representative in New York to handle the shipping accounts directly, allowed London to alter the administrative arrangements governing the Canadian transport director's functions. As the British ministry advised Kingsmill, "the general effect of the proposed administrative and financial arrangements would be that Sir Arthur Harris as this ministry's representative, would be directly responsible for all shipping questions and all land routing questions in connection with shipping while you would remain responsible for all matters relating to protection, escort and naval questions generally, taking such steps as may be necessary in emergency as regards salvage and assisting Sir Arthur Harris as and where necessary in matters relating to dry docking and

---

186. Kingsmill, "Memorandum for the Minister," 26 February 1918, ibid It was not until May 1918 that Harris instituted new rules for the loading of munition ships at the port of Montreal, although explosives continued to be stored in the harbour sheds in the centre of the city. Harris to Transports Admiralty, 13 June 1918, 1048–17–30, LAC, RG 24, vol. 3713.

repairs. Telegraphic reports would not be necessary from you except on convoy and such other matters."[187] Since the proposal would pass control of Canadian rail lines to a representative of the British government—albeit the same Canadian who had been exercising that control for several years—Kingsmill could only inform London that "the whole question of the status of Sir Arthur Harris is now being taken up by the minister of the naval service with the prime minister."[188]

The question of Harris's status was discussed with Grant and Royden during their 21 May meeting with Borden, Ballantyne, and Kingsmill in Ottawa. As a result, Royden submitted a written proposal of the organizational changes for the Canadian government's consideration. As the Ministry of Shipping's representative in Canada, Harris would now report directly to London, while continuing to control the movement of war supplies in Canada on behalf of the British government, allotting cargoes to ships and routing all munitions and supplies on the nation's railways. All Canadian transport accounts would be sent directly to the Ministry of Shipping's financial representative in New York for payment from imperial funds. The Royal Navy's Captain J.D. Greenshields was to be appointed to Canada by the British shipping ministry to serve as a *de facto* shipping agent for all imperial transports loading in Montreal under Harris's direction.[189] In forwarding the proposals to Ballantyne, Royden insisted that Greenshields "will keep himself fully posted concerning the vessels and will be only too glad to run over to Ottawa at any time to discuss any special matters with you or with the militia department."[190]

Commander G.C. Holloway, an RNR officer serving in the RCN, had already been transferred from his duties in Halifax to serve as the naval transport officer and senior naval officer at Montreal. In addition, Royden proposed that Holloway would also act as the liaison with the American embarkation staff that was to be established at the port for all US Army troopships departing overseas from Montreal. As both the militia and naval departments had insisted, "all information as to vessels allocated to lift Canadian troops will be sent direct to the director of naval services [sic], Ottawa, who would pass them on to Commander Holloway, and who would arrange direct with him the dates of embarkation. Commander Holloway would be responsible for seeing that the vessels are ready and in a fit state to receive the number of troops which they are expected to carry."[191]

Although Royden had hoped to receive a quick reply from Ballantyne, the question of Harris's status was left in abeyance for most of the summer. The urgency for formal approval of the change was reduced when Captain Greenshields reported to NSHQ "that the work was going along extremely well at Montreal under the present arrangement." It was decided not to answer Royden's letter until after Ballantyne had had a chance to

---

187. Kemball Yorke to Kingsmill, 13 April 1918, 1048–18–2, LAC, RG 24, vol. 3714.

188. Kingsmill to Graeme Thomson, 4 May 1918, ibid.

189. Sir Thomas Royden to C.C. Ballantyne, 28 May 1918, ibid.

190. Sir Thomas Royden to C.C. Ballantyne, covering letter, 28 May 1918, ibid.

191. Sir Thomas Royden to C.C. Ballantyne, 28 May 1918, ibid.

consult with Admiralty officials in London in July.[192] In the event, it was not until early September that Prime Minister Borden relented to Ballantyne's urging and approved the transfer of his Montreal friend—the PM reported that he had "warmly opposed" the move—to the British Ministry of Shipping.[193] Although Harris would continue to work in conjunction with the naval department, and provide NSHQ with reports of shipping movements as he had in the past, for the remainder of the war he did so as director general, British Ministry of Shipping (Canada).[194]

Nonetheless, the arrangements made in Ballantyne's office in May to remove responsibility for the overseas transport organization from NSHQ relieved the navy of its long-standing frustration at being accountable for a strong-willed businessman over whom the department had no tangible control. As the Halifax explosion had demonstrated, the public was only too willing to pin the blame for mishaps or mismanagement on the fledgling Canadian navy even if the service was itself no more than an impotent bystander. In passing bureaucratic and financial responsibility for Sir Arthur Harris onto the British Ministry of Shipping, the naval minister cleared the decks in time for the navy to concentrate on its primary task of defending Canada's shipping lanes from the long-range German submarines that were about to make North American waters their newest hunting grounds.

---

192. G.J. Desbarats, "Memo for file no. 48–18–2," 4 July 1918, ibid.

193. R.L. Borden, *Robert Laird Borden: His Memoirs* (Toronto 1938), II, 855.

194. Department of the Naval Service, *Report of the Department of the Naval Service for the Fiscal Year Ending March 31, 1919* (Ottawa 1920), 15; and Harris to J.A. Wilson, 20 September 1918, 1048–18–1, pt. 5, LAC, RG 24, vol. 3714.

CHAPTER 10

Defending Against the U-Boats, June to August 1918

On 14 April 1918 a converted mercantile submarine of the Deutschland class departed Kiel, Germany, with a crew of eight officers and sixty-five seamen. Commanded by *Korvetten-kapitän* Heinrich Van Nostitz und Janckendorf, a twenty-year veteran of the German Navy, *U 151* was bound for the East Coast of the United States using the North Sea route around the north of Scotland. On 22 April the British intercepted a radio signal from the station at Nauen, Germany that clearly indicated that a U-boat was on her way to North America. The signal provided its U-boat recipient with a description of the troop transport sailings from both Newport News and New York along with their normal escorts and routes east. Another message intercepted on the 27th specifically identified the North American-bound submarine as *U 151*, which was known to have been at sea at least since 18 April. Two days later, further intercepts suggested that both *U 151* and *U 155* were probably heading across the Atlantic, the former proceeding at five knots on the more northerly route, to attack troop transports and cargo vessels off the coast of the United States.[1]

The first visible indication that a German U-boat was making her way across the Atlantic came when Kingston, Jamaica, relayed a report that an American merchant ship had engaged an enemy submarine on 2 May about 650 kilometres north of the Azores.[2] That same day, the British commander-in-chief, North America and West Indies Station, Vice-Admiral W.L. Grant, informed Ottawa of an Admiralty message "that information from reliable source states that submarine of *Deutschland* type sailed from Germany about 19th April to attack either troop or cargo steamers from the United States."[3] As the Admiralty message reminded the North American station, Deutschland-class submarines "generally operate long distance from shore and seldom in less than 100 fathoms. Their single hulls are very vulnerable to depth charge attack. They rarely attack submerged. There is but one known instance of attack against convoy and but two of torpedo attack against single

---

1. Richard Compton-Hall, *Submarines and the War at Sea, 1914–1918* (London 1991), 278; and Robert M. Grant, *U-Boat Intelligence, 1914–1918* (London 1969), 150–51.

2. US Navy Department, Office of Naval Records and Library, Historical Section, *German Submarine Activities on the Atlantic Coast of the United States and Canada* (Washington 1920), 23; and "Submarine Activities off Atlantic Coast of the United States: Cruise of the German 'U-151' from May 25 to June 18 1918," nd, 5, United Kingdom National Archives (hereafter UKNA), Admiralty (hereafter ADM) 137/4136.

3. C-in-C, NA&WI to Naval Ottawa, 2 May 1918, 1062–13–2, pt. 2, Library and Archives Canada (hereafter LAC), Record Group (hereafter RG) 24, vol. 4021.

vessels, one being unsuccessful. They attack by gunfire almost exclusively. Most effective type to oppose them is the submarine. They shift operating area as soon as presence of submarine is discovered."[4]

London's advice that submarines were the "most effective" naval vessels to cope with a U-cruiser undoubtedly reflected the Allied Naval Council's somewhat wishful thinking on the subject, a view that had itself been conditioned by the Admiralty's insistence on concentrating all available destroyers in British home waters. Indeed, the Naval Council's willingness to class the threat posed by long-range submarines in the same category as surface raiders was not based on any practical experience or operational analysis of the type's capabilities, and it is difficult to discover any rationale behind the Admiralty's advice other than to exclude the need for destroyer forces in waters distant from Britain and so circumvent demands for them. In the event, the use of submarines to combat U-cruisers quickly proved to be more of a nuisance than a help as their very presence in waters where U-boats were operating unnecessarily frightened any merchantmen that spotted them, resulting in false reports of enemy submarines and indiscriminate friendly fire. Nonetheless, the suggestion that submarines would prove useful, even if they were not the "most effective" vessels, provided the RCN with some reassurance since the Canadian navy had already brought *CC 1* and *CC 2*, along with *Shearwater*, around to Halifax from Esquimalt in the fall of 1917 and the USN had promised to send an additional submarine soon.[5]

Two weeks after the first Admiralty warning of a possible U-cruiser heading for North America, *U 151* gave her position away when she unsuccessfully attacked a British merchant ship, in disregard of the orders she had been given not to do so while en route. On 15 May the *Huntress* of 4,997 tons reported an unsuccessful torpedo attack by an enemy submarine some 800 kilometres east north east of Bermuda and some 1,000 kilometres east of Cape Hatteras. Apparent confirmation of a U-boat's presence in North American waters was received on 19 May when the American merchantman *Nyanza* of 6213 tons radioed a New Jersey wireless station that she was being fired upon by a submarine some 480 kilometres off the Maryland coast.[6] A message warning all naval authorities and merchant ships in Canada and the United States of the approaching U-cruiser had been disseminated three days earlier, stating that the enemy warship probably would use her guns or mines rather than torpedoes in her attacks and that merchant ships "should keep in as deep water as possible without going far out and should give all headlands and lights on frequented routes as wide [a] berth as possible consistent with safe navigation."[7] The tracking of a U-cruiser's progress westward continued when the Canadian steamship *Montcalm* relayed a radio report from a British merchantman on 21 May that she had been fired upon six times by a surfaced enemy submarine only 130 kilometres off the Maryland coast.[8]

4.   C-in-C, NA&WI to Naval Ottawa, 2 May 1918, ibid.

5.   C-in-C, NA&WI to Naval Ottawa, 28 April 1918, Naval Ottawa to Britannia [C-in-C, NA&WI], 30 April 1918, Naval Ottawa to Britannia, 3 May 1918, 1065–7-6, LAC, RG 24, vol. 4031; and Allied Naval Council minutes, January 1918, 25, UKNA, ADM 137/836.

6.   US Navy Department, *German Submarine Activities*, 23–24; and Grant, *U-Boat Intelligence*, 151–52.

7.   C-in-C, NA&WI to Naval Ottawa, 16 May 1918, 1062–13–2, pt. 2, LAC, RG 24, vol. 4021.

Arriving off the coast of the United States on 22 May, *U 151* entered Chesapeake Bay and—contrary to the Admiralty's expectations that minelaying by submarines was "not a paying concern"[9]—laid mines off Baltimore, using the American coastal navigation lights to help establish the U-boat's position.[10] Returning to the open sea, the German submarine sank her first victims on the 25th, sending the schooners *Hattie Dunn* and *Hauppauge*, of 435 and 1,446 tons respectively, to the bottom with bombs placed in the hold after stopping and boarding the wooden vessels. A third schooner, *Edna* of 325 tons, remained afloat and was later salvaged when the German bombs failed to explode.[11] All three schooners lacked radio equipment and were unable to broadcast a warning signal. The action against the *Hattie Dunn* was typical of the type of surface action the U-cruisers would favour in attacking smaller vessels in North American waters. According to the schooner's master, his ship was southbound from New York to Charleston, South Carolina about 1010 hours when:

> I heard a cannon go off; I looked and saw a boat and thought it was an American. That boat fired once; I started my ship full speed to the westward. He fired again and finally came alongside and said: "Do you want me to kill you?"
>
> I told him I thought his was an American boat. He told me to give him the papers and get some foodstuff. He then wanted me to get into his small boat but I was anxious to get ashore, so I immediately got into one of my own boats and shoved off. He halted me because he did not want me to get ashore. He then put a man into my boat so that I would come back to the submarine. An officer and other men from the German submarine then boarded the schooner and after placing bombs about ordered the crew of the *Hattie Dunn* to row to the submarine which we did. The schooner was sent to the bottom by the explosion of bombs in latitude 37 degrees 24 minutes N, longitude 75 degrees 5 minutes W. The second officer in command aboard the submarine gave me a receipt for my ship. There were no casualties. The weather was fine and clear, the sea was calm.[12]

The twenty-three crewmen from the three schooners were taken aboard *U 151* and held prisoner until the morning of 2 June. In the meantime, the U-boat headed north, where

---

8. US Navy Department, *German Submarine Activities*, 24. The speculative assertions in *Submarine Activities* that the reported actions on 19 and 21 May were genuine attacks by *U 151* are not supported by the U-cruiser's log. Michael L. Hadley and Roger Sarty, *Tin-pots and Pirate Ships: Canadian Naval Forces and German Sea Raiders, 1880–1918* (Montreal and Kingston 1991), 353.

9. Admiralty to Undersecretary of State, Colonial Office, 3 January 1918, 1017–10–1, pt. 1, LAC, RG 24, vol. 3831.

10. US Navy Department, *German Submarine Activities*, 123; Compton-Hall, *Submarines and the War at Sea*, 279; and Edwyn A. Gray, *The Killing Time: The German U-Boats, 1914–1918* (New York 1972), 193.

11. Ibid, 24–25.

12. Ibid, 26.

she laid mines off the mouth of Delaware Bay before proceeding to the eastern end of Long Island, New York. On 28 May the submarine cut both the Commercial Cable Company's Nova Scotia-New York telegraph cable and the Central and South American Cable Company's New York-Colon cable.[13] Heading south once again, on 2 June *U 151* stopped and sank the 776-ton schooner *Isabel B. Wiley* and the steamship *Winneconne* of 1,869 tons some fifty miles off the coast of New Jersey. Putting their prisoners aboard the merchant ship's lifeboats and instructing them to row for shore, the sailors of the sunken vessels were finally picked up by a passing steamship on the morning of the 3rd. Following the sinking of the *Winneconne*, the U-cruiser continued a busy afternoon by stopping and sinking the cargo schooners *Jacob M. Haskell* and *Edward H. Cole*, of some 1,800 tons each. All four ships were engaged in the US East Coast coal trade. The master of the *Jacob M. Haskell* described the German submariners that sank his ship as going "about their work in a business-like manner; the officer was so polite that he almost got on our nerves."[14] The U-boat's final victims of the day were two larger merchant ships, the 3,210-ton *Texel* and the 5,093-ton *Carolina*, both bound for New York from Puerto Rico with cargoes of sugar. The *Carolina* also carried 218 passengers and a crew of 117. Stopping both vessels with shots across the bow, the *Texel* was boarded by the Germans and sunk by bombs, while the larger *Carolina* was sunk by shellfire from the submarine's 5.9-inch guns after all passengers and crew had taken to their boats. Unfortunately one of the boats capsized in a heavy squall that night, drowning her occupants, nine passengers and four crew, the first casualties of the war resulting from enemy action in North American waters.[15]

Lacking definite evidence of a U-boat's presence until 3 June—the crews of the schooners sunk on 25 May remaining prisoners until then—Vice-Admiral Grant had informed the Admiralty at the end of May that it was his belief that there were "no enemy submarines this side, but in view of the inexperience of patrols and the lack of realisation of what measures were really necessary in the event of their appearance off the coast, the uneasiness caused has been of the utmost value [in preparing anti-submarine defences]. Patrols have more realised a probable danger, submarines have been placed under better control, I have been able to initiate some measures for the protection of, at any rate, important British coast traffic and to safeguard it against enemy minelaying, and the issue of warnings has to a certain extent prepared the press and public against any scare when the danger really arises."[16] The peril arose faster than the British admiral had apparently contemplated when the rescued crewmen and passengers began landing on the US East Coast on 3 June. That same day, Grant telegraphed NSHQ to warn that a "submarine has been this side for some days and may have laid delay action mines anywhere."[17] As the

---

13. Ibid, 29, 119–21; and Compton-Hall, *Submarines and the War at Sea*, 279.

14. US Navy Department, *German Submarine Activities*, 30–33; and "Submarine Activities off Atlantic Coast from May 25 to June 18 1918," nd, 15–16, UKNA, ADM 137/4136.

15. US Navy Department, *German Submarine Activities*, 34–38.

16. Grant to Admiralty, General Letter No. 4, 1 June 1918, UKNA, ADM 137/504.

17. C-in-C, NA&WI to Naval Ottawa, 3 June 1918, 1062–13–2, pt. 3, LAC, RG 24, vol. 4021.

Canadians attempted to put their own limited anti-submarine resources into place, they could at least take some consolation that the U-cruiser was operating primarily against the soft targets presented by the unconvoyed coastal traffic south of New York.

The United States Navy had received the same Admiralty warnings at the start of the year as Ottawa concerning the likelihood of long-range German submarines operating in the western Atlantic in 1918. Unlike the RCN, however, the Americans were much better placed to provide the warships they needed for their own defence. Although Admiral Benson and the Navy Department endorsed the policy of sending the bulk of the USN's destroyer strength overseas, the chief of naval operations later explained to Congress that his "first thought in the beginning, during, and always, was to see first that our coasts and our own vessels and our own interests were safeguarded. Then ... to give everything we had ... for the common cause."[18] Nonetheless, Benson's nationalism was tempered by pragmatism and the USN had responded to the desperate pleas of both the Admiralty and Vice-Admiral Sims following America's entry into the war, by deploying a total of thirty-five destroyers to Queenstown, Ireland by mid-July 1917. These included almost all of its thirty-one "Thousand Tonners"—modern 4-inch gunned destroyers built in the 1913–16 programs. The rest of the American destroyers based at Queenstown were from the twenty-one-ship 740-ton Drayton class armed with five 3-inch guns that had been built under the 1910–12 programs. The USN also sent five of its oldest destroyers, the 420-ton Bainbridge-class warships of the 1900–02 period, armed with two 3-inch guns, for anti-submarine duties at Gibraltar. Although Sims complained about the small number of older destroyers the navy department insisted on retaining in American waters, further reinforcements for Europe would not be available until the first of the new flush-deck destroyers, some 270 of which were ordered as part of the USN's wartime construction programs (although only fifty or so were actually completed by the Armistice), which began to be commissioned in late 1917 and early 1918.[19]

Once the introduction of the convoy system reduced shipping losses to the point where it no longer appeared that Britain could be defeated by submarine attack alone, Washington's view of its overseas anti-submarine forces changed. As early as May 1917, when the first American destroyer divisions had been sent overseas, President Woodrow Wilson had cautioned the navy not to become so involved in the British anti-submarine campaign that it would be unable to use its destroyers at Queenstown to protect the US troopships that were carrying the AEF to the ports of western France. By July 1917, the navy department was sending repeated instructions for Sims to assign the USN destroyers the primary task of protecting the AEF's lines of communication to France rather than their original mission of escorting supply convoys into British ports. Washington recognized that neither the Admiralty nor Sims fully appreciated the importance the United

---

18. Benson testimony to Senate Naval Affairs Committee quoted in Dean C. Allard, "Anglo-American Naval Differences During World War I," *Military Affairs*, April 1980, 76–77.

19. Paul G. Halpern, *A Naval History of World War I* (Annapolis 1994), 359, 394; Henry Newbolt, *Naval Operations* (London 1931), V, 35n, 55n, 81n; and O. Parkes and M. Prendergast, eds., *Jane's Fighting Ships 1919* (London 1919), 210–12.

States government attached to the establishment of a sizable American army on the Western Front. As Benson's assistant chief of naval operations, Captain W.V. Pratt, explained to Congress, the USN's greatest "contribution to the war lay not in the fighting ships we could throw to the front, but in our ability to mobilize and transport America's great reserve [of man]power quickly to the European war front." This, Pratt asserted, was in contrast to the priorities of the Admiralty and Sims: "The impelling reason of the British was protection to food and war supplies in transit. Our basic reason was protection to our own military forces in crossing the seas."[20]

Washington's emphasis on troopship protection was given greater urgency following the success of the Germans' March 1918 offensive. On the heels of Sir Douglas Haig's "backs to the wall" order following the near-collapse of the British Fifth Army, the movement of AEF reinforcements to France finally became a top priority for both Sims and the Admiralty. The transfer of the fast HX convoys to New York coincided with a large increase in the number of American troops being transported overseas. This effort was aided by the Admiralty's assignment of three of Britain's largest passenger liners, *Olympic* (sister ship to the *Titanic*), *Mauretania*, and *Aquitania* exclusively to transporting American troops to Europe. The United States, which had only a limited number of suitable liners in its own merchant marine, seized and recommissioned eighteen large German liners that had been interned in American ports, including the largest passenger liner in the world, the 54,282-ton *Vaterland* of the Hamburg-Amerika line. Renamed the *Leviathan*, the ship could carry more than 10,000 troops on each passage. Over 120,000 AEF soldiers were carried overseas in April, rising sharply to 247,000 in May, and reaching a peak of 311,000 in July 1918. By war's end, 2,079,880 American troops had been transported to Europe, 51.25 percent in British ships and 46.25 percent in US liners. In keeping with Washington's view of the employment of the American naval forces, the USN provided 83 percent of the escorts for their troop convoys. This escort force, based primarily in the United States, covered the troopships throughout their trans-Atlantic passage and included most of the USN's thirty-one cruisers and some thirty modern destroyers fresh from the builders' yards. By early August 1918, as the U-cruiser offensive in American waters intensified, the US navy department decreed that a USN destroyer would escort each troop convoy proceeding to Britain.[21]

Although Admiral Benson and the navy department gave top priority to guarding America's trans-Atlantic troopships, they did not ignore their responsibility for providing some measure of protection to the US East Coast. A special board convened by Benson in January 1918 to formulate a defence plan for the eastern seaboard supported the chief of naval operation's views by insisting that the protection of America's trans-Atlantic shipping "is the chief task of the naval force based on America." As a result, the board concluded

20. Pratt testimony to Senate Naval Affairs Committee quoted in Dean C. Allard, "Anglo-American Naval Differences," 76–77.

21. Commander-in-Chief, North America and West Indies Station to Admiralty, 4 August 1918, UKNA, ADM 137/903; Halpern, *A Naval History of World War I*, 435–36; Allard, "Anglo-American Naval Differences," 76; and Navy Department to Admiralty, 5 September 1918, quoted in Michael Simpson, ed., *Anglo-American Naval Relations, 1917–1919* (Aldershot, UK 1991), 469–70.

that "the force retained in American waters cannot with reasonable military prudence be reduced below the minimum required for meeting the emergency here being considered. It has devolved upon this board to determine what that minimum is; and such determination should be held to against the repeated urgings, to send all force abroad, of individuals who have not fully considered the situation as a whole.... Emphasis is laid upon it as the basis for any plan for defense against hostile operations near our coast."[22]

The officers of the board embraced the fact that "the general policy of the United States is to send the maximum possible force abroad for offensive operations in the active theater of war. This policy the board has kept constantly in mind to the end that there might be no weakening of it." Nevertheless, with the chief of naval operations' approval, the board concluded that new US destroyers should be kept on the American East Coast for the one month period of their "shakedown after commissioning." It also stipulated that at least nine newly commissioned destroyers were to be retained on the East Coast, with four of them assigned to the third naval district at New York, and four to the Fifth Naval District at Hampton Roads. (While the point had not been raised by the Admiralty in its correspondence with NSHQ, the fact that there would always be at least four modern destroyers based at New York—compared to the lack of destroyers in Canadian waters— would have counted in favour of the American port as the assembly point for fast convoys.) The ninth new destroyer was assigned to the first naval district headquartered at Boston for her shakedown training, while a second modern destroyer "permanently employed in experimentation" would be available to the New England command. The board members also stated that these numbers were "the minimum increase needed," and anticipated "more destroyers being under shakedown" and available for anti-submarine operations "after the building program shall have begun to yield more frequent deliveries." The commandants of the three naval districts were instructed to employ the new destroyers "as necessary in the event of hostile submarines appearing on this coast; otherwise not to employ them, but instead to allow them all possible freedom in their training for active service." They pointed out that the altered shakedown schedule would have little impact on "the ultimate date of beginning service in the [European] war zone" since the previous "slow passage for shakedown en route" would now be replaced by the "somewhat longer shakedown time on our coast together with a quick run across" to Britain.[23]

Besides a minimum of four modern destroyers, New York and Hampton Roads were each to have at least five modern submarines available to counter any U-cruisers operating in their districts. The new submarines would be available, while they were undergoing a two-month shakedown period before heading overseas. The two convoy assembly ports were also assigned a force of thirty submarine chasers each "for convoy escort and listening service." While the utility of the subchasers as convoy escorts was somewhat dubious, they could at least provide an anti-submarine listening screen in the approaches to the ports or

22. Office of Naval Operations, A Special Board to formulate a plan of defence in home waters to Chief of Naval Operations, "Defense against Submarine attack in home waters," 6 February 1918, in US Navy Department, *German Submarine Activities*, 143–50.

23. Ibid, 148–49.

The USN submarine chaser *SC 242* spent the summer of 1918 escorting convoys from Sydney, Nova Scotia. At 110 feet long, the wooden sub chasers had a top speed of sixteen knots when fully loaded. In addition to a 3-inch short-range 23-calibre gun, it also carried depth charges. *SC 242*'s "Y" gun, which fired charges off either side, is visible between the three sailors at the rail and the chaser's stern. (DND CN 3279)

be despatched to the scene of reported submarine sightings. New York and Hampton Roads were also each allocated eighteen minesweepers to maintain the approach channels. The air stations at Rockaway Inlet, New York, and Hampton Roads were to have at least one squadron of twenty aircraft available for convoy escort, as soon as possible, without interfering with the deliveries of American-made aircraft to France.[24]

The nine new-construction destroyers to be kept in US waters for their one-month shakedown period were not, however, the only such vessels available to the East Coast naval districts. Although the most modern American destroyers had been sent to Ireland by the spring of 1918, the navy still retained over a dozen older destroyers and coastal torpedo boats along the eastern seaboard, several of which were used in the search for *U 151*. The largest of the older warships were the 840-ton Drayton-class destroyers of the 1910–12 building programs (only half of which had been sent to Europe) and five Flusser-class 800-ton destroyers of the 1909 program. While five of the ten 1900–02 Bainbridge-class had been sent to Gibraltar for anti-submarine duties, the remainder were available for service on the East Coast. The USN also had seven large coastal torpedo boats that had been built in 1900–02. At 400 to 430 tons and carrying the same two 3-inch and four 6-pounder gun armament as the 420-ton Bainbridge-class (except *Lawrence* and *Macdonough*, which each carried seven 6-pounders), the seven torpedo boats served a role similar to that of the USN's older destroyers. As a result, the East Coast naval districts had some twenty-five older, 3-inch-gunned destroyers/torpedo boats available to patrol in search of enemy U-boats. The naval districts also had seventeen old torpedo boats still in commission. Built between 1895 and 1902 and varying in size from 105 to 280-tons, the old torpedo boats were, however, of little value beyond a port's immediate approaches.[25]

The availability of these naval assets was evident during the search for *U 151* in early June. In a coastal sweep conducted on the morning of 3 June, the 420-ton destroyer USS *Preble* reported firing on an enemy submarine. A Drayton-class destroyer, USS *Henley*, was despatched to the *Preble*'s position but could find no sign of a U-cruiser. *U 151* was actually well to the south of the position given by *Preble*, however, where she sank the 915-ton American schooner *Sam C. Mengel* by bombs that same evening. Early the following morning the U-cruiser had just sunk a small American schooner and was shelling the French tanker *Radioleine* when the torpedo boat USS *Hull* arrived on the scene and forced the enemy to break off his attack and submerge to escape. Another Bainbridge-class destroyer, USS *Paul Jones*, picked up the survivors of a Norwegian sailing ship sunk by the U-cruiser on the morning of 14 June, off the coast of Delaware, while the Drayton-class destroyer *Patterson* picked up the survivors of a second Norwegian vessel, the *Kringsjaa*, sunk later that afternoon.[26] A third Drayton-class destroyer, USS *Jouett*, was the lead ship for a "naval hunt squadron" the USN formed in conjunction with six submarine chasers. As one American naval historian has commented, the subchasers were eventually equipped

24. Admiral W.S. Benson, "Modifications and Changes or Alterations—Outbound Shipping," 6 March 1918, in US Navy Department, *German Submarine Activities*, 150–51.

25. *Jane's Fighting Ships 1919*, 214–17.

26. US Navy Department, *German Submarine Activities*, 41–48.

with hydrophones to aid in their searches "but, not surprisingly as the experience of war in European waters had shown, these methods achieved little success." Following the sinkings on 3 June, the navy department placed coastal shipping under the direction of the naval districts and instituted a system of coastal convoys between Rhode Island and Cape Hatteras. Most of this shipping was escorted by submarine chasers (even though the motorboats often had difficulty keeping up with the faster convoys), thus allowing the naval districts to use their available destroyers and torpedo boats on sea patrols, supplemented by the less-effective subchasers.[27]

Despite the USN efforts at defence, *U 151* continued to operate seaward of Chesapeake Bay until the middle of June. The German U-boat sank another nine ships, totalling 16,800 tons, between the 3rd and the 14th, of which the Norwegian merchant ships *Vindeggen* and *Henrik Lund*, of 3,179 and 4,322 tons, respectively, were the largest. In addition, a mine laid by the U-boat early in her cruise sank the American tanker *Herbert L. Pratt*, of 7,145 tons on 3 June, 2.5 miles southeast of Overfalls Lightship at the mouth of Delaware Bay.[28] By the second half of June it was obvious that *U 151* was making her way home as the final two victims, the Belgian transport *Chillier* of 2,966 tons and the Norwegian steamer *Augvald* of 3,406 tons, were sunk on the 22nd and 23rd respectively well out in the Atlantic over 800 kilometres south of Cape Race.[29] For the British C-in-C observing the situation from his base in Washington, the "most noticeable features of this submarine's operations have been her avoidance of the New York routes and of attacks on convoys, also her small use of torpedo attack, there being at present only record of three having been fired."[30] On both 20 and 28 June, the radio station at Nauen, Germany had signalled the U-boat with instructions for her return route home. Although the Royal Navy mounted a strong hunting patrol off the Shetland Islands based on the intercepted messages, *U 151* reached Germany in mid-July.[31]

In stark contrast to the American navy's more numerous anti-submarine forces—even given the navy department's emphasis on European waters—the RCN was being asked to protect Canada's shipping lanes from the same U-cruiser threat with only its auxiliary patrol vessels, trawlers, and drifters. While *U 151* was making her presence known along the US eastern seaboard, the RCN at least received a few needed reinforcements when the six USN submarine chasers promised by the Americans in April arrived at Halifax on 15 May, accompanied by two of the old USN torpedo boats *DeLong* and *Tingey*.[32] Launched in 1900 and 1902 respectively, they were 196-ton boats with a design speed of twenty-six

27. Halpern, *A Naval History of World War I*, 431–32.

28. US Navy Department, *German Submarine Activities*, 41–48, 139. In addition, the crew of *U 151* transferred seventy tons of copper bars from *Vindeggen* to their U-cruiser before scuttling the merchant ship. Hadley and Sarty, *Tin-pots and Pirate Ships*, 244–45.

29. US Navy Department, *German Submarine Activities*, 49–50, 139.

30. Grant to Admiralty, General Letter No. 5, 1 July 1918, UKNA, ADM 137/504.

31. Grant, *U-Boat Intelligence*, 152.

32. C-in-C, NA&WI to Naval Ottawa, 28 April 1918, Naval Ottawa to Britannia [Grant], Naval Ottawa to Navyard Halifax, 30 April 1918, C-in-C, NA&WI to Naval Ottawa, 10 May 1918, 1065–7-6, LAC, RG 24, vol. 4031.

knots, armed with three 1-pounder guns and three 18-inch torpedo tubes, making them almost 100 tons smaller, four knots slower, and more weakly armed than the much newer HMCS *Grilse*.[33] Soon after the Americans' arrival, Captain Hose informed NSHQ that the "two torpedo boats are old vessels and unsuitable for convoy work and it is considered they could be most usefully employed in augmenting the inner patrols at Halifax and Sydney. T[orpedo] B[oat] *DeLong* has sustained some damage and is not available for duty at present. She would be attached to Sydney Base and the TB *Tingey* to Halifax."[34] After several months experience with the old torpedo boats, however, the admiral superintendent, Vice-Admiral W.O. Story, realized that even in assigning them to the Halifax inner patrol they were "unsatisfactory. *DeLong* and *Tingey* are useless. It is essential two good vessels of our own service should always be on this patrol."[35]

With few other patrol craft capable of escorting a convoy to seaward of the port approaches, Hose had to rely heavily on the USN motorboats to handle most of the convoy escort duties. Soon after the Americans' arrival at Halifax, the captain of patrols instructed the chaser division's senior officer, Lieutenant (jg) G.B. Schmucker, to inform him "of the date on which the flotilla will have completed any defects and any preliminary exercises you consider necessary and will be ready to take up its duties." In the meantime, Hose assured Schmucker that the senior officer of the local patrol at Halifax, Commander P.F. Newcombe, would "arrange to meet such requirements of your flotilla as you bring to his notice."[36] Once the American subchasers were ready for operations, Hose planned to organize them into two divisions of three chasers each, with one division assigned to the escort of the medium convoys departing Halifax and the other to the slow convoys, initially at Halifax until the shift to Sydney for the summer season. The captain of patrols expected the subchasers to escort convoys for the first "200 to 300 miles from shore, weather permitting" with the divisions taking their orders from the commanding officer of the cruiser escort while in company. With each convoy cycle lasting eight days and their escort duties only taking some twenty-four hours, the USN divisions would each have seven days off between escorts for maintenance and refuelling. Nonetheless, while in harbour each division was to detail one of its chasers as a ready boat with "all ranks and ratings on board ... ready to proceed to sea instantly if necessary." A second chaser in each division would be designated as stand by boat, "ready to proceed at two hours notice." Commander Newcombe, meanwhile, would keep Schmucker informed of the dates and times for all convoy sailings, an arrangement to which the American lieutenant readily agreed.[37]

The arrival of the American subchasers and torpedo boats at Halifax was not the only aid being exchanged between the North American allies, however. At the same time that Hose

---

33. Fred T. Jane, ed., *Jane's Fighting Ships 1914* (London 1914), 191; and Ken MacPherson and Ron Barrie, *The Ships of Canada's Naval Forces, 1910–2002* (St Catharines, Ontario, 2002), 20.

34. Captain of Patrols to NSHQ, 22 May 1918, 1065–7-6, LAC, RG 24, vol. 4031.

35. Story to Kingsmill, 5 August 1918, ibid.

36. Captain of Patrols to Lieutenant Schmucker, 22 May 1918, ibid.

37. "Medium and Slow Convoy Escort Flotilla," 16 May 1918, Hose to Admiral Superintendent, Halifax, 22 May 1918, ibid.

was sorting out the escort arrangements for the subchasers, the US Secretary of the Navy, Joseph Daniels, was writing to the RCN asking if it would be willing to detail six of the Canadian-built imperial drifters "fully manned and equipped by the Canadian government" to the First Naval District's coastal patrol based at Shelburne, Nova Scotia, covering the waters west of the 65th meridian. Daniels asserted that assigning the six drifters to the American patrol at Shelburne would "greatly increase its effectiveness." Apparently ignorant of Canadian naval organization, Daniels had written directly to the admiral superintendent at Halifax in the mistaken assumption that he was the senior Canadian naval authority.[38] Story, of course, had to refer the matter to Ottawa, which, in turn, had to ask the Admiralty, since the drifters being built in Canada belonged to the British government.[39] After London had agreed to increase from thirty-six to forty-two the North American allocation of the 100 drifters being built in Canada, Kingsmill offered six completed vessels waiting at Quebec City to the Americans, but regretted that the RCN could not provide crews for them. He also sought to correct Washington's misunderstanding that the admiral superintendent at Halifax was the head of the RCN by asking "that communications from the navy department or the commandant at Boston be addressed to this department [in Ottawa] in order to save unnecessary delay, except in case of emergency when the admiral superintendent at Halifax should be addressed."[40] Six wireless-equipped drifters departed Quebec bound for Boston, with USN crews, on 14 July.[41]

The transfer of the six drifters to the USN was but a small gesture of compensation for the American navy sending six of their submarine chasers to Halifax. It was also easily accommodated by the RCN since the marginally useful vessels were already in relatively plentiful supply to the captain of patrols. Thirty-nine imperial drifters had arrived at Halifax before the winter freeze-up of the St Lawrence, while only three Admiralty trawlers and six of the twelve Canadian Battle-class trawlers had done so.[42] Most of the remaining vessels had been delivered from the builders and were completing their fitting out and painting at Quebec. As of 21 May, there were fifty-three drifters and nine trawlers waiting there and another twelve trawlers completed and ready to go into service at Montreal, Toronto, and Sorel. Seven other trawlers had already departed Quebec and were en route to Halifax.[43] By mid-summer, another thirteen drifters had been delivered to the East Coast—for a total of fifty-two, of which fourteen had been sent on for service with the

38. Joseph Daniels, Secretary of the Navy, Washington to Admiral Superintendent, Halifax, 22 May 1918, ibid.

39. Story minute to The Secretary, Naval Service, 29 May 1918, Naval Ottawa to Admiralty, 12 June 1918, ibid.

40. Kingsmill to C-in-C, NA&WI, 18 June 1918, Admiralty to Naval Ottawa, 12 June 1918, Kingsmill to Rear-Admiral Spencer Wood, USN, 19 June 1918, ibid.

41. First USN District, Boston to Naval Ottawa, 19 June 1918, C-in-C, NA&WI to Naval Ottawa, 29 June 1918, Naval Ottawa to Britannia, 30 June 1918, Naval Ottawa to Admiralty, 13 July 1918, Navyard, Halifax to Naval Ottawa, 15 July 1918, Naval Ottawa to Admiralty, 15 July 1918, ibid.

42. Assistant to Director of Ship Construction to G.J. Desbarats, 31 May 1918, 29–16–1, pt. 4, LAC, RG 24, vol. 5605; and Captain of Patrols to NSHQ, 16 April 1918, 1065–7-6, LAC, RG 24, vol. 4031.

43. A.A. Wright, Assistant to Director of Ship Construction to G.J. Desbarats, 31 May 1918, 29–16–1, pt. 4, LAC, RG 24, vol. 5605.

Royal Navy at Jamaica and Gibraltar—while six of the wooden vessels had been handed over to the USN's First Naval District and another twenty were laid up in the inner basin at Quebec awaiting crews. Thirty-five of the thirty-six Admiralty trawlers had also been delivered to the navy, while the last such vessel, *TR 20*, was awaiting a crew at her Kingston, Ontario, shipyard.[44] The last of the twelve Canadian Battle-class trawlers to be commissioned—*Arleux, Armentieres, Arras, Givenchy, Loos,* and *Thiepval*—entered service between 5 June and 1 August 1918.[45]

In the absence of any, more powerful, anti-submarine vessels, however, the trawlers and drifters being produced in Canadian shipyards were to be the main reinforcement to Hose's patrol organization. Having been hurriedly built by firms suffering from wartime shortages of material, machinery, and skilled labour, they arrived at Halifax and Sydney with varying degrees of defects. A report on the first nine trawlers to arrive at Halifax in the spring showed the engine machinery to be consistently "in good order" with "only fair wear and tear adjustments required ... as will be expected in any vessel after her first run." Any defects with the deck and hull were "not of a serious nature, being minor alterations in some places and caulking." All the windlasses used to haul in the anchor, however, were unable to function properly because of mismatched chain cables and gypsies, requiring replacement of the latter. More troubling still, almost all the boilers were only "in fair condition" after the run from Quebec City, and showed "small leakages in shell and combustion chambers which may take up or develop into more serious leakages." The leaks had been sealed and the trawlers made ready for duty within days but the problem had the potential to require more extensive work in future. Only *TR 6*, "by far the best TR vessel which has arrived to date," had engines and boilers that were "in good running order and condition on arrival."[46] There was also a design problem with the Admiralty trawlers in that the wireless operator could not easily communicate with the bridge. "In all the numbered trawlers the wireless cabin is below the main deck and there is no method of getting to the bridge except by coming up the hatchway on the deck," explained the RCN's fleet wireless officer in late July. "In rough weather this hatchway is closed and the wireless operator has considerable difficulty in communicating with the captain should the necessity arise." It was not a problem that arose in the Canadian Battle-class trawlers, where the wireless cabin had been placed "within easy access of the bridge," the solution being to install an interphone in the numbered trawlers.[47]

The wooden drifters also had a number of defects, although, after going over the list of these, the director of ship construction, J.W. Norcross, believed "that they are only what could be expected in new vessels, particularly when such a number have been constructed in a country where skilled labour is so scarce." Leaks in the wooden decks were the main problem, one Norcross felt was "entirely due to the extreme climatic conditions [in

44. A.A. Wright, Assistant to Director of Ship Construction to G.J. Desbarats, 15 July and 3 August 1918, ibid.

45. K. MacPherson and J. Burgess, *The Ships of Canada's Naval Forces, 1910–1985* (Toronto 1985), 22–25.

46. Commander P.F. Newcombe, Senior Officer of Patrols, Halifax to Captain of Patrols, 7 June 1918, 29–16–1, pt. 4, LAC, RG 24, vol. 5605.

47. Fleet Wireless Officer to Admiral Superintendent, Halifax, 29 July 1918, ibid.

Canada] and one must expect to re-caulk the whole of the decks after having been exposed to the heat and sun." As was the case with the trawlers, the windlasses used to haul in the drifters' anchors also had to be replaced, an installation that could "be put in place by the crews in two or three hours."[48] The captain of patrols also objected to the fact that "accomodations for officer is very unsatisfactory in the CD's not fitted with W/T." Arguing that the absence of separate cabins for officers was "detrimental to naval discipline," Hose received NSHQ's approval to have cabin accommodation for skippers and mates built in "a portion of the large amount of space in the fish hold," the work to be undertaken by local shipbuilders "during the periodical lie-ups of these vessels."[49] In the case of one particular drifter, *CD 87*, the leakage through the bottom planking was so bad that two representatives sent to Halifax by her builder, Canadian Vickers, concluded "that a considerable proportion of the work of fastening the bottom planking has not been done in a proper and workmanlike manner." Assuring Hose that they regretted "exceedingly that work of this description should have left our yard," Vickers informed the captain of patrols that they would "esteem it a favour if you would have the defects remedied at our expense by some local boatbuilder in Halifax."[50]

When the state of the Canadian shipbuilding industry during the First World War is taken into account—particularly its lack of familiarity with the construction of wooden-hulled vessels, shipyards having built primarily steel vessels in the immediate pre-war years—such defects as were exposed on arrival at Halifax should not have come as much of a surprise. A.A. Wright, the assistant director of ship construction, suggested to Desbarats in September 1918 that, in his judgment, the Admiralty's "urgent call" to build 100 drifters and thirty-six trawlers in the fall of 1917 had been "entirely beyond the capacity of the Canadian shipyards between Quebec and Port Arthur, to build in less than three years, working at their limit."[51] Purchasing the timber for the drifters from British Columbia had been the most satisfactory part of the process since "none of the yards had to wait an hour for timber" as the lumber mills "more than lived up to their promises in connection with the furnishing of the timber, both as to time, quality and price. Outside of them, our troubles were without limit." In the case of the drifters, Wright explained that "wooden shipbuilding, with the exception of a few small tugs, has been virtually a lost art for over twenty-five years, and only a few old men were left, mainly in the province of Quebec and the maritime provinces." As a result:

> In the construction of the wooden hulls, we had to force these on firms between Montreal and Quebec, and had to distribute the few competent wooden shipbuilders, and have them teach common labourers how to do the work, under the supervision of an exceptionally competent lot of surveryors, assisted

48. J.W. Norcross, Director of Ship Construction to G.J. Desbarats, 31 July 1918, 29-6-1, pt.5, ibid.

49. Captain of Patrols to NSHQ, 30 July 1918, 29–16–1, pt. 4, ibid.

50. M.R. Miller, Canadian Vickers Ltd., to Captain of Patrols, nd, ibid.

51. A.A. Wright, Assistant to the Director of Ship Construction to G.J. Desbarats, 18 September 1918, 29–16–1, pt. 6, ibid.

by Commander Skentelberry and the writer [Wright], and while we are fully aware of all the defects in these boats, particularly a few which got away last fall, the majority of them were good sea-worthy boats, and considering the conditions prevailing and the lack of skilled labor, I consider the building of them a wonderful performance.[52]

The shortage of skilled labour was in part a function of the lateness in the war when a shipbuilding contract was let, as most skilled tradesmen were already engaged working on munitions contracts for the army. The firm of Goldie and McCulloch in Galt (now Cambridge), Ontario, for instance, was "probably the best firm in Canada for stationary engines and boilers but their boiler shop was out of business because they were engaged on shell forgings and the same thing applied at that time to the Canadian Allis-Chalmers Limited at Toronto.... When it came to getting auxiliaries, boiler mountings, valves and fittings, the shops in this country had never made these in the quantities necessary for contracts of this kind, and we found it impossible to get deliveries of these articles. We could not even get compasses, and finally had to take them from firms in the United States, whom we were led to believe, could make compasses but these proved to be defective." With Canadian shipyards that were, at best, only building one or two vessels a year, and doing repair work, it had not been possible to maintain a skilled work force given the labour shortages associated with a modern, industrial war, especially so when those firms had not previously received government contracts to keep their yard workers profitably employed. Canadian Vickers in Montreal, established to give the dominion a firm capable of naval construction and equipped with "machinery fit to build battleships," had hired a large, skilled workforce to build submarines and motor launches for the Admiralty in 1915–16, but with no warship contracts—such as the destroyers Kingsmill had proposed in the spring of 1916—coming from the Canadian government, even that firm "had not the men to carry out any large volume of work" as their work force was lured away to other war industries by the summer of 1917. Unable to obtain all the required machinery from Canadian companies, the director of ship construction had been forced to turn to the United States for some 40 percent of the vessels' engines and boilers. According to Wright, the latter "were more or less defective ... and we found wrenches and nuts in cylinder and valves, and had to open up, after their arrival at Quebec, and overhaul every engine and pump, besides having to replace rivets, and re-caulk boilers." Even though every shipyard working on the steel trawler contract had been "held up for lack of material necessary," the yards were still able to exceed Wright's "most sanguine expectations."[53]

Despite the underdeveloped nature of the Canadian shipbuilding and steel industries—and the fact that they had largely been left to languish without substantial Canadian government contracts since the outbreak of war—the shipping losses incurred in the 1917 unrestricted submarine campaign prompted the British government to seek to exploit

---

52. Ibid.

53. Ibid.

whatever underutilized industrial capacity remained in the empire. In February 1917, at the same time that the Admiralty was proposing to place a contract for the thirty-six trawlers and 100 drifters, the colonial secretary informed Ottawa that the British government had recently adopted a scheme to secure as much of the mercantile output of American shipyards as they could, and were now anxious to extend the scope of the scheme to secure as large an output of steamships as possible from Canadian shipyards.[54] Unlike the trawler and drifter contract, that was supervised by the naval service, the construction of merchant shipping was overseen by the Imperial Munitions Board. An initial order for wooden steamships was explored in the summer of 1917,[55] but it was not until late in the year that the IMB was asked by London to place contracts for the construction of steel-hulled merchant ships. In December 1917, the British government proposed a program for building up to 400,000 tons of steel, and 300,000 tons of wooden merchant ships in Canada at a cost of some $150,000,000, the vessels to be delivered before the end of 1919.[56]

Although the Canadian-built merchant ships would be the property of the British government, the British treasury had no means of financing payments while the fighting continued. As a result, Ottawa was asked to fund the scheme and be reimbursed by Britain sometime after the war. The merchant ship construction program was to be supplied with steel plate purchased from recently expanded steel plants, and a contract for rolled steel plate was awarded to the Dominion Steel Corporation of Sydney, Nova Scotia.[57] Because contracts for the Canadian-built merchant ships were not awarded until 1918—and delivery was not expected until sometime in 1919—most of the vessels were not completed until after the Armistice. Given names beginning with "War," Canadian shipyards built forty-six wooden steamships totalling 141,600 tons, all of which were a standard 3,080 tons each, as well as forty-one steel merchant ships, ranging in size from 1,800 tons (*War Wasp*), to nine vessels of 8,800 tons each built by J. Coughlan & Sons of Vancouver, British Columbia.[58]

At the same time that the British government was arranging the production of merchant ships in Canada, the ability of the country's shipyards to overcome the shortages of material and skilled labour and build anti-submarine trawlers, in reasonable time, convinced the Admiralty to order a second batch of twenty-four.[59] Known as lot B, the second group of trawlers was to be delivered by the fall of 1918, but shortages of labour,

---

54. "Paraphrase of cypher telegram from Mr Long to the Governor General," 12 February 1917, 1048–42–2, LAC, RG 24, vol. 3766.

55. Wooden Shipbuilding Department, Imperial Munitions Board to Commander R.L. Stephens, 29 May 1917, ibid.

56. "Paraphrase of cypher telegram from Mr Long to the Governor General," 11 December 1917, ibid; and PC 758, 26 March 1918, copy in 1048–42–1, ibid.

57. Ibid.

58. Director of Steel Shipbuilding, Imperial Munitions Board to NSHQ, 12 June 1919, 1048–42–2, LAC, RG 24, vol. 3766.

59. PC 3476, 5 January 1918, copy in 29–16–1, pt. 4, LAC, RG 24, vol. 5605.

material, and equipment, primarily the supplies of boilers, meant that only a handful of trawlers were available on schedule. The last of the steel needed for the hulls and boilers, meanwhile, was only supplied to the shipyards in August 1918. Shortages were exacerbated by the contract for merchant ship construction, which, as Commander Skentelbery explained to NSHQ in September, meant that shipyards building merchant tonnage were "attracting the men from the other yards, by giving them higher rates of pay, and the result is that several vessels are being launched which it is utterly impossible to complete for many months, whilst those which could have been completed are delayed for want of riveters."[60]

Since it was rather unlikely that U-boats would operate off the Canadian coast again until the following spring, by September 1918 the assistant director of ship construction was wondering if the merchant ships might not be more urgently required than the extra trawlers.[61] Kingsmill, however, wanted "all possible pressure [to] be brought to bear upon the firms" to complete the lot B trawlers, if for strictly service reasons. "It is quite realized that these are Admiralty trawlers, but they will meet our wishes and lend what we require. Another reason for hastening the completion is that they are an Admiralty order and the Admiralty have treated us well by the loan of those first completed." The naval director was also aware of the vulnerability of the weakly armed trawlers to attack by U-cruisers, and felt it fortunate that the RCN had "not lost any up to date but at any time a submarine may sink a whole division."[62]

The arrival of the completed trawlers and drifters at Halifax and Sydney in June and July 1918, finally allowed Hose to expand his patrol schemes for the approaches to the two convoy assembly ports—even if Kingsmill had grave doubts about their chances of surviving a confrontation with an enemy submarine. Although Hose had been in charge of the East Coast patrol force since the previous August, the small number of vessels available meant that the 1917 defences he inherited from Coke were little altered from previous years. The arrival of the remaining Canadian Battle-class trawlers, as well as the Admiralty trawlers and drifters assigned to the East Coast, meant that the captain of patrols had to draft yet another defence scheme in early June to incorporate the increased number of small vessels. While the navy would not have the twelve destroyers and fast trawlers that had been central to the scheme devised by Hose and Kingsmill in March, the latest plan was drawn up with a renewed sense of the very real threat that existed to Canada's East Coast shipping lanes, as demonstrated by *U 151*'s successful operations off the US eastern seaboard in late May and early June.

However, having spent most of the war conducting cruiser operations in the backwater of the northeastern Pacific as captain of HMCS *Rainbow*, Hose had little practical anti-submarine experience to draw upon beyond his now-defunct March patrol plan. As a

60. Commander J.W. Skentelbery to NSHQ, 24 September 1918, A.A. Wright, Assistant to the Director of Ship Construction to G.J. Desbarats, 18 September 1918, 29–16–1, pt. 6, ibid.

61. A.A. Wright, Assistant to the Director of Ship Construction to G.J. Desbarats, 3 September 1918, 29–16–1, pt. 5, ibid.

62. Kingsmill, "Memorandum for the Deputy Minister," 6 September 1918, 29–16–1, pt. 6, ibid.

result, the 19 June defensive scheme for patrolling the approaches to Halifax and Sydney—far more difficult to draw than his March proposals that had included destroyers and fast trawlers—was "based on that now employed in European waters."[63] The captain of patrols proposed establishing a series of rigid shipping lanes in the approaches to the two convoy assembly ports, a method of protection that he believed was "more economical and more efficient than any scheme which does not tie shipping down to certain rigid lines." Although he acknowledged that the new "system differs considerably from that previously proposed," Hose argued that "in laying down definite lines of approach and departure of vessels it limits the areas over which protection has to be provided, gives a greater measure of protection in those areas, considerably enhances the chance of locating enemy craft and reduces the work to be done should mines be laid as no areas need be cleared beyond the traffic lines." The key to the system lay

> in the rendezvous patrol vessels (RP vessels) who are responsible for the section of the traffic lines in use between them and the next RP Vessel, and who meet all shipping and pass it on through their section, diverting the shipping to one of the alternative lines if there are mines or dangers in the section for which they are responsible.
>
> It is most essential that the RP vessels do not leave their posts *for any reason whatever.* [Hose's emphasis]
>
> Arrangements have been made for the necessary reliefs, etc., of vessels employed in accordance with this scheme.
>
> Shipping leaving US ports or Quebec for Halifax or Sydney would be given route orders, detailing the RP vessels they are to speak [i.e., contact] and the entrance routes to be followed into port.
>
> A very great check is kept on shipping in this manner and suspicious vessels are more easily detected.
>
> Each section is under constant patrol or sweeping, also large extents of what may be called "useless water" can be left without anxiety, the chances of perhaps coming across a supply vessel assisting a submarine is considered so slight as not to warrant the withdrawal of vessels from the work of rendering certain routes as safe as practicable, particularly when the mining facilities [i.e., ease of mining] of coastal routes on the Canadian seaboard are considered.[64]

Once submitted to Ottawa, however, Hose's proposal quickly came in for criticism. The recently appointed director of operations at NSHQ, Acting Commander John P. Gibbs, a Royal Navy officer on loan to the RCN, explained that "a scheme somewhat like [Hose's proposal] is in operation in the English Channel, but all R[endezvous] V[essel]s are in sight of land, and destroyers, lightships, buoys, etc., are kept to check positions. The traffic lane

---

63. Captain of Patrols to The Secretary, Department of the Naval Service, Ottawa, 19 June 1918, 1065–7-6, LAC, RG 24, vol. 4031.

64. Ibid.

passes close to the coast always." The director of operations believed that circumstances in Canada made a similar system of protection impractical for the East Coast patrols. "This would require an enormous number of patrol vessels with considerable numbers of highly[-]trained officers and is quite impracticable.... The only possible way of protecting these large distances seems [to be] by keeping hunting units when available."[65] Nor did the director of operations like Hose's approach of positioning escorts 300 yards off the seaward bow of merchant ships, bluntly stating that "it would seem necessary to point out to the captain of patrols that submarines practically always attack slow ships from abaft the beam. His escort order had been found in practice to be wrong."[66] Above all, Gibbs argued that "absolute simplicity is necessary where the personnel is not highly trained."[67]

The views of the director of operations were echoed by Kingsmill's newly appointed chief of staff, Acting Commander Stephen H. Morres, who had taken over from Commander Stephens when the latter officer was loaned to the Royal Navy.[68] Morres also believed the "scheme too complicated for practical use with our inexperienced patrol," and that "RP vessels would not be able to constantly and accurately maintain their positions." Moreover, the new chief of staff considered "drifters too slow to escort vessels in their sections"—a rather damning indictment given that Sydney was the convoy collecting point for the very slowest merchant ships—and that the entire scheme would require keeping a total of twenty-one RP vessels on station.[69]

In asking the captain of patrols to redraft his patrol scheme, NSHQ closely followed Gibbs's recommendations, though phrased in a more diplomatic tone: "the department considers [Hose's 19 June plan] ... most valuable in theory but regrets its inability to approve for the reason that a scheme along the same lines was tried in home waters and found to be too complicated in practice. The basis of any scheme to be adopted will have to be simplicity, this being vital when the personnel is not highly trained. Relative to escort orders, it should be borne in mind that submarines nearly always attack slow ships and convoys from abaft the beam; escorts should therefore be disposed accordingly. You should, in the first place, satisfy the requirements of standing patrols for the entrances to harbours, etc., and when this has been done the question of the establishment of hunting units should be considered."[70] NSHQ's rejection of Hose's scheme of patrolled shipping lanes forced him to revert to the previous policy of maintaining outer patrols off harbour entrances, forming-up patrols to cover convoys as they sorted themselves into position in the approaches, and limited seaward escort by the faster auxiliary patrol vessels and USN subchasers.

---

65. Acting Commander J.P. Gibbs minute, 5 July 1918, ibid.

66. Acting Commander J.P. Gibbs minute, 5 July 1918, Captain of Patrols to The Secretary, Department of the Naval Service, Ottawa, 19 June 1918, ibid.

67. Acting Commander J.P. Gibbs minute, 10 July 1918, ibid.

68. Department of the Naval Service, *The Canadian Navy List for July 1918* (Ottawa 1918), 11, 24.

69. Acting Commander S.H. Morres, "Remarks," nd, 1065–7-6, LAC, RG 24, vol. 4031.

70. Acting Staff-Paymaster J.R. Hemsted, Naval Secretary to Captain of Patrols, 12 July 1918, ibid.

The addition of the Admiralty trawlers and drifters to the East Coast patrol force also meant adding RCN personnel to man them, though the number was less than the 2,250 sailors Hose had estimated were required for the job in his February manpower assessment.[71] At the beginning of August, the captain of patrols said that manning the 100 vessels of the East Coast patrol force—nine auxiliary patrol vessels, seven New England trawler/minesweepers, twelve Battle-class trawlers, thirty-six Admiralty trawlers, and thirty-six Admiralty drifters—required a total of 1,550 seamen. As a margin to allow for casualties and spare crews, Hose also recommended the creation of an additional pool of 160 ratings, bringing the total patrol force requirement to some 1,710 sailors.[72] As NSHQ had anticipated in February, the RCN was able to provide the vast majority of these sailors from its own RNCVR manpower pool, a source that had been substantially increased with the decommissioning of HMCS *Rainbow* the previous year and the transfer of her experienced seamen to the East Coast. These included a significant number of trained gun crews, both the ship's regular gunners, and those that NSHQ had arranged to be trained on the cruiser's guns before their removal.[73]

Nevertheless, the Canadian patrol still required Admiralty assistance in the form of skilled trades such as skippers, mates, and engineers.[74] In February 1917, their lordships had directed the commander-in-chief, North America and West Indies Station, to lend the Canadian navy forty-six trained gunnery ratings from both the Royal Navy and the Newfoundland RNR.[75] Twelve months later Ottawa also asked the Admiralty to return a small portion of the RNCVR sailors of the Overseas Division to Canada. Specifically, NSHQ requested the Royal Navy to supply "twenty-five skippers and one hundred engine men," but were informed the British "could only supply four skippers and twenty-eight engine men." As Ottawa explained in mid-May, "every effort is being made to secure the balance of men required in Canada and it is hoped that no further appeal for personnel will have to be made to Admiralty. It is the wish of this department that any ratings sent out [from Britain] may be transferred to the Royal Canadian Navy."[76] By the beginning of July, five skippers, twenty-four leading deck hands, thirty-eight engine men, and thirty-six engine room hands, all experienced RNCVR ratings trained in trawler work, had been sent to Canada, and an additional thirty-seven leading deck hands, thirteen deck hands, and twenty-five trimmers were scheduled to depart Britain "in a few days."[77] London was advised of the remaining number of RNCVR seamen the RCN wanted returned from

71. Hose, "Memorandum for DNS," nd [February 1918], 1017–10–1, pt. 1, LAC, RG 24, vol. 3831.

72. Captain of Patrols to NSHQ, 1 August 1918, 1065–7-6, LAC, RG 24, vol. 4031.

73. Naval Ottawa to Admiralty, 13 February 1917, Naval Ottawa to Navyard, Esquimalt, 13 February 1917, NSC 1065-7-2, pt 1, ibid.

74. Kingsmill, "Memorandum for the Minister," nd [February 1918], 1017–10–4, pt. 1, LAC, RG 24, vol. 3832.

75. Enclosed, W. Graham Greene, Admiralty to Vice-Admiral Sir Chas. H. Coke, 21 February 1917, 1065–7-2, pt. 1, LAC, RG 24, vol. 4031; and Vice-Admiral M.E. Browning to Captain Superintendent, Halifax, 21 March 1917, 1065–7-3, ibid.

76. Desbarats to Undersecretary of State for External Affairs, 23 May 1918, 1065–7-6, ibid.

77. Admiralty to Naval Ottawa, 4 July 1918, ibid.

overseas the following month after all seventy-two of the Admiralty trawlers and drifters had been commissioned. The "total requirement" came to 129 sailors, consisting of a carpenter, two chief petty officers, five stoker petty officers, nine signalmen, fourteen petty officers or leading seamen, twenty-two engine room artificers, thirty-four stokers, and forty-two able or ordinary seamen.[78]

Since the RCN's auxiliary patrol vessels and minesweepers were already fully manned, the RNCVR trawlermen returning from Britain provided a much-needed pool of experienced sailors to crew the seventy-two Admiralty trawlers and drifters. That leavening of experience was of great importance given the small size of the trawler and drifter crews—twelve ratings on the former and ten on the latter—and the fact that trawler-training for new RNCVR ratings was mostly handled on board ship by the skippers and more experienced members of the crew. With only two engine room artificers (ERAs) on each trawler or drifter, for instance, the thirty-eight RNCVR engine men returned from Britain's patrol service, together with the civilian sailors the RCN recruited from the East Coast fishing fleet, meant that half of the engine room personnel would be fully experienced.[79] The fact that the chief skippers were qualified professional seamen in civilian life, became an issue when it was found that the poorly made compasses fitted in the steel wheelhouses of the trawlers were difficult to adjust properly. As Commander Eliott explained to Kingsmill in late May, "the chief skippers' principal fear was that their certificates, upon which they depended upon for a living [when not in the navy], were at stake as well as their reputation," should they run aground or be involved in a collision because of faulty headings.[80]

Simply having a few experienced seamen who were capable of handling a trawler or drifter on board did not mean that the vessel's crew was fully trained to naval standards, however. Rigid station keeping in a formation of ships on patrol or knowing how to fight their ship in anti-submarine warfare—rudimentary as such techniques were for the lightly armed trawlers and drifters of the patrol service—were not skills that even the most experienced civilian sailors brought with them. It will be recalled that one of the Royal Navy's initial objections to the introduction to convoy had been its conviction that merchant captains, even those with decades at sea, would not be able to keep station. Even with sea-experienced skippers in command of its trawlers and drifters, therefore, the East Coast patrol fleet had only a small core of naval-trained officers and petty officers to guide the RNCVR men that made up the bulk of its sea-going personnel. The need for "simplicity … where the personnel is not highly trained" was a primary reason Gibbs offered in rejecting Hose's scheme for patrol vessels to pass merchant ships up and down swept shipping lanes.[81]

The captain of patrols also recognized that the lack of training handicapped his force and urged NSHQ to implement a proper program of training for all of its personnel.

---

78. Naval Ottawa to Admiralty, 10 August 1918, ibid.

79. Captain of Patrols to NSHQ, 1 August 1918, ibid.

80. Commander Eliott to Director of the Naval Service, 28 May 1918, 29–16–1, pt. 4, LAC, RG 24, vol. 5605.

81. Acting Commander J.P. Gibbs minute, 10 July 1918, 1065–7-6, LAC, RG 24, vol. 4031.

Writing to Ottawa in September 1918 "after carrying out the work of Canadian coast patrol for one year," Hose had two recommendations that he felt were priorities:

> *First.* That a considerable reserve of both officers and men is needed.
>
> *Second.* That a proper training establishment is absolutely necessary, through which officer and men should *all* be passed with regulation courses before being drafted to the sea-going patrol, and that as soon as one batch of officers and men has passed through the prescribed courses they should relieve an equal number of untrained officers and men at present serving afloat.
>
> The depots are short of their requirements for harbour duties of all sorts, and the examination service and patrol services are barely manned and the greatest difficulty is found in filling vacancies when they occur....
>
> In the case of officers, the shortage is getting worse. There are not sufficient commissioned officers to fill the present vacancies; as regards skippers and chief skippers, there are just the number that there are vessels with the result that whenever a vacancy occurs for command of a trawler or drifter, many changes of appointments have to be made to fill in the vacancy.... Also, if seniority is to be taken at all into account in advancing men from mate RNCVR to skipper (temp) RCN, a promotion which all mates reasonably hope for, the mates serving in the examination service and other services must be taken into consideration, but the officers in charge of those services are naturally loath to part with subordinates trained especially for these duties. The same applies to capable mates in charge of tugs, and tug work with large vessels needs considerable experience.
>
> In order to meet calls to fill temporary vacancies of mates in sea-going ships at present it is very frequently necessary to take a mate out of a ship which has just come in from sixteen to twenty days patrolling for periodical lay-up and send him to sea again at once.
>
> The officers and men of the vessels are untrained, not only in the technical knowledge required to handle the weapons and offensive appliances on board the ships, but also in service discipline, being drafted to ships as hardly more than raw recruits.
>
> The commander (G) [gunnery] and officers in charge of signals, minesweeping, etc., have all worked most energetically and systematically but when only eight days in about twenty are spent in harbour, the remainder being actually on patrol work at sea, it will be realized that it is impossible to fit in hydrophone, signal, minesweeping, depth charges, and gunnery instruction, clean and refit, coal and store the ships, and also provide working parties which has constantly to be done.

It is submitted that the two requirements started at the commencement of this submission are very urgent necessities, and that at least 10 per cent more skippers than are actually needed for command of vessels should be made from the existing mates to form a reserve for training and filling vacancies, also that every endeavour should be made to enter thirty more certificated mates....

That one AP [auxiliary patrol] ship and one tr[awler] should be detailed entirely as gunnery and stoke hold training ships.

That barracks should be built to accommodate the necessary additional officers and men and that proper courses of instruction should be laid down and officer and men [should be] drafted to sea-going ships after completing the courses....

It is further submitted that if taken in hand promptly, the necessary training could be given to sufficient officers and men before full patrol activities are required in 1919.[82]

The absence of the sort of Canadian training establishment recommended by Hose is in part explained by the nature of Britain's own auxiliary naval forces. From the beginning of the war the Royal Navy had attempted to exploit the seafaring experience of its large fishing community to create a force of minesweepers and submarine detectors by employing the same type of vessels with the same equipment that British fishermen used in peacetime. Although many regular naval officers were skeptical of the results, it was thought that with the same drifter and trawler-net techniques to sweep mines and entrap U-boats that civilian fishermen used for their catch, an extensive training program for the fishing reservists would be unnecessary. Indeed, during the early years of the war, the trawlers and drifters continued to display their civilian fishing numbers on their hulls and their crews continued to wear their peacetime fishing gear in an attempt to lure unsuspecting U-boats toward them.[83] As one of the RN officers involved in Britain's auxiliary patrol, E. Keble Chatterton, has recalled:

To think that untrained men in peace-built craft should become, not a nuisance, but a necessity to the Royal Navy—to be not merely the assistants, but the protectors of the capital ships, was a tremendous mental shock. No one was more astounded than the Admiralty, and for quite a time the daring experiment was regarded with suspicion, at times even with amusement.... From the most modest beginnings of a very few trawlers and yachts, this Auxiliary Patrol force grew until at the time of Armistice there were about five thousand yachts, patrol gunboats, trawlers, whalers, motor-launches, drifters, motor-boats, paddle or screw mine-sweepers and boom-defence vessels. A

82. Captain of Patrols to The Secretary, Department of the Naval Service, 24 September 1918, 1065–7-12, pt. 1, LAC, RG 24, vol. 4032.

83. E. Keble Chatterton, *The Auxiliary Patrol* (London 1923), 43; and Nigel Hawkins, *The Starvation Blockades: Naval Blockades of WWI* (Barnsley, South Yorkshire 2002), 61–62.

truly marvellous organization, even if we except a few of the mine-sweepers which were commanded by Royal Naval officers retired or active.[84]

Nonetheless, Chatterton was forced to concede that the fisherman-turned-naval reservist proved to be "a rough, tough, hardcase fellow who did not take kindly to naval discipline at first. During that first autumn and winter [of 1914–15] not a few of them received sentences of ninety-days, and I recollect one trawler where the whole crew (the skipper excepted) were put into cells. Many of the skippers used to get drunk and become unsatisfactory in other ways.... On the other hand, it may be stated at once that many naval officers foolishly attempted to use the methods on independent fishermen which had been devised only for men accustomed to the life and discipline of the Royal Navy. As time went on, and naval officers began to realize what a magnificent, plucky, hard-working, resourceful body of men these were, greater tact and latitude were employed, with most satisfactory results.... You can lead a fisherman, but if you try to drive him you only put his back up. The result is an unhappy ship, and still more trouble on reaching shore." Although the original intention had been that the auxiliary patrol would not require much in the way of naval training, the size of its wartime expansion, to more than 39,000 reservists,[85] meant that training courses had to be instituted for naval equipment such as gunnery, hydrophone, and depth charges. For the most part, however, sufficient seafaring personnel were available in the British Isles so that reservists "were for the most part taken from the fishing industry, the mercantile marine, or the professional hands accustomed to serve in yachts."[86]

On the other side of the Atlantic, the RCN was compelled to pattern its own coastal patrols after the example of the Royal Navy's auxiliary force by the Admiralty's decisions regarding the type and quantity of vessels Canada's coastal navy was to employ. The British example, however, was not as readily adaptable to Canadian conditions. For one thing, the standard British techniques of drifter and trawler-net fishing were completely foreign to Canadian fishermen, who sailed to the various banks in schooners and fished from dories using hand-held lines. The Admiralty's decision to supply the Canadian patrol with the same standard trawlers and drifters that were second nature to British seafarers was taken without thought as to the very different experience of the Canadian maritime community. The far smaller size of the RCN did offer some compensation, however. Since the navy did not have to man any large warships following the decommissioning of HMCS *Rainbow*, the trained crews of the two Canadian cruisers were freed to provide a large nucleus of experienced seamen to complement the RNCVR ratings that had been trained in gunnery aboard *Rainbow* in 1917.[87] The Canadian patrol force was also fortunate in having three full shipping seasons free of enemy interference in which its small establishment could gain experience.

---

84. Chatterton, *The Auxiliary Patrol*, 2, 6.

85. Ibid, 3.

86. Ibid, 105–06.

87. Naval Ottawa to Admiralty, 13 February 1917, Naval Ottawa to Navyard, Esquimalt, 13 February 1917, NSC 1065–7-2, pt 1, LAC, RG 24, vol 4031.

Niobe, missing two of its funnels after the Halifax explosion, alongside the dockyard in 1918. (LAC PA-209548)

Since RNCVR ratings were recruited from across Canada, a high proportion of Canadian naval recruits lacked any kind of maritime experience, in contrast to the seafaring men the British auxiliary service deliberately attracted. Courses of instruction for novice sailors were given to RNCVR recruits after being posted to HMCS *Niobe* in Halifax. As one of the RNCVR ratings assigned to "Hotel Niobe" has recalled: "not only was she a receiving ship but a training ship as well for all branches of the service. At times she would have over a thousand men aboard not to mention officers of different rank. Also there were the usual amount of midshipmen aspiring to become officers of rank. There was [sic] classrooms for the different branches, such as signal, torpedo, writers and even cooks and sick bay assistants, the gunners to be messed in the gun rooms in the close proximity of the six inch guns where the trainees' classes were held. The stokers and those aspiring to become ERAs or electricians had there [sic] facilities a[d]jacent to the engine rooms."[88] Command experience, of course, could not be taught in a classroom and, as Hose was aware, one of the greatest needs of the East Coast force throughout the war would be for experienced skippers and mates to captain the RCN's trawler and drifter fleet.

As the Canadian navy was updating its arrangements to defend Canada's East Coast shipping, reports continued to come in throughout June of the depredations of *U 151*. The sinkings off the American coast, and the greater USN involvement in organizing and escorting convoys from American ports to Europe, undoubtedly left Vice-Admiral Grant feeling somewhat isolated from the cruisers of the North America and West Indies Station and the convoys being assembled at Halifax under direct British control. Having been instructed by the Admiralty to base himself in Washington, DC, in order to maintain close contact with the US navy department, the British admiral sent his chief of staff, Captain V.H.S. Haggard, to Halifax in June to help sort out the question of coal supplies at that port. Grant was concerned that the Dominion Coal Company on Cape Breton Island and the Canadian government were not taking sufficient steps to ensure that enough coal was being stockpiled at Halifax and Sydney for the winter of 1918–19. Maintaining the same Halifax-centric view that dominated the thinking of many Royal Navy officers, the British C-in-C believed that it would be beneficial to assign Haggard permanently to the Nova Scotian capital:

> There are so many questions at Halifax such as protection of fisheries, patrol and minesweeping services, institution of an air service, coastal and ocean escorts, diversion of shipping and its effect on shipment of cargoes and troops, etc., which involve imperial navy, shipping ministry, Canada, Newfoundland and United States, that the presence of an officer fully in touch with myself and acting under my authority in all these matters, also recognized as such by Ottawa and the other authorities concerned, appears most desirable, if not essential.... I can usefully spare the chief of staff from here for the purpose and have directed him to make his headquarters at Halifax in *Highflyer* with the other technical officers on the staff. This will bring me into touch with the men of war employed on the [NA&WI] Station and ensure their requirements

---

88. A.H. Wickens to E.C. Russell, 16 November 1955, DHH 81/520/8000/Stadacona, vol. 1.

being adequately dealt with, and will also I hope, when coupled with monthly visits of Captain Haggard to myself at Washington, create a decentralization from Washington and a guiding and co-ordinating energy at Halifax which should produce excellent results both in existing organizations and in the carrying through of proposed measures.[89]

The British admiral's proposal was rooted in his concern that the various naval authorities at Halifax—the convoy officer in charge of organizing the merchant ships and ocean escorts, Rear-Admiral Chambers; the admiral superintendent in charge of the port's defences and administration, Vice-Admiral Story; and the officer in charge of the seaward patrols, Captain Hose—did not have either sufficiently defined powers or the personalities to achieve the required coordination of effort. The Admiralty staff, however, which not only deprecated the designation of HMS *Highflyer* as a headquarters ship, but also turned down the proposal to post Haggard to the Canadian port, informed Grant that "the necessity for another naval authority at Halifax is not apparent. Any questions which cannot be settled by those now there can be referred to you and periodical visits by you or officers on your staff would seem to be sufficient."[90] Haggard's presence in Halifax would also have done nothing to make the three USN subchasers assigned to that port any larger or better-armed, nor would it have increased the speed or armament of the trawlers that formed the core of Hose's patrol force.

Grant's concerns about North America's inadequate anti-submarine defences were heightened when intelligence was received from the Admiralty that a second U-cruiser had departed Germany for North American waters. The converted mercantile submarine *U 156* left Kiel on 16 June under the command of *Korvettenkapitän* Richard Feldt with instructions to lay mines in the approaches to New York. He was then to head north to operate in the Gulf of Maine and cover the approaches to Boston, Saint John, and Halifax. Feldt had also been instructed to cut the overseas telegraph cables at Canso, Nova Scotia, and, if possible, convert a suitable prize vessel into an auxiliary warship to support further operations.[91] Once again, an intercepted radio message forewarned the Admiralty of the U-cruiser's departure, while a second message a week after her departure provided her with the latest information on the shipping routes off New York. It was not until 29 June, however, that Sims cabled the navy department in Washington to inform them that a second cruiser submarine was at sea off the coast of Ireland and possibly headed for North America. Ever fearful of compromising security, the Admiralty insisted that Sims word his warnings rather vaguely so as not to betray the fact that the British were reading German radio messages. As a result, Sims only informed Washington on 6 July that "the Admiralty thinks it possible that one and possibly two cruiser submarines of later type are at sea" despite having been told that *U 140* had also departed Germany on 2 July.[92]

---

89. Grant to Admiralty, General Letter No. 5, 1 July 1918, UKNA, ADM 137/504.

90. Admiralty to C-in-C, NA&WI, 6 August 1918, ibid.

91. Hadley and Sarty, *Tin-pots and Pirate Ships*, 247.

92. Grant, *U-Boat Intelligence*, 152.

Making her way north of the Shetland Islands, on 26 June *U 156* had torpedoed and sunk the British merchantman *Tortuguero* of 4,175 tons some 450 kilometres west of Ireland. Her track across the Atlantic was marked by an unsuccessful attack on the US transport *Lake Bridge* on 5 July some 350 kilometres south of the Flemish Cap. The American ship was bound from Lamlash, Scotland for Hampton Roads, Virginia when the U-boat, disguising herself with a false funnel to appear as a steamship, headed for the transport at high speed before opening fire at 10,000 yards range. Fortunately for the *Lake Bridge*, the faster American ship was able to escape after engaging in a running gun battle with the U-cruiser. Continuing toward the US East Coast, the German submarine stopped and sank the 1,987-ton Norwegian schooner *Marosa* with bombs on 7 July and the Norwegian schooner *Manx King* of 1,729 tons the next day, 550 kilometres south of Cape Race. Instructed by the German submariners to "head west," both Norwegian crews were left to make the 1,200 kilometre voyage to the American coast in their open life boats. The crew of the *Manx King* reached land to report the sinking of their ship on 12 July, while the crew of the *Marosa*, with farther to go, did not reach port until the 16th.[93]

For the next nine days the U-boat remained unsighted as she headed for the waters off the entrance to the port of New York where she laid mines in the approaches. On 19 July the 13,680-ton American armoured cruiser USS *San Diego* struck one of *U 156*'s mines approximately ten miles southeast of Fire Island off the Long Island shore. The cruiser sank with the loss of only six sailors, but she was the largest American warship lost during the war.[94] The appearance of a second U-cruiser in North American waters, and the sinking of the *San Diego*, convinced the British C-in-C that the danger posed to shipping in his area of responsibility was greater than the Admiralty apparently realized. Two days after the American cruiser went to the bottom, Grant telegraphed London with an urgent call to reinforce the anti-submarine forces available on the US eastern seaboard:

> Having regard to the present military and food position in France and England and the increasing relative importance to Germany of checking the vast movement of troops, munitions and supplies from North America, also the increased difficulties and losses to submarines operating in home waters, am of the opinion present inadequate anti-submarine forces on this side can no longer be justified and that they should be gradually increased by retention of US destroyers as completed for sea if they can possibly be spared from home forces. I have, of course, not mentioned this in any way to US nor has point been raised by them.[95]

---

93. US Navy Department, *German Submarine Activities*, 50–54; and Grant to Admiralty, General Letter No. 6, 1 August 1918, UKNA, ADM 137/504.

94. US Navy Department, *German Submarine Activities*, 53–54, 124, 141; and Paul G. Halpern, *A Naval History of World War I* (Annapolis 1994), 432.

95. Grant to Admiralty, General Letter No. 6, 1 August 1918, UKNA, ADM 137/504.

The C-in-C's concern met with a rather severe reply from London, where the Admiralty remained on guard against any call to disperse anti-submarine forces away from British waters. In a decidedly condescending tone, their lordships scolded the British admiral that "as you are not in a position to form a true appreciation of the submarine situation generally, it is essential that you should not express any opinion to the US authorities on the subject of retention or otherwise of US destroyers in American waters."[96] The Admiralty's sensitivity to the issue had undoubtedly been aroused to a greater degree than it might otherwise have been by the fact that the USN, as already mentioned, had begun assigning a greater number of its modern destroyers to trans-Atlantic duties escorting American Expeditionary Force troopships from New York to Europe.[97] Nonetheless, the harsh tone of the Admiralty's response prompted Grant to express his indignation in his monthly report, particularly since his own telegram had clearly stated that he had "not in any way mentioned this to US." The British admiral assured London that he "of course loyally accept their lordships' decisions as to the disposition of forces and in the present instance I am fully aware that they with their full knowledge of the forces at our disposal and their employment are in a far better position than myself to weigh the relative dangers and requirements"; but added "that as commander-in-chief it is my duty to express my views whether asked for or not as to the military situation and requirements of the station under my command, and that those views when offered should receive courteous consideration."[98] Although the contretemps did not lead to any redistribution of forces by the Royal Navy, it did reflect the renewed sense of vulnerability felt along the eastern seaboard following the sinking of the cruiser USS *San Diego*. It also made clear to Grant that the RCN's anti-submarine defences off Halifax and the Gulf of St Lawrence would not be receiving any reinforcement from Britain.

The appearance of U-cruisers off the American East Coast in June and July was widely reported in the Canadian press and had already led to an increased nervousness throughout the maritime provinces. From the time of the first reports of *U 151*'s operations in early June, Canadian naval officials had received frequent U-boat sighting reports. On 9 June, for instance, HMC Ships *Hochelaga* and *Margaret* were despatched to Saint Paul Island to investigate a report of firing heard to seaward but, finding nothing suspicious, could only conclude that a steamer had been practice firing her gun.[99] Throughout June, Kingsmill passed to naval minister Ballantyne the numerous submarine sighting reports that were flooding into the navy, most of them beginning with "fisherman spotted" or "four fishermen spotted."[100] Nor were Canadian fishermen the only seamen to demonstrate vivid

---

96. Ibid.

97. Halpern, *A Naval History of World War I*, 435–56; Allard, "Anglo-American Naval Differences," 76; and Navy Department to Admiralty, 5 September 1918, quoted in Michael Simpson, ed., *Anglo-American Naval Relations, 1917–1919* (Aldershot, UK 1991), 469–70.

98. Grant to Admiralty, General Letter No. 6, 1 August 1918, UKNA, ADM 137/504.

99. Patrols Sydney to Naval Ottawa, 9 and 10 June 1918, 1062–13–2, pt. 3, LAC, RG 24, vol. 4021.

100. Many of the sighting reports passed by Kingsmill to Ballantyne are contained in file 1062–13–2, pt. 3, ibid.

imaginations when it came to identifying objects seen on the surface as definite German U-boats. On 1 July the US subchasers escorting convoy HS 46 some 105 kilometres east of Halifax made a depth charge attack on a suspected U-boat that the Americans reported had fired a torpedo at the convoy. According to the report sent to NSHQ four days later:

> Chaser *240* stationed 400 yards ahead of convoy. Chaser *241* on wing and *247* on left wing about half mile distant. Weather foggy but clearing to visibility one mile. At 1510 latitude 44 degrees 22 minutes North, longitude 62 degrees 58 minutes West, Chaser *247* sighted submarine on starboard quarter making for leading ship of convoy getting into position to attack, speed about 10 knots. Chaser fired two depth charges, one fell on starboard bow, other on port quarter of submarine exploding within few feet of her. Surface water covered with oil. Chaser *241* not yet returned to harbour. Reported to Senior Officer in *240* as follows, (begins) at 1540 observed torpedo fired at ship abreast of her, who at same time altered course sharply, *241* followed wake of torpedo sighted submarine with periscope up. Chaser straddled her with two depth charges which exploded as submarine was submerging.[101]

Despite the certainty with which the inexperienced American sailors made their report, the nearest enemy submarines, *U 156* on her trans-Atlantic passage to North America and the homeward-bound *U 151*, were both some 1,500 kilometres to the east of the Nova Scotian port at the time of the reported attack. A more reliable account of the incident was provided in the convoy report of HS 46 herself: "The convoy was escorted from Halifax by US submarine chasers. Weather was foggy and rainy. One of them reported that she sank a submarine with depth charges which was getting into position to attack the convoy, but as one of the ships in convoy reported that a depth charge had been exploded alongside her fog buoy and shots fired at it, it is somewhat doubtful as to whether this was a submarine."[102]

Although NSHQ regularly received Admiralty intelligence updates on the likely tracks of U-boats in the Atlantic—as in the case of Sims's reports to Washington, vaguely phrased so as not to compromise the source of the intelligence—the definitive tone of the subchaser report created some uncertainty in Ottawa regarding the likelihood that a German submarine was actually operating in Canadian waters. On 2 July NSHQ was informed that Halifax had intercepted the SOS calls of a Greek steamer that had accidentally run aground on the Nova Scotia coast sixty-five kilometres south of Chebucto Head, while taking evasive action "after a crewman reported sighting a torpedo passing close by."[103] Given the evidence, an alarmed Ballantyne cabled the British commander-in-

---

101. Navyard Halifax to Naval Ottawa, 4 July 1918, 1048–48–12, LAC, RG 24, vol. 3775; and Kingsmill to acting Prime Minister, 2 July 1918, 1062–13–2, pt. 3, LAC, RG 24, vol. 4021.

102. "Convoys from Sydney (C.B.) (HS Convoys)," nd, HS 46, UKNA, ADM 137/2656.

103. Kingsmill to Acting Prime Minister, 2 July 1918, Canadian Naval Staff Officer Halifax to Admiral Superintendent, Halifax, 15 July 1918, 1062–13–2, pt. 3, LAC, RG 24, vol. 4021.

chief that day asking if "in view of proximity of submarine to Halifax would it not be desirable to approach US authorities with a view to despatch of some destroyers if available for protection of shipping off Nova Scotian coast."[104] As we have seen, however, it was not until the *San Diego* was sunk two weeks later that the Canadian naval minister's concern would infect Grant sufficiently to convince him to approach London about the possibility of retaining more US destroyers in North American waters.

In the meantime, the lone U-boat operating off the American coast, *U 156*, had been keeping out of sight. After sinking the Norwegian schooner *Manx King* on 8 July, the German submarine was not spotted again until the 17th when the American transport USS *Harrisburg* reported seeing her some 100 kilometres south of Nantucket. The U-boat made no attempt to attack the USN vessel but remained on the surface for some ten minutes at a distance of 10,000 yards.[105] Three days after the alarming sinking of the USS *San Diego* on the 19th, however, the North American public's concern was further aroused when *U 156* made one of the boldest attacks of any German submarine in US waters. In front of thousands of sunbathing onlookers trying to escape the summer heat on Cape Cod's beaches, the U-boat attacked the tug *Perth Amboy* and the four barges she was towing only three miles from shore. In a one-sided battle that lasted for ninety minutes, the tug was heavily damaged, while her four barges were sunk. According to the war diary of the First Naval District in Boston:

> A fog bank lying four miles offshore hid the U-boat from her approaching victims. The *Perth Amboy*, steaming leisurely through the calm summer sea, [the tug was bound from Gloucester, Massachusetts to New York] was unaware of the presence of danger until a deckhand sighted a streak in the water shooting by the stern.
>
> Before he realized that it was a torpedo [in fact, a passing shell], two other missiles sped by, wide of their mark. He shouted a warning. At the same time there was a flash from the fog and a shell crashed through the wheelhouse. A fragment of steel took off the hand of a sailor as he grasped the spokes of the steering wheel. In quick succession came other shots, some of which were wide and some of which struck home....
>
> The bombardment set the tug on fire, and the German then turned his attention to the helpless barges.... The shooting of the enemy was amazingly bad. For more than an hour the blazing tug and the drifting barges were under fire before the enemy succeeded in getting enough shots to sink them. In the meantime, the submarine crept nearer until her range was only a few hundred yards. This at length proved sufficient and the barges disappeared beneath the surface one by one until only the stern of the *Lansford* [second barge in tow] was visible. The tug was a burning hulk....

---

104. Naval Ottawa to Britannia, Washington, 2 July 1918, 1065–7-6, LAC, RG 24, vol. 4031.

105. US Navy Department, *German Submarine Activities*, 54.

Some of the summer residents grew uneasy when they saw how wild the German gunners were shooting and feared stray shells would hit their cottages. Many of these residents went to cottages that had substantial cellars and watched the firing there, ready to seek shelter should the German try his marksmanship on shore targets. Some residents reported shells falling on shore.[106]

The U-boat's attack was made only a few miles from the naval air station at Chatham, Massachusetts. Four USN aircraft despatched to the scene managed to engage the submarine but all their bombs failed to explode and the raider was able to submerge and escape unscathed Although only three American sailors were wounded in the attack, the boldness of the daylight bombardment so close to shore created a stir among both the American and Canadian public and press. On 18 July, the *Ottawa Journal* reported the landing of the twenty-two crewmen of the Norwegian *Marosa*, sunk by *U 156* on 7 July, at Canso, Nova Scotia, after a 1,100-kilometre voyage in open lifeboats.[107] After reporting the U-boat's audacious attack off Cape Cod on the 21st, the *Ottawa Citizen* remarked that "in contrast to the tactics adopted by the submarines which last raided the American waters, the German sea-wolf which appeared today off the Massachusetts coast torpedoed and shelled vessels without giving the crews opportunity to seek safety in small boats. This fact was accepted in some quarters as indicating that the Germans were undertaking to bring their campaign of 'frightfulness' directly home to Americans in hope of shaking the morale of the nation. That this attempt would have no more success than the raid of last May and June was the firm conviction of official Washington."[108] That resolve would quickly be tested as the U-boat stepped up the pace of her attacks.

Making her way northward into the Gulf of Maine, *U 156* sank the American schooner *Robert and Richard*, 100 kilometres east northeast of Boston on 22 July. Stopping the fishing vessel with a shot across her bow from a distance of two miles, the Germans sent the *Robert and Richard* to the bottom with a single bomb placed amidships below the hull. The fishermen reported that the Germans "acted as though they had plenty of time," and that the officer in charge of the boarding party spoke English well and informed the Americans that "he had a big house in the States." When asked what the Germans were going to do with the captured crew, the officer instructed the fisherman "to tell the authorities that we do not do anything to those on the vessels we sink."[109] News of the sinking was announced after the American crew reached shore three days later by a *Halifax Herald* headline of "Huns Sunk Schooner Off The Coast of Maine."[110] On 26 July, NSHQ received

---

106. "War Diary of the First Naval District," nd, quoted in US Navy Department, *German Submarine Activities*, 54–55.

107. *The Ottawa Journal*, 18 July 1918, copy in 1062–13–2, pt. 3, LAC, RG 24, vol. 4021.

108. *The Ottawa Citizen*, 22 July 1918, copy in ibid.

109. Quoted in US Navy Department, *German Submarine Activities*, 55–56.

110. *Halifax Herald*, 25 July 1918, copy in 1062–13–2, pt. 4, LAC, RG 24, vol. 4021.

word from Washington, by way of Halifax, that "information has been received that the probable area of operations of *U 156* will be Gulf of Maine unless fog too thick. Information has been received which would lead to belief second submarine may be expected in the area."[111] The second boat was *U 140* which had departed Germany on 2 July under the command of *Korvettenkapitän* Waldemar Kophamel, a submarine veteran who had served as first officer of the *U-Deutschland* during her 1916 voyage to the United States. On the 26th, Kophamel attacked a pair of British merchantmen, *Melitia* of 13,967 tons and *British Major* of 4,147 tons, but both vessels managed to escape. Word of both attacks, which were made some 500 to 580 kilometres southeast of Cape Sable, was passed to NSHQ on 27 July.[112]

The arrival of the two U-cruisers in North American waters gave greater urgency to efforts to organize air patrols off the Canadian coast. During Captain Hose's visit to Washington in April, the US navy department had agreed to supply Canada with the dirigibles, kite balloons, and seaplanes needed to set up air stations at Halifax and Sydney, and to lend the RCN American pilots until Canadian aircrew could be trained to replace them. Following the naval minister's agreement to set up two East Coast air stations in early May, the Admiralty informed Ottawa that Lieutenant-Colonel J.T. Cull had been named the overall commander of the proposed air service.[113] The despatch of Cull and the two officers who were to command the air stations was delayed, however, by administrative difficulties occasioned by the amalgamation, on 1 April 1918, of the Royal Flying Corps and the Royal Naval Air Service into the Royal Air Force (RAF). With the former RNAS officers now part of the RAF, the Admiralty had to obtain Air Ministry approval for their secondment to the RCN. On 5 June the British secretary of state for air agreed that, provided the first sea lord was "satisfied that anti-submarine patrols are needed on the Canadian coast and that Canada can arrange for materiel and personnel other than the OC s stations and one organization officer ... then we must do what we can to help and send off the officers." Cull, the two designated station commanders, Major H. Stewart and Captain J.W. Hobbs, the latter a Canadian serving in the RAF, accompanied by an administrative and a technical officer sailed for Canada on 15 June.[114]

In the meantime, NSHQ had been attempting to make progress in organizing an air service within the naval department and in going ahead in constructing the proposed air stations. In view of the government's approval to establish air stations at Halifax and Sydney, Commander Stephens prepared a memorandum on 7 May that estimated the cost

---

111. Navinet, Halifax to Naval Ottawa, 26 July 1918, Navinet to Naval Ottawa, 27 July 1918, 1062–13–2, pt. 3, ibid.

112. J.P. Gibbs for Director of the Naval Service to Acting Prime Minister, 27 July 1918, ibid; and US Navy Department, *German Submarine Activities*, 71.

113. C-in-C to Naval Ottawa, 2 May 1918, Kingsmill to Ballantyne, Ballantyne's minute, 3 May 1918, 1034–3-4. pt. 1, LAC, RG 24, vol. 3894; "Naval Aviation in Canada during the First World War," nd, 11–12, DHH 74/25; and S.F. Wise, *Canadian Airmen and the First World War* (The Official History of the Royal Canadian Air Force, I; Toronto 1980), 605.

114. Air Minister quoted in F.H. Hitchens, "The Royal Canadian Naval Air Service," February 1958, 5, DHH 81/520/1700–219, box 116, file 10.

of the stations at nearly $2.2 million including provision of aircraft, buildings, stores, and the first year's maintenance. The chief of staff believed the new air service would "add about 500 officers and men to the Canadian naval forces."[115] Stephens submitted his recommendations to Kingsmill two days later. Arguing that it was desirable to avoid creating an entirely new organization, the chief of staff recommended that the air personnel be enrolled directly in the RCN at ordinary RCN rates of pay although all officers and men employed on air duties would receive a special "air allowance." Officers would belong to the executive branch but with an "(A)" added after their rank and all members of the air service would wear ordinary RCN uniform with the addition of an eagle on the cuff. Officers and men employed on air duties would be "considered as not available for ordinary naval duties until they are permanently detached from air duties." Stephens believed that "an organization based on these principles would be very simple and the preliminary work such as establishing rates of pay, etc., can be proceeded with immediately pending the arrival of the officer for organization being sent from the Admiralty." Based on the chief of staff's recommendations, the naval director agreed that "the proposition seems exceedingly simple," and forwarded the air service proposal to London for comment. The Admiralty quickly concurred with Ottawa's scheme, which they believed "should form sound basis for new service."[116]

At the same time that NSHQ was drawing up an outline plan for the formation of a Canadian naval air service, Kingsmill approached the head of the Toronto-based RAF Canada training program, Brigadier-General Cuthbert Hoare, to ask him to provide the navy's airmen with the first part of their training course there. The British general, who had held his position since January 1917, did not believe the navy's plan was a practical proposition, however, and rejected it on the grounds that the naval airmen would eventually have to be qualified on US seaplanes. Since the navy's pilots still had to receive their initial flight training, something which they could easily have done on the landplanes of the RAF Canada organization, Hoare's resistance to NSHQ's practical suggestion was rooted in his own apprehensions of the effect an established naval air arm would have on the RAF Canada's recruiting program. As he acknowledged in his response to Kingsmill, the air force general wanted an assurance from the navy "that no men from the Royal Air Force will be taken on for this new service."[117]

Although the importance of establishing a naval air service did not appear to be shared by the RAF training organization in Canada, throughout May the RCN pressed ahead with its attempts to assemble the new organization. Contrary to the statement made in the first volume of the Royal Canadian Air Force official history that "up to this point the Canadian authorities had been following rather ineffectually in the wake of the Admiralty and the

---

115. Stephens, "Memorandum," 6 May 1918, 63–10–1, pt. 1, DHH 77/58, vol. 20, file 2.

116. Stephens, "Air Service—Organization," 8 May 1918, Kingsmill, "Memorandum for Chief of Staff," 8 May 1918, Naval Ottawa to Admiralty, 11 May 1918, Admiralty to Naval Ottawa, 15 May 1918, ibid.

117. Hoare to Kingsmill, 15 May 1918, 1034–3-4, pt. 1, LAC, RG 24, vol. 3894; Headquarters, RAF Canada to Director of the Naval Service, 13 May 1918, 63–10–1, pt. 1, DHH 77/58, vol. 20, file 2; and "Naval Aviation in Canada during the First World War," nd, 14, DHH 74/25.

United States Navy," and that "no real progress had been made in organizing an east-coast system,"[118] naval headquarters had, in fact, been quite active in its efforts to prod the British authorities into proceeding with the scheme. On 4 May, NSHQ had asked London to have Flight Commander John Barron, the Canadian airship pilot stationed in Washington, DC, transferred to Ottawa to help in setting up the new air service and requested more information as to when Wing Commander Cull might be expected to arrive in Canada.[119] Despite a further telegram from NSHQ to the Admiralty on 29 May asking for answers to their earlier queries, it was not until 8 June that Admiral Grant in Washington finally informed the RCN that Barron was "being instructed to proceed to Ottawa until further orders."[120] As we have seen, it was not until 11 June that the Admiralty informed NSHQ that Cull and his party would be leaving England on the 15th.[121]

In the meantime, the naval deputy minister was making the necessary arrangements with the Department of Public Works for the acquisition of the land needed for the two East Coast air stations and for awarding contracts to build the facilities. In mid-May, an architect from Public Works was accompanied by Flight Commander Barron and two other naval air officers, one of which was from the USN, to select suitable sites at both Halifax and Sydney.[122] Once the sites had been selected, Desbarats wrote to the deputy minister of Public Works on 25 May asking that department "to acquire the land and proceed with any necessary surveys." The "plans and specifications of the necessary hangars" were being supplied by the US navy department and would be passed on to Public Works as soon as NSHQ received them. Desbarats tried to speed his fellow deputy minister along by reminding him that "the work is of an urgent nature and should be pushed forward as rapidly as possible."[123] The construction of the air stations at Halifax and Sydney received formal government approval on 5 June, at an estimated cost of $2,189,600.[124]

With an outline drawn up for organizing the Canadian naval air service and arrangements in place with Public Works for building the air stations, further decisions had to await the designated commander's arrival from Britain. Lieutenant-Colonel Cull did not finally make his appearance in Ottawa until early July, having travelled to Canada through Washington, DC, so he could consult with Vice-Admiral Grant and the aviation section of the US navy department about the current air situation.[125] While in the American capital, Cull was informed of the earlier agreement that the Canadian air stations

---

118. Wise, *Canadian Airmen and the First World War*, 605.

119. Naval Ottawa to Admiralty, 4 and 7 May 1918, 63–10–1, pt. 1, DHH 77/58, vol. 20, file 2.

120. C-in-C, NA&WI to Naval Ottawa, 8 June 1918, ibid.

121. Admiralty to Naval Ottawa, 11 June 1918, ibid.

122. Deputy Minister, Public Works to Commander R.M. Stephens, 10 May 1918, Naval Ottawa to Navyard Halifax, 9 May 1918, Sydney to Naval Ottawa, 12 May 1918, ibid.

123. Desbarats to Deputy Minister, Department of Public Works, 25 May 1918, ibid.

124. PC 1379, 5 June 1918, copy in ibid.

125. Grant to Admiralty, General Letter No. 6, 1 August 1918, UKNA, ADM 137/504; and "Naval Aviation in Canada During the First World War," nd, 14–15, DHH 74/25.

would initially be manned by USN airmen until they could be replaced by RCN aviators—Canadians who had yet to be recruited, let alone trained. The navy department stipulated to Cull that the American airmen were to remain under the command of USN officers while operating from the Halifax and Sydney air stations. As early as 13 July Cull noted to NSHQ that it had already been arranged that the two designated station commanders, Stewart and Hobbs, would be placed on Admiral Story's staff at Halifax and would only act as liaison officers between the American officers commanding the air units at the two stations and the naval officers—Hose, Story, and Chambers—in charge of running the sea patrols. Stewart and Hobbs would not live on the air stations themselves but would remain in telephone communication with the USN officers at the air bases.[126]

After making the rounds of NSHQ in early July, Cull travelled to Nova Scotia to examine the sites Barron had selected in May for the East Coast air stations. Although the RAF officer found the Halifax site at Baker Point "suitable in every way," he recommended shifting the Point Edward site across from Sydney to Kelly Beach, north of North Sydney. At the same time, Cull—based on his earlier consultations in Washington—recommended "that the United States be approached with a view of releasing some of their smaller flight machines for use at Halifax until the larger machines are ready and the stations properly built." The Americans would also "be asked to provide sufficient canvass hangars to accommodate machines and sufficient personnel to run them for the time being." He also proposed sending Stewart and Hobbs to the USN air station at Pensacola, Florida, to test various aircraft that might be suitable for the Canadian service once it had come into operation.[127]

Having settled on the location of the East Coast air stations, Cull proceeded to Washington on 22 July to take up the question of manning them with American personnel for the 1918 season.[128] The need for USN assistance was evident when the Canadian naval minister cabled Kingsmill from London with the Admiralty's latest proposals for training Canadian airship officers in Britain. Ballantyne concluded his telegram with the instruction that "every effort should be made to have air stations in full working order and manned by Canadian personnel by opening of navigation next year."[129] The call for Canadian recruits for the new air service was not sent out to newspapers until 8 August, while the Royal Canadian Naval Air Service (RCNAS) was not officially approved by the government until 5 September.[130] Sixty-four RCNAS volunteers were sent to the Massachusetts Institute

126. Wing Commander J.T. Cull, Department of the Naval Service—Air Section, "Note," 13 July 1918, 63–10–1, pt. 1, DHH 77/58, vol. 20, file 1.

127. J.T. Cull, "Memo: To Director of the Naval Service," 11 July 1918, Cull, "Memo: For Director of the Naval Service," 11 July 1918, DHH 81/520/1700–219, box 116, file 10; and Brian Tennyson and Roger Sarty, *Guardian of the Gulf: Sydney, Cape Breton, and the Atlantic Wars* (Toronto 2000), 139, 180–1, 210.

128. Naval Ottawa to Lieutenant-Commander Towers, USN, 16 July 1918, Naval Ottawa to Opair, Navy Department, Washington, 17 July 1918, Naval Ottawa to Cull, 19 July 1918, 63–10–1, pt. 1, DHH 77/58, vol. 20, file 2.

129. Borden to Ottawa, Ballantyne for Naval [Kingsmill], 31 July 1918, ibid.

130. "Department of Naval Service," nd, J.A. Wilson minute, nd, J.A. Wilson to J.M.S. Carroll, 8 August 1918, ibid, file 1; PC 2154, 5 September 1918; and "Naval Aviation in Canada During the First World War," nd, 21, DHH 74/25.

of Technology (MIT) in Boston in late September and early October to commence aircrew training, while a third contingent of RCNAS cadets followed at the end of October. The MIT curriculum given the Canadian recruits was identical to the USN's air training, with instruction being provided by US officers from Pensacola and West Point. Another twelve RCNAS cadets and six RCN petty officers sailed to Britain in early October to start airship training.[131]

In Washington, meanwhile, Cull discovered that the US navy department was initially reluctant to send air units to Canada in 1918 because the lateness of the shipping season meant its airmen would have to spend a winter in Nova Scotia sitting idle until U-cruisers returned in the spring. The American chief of naval operations, Admiral W.S. Benson, finally agreed to implement the April agreement with the additional requirement that the Canadian government guarantee that its airmen would be housed in permanent buildings by 15 October. It was also arranged, as Cull had indicated on 13 July, that the American airmen would remain under USN commanders with the RAF station commanders acting as liaison officers on the staff of Vice-Admiral Story, the senior Canadian naval officer on the Atlantic coast. As well, agreement was reached that Washington would supply and pay for all air equipment, while the Canadian government would pay for all ground installations.[132]

An advance party of USN airmen arrived at Halifax on 5 August. They brought portable hangars with them to begin the task of establishing a temporary aerodrome at Baker Point on the Dartmouth side of the harbour across from McNab Island. Ten days later, USN Lieutenant Richard E. Byrd (who in post-war years would gain fame as an aviation pioneer and polar explorer) arrived to take command of the station with the additional title of commanding officer, US Naval Air Forces in Canada. Byrd's immediate problem was to get the four Curtiss HS-2L flying boats, with which his unit was to be equipped, through the supply bottleneck represented by the single-track railway that served Halifax. With much energy, the USN airmen managed to assemble and fly two of the machines by 25 August, at which time Byrd declared his airmen ready to begin air patrols.[133]

A conference was held in Halifax the following day to set out a general policy governing the American air patrols for the remainder of the 1918 season. In attendance were the principal commanders, Hose, Chambers, Cull, and Byrd, as well as the two RAF liaison officers attached to the admiral superintendent's staff, Stewart and Hobbs, along with Lieutenant Robert Donoghue, the designated USN station commander for the North Sydney air base. With four American flying boats expected to be assigned to each of Halifax

---

131. "Naval Aviation in Canada During the First World War," nd, 22–23, DHH 74/25.

132. C-in-C, NA&WI to Chief of Naval Operations, 23 July 1918, C-in-C, NA&WI to Director of Naval Service of Canada, 31 July 1918, Director of Naval Service to C-in-C, NA&WI, 3 August 1918, Cull to Director of Naval Service, 3 August 1918, Benson to C-in-C, NA&WI, 13 August 1918, Kingsmill to C-in-C, NA&WI, 15 August 1918, 63–10–1, pt. 1, DHH 77/58, vol. 20, file 1; "Naval Aviation in Canada During the First World War," nd, 15, DHH 74/25; and F.H. Hitchens, "The Royal Canadian Naval Air Service," February 1958, 8, DHH 81/520/1700–219, box 116, file 10.

133. "Naval Aviation in Canada During the First World War," nd, 16, DHH 74/25; and F.H. Hitchens, "The Royal Canadian Naval Air Service," February 1958, 9, DHH 81/520/1700–219, box 116, file 10.

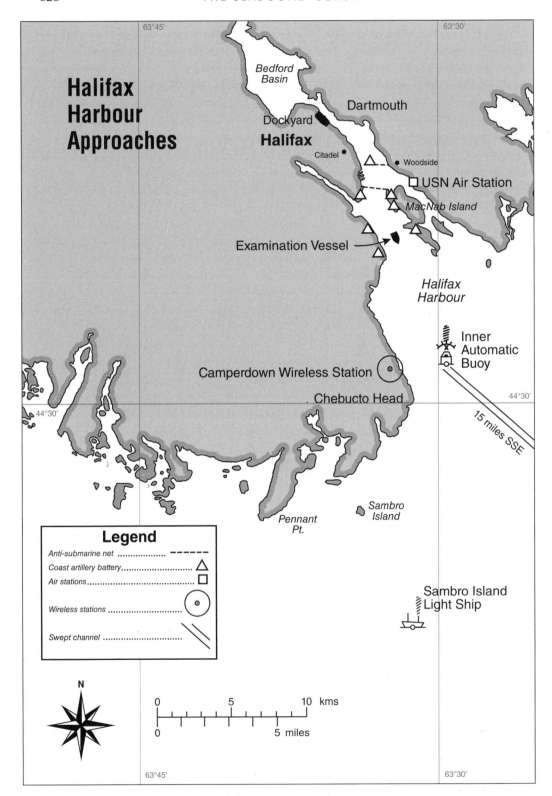

**Halifax
Harbour
Approaches**

Bedford
Basin

Dartmouth

Dockyard

Halifax

Citadel

Woodside

□ USN Air Station

MacNab Island

Examination Vessel →

Halifax
Harbour

Inner
Automatic
Buoy

Camperdown Wireless Station

44°30'

Chebucto Head

15 miles SSE

44°30'

Sambro
Island

Pennant
Pt.

Legend

Anti-submarine net ....

Coast artillery battery........................... △

Air stations.. □

Wireless stations .... ⊙

Swept channel ....

Sambro Island
Light Ship

N

| 0 | 5 | 10 kms |

0   5 miles

63°45'   63°30'

63°45'   63°30'

and Sydney, it was agreed that two aircraft at each station would be assigned to operate escorting convoys, while another machine was held in readiness to investigate any reliable submarine sighting reports. The fourth flying boat would be laid up for maintenance. Outward-bound fast convoys were to be provided with air escort out to sixty-five miles from the harbour entrance, the two HS 2Ls alternating patrols during their four-hour endurance, while inward bound fast convoys were to be met eighty miles out and escorted until they reached the harbour mouth. Slow convoys were to be escorted for the first fifty miles upon departure and would be met sixty miles from port when inbound. The port patrol offices would keep USN commanders informed of the departure of convoys, providing particulars a day in advance of its speed, size, and course as well as the timing and position for rendezvous with the aircraft. Detailed orders would then be given to the USN pilots by either Byrd or Donoghue. It was also emphasized by the Canadian authorities that "in view of the importance of Sydney" the first two flying boats at Halifax should be transferred to the Cape Breton port as soon as Byrd was satisfied that they were ready for operations.[134]

While the USN began operating air patrols from Halifax at the end of August, a considerable amount of work in building slipways still had to be completed at the North Sydney air station and it was not until 21 September that Captain Hobbs reported its four flying boats ready for convoy duty.[135] Nonetheless, the eight USN aircraft at Halifax and Sydney represented the most significant reinforcement that Canada's anti-submarine forces had yet received. Air cover had already proven its worth in British waters where, in the words of the RCAF official history, air patrols over convoys had "a most decisive effect— they rendered convoys virtually immune from successful attack."[136] The presence of air patrols forced U-boat commanders to alter their tactics, either by attacking ships at night after aircraft had returned to base or beyond the one- to two-hundred mile limit of a flying boat's range. Ironically, the success of aircraft cover based in Britain was also a contributing factor to the German decision to send U-boats across the Atlantic to operate off the American and Canadian eastern seaboards.[137]

It would certainly have been understandable if the number of naval authorities, both RN and RCN, who had responsibility for various aspects of convoy escorts—the captain of patrols, the admiral superintendent, and Chambers's rather unwieldy title of port convoy officer and senior officer of escorts Halifax—had left the USN's Lieutenant Byrd somewhat confused as to who was in charge on the Canadian East Coast. Even within the RCN, Story's transfer to the East Coast now meant that the superintendent of the port of Halifax outranked the commander of the navy's patrol vessels, a fact that created some dispute over the extent of command authority each officer would exercise. By June 1918, however, a clear delineation of their respective areas of responsibility had become necessary when

---

134. Captain of Patrols to The Secretary, Department of the Naval Service, 27 August 1918, and enclosure, 63–10–1, pt. 1, DHH 77/58, vol. 20, file 1.

135. "Naval Aviation in Canada During the First World War," nd, 17, DHH 74/25.

136. Wise, *Canadian Airmen and the First World War*, 226.

137. Ibid, 225.

the increased number of personnel required for the expanded patrol service led to a reorganization of the service's shore establishments. Whereas all patrol personnel had previously been carried on the books of HMCS *Stadacona*, commencing on 1 May 1918, the sailors of patrol vessels based at Halifax and Sydney were given their own organizations. At Sydney, the drifter *CD 74* was designated HMCS *Seagull* to represent the patrols depot afloat and was placed under the command of the RCN's Lieutenant-Commander J.H. Knight. All other Sydney personnel remained with the port's shore establishment, HMCS *Lansdowne*, while gate and examination vessels, harbour tugs, and motor launches were carried as tenders to *Lansdowne*, herself under the command of Captain F.C.C. Pasco, the captain-in-charge at Sydney. Patrol personnel based at Halifax, meanwhile, had been transferred to the books of HMCS *Guelph*, represented afloat by drifter *CD 20*, commanded by acting Commander P.F. Newcombe. Harbour vessels at Halifax, plus any patrol vessels that were undergoing extensive repairs or refits in the dockyard, were carried on the books of HMCS *Niobe*. Both commanding officers of the two patrol depots were under Hose's command, while the captain of patrols himself held an independent command and reported directly to NSHQ.[138]

Ottawa sought to further clarify the responsibilities of the various authorities by issuing a confidential naval order on 19 June. Although the order stated that Newcombe and Knight represented Hose at Halifax or Sydney whenever the captain of patrols was absent, the order also stipulated that they were "not to make any alterations in disposition of ships, etc., etc., without consulting and obtaining the approval of the senior officer present." Their powers were further circumscribed by the decision that "in the event of any occurrence which has not been foreseen or arranged for by the captain of patrols, the senior officer of the area affected is at once to assume command."[139] The powers that Story and Pasco, the senior officers at Halifax and Sydney, respectively, held in relation to the captain of patrols were reinforced the following month in a memorandum issued by NSHQ after "a question ha[d] arisen as to the control of the patrol forces as between yourself [Hose] and the local senior officers." Claiming it was setting out "broad principles" for Hose's guidance, NSHQ reiterated that the captain of patrols was "responsible in every respect for the efficiency of all ships, their equipment and their personnel" as well as for "the training of all men, and the replacement of casualties." Hose was reminded that he was to "arrange for the normal patrols, escorts, etc.," while working "in close cooperation" with the local senior officer. "A scheme of offensive action against submarines, raiders, etc., having been prepared by you in cooperation with the local senior officers, you should take charge of operations when present. If you are absent, the senior officer would take charge. At all times you should refer your arrangements insofar as they affect the local senior officer, to him, and work in the closest possible cooperation with him."[140]

---

138. "RCN Shore Establishments on the Canadian East Coast, 1910–1919," nd, 24–25, DHH 81/520/8000/*Stadacona*, Armed Yacht, vol. 2.

139. "Extract from Confidential Naval Orders, Department of the Naval Service, 19th June 1918," nd, 1065-7-1, pt. 1, LAC, RG 24, vol. 4031.

140. J.R. Hemsted, Naval Secretary, to Captain of Patrols, 10 July 1918, ibid.

U 156 was the most active German submarine in Canadian waters. After attacking the Canadian fishing fleet in late-August, *U 156* sank during its return voyage to Germany, most likely in a minefield while rounding the British Isles. (DND U156-003)

The desired co-operative relationship set out by Ottawa was more easily instituted at Sydney, where Hose spent most of his time during the summer shipping season. The captain of patrols and Captain Pasco managed to work together in reasonable harmony, with Hose controlling the operations of all active vessels, including Sydney's minesweeping force, and Pasco confining himself to the running of the port organization. It was probably no coincidence that the two captains were co-located, with the patrols depot HMCS *Seagull* and the port authority's ship *Lansdowne* headquartered at 145 Esplanade in Sydney. Such a relationship proved to be more complicated in Halifax, where the admiral superintendent was not only the senior naval officer on the East Coast but occasionally demonstrated a rather prickly character as well. Although Commander Newcombe of HMCS *Guelph* was designated the "senior officer of patrols, Halifax" in command—in Hose's absence—of all patrol forces at the port, friction quickly developed between Newcombe and the admiral superintendent when Story insisted on asserting his authority over everything naval at Halifax.[141]

The Canadian admiral's fractious nature was not confined to his relationship with his fellow RCN officers, however. By August, the command situation at Halifax had convinced the British commander-in-chief to revive his earlier proposal to have "a carefully selected and experienced naval captain" assigned to Halifax as his representative. One of the reasons Vice-Admiral Grant gave to the Admiralty for his renewed request was an awareness "of possible friction between admiral superintendent and senior officer of escorts, Halifax," Rear-Admiral Chambers. The need for such an appointment to reduce the friction between Story and Chambers had, in the commander-in-chief's view, "become more acute with the increased importance of the sea and air patrols and the augmentation of these by US forces."[142] Grant's proposal had been endorsed by Kingsmill, who was well-aware that the limited naval staffs at both Sydney and Halifax were being overworked.[143] As the British admiral explained to London:

> The director of the naval service of Canada, admiral superintendent and senior officer of escorts are very good friends but ready to rend one another on small provocation. This triangular system of potential eruption frequently comes to a head either in sections or all together with the emission of steam, generally in the direction of the commander in chief, the safety valve opens and pressure subsides.
>
> The remedy lies in prevention of overlapping of duties and for this reason I desire to have machinery which renders it unnecessary for the senior officer of escorts to encroach into the sphere of the local defence forces and at the same time provides the admiral superintendent with expert advice and executive machinery to control the component parts of the defence forces.[144]

---

141. "RCN Shore Establishments on the Canadian East Coast, 1910–1919," nd, 27, DHH 81/520/8000/*Stadacona*, Armed Yacht, vol. 2.

142. Grant to Admiralty, General Letter No. 7, 3 September 1918, UKNA, ADM 137/504.

143. Hadley and Sarty, *Tin-pots and Pirate Ships*, 258.

144. Grant to Admiralty, General Letter No. 7, 3 September 1918, UKNA, ADM 137/504.

A large part of the problem between Story and Chambers was the result of the utter lack of convoy escort forces beyond those of the local defence force. While Chambers had been designated the senior officer of escorts in addition to his duties as port convoy officer, the only escorts he controlled were British cruisers, vessels capable of guarding against attack by German surface raiders but completely inadequate as anti-submarine vessels. The friction resulting from complicated East Coast command relationships added further stress to the staff and senior officers of the patrol service as they desperately tried to organize an inadequately equipped force to face the U-cruisers already operating in US waters. By late July, the pressure he felt as captain of patrols took a sufficient toll on Captain Hose's health to render him too exhausted to continue carrying out his naval duties. As he explained to Kingsmill on 4 August, "the machinery needs a rest" and he asked for fourteen days leave to recover.[145]

Having spent the first three years of the war in the relative calm of the northeastern Pacific commanding HMCS *Rainbow*, aside from his patrols down the California and Mexican coasts, Hose had been exposed to far greater stress since assuming command of the navy's East Coast patrols. After taking over from Coke partway through the 1917 shipping season, he had experienced first-hand the heavy price the Canadian public could exact on naval officers for any perceived failings, while serving as a nautical assessor on the Drysdale inquiry into the Halifax explosion. Although his own role in the disaster had been non-existent, his mere presence in Halifax at the time of the explosion had made Hose the subject of daily attack in local newspapers, with repeated calls for his resignation from the inquiry. He was also well-aware of the public vilification and manslaughter charges, which had befallen the unfortunate Commander Wyatt—a fate that the captain of patrols himself had had a hand in. As we have seen, Hose surrendered to the immense public pressure within Halifax to find a scapegoat and went along with the inquiry's conclusions that falsely implicated the RCN as being negligent in the events leading up to the disaster. The lessons he had drawn from his disturbing experience as a member of the inquiry had been voiced at the end of March when the Admiralty suddenly withdrew its promise of destroyers and fast trawlers for Hose's patrol service and left the RCN to fend for itself. With the local search for scapegoats still undoubtedly fresh in his mind, Hose had strongly reminded NSHQ of the public wrath that would await the navy—and himself— for any failure in defending the nation's shipping: "if shipping is attacked this summer off the Canadian coast and the full measure of defence of which the dominion is capable is not provided ... it will reflect seriously on the patrol service.'[146] Forced to cobble together a coherent patrol scheme using only the collection of ill-suited vessels the Admiralty insisted were adequate to the task, Hose would have had difficulty putting the nasty

---

145. Captain-in-Charge, Sydney to Naval Ottawa, 3 August 1918, Hose to Kingsmill, 4 August 1918, O-44178, pt. 1, LAC, National Personnel Records Centre [hereafter NPRC], quoted in Hadley and Sarty, *Tin-pots and Pirate Ships*, 258.

146. Captain of Patrols to Secretary, Department of the Naval Service, 25 March 1918, 1017–10–4, pt. 1, LAC, RG 24, vol. 3832.

Halifax inquiry experience out of his mind as he contemplated his own fate should the U-cruisers that were sinking ships in US waters move north.

In that light, it is probably not surprising that the overworked and overstressed captain of patrols suffered the effects of exhaustion after receiving word of *U 156*'s attacks in the Gulf of Maine on 21 and 22 July. Any doubts that the German submarine was moving into Canadian waters rather than returning to the busy shipping lanes off New York were removed on 2 August when the U-boat sank the Canadian four-masted schooner *Dornfontein* of 695 tons forty kilometres south-southwest of Grand Manan Island at the mouth of the Bay of Fundy. The recently launched vessel had departed Saint John on 31 July with a load of lumber destined for Natal, South Africa when:

> the submarine rose from the water and fired two shots across her bow. The schooner quickly came to and a few minutes later was boarded by a party of Germans who left the submarine in a small boat.
>
> The Germans wasted no torpedoes, shells, or bombs, but set the vessel afire. Every stitch of available clothing owned by the crew, together with a six-months' stock of provisions, was taken off by the German raiding party. The officers and crew of the schooner made the best of their time while in contact with the Germans and brought in the best account of the vessel and her crew that had been obtained up to date. Part of their report is as follows: "The submarine was the *U 156*, and the crew numbered seventy-three. Their ages would run from twenty to thirty-five. They were well clad and appeared to be in good health and condition. The men stated that the only thing they suffered from was a lack of vegetables. The captain of the submarine was a stout man, apparently about thirty-two years of age and about five feet seven inches tall, and the crew were pretty much the same type of men. The captain spoke only broken English, while the second lieutenant spoke English fluently. Nearly all the crew spoke English."[147]

U 156's fluently English-speaking second lieutenant had told the master of the *Robert and Richard*, sunk by the submarine in the Gulf of Maine on 22 July, "that he [or his family, given that the officer was described as being about thirty-five years old by American witnesses] had maintained a summer home on the Maine coast for twenty-five years before the war." US naval authorities believed numerous reports they had received that the German officer's familiarity with the East Coast probably explained why the U-boat appeared to know local waters so well and had been willing to venture close inshore in her operations.[148]

Further information on the German submarine was gathered by naval intelligence after the *Dornfontein*'s crew rowed ashore on Grand Manan Island early the next morning. The RCN's naval transport officer at St John, Lieutenant A.J. Mulcahy, RNCVR, immediately

---

147. USN, First Naval District War Diary, nd, quoted in US Navy Department, *German Submarine Activities*, 56–57.

148. USN, First Naval District War Diary, nd, quoted in ibid, 56, 64.

cabled Ottawa with the initial report of the attack and that the "cargo of lumber, vessel, burned. Crew removed and landed at Gannet Rock by submarine which had crew of seventy-three men and was 225 feet long and had two guns on deck. Trawler *Festubert* proceeding forthwith."[149] Aside from a small USN patrol boat, the Canadian Battle-class trawler was the only naval vessel in the vicinity of the attack, having just completed a fisheries patrol in the Bay of Fundy. Further details were provided from St John after the *Dornfontein*'s crew was brought to the Canadian port at 9:00 pm on the 3rd. According to the naval transport officer:

> Crew taken aboard submarine held four and half hours while Germans removed everything possible from schooner then put crew back in schooner life boat who proceeded to Gannet Rocks [*sic*] landing here six am on August 3rd. Submarine still at schooner when last seen by crew August 2nd. Schooner still burning this afternoon from end to end. Submarine sighted on the surface one hour before attack but not recognized as such. Submarine two hundred and seventy long, able to submerge twenty seconds. Engine room plates marked U fifty-six. Vessel painted black on top, grey underneath, old paint. Two guns on deck. 5.9 fore and one aft. Decks rounded out to meet ships sides. Bow gun on deck not in well. All [ship's] papers taken.[150]

The fact that *Dornfontein*'s master had allowed the German submariners to get hold of his confidential naval papers was not taken lightly by the naval authorities who believed that he "must have been excited, forgetting all about his instructions to destroy his papers if attacked by the enemy, until too late. After being ordered by the commander of the submarine to bring his papers, he got frightened and complied with the request." *Dornfontein*'s unfortunate captain subsequently had his master's certificate suspended for the duration of the war.[151]

HMCS *Festubert*, of course, found no trace of *U 156* by the time she reached the scene of the attack, since the submarine had already moved south-eastward across the mouth of the Bay of Fundy and down Nova Scotia's southern coast. On 3 August, the German submarine struck again, sinking four American fishing schooners off Seal Island, thirty-two kilometres west of Cape Sable. Once again the submariners were reported to have boarded the vessels and removed all the provisions they could find before scuttling the schooners with bombs.[152] On 4 August crewmen from the German submarine boarded and sank the

---

149. Transports, St John to Naval Ottawa, 515, 3 August 1918, 1062–13–2, pt. 4, LAC, RG 24, vol. 4021.

150. Transports, St John to Naval Ottawa, 519, 3 August 1918, ibid.

151. "Particulars of Attacks on Merchant Vessels by Enemy Submarines," Dornfontein, 2 August 1918, 1062–13–10, pt. 3, LAC, RG 24, vol. 4023; *Sydney Post*, 17 September 1918; and Hadley and Sarty, *Tin-pots and Pirate Ships*, 252.

152. US Navy Department, *German Submarine Activities*, 57–58; and Navinet to Naval Ottawa, 4 August 1918, 1062–13–10, pt. 3, LAC, RG 24, vol. 4021.

Battle-class trawlers and Imperial trawlers and drifters of the Halifax escort fleet in 1918. (LAC PA-167307)

An Imperial trawler escorting a merchant ship. (DND S-45)

The Imperial drifter *CD 49*. The drifter design was more suited to British reservists employing the drift nets that were commonly used by British fishermen. It lacked the speed and armament to be of much value in Canadian waters. (DND CN 3271)

The Imperial trawler *TR 8*. (LAC e007140919)

72-ton Canadian schooner *Nelson A.* some forty kilometres southeast of Shelburne. Two more Canadian fishing vessels, *Agnes B. Holland* and *Gladys M. Hollett*, of 100 and 203 tons respectively, were attacked by the U-boat on the morning of the 5th, twenty-five kilometres southeast of the Lahave Banks and eighty kilometres east southeast of where the *Nelson A.* met her fate the previous day. While *Agnes B. Holland* was sunk, the scuttling charges set in *Gladys M. Hollett* only damaged the vessel and she was eventually towed into Halifax.[153]

Since none of the fishing schooners carried a wireless set, word of the sinkings did not reach naval authorities until the fishermen managed to row ashore. Once they reached land, however, the disquieting news quickly made its way up and down Nova Scotia's southern coast. After the first two American fishing crews landed at Woods Harbour on the morning of 4 August, the news was relayed by the naval intelligence staff at Halifax to NSHQ and the British commander-in-chief at Washington. Word of the sinking of the *Nelson A.* on the 4th was given to the naval authorities by the lighthouse keeper at Lockeport, Nova Scotia, the following day and immediately passed on by NSHQ to the acting prime minister in Ottawa.[154]

A sense of the dire public mood consequent to the sinkings was conveyed by the member of parliament for Yarmouth, E.K. Spinney, who sent both a telegram and a letter to the deputy minister of the naval service on the 5th to express his concern. Stating that the sinkings had resulted in all steamboat coastal service being suspended from Yarmouth, Spinney's telegram informed Desbarats that "no protection service in evidence operating on this coast. Granting submarines absolute freedom. Strongly urge prompt action extending that protection on the present perilous condition demands keen anxiety. Reply."[155] Desbarats simply assured the Yarmouth MP that the "situation [was] receiving joint attention Canadian and United States authorities."[156] The member's letter of the same date—as Hose had predicted—emphasized the public's concern that an enemy submarine was operating off their coastline with no apparent response from the Canadian navy.

> An active German submarine off this coast has been a matter of public knowledge during the past two weeks. Until Saturday no serious results were apparent in our waters. I interviewed the crew of one of the vessels on Saturday and he informed me that the captain of the submarine which destroyed their vessels, informed him that he was operating in these waters with instructions to destroy shipping of all classes or description in evidence. He had been carrying on his operations for three weeks on the coast of the United States and the maritime provinces without any restrictions whatever.
>   I do not know what system of protection the federal government has

---

153. Hadley and Sarty, *Tin-pots and Pirate Ships*, 358; and US Navy Department, *German Submarine Activities*, 58, 140.

154. Navinet to Naval Ottawa, 4 August 1918, S.H. Morres for Director of the Naval Service to Acting Prime Minister, 5 August 1918, 1062–13–10, pt. 3, LAC, RG 24, vol. 4021.

155. E.K. Spinney to Deputy Minister of Naval Service, 5 August 1918, ibid.

156. Desbarats to Spinney, 5 August 1918, ibid.

organized but naturally assume that the knowledge of the menace to our shipping by the appearance of submarines, would have influenced them to make some provision for our protection. The people in this section of Nova Scotia, as you may well imagine, are filled with keen anxiety.

In sending you the above telegram I have put you in the possession of all the facts available and have every confidence that some action will be taken on the part of the department which will insure the public that their safety and interests are not being neglected.[157]

As Desbarats's reply correctly pointed out, the anti-submarine effort off Nova Scotia's southern coast was a joint RCN-USN responsibility. The four American fishing schooners had all been sunk in the USN's patrol zone, which extended to the 65th meridian east of Shelburne. The submarine chasers from the First Naval District based there were also the naval force closest to the three Canadian schooners sunk by *U 156* on the 4th and 5th. In keeping with their responsibilities, the USN had despatched its "naval hunt squadron" (consisting of the destroyer USS *Jouett* and eighteen submarine chasers), which had been searching for the German U-boat in the approaches to New York, from Provincetown, Massachusetts to the scene of *Dornfontein*'s sinking. Arriving at the mouth of the Bay of Fundy on 4 August, the hunt squadron patrolled southeast to cover the south coast of Nova Scotia off Yarmouth but turned back toward the coast of Maine late on the same day. *Jouett* and her subchasers, therefore, remained some fifty kilometres to the west of the vicinity where *Nelson A.* had been sunk and some 130 kilometres west of where *U 156* sank *Agnes B. Holland* and *Gladys M. Hollett* on the morning of 5 August.[158]

The local naval forces at Halifax, meanwhile, were preoccupied escorting convoy HC 12 out to sea on 4 August. The convoy—consisting of the cruiser HMS *Roxburgh* and eighteen transports carrying, in addition to their cargo, 14,685 Canadian and 6,495 US soldiers to Europe—had made an uneventful departure from Halifax in the early afternoon in fine weather. As was the usual practice, two hours before the convoy was scheduled to depart it had been preceded to sea by the three submarine chasers of the USN chaser division under the command of Lieutenant Chester. The subchasers then waited for the convoy "well outside the harbour with their listening tubes down." The convoy itself was escorted out to sea by three RCN escort divisions, each normally consisting of a trawler and two drifters. On this occasion, however, the 1st Division was short one drifter when *CD 19* was withdrawn to augment the other vessel conducting the harbour's inner patrol, the torpedo-boat USS *Tingey*. Rear-Admiral Chambers later admitted that the growing number of reports of schooner sinkings to the south were a cause for concern and he was "much relieved that this convoy got away in safety," having cleared the harbour in only seventy-five minutes, "a fine performance considering the scattered nature of the anchorage" in

157. Spinney to Desbarats, 5 August 1918, ibid.

158. Halpern, *A Naval History of World War I*, 432; "Estimate of the Submarine Situation in Western Atlantic from July 1 to and including 4 August 1918, file JA-2, United States National Archives, RG 45, subject file 1911–1927, box 185; and Hadley and Sarty, *Tin-pots and Pirate Ships*, 251, 253, 255.

Bedford Basin. Their only concession to the submarine threat lurking off the southern coast of Nova Scotia was to maintain a constant zig-zag course. The three RCN divisions and the submarine chasers continued to escort HC 12 out to sea during the night of 4/5 August before parting company to return to Halifax.[159]

While the convoy's local escort forces were returning to port the next morning, the Canadian tanker *Luz Blanca* of 4,868 tons steamed out of Halifax sometime before 0800 hours, bound for Mexico. In doing so, the ship's master ignored the advice of the port's shipping control officers who suggested, in view of the submarine activity off southern Nova Scotia, that the tanker delay her departure until dusk and maintain a zigzag course once she had cleared the harbour entrance. With no specific information that the U-boat was operating in the Halifax approaches, the naval authorities had no reason to close the port and *Luz Blanca*, whose course south would take her eighty kilometres to the east of where *Nelson A.* had been sunk the previous day, was free to proceed. Unknown to either the naval staff in Halifax or the tanker's master, however, *U 156* had moved eastward during the night of 4/5 August to sink the Canadian fishing schooners *Agnes B. Holland* and *Gladys M. Hollett* directly south of *Luz Blanca*'s intended course. The German raider would have been looking for just such a target as the lone tanker when she turned north on the morning of 5 August and set course directly for the Halifax approaches.[160]

At 1140 hours *Luz Blanca* was struck in the stern by a torpedo, while steaming fifty-eight kilometres south-southwest of the Sambro lightship. Uncertain if she had been torpedoed or had struck a mine, the damaged tanker was able to turn back and make for Halifax for repairs. The vessel was heading north at a speed of twelve knots when a surfaced *U 156* opened fire from a range of some seven or eight kilometres off the port quarter. *Luz Blanca*, which carried a 12-pounder gun aft manned by two Royal Naval reservists, began a running battle with the submarine but was easily out-ranged by the U-boat's 5.9-inch deck guns. Remaining beyond the reach of the tanker's 12-pounder in the "thick and hazy" weather, *U 156* fired some thirty rounds into the vessel, killing two of her crew and wounding several others, before finally bringing the ship to a stop some seventeen miles south of the Sambro lightship. Abandoning the tanker, which was ablaze in several places, her crew made off to the north in three boats shortly after 1500 hours. When they last saw her through the afternoon haze, the tanker was settling rapidly as the German submarine continued to shell the hulk.[161]

159. Commander P.F. Newcombe to Captain of Patrols, Sydney, 13 August 1918, 1065–7-1, pt. 1, LAC, RG 24, vol. 4031; Port Convoy Officer and Senior Officer of Escorts, Halifax to Commander-in-Chief, NA&WI, 2 December 1918, 22, and enclosure No. 5, "Statistics of HC Convoys," HC 12, UKNA, ADM 137/2658; and "Mercantile Convoy No. HC 12," 15 August 1918, UKNA, ADM 137/2566.

160. US Navy Department, *German Submarine Activities*, 58–59; Hadley and Sarty, *Tin-pots and Pirate Ships*, 255–56; and "Subchasers Are Seeking U-boat in Bay of Fundy," *The Ottawa Citizen*, 6 August 1918, copy in 1062–13–10, pt. 3, LAC, RG 24, vol. 4021.

161. The timings in the various accounts of the action vary with some suggesting a three hour running gun-battle that commenced at 1200 hours or a one-hour battle with the U-boat appearing on the surface at 1400 hours. US Navy Department, *German Submarine Activities*, 58–59; "Subchasers Are Seeking U-boat in Bay of Fundy," *The Ottawa Citizen*, 6 August 1918, copy in 1062–13–10, pt. 3, LAC, RG 24, vol. 4021; and Hadley and Sarty, *Tin-pots and Pirate Ships*, 255–56.

At 1345 hours, the naval staff office aboard *Niobe* received word of *Luz Blanca*'s plight and quickly relayed the report to Commander P.F. Newcombe, the senior officer of patrols whenever Hose was absent from the port. The dispersed forces Newcombe had available to respond to the distress call reflected the inadequate resources the RCN had been given to defend the shipping lanes. A radio call to proceed to the scene was quickly sent out by the naval staff office to the antiquated American torpedo-boat USS *Tingey*, conducting an inner patrol off the harbour entrance and to the 1st and 2nd Divisions returning from escorting HC 12. Newcombe also had a general call sent to the USN chaser division, the last of the escorts to part company with the convoy. Forty-five minutes after first being told of the attack, the senior officer of patrols was informed that *TR 11* of the 1st Division had received the wireless message and was proceeding with *CD 9*, the only other vessel in her formation, to the reported area of the attack. Although Newcombe had hoped that the 2nd Division would still be at sea and able to respond, its trawler and drifters had already reached Halifax and were preparing for their regularly scheduled layup period.[162]

The naval staff's message had also been received by Lieutenant Chester aboard *SC 240* but no acknowledgement was heard at Halifax and Newcombe did not find out about the subchaser's actions until Chester reported to the patrols office at 2030 hours that night. According to the American lieutenant, his subchaser "had picked up the message sent out by naval staff and at once altered course to the position given and though the weather was thick and hazy his course took him direct to the two boats containing captain and eighteen men of *Luz Blanca* practically without search or further alteration of course. There being then neither sight nor sound of the submarine, he proceeded back to harbour with the rescued crew." The senior officer of patrols at Halifax, meanwhile, was spending a trying afternoon attempting to round up all the available escort trawlers and drifters that could be made ready for sea. Newcombe's problems were compounded by difficulties in communication within the harbour organization.

> Further inquiry showed that 3rd Division had reported to officer in charge of outer escorts at 10:30 am and in accordance with usual procedure, he had sent them for water and to make good small defects, prior to proceeding on patrol again, on the following morning. All four vessels comprising this division had small engine room defects needing dismantling of certain parts and proceeded to carry out this work. Both 2nd and 3rd Divisions were ordered to prepare for sea forthwith, quick engine room adjustments were made and plus [the Battle-class trawler] *St Eloi* (who I took out of dockyard hands on my own responsibility), were all under way to scene of action by 5 pm.[163]

Subchaser *SC 247*, meanwhile, had also returned to harbour, having left HC 12 early because of a shortage of fuel. After refuelling, Newcombe ordered the vessel "to proceed at once to the

---

162. Commander P.F. Newcombe to Captain of Patrols, Sydney, 13 August 1918, 1065–7-1, LAC, RG 24, vol. 4031.

163. Ibid.

area, get listening tubes out, and try to locate the submarine." Through his efforts, the senior officer of patrols had *Tingey, SC 247, St Eloi* and the three escort divisions of trawlers and drifters combing the area of the attack by last light that evening. Of these, *CD 14* picked up the last of *Luz Blanca*'s lifeboats, with twelve crewmen, at the Sambro lightship and returned them to port at 2335 hours that night. Not surprisingly, given the extreme difficulty of locating a submerged submarine with listening tubes, the dozen escort vessels despatched to the scene did not make contact with *U 156*. *SC 247*, the last of the escorts to return to Halifax, claimed to have heard submarine noises through her listening tubes until 2300 hours on the 5th and, while possible, it would seem more likely to have been the sounds of the many other escort vessels in the area. In all probability, *U 156* left the scene soon after sinking the Canadian tanker, although the U-boat's next confirmed encounter was not until 8 August, when she stopped and sank the Swedish steamer *Sydland* 250 kilometres to the southwest of the *Luz Blanca* action.[164] Newcombe also had the ten trawlers of the minesweeping division prepared for sea at thirty minutes notice with all crews on board and fires banked. The minesweepers departed at 0330 hours on 6 August to make a "protracted and careful sweep" of the main shipping channel for a distance of twenty-five miles to seaward.

Having cabled NSHQ on 3 August to request fourteen days leave to recover from his exhaustion brought on by the burden of command, word of the sinking of *Luz Blanca* in the Halifax approaches convinced the captain of patrols to return to his duties immediately.[165] Late on the night of 5 August, after Newcombe had placed all of his available patrol vessels south of the Sambro lightship, Hose informed Ottawa of his intended dispositions to meet the submarine threat along the eastern Nova Scotian coast. With the trawlers and drifters evenly divided between Sydney and Halifax—six Battle-class, seventeen imperial trawlers, and twenty-two drifters at the former; and six Battle-class, sixteen imperial trawlers, and fourteen drifters at the latter—the captain of patrols had a slightly larger force at his disposal if the RCN's nine auxiliary patrol vessels are included. Hose detailed one of the Halifax escort divisions, consisting of one trawler and two drifters, to patrol to the southwest of the Sambro lightship down to Gull Rock, near the 65th meridian that divided the Canadian and American patrol zones. A second Halifax division, also of one trawler and two drifters, was to patrol to the northeast of Halifax up to Hawbolt Rock. Hose also assigned two of the Sydney escort divisions, each consisting of two trawlers and two drifters, to patrol the coast between Sydney and Hawbolt Rock, with one division covering the area to the southwest of the Fourchu Light and the other the coast of Cape Breton Island between the light and Sydney.[166]

While the six trawlers and eight drifters assigned by Hose to the patrol sweep along the Nova Scotia coast may appear to represent but a small fraction of the forty-five trawlers (both Battle-class and imperial) and thirty-six drifters present on the East Coast, in fact the four

164. Ibid; and US Navy Department, *German Submarine Activities*, 59–60.

165. Captain-in-Charge, Sydney to Naval Ottawa, 6 August 1918, 0–44178, pt. 1, LAC, NPRC; and Hadley and Sarty, *Tin-pots and Pirate Ships*, 258.

166. Captain of Patrols to Naval Ottawa, 801, 5 August 1918, Captain of Patrols to NSHQ, 1 August 1918, 1065-7-6, LAC, RG 24, vol. 4031.

trawlers from Sydney represented half of the available trawler strength at that port. As Hose explained to Ottawa, of the twenty-three trawlers at Sydney "ten trawlers here unable to patrol on account of no guns and defects on arrival. Two trawlers and three drifters which should be on patrol laid up with boiler and engine defects. These are in addition to three trawlers, five drifters in harbour for routine lay up."[167] The fact that ten of the Sydney trawlers had no guns or were defective upon arrival was a consequence of having the majority of the most recently commissioned trawlers assigned to the Cape Breton port. As of 1 August, sixteen of the trawlers had been in commission for less than two months and six of those for less than a week.[168] With 12-pounder guns in short supply, the newer vessels could only wait alongside until the necessary armament could be delivered. Unlike at Sydney, where the minesweeping flotilla consisted of the seven New England fishing trawlers, *PV I* to *PV VII*, the minesweeping force at Halifax was made up of the ten imperial trawlers *TR 1* to *TR 10*, leaving only twelve trawlers, including the six Battle-class, for patrol and escort duties.[169] Up to half of these might be expected to be on routine lay up to rest the crews, reprovision, and make minor repairs or were in the dockyard for more substantial work.

On the other hand, the locations of the RCN's nine auxiliary patrol vessels on 5 August, while reflecting the difficulty of keeping a tiny fleet of makeshift warships ready for immediate operations, did not demonstrate the best judgment on the part of the captain of patrols. The two most effective anti-submarine vessels in the East Coast patrol force, HMC Ships *Canada* and *Grilse*, were in dockyard hands for repairs, the former at Pictou and the latter at Halifax. Hose's flagship *Stadacona*, meanwhile, was also alongside at Halifax repairing defects, while *Acadia*, whose ability to mount a valuable 4-inch gun was offset by her paltry top speed of only eight knots, had gone to Pictou for docking. Two of the more useful of the remaining APVs, however, were immediately unavailable because Hose had assigned them to routine local duties. Despite the fact that *U 156* was operating in the Gulf of Maine and could easily move into Canadian waters at any time, the armed-yacht *Hochelaga* was attending to a shipwreck near Guion Island on the east coast of Cape Breton Island, while *Cartier*, whose twelve-knot top speed and three 12-pounder guns made her valuable in an anti-submarine role, was making routine calls on life-saving stations along the coast. The other auxiliary patrol vessels, although they were generally too slow or too weakly armed to pose much of a threat to a U-boat, had also been given mundane tasks. The ex-fisheries patrol vessel *Margaret* was taking coal to a fog station in Newfoundland, *Laurentian* had just arrived back at Halifax after taking coal to stations in the Bay of Fundy, while *Lady Evelyn* was taking Commander J.T. Shenton, Story's flag commander at Halifax, to the war signal station.[170]

On receiving word from Hose of the disposition of his auxiliary patrol vessels, an

167. Captain of Patrols to Naval Ottawa, 801, 5 August 1918, ibid.

168. Captain of Patrols to NSHQ, 1 August 1918, ibid.

169. Kingsmill to Admiralty, 18 July 1918, ibid; and Grant to Admiralty, General Letter No. 6, 1 August 1918, UKNA, ADM 137/504.

170. Captain of Patrols to Naval Ottawa, 801, 5 August 1918, 1065–7-6, LAC, RG 24, vol. 4031; and Ken MacPherson and John Burgess, *The Ships of Canada's Naval Forces, 1910–1985: A Complete Pictorial History of Canadian Warships* (Toronto 1985), 206.

HMCS *Grilse* at Halifax with cruisers of the North America and West Indies Station and a passenger liner in the channel. (LAC PA-209546)

alarmed Kingsmill immediately issued direct orders to the captain of patrols on the course of action he should already have taken. In a 6 August telegram marked "urgent," he directed Hose to "recall all patrol vessels now employed on services other than anti-submarine patrol and use them for patrol. Hasten completion defects. Work to be carried on continuously.... Have you any patrol between Cape Ray and Cape North [covering the Cabot Strait]? If not, place one as soon as you have ships available."[171] That the naval director was less than pleased that Hose had allowed his APVs to be sent to dispersed locations on relatively menial tasks at a time when an enemy submarine was known to be south of Nova Scotia, was made clear in his subsequent telegram to Sydney that same day: "re APVs on special service. It should be understood that these duties, while essential when possible owing to war conditions, should be dropped on any emergency. Report what orders you gave on becoming aware of submarine in close proximity of Canadian ports."[172]

After a year in his position, the captain of patrols may not have enjoyed being taken to task by the naval director for his lack of judgment, but his explanation did not admit that any mistake had been made: "No special orders were issued on becoming aware of submarines in close proximity to Canadian ports as patrol off Canadian ports had already been organized to meet this possibility and was in operation as organized."[173] While there was little Hose could have done about the four patrol vessels that were in dockyard hands, there was no excuse for dispersing the five remaining auxiliaries on housekeeping duties when the threat of attack appeared imminent. It is perhaps not surprising, therefore, that the captain of patrols emphasized the operational nature of the APV's tasks when he reported their subsequent assignments to NSHQ on the 9th. HMCS *Hochelaga* had been ordered from attending to the wreck of the steamer *Afghan Prince* at Guion Island to escort the steamer *Takada*, en route from Montreal to Sydney, while *Lady Evelyn* was also escorting another merchant ship, the *Lord Kelvin*. *Cartier* had been assigned to the Halifax inner patrol as had *Margaret*, although the latter was still en route after taking coal to the fog station at Cape Norman. *Canada*, *Grilse*, *Stadacona*, and *Acadia*, however, were still laid up with defects although the latter was expected to be out of dockyard hands at Pictou in a few days.[174] Whatever doubts Kingsmill may have had about his subordinate's handling of his forces, while *U 156* was lurking off southern Nova Scotia, his only rebuke was the reproach implicit in his telegrams of 6 August querying Hose's allocation of his auxiliary patrol vessels and directing that they be properly employed to meet the threat.

The sinking of *Luz Blanca* in the Halifax approaches on 5 August also had an immediate impact on the movement of shipping from American to Canadian ports for convoy. Ships bound from New York or Hampton Roads to Sydney for inclusion in the HS convoys had always been routed independently along the coast until after HS 50 sailed from the Cape Breton port on 3 August. On the day *Luz Blanca* was attacked, Vice-Admiral Grant instructed the British port convoy officer at New York, Commodore L. de L. Wells, to detain all ships

---

171. Naval Ottawa to Transports, Sydney, 44, 6 August 1918, 1065–7-6, LAC, RG 24, vol. 4031.

172. Ibid.

173. Patrols to Naval Ottawa, 7 August 1918, ibid.

174. Patrols to Naval Ottawa, 9 August 1918, ibid.

destined for HS convoys at the US port. At the same time, the C-in-C telegraphed NSHQ to inform the Canadians that "any measure possible should be taken to protect incoming ships now en route from Hampton Roads to Sydney ... Are you in position to protect incoming ships on approach route to Halifax and Sydney if not diverted? Also to escort outgoing convoys beyond dangerous area?"[175] A direct inquiry to Rear-Admiral Story forcefully demonstrated the extent to which the senior Canadian officer on the coast felt that the naval forces available at Halifax were insufficient to meet the situation: "Am not in position to protect incoming ships and outgoing convoys. Have only two United States chasers in proper order. Remaining vessels, trawlers and drifters, too slow." In Story's opinion, any "attempt to give adequate protection to outgoing HC convoys requires at least six more chasers."[176] Even before he was asked for his views on 6 August, the Canadian admiral had already provided an indication of his response in telegrams to both Hose and Kingsmill the previous night: "I consider the vessels on inner patrol [at Halifax] unsatisfactory. *DeLong* and *Tingey* are useless. It is essential two good vessels of our own service should always be on this patrol."[177]

Story was not, of course, stating anything new about the weakness of the RCN's forces. Kingsmill had long held the view that the East Coast fleet was too slow and underarmed to provide any sort of effective defence against U-cruisers, while Grant had already been sharply criticized by the Admiralty for expressing his private opinion that the naval forces all along the eastern seaboard, in both the United States and Canada, were inadequate. It had been their lordships who had saddled Canada's East Coast with a fleet of ten- and nine-knot trawlers and drifters armed with 12- and 6-pounders rather than the handful of fast, 4-inch gunned destroyers that were needed to combat a U-cruiser. While the trawlers and drifters had a "scarecrow" value in protecting convoys, their presence perhaps discouraging a timid U-boat commander from closing in for an attack, the East Coast patrol was most desperately in need of vessels with an armament large enough to take on a surfaced U-boat's 5.9-inch guns. After inquiring of Ottawa if any of the RCN's present patrol craft could take a heavier armament, and whether any heavier guns or mountings were available in Canada if larger vessels were supplied from elsewhere, Grant was bluntly told that the answer was "no to both questions."[178] Despite his earlier dressing-down by the Admiralty for giving expression to the need for destroyers in the western Atlantic, the C-in-C reminded London at the end of August of the inadequacy of the patrol craft available in Canadian waters: "There is a great need ... for craft with a heavier armament than that at present possessed by the patrols, none of which have anything to compete with the large guns now carried by the enemy submarines.... The fitting of the present patrol craft with a heavier armament is, I fear, out of the question as the vessels cannot carry it," because of the light structure of their original construction as civilian vessels.[179]

---

175. Britannia to Naval Ottawa, 5 August 1918, ibid.

176. Navyard, Halifax to Naval Ottawa, 6 August 1918, ibid.

177. Story to Kingsmill, 5 August 1918, Patrols to Naval Ottawa, 6 August 1918, ibid.

178. Britannia to Naval Ottawa, 15 August 1918, Kingsmill to Britannia, 16 August 1918, ibid.

179. Grant to Admiralty, General Letter No. 7, 3 September 1918, UKNA, ADM 137/504; and Captain L.G. Preston, "Report by DMS Re Canadian Waters," 28 October 1918, UKNA, ADM 137/1619.

The Canadian naval minister, in London attending an imperial conference with the prime minister during August, was also being reminded by NSHQ of the importance of obtaining better-armed reinforcements for the East Coast patrols. Although Ballantyne had already informed Ottawa that the "Admiralty promises immediate action and will at once confer with Admiral Grant in Washington," he was urged to "press strongly [for] some assistance here against submarines, even for one boat with longer range [guns] than submarine."[180] No amount of pressure from the Canadian naval minister, however, was going to change the Admiralty's view that any diversion of anti-submarine forces to North American waters was a waste of resources. Before leaving England, Ballantyne met with the British assistant chief of naval staff, Vice-Admiral Sir Alexander L. Duff, to discuss the lack of effective anti-submarine vessels in the RCN. At the Canadian minister's urging, Duff cabled Grant in Washington "to use his best influence with the United States government to send a boat to Halifax."[181] It certainly would not have come as any surprise to NSHQ that, as usual, the Admiralty's "immediate action" for reinforcing Canadian patrols consisted entirely of directing Grant to seek further assistance from the US navy department.

The British C-in-C's efforts in Washington had, at least, been making some progress. By the beginning of August, the Americans were already supplying Canada with the air units and submarine chasers at Sydney and Halifax and further USN support was at hand. On the 10th, NSHQ was informed that the destroyer USS *Jouett*, together with her hunting group of eighteen submarine chasers, was being sent to Halifax after her recent, fruitless search for *U 156* in the Bay of Fundy area. The American destroyer and her subchasers would not arrive at Halifax to operate, "temporarily," in Canadian waters until two more weeks had passed, and then only after a further appeal from Grant after the U-boat had returned to strike off Nova Scotia for a second time.[182] On 16 August, the C-in-C cabled Ottawa with the information that the American navy department was despatching the USS *Yorktown* to Halifax "to reinforce your patrol services against powerful submarines." By any stretch, the *Yorktown*, an obsolete 1,700-ton gunboat launched in 1888, albeit one that mounted six 5-inch guns, was a disappointing response to Ottawa's appeal "even for one boat with longer range [guns] than submarine." In the absence of any meaningful British aid, Grant could only offer further assurances to NSHQ that the "United States will do everything possible and anticipate they can supply heavier guns for such of your patrol craft as you desire to rearm."[183]

NSHQ, of course, had already told Grant that their auxiliary patrol vessels, originally designed for civil rather than naval use, were incapable of mounting larger guns. The

180. Ballantyne to Acting Minister Naval, 14 August 1918, 1065–7-6, LAC, RG 24, vol. 4031.

181. Ballantyne to Admiral Sir Rosslyn Wemyss, First Sea Lord, 11 September 1918, 1017–10–1, pt. 1, LAC, RG 24, vol. 3831.

182. Navinet to Naval Ottawa, 10 August 1918, Britannia to Naval Ottawa, 14 August 1918, 1048–48–1, pt. 4, LAC, RG 24, vol. 3772; and Britannia to Naval Ottawa, 22 August 1918, Navyard, Halifax to Naval Ottawa, 25 August 1918, 1065–7-6, LAC, RG 24, vol. 4031; and Grant to Admiralty, General Letter No. 7, 3 September 1918, UKNA, ADM 137/504.

183. Britannia to Naval Ottawa, 16 August 1918, 1065–7-6, LAC, RG 24, vol. 4031.

relative abundance of trawlers in Canada and submarine chasers in the United States, however, did raise the possibility that American aid might take the form of exchanging twelve imperial trawlers for an equal number of USN subchasers. Having heard of the possibility of acquiring more of the American motorboats for Canadian service, Kingsmill immediately cabled Hose to ask his opinion on an exchange of vessels with the USN. The trawlers would have to be taken from the TRs already in commission on the East Coast rather than from the second batch being built in Canada to Admiralty order. The naval director planned to propose to the navy department that USN personnel would continue to operate the subchasers in Canadian service, while the RCN would offer to man the TRs for the USN "if they wish."[184] The captain of patrols responded immediately that the proposed exchange was " desirable." As Hose pointed out, although twelve trawlers would be sent south, the actual reduction in the number of TRs available to the mobile patrol in the Gulf of St Lawrence would only be seven since the five trawlers then serving in the patrol organization escorting slow convoys from Sydney "would not be needed" after being replaced by faster USN submarine chasers.[185]

After relaying word of the proposal to Hose, however, the naval director had to proceed through regular channels to explore the opportunity further. Although the imperial trawlers were manned by the RCN, they technically belonged to the Admiralty, and any change in their status would require British approval. On 18 August, therefore, Kingsmill cabled Grant to see if it would "be possible to exchange a division [of] twelve trawlers for some submarine chasers?"[186] In reply, the C-in-C asked if NSHQ was proposing a permanent exchange of vessels, with the RCN manning the subchasers and the USN providing the sailors for the twelve trawlers.[187] Although this was not the short-term, immediate exchange that Kingsmill had envisaged as a quick solution to Canada's patrol weakness, the director was willing to consider manning the subchasers with RCN sailors provided the US navy department was also agreeable, and "if Admiralty approve of permanent exchange of twelve TRs for [an] equal number of chasers."[188] Such is the friction of bureaucracy, however, that a formal exchange of vessels requiring both US navy department and Admiralty approval was bound to take weeks, if not several months, to come to fruition. With the submarine threat decreasing sharply after September, the exchange was not pressed forward as NSHQ turned to other solutions in developing its plans for the 1919 shipping season.

Nonetheless, the enthusiasm Canadian officers—Kingsmill, Hose, and Story—demonstrated for acquiring submarine chasers reflected their acute awareness of the weaknesses inherent in having a predominantly trawler force. As Story frankly told the C-in-C immediately after the sinking of *Luz Blanca*, trawlers were "too slow" to protect the HC

---

184. Naval Ottawa to Transports, Sydney, 16 August 1918, ibid.

185. Patrols to Naval Ottawa, 16 August 1918, ibid.

186. Naval Ottawa to Britannia, 18 August 1918, ibid.

187. Britannia to Naval Ottawa, 19 August 1918, ibid.

188. Naval Ottawa to Britannia, 21 August 1918, ibid.

convoys departing Halifax.[189] Their speed was barely sufficient to keep up with the slow HS convoys that assembled at Sydney and they were primarily used as a screening force when the merchant ships steamed out of harbour and commenced forming into columns. The USN submarine chasers, on the other hand, did have a sufficient margin of speed over their merchant ship charges to allow them to escort the Halifax and Sydney convoys to seaward but their short barrel 3-inch gun gave them little chance of surviving a gun-battle with a determined U-boat. Moreover, while there is no question that their speed advantage over trawlers made them more useful as escorts, their top speed of sixteen to seventeen knots gave them little margin over a surfaced submarine. Despite being equipped with hydrophone listening tubes and depth charges, providing a theoretical ability to attack a submerged enemy, none of the 129 American subchasers that served in European and Mediterranean waters during the war was ever able to make a successful attack. As highly prized as the American subchasers were viewed by a destitute RCN—and in contrast to the low regard in which they were held by most US and British officers—the boats needed to be grouped with a destroyer if they were to have any chance of effectively engaging enemy submarines. In Canadian waters, the subchasers' real value, like that of the trawlers, was to act as a "scarecrow" and dissuade timid U-cruiser commanders from closing with a convoy.[190]

Of course, an alternative means of defence was to close threatened ports and shift convoy assembly points away from areas where U-boats were operating, and in that regard NSHQ was informed by the Admiralty on 8 August that it had "been decided to divert all HC vessels to Montreal and organize HC convoy from Quebec. This diversion will take about three weeks.... General arrangements for Quebec convoy re: [their division into] east and west coast [convoys] and time of arrival of destroyer rendezvous to remain as for existing procedure."[191] Acting on London's decision, Vice-Admiral Grant "considered it desirable in view of the submarine activities for the ships for HC convoys from the St Lawrence to assemble at Sydney instead of Halifax and to proceed thence to meet the New York section at a sea rendezvous" until the diversion of incoming traffic to Montreal and Quebec was completed. To that end, he urged NSHQ that "it is of utmost importance convoys should not be delayed. Drifters and trawlers should suffice for HS convoys. Cannot you concentrate [the drifters and trawlers at] Sydney for departure of wing of HC 13 and dispose available forces to give maximum of possible protection."[192] On 10 August Ottawa was informed that the US navy department planned to provide a destroyer escort for the New York section of HC convoys and to have the destroyer remain with the convoy throughout its trans-Atlantic passage.[193]

In the event, Washington's plan to provide a destroyer escort for the HC convoys was

---

189. Navyard Halifax to Naval Ottawa, 6 August 1918, ibid.

190. Dwight R. Messimer, *Find and Destroy: Antisubmarine Warfare in World War I* (Annapolis 2001), 112–13, 125.

191. Admiralty to C-in-C, NA&WI, repeated to Naval Ottawa, 8 August 1918, 2035, 1048–18–1, pt. 1, LAC, RG 24, vol. 3772.

192. Britannia to Naval Ottawa, 8 August 1918, ibid.

193. Navinet to Naval Ottawa, 10 August 1918, ibid.

not entirely implemented. Until June 1918, ships for the HC convoys had been routed independently from American ports to Halifax. The number of US troops being carried on HC transports and the operations of *U 151* during late May and early June, however, convinced the authorities to group the ships of the American section into a local convoy every eight days under USN cruiser escort to Halifax. Although HX convoys from New York were given US destroyer escort overseas beginning with HX 45 on 16 August, only the first three of the American sections for the next four HC convoys, HC 13 to HC 16, had a destroyer join the USN cruiser in escorting them to the ocean rendezvous with the Canadian HC section, despite carrying a total of 63,570 US troops in the four American sections. In each case, HC 13 to HC 15, the USN cruiser returned to New York following the ocean rendezvous, while the destroyer continued to escort her charges across the Atlantic. HC 16 in early September was the last convoy to have an American section join at sea since by that time all incoming merchant ships destined for HC convoys had been diverted to the St Lawrence for loading.[194] With no destroyers of its own, of course, the RCN could only provide its local escort of submarine chasers, trawlers, and APVs to supplement the RN cruiser that accompanied subsequent HC convoys to Britain.

Besides closing Halifax as a convoy assembly port and shifting all Canadian convoy traffic to Quebec City and Sydney, the sinking of *Luz Blanca* also resulted in a rearrangement of command responsibilities between Hose and Story. In this instance, Hose's unwillingness to support a subordinate resulted in Kingsmill's decision to reduce the patrol force under his command. One week after the attack on the Canadian tanker, the subordinate in question, Commander P.F. Newcombe, the senior officer of patrols at Halifax, submitted his report on the actions of the port's patrol vessels during the action. In doing so, Newcombe explained some of the difficulties he had experienced on 5 August in communicating with his dispersed escort forces and despatching them to the scene of the attack: "On the afternoon of the attack, it was wet and misty. Visual signalling was impossible even in the Harbour, verbal messages often incorrectly delivered were a necessity. Vessels at Dartmouth, Marine and Fisheries wharf and the [Northwest] Arm were impossible to reach except by motor boat. My boat was in dockyard hands for repairs. A harbour drifter became the only means of communication. It was rather like using a cart horse for a general's galloper before an attack."[195]

Although the USS *Tingey* on the harbour inner patrol had been closest to the scene of *Luz Blanca*'s sinking, the Halifax authorities had been unable to reach the American torpedo boat by wireless for several hours, while fog prevented Newcombe from visually signalling the trawlers and drifters across the harbour at Dartmouth. In view of his communications problems, the senior officer of patrols promised to "submit a feasible scheme of communication which ... will meet all emergencies" and recommended "the urgent necessity of constant inspection and tests of all vessels by a wireless officer, so that

194. Grant to Admiralty, 28 December 1918, enclosure 12, SNO, New York to Grant, 6 December 1918, enclosure 7, UKNA, ADM 137/2658; and HC convoy reports, nd, UKNA, ADM 137/2657.

195. Commander P.F. Newcombe to Captain of Patrols, Sydney, 13 August 1918, 1065-7-1, LAC, RG 24, vol. 4031.

this extremely important department may be kept constantly efficient." Newcombe also took the opportunity to repeat his previous complaints concerning the amount of administrative work he was forced to undertake with only "one assistant paymaster, entirely new to the requirements and work of naval or sea service, and one stenographer" to assist him in his duties:

> I naturally consider that the whole of my available time is at the disposal of the department, but if I am to render useful and efficient service, I submit most strongly that I might be relieved of a mass of this clerical supervision as with it, though trying my utmost, I cannot be responsible to you at this most important juncture, for the fighting efficiency of the officers and men under my command and the practical observance of your orders, issued to meet active service conditions.
>
> I am not at the moment in a position to take hold and get real results from the Halifax patrols on an emergency arising.... Everything points to far bigger efforts yet being required from this office.
>
> In short, I would ask for the opportunity to try and turn a paper organization into a practical one of as nearly as possible equal efficiency.[196]

Although the sinking of *Luz Blanca* took place four years and a day after the declaration of war, it was the first time that an enemy warship had ventured into Canadian waters. Despite it being the RCN's first real operational experience, and aside from the obvious communication problems Newcombe experienced in rounding up his available patrol forces, he managed to deploy his vessels about as well and as quickly as could reasonably have been expected under the circumstances. Contrary to the negative impression of naval incompetence suggested by some historians that "almost everything that could go wrong did go wrong,"[197] by 1700 hours the senior officer of patrols had despatched a torpedo boat, a subchaser, a Battle-class trawler, and the three escort divisions of trawlers and drifters to comb the area of the attack. The escort vessels themselves, once they received word of the emergency, had responded without hesitation even though none of the mixed bag of trawlers, drifters, subchasers or decrepit torpedo boats had any realistic chance of successfully engaging a U-boat should they make contact. Moreover, by flooding the scene of the attack with over a dozen patrol vessels that first night, the senior officer of patrols made it unlikely that *U 156* would attempt to move closer to the Halifax approaches— indeed, the U-boat quickly retraced her path to the south—unless it was more boldly handled than the U-cruisers sent to operate in North American waters were to prove.

The naval defences of the port, moreover, were focused on and organized primarily for convoy protection, not responding to a distress signal from a solitary tanker, and it was from the former task that the escorts were returning when the emergency call was received. It could not be said, therefore, that they had in any way been misemployed even though

---

196. Ibid.

197. Hadley and Sarty, *Tin-pots and Pirate Ships*, 256.

the presence of a German submarine in Canadian waters was suspected. On the other hand, although one of Newcombe's main recommendations for improvement of the Halifax defences was "the great necessity for vessels of speed to be in reserve and always ready," the suggestion itself, while applicable in ideal circumstances, was quite impractical. Even if the Admiralty had lived up to its January commitment and supplied the twelve destroyers and fast escorts deemed necessary, such a force would also have been used almost exclusively as convoy escorts and would, therefore, have been similarly in the process of returning from HC 12 when the emergency call came in. Furthermore, had enough vessels been available to allow for a secondary force of destroyers or fast trawlers to be held in Halifax at short notice to steam, it is unlikely that the warships could have reached the vicinity of the attack in time to alter the outcome. From the time that word of the attack was received in Halifax at 1345 hours until the tanker was abandoned shortly after 1500, any supporting warship would have had only seventy-five minutes to put to sea and cover the more than thirty miles from the dockyard to the scene of the sinking. Having already advised the captain of *Luz Blanca* not to proceed to sea until after dark to evade the U-cruiser that was known to be operating off southern Nova Scotia, the Halifax naval authorities had done all they could to protect the ship. Vessels proceeding independently were, after all, always at the most risk of attack, even in British home waters where the Royal Navy had concentrated a vast auxiliary fleet and almost all the Allies' destroyer strength.

Despite Newcombe's creditable performance in rounding up and despatching sufficient vessels to dissuade the U-boat from moving closer to Halifax, Hose—undoubtedly still smarting from Kingsmill's rebuke for his disposition of the APVs—exhibited little sympathy for his overworked subordinate when he forwarded his report to NSHQ on 15 August. The captain of patrols understandably endorsed Newcombe's recommendation that "vessels of speed to be in reserve and always ready" at Halifax to respond to an emergency, but otherwise did not offer any support or encouragement for his subordinate's efforts. Although a general shortage of trained naval officers capable of handling staff work made Newcombe's grievance about a lack of administrative personnel a common one throughout the East Coast navy, Hose informed NSHQ that "this is the last of a series of complaints, mostly written in personal letters, of the amount of work which he is called upon to carry out and the inadequacy of the staff at his disposal. I am of opinion that this officer is really lacking in the organizing ability necessary for the position he holds and, while zealous and energetic, lacks the ability to cope with varied and numerous responsibilities." Hose's rather uncharitable assessment is particularly surprising given the fact that the captain of patrols had himself recently asked for two weeks leave to recover from exhaustion just as *U 156* was making her way into Canadian waters. Hose proposed to NSHQ that Newcombe's responsibilities be reduced to the administrative command of the *Guelph* depot, while Commander J.T. Shenton (who, like Hose himself, had been brought east from Esquimalt and was now serving as Story's flag commander) be appointed as Newcombe's replacement as senior officer of escorts at Halifax. Hose made it clear in his report, however, that he expected Shenton to serve under the command of the captain of patrols and report directly to him.[198]

What the captain of patrols wanted and what Kingsmill was willing to agree to, however, proved to be two different things. With two separate naval commands functioning at Halifax, the seaward patrols organization under Hose and the port defence organization under Story, both of whom reported directly to the naval director, Kingsmill had some flexibility in rearranging the relative responsibilities of his two senior officers on the East Coast. Whether concerned about the state of Hose's health or whether he lacked confidence in the captain of patrol's judgment in view of his earlier mishandling of the APVs, the naval director opted to implement a proposal put forward by Admiral Story that his command be extended to include control of the seaward patrol forces based at Halifax. With the shift of HC convoy assembly to the St Lawrence, Kingsmill also knew that Hose already had his hands full controlling the Sydney patrol forces and would not have wanted him distracted by his responsibility for Nova Scotia's East Coast as well. Under the admiral superintendent's plan, Shenton would still replace Newcombe as senior officer of escorts at Halifax but would report directly to himself and only "forward to the captain of patrols the duplicates of all reports received from patrol officers." Shenton would "be responsible that the patrol and minesweeping vessels are detailed for their respective duties, and maintained thereon, in accordance with the approved programme. In case of emergency he is to detail the necessary vessels to meet the same. He is to coordinate the working of the patrol and air service.... He is to submit to the admiral superintendent all arrangements made, reports received, and draw up reports of operations." For his part, as the commanding officer of *Guelph*, Newcombe would continue to be "responsible to the captain of patrols for the up-keep, training and discipline of the patrol vessels [and their personnel] on his books. He is to report to the admiral superintendent, through the flag commander, the names of the vessels detailed for duty at Halifax by the captain of patrols."[199]

Although Story assured the naval director that "the captain of patrols concurs in these orders," Kingsmill's approval of the change the following week significantly reduced the scope of Hose's command.[200] As of 27 August, Commander Shenton became the head of all patrols at Halifax under the command of the admiral superintendent. The flag commander submitted all patrol reports directly to Story, and, although copies of reports were passed to Hose at Sydney, Shenton was in no way responsible to the captain of patrols for his actions. It does not appear that Hose immediately appreciated the extent to which he had been eliminated from the Halifax patrol organization, but any doubts he may have had were forcefully removed by the admiral superintendent in mid-October. Following a

---

198. Hose to The Secretary, Department of the Naval Service, 15 August 1918, 1065-7-1, LAC, RG 24, vol. 4031.

199. Admiral Superintendent to Kingsmill, 20 August 1918, and attached "Halifax Patrol Duties of Officers," nd, ibid.

200. Admiral Superintendent to Kingsmill, 20 August 1918, Kingsmill to Navyard, Halifax, 27 August 1918, ibid.

report by an American merchant ship that she had sighted a submarine periscope off Halifax on the 17th, the captain of patrols requested Shenton to advise what action had been taken by the Halifax patrols organization in response, the senior officer of patrols refused to do so, however, informing Hose that the "admiral superintendent instructs me to reply that he is in charge of naval defences at Halifax."[201]

An outraged Hose immediately complained to NSHQ, arguing that "as captain of patrols, it is entirely in order for me to call on the senior officer of patrols, Halifax, for information as to what action is being taken by patrol vessels based on Halifax in the event of suspected enemy craft being sighted off the Nova Scotia coast. The admiral superintendent's action in not permitting the senior officer of patrols to forward me this information is not understood. I am at the present moment entirely ignorant of what was done by any patrol vessels inside or outside the harbour of Halifax on this occasion."[202] Hose would not receive any satisfaction from Ottawa, however. Despite Story's churlish behaviour in denying that Hose had any right to be kept informed, Kingsmill, who was apparently content with Hose's reduced responsibilities, minuted "no action required" on the complaint.[203] The department simply referred the captain of patrols to previous memoranda issued on the relationship between himself and the cantankerous admiral superintendent. Whatever he may have thought, from mid-August until the end of the war Hose served only as captain of the Gulf of St Lawrence patrols and was no longer responsible for the RCN's entire East Coast patrol force. Even with a reduced command—though one of increased importance following the shift of all trans-Atlantic convoy traffic to the St Lawrence—Hose's dispositions and escort arrangements were carried out under Kingsmill's close supervision until the last of the U-cruisers left North American waters later that autumn.

The Admiralty's decision to use Quebec as the assembly port for HC convoys should, in theory, also have allowed the RCN to shift many of its Halifax vessels to Cape Breton, and on 19 August Vice-Admiral Grant cabled NSHQ to ask that they reconsider a redistribution of patrol forces to the Gulf. As the C-in-C pointed out, once the shift was carried out "Halifax [would] then [be] practically unused and would suggest that temporary transference to St Lawrence of large proportion of minesweepers, et cetera, and perhaps Sydney could spare some, especially after introduction of air patrol."[204] Grant's interest in freeing up minesweepers related to an earlier request he had made that NSHQ send two trawlers to St John's to provide the Newfoundland port with a limited minesweeping capability. The Sydney minesweepers were, in turn, to be replaced by a pair taken from Halifax.[205] Kingsmill acted upon Grant's request on the same day it was received. The

201. Patrols, Halifax to Transports, Sydney, 19 October 1918, 1062–13–2, pt. 6, LAC, RG 24, vol. 4021.

202. Captain of Patrols, Sydney to NSHQ, 21 October 1918, ibid.

203. Kingsmill minute, nd, ibid.

204. Washington [Grant] to Naval Ottawa, 18 August 1918, 159, 1048–48–1, pt. 1, LAC, RG 24, vol. 3772.

205. C-in-C to Naval Ottawa, 10 August 1918, 117, Naval Ottawa to Transports, Sydney, 11 August 1918, 93, 1065–7–6, LAC, RG 24, vol. 4031.

naval director instructed Story to confer with Hose and forward his proposals as to what forces should be kept at the Nova Scotian capital and what forces could be reassigned to Sydney, pointing out that if the shift of HS convoys to Quebec was carried through, "every ship that can possibly be spared will be needed in the St Lawrence"[206]

Nonetheless, the admiral superintendent's definition of "every ship that can possibly be spared" proved somewhat more constrained than the circumstances would appear to have warranted. Despite the fact that Halifax was no longer part of the trans-Atlantic convoy system—although it remained an important port for coastal convoys and for ship repairs at the dockyard—Story proposed keeping the division of three US submarine chasers, the auxiliary patrol vessels *Grilse* and *Stadacona*, the Battle-class trawlers *St Eloi* and *Vimy*, two of the *PV* trawlers, three escort divisions of one trawler and two drifters each, and an additional flotilla of three drifters. The admiral superintendent's parsimonious attitude would only release the APVs *Margaret* and *Canada*, an escort division of one trawler and two drifters and a pair of minesweepers to join Hose's Gulf of St Lawrence forces at Sydney.[207] Story's caution is all the more curious given that the destroyer USS *Jouett* and her hunting group of eighteen submarine chasers was expected at Halifax shortly, arriving at the port a mere four days after the admiral superintendent's reply.[208]

As the fallout from the sinking of *Luz Blanca* was percolating its way through the naval chain of command, the submarine that had caused all the trouble in the first place had reversed course and made her way south across the Gulf of Maine. On 8 August *U 156* stopped and sank the Swedish merchant ship *Sydland* of 3,031 tons some 160 kilometres south of Cape Sable and 230 kilometres due east of Cape Cod. Continuing southward, the U-boat torpedoed and sank the British merchantman *Pennistone* of 4,139 tons, three days later, 110 kilometres southeast of Cape Cod. *Pennistone* had been part of an eighteen-ship convoy that departed New York on 9 August but, unable to keep up with a nine-knot pace, she had fallen well behind the other vessels by the time she was torpedoed. The precise movements of *U 156* are unknown for the next five days as the submarine remained out of sight. According to *Pennistone*'s captain, as he was held prisoner on board the U-boat with the rest of his crew, *U 156* "ran on the surface all the time and they did not submerge from Sunday [11 August] till Thursday afternoon. We just ran along slowly, and two or three nights we just lay to. We never sighted anything from Sunday till Thursday afternoon. We were probably somewhere around the entrance of New York. After that we started north, then south again. We did not sight land at all."[209] On 16 August the submarine attacked the British merchant ship *Lackawanna* with both torpedoes and gunfire some 300 kilometres east-southeast of Cape Cod but the vessel managed to escape after successfully returning fire and forcing the U-boat to break off action. Moving due north toward Canadian waters the following day, *U 156* stopped and sank the Norwegian steamer *San*

206. Naval Ottawa to Navyard, Halifax, 19 August 1918, 1048–48–1, pt. 1, LAC, RG 24, vol. 3772.

207. Admiral Superintendent to Kingsmill, 20 August 1918, ibid.

208. Navyard, Halifax to Naval Ottawa, 25 August 1918, 1065–7–6, LAC, RG 24, vol. 4031.

209. Captain David Evans of SS *Pennistone* quoted in US Navy Department, *German Submarine Activities*, 64.

Jose of 1,586 tons, running in ballast from Bergen, Norway to New York, some 120 kilometres south-southeast of Cape Sable. *San Jose*'s crew was joined in her lifeboats by the men captured from *Pennistone* and told to make for the Nova Scotian coast.[210]

Much of the intelligence picture about a U-boat's movements was built up from information obtained by naval officers debriefing the crews of ships attacked or sunk by enemy raiders, even though that information was usually at least several days old by the time the merchant seamen had reached shore and could be questioned. Further reports on *U 156*, for instance, had been forwarded to NSHQ on 10 August by the RCN's naval transport officer in St John, Lieutenant Mulcahy, intelligence the officer had gleaned from debriefing one of *Dornfontein*'s crewmen who spoke fluent German. Among the many pieces of information the Canadian sailor had picked up on 2 August in conversation with the submarine's crew—some false and most of it exaggerated—was that their vessel had a speed of eighteen knots on the surface and twelve knots submerged, could dive in twenty-seven seconds and reach a depth of 150 feet. The Germans also claimed to have thirty-six torpedoes on board, stating that they "would be operating here for ten months more" before returning to Germany. They also suggested that there were six other submarines operating on the North American coast.[211]

The submariners' assertion that others would soon be joining them for a U-boat offensive on this side of the Atlantic was overstated (there were, in fact, only three submarines, including *U 156*, operating in North American waters in August), but it certainly appeared to be borne out by the number of attacks and sinkings taking place to the south. On 26 July, *U 140* made her presence known by attacking two large British merchantmen with gunfire some 500 kilometres south of Halifax. Although both vessels were able to escape, the German submarine sank the Portuguese bark *Porto*, of 1,079 tons, the following day. The U-boat's next victim was the Japanese steamship *Tokuyama Maru*, of 7,029 tons, torpedoed and sunk 260 kilometres southeast of New York on 1 August. Three days later, *U 140* struck again, sinking the American tanker *O.B. Jennings*, of 10,289 tons, after a two-hour gun battle off the entrance to Chesapeake Bay. Moving south to operate off Cape Hatteras, North Carolina, the U-boat sank two vessels totalling 4,084 tons and the Diamond Shoals Lightship over the course of the next two days. On 10 August *U 140* was attacking the Brazilian steamship *Uberaba* when she was intercepted and engaged by the destroyer USS *Stringham*, one of the new "flushdeck" ships that had just been completed in July; although the American destroyer dropped fifteen depth charges, the submarine escaped. After being attacked by *Stringham*, the U-boat moved further out to sea where she engaged in an ineffective gun-battle with a passing USN transport, USS *Pastores*, on the 13th. Remaining out of sight for the next week as she moved north into the New York shipping lanes on her return passage to Germany, *U 140* sank the British merchantman *Diomed*, 7,523 tons, in a surface action 220 kilometres south of Cape Sable and almost due east of New York. *Diomed* had departed Liverpool in an eight-ship convoy, escorted by eight destroyers to 15 degrees west where, in keeping with Admiralty

210. US Navy Department, *German Submarine Activities*, 64–65.

211. Naval Transport Officer, St John to Secretary, Department of the Naval Service, Ottawa, 9 August 1918, 1062–13–2, pt. 4, LAC, RG 24, vol. 4021.

policy and despite the presence of U-boats operating off North America, the convoy dispersed onto routes prescribed in ships' sailing instructions. Remaining in the New York trans-Atlantic lanes on her return voyage, *U 140* made two further unsuccessful attacks on independently routed merchant ships, one heading for New York and the other to Halifax.[212]

A third U-boat, *U 117*, departed Germany earlier in July and on the 26th made an unsuccessful attack on a British merchantman, *Baron Napier*, in mid-Atlantic. The German raider made her presence felt with a vengeance on 10 August when she sank nine American fishing schooners, many based in Gloucester, Massachusetts, in a single day's action off the Georges Bank in the Gulf of Maine. With New England fishing communities alarmed by the losses, the assistant state administrator for Massachusetts, at the prompting of the mayor of Gloucester, reported the furor to Washington and asked the Navy Department for additional protection for the fishing fleet. Since German submariners questioned the fishermen about the attitude of the American public to the war, the Navy Department suspected that the attack on the fishing fleet was evidence of a "German plan of breaking the morale of the American people," and an attempt to have the public "demand for the recall of the destroyer division" from European waters. [213] Although they were "soft" targets easily stopped and sunk, the destruction of small, unarmed fishing schooners had a negligible economic impact on the Allied war effort, as compared to an attack on a convoy of merchant ships laden with war supplies for Europe, leaving influencing North American public opinion against the war as the only plausible motivation for the U-cruisers' campaign. *U 117* returned to more conventional targets as she made her way into the approaches immediately south of New York two days later, torpedoing and sinking the Norwegian *Sommerstadt*, 3,875 tons, on the 12th, and the American *Frederick R. Kellogg*, 7,127 tons, on the 13th. Working her way toward Cape Hatteras, where *U 140* was also operating, *U 117* sank three more merchant ships in the next four days.[214]

The absence of U-boats in Canadian waters for a two-week period in mid-August gave the naval authorities a badly needed breathing space free of enemy interference in which to shift the HC convoy assembly port to the St Lawrence. One of the first obstacles that needed to be cleared was the opposition of the US Army's chief of staff, General Peyton C. March, to the embarkation of American troops for HC convoys at Montreal rather than, as previously, at New York. As Grant explained to London, the British admiral had expected that "some [American] opposition to the transference to Canada was inevitable," but "did not anticipate such as has arisen. As to the motives which prompt it ... I fancy that an excuse, founded on our action, for diminishing the large number of [US] troops now sent monthly will [be made].... Admiral Benson, at my request, personally represented the expediency of the change in support of my arguments but with no result." Washington's attitude was not improved by the fact that the Admiralty had once again made a decision that greatly affected North America without asking for input from the other side of the

---

212. US Navy Department, *German Submarine Activities*, 70–82; and F.T. Jane, ed., *Jane's Fighting Ships 1919* (London 1919), 210.

213. US Navy Department, *German Submarine Activities*, 82–83, 89.

214. Ibid, 91–95.

Atlantic. In yet another instance of confusion at the Admiralty, London interpreted a signal from Washington in which the C-in-C had "merely outlined general policy to which I thought US would agree," a telegram that had "specifically stated I had consulted neither US nor Canada," as confirmation that Britain was free to shift the HC convoys to the St Lawrence without further reference to Ottawa or Washington. According to the Admiralty, they had "assumed that you [Grant] had consulted the [US and Canadian] authorities before sending your wire."[215] While the C-in-C regretted "that the decision should have been made and ships diverted without previously consulting United States or Canada," he was sufficiently conscious of London's earlier displeasure with his request for greater defences on the North American side of the Atlantic that he made a point of assuring his superiors that he had "endeavoured that this fact [of British miscommunication] should not be apparent and can only say that, in all my conversations [with the Americans] on the subject, no hint was given of a grievance in this respect."[216]

In any event, Grant was very doubtful that the US Army would agree to send large numbers of troops overseas in HC convoys organized at Quebec and thought it as well that the shift to the St Lawrence was presented to Washington officials "as a more or less accomplished fact." Far from apologizing for the lack of advance warning, the C-in-C felt that such actions "are not appreciated and are liable to misconstruction in this country" where the Americans were becoming increasingly aware of their growing military might and asserting a greater independence from British direction.[217] Indicative of the US Army's resistance to sending its troops to Europe through Canada, only 17,894 American soldiers embarked for overseas from Canadian ports in convoys HC 13 to HC 24. This compares to the 63,570 US troops carried on the four New York sections of convoys HC 13 to HC 16 in August and early September, and the 132,194 US soldiers taken overseas on the first twelve HC convoys between 11 May and 4 August 1918. New York continued to serve as the US Army's main port of embarkation for France, with 214,338 American troops travelling to

---

215. Admiralty to C-in-C, NA&WI, 13 August 1918, C-in-C, NA&WI to Admiralty, 14 August 1918, UKNA, ADM 137/903.

216. Grant to Admiralty, General Letter No. 7, 3 September 1918, UKNA, ADM 137/504. Although Hadley and Sarty in *Tin-pots and Pirate Ships*, 281 refer to "the Canadian staff's long-standing reluctance to dispatch fully loaded, high-value ships through the Gulf," there was, in fact, no such reluctance on the part of either NSHQ or the director of overseas transport. As discussed earlier, the intersection of Canada's rail lines at Montreal made that city the predominant port for all of eastern Canada, and the port from which the over-whelming majority of Canada's war supplies were shipped overseas. During the seven-month summer season, most Canadian shipping transited through the St Lawrence, a fact that could not be altered whether the convoy assembly port was at Quebec, Sydney, or Halifax. As we have seen, Harris strongly objected to the HX convoys being assembled at New York in the spring of 1918 because it meant diverting the large ocean liners away from Montreal. The DOT also repeatedly sought to have as much American traffic as possible, particularly from the US Midwest, transshipped through Montreal so as to maximize as much as possible the port's often underutilized capacity. Both Grant and Kingsmill were also well aware of the great strategic advantage the St Lawrence provided in offering an alternate access route to the Atlantic using the Strait of Belle Isle. Any suggestion that anyone in Ottawa was at all reluctant to use the port of Montreal to the fullest extent possible is incorrect and confuses a desire to protect Canada's most important shipping lane with a non-existent reluctance to use it.

217. Grant to Admiralty, General Letter No. 7, 3 September 1918, UKNA, ADM 137/504.

Europe on HX convoys between August and November 1918.[218] Whether or not the Americans chose to make use of the HC convoys to move troops overseas, Grant was in no doubt of the wisdom of the shift to the St Lawrence.

> The disadvantages of Halifax as an assembly port were obviously those of coaling facilities and the dangerous approach in the fogs so often prevailing....
>
> The transferring of the HC convoys from Halifax to Quebec, although leading to difficulties with the United States Army authorities regarding the embarkation of their troops, was, in my opinion, an eminently wise decision, and I have no doubt that Quebec, with its two approaches through Cabot Straits or Belle Isle Straits, is the best possible assembly port in Canada during the months when navigation in the Saint Lawrence [*sic*] remains open.
>
> The organization of the convoy office at Quebec was most efficiently and expeditiously carried out, and the transfer of the HC convoys to that port effected in a remarkable smooth manner.[219]

Much of the initial work at Quebec was carried out by the RCN's naval transport officer at the port, Commander G.O.R. Eliott, after he was "appointed port convoy officer for port of Quebec, under the direction of Rear-Admiral Chambers, RN, senior officer of escorts, who came up from Halifax for a short while to inaugurate the convoys sailings from Quebec." Eliott, who was already responsible for getting the Admiralty trawlers and drifters into commission as they arrived from the inland shipyards, quickly found that the convoy work "would require a very much larger staff to carry on the combined duties" than his small staff of only two writers and one messenger.[220] Despite the small size of the Canadian staff at Quebec available to organize the first HC convoys, Rear-Admiral Chambers was initially reluctant to transfer his offices from Halifax. In his report to Grant on 22 August, the British convoy officer preferred simply to send an assistant to Quebec and suggested "that all sailing orders should be made out at Halifax and I could keep in touch with the officer at Quebec without much difficulty.... Even assuming that the convoys continued to run from Quebec until the close of the season, the period of working from that port would be only about two months and at the expiration of that period they are bound to revert to Halifax, as will also the Sydney slow convoys."[221] It was not until 24 August that Chambers received definite instructions from Grant to proceed to Quebec to oversee setting up the convoy office there.[222]

---

218. Grant to Admiralty, 28 December 1918, UKNA, ADM 137/2658.

219. Ibid., enclosure 3.

220. Commander G.O.R. Eliott, "History of Work Carried Out At Quebec From Naval Transport Office," 1 December 1918, 1049–2–40, LAC, RG 24, vol. 3981.

221. Chambers to C-in-C, NA&WI, 22 August 1918, UKNA, ADM 137/1620.

222. Chambers to C-in-C, NA&WI, 2 September 1918, ibid; and Grant to Admiralty, 28 December 1918, Enclosure 21, Port Convoy Officer and Senior Officer of Escorts, Halifax to C-in-C, NA&WI, 2 December 1918, UKNA, ADM 137/2658.

Arriving on 31 August with some of his Halifax personnel, Chambers added his officers to Eliott's own staff, putting together a convoy organization to administer the HC sailings. Although Chambers reported directly to the Admiralty through the C-in-C, it was the RCN who supplied most of his convoy personnel. As he explained to Grant soon after arriving at Quebec, the British admiral had "asked Ottawa for a coding staff and for a routing officer but there does not seem to be any undue haste on their part to furnish these essentials. The routing officer is particularly important as this work cannot be very well doubled with any other duty.... The routing at Sydney and Halifax has always been carried out by Canadian officers under my personal supervision and has been very satisfactorily performed by Lieutenant Cane [sic, J.C. Caine], RNCVR, Commander Unwin, RNR [a retired officer serving in the RCN], and Lieutenant Dart, RNCVR. I have asked Ottawa that the first named officer, now in Montreal, may be sent here at least temporarily for routing duties."[223] Having received only a small number of RN staff officers from the Admiralty, Chambers seems not to have appreciated the extent to which the RCN was experiencing a similar shortage of trained officers to carry out the many administration tasks associated with both the convoy system and the East Coast patrols. Nonetheless, the RCN supplied ten of the fourteen naval personnel at the Quebec office, including Commander Eliott, and three of the four civilian staff.[224]

After a mere two weeks at Quebec, Chambers was sufficiently satisfied that "everything was running smoothly" for him to return to Halifax, which—in an unintended echo of the ill-fated Commodore Coke—he found "more central and more in touch with naval matters generally," even though the convoy work he was in charge of was being performed at Sydney and Quebec, while Halifax was, in Grant's opinion, "then practically unused." Leaving Eliott and his predominately Canadian staff to run the HC convoys in his absence, Chambers reported that "the work of dispatching the convoys was well and efficiently performed by him [i.e., Eliott], until the discontinuance of the convoy system."[225] While the Canadian sections of convoys HC 13, HC 14, and HC 15 had been organized at Sydney, departing that port on 14, 21, and 29 August respectively, the Quebec convoy organization was able to despatch its ten-ship section on 4 September to rendezvous with the eleven ships of the New York section 200 kilometres east of Cape Race on 9 September. The fifteen ships of convoy HC 17, the first of the series to be organized and despatched entirely from Quebec, left port on 13 September for a passage through the Straits of Belle Isle.[226]

The Canadian naval staff at Halifax, meanwhile, was not entirely free of convoy duties. As submarine activity increased during the summer, the RCN organized into small coastal

223. Chambers to C-in-C, NA&WI, 2 September 1918, UKNA, ADM 137/1620.

224. Commander G.O.R. Eliott, "History of Work Carried Out At Quebec From Naval Transport Office," 1 December 1918, 1049–2-40, LAC, RG 24, vol. 3981.

225. Grant to Admiralty, 28 December 1918, Enclosure 21, Port Convoy Officer and Senior Officer of Escorts, Halifax to C-in-C, NA&WI, 2 December 1918, UKNA, ADM 137/2658; Washington [Grant] to Naval Ottawa, 18 August 1918, 159, 1048–48–1, pt. 1, LAC, RG 24, vol. 3772; and Commander G.O.R. Eliott, "History of Work Carried Out At Quebec From Naval Transport Office," 1 December 1918, 1049–2-40, LAC, RG 24, vol. 3981.

226. HC Convoy reports, nd, HC 17, UKNA, ADM 137/2657.

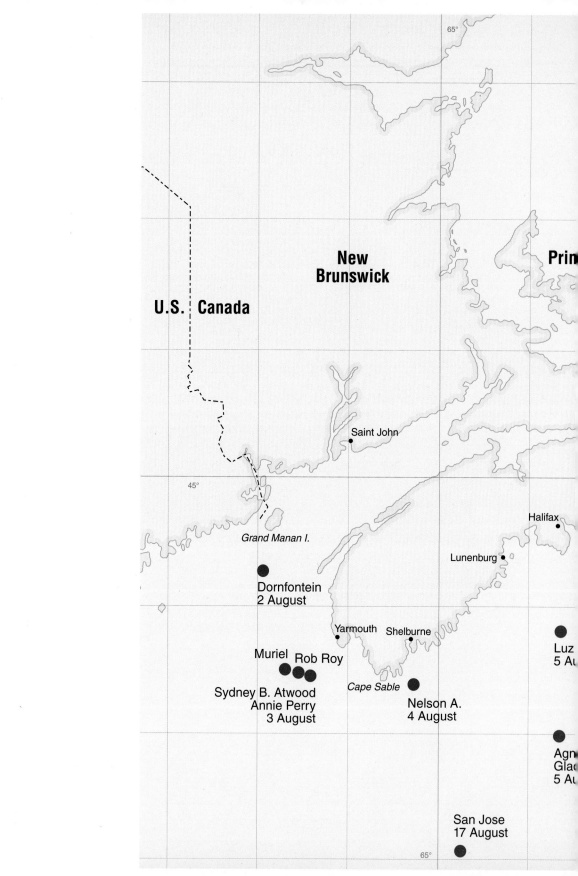

65°

New
Brunswick

Pri

U.S. **Canada**

Saint John
●

45°

Halifax
●

Grand Manan I.

Lunenburg ●

●
Dornfontein
2 August

Yarmouth   Shelburne
●   ●

●
Luz
5 Au

Muriel   Rob Roy
● ● ●

Sydney B. Atwood
Annie Perry
3 August

Cape Sable

●
Nelson A.
4 August

●
Agn
Glad
5 Au

San Jose
17 August
●

65°

convoys all the coastwise shipping that called at Halifax, including those vessels proceeding across the Gulf of Maine to US ports. The Canadian naval staff office aboard *Niobe* organized the convoys and provided the ships with their route instructions. The Canadian coastal convoy system remained in place until German submarine operations ceased in late October, when it was concluded that coastal shipping from the Gulf of St Lawrence destined for the Bay of Fundy or the Gulf of Maine could proceed safely without calling at Halifax. However, ships would be "warned to put into port if war warnings indicate danger. Much delay is being caused at present [waiting for a convoy] without corresponding increase of safety to shipping. In most instances ships are sent on from here alone for lack of convoying [escort] vessels."[227]

Although the nearest of the three U-cruisers operating off the North American coast spent the middle days of August cruising east of Cape Cod—and some 200 kilometres south of Cape Sable—the knowledge that enemy submarines were loose in the western Atlantic and had sunk a Canadian tanker in the approaches to Halifax prompted an outbreak of "periscopitis" among both the RCN and USN sailors operating in Canadian waters. On 9 August NSHQ received word that the superintendent on Sable Island had spotted an enemy submarine five miles to the south, while the USS *Tingey*, on the Halifax inner patrol, reported an "enemy submarine operating ten miles south south-east of Chebucto Head."[228] On the 14th, the captain of patrols cabled Ottawa with news that HMCS *Lady Evelyn* had dropped depth charges and called in all available trawlers after spotting a periscope shortly after 2300 hours on the 13th. Hose quickly instructed "*Lady Evelyn* and trawlers to patrol on track of outgoing HC convoy until dark Wednesday evening of 14th August."[229] A dubious headquarters asked for a "most careful inquiry" to be made of the *Lady Evelyn*'s CO and was told that the "commanding officer [was] convinced that it was [a] periscope he sighted forty feet off. G depth charge [a small depth charge containing only thirty-five pounds of Amatol explosive adopted for dropping by hand] was dropped instead of D star [normally used by slower vessels such as trawlers, it was a smaller version of the D depth charge] owing to proximity of trawler astern in the fog. Commanding officer states submarine appeared just on the surface shortly after and thinks he scored one hit each with 4-inch and 12-pounder. No sign of oil or other evidence of successful attack."[230]

False sightings were also made by the USN subchasers assigned to the departing convoy, HC 13, the first of the HC series to be despatched from Sydney. The convoy, five merchant ships escorted by HMS *Victoria*, carrying 2,599 Canadian and 1,958 American troops to Europe, departed Sydney on the morning of 14 August for an ocean rendezvous with the

227. Navinet Halifax to Naval Ottawa, 21 October 1918, Naval Ottawa to Navinet Halifax, 22 October 1918, 1048–48–1, pt. 1, LAC, RG 24, vol. 3772; and Canadian Naval Staff Officer to Admiral Superintendent, Halifax, 13 December 1918, 1049–2–40, LAC, RG 24, vol. 3981.

228. J.P. Gibbs to acting Prime Minister, 9 August 1918, 1062–13–2, pt. 4, LAC, RG 24, vol. 4021.

229. Navinet to Naval Ottawa, 14 August 1918, Patrols, Sydney to Naval Ottawa, 14 August 1918, ibid.

230. Patrols, Sydney to Naval Ottawa, 15 August 1918, ibid.

seven-ship New York section to the east of Newfoundland. The three subchasers, *Chaser 51*, *Chaser 183*, and *Chaser 242*, departed Sydney at 0900 hours, one hour ahead of the convoy they were escorting and proceeded out to sea for four miles, where they put their long distance listening tubes into the water until the convoy arrived. After hauling them in, the three subchasers formed up ahead and on either beam of the leading merchant ship. After fifteen miles, however, "*Chaser 51* saw periscope of submarine on his port beam about two hundred yards distance and gave chase immediately."[231] According to the subchaser's commanding officer, Ensign Hayllar:

> At 1:16 pm lookout reported object resembling periscope on port bow about 200 yards distant. While trying to determine positively that object was a periscope it disappeared. We immediately altered course and ran over spot where last seen and stopped to put down listening tubes. Listener reported submarine moving very fast bearing dead ahead. We followed for 15 minutes and listened again. Listener reported submarine one point on starboard bow. At 1:20 general quarters sounded, at 2:20 secure. At intervals of 15 minutes tube was lowered each time listener reporting submarine. At 1:35 listener reported that submarine was sending message by oscillator. Submarine bore to right and passed astern of convoy which had increased speed. At 3:20 Listener reported submarine growing fainter and 3:35 lost sound. We stayed in vicinity until 4:20 listening frequently then followed convoy.[232]

After rejoining their charges following the fruitless search for a non-existent U-boat, the three chasers resumed their positions ahead and abeam of the convoy. As reported by the chaser division's commander, Ensign William Hauck, the subchasers: "zigzagged [the] entire time of escort. Chasers would stop, put down hydrophones and listen in at frequent intervals. Division left convoy at 10 pm August 14th, having authority to return from captain of ocean escort, arriving back at wharf 12:55 pm August 15th. Convoy escorted for distance of 103 miles."[233] In forwarding the USN report to Ottawa, Hose

> regretted that Mr Hayllar stopped to examine the object supposed to be a periscope instead of altering course immediately for it and dropping depth charges. This incident was reported to me at midday the following day on return of the chaser division from their escort duty and I dispatched them immediately for a listening search. The chaser division returned from this search at 11.30 pm having heard nothing. It is submitted that there is considerable reason to doubt the presence of a submarine on the 14th; first,

---

231. Ensign William Hauck, Division Commander, US Submarine Chasers, Division 2 to Senior Officer of Patrols, Sydney, 16 August 1918, "Report of Commanding Officer of Chaser Escort," ibid.

232. Commanding Officer of Chaser 51 to Captain of Patrols, 16 August 1918, ibid.

233. Ensign William Hauck, Division Commander, US Submarine Chasers, Division 2 to Senior Officer of Patrols, Sydney, 16 August 1918, "Report of Commanding Officer of Chaser Escort," ibid.

on account of its having taken no offensive action, second, because neither of the other chasers in the division heard any submarine though all had their tubes down at frequent intervals.[234]

With naval sightings and attacks on imagined periscopes on the rise, it is not surprising that civilian reports of U-boats lurking off the coast also became more prevalent. Typical was the sighting report from the master of the British schooner *Klondyke* of a submarine on the surface five miles southeast of Bay Bulls, Newfoundland, on 18 August. According to Master C.N. Dane, the submarine had a "conning tower painted grey," carried "no number," and was "last seen lying leeward of an iceberg and stopped." Why she was stopped and carried no number was explained the next day when the trawler HMCS *Armentieres* was sent to investigate *Klondyke*'s report: "Dead whale observed five miles southeast by south of Bay of Bulls."[235] On 19 August submarines were also reported to have been sighted three miles southeast of Guion Island and off the Nova Scotia coast between Shelburne and Lockeport.[236] Of the alleged sightings, only the report suggesting a submarine was off the southeast coast of Nova Scotia had any merit. After cruising in the shipping lanes to the east of Cape Cod since sinking *Luz Blanca* on 5 August, *U 156* was once again heading into Canadian waters—this time with the intention of striking at the fishing fleet.

---

234. Hose to NSHQ, 16 August 1918, ibid.

235. Navinet to Naval Ottawa, 18 August 1918, Navinet to Naval Ottawa, 19 August 1918, ibid.

236. Naval Intelligence Report No. 87, 26 August 1918, DHH.

CHAPTER 11

Attacking the Fishing Fleet, August to November 1918

Ever since the Admiralty informed NSHQ in early 1918 that U-boats could be expected on the North American side of the Atlantic that spring, the possibility of a German attack on Canadian fishing trawlers had been a concern of both the naval authorities and the government as a whole. Although the convoy traffic carrying vital war supplies to the war fronts was a more logical target for the U-cruisers to engage, experience in European waters indicated that the Germans saw value in attacking soft targets as well. They had launched attacks against the British fishing fleet in the North Sea from the very outbreak of war, sinking twenty-six vessels in August 1914 alone. Although only twenty-two more were sunk over the next seven months, the enemy began a more concerted effort in April 1915 when eleven fishing vessels were destroyed, an activity that the British official naval history, published soon after the war, labelled as "a new development in inhumanity" in as much as such boats were "a class of vessel which the French and ourselves, even in our bitterest days [during the Napoleonic wars] had always held immune."[1] From May to August 1915, German warships, primarily U-boats, sank another 169 fishing vessels, with sixty British trawlers being sunk during June, including sixteen on the 23rd by a single submarine. Despite British attempts to counter the enemy offensive using trawler patrols and coastal submarines working in tandem with disguised auxiliary trawlers, the U-boats continued to sink large numbers of British fishing vessels throughout the war. By the time German U-cruisers first entered Canadian waters at the beginning of August 1918, the enemy had sunk a total of 660 British fishing vessels, averaging 103 tons in size, and killed 434 British fishermen.[2]

That the Germans were prepared to engage in a similar campaign in North American waters was apparent when *U 156* sank four American and three Canadian fishing vessels off southern Nova Scotia from 3 to 5 August 1918. The sinkings prompted the acting minister of the naval service (while Ballantyne was in London attending the imperial conference), A.K. Maclean, to look into the navy's arrangements for protecting the

---

1. Sir Julian S. Corbett, *Naval Operations* (History of the Great War; London 1921), II, 385.

2. Sir Julian S. Corbett, *Naval Operations* (History of the Great War; London 1923), III, 45–48, 129; E. Keble Chatterton, *The Auxiliary Patrol* (London 1923), 108, 153; and Sir Archibald Hurd, *The Merchant Navy* (History of the Great War; London 1929), III, 378–79.

Canadian fishing fleet on the banks. Maclean, a Liberal member from Halifax brought into Borden's Union government as a minister without portfolio, reminded the naval authorities on 7 August of the "great anxiety concerning safety of Nova Scotia fishing vessels," and sought some reassurance that the navy was adopting adequate measures to protect the fishing fleet.[3] Perhaps hoping to placate the acting minister, Deputy Minister G.J. Desbarats, referred him to the "programme in department [files] of arrangements for protection of fishing fleet on banks. Protection vessels are equipped with wireless and receive war warnings so that fishing vessels in their vicinity are advised. Patrols at Sydney have been instructed to inform fishing vessels returning from banks of submarine menace."[4] Maclean's check of the appropriate departmental files, of course, would have revealed that the protection of fishing vessels had concerned NSHQ in the spring but British and American indifference had forced Kingsmill to concur with Vice-Admiral W.L. Grant's July proposal that allocating escort vessels to the fishing banks was "inadequate to fill any useful purpose" and that the RCN's ships "would be more profitably employed on coastal patrol and escort duties, whence they could be diverted for patrol of the banks when the need arises."[5]

Further evidence of German intentions was provided on 10 August when, in a single day's work, *U 117* easily sank nine more American fishing vessels on the Georges Bank. That same day, an increasingly nervous Maclean prompted Kingsmill to contact Grant in Washington and inquire "what American and French vessels are patrolling the Banks for protection of fishing craft and if any arrangements can be made to warn homeward bound fishing craft of enemy activities on the coast."[6] The British C-in-C was as unconcerned as he had been in May when he had told Kingsmill that the United States did not plan to provide any protection to their fishing fleets.[7] Grant responded to Kingsmill's fisheries enquiry a week later to inform him that the "protective forces are now as then but Americans may increase of which I will inform you." Grant did take steps, however, to have the Royal Navy authorities in St John's, Newfoundland, supply the wireless-equipped French armed schooners with the latest U-boat intelligence. More optimistic information came from the C-in-C the following day, 19 August, with word that the United States Navy was sending patrol craft from Boston for the Newfoundland fishery. He also suggested Kingsmill consult with Rear-Admiral Spencer S. Wood of the First Naval District to coordinate arrangements for the protection of the fishing fleet.[8] Hose, meanwhile, was implementing the previously agreed upon plan to spread submarine warnings throughout the fishing banks: "All Canadian patrol vessels have been instructed to inform all fishing

---

3. Maclean to Desbarats, 7 August 1918, 1017–10–1, pt. 1, Library and Archives Canada (hereafter LAC), Record Group (hereafter RG) 24, vol. 3831.

4. Navyard Halifax to Naval Ottawa, 8 August 1918, 109, for acting minister from deputy minister, 1017–10–6, pt. 1, LAC, RG 24, vol. 3832.

5. C-in-C, NA&WI to Director of Naval Service, 3 July 1918, Kingsmill minute, 13 July 1918, ibid.

6. Naval Ottawa to Britannia, 10 August 1918, 1065–4–3, LAC, RG 24, vol. 4030.

7. Grant to Kingsmill, 14 May 1918, 1017–10–6, pt, 1, LAC, RG 24, vol. 3832.

8. Britannia to Naval Ottawa, 18 and 19 August 1918, 1065–4–3, LAC, RG 24, vol. 4030.

vessels met that submarines are operating in vicinity and to give them any war warnings. Propose that Commander Ferlicot [commanding the French armed schooners] should be requested to instruct French bank patrol vessels to issue all war warnings to any allied fishing vessels met."[9]

With the U-cruisers still operating well south of Nova Scotia throughout the middle of August, Canadian concerns regarding the safety of the fishing fleets were more precautionary than immediate. It was not until the 17th, when *U 156* sank the Norwegian steamer *San Jose* some 120 kilometres south-southeast of Cape Sable, that a submarine attack had taken place within 150 kilometres of Canada since the sinking of *Luz Blanca* on the 5th. Although the crew of *San Jose* had been ordered into lifeboats and told to row for the Nova Scotia coast, word of the sinking was received ashore soon thereafter when the crew was picked up by the passing British merchantman *Derbyshire*. Even then, naval authorities could only guess whether the U-boat would continue to operate against New York-bound shipping or continue further north into Canadian waters. With the Halifax shipping lanes virtually empty following the shift of convoys to the St Lawrence, the only ships left in the area that *U 156* could attack were the many fishing vessels plying their trade on the Canadian and Newfoundland banks. These were, in fact, a target, and the German submariners had come prepared to adopt an entirely new tactic in their attacks.

Moving northeast parallel to the Nova Scotia coast throughout 18 and 19 August, the German submarine may well have lingered in the shipping lanes off Halifax—perhaps in the hope of finding another merchantman proceeding independently as *Luz Blanca* had been—before proceeding to the northeast to look for easier targets on the fishing grounds between Sable and Cape Breton Islands. By noon on 20 August, *U 156* was some 110 kilometres south-southwest of Cape Canso when her crew spotted the 239-ton Canadian steam trawler *Triumph* cruising slowly with her nets out:

> At 12:10 pm, August 20, 1918, ship's time, approximately sixty miles S by W off Canso, Nova Scotia, the captain and crew of the *Triumph* sighted the conning tower of a submarine, coming out of the water astern, one-and-a-half to two miles away.
>
> Five minutes later a shot was fired, landing in the water over port side about amidships. Engines were stopped, lifeboats manned, and hasty preparations were made to shove off, taking practically no belongings except a box of biscuits for each boat.
>
> After putting off, the submarine came up to within fifty yards of the trawler and Capt. G. Myhre proceeded for the side of the submarine in a dinghy with the ship's papers and articles, while the other boats laid by. The commander of the submarine took the papers from the captain and ordered him aboard. He then ordered another one of the lifeboats to come alongside. The eleven men in this boat were ordered aboard the sub.

9.   Captain of Patrols to Naval Ottawa, 20 August 1918, ibid.

The Germans then put armament into the lifeboat and proceeded with two of the *Triumph* crew to board the ship. The armament taken aboard consisted of the following:

(a) Either one or two 3-pounders, not assembled, including base and all.

(b) Approximately twenty-five high-explosive bombs, about one to one and-a-half feet in height and six to nine inches in breadth, with time attachment visible.

(c) A large sea bag, the contents of which were not visible or possible to learn, it being about twice the size [of] the navy regulation sea bag.

(d) Two large boxes of 3-pound shells. Three or four members of the submarine's crew spoke Norwegian and English, while others spoke English; one petty officer who spoke excellent Norwegian and English stated that he had been sailing on Norwegian ships previous to the war.

It was 12:35 pm when the crew (new [German] crew) was aboard the *Triumph* and had the engines running, but they did not move until 1:15 pm, the time that the *Triumph* crew left the submarine.[10]

Even as the Canadian trawlermen began rowing for the Nova Scotian coast, it was obvious that the Germans were planning to use the captured trawler to attack other fishing vessels. After reaching Canso the next morning, Myhre and his crew were interrogated by RCN intelligence officers who reported "that nobody ever dreamed [the Germans] would do other than sink the trawler; the idea of her being captured and made use of not entering their minds as they had never heard of such a thing."[11] The fact that the crew of *U 156* had brought the 3-pounder guns with them from Germany clearly indicated that the possibility of using a captured trawler against fishing vessels had been planned well in advance. Just how successful the new tactic would prove was demonstrated shortly after *Triumph's* Canadian crew began pulling for the Nova Scotia coast. Continuing east-northeast for the next hour and a half, the submarine and her newly acquired surface consort eventually spotted several fishing schooners some ninety-five kilometres south-southeast of Cape Canso. With the Canadian trawler known by sight to most fishermen working in the area, it was able to approach unsuspecting fishing schooners while the submarine remained partially submerged some three miles distant.

Beginning at 1445 hours with an attack on the American schooner *A. Piatt Andrew*, *Triumph* stopped and sank two American and two Canadian fishing schooners ranging in size from 117 to 141 tons.[12] The ease with which *Triumph* carried out the sinkings was

10. Navinet Halifax to Naval Ottawa, 21 August 1918, Directorate of History and Heritage (hereafter DHH) 81/520/1440–6, vol. 7, Halifax, Nova Scotia—1905–1920; and Intelligence report on *Triumph* crew quoted in US Navy Department, Office of Naval Records and Library, Historical Section, *German Submarine Activities on the Atlantic Coast of the United States and Canada* (Washington 1920), 65–66.

11. "Particulars of Attacks on Merchant Vessels by Enemy Submarines," *Triumph*, nd, 62–13–2, pt. 4, LAC, RG 24, vol. 4023.

12. US Navy Department, *German Submarine Activities*, 66, 140.

demonstrated by the report of the master of the American schooner *Francis J. O'Hara Jr.* who spotted the Canadian trawler soon after she had stopped *A. Piatt Andrew:*

> With my glasses I could see that they were fishing.... so I decided that I would go up and speak to the vessel which was laying to and find out what kind of fishing they were having. On getting nearer, I made out that the vessel was the schooner *A. Piatt Andrew* of Gloucester, and I was going up alongside her to speak to the captain when the beam trawler approached us under full steam. I could see that it was the trawler *Triumph* of Halifax, as we had fished alongside of him on our last trip and I know the captain of her quite well. I did not mistrust anything out of the way until they got within 150 yards of us, when they stopped their vessel and the captain, through a megaphone, ordered us to heave our vessel to. I thought the captain was joking with us and kept on toward the *A. Piatt Andrew*, and the first thing we knew four shots were fired across our bow from rifles. We brought our vessel up in the wind and the beam trawler came up alongside of us and I then saw that she was manned by a German crew and had a German flag at her masthead.[13]

The two American crews watched their schooners being sunk by bombs before beginning the ninety-five kilometre row to shore, arriving at Canso, Nova Scotia, at 0900 hours the next morning. While *Triumph* continued on to capture and sink the Canadian schooners *Lucille M. Schnare* of 121 tons and *Pasadena* of 119 tons, using the same tactics, *U 156* acted alone in overtaking the 124-ton Canadian schooner *Uda A. Saunders.* As the *Uda A.*'s captain later described:

> The submarine came up on our bow and came right alongside, her decks awash. She was about 280 feet long, with guns fore and aft. I was practically alone on the vessel, all but three of the crew being out in the boats from half mile to a mile away. The Huns hailed us and ordered a dory alongside. I sent two men out to her in a dory and three of the raider's crew came aboard. "Don't be afraid," said the one who appeared to be in command. "We are going to sink your vessel. I will give you ten minutes to gather up food and water enough to last you until you get ashore." One of the Boches set about storing bombs below and soon after we left the *Uda A.*, I heard a muffled explosion, the two masts broke off short, she seemed to crumple in the center and immediately went under. We had enough food and water, but the men in the other dories had only their working clothes and we who were on board had only the barest necessities. The Hun commander took all my papers and the flag. We set out for the nearest shore and rowed eighteen hours before landing.[14]

---

13. Joseph P. Mesquita, master of the *Francis J. O'Hara Jr.* quoted in ibid, 66–67.

14. Captain Publicover of the *Uda A. Saunders* quoted in ibid; 67.

While the fishermen of the sunken schooners were making their way toward land, *U 156* and *Triumph* hurriedly steamed 150 kilometres to the northeast throughout the evening. The Germans drove the Canadian trawler at top speed undoubtedly in the hope of throwing off any pursuing naval forces by putting as much distance as they could between themselves and the vicinity of the sinkings on the afternoon of the 20th. Arriving on the Banquereau Bank some eighty kilometres east-southeast of Scatari Island during the early morning hours of the 21st, three German submariners quietly boarded the 145-ton French fishing schooner *Notre Dame de la Garde* from one of *Triumph*'s dories, taking the sleeping crew by surprise. After ordering her crew into their boats, the French schooner, loaded with some 320 tons of fish, was quickly sent to the bottom. Three hours later *Triumph* steamed alongside the 136-ton American schooner *Sylvania* shortly after dawn, fired a shot across her bow and demanded the crew take to their boats as well. With the French fishermen of *Notre Dame de la Garde* looking on from a distance, the American schooner was also sunk. When last seen by the stunned fishermen, both submarine and trawler were slowly making off to the east.

Alerted as to what the Germans were up to by the numerous fishermen landing along the coast of Cape Breton throughout the 21st, the navy moved quickly to inform the fishing fleet. HMC Ships *Stadacona*, *Cartier*, and *Hochelaga* and two escort trawlers were immediately despatched from Halifax to search the Artimon Bank, while a submarine chaser was sent to the Banquereau Bank—the naval authorities were as yet unaware that the raiders had already sunk two schooners there by early morning—with "instructions to warn all fishing vessels met of presence of trawler *Triumph* as German raider and of presence [of a] submarine on the banks." The submarine chasers and trawlers that had just returned from escorting convoy HC 14 from Sydney, meanwhile, were sent to assist in the search on the Misaine Banks, off Canso, later that same day.[15] After sinking *Sylvania* at dawn on the 21st, the submarine remained out of sight for the next three days, unable to find any other vessels to engage. The only indication of *U 156*'s presence was an incomplete radio signal from the U-boat to Germany, intercepted by the Admiralty on the 23rd, asking "Why do you not give ... ?" The intent of the partial message remains unclear.[16]

The ninety-hour reprieve between *Sylvania*'s sinking and *U 156*'s next attack allowed the RCN to redirect its patrol forces from convoy escort to fishing fleet protection. The Canadians would have to distribute their forces to cover the various fishing banks with little in the way of useful aid from the United States, however. On 22 August Grant informed NSHQ that the Americans were finally sending the destroyer USS *Jouett* and her hunting group of eighteen submarine chasers—previously promised on 10 August in the wake of the *Luz Blanca* sinking—to Halifax "to search area east of Nova Scotia," while the ancient gunboat USS *Yorktown*, promised to the Canadians one week earlier, was now "en route." The only new assets made available were the US Coastguard's fishery patrol vessel

15. Patrols to Naval Ottawa, 21 August 1918, 342 and 351, S.H. Morres to acting prime minister, 21 August 1918, Naval Ottawa to CO HMS *Briton*, St John's, 21 August 1918, 1062–13–2, pt. 4, LAC, RG 24, vol. 4021.

16. US Navy Department, *German Submarine Activities*, 67–68; and Robert M. Grant, *U-Boat Intelligence, 1914–1918* (London 1969), 154.

Androscoggin and the patrol vessel USS *Aztec* "to patrol Great Banks" and, to a lesser extent, the destroyer USS *Bell* (one of the new flush deck destroyers completed at the Fore River shipyard on 1 August), returning to New York from St John's. The American destroyer had been part of the escort for convoy HX 45 that departed New York on 16 August but had been forced to put into the Newfoundland capital owing to condenser defects. Nonetheless, she was nominally made available to "assist if necessary," while steaming southwest off the Nova Scotia coast on the homeward voyage for repairs.[17] Both the gunboat *Yorktown* and the destroyer *Jouett* and her subchasers arrived at Halifax on the 24th. While the latter immediately began a ten-day patrol along the Nova Scotia coast, the former did not depart for the Newfoundland fishing banks until 28 August. Despite the concerns of fishing communities both north and south of the border, the warships made available by the American navy department indicated that neither Canada nor the United States was going to allow an attack on a few fishing vessels to deflect their navies away from their main task of convoy protection.[18]

While there was a sense of urgency in despatching patrol vessels to the various fishing banks, even as NSHQ was concerned about its ability to protect convoys traversing the long Gulf of St Lawrence route,[19] there was no panic among Canadian naval authorities. Responding to a 21 August cable from NSHQ directing Hose to proceed to Boston to consult with Admiral Woods of the First Naval District (sent before the news from *Triumph*'s crew that *U 156* was operating in Canadian waters), the captain of patrols explained his proposed course of action to counter the German raiders' presence: "in view of present situation off Canso which requires my constant attention, and also that air conference is to be held here, submitted that discussion re protection of bank fishers may be held here with officer from Admiral Wood's staff due here Wednesday, August 28th. Commander Ferlicot [commanding the French armed schooners on the banks] will be kept constantly informed of situation on banks as far as known here. Propose utilizing six trawlers in meantime for patrol purposes on Nova Scotia banks. These are distinct from flotilla now searching."[20] Even though Hose's proposal put off the meeting with the Americans for another week, the suggestion was readily concurred in by Kingsmill.[21]

Though not completely ignoring the need to provide convoy protection, the Canadian navy had sent a large proportion of its available strength to patrol the various fishing banks

---

17. C-in-C to Naval Ottawa, 22 August 1918, 1062–13–2, pt. 4, LAC, RG 24, vol. 4021; HX Convoy reports, nd, HX 45, United Kingdom National Archives (hereafter UKNA), Admiralty (hereafter ADM) 137/2657; Grant to Admiralty, "General Letter No. 7," 3 September 1918, UKNA, ADM 137/504; and O. Parkes and M. Prendergast, eds., *Jane's Fighting Ships 1919* (London 1919), 210.

18. Navyard, Halifax to Naval Ottawa, 25 August 1918, 1065–7-6, LAC, RG 24, 4031; and Michael L. Hadley and Roger Sarty, *Tin-pots and Pirate Ships: Canadian Naval Forces and German Sea Raiders, 1880–1918* (Montreal and Kingston 1991), 264–65.

19. Commander J.P. Gibbs, Director of Naval Operations, "Memo: To the Director of the Naval Service," 29 August 1918, 1048–48–1, pt. 1, LAC, RG 24, vol. 3772.

20. Captain of Patrols to Naval Ottawa, 22 August 1918, Naval Ottawa to Transports, Sydney, 21 August 1918, 1017–10–6, pt. 1, LAC, RG 24, vol. 3832.

21. Naval Ottawa to Transports Sydney, 22 August 1918, ibid.

and warn schooners of the presence of *Triumph* and *U 156* acting in concert. They were aided in their efforts by the fact that convoy HS 52 had departed Sydney and proceeded through the Cabot Straits on the 20th and was well out to sea by the time naval authorities received word the following day that *U 156* had captured the Canadian trawler and was using her to attack the fishing fleet off Canso. With HC 14 setting out from the Cape Breton port on the 21st and the next two convoys, HS 53 and HC 15, not scheduled to leave Sydney until the 28th and 29th respectively, Hose had a full week to send out his escorts in search of the marauding Germans.

The acting naval minister's concern for the safety of the fishing fleet—and the political repercussions of that community's "great anxiety" over possible attacks—had already prompted him to travel to Halifax a few days before *Triumph*'s capture, and he was rather more agitated than the navy. Maclean's anxious mood was demonstrated in the curt telegram he sent to the deputy minister in Ottawa on 22 August, the day after word of the sinkings off Canso had spread throughout the maritimes: "Did you direct anybody at Dockyard [in Halifax] that word be sent to fishing fleet that submarines were operating here. So far as I can ascertain no word was ever sent and I understood from you that you gave such directions when here. Would like to be advised as to the facts if this was not done it would seem to be indefensible."[22] Having already dispersed its patrol vessels across the fishing banks "to warn all fishing vessels met of presence trawler *Triumph* as German raider and of presence submarine" as soon as word of the Canadian trawler's capture reached them on the 21st, NSHQ took the acting minister's implied criticism in stride.[23] Accordingly, Desbarats's reply, though short on details (and failing to mention the American patrol vessels *Androscoggin* and *Aztec* being sent to the fishing grounds by the United States), simply tried to reassure Maclean that a "special patrol was sent to warn fishermen on banks south of Cape Breton and special patrol to be maintained on these banks. French patrol on Grand Banks protects and warns our vessels."[24]

Maclean's anxiety would not have eased over the next several days as further reports were received from the fishermen of the sunken schooners as they finally reached shore. Preliminary information about the American and French schooners sunk on the Banquereau Bank on the 21st was forwarded from Sydney to Ottawa on 23 and 24 August.[25] This was followed by a more detailed report from Captain Pasco later on the 24th:

> Submitted for the information of the department, the following account of the sinking of the French schooner *Notre Dame de la Garde* and the American schooner *Sylvania* on the morning of Wednesday, August 21st. These schooners were at anchor on the Bankquereau [*sic*] Bank.
> At 2.30 AM the French schooner was boarded by three men from a dory. The fishermen were taken by surprise and the Germans holding revolvers to

22. A.K. Maclean to Desbarats, 22 August 1918, 1065-4-1, LAC, RG 24, vol. 4030.

23. Patrols to Naval Ottawa, 21 August 1918, 342, 1062–13–2, pt. 4, LAC, RG 24, vol. 4021.

24. Naval Ottawa to Dockyard, 23 August 1918, 1065-4-1, LAC, RG 24, vol. 4030.

25. Transports, Sydney to Naval Ottawa, 23 August 1918, Captain in Charge, Sydney to Naval Ottawa, 24 August 1918, 1062–13–2, pt. 5, LAC, RG 24, vol. 4021.

their heads ordered them to leave their vessel at once, a submarine was then seen lying a half mile off with her guns trained on the schooner. The fishermen abandoned the ship in their dories, the Germans then proceeded to place a bomb on board the schooner with which they blew her up. The Germans took one life buoy from the schooner before sinking her. This vessel was on a fishing voyage from St Pierre. The name of her master was Royer Raoul and her owner's name was Mrs Le Moine, St Malo, France.

At the time of this schooner being sunk there were two other schooners in sight, one of which the men saw destroyed about 5.30 AM. The trawler *Triumph* was also in sight at a distance, the master of the schooner estimated as being ten miles (probably much closer).

The crew of the American schooner *Sylvania* owned by the Gordon Pew Co. of Boston, state that they were on the Banquereau Bank baiting their trawls when they noticed a trawler coming from the westward at full speed.

It stopped one hundred yards from the *Sylvania* and hailed them, then fired a shot across her bow. The schooner then lowered a dory which went alongside the trawler. An officer in uniform asked, "Are you the skipper?" "You have to leave your ship. I'll give you ten minutes to get back and leave your ship." Three Germans, one petty officer and two men, jumped into the dory and returned to the schooner with them, taking bombs in a bag, which they placed under her quarter. The ship's papers and flags were asked for and given. The Germans took one dory and the schooner's crew abandoned their vessel in the others. The schooner was seen to sink when the dories were a mile and a half away, no explosion was heard. A submarine was seen after the crew had left the schooner, lying on the surface about three or four miles to the westward, appeared to be painted grey, newly painted, 250 feet or more.

When last seen both trawler and submarine were going slowly eastward. When twenty miles off the land, the *Sylvania*'s crew were picked up by the *Catherine Burke*, bound for Ingonish, who transferred them to the *Restless* when off Flat Point, in which ship they were conveyed to Sydney.[26]

Although it has been claimed that "*Triumph* went silently about her business of raiding for the next three days,"[27] in fact the crew of the American schooner were the last to see the trawler. In the absence of any records as to her exact fate, her operational career in the German navy would appear to have lasted less than twenty-four hours. As no further attacks were made by her, it is most likely that, aware of the alarm that would be raised by *Triumph*'s crew once they reached shore, the Germans simply scuttled her soon after sinking *Sylvania*. Better that than run the risk of taking on an Allied patrol vessel with the 3-pounder they carried aboard or having the trawler betray the whereabouts of their

---

26. Captain Pasco, Captain in Charge Sydney to NSHQ, 24 August 1918, ibid.

27. Hadley and Sarty, *Tin-pots and Pirate Ships*, 266.

submarine. Ironically, even as *Triumph*'s Canadian crew were informing the naval authorities on the morning of 21 August that their trawler was being used to attack the fishing fleet, the vessel herself was probably already resting on the floor of the Atlantic.

With *U 156* remaining out of sight from dawn on the 21st until the early morning hours of the 25th, naval authorities could only guess as to where she might strike next. The absence of any sort of radio equipment among the fishing schooners inevitably meant long delays before naval authorities received information on a U-boat's latest attacks or movements, the crew of a sunken vessel usually requiring at least twenty-four hours to row ashore. Forced to operate on the basis of day-old intelligence, the RCN continued to send out escort ships as they became available in an ever-widening search across the fishing banks for the German submarine and her presumed consort. As the hunt for *U 156* entered its third day on the 23rd, Hose added the Battle-class trawler *Armentieres* and *TR 23*, both sent to search the St Pierre Bank near the French islands south of Newfoundland, and the drifters *CD 38* and *CD 48*, sent to patrol the Gut of Canso, to the list of patrol vessels looking for the enemy raider.[28]

As the RCN's ships spread across the fishing banks, however, no one in the navy was under any illusions regarding the relative chances Canada's under-sized, under-gunned, and under-powered patrol vessels would have in a clash with a U-cruiser. As we have seen, the RCN's senior officers already harboured serious misgivings about the effectiveness of the 12-pounder to engage a surfaced U-boat,[29] and Kingsmill would reiterate his concerns about the inadequate armament of the East Coast fleet in a memorandum to Desbarats in early September, declaring that "at any time a submarine may sink a whole division" of Canadian patrol vessels.[30] Nonetheless, in a memorandum sent to the captain of patrols on 7 August, Kingsmill laid down what was expected of the patrol fleet in an encounter with a U-cruiser. Much of the memorandum dealt with the procedures to be followed while hunting a submerged submarine, and the possible ruses the enemy would use to escape once he was below the surface. A submarine that was forced to dive "often goes as deep as 200 feet, seldom less than 120 feet, and he generally makes a very sharp alteration from his surface course," he advised, adding that if a submerged U-boat was unable to get outside effective gun range before resurfacing to make her escape on the surface, she was capable of lying on the sea floor for up to forty-eight hours. If hydrophone contact with a submerged U-boat was lost, patrol vessels were to "drop a buoy on the spot where he dived, take a sounding, and then drop a pattern of depth charges.... Watch the position for at least thirty-six hours if you cannot hear any movement in the hydrophones, and drop an occasional depth charge."[31] The naval director did not hide the fact that the RCN's ships would be badly out-gunned in any surface encounter but indicated that all vessels were still expected to press an attack in an attempt to inflict damage:

28. Captain of Patrols to Naval Ottawa, 23 August 1918, 1062–13–2, pt. 5, LAC, RG 24, vol. 4021.

29. Captain of Patrols to The Secretary, Department of Naval Service, 25 March 1918, Stephens minute, nd, Stephens to Kingsmill, 28 March 1918, 1017–10–4, pt. 1, LAC, RG 24, vol. 3832.

30. Kingsmill, "Memorandum for the Deputy Minister," 6 September 1918, 1029–16–1, pt. 6, LAC, RG 24, vol. 5605.

31. Kingsmill to Captain of Patrols, 7 August 1918, DHH 81/520/1000–973, vol. 2.

Enemy submarines operating in Canadian waters are very heavily armed, either with 5.9-inch or 4.1-inch guns, which are usually of high velocity and long range.

They will seldom hesitate to attack a single trawler, if they think that no assistance is near, so ships should never be out of supporting distance from each other.

If attacked by a submarine, close at full speed *and zig-zag* to throw the enemy off his aim. If you attack with determination the enemy will almost certainly dive when your shell commences to drop close to him, and you then have the advantage.

The surface speed of the enemy is probably twice your own, but his submerged speed is very slow except for short distances, when it about equals yours....

Remember that an enemy submarine in Canadian waters is a very long way from his base. He will make every endeavour to prevent getting damaged, and even if you can damage him only slightly, it is going to make his home trip very uncomfortable.

If you have damaged him enough to prevent him diving, he is very likely to be sunk when in British waters.[32]

Although an aggressive attack was itself a form of defence for the RCN's patrol vessels— in view of the likelihood that a submarine would break off action and submerge rather than risk damage so far from home—Kingsmill also knew that a determined U-boat was likely to destroy the Canadian ship. Betraying his long-standing pessimism about the quality of the vessels that made up the East Coast navy, the naval director reminded his patrol force of where their duty lay in the likely event of an unsuccessful encounter:

It is *imperative* that no confidential books or papers should fall into the hands of the enemy.

If you are in danger of being captured or sunk, see that everything confidential is burned or thrown overboard. If thrown overboard, everything must be in a bag, and *heavily weighted* to make certain that the bag sinks.

Every man in the ship must be told where the books are kept in action, so that if the officers are killed the books will be destroyed....

Your ship must never be allowed to fall into the hands of the enemy. If you have been made defenceless, no help is at hand, and the submarine is still attacking you, scuttle the ship by opening the seacocks, breaking the inlet, etc. Explosive charges are not to be used, as they usually fail at the critical moment, but the engineers are to make quite certain that they can sink the ship quickly.[33]

---

32. Ibid.

33. Ibid.

With the patrol forces hunting *U 156* growing in number in the days following *Sylvania*'s sinking on 21 August, Kingsmill's sombre directions were eventually put to the test. After nearly four days without making any attacks or being spotted by Allied vessels, the German submarine finally reappeared at 0130 hours on 25 August when she attacked the British steamer *Eric* some 115 kilometres west-northwest of the French island of St Pierre. Under charter to the Newfoundland government, the 610-ton freighter was en route from St John's to Sydney on a moonlit night when she was struck by five shells in rapid succession, slightly wounding five, including the captain, mate, and chief engineer. According to the RCN intelligence report made to the Admiralty: "A few minutes after the firing ceased the submarine was seen by *Eric*'s crew right alongside by the stern. Someone aboard the submarine hailed the crew of the *Eric* and asked if anyone had been killed by the shells fired; on being told that no one was killed, the man aboard the submarine said that he was glad, as he was after ships and not lives." With only one small lifeboat undamaged, *Eric*'s eighteen-man crew was taken aboard the submarine and the steamer sunk by bombs, while the U-boat commander informed the captain that "he would keep them aboard the submarine until he found a vessel with sufficient boats to accommodate them." Around 0600 hours *U 156* overtook the Newfoundland schooner *Wallie G*, forty kilometres west of St Pierre. Going alongside, "the submarine commander inquired regarding the number of boats she carried. On being informed that she only carried six small dories, he said that these were not enough to accommodate the crew of the *Eric* and the crew of the *Willie G*. [*sic*] and that therefore he would send the *Eric*'s crew aboard the *Willie G*. [*sic*] and would not sink her, as he had intended doing." As promised *Wallie G*. was allowed to proceed to St Pierre where she landed *Eric*'s crew—despite the relatively short distance to be travelled—at 0930 hours the next day.[34]

Turning south-southwest, the U-boat travelled some thirty kilometres when she spotted a group of four fishing schooners at anchor about a kilometre apart from each other. The Canadian crews of the first three schooners, *E.B. Walters*, *C.M. Walters*, and *Verna D. Adams*, were all on board their vessels since, in the words of the naval report, "Canadian fishermen do not fish on Sundays." The fourth schooner, the largest of the group, was the 162-ton American, *J.J. Flaherty*. As the U-boat approached *E.B. Walters* slowly on the surface, the Canadians were unconcerned "as they mistook it for a Canadian patrol boat." Ordering the captain of the schooner, Cyrus Walters, to row over to the submarine, four of the Germans jumped into the dory and boarded the fishing vessel. After over two months at sea, the U-boat was apparently running low on supplies, Walters reporting "that the men from the submarine ransacked the ship, even going through the chests of the crew in the forecastle. He saw them pile up a quantity of canned goods from the vessel's stores near the dory in which they had come aboard. Capt. Walters and his crew hastily packed up a few personal belongings and got into the dories and pulled away from the vessel. About ten minutes after they had left the vessel they heard an explosion aboard the schooner and in about five

---

34. Intelligence report to Admiralty quoted in US Navy Department, *German Submarine Activities*, 68–69; and Transports Sydney to Naval Ottawa, 26 August 1918, DHH 81/520/1440–6, vol. 7, Halifax, Nova Scotia—1905–1920.

35. US Navy Department, *German Submarine Activities*, 69–70.

Canadian fishing schooners in Lunenburg, Nova Scotia. (LAC PA-211340)

minutes they saw the schooner sink." After sinking *E.B. Walters*, the four submariners in the dory were towed by *U 156* to the schooner *C.M. Walters* lying at anchor only a half-mile away. Within half-an-hour of boarding the second Canadian schooner, she too was sent to the bottom. The captured dory was then towed over to the already-abandoned *Verna D. Adams*, her crew watching the same four Germans board their vessel. The Canadian fishermen noted that "the men from the submarine stayed on board the *Adams* longer than aboard any of the other vessels. Captain Mosher of the *Adams* says that he had a large supply of stores aboard, especially of canned foods, and believes many articles were removed from the schooner and taken aboard the submarine. The *Verna D. Adams* was sunk by a bomb placed aboard in the same manner as was done with the other two vessels."[35]

The submariners were still in the process of replenishing their food reserves at 1345 hours when *Verna D. Adams* and *J.J. Flaherty* were spotted by a passing Canadian patrol. The RCN vessels, HMC Ships *Cartier* and *Hochelaga* and the trawlers *TR 22* and *TR 32*, had departed Louisbourg at 1950 hours the previous evening to patrol the fishing banks south of Newfoundland, and "warn all vessels that submarine was operating on banks, also *Triumph* captured by enemy submarine and now operating as an enemy raider."[36] Beginning at a point seventy kilometres west-southwest of Miquelon, the RCN flotilla were to patrol southeast past the French islands toward the Green Bank fishing grounds.[37] With the RNCVR commander of *Cartier*, Lieutenant H.F. McGuirk, serving as senior officer, the four patrol vessels reached the rendezvous point at 1200 hours on 25 August, and deployed five to seven kilometres apart before proceeding in a rough line abreast to the southeast. *TR 22* was on *Cartier's* starboard beam while *Hochelaga* was on her port beam with *TR 32* steaming as the eastern-most vessel in the formation. One hour and fifteen minutes after sighting the Miquelon Islands, the signalman of the watch aboard *Hochelaga* spotted two schooners—*Verna D. Adams* and *J.J. Flaherty*—some ten kilometres to the east. The officer of the watch, Mate Elcho Ross-Ross then called the patrol vessel's commander, Lieutenant R.D. Legate, to the bridge and course was altered to the east to intercept the two schooners and warn them of the submarine danger. With *TR 32* following *Hochelaga* toward the fishing schooners, the two ships increased to full speed.

> At about 2 PM, when *Hochelaga* was about four miles away from the schooners, an object was sighted from her close to them, which on examination appeared to be a hostile submarine. This was observed by Lieutenant Legate, Lieutenant Cyril McLean Fry, ... Mr Ross-Ross, ... Harold Gates, signalman, signalman of the watch, and Petty Officer George Hilton ... quarter-master of the watch. At about the time the submarine was sighted, one of the schooners disappeared, sunk or cap[s]ized, presumably by the action of the submarine. Lieutenant

---

36. Lieutenant H.F. McGuirk, Commanding Officer *Cartier* to Captain of Patrols, Special Report, 1 September 1918, DHH 81/520/8000, Stadacona, vol. 2.

37. Lieutenant-Commander R.A. Barber, *Stadacona* to *Cartier*, 24 August 1918, ibid.

Legate then ordered "action" to be sounded and altered *Hochelaga*'s course to southeast towards *Cartier*, who, with *Trawler No. 22* had continued on her original course. At about the same time, he hoisted "B" flag and signalled to *Trawler No. 32* "follow me." Legate also sent a W/T message "allo port beam" to *Cartier*, who was then distant about five miles from *Hochelaga*.[38]

Legate's "allo" radio message, the standard signal sent by all Allied vessels upon sighting an enemy submarine, was also intercepted by the Canadian naval staff at Halifax and Captain Hose at Sydney. After spending four days anxiously waiting while the various patrol vessels searched for the elusive U-boat, both quickly relayed the report to NSHQ in Ottawa. It was then passed on to the acting prime minister, although there were "no further particulars" to report beyond the sighting message itself.[39] Such widespread knowledge of *Hochelaga*'s sighting of a U-boat, however, would make Legate's subsequent actions difficult to ignore.

> On seeing *Hochelaga* make this last alteration in course and hoist a flag, Lieutenant McGuirk in *Cartier* altered course to North 25 degrees East (Magnetic) to meet her. The time during which *Hochelaga* was steering towards *Cartier* was approximately seven or eight minutes. At the expiration of this period, when the vessels were about a mile apart, *Cartier* signalled to *Hochelaga* "What is your signal and what have you seen?" *Hochelaga* replied "submarine bearing east," *Cartier* then altered course to the east, *Hochelaga* and *Trawler No. 32* altering to the same course and coming up *Hochelaga* on *Cartier*'s port quarter, and *Trawler No. 32* on *Hochelaga*'s port quarter. *Cartier* then signalled to *Hochelaga* to increase to full speed. Shortly after *Hochelaga* signalled to *Cartier* "Do you see reinforcements astern, don't you think it better to wait for them?" *Cartier* replied "Negative."
>
> The submarine had by this time submerged, while the schooner which had been seen from *Hochelaga* to disappear had cap[s]ized and could be seen on her side. *Cartier*, *Hochelaga* and *Trawler No. 32* came up to her and cruised round; some empty dories were seen, but no signs of the submarine. Some smoke was then seen on the horizon, which it was thought by the senior officer might be from the captured trawler *Triumph*, the ships accordingly shaped course for it; it was found to come from a Newfoundland sealer.[40]

The "reinforcements" Legate had spotted to the west turned out to be a five-ship coastal convoy being escorted along the south coast of Newfoundland by *TR 25* and *TR 28*. With

---

38. Lieutenant-Commander J.H. Knight, Commanding Officer *Seagull* Depot, Sydney to Captain of Patrols, 17 September 1918, DHH 81/520/1440–6, Halifax, Nova Scotia—1905–1920, vol. 7.

39. Navinet, Halifax to Naval Ottawa, 25 August 1918, Patrols, Sydney to Naval Ottawa, 25 August 1918, J.P. Gibbs to Acting Prime Minister, 26 August 1918, 1062–13–2, pt. 5, LAC, RG 24, vol. 4021.

40. Lieutenant-Commander J.H. Knight, Commanding Officer *Seagull* Depot, Sydney to Captain of Patrols, 17 September 1918, DHH 81/520/1440–6, Halifax, Nova Scotia—1905–1920, vol. 7.

HMCS *Hochelaga* and HMCS *Margaret*, inboard, alongside the dockyard in Halifax. (LAC e007140904)

Typical of the RCN's escort fleet in 1918 are, from left to right, the drifters *CD 16* and *CD 22*, the Battle-class trawler *Givenchy*, and the auxiliary patrol vessel *Cartier*, alongside in Halifax. (DND CN 2902)

no sign of the U-boat or any knowledge as to what direction she had headed, McGuirk wisely decided to close with the convoy at 1600 hours to warn them of the presence of a submarine and have his flotilla join in escorting them 300 kilometres east to Cape Race before breaking off to continue his patrol of the fishing banks shortly after noon on 26 August.[41] Lieutenant Legate's actions in turning away after sighting the German submarine and heading for *Cartier*, and his subsequent attempt to dissuade McGuirk from heading for the U-boat's reported position, had not gone unnoticed, however.

Having easily evaded the Canadian flotilla, *U 156* travelled southwest away from the well-escorted coastal convoy. On the morning of the 26th, the U-boat once again boarded and sank another Canadian fishing schooner, *Gloaming* of 130 tons, 130 kilometres southwest of Miquelon Island.[42] Undoubtedly running short of supplies, the German submarine began her homeward voyage within the next few days, making an unsuccessful gun attack on the American naval transport USS *West Haven* 220 kilometres southeast of Cape Race on 31 August.[43] Alone among the U-boats that operated off the North American coast in 1918, however, *U 156* failed to return safely to Germany. On 6 September the submarine radioed Germany from mid-Atlantic that she had sunk 41,000 tons of shipping, including the American cruiser *San Diego*, and cut five telegraph cables. Two weeks later the inbound submarine radioed the outgoing *U 139* with information about North American shipping lanes. Once again intercepted by the Admiralty, *U 156* told the other U-cruiser that there was no merchant traffic in the Gulf of St Lawrence but considerable shipping between Halifax and New York. On 24 September the U-boat radioed Germany that she intended, next day, to pass through the Royal Navy's mine barrage near Fair Isle between the Shetland and Orkney Islands north of Scotland and was told to make the attempt only in daylight and on the surface. Alerted by the radio intercept, the Royal Navy despatched the destroyer *Marksman* and submarine *L-8* to *U 156*'s anticipated position where, at 0740 hours on the 25th, *L-8* "sighted vessel nature undistinguishable" before diving to move in closer. The British submarine could not, however, re-establish either visual or hydrophone contact. *L-8* was, in all probability, the last warship to sight the U-cruiser. *U 156* disappeared that same day, most likely a victim of the British mine barrage to the west of Fair Isle.[44]

The Canadian patrol flotilla that had sighted *U 156* on 25 August, meanwhile, had resumed patrolling Green Bank after detaching the coastal convoy off Cape Race on the 26th. *Cartier* later parted company with the rest of the flotilla and returned to patrol off Cape Race before heading to St John's on the 28th to escort another coastal convoy bound for Sydney. *Hochelaga*, meanwhile, continued to patrol the Green, Banquereau and Misane fishing banks before returning to Cape Breton, entering Louisbourg Harbour on the afternoon of 29 August. With the fact of his having sent an "allo" submarine sighting

---

41. McGuirk, "Weekly Report on Proceedings," 31 August 1918, Legate, "Special Report of Proceedings," 30 August 1918, DHH 81/520/8000, Stadacona, vol. 2.

42. Navinet Halifax to Naval Ottawa, 28 August 1918, 1062–13–2, pt. 5, LAC, RG 24, vol. 4021.

43. US Navy Department, *German Submarine Activities*, 70.

44. Robert M. Grant, *U-Boat Intelligence, 1914–1918* (London 1969), 103, 155–56.

message on the 25th being widely known, Lieutenant Legate had to answer the questions of curious naval authorities once he returned to port. Asked to file a "special report of proceedings" covering the period of *Hochelaga*'s patrol, Legate was unwilling to volunteer much detailed information about his actions on the 25th. His summary was deliberately vague: "Sighted large submarine near schooner. Sounded 'action,' courses various to cooperate with flotilla. Submarine submerged on being sighted."[45] The report of proceedings that Lieutenant McGuirk submitted when he reached Sydney on the 31st was also deliberately uninformative about Legate's hesitant actions in the face of the enemy. *Cartier*'s commanding officer merely stated: "*Hochelaga* reported sighting submarine. Actions stations. Closed *Hochelaga* at full speed. *Hochelaga* reports submarine bearing due east. Proceeded in that direction five miles and sighted schooner laying on her side. Cruised around and did not see submarine again."[46]

Based on the written information provided by Legate and McGuirk, Captain Hose had little reason to question the actions of his skippers. However, whether it was an individual present on *Hochelaga*'s bridge who was embarrassed by his commander's timidity or some other officer from the flotilla, it is apparent that someone who had witnessed the incident on the 25th candidly informed the captain of patrols of the actual circumstances. Not satisfied with McGuirk's initial report of proceedings, Hose had *Cartier*'s commander submit a second, "special report" the next day, 1 September, covering the three day period from 24 to 26 August. Once again, McGuirk remained unwilling to provide any indictment of Legate's actions: "*Hochelaga* signalled by W/T 'allo port beam.' Full speed and action stations. *Hochelaga* and *Cartier* closing. Signalled *Hochelaga* for direction of submarine and bearing. Bearing east. Proceeded at full speed, *Hochelaga* coming up on quarter, TRs following at full speed. Steamed about five miles on easterly course and found schooner laying on her side. Cruised about and did not sight submarine again."[47] The lieutenant's attempt to obfuscate the facts, however, did not dissuade the captain of patrols from pursuing the matter further.

With more accurate information apparently being provided to him by other members of *Cartier*'s flotilla, Hose ordered Legate to be placed under arrest in *Cartier* on 2 September "on account of movements of *Hochelaga* on 25th August."[48] Kingsmill was taken aback when news of the arrest was forwarded to NSHQ the following week and he promptly ordered Hose to "inform me fully [and] immediately [of] circumstances necessitating putting commanding officer of *Hochelaga* under arrest."[49] The captain of patrols replied that "not being satisfied at action of commanding officer *Hochelaga* on sighting enemy submarine on 25th August, I ordered him to be put under arrest and application for court

---

45. Legate, "Special Report of Proceedings," 30 August 1918, DHH 81/520/8000, Stadacona, vol. 2.

46. McGuirk, "Weekly Report of Proceedings," 31 August 1918, ibid.

47. Commanding Officer, *Cartier* to Captain of Patrols, 1 September 1918, ibid.

48. Patrols Sydney to NSHQ, 11 September 1918, quoted in "War Services Legate.... Robt. D. Lieut. RCNVR [sic]," nd, DHH 81/520/1440-6, vol. 8, Halifax, Nova Scotia—1905–1920.

49. Kingsmill to Patrols Sydney, 11 September 1918, quoted in "War Services Legate.... Robt. D. Lieut. RCNVR [sic]," nd, ibid.

martial is being made."[50] Readers, of course, will recall that Hose had reacted almost exactly as Legate had done when he believed he had spotted the German cruiser *Leipzig* off the West Coast of the United States on 12 August 1914 (i.e., he had turned *Rainbow* onto a reciprocal course and made off at high speed away from the presumed enemy). The decision to court martial the commander of *Hochelaga*, therefore, seems hard-hearted and that was certainly the view of E.C. Russell, the navy's official historian in 1961, who candidly pointed out the hypocrisy of Hose's lack of mercy in 1918 given his own lack of nerve four years earlier.[51]

Such a conclusion ignores context, however, as Hose may well have had less room for discretion in charging Legate than would first appear. If the timid nature of the lieutenant's behaviour in the face of the enemy had become the subject of gossip among the escort crews at Sydney—and the fact that the captain of patrols apparently learned the details of *Hochelaga*'s actions from sources other than official reports would indicate that at least some of the sailors who witnessed the incident were talking when they reached port—then Hose would have been perceived within the escort fleet as condoning cowardice if he had not arrested the patrol vessel's commander. Any attempt by Hose to sweep the entire matter "under the rug" would have been prejudicial to the good discipline of his sailors at the very time when any of them might be called upon to engage an enemy submarine. Nevertheless, after Hose's own less-than-creditable performance on *Rainbow*'s bridge in August 1914, and in view of the way he crumbled under public pressure as a member of the Halifax explosion inquiry, it is difficult not to share some of E.C. Russell's disdain for the captain of patrols' decision.

Lieutenant Legate's court martial took place at Halifax on 5 October 1918 with Hose in attendance.[52] *Hochelaga*'s commander was charged under the Naval Discipline Act with "when in sight of a ship of the enemy which it was his duty to engage, did not use his utmost exertion to bring his ship into action."[53] Sitting in judgment were Captain Pasco from Sydney, Commanders J.T. Shenton, D. Tatton Brown, and H.E. Holme, and acting Captain Eldridge, the naval staff officer aboard *Niobe*. With the prosecution's witnesses consisting of the main actors who were present on *Hochelaga*'s bridge at the time, as well as Lieutenant McGuirk of *Cartier* and Chief Skipper R. Davidson of *TR 32*, it was not difficult for the court to find "the charge against the accused proved."[54] Had Legate simply altered course to close with *Cartier* after first sighting *U 156* on 25 August, the unfortunate lieutenant would have been in a better position to defend himself against the charge. The most damning piece of evidence of the extent to which Legate had lost courage was his

50. Patrols Sydney to DNS, 12 September 1918, quoted in "War Services Legate.... Robt. D. Lieut. RCNVR [*sic*]," nd, ibid.

51. E.C. Russell, "*Rainbow*," 10 April 1961, DHH 81/520/8000, "HMCS *Rainbow*," vol. 2.

52. Notes 16 and 23, nd, "War Services Legate.... Robt. D. Lieut. RCNVR [*sic*]," nd, DHH 81/520/1440–6, vol. 8, Halifax, Nova Scotia—1905–1920; and Hadley and Sarty, *Tin-pots and Pirate Ships,* 269.

53. Note 17, nd, "War Services Legate.... Robt. D. Lieut. RCNVR [*sic*]," nd, DHH 81/520/1440–6, vol. 8, Halifax, Nova Scotia—1905–1920.

54. "Finding," 5 October 1918, ibid, vol. 7; and Note 18, nd, "War Services Legate.... Robt. D. Lieut. RCNVR [*sic*]," nd, ibid, vol. 8.

subsequent signal to *Cartier*, made after *Hochelaga* had closed with the flotilla leader, asking: "Do you see reinforcements astern? Don't you think it better to wait for them?" McGuirk's curt reply of "negative" as he steamed full speed toward the submarine's location only emphasized the *Hochelaga* commander's own loss of nerve.[55] As the court martial correctly decided, the evidence clearly showed that on the afternoon of the 25th Lieutenant Legate demonstrated he had no interest in closing with the enemy, whether his ship was alone or was following the rest of the patrol flotilla to the attack.

Although some have viewed the verdict as "rough justice,"[56] the RNCVR lieutenant's actions could not be tolerated in an active service force, particularly in an officer of Legate's experience. The son of a Royal Navy fleet engineer with two brothers serving as RN engineer commanders, Legate had joined the RNCVR in September 1914 and been promoted to sub-lieutenant in June 1915. After serving as the navigation officer on *Stadacona* in 1916, he was given command of *Tuna* in April 1917 and command of *Hochelaga* the following September.[57] With his conviction, Legate was sentenced "to be dismissed from his majesty's service" as of 5 October 1918 with the forfeiture of his commission, war service gratuity, medals, and other benefits. When Legate applied to the naval secretary in December 1918 for a certificate of service and a war service gratuity, he received only the former.[58]

Even as the East Coast escort fleet was fanning out across the fishing banks to warn schooners of the presence of *U 156* and *Triumph*, a second U-boat had entered Canadian waters off Nova Scotia. After operating south of New York since first making her presence felt with a highly successful attack against the New England fishing fleet on the Georges Bank on 10 August, *U 117* began her homeward voyage from the shipping lanes southeast of Cape Cod on the 22nd. The U-cruiser spent the next week moving northeast parallel to the Nova Scotia coast and from 100 to 200 kilometres out to sea, travelling south of Sable Island before passing within twenty-five kilometres of Cape Race. On 24 August the submarine shelled the Canadian schooner *Bianca* of 408 tons some 275 kilometres

---

55. "Finding," 5 October 1918, ibid, vol. 7.

56. Keith Calow, "Rough Justice: The Court Martial of Lieutenant Robert Douglas Legate," *The Northern Mariner*, XV, No. 4, (October 2005), 1–17.Calow argues in Legate's favour and points to a number of legal technicalities to support his contention, including the argument that RCN personnel were not governed by any legal authority, either British or Canadian, once HMC ships moved beyond the twelve-mile territorial limit. The article also suggests that Legate was sacrificed for political reasons by "the RCN command," an interpretation that ignores the fact that Legate was arrested strictly on Hose's own initiative on 2 September, with no reference to NSHQ, and that a failure to do so would have had serious repercussions for naval discipline within the Sydney escort fleet. The political argument is also unconvincing because the incident was not reported in the press at the time, although it appears to have been public knowledge in Sydney. When the court martial was revealed in the Sydney Daily Post at the end of November 1918, the newspaper misidentified the *Hochelaga's* commander as a W.G. Tudor. Brian Tennyson and Roger Sarty, *Guardian of the Gulf: Sydney, Cape Breton, and the Atlantic Wars* (Toronto 2000), 168–69, 413. Whatever the legal technicalities, there can be no question that on 25 August the commander of an RCN warship suffered a loss of nerve in the face of the enemy and that his subsequent dismissal from the naval service was justified.

57. Notes 29 to 39, nd, "War Services Legate…. Robt. D. Lieut. RCNVR [*sic*]," nd, DHH 81/520/1440–6, vol. 8, Halifax, Nova Scotia—1905–1920.

58. Notes 25 to 28, Note 39, nd, ibid.

southeast of Halifax. Carrying a cargo of tobacco on passage from Brazil, the vessel was abandoned by her crew soon after the Germans opened fire and they did not wait to see the raiders board the schooner and attempt to sink her with bombs. Although the latter exploded, *U 117*'s crew also did not wait to see if the vessel actually sank. Ironically, she was saved by her tobacco cargo, which swelled with sea water and plugged the holes in the hull. *Bianca* was taken in tow by a Boston fishing schooner three days later, and successfully brought into Halifax.[59] Not having bothered to see what became of their schooner, *Bianca*'s crew reached shore and reported that they had been overhauled by an enemy submarine but had not seen their ship sink. With *Triumph*'s capture fresh in their minds, naval intelligence in Halifax reported to NSHQ on the 29th that *Bianca* was "possibly being used" by her German captors as a surface raider and promptly informed all Canadian auxiliary patrol vessels to be on the lookout for her.[60]

While *Bianca*'s arrival at Halifax precluded her being used by the Germans as a raider, the several-days' delay in survivors reaching shore, occasioned by the greater distance *U 117* was operating from the coast, meant that naval authorities could not organize an effective response to her activities. By the time Halifax received word of the attack on *Bianca*, for instance, the U-cruiser had already sunk the American fishing trawler *Rush* on the morning of the 26th. The trawler was sunk some 260 kilometres east-southeast of Canso, and some 170 kilometres south-southwest from where *U 156* sank *Gloaming* that same morning. The next day *U 117* torpedoed and sank the Norwegian merchant ship *Bergsdalen* some 175 kilometres southwest of Cape Race. Hit without warning, the 2,550 ton steamer sank so rapidly that some members of the crew had to leap into the sea to save themselves and not all lifeboats could be launched. Fortunately, only one of the sailors died. The U-cruiser's final attack came after passing Cape Race. On the evening of 30 August *U 117* overhauled two Canadian fishing schooners travelling in company, *Elsie Porter* and *Potentate*, both of 136 tons, and sank them with bombs 450 kilometres northeast of St John's. The fishermen were picked up by the steamer *Solberg* two days later and brought ashore. The submarine later rendezvoused with the homeward-bound and leaking *U 140* west of Ireland to provide assistance. Both U-boats arrived safely back in Germany in late October, although *U 117* had to be towed into port by German destroyers after running out of fuel oil.[61]

Even though intelligence concerning *U 117*'s attacks arrived ashore too late to be of practical operational use, the defence of the Nova Scotia coast received a further boost at the end of August with the inaugural flights by the American air detachment at Baker Point. One day after *Bianca*'s sinking, the USN detachment commander, Lieutenant Byrd, reported his HS2L flying boats as ready for action, the Halifax station having a "full complement of experienced men and officers" available. As we have seen, a plan of operations had been worked out with Hose, Chambers, and Cull on the 26th for the eventual employment of four aircraft at both Halifax and Sydney.[62] For the first three

---

59. US Navy Department, *German Submarine Activities*, 97–98.

60. Navinet to Naval Ottawa, 29 August 1918, 1062–13–2, pt. 5, LAC, RG 24, vol. 4021.

61. US Navy Department, *German Submarine Activities*, 82, 99–100.

62. "Naval Aviation in Canada During the First World War," nd, 16, DHH 74/25.

weeks the air detachment at Halifax averaged one or two flights per day, either flying to seaward as air cover for coastal convoys or along the coast "making a thorough investigation for possible submarine bases." Although they did not sight a U-cruiser during any of their patrols, operations could still prove hazardous. During the first week of September, for instance, two flying boats were on convoy patrol when, "twenty-five miles out, the propeller of one machine burst, severing a control and cutting a hole through the boat and right wing. Pilot landed safely and was towed in by TBD *DeLong*." On another convoy patrol two weeks later, "one of the machines had to [force] land on twelve-foot waves. The pontoon was smashed and the machine slightly strained, but the pilot got off safely and returned to the station." Preparations at the Sydney air station, meanwhile, were a month behind those at Baker Point and it was not until the final week of September that the Cape Breton base was able to undertake its initial convoy air patrols.[63]

As comforting as the added measure of security provided by the air patrols at Halifax was, by the time the USN's flying boats were operational the port was primarily used for convoy assembly by coastal shipping proceeding between the Gulf of St Lawrence and the Gulf of Maine.[64] The RCN's main focus remained on the trans-Atlantic HC and HS convoys moving through the Gulf of St Lawrence and its main concern was the weakness of the escort forces it had available to provide protection along its considerable length. In late August, Kingsmill sent his director of the operations division, Commander J.P. Gibbs, to Washington to confer with Vice-Admiral Grant about the precarious situation. As Gibbs informed Kingsmill upon returning Ottawa, he had given the C-in-C the "full details of the organization of the Canadian patrols" whereupon "the commander-in-chief adhered to his decision that HC convoys would sail from Quebec until the close of navigation and informed me that the Admiralty would not hear of any alteration."

> I pointed out the weakness of the Canadian patrols taking into consideration the great length of the traffic lane, but the commander-in-chief considered that the risk must be accepted. He offered, however, to supply a certain number of drifters now, and some of the new trawlers of lot B later, to patrol the most dangerous points.
>
> He informed me that the route south of Anticosti would always be used except under exceptional circumstances, when I pointed out the danger of mines in the northern channel, owing to the shortage of sweepers.
>
> The points which the commander-in-chief considers to be most important are the Straits of Belle Isle and between Gaspé and Anticosti, and at these places he wishes to place his patrol.

---

63. Lieutenant-Colonel J.T. Cull, "Royal Canadian Naval Air Service Events for Week Ending September 9th, 1918," nd, "Royal Canadian Naval Air Service Events for Week Ending September 14th, 1918," nd, "Royal Canadian Naval Air Service Events for Week Ending September 22nd, 1918," nd, "Royal Canadian Naval Air Service Events for Week Ending September 30th, 1918," nd, Wing Commander F.H. Hitchens, "The Royal Canadian Naval Air Service," February 1958, DHH 81/520/1700–219.

64. Navinet Halifax to Naval Ottawa, 21 October 1918, Naval Ottawa to Navinet Halifax, 22 October 1918, Naval Ottawa to Examine, Quebec, et al., 22 October 1918, 1048–48–1, pt. 4, LAC, RG 24, vol. 3772.

For that purpose he is lending to us the following ships *temporarily*—Eight drifters, now ready, detailed for Gibraltar. These are to proceed to the Straits of Belle Isle, with base at Mutton Bay.

When the remaining Admiralty drifters are ready he proposes that the following procedure be carried out. (The crews for these have arrived at Quebec, but the ships are not quite ready for sea.) Six to proceed to Gaspé and patrol between there and Anticosti on radial lines. Six to replace those temporarily in the Straits of Belle Isle. Three to reinforce the Cabot Straits patrol. The eight detailed for Gibraltar will then leave for Halifax and their destination. The remaining twelve drifters will be turned over to the United States authorities, and manned by them. They will be used as necessary, but I understand, unofficially, that they will work in the Gulf of Maine, and near Canadian waters....

The commander-in-chief asked that every possible means should be taken to keep a watch on the Cabot and Belle Isles Straits from the shore side, so that instant information could be sent if a submarine was sighted. By this means a troop convoy could be diverted if necessary.

I gave him the details of the present organization, and informed him that everything possible would be done, pointing out the difficulties of the country, and the lack of land lines. The superintendent of radio is forwarding proposals on this.

I pointed out the difficulty of providing ships to coal the patrols in the St Lawrence, and the commander-in-chief hoped that arrangements could be made by us, as he had nothing available. I informed the commander-in-chief that we had great difficulty in getting guns for our patrol vessels, and that some were still unarmed. The commander-in-chief sent a telegram to the Admiralty urging immediate action.

The commander-in-chief hoped that this department would work in the closest possible cooperation with him, and impressed upon me that he would always give all possible assistance.[65]

Although Grant confirmed that Quebec would continue to serve as the assembly port for all HC convoys until the close of navigation in 1918, the limited reinforcement he could offer Ottawa amounted to only seven additional drifters—fifteen Admiralty drifters less the eight sent on to Gibraltar—a rather meagre augmentation of the RCN's already inadequate force. Kingsmill was not only concerned by the lack of suitable escorts over the lengthy St Lawrence shipping lane but also with the performance of the captain of patrols in ensuring that a proper protection was organized with the forces available. Having already reduced Hose's area of responsibility to the Gulf of St Lawrence alone, the naval director maintained a close supervision of his escort arrangements for the protection of HC 16, the first of the HC series to be organized at Quebec. Hose had informed NSHQ on 29

---

65. Commander J.P. Gibbs, "Memo: To The Director of the Naval Service," 29 August 1918, ibid.

HMCS *Canada* at Davie Shipbuilding in Lauzon, Quebec. The company's shipyard, located across the St Lawrence River from Quebec City, had been founded in 1825 by British ship captain Allison Davie. (PAC e007140918)

Captain Walter Hose's flagship, HMCS *Stadacona*, in Sydney Harbour, 1918. (DND CN 6371)

August that he planned to use four auxiliary patrol vessels, *Lady Evelyn*, *Acadia*, *Stadacona*, and *Cartier*, to escort the convoy from the Gaspé to the Cabot Strait "and as far to seaward as coal supply will admit," with the Sydney subchaser division joining the convoy off St Paul Island.[66]

Only one day before the convoy was scheduled to sail from Quebec on 4 September, however, a still wary Kingsmill wanted to confirm Hose's specific plans for HC 16's protection. The naval director cabled the captain of patrols on the 3rd with a terse demand that a "full report as to your dispositions of all vessels for protection HC sailing 4th to be wired [to Ottawa] immediately."[67] The captain of patrols responded that same day with the news that the 8-knot "*Acadia* cannot keep up with HC [convoys], consequently *Lady Evelyn* only vessel available for HC 16 as far as Saint Paul's Island. Chasers will join convoy there and escort. Straits will be patrolled by six trawlers prior to arrival of convoy. *Acadia* with five trawlers will be escorting HS convoy leaving Sydney September 5th. *Hochelaga* in dock at Saint John's (Nfld) [after escorting a coastal convoy to that port while under the command of her navigating officer, Lieutenant C.McL. Fry[68]]. *Cartier* routine lay up cleaning boilers."[69]

Kingsmill was taken aback to find that the captain of patrols did not seem to appreciate that a maximum effort was required to protect the valuable convoys from Quebec. Bluntly telling Hose that his response was "quite inadequate," the naval director wanted to know why he was not making use of the auxiliary patrol vessels *Margaret*, *Canada*, and *Stadacona*, and insisted that the focal points for shipping off both Bird Rock and the waters nearer the Magdalen Islands had to be patrolled. Reflecting his dismay at the apparent lack of preparation—the second time within the month that the naval director was disturbed by Hose's casual patrol dispositions—Kingsmill emphasized that the captain of patrols was to "make best arrangements possible and report fully [to NS]HQ."[70]

A chastened Hose quickly reordered his deployments, sending *Stadacona* to sweep from Bird Rock to the west of the Magdalens, and *Margaret* to make the same patrol to the east of the islands. *Lady Evelyn*—replacing *Canada* which was still laid up at Pictou repairing defects—would patrol in the vicinity of Bird Rock, the most northeasterly of the Quebec islands, for the twenty-four hour period before the convoy's arrival. All three vessels would attempt to intercept the convoy off Bird Rock "and accompany them as far out as coal capacity will admit." Hose also emphasized to NSHQ that he had not been kept informed of either the timing or route that HC 16 would be taking, and pointedly asked that he "may be informed in future of convoy sailing and route sufficiently to arrange meeting them."[71] As he subsequently explained to Kingsmill in his own defence, "the only information I had

66. Hose to Naval Ottawa, 29 August 1918, ibid.

67. Naval Ottawa to Transports, Sydney, for Patrols, 3 September 1918, 1065–7-6, LAC, RG 24, vol. 4031.

68. Note 39, nd, "War Services Legate.... Robt. D. Lieut. RCNVR [sic]," nd, DHH 81/520/1440–6, vol. 8, Halifax, Nova Scotia—1905–1920.

69. Captain of Patrols to Naval Ottawa, 3 September 1918, 153, 1065–7-6, LAC, RG 24, vol. 4031.

70. Naval Ottawa to Transports, Sydney, for Patrols, 3 September 1918, ibid.

71. Patrols to Naval Ottawa, 4 September 1918, ibid.

re HC 16 was that Rear-Admiral Chambers was telegraphing commander-in-chief that if HC 16 was to keep programme time on the other side [of the Atlantic] it would have to leave Quebec on the 4th. Port convoy officer here [Sydney] when asked had no information of HC 16 leaving on the 4th and told me as far as he knew it was leaving on the 5th."[72] The naval director was understandably nonplussed at the lack of coordination between senior officers on the East Coast, and questioned both Hose and the RCN's senior officer at Halifax, Admiral Story, if they had conferred with each other as planned.[73] Responsibility for the failure to keep the captain of patrols informed concerning the movements of HC 16, however, lay with Rear-Admiral Chambers and his convoy staff at Quebec. Nonetheless, the lack of communication between the East Coast's three senior naval officers responsible for convoy defence could only reinforce Kingsmill's desire to maintain his oversight of operations in Canadian waters.

With the naval director's criticism in mind, Hose proposed using the auxiliary patrol vessels *Stadacona*, *Margaret*, *Lady Evelyn*, and *Canada* to escort all future HC convoys from Quebec, if they were being routed through the Strait of Belle Isle, meeting them off Pont des Monts at the mouth of the St Lawrence and accompanying them as far as Belle Isle. The Sydney-based submarine chasers were "not much value for convoys proceeding via Belle Isle but can meet them off Birds [*sic*] Rock if proceeding via Cabot Strait." He warned Kingsmill, however, that if it was also necessary to maintain a patrol at the mouth of the St Lawrence, "more vessels will be needed as I can only just maintain patrol and coastal and slow convoy requirements, fishery protection and emergency call[s]" with the ships he had available at Sydney.[74]

With HC 16 required to make an ocean rendezvous with its New York section of eleven ships, the convoy was routed through the Cabot Strait for a planned junction with the other half of the convoy at 49° West at 1400 hours on 8 September. Fortunately, the passage through the strait was made following the departure of both *U 156* and *U 117* from the area at the end of August and, although *U 155* was heading toward North America at the time, she passed some 300 kilometres to the south of the rendezvous point. Even in the absence of any submarines in the convoy's vicinity, the difficulties associated with an ocean rendezvous were amply demonstrated when fog and icebergs prevented the two sections from joining until 2000 hours on the 9th.[75] With all fifteen ships of HC 17 departing Quebec together on the morning of 13 September, Chambers's staff was able to route the convoy through the Strait of Belle Isle, well clear of U-boat interference. After meeting its three-ship RCN escort off Cape Gaspé, HC 17 passed through the strait and into the open ocean north of Newfoundland on the night of 15/16 September.[76] In a similarly successful

---

72. Patrols to Naval Ottawa, 7 September 1918, ibid.

73. Kingsmill to Story, Hose, 4 September 1918, ibid.

74. Patrols to Naval Ottawa, 5 September 1918, ibid.

75. Britannia, Washington to Naval Ottawa, 3 September 1918, 1048–48–1, pt. 1, LAC, RG 24, vol. 3772; US Navy Department, *German Submarine Activities*, 70, 99–101; and HC Convoy reports, nd, HC 16, UKNA, ADM 137/2657.

76. HC Convoy reports, nd, HC 17, UKNA, ADM 137/2657.

attempt to avoid the U-cruisers operating off the entrance to the Cabot Strait, incoming shipping bound for Montreal was also routed to the north of Newfoundland through the Strait of Belle Isle.[77]

Despite the primacy of convoy protection among the RCN's tasks, the navy could not forget the political importance of protecting the fishing fleet, even if those concerns had not prompted the acting naval minister to visit Nova Scotia as he had in August. As difficult an undertaking as guarding dispersed fishing vessels was for any navy, even one equipped with destroyers capable of engaging a U-boat, there was a public expectation that the RCN should provide protection. With its meagre forces already stretched thin escorting both ocean and coastal convoys as well as patrolling the focal points of shipping, the RCN had to press all of its assets into service. These included the two submarines *CC 1* and *CC 2* that had been brought around to Halifax from Esquimalt in the fall of 1917. Unfortunately, both boats had arrived in October following their gruelling sea voyage with their engines in desperate need of overhaul.[78] It was not until mid-August 1918 that either of the two boats was ready for sea. Nonetheless, in anticipation of one of the boats becoming operational, Kingsmill instructed Hose to employ *Shearwater* and one of the submarines in Bras d'Or Lake on Cape Breton Island to train the trawlers and drifters "in hunting by hydrophone, first with single ship, and afterwards by units, until units of six ships can be handled effectively. Every endeavour should be made to pass all trawlers and drifters through this course, the sea patrols being reduced as necessary, provided that the submarine situation at the moment warrants it. The necessary adjustments should be made between the patrols at Halifax and Sydney to enable *all* ships to go through the hydrophone course, as it is considered of the highest importance."[79] Although the arrival of U-cruisers in Canadian waters later in August made it impossible to train as many of the trawlers and drifters as Kingsmill had hoped, a program was established on Bras d'Or Lake using CGS *Petrel* to train hydrophone operators in mock attacks on *CC 2*.[80]

The attack by *U 156* on the fishing fleet, however, raised the possibility that *CC 2* might be sent to the fishing banks to attack the German raiders. Although small, the torpedo armament of the two Canadian submarines made them the only vessels in the RCN that were capable of engaging a U-cruiser on anything approaching even terms. With a view to their possible employment against U-boats, Kingsmill had emphasized in early August that "every possible opportunity should be taken" once *CC 1* and *CC 2* were on Bras d'Or Lake "to practice 'submarine v. submarine.'"[81] On 28 August, three days after *U 156* sank the schooner *Gloaming* in the Cabot Strait between St Pierre and Sydney and with the German offensive apparently intensifying, the captain of patrols proposed despatching the Canadian boats to the fishing banks "accompanied each by a schooner to act both as a decoy and as

77. Admiralty to Grant, 401, 22 August 1918, Port Convoy Officer, Halifax to Grant, 711, 25 August 1918, UKNA, ADM 137/903.

78. Dave Perkins, *Canada's Submariners, 1914–1923* (Erin, Ontario, 1989), 168–71.

79. Kingsmill to Captain of Patrols, 4 August 1918, DHH 81/520/1440–6, vol. 7.

80. Hadley and Sarty, *Tin-pots and Pirate Ships*, 279.

81. Kingsmill to Captain of Patrols, 4 August 1918, DHH 81/520/1440–6, vol. 7.

The crews of *CC 1* and *CC 2*, with drifters in the background, at Halifax, 1918. (DND CN 509)

HMCS *Shearwater* at Halifax, 1918. The former British sloop accompanied the submarines *CC 1* and *CC 2* to the Atlantic port in October 1917. (LAC e007140913)

The submarines *CC 1* (left) and *CC 2* after their arrival at Halifax via the Panama Canal. (DND DHH file CC-1)

Staff and students of the Naval Wireless Telegraph School in Ottawa on the front steps of the Parliament buildings' reconstructed Centre Block in May 1918. The telegraph school was transferred from Halifax following the December 1917 explosion, graduating 140 fourth-class operators for service as warrant officers in Canadian and British ships. (LAC PA-122251)

supply ships for the submarines." Commander Bertram Jones of the *Shearwater* considered "that each of the submarines would be in a position to remain on the banks for a period of two weeks under these conditions." As Hose explained, "the attendant schooner should lie at anchor on the banks, equipped with all the proper fishing requisites and that the submarine should lie in close proximity, both submarine and schooner being equipped with directional hydrophones. The schooner should have auxiliary power capable of giving her a speed of seven knots. The schooner is to be manned by naval ratings specially selected from men previously fishermen."[82] Although the American navy eventually decided that the tactic of using a schooner to lure an enemy submarine into torpedo range was ineffective,[83] it was one of the very few offensive options available to the weakly armed vessels of Canada's East Coast.

As important as hydrophone training was for an anti-submarine fleet, it was Hose's opinion that "owing to present probability of fairly frequent U-boat activities off the Nova Scotian coast and on the Grand Banks, during which every available vessel at our disposal will be required for escorting convoy[s] in all directions, both coastal and ocean-going, protection of fishing fleets, mine-sweeping, and patrols generally, that little opportunity is likely to exist for training of organized divisions of trawlers." Stating that training for individual hydrophone operators would continue unabated in the meantime, the captain of patrols reasoned that "the season for U-cruisers activities in these waters will in all probability have come to an end" by the time "a sufficient number of divisions had been trained to the full." Because "the speed, armament, etc, of trawlers" limited their "full measure of utility," Hose recommended "that the employment of our submarines in any offensive operations ... is of the greater importance at the present time."[84] Well aware of the political pressure to defend the fishing fleet from attack, Kingsmill did not hesitate to endorse the submarine scheme, directing Hose to "take immediate action to obtain one suitable schooner and to collect the necessary stores and supplies. One schooner only is necessary for the present, as only one submarine is available. The utmost care should be taken to keep the disguise of the ships perfect, and armament should be carefully hidden."[85]

Both Hose and Kingsmill moved quickly to implement the decoy plan, with the naval director recommending the appointment of Lieutenant Geoffrey Lake to command the vessels. An RNCVR officer since 1914, Lake had spent most of the war with the Canadian submarines and, as the commanding officer of *CC 2*, had brought the boat from Esquimalt to Halifax.[86] The captain of patrols made inquiries into suitable schooners available for

82. Hose to NSHQ, 28 August 1918, ibid.

83. Carroll S. Alden, "American Submarine Operations in the War," *United States Naval Institute Proceedings,* No. 46, June 1920, 820–27.

84. Hose to NSHQ, 28 August 1918, DHH 81/520/1440–6, vol. 7.

85. Kingsmill to Captain of Patrols, 4 September 1918, Naval Ottawa to Transports Sydney, 4 September 1918, ibid.

86. Kingsmill to Captain of Patrols, 5 September 1918, ibid; and Department of the Naval Service, *The Canadian Navy List for November 1914* (Ottawa 1914), 30; and Perkins, *Canada's Submariners,* 104, 168.

purchase and suggested two possibilities, one in Boston and one in Louisbourg. Planning for the scheme continued at both Ottawa and Sydney through much of September. Before privy council approval was received for a schooner purchase, however, *CC 2* developed a defective armature that required several weeks to repair and the boat was not available for service again until later in October. *CC 1*, meanwhile, did not complete her sea trials and join her sister boat and *Shearwater* at Baddeck until the 26th.[87] By that time, the U-cruiser threat had ended for the 1918 season, the European war appeared to be concluding, and the entire decoy schooner scheme to protect the fishing fleet was shelved.

Although the use of the two Canadian submarines did not materialize, NSHQ remained aware of the need to address the fishing industry's concerns. Even as word of *Triumph's* capture was spreading in Nova Scotia, the acting minister, A.K. Maclean, had supported a request by the trawler's owner that the vessel be replaced by one of the navy's escort trawlers. In early September, Kingsmill agreed that the Admiralty trawlers being built in Canada—a design based on British fishing vessels—might be turned over to Canadian fishermen as compensation for vessels, such as *Triumph*, sunk by the Germans. Based on the naval director's suggestion, Desbarats mentioned the possibility of transferring RCN patrol vessels as compensation for war losses in urging the director of ship construction to complete as many of the second batch of twenty-four imperial trawlers as possible before the end of the year.[88]

From the time of *Triumph's* capture, NSHQ had been urging Hose to meet with the USN's Admiral Wood at Boston to coordinate a plan for protecting the fishing fleets. As the toll of sunken fishing schooners continued to rise during the last week of August, a plan was developed for a general conference to be held between the captain of patrols and representatives of the American and French navies and of the fishing interests of Newfoundland, Nova Scotia, and New England. Although the naval minister, C.C. Ballantyne (recently returned from London), issued the call for the conference to convene on 7 September, NSHQ left most of the arrangements in the hands of Rear-Admiral Story at Halifax and Captain Hose at Sydney. As a measure to reassure the Canadian fishing industry of the navy's continuing concern for the safety of the fishing fleet, the deputy minister contacted an anxious A.K. Maclean at Halifax to seek his input in nominating a representative of the Nova Scotia fleet, assuring the former acting minister that the

---

87. Transport Sydney to Naval Ottawa, 10 September 1918, Kingsmill, "Memorandum for the Minister," 11 September 1918, Joseph Salter and Sons to Hose, 7 September 1918, Patrols to Naval Ottawa, 13 September 1918, Hose to NSHQ, 13 September 1918, NSHQ to Captain of Patrols, 18 September 1918, Patrols to Naval Ottawa, 20 September, 21, 24 and 26 October 1918, Naval Ottawa to Navyard Halifax, 23 October 1918, DHH 81/520/1440-6, vol. 7.

88. Maclean to Desbarats, 22 August 1918, 1029-16-1, pt. 5, LAC, RG 24, vol. 5605; and Kingsmill, "Memorandum for the Deputy Minister," 6 September 1918, A.A. Wright to Desbarats, 18 September 1918, 1029-16-1, pt. 6, LAC, RG 24, vol. 5605; and Hadley and Sarty, *Tin-pots and Pirate Ships*, 278.

89. Naval Ottawa to Transports, Sydney, 21 August 1918, Captain of Patrol to Naval Ottawa, 22 August 1918, Naval Ottawa to Transports Sydney, 22 August 1918, Captain of Patrols to Naval Ottawa, 28 August 1918, Naval Ottawa to Navyard Halifax, 29 August 1918, Naval Ottawa to Navyard Halifax, 4 September 1918, 1017-10-6, pt. 1, LAC, RG 24, vol. 3832.

conference had the prime minister's approval.[89] If Ottawa hoped that the conference would help calm anxiety in Nova Scotia in regard to the RCN's ability to protect the fishing fleet, however, its purpose was undermined when the conference plans totally miscarried.[90] While in itself a rather small matter—a successful conference would not have altered the number of fishing vessels that had already been sunk—it does present yet another example of Hose's often mediocre performance as captain of patrols.

In what would soon prove to have been a mistake, the captain of patrols agreed to hold the meeting at Hawkesbury on the southern tip of Cape Breton on the dubious suggestion of Lieutenant H. White, a USN naval intelligence officer who had recently arrived at Halifax. The American officer was apparently unfamiliar with the area, and chose Hawkesbury off the map "as being central between Boston and Newfoundland" when, in fact, it was somewhat out of the way and the Newfoundland representative, the colony's minister of shipping, J.C. Crosbie, would have to land at Sydney first before taking the train south.[91] As H.R. Silver of Halifax, the Canadian fishing representative, explained to naval minister C.C. Ballantyne shortly after the planned conference failed to materialize, "it was a pity that some more central place than Hawkesbury could not have been chosen at first, either Sydney or Halifax, would have been far preferable from every point of view, as at Hawkesbury, it is impossible to get any information as to what is going on, or what can be done in the event of plans miscarrying."[92] After agreeing to the dubious location, Hose decided to travel to Hawkesbury in HMCS *Cartier*—"in order to have a suitable place for the conference where the necessary charts, etc., would be easily obtainable"[93]—by crossing Bras d'Or Lake. Although both Hose and Crosbie were in Sydney on the afternoon of the 6th, and had a telephone conversation to confirm the meeting at Hawkesbury the next day, the Newfoundland minister of shipping travelled there by train that evening, while the captain of patrols proceeded into Bras d'Or Lake aboard *Cartier*.[94]

As Hose subsequently explained to Ottawa, "by midnight an exceptionally heavy gale sprang up and although every endeavor was made to push on, it became necessary at 4 am to heave the ship to until noon" on the 7th, the day the conference was supposed to have taken place. By the time Hose arrived at Hawkesbury at 2200 hours that evening, he "found that Messrs Crosbie and Silver had decided not to wait, but had returned to Sydney at 4 pm." After waiting overnight to see if the USN representative to the conference—who had also failed to appear on the 7th—would arrive on the following morning's train from Halifax (he did not), Hose decided to reboard *Cartier* for a return voyage rather than try to catch up to Crosbie and Silver by train. Hose departed Hawkesbury at 0900 hours on the 8th but was delayed in his attempts to re-enter Bras d'Or Lake by the attendant at St Peter's. The captain of patrols "informed the lock-keeper that urgent work for the Department of the Naval

90. H.R. Silver to C.C. Ballantyne, 9 September 1918, Ballantyne to Silver, 13 September 1918, ibid.

91. Captain of Patrols to NSHQ, 20 September 1918, ibid.

92. H.R. Silver to C.C. Ballantyne, 9 September 1918, ibid.

93. Captain of Patrols to NSHQ, 12 September 1918, ibid.

94. Ibid.

Service made it most important that I should go through, the lock-keeper however refused to do anything to enable the *Cartier* to go through and I was held until 7 am on Monday, 9th."[95] As a result, Hose did not finally return to Sydney until late on the afternoon of 9 September when he discovered that the lock-keeper's disdain for the RCN was now shared by the Newfoundland minister of shipping. According to Admiral Story's report on the matter, the captain of patrols found "a very rude message" from Crosbie waiting for him when he arrived back at the Sydney patrol office.[96] When called upon to explain the conference fiasco to Ottawa, Hose placed most of the blame on the Newfoundland minister's impatience, failing entirely to appreciate the extent to which Crosbie's anger at being badly inconvenienced was the result of Hose's own errors:

> I then tried to get into communication with Mr Crosbie at the Sydney Hotel but found that he had left for North Sydney.
>
> Lt. Commander Knight informed me that Mr Crosbie had come into the patrol office at 1:30 and had said he was going to North Sydney. Mr Knight informed him that a message had arrived saying that I expected to arrive at 2 pm, however Mr Crosbie said that if anyone wanted to see him they could go across to North Sydney.
>
> Since Mr Crosbie could not wait any time at Mulgrave or at Sydney for the Canadian captain of patrols, it appeared to me that he was not particularly anxious as to whether the Canadian naval forces protected the Newfoundland fisheries or not and as there was much very urgent and important matter[s] from the department awaiting my attention, I did not proceed to see Mr Crosbie at North Sydney....
>
> I am at a loss to understand why neither any fishery representative from the United States nor Lt. Commander Snow [the USN representative] arrived at Mulgrave.
>
> Commander Ferlicot, who has a considerable force on the banks, sent me a message to say he could not leave the banks to attend the conference.
>
> Without such a conference no co-ordinated work can be done by the combined US, French and Canadian forces.
>
> As matters stand at present, with the many calls that there are on the Canadian patrol squadron for convoy escorts, coastal and ocean going, minesweeping and trade route patrols, that very little can be done in the matter of a constant patrol on the banks.[97]

If the captain of patrols was unwilling to recognize the degree to which his failure to arrive for the conference at the appointed time had annoyed Crosbie and Silver, the point was certainly appreciated by the naval minister who had to apologize for the naval officer's

---

95. Ibid.

96. Story to NSHQ, 11 September 1918, ibid.

97. Captain of Patrols to NSHQ, 12 September 1918, ibid.

blunder. Silver wrote to Ballantyne on 9 September out of a genuine concern for the safety of the fishing fleet and was not harbouring any recriminations, but did explain that Crosbie "was very much annoyed with his experience. He came 700 miles to attend this conference at a time when his duties at home needed his presence there."[98] The naval minister responded that he was "extremely sorry that you ... should have been obliged to waste so much of your valuable time without any result, and I am very much put out at Mr Crosbie taking such a long trip and not finding the other members of the conference at Hawkesbury." Dismayed by his officers' inability to arrange a simple conference "so that measures can be taken to extend proper protection to the fishing fleets," Ballantyne demanded that the senior Canadian officer on the East Coast, Vice-Admiral Story, "submit an explanation of the failure."[99]

Both Hose and Story were willing to dismiss the whole affair as the result of *Cartier* being "unfortunately delayed by the heavy gale" but both Silver and a very angry Crosbie—who insisted upon returning to St John's that the governor of Newfoundland pursue the matter with the governor-general of Canada—provided information that seriously questioned Hose's judgment. Silver informed Ballantyne that "it is difficult for a civilian like myself to understand why Capt. Hose could not have come from Sydney to Hawkesbury by rail same as Mr Crosbie did, especially when the Meteorological Bureau had advised two days previous that a severe tropical storm was moving north, and all vessels were warned to keep in harbour, however, that is for him to explain."[100] The Newfoundland shipping minister was equally baffled, making it clear in his letter to the Canadian government that "it cannot be suggested that this gale was unexpected as the chief topic of conversation in North Sydney on Friday, the 6th instant was the tropical storm which had been forecasted and which was expected at any moment. In the report of the storm the 'Sydney Daily Post' of the 9th instant states 'the mariners of Nova Scotia were warned as early as Thursday morning that a tropical storm was brewing.'"[101] When questioned directly by NSHQ about the weather forecast, however, Hose replied that "at the time I embarked in *Cartier* [on the evening of the 6th], I ha[d] not seen the storm warnings."[102] Coming from the Canadian naval officer responsible for making all escort and patrol arrangements in the Gulf of St Lawrence, his claimed ignorance of the approach of a major storm, one that was well-known on the streets of Sydney and which had the potential to seriously affect naval operations, was a rather stunning admission indeed.

Whatever concerns Ottawa may have had that the man-in-the-street was better informed of the weather than the captain of patrols—and Hose's explanation was passed to the minister—an embarrassed naval department preferred to downplay the entire matter. St John's was simply informed that another conference on fishing fleet protection

---

98. H.R. Silver to C.C. Ballantyne, 9 September 1918, ibid.

99. Ballantyne to Silver, 13 September 1918, ibid.

100. H.R. Silver to C.C. Ballantyne, 9 September 1918, ibid.

101. "From the Governor of Newfoundland to the Governor General," 5 October 1918, and enclosed "Extract from Mr Crosbie's letter," ibid.

102. Captain of Patrols to NSHQ, 20 September 1918, ibid.

would be held "during the winter or early spring so that all arrangements may be made before next season."[103] There is no question that Hose was burdened with a great deal of work in carrying out his duties as captain of patrols and that he had only a minimum of staff officers to assist him. His heavy workload suggests, however, that it would have been far wiser for Hose to have held the conference at Sydney, where it would have taken only a few hours of his time, or travelled by train as Crosbie did, rather than taking several days out of his schedule to sail *Cartier* (herself a valuable escort) across Bras d'Or Lake and back. It is difficult to see how Hose's explanations of his mismanagement, particularly his professed ignorance of an impending major storm, could have done anything to allay Kingsmill's doubts about his performance as captain of patrols.

As Hose's memoranda of explanation to NSHQ demonstrate, he was more concerned with his responsibilities for escorting both coastal and ocean convoys and patrolling the shipping lanes generally than he was in providing armed vessels to protect the fishing fleets. Although both *U 156* and *U 117* had departed Canadian waters at the end of August, the Admiralty had already passed word to North America that the converted mercantile submarine *Deutschland*, refitted and recommissioned as *U 155*, would be arriving sometime in mid-September to lay mines off St John's and Halifax.[104] Departing Kiel on 11 August, the former U-freighter made her first attack on the 27th to the northwest of the Azores, engaging in an inconclusive gun battle with the American steamships *Montoso* and *Ticonderoga*. *U 155* continued to operate in the waters northwest of the Azores for the next several days, making an unsuccessful attack on the American transport USS *Frank H. Buck* on 1 September, and sinking the 315-ton Portuguese schooner *Gamo* on 31 August and the Norwegian steamer *Shortland* of 2,560 tons on 2 September. Heading west over the next several days, the U-cruiser chased and shelled the British merchant ship *Monmouth* on the 7th some 650 kilometres southeast of Cape Race.[105] Four days later, *U 155* torpedoed and sank the Portuguese merchant ship *Leixoes* of 3,345 tons, steaming in ballast from England to Boston, 300 kilometres southeast of Canso, Nova Scotia. Word of the sinking did not spread, however, until a portion of the crew landed at Canso on 16 September.[106] By that time NSHQ had been fully informed of the presence of *U 155* by her attack on the wireless-equipped British merchant ship *Newby Hall* on 13 September some 150 kilometres southeast of Sable Island. As the Admiralty informed NSHQ the next day, the attack on the *Newby Hall* "would be by converted mercantile type submarine which is expected to mine the entrance of Saint John's and western entrance of Halifax."[107]

As the Admiralty's intelligence network had ascertained, *U 155* had indeed been tasked

103. Desbarats minute, 27 September 1918, on Captain of Patrols to NSHQ, 20 September 1918, Desbarats to Acting Undersecretary of State for External Affairs, 18 October 1918, ibid.

104. Grant, *U-Boat Intelligence*, 154–55.

105. J.P. Gibbs to Kingsmill, 11 September 1918, 1062–13–2, pt. 5, LAC, RG 24, vol. 4021; and US Navy Department, *German Submarine Activities*, 100–01.

106. Navinet to Naval Ottawa, 16 September 1918, 1062–13–2, pt. 5, LAC, RG 24, vol. 4021.

107. Navinet to Naval Ottawa, 14 September 1918, ibid.

with mining the approaches to both St John's and Halifax, the former assignment indicating the German navy's sketchy knowledge of Canadian geography and its inability to distinguish between the fishing port of St John's, Newfoundland, and shipping port of St John, New Brunswick. It was up to the commander of *U 155* himself to figure out the error: "Studying the nautical material, together with statements of the Englishman aboard the Portuguese sailing vessel *Gamo* [which I] sank on 31 August, lead me to believe that the harbour of St John's w[h]ere I am supposed to lay mines is really St John in the Bay of Fundy."[108] As a result, the U-cruiser ignored the Newfoundland port and proceeded directly to the Halifax approaches to carry out her minelaying and cable-cutting tasks. On 17 and 18 September *U 155* laid a series of mines some ten to fifteen kilometres off the coast between Betty Island to the southwest of Chebucto Head, the Sambro lightship, and Sambro Island. As well as being hampered by the fog that normally occurred off the Nova Scotia coast during the summer months, the German submarine recorded having to interrupt her work after spotting "destroyers, patrol vessels" in the shipping lanes off the Sambro lightship. The "destroyer" was undoubtedly HMCS *Grilse*, deployed by Admiral Story in the approaches along with the three USN subchasers as part of his defensive measures. Although no aircraft were sighted by *U 155*'s commander, the flying boats from the USN air station at Baker Point accompanied each of the coastal convoys to and from Halifax, an average of one flight per day.[109] A Halifax patrol vessel also destroyed an "apparently new" mine four kilometres southeast of the Sambro lightship only a couple of days after it was laid. None of the mines laid by *U 155* caused any damage and most were soon rendered unreliable after breaking their moorings and drifting ashore. Several of them were subsequently discovered by local fishermen.[110]

After lying some twenty kilometres off the coast during the night of 18/19 September, the U-cruiser made her way to Sable Island in an effort to cut some of the telegraph cables linking Canada to Britain. *U 155* did not waste much time on the effort, apparently cutting only one cable, before heading for US waters. On 20 September *U 155* stopped and sank the American fishing trawler *Kingfisher* 100 kilometres west-southwest of Sable Island, the last vessel sunk in Canadian waters during the war.[111] For the next three weeks the converted U-freighter operated well out to sea in the shipping lanes 200 to 600 kilometres southeast of Cape Cod. Her lack of surface speed betrayed her during several running gun battles, however, as merchant ships were eventually able to outdistance their pursuer. The German submarine was able to capture and scuttle the British schooner *Industrial* on 4 October but, as her operations in Canadian waters demonstrated, she was only able to

---

108. U-155 War Diary translation, quoted in Hadley and Sarty, *Tin-pots and Pirate Ships*, 284.

109. Lieutenant-Colonel J.T. Cull, "Royal Canadian Naval Air Service Events for Week Ending September 22nd, 1918," nd, DHH 81/520/1700–219.

110. J.P. Gibbs, "Memorandum: For the Prime Minister," 20 September 1918, 1062–13–2, pt. 5, Gibbs to PM, 11 October 1918, 1062–13–2, pt. 6, LAC, RG 24, vol. 4021; and Hadley and Sarty, *Tin-pots and Pirate Ships*, 286–7.

111. Navinet to Naval Ottawa, 21 September 1918, 1062–13–2, pt. 5, LAC, RG 24, vol. 4021; US Navy Department, *German Submarine Activities*, 103; and Hadley and Sarty, *Tin-pots and Pirate Ships*, 287.

achieve success against larger merchant ships when she attacked with torpedoes. On 3 October, *U 155* torpedoed and sank the 3,838-ton Italian steamship *Alberto Treves* and, on the 17th, attacked the 6,744-ton freighter *Lucia*, owned by the United States Shipping Board, as she was steaming in an unescorted convoy from New York to Marseilles, France. The *Lucia* was the last ship sunk in North American waters as the U-cruiser made her way toward the Azores before finally returning to Kiel on 15 November.[112]

The departure of the last enemy submarine from North American waters did not, however, cause any relaxation of the convoy organization process at either Quebec or Sydney. From the sailing of HC 16 from Quebec on 4 September until HC 24 steamed down the St Lawrence on 7 November, a total of ninety-two merchant ships departed for Europe in HC convoys. Another 419 merchant ships were organized into the thirteen HS convoys, HS 50 to HS 62, that weighed from Sydney between 3 August and 8 November. Including the thirty-two ships in the Canadian portions of convoys HC 12 to HC 15 organized in August, 543 merchantmen were safely escorted through Canadian waters without being attacked by enemy raiders.[113] Indeed, the final four months of the war saw an increase of over 550,000 tons of war materiel shipped from Montreal compared to the same period in 1917. The new director general, British Ministry of Shipping (Canada), A.H. Harris, and his overseas transport organization loaded a total of 1,788,575 tons of supplies at the port of Montreal from August to November, 83 percent of the total volume of war supplies shipped overseas from Canadian East Coast ports during that period.[114]

By the end of September the most immediate problem facing the convoy staffs ashore— aside from the chronic shortage of anti-submarine escorts—was the growing threat posed by the spread of Spanish influenza. At Quebec, three of Commander Eliott's small convoy staff were absent with the flu in mid-October and he had to scramble to find officers to handle the coding and routing duties. Delays also resulted from influenza cases among various ships' crews and especially among the soldiers being sent overseas. Eliott informed Chambers on 23 October, for example, that "there were no troopships in HC 22 owing to quarantine restrictions, for which I was personally glad, as the HC 20 had so many troopships with infectious cases that it kept the tugs busy taking off the most serious cases."[115] A portion of the convoy work was alleviated on 22 October when NSHQ decreed that coastal shipping proceeding between the Gulf of St Lawrence and the Bay of Fundy "may now be despatched coastwise … without being ordered to Halifax for convoy. Such vessels, however, are to be instructed to put into port if war warnings indicate danger in

112. US Navy Department, *German Submarine Activities*, 104–06.

113. HC and HS Convoy Reports, nd, UKNA, ADM 137/2657.

114. A.H. Harris, Director General, British Minister of Shipping (Canada) to J.A. Wilson, Director of Stores, 20 September 1918, Harris to Wilson, 16 October 1918, Harris to Wilson, 13 November 1918, Harris to Wilson, 4 December 1918, 1048–18–1, pt. 5, LAC, RG 24, vol. 3714.

115. Eliott to Chambers, 23 October 1918, quoted in Port Convoy Officer and Senior Officer of Escorts, Halifax to Commander-in-Chief, NA&WI, 11 and 26 October 1918, UKNA, ADM 137/1620.

116. Naval Ottawa to Examination Service, Quebec, et al., 22 October 1918, 1048–48–1, pt. 1, LAC, RG 24, vol. 3772.

their locality."[116] As Halifax had explained to Ottawa in requesting the change, "much delay is being caused at present without corresponding increase of safety to shipping. In most instances ships are sent on from here alone for lack of convoying vessels."[117]

The lack of escorts for coastal convoy work was an indication of just how thinly the RCN's anti-submarine forces were stretched. While HMCS *Grilse* was employed in the approaches to Halifax, most of the navy's remaining auxiliary patrol vessels, particularly *Margaret* and *Canada*, were being used in the Gulf escorting the HC convoys on their passage from the Gaspé through the Strait of Belle Isle. Of the remaining APVs, only *Lady Evelyn*, *Stadacona*, *Hochelaga*, and *Cartier* had sufficient speed to be of any use as convoy escorts, but with such a small margin over the speed of the merchant ships that Hose normally employed them patrolling set areas along the convoy route.[118] In view of the inadequacy of the East Coast patrols' anti-submarine vessels, and the complete absence of destroyers, the fact that the German raiders did not sink a single ship in convoy is a testament to the effectiveness of the shift of HC convoys to Quebec, and to the navy's ability to get the most out its armed yachts, submarine chasers, trawlers, and drifters. The three merchant ships that were sunk in Canadian waters—the *Luz Blanca*, *Eric*, and *Leixoes*—were all attacked while proceeding independently as, indeed, were most of the ships sunk in US waters. The only other U-cruiser victims off the Canadian and Newfoundland coasts were the fifteen small fishing schooners and trawlers sunk by *U 156* and *U 117* between 20 and 30 August. (The schooner *Bianca*, although abandoned to the enemy, was later salvaged while the schooner *Dornfontein* and the seven fishing vessels sunk by *U 156* in early August were attacked off southern Nova Scotia in waters that had been designated the USN patrol's responsibility.) Although there is no denying the success achieved by shifting the assembly port for HC convoys from Halifax to Quebec, the decision was an obvious one for the naval authorities to have made and, indeed, was a strategy Chambers had already suggested in March.[119] With over 80 percent of Canadian-bound transports and liners having to journey up the St Lawrence to load at Montreal in any event, the use of Halifax as an assembly port made little sense within the Canadian transportation network—of which the convoy system was an extension—and simply added some 650 kilometres to a merchant ship's voyage, all of it in the very waters that were most exposed to U-boat attack.

An equal portion of the "credit" for the RCN's success, however, must go to the timidity of U-cruiser commanders in making their relatively feeble efforts to disrupt North American shipping. Attacks on ships in convoy were avoided even when their assembly ports were well-known—for example, the HX convoys that continued to sail from New York throughout the summer and autumn of 1918. The Americans, of course, were in a position to ensure that HX shipping had a destroyer escort for its entire trans-Atlantic crossing, something the RCN was incapable of providing. As demonstrated by *U 155*'s

---

117. Navinet Halifax to Naval Ottawa, 21 October 1918, ibid.

118. Captain of Patrols to Naval Ottawa, 3, 4, and 7 September 1918, 1065–7-6, LAC, RG 24, vol. 4031.

119. Port Convoy Officer and Senior Officer of Escorts, Halifax to Commander-in-Chief, NA&WI, 11 March 1918, UKNA, ADM 137/1620.

references to the many "destroyers" and "patrol vessels" in the Halifax approaches that interrupted her work, German submarine commanders, prone to see what they expected to see, habitually overestimated both the strength and the capabilities of the anti-submarine forces opposing them.

German timidity was further evident in the fact that so much of their effort was directed against fishing schooners, a target that presented little risk to U-cruisers but also one that contributed little of direct value to the war effort. With food in abundant supply throughout North America, such attacks would have had little impact on the general public (except perhaps for Newfoundland) even if fish was completely removed from their diet. Whether the potential psychological or moral impact was worth the effort is debatable, but as we have seen, the reaction of maritime politicians to the attack on fishing vessels made it all the more frustrating for the US and Canadian navies because they were rarely able to respond to individual sinkings. Lacking radios, the unarmed schooners could not alert naval authorities of events on the fishing banks until the crews rowed ashore, twelve to twenty-four hours—or longer—after they had been attacked. Reacting to outdated intelligence and with the fishing fleets spread over vast areas of ocean, the two navies could only see that word of a U-cruiser's presence was promulgated among the various banks. Of the thirty-four fishing vessels sunk in North American waters in 1918, twenty were American, with the greatest single-day toll coming on 10 August when *U 117* destroyed nine US vessels on the Georges Bank. Only thirteen of the fishing vessels sunk were Canadian, a total that represented only one percent of the 1,270 steam and sailing vessels in the Canadian salt-water fishing fleet.[120] It was also only a tiny fraction of the 675 British fishing vessels that were sunk by the enemy in United Kingdom waters during the war.[121]

Acutely aware of the inadequacy of their patrol force, Canadian naval officers were privately relieved that U-cruiser commanders had attacked fishermen, while assiduously avoiding interfering with far more valuable Canadian convoys. In submitting his 21 October recommendations for naval defence during the 1919 season, Captain Hose was also aware that the U-cruisers used in the 1918 campaign were not of the latest pattern and had included the less-effective, converted mercantile submarines. With their attacks "confined almost entirely on fishing craft," he believed "that the U-cruisers which operated off the Canadian coast were homeward bound after having spent some considerable time in the more southern waters ... where they had been considerably more active." The captain of patrols believed that "the probable reasons for the U-cruisers acting with such discretion" in their attacks was because of "the inherent weakness of the [mercantile] type and vulnerability increased by the foul condition of the outside plating after several months at sea which had probably decreased their speed both on the surface and submerged. The fact that the commanders of the vessels had very important information

---

120. Canada, Dominion Bureau of Statistics, *The Canada Year Book, 1920* (Ottawa 1921), 294; and Director of the Naval Service of Canada to Commander-in-Chief, NA&WI, 29 April 1918, 1017–10–6, pt. 1, LAC, RG 24, vol. 3832.

121. Hurd, *The Merchant Navy*, III, 379.

of the condition of the operations of shipping over [on] this side and of the extent and conduct of US and Canadian defenses (which it was an important part of their mission to obtain)" also explained their tentativeness since they needed to return safely to Germany for debriefing. It was Hose's opinion that the 1919 submarine campaign in Canadian waters would "be organized to a considerable extent on the information taken to Germany by the vessels which have been here this year."[122]

In looking toward the 1919 shipping season, the captain of patrols expected that the German submarines arriving in Canadian waters would be "of the latest pattern," and warned his superiors—a rhetorical warning since NSHQ was already keenly aware—that "in the event of a U-cruiser of this type appearing off Canadian coasts, that there is not one vessel or any combination of vessels which it would be the slightest use to despatch to the attack even if it were known exactly where to find and pick up with the U-cruiser." The 1919 defensive plan envisaged by Hose relegated the trawler fleet, which had made up the bulk of the RCN's East Coast escorts in 1918, to primarily a minesweeping role. The numbers of trawlers would be expanded, however, from forty-six to fifty-five to allow for a regular sweep to be maintained along both the coastal routes and shipping lanes around Newfoundland, Nova Scotia, and the Gulf of St Lawrence. The only employment Hose could come up with for the thirty-six drifters he had been saddled with by the Admiralty was to distribute them between Halifax, Sydney, St John's, Gaspé, and Port Saunders at the southern entrance to the Strait of Belle Isle, and have them operate "E.C. nets"—drift nets strung with forty-five-pound electro-contact mines. Although their chances of actually damaging a U-boat were so limited as to barely justify the expenditure in personnel to man them, the only possibility of success would come at the shipping choke points Hose suggested.[123]

Should the U-cruisers return to attack the fishing fleets in 1919, Hose proposed outfitting six "Q" schooners to operate on the banks as a means of ambushing unsuspecting raiders. Since "these 'Q' schooners cannot well be fitted with a gun armament capable of coping with a U-cruiser," the captain of patrols suggested that they "be fitted with 14-inch torpedoes with 12 pdr. gun (or 4-inch if procurable) as auxiliary armament." He also recommended stationing two submarines each at Halifax and Sydney but did not specify their role, whether to guard the port approaches or operate with the "Q" schooners. The navy's auxiliary patrol vessels, the most effective of the RCN's 1918 escorts, would merely "be utilized for kite balloon work." Hose apparently did not foresee any role for the USN's six submarine chasers and made no mention of them. In fact, the only part of the 1918 defences that Hose felt should be kept in the same role for 1919 were the air patrols—by which time they would be flown by the navy's own RCNAS—"but with the number of planes increased to allow of daily patrols with two planes for a radius of 100 miles from Halifax and Sydney. The Magdalen Island sub-base should also send up two planes daily."[124]

---

122. Captain of Patrols to NSHQ, 21 October 1918, 1065–17–12, pt. 1, LAC, RG 24, vol. 4032.

123. Ibid.

124. Ibid.

Having shown his utter lack of confidence in virtually his entire 1918 patrol force by relegating it to the margins of anti-submarine operations in the coming season, Hose was convinced that an effective counter to a U-cruiser offensive in Canadian waters would require an entirely new force of thirty-three destroyers. The captain of patrols believed that the warships could be built over the winter as part of the large American destroyer program, supplemented by some construction in Canadian shipyards. Hose suggested dividing the force into five groups of five destroyers each, with one group each to escort the HC and HS convoys. The remaining three destroyer groups would provide local escort: one group of five operating between Sydney and Newfoundland, primarily guarding the ore trade; another group escorting coastal traffic between Sydney and Halifax; and a third group operating between Halifax, St John, and Boston. There would also be two hunting groups of four destroyers each, one at Halifax and one at Sydney. To man the new warships, Hose was confident that the Royal Navy would be able to lend Canada the required number of captains, while "a considerable number" of the other officers required "could be drawn from young Canadian officers now serving in the Grand Fleet who might be detailed forthwith to destroyers in British waters for special training in destroyer work." Ratings for the destroyer crews could similarly be drawn in "sufficient numbers" from the thousands of RNCVR men that Canada had sent overseas and they could also "receive special training in England during the coming winter." In the case of engineer officers, Hose felt that "the majority of chief artificer engineers and artificer engineers now in the Canadian service could be made quite capable of taking charge of the engines of a T[orpedo] B[oat] D[estroyer] if specially trained between now and next April." In summing up his plans for 1919, the captain of patrols clearly restated the utter inadequacy of the force he had been compelled to employ against the U-cruisers in 1918:

> I would submit that the enemy to be faced is the enemy of 1919 and that the equipment at present available is the equipment of Europe in 1914, that at the time when the Admiralty placed an order for the trawlers and drifters now operating in Canadian waters, that this order was not placed with a view to meeting enemy cruisers which have the power of submerging.
>
> Our trawlers still have an important duty to fulfil in minesweeping, but otherwise, they and the drifters and the A[uxiliary] P[atrol] ships are powerless to prevent the enemy from acting when and where he pleases against the shipping off Canadian coasts.
>
> It is considered that if the enemy do send U-cruisers ... to this coast next summer that the losses in shipping, men and material in Canadian waters will be very serious unless a force, of which the above should be the minimum, is available as a defence.[125]

At NSHQ, the captain of patrols's recommendations for the 1919 naval defence scheme were passed to the director of operations, Commander J.P. Gibbs, for his comment and

---

125. Ibid.

analysis. Certainly no naval officer at headquarters would argue against the proposition that the patrol force of 1918 had been horribly inadequate for the task of protecting Canada's shipping lanes. Gibbs had a great deal of sympathy for the strong position Hose advocated, stating at the outset that "in theory" he would "entirely concur with the captain of patrols, and he, in no way, exaggerates the seriousness of the situation. But his demand for thirty-three destroyers is considered to be quite outside the realm of practical politics." In Gibbs's view, there were three overwhelming reasons why Hose's plan could not be implemented: "it is impossible to get this number of destroyers built"; "the personnel question is insuperable"; and "we have no dockyard capable of keeping even our present force in repair." American shipyards were already so far behind in their destroyer construction program that the British first lord had visited Washington to urge an increased effort at the expense of merchant ship construction, while British shipyards were having difficulty meeting the needs of the Royal Navy. Gibbs, a Royal Navy officer on loan to NSHQ, was also less sanguine than Hose regarding the RCN's ability to man a large destroyer force with its own personnel, pointing out that the thirty-three warships would require over 700 additional officers and ratings, "all of whom require high training to be of use in the modern destroyer. All this is necessary at a time when the shortage of destroyer personnel has come to a critical stage in England. I say this with complete first hand knowledge, having been in the closest possible touch with the administration of destroyers for the past three years."[126] Perhaps the greatest impediment to obtaining a large Canadian destroyer force, however, was the lack of repair facilities:

> After three years' experience I have found that, under the most favourable conditions, one third of the destroyer force is always under repair at any one time. This would mean that eleven destroyers would be always under refit, and practically the whole of the work requires highly skilled mechanics. Judging by the history of our submarines, one can only form the opinion that we have no skilled workmen in Halifax yard. It is improbable that we can call on the US to repair our ships, and Bermuda is too far off for any case of serious injury or breakdown.[127]

In place of Hose's ambitious scheme, the director of operations proposed a more modest undertaking to build six destroyers and eight submarines at the Vickers's shipyard in Montreal. The vessels Gibbs suggested would be patterned after the modified V-class ships being built as part of Britain's 1919–20 construction program. At 1,500 tons with a top speed of thirty-six knots and mounting three 4.7-inch guns and two triple 21-inch torpedo tubes, the "magnificent seaboats" would have been capable of matching any surfaced U-boat. Four of the eight submarines would be seagoing L-class boats "for service on the Canadian side of the trade routes," while the remaining four would be slower R-class

---

126. Commander J.P. Gibbs, "Memorandum for the Director of the Naval Service," 28 October 1918, 1065-1-1, pt. 1, LAC, RG 24, vol. 4029.

127. Ibid.

submarines "for anti-submarine work." The director of operations believed "that all the destroyers and probably all the submarines can be built in Canada by Vickers, provided that the firm is given a reasonable guarantee of future work to justify the expense of their outlay on the slips, tools, etc. They may have to sub-contract for all or some of the submarines, but submarine construction in the United States is nearer to the British standard than their destroyer construction." Building as many of the ships in Canada as possible would, moreover, have the added advantage of giving "the people a greater pride in their navy."[128]

The reduced number of warships would also mean that "practically no personnel would be required from the imperial service to man the destroyers." Gibbs believed that the RN would only have to lend four officers, three of them engineers, for the destroyers since "there are sufficient lieutenants in the RCN (lent to the imperial service) to provide the commanding officers and watchkeeping officers in the destroyers, several of them having had a large amount of destroyer experience during the war." The six warships would also need twenty-eight other petty officers and specialists, principally ERAs and torpedomen. The eight submarines, meanwhile, would need eight experienced officers and sixteen ERAs from overseas to supplement the submarine personnel already in Canadian service. Gibbs did "not consider ... that any other imperial ranks or ratings would be required, as the standard of education is so high in Canada that the men should be able to be trained with comparative ease and quickness." At most, a number of ratings would have to be sent to Britain over the winter for some torpedo, steam turbine, and oil-fuel courses.[129] In emphasizing the importance of having proper repair facilities at a naval dockyard, he also offered a possible solution to help defray costs:

It would be useless to build good ships, as these are, if there was not a thoroughly efficient dockyard to keep them in repair. The size of the navy in itself, is not sufficient to warrant a large dockyard, but, on the other hand, very great docking and repairing facilities are necessary in time of war.

To make a dockyard large enough for all war purposes, and at the same time to keep it for purely naval use in time of peace would be ruinously extravagant. But a very small part of any naval dockyard is of a description which necessitates special guarding or secrecy, and the remainder can be made available for either naval or mercantile ship building and repairs.

There is now a great opportunity to make Halifax a first class port, as the dockyard will have to be rebuilt.

At present the yard is unable even to keep our small patrol force in repair, and trawlers and drifters do not require any delicate machine work or great accuracy.

It is considered that the new dockyard should be so laid out that the great majority of the space and plant can be used for building and repairing either

128. Ibid.

129. Ibid.

naval or mercantile ships, and only a small part kept as a purely naval yard, the latter to contain the gun-mounting shops, torpedo stores, ordnance stores, victualling stores, etc., and any other buildings of a nature which makes it desirable that they should be kept separate.

In this way the dockyard, with efficient management, would not only pay for itself, but would probably make a profit for the dominion government, which would help to pay for the upkeep of the navy.

In every yard in Great Britain, including even the royal dockyards, merchant ship repairs are being carried out in conjunction with warship repairs, and everything works quite smoothly.[130]

In submitting his proposals to Kingsmill, Gibbs stressed that "the destroyers especially are considered to be an urgent necessity, as German submarines consider them to be by far their most dangerous enemy." The director of operations made it clear, however, that he had kept his recommendations "as moderate as possible to fit in with the present resources of Canada," and limited the number of destroyers to a figure he believed the country could realistically hope to build, man, and maintain from its own resources during 1919.[131] Hose, on the other hand, had submitted a statement of the resources he believed the RCN would actually need to provide a reasonable measure of security for Canada's shipping lanes in the face of a more determined U-cruiser offensive. While outwardly appearing to be "extravagant," Hose's "mad dreams"[132] did not, in fact, represent a gross over-insurance against the increased U-boat threat the Allies were facing in 1919. The captain of patrols was planning to assign only one group of five destroyers (of which four would serve as escorts at any one time) to each of the valuable HC and HS convoys, the same ships that were routinely met by at least that number of destroyers once they reached British waters. The extent of ocean to be searched for U-cruisers operating in Canadian waters made his proposal to maintain two small hunting groups at Sydney and Halifax prudent while the RCN's difficulties in 1918 in providing sufficient escorts along the hundreds of miles of coastal shipping lanes suggested that assigning a destroyer escort group to each of the three main sections was similarly reasonable.

It also cannot be ignored that in a moment of inadvertent candor, in January 1918, the Admiralty had admitted that Canada required six destroyers and six fast, 4-inch-gunned trawlers to meet the lesser threat posed by armed U-freighters during the 1918 shipping season. A more concerted German effort made by modern U-cruisers in 1919 would undoubtedly have doubled the numbers required in the earlier British assessment. The refusal of the Admiralty to contemplate sending even a handful of British destroyer reinforcements to Canada seems all the more short-sighted, because at the time of the armistice in November 1918 the Royal Navy had twenty-one destroyer leaders, 412

---

130. Ibid.

131. Ibid.

132. The description used by Hadley and Sarty, *Tin-pots and Pirate Ships*, 292.

133. Edgar J. March, *British Destroyers: A History of Development, 1892–1953* (London 1966), 233.

destroyers, and ninety-four torpedo boats in commission.[133] Given the importance of the war supplies being transported to Britain in the HC and HS convoys, the large numbers of destroyers being kept in British waters to protect the valuable trans-Atlantic merchant ships and liners in the presumed danger zone would have made even less sense in 1919 if those same ships had already been sunk in the relatively undefended waters of North America. While it would certainly have been possible for the Admiralty to have despatched a dozen or more RN destroyers to Canada within a few weeks if U-cruisers began sinking large numbers of trans-Atlantic transports in 1919, the infrastructure needed to support them, as Gibbs pointed out, would not be available without advanced planning and preparation.

The captain of patrols' optimism about the availability of sufficiently large numbers of American-built destroyers to allow for the supply of some of them to the RCN also reflected his anxiety at being directly responsible for protecting Canada's East Coast shipping rather than resulting from a practical appreciation of the problems being encountered by the US destroyer construction program. As the director of operations had pointed out in his memorandum to Kingsmill, the United States had fallen behind in their construction schedule. By the beginning of May 1919, American shipyards would complete only eighty-six of the more than 250 wartime destroyers they had been contracted to build. Together with the thirty 4-inch-gunned destroyers of their pre-war programs, the USN would have had only 116 destroyers in commission by the time U-cruisers began arriving in North American waters in 1919.[134] Those totals would probably have precluded Washington from giving the RCN any more than a half-dozen destroyers by the time the St Lawrence reopened to traffic that spring—if, that is, an expanded U-cruiser offensive off the US eastern seaboard did not frighten the US navy department into keeping all available USN destroyers in American waters.

On the other hand, if the Vickers's shipyard in Montreal were able to build six destroyers for the RCN over the winter of 1918–19, as had been stated in both the Hose and Gibbs memoranda and been repeatedly expressed by Vickers's officials throughout the war, then it would have been possible for the RCN to have had twelve destroyers (six US-built and six Canadian-built) in operation by the following summer. The Ford Motor Company in Detroit, Michigan was also building sixty "Eagle" boats for the USN and had a second contract to build a similar number for the Italian navy. Based on the British patrol boat design and roughly equivalent to the "fast trawlers" recommended by the Admiralty, the American Eagle boats were 500-ton, eighteen-knot convoy escort vessels that mounted two 4-inch guns, two 3-inch guns, and carried twelve depth charges. In view of the importance of the HC and HS convoys, it is not unreasonable to suggest that Washington might have diverted a dozen Eagle boats, either their own or from those meant for Italy, to help meet the RCN's escort needs had a serious U-cruiser offensive developed in Canadian waters.

In making his "mad dreams" assessment of Canadian needs for 1919, Hose could also have looked south at the scale of naval assets the USN was maintaining to protect its trans-

134. O. Parkes and M. Prendergast, eds., *Jane's Fighting Ships 1920* (London 1920), 203–14.

Atlantic and coastal convoys. Whereas the two most useful RCN vessels for escorting the HC convoys through the Gulf of St Lawrence were the two ex-fisheries patrol ships *Canada* and *Margaret*, neither of which mounted guns that were capable of effectively engaging a surfaced U-boat, the American navy deployed a vastly greater force against U-boats in the western Atlantic in spite of its stated primary commitment to anti-submarine warfare in European waters. As of 1 September 1918, the USN were using twenty cruisers and thirty ocean-going destroyers to escort their trans-Atlantic convoys, with a pair of destroyers covering each of the HX troop convoys during its entire passage to Europe before escorting a westbound convoy on its return voyage. The eight US naval districts on the eastern seaboard had another eight destroyers, ten torpedo boats, twenty-three coastguard cutters, and 105 submarine chasers to cover the coastal shipping lanes. There were, in addition, three U-boat hunting groups, with one destroyer, the USS *Jouett*, and nine subchasers based at Boston, one destroyer, and eleven subchasers based at Delaware Bay, and a light cruiser and twelve subchasers based at Key West, Florida. The USN also had twenty-five submarines available for anti-submarine patrol, a minesweeping force of sixty-eight vessels, and 108 seaplanes for coastal patrols and escort duties.[135]

As much as Hose was hoping that the large American destroyer construction program would be able to provide the RCN with effective escorts, Gibbs's position that Canada should look to Vickers to construct Canadian warships reflected Kingsmill's own long-held view that the navy should have its own destroyers built at the Montreal shipyard. After exploring the possibility in the spring of 1916, only to have the Admiralty discourage the idea, the naval director remained convinced that if the Canadian navy's east coat patrols were to receive any meaningful reinforcement, it would have to come from the nation's own resources. In the immediate wake of the German attack on the Canadian fishing fleet, another destroyer proposal was put forward by the naval minister in a letter to the first sea lord in London on 11 September. Stating that "it is most essential that we should have better naval defence on our Atlantic coast," Ballantyne referred Admiral Sir Rosslyn Wemyss to an enclosed RCN order of battle that did not include a single effective anti-submarine vessel. He also reminded the first sea lord of the plea he had made for warships capable of combating a U-boat in Canadian waters during his visit to London a few weeks earlier, an appeal that had only resulted in the ancient USN gunboat *Yorktown*—politely referred to by the Canadian minister as a "cruiser"—being sent to Halifax. After conceding that he did "not suppose that it is possible for the Admiralty to spare any torpedo destroyers or cruisers to operate off Halifax," and that their American ally "could not give us anything more in the way of protection than what they have done," Ballantyne enquired:

> what your opinion would be regarding the advisability of the Canadian government undertaking the building of torpedo destroyers in Canada; and if this should be decided upon could Canadian builders such as Vickers Company get the necessary armament, engines, boilers, etc. from England? If

---

135. US Navy Department to Admiralty, 5 September 1918, "Distribution of US Naval Forces Employed Against Enemy Submarines in West Atlantic Waters, 1 Sept. 1918," UKNA, ADM 137/1619.

this proposition is not feasible what would you think about the Canadian government getting from the United States their plans and specifications for the type of destroyers that they are building there, and enquiring if we can get the necessary guns, etc. from them.

Your advice on such matters as this would be of the greatest assistance to me and the Canadian government, and I would be under a debt of gratitude if you would give me freely your opinion in order that I can discuss the matter officially with the Canadian government.[136]

It was not until 28 October, over six weeks after Ballantyne wrote to London and the same day that Gibbs submitted his views to Kingsmill, that the first sea lord finally managed to send off a reply to the Canadian minister's urgent enquiry. After offering a token platitude that the Admiralty "quite realize the necessity for better naval defence on your coast and will be glad to do what we can in the matter," Wemyss insisted that the RCN already had "sufficient armed small craft to provide for the necessary escort, patrol and minesweeping services." He did concede that "the need for more fast craft, such as destroyers, is evident," and finally offered some good news to Ottawa. "Arrangements have accordingly been made with the United States that they will provide six destroyers for Halifax early in the next year." He also assured Ballantyne that German submarine activity had ceased in North American waters for the season and was unlikely to recommence until next May, by which time "the American destroyers should be at Halifax."[137] As encouraging as was the promise of American destroyers, there was no mention in Wemyss's letter of the six fast trawlers the Admiralty had stated in its January 1918 assessment were needed to meet Canada's defence requirements. Since it was fully expected that the improved U-cruisers would pose a greater threat in 1919 than the converted U-freighters had presented in 1918, NSHQ could hardly have been as sanguine as the first sea lord that the six American destroyers—if, in fact, they ever materialized—would assure Canada's maritime security. As it had when Kingsmill had proposed the idea in 1916, London remained reluctant to support any Canadian effort to build destroyers at Vickers in Montreal.

With regard to Canada building destroyers, I do not think that it would be advisable at present, in view of the difficulties in providing the engines, boilers, etc., as we shall require all of these that we can get on this side; and since the United States are going to send destroyers to Halifax, there does not seem to be any urgent necessity, especially as they could not be completed probably until after the war is over. If, however, you decide otherwise, you may be sure that the Admiralty will be ready to give you all possible assistance.[138]

136. C.C. Ballantyne to Admiral Sir Rosslyn Wemyss, First Sea Lord, 11 September 1918, 1017–10–1, pt. 1, LAC, RG 24, vol. 3831.

137. Wemyss to Ballantyne, 28 October 1918, ibid.

138. Ibid.

Although the Admiralty had presented the same excuse in dismissing Kingsmill's destroyer proposal in 1916—namely, that the war would be over before the ships could be completed—by October 1918 the prophesy seemed far more certain of being fulfilled. With the Canadian Corps, among others, serving as the shock troops of the British armies in northern France, fighting skilful battles to break through the strongly defended Drocourt-Queant Switch Line in early September, cross the Canal du Nord by month's end, and capture Cambrai by mid-October, Field Marshal Haig's forces had successfully breached the Germans' Hindenburg Line of fortifications. Accompanied by Franco-American offensives to reduce the St Mihiel salient in September and a further offensive in the Meuse-Argonne launched later that month, the enemy was in retreat across the Western Front by late October and the German high command was privately conceding defeat. With both the German and Austro-Hungarian empires facing internal collapse, the two governments had sent notes to US President Woodrow Wilson in early October requesting an armistice based on his stated "Fourteen Points." While the Allied governments debated the terms of peace they would be willing to offer and the Canadian Corps continued its advance in the direction of Mons, Belgium, the naval war effectively came to an end with the mutiny of the High Seas Fleet on 29 October. Franz von Hipper, who had succeeded Admiral Scheer in command in August, ordered the fleet to make a desperate sortie into the North Sea to seek a final battle with the Grand Fleet only to have his crews seize control of their ships and refuse to sail.

Despite the Admiralty's discouragement of Canada's latest destroyer construction scheme, Kingsmill forwarded both the Hose and Gibbs memoranda to Ballantyne on 5 November. In commenting on the defence scheme submitted by the captain of patrols, the naval director acknowledged that "it is a practical impossibility to carry out his views" but supported Hose's call for reinforcement by cautioning the minister that "we shall be in a very poor position next summer to protect the trade routes to and from our ports with our present defence force." As a more realistic alternative, Kingsmill recommended the adoption of Gibbs's suggestions, pointedly remarking to the Liberal politician that the Gibbs "proposal is generally that proposed in 1910 by the Laurier government excepting that the light cruisers proposed are left out and submarines suggested. We could operate cruisers but would find some difficulty, unaided, in operating the submarines. With reference to Commander Gibbs' remarks re Halifax Dockyard, I concur and submit that it is a waste of money doing anything to bolster up the present yard. All this has been brought forward before. As to the primary necessity of docks and repairing plant in connection with a naval programme, I represented in 1908–09 to the minister that the first consideration should be given to such works."[139] Kingsmill recommended proceeding with the proposal to build destroyers at Vickers one week after the Admiralty had once again discouraged the latest Canadian suggestion that such warships be laid down at the Montreal shipyard. With the war in Europe rapidly coming to an apparent conclusion, however, Ballantyne wasted little time in deciding upon inaction: "I would suggest that nothing be done for a few days until we see what will be the outcome of the terms that the

139. Kingsmill, "Memorandum for the Minister," 5 November 1918, 1065–1-1, pt. 1, LAC, RG 24, vol. 4029.

Allies will be submitting to Germany within a day or two. If Germany decides to continue the war then we will have to go ahead vigorously and, on the other hand, if she accepts the Allies' terms—which I am convinced she will be compelled to do—then we have only to consider what is required for peace conditions."[140]

With the signing of the armistice six days later, the naval minister's response was the obvious one for him to have made. Despite its timing, it was in keeping with the manner in which the Borden government had handled naval matters throughout the war by refusing to commence any naval undertaking unless it had the Admiralty's approval. The Canadian prime minister had always held to the view, as he stated at the imperial war conference in March 1917, that "for the purpose of obtaining expert advice, there is no authority that can be consulted with greater advantage than the Admiralty."[141] Unfortunately for the RCN's wartime fortunes, they were always held hostage to the whims of the Admiralty. Borden was never able to shake his bias in favour of advice provided by British officers, no matter how narrowly focused on British waters they might be, over the opinions being offered by the Canadian naval officers at NSHQ, men who were far more attuned to local conditions, the circumstances of the nation's shipping and the naval assets needed for its defence. And, as Kingsmill had pointedly reminded the naval minister, the minimum naval force Canada would need to defend the East Coast in 1919 was the little navy that Laurier had proposed and that Borden had cancelled.[142]

While the naval director harboured few doubts as to where the political responsibility lay for the feeble position in which the Canadian navy still found itself after four years of war, British naval officers were more likely to form a rather different opinion of the abilities of their dominion colleagues. One British officer who visited Ottawa during the war's final weeks was the Admiralty's director of minesweeping (DMS), Captain L.G. Preston, who made a cursory tour of Canadian naval establishments in October. Although Preston was unable to meet with either Kingsmill, who was on a tour of Esquimalt, or Hose, he received a briefing on the RCN's minesweeping organization by Commanders Morres and Gibbs, and met with Desbarats. Despite being accurately informed in Ottawa that the minesweepers at Halifax and Sydney were under the orders of the senior naval officers at those ports, Admiral Story and Captain Pasco, respectively, Preston preferred to rely on the information provided to him by a disgruntled RNR lieutenant who had been sent to Halifax in 1917 for service with the port's minesweeping forces. The RNR officer in question, Lieutenant Alick Purdon, was the commanding officer of drifter *CD 23* but, as Preston explained to the Admiralty, the British lieutenant complained that he "obtains no access to the senior naval officer [i.e., Story], and appears to be employed in extraneous duties under various officers and seldom, if ever, takes any practical part at sea in minesweepers." Although the authorities in Halifax were apparently utilizing Purdon's

---

140. Ballantyne to Kingsmill, 5 November 1918, ibid.

141. "Minutes of the Imperial War Conference, 4th day," 28 March 1917, quoted in Nicholas Tracy, ed., *The Collective Naval Defence of the Empire, 1900–1940* (Publications of the Navy Records Society, vol. 136; Aldershot, Hants, England 1997), 228.

142. Kingsmill, "Memorandum for the Minister," 5 November 1918, 1065–1-1, pt. 1, LAC, RG 24, vol. 4029.

RNR experience to help offset the shortage of staff officers on the East Coast, that fact did not ease his preference for employment sweeping the shipping channels in the approaches to the port. Based solely on Purdon's misinformation as to which officers held the various appointments at the port, the British director of minesweeping related to London that "the allocation of duties did not appear to be thoroughly known by the navy department at Ottawa," and then proceeded to misidentify the Canadian naval staff officer at Halifax, Commander Eldridge, as the port's operational officer:

> As regards the navy department, Ottawa … the officers whom I saw did not appear to be in touch with the bases, and the organization which they believe to be in force at Halifax as regards the port minesweeping operations is not apparently in force. The status of the Canadian navy is certainly not, in the eyes of the Canadian public, the same as the status of its army. The naval officers employed at the navy department do not appear to have any confidence in their position, and their whole attitude shows a lack of co-ordination. Social and political matters appear to present to them greater interest than the conduct of the dep[artmen]t on Admiralty lines. It is noticeable that no officer employed in Canadian waters has had any war experience; and if any efficiency is to be obtained, in my opinion it is most desirable that [some] such senior [RN] officer is sent to the navy department. This officer should be one whose future in the imperial service will not be jeopardised by the appointment, and who consequently will not be seeking permanent employment in Canada at a later date. The difficulty of dealing with Canadian bases which receive their orders from the navy department, Ottawa, can only be surmounted by the appointment of an energetic, tactful and war-experienced naval officer.[143]

Neither Preston nor Purdon seemed even remotely aware that Halifax was no longer being used as a convoy assembly port, following the transfer of the HC convoys to Quebec City in August, and that only coastal traffic called at the port for convoy, a requirement that was also about to be cancelled.[144] Once again reflecting the Royal Navy's preoccupation with Halifax, Preston insisted that four pairs of minesweepers be maintained at that port but only two pairs at Sydney, even though the Cape Breton port continued to be the assembly point for HS convoys. In view of Preston's ignorance of both the East Coast's organization and its operations, his recommendation to replace all senior RCN officers, including the director of the naval service itself, with British officers—euphemistically categorized as "war-experienced"—smacked of ill-informed bias against all things dominion. That attitude was particularly evident in the British DMS's spurious contention concerning "the difficulty of dealing with Canadian bases," a problem he apparently presumed to exist based on Admiral Grant's earlier call for the appointment of

---

143. Captain L.G. Preston, "Report by DMS re Canadian Waters," 12 October 1918, UKNA, ADM 137/1619.

144. Navinet Halifax to Naval Ottawa, 21 October 1918, 1048–48–1, pt. 1, LAC, RG 24, vol. 3772.

an imperial staff officer to Halifax.[145] By the time the DMS made his partial inspection of Canadian naval establishments, however, Grant had already concluded that the time for such an appointment was "rapidly passing." Contrary to Preston's imperious assessment, the more astute and experienced C-in-C had stipulated that such an appointment would require an officer with "an intimate knowledge of local conditions and difficulties and of Canadian and United States susceptibilities."[146] In making his rounds of the Canadian capital, Preston's anti-dominion stance may have been exacerbated by the fact that the most senior departmental official he had contact with in Ottawa—Kingsmill and Ballantyne being unavailable—was the deputy minister. Although an experienced bureaucrat, Desbarats was not a man who was likely to impress anyone in authority—as Borden had discovered at the end of August. After meeting with the deputy minister to discuss the proposed naval air service, the prime minister confided in his diary that "he seems to have little drive and to be rather casual."[147]

Nonetheless, the DMS's dismissive attitude toward NSHQ and dominion navies was clearly shared by many of the British officers at the Admiralty, where the idea of forming an imperial naval staff with dominion naval representation as part of a more integrated imperial navy was being generally discussed during the war's final months.[148] The assistant chief of the naval staff in Whitehall, Admiral Duff, for instance, concurred in Preston's ill-informed view with the comment that he was "convinced that no sound organisation of the forces in Canadian waters can be expected so long as the present regime at Ottawa continues."[149] Duff's opinion was echoed by the DOD (F), Captain Charles Coode, who misinterpreted Admiral Grant's request (the C-in-C wanted a captain appointed primarily to act as a liaison between Chambers and Story) as being for "an officer of captain's rank at Halifax to be under SNO (Admiral Storey [sic]) and to run imperial as distinct from purely Canadian local operations" without realizing that the Canadian admiral was already only responsible for "purely Canadian and local operations," while Chambers's operational responsibilities consisted of organizing the trans-Atlantic convoys (with most of his convoy staff being Canadian), and providing them with RN cruiser escorts, activities which, in any event, had not been carried out at Halifax since the transfer of the HC convoys to Quebec in early September. Despite an utter lack of understanding of the actual situation in Canada, it was accepted as fact within the Admiralty that "the present organisation both at Ottawa and in the ports appears to be in need of attention.... but it may be doubted whether any real improvement can be looked for under the present regime at Ottawa."[150]

An opinion on Preston's report that was more sympathetic to the RCN's position was provided by the director of training and staff duties (DTSD) at the Admiralty, Captain

145. Grant to Admiralty, General Letter No. 5, 1 July 1918, UKNA, ADM 137/504.

146. Grant to Admiralty, 1 October 1918, ibid.

147. Borden diary, 29 August 1918, LAC, reel C-1864.

148. Captain Herbert Richmond minute, 22 November 1918, UKNA, ADM 137/1619.

149. Duff minute, 27 October 1918, DOD (F) minute, 30 October 1918, ibid.

150. DOD (F) minute, 30 October 1918, ibid.

Herbert Richmond. The British DTSD had been part of the small group of Royal Navy officers who had launched the professional journal *Naval Review* in 1912 as a forum for the free interchange of opinion without fear of reprisal. Richmond hoped that the new journal would serve to further a naval officer's education, an area of development he viewed as being badly handled by the RN officer training system. A long-time critic of the Admiralty's ineffective staff work, he had been appointed to head the training and staff duties division in April 1918 to help reorganize the system.[151] Although Richmond was as ignorant of the RCN's organization as any of his colleagues, he was also the only Admiralty officer who was willing to preface his comments with the word "presumably." The DTSD recognized that in Canada's "endeavour to raise a comparatively insignificant naval force there was no such carefully thought out naval system to be obtained from home [i.e., Britain] as a model" as had been the case in putting together the command structure of the much larger CEF and patterning it on the British Army's more advanced staff system.

> It is hardly fair to expect officers untrained in staff work and possibly with a very limited experience of administrative organisation outside of ship-work to compete with the political and other difficulties extant in Canada.
>
> There appear to be strong party differences of opinion on the Navy question in Canada, and in consequence whole-hearted support for the Naval Administration is not obtainable.
>
> If this be so it would require an officer of the very greatest ability to occupy the post of director of the naval service and he would have to be supported by a staff of highly trained officers competent to represent their requirements unequivocally and to realise to the full what these requirements were.
>
> At the same time, the ablest directorate and staff will be powerless against a policy of laissez-faire or deliberate obstruction on the part of the government.[152]

Richmond's acerbic reference to the Borden government posing a "deliberate obstruction" to the RCN's development reflected a general British disdain for Canada's shifting naval policies—neither making a financial contribution to the Royal Navy nor building a local Canadian navy—in the years immediately before the outbreak of war.[153] Indeed, the 1914 issue of the British publication *The Naval Annual* had described "the present position" of Ottawa's naval policy as "not creditable to this great dominion," particularly in light of the battle cruisers that the smaller dominions of Australia and New Zealand were contributing to the Royal Navy.[154] It is possible to suppose, therefore, that Whitehall's view of Canada as having failed to play its proper role in providing for the

---

151. Barry D. Hunt, *Sailor-Scholar: Admiral Sir Herbert Richmond, 1871–1946* (Waterloo, Ontario, 1982), 90–96; and D.M. Schurman, *The Education of a Navy: The Development of British Naval Strategic Thought, 1867–1914* (London 1965), 127–8.

152. Richmond minute, 22 November 1918, UKNA, ADM 137/1619.

153. "BX," "Canada and the Navy," in The Naval Society, *The Naval Review* (1913), 96–100.

154. Viscount Hythe and John Leyland, eds., *The Naval Annual 1914* (London 1914), 24.

empire's naval defence before 1914 may have contributed to a lack of sympathy for the RCN's wartime struggles. Nonetheless, it must also be recognized that British officers needed no encouragement to subscribe to a belief in the natural inferiority of any colonial organization. That attitude is evident in the fact that even an officer of Richmond's considerable intelligence could effortlessly suggest, with no direct knowledge of the actual situation in Ottawa, that the RCN's problems must have resulted from shortcomings at NSHQ.[155]

As much as the Borden government's resistance to building a Canadian navy had forced the RCN to embark upon war with only the two obsolescent cruisers carried over from Laurier's naval policy, it was the Admiralty itself that had posed the biggest obstacle to Canadian naval development throughout the conflict. From 1914, when London had instructed Ottawa to concentrate the Canadian war effort on providing an expeditionary force to fight in France rather than building up its navy, Whitehall had demonstrated a relative indifference to Canada's naval defence. Beginning with Ottawa's initial enquiry in August 1914 about using the Canadian Vickers's shipyard in Montreal to build submarines for the RCN—followed by further Canadian proposals in 1914, 1916, and 1918 to build destroyers at Vickers—the Admiralty consistently advised against these initiatives, and, simultaneously used the Montreal shipyard's facilities to place orders for its own submarines, motor launches, and trawlers (although most of the trawlers, marginal warships at best, were eventually loaned to the RCN). In view of the general shortage of anti-submarine destroyers among all Allied navies, the British advice against Kingsmill's repeated proposals to build anti-submarine destroyers in Canada appears inexplicable. As we have seen, however, such advice was routinely offered without benefit of a proper staff appraisal as to the importance of the North American shipping being protected, the probable scales of enemy attack, or the actual requirements of the Canadian navy to meet it, and was more likely to be based simply on some senior British officer's uninformed intuition.

In that light, Captain Richmond's supposition that the RCN's high command must somehow have failed "to represent their requirements unequivocally and to realise to the full what these requirements were," is entirely misplaced. The DTSD's criticisms are, in fact, more applicable to the Admiralty's own staff procedures—a system of which, ironically, Richmond was himself sharply critical—rather than the realistic appreciations of Canadian naval needs that NSHQ repeatedly produced during the war. Far from failing "to realise to the full what these requirements were," Kingsmill and Hose had a very clear idea of exactly what the East Coast patrol force needed, a realization that bordered on the desperate by the summer of 1918 when U-cruisers began operating in the western Atlantic. As we have seen, both Canadian officers fully recognized that the RCN had been left virtually powerless to defend against the U-cruiser threat once London withdrew its January 1918 promise of twelve destroyers and fast trawlers, leaving Canada's East Coast patrols saddled with an ineffective force of Admiralty trawlers and drifters. The fact that Whitehall had inexplicably provided Ottawa with a candid assessment that Canadian naval defence required six destroyers and six fast trawlers—a telegram that Kingsmill and Hose immediately embraced with huge relief—

---

155. Richmond minute, 22 November 1918, UKNA, ADM 137/1619.

only subsequently to abandon the RCN to its own fate with no British reinforcement at all, makes Richmond's criticism of NSHQ's presumed inability to appreciate Canadian defence needs all the more ironic. Similarly, Kingsmill's destroyer proposals, NSHQ's patrol plans, Grant's desire to divert some US destroyers to Canadian waters, and Hose's urgent calls for reinforcement of the East Coast patrol—"get seven modern torpedo boat destroyers out here"[156]—completely refutes Richmond's slanderous presumption that NSHQ must somehow have failed "to represent their requirements unequivocally" to their political masters.

The RCN was not, of course, privy to the ill-informed speculation masquerading as analysis that was being circulated through Admiralty corridors at war's end. For the navy's senior officers that was undoubtedly fortunate given the frustrations that had plagued the Canadian naval project from its outset. The election of the Borden government in 1911, and its decision not to proceed with building a Canadian navy would not have had serious consequences for national defence had not a European war broken out three years later. Throughout the First World War, the RCN was squeezed between Whitehall's indifference to Canadian naval defence—a lassitude that was compounded by the inability of the Admiralty staff to provide coherent advice to Ottawa—and Prime Minister Borden's unwillingness to undertake any of NSHQ's proposals unless they had the Admiralty's stamp of approval. In that sense, the main political interference the Canadian navy experienced during the war was the government's insistence that the RCN do whatever the Admiralty suggested. The result was the situation in which the navy found itself in 1918, facing 6-inch gunned U-cruisers with a fleet composed primarily of slow trawlers and drifters armed with 12- and 6-pounder guns, weapons half the size of the enemy's. Although the Canadian government spent less than $600,000 on the navy in 1913–14, wartime expenditures increased from just over $3,600,000 in 1914–15, to slightly less than $10,000,000 in 1917–18, and to some $11,500,000 in 1918–19. In contrast—and reflecting the British government's expressed desire for Canada to concentrate on sending an expeditionary force overseas—the naval amounts were dwarfed by the financial outlay of the Borden government to support the nation's main war effort on the battlefields of France. For the fiscal years 1917–18 and 1918–19 alone, the war expenditures of the Militia and Defence department totalled more than $800,000,000 and $1,200,000,000 respectively, a sum that was a hundred-fold larger than the RCN budget.[157]

Despite the handicaps imposed on it by both the Admiralty and the Borden government, however, the RCN's war experience was not without some success. From the tiny, prewar remnants of Laurier's navy, a total of 8,826 Canadian personnel served in the RCN during the war: 388 RCN officers and 1,080 RCN ratings, and 745 RNCVR officers and 6,613 RNCVR ratings. Another 90 RN and RNR officers and 583 ratings served with the RCN for a grand total of 9,499 sailors. Of these totals, 190 men in RCN service were killed

---

156. Captain of Patrols to Secretary, Department of the Naval Service, 15 January 1918, 1017–10–4, pt. 1, LAC, RG 24, vol. 3832.

157. "Naval Expenditure," nd, DHH 81/520/1000–5-5; Canada, Dominion Bureau of Statistics, *The Canada Year Book 1919* (Ottawa 1920), 604–06; and Canada, Dominion Bureau of Statistics, *The Canada Year Book 1920* (Ottawa 1921), 674–76.

158. Director of the Naval Service, "Memorandum for Director of Historical Section," 31 January 1928, DHH 81/520/1000–5-5.

in action, died of wounds, or died of disease or accident, the later category including those sailors who were killed in the Halifax explosion.[158] Although a much smaller service, the navy's fatality rate of 2 percent was, in fact, identical to that sustained by the RCN in the Second World War.[159] While the prewar cruisers *Niobe* and *Rainbow* were the navy's largest warships, the RCN employed 130 commissioned vessels on the East Coast during the war and another four in the Pacific.[160] Unfortunately, the size of the Canadian fleet was not matched by the effectiveness of its warships, only HMCS *Grilse* having the required margin of speed, but not the armament or seakeeping qualities, to counter a surfaced U-cruiser.

In view of the Admiralty's unwillingness either to send effective anti-submarine vessels to reinforce the East Coast patrol force or—and far less explicably—encourage the Canadian government to undertake the construction of destroyers or fast trawlers in Canadian shipyards, the navy's shore establishments were among the most important assets the RCN contributed to the Allied victory. The naval department's work with the overseas transport organization headed by A.H. Harris provided it with a detailed knowledge of the Canadian transportation network, and the challenges that had to be surmounted in moving vast quantities of war supplies from the continent's interior to its eastern shipping ports. In contradistinction to the Royal Navy's dominant view of Halifax as "the naval centre in the east,"[161] NSHQ was aware of the prominence of the Gulf of St Lawrence as the nation's primary shipping artery and the strategic importance that it gave to Sydney as the RCN's main operational base.

Even after the introduction of convoy in the summer of 1917 gave an added significance to Halifax as an assembly port, the Canadian naval command remained aware that the convoy system was still an extension of the country's entire transportation network. That fact was not always readily appreciated by Admiralty staff, accustomed to Britain, a comparatively small country with an extensive rail network that linked numerous ports at which to unload cargoes from overseas, and that had a relatively easy time shifting ships from one port to another. In Canada the national rail network intersected at only one major seaport: Montreal. With few exceptions, British naval officers did not fully understand the vast distances covered by North American railways or the extreme weather conditions that added to the difficulty of moving hundreds of thousands of tons of war supplies by rail each month. It was fortunate that the two most senior British officers in North America in 1918, Grant and Chambers, shared NSHQ's understanding of Canadian shipping lanes and that the three authorities were able to offset the weakness of the RCN's patrol forces by diverting the convoys away from areas threatened by U-cruisers.

The dominance of Montreal as Canada's main East Coast shipping port also made it a relatively straightforward proposition to shift the HC convoy assembly port from Halifax to Quebec in 1918. The British commander-in-chief, Vice-Admiral Grant, had "no doubt

---

159. C.P. Stacey, *Arms, Men and Governments: The War Policies of Canada, 1939–1945* (Ottawa 1970), 66, 590.

160. Desbarats to The Dominion President, Navy League of Canada, 27 September 1919, DHH 81/520/1000-5-5.

161. C.H. Coke, "Memorandum for the Director of Naval Service," 23 March 1917, 1065-7-3, LAC, RG 24, vol. 4031.

that Quebec, with its two approaches through Cabot Straits or Belle Isle Straits, is the best possible assembly port for Canada during the months when navigation in the Saint Lawrence remains open," while "the disadvantages of Halifax as an assembly port were obviously those of coaling facilities and the dangerous approach in fogs so often prevailing" during the summer months.[162] Even before the U-cruisers had appeared in North American waters in 1918, Chambers had objected to the need to assemble Canadian shipping at Halifax for convoy. Writing to the Admiralty that March, he had argued: "Practically the whole of the Canadian fast traffic (in summer) comes down the St Lawrence and the loss of efficiency through concentrating at Halifax is far greater than in the case of the United States vessels. The actual increase in distance for those is approximately 400 miles and the whole of this will be in water where they will be singularly open to attack. The question therefore arises whether this procedure [of assembling at Halifax] cannot be avoided."[163] As we have seen, the relative importance of Sydney as a base for protecting the shipping lanes in the Gulf of St Lawrence over that of the naval dockyard at Halifax was a well-accepted fact at NSHQ and had been the basis for much of its disagreement with Commodore Coke in 1917. With Halifax's poor rail connection to the Canadian transportation network rendering it only a minor shipping port and being inconveniently located to serve as a point of assembly for the St Lawrence traffic, it is easy to see why there had been no hesitation in shifting the HC convoys to Quebec at the first appearance of German submarines in the Nova Scotia approaches the following year.

Although the Canadian navy was successful in asserting national control over its own ports and shore establishments—most notably in keeping the Halifax intelligence centre as an RCN organization and in fending off the efforts of Admiral Browning in the spring of 1917 to sideline Kingsmill and establish an independent command for Coke on the East Coast—it had to struggle throughout the war with being placed in a position of responsibility without being given either the power or resources needed to carry out the tasks assigned to it. Such was the case with NSHQ's repeated attempts to have its responsibility for the overseas transport organization clarified, aware that its director, an employee of Canadian Pacific, was in a clear conflict of interest by virtue of his control over the Canadian transportation network, including CPR's competitors. The RCN was also saddled with much of the public's anger over the Halifax explosion when responsibility for the disaster would more accurately have been laid at the door of the Admiralty and the Halifax pilotage authority. Similarly, senior RCN officers were acutely aware of the weakness of the navy's East Coast patrol force but were unable to convince either the Admiralty or Borden to provide it with effective anti-submarine vessels. While the HC and HS convoys were successfully diverted away from the U-boat threat, the German navy's willingness to attack the strategically insignificant East Coast fishing fleet amounted to a direct, if unintended, attack on the RCN and its already limited credibility with the Canadian public. As the officer who would lead the Canadian navy for a decade and a half, Captain Walter Hose, recalled

---

162. Grant to Admiralty, 28 December 1918, enclosure 3, UKNA, ADM 137/2658.

163. Port Convoy Officer and Senior Officer of Escorts, Halifax to Commander-in-Chief, NA&WI, 11 March 1918, UKNA, ADM 137/1620.

in later life, the Canadian navy had to endure "scathing—you might say scurrilous—ridicule for years in the press and in parliament, against the navy itself, which was trying its best, making bricks without straw, to maintain the highest efficiency possible and which could not defend itself, it was indeed discouraging."[164] Although the immediate goal of the nation's three armed services for the next two decades would be mere survival, the discouragement engendered by the navy's war record would help to foster a determination among many of the RCN's younger officers to see that the navy would never again be relegated to the status of afterthought in any future Canadian war effort.

---

164. Hose, "The Early Years of the Royal Canadian Navy," 19 February 1960, Hose Papers, DHH 2001/12.

SECTION 3

The Interwar Years

CHAPTER 12

War's End, 1918–1922

"I arrived in London by train on the morning of November 11th, 1918," an RCN officer remembered decades after the event. "As my taxi drove past Selfridge's, a large sign was being hoisted into place, 'Armistice Signed at Five A.M.' This news took some time to circulate, and it wasn't until 11 am, when the Armistice actually came into force, that all hell broke loose … With one accord, everyone in sight broke into wild cheering, women wept openly, flags appeared in all directions. London literally went mad! Every taxi, every passing car, were boarded by men in uniform, in civvies, by girls of all shapes and sizes—anyone who could get in, or even on the roofs. Motor lorries and trucks were commandeered and careered [i.e., careened] through the streets, the clinging passengers cheering and waving flags, palm leaves snitched from hotel lobbies, their own hats, other people's hats, even articles of underwear. A remarkable example of spontaneous relief and joy."[1]

An armistice is not, however, a peace treaty, and to the sailors of the Royal Canadian Navy peace would not be official until—like the changes of the seasons—higher authority said it was. Negotiations with Germany, Austria-Hungary, and Turkey lasted many arduous months, and it was not until 1919 and 1920 that peace treaties were signed with the major belligerents. It was not until 17 March 1920, therefore, that "the technical officers of the Department of the Naval Service report that this emergency has now ceased to exist and they recommend that the naval forces of Canada, including the naval volunteer forces be placed on a peace footing."[2] The recommendation being acceptable, war's end could be deemed official, and worthy of the ritual that normally accompanied important naval events, the director of the naval service issuing orders to the effect that on 31 March the white ensign, designating a vessel as an RCN ship, was to be hauled down on board *Stadacona*, *Malaspina*, *Thiepval*, and *Armentieres*. Next day the blue ensign would be hoisted, indicating that although they were in government service, they were no longer naval units. Furthermore, all officers and ratings of the naval reserves who were part of the ships' crews "will be considered demobilized on that date." Commanding officers were to take steps to provide their ship's companies with the proper government—as opposed to navy—uniform."[3]

An obvious issue with the coming of peace was to determine the role the RCN, as an institution, would play in national defence when the country was not at war. Given that

---

1. F.L. Houghton, "Memoir," nd, 29, Library and Archives Canada (hereafter LAC), Manuscript Group (hereafter MG) 30 E444.

2. PC 559, 17 March 1920, 26–2-4, LAC, Record Group (hereafter RG) 24, vol. 5597.

3. DNS to Navyard Esquimalt, 19 March 1920, 133–1-1, LAC, RG 24, vol. 5682.

Canada was not an independent nation, but part-and-parcel of the British Empire, such deliberations had to take the metropole's intentions and wishes into account, though it was sufficiently autonomous to reject them if it so chose. The British, meanwhile, who had found themselves at war in 1914 in part because of fears aroused by German naval construction, emerged from the conflict to find that their position had not necessarily been improved by the enemy fleet's internment at Scapa Flow. As one historian has explained, "in the years immediately following World War I, the concept of 'imperial defence' acquired a sharpened focus and renewed strategic significance. Foremost were indications of an alarming disjunction between British imperial ends and British imperial means. Whatever the suspicions of particular dominion nationalists, this reality underlay the British Admiralty's attempts to resurrect its controversial proposal for some kind of empire naval defence structure based on centralized operational control and on specific role- and cost-sharing agreements."[4]

As a result, London would seek to continue the kind of wartime unity that had seen the ships of the self-governing dominions serving under the direction of the Admiralty. In attempting to achieve a "one-power standard," where the Royal Navy would be able to defeat its main opponent, no matter how large, Canada, Australia, New Zealand, and South Africa were expected to play increasingly important roles. As has been noted elsewhere, it was not just a matter of preparing for war, as "the one-power standard was necessary for British prestige. As Churchill wrote, any external perception that the RN was 'definitely inferior' in strength to the United States Navy would 'undoubtedly affect our whole position and indicate to our dominions that a new centre has been created for the Anglo-Saxon world.'"[5]

The United States was thus a crucial variable in the equations that would govern postwar strategic planning. Shortly after the Armistice, the secretary of the Admiralty, Sir Oswyn Murray, noted that "the two next strongest naval powers will now be the United States and France, the latter our closest ally, and the former the nation that the Liberal government of which the present prime minister was a prominent member declared we could never contemplate as a naval rival." Such contemplation, however, was not long in beginning, and in mid-1919, as the Treasury planned substantial reductions in spending, "the Admiralty, which expected the United States to keep eighteen dreadnoughts and eleven pre-dreadnoughts in full commission, denounced this proposal, which it believed would 'be regarded generally as the handing over of sea-supremacy by the British empire to the United States of America.' The issue was Britain's status as a great power, which rested on its maritime supremacy."[6] It was not necessary for the USN to make threatening noises for the Admiralty to consider it a potential opponent—its existence as an effective force, complete with modern battleships, was sufficient.

---

4. Barry D. Hunt, "The Road to Washington: Canada and Empire Naval Defence, 1918–1921," James A. Boutilier, ed, *The RCN in Retrospect, 1910–1968* (Vancouver 1982), 44.

5. John R. Ferris, "The Symbol and the Substance of Seapower: Great Britain, the United States and the One-Power Standard, 1919–1921," B.J.C. McKercher, ed, *Anglo-American Relations in the 1920s: The Struggle for Supremacy* (Edmonton 1990), 74.

6. Christopher M. Bell, *The Royal Navy, Seapower and Strategy Between the Wars* (Stanford 2000), 6.

Also, there had indeed been disagreements between the British and Americans, the latter having entered the war as an "associated power," and not as a member of the alliance against the Central Powers. Furthermore, by the end of the war British-US disagreement concerning belligerent and neutral rights had brought relations between the two allies to a state of open tension, that had not been eased by President Woodrow Wilson's persistent criticisms of British blockade practices and the American government's decision to implement its "navy second to none" building program. In August 1918, with victory over Germany becoming a distinct possibility, trade competition between the British and Americans became more evident. Eric Geddes, the first lord of the Admiralty, believed that Britain was clearly in danger of losing its supremacy with respect to the merchant marine, suggesting that the United States was taking advantage of Britain's focus on the war to build up a merchant fleet that would allow it to dominate overseas markets after the conflict. Britain's Board of Trade agreed, suggesting that the repair work of allied ships undertaken in British yards further reduced Britain's ability to compete in the production of new tonnage.[7]

Even the internment of Germany's High Seas Fleet in November 1918, and its subsequent scuttling in June 1919, did little to lessen their mutual distrust, antagonism coming to a head at the Paris peace talks, where the second of Wilson's Fourteen Points, the freedom of the seas, threatened Anglo-American co-operation. Such were the underlying causes of Anglo-American naval and commercial rivalry, which remained unresolved in the immediate post-war period. One historian has gone so far as to refer to "an Anglo-American commercial/maritime 'cold war' spanning much of the inter-war era,"[8] while another has pointed out that in developing its concept of a mobile naval base organization the Royal Navy was not only thinking in terms of possible war with Japan, where six such units would be needed, but against the US, where four would be required. In the end, Britain would eventually accept parity with the United States in battleship numbers under the terms of the Washington Naval Armaments Limitation Treaty of 1922, not out of any spirit of international altruism but as the lesser of two evils. The alternative, that of being "outbuilt" by the United States in the course of the armaments race then burgeoning, would have been even less palatable.[9]

Rivalry between the British Empire and the United States might be of some interest to the Canadian government—and the RCN—but it did not necessarily mean conflict, and when in August 1919 the British Cabinet decreed that US shipbuilding would not be an excuse for increased RN construction, the decision "virtually ended talk of war with the United States within naval circles," though according to Vice-Admiral Sir Osmond Block

---

7. Hunt, "The Road to Washington," 45; and Keith Nelson, "Reinforcements and Supplies from Overseas: British Strategic Sealift in the First World War," Greg Kennedy, ed, *The Merchant Marine in International Affairs, 1850–1950* (London 2000), 46–47.

8. Kevin Smith, "Maritime Powers in Transition: Britain's Shipping Capacity Crisis and the Mobilization of Neutral American Power, 1940–41," Greg Kennedy, ed, *The Merchant Marine in International Affairs*, 159.

9. Hunt, "The Road to Washington," 45; and Richard Harding, "Amphibious Warfare, 1930–1939," Philip Pugh, "Managing the Aerial Threat," Richard Harding, ed, *The Royal Navy, 1930–2000: Innovation and Defence* (New York 2005), 23, 47.

"the United States has become our rival for the carrying trade of the world." A possible scenario for that rivalry leading to armed conflict would be if the British interfered with American trade while at war with a third power. In such a situation "a powerful fleet would be sent across the Atlantic at the earliest possible moment to neutralize the US fleet, while British cruisers based in Canada and the West Indies protected imperial trade routes and disrupted the enemy's trade." The rather fanciful thinking behind such an approach was that "as long as American capital ships did not have easy access to the Atlantic trade routes, it was thought that cruiser forces could provide a reasonable level of protection to British commerce. Trade with Canada, however, would almost certainly be cut off," by US heavy artillery near the St Lawrence. Still, "the complete loss of both Canadian and South American trade was not regarded as fatal to Britain." Even worse outcomes could be tolerated—at least in British eyes—and given US preponderance on land in North America, Canada was expected to fall. However, "naval opinion hoped, at the very least, to hold Halifax for use as a naval base. Indeed, this was considered to be essential if the navy were to support a land campaign in Canada. As a precaution against failure, however, one Admiralty memorandum recommended that 'the possibility of obtaining a large ice-free anchorage elsewhere should be investigated by the Canadian authorities.'"[10]

Peace was therefore not to be taken for granted, and it was against such a background that Canadian policy makers attempted to determine the proper role—if any—for the RCN. The atmosphere was not friendly toward such endeavours, however, and in the immediate post-war period Prime Minister Sir Robert Borden would find that "he could not buck the deep, pervasive hostility in post-war Canada to military expenditure in general and the navy in particular." The deaths of 60,000 Canadians on the battlefields of Europe had touched untold numbers of families, who were understandably skeptical of what had been purchased for the price, and hesitated to make any further sacrifice, whether on land or at sea. The RCN had performed its duty during the war with the meagre resources allowed it, but had not captured the public imagination, and had even taken much of the blame for both the Halifax explosion of 1917 and the sinking of Canadian fishing vessels in 1918. The navy's performance was the subject of "harsh scrutiny and often unjustified scorn" during the May 1919 parliamentary debates on the naval estimates when, "offering an unsensational past, the navy seemed to provide no justification whatever for future development. Naval prestige was not a Canadian issue."[11]

It should be noted, however, that although the army's Canadian Expeditionary Force had earned much distinction on European battlefields, a large regular army did not survive into the post-war era. Even if the minister of militia and defence could say that its members "have made a splendid history for Canada and I would like something to be done to continue them," while other members referred to the gallantry of the CEF and the "gallant Canadian soldiers," the Canadian Expeditionary Force disappeared, its battle honours

---

10. Bell, *The Royal Navy*, 49, 51–54.

11. Michael L. Hadley and Roger Sarty, *Tin-pots and Pirate Ships: Canadian Naval Forces and German Sea Raiders, 1880–1918* (Montreal and Kingston 1991), 301.

perpetuated by units of the militia. On the other hand, when William Duff asked "have any of the vessels of the Canadian Naval Service ever been in action?" the reply, from A.K. Maclean, minister without portfolio, was a simple, if somewhat inaccurate, "no."[12] If a brilliant history failed to protect the CEF, the RCN would do no better unless the Canadian government was convinced it could provide a useful service in the post-war era.

It was in that less than auspicious environment that the staff officers at NSHQ began planning the future of the Royal Canadian Navy. A Naval Committee, with Kingsmill, Hose, and Desbarats as its only members, was formed in February 1919 to "discuss and make recommendations to the minister" on questions of general policy, organization and regulations. At its second meeting on 13 March, the committee discussed "the probable development of the Canadian navy during the next two years" with the consensus opinion being "that the present service should be reduced as far as possible to the minimum with a view to making a fresh start after the report of Lord Jellicoe [of which more later] had been presented. It was agreed that it was desirable to continue the training of boys and obtain as many as possible as a nucleus for a new service, the present services being very deficient of the right type of men for petty officers, this having been one of the difficulties in running the patrol service during the war.... The young officers from the [Royal Naval] College [of Canada] now with the Grand Fleet would also provide a good nucleus for the future. It was felt, however, that no great activity could be expected for several years, but that the problem of providing a modern base on each coast would probably have to be faced soon."[13]

In response to the naval minister's request for definite proposals for a discussion of future naval policy during June 1919, the Naval Committee set about committing its views on the Canadian navy's future to paper. On the issue of whether the RCN should be maintained or if Canada should simply make financial contributions to the Royal Navy, Hose believed that it was "unnecessary to say much on this question, as in the political struggles of the past ten years nothing has been left unsaid either on one side or the other. The war has proved conclusively that some form of Canadian naval service is necessary," since the conflict at sea had reached Canadian shores. The threat, the assistant naval director believed, would most likely be in the form of one or two cruisers operating against Halifax, and one or two unarmoured cruisers against Esquimalt and Prince Rupert. An effective defence would thus require three cruisers and supporting vessels "stationed either on the Atlantic or Pacific, as a matter of course, the whole area should be one station, the ships proceeding from Atlantic to Pacific, and vice versa periodically."[14] Hose also asked the chief accountant to "prepare an estimate of the cost of pay—officers and men—for three cruisers of the 'D' class and eighteen 'PC' boats and *Rainbow* with half a crew." Of the consulting naval engineer he asked for estimates of the cost of additional buildings at Halifax and

---

12. Canada, Parliament, House of Commons, *Debates*, 12, 14, and 19 March 1919, 29 April 1919. As we have seen, *Rainbow* did capture two enemy merchant ships off the coast of Mexico in 1916.

13. Naval Committee minutes, 13 March 1919, 1078–1-1, pt. 1, LAC, RG 24, vol. 4044.

14. ADNS to Naval Committee, 10 June 1919, 1017–10–8, LAC, RG 24, vol. 3833.

Walter Hose, director of the naval service and chief of the naval staff, 1921–1934. (LAC PA-142594)

Esquimalt in light of the possible procurement of cruisers and other vessels, as well as the necessary increase in personnel at the two bases.[15]

The resulting occasional paper No. 2 on "Proposals for Canadian Naval Expansion" urged the government to give naval policy the permanency it had previously lacked and suggested "that a certain sized naval service should be aimed at in say fifteen or twenty years, the whole scheme being sealed by a special act of parliament. The effect of such a policy would greatly tend to economy in the prevention of hurried and ill-considered annual programmes, and it would give stability to the whole service." In terms of ships, the naval staff broke its requirements down into two seven-year construction programs. At the end of that time—i.e., by 1934—the navy would be composed of seven cruisers, twelve destroyers, six submarines, eighteen "PC" patrol boats (similar to the P-boats used by the Royal Navy in the First World War), and three depot ships for the submarines. The paper also presented suggestions for making the necessary upgrades to the naval facilities at both Halifax and Esquimalt.[16] At its meeting on 9 July, the Naval Committee endorsed the paper's conclusions "as providing a good basis for future development." In all, the naval staff prepared thirty-six occasional papers covering all aspects of naval development, twenty-three of which had been completed in time for Lord Jellicoe's arrival in Canada that fall.[17]

In attempting to determine the RCN's proper role, Canada's naval officers had certainly anticipated receiving input from London. In fact a formal method of rendering such advice had been promulgated at an imperial war conference on 30 March 1917, attended by Britain and the dominions. It had been resolved that "the Admiralty be requested to work out immediately after the conclusion of the war what they consider the most effective scheme of naval defence of the empire, for the consideration of the several governments summoned to the conference, with such recommendations as the Admiralty consider necessary in that respect for the empire's security." Such was the genesis of what came to be called the Jellicoe Mission, led by Admiral of the Fleet Earl Jellicoe. The Admiralty's view was clear, "convinced as they are that a single navy is necessary for the security of the whole empire." More junior members of that empire might beg to differ, Prime Minister Sir Robert Borden stating that "the proposals set forth in the Admiralty memorandum for a single navy at all times under a central naval authority are not considered practicable."[18] The exchange was part of a very long argument.

Jellicoe's role was not to resolve the debate, and when Ballantyne told him that he was willing to abolish the RCN unless "a serious start" was made toward a settled policy, Jellicoe simply agreed.[19] The admiral's main role, rather, was to visit the dominions and

---

15. Hose to Chief Accountant, 12 June 1919, Hose to Consulting Naval Engineer, 12 June 1919, ibid.

16. Naval Committee, "Proposals for Canadian Naval Expansion," 3 July 1919, 1017–31–2, pt. 1, LAC, RG 24, vol. 5696.

17. G.N. Tucker, *The Naval Service of Canada, Its Official History, I: Origins and Early Years* (Ottawa 1952), 306–09; and James Eayrs, *In Defence of Canada: From the Great War to the Great Depression* (Toronto 1964), 151–54.

18. A. Temple Patterson, ed., *The Jellicoe Papers: Selections from the Private and Official Correspondence of Admiral of the Fleet Earl Jellicoe* (London 1968), II, 284, 285, 287.

19. Stephen Roskill, *Naval Policy Between the Wars* (London 1968), I 285.

advise on such issues as bases, administration, personnel, works, naval aviation, and intelligence. In late October 1919, Admiral Kingsmill provided him with a series of questions, although "the government will also be glad to have your opinion on any point connected with naval defence on which you may care to express an opinion." There were fourteen topics in all, the first one concerning a Canadian Pacific naval base, of which the first of five questions was: "is a naval base considered on the Canadian Pacific coast on account of either Canadian or imperial interests." The second topic related to shipbuilding, followed by personnel, "works," the reconstruction of Halifax dockyard, and naval bases on the East Coast. As for the latter, the report asked: "do you consider that any ports on the east coast should be fortified, other than Halifax and Quebec, for naval purposes." Other topics included mining and aviation, with questions such as "in the event of the Canadian government deciding to create a separate air force, what method of cooperation between navy and air force, do you recommend in regard to training, discipline, control and operations." Under anti-submarine measures, there was only the question of what preparations might be necessary. Still other topics covered defensively armed merchant ships, a naval intelligence organization, wireless communications, and the RNCVR. For the latter, the report simply asked: "have you any suggestions for the re-organization of the Royal Naval Canadian Volunteer Reserve?" Final topics included minesweeping, and mining Canadian ports as a defensive measure.[20]

Jellicoe also served in a proselytizing capacity, later reporting how "during my stay in Canada ... the several branches of the Navy League in the Dominion were particularly desirous that I should address meetings in the principal cities with the object of emphasizing the supreme importance of sea-power in the empire, and this was done."[21] This was, no doubt, appreciated as the league's three-fold mission was to produce "a thoroughly organized educational campaign," "to raise funds for the relief of British and Canadian sailors and their dependents," and "to encourage volunteer naval brigades for boys and young men." The educational aspect of the league's goals would aim "to disseminate among the people of Canada a knowledge of the necessity and use of sea power as the keystone of empire and national defence and commercial prosperity." It would also engage in lobbying in favour of "a policy that Canada shall assume her proper share of the cost and maintenance of protecting her own trade routes and coast defences." The league would also see to "the application of steady pressure upon parliament and the government for the most efficient administration of the Department of Naval Service, and the abandonment of the present system of the portfolio of marine, fisheries and naval defence being under one minister." The navy, it was argued, was of sufficient importance to deserve a minister of its own.[22]

The Navy League played its part, advising the government that it was "of the opinion that the time has arrived when Canada must earnestly turn its attention to its future on the sea and what position it will take in the British empire to insure a free intercourse

20. Kingsmill to Jellicoe, 31 October 1919, 78-1-13, LAC, RG 24, vol. 5669.

21. Patterson, ed, *The Jellicoe Papers*, II, 370–71, 374–6, 378.

22. Dominion President, Navy League of Canada to George Foster, 14 November 1919, LAC, MG 26 H, mfm reel C4350.

between the various member nations of the empire." Its earnestness was evident in a resolution passed in Victoria in February 1919, to the effect that "the Navy League of Canada
is in favour of a naval policy for Canada which will have regard to the needs of the whole
British empire and, in deciding upon such policy, political exigencies will be disregarded
and the opinion of the most eminent naval strategists shall be alone considered, and the
fundamental idea shall be EMPIRE NAVAL DEFENCE, and that the fleet units may be either
acquired or built, and that the dominion shall retain control of their ships, and that there
shall be a complete standardization of personnel, ships and equipment, and that the whole
shall be of the best, and that in time of war all the fleets shall be under one supreme command."[23] The British admiral could not have asked for a more loyal ally in Whitehall's quest
for an imperial navy.

Still, as one historian has noted, although Jellicoe toured the empire in HMS *New
Zealand* "with an Admiralty mandate to persuade the empire to accept centralized naval
control," he found that "he had to yield something in each dominion that he visited, even
in India." New Zealand alone was willing to style its warships as "the New Zealand division of the Royal Navy." The other dominions "insisted upon the same autonomy in naval
matters that they had long possessed in military affairs. Nevertheless, for a generation, naval
imperialists were to continue to press for unity in the empire based on a single imperial
navy or a single strategic doctrine and control."[24] On the other hand, there were areas
where Jellicoe and the dominions were in easy agreement. For example, the British admiral agreed with the recommendations of the Canadian services that the coastal fortifica-
tion system at British Columbia ports should be completed with permanent defences at
Vancouver and Prince Rupert, the principal mainland ports and railheads on the West
Coast, and at Saint John and Sydney on the East Coast. He also accepted the Canadian
navy's argument that fixed artillery had to be the final link in a combined coastal defence
system whose primary elements would be fast well-armed patrol vessels and aircraft. On
the West Coast, the only danger was from hit-and-run attacks from unarmoured, long-
range, Japanese vessels. Quite probably on the advice of Canadian staff officers, Jellicoe
argued that Sydney was a special case because both the coal mines and the steel plant were
conspicuously situated at the water's edge, providing "excellent targets for bombardment." Similarly, the destruction of the large transatlantic wireless station at Glace Bay
would be a very serious matter. He therefore recommended that Sydney be designated a
defended commercial port and be provided with defences similar to those that had existed
during the war, but more substantial and better equipped, including three batteries, each
of two 6-inch guns, as well as a field of anti-ship mines covered by two batteries of 4.7-inch
guns. In addition, defences would incorporate eight minesweepers, armed with guns in
addition to their sweeping gear, and other vessels. It was but one issue among dozens,
though one rendered of no little importance by Jellicoe's warning that, given planned

23. Navy League of Canada to Borden, 28 November 1919, LAC, MG 26 H, mfm reel C4349.

24. Richard A. Preston, *Canada and "Imperial Defense": A Study of the Origins of the British Commonwealth's Defense
Organization, 1867–1919* (Toronto 1967), 502–03.

reductions within the Royal Navy, the latter would not be able to convoy reinforcements to Canada should war break out with the US. On the other hand, he found that policy makers in the dominion were waiting to see what funds the British government would provide the Royal Navy before determining what was to be done in regard to the RCN.[25]

With his investigation completed, Jellicoe recommended that, if Canada was to protect its trade and ports, it needed three light cruisers, a flotilla leader, a dozen torpedo craft, and eight submarines with a parent ship. For the larger task of general co-operation within the Royal Navy, the requirement rose to a battle cruiser, two light cruisers, six destroyers, four submarines, and two fleet minesweepers. Generally, "it is of great importance that the Royal Canadian Navy and the Royal Navy should hold themselves in the very closest relationship. The ships should be of similar types, the personnel actuated by the same motives, trained on the same lines, imbued with the same traditions, governed by a practically common discipline and aiming at the same high standard of efficiency."[26]

In effect, Jellicoe had broken down imperial co-operation into the numbers and types of ships Canada would need. The Canadian view was that such advice was offered "in the event of the Canadian government deciding to adopt a policy of a local navy," language that hardly guaranteed the RCN would survive into the post-war world. The British admiral would try to convince the dominion that it should, noting that on 30 November 1919 there were 8,631 merchant vessels with Canadian registry, with a gross tonnage of almost 1.5 million. "It will thus be seen that Canada has great interests on the ocean, for which in war naval protection would be necessary," Jellicoe insisted. He was also sufficiently thorough to put a price on security, calculating that for five million pounds Canada could put to sea a force of two battle cruisers, seven light cruisers, two aircraft carriers, and fifty-one other vessels, almost all of which would have to be built in Britain given Canada's limited shipbuilding capacity. The lesser sum of £3.5 million sufficed for a single battle cruiser, five light cruisers, an aircraft carrier, and thirty-five smaller ships. If such sums frightened Canadian policy makers, for two million pounds the country could have three light cruisers and twenty-six sundry vessels, and for one million it could acquire eight submarines and sixteen miscellaneous craft.[27]

The numbers contained in Jellicoe's report were more than those put forward by NSHQ in July 1919 and were well beyond what some Canadians were willing to contemplate. Henri Bourassa, who had opposed contributions to the Royal Navy in 1911, had not changed his views in the intervening years. Relating his version of Canadian-imperial relations in a pamphlet entitled *La mission Jellicoe: Nouvelle poussée d'impérialisme*, he suggested that "the contribution to the war of Africa was established by the scent of poppies distributed in abundance by Chamberlain to the colonial premiers in the festive atmosphere

25. Brian Tennyson and Roger Sarty, *Guardian of the Gulf: Sydney, Cape Breton, and the Atlantic Wars* (Toronto, 2000), 192; "Memorandum on Coast Defence, Halifax," 7 October 1936, HQS 66, pt 14, LAC, RG 24, vol. 2325; and Roskill, *Naval Policy Between the Wars*, I, 285.

26. Patterson, ed, *The Jellicoe Papers*, II, 370–71, 374–6, 378.

27. Jellicoe report, nd, 78-1-14, LAC, RG 24, vol. 5669.

of the jubilee celebrations of 1897. Naval contribution projects, aborted in Canada and partially completed in Australasia, were born from the 'panic' created in 1909 by the English shipbuilders, Krupp associates. The shocking swath cut through the ranks of young Canadians came about as a direct and anticipated result of the misleading and artificial flattery lavished on our 'statesmen' for some twenty years—and the money thrown at and welcomed by the malevolent characters who control the press and shape opinion." Insisting that the fleet Jellicoe recommended would cost $50 million, he added that Sir Percy Scott, in *The Times*, "clearly stated that the era of huge combat units was over," and that the money would be wasted on an obsolete force. To buttress his general argument, he opined that no fleet would help in a war against the United States,[28] an opinion held by many within the Admiralty. Bourassa's views reflected not only those of *nationalistes* Canadians, but those of many late nineteenth century radicals in Britain, who "saw the Naval Defence Act as a plot to involve Britain in European power politics and said it would ignite an arms race among the great powers."[29]

The Navy League, not surprisingly, supported Jellicoe's proposals. As we have seen, the RCN was never given the resources to conduct operations in the First World War in a manner that would have captured public imagination, so the league referred to one of the Royal Navy's most famous victories in making its point. In a pamphlet entitled "Canada expects this day that every man will do his duty," a paraphrasing of Nelson's message to the fleet of 21 October 1805, it insisted that the "freedom of the empire" and "the safety of the world" depended on the Royal Navy, noting that British success at the battle of the Plains of Abraham was because of the RN's control of the sea. In a more prosaic vein, it pointed out how Canada's foreign trade amounted to more than $2.3 billion, of which over a billion was sea-borne. One conclusion was clear, that "the Canadian public's responsibility is to insist upon the development of our sea heritage." The league was doing far more than proselytizing and providing Jellicoe with moral support; it was also training some 2,000 boys for a life at sea, with naval brigades in Montreal, Toronto, London, Windsor, Hamilton, Port Arthur, Fort William, Sault Ste Marie, Haileybury, Cobalt, Nanaimo, Trail, Kaslo, Saskatoon, and Calgary. In a wider context, it worked on the "promotion of national sea consciousness spirit" in that Trafalgar Day was adopted as "our day," or "the great anniversary of our security on land established by supremacy on sea." Trafalgar had also ensured "the future protection of Canadian national prosperity." The British Navy League promoted Trafalgar Day in a similar manner, so the Canadians were not unique in incorporating the battle into their literature and traditions.[30]

The period immediately following the First World War was thus characterized by the interplay between three main actors: a Canadian government investigating whether or not it wished to maintain a navy; the RCN, which made plans in the expectation that it would

28. Henri Bourassa, *La mission Jellicoe: Nouvelle poussée d'impérialisme* (Montreal 1920), 6, 9, 12, 24.

29. Marshall J. Bastable, *Arms and the State: Sir William Armstrong and the Remaking of British Naval Power, 1854–1914* (Aldershot, England 2004), 191.

30. Navy League of Canada pamphlet, *Canada Expects This Day That Every Man Will Do His Duty* (np 1920); and Bastable, *Arms and the State*, 210.

not only survive, but would do so with powerful vessels such as cruisers; and the Admiralty, which hoped Canada would be part of a larger whole when it came to naval issues, even if the country operated its own ships, themselves possibly gifts from Britain. Allied with the latter was the Navy League, which advised on "the necessity of adopting the higher estimate submitted by Lord Jellicoe as being the only policy compatible with our national honour."[31] At one level, at least, the RCN prepared for the eventuality that it would not serve as a substantial force within the Royal Navy, the assistant director providing cost estimates in January 1920 "if it is decided not to carry out any of Lord Jellicoe's proposals." These "provided for a reserve force of 5,000 officers and men, needing a permanent instructional force of 126 officers and men ... The estimated annual cost for this reserve force and permanent staff is $2,500,000 which includes maintenance of college and dockyards," not an insubstantial sum. The figure would be used to keep much of the wartime auxiliary fleet in operation, including the vessels *Canada*, *Acadia*, *Cartier*, *Malaspina*, *Hochelaga*, *Stadacona*, *Arleux*, *Armentieres*, *Arras*, *Givenchy*, *Loos*, *Thiepval*, *Gulnare*, *Petrel*, and *Grilse*, as well as the submarines *CC 1*, *CC 2*, *H 14*, *H 15*—the latter two post-war acquisitions—with personnel totalling 610.[32]

The Jellicoe report, meanwhile, came up for discussion by Borden's Cabinet in early 1920, with the politicians agreeing to a reduced version of the British admiral's most modest proposal, one that called for a Canadian navy of eight submarines, four destroyers, eight patrol boats, and four trawler minesweepers. Cabinet approval was contingent upon the Admiralty offering some of the required ships from its war surplus vessels. When a British offer was indeed put forward in March, Ballantyne placed the Cabinet's proposal before the Union government caucus on the 16th for what, he assumed, would be automatic approval. As he explained to the prime minister, who was away from Ottawa on vacation at the time, the naval minister's expectations were quickly dashed when caucus firmly rejected his naval plan.

> I was personally much disappointed, because I considered, and so did the majority of the members of the government, that it is time that Canada adopted a permanent policy, and more particularly, when Great Britain made such a generous offer of ships and the maintenance and upkeep was not more than $4,500,000 per annum. If the matter had been handled differently before caucus, I am sure it would have carried. Owing to some of the ministers desiring delay, it was decided that I would be the only one to speak and I was not permitted to say it was the policy of the government; and, rightly or wrongly, caucus got the opinion before being called together that the government did not wish to proceed with the $4,500,000 expenditure and therefore turned it down.[33]

---

31. Dominion Secretary, Navy League of Canada to Robert Borden, 14 June 1920, LAC, MG 26 H, mfm reel C4350.

32. Hose to Kingsmill, 23 January 1920, 1017–10–8, LAC, RG 24, vol. 3833.

33. Ballantyne to Borden, 12 April 1920, quoted in Eayrs, *In Defence of Canada*, I, 164.

According to Sir George Foster, the minister of Trade and Commerce, Ballantyne emerged from the caucus meeting "wilted and discouraged and mad—and said nothing." Also writing to Borden to inform him of the events, Foster described the results of the rejection.

> Next day the wires were hot over orders said to have been given by minister [Ballantyne] to demobilize the whole force (naval), scrap the old *Rainbow* and *Niobe*, and demobilize the [Naval] College. The mouse was in the soup sure. The Navy League spent half its revenue on messages, H[ali]f[a]x and Esq[uimalt] were up in arms and the rest of the ministers were asking "who did it?"
>
> B[allantyne] was in Montreal when all this rumpus broke out. When he came back, having fought off the reporters during the interval, we found out the facts—that B had sent such orders to dismiss most of the officials and had sent Kingsmill his letter of dismissal with the idea of scrapping the old if he could not get the new. Well, we had a talk over it, and ended with a compromise. (a) To give the minister a free hand to reorganize by notice of discontinuance of present staff. (b) Accept two destroyers and one cruiser from G[reat] B[ritain] to replace the *Rainbow* and *Niobe* for training and protection purposes. (c) Keep up the college. (d) Defer permanent navy policy for the present. This I took to caucus ... and in less than half an hour got their unanimous consent.[34]

Ballantyne informed the House of Commons on 25 March that "in view of the heavy financial commitments and the fact that Great Britain has not yet decided on her permanent naval policy and of the approaching imperial conference at which the question of naval defence of the empire will come up for discussion ... it has been decided to defer in the meantime action in regard to the adoption of a permanent naval policy for Canada." As a result, the government had "decided to carry on the Canadian Naval Service along prewar lines," and had accepted the British offer of one light cruiser and two destroyers to replace "the present obsolete and useless training ships" *Niobe* and *Rainbow*. The naval minister also announced that "in order to be free to thoroughly reorganize and place the present service on an economical and efficient basis," he had "issued orders for the demobilization of all officers and naval ratings.... The Canadian officers who are in the imperial fleet and who are now being paid by the Canadian government will be recalled and placed on duty with the Canadian Naval Service. The naval college will also be continued. After reorganization has been completed, only those officers and other ratings and civilians will be taken on who are absolutely necessary and possess the qualifications desired." As part of the proposed personnel reductions—done quite sensibly by releasing all officers and men before re-engaging the most efficient so as to eliminate the issue of seniority—Ballantyne also announced that Admiral Kingsmill would be retiring as naval director.[35]

---

34. Foster to Borden, 25 March 1920 quoted in ibid.

35. Canada, Parliament, House of Commons, *Debates*, 25 March 1920.

Kingsmill advised both Desbarats and the chief accountant of his retirement decision the next day. He would be on leave from 1 July to 31 December, during which time Captain Walter Hose, the naval assistant to the minister of the naval service, would also act in the capacity of DNS.[36] On 21 June 1920, the Admiralty was advised that Kingsmill would be proceeding on leave on 1 July "and has resigned the appointment of Director of the Naval Service with effect from 31st December 1920."[37] Kingsmill would turn sixty-five on 7 July, and one can speculate that, after seeing the Canadian naval project to fruition and then guiding the RCN through the four difficult years of the First World War, he felt the time had come to leave to a younger officer the bureaucratic battles that would inevitably result during the transition to peace. In a memorandum to the heads of NSHQ's various branches, he acknowledged that "the times have been difficult and would have been far more so for me personally, had I not received loyal support from those working with me."[38] It was a fitting recognition of the efficient service that NSHQ's relatively small number of staff officers had rendered during the war. While there was no questioning the support the officers at NSHQ had provided—particularly the energy and advice that the navy's chief of staff, Commander R.M.S. Stephens, had supplied throughout the war—it is equally clear that the most important guiding hand in the RCN's early development belonged to the outgoing naval director himself. Although Kingsmill's efforts to provide an adequate defence for Canada's shipping lanes had been complicated by the Borden government's willingness to adhere to the Admiralty's inconsistent advice, the naval director entered retirement on friendly terms with the prime minister. According to Borden's memoirs, he and his wife enjoyed "several delightful visits with friends," while on vacation in the summer of 1920, including "ten days in July at Grindstone Island, the summer home of Admiral and Lady Kingsmill" shortly after the Canadian admiral began his retirement.[39]

The younger man chosen to fight the navy's post-war policy battles was Walter Hose, the senior permanent officer of the RCN and, since 30 March, the naval assistant to the minister. He took up his acting director duties on 1 July, the same day Kingsmill began his holiday, it being announced on 27 October that he would be appointed as DNS on 1 January 1921, the day after his predecessor's official resignation (the expression "retirement" not yet in official use in the RCN).[40] It was a straightforward promotion. Although Story, Pasco, and Martin had been senior to Hose on the wartime navy list, they were all close to retirement themselves and none of them could match Hose's RCN command experience. Having been captain of *Rainbow* for almost six years before moving east to become captain of patrols in August 1917, the new naval director had an unparalleled knowledge of both

---

36. Admiral C.E. Kingsmill, LAC, RG 24, Acc 92–93/169, box 116.

37. "Admiral Sir Charles E. Kingsmill," nd, C.E. Kingsmill biographical file, file 1, Directorate of History and Heritage (hereafter DHH).

38. Admiral C.E. Kingsmill, LAC, RG 24, Acc 92–93/169, box 116.

39. Robert Borden, *Robert Laird Borden: His Memoirs* (Toronto 1938), II, 1042–43.

40. Walter Hose RCN Service Record, DHH 2001/12, file A-2; and William Glover, "Commodore Walter Hose: Ordinary Officer, Extraordinary Endeavour," Michael Whitby, Richard H. Gimblett, and Peter Haydon, eds., *The Admirals: Canada's Senior Naval Leadership in the Twentieth Century* (Toronto 2006), 56.

Esquimalt and Halifax. Nonetheless, his First World War record had, at times, been less than stellar. Although Kingsmill had never expressed criticism of Hose's role in the conclusions Judge Drysdale had reached as to the extent of the RCN's responsibility for the Halifax disaster, the outgoing director had kept a close eye on the decisions and escort assignments his captain of patrols had made over the summer of 1918 as German U-boats moved into Canadian waters. Given the shortcomings Hose had demonstrated as an operational commander, the fact that his selection as DNS was an obvious one for Ballantyne to have made was more a reflection of the thin talent pool in the fledgling navy's senior officer ranks than it was a positive demonstration of confidence in his abilities. As we shall see, however, Walter Hose's fourteen-year term at the head of the Royal Canadian Navy—during which he would have to struggle against small budgets that would occasionally bring the navy's very existence into question—would turn out to be the most professionally successful period of his forty-four years of service in both the British and Canadian navies.

The post-war navy that Hose inherited from Kingsmill continued to be administered by the Department of the Naval Service, which, for a time, would still have the same minister as the Department of Marine and Fisheries. The department's organization remained unchanged from the First World War, with its civilian branches, such as the Radiotelegraph Service, the Hydrographic Survey, and the Tidal Survey, being under the same ministerial umbrella for administrative convenience, while the Fishery Protection Service, the Life Saving Service, and Fisheries were institutions distinct from that of the navy but part of the same department for similar reasons. As for the navy, its leadership continued to comprise a minister, a deputy minister, a director, and a naval board, though the latter existed only on paper. The naval staff was composed of the director, an assistant director responsible for such things as mobilization and war plans, a consulting naval engineer to take care of materiel, and a secretary to deal with administration.[41] Although it would grow in years to come, especially during the Second World War, the naval staff retained the same basic structure until Canadian Forces unification in the late 1960s.

For some members of the official opposition, however, even the reduced naval strength proposed by Ballantyne was more than they were willing to approve. During a June 1920 debate on supplementary naval funding, William Duff, the Liberal member for Lunenburg, suggested that "instead of voting $2,000,000 odd for naval purposes this year we should vote only the exact amount required to settle up naval matters in Halifax, Esquimalt and elsewhere; and we should sell off the *Niobe*, the *Rainbow* and other ships and generally clean up the nasty, dirty mess in which matters stand at present." Nor was he done, stating later that "I do not think we can afford a navy," that even the large amounts requested "will be inadequate for defensive purposes." And there was icing on the cake, as "I am convinced that public opinion is strongly adverse to the proposal." For those seeking to build a viable naval service, these were not encouraging words, especially since they were not entirely without logic. The federal government's debt was in the two to three billion dollar range, a previously unheard of number, and it was difficult to argue that five ships would be able to defend Canada's long coastline. Even gifts from Britain, to be discussed later, might prove

---

41. Organisation of the Department of the Naval Service, 15 September 1919, 1017–31–2, LAC, RG 24, vol. 5696.

too expensive for a grossly indebted country and yet insufficient to put up a proper defence. Mackenzie King, leader of the opposition, added a pointed question to his colleague's comments. "What is the government naval policy?" he asked. "Has it a naval policy or has it not a naval policy?" Ballantyne simply reiterated what he had stated in March, namely, that "no definite naval policy will be decided upon until after the naval conference that will be called in 1921."[42]

Determining either Britain's or Canada's post-war naval policy was complicated by both the need to renew the 1902 Anglo-Japanese naval alliance and the Americans' willingness to continue the large naval building program begun during the war. As a result, the United States Navy figured prominently in Admiralty thinking though, to be fair, it was more of a consideration than an obsession, and even then not one that all policy makers in Britain shared. Sir George Bastow, for one, the Admiralty's controller of supply and services, suggested that it was not necessary for the RN to be equal in numbers with the USN, since "Britain is absolutely secure by its distance ... that Canada could not be secured by any fleet however large: and that the West Indies could not be secured on the One Power standard owing to their geographical position."[43] His was, however, not the voice of the majority—far from it—and the Admiralty set out to determine how to defend the empire, though in doing so it found the post-war world a much more hazardous place for the Royal Navy than it had been a few short decades before. In fact, "the worst situation the empire could face," the naval staff warned, would be any double threat of a crisis in Europe combined with Japanese "aggressive action in the Pacific at a time when ... reinforcements capable of dealing with the whole of Japan's main forces could not be immediately spared."[44] Unlike the USN in 1942–45, the Royal Navy of the 1920s could not fight a two-ocean war, and British policy throughout the interwar years reflected that very reality.

The Canadian navy's view of the Japanese empire, meanwhile, had been laid out in a May 1919 occasional paper prepared for the Naval Committee. Entitled "Remarks on a Canadian Naval Base in the North Pacific," which noted that "the strategic situation in the Pacific is dominated by the Anglo-Japanese Alliance," which was due to expire in July 1921. "By the elimination of Germany from the Pacific the Alliance, however, appears to have lost its main value for us, and may be even looked upon more in the light of an encumbrance, as it is a potential means of embroiling us with the United States. We are, therefore, confronted with Japan as a possible and even probable future enemy. This problem of the Pacific may be approached from other points of view but always it leads to the same conclusion, namely, that Japan is the enemy."[45] The RCN's position on the issue could not have been clearer.

As for its political masters, the Canadian government had concerns of its own, though being a small country next to a major power tended to focus them in one direction—

---

42. Canada, Parliament, House of Commons, *Debates*, 26 June 1920.

43. Bell, *The Royal Navy*, 16.

44. Hunt, "The Road to Washington," 52.

45. Naval War Staff, Occasional Paper No 1, 28 May 1919, 1017–31–2, LAC, RG 24, vol. 5696.

avoiding conflict with the United States. In the navy's view, "the American lobby against renewal of the alliance" was "active," and "pressure was being exerted on Mr Meighen, the Prime Minister of Canada, to come out wholeheartedly" against renewing the alliance, "at the forthcoming imperial conference."[46] During the conference, in the summer of 1921, Arthur Meighen, who had succeeded Borden as Conservative leader and prime minister in July 1920, indeed weighed into the agreement, signed in 1902, which he considered to be "undoubtedly the most important subject of discussion at this conference," but not because of the relationship between the signatories. He announced that "I feel compelled to oppose the renewal of the Alliance. I would regret to see the Treaty continued in any form at all." He first argued that it had already served its purpose when Russia was a major threat, then again when Germany was the main concern. He also proposed that Japan had "exceeded her rights" in the "invasion of th[e] very independence and integrity of China." It was, however, in the area of relations with the United States, which had its own interests in China, that Meighen felt that "we have a special right to be heard," since, should war break out between the US and Japan, "Canada will be the Belgium." The Japanese government, Meighen opined, would seek to use its alliance with Britain to manoeuvre that country "into a position of opposition to American interests."[47]

Even if that did not result in war, it could lead to a situation short of war in which Canadian interests, such as trade with the United States, could be seriously undermined. Preparing to attend a conference in Washington, DC, in the final months of 1921, Sir Robert Borden, who was to represent Canada in meetings that would include, among others, Britain, the United States, and Japan, noted how a British representative felt that "the continuance of the Anglo-Japanese Alliance would produce a most unfortunate impression upon public opinion in the United States." Referring to his prime minister's views, Borden told the British representative that "I believed public opinion in Canada strongly supported the stand taken by Mr Meighen."[48] In discussing Britain's decision to abrogate the Anglo-Japanese alliance, which had held firm through the First World War, one analyst has gone so far as to suggest that it "stemmed from a desire to appease not Washington but rather Ottawa," Britain perhaps deferring to the dominion as the latter attempted to maintain good relations with its southern neighbour.[49] It should be noted, however, that British planning from at least 1920 "centred almost exclusively on fighting a marine war against Japan." With the elimination of Germany as a threat, "the Admiralty staff began to consider Japan as the next possible enemy which it might have to face, despite the fact that

---

46. Roskill, *Naval Policy Between the Wars*, I, 293.

47. Lovell C. Clark, ed., *Documents on Canadian External Relations* (hereafter *DCER*), III: *1919–1925* (Ottawa 1970), 174–80.

48. "Notes by Sir Robert Borden Upon the Disarmament Conference at Washington," nd, 7(1)(A), 4, LAC, MG 26 H, vol. 297.

49. John R. Ferris, "The Symbol and the Substance of Seapower: Great Britain, the United States and the One-Power Standard, 1919–1921," B.J.C. McKercher, ed, *Anglo-American Relations in the 1920s: The Struggle for Supremacy* (Edmonton, 1990), 63; and A.G.L. McNaughton, "The Principles of Imperial Defence, A Canadian Aspect," 25 March 1933, LAC, MG 27 III B-5, vol. 30, file X-16.

the Anglo-Japanese Alliance remained in place."[50] The latter was soon brought to an end, however, replaced with a multinational naval limitation treaty involving the United States, Japan, the British Empire, France, and Italy.

Another potential area of contention in this period was the Soviet Union. Specifically, the area in question was Petropaulski, in Kamchatka, which it was rumoured in 1921 might be sold to the United States. That such was considered at all possible in the midst of the "Red Scare," a reaction to the 1917 October Revolution in Russia, was itself evidence of how the potential rivalry between the US and the British Empire was taken seriously. According to the RCN's naval staff, "possession of Kamchatka by the United States would not be at all to the advantage of Canada or the British empire. As hitherto imperial foresight with regard to the Pacific has been conspicuously absent, it is considered that this matter be drawn with advantage to the attention of the imperial government at the approaching imperial conference, supported by a statement of Canadian views on the subject." Petropaulski was 4,728 kilometres from Seattle, 4,028 from Prince Rupert, and 2,285 from Yokohama, making it strategically valuable, and "if its occupation and defence were conducted with energy from the very commencement of the war, there seems reason to think it could be maintained." On the other hand, if "either Japan or the United States occupy this place by treaty or otherwise in peace time, it will immediately be developed as a naval defended port, and will be lost to British use. It is therefore of great importance to Canada that the Kamchatka peninsula be retained in the possession of Russia."[51]

A different study, of Wrangel Island, 185 kilometres off North Cape, Siberia, argued that sovereignty over it was in doubt and the island might provide facilities for operations against Petropaulski in case of a war against Japan. The island had been discovered in 1849 and given its modern name in 1867. Located between Siberia and Alaska, its links to Canada were somewhat tenuous, the Canadian government's exploration vessel *Karluk* having been wrecked there, leading to unsubstantiated stories that Ottawa had laid claim to the territory. In 1919 Vilhjalmur Stefansson, a well-known explorer, lobbied the Canadian government, insisting that the island "should be British territory" to ensure freedom of movement in the region "in the next great war." His proselytizing was not well received, however, Ottawa not wanting to set a precedent by which the US could claim islands in the Canadian Arctic. The British armed services showed no interest in the desolate island, and a Soviet claim to it in 1923 further encouraged Canadian authorities to leave well enough alone.[52]

Back in Canada, the Navy League, unsurprisingly, considered the reduced naval force approved by the Borden government in 1920 to be insufficient; nor did its members agree

---

50. Orest Babij, "The Royal Navy and Inter-War Plans for War Against Japan: The Problem of Oil Supply," Greg Kennedy, ed., *The Merchant Marine in International Affairs, 1850–1950* (London 2000), 101.

51. Naval War Staff, Occasional Paper No 26, 11 February 1921, 1017–31–4, LAC, RG 24, vol. 5696.

52. Richard J. Diubaldo, *Stefansson and the Canadian Arctic* (Montreal 1978), 161; and Undersecretary of State for External Affairs to Prime Minister, "Claim to Certain Islands within the Arctic Circle," 25 November 1920, *DCER*, III, 568–69; and Naval War Staff, Occasional Paper No 30, 13 April 1921, 1017–31–4, LAC, RG 24, vol. 5696.

with the decision to await the 1921 imperial conference before finalizing the relationship between the RCN and the RN. The League's Ontario division passed a resolution, unanimously, to the effect that "whereas the question of Canada's naval defence has been under imperial and national review since the Colonial Conference of 1902—eighteen years ago," and "whereas the great war of 1914–1918 demonstrated the pitiful inadequacy of Canadian co-operation in the duty of bearing a just share with other nations of the empire, in the naval defence of the empire," the meeting agreed that "the question of Canada's naval policy is insistent and pressing, honour and common sense alike urging its early consideration and solution, and that to delay reaching a decision on the matter until the forthcoming meeting of the imperial conference is tantamount to a confession that Canada is as unappreciative of her high national and imperial obligations to-day, as she was eighteen years ago." Furthermore, the League had the support of the Ontario government, which voted $50,000 to the organization so it could continue its work.[53]

The RCN, meanwhile, seemed less angst-ridden over recent developments, though the Admiralty suffered disappointment. Still convinced of the need for central control of naval forces, it nevertheless would not achieve its goals, the 1921 imperial conference resolving "that while recognizing the necessity of co-operation among the various forces of the empire to provide such naval defence as may prove to be essential for security and while holding that equality with the naval strength of any other power is a minimum standard for that purpose, this conference is of opinion that the method and expense of such co-operation are matters for the final determination of the several parliaments concerned." Dominion autonomy had won out over naval efficiency, and the best the Royal Navy could get at the time were "a number of useful consultations" with several dominions and India "at which were discussed such matters as local co-operation of each dominion in regard to the provision of oil tanks, local naval defence, etc."[54] Until another world conflict made centralization of force more appealing, it would have to do, though staff officers co-operating on issues such as logistics ensured that the various navies kept in touch at a basic level. "Important information on oil usage and supply, for instance, was exchanged yearly."[55]

The Navy League of Canada, having apparently failed to fulfill one part of its mission, could still shift focus onto the other two. In the mistaken expectation that the government's recent decision would mean "closing-up of activities of the Canadian naval service and the carrying on of the work on a pre-war basis, it is thought that there will be a considerable amount of naval stores probably for disposal." Since the navy was training adolescent boys for careers in the navy or merchant marine, it needed equipment suitable for instructional purposes.[56] If the Navy League was expecting a windfall, it would be disappointed, for as we have seen Cabinet had decided to fund a smaller navy than many might have wanted,

53. Ontario Secretary, Navy League of Canada to Robert Borden, 14 May 20, LAC, MG 26 H, mfm reel C4350.

54. "Summary of Discussions and Conclusions of Colonial and Imperial Conferences, 1887–1921," nd, LAC, MG 30 E133, vol. 6, file 14.

55. Babij, "The Royal Navy and Inter-war Plans for War against Japan," 101.

56. LCol Cecil Williams, Navy League of Canada, to Director of Stores, 20 April 1920, 59–2-2, LAC, RG 24, vol. 5666.

but had not shut it down. As the director of stores explained, "it is not the intention of the department to sell stores to any appreciable extent. For the information of your organization, however, I am to state that the department is prepared to issue small quantities of stores to the Navy League of Canada on repayment whenever such stores can be spared." If the League could provide a list, the naval department would "immediately inform you whether such are available and at what prices they can be supplied."[57] The RCN, therefore, provided the Navy League with some logistical support but it would go no further. Responding to a request for funding on the part of branches and divisions from across the country, C.C. Ballantyne responded negatively. "The work being done is of great value to the boys under training and prepares a certain number of them for service at sea ... but I regret that at the present time such a thing is not possible." Although CGS *Canada* was allocated to League use free of charge, the organization could not afford the insurance and other associated costs.[58]

For the Royal Canadian Navy, generally speaking, Cabinet decisions in this period were more cause for optimism than otherwise, and though the fleet of 1920 would not have an aircraft carrier, which had figured in some of Jellicoe's recommendations, it could still expect to develop a naval aviation branch. Its beginnings, interestingly enough, could be found in the USN's wartime air stations at Halifax and Sydney. A month after the armistice, American representatives asked if the facilities, which had reverted to Canadian control, would be maintained into the post-war period. As Desbarats explained, "while policy was indefinite stations would probably be reopened later either on naval or Royal Air Force basis." As it turned out, facilities had only been closed down for the winter season, and the deputy minister was instructed to "inform American government it is intention Canadian government [to] permanently continue Naval Air Service."[59]

The next step was to acquire the necessary materiel, not a difficult matter since discussions with the Americans, represented in part by Assistant Secretary of the Navy Franklin D. Roosevelt, were described as "extremely friendly and pleasant." The bottom line was that "Canada should pay for all the ground material furnished by the United States and retained by Canada—that the United States would leave at the stations all the flying material which they had furnished," including a dozen seaplanes, with spares, four kite balloons with winches, and twenty-six spare Liberty engines, "as well as the armament needed for the flying machines, instruments, clothing for flying men, and stock of various articles needed for the upkeep and repair of the seaplanes and kite balloons."[60]

It was, however, a beginning that might not have a future. Ottawa was willing to maintain the nucleus of an air service for the time being but would make no guarantees regarding the subsequent fiscal year. The director of stores felt obligated to report in early 1919 that

57. F. McVeigh to Cecil G. Williams, 20 May 1920, 59–2-2, LAC, RG 24, vol. 5666.

58. Ballantyne to Aemilius Jarvis, Dominion President, Navy League of Canada, 18 May 1921, Secretary, Boys Naval Brigade Winnipeg to Ballantyne, 10 January 1921, 59–1-3, Ballantyne to G.B. Jackson, Dominion Secretary, Navy League of Canada, 11 March 1921, Ballantyne to Aemilius Jarvis, 16 June 1921, 59–2-2, LAC, RG 24, vol. 5666.

59. Desbarats to Ballantyne, 9 December 1918, Ballantyne to Desbarats, 10 December 1918, 63–1-1, ibid.

60. Desbarats to Ballantyne, 9 December 1918, Ballantyne to Desbarats, 13 December 1918, ibid.

if the machines were not needed the following summer, it would be best to dispose of them, as they would, "within eighteen months, become obsolescent ... The progress in flying has been so rapid that engines and planes will rapidly become obsolete and it is considered that if any return is to be obtained from the disposal of the gear it should be disposed of forthwith while it is comparatively up-to-date and in good order." One possibility might be to sell the materials to the Air Craft Manufacturing Company of Montreal.[61] In August 1919 the assistant director of the naval service, Walter Hose, reported that "both Stations are in a semi-completed state. Barracks for one hundred men, mess and recreation buildings for three hundred men, a spacious store building and a temporary steel seaplane hangar have been completed at each station. Nothing has been done on the construction of airship or kite balloon accommodation. A few men have been engaged at each station for overhauling equipment, and for care and maintenance purposes." In the meantime, however, legislation in 1919 had created a federal Air Board, of seven members, "to regulate and supervise all matters connected with aeronautics."[62] There was now an interested body specifically mandated to deal with such issues as the air stations at Halifax and Sydney.

The history of the latter as a naval station in the interwar period has been encapsulated in the title, "The Years of Neglect," given to that period by two historians of the city. They note how "there was some local concern about the unseemly haste of the military withdrawal" from Sydney. At one point "the mayor of North Sydney 'got the wind up' about bombs and ammunition stored at the nearby naval air base, warning that if guards were not posted he would throw them into the river. In fact, as one officer sardonically observed, such action 'would be convenient to us and save trouble,' except for the fact that the navy was required by its agreement with the US Navy to return the munitions to the United States."[63] Sydney's role in naval aviation was therefore cut short until it once again became an air base in the Second World War.

Meanwhile, the RCN, in the form of a naval war staff occasional paper, made its bid for what it called a "Naval Air Force." One of its many arguments was that "in war time, as soon as an airman alights on land he becomes dependent on the military for almost everything, and therefore, he must come under the orders of the military Commander-in-Chief, otherwise, there would be two Commanders-in-Chief exercising authority in the same area. The argument is equally applicable to an airman alighting on board a ship. He must then necessarily come under the orders of the naval Commander-in-Chief. Still greater is the necessity when the airman lives on board a ship or is working in conjunction with a ship." Ignoring the British example of combining the RFC and RNAS into a unified Royal Air Force, Canadian naval planners argued that the principle of unity of command called for the navy to control aircraft and personnel working in its interests.[64]

---

61. Director of Stores to Desbarats, 10 January 1919, ibid.

62. ADNS to Acting Director Air Service, 29 August 1919, 78–1–13, LAC, RG 24, vol. 5669. For more on this issue, see W.A.B. Douglas, *The Creation of a National Air Force* (Toronto 1986), 603–08, 614–15.

63. Tennyson and Sarty, *Guardian of the Gulf*, 189.

64. Naval War Staff, Occasional Paper No 24, "Remarks on a Canadian Naval Air Force," 26 January 1920, 63–1–1, LAC, RG 24, vol. 5666.

They were aware, however, of the argument to be made for a unified air force. "The work of the air force is to obtain command of the air. Command of the air is necessary to prevent towns, dockyards, camps, etc, from being bombed, to admit of [i.e., to allow for] troops being convoyed from one point to another rapidly, and to keep open imperial communications in the air. In these matters the air force should be entirely independent of the navy, except insofar as their strategy is co-ordinated to that of the general plan of campaign.... On the other hand when necessary to use aerial force in connection with work for which the navy is responsible, that is to say, for gaining or keeping command of the sea, then that force should be part of the navy." In way of analogy, the paper noted that "although the army is responsible for operations on the land and the navy on the sea, this does not prevent the army from having its own inland water transport or the navy from having its own battalions of seamen for land warfare, because these are found necessary on certain occasions to the efficient performance of the work of army and navy, respectively, in their own particular spheres."[65]

To arguments of principle the Air Board responded with practicalities. Its vice-chairman, the naval department's G.J. Desbarats, argued "that it is yet too early in Canada to subdivide the air forces. The total personnel available for air services (about 200 by the end of 1920) with the naval forces, with the land forces and for independent operations will be so small that to divide them into three groups at present would be a very serious handicap to general aerial development."[66] That did not, however, exclude the navy from such development, and in fact the acting naval director, Walter Hose, was a member of the Air Board. As such he was in touch with the Admiralty to see "that the Canadian naval air work should be conducted in a manner to ensure complete co-operation in this, as in other naval operations with the Royal Navy." To that end, he asked for information "on the relations between the navy and the Royal Air Force, observing that there appears to be a very similar situation as regards the Royal Canadian Navy and the Air Board of Canada; consequently, any remarks on what is considered desirable in the way of liaison between the two departments and the conditions of control of material and personnel when employed by the navy, would be very desirable. I would further request that I may be kept informed at Ottawa of any developments in naval air work in England and abroad in order to try and arrange for as complete co-operation as possible in Canada."[67] Although the RCN did not yet have its own air element, there was still a possibility it could develop some form of aerial capability.

Still, for the time being the focus would be on ships and the facilities necessary to keep them at sea. At war's end the RCN's infrastructure was centered on its two main bases at Halifax and Esquimalt. The Halifax dockyard conducted its work in a similar fashion to the imperial yards in Britain, that being through such individuals and organizations as the captain superintendent, the captain dockyard, the chief constructor, the chief engineer, the works department, the electrical engineer, the naval store officer, the expense accounts

65. Ibid.

66. Vice-Chairman Air Board to Desbarats, 1 March 1920, 63–1-1, LAC, RG 24, vol. 5666; and Douglas, *The Creation of a National Air Force*, 52.

67. Hose to Admiralty, 24 September 1920, 31–9-9, LAC, RG 24, vol. 5632.

officer, the cashier, the principal medical officer, and a secretary, the latter a naval officer. It was thus a sophisticated organization with administration to match, though at times more burdensome than necessary. For example, in 1920 it was found that General Order No 1, conduct of correspondence, needed revising. Until then it had been customary for the dockyard to submit requests to higher authority in duplicate, so the response could simply be written on one copy and returned. Elsewhere in the naval service, however, the custom had developed by which responses were provided in a separate letter, so the duplicate requests were simply destroyed. "It is therefore obvious that there must be considerable waste of paper and unnecessary work in the records branch in stamping, filing and subsequently destroying the duplicates."[68]

Logistics and administration were thus complex tasks rife with potential pitfalls, though practitioners of such arcane arts also had to be on the *qui vive* for opportunity. When war ended and it was decided that Germany would pay reparations, RCN staff jumped at the opportunity of acquiring sophisticated materiel. By way of the chain of command, the governor general communicated to the Admiralty their interest "in obtaining two small floating docks, one for use at Halifax and one at Esquimalt, capacity of these docks to be sufficient to take large destroyers and light cruisers. [Naval] department would also be interested in acquiring two floating cranes of about ten tons capacity."[69] There is no record of the RCN having been successful in its bid, but the attempt is exemplary of its logistics officers' manner of operating.

The dockyard also relied heavily on contractors, agreements usually calculated based on estimates of labour, material, plus a percentage for profit. Determining the latter could, however, be something of a challenge given that overheads could vary widely, especially between small and large firms. As of early 1919 rates were labour plus 20 percent and material plus 10 percent, with an additional charge of 15 percent to cover overhead. One of the larger firms was Halifax Shipyards Limited, "the only firm at Halifax who have the facilities for undertaking extensive repairs involving docking," reported Desbarats. Entering into a contract with the company was thus a tricky matter, as there was really nowhere else to go. The firm does not seem to have attempted to take undue advantage, however, no doubt to avoid killing the goose that was laying its golden eggs. When it was decided in 1920 to close the naval workshops at the dockyard, Halifax Shipyards offered to repair government ships (not just those of the RCN) for the cost of labour plus 60 percent, with an additional five percent to cover overhead, and another 25 percent for profit.[70]

Hiring dockyard staff offered different challenges and complexities. As one engineering officer reported three months after the armistice, skilled labour was scarce, and what labour was available lacked the necessary skills, so much so that "the serious consequences that might be incurred through a breakdown while at sea" had to be considered. As a result, it

68. Proposed Memo for Deputy Minister, 25 September 1920, 1700–100/76, LAC, RG 24, vol. 8166; and Captain Superintendent, Halifax to NSHQ, 10 July 1919, 78-1-13, LAC, RG 24, vol. 5669.

69. Governor General to Lord Milner, 3 January 1919, LAC, MG 26H, mfm reel C4349.

70. Desbarats to War Purchasing Commission, 15 May 1919, Cdr (E) Phillips to Desbarats, 10 January 1919, 44-3-2, LAC, RG 24, vol. 3592.

was "of great importance to get the very best workmen to carry out the work of repairing, overhauling, and perhaps eventually constructing the hulls and machinery of vessels belonging to the navy." If necessary, "special privileges and attractions" were to be offered to entice the "highest class required." Such inducements would include pay at five to ten percent above union rates. Furthermore, "the workshops should be large enough to avoid overcrowding, should be light, well ventilated and well heated in winter and above all kept clean. The provision of coat rooms with sanitary lockers and a well equipped wash room and lavatories also adds to the efficiency of the man and makes him take an interest in his work."[71]

Providing the necessary facilities would not be easy, however, since the dockyard had not yet been fully repaired after the Halifax explosion and was, as the navy had explained to the government, completely inadequate in any case. For example, in reporting on the blacksmith's shop, the civil engineer noted in 1920 how the "roof has not been repaired since the explosion," and was old and rotten in any event. Similarly, of thirteen houses in one section of the dockyard, one had been destroyed by fire and only five of the remainder were considered to be in good condition. Of the stores buildings, one was "a very light building on temporary foundation which has badly settled in places," another was "a useful building but badly racked in the explosion," while a third was in good condition. A fourth was "an old building badly shaken in the explosion," and one nearby was "troubled with water on the floor." Yet another was best abandoned, while two more needed new roofs, and four others were temporary structures that had been erected after the explosion and would only last two years or so because of wooden foundations. Similarly, though the electrical shop was in good condition, it was deemed best to abandon the submarine depot.[72]

On Canada's opposite end, Esquimalt had not suffered the kind of catastrophe that had befallen Halifax, but it had challenges enough to face as it entered the post-war period. One order of business, quickly disposed of, was the return of the Naval Hospital, temporarily loaned to the Department of Soldier's Civil Re-establishment.[73] More complicated was the construction of a dry dock, a project that dated to 1914 but which had been interrupted by the war. By 1919, however, Esquimalt's very existence as a naval base was in doubt, as was evident in an RCN submission to the minister, which noted that "the Colonial Defence Committee, as far back as 1905, recommended the abandonment of Esquimalt as a defended port." Esquimalt survived as a naval facility, but activity on the base was noticeably reduced.[74]

---

71. "Suggested Scheme of Organization for Home Dockyards in Canada," 18 February 1919, 37–26–11, LAC, RG 24, vol. 5635.

72. Civil Engineer HMC Dockyard to Captain Superintendent, 9 July 1919, Commander in Charge HMC Dockyard to NSHQ, 8 April 1920, 14–2-1, LAC, RG 24, vol. 3602; and Kingsmill, "Memorandum for the Minister," 5 November 1918, Gibbs, "Memorandum for the Director of the Naval Service," 20 October 1918, 1065–1-1, pt 1, LAC, RG 24, vol. 4029.

73. Naval Committee Proceedings, 9 July 1919, Deputy Minister Militia and Defence to Desbarats, 25 July 1919, 1017–10–8, LAC, RG 24, vol. 3833.

74. Memorandum for the Information of the Minister, Proposed Drydock at Esquimalt, 31 October 1919, 78–1-13, LAC, RG 24, vol. 5669; and T.C. Phillips, Consulting Naval Engineer, to Desbarats, 31 March 1921, 14–3-1, LAC, RG 24, vol. 3603.

Warships were no longer of interest to a government that had gone through a bloody and divisive war, but it was only a little over a year later that Cabinet, as we have seen, decided to follow the counsel of its naval advisers and acquire new vessels. On 24 March 1920, therefore, it accepted the British offer of a light cruiser and two destroyers.[75] Superficially, this may seem to be a contradiction of the Admiralty's preference for a centrally controlled imperial navy, but the Royal Navy's thinking was more sophisticated. Its aim was the establishment of a force or forces that, in a time of crisis, would be available for deployment. A single naval service with headquarters at Whitehall would, of course, achieve that purpose, but it had been clear since the late nineteenth century that colonies or dominions such as Canada and South Africa were not willing to go along with the establishment of such an organization. Providing more autonomous-minded parts of the empire with ships so they could form their own navies could still benefit the Admiralty so long as they were trained in RN procedures and might be available when needed. It was, perhaps, more of a muddle than British naval authorities would otherwise have liked, but it would pay certain benefits when Great Britain went to war again, in 1939.

As for the British gift of vessels, the Royal Navy had also demobilized and did not have surplus sailors to take the ships across the Atlantic. It was one detail among many that the RCN would have to resolve, though its experience in the First World War and the availability of British advice would make the procurement relatively smooth sailing. The light cruiser being offered, one of the Bristol class, was not fitted with director firing for its guns, and though the destroyers had such equipment, they were not fitted with the more modern Evershed Bearing Indicators, required for accurate fire. As one high-ranking but anonymous staff officer remarked, "if it is intended that the ships to be acquired by the department should act as training ships for personnel of future ships, it is very desirable that they should all be fitted with director firing and Evershed Bearing Indicators."[76]

The entire issue of obsolescence was an important one for the RCN, since it wanted the ships to train sailors in the conduct of modern naval warfare. More crucial than director finding, which could be fitted by a British shipyard, was the propulsion system, which in the Bristol-class light cruisers ran on coal. As T.C. Phillips, the consulting naval engineer, advised, "there has been no light cruisers or destroyers designed for coal burning since 1912." Oil burned more efficiently than coal, allowed an increase in a ship's radius of action of 40 to 50 percent for a given weight of fuel, was much easier to bunker, and allowed "an appreciable reduction in stokehold compliments [sic]." Furthermore, "on both east and west coasts of Canada, fuel oils are easily procurable today." The consulting naval engineer also argued that, "the advent of geared turbines in lieu of direct running installations dates back to 1914, the benefits resulting being so marked that this design has been proceeded with to date to the exclusion of all others in vessels of the light cruiser and destroyer classes. In all some 600 sets of geared turbines have been fitted to new ships constructed for the Admiralty during the past six years, and of these no serious defects or breakdowns have resulted.

---

75. Desbarats to Undersecretary of State for External Affairs, 24 March 1920, 1017–10–8, LAC, RG 24, vol. 3833.

76. Chief of Staff to Naval Assistant, 28 April 1920, Milner to Governor General, 23 April 1920, ibid.

The cruiser HMCS *Aurora* at San Diego on 3 March 1921 during her training cruise from Halifax to Esquimalt. *Aurora* mounted two 6-inch, six 4-inch, and two 3-inch guns, and eight 21-inch torpedo tubes. After serving in the Grand Fleet during the First World War, she was presented to the RCN in 1920 but was paid off two years later and sold for scrap in 1927. (LAC PA-041129)

The destroyer HMCS *Patrician* spent most of her RCN career on the West Coast, training officers and men of the naval reserve. (LAC e-007140907)

The battle cruiser *Hood* has been fitted with geared turbines," and that warship was the pride of the post-war British navy. "It is calculated that a fair average of increase in efficiency of geared turbines over direct connected installations may be stated to be 16% in the case of light cruisers and 20% in the case of flotilla leaders and destroyers at all power speeds, that means considerable economy in fuel and a consequent saving in maintenance costs."[77]

The issue was quickly disposed of when the Admiralty replied in June that an oil-burning cruiser would be provided. The question of the RCN's strategic orientation was addressed in a July 1919 paper on naval expansion. Regarding "Japan as the most probable enemy of the future," the paper noted that her navy "at present possesses six battle cruisers and a number of light cruisers." Given the composition of the potential enemy's fleet, and the long distances involved in operations in the Pacific, a ship of the Frobisher class was suggested as being appropriate. What remained were simple matters of detail, such as the expenditure of £105 to install pipes so the oil in the ship's bunkers could be kept warm.[78] As for the destroyers, they would be *Patriot* and *Patrician*, each of which needed to have three main items installed: an additional electrical engine for manoeuvring in harbour, an oil fuel galley to avoid having to store coal for cooking, and an enclosed bridge given that the vessels would spend at least part of their working lives in northern climes. For a time, at least, the RCN would be operating with modern, effective ships of war, though the work required to render *Patriot* and *Patrician* "efficient fighting units" would total £14,000. That amount would not, however, include the cost of "Canadianizing" the ships, as "the department has under consideration the question of heating arrangements in the *Aurora*, *Patriot*, and *Patrician*, in order that the ships may be maintained at a satisfactory temperature without the assistance of temporary heating stoves during the winter season." To that end, it was "proposed that an arrangement of heating for the mess decks and other large compartments if necessary be effected by the ships' company." For *Patriot* and *Patrician*, "electrical radiation" elements would suffice.[79]

Besides acquiring modern vessels and making them habitable, the RCN was also open to new developments in maritime technology, including some that were downright futuristic in nature. The most noteworthy from this period was a craft being tested by Alexander Graham Bell, of telephone fame, and F.W. Baldwin. As they reported in October 1918, the two inventors had "been making experiments here with the assistance of the Navy Department of the United States on a new model of a hydroplane boat that may perhaps be of use for war purposes. The boat has been launched and is now ready for trial…. It would give us great pleasure should the Department of Naval Service care to detail an officer to observe our experiments."[80] The RCN was, in fact, very much interested, Hose relating how

---

77. T.C. Phillips to Hose and Desbarats, 30 April 20, 31–9-1, LAC, RG 24, vol. 5632.

78. Capt H.G.H. Adams to DNS, 31 August 1920, ibid; and Naval War Staff, Occasional Paper No 2, 3 July 1919, 1017–31–2, LAC, RG 24, vol. 5696.

79. Naval Secretary to Commander in Charge HMC Dockyard Halifax, 29 April 1921, 31–1-1, Cdr (E) Studsen to Capt H.G. Adams, 3 September 1920, 31–9-1, LAC, RG 24, vol. 5632; and McVeigh to Ballantyne, 21 July 1920, 1017–10–8, LAC, RG 24, vol. 3833.

80. Alexander Graham Bell and F.W. Baldwin to Naval Minister, 15 October 1918, 1077–1-4, LAC, RG 24, vol. 3789.

HMCS *Patriot* towing Alexander Graham Bell's experimental hydrofoil on Bras d'Or Lake, Cape Breton, in September 1921. (LAC e007140908)

Patriot working up to speed. (CWM 19910109-190)

he attempted "to get Mr F.W. Baldwin, who is the real manager of the Hydroplane business, on the long distance phone at Baddeck.... I learnt however that he is at New York—which looks bad.... I have written him personally that the Admiralty are making enquiries and asked him not to let the Hydroplane get into the hands of other parties until the Admiralty are more fully informed."[81]

Although the US Navy was still being perceived as a potential rival in staff circles, it is unlikely that Bell and Baldwin were aware of such concerns as they worked on what would now be called a hydrofoil. Bell, for instance, responded to Hose's requests for information with encouraging words: "I am very glad to know that the Admiralty are evincing interest in our hydroplane boat the HD-4 and shall of course be glad to furnish them with every information concerning our work here." He added, however, that he had "just made a report to Admiral Griffin, Chief Engineer of the US Navy, on the recent experiments with the HD-4 equipped with the Liberty motors loaned to us by the Navy Dept," and suggested that "a copy of the report be forwarded to Canada's naval minister," though the inventors were "already in communication with the United States Navy department in relation to the building of boats of this design." The United States did, however, have a claim on Bell's work, for though he had personally borne the costs of construction work and experiments, the engines had been provided, on loan, by the USN. In fact, Admiralty officers had been allowed to witness experiments, and they commented favourably on the outcome; by the autumn of 1921 the British were conducting towing trials of their own.[82]

The RCN ran a series of tests at about the same time, HMCS *Patriot* called upon to support Bell's work. The ship's captain, Lieutenant Charles Beard, reported how "the object of the experiment was to determine horse-power consumed by this type of boat at various known speeds, and to note behaviour when towed at high speeds for target purposes." Therefore, "I think this type of boat would be an ideal target, as hull need only consist of a T frame connecting the three hydrofoils, and on top of this could be erected the two masts for stretching the canvas between ... The great advantage of this type of target would be that speed is not restricted, it has exceptional stability, it can be constructed so that it can be taken to pieces, and reconstructed on board ... also there is no appreciable reduction in speed to the towing ship."[83] There the matter stood, and though there is no record of the hydrofoil targets being used, and though hydrofoils themselves would not be the subject of experiment until another world war had consumed the service's attention, the episode nevertheless demonstrates the institution's openness toward technological development.

At the other end of the technical scale was the need to maintain the technologies the RCN already possessed—and to explain their loss when accident led to destruction or damage. When on 14 August 1919 the tug *Becancour* sank in Halifax Harbour, a court of enquiry was assembled to look into the circumstances surrounding its loss, leading to the tabling of a twenty-four-page report. It was a wonderful example of how the procurement of

81. Hose to Stephens, 5 March 1920, ibid.

82. Bell to Hose, 11 March 1920, Capt Superintendent, Halifax to NSHQ, 23 March 1920, Bell and Baldwin to Hose, 19 September 1921, ibid.

83. Charles Beard, Lt in Command HMCS *Patriot*, 5 October 1921, ibid.

effective technologies can be nullified by human error. In this case it was found "the sinking of the Tug *Becancoeur* [*sic*] was due to the fact, that the scuttles in the forecastle were not properly closed, and secured before the vessel commenced coaling, and that the responsibility for this omission rests upon Mr Richard Huelin, Mate, RCNVR, [Royal Canadian Naval Volunteer Reserve, of which more later], the officer in command of the ship. While he appears to have been aware, that it was necessary to secure these scuttles whilst coaling, he seems to have taken no steps to insure that such a precaution was taken, and to have been content to accept a general assurance that his ship was 'prepared for coaling,' without attempting to ascertain what such a report implied." Worse, "the court also consider that there was great laxity in the general organization of the vessel under his command. No definite responsibility for the performance of any specific duty seems to have been placed upon the mates of the ship, who indeed appear never even to have settled the question of their relative seniority, nor—to take this particular occurrence—was the responsibility for seeing that the forecastle scuttles were properly secured, laid upon either of these officers."[84]

Huelin and another officer "incurred the severe displeasure of the department," while "Engine Room Artificer 3rd Class Allan White ... is to be informed of the appreciation of the department for his promptitude and discretion in the performance of his duties on the occasion in question. A notation is to be made in his service certificate that he received the commendation of the department on the 5th September, 1919."[85] Similarly, the captain superintendent of HMC Dockyard reported a few months later on the "action taken for the preservation of trawlers, drifters, and other vessels in the Dockyard Reserve at Halifax during a heavy gale on November 5th," a more comprehensive example of the lengths sometimes necessary to protect the navy's surplus assets. About noon on that date the wind was blowing from the south east with a force of eight or nine (a gale or strong gale at seventy-five to 102 kilometres per hour), and eighteen trawlers "were observed to be dragging their moorings and drifting in batches of three up towards the Narrows. A working party was at once sent off to let go anchors from each trawler, and they were finally brought up, the nearest within about fifty feet from the wharf at the Halifax Shipyards." Then, in the early morning of 6 November, *Grilse* parted her stern mooring, but the armed yacht was rescued soon after, though drifters suffered considerable damage when their mooring ropes parted.[86] It was only the beginning, and in a final accounting it was found that twenty-two drifters and eighteen other vessels had suffered damage, though "of a minor nature." Still, repairs were estimated at $3,978, most of which would be deferred given that many of the vessels concerned were to be sold off the following spring.[87]

Such sales were, in fact, an important government endeavour after the war, though *caveat emptor* seemed to dominate such operations, which included vessels being disposed of on behalf of the Admiralty. Referring to the Canadian-made imperial trawlers, one of the British representatives noted that vessels would be sold "as they lie, without guarantee or

84. Lt (E) G.L. Stephens, Cdr H.E. Holme, and Lt J.E.W. Oland to Hose, 23 August 1919, 80–5-56, LAC, RG 24, vol. 5671.

85. Captain Superintendent, "Memorandum," 5 September 1919, ibid.

86. Captain Superintendent to NSHQ, 12 November 1919, 85–9-1, LAC, RG 24, vol. 5657.

87. CNE to DM, 5 December 1919 and 13 January 1920, ibid.

any allowance for necessary repairs." The RCN, however, through its dockyard at Halifax, had to provide some form of help, as almost all the 125 vessels in question had defects requiring work before they could even leave port and potential buyers might not be willing to pay for exorbitant repairs just to get the vessels ready for sea. It was decided to approve the necessary modifications.[88]

Another possible client for surplus vessels was the Navy League of Canada, which, as we have seen, supported a form of sea scout movement for boys for which it needed equipment of all kinds to teach seamanship and other sailing skills. In 1921, its Ontario Branch asked for the use of an RCN vessel on the Great Lakes, and Desbarats noted that the department still had on hand vessels that had been used during the war and that had been placed on the sales list. The easiest to sell had already been disposed of and "the ships now on hand are those which are not easily adaptable for commercial purposes." Since they cost the service money to maintain, the deputy minister suggested loaning one to the Navy League, since its work "is of value to the boys and leads a certain number of them to either enlist in the Navy or take service in the Mercantile Marine."[89] Desbarats's suggestions included the not-insubstantial HMC Ships *Canada* and *Shearwater*, and the RCN's twelve Battle-class trawlers, but none of the warships were ever lent to the League.

Unlike the trawlers, tenders, and other vessels that could easily be taken up by the fishing industry, submarines had little commercial use, but even then they represented a considerable dollar value. When *CC 1* and *CC 2* went on the market in the summer of 1920, John Simon of Halifax offered $6,000 for each, but the consulting naval engineer balked. The bid "cannot be considered as even approaching their present actual value," he wrote to the deputy minister, their worth determined in part "by the ability to utilize the diesel sets and motors for operating plants ashore, although considerable outlay would need to be made to fit them up for operation. There are also valuable pumps, electrical fittings and numerous accessories. The torpedo tubes—five in *CC 1* and three in *CC 2*—are of solid gun metal, as are also both conning towers, these parts alone weighing approximately 70,000 lbs." They were not sold to Simon, but instead were packaged with HMCS *Niobe*, for which New Brunswick Rolling Mills offered $130,000. The company subsequently went bankrupt, but the entire episode, in conjunction with the sale of other vessels, demonstrated that getting rid of ships could be no less complicated than procuring them in the first place.[90]

The RCN was not, however, divesting itself of all of its vessels, and those remaining needed some minimum level of manning if, for nothing else, to keep them at a reasonable level of care. That itself proved something of a challenge, the reservists the navy had enrolled for the First World War having already been demobilized. The naval minister reported to a committee of the Privy Council in May 1919 how "the technical officers of the department have reported that approximately 500 officers and men are necessary for

88. Naval to Captain Superintendent Halifax, 30 January 1920, 29–22–18, LAC, RG 24, vol. 5607; and CNE to DM, 24 March 1920, 85-9-1, LAC, RG 24, vol. 5657.

89. Desbarats to Minister, 15 February 1921, 132-1-1, LAC, RG 24, vol. 5682.

90. Consulting Naval Engineer to Desbarats, 25 August 1920, Clerk of the Privy Council to Minister of Naval Service, 23 October 1920, 29–22–23, LAC, RG 24, vol. 5607.

HMCS *Ypres*, one of the twelve Battle-class trawlers built for the RCN during the First World War, photographed in 1924. The trawlers remained an important part of the Canadian navy's fleet throughout the 1920s. (DND E-35756)

the care and maintenance of ships and establishments of the Canadian Naval Service now in existence. Service at present time consists almost entirely of officers and men who volunteered for war service and it is, therefore, necessary to enter sufficient officers and men to meet present requirements." New entries would "sign an engagement to serve for a period of one year from date of entry, pay and allowances to be not less than those at present in force in the Royal Canadian Navy." The committee concurred,[91] but getting the necessary people and, more to the point, training them, would be one of the RCN's major preoccupations in the interwar period.

For those who joined as officers, their professional education began at the Royal Naval College of Canada, which had been opened in Halifax in 1911 but moved to Kingston following the catastrophic Halifax explosion and then to Esquimalt. Whereas previously it had incorporated a small electrical laboratory, engineering workshops, a drawing office, a gymnasium, sick quarters, and a boat house, its new surroundings were somewhat more spartan. As its commander in charge reported in mid-1919, "the accommodation at Esquimalt is suitable for a maximum of forty-eight cadets and would then be somewhat cramped in the living quarters." The school, though "apart from the main building," and with laboratories in the basement, "is quite suitable as a temporary expedient," though the C-in-C was unaware of how prophetic his words were. As for other courses on the curriculum, "the engineering instruction and workshop practice takes place in various scattered structures." Rounding out the picture was the fact that "the cadets use the canteen grounds for playing field. This is a mile away. In addition two tennis courts have been made for the college in the dockyard." The costs of running the facility increased from less than $50,000 in 1911 to over $195,000 in 1921.[92]

Some of those funds were needed to pay the college's instructional and administrative staff, which included a retired commander from the RN, an engineer commander on loan from that same service, a paymaster lieutenant-commander RCN, two Canadian lieutenants, an engineer lieutenant RCN, an instructor commander director of studies on loan from the Royal Navy, two instructor commanders RCN, two masters, one in mathematics and the other in physics, as well as a master in English and other languages. Other staff members included three warrant officers, a boatswain, and a warrant writer, all of them RCN. The commander in charge noted that "the staff under the director of studies has only been varied by the exchange of sea going duties by the two naval instructors, RCN, one being at sea and the other at the College alternately." Also, "the master in English subjects and languages is an Oxford man and Rhodes scholar." Student strength had varied considerably over the years, with nineteen graduating (or "passing out" to use the institution's expression) in 1911, and eight, six, six, eight, three, and eleven in later promotions. There were thirty cadets at the college in mid-1919.[93]

---

91. PC 1008, 15 May 1919, 1–24–1, LAC, RG 24, vol. 5586.

92. Commander in Charge Royal Naval College of Canada to NSHQ, 25 June 1919, 78–1-11, LAC, RG 24, vol. 5668; and "Historical Synopsis of the Organization and Development of the Royal Canadian Navy," nd, LAC, MG 27, III B-5, vol. 38, file 42.

93. Commander in Charge Royal Naval College of Canada to NSHQ, 25 June 1919, 78–1-11, LAC, RG 24, vol. 5668.

Retaining staff to instruct the cadets and support the various activities of the college could be a headache at times. Kingsmill, while still DNS, had advised in early 1919 that "I fear we are going to have difficulty providing stewards and cadets' servants for the RNC. We cannot retain those we have as the wages they can obtain outside are higher than service pay." The cadets being naval officers, such stewards and servants were considered of no little importance, so Kingsmill related how "I have been talking the matter over with the deputy and he agrees to the employment as cooks, stewards etc, of Chinese," no doubt from the local community around Esquimalt, "if it becomes necessary. The best thing to do would be to get someone who understands the Chinamen [sic] to go down and see the situation and tell you what number of stewards, cooks etc would be necessary to run the whole show." One potentially fruitful locale for recruiting was the Oak Bay Hotel in Victoria, whose manager "employs no one but Chinamen, some of whom have been with him for twenty-five years."[94]

The cadets such staff members supported entered between the ages of fourteen and sixteen, and "all the instruction, training and the syllabus including engineering have, in a broad way and so far as facilities allow, been arranged and carried out in a manner very similar to the practice in the Royal Navy." Such education was primarily meant to prepare the candidate for a career in the RCN, but such was not compulsory, and it had been possible to obtain from Canadian universities "concessions which allow of cadets who do not elect for a naval career, to enter the universities in the 2nd year of the science course." (That meant, of course, that RNCC graduates had completed the rough equivalent of the first year of university whereas the three-year RMC program allowed graduates to receive a bachelor degree after completing their fourth year at a civilian university.) Since 1914 the naval college had run a three-year curriculum, testing being conducted by examination, usually four times per term with one to cover all the material learned in that term.[95]

Upon graduation, those who chose to make a career in the RCN's executive branch could expect to spend three years as midshipmen, two as sub-lieutenants, eight as lieutenants, four as lieutenant-commanders, six as commanders, and twelve as captains before reaching retirement age. According to the assistant naval director, "it is further assumed that whilst all officers are eligible to reach the rank of lieut-commander, that fifty per cent of entries fail to be promoted to commander. The wastage includes deaths, resignations, withdrawals and failure to be promoted owing to lack of vacancies. It is also assumed that of those who reach commander rank only 50 per cent are promoted to captain owing to further wastage."[96] All graduates were Canadian, as there were more candidates within the country than there were vacancies, so requests for positions within the RCN coming from Britain had to be turned down. Furthermore, "as matters stand at present we are obliged to request the Admiralty to place a considerable number of our surplus officers."[97]

94. Kingsmill to Nixon, 20 January 1919, LCdr (Pay) Haddon to Cdr Nixon, nd, LAC, MG 30, E218, vol. 1, file 13.

95. Commander in Charge Royal Naval College of Canada to NSHQ, 25 June 1919, 78-1-11, LAC, RG 24, vol. 5668.

96. ADNS to Naval Committee, 10 June 1919, 1017–10–8, LAC, RG 24, vol. 3833.

97. DNS to W.O. Rooper, 6 September 1920, 31–9-9, LAC, RG 24, vol. 5632.

Whether surplus or not, all officers had to serve with the Royal Navy given the RCN's limited size and concomitant opportunities. As one, Frank Llewellyn Houghton, who underwent such a process, later wrote in his memoirs, "during World War I and for some years thereafter I was, together with many other RCN officers, 'lent to the Royal Navy,' where our ranks and seniority were recognised as though we were RN. My own spell of service with the Royal Navy lasted from the age of eighteen until I was twenty-six, a formative period during which I absorbed the 'spirit of the Royal Navy' in more ways than one." In fact, in his thirty-nine years in the RCN the Canadian officer and his comrades "flew the White Ensign and did our best to uphold the glorious traditions of the Royal Navy."[98] As the Canadian naval minister explained in June 1919, those who had completed their education at the Royal Naval College of Canada before the war "have been continuing their training on the ships of the imperial navy. A very few of them have reached the rank of lieutenant, but they are beginning to be available for junior appointments. An arrangement was made whereby these officers were to be transferred to the imperial navy but the war intervened and the arrangement was never carried out. They are however, as I stated above, serving with the imperial navy getting the very best experience which men in their profession could be given and fitting themselves for advancement in their career. They have been paid by the Canadian government and are borne in the ranks of the Canadian navy," to which they returned, in effect, as Royal Navy officers.[99]

One of those to have undergone a Royal Navy education in the post-war period was Horatio Nelson Lay, who kept a detailed journal of his experiences. Joining the battleship HMS *Resolution* in 1921, he noted that of thirty members of his mess, four were from the RCN and three were Australians. After such routine elements as lessons in navigation, re-ammunitioning ship, and going ashore for tea with a high-ranking RCN officer, Lay was part of an impressive training exercise in November 1921. Its objects were: "to investigate the situation when destroyers of two opposing fleets each attempt to deliver a torpedo attack the fleets and flotillas on each side being about equal"; "to investigate the situation when the opposing battle fleets are being manoeuvered so as to obtain the maximum gunnery advantage from the attacks that are being delivered by their flotillas. Both CinCs must also endeavour to develop the torpedo fire of the battle line, either during the destroyer attacks or subsequently"; "to exercise aircraft in reconnaissance"; and "to exercise casualties amongst the destroyers." On one side were the battleships *Revenge*, *Ramillies*, and *Royal Oak*, the battle cruisers *Hood* and *Repulse*, the cruisers *Curacoa*, *Caledon*, *Cardelia*, and *Coventry*, and various destroyers, and, on the other, the fast battleships *Queen Elizabeth*, *Valiant*, *Warspite*, and *Malaya*, the cruisers *Delhi* and *Castor*, the aircraft carrier *Argus*, and their accompanying destroyers.[100]

Lay's role was to act as a torpedo observer, but it turned out to be too windy for the practice torpedoes to be picked up easily, so that part of training had to be put off. That night his ship was part of a gunnery action against a light cruiser. Then came more routine, including make and mend, a rugger match, physics lessons, and gunnery exercises; there

---

98. F.L. Houghton, "Memoir," nd, i-ii, LAC, MG 30 E444.

99. Ballantyne to N.W. Rowell, President of the Privy Council, 10 June 1919, 1017–10–8, LAC, RG 24, vol. 3833.

100. H.N. Lay, Midshipman's Journal, 26–28 October, 9 November 1921, LAC, MG 30 E420, vol. 1.

were also movies in the wardroom. In January 1922 he participated in another series of manoeuvres "to exercise the fleet cruising under war conditions," "to investigate problems connected with the defence by a powerful but slow fleet, of a valuable convoy including a mobile base, on an ocean passage when attacked by a weaker but faster force," and "to exercise air reconnaissance from an aircraft carrier." Eight capital ships, an aircraft carrier, five cruisers, and various other vessels were involved, but weather may have proved of greater interest to the midshipman than fleet action. On the 19th, the "wind blew very hard from the SW all night with occasional heavy showers of rain," while on the 20th, the "wind was still strong and ship was rolling heavily." At 0540 hours one of the davits holding the starboard cutter let go, so "ships head was put up into the wind but as the cutter was badly damaged it was cut away. At daybreak action stations were closed up and the exercise was finished at 0815."[101]

One whose interwar experience with the Royal Navy began at a higher rank was Llewellyn Houghton, who had joined the destroyer HMS *Tumult* in 1918 as the ship's navigating officer. "As she would not be ready to commission for three weeks, I put up in a boarding-house nearby and was fully occupied in trying to bring her six hundred Admiralty charts up-to-date." Upon leaving Scapa Flow in January 1919, Houghton commented that "due to the general post-war confusion we had only a reduced crew, and most of them appeared to be thoroughly untrained." Demobilization had obviously had a greater impact on personnel than on the number of ships. Still, "as navigator, it was my job to pick four quartermasters for steering duty. I obtained four able seamen from the first lieutenant, all of whom soon proved demonstrably un-able. The captain immediately blew his top—a common occurrence—and in final desperation I canvassed the whole crew for anyone who had ever steered a ship before. A leading stoker—of all people—turned out to be far and away the best steersman we could find; and so the unfortunate Ldg Sto. Jones spent most of his time on the bridge all the way to Scapa."[102]

Houghton's first post-war commission was not his best, having a captain who "was without doubt the most unpleasant officer with whom I ever had the bad luck to serve," and who, among other things, tended to criticize his officers in front of their men. Still, it was eventful and interesting; following a cruise in the Mediterranean, "after three solid months of gunnery and torpedo exercises, manoeuvres, communication exercises, general drills and heaven knows what else—anything they could think of to keep us fully occupied from dawn to dusk and often for half the night as well, we had a short period for cleaning up and finally Captain (D[estroyer])'s inspection, from which we emerged with flying colours. At last, I thought, we can sit back and do nothing for a pleasant change. Instead, we suddenly received orders to proceed to the Baltic immediately, there to report to senior naval officer, Baltic for orders. We sailed within twenty-four hours, and a thousand miles later we secured alongside the Langelline in Copenhagen." Then, "two days later we were in Danzig, where the heat was appalling and the mosquitoes unbelievably ferocious."[103]

---

101. Ibid, 9, 14, 19–20 November 1921.

102. F.L. Houghton, "Memoir," nd, 30–31, LAC, MG 30 E444.

103. Ibid, 31, 39.

Given his position within the ship, Houghton was of course interested in matters navigational, and later related how "navigation—or more correctly, pilotage—in the Baltic just after the First War posed many problems. One had to steer extremely accurate courses between unmarked sandbanks on the landward side—most of the spar-buoys and markers were absent or out of position—and a series of minefields on the seaward side, also unmarked. It was a constant challenge and I rarely left the bridge while we were at sea. We came across a good many floating mines which we sank by gunfire, and we managed to keep to deep water." The ship then steered for Libau, Latvia, which had been held from February to November 1919 by German forces, before they were forced out by Latvian, British, and French units. By the time Houghton's destroyer, HMS *Valhalla*, arrived, the fighting was over. After an official visit to Riga, the vessel returned to Copenhagen.[104]

After a period back in Canada, Houghton returned to England in September 1920, being appointed first to the destroyer HMS *Saumarez*, then to *Valhalla*. "I was instructed to 'join forthwith' as though she was on the verge of leaving for parts unknown. To my surprise (though I should have known better by this time) I found she was in dock for three weeks. There was only one officer on board—the Engineer—and half-a-dozen bluejackets. The Captain, I was told, lived ashore and rarely came down to the ship, so to all intents and purposes I was temporary CO." Soon thereafter promoted to lieutenant, Houghton "became navigator, confidential book officer, torpedo control officer, and—voluntarily—mess secretary, all in addition to my normal duties as a watchkeeper at sea and in harbour. Because we were expecting to go to the Mediterranean I had no less than 1,250 Admiralty charts to keep up-to-date with the innumerable corrections issued weekly in Admiralty notices to mariners." The ship sailed in mid-January, and after tactical manoeuvres anchored at Gibraltar, where "the Second Flotilla—that's us—carried out torpedo practice just inside the western Mediterranean, behind the Rock, so to speak.... We fired three 'fish' in the forenoon and retrieved them, anchored for lunch, and did three mock attacks in the afternoon, mainly for the edification of soldiers from the garrison who came along as our guests."[105]

An idea of the challenges Houghton faced might best be described by relating one of his many tasks, that of torpedo control officer. In that capacity, "it was my job to aim and fire the tin fish and hope they would cross the target-line at the right spot. After this was over, I then had to prepare frightfully accurate plots of each firing on tracing-paper with different coloured inks for the edification of the experts who would then promulgate—as they termed it—their criticisms to the fleet. This is probably one of the most frustrating tasks I have ever attempted. The total amount of tracing-paper to be used should have been one and a half square feet; but by the time I had finished struggling with scratchy pens, crooked rulers, blunt dividers and constantly breaking pencils I had used up six square yards of it and most of my patience."[106] The latter, thankfully, seemed to be a renewable resource.

In common with most sailors, weather was often the topic of greatest interest. Leaving Gibraltar, Houghton's ship "ran into a real Atlantic blow, the worst gale of the trip. We had

---

104. Ibid, 39–40.

105. Ibid, 34–36.

106. Ibid, 42.

two whole days of it; it was impossible to sleep because of the severe rolling and pitching; and though I had carefully stowed much of the moveable gear in my cabin, by morning the whole place was littered in debris about a foot deep—books, clothes, boots, chairs—nothing was spared. To add to the discomfort a couple of hissing seas came pouring down the after hatch and helped to form a kind of soupy mess all over the deck through which I had to wade while trying to balance and dress myself at the same time. Breakfast consisted of a boiled egg—which I ate standing up—supplemented by a piece of cold toast which had suffered a sea-change by accidental immersion in the none-too-clean mixture of seawater and dirt on the deck; and a couple of mouthfuls of tepid coffee tinged with salt. Then I spent seven hours on the bridge, dodging the spray—quite ineffectively—hanging on for dear life, looking after the ship and praying for harbour—which we at last reached—Vigo Bay. I made my way aft to eat what was left of lunch and to wash myself, as by then I had 'dried up' to some extent and was literally caked in salt—eyes, ears, nose, mouth, clothes, boots, everything."[107]

Of course, being in service with the Royal Navy meant engaging in operations to support the policies of the British Empire, which at the time were perceived by many to be benevolent in that they brought civilization to the far-flung corners of the world. Houghton certainly never questioned them. In April 1921, according to his memoir, "we were suddenly ordered to Ireland, where the Sinn Fein trouble was in full swing. We were told that our principal job was to carry mails between Kingstown, the port for Dublin, and Queenstown in the south." As the Canadian officer explained, "Irish volunteers became the Irish Republican Army (the IRA). Large numbers of the Irish police resigned and were replaced by recruits from England who, from the colour of their uniforms, became known as the Black and Tans. The sorry conflict was in full spate by the time we arrived there." In a letter home, he related how, as officer of the night one evening, "the Quartermaster came down and reported a lot of firing ashore. As this is more or less common occurrence, I said 'All right' (such a useful phrase when one is snug in one's bunk). However, on this particular night the Sinn Feiners seemed to be more determined than usual and the fusillade ashore assumed quite extraordinary dimensions. I slipped on my coat and went on deck. The guard destroyer was made fast alongside us and had her searchlight on so I decided to go over there and have a look with my glasses. Hardly had the idea occurred to me when an excited signalman came pelting aft with the news that the wireless station ashore, which the Sinn Feiners were attacking, was making frantic SOS signals to all destroyers."[108]

It looked like Houghton's RN experience would include a taste of battle, though perhaps not of the type a naval officer expected or preferred. He gave orders to turn out the guard, got dressed, and joined a landing party:

> The first lieutenant was in charge of the party and of course I should have remained on board as duty officer; but I couldn't resist such a heavensent opportunity and fortunately no one noticed this slight dereliction of duty. We

---

107. Ibid, 36.

108. Ibid, 42–43.

landed on the breakwater with the intention of doing a little counter movement of our own and arriving *behind* the attackers instead of meeting them
head on as the other destroyers appeared to be doing. We found we had ten
bluejackets, with number one and myself. Pausing a moment to load rifles and
revolvers, we doubled silently off the breakwater into the darkness of an
unlighted street. I'm not quite sure what might have happened to us had we
arrived a few minutes earlier; as it was, by the time we arrived most of the firing had stopped. However, we continued to advance, but taking considerable
care as we were, of course, arriving on the scene from the same direction as
the attackers. We were challenged, answered just in time, and proceeded to assist
the military and the Royal Irish Constabulary in searching for bodies. We found
none, though we learnt later that several Sinn Feiners had been wounded.[109]

A later appointment, beginning in January 1922, was to HMS *Cairo*, "a piece of outstanding luck for an RCN officer." The ship was a light cruiser, where life was less formal
than in a battleship but more comfortable than in a destroyer. "As the senior lieutenant
on board I automatically became senior watchkeeper, a job which also involved taking complete charge of the instruction of ship's boys and ordinary seamen, principally in seamanship. In addition, I was torpedo control officer, member of the soccer, dance and regatta
committees, and 'chief adviser' to the jazz and fife-and-drum bands—these latter, I suspect,
because the commander saw me coming over the side with my mandolin and banjo-
ukulele. Finally, I was appointed official swimming instructor and warned that I would
probably have to organise the ship's concert party in due course. I gained the impression
that I was unlikely to suffer from boredom for lack of something to keep me occupied." He
described his fellow officers as a "grand lot."[110]

One task came up while making way from Shanghai to Hong Kong, as the voyage "was
unexpectedly interrupted when we were diverted by signal to Swatow, a small port on the
Chinese mainland about 170 miles northeast of Hong Kong. Apparently there was a strike
on in Hong Kong and the Island was rapidly running short of fresh vegetables, and we were
ordered to purchase forty tons of potatoes and rush them to Hong Kong." Owing to the
confused political situation, the usual civilian supplier balked at providing the necessary
food, "but by the judicious greasing of a few palms we managed to obtain twenty tons from
up-country and had to be content with that." Another incident was far closer to home. "I
was officer of the day, and in the middle of dinner I was sent for by the master-at-arms to
investigate an urgent case on the quarterdeck. A young seaman had apparently got a touch
of the sun plus religious mania, and he told me, among other things, that he was 'finished
with life.' While we were waiting for some witnesses I had sent for, the unhappy lad suddenly took it into his head to dash to the guardrail and leap over the side into the drink.
It was immediately obvious that he couldn't swim so there was nothing to do but go in after
him, and in I went, mess dress and all—which was the only thing that bothered me because

---

109. Ibid, 43.

110. Ibid, 48.

of the nice new and shiny shoulder-straps. I managed to get him to the ladder—he was pretty well 'out' by then—where willing hands hauled him to safety. He recovered in due course and soon thereafter was sent home, from where he wrote me a letter of thanks." Later, and more tragically, a stoker was lost when he fell overboard attempting to jump to the fleet oiler.[111]

Based in Colombo, Ceylon (now Sri Lanka), Houghton's ship travelled to dozens of ports from Rangoon to Mauritius and from Aden to Zanzibar, the voyage characterized by varying levels of discomfort because of heat. Gunnery and torpedo training predominated, Houghton encapsulating the main goal of all such work in his memoir.

> Life in a warship is largely a matter of discipline and routine. The naval motto …"In time of peace prepare for war," continually reminds us that we are, first and foremost, a fighting ship. Every officer and man on board has his own particular job or jobs and his own special responsibilities. If but one member of the team should fail at a critical moment, the whole ship could well be endangered. All peacetime training is devoted to producing maximum fighting efficiency at all times. The whole ship's company, from captain down to the youngest seaman, make up a well-drilled team, bound together by a single purpose. Routine, Sysyphean perhaps, but well understood by all, might be described as the horizontal component of this teamwork while discipline, strict but withal beneficent [sic], is the vertical element, working both ways, from senior to junior and *vice versa*. When the officers respect the men, they will in turn respect their officers, and all will work cheerfully together to achieve that vital goal of fighting efficiency.[112]

Officers, Lay and Houghton among them, represented only a minority of those few hundred who served in the RCN (or, for most officers, in the RN) in the interwar period, the bulk of the personnel in Canada's naval service being ratings. As Lay himself noted decades later, "I would say they were first class. Primarily we'd get people with reasonably good education, perhaps I think probably the lowest standard that was allowed was perhaps grade nine but frequently we would have people who were grade twelve or thirteen and many of these people were quite good at picking up not only their job in the navy but going on for extra-curricular training, several, not several, but many Canadian sailors became officers, got higher education, either in their own time or through service arrangements, and in fact, two of the officers who I served with many years during the navy started on the lower deck and became rear-admirals. I would also mention that I think the Canadian sailor had a great deal more initiative than the average British sailor."[113]

Lay may have been biased to no little degree, but the RCN did go to considerable effort to ensure its lower deck personnel would be well-prepared for their tasks. With the acquisition of *Aurora*, *Patriot*, and *Patrician*, as well as the submarines *CH 14* and *CH 15* (the latter

---

111. Ibid, 56, 62.

112. Ibid, 64.

113. Lay interview transcript, 14 January 1974, LAC, MG 30 E420, vol. 2.

given over by the Admiralty in February 1919), "it was decided to develop as soon as possible a Naval Service composed of personnel recruited in Canada." To that end, "a youths training establishment was established in the building previously used as a naval college," in Halifax. "The establishment was put into operation in October, 1921, with a teaching staff loaned from the Admiralty." Fifty-eight recruits were entered as seamen or stokers, each having signed an engagement for seven years. The course of instruction included algebra, mensuration (which is to say measuring the area of a rectangle), plotting, logarithms, triginometry, navigation, magnetism, mechanics (e.g., the equilibrium of forces), all in the first month, subsequent courses building upon these until such subjects as electricity, electroplating to be precise, entered the curriculum, the whole, no doubt, to ensure recruits would have the equivalent of a high school education.[114]

All such work was ashore, an approach considered necessary, in the words of one officer, unfortunately anonymous, because, "owing to the conditions existing in the country, they must be coaxed rather than forced at first, until the idea of discipline is firmly implanted, when the best in them may be brought out by gradual accustoming and stimulating of interest. The good points of the Canadian youth may then be fully utilized, instead of being mere obstacles to efficiency and discipline." Such had been learned through hard experience, and "it is impossible to achieve these results if boys are sent to a ship without previous training, as was found in the instance of the *Niobe*'s first commission," before the First World War. Though a ship might seem like an ideal learning environment for someone about to make a career in the navy, "officers and petty officers on board ship cannot give the time or minute attention essential to the preliminary training of Canadian boys. Ship routine is not strenuous enough, not sufficiently detailed, and too slackly carried out to impress or in any way be good for boys. They are apt to see only the seamy side of navy life, and that, in Canada, means wholesale desertion and dissatisfaction, unless efficiency is slaughtered to 'give them a good time.'"[115]

A related consideration was that "the mixing with older ratings, which would inevitably take place in a ship, is among the most undesirable features. This alone is enough to annul a great part of the efforts of those in charge of the boys," though such comments did not reflect well on ratings then serving in the RCN—or on the officer penning the report. Still, the argument could be made that "a shore training establishment is undoubtedly the most important part of a young navy, where material counts for little, and men are all important. If the boys entering now, who will be the petty officers and warrant officers of the future do not have the advantage of a good thorough training, the navy will suffer for years in consequence, and might conceivably never recover."[116]

The point was well taken, and confirmed by Warrant Engineer A.E.L. Thomas in relation to artificers (responsible for keeping the engines running), who had been undergoing

114. Historical Synopsis of the Organization and Development of the Royal Canadian Navy, nd, LAC, MG 27, III B-5, vol. 38, file 42; and CO Youths Training Establishment to Naval Secretary, 20 March, 11 April 1922, 93–1-4, LAC, RG 24, vol. 5677.

115. 1st Lt to CO Youths Training Establishment, 10 April 1922, 93–1-4, LAC, RG 24, vol. 5677.

116. Ibid.

training in HMCS *Aurora*. "The general atmosphere of a sea-going ship is highly derogatory to a specialist training," he wrote in the spring of 1922, "and not at all conducive for the boy artificers to put their best effort forward, which effort is absolutely necessary." For instance, "the general atmosphere of a ship detracts from study…. It is my experience that study afloat is an impossibility and these Boys must not merely study—they must 'saturate.' To this end entire segregation from all other elements must be the ideal condition. They must live amongst themselves, compete amongst themselves, maintain a healthy rivalry amongst themselves, to excell in all things appertaining to their own training. This state is impossible in a sea-going ship where so many various elements with totally different aims are at work."[117]

The problem the warrant officer faced, however, was the possibility that the Youth's Training Establishment would be closed down to reduce expenses. He suggested that, "as a purely temporary expedient, if the present establishment is to close down, it might be possible to continue the boys in their training using the *Aurora*." Instruction in the cruiser was already being conducted in a lecture room and machine shop, but "this arrangement is unfortunate, inasmuch as it is purely makeshift, and the correct atmosphere … cannot be effected. Under the foregoing conditions, it is considered of the highest importance that the position of the staff should be made quite definite. It is necessary that the staff should be left quite free and unfettered to devote their whole time and energy to the training of these boys, and not interfered with by any outside source," such as duties as members of the ship's complement.[118]

Education, whether for officers or ratings, was thus a complex endeavour, as would be expected given that they worked within a service attempting to operate reasonably modern equipment as represented by *Aurora*, *Patriot*, and *Patrician*. Other aspects of personnel management were no less complicated, such as the provision of health care, especially in the immediate post-war period. One medical issue of the time was the provision of treatment for those who had served overseas and were being demobilized. Dental work seemed to figure rather prominently, one potential patient in the spring of 1919 enquiring into the issue. "I lost several gold fillings and three teeth broken while in the service. Will I be reimbursed in any way in having these repaired?"[119] He certainly had a good case, and the naval secretary related how the work required would cost eighty-five dollars, a certificate from a dentist having been forwarded. "It appears to me … from the details given in Edward's letter that there is little doubt that he actually received the injuries as stated, and it is recommended that dental treatment be authorized, observing that the department is responsible for dental treatment arising out of accidents incurred during service."[120]

As for those who remained in the navy, or who joined in the first years of peace, pay

117.　Warrant Engineer A.E.L Thomas RN to Youths Training Establishment, 10 April 1922, 93–1–4, LAC, RG 24, vol. 5677.

118.　Ibid.

119.　George M. Edwards to NSHQ, 4 April 1919, 799–2–1, LAC, RG 24, vol. 5689.

120.　Naval Secretary to Deputy Minister, 6 May 1919, ibid.

and benefits ranged widely depending on one's rank and specialty. A midshipman received two dollars a day, his pay doubling when promoted to acting sub-lieutenant, then rising to five dollars, $7.50, ten dollars, and fifteen dollars for the ranks of lieutenant, lieutenant-commander, commander, and captain. One also received higher pay for seniority within one's rank, while engineer lieutenant-commanders were paid more because of their specialty, as were submariners (in those periods when the RCN operated submarines). Pay for ratings ranged from fifty cents for a boy to $1.65 for an ordinary seaman, $1.85 for an able seaman, $1.95 for a leading seaman, $2.40 for a petty officer, and $2.80 for a chief petty officer, meaning that the highest ranking rating made less than an acting sub-lieutenant. Specialist ratings also received more, there being separate pay lists for signallers, telegraphists, sailmakers, stokers, mechanicians, engine room artificers, shipwrights, "blacksmiths, plumbers, painters, joiners, coopers," armourers, sick berth staff, writers, victualling staff, ship's cooks, members of the regulating branch, officers' stewards, and cooks. Mechanicians and engine room artificers earned the most, at a maximum of $4.05 a day. Possible allowances filled four-and-a-half pages of regulations, ratings being paid more if they were working as naval school-masters or in a harsh climate, to give just two examples. By way of comparison, an electrician in Toronto earned seventy cents a day, a plumber in Winnipeg a dollar, and a carpenter in Vancouver also earned a dollar, so ratings at all ranks were relatively well paid.[121]

As for other benefits, according to the naval secretary "the question has arisen as to whether the department will pay for dental treatment for officers and men. The supply of dentures to ratings in order to fit them for retention in the Service has already been approved." As with so many issues, the RCN looked to the parent service for precedents, and the Admiralty procedure in regard to urgent cases, where it was not possible to obtain the services of a dental surgeon at a naval establishment, was to allow "reasonable expenses" for extractions or fillings. They were, for extractions, no more than four shillings per tooth, and eight shillings for fillings (to a maximum of one pound). The naval secretary suggested a similar schedule of eligible reimbursements be instituted for the RCN, though cadets at the Royal Naval College of Canada in Esquimalt would pay for their own dental work.[122]

More general medical care, on the other hand, was provided at taxpayers' expense, which no doubt encouraged the naval service to institute preventive measures. These could only be imperfect, however, as became evident in February 1922 when an epidemic of influenza (of a mild form, not the killer of 1918–19) broke out in the naval college. One cadet developed nephritis, a condition affecting the kidneys, and his mother was kept apprised of his condition. To deal with the outbreak, the commander-in-charge related how "it has been necessary to engage the services of a hospital nurse for night duty." When the situation had returned more or less to normal, he reported how the flu "spread through the college with great rapidity; nearly all the cadets and more than half the officers and ships company have suffered or are suffering from it.... On 24th February it became

---

121. Department Naval Service, *Pay and Allowances, 1920* (Ottawa 1920), 5, 8, 13–17; and F.H. Leacy, ed., *Historical Statistics of Canada* (Ottawa 1983), E249, E256, E258, E260, E262, E265–6.

122. Naval Secretary to DNS, 3 March 1919, Desbarats to Dr H. Le Roy Burgess, 1 March 1919, 799–2-1, LAC, RG 24, vol. 5689.

necessary to use one of the dormitories as an extra sick room for cadets and to engage the services of two additional hospital nurses.... All patients are progressing favourably."[123]

Health care was thus no small matter, and on the East Coast the navy in Halifax had its own hospital, with "accommodation for thirty ratings, and an additional ten beds on the veranda, during the summer months. Also ten beds for officers," who, given the navy's official social hierarchy, needed to be segregated from ratings in illness as in health. Regardless of rank, however, all who suffered from venereal disease, which required lengthy treatment in the days before sulfa drugs and antibiotics, were sent to the nearby Rockhead Military Hospital. Also, "the Nova Scotia Hospital has so far provided accommodation for naval infectious diseases, as many as twenty having been treated there at one time. This hospital will close in the near future. From then on naval infectious disease cases will be received in the civic infectious hospital. In a submission of January 4th 1918, item eight, it is suggested that the question of huts for infectious diseases on RCN hospital grounds be considered." Other available facilities included the Camp Hill Military Hospital, where 550 patients could be accommodated, and the Cogswell Street Military Hospital, with a capacity of 150, both of which were open to naval personnel.[124]

The navy could not, however, rely exclusively on the kindness of other agencies, and needed to recruit medical personnel of its own. As Desbarats explained, "at the present time two medical officers are required for the Canadian service, viz one surgeon lieutenant-commander and one surgeon lieutenant. Under the regulations for the entry of medical officers ... they are entered for a period of three years which may be extended to five years. Both medical officers at present have now served for the full term authorised. It is recommended that authority be obtained by order-in-council to extend the service of one medical officer for a further period of three years from 1st July, 1920, and that Surgeon Lieutenant Commander Rousseau be offered this appointment, Surgeon Lieut-Commander Irwin being discharged."[125]

One who hoped to join the service's medical branch was Surgeon Lieutenant Archie McCallum, who was serving in the Royal Navy at the time and who in September 1920 applied to join HMCS Aurora. That appointment had already been filled, "but from conversation with Captain Hose, RCN, I learn that there is still a shortage of surgeons in the Royal Canadian Navy ... I am still very desirous of having my name kept to the fore in case any other vacancy should arise in either the Royal Canadian dockyards, or ships, for which I might be eligible for service.... I am Canadian-born, a graduate of the medical faculty, University of Toronto, and my parents are resident in Canada, all of which increases my desire to serve in, or near Canada." He would, of course, transfer from British to the Canadian navy, presuming approval from the Admiralty, and he had only entered the British service as a second choice, as "when I joined the Royal Navy, Sept 24th 1917, there were no

123. Commander in Charge Royal Naval College of Canada to NSHQ, 23 and 28 February 1922, 24–11–7, LAC, RG 24, vol. 5597.

124. Surgeon LCdr RCN to Capt Superintendent, 1 August 1919, 78–1–13, LAC, RG 24, vol. 5669.

125. Desbarats to Minister, 14 May 1920, 1078–2-1, LAC, RG 24, vol. 4044.

vacancies for surgeons in the Canadian navy."[126] Either then or later his request was approved, McCallum eventually rising to become the RCN's surgeon general.

At the other end of the personnel services scale was discipline, the RCN having its own laws, which it could, if necessary, uphold through punishment, including incarceration in prison. For that purpose, a detention quarters at Melville Island, near Halifax, was available, though of its capacity of thirty prisoners only ten cells were set aside for naval ratings, a reflection of the navy's small size and, perhaps, a sign that disciplinary problems were neither severe nor widespread. Corporal punishment, which had been a mainstay in the Royal Navy until the late nineteenth century, was limited to the younger members within the RCN, but even then was sometimes the subject of controversy. Responding to allegations of the ill-treatment of boys in HMCS *Aurora*, which as we have seen was the training facility for artificers, among others, the ship's captain was adamant: "I may at once state that I have recognized that the welfare of the boys in this ship was a matter of vital importance and have done all in my power to make life popular and to see that their training should be such as to increase their morale to the highest pitch." Responding to the accusation that some of his charges had been flogged, he answered that "since the date of commissioning, two boys have been caned, viz D.K. McDonald on the 5th March and L.R. Fedderson on the 29th April. Both boys were caned with the express authorization of the Department of Naval Service. The charges in each case was theft, and though they related to different occasions, the offences were similar in nature. Each boy was found in possession of a stolen article, each boy denied the offence, both cases were proved and the boys admitted the offences after the case was proved." As for retribution, "the punishment in the case of a man would have been detention but as the ages of these boys were only sixteen, I was unwilling to inflict this and wired and obtained sanction to punish them as above stated."[127] The ship's captain may well have felt vindicated, since his actions were consistent with Canadian attitudes generally. They had also followed RCN procedure, J.M. Hemsted, the naval secretary, later advising that "no punishment of caning is to be awarded in the Youths' Training Establishment without specific authority, in each case, from headquarters. Should it be necessary to recommend the infliction of this punishment, full particulars are to be reported to headquarters in writing."[128]

Disciplinary issues could cover a wide range of offences. In May, 1921, for example, the RCN sent a telegram to the Admiralty noting that "appendix twenty-two KR being now in operation as between Royal Navy and Royal Canadian Navy please inform me by telegraph whether Admiralty have any objection to Minister of the Naval Service of Canada issuing court martial warrant to commander-in-chief North America and West Indies Station authorizing him to convene courts for trial of Canadian offenders serving in Canadian ships. Matter is important as department desires to ask commander in chief to order court

126. Surg Lt Archie McCallum to Capt A.J.B. Stirling, HMS *Argus*, 17 September 1920, McCallum to Hose, 25 September 1920, 31-9-9, LAC, RG 24, vol. 5632.

127. CO *Aurora* to DNS, 7 May 1921, 31-1-1, ibid; and CO *Niobe* to Captain Superintendent, 22 August 1919, 78-1-13, LAC, RG 24, vol. 5669.

128. Naval Secretary to CO Youths Training Establishment, 13 October 1921, 93-1-1, LAC, RG 24, vol. 5677.

martial for trial of commanding officer and navigation officer of HMCS *Patriot* in connection with grounding of that ship 10th May. Squadron due Bermuda twenty-second July."[129] Worse, perhaps, was an incident in *Aurora* during the same time period, the captain writing that "I regret to report that malicious damage has been done to two Dumaresqs," instruments the ship needed for accurate gunnery. "The damage was indisputably inflicted with a hammer." Investigation was through deductive reasoning rather than by gathering facts. There was no direct or circumstantial evidence that could convict the offender, but suspicion rested on one individual in the gunnery department who was known to have a grudge. To be considered was the fact that the type of hammer used was only available to a few of the ship's company, while the nature of the damage tended to indicate that the perpetrator knew what he was doing. Furthermore, "the position and knowledge of the existence of these two Dumaresqs would not be known to the majority of the ship's company," and the suspect's duties gave him access to them. Finally, "it is a subject of talk that the above mentioned individual is known to harbour malicious sentiments." The captain had to admit, however, that deduction was insufficient evidence for dismissing a man from the service.[130]

All the above personnel issues, whether relating to recruiting, education, health care, or discipline, pertained to members of the Royal Canadian Navy, but there was also a substantial Royal Navy presence in Canada and in Canadian ships, men whose services were needed to keep the dominion's service afloat, but whose presence added an extra level of complexity to its administration. In fact, the main reason for the creation of the youth training establishment in Halifax was because the RCN perceived that "the system of borrowing ratings from the Admiralty, or of recruiting ex-service men in the British Isles for special service, is not satisfactory. Moreover, when such ratings leave the Canadian service for one reason or another, their replacement from the same source, is a matter of great difficulty, since there is no proper recruiting organizations in England for the purpose."[131]

British personnel could not be dispensed with entirely, however, and many had come to the RCN to help the fledgling navy in wartime. They could only, according to RN regulations, count five years of such service toward their pensions, however, and would have to be returned home, and possibly replaced, or offered positions within the Canadian navy at the end of that period. Nor could the RCN do without such men, and in 1922 the naval director advised the minister that, consequent to a recent reorganization, "a senior naval officer will be required for the Halifax station to be responsible for the naval portion of the defence scheme, together with current responsibilities and general disciplinary charge of the naval forces stationed there." However, "this officer should be of commander's rank and since we have no officer in the Canadian navy with the necessary rank or experience I propose, with your concurrence, to retain the services of Commander Jermain, RN, for the balance of his two years' loan from the Admiralty, which will be till the 21st May 1923." In addition, "we shall also require the services of Paymaster Lieut Commander Tyers, RN, for the naval accountant work," while "Paymaster Commander Eves, RN, in charge of naval

129. Naval Ottawa to Britannia Bermuda, 30 May 1921, 80–1-1, LAC, RG 24, vol. 5671.

130. Senior officer commanding Canadian Squadron to NSHQ, 27 February 1912, 1055–2-1, LAC, RG 24, vol. 3984.

131. Hose to Minister, 25 January 1921, 93–1-1, LAC, RG 24, vol. 5677.

intelligence at headquarters and Paymaster Commander Woodhouse, RN, the naval secretary will be the other imperial commissioned officers whom it is necessary to retain."[132]

Holding on to them may have been necessary, but the conditions under which they served in the RCN were not always clear-cut, at least as far as the Admiralty was concerned. When in mid-1919 Sub-Lieutenant A.E.L. Williams of the Royal Naval Reserve was found guilty by an RCN court martial of three offences involving borrowing money, the response from London must have come as something of a shock. "Admiralty consider that courts which tried this officer had no jurisdiction to do so as he is not an officer of the Royal Canadian Navy. He is an officer of the Royal Naval Reserve subject to the Naval Discipline Act and liable to be tried by a court convened under that act.... Admiralty are therefore of opinion that there is no option but to ask that the proceedings of this court martial should be quashed.... Questions of remedying legality of position involved will be raised through Colonial Office."[133]

The sentence was indeed "quashed," though the Admiralty was contacted so "immediate steps be taken to remedy the state of affairs created." A solution was needed soon, Hose reporting to the minister on 27 January 1920 how "a few days ago a telegram was received from Halifax reporting that three imperial ratings borne in *Niobe* and awaiting passage to HMS *Mutine* at Bermuda had refused duty. The commanding officer of *Niobe* asked whether he should deal with them summarily. Under the ruling given by the Admiralty ... it is clear that no officer of the Canadian navy has any jurisdiction whatsoever over these ratings."[134] The RCN had to wait until April for the Colonial Office to provide encouraging words, which came in the form of a bill in parliament to the effect that "an officer or man in or belonging to his majesty's navy and who by order of Admiralty is serving in navy of any self-governing dominion o[r] under orders from officer of a self-governing dominion shall be subject to the laws and customs for the time being in force of such self-governing dominion." The Canadian government found the wording acceptable.[135]

There was, however, another solution, which was adopted over a year later. As the naval secretary explained, "it is to be noted that the Admiralty, by telegram of the 30th September, informed the department that they are of opinion that officers and men of the RN lent to the RCN will be amenable to Canadian naval discipline if legally entered into the Canadian navy under the Canadian Naval Service Act. There can be no question but that all officers and men on loan from the RN to the RCN have been in the past, and are now, legally entered into the latter service in accordance with the Naval Service Act. Accordingly all officers and men lent from the RN are subject to Canadian naval discipline as from the date of being loaned, and ratings are accordingly, liable to summary punishments, and both officers and men to Canadian courts martial." Should an officer attempt to defend himself on the grounds that he was not a member of the Canadian service, then he was to be advised that "all RN officers loaned

132. Hose to Minister, 1 May 1922, 64-1-3, ibid; and Naval Secretary to Hose, 6 August 1919, 53–6-1, LAC, RG 24, vol. 5651.

133. London to Naval Ottawa, 17 June 1919, Naval Secretary to DNS, 20 June 1919, 80–1-1, LAC, RG 24, vol. 5671.

134. DNS to Minister, 27 January 1920, ibid.

135. Colonial Secretary to Governor-General, 1 April 1920, 53–6-1, LAC, RG 24, vol. 5651.

to the RCN have their names included in the Canadian Navy List, and that is proof that they belong to the Canadian navy unless they can prove to the contrary." Though the ruling did not cover RN personnel temporarily accommodated in RCN facilities, such as the three ratings mentioned above, it was nevertheless sufficient to cover Canada's naval operations.[136]

The issues discussed above, whether they focused on materiel or personnel, were all related to one common goal—operating a navy at sea. And such operations (described in detail below), whether they were of a diplomatic, instructional, or enforcement nature, needed the guidance of timely and accurate information, in the form of naval intelligence. An example of the latter was the Callao report, which provided information under such headings as "wireless telegraphy," "shipping," "naval military and aviation," "oil and coal," "foreign agents and suspects," and "political." It originated from the British consulate in Callao, Peru, and covered southern waters in which the RCN might sail to conduct training or to show the flag. The monthly summary for March 1923, to give just one example, provided details on the region's navies, such as establishments, personnel, materiel, war vessels, movements, strategy, policy, and spending. Perhaps of greater importance in times of diminished international strain were the incorporated coast reports, which discussed such matters as ports and bases as well as coastal defences and arsenals. Such material was distributed not only to the directors of naval intelligence in Ottawa and Melbourne but to district intelligence officers in Esquimalt, Bermuda, and Wellington.[137]

Nor was the RCN merely a consumer of such data; it also gathered intelligence of its own, which it passed on to the Admiralty. For example, in March 1921 the director of naval intelligence in Ottawa sent to the district officer in Bermuda extracts from a report prepared by HMCS *Aurora* during and after a cruise. One point of interest was that "oiling is very slow at Colon (Commercial Texas Oil Company). It took *Aurora* 17 hours to complete and the passage through the canal in her case had to be delayed $5\frac{1}{2}$ hours.... The passage through the canal took *Aurora* $8\frac{1}{2}$ hours. From this time should be deducted three quarters of an hour casting off and securing to wharves," information that, if somewhat mundane, could still be of use to other commonwealth warships. Similarly, the report noted that, in Salina Cruz, "the consul came off and had made the necessary arrangements for the ship entering the inner harbour. The access to this harbour is very difficult for a ship of the length of *Aurora*, especially at this period of the year when the Tehuantepecer [the isthmus of Tehuantepec is in southern Mexico] may be blowing for several days on end and it would be highly inadvisable to move the ship in a high wind." In a different vein, *Aurora* related how in San Salvador "the president speaks English fluently and was educated in England. The president accepted my invitation to visit the ship, but shortly before my departure he cancelled it owing to pressure of business. He appears in some danger of assassination and extraordinary precautions are taken to guard him."[138] It was all part of naval headquarters

136. Naval Secretary to SNO, Esquimalt, 6 October 1921, LAC, MG 30 E218, vol. 1, file 15.

137. HMC Dockyard Esquimalt to Naval Secretary, 6 August 1919, Kingsmill to Vice Consul, HBM Consulate, Callao, Peru, 22 June 1920, Monthly Intelligence Summary, Callao Area, March 1923, 1023-7-14, LAC, RG 24, vol. 3858.

138. District Intelligence Officer, Ottawa to District Intelligence Officer, Bermuda, 17 March 1921, 1031-7-5, LAC, RG 24, vol. 3887.

in Ottawa playing its role as "a regular intelligence centre in the Admiralty world-wide intelligence organization."[139]

Naval operations, however, were not always international in scope, and especially until the acquisition of *Aurora*, *Patriot*, and *Patrician* tended to be focused rather close to home. In the months immediately following the armistice, in fact, the RCN found its operational capability severely limited, as exemplified by its response to a request from the radiotelegraph branch, which maintained communications with other parts of the commonwealth and foreign countries. As it explained in regard to West Coast facilities, "in the case of the W/T stations located at Pachena Point, Estevan Point, Triangle Island, Ikeda Head and Dead Tree Point, we are under a severe handicap in that they can only be supplied with stores by a government or chartered steamer.... We endeavour to make use of the marine department ships when they are proceeding to these points, but their movements can only be classed as spasmodic. It would be of the utmost value to us and would greatly increase our efficiency, if arrangements could be made for each station to be visited regularly every six months, and a regular schedule established." It asked if navy patrol boats could undertake the task, each complete trip requiring about two weeks.[140] Admiral Kingsmill felt the need to reply that the vessels in question "are not of sufficient size to cope satisfactorily with the landings which have to be made from time to time at Estevan, Triangle Island, Ikeda Head and Dead Tree Point."[141]

The RCN was not idle, however, and over a year into the post-war period listed a variety of responsibilities it needed to attend to, including examination services at Halifax, Sydney, Quebec, St John, Esquimalt and Victoria, Vancouver, and Prince Rupert. At the same ports, the service was responsible for minesweeping services and patrols. Further duties included running naval wireless stations, a naval intelligence organisation (including signal stations), defences such as mines, booms, and nets, dockyards, small depots, the naval college, the headquarters, gun crews for defensively armed merchant ships, and the maintenance of guns and ammunition in storage. "Miscellaneous duties on the outbreak of war," filled out the list, since its role was to serve as a nucleus in time of peace that could be expanded when an emergency arose.[142] On 1 October 1921, for example, HMCS *Thiepval*, operating off Canada's West Coast, began a fisheries patrol (of that more later), cruising Dixon's Entrance, Hecate Strait, and adjacent waters. On the 21st she received a message from the collector of customs advising that the US steamer *Spokane* was disabled in Carter Bay. "I immediately proceeded to Prince Rupert, and embarked Mr McLeod, and left at midnight for Carter Bay, but about noon on the 22nd, picked up a W/T that the Spokane had made repairs and proceeded, so I returned to Prince Rupert and landed customs officer." It was all a matter of routine.[143]

---

139. Intelligence Division, 20 June 1922, 93–1-4, LAC, RG 24, vol. 5677.

140. Superintendent Radiotelegraph Branch to DNS, 21 June 1919, 133–1-1, LAC, RG 24, vol. 5682.

141. Kingsmill to Superintendent Radiotelegraph Branch, 23 June 1919, ibid.

142. ADNS to Director of the Naval Service, 1017–10–8, 13 January 1920, LAC, RG 24, vol. 3833.

143. Captain's Monthly Report, October 1921, 324–16–4, LAC, RG 24, vol. 5687.

For the submarines *CH14* and *CH15*, the normal could be blended with the exotic. Arguing that remaining at Halifax during the winter months "is decidedly detrimental to the efficiency of both the boats and personnel," then director of the Naval Service Walter Hose recommended the boats be sent to Bermuda. "Lieut Watson, senior officer of submarines is a thoroughly reliable officer, very keen on working up the efficiency of our submarine service and can be relied upon to take advantage of the winter months in Bermuda to further the best interests of the service." Having already discussed budgetary issues with the deputy minister, the DNS had little trouble getting the minister's concurrence.[144]

For the immediate post-war era, the submarines were a marked exception to a rule that kept RCN vessels close to home for training and operations, with fisheries patrols a large part of the latter. The navy had taken over responsibility for some of this work from the Department of Marine and Fisheries in the early days of its existence, and would play an important role in protecting natural resources at sea for the remainder of the century and beyond. It did so at its own expense, since it was an opportunity for training, so that in 1921–22 it spent $325,000 on such duties, while Marine and Fisheries expended $350,000. In early 1920 the superintendent of fisheries wrote the DNS to inform him that "it is necessary for the Fisheries Branch to now complete its arrangements for Fisheries Patrol work in British Columbia next summer." Although "there is comparatively little danger of inroads to our fisheries by United States fishing vessels during the summer months," there was still a need for patrolling. Therefore, "if you can arrange for the *Thiepval* or other suitable vessel to be so detailed, it will be of great service and at the same time an efficient supervision of the coast from a fisheries protection standpoint can be carried on as this vessel will be moving up and down, and also the smaller fisheries patrol boats can be continuously reporting to her."[145]

Thiepval, one of the RCN's wartime Battle-class trawlers was indeed on fisheries patrol a few months later, as "ship transferred to Fishery Patrol Service under orders of chief inspector of fisheries. Cruising on West Coast of Vancouver Isl[and] issuing salmon trolling licenses." Such was her main task in May, the following month turning her attention to "visiting and inspecting cannerys," followed by "duty in northern waters" in July and cruising to the Queen Charlotte Islands in August. Her tasks ended temporarily in early September, the vessel returning to Esquimalt, but they resumed in October, when she proceeded to cruise off the north end of Vancouver Island and Queen Charlotte Sound. However, "weather very unsettled and only one halibut fisherman was seen [—] a Canadian boat."[146]

There was no such work from November to January, but in February it started again. On the 6th *Thiepval* had to put into Bull Harbour for shelter, where she "found the US fishing boat *Woodrow* of Seattle in for shelter, and permission given him to remain until weather moderated." On 8 February, "at Swanson Bay, US fishing boat *Clara* of Tacoma entered and requested permission to make good defects in engine room." Later, on the 14th, "spoke to

---

144. Hose to Minister, 20 September 1921, 45–6-1, LAC, RG 24, vol. 3595.

145. Superintendent of Fisheries to DNS, 2 March 1920, 133–1-1, LAC, RG 24, vol. 5682; and Historical Synopsis of the Organization and Development of the Royal Canadian Navy, nd, LAC, MG 27, III B-5, vol. 38, file 42.

146. Captain's Monthly Report, 31 May, 30 June, 31 July, 31 August, 30 September, 31 October 1920, 324–16–4, LAC, RG 24, vol. 5687.

US fishing boat *H&R* of Tacoma fishing off Dundas Isl[and], out ten days, 1,500 lbs of halibut. On the 15th, spoke [to] *Rosepit* and *Alliance* both of P[rince] Rupert, fishing in Hecate Straits, report of poor fishing." On 17 February, "found the US fishing boat *Seneca* of Seattle at anchor in Brundige Inlet, had her alongside and examined her, as she had no clearance papers, ordered her out, went with her, and saw her across the boundary, and into US waters." Such were the highlights of the February patrol, which ended on the 19th.[147]

Given the nature of the laws that governed resource exploitation, enforcement could be extremely intricate. On 5 March, for example, "while cruising off Cape Scott, a fishing boat was sighted picking up her dories, she was stopped and the capt[ain] ordered on board as she proved to be the *La Paloma* of Seattle, capt[ain] informed that he was suspected to be inside the three mile limit, took the boat in tow, and proceeded to the inside buoy, and by careful sextant angles fixed her at three and one half miles from the West Haycock Isl[and]. The ship was then released, and told to get farther off shore, as this was the same man Capt Hurley, who in 1914, in the US boat *Malola*, was warned off Rose Spit, by the *Malaspina*."[148]

Protecting fish sometimes called for far more drastic measures, and in early 1922 one staff officer reported how "this department is endeavouring to have an onslaught made on sea lions along the coast of British Columbia, as these animals are very destructive of salmon." The chief inspector of fisheries had been in touch with the captain of *Malaspina*, "with a view to having that boat and the *Thiepval* shell the rookeries from time to time. Captain Newcomb replied stating that it would be an easy matter for these vessels to practically exterminate the sea lions on this coast during the pupping season if they are supplied with explosive shells as at present. In view of the importance to the salmon industry of destroying these sea lions, could arrangements feasibly be made to supply these boats with the proper shells and to instruct them to do all they can towards killing the sea lions."[149] There is no record to show the operation was actually carried out, but everyone's intentions were clear.

Such was, in part, the nature of operations for the RCN's trawlers; for *Aurora*, *Patriot*, and *Patrician*, not unexpectedly, operations and training were more elaborate—and more warlike. All three ships were commissioned on 1 November 1920, *Aurora* having cost £10,495 to fit out, exclusive of machinery and a refrigeration plant. In Canada, other arrangements also needed to be made, as "no longer was it a question of dealing with coal-burners; hence, provision would have to be made for the supplying of fuel oil on both coasts. A proposal was made to the lords commissioners of the Admiralty that they should furnish to the Department of the Naval Service from their reserve, supply sufficient to meet immediate requirements. This they consented to do on condition that the Canadian government made arrangements for her storage at Halifax and Victoria and that she be used exclusively for Canadian and imperial naval purposes. The erection of tanks was not held to be justifiable at the time by the department's officials, because of the expense involved and the uncer-

---

147. Captain's Monthly Report, 28 February 1921, ibid.

148. Captain's Monthly Report, March 1921, ibid.

149. "Memorandum for Director of the Naval Service," 18 April 1922, 133–1-1, LAC, RG 24, vol. 5682.

tainty of the future. Arrangements were therefore made to rent tanks on both coasts from Imperial Oil Ltd."[150]

Equipment having been installed and tested, the three vessels sailed from Britain on 1 December, though by 1800 hours "all ships were hove to with a southerly gale blowing.... The sea-going behaviour of all ships was a matter of congratulations, but a good deal of discomfort was experienced by small leaks in upper deck, etc which were easily put right by the ships staff." Reaching Fayal, in the Azores, on the 6th, it was found that "the estimate of expenditure of oil fuel was however largely underestimated. The *Patrician*'s expenditure corresponded nearly to that expected, but both *Aurora* and *Patriot* were largely in excess." The cause was difficult to determine, as "no reliable data was available. The *Aurora* and *Patriot* were practically out of commission after the war, while during the war high speeds were always maintained and so no comparison for 10 to 12 knots could be accurately forecasted." Five-and-a-half days of steaming had left the vessels with a reserve of between 30 and 48 percent, one possible reason for the excess consumption being the "unfamiliarity of engine room staff with ship under steaming conditions and the tuning up of the auxiliary machinery." One consequence was the need for 620 tons from the oiler instead of the predicted 350.[151]

"Unfamiliarity" was a common theme in reports on the ships' personnel, *Aurora*'s complement of 323 including forty-seven ordinary seamen and boys recruited in Canada who had no previous experience. "This number is practically as high as there is room for in the Ship." The latter was sailing with less than the optimum complement of artisans, being short two ordnance artificers, one electrical artificer, one plumber, one joiner, and one light director layer, the latter for *Patriot*. Furthermore, *Aurora*'s CO, Captain H.G.H. Adams, felt that "it is necessary for efficiency of the destroyers that one ordnance artificer, one electrical artificer and one shipwright be carried in addition as the work on the destroyers is more than the staff of *Aurora* can cope with." Such work, in this part of the cruise, included range finding exercises on all working days, though "the gun circuits, etc, have still a good deal of work to be carried out before firing can safely take place, and ... I do not anticipate being ready for any serious firing programme before two months. Meanwhile training is taking place daily."[152]

The squadron's first cruise ended in Halifax, where it was inspected by Captain Hose. On 23 December he informed *Aurora*'s commanding officer "that the appearance of the *Patrician* and *Patriot* and of their ships' companies was entirely satisfactory, particularly in view of the large amount of steaming they had just completed. The upper decks and mess decks were clean and showed evidence of good organization." Far less favourable, the naval director was "unable to say the same of the HMC ship under your command. While very ready to make a generous allowance for the fact that the ship had only just arrived in harbour at 8 A.M. and that a certain number of men were necessarily required to attend on

---

150. Naval Historical Section, Brief History of HMCS *Aurora*, 23 January 1962, Naval Ottawa to Ballantyne, 25 August 1930, ibid.

151. CO *Aurora* to NSHQ, 17 December 1920, 1031–7-5, LAC, RG 24, vol. 3887.

152. Ibid.

HMCS *Patrician* ... still these same disabilities applied equally to the smaller ships, who had overcome them very well."[153]

The details Hose provided must have made Adams distinctly uncomfortable, as "at 11.30 A.M. the boats' falls and ropes on the upper deck were in tangled masses and in spite of their being stiff with frost I cannot admit that there was any reason why a better attempt could not have been made to clear up the upper deck." Furthermore, the naval director could "only describe the condition of the mess deck as filthy, with heaps of food stuff and other dirt in half swept up heaps, and a number of men in a half-dressed condition about the deck." Generally, "taking all adverse conditions well into consideration such a state of affairs is very unsatisfactory and cannot but very detrimentally reflect on the organizing ability of the executive officer and he is to be so informed." Contrarily, "the commanding officer[s] of *Patriot* and *Patrician* are to be commended for the satisfactory condition of their vessels."[154]

Perhaps improvement would come with experience, the squadron leaving on its second cruise in January 1921. One task would be to deliver secret documents from the Admiralty to consuls at Colon, Panama, Managua, San Salvador, Guatemala, Salina Cruz, Colima, San Diego, San Francisco, Portland (Oregon), and Seattle. "These documents are to be handed over to the consuls personally, either by you or an officer selected for the purpose. In the event of its being impossible for any reason to hand over a document to one of the consuls, it is to be retained on board the ship, and the department informed by telegraph."[155] Somewhat more routine after the ships left Halifax on 8 January was how "advantage was taken of fine weather on Monday 10th January by range finding exercises AM and PM, followed by manoeuvres, general drill and burning searchlights." Arriving in Bermuda on the 11th, they remained four days before leaving for Port of Spain, conducting night defence and night attack exercises with star shell and searchlights along the way. At their destination, Adams soon discovered how accommodating British officials could be, and "found the rear admiral entirely desirous in framing the programme to meet my wishes. I had with regret to exclude any torpedo programme." The Canadian ships had had no opportunity to carry out test runs, the water was too muddy to easily retrieve practice torpedoes, and "the whole Gulf is covered with oil tracks," making it difficult to determine where a ship's torpedoes had gone. "I may add that imperial ships have lost five torpedoes in these waters during the winter months."[156]

Reporting on the Canadian squadron's training, the commanding officer of the 8th Light Cruiser Squadron noted that he had taken into account the fact that the three ships had already steamed 6,000 miles and had another 5,200 to go before arriving at Esquimalt. "I cannot help being of the opinion that there is some danger in making this young squadron do such an excessive amount of running before they can have humanly found their feet,"

---

153. Hose to Capt H.G.H. Adams, 23 December 1920, 33–1–1, LAC, RG 24, vol. 5633.

154. Ibid.

155. Naval Secretary to Senior Officer Commanding Canadian Squadron, 4 January 1921, 31–7–1, LAC, RG 24, vol. 5632.

156. Senior Officer Commanding Canadian Squadron to Naval Secretary, 3 February 1921, 1031–7–5, LAC, RG 24, vol. 3887.

the voyage to the West Coast and back perhaps being an excessive demand on the part of the Canadian government. It seemed to him that "too much strain is being imposed on both the materiel and personnel by not allowing them more time in harbour to settle down, get clean and thus inculcate their self-respect." Perhaps *Aurora* had failed inspection in Halifax because too much was being demanded, but at least "Captain Adams realizes the great responsibility which rests on him on the re-creation of a Canadian navy, and it is naturally very much to the interests of the empire (and, incidentally, the English tax payer) that its development and efficiency should be encouraged as much as possible. I therefore trust that such-like reunions between imperial and Royal Canadian ships may be perpetuated."[157]

That training was limited was therefore acceptable to all concerned. As Adams explained, "the smallness of the programme was largely determined by the necessity of giving each ship sufficient time to carry out engine room repairs, the intense damp heat varying between 110° to 130° in each engine room rendering work decidedly oppressive." Thinking ahead, *Aurora*'s captain suggested "that it would be prudent to enlist a certain number of stokers to meet any shortage that may arise owing to desertion at Esquimalt, as I consider that in addition to the usual reasons for desertion, the proposed return through the tropics may have a bearing on the subject, the conditions of heat so far having been trying and will no doubt be aggravated on the Mexican coast." Other than the heat, restrictions to training "were caused by seizing up of gun bearings due to cold weather at Halifax," and a breakout of gastroenteritis did nothing to help matters. Still, signal and wireless telegraphy training was carried out every day, and a full-calibre shoot was conducted by all three ships on the 28th.[158]

An important part of the squadron's training was in torpedo and gunnery (*Aurora* was armed with two 6-inch and six 4-inch guns, while the destroyers each carried three 4-inch), which represented the main weapons it would use in time of war. Before the light cruiser and the destroyers had even commissioned, the RCN had recognized that "it will be impossible for Canadian ships to carry out efficient gunnery and torpedo practices by themselves,"[159] hence the need for the southern cruises to take advantage of British facilities. In fact, in Admiralty regulations no less than a full month of firing and preliminary practices were considered necessary to bring a ship up to the minimum level of efficiency. As *Aurora* related in her first annual report on gunnery exercises, however, "it was not possible at the beginning of the ships commission to work the requisite amount of time to working up the gunnery efficiency as laid down in Part V Chapter II of the Firing Manual. The practices carried out at Trinidad in January, in conjunction with the N. American & West Indies Squadron, were of great value but the stay of the squadron was too short to allow of all the preliminary instruction, drills and firing practices to be completed. The practices carried out at Esquimalt and Magdalena Bay were of an elementary character but on each occasion sufficient time was not allowed to enable the personnel to be thoroughly trained.... Gunnery instruction and training classes have been going on steadily through-

157. CO 8th Light Cruiser Squadron to C-in-C, NA&WI, 16 February 1921, 1057–50–11GE, LAC, RG 24, vol. 4008.

158. Senior Officer Commanding Canadian Squadron to Naval Secretary, 3 February 1921, 1031-7-5, LAC, RG 24, vol. 3887.

159. Stephens to Hose, 7 October 1920, 1057–50–11GE, LAC, RG 24, vol. 4008.

out the year. It is hoped that during the coming cruise to the West Indies, the gunnery progress of the ship will be accelerated."[160]

One goal for such training was to defend Canadian harbours against raiders and at least one exercise was conducted in this period to put all the elements necessary for such a defence through their paces. Carried out from 22 to 24 August, 1921, its object "was to act out the defence of Halifax Harbour during, first, a pre-supposed period of strained relations and, second, after hostilities had broken out." The attackers, called Blue Force, consisted of the submarines *CH 14* and *CH 15*, while the light cruiser, the two destroyers, and two trawlers, fitted out for minesweeping, made up Red Force. It was a combined arms exercise, where "the air force was represented by three flying boats which patrolled one at a time. The army had guns manned along the shores to resist invasion from the sea." The first day concentrated on relearning basic skills, and "the submarines were exercised in attacking *Aurora*, directing their torpedoes at the cruiser both on her leaving and entering harbour."[161]

Then began the exercise proper, and "daytime of the 23rd was supposed to be a period of strained relations. The submarines, as the Blue Force, patrolled the entrance of the harbour, observing shipping arriving and leaving port. Ships of the Red Force entered and left harbour … while the aircraft kept up a patrol looking for them." War was declared that night. "The examination service was now on duty and the approaches to the harbour were patrolled by imaginary auxiliary patrol vessels, it being understood that no boom had yet been set across the entrance to protect it. *Patriot* was instructed to endeavour to enter the harbour by a 'ruse de guerre,' making a signal as if she belonged to the defending force and wished to come in to make good urgent defects. *Patrician* was ordered to attempt to enter without lights or making signals." Clearly, a potential enemy was not expected to play fair—nor did *Patriot*. "The commander-in-charge and the port war signal station at Camperdown were taken in by *Patriot*'s 'ruse de guerre' and the destroyer would have succeeded in her attempt but for an examination vessel stopping her. The smaller ship signalled to the shore defences which switched on searchlights and opened fire with blank shells." *Patrician*, without resorting to tricks, avoided observation by the port war signal station, but was also intercepted by an inspection vessel, which gave the alarm while turning on searchlights and opening fire.[162]

Next day *Aurora* played the part of a convoy. "Submarines were known to be in the vicinity and the destroyers were sent out to meet her. *CH-15* sighted the supposed convoy and attacked. As *Aurora* was zig-zagging and the range was outside 4,000 yards, it was considered unlikely that a hit would have been registered. It was felt, however, that with more practice the submarine would have been able to deliver an attack at a closer range." There were other lessons, as "the ships did not sight the attacker. Although a flying boat located both submarines, communications, both radio and lamp flashing, between *Aurora* and the aircraft were never satisfactory. The latter patrolled fifty miles out to sea and they maintained wireless communication, both Morse and voice, with the base. They also released carrier pigeons and these birds

160. "Annual Report of Gunnery Exercises … *Aurora*, 1 November 20 to 1 November 21," nd, ibid.

161. "Combined Exercises by Navy, Army and Air Force, 22–24 August 1921," 30 August 1922, 33–1–1, LAC, RG 24, vol. 5633.

162. Ibid.

conveyed their messages safely to base."[163] Still, the main lesson of the exercise was that all three services had much to learn and practice if they were to carry out their common duty effectively.

The whole purpose of cruises and training was to prepare the navy to play a role on the international stage, which the three Canadian warships did once in this period. The place was Costa Rica, during a cruise by *Aurora*, *Patriot*, and *Patrician* in the spring and summer of 1921. A hint of things to come came in a message of 6 June, when the Admiralty advised that "Costa points out that Puerta Culebra," a possible port of call for the Canadian warships, "is unsuitable for visit of His Majesty's Canadian Ships as usual salutes and other international courtesies cannot be accorded at that port. British Minister at Costa Rica suggests Punta Arenas as port of call which is in direct railway communication with capital." The ships arrived on 6 July, and after the usual courtesies, including an exchange of salutes, "the British minister arrived down in a special train during the afternoon with a deputation from the British residents of San Jose and was my guest on board during his stay at the port," reported *Aurora*'s captain. "An invitation was extended to twelve officers of the squadron to visit San Jose the following day and remain up there for two nights, which I accepted especially as the minister thought that this visit would strengthen his hands in negotiations with the Costa Rica government over claims of the Royal Bank of Canada and the re-granting of oil concessions to a British company which had been taken away."[164]

Strictly speaking, this was not gunboat diplomacy, since the Canadian ships were not prepared to use force in resolving the dispute, but the dozen officers in uniform would be evidence that the British were interested in serious negotiations—otherwise why pay for their visit? It was all part and parcel of a large tea ceremony that was diplomacy in the 1920s, where the backdrop, in this case Canadian naval officers, was an important part of proceedings. They certainly had no cause to regret the role they were to play, being invited to the opera, where the president of Costa Rica invited them into his box. He and his ministers also received the Canadians at their official residences "with great cordiality." Furthermore, there was a ball held in the sailors' honour by the British residents of San Jose, which the president and his ministers attended. Finally, "the minister of war arrived personally at the station at an inconvenient hour [to himself] to wish farewell to the officers and sent his ADC in the train as a mark of affection." A letter of thanks was sent by way of the British minister to Costa Rica thanking that nation's government for its hospitality. As for the ships concerned, a pamphlet later issued by HMCS *Skeena* (acquired in the 1930s) claimed that "the chance visit of our three ships [in 1921] provided visual proof of Canada's status as a powerful nation."[165]

In this period, however, the relationship between the army, navy, and air force could be as complicated as that between nations, tradition looming large as a means of giving a service's members a sense of belonging that could aid in the creation of unit cohesion and

163. Ibid.

164. London to Ottawa, 6 June 1921, "Extract from Letter of Proceedings 14th July 1921," nd, 31-7-1, LAC, RG 24, vol. 5632.

165. SNO, Canadian Squadron to NSHQ, 14 July 1921, Desbarats to Undersecretary of State for External Affairs, 27 July 1921, ibid; and F.L. Houghton, *HMCS Skeena, 1931–1932: Commemorating Her First Year in Commission* (Victoria 1932), 30.

hence combat effectiveness, though sometimes to the detriment of inter-arm relationships. One issue creating animosity between the RCN and the Canadian militia was that of precedence—in effect who came first on the order of battle and thus who marched first on parade. To outsiders, it might seem to be an irrelevant or even silly debate, but the navy was more than an institution: it was and is a society which felt the need to set itself apart from the larger, Canadian, society and from other services if it was to legitimately demand loyalty from its members. As R.M. Stephens, the assistant director of the naval service, related in early 1919, "the question of precedence between the Royal Canadian Navy and militia has been allowed to drop during the war. The near approach of peace and the certainty of many official functions taking place in connection therewith, makes it desirable that the matter should now be finally settled, if possible."[166]

Past discussions did not leave much room for optimism, however, as "we have long been at a deadlock, and neither party is likely to give way entirely, but it seems to me possible that a compromise might be effected without endangering the rights of the RCN." The question at issue was a simple one: "Is the RCN to have the same precedence accorded to it as the RN, that is to say, to come before the Canadian militia?" To Stephens, the answer was somewhat ambiguous. On the one hand, "the RCN is by the Admiralty accorded equal rights and privileges with the RN in every respect similarly it is understood that the War Office accords equal rights and privileges to the Canadian militia as to the regular army. It seems clear, therefore, that when all these four services are acting in conjunction, that the RN and RCN are one and the imperial army and the Canadian militia are also one. As the navy admittedly takes precedence of the army, the RCN would under such circumstances take precedence of the militia." On the other hand, "the precedence of the RN rests on historical ground in which the RCN participates insofar as the two services are one. But in certain circumstances the RCN acts as a separate service, and in particular in Canadian waters, when its status is not so clearly defined. It appears to me exceedingly doubtful if claim to precedence in Canada for the RCN can be substantiated."[167]

Stephens therefore recommended a compromise whereby "in Canada militia takes precedence of RCN," though "outside Canada RCN takes precedence as part of RN." In practice, "when RCN officers or men are on duty conjointly with officers or men of the RN, they will then take precedence as part of RN irrespective of whether the occasion is within or without Canada," while naval reservists were "to be considered as part of the RCN," for purposes of precedence. Either Stephens's arguments were even more convincing than he himself expected, or the militia had other battles to fight, but a little over a month later the militia secretary advised that "the Minister of Militia concedes seniority to the Royal Canadian Navy."[168]

It would concede little else in the years that followed, especially when, after a December 1921 general election fought mainly on tariff issues, the newly elected government of Mackenzie King decided to place all the fighting services under a single ministry, no

---

166. Stephens to Hose, 20 February 1919, 1–1–15, LAC, RG 24, vol. 5585.

167. Ibid.

168. Ibid; and Military Secretary to Naval Secretary, Naval and Military Committee, 26 March 1919, ibid.

doubt to reduce the costs of administration, but perhaps also to avoid having several ministers lobbying for funds within Cabinet. King himself was not sympathetic to spending more money on the armed services, having, while leader of the opposition, denounced the government's naval proposals in September 1920 and proposed in April 1921 a resolution that there be no new expenditure for naval or military purposes. It was defeated, ninety-six to sixty-four. In the 1921 election, defence issues had not been on the agenda, tariffs looming large instead, as they had in 1891 and 1911, though this time with a different result, the Liberals winning at the polls. Although national development was the new government's priority, as it had been from 1896 to 1911, it was not long before it turned its attention to the armed services. At a meeting on 15 February 1922, Desbarats noted that "we were not given any information but were allowed to air our views," the scheme at the time calling for a department with a board representing the militia, air force, RCN, and the RCMP (although the latter was later dropped).[169] An act of parliament would transfer the various powers allocated to these forces to the new organization, as well as "all the powers, duties and functions vested in the Minister of Marine and Fisheries by the Naval Service Act."[170]

For those fearing the "abolition" of the navy, leader of the opposition Arthur Meighen had encouraging words, though they were not couched that way. "I observe ... that the new government, though they pretend to be amalgamating the naval service with the militia, are taking care to retain the chief officers of both, and I fear the amalgamation is more a matter of advertisement than reality." The goal of the exercise was to consolidate the political and higher-level bureaucratic echelons of the different services into a single department with a single minister, a single deputy minister, and a single advisory committee or council of national defence.[171] The new department came into being on 1 January, 1923, in effect amalgamating the army, navy, and air force only within Cabinet without affecting their separate organizations. The RCN ceased to be a part of a general seagoing Department of Marine and Fisheries and of the Naval Service and instead joined the other armed services in the new Department of National Defence. It is doubtful that any officer or rating outside of headquarters in Ottawa noticed the change.

Of far greater import, and preceding the formation of the Department of National Defence, was the Mackenzie King government's reappraisal of the resources that would be allocated to the RCN. Interestingly, Canada had spent more on its navy in its first year than in any subsequent period, expenditures totalling more than $2.2 million on estimates (in essence, the service's request for money) of $3 million. The following year the RCN's estimates remained the same, but expenditures dropped to $1.9 million; by 1919 they were less than $1.2 million. Actual debentures then rose to almost $2 million in each of 1920–21 and 1921–22. It was thus normal for the navy's request for money, in the form of estimates, to be reduced substantially by the time it had been transformed into a budget. When the incom-

---

169. Notes on 15 February meeting, 22 February 1922, LAC, MG 30 E89, vol. 6; John Herd Thompson and Allen Seager, *Canada: 1922–1939, Decades of Discord* (Toronto 1985), 63; and Mason Wade, *The French Canadians, 1760–1967* (Toronto 1968), II, 784.

170. PC 331, 10 February 1922, 10–1-83, LAC, RG 24, vol. 5590.

171. Meighen to John Regan, 30 May 1922, LAC, MG 26I, vol. 116, file 119; and Eayrs, *In Defence of Canada: From the Great War to the Great Depression*, 232.

The H-class submarines *CH 14* and *CH 15* saw only limited service in the RCN before being paid off in June 1922. (LAC PA-139976)

ing government received the navy's funding request for 1922, totalling $2.5 million, it had no reason to think that it was doing anything new in arranging a meeting of the Naval Committee to discuss "possible cut in naval estimates," so that the RCN's actual budget would be $1.5 million. (Actual expenditures would be just under $1.4 million in 1922–23, and 1923–24, according to the department's annual report). The naval director sought to avoid any reduction of the fleet, which as we have seen was pretty much the minimum he felt the country needed; it was also suggested that shutting down the base at Halifax would cost more than keeping it in operation.[172] Other savings, however, would have to be sought immediately, Hose advising the naval minister that "in view of the fact that the present programme of HMC squadron carries them into the coming financial year, I would suggest that it should be cancelled and that I should send instructions to the squadron to return to Halifax, arriving there by the 31st March or as near that date as possible. This is in order that oil fuel and other expenses should not be incurred outside of Canada after this financial year."[173]

Hose's language masked the trepidation he must have felt, but with the passage of another month he found a way to salvage a Royal Canadian Navy, although the resulting organization would be unable to fight even the most limited naval battle. The service would rely on reserves to maintain its existence, a plan that naval officers submitted on 19 April and that was swiftly approved on the 24th. As he reported to the Admiralty on the 27th, Ottawa had "decided that, owing to the financial condition of the dominion, they are unable to appropriate more than one and a half million dollars for naval defence this year," which was more than in most previous years but insufficient to operate its new, though small, fleet. "After careful consideration it has further been decided that to attempt the continuation of a sea-going navy for such a sum is impracticable, particularly in view of the fact that any definite increase in funds available cannot be guaranteed in the immediate future." Important choices had to be made, and "the only sea-going force which could be maintained for $1,500,000 would be one light cruiser and since this would offer no scope or prospects for the personnel and, further, would entail overhead expenditures which would be out of all proportion to the defence value obtained, such a policy is deemed inadvisable."[174]

It was decided, therefore, "to organize the naval defence measures of the dominion on a reserve or naval militia basis, having a small permanent force as a training nucleus," it being estimated that funds would be available to train 1,500 reservists. Also, "a short service system is being considered for the ratings, terms of engagement being increased when men accept promotion to leading and petty officer grades," where "minesweeping, examination service, manning of port war signal stations, patrols and the other coast defence responsibilities of the Navy will be met by this system." As for the fifty-nine officers in the

172. Desbarats journal, 23 and 25 February 1922, LAC, MG 30 E89, vol. 6; Canada, DND, *Report of the Department of National Defence (Naval Service) for the Fiscal Year Ending March 31, 1923* (Ottawa 1923), 18–19; Canada, DND, *Report of the Department of National Defence (Naval Service) for the Fiscal Year Ending March 31, 1924* (Ottawa 1924), 18–19; and "Canadian Naval Service," nd, LAC, MG 26 I, vol. 116, file 119.

173. Hose to Minister, 20 March 1922, 31–7-1, LAC, RG 24, vol. 5632.

174. Hose to Admiralty, 27 April 1922, 64–1-3, LAC, RG 24, vol. 5667; and Desbarats journal, 19, 21 and 24 April 1922, LAC, MG 30 E89, vol. 6.

executive and engineering branches of the RCN, only twenty-six could be retained, it being "desirable that there should be a surplus above these twenty-six who should be serving in the Royal Navy and who should be exchanged from time to time with the officers serving in Canada…. The Department of the Naval Service has very much appreciated the action of their lordships in giving appointments to RCN officers in the Royal Navy and hopes that their lordships will be able to continue to place the surplus officers in the fleet for training as heretofore, being paid from Canadian funds." It was not expected that there would be more than thirty such officers in any case.[175]

Meanwhile, Desbarats attempted to work out the consequences of the King government's decision at a pace that can only be described as hectic. Referring to the budget figure of $1.5 million, he wrote in his diary on 4 May how the service "will have difficulty to keep within these figures unless authority given immediately to demobilize. Reports to council before minister but not signed. Have not been able to see minister for quite a while. Cannot get tenders for sale of ships before him and being passed for decisions." Trying to do the best he could for the RCN's employees, he discussed the possibility with the Department of Marine of transferring them there, but its staff was "doubtful as to legality," forcing him to send someone to the Department of Justice for a ruling. Finally getting in to see the minister, the latter would not however sign off on closing ships and establishments, and "will not make announcement" before the estimates were actually tabled in parliament. Officers working on salvaging what they could reported on 16 May that even with the limited funds available *Patriot* and *Patrician* could remain in commission, so the navy would be more than a reserve force, and on 23 May the budget was brought down in the house.[176]

There was no lack of opposition to the government's decision, with one resident of Halifax, though admitting there was little chance of changing the budget, willing to fight for "better terms," especially for those being discharged as a result of the cuts. "The midshipmen who went to sea last year will of course be the least affected. Their training is such that they can enter the second year at McGill in engineering and the break will not be severe and they can more easily adapt themselves to some other line of work. Take, however, the officer who has put in five years or more at sea after his college course; it will take at least three years of hard work to fit him for some other work and the officer who has served from the outset will find it will take him longer. It may well turn out that he will find it impossible to fit into something else. That will be his misfortune. All the country can do and what it ought to do is to start these officers towards any new calling they might choose."[177]

Leader of the opposition Arthur Meighen, for his part, noted that "there are signs of growing realization throughout the country of the humiliating position Canada is getting into on the matter of naval defence." They were strong words, Meighen adding that he and his party "are making every effort in our power to bring home to the minds of the Canadian people the utterly indefensible conduct to which the government is committing this country. The money being voted is paltry, and for the purpose for which it is being voted

---

175. Hose to Admiralty, 27 April 1922, 64–1-3, LAC, RG 24, vol. 5667.

176. Desbarats journal, 4, 5, 16 and 23 May 1922, LAC, MG 30, E89, vol. 6.

177. W.E. Thompson to Arthur Meighen, 15 May 1922, LAC, MG 26I, vol. 116, file 119.

will be as good as wasted. If we cannot pay our way on a reasonable basis in the matter of defence, it would be more honourable on our part to step out of the empire and stand on our own feet."[178] Though it had been the Meighen government that had opted for a navy capable of no more than defending Canadian ports, his imperialist credentials were not in doubt. Just as obviously, however, the King government had far more parochial views of the relationship between Canada, the British Empire, and the RCN.

Aurora was to be laid up until the manner of her disposal could be decided, the ship's guns sealed with lacquer at the muzzle and breach, while the submarines were to be similarly treated. The destroyers, as we have seen, would remain in commission. The Royal Naval College of Canada was to be closed and the British ratings on loan to that institution for support functions returned home. Four drifters at Halifax were put up for sale, though one of them had to be removed from the sale list when it was found that it was needed to fill water tanks at the magazine for fire fighting purposes (it was later replaced by a contractor to perform that task). By 10 August there remained Naval Service Headquarters in Ottawa, the RCN barracks in Halifax, *Patriot*, *Patrician*, the district intelligence offices in Esquimalt and Halifax, the dockyards in both bases, and personnel totalling eighty officers and 250 ratings. It was planned to use the college building at Esquimalt to train reservists. As for educating men in the Royal Navy, "Admiralty will continue to give facilities for training and suitable appointments to Canadian naval officers."[179]

It was at that time that Llewellyn Houghton returned from eight years of service with the Royal Navy, joining *Patriot* as first lieutenant and second-in-command. The captain was Lieutenant Howard Emerson Reid, "one year older and six months senior to me." It was not a happy moment, as "I was returning to the RCN at a time when it was at its lowest ebb. I shall always remember the farewell party given to my predecessor, Lieutenant Cuthbert Robert Holland Taylor.... I can still hear in my mind the last words he managed to articulate before he quietly and appropriately passed out: 'I've seen a navy die, boys! I've seen a navy die!' "[180] Such words may seem melodramatic, but the RCN was not just an institution, it was a society and community as well. Still, one member of that society, Walter Hose, seemed far less angry and far more optimistic, at least after some time had passed. In August he wrote one of his colleagues, who had retired before the cuts, that, "as you may imagine, we have had to go through an anxious time as regards the Canadian navy, but although I very much deplore the arbitrary cut of $1,000,000 in our appropriation, still I have by no means lost hope as regards the future, and I hope within the next couple of years to have an efficient reserve of at least 1,500 men organized and trained by the nucleus of the permanent force, and I still believe that from that we shall expand into a seagoing service again."[181]

He was right.

178. Meighen to John Regan, 19 May 1922, ibid.

179. Admiralty to Naval Ottawa, 24 May 1922, Hose to Admiralty, 10 August 1922, NSHQ to CO *Aurora*, 23 May 1922, Naval Ottawa to RN College of Canada, 23 May 1922, 64–1-3, LAC, RG 24, vol. 5667; and Acting Director of Stores to Desbarats, 23 May 1922, T.C. Phillips, Consulting Naval Engineer, to Desbarats, 7 June 1922, 842–3-3, LAC, RG 24, vol. 5696.

180. F.L. Houghton, "Memoir," nd, 91, LAC, MG 30 E444.

181. Hose to Capt H.E. Holme, 10 August 1922, DHH 2001/12, file C11.

CHAPTER 13

Survival, 1922–1927

With the 1922 government decision to limit the RCN's budget to $1.5 million, the service in effect demobilized, limiting itself to a few destroyers and other, smaller vessels (the fleet being divided almost equally between the East and West Coasts) and relying on reservists to maintain basic skills—and keep up tradition. The navy's core, its permanent, full-time personnel, would increase in this period, but only modestly, from 467 in 1923–24 to 500 the following year, then to 516 in 1926–27[1] but these numbers would be insufficient to conduct operations, and would force the RCN to focus simply on maintaining its own and the reservists' knowledge until funding might increase.

Given the political philosophy of Liberal governments until 1930 and of the Conservative government until 1935, the navy could not hope for much more, for if isolation from world affairs was not Canada's only priority at this time, it was certainly one of the most important influences on the country's foreign policy and defence doctrine. In January 1922, for example, O.D. Skelton attacked the concept of a unified imperial foreign policy in a speech to the Ottawa Canadian Club. Mackenzie King, soon to be prime minister, did not disagree, and would consistently defend Canada's autonomous status within the empire (and commonwealth) and other institutions such as the League of Nations. Clifford Sifton, another influential Liberal, called for the removal of remaining formal limitations on Canadian sovereignty, in effect calling for the patriation of the constitution, something that would not occur for another six decades.[2]

In the meantime, although British signatures on international treaties bound the empire as a whole, in Canada parliament would decide exactly how the country would fulfil such obligations. Article 10 of the League of Nations Charter was a case in point. Calling for all members to act should one be the victim of aggression, Canadian authorities never doubted that they opposed it, but merely disagreed on whether to seek its suppression or merely an amendment to water it down. As King himself pointed out years after the end of the First World War, no party in the Commons called for preparations for overseas operations so, logically, it made no sense to commit to even the possibility of such expeditions. Also, the King government was well aware that the United States had become

---

1. Canada, Department of National Defence, *Report of the Department of National Defence (Naval Service) for the Fiscal Year Ending March 31, 1924* (Ottawa 1924), 13; Canada, DND, *Report of the Department of National Defence (Naval Service) for the Fiscal Year Ending March 31, 1925* (Ottawa 1925), 12; and Canada, DND, *Report of the Department of National Defence (Naval Service) for the Fiscal Year Ending March 31, 1927* (Ottawa 1927), 17.

2. C.P. Stacey, *Canada and the Age of Conflict, II* (Toronto 1981), 8, 12, 14.

a world power before the end of the First World War, and it made little sense to join in the application of sanctions against a wrong-doing nation if the United States was opposed. If Canada chose to embargo some distant country, its southern neighbour could simply purchase the necessary goods and export them itself. Only much later in this period, after the Liberals defeated R.B. Bennett's Conservative government in 1935, would King advise British authorities that Canada would come to their assistance if Britain was threatened, or even if any part of the empire was at serious risk.[3]

In this atmosphere the navy would amount to far less than it had hoped to be in the period immediately following the Armistice, but far more than it had feared to be in the immediate aftermath of Mackenzie King's first budget. It would continue to operate in accordance with its role and responsibilities, and those would continue to be determined by an interplay between the naval service, the government, and, in spite of the conclusions of the 1921 Imperial Conference, the Admiralty. For the RCN still had a role to play in the eyes of the Royal Navy, which would not give up its vision of an imperial or commonwealth force, regardless of any conciliatory statements it might make at meetings with the dominions, until another world war intervened to remove Great Britain from the first tier of world powers.

An excellent statement of the Admiralty's outlook—and, perhaps, ambitions—followed a meeting of the Committee of Imperial Defence in August 1922. "A war between the British empire and any of the great naval powers is considered unlikely during the next ten years," it suggested in a comment that would remain true for more than half a decade, "but it would not be safe to gamble on this when making provision for the naval defence of the empire." Given the abrogation of the alliance with Japan and the reductions in naval armaments accepted at the Washington Naval Conference of 1922, "the strategic situation in the western Pacific has changed for the worse, and the necessary preparations for a possible rapid concentration of the main fleet in the east must be pressed on with." Such preparations needed to be in place in time of peace if they were to be available should war break out, and "naval defence can only be assured by adequate naval forces, capable of offensive action and endowed with full freedom of action, which in its turn can only be maintained by adequate fuelling and base facilities."[4]

In a comment that may well have had the RCN in mind, the committee stated, "it therefore follows that, as the mother country cannot unaided maintain the fleet necessary for the safety of the empire, with the requisite bases and oil-fuel reserves, the dominions and colonies must be depended upon not to confine their co-operation in naval defence to purely local measures." Since direct financial contributions had been ruled out by successive Canadian governments, it recommended, "during this period of financial stringency, maintenance, by the dominions which have hitherto possessed navies, of a healthy nucleus of a sea-going squadron which, when times are better, can be rapidly expanded." Still, it knew it had a difficult row to hoe, as "the Canadian government, when explain-

---

3. Stacey, *Canada and the Age of Conflict*, II, 41, 57, 63, 80, 206, 211–12.

4. Committee of Imperial Defence, "The Washington Conference and Its Effect upon Empire Naval Policy and Co-operation," August 1922, Library and Archives Canada (hereafter LAC), Manuscript Group (hereafter MG) 26 J4, vol. 124, file 913.

ing their decisions as to the recent abolition of their seagoing fleet, stated that, had the latter been maintained, overhead charges would have been out of all proportion to the defence value obtained."[5] One can almost hear the tone of disappointment in the last sentence.

The situation would not markedly improve, from the Admiralty's point of view, in the years to follow. Future Chief of the General Staff A.G.L. McNaughton, for one, wrote a report on the 1923 conference. Although noting the need "to provide for the adequate defence of the territories and trade of the several countries comprising the British empire," the conference had repeated a previous resolution "expressly" recognizing "that it is for the parliaments ... upon the recommendations of their respective governments, to decide the nature and extent of any action that should be taken by them." It noted "the primary responsibility of each portion of the empire represented at the conference for its own *local defence*," but also the requirement for "adequate provision for safeguarding the maritime communications of the several parts of the empire and the routes and waterways along and through which their armed forces and trade pass." Furthermore, the conference recognized the need for "the provision of naval bases and facilities for repair and fuel so as to ensure the mobility of the fleets," as well as "the desirability of the maintenance of a minimum standard of naval strength, namely, equality with the naval strength of any foreign power, in accordance with the provisions of the Washington Treaty on Limitation of Armaments as approved by Great Britain, all the self-governing dominions and India." McNaughton, being a strong proponent of air power, could not fail to note "the desirability of the development of the air forces of the several countries of the empire upon such lines as will make it possible ... for each part of the empire as it may determine to co-operate with other parts."[6]

Applying such principles to the realities of the day, the conference noted "the deep interest of the Commonwealth of Australia, the Dominion of New Zealand, and India, in the provision of a naval base at Singapore, as essential for ensuring the mobility necessary to provide for the security of the territories and trade of the empire in eastern waters," an issue to be revived often in the coming years until the base was taken by Japanese forces in 1942. Also, the conference agreed on "the necessity for the maintenance of safe passage along the great route to the east through the Mediterranean and the Red Sea," as well as "the necessity for the maintenance by Great Britain of a Home Defence Air Force of sufficient strength to give adequate protection against air attack by the strongest air force within striking distance of her shores."[7] There was no recognition, however, of the need for a centralized imperial navy, principles of defence having in effect been broken down into local issues. As Prime Minister Mackenzie King stated at the conference's ninth meeting, "we in the dominions have most in mind in seeking co-operation rather than centralisation in these matters of defence. The original point of view of the Admiralty was that the more centralised in every particular matter of defence could be, the more effective and better the outcome. I think we might admit at once that, from the point of view of strategy, efficiency

---

5. Ibid.

6. A.G.L. McNaughton, "The Principles of Imperial Defence, A Canadian Aspect," 25 March 1923, LAC, MG 27, III B-5, vol. 30, file X-16.

7. Ibid.

and economy, the Admiralty were perhaps right, speaking of the defence of the empire as a whole. On the other hand, there is always the difference between the political point of view and the technical point of view, and the political point of view, inasmuch as it lies at the basis of all the rest, cannot receive too full consideration. I do not think it would be possible for the dominions, whether in relation to naval, military, or air forces, to concur in any policy in the nature of a highly centralised policy. The question in the end comes back to one of taxation. All these matters in the last analysis are questions of taxation, and those of us who are really interested in the defence of the empire have to ask ourselves, above every other question: How can the taxes be raised for the purposes for which we require them?" The Royal Canadian Navy had been founded by Canadians in 1910 as "the natural outgrowth of their national standing and national status," and so it would remain.[8]

According to member of parliament L.C.M.S. Amery in a letter to King (which the latter concurred in), the government of the day was willing to build up a Canadian unit, but "the present political position precluded you from actually announcing any such scheme and that you would not be in a position to do so until you had had more time to educate public opinion and had also more effective Parliamentary backing. Consequently that the only thing you could do at this moment was to consider such moderate programme of expansion in personnel and other arrangements as would make it possible for you to initiate a larger policy when in a position to do so." Taking over a cruiser might be a possibility in future, but not at the time, though Liberal policy aimed at the not unambitious goals of "the creation," though perhaps *recreation* would have been a better word, "of a naval department, the establishment of a naval reserve, the creation of a volunteer naval force, and the construction of ships to act in co-operation with the British navy at such times as the government of Canada may place them at the disposal of the Admiralty. That is a broad policy: it is a policy not for one day or one month or one year: it is a policy for the years that lie ahead."[9] At the 1923 Imperial Conference, as things turned out, though it was noted that Australia and New Zealand had contributed to the development of the base at Singapore, British Prime Minister Stanley Baldwin also announced "the end of the controversy 'between the advocates of dominion navies and dominion contributions to a single imperial navy,' and he stated that 'the principle of dominion navies is established, and is not merely accepted, but is wholeheartedly endorsed, by the Admiralty.'"[10]

The word "wholeheartedly" was perhaps not an accurate reflection of the Admiralty's views, since they had been insisting on the need for imperial coordination since before the end of the First World War, though they had had to admit soon after that conflict that "any system which attempts to dictate the naval policy of the dominions ... will meet with grave difficulties in practice." In February 1921, however, the Admiralty noted to Cabinet that it still adhered to the "ideal" of a "unified navy under a single command," and went so far as to suggest that it would be "equitable" for each dominion to provide a portion of its

8. Lovell C. Clark, ed., *Documents on Canadian External Relations*, III: *1919–1925* (Ottawa, 1970), 252.

9. L.C.M.S Amery to Mackenzie King, 12 October 1923, LAC, MG 26 J1, vol. 88.

10. McNaughton, "The Principles of Imperial Defence, A Canadian Aspect," 25 March 1923, LAC, MG 27, III B-5, vol. 30, file X-16.

budget for imperial defence, "and the Admiralty accepted that this might well be less than the normal British proportion." It had to be admitted, however "the truth was that in 1921, when Britain herself was doing her utmost to economise on defence expenditure, to expect the dominions to accept increased contributions was highly optimistic." Still, centralization continued to be an Admiralty goal, and when at the 1926 conference Mackenzie King focused his comments on the local defence of coastal waters and approaches to ports, they "scarcely accorded with the Admiralty's repeated urgings that naval defence should be regarded as a global matter."[11]

One reason the Admiralty may have been seeking centralized authority over all dominion navies in the post-war period was that it was itself shrinking, the South America cruiser squadron, for one, being abolished in this period. Co-operation with dominion navies was thus essential, and if this could not be achieved through the creation of a single headquarters then it would have to come about through other means. The logical response was to proceed to liaison activities, such as those leading to an agreement between the RN and the RCN on the coordination of the two navies, in time of war, on the North America and West Indies Station. As had been the case in the First World War, Canada would be responsible for its coasts and coastal waters, including "any imperial craft definitely assigned for such work." Seagoing forces would be a British responsibility. Also, "the Canadian Naval Board will control all war services operated on shore, e.g., promulgation of navigational warnings relating to Canadian and adjoining waters. The Canadian Naval Board will act in concert with the Admiralty, and, as far as local circumstances permit, will adopt procedures and systems which the Admiralty are putting into force in other parts of the world," standardization being achieved through prior agreement rather than through a single chain of command. Any issues involving Newfoundland would be for that colony and Canada to resolve, with the commander-in-chief North America and West Indies acting as an Admiralty representative in any such discussions. In the same period the RCN and the Admiralty agreed on the organization of a convoy system, local authorities providing escorts for the first and last parts of the voyage, while the British took responsibility for escort on the high seas; Canada and Newfoundland approved the plan in early 1924, while the commander-in-chief, North America and West Indies, worked out the necessary mercantile convoy instructions.[12]

From the Admiralty's point of view, such coordination was made all the more crucial by the decision at the 1921 Imperial Conference, confirmed at the 1923 meeting, to apply Britain's one power standard to the Commonwealth in its entirety, though the resulting whole might not be as large as its various parts. One way to ensure the close co-operation necessary to fight a war together might be "the appointment of dominion naval officers to the Admiralty naval staff and British naval officers to the dominion naval staffs, and by arranging the free interchange of advice being maintained between the naval advisers at the Admiralty on the one hand and the naval advisers of the dominions on the other. The

---

11. Stephen Roskill, *Naval Policy Between the Wars*, I (London 1968), 282, 294, 295, 409, 465.

12. Devonshire to Governor General, 15 December 1923, 1015–3-6, LAC, Record Group (hereafter RG) 24, vol. 3828; Christopher M. Bell, *The Royal Navy, Seapower and Strategy Between the Wars* (Stanford 2000), 146; and Roskill, *Naval Policy Between the Wars*, I, 407–08.

organization would be analogous to the Imperial General Staff, agreed to in principle at the 1907 Imperial Conference." Such a scheme would, of course, require that the officers in question receive staff training, preferably at the Royal Naval Staff College in Greenwich. Also, for the sake of standardization and to reflect their status within the larger, if not centralized, whole, the first naval members in Australia and New Zealand, as well as the director of the naval service in Canada, would each take on the title of chief of the naval staff.[13]

With decentralization the accepted norm, if rather reluctantly on the part of the Admiralty, then any and all contributions the various dominions made to their own defence were in effect part of the general effort—or at least that was how it could be portrayed. In the course of a debate in Britain's House of Commons in 1926, a member of the government noted that "the contributions of the dominions towards naval defence take the form of maintenance of their own forces and establishments by the governments of Canada, Commonwealth of Australia, New Zealand and the Union of South Africa. In addition to these the government of India maintains the Royal Indian Marine and pays a cash contribution towards the expenses of the East Indies Squadron, and the colony of Hong Kong is paying during the current year a cash contribution towards the cost of the Singapore base." Totals amounted to £1.4 million for Canada, £3.9 million for Australia (with an additional special appropriation of £1 million), £538,325 for New Zealand, £159,985 for South Africa, and £120,000 for Hong Kong.[14]

Liaison therefore continued, and by the summer of 1926 many of the details necessary for the Royal Navy to operate as it had before the First World War were in place. For example, Canada's West Coast was the subject of discussion in relation to victualling "in the event of war in the Far East," where "each of dominion governments concerned should undertake full responsibility for the supply of victualling stores to the minesweepers and patrols operating from their ports." As for Canada more specifically, "the Canadian government should fit out an issuing ship for, and undertake the victualling of, the naval forces based on the west coast of North America."[15] If ratified, the agreement would be one among many between the RCN and the RN, but O.D. Skelton of the Department of External Affairs, who was always suspicious of British intentions in such matters, suggested that "it might be well to take stock of the various more or less hypothetical commitments that have been made with regard to co-operation with the imperial forces in time of war," given that "I do not know how many hypotheses it takes added together to make an established fact."[16] Was the Admiralty achieving centralization by other means?

As for the Canadian naval director, Hose's thinking had been focused by the Canadian federal budget of 1922, but he also analyzed the situation from the standpoint of Canadian interests, the possibility of war in the 1920s not being sufficiently remote to preclude the need for armed forces, and even neutrality might need to be defended. The latter was not a recent issue,

---

13. Committee of Imperial Defence, "Empire Naval Policy and Co-operation," February 1924, LAC, RG 25, vol. 1375, 566.

14. Extract from Official Report Parliamentary Debates, House of Commons, 9 March 1926, LAC, RG 25, vol. 755, 238.

15. L.S. Amery to Governor General, 8 July 1926, LAC, RG 24, vol. 1475, file 743.

16. Skelton to Desbarats, 4 August 1926, LAC, RG 24, vol. 1475, file 743.

since after Confederate troops used Canadian soil to launch a raid against the Vermont town of St Alban's during the US Civil War, the governor of Quebec called out fifteen companies of volunteers for just that purpose, ensuring Canada did not get involved in the conflict between north and south. In the early days of the century German staff officers had proposed landing forces in Canada to attack the US across the border, and somewhat more realistically, "the gunboat SMS *Panther* had in 1905–06 undertaken lengthy voyages in the Atlantic and Pacific oceans and along the east and west coasts of Canada and the United States in search of secret anchorages, in which cruisers could replenish with coal from friendly steamers and prepare for combat. She submitted a report from Seattle on 16 September 1905 covering her voyage along the BC coast to Alaska," in which many "hiding places" were mentioned.[17]

Defending Canada's neutrality was therefore not a purely theoretical matter. Furthermore, in his report the DNS asked policy makers to consider that "our geographical position, particularly on our Pacific coast, makes the advent of assistance from the remainder of the empire a matter for considerable time. This applies even more forcibly to our maritime enterprises, the immense capital embarked in our fisheries, our merchant ships, our sea commerce and their allied industries on shore, than to our territory," the need to defend trade rather than land being a recurring theme in Hose's analysis. He noted, for example, that economic relations with countries other than the United States were worth $695 million. "This sum is just the actual value of the goods and takes no account of the distress occasioned all over the dominion—to the farmer and the lumberman, the artisan and the fisherman, resulting from the dislocation of such an immense volume of trade in all commodities." All such endeavours together added up to $796.5 million. Similarly, the navy had to take militia requirements into account, since the transportation of troops overseas, as had occurred during the First World War, required naval escort.[18]

Among the principles that would guide the creation and maintenance of a naval service to protect trade, natural resources, and the operations of the army was that the Canadian navy was "to be under the complete control of the dominion government," though "the closest co-operation of the Royal Navy and Royal Canadian Navy [was] to be considered of primary importance." The service's first priority would be the defence of bases and ports, followed by the efficient escort of merchant vessels and fishing fleets. A third priority, linked to the second, was the protection of trade routes, with the provision of defensive armament to merchant ships coming fourth. Achieving that aim would take time and planning, a period of ten to twenty years perhaps being required, "the whole scheme being sealed by a special act of parliament." The latter's purpose would be the "prevention of hurried and ill considered annual programmes, and it would give stability to the whole service, as personnel joining (especially officers who make the navy their life's career) would fully understand what prospects were before them."[19]

---

17. Michael L. Hadley and Roger Sarty, *Tin-pots and Pirate Ships: Canadian Naval Forces and German Sea Raiders, 1880–1918* (Montreal 1990), 47; and Jacques Castonguay, *Les Voltigeurs de Québec: Premier régiment canadien-français* (Quebec 1987), 50.

18. Hose to Mackenzie King, 26 October 1922, LAC, MG 26 J1, vol. 77.

19. Ibid.

The navy as it then existed, with its two destroyers and other vessels, was insufficient to meet the first priority, the defence of bases and ports, though it was a better nucleus than a light cruiser and destroyers lacking a naval reserve. Its one basic flaw was that "the permanent force is too small to offer reasonable opportunity to young men to embark in it as a life career, and consequently real efficiency cannot be looked for in a very few years' time." It needed new submarines—the wartime boats *CC 1* and *CC 2* having been sold for scrap in 1920, while *CH 14* and *CH 15* were paid off in June 1922—in order for the RCN to practice anti-submarine warfare, as well as patrol boats for harbour protection. As for the force required to meet all four priorities, that would take about eight years to build and train.[20]

It would also cost about $5 million annually, and in terms of funding Hose was fortunate in the individual Mackenzie King chose to be minister of national defence after the election of 1926. Though the King government had reduced the navy's estimates by a million dollars in 1922, it was in the expectation of building the service up in the years that followed (total appropriations for defence added up to $12.5 million that year). James Ralston's role would be to stand up to other members of Cabinet to ensure all three services could be placed on a firm financial footing, and he succeeded, total appropriations for defence rising from the low of $12.5 million mentioned above to $21 million the year the government fell, in 1930. By comparison, total government expenditures in this period rose from $359 million in 1926 to $442 million in 1930.[21]

The King government might have seen the 1922 budget as a beginning from which the RCN could expand, and indeed expenditures rose steadily in this period, from a low of $1.4 million in 1924–25 to a high of almost $3.6 million in 1930–31. But the service was nonetheless concerned about its future, and took steps to ensure its survival. Hose, promoted to the rank of commodore on 14 August 1923, was part and parcel of this process. As one historian has explained, "a typical luncheon was held in his honour at the Canadian Club of Quebec City on 22 April 1924. Nicely shaping his argument to the interests of his audience (being mainly composed of the local financial community), Commodore Hose told how useful the Canadian navy had been to the Royal Bank of Canada. It seemed that the Royal Bank had experienced great difficulty 'in a certain foreign capital to get its just claim recognized, despite the efforts of the British consul stationed there. It so happened that a squadron of the Canadian Navy was reported to be on the seas in that vicinity. There was no threat made, but ... the arrival of the squadron created just enough impression on the officials of the foreign capital to tip the scales in favour of the Royal Bank.' He concluded in masterful fashion by declaring that 'he had always considered the French to be the finest race of sea-going people of the world.'"[22]

---

20. Ibid; and Ken MacPherson and John Burgess, *The Ships of Canada's Naval Forces, 1910–1985: A Complete Pictorial History of Canadian Warships* (Toronto 1981), 14.

21. Hose, "Memorandum on Naval Policy," 30 July 1926, LAC, MG 26 J4, vol. 124, file 913; B.J.C. McKercher, "Between Two Giants: Canada, the Coolidge Conference, and Anglo-American Relations in 1927," B.J.C. McKercher, ed, *Anglo-American Relations in the 1920s: The Struggle for Supremacy* (Edmonton 1990), 87; and F.H. Leacy, ed, *Historical Statistics of Canada, Second Edition* (Ottawa 1983), H19-H34.

22. James Eayrs, *In Defence of Canada*, I: *From the Great War to the Great Depression* (Toronto 1964), 107; and Canada, Department of National Defence, *Annual Report* (Ottawa 1925–1930).

As we have seen, the visit had been to Costa Rica, and the squadron in question had been made up of *Aurora*, *Patrician*, and *Patriot*, and with the light cruiser having been paid off in the meantime Hose's point was clear. The remaining destroyers, however, could still do their bit to ensure the navy's interests were not forgotten (they would remain in commission until 1929), such as an occasion in 1924 when *Patrician* embarked Prime Minister Mackenzie King in Prince Rupert, as he "was desirous of reaching Nanaimo with the utmost despatch." Sailing at two in the morning, "speed of fifteen knots was maintained until 7 A.M. and then increased to thirty knots." The ship could not, however, show herself off to the full, "owing to bad visibility on account of rain squalls," which forced a reduction in speed to ten knots. The prime minister went ashore in Comox, spending the night in a hotel before continuing to Nanaimo. He later sent a letter of thanks.[23]

With experience came greater sophistication in getting the navy's message across, the naval secretary suggesting in 1927 that "the naval education of the people being the keystone of future naval development, it may be of interest to develop more fully what is being done in this respect." He saw three target audiences: parliament, the press, and the business community. Since the first was the responsibility of the government, there was little to be said there; still, in order "to educate parliament, the press, and business men, the story to be told must appeal primarily to common sense, and to commercial interest; secondarily to sentiment—the idea that Canada, as an autonomous nation within the empire, should provide for the defence of her shore and territorial waters, and eventually should take her share in the defence of the empire. The latter idea though it may appear to be an excellent argument carries least weight when advocating naval needs." Furthermore, "the story must be a consistent story which will appeal in great or less degree to all. One cannot safely use one argument in the imperialistic centres (Toronto and Hamilton) and another argument in Quebec or the prairie provinces.... One must bring opponents and friends to a single line of thought."[24]

Therefore, "the story must avoid all political questions; it must be such that Liberal or Conservative or Progressive can adopt it without prejudice to the policies of their respective parties." The essence of that story was to propound "the policy adopted by the high authorities of the RCN," which was "to emphasize defence not offence—defence of Canadian shipping and territorial waters," a recurring theme in Hose's papers of the early 1920s. "The story told hitherto relates how Canada has two million dollars worth of shipping on the ocean every day of the year; outlines the dangers to shipping at focal points of trade routes in time of war; gives a typical example of the effectiveness of stopping trade in a seemingly unimportant article (tin); and appeals to the business man's appreciation of the value of insurance against commercial risks." Furthermore, "it explains that the RN can only protect the trade routes vital to the empire as a whole and leaves it to the imagination to picture what would be the situation if outgoing and incoming trade were stopped." In spite of what the naval secretary may have said concerning the necessity for universality in the navy's position, in one area it needed to be specifically targeted. "As given to the government

23. Naval News Letter, 15 December 1924, 10–1–9, LAC, RG 24, vol. 3579.

24. Eayrs, *In Defence of Canada*, I, 107.

only, the story concludes with an explanation that an annual naval vote increasing gradually to six million dollars after five years would give Canada a naval force capable of providing for shipping in time of war safe egress and ingress within Canadian territorial waters."[25]

The Navy League, for its part, lobbied for the acquisition of four light cruisers, but given the budgets of the day the RCN was hard pressed maintaining the infrastructure and ships it already had. Even Esquimalt, which was essentially in mothballs, needed constant work just to prevent irreversible deterioration. The dockyard, for one, in the spring of 1924 asked that two painters, a carpenter, and a labourer "be entered and employed continuously in seasonable weather." The problem was that such would mean "no less than an increase in permanent staff," and Commander (Engineering) T.C. Phillips therefore suggested spreading the work over several years, costing $5,642, $5,608, $4,721, and $2,969 as a result. Thus, instead of a regular program of painting, such work would only be carried out when absolutely necessary, though who would make that determination was not clear. The scheme would also avoid another difficulty, as "it has been shown that better results have been reached by dealing with painting work on the lines of repair work, that is to say, estimates and costs to be prepared for headquarters authorization, the work to be performed by contract or by men entered by the dockyard—whichever is the cheaper—and carried out to completion in reasonable time, the other means tend to the enlarging of the dockyard staff, giving to such workmen a feeling of permanence not good, and not in the interests of good dockyard operation."[26]

There were also costs associated with the routine inspection and testing of Esquimalt's facilities should they ever be required for operations, as well as for the "care and maintenance" of *Aurora* and the submarines, which had been paid off but not yet disposed of. This included heating certain spaces and ensuring selected pieces of machinery were "turned." Another drifter due for eventual disposal, *Guelph*, posed greater difficulties, Desbarats having to inform potential buyers that "a report has been received from HMC Dockyard, Halifax, that this vessel has recently developed some rather serious leaks and that in order to prevent her sinking, a considerable amount of pumping has been necessary. The dockyard authorities recommend that authority be given to haul out and repair the *Guelph* as early as possible. Unless early action is taken in this matter, ice will form inside the vessel, preventing pumping out, in which case only beaching can then be adopted as an alternative to sinking, and this will only result in more serious damage to the hull." The purchasers graciously agreed to take the ship away for repairs.[27]

And then, of course, there were vessels still in service to take care of, the RCN operating, besides the two destroyers, four Battle-class trawlers: *Festubert, Ypres, Armentieres,* and

25. Ibid, 108.

26. Phillips to DNS, 20 May 1924, 14–3-1, LAC, RG 24, vol. 3603; and Navy League of Canada, BC Division, to Arthur Meighen, 5 February 1925, LAC, MG 26I, vol. 116, file 119.

27. Desbarats to McGivern, Haydon, and Ebbs, 17 October 1923, Director of Naval Stores to DNS, 21 November 1923, 842–3-3, LAC, RG 24, vol. 5696; Consulting Engineer's Report for the Quarter Ending 31 December 24, nd, 38–5-16, LAC, RG 24, vol. 3591; and Naval Secretary to Senior Naval Officer, RCN Barracks and Manager HMC Dockyard, 15 November 1922, 45–6-1, LAC, RG 24, vol. 3595.

Thiepval. As of November 1922 they were officially designated as minesweepers, and orders were that they "should be kept in a seagoing condition in all respects, stores, ordnance, etc."[28] Although the original intent was to have their crews accommodated in barracks, it was found that, in *Festubert* at least, when the ship "was in commission and her crew living on board, the ship has benefitted to a very great extent, and has improved greatly in appearance; the ship's company have taken a real interest and pride in their ship, and both the officers' and men's quarters have been kept in a state of cleanliness and order not obtainable when the crew work on board as a working party from the RCN Barracks." Therefore, Commander M. Goolden, RN, the senior naval officer for HMCS *Stadacona* (as the base in Halifax was now designated, the armed yacht having been paid off in 1920 and sold four years later), reported "that by having the crews living and continually working service routine in their ships that an appreciable amount of wear and tear and general dilapidation is saved."[29] His recommendation was approved by higher authority.

The RCN's destiny would thus be determined in large part by the intertwined issues of technology and personnel. The latter, at the officer level, posed few difficulties after the budget of 1922, since the navy had only twenty-six positions for executive officers with forty-nine men in service. This did not, however, take into account the need to send many of them to the Royal Navy to advance their education and qualify them for higher positions. Staff officer Victor Brodeur suggested "that every two years we could make a complete shift around of appointments, as we could divide the officers into three equal groups to fill up the three different types of appointments, i.e., shore in Canada, ship in Canada, ship in RN. In addition to this surplus we should have about four officers to meet any contingencies such as death, accidents, etc. This would bring the total of executive officers to forty-three, leaving still a surplus of six officers who can be retired before next April."[30]

Others would retire from time to time, so there was a continuing need to recruit new officers, if only a handful a year. One who came forward in 1923 was René Coulombe, who detailed his qualifications to Victor Brodeur: "My six years of classical education are complete and I am a Bachelor of Arts; I am presently in my first year of studies in philosophy." His question, "I would like to join the navy. What education do I need? Can I enter military college without further preparation? Which college do I need to attend? How long will these studies take? How many years of schooling do I need before I am promoted to the rank of officer? How much does boarding cost at this college? Will I need to sit for an examination for admission to this college? If so, what subject areas does the examination cover?"[31] In subsequent correspondence, he added that "I speak English sufficiently well," the RCN being an English-speaking institution like the Royal Navy it sought to emulate. Coulombe applied and was rejected on the grounds that he lacked knowledge of physics

28. NSO to NSHQ, 22 March 1923, 58–27–1, LAC, RG 24, vol. 5659; and Naval Secretary to Distribution List, 25 November 1922, 58–1–1, LAC, RG 24, vol. 5654.

29. Goolden to NSHQ, 14 June 1925, 132–1–1, LAC, RG 24, vol. 5682.

30. Brodeur to NSHQ, 5 October 1922, LAC, MG 30 E312, vol. 1, file 2.

31. René Coulombe to Victor Brodeur, 16 October 1923, LAC, MG 30 E312, vol. 5, scrapbook no. 2.

and chemistry and was not sufficiently proficient in English. Brodeur stepped forward to defend the potential new entry. On the issue of the science requirements, he argued that "the similarity between the first term of Canadian naval officers and this last term will be used to illustrate that reason of 'lack of knowledge in chemistry and physics' is no handicap whatever. Most of the officers in the first term had never heard a word of physics and chemistry—still they were trained in RN ships and passed examinations for the rank of lieutenant in the RN, including courses in the RN schools, and none of them were handicapped by that lack of knowledge in chemistry and physics." Also, "the instructions given to sea-cadets consist mostly of seamanship, navigation, gunnery, electricity and mathematics; physics and chemistry are very seldom mentioned till these officers proceed to Greenwich for the lieutenant courses, where every instruction starts in the most elementary parts of all subjects."[32]

On the second issue, Brodeur wrote that "the objection raised as to this gentleman being handicapped by his little knowledge of the English language is not considered very sound, considering that the present naval staff officer could not speak a word of English when he joined the navy and passed all his examinations in the RN, besides qualifying as a specialist in gunnery, where a very high standard of knowledge in physics and chemistry is essential, but this officer had never heard a word of it before joining the RCN." Perhaps more important, "considering that Mr Coulombe was interviewed by Lieut. Hibbard and that the interview was held in English, this should have been considered sufficient knowledge for any future education in that language."[33] The refusal to admit Coulombe stood, however, in spite of a rather petulant memorandum from Brodeur advising that "the naval staff officer," namely himself, "whose duties include those of appointment and training in the Royal Canadian Navy, was not consulted in any way in this matter."[34]

That was not, however, the end of the story, and an article in *La Presse* of 24 September 1924, entitled "Are French Canadians being held back?" claimed that "recently, in the Naval Service of Canada, an act of favouritism was committed to the detriment of French Canadians. This is a serious matter, because not only is it a grave injustice to one of our own, it does nothing less than exclude French Canadians from the naval service." Repeating the navy's argument that he had insufficient knowledge of the sciences and spoken English, and in addition that he was not "fit for service," the newspaper claimed that physics and chemistry were not, in fact, required, that the interviewing officer spoke no French, so Coulombe's English must have been up to par, and that Hibbard had declared Coulombe to be "fit for service" in any case. The story suggested that no less a person than the naval director had turned down the candidate's request for entry.[35]

An RCNVR officer in Montreal, Lieutenant Alexandre Brodeur (no relation to the naval staff officer), sent a copy of the article to Hose, warning that "unless the campaign outlined in said article is immediately checked, it will become impossible for me and my officers to

---

32. Brodeur to DNS, 11 September 1924, ibid.

33. Ibid.

34. Brodeur to DNS, 19 September 1924, ibid.

35. "Les Canadiens-français sont-ils mis à l'écart?" *La Presse*, 24 September 1924, ibid.

keep our men and will make our position almost unbearable," the RCN attempting to build up a reserve unit in that city. "May we expect from you without delay a denial of the motives attributed to you in refusing Coulombe's application?"[36] Hose had paid lip-service to the abilities of francophones, as we have seen, and though his reply would be seen as patronizing today, it was in keeping with the nature of discourse in the 1920s and would have been seen as sincere at the time. In a letter to Lieutenant Brodeur, he expressed the view that "of course I am very sorry to see such an article, more particularly on account of the disastrous effect that it will have on the Canadian navy if the French Canadians feel that the director of naval service is anti-French Canadian." He could not, however, provide a defence in the press as such interventions were the responsibility of the minister. "I have laid the matter before the deputy minister and he is taking it up to the minister. Of course the opinion may be held that it would be undesirable to have a controversy in the press (much as newspapers would like that)."[37]

Clearly, Hose was allowed to move ahead with a defence, which was reported in a 26 September article in *La Presse*. Explaining that, although from 1910 to 1914 only twenty francophones had joined the RCN, a greater number of opportunities had opened up for that community during the First World War. Furthermore, some 155 had joined in the period from 1920 to 1924, when Hose became naval director. "I was very happy when a French Canadian, Mr Coulombe, applied for admission, and I was very sorry when he withdrew his application because his parents disapproved. When they consented, I sent Lieutenant Hibbard to interview the young man. Hibbard showed him copies of the examinations the admiralty administers to cadets. Coulombe had not written these examinations, but he had to have comparable qualifications before leaving. Mr Coulombe explained to Lieutenant Hibbard that he did not have broad enough knowledge of mathematics, chemistry, and physics." There was no Privacy Act at the time, so Hose could release to the press information about Coulombe that the latter must have found deeply personal. "Young Coulombe's father was against his leaving; it was not right to send him to England, in these circumstances."[38]

Chemistry and physics were, in fact, required subjects, though some confusion may have arisen in that though they were necessary for entry into the RCN, they were not required for the Royal Military College in Kingston, Ontario. Suggesting that "we do not have a Canadian navy if French Canadians are not a part of it." Hose added that "it would be unfortunate if they could not join. Early in the year, we had eight French Canadians from Sorel in the volunteer reserve in Halifax. Two of them qualified for service, but the other six were unsuccessful. I immediately instructed the Halifax officers to keep the unfortunate candidates, because their failure to qualify was not their fault. I announced that a special instructor would be assigned to these young men so that they would receive their instruction in Halifax in French." The naval service was at the time searching for such an instructor.[39]

---

36. [Lt A. Brodeur] to Hose, 24 September 1924, ibid.

37. Hose to Lt A. Brodeur, 25 September 1924, ibid.

38. "Le Commodore Hose explique le cas du jeune René Coulombe," *La Presse*, 26 September 1924, ibid.

39. Ibid.

Lieutenant Alexandre Brodeur also came to Hose's defence in his capacity as commander of the French-language company of the RCNVR in Montreal (there was also an English-language company in that city). Stating that he had no direct knowledge of Coulombe's situation, he insisted that "Commodore Hose was unfairly attributed sentiments toward French Canadians that I have never known him to harbour in my dealings with him as the commanding officer of the Montreal navy reserve's French Canadian company. It was upon his very insistence that I agreed to organize this company, and I clearly recall the one point about which he was adamant: because the authorities wanted French Canadians to enlist, he felt it would be fairer and more effective to group them together under the command of officers of their own nationality." Furthermore, "I cannot imagine how Commodore Hose could have possibly treated my men and me any more impartially if we had been of English nationality"[40]

It was not the end of the affair, with further arguments as to the need for physics and chemistry (one naval circular said its candidates must have the same qualifications as those entering RMC, which did not call for those two sciences), but even the nationalist *La Presse* accepted the need for knowledge of the English language if one was to do extensive officer training in the Royal Navy. *Le Droit*, for its part, noted that about 100 of 1,000 members of the RCNVR were French-Canadian, as were eighty of 500 members of the Royal Canadian Naval Reserve (RCNR), and 5 percent of the RCN, an overall percentage of 6 percent for the service as a whole.[41] That francophones might be allowed to join the navy as such was left for a future generation to implement. For the time being, and for the half-century to follow, the RCN would be an English-speaking institution.

As for those who successfully entered the RCN as officers (there were six the year the *affaire* Coulombe hit the press), according to Desbarats, "training of officers and men of the Royal Canadian Navy is the same as in the Royal Navy." Some aspects of educating the former we have already seen, but a short comprehensive explanation of the system as a whole might be useful here. Midshipmen were lent to the RN until they were qualified for promotion, while sub-lieutenants (one rank higher) were employed, as far as possible, in Canadian destroyers; some went into RN ships of the same type. "Royal Canadian Navy officers of the rank of lieutenant and above are employed in HMC ships and establishments as far as possible. Those for whom no appointments are available in HMC ships and establishments are lent to ships of the Royal Navy," while "officers specializing in gunnery, torpedo, etc, and men qualifying for higher rating or for non-substantive ratings in gunnery or torpedo, join the Royal Naval Schools of Gunnery, Torpedo, etc, with the permission of the Admiralty."[42]

Llewellyn Houghton, whom we met in the previous chapter, left a detailed account of his experiences in the RN. By 1925, as an officer in the executive branch, "at various times during my career to date I had given consideration to specialising in one particular line.

40. Ibid.

41. "Explications qui n'en sont pas," *Le Droit*, 1 October 1924, "Une réponse au Commodore Walter Hose," *La Presse*, 1 October 1924, ibid.

42. Desbarats to Undersecretary of State for External Affairs, 10 August 1923, 21-1-1, LAC, RG 24, vol. 3610.

There were five main choices: gunnery, which I have to admit held no appeal for me; torpedo, involving not only a knowledge of the weapon but also of all electric installations in a ship; navigation, which did appeal to me a great deal; signals, which involved a close knowledge of all methods of communicating at sea; and anti-submarine, that would clearly be of prime importance in any future war," as it had been in the 1914–18 conflict. "Of most of these subjects I already possessed a reasonable groundwork of knowledge, having done 'short courses' and passed the necessary exams. However, the one thing I knew nothing about was wireless telegraphy, which was still in the relatively early stages of importance as a means of communicating at sea. It irked me that when a telegraphist reported, for example, that he couldn't get a message through, I was unable to argue with him and to point out that if he would do such and such he would have no trouble. I pictured myself as a future signal officer, surrounded by a maze of dials, switches and wires, tapping out or receiving the Morse code at incredible speeds, the admiration and envy of all. So that was what I finally decided upon, and to my surprise my application for a course at HM Signal School was immediately approved." The necessary studies would take nine months, a testament to the complexity of just one aspect of interwar naval operations.[43]

Officers like Houghton seemed to be up to the task, and it was even hoped that they would be able to contribute not just through their work at sea, but through their ability to manage and develop the technology of the day. The senior naval officer in HMCS *Stadacona*, for one, suggested in 1927 that "the specialist officers of the Canadian naval service be given every opportunity and assistance to further the development of the naval service by means of inventions and experiments of service appliances." He went so far as to recommend that "a yearly grant be made to each specialist branch of the service in order to enable experiments of a nature to help the navy, being carried out." Interestingly, part of his thinking was that, in a service much reduced in scope since 1922, many officers could not apply their knowledge to the fullest, and his scheme would thus offer them an opportunity to work to their full potential. "The approval of this recommendation will greatly benefit our specialist officers, who, owing to the very limited amount of specialist work in the Canadian naval establishments, do not get sufficient opportunities to give to the service all the advantages of their highly technical qualifications."[44] There is no record, however, of higher authority having approved the project.

More basic issues were the order of the day, such as Canada's lack of any kind of naval pension act, a topic Hose felt was so important in the spring of 1926, perhaps not coincidentally soon after the Liberal government had adopted a pension plan for Canadians generally, that he wrote the prime minister directly. He apologized for doing so, but insisted that "the situation has reached an acute stage which has not obtained in previous years," and that "there is undoubtedly a growing conviction right through the Canadian navy that the government takes no interest whatsoever in it, and that the hard and efficient work done by all to make it truly Canadian and really efficient is not in the least appreciated by the cabinet." Though he did not say so in his letter to King, the naval director may have

43. F.L. Houghton, "Memoir," nd, 98–99, LAC, MG 30 E444.

44. Senior Naval Officer, *Stadacona* to NSHQ, 11 March 1927, 21-1-18, LAC, RG 24, vol. 3613.

been aware of how difficult it could be to save enough money for retirement given the severe inflation of the First World War and the milder, but not negligible, inflation of the 1920s. "Every time that I visit the naval centres for inspection it is a necessary phase of that inspection that I call for any officers and men who wish to do so to lay before me any complaints or grievances.—It is always the same question from both officers and men.'What is being done about our pensions?' and they are now tired of the answer, 'The minister has promised to bring the matter before cabinet as soon as possible.' "[45]

As for timing, "during 1927 some fifty odd ratings out of a total of 500 composing the permanent naval force are due to complete their first period of engagement…. It has taken a large sum of money and much careful and intensive training to make these ratings efficient…. The greatest inducement to re-engage in the navy is always the prospect of a pension." The conclusion was obvious, and "there is great danger of these men, many of whom have been trained to engineering and artisan qualifications by the service, taking their discharge if no pension bill has been passed." There was already a working model in the form of the Militia Pension Act, so the legislation would not be difficult to draft. Hose informed the minister of his direct approach to King, but his tactics failed to bear fruit. Officers and ratings would have to continue to rely on their own savings to prepare for retirement or early release.[46]

In the context of the time, such was not completely unexpected, and though pension issues might be of some importance to members of the RCN, they could still join and serve for other reasons; for the officers that might include operations with the Royal Navy, which still played an important role in the British Empire and attempted to keep abreast of modern technical developments. One Canadian, future admiral L.W. Murray, recalled his transfer from the battleship *Revenge* to the battleship *Queen Elizabeth.* "We were at that time, just beginning to evolve a system of direction finding by radio, the ordinary radio. We had an experimental one fixed in the *Queen Elizabeth* and a destroyer went with us, practically everywhere we went, and she spent her time going round us from one side to the other, and we tried to get a bearing by the radio RDF arrangement and compare it with the actual compass bearing we would take from the bridge. That went on for a whole year and the last trip I did in the *Queen Elizabeth* was coming back from Gibraltar from the spring cruise with the whole fleet, coming up Channel we ran into fog and we started using RDF bearings. And they were coming along—as the British sailor would say 'they were coming along a treat'—suddenly, the line of bearings branched off to seaward about three miles and continued, and there was some consternation about this, because we couldn't make it out until we realized that a carpenter's hut, a metal carpenter's hut, had been built during this time" on the superstructure of *Queen Elizabeth*, "and that was the direction of which these bearings were then being taken."[47] It was another lesson learned, and one that would recur with respect to radar in the Second World War.

---

45. Hose to King, 19 May 1926, LAC, MG 26 J1, vol. 154.

46. LCM [L.C. Moyer, Mackenzie King's private secretary], Memo, 21 May 1926, Hose to King, 19 May 1926, ibid.

47. L.W. Murray, "Recollections," nd, 20, LAC, MG 30 E207, vol. 4.

Aside from the purely technical, time in the RN could also be a learning experience in terms of training and operations. Houghton recalled some three decades later how, while in *Southampton* of the East Indies Squadron in 1922, the cruiser made way to Karachi to meet colleagues from all three services attending the staff college at Quetta. "The staff 'scheme,' designed to train the three services to work together was, in brief, to land 20,000 men on Karachi's Clifton Beach, together with all their impedimenta, paraphernalia and what-have-you; a modest forerunner of the Operation Overlord landings on D-Day twenty-two years later. It is quite extraordinary how much detail is necessary for such an apparently simple operation. To begin with, we spent a week in Karachi, living in tents, carrying out a thorough reconnaissance, mostly on horseback; but in that time, working in a minimum of ten hours a day, we were only able to produce about half the necessary orders and instructions—over a hundred pages of foolscap with single-spacing, seven maps and charts and four very intricate diagrams." To foster interservice co-operation, "we were all divided into syndicates, with three sailors and seven soldiers and airmen in each. Our syndicate's effort comprised sixty pages—mostly typed by me on my portable—and four maps."[48]

Of greater interest still was to be a participant in and a witness to the Royal Navy's work in policing the empire, which reached a climax in this period during the Chanak crisis. The Ottoman empire having been defeated in the First World War, it had been stripped of most of the lands it had conquered in previous centuries; a subsequent revolution brought a secular government to what was now called Turkey, which found itself in a confrontation with Great Britain over demarcation lines and borders. The Treaty of Sèvres had handed over a slice of territory, centered on Smyrna, to Greece, but the government of Mustapha Kemal Pasha (Attaturk) invaded the area and defeated Greek forces, threatening British units in Constantinople. The British turned to the dominions for help, asking if they each wished to send a contingent. A message was duly sent in cipher, but later the newspapers were also advised of the British request, and in Canada they were able to print it before the government's clerks, who did not work weekends or evenings—the country was not at war, after all—had deciphered it. Canada replied, to the press and to London, that it would not send a contingent to Chanak without a parliamentary vote, and there the King government stood, the incident having turned into a conflict between imperial centralization and Canadian autonomy—at least superficially. In the event, Turkish troops did not attack British positions.[49]

It is, however, the presence of Canadian naval personnel at Chanak that is especially of interest here. For instance, the RCN's L.W. Murray was in *Revenge* in late 1922 and early 1923, "two months of this great battle of wits with Kemal," or Kemal Attaturk, leader of the "Young Turks" who were attempting to westernize their country. The British had 4,000 troops on the Ismid Peninsula "and considerable hope was extended that he wouldn't want to come in. On the other hand, the army that was there, had no artillery, and we stationed the ships around the end of the Ismid Peninsula from the Island of Prinkipo up to, halfway up the Bosphorus in suitable places to provide artillery fire and support for the soldiers on shore. As assistant navigator, I had no very difficult duties to undertake connected with

---

48. F.L. Houghton, "Memoir," nd, 74, LAC, MG 30 E444.

49. Stacey, *Canada and the Age of Conflict*, II, 18–20, 23, 25–6.

the ship, so I got handed over to the staff and we had to find suitable places to anchor these ships in case there was an attack. The places where we could enfilade attacks up the side of a hill and that sort of thing. We had to arrange to fire naval guns at fixed objectives unseen using reduced charges and shooting over the hill, and with aiming points somewhere near the ship and the ship waving about in the current of the Dardanelles, but we felt we had a pretty good arrangement. And having been connected with setting this up and when we exercised occasionally, it fell upon me to direct the fire. If the army called for fire on a certain square on the map, I was able, sitting in the conning tower of the *Revenge*, to decide which ship would be able to reach that spot to the best advantage, and then we sent out a signal, detailing that ship to open fire on that square. So, I found myself as a CRA"—commander Royal Artillery, usually a lieutenant-colonel (equivalent to a commander in the navy) in charge of all the guns of a division—"of the army ashore on the Ismid Peninsula." It was thus an important responsibility, but Murray never fired a shot,[50] diplomacy winning out over force.

Horatio Nelson Lay, for his part, began his Chanak adventure in Rosyth, Scotland before sailing to Chanak by way of Gibraltar and Malta. On 28 February 1923, Lay "arrived at the Narrows and anchored on the Gallipoli side.... The ships in company are: *Royal Sovereign*, *Emperor of India* (RA IV), *Centaur*, and the 1st and 4th Destroyer Flotillas.... In the afternoon I attended a lecture given by General Marden on the events since December, 1920. This lecture was held in an army hut at Khelia and was very interesting. It told of the various campaigns which comprised the Greek advance into Asia Minor and their subsequent defeat and retreat to Kios, Mitylene and Thrace." On 1 March his ship took up a bombardment position commanding the northern approach to Chanak, and in the afternoon the ship's captain and two other officers "landed to look over this ground and to decide on a suitable spot for an observation post," which would correct the vessel's shooting if necessary. Next day, "general quarters were exercised during the forenoon. Afterwards Lieut Com Mends gave a short lecture to officers about 'preparing for war,' the various stages in 'defence stations,' 'preparing for immediate action,' and the procedure during a 'lull in action.' ... During the evening searchlights were exercised in co-operation with the troops ashore." Similar exercises were conducted in the weeks and months that followed.[51]

Like officers, ratings were trained very much along Royal Navy lines, Desbarats reporting in 1923 that "the educational system is the same as in the Royal Navy and the same qualifications for advancement are required." At that time, most members of the lower deck were serving seven-year engagements, though some were under special two to five-year contracts, while a few gunnery and torpedo specialists were on loan from the Royal Navy.[52] Seven-year engagements were, in fact, the RCN's preferred mode of entry, as opposed to recruiting members of the RN's Royal Fleet Reserve or naval long service pensioners, as had been the case in the pre–First World War era. Entrants needed to be between the ages of sixteen and a half and seventeen and a half, with their seven-year engagement actually

---

50. L.W. Murray, "Recollections," nd, 19, LAC, MG 30 E207, vol. 4.

51. H.N. Lay, "Midshipman's Journal," 26 October 1921 to 10 December 1923, LAC, MG 30, E420, vol. 1.

52. Desbarats to Undersecretary of State for External Affairs, 10 August 1923, 21–1-1, LAC, RG 24, vol. 3610.

beginning at age eighteen. They were of special concern in the months following the 1922 budget, for, in contrast to the situation regarding officers, it looked as if the reduced RCN would have an insufficient number of ratings. Staff officer Victor Brodeur filled in the details in September. "Having studied the duties and needs of the Royal Canadian Navy as at present established, I beg to report that I do not consider the present complement of able seamen, ordinary seamen and boys sufficient.... The present complement is supposed to represent a nucleus crew for emergency. I do not think it does fulfill that primary condition.... At present should an emergency arise we could just man the two destroyers only with a four-fifths complement as the total number of the above ratings in the Canadian service is only seventy-seven and eighty-eight is the full complement for the two destroyers at present in the RCN.... This means that in emergency all these ratings would have to be used leaving the barracks devoid of any lower ratings, and no reliefs to meet cases of sickness, death, deserters, incompetency [sic], etc." Perhaps worst of all, "on the outbreak of hostilities the barracks would have no complement except partly trained ratings."[53]

Sending men to the British schools for training was beneficial and inexpensive, but "this reduces our complement of lower seamen ratings below the minimum set down to obtain any efficient results from a nucleus navy." Brodeur calculated that the RCN needed to enrol a further thirty-six ordinary seamen and boys, at a yearly expenditure of about $30,000. "This under our present financial conditions can be easily afforded without interfering in any way with our future developments," though "even the number mentioned would not allow any ratings for the four trawlers mentioned in the new re-organisation." Brodeur suggested there would be little difficulty finding recruits from among the boys discharged from the Youths' Training Establishment, which had been shut down the previous July.[54]

Dealing with wastage, as it was called, was an ongoing effort, and months later Brodeur was still reporting that the RCN's complement for ratings failed to account for those who were temporarily not available for service. He advised adding twelve percent to establishment for that purpose, as was done at the Admiralty. "Evidently the RCN is bound to be very short-handed always, owing to the comparatively large number of the permanent personnel who have to undergo continual courses to be able to give up to date instructions to the active and reserve forces, so this twelve per cent would be inadequate if the ships were always kept steaming, but with a restricted sea-going scheme it would be sufficient to meet our present needs." As things stood, "if a destroyer must be sent to sea for any reasons the barracks complement must be reduced owing to ratings away on courses, and therefore the training of reservist force will suffer considerably." Brodeur recommended adding twenty seamen to a branch that at the time numbered 178.[55] A later memorandum suggested increasing the complement of the barracks on each of the East and West Coasts from sixty-two to seventy-four, though continuing to operate with seventy-seven in each

53. Brodeur to DNS, 18 September 1922, LAC, MG 30 E312, vol. 1, file 2; NSHQ to Admiralty, 19 May 1923, 53-6-1, LAC, RG 24, vol. 5651; and Canada, Department of National Defence, *Report of the Department of National Defence (Naval Service) for the Fiscal Year Ending March 31, 1928* (Ottawa 1928).

54. Brodeur to DNS, 18 September 1922, LAC, MG 30 E312, vol. 1, file 2.

55. Brodeur to DNS, 11 April 1923, LAC, MG 30 E312, vol. 1, file 2.

of the destroyers and sixty in each of the four minesweepers. "The number to be sent to England every year for qualifying and re-qualifying courses will be an average of about thirteen from each coast."[56]

By the end of 1923 the situation was clearer still, as not only was the overall complement of seamen in the RCN deficient, but "about 70 per cent of the RCN personnel being young Canadians, they are still under training for advancement in the lower ratings, so the shortage in higher ratings is becoming more and more pronounced." A second problem was that "the size of the present RCN complement does not give a large enough field of selection for higher ratings," in that "all men entered in the service are not above the average ability, and to be eligible for advancement a man must show signs of superior ability in all subjects, and education is proving a great stumbling block to the young Canadians as the educational standard of young Canadian seamen is lower than that experienced in other dominion navies." Furthermore, "owing to the very limited type of sea training which can be given in Canadian ships at present, it is impossible to expect any Canadian ratings to be able to pass successfully examinations for advancement to leading rates and above. This can only be remedied by sending Canadian ratings for service in imperial ships, but the present complement is too small to allow for the sending away of any ratings for a length of time without seriously hampering our present training organisation."[57]

The situation was not helped by the permanent force's role of training reservists, and "during the past summer the training classes of the RCN personnel had to be practically abandoned owing to the training of the RCNVR officers and ratings, who kept our present instructional staffs fully occupied, and the same results must be anticipated during the training periods of the RCNR force. Therefore under present conditions a Canadian rating will take about three times as long as an imperial rating before he can pass for AB and once there, owing to lack of sea experience, he will probably never be eligible for further advancement. This will mean always having on loan from the RN nearly all the higher ratings of the RCN, thereby discouraging Canadians, who cannot foresee any future chance of advancement, though not due to any causes under their control." To rectify the situation, Brodeur recommended increasing the RCN's complement by two petty officers, six leading seamen, and twenty seamen, with consequent increases in other branches of two writers, two cooks, and two victualling assistants. Also, an additional shipwright should be added to each coast.[58]

Order-in-Council 1008, however, which had set the complement of the permanent force RCN at 500, remained unamended, though in October 1924 the minister of National Defence requested it be increased to 550, based on estimates provided by the naval director, himself relying no doubt on the work of Victor Brodeur over the previous year and a half. The additional fifty men were required for two destroyers, four minesweepers, and the two RCN barracks, where reservists trained during the summer and permanent force

---

56. Brodeur to DNS, 26 April 1923, ibid.

57. Brodeur to DNS, 10 December 1923, ibid.

58. Ibid.

sailors received instruction year-round. The increase was approved, but that did not put an end to demand, the senior naval officer for the RCN barracks in Esquimalt insisting in October 1925 that the complement on the West Coast needed to be increased by 14 percent. "Experience has shown that generally speaking the only leading seamen who can pass for petty officer professionally are those who have done training afloat in one of HM ships," he wrote to the naval secretary, but such a scheme could not be practicable unless these candidates for higher rank were replaced while undergoing training and experience.[59] And so the cycle of personnel demand and supply began once again.

It was one where the devil was indeed evident in the details, whether it was a signals officer asking for an increase in complement "to be able to maintain regular watches, and to form signal classes whereby all signal and W/T ratings may be brought on a par to ratings of the Royal Navy," or an engineer officer requesting additional engine room artificers to cover for those training in England and to allow for a more extensive use of minesweepers off the West Coast.[60] Similarly, "owing to our destroyers carrying out cruises as separate commands, it is considered essential that one sick berth rating should be drafted for these cruises. The present complement shows one rating at each base and it is therefore considered that a minimum of two sick berth ratings for each coast is essential."[61] In one final example, in September 1924 acting Commander Charles Beard, the senior naval officer for the RCN barracks at Esquimalt, asked "that the complement of ship's cooks be increased by one, in order that one shall always be available for duty in minesweepers.... Fourteen months of continuous difficulty has been experienced in the question of cooks in minesweepers. As this duty must be performed by somebody, it is better that a rating skilled at cooking should be employed to add appreciably to the comfort and well being of the officers and ratings serving in these ships."[62] And it was but one request among many.

Numbers were but one issue—pay was another, and it would seem that it too was difficult to resolve. As Brodeur reported at the end of 1924, "it is considered that the present RCN pay and allowances are not satisfactory for the present or any future naval organisation in Canada." Based on Admiralty regulations, they did not "take into account Canadian requirement," where the cost of living was higher; they were also noticeably lower than in the army or Royal Canadian Air Force. "Surely a naval officer is entitled to have a home the same as any other human being; he is the only one in Canada not allowed to because he would have to keep up two separate establishments and he cannot do so on his present salary. Canada is a young country and can only hope to further develop by early marriages, whatever anyone may say. It is not when a man is forty and getting sufficient salary to have a wife that he can start a home." Also, "the naval officer is at a great disadvantage in that in Canada his appointment changes every two or three years, and if married

59. SNO, RCN Barracks Esquimalt to NSHQ, 15 October 1925, Minister to Governor General, 21 October 1924, DNS to Minister, 21 October 1924, 1–24–1, LAC, RG 24, vol. 5586.

60. SNO, RCN Barracks Esquimalt to NSHQ, 15 October 1925, ibid.

61. Brodeur to NSHQ, 4 January 1923, ibid.

62. A/Cdr Charles Beard, SNO, RCN Barracks Esquimalt, to NSHQ, 16 September 1924, 58–27–1, LAC, RG 24, vol. 5659.

and intends to remain so he must be prepared to meet very heavy expenses at the end of nearly every appointment; whilst the military officer is practically permanent in his regiment and now wherever he moves all his expenses are paid, though he is already better off than the naval officer."[63]

If pay was the carrot, though not a large one, then punishment was the stick, though as with caning and similar sanctions awarded to boys in the early part of the post-war period, the RCN as an institution did not wish to be overly harsh. Brodeur, in his capacity as naval staff officer, noted in September 1924 how "during the present year a comparatively large number of detention punishments have been awarded in the Royal Canadian Navy, most of them being awarded to the West Coast personnel." He wondered whether some procedure "should be brought into force to prevent such a serious punishment being given too lightly, as appears to have been the case on the West Coast." In a somewhat sarcastic reference to "the apparent wave of crime passing through the RCN personnel on the West Coast," he seemed to lean more toward defending delinquent sailors than supporting the system of which he was a part. He felt that disciplinary problems could be attributed to "over-strict discipline in small matters," or "alternating disciplinary waves." In his opinion, "the latter would appear the predominant factor if one can judge from the great disparity in the punishments awarded for similar offences by different ratings."[64]

An example in point was Ordinary Seaman James Robert Miller, a member of a minesweeper crew on the West Coast. "The award of detention to this rating for the offence indicated appears, on paper, to be a most unjustified punishment when the age, 18½, and the naval service experience of that young rating (he joined the service in April, 1923) are taken into consideration." With only five months in the navy, perhaps a lesser sanction would have been just as effective in convincing a young mind of his wrongs, and Brodeur was willing to advance that concept to a general principle. "In view of the fact that nearly seventy per cent of the RCN personnel consist of very young men, the award of such punishment as detention should be finally decided by headquarters who are disinterested personally, but interested in the general welfare and future of the RCN personnel. The result of 'detention' on a young man under twenty never had any improving results, if one can depend on the opinion of judges in nearly all the civilian courts, who have had more experience in these matters than the naval service. The reason is very sound and has been proved; a young man sent to detention who cannot reason fully like a person of twenty-four years or more, will only think that the punishment is a disgrace and the proof is that on coming out from prison he immediately leaves his surroundings to start afresh elsewhere, or goes from bad to worse, thinking his reputation and future soiled forever."[65]

Though he provided no evidence, such as testimony from one of the judges in question, Brodeur nevertheless pursued his argument. Whereas in civilian life a young man leaving prison could simply move to a different community, in the RCN he returned to his ship a

63. Brodeur to DNS, 2 December 1924, LAC, MG 30 E312, vol. 1, file 2.

64. Brodeur to DNS, 13 September 1924, LAC, MG 30 E312, vol. 2, file 19.

65. Ibid.

marked man. "It is admitted that there are cases, such as theft, immorality, etc, when such a punishment is justified, but asleep on duty does not justify such drastic action to punish a young and inexperienced rating."[66] The naval staff officer, however, was not in tune with his peers, and his comments are of most interest in that they were exemplary of the level of frank commentary allowed at the higher levels of the RCN. The latter's view, institutionally, was evident in the response to Brodeur, to the effect that it was "not considered desirable to change usual naval procedure in awarding punishments. Should an apparently unduly severe punishment be awarded full particulars of the case should be called for. If an officer cannot administer naval discipline in his position as commanding officer of a naval establishment in accordance with the KR&AI [Kings Regulations & Admiralty Instructions] and usual naval custom he should be relieved."[67] That did not necessarily mean that detention was the punishment of choice, and in regard to theft it was felt in some quarters that dismissal, as services no longer required, was in order. The offence "is considered a very serious one in the service, owing to the great number of opportunities for persons inclined to thieving and due to the very limited amount of protection afforded against this crime," wrote Brodeur, and there seemed to be no contradictory voices.[68]

The whole purpose behind such administrative infrastructure as pay and discipline was, of course, to train Canadian men in time of peace so they would be available in time of war. One evident challenge in the early post-war years, however, was the junior status of most of the RCN's ratings, the result being a shortage of more senior men to act as instructors. In 1924, Hose proposed borrowing, from the Admiralty, two petty officer physical and recreational instructors, and six leading seamen, for a two-year period. Of other challenges there were many, as the senior officer of *Stadacona* related later that fall. Recruits were arriving not in batches, but singly, so work had to be found for early arrivals until classes could be organized. Also, petty officers and leading seamen acting as instructors had other duties, so that "when a minesweeper is sent away it takes a petty officer and leading seaman" away with it, reducing the pool of instructional staff.[69]

The school had nevertheless managed to put together a routine, so that "as soon as possible after arrival in barracks, they are given their kit, and shown how to mark, wear, and stow it. Then they are given a two weeks disciplinary course under the gunnery staff. On completion of this they are given instruction in seamanship, that lasts about ten days and includes a run through the seamanship manual, vol 1, and (depending on the season) boat pulling and practical instruction in minesweeper. After that they are considered available for duty in minesweepers or barracks as required, being employed in working parties, or put into training classes as circumstances permit. As a rule they are not drafted to *Patriot* until they have been three months or so in the barracks." On the job training was thus an important part of a rating's early education. If he was a stoker, he was turned over to the

---

66. Ibid.

67. Minute by WH, 17 September 1924, LAC, MG 30 E312, vol. 2, file 19.

68. Brodeur to DNS, 20 October 1924, LAC, MG 30 E312, vol. 1, file 13.

69. Senior Naval Officer, *Stadacona* to NSHQ, 28 October 1924, 21–1-1, LAC, RG 24, vol. 3610; and Hose to Minister, 25 March 1924, 1–24–1, LAC, RG 24, vol. 5586.

An aerial view of the east coast destroyer HMCS *Patriot*. (LAC e-007140909)

engineer officer for technical instruction after the two-week disciplinary course. As for signalmen and telegraphists, "there has been no new entry signalmen or telegraphists entered direct as such, for over a year now, but they would carry out the same training as seamen for their first month, after which they would be turned over to the signal officer for instruction in their branch, in accordance with 'signal training instructions.'"[70]

Of these specialists stokers seemed to be entering in larger numbers, so their initial training will be followed in some detail as an example of what was entailed in preparing a young Canadian for service in the RCN. As the engineer officer for HMCS *Naden* related, the syllabus of training for a second class stoker began with "ten days under personal instruction of a stoker petty officer," itself beginning with "five days elementary engineering lectures on machinery in use in ships and naval establishments, elementary knowledge of their construction and principles and materials used, general arrangement and use of machinery in a ship, course taken by steam and water in passing from the boilers through engines and back again to boilers, general duties of a stoker.... The stokers manual is followed as far as practicable in this instruction supplemented by use of models and sketches." Another two days focused on "practical instruction in use of shovel and firing coal burning furnaces," although another day was spent in a minesweeper and two in a destroyer, "locating machinery, tracing pipes and connections etc." Next came a month in the depot workshop "as ERA's mates, special attention being given that they are afforded every facility to learn names and use of tools, various machines in use for repair work, and the names, parts and uses of engines and fittings under repair both in workshop and on ships. During this period instruction is given in running and maintenance of motor boat." From there the stoker was drafted to a minesweeper for a few weeks, the chief engine room artificer having special orders to attend to his instruction. Finally, "As soon as qualified in watchkeeping in minesweepers, drafted as vacancies occur to HMCS *Patrician.* (Average period in minesweepers, four months.)"[71]

The above refers, of course, to members of the RCN, but as we have seen following the 1922 budget the naval service created two reserve systems to train potential sailors and to create a link between the navy and the community at large. One of them was the Royal Canadian Naval Reserve, which would be made up of men who already had training and experience in the merchant marine but who would be available for short periods of time to learn the purely naval aspects of their trade. In 1926–27 they reached a strength of 123 officers and ratings. To recruit them, "a gentleman will be selected in each town to act as registrar of the RCNR. This gentleman will, if possible, be a master of shipping or assistant master of shipping, and will thus have an intimate knowledge of, and be in close touch with the sea-faring population of the town." Himself enrolled in the RCNR as a paymaster sub-lieutenant, "he will be given the opportunity of performing, every year, fourteen days' naval training in RCN barracks, to acquire a knowledge of naval life and conditions, which should be most useful to him in the course of his duties with the RCNR." His task was straight-

70. Senior Naval Officer, *Stadacona* to NSHQ, 28 October 1924, 21–1–1, LAC, RG 24, vol. 3610.

71. Engineer Officer *Naden* to Senior Naval Officer, HMC Ships and Establishments, Esquimalt, 11 November 1924, ibid.

HMCS *Patrician* at Esquimalt in 1924 with three British D-class cruisers, including, at left, one of two such cruisers fitted with an aircraft hangar under the bridge. (DND E-12820)

forward, to "arrange to call for recruits, prepare and send to headquarters questionnaires, and attest men, etc," who, in 1923–24, could train either from 12 November to 23 December, from 14 January to 24 February, or from 3 March to 14 April. The hope was that about fifty or sixty men would be available for the second and third courses, time being insufficient to recruit the first course to full complement.[72]

By the autumn of 1923 there were registrars in such potential recruiting areas as Charlottetown, Quebec City, St John, Halifax, Montreal, Lunenburg, Prince Rupert, Victoria, and Vancouver. Many of them would be kept busy, since managing a group of people whose primary employment was with some other organization required no little flexibility and imagination. The registrar in Montreal, for one, noted that "it would appear that the great difficulty to face is the fact of seamen filling in their questionnaires, and a day or so later, joining and sailing in a ship, being unable to wait for the training period." Still, "the benefits to be derived by members of the RCNR (pay and board during period of training, retainer after twelve months' service, and free kit) and the nature of the training to be given, are considered to be such that the department may expect to obtain good candidates for enrolment from amongst the best type of the sea-faring population of Canada." The problem of men signing up only to go to sea in merchant ships was thus not a major concern, and "the department may expect, also that men who wish to enrol in the force, and who fill in a questionnaire, if compelled by circumstances to leave the port on a voyage in the ordinary course of their profession, (1) will keep in touch with the registrar of their district, and obtain information from him as to whether their applications to enrol have been accepted; and (2) will consult the registrar as to period when they can be received for training."[73]

Signing on to a merchant ship after enrolling in the RCNR was not irresponsible on their part, and "it is appreciated that members of the RCNR desire to be continuously employed, and in receipt of wages, and though naval training, if accepted for enrolment, will give them steady pay for three weeks, and probably for forty-two days on the assumption that they will be finally accepted after the first three weeks of training, yet they must take into account the possibility that their applications may not be approved. Must therefore take advantage of the opportunity of signing on for a voyage." Authorities would just have to be accommodating, at least to a certain extent, and instead of a few periods of training with fifty men, the service should, according to NSHQ, organize more frequent training periods, even if only twenty men could attend each. The standard was that a member of the RCNR undergo forty-two days of training within a year of enrolment and twenty-eight days a year subsequently.[74] Logically, the RCN kept in touch with the minister of Customs and Excise, noting that it "should much appreciate it if you could see your way to encouraging the seafaring men of your department, both deck and engineroom [sic], to join up with this force."

72. Naval Secretary to SNOs, RCN Barracks Halifax and Esquimalt, 26 October 1923, 121-1-1, LAC, RG 24, vol. 5680; and Canada, DND, *Report of the Department of National Defence (Naval Service) for the Fiscal Year Ending March 31, 1927* (Ottawa 1927).

73. Naval Secretary to Registrars, RCNR, 30 November 1923, E.M. Hiney, i/c Naval Section, to NSHQ, 27 October 1923, 121-1-1, LAC, RG 24, vol. 5680.

74. Naval Secretary to Registrars, RCNR, 30 November 1923, 121-1-1, LAC, RG 24, vol. 5680.

They were required to undergo only one long period of training their first year, with shorter periods thereafter, and "it has been very abundantly proved that men who enrol in a reserve force are a great asset to both their employers and the masters of the vessels in which they serve, as they acquire a sense of smartness, pride and discipline difficult otherwise to attain."[75] Just as logically, the RCN sent similar calls for volunteers to the ministers of Railways and Canals and Marine and Fisheries, who promised to co-operate.

By early 1924 the system was, in essence, up and running, though its first few years would obviously be a learning process for its paymaster sub-lieutenants. One reported how "very few of the applicants have a certificate of birth, and they all object to the trouble and expense of declaring an affidavit before a notary," while "the young fellows do not seem inclined to enlist, but I have had numerous applications from men over the prescribed age, who have nearly all seen service in some naval unit." Another issue was that "only those out of employment have applied. Men who are working will not quit their jobs to do their training."[76] There was little to be done regarding the age limit, since "it is essential that the Force in its early days should be composed of younger men who can continue to serve during several periods of enrolment and qualify for advancement before attaining the age where discharge is necessary." Under the circumstances, however, "applications from men who have had former service with the naval forces, and who are only a year or two years over the prescribed age, may be forwarded for consideration as to whether in view of their war service the age limit can be extended. Certification of service in the naval forces must be forwarded with all such applications," their experience being no doubt considered of much value in the RCNR's formative period.[77]

Recruiting was not a simple matter of waiting for eager young men to enter one's office, registrars having to go some distance afield on one-man campaigns to locate potential naval ratings. H.T. Preedy, the registrar in Halifax, thought visiting Pictou, eighty miles away, would be worthwhile, as some men there had already indicated a willingness to volunteer.[78] Similarly, the registrar for Quebec City visited Sorel in 1923 after NSHQ suggested that "it would seem quite worth while to establish the RCNR in any town in which interest in the force is shown, and the visit of the registrar would accomplish this."[79] Much like a missionary, a successful registrar needed to bring no little amount of dedication to his work, Preedy later advising that "I have had a number of enquiries from young men whising [sic] to join the RCNR from the vicinity of Cape Sable and Shelburne. Of course these I have replied to and forwarded them conditions of service and questionaire forms with the request that they renew their application in September, whether they will do so or not remains to be seen. Unfortunately they do not seem to be able to 'take in' these conditions without a personal interview."[80]

75. E.M. Macdonald to Minister of Customs and Excise, 13 December 1923, ibid.

76. Geo Kirkendale, Registrar Victoria, to NSHQ, 16 January 1924, 124–15–1, LAC, RG 24, vol. 5681.

77. Naval Secretary to SLt (Pay) Geo Kirkendale, 29 January 1924, ibid.

78. H.T. Preedy, Registrar RCNR Halifax, to NSHQ, 3 October 1924, 124–2–1, ibid.

79. Naval Secretary to DNS, 14 October 1924, ibid.

80. H.T. Preedy, "Memorandum re Naval Training," 7 July 1925, ibid.

Another area of recruiting in which some registrars were willing to put in an extra effort concerned language. Though instruction would be in English, the number of potential candidates could still be increased if initial contact could be made in the sailor's mother tongue. As J.A. O'Dowd, the registrar in Quebec City, explained, "as many requests are made to me for French literature concerning the Royal Canadian Naval Reserve, I would appreciate it very much if you would send me, as soon as possible, all information concerning the organization of the force that you have written in the French language.... I feel certain that if I were furnished particularly with posters and pamphlets explaining 'conditions of service' written in French it would stimulate my recruiting work. If I had also the detailed regulations for the RCNR, amplifying or amending as necessary the RNR regulations written in the French language, this would be of very valuable assistance, indeed, to me." Though preparing the necessary materials might "take considerable time," the navy was willing to accommodate O'Dowd's request.[81]

Though not a thankless task, the role of registrar provided little in the way of job security, one's position being at the mercy of the cycle of government revenue and expenditure. In the fall of 1925 Naval Staff Officer G.C. Jones warned the naval secretary that expenditures for the rest of the fiscal year had to be curtailed. "Accordingly I do not feel able to recommend that any recruits be entered for the RCNR THIS year. This is undesirable, but cannot be helped. It will be essential to enter recruits next year in order to keep the reserve alive," it not having yet become a viable institution. Furthermore, Jones recommended "that approval be obtained to dispense with the services of the registrars at Lunenburg and Charlottetown. Considerable notice should be given these two gentlemen in order to convince them that their services are being dispensed with for no other reason than that of economy." No registrar would be appointed at Prince Rupert for the same reason. The freeze lasted only from October 1925 to March 1926, however, and by the fall of 1926, the senior officer naval reserves was calling for the recruiting of fifty men in addition to the sixteen already attested in Halifax, two in Lunenburg, six in Charlottetown, seven in St John, thirty-four in Quebec, twenty in Montreal, eight in Prince Rupert, thirteen in Vancouver, and six in Victoria. In the training season that ran from October 1926 to March 1927, a dozen officers performed their required twenty-eight days' training, and one did fifty-six days, while ninety-four ratings completed either fourteen-days' training or thirty days of volunteer service (or on-the-job training).[82]

Such indoctrination was necessary, since sailors' education and experience in the merchant marine only partly prepared them for operations within the navy. One facility for such training would be at Halifax, which would also serve to prepare members of the RCNVR, of which more later. Issues to be resolved before training could begin were the construction of a suitable parade ground, drill being part of the syllabus, as well as a gun battery and a torpedo and electrical shed to cover some of the more warlike aspects of a

---

81. J.A. O'Dowd, Registrar Quebec, to NSHQ, 31 January 1924; and Naval Secretary to SLt (Pay) J.A. O'Dowd, 8 February 1924, 124–15–1, LAC, RG 24, vol. 5681.

82. G.C. Jones to Naval Secretary, 22 September 1925, 124–3–1, LAC, RG 24, vol. 5681; and Lt (G) A.M. Hope to DNS, 13 September 1926, Hope to NSHQ, 9 April 1927, 121–1–1, LAC, RG 24, vol. 5680.

reservist's education. Prioritizing was important, Victor Brodeur warning in late 1922 that "a good many instructional appliances are required to render our naval training establishments efficient and they can only be purchased by small quantities each year owing to very limited appropriations."[83]

An excellent example of the effort involved in setting up and running a unit of the RCNR was the one in Quebec City, though it may have been exemplary in facing more difficulties than the others. The story begins in late 1923, when Desbarats contacted Théophile Béland, an agent for the Department of Marine and Fisheries in that city. It was not an entirely friendly letter, relating how "upon returning from his trip to organize the navy reserve, Lieutenant Hibbard reported to me that in every port except Quebec, the shipping master or his deputy accepted to be the reserve recruiting officer. He also reported that you objected to the shipping master's acceptance and that, consequently, he made arrangements with a lawyer who was prepared to do the job."[84]

Placing a lawyer in charge of recruiting for a service he knew little about, from a community with which he had little contact, struck Desbarats as being counterproductive. He attempted to convince Béland that the task was not too onerous, especially for a shipping master already aware of the needs of the service and the nature of a merchant mariner's work. "I am afraid you may have been given a somewhat overstated view of the work to be done, and perhaps, of some potential disruptions to your office. Because the shipping master must ensure that the ship's company's agreements are signed, he comes into contact with the men, yet he can easily handle the very limited number of agreements to be prepared for the reserve. He may register fifty men during the first year, and in subsequent years, record the few changes that may occur among this small number of sailors. As you can see, there is very little actual work; it can easily be incorporated into daily work and affects those men enlisted as the ship's company." As for the men he would be recruiting, "the training these men will receive in the reserve will benefit them and produce results that will advance commercial navigation a great deal. It would be regrettable should the port of Quebec not contribute to the movement." Béland took on the burden.[85]

The duty may have been a logical extension of what the shipping master was already doing, but it still required a certain amount of work, and that might call for a certain increase in infrastructural and logistical support. For example, in the spring of 1924 the registrar in Quebec City requested that a telephone be installed in his office. "I may say that I devote myself to the duties of the position of registrar for about two hours every day in the week, from 5 to 7 p.m. excepting Saturday and legal holidays.... This condition exists even at this time of the year, but more especially so when the training season is in full swing.... As we are now in the early days of the formation of the force and as I have been appointed only since the middle of December last, it is essential that I keep myself well posted to answer queries that are made on all sides.... Here at the marine department, where I am employed, we have a switchboard affording telephonic connection with every office

---

83. Brodeur to Hose, 6 September 1922, 1078–2-1, LAC, RG 24, vol. 4044.

84. Desbarats to Théophile Béland, 10 November 1923, 124–5-1, LAC, RG 24, vol. 5681.

85. Desbarats to Théophile Béland, 10 November 1923, Béland to Desbarats, 15 November 1923, ibid.

in the day time, but there is no phone in mine. The operator leaves the board at 5 p.m. daily, excepting Saturday when she leaves it at 1 p.m," meaning that he was without service at exactly the times when he carried out his work as registrar. The night watchman was available to take calls, but also had patrols to conduct. Cost of a telephone would be $4.82 monthly, and the entry in the phone book would refer to the RCNR. No less a personage than the director of the naval service approved the installation, with concurrence from the deputy minister and a written statement from the Department of Marine and Fisheries that it had no objections.[86]

Similarly, later in the summer the registrar requested a letter box, but was refused, though he would repeat the request in the years that followed. Other impediments to his work included boxing exhibitions at the local drill hall, which forced the closure of his recruiting quarters there, though only for a week. As we have seen, he made up for these difficulties by working in the field, including a trip to Sorel in early 1924. As a result, that year, "though the season is getting late, I feel that it will be possible to recruit a few more men from Quebec, and if a few can be had in Sorel this will bring my number pretty well up towards the quota allotted to me."[87] He did even better than that, and the naval secretary had to advise that "your recruiting campaign in 1923–24 was so successful that you obtained the number of members of the force who are allotted to your district. It is necessary to give the other districts the opportunity of obtaining their quota of men, and it is not, therefore, possible to accept, for the present, a large number of recruits from Quebec." However, "if you receive any applications for enrolment from any exceptionally suitable men, the department will be prepared to consider their names, but it is not desired to receive questionnaires from men in the Quebec district as to whose suitability there is any doubt in your mind."[88] In Quebec City, at least, the RCNR seemed to be doing well.

Another active RCNR division was in Halifax, where the registrar was also successful in getting a telephone installed, though only after considerable correspondence. In Charlottetown, meanwhile, Registrar G.H. Holbrook "distributed some posters in the outlying ports of George Town, Souris Montague and Tracadie, unfortunately practically all of the young fishermen had left early for the lumber woods but they will be back in the spring." Still, Holbrook was "negotiating with some young men with sea experience hoping to secure a few at least suitable for the service, and no doubt in the early spring I can complete my compliment [*sic*]."[89] The complement, or quota, was something of a controversy in New Brunswick's main port, since "nearly all the men of the St John Division ship out of St John during the winter months, and Montreal during the summer, and it would appear to me that if they are transferred to Montreal Division, St John will make a poor showing."[90]

---

86. Registrar RCNR Quebec to NSHQ, 27 May 1924, ibid.

87. J.A. O'Dowd, Registrar, to NSHQ, 24 February 1924, Registrar RCNR *Quebec* to NSHQ, 21 November 1923, NSHQ to Sub-Lieutenant (Pay) J.A. O'Dowd, 11 August 1924, ibid.

88. NSHQ to Sub-Lieutenant (Pay) J.A. O'Dowd, 12 September 1924, ibid.

89. G.H. Holbrook to NSHQ, 26 December 1923, 124–3-1, H.T. Preedy, Registrar RCNR Halifax, to NSHQ, 21 July 1924, 124–2-1, LAC, RG 24, vol. 5681.

90. B.S. Purdy, Registrar, to NSHQ, 26 May 1924, 124–4-1, ibid.

Though at headquarters total numbers were far more important than the strengths of individual divisions, that registrars were in a sense competing with one another might be taken as a sign of dedication and conscientiousness.

The RCNR was only one means of training men part-time so they might be available in an emergency; another was the Royal Canadian Naval Volunteer Reserve (RCNVR), which, unlike its counterpart, accepted volunteers right off the street, as it were. In 1926–27 their strength reached twenty-four officers and 577 ratings, only counting those who actually attended training. Since indoctrination was the main purpose of the scheme, instructors would of course form its nucleus, but where these men would be found, and whether the RCN could provide them, was not clear in the Volunteer Reserve's early days. One possibility, broached by Victor Brodeur in early 1923, was that they "may be recruited as a special branch of the naval service and called reserve instructors.... As these ratings are not liable to sea service they cannot therefore form part of the RCN, which is a permanent and sea-going force."[91] Clearly, Brodeur was attempting to avoid having the RCNVR become a drain on the RCN, one approach toward this end being to make the former more autonomous of the latter. As with the early days of the RCNR, however, which chronologically paralleled those of the RCNVR, everyone was learning as they went in organizing a reserve system.

Such was clear in Quebec City, where at the end of 1923 Acting Lieutenant Gauvreau, the company commanding officer for the division there, complained that "it has been brought to my notice that a position of lieutenant RCNVR was offered by the Department of Naval Service to Mr G. Coote, advocate of this city." The problem, though couched as a question, was whether it was "always the rule of the department to appoint officers directly from head-quarters; before advising the commanding officer who are in charge of companies.... I feel that it would be better for the success of this reserve if we were consulted before giving new appointment."[92] Brodeur, as naval staff officer, had to explain that Mr Coote had in fact been the lawyer temporarily, as it turned out, appointed to be registrar for the RCNR in Quebec City. As we have seen, the shipping master took over those duties, but in the meantime, "this young gentleman, while only under probation awaiting the department's final approval of his enrolment [sic], did quite a lot of good work and published several articles in the papers to help our recruiting." He was offered a commission in the RCNVR, the naval secretary reminding Lieutenant Gauvreau that "appointments of officers in the RCNVR are made at the discretion of the Honourable the Minister of National Defence, and whilst in certain cases, it is convenient to obtain the recommendation of the company commanding officer, such procedure is in no way necessary."[93] There the matter stood.

As well as issues pertaining to personnel company commanding officers and headquarters in Ottawa had to deal with equipment and supply. Each division would need

---

91. Brodeur to DNS, 5 January 1923, LAC, MG 30 E312, vol. 2, file 14; and Canada, DND, *Report of the Department of National Defence (Naval Service) for the Fiscal Year Ending March 31, 1927* (Ottawa 1927)

92. Act/Lt Gauvreau, CCO Quebec to NSHQ, 4 December 1923, 124–5-1, LAC, RG 24, vol. 5681.

93. Brodeur to DNS, 11 December 1923, NSHQ to Lt. Léon Gauvreau, 15 December 1923, ibid.

certain items to carry out the basic training that was its *raison d'être*, such as the webb equipment in which a sailor carried water, food, ammunition, and other necessities for operations ashore. "The Webb equipment is now the recognised equipment throughout the British forces," wrote Naval Staff Officer Victor Brodeur to both the director of the naval service and the deputy minister, "and I consider that it would be very unfair if our volunteer rating were allowed to be trained with discarded equipment from other forces when the militia man alongside him in the same town is fitted up to date. All naval field training books are now written to meet the requirements of the Webb equipment." In addition, each unit would need instructional mock-ups of fuse boxes and similar ship-board items to learn their trade. Ordnance in the form of the 12-pounder gun, which "can be purchased from Admiralty stock at Halifax," would serve a similar purpose. Also on Brodeur's list were Lewis guns for anti-aircraft training and .303 rifles with .22 inserts to practice musketry. It might seem like a lot, but the naval staff officer warned that "the great attraction to the naval service, especially for a civilian element such as a volunteer force, is the great variety of instructions it is comprised of, and once you prevent these various instructions from being given, the attraction disappears."[94]

Whether or not they obtained the equipment they thought they needed—and it would seem that in the main they did not—the RCNVR companies nevertheless managed to recruit young Canadian men interested in what the navy had to offer. They were entering a world which, like the RCN it was supposed to support, was hierarchical and far more focused on a sailor's obligations than on his rights. For example, when at the end of 1924 Brodeur held a court of enquiry into activities of the Quebec half company, he found discipline "below normal." Some of the apparent reasons for this state of affairs may have reflected his own personality rather than the exigencies of the service, such as "the company commanding officer at times has been inclined to enforce most strict discipline" or "the effect of this over-strict discipline on raw recruits has evidently caused a state of antagonism of the ratings towards their superior officers." Other reflections, however, were very much in tune with the navy's institutional views. For instance, "the present petty officer has not been of any assistance to his commanding officer by not properly carrying out his duties of interpreter between the ratings and their commanding officer. On occasions he has decidedly sided with the ratings instead of strongly supporting his superior officer." Another comment reflected the RCN's perceived need to maintain class divisions within its ships, as "the nomination of Beaudoin Lemieux to acting sub-lieutenant after he had failed to pass as able seaman seems to have caused a certain amount of discontent, as the gentleman in question is certainly not above the average. This has undoubtedly assisted in lowering the respect of the ratings for their superior officers."[95]

Quebec City was not the only division to experience such difficulties, Lieutenant E.R. Mainguy reporting in early 1927 how "there is a certain amount of friction in Regina between the CCO [company commanding officer] and the remainder of the officers, principally Lieut Hall." The details are of some interest, as they exemplify how the conflicts that

---

94. NSO to DNS, 20 April 1923, LAC, MG 30 E312, vol. 2, file 20.

95. Brodeur to DNS, 17 January 1925, ibid, file 16.

could build up within a reserve division differed from those in the RCN. As Mainguy related, "the CCO is the deputy attorney general for Saskatchewan and has his office in the parliament buildings which are far removed from the RCNVR headquarters. He is a very conceited gentleman and has continually informed me what a success he has made of everything he has undertaken in his life, starting from office boy. He is inclined to look down on anyone in a position below him, but is always charming and very flattering to those above or of an equal standing. He has told me that he really hasn't got much time to bother with the RCNVR as he is far too busy. He is extremely fond of advertising and in this way has done a lot for the RCNVR which has an excellent name in the town. He objects to sending in returns etc, and has his own ideas as to how the RCNVR should be run, taking very little notice of his officers or their opinions."[96]

Such were not the characteristics of the ideal naval officer, and the result was resentment on the part of the division's junior officers, especially Lieutenant Hall. The latter, "being an extremely talkative and loud-voiced man, is very prone to getting up and telling the CCO exactly what he thinks of him, his ideas, and ancestors. The CCO feels it is beneath his dignity to quarrel with a man who has not made much of a mark in the world." Arrogant he may have been, but the commanding officer seemed unable to establish his authority, not exactly the recipe for a happy ship. There was hope, however, in that "most of the real work of the half company is done by Lieut Ellison who is a quiet, unassuming type of man, and endeavours to act as mediator between the CCO and Lieut Hall. He has been trying to do everything but badly needs the assistance of a paymaster. I interviewed Mr Poyntz who is a writer in the half company, and consider he would be suitable for enrollment as an acting paymaster sub lieutenant. At present he is in charge of two departments in 'Simpsons,' and has an excellent knowledge of accounting etc." Also cause for optimism was that "in spite of the state of records of the half company and the lack of co-operation between the officers, the ratings and general appearance of the CHQ [company headquarters] show up well. They have enrolled a splendid type of rating, mostly boys attending the university."[97] It would seem that intelligent recruiting and a few dedicated junior officers could go far toward creating an effective environment for training.

Within months, Ellison was recommended for appointment as acting company commanding officer, and a month after that the naval director was reporting that "experience during the past four years (since the RCNVR was organised) shows that it is very desirable that the commanding officers of companies and half companies of the RCNVR should hold the acting rank of lieutenant-commander (corresponding to major in the militia)." Responsible for "the efficiency and upkeep of their units," these officers had to see to the drill and training of fifty to 100 officers and men, manage the storage and use of stores, arms and clothing, arrange for the care of a company headquarters building, as well as personally supervise "a considerable volume of correspondence with the various branches of Naval Service Headquarters in connection with entry, advancement, drill, pay, recreations, etc,

96. Lt E.R. Mainguy to DNS, 14 January 1927, 114–11–9, LAC, RG 24, vol. 5680.

97. Ibid.

of their unit."[98] Desbarats concurred, but was not in favour of promoting lieutenants who only had four years seniority, eight years in rank being the RCN norm. Company commanding officers would continue to be the lowest-ranking unit commanders in their districts, as those commanding infantry battalions were lieutenant-colonels, the equivalent of commander in the navy. The expectation was that, in time, the sailors would achieve the necessary seniority for promotion.[99]

While they waited they still had their varied duties to perform, recruiting always being a high priority. By the spring of 1923 the RCNVR seemed to be doing well in that regard, "as the seaman branch is getting rapidly filled up in some of the recruiting towns," but the engineering branch was noticeably under-strength. Victor Brodeur suggested all recruiting officers be advised.[100] It should be noted here that reserve divisions were not only seeking new men for their own units but for the RCN as well, the permanent force institution hoping that "all provinces of Canada may be represented in the RCN." A scheme mooted near the end of 1923 would advise company commanding officers in the western provinces when there were vacancies in the permanent force, and instruct them "to select volunteers either from the RCNVR or outside." The aim would be to get four recruits from Winnipeg and two from each of Saskatoon, Edmonton, Regina, and Calgary. "Once this system is established, there should be no difficulty in recruiting any required number of ratings."[101]

Those who opted to join the RCNVR underwent training on the odd evening and weekend during autumn and winter. In the spring of 1925, for instance, Lieutenant F.R.W.R. Gow, a naval intelligence officer, was asked to attend drill at the RCNVR company in Prince Rupert. "I had no connection whatever with the RCNVR movement," he related to the RCN barracks in Esquimalt, but the unit's commanding officer insisted, as "I was the first RCN officer to visit Prince Rupert since the movement had got well under way, that I should make an impartial report of my observations." Gow found quarters very cramped, though "new quarters, to which unit will move, appear to be ideal." The company held well-attended drills three times a week for promising officers and men. The engineering officer owned a large motor boat, which was used for instruction in addition to the government-issue whaler.[102]

In contrast, the company in St John, New Brunswick, seemed to face rather severe difficulties, as reported by Lieutenant (Gunnery) A.M. Hope: "The quarters are such that it is impossible to mount the 12-pdr.... gun supplied and this is kept mounted in the armouries, some distance outside the centre of the city. The officers claim that this is a difficult position to get the men to go to, and as a result, very little has been done as regards giving

98. Hose to Minister, 22 March 1927, 101–1-2, LAC, RG 24, vol. 5678; and Mainguy to DNS, 21 February 1927, 114–11-9, LAC, RG 24, vol. 5680.

99. Desbarats to DNS, 28 March 1927, A. Eveleigh Eagar, "RCNVR Memorandum No 13," 12 January 1928, NSHQ to Lt C.A. Pettigrew, RCNVR, 30 January 1928, 101–1-2, LAC, RG 24, vol. 5678.

100. NSO to DNS, 10 April 1923, LAC, MG 30 E312, vol. 2, file 14.

101. Brodeur to DNS, 16 November 1923, 1–24–1, LAC, RG 24, vol. 5586.

102. Lt F.R.W.R. Gow to RCN Barracks Esquimalt, 7 April 1925, 114–16-9, LAC, RG 24, vol. 5680.

The rebuilt Esquimalt dry dock in 1926. At 1,173 feet long and 126 feet wide, the reopened facility was able to accommodate the largest ships of any fleet. (LAC PA-800458)

instruction in gun drill, field training, etc. This fact was noticeably apparent this year at Halifax barracks, where it was reported to me that the St John company, RCNVR, was a long way behind the other eastern units, RCNVR in all gunnery matters. Their seamanship knowledge was equal to any other unit, taken as an average, but the deficiency in gunnery was not made up by this." At least the condition of the 12-pounder was "fair," as were the rifles and other armament, while "the spirit of the men on parade on the evening of 8th July was good, the seamanship and signalling classes deserving special mention." Out of a strength of eighty-one, however, only twenty-eight had been present.[103]

In worse condition in these early years, perhaps reflecting some of the other difficulties it faced (as described earlier in this chapter), was the Regina half-company. Commander Percy Nelles inspected the unit in December 1925, and the future chief of the naval staff found little to be impressed with. "As this half company has no building in which to drill it was stated that it was impossible to hold an inspection of the personnel—the last drill carried out by this half company was 'some time in August,'" a less than encouraging state of affairs. It was hoped the Saskatchewan Mortgage Building Company building would become available for rent, though Nelles noted that "I instructed the company commanding officer to endeavour to find some place in which to stow the whaler during the winter months—on the 20th November it was on the jetty," nor had it been possible to properly inspect stores as many were still in packing crates.[104]

Nelles's report cannot be put down to overly exacting standards, as his comments concerning the Calgary half-company were generally favourable, even though there were too few sailors to provide the commander with a decent guard of honour. "Ratings were put through the movements of the rifle, W/T receiving instructions, knots and splices, 12 pdr loader, and did a trick at the wheel of the steering model. All the personnel are keen and, with the exception of two recent recruits, had a good working knowledge of subjects and drills." Headquarters, store rooms, etc, were found to be ship shape, though the unit needed paymasters.[105] Two years later the unit was better still, as "the Calgary half company is up to strength and doing well. Their headquarters is the best I have seen and the PO instructor—Petty Officer Mitchell—takes a great pride in its appearance.... All the officers get along well and work together, taking an interest in the half company.... The ratings—again mostly university boys—are keen and anxious to learn all about the navy ... The company commanding officer informed me that he could easily raise a full company if it were allowed."[106]

Most reserve half-companies and companies were in good condition, if inspection reports were any indication, and after the evening drills of autumn and winter came two weeks of indoctrination sometime in the spring or summer, the first such course beginning in April 1923. By 1926 headquarters staff could report how eleven officers of the executive branch had completed annual training that year. "These officers took general courses in

103. Lt (G) A.M. Hope to DNS, 23 July 1925, 114–1-4, ibid.

104. Cdr Percy Nelles, "Regina, Sask, RCNVR Half Company—Inspection of," 20 November 1925, 114–11-9, ibid.

105. Nelles, "Calgary, Alberta, RCNVR Half Company—Inspection of," 21 November 1925, 114–14-9, ibid.

106. Mainguy to RCN Barracks Esquimalt, 26 January 1927, ibid.

navigation and pilotage," while "two surgeon lieutenants reported for one week's training and were attached to the district medical officer for training and experience in naval methods of medical procedure." Also, "two paymaster lieutenants reported for fourteen days' training. These officers were given instruction in general accounting," and "all officers were given opportunity of going to sea in vessels attached to the base." Some 226 ratings also reported for annual training, of whom thirty-seven qualified as able seamen, twenty as seamen torpedomen, eight as seamen gunners, eight as signalmen, four as telegraphists, eleven as stokers first class, and two as leading stokers. In general, therefore, "the training season was a successful one."[107]

The ultimate experience for a member of the RCNVR, however, was to attend an RCN cruise. In September 1924, for example, about fifty of them embarked in ships of the North America and West Indies Squadron while they were cruising in Canadian and Newfoundland waters. These were not mere destroyers along the lines of *Patriot* and *Patrician*, but British cruisers, with thirty RCNVR men going into HMS *Constance*, eleven in *Calcutta*, and a dozen in *Capetown*. "These ratings … during their time in the ships take duty as part of the ship's company in which they serve, and take part in all drills and exercises carried out during the cruise." Some of their colleagues, however, had already done better still, an executive officer, ten seamen, four engine room artificers, four motor mechanics, six stoker petty officers, and ten stokers having served in the battle cruiser *Hood*, with an officer and ten seamen joining the battle cruiser *Repulse*.[108]

One of those in *Hood* was Ernest Fecteau, a member of the Quebec half-company, who left headquarters on 25 June 1924, to serve in the Royal Navy's showpiece. "The first two days were spent in seeing the principal parts of the ship," he reported in December. "They left Vancouver on July 5th escorted by four destroyers, HMS *Repulse* and HMAS *Adelaide*, going to San Francisco arriving there on July 7th at 4 o'clock, when they passed through the Golden Gate an American destroyer came to meet the squadron." Hospitality in San Francisco was excellent, then, "during the cruise from San Francisco to Panama for which lasted twelve days the *Hood* and *Repulse* held battle practice with their big guns also torpedo firing this was quite interesting." Sailing through the canal, the ship underwent a "tropical medical examination" in Colon before arriving in Jamaica, which Fecteau found "very hot." Then, on "1st of August speed trial between the *Hood* and *Repulse* was made and tested and lasted for four hours at full speed at the rate of thirty-two knots during that time torpedo firing was held, very interesting work and good instructions for the RCNVR ratings." Fecteau's cruise ended in Halifax on the 5th, and the program was repeated in subsequent years.[109]

The RCN, of course, had ships of its own, even if they were not of the type and numbers it would have preferred. Though *Aurora* had been paid off, there still remained *Patriot*

---

107. "RCNVR Training," nd, 10–1-9, LAC, RG 24, vol. 3579; and Desbarats to Undersecretary of State for External Affairs, 10 August 1923, 21–1-1, LAC, RG 24, vol. 3610.

108. "Men of the Royal Canadian Naval Volunteer Reserve Cruising in Ships of the North America and West Indies Squadron," 16 September 1924, 10–1-9, LAC, RG 24, vol. 3579.

109. Report by Ernest Fecteau, nd, ibid.

and *Patrician* as well as the four minesweepers, and since cruises into foreign waters had been part of the navy's operational routine before the 1922 budget, there was no suggestion that they should cease simply because the squadron had been reduced in size. The starting point for any cruise or operation, whether in home waters or overseas, was information, hence the need for the naval intelligence section of the Department of National Defence. One order of business was "a Canadian coast report," which "will present an adequate conception of the status and facilities of the principal Canadian ports." Such a system of reporting had, in fact, been established after the war, but abandoned when the RCN's staff was reduced. As described by Desbarats, procedure would call for district intelligence officers in Ottawa, Halifax, and Esquimalt to prepare reports on the ports within their areas, for which purpose they would be authorized to conduct visits and interview local authorities. "While this coast report is being undertaken primarily in connection with the Admiralty intelligence system, it is also hoped that it will form a useful book of reference for certain government departments, as it will present in concise form the commercial facilities of the Canadian ports and record of their development."[110]

Other government departments (as well as the army and air force) could also provide useful information, such as a report by J.B. Hunter, deputy minister of Public Works, on the facilities at Union Bay, BC, including a general description of the port, the length and width of the outer harbour, quayage, warehouses, lifting appliances, docks, patent slips, building slips, coal, oil, harbour craft, water supply available to shipping, shipbuilding and repair firms, the town itself, the wireless station, steamship services, naval establishments, the government arsenal, the garrison, defences, and aerodromes or seaplane stations. Subsequent reports covered Ladysmith (Oyster Harbour) and Nanaimo. There was thus plenty to keep investigators busy, with twenty-eight such ports in the Ottawa intelligence area, twenty-one for the Halifax office, and ten within Esquimalt's jurisdiction. In late 1925 Desbarats asked the deputy minister of Health for information, specifically for the naval intelligence division, on the number of hospitals at each port, along with details as to whether they were naval, military, government, or civilian, whether they treated general conditions or focused on infectious diseases, where they were located, whether they were suitable for officers or ratings, the approximate number of staff, the extent of laboratory facilities, whether they contained special departments such as x-ray, as well as general sanitary conditions in town and what diseases were prevalent. Similar requests went to the dominion statistician, on power plants, and to the Dominion Arsenal at Quebec.[111]

As for the more general duties of district intelligence officers, Halifax can be taken as an example of what was expected of them. The area of observation was bounded in the east by the 40th meridian, and on the south by a line drawn from Savannah to Bermuda to 40° west. "The Halifax Intelligence Office is in effect a sub-centre, the recognized district intelligence officer for Canada being at Ottawa," and hence in contact with the Admiralty, as

---

110. Desbarats to Commissioner Dept. of Customs and Excise, 12 January 1923, 1017–35–2, LAC, RG 24, vol. 3846.

111. Deputy Minister Public Works to Desbarats, 26 July 1923, Desbarats to R.H. Coats, Dominion Statistician, 11 August 1923, Desbarats to Deputy Minister of Health, 6 November 1925, 1017–35–2, LAC, RG 24, vol. 3846.

well as the Canadian navy. "Within this area efforts are made to collect all information of naval interest, information of military and air force importance also being forwarded." To that end, "the district intelligence officer is assisted by eight reporting officers at Sydney, North Sydney, Louisbourg, Canso and Yarmouth in Nova Scotia; St John and Chatham in New Brunswick; Charlottetown in Prince Edward Island." There was little cloak and dagger involved in these officers' activities, and "the main source of information at Halifax Intelligence Centre, is from the press," mainly the New York *Commercial*, the *Halifax Herald*, and the *Daily Telegraph Journal*. As well, "a certain amount of information is also obtained from government officials in the Customs, Public Works and Marine and Fisheries Departments, and from private commercial concerns, but there is no organization for obtaining a continuous flow of such information. Consequently repeated requests for information from these officials, which are necessary to keep existing information up to date, are not usually received very kindly and replies are often received many months after the request, and then only after repeated visits to the officials concerned. This is inclined to make district intelligence officers most unpopular."[112] Intelligence offered few opportunities to cover oneself with glory.

Headquarters therefore had to rely on the officers' sense of duty, and there is no evidence that they failed in that regard, visiting British merchant vessels, in part to "remind captains of the importance of keeping in touch with the naval service, and endeavour to impress upon them the importance and usefulness of information contained in forms," which the captains were expected to fill out, "and the excellent means these forms afford of maintaining liaison with the naval service. The customs service also carry out this work at Halifax, occasional ships being visited by the district intelligence officer as opportunity affords." The work load was thus one to prohibit idleness, the staff of the district intelligence office consisting of a senior clerk, a clerk stenographer, and a messenger (later dismissed as unnecessary). In 1924 their output included a Canadian coast report, for the Halifax area, a guide to Atlantic shipping, a report on the coal areas of Nova Scotia, another on the press in that same area, the compilation of "war organization of district intelligence office," "corrections and amendments to senior naval officer's confidential book set," as well as a wide variety of weekly, monthly, quarterly, annual, and "from time to time" returns.[113]

On the West Coast in this period, Lieutenant F.R.W.R. Gow prepared a monthly intelligence report, that of 17 December 1923 being reasonably typical. It provided information on American war vessels in the area, the USN's winter manoeuvres, the construction of new oil bunkering facilities in Seattle, the despatch of US aircraft to Asia, and plans for a long flight by the US Navy. It also provided intelligence on merchant vessels in the area, a strike by Vancouver longshoremen, and the opening of a seamen's institute in Vancouver. The report also discussed the state of supplies on the West Coast, breaks in trans-Pacific cables, US fisheries protection along the coast of Alaska, and an investigation into the death of an

---

112. District Intelligence Officer Halifax to DNI, Admiralty, 12 December 1924, 1920–152/1, LAC, RG 24, vol. 8200.

113. District Intelligence Officer Halifax to DNI, Admiralty, 12 December 1924, Annual Report by the District Intelligence Officer, Halifax, 1926, ibid.

American marine officer in the Caroline islands.[114] It was all, however, perhaps more eclectic than comprehensive.

Ships on operations thus had access to certain types of useful information, if necessary, and though the RCN was a small navy after the 1922 budget, its vessels were no more idle than the intelligence officers. In the course of 1923 West Coast ports visited by minesweepers included Hubbard, St Margaret's Bay, Vancouver, Esquimalt, Comox, Safety Cove, Alert Bay, and Bamfield. In July 1925 G.C. Jones, the naval staff officer, drew up a program for West Coast operations in consultation with the director of the naval service, which, for the minesweepers, included customs patrols, RCNVR training, more customs patrols, towing targets, boiler cleaning, towing a target for *Patrician*, gunnery exercises, yet more RCNVR training, standing by in case customs needed them for any kind of emergency, and operations "with military," all from mid-July to early September. In one East Coast cruise, *Festubert*, with a lieutenant-commander (navigation) on board, first adjusted her compasses and wireless telegraphy gear, then landed the senior officer before making way to Hubbard's Cove, then to Chester and Halifax. "During the passage from Halifax to Hubbard's Cove the W/T set was tested by communication with RCN barracks and Chebucto Head DF station. Chebucto Head reported that set was not tuned correctly.... Soon after this W/T set broke down and was not in action again." The ship experienced no other defects.[115]

In Halifax Harbour, RCNVR ratings were used as boat's crew "and received instruction in the use of lead line at helm at sea as well as general duties of a seaman." Even so simple a task could reveal important lessons, however, and *Festubert*'s commanding officer asked "that new boats be supplied to the ship of a type similar to a service gig but of a smaller size to take the davits in ship. Boats at present in ship are not considered sea-worthy and are too cumbersome to be of any use for instruction of RCNVRs in pulling. Also it is submitted that dropping gear be fitted to each as it is not safe to lower a boat in a seaway at present without this gear."[116] Later, *Ypres* was given the task of recovering an anchor and cable that *Patriot* had slipped, but such operations were halted because of "the dangerous nature of the coast, the uncertain weather conditions prevalent in that vicinity, and the small probability of being able to locate and pick up the lost cable owing to the rocky nature of the bottom."[117] It should be noted that work for the minesweepers, on the East Coast at least, was somewhat seasonal, Commander M. Goolden, the senior naval officer in HMCS *Stadacona*, recommending that one of them be laid up during the winter as "it is not anticipated that both minesweepers will be required for gunnery or minesweeping instruction."[118]

Interestingly, the RCN seems to have played little or no role in the attempt to halt rum-running to the United States, where alcohol was prohibited from 1919 to 1934, the navy

114. Lt F.R.W.R. Gow, Monthly Intelligence Report, Esquimalt, BC, Area, 17 December 1923, E57–63–3, LAC, RG 24, vol. 11,918.

115. Hose to DNI Admiralty, 26 May 1924, 58–1–1, LAC, RG 24, vol. 5654; and G.C. Jones to NSHQ, 20 July 1925, Lt-in-Command *Festubert*, Letter of Proceedings, 27 July 1926, 132–7-5, LAC, RG 24, vol. 5682.

116. Lt-in-Command *Festubert*, Letter of Proceedings, 27 July 1926, 132–7-5, ibid.

117. Cdr M. Goolden, SNO, *Stadacona*, to NSHQ, 17 August 1926, 134–7-5, LAC, RG 24, vol. 5683.

118. Cdr M. Goolden, SNO, HMCS *Stadacona*, to NSHQ, 30 November 1926, 134–1-1, ibid.

limiting itself to inspecting vessels before they were purchased by enforcement agencies such as the RCMP. More local problems were another matter, however, the general officer commanding the area next to the East Coast requesting, in the summer of 1922, that *Patriot* and *Patrician* make way for Sydney, "on account of strike there." The senior naval officer in the region issued the necessary instructions, "unless Dept Naval Service, Ottawa, orders otherwise."[119] There was something of a hitch, however, the defence department's judge advocate general advising that "there is nothing contained in the Naval Service Act similar to that contained in the Militia Act with regard to the employment of naval forces in aid of the civil power. The act, however, provides that the governor-in-council may place the naval forces, or any part thereof, on active service at any time when it appears advisable so to do by reason of any emergency. (Emergency meaning—war, invasion, or insurrection, real or apprehended)." Emergency was thus defined rather strictly, and a coal miner's strike might not count, especially since it was up to parliament to determine whether "war, invasion or insurrection" was indeed staring the Canadian people in the face. In the case of a riot, however, a naval (or air force) officer could act in accordance with common law.[120]

The navy would thus play little or no role in strike-breaking and similar activities, though it would occasionally provide aid to civil authority in other ways. One of *Patrician*'s more unusual operations was conducted at the end of 1924, when on 12 December it raised steam, prepared to make twenty knots, "in order to proceed in search of the Nanaimo Bank robbers." Before leaving the dockyard jetty in Esquimalt, the captain consulted with the chief of provincial police, and "as the bank robbers had by now sufficient time to get into American waters it was considered that the *Patrician* could be of more use inside the American islands in Rosarie Strait. With information at our disposal it was to be our duty to report suspicious craft to both American and Canadian police. Our activities in these waters were hampered by not having the right of search." The task was further complicated by rain squalls, and for her labours the destroyer could do no more than report a suspicious "fast motor boat" that was sighted once but could not be found subsequently. The patrol continued until 1130 hours on 13 December, when *Patrician* was recalled to Esquimalt.[121]

Some tasks were thus unique, and one that fit that category best was support for a "Round the World Aeroplane Flight" by the Royal Air Force's Squadron-Leader A. Stuart McLaren in a Vickers Viking flying boat in the spring of 1924. Specifically, Lieutenant-Colonel L.E. Brome, the British representative for the project, asked for help in that portion of McLaren's route lying between the northern island of Japan and Canada's West Coast. "His request is for a vessel to proceed along the route which follows the line of the Kurile Islands and the Aleutian Islands to Alaska, leaving dumps of motor fuel approximately every 300 miles along this route." The minesweeper *Thiepval* was deemed to be "an entirely suitable vessel," and though "undoubtedly her absence during the first half of the summer will interfere to a certain extent with the training of the Royal Canadian Volunteer

119. Senior Naval Officer, to Naval Ottawa, 19 August 1922, 33–7–1, LAC, RG 24, vol. 5633; and F.W. Cowan, Chief Narcotic Division, Dept of Health, to Cdr T.C. Phillips, 2 March 1927, 91–7–2, LAC, RG 24, vol. 5676.

120. LCol R.J. Orde, JAG, to CGS, 7 September 1922, LAC, MG 30 E133, vol. 108.

121. Senior Naval Officer, RCN Barracks Esquimalt to NSHQ, 2 January 1925, 34–7–5, LAC, RG 24, vol. 5633.

Reserve officers and men," Hose noted that "there are still two other vessels available to carry on this work and it is recommended that HMCS *Thiepval* should be detailed for this work."[122]

Clearly, the naval director was eager for the RCN to take on the task, as he argued enthusiastically in its favour. First, "without Canadian government assistance at this stage, it is highly problematical, in fact really doubtful whether the proposed round-the-world flight could be carried out and there would be serious prospect of the flight coming to an end in Japan." There was also the matter of prestige to consider, and "the Royal Canadian Air Force, it is understood, has the sanction of the minister to afford the proposed aeroplane flight all the facilities of their stations and plant. If this naval assistance is given as well, it will result in the flight being carried out owing to Canadian assistance for at least 170[degrees] of longitude or practically half way round the globe." Related to the above were other international considerations: "In view of the Canadian acceptance of a share of the Pelagic sealing patrol at the entrance to the Behring [*sic*] Sea, which has been in force for approximately ten years and to which practical effect has never, so far, been given, it would be very desirable to show the Canadian naval flag in these waters." The RCN would benefit in more practical ways, as "the actual cruise of HMCS *Thiepval* from Canada to the northern island of Japan will be exceedingly valuable experience for the officers and men of the Canadian naval service engaged." Finally, though perhaps less relevantly, Hose noted that "the United States are also undertaking a round the world flight and for this flight all the resources of the United States Navy considered necessary to assist it are being tendered by the United States Navy Department."[123]

Permission was granted and headquarters in Ottawa issued the necessary orders to the effect that *Thiepval* was to make way to the island of Yezo, Japan, by way of Alaska, the Aleutian Islands, and the Kuriles, taking Lieutenant-Colonel Brome as a passenger. The ship was to deposit fuel every two to three hundred miles, the operation beginning no later than 1 March. The number of sites involved numbered about twenty and required permission from either the US, Japan, or the USSR, and diplomacy proved to be the cruise's greatest challenge. A few weeks after receiving his orders, the senior naval officer at Esquimalt was warned that, according to Britain's Colonial Office, "Japanese minister foreign affairs regret cannot grant permission for *Thiepval* to call at ports mentioned in Japanese territory, Hakodate excepted.... Hakodate may be visited by *Thiepval* but at other places Japanese vessel must be chartered for supplies."[124] More encouraging was the Soviet response, which allowed the ship to carry out her work "provided pilot and local officials are on board." After much to-ing and fro-ing, the Japanese agreed to *Thiepval*'s visits under similar conditions.[125]

Other preparations focused on the ship herself, as it might require "reconditioning" at such places as Nemora, and upon its return to Esquimalt. Since the Shell Oil Company was

---

122. DNS to Minister, 7 February 1924, 133–1-5, LAC, RG 24, vol. 5682.

123. Ibid.

124. Naval Ottawa to SNO, Esquimalt, 8 and 27 February 1924, Desbarats to Under Secretary of State External Affairs, 9 February 1924, ibid.

125. Colonial Secretary to Governor General, 3 March 1924, Ambassador Tokyo to Navy Department Ottawa for Col Broome, 25 March 1924, ibid.

at least in part sponsoring the flight, it was deemed fair that it pay for some of the work *Thiepval* would need following the wear and tear of her cruise. Similarly, the RCN's accountants requested "a decision whether any proportion of the pay or victualling of the officers or men of *Thiepval* during her cruise to Japan should be charged to the Company concerned in the British round-the-world flight.... The argument for making such charge is that *Thiepval* probably carried a larger complement than she would have carried if employed in Canadian waters." The naval secretary, however, noted that there was also a counter-argument, to the effect that "a main object of the cruise was that, in addition to rendering assistance ... the officers and men of *Thiepval* would gain useful sea training and the department would obtain full value in this respect from the experience gained by Lieutenant Shipley and the reserve men embarked in addition to complement, their service being very useful voluntary service afloat."[126] Similarly, as with so much else related to the cruise, who would pay for food was the subject of no little negotiation.

Thiepval returned from the operation on 21 August, her adventures described in detail by Frederick B. Watt of the *Edmonton Journal*. The flight itself had been a failure, the aircraft never reaching Canada's West Coast, but the ship's crew still had good stories to tell. The Battle-class trawler, "only a few tons heavier than Columbus's *Santa Maria* ... had covered over ten thousand miles of dangerous and uncharted seas, had crossed the Pacific Ocean to Japan and had passed through enough thrilling experiences to last an ordinary man a lifetime." Because of her size, "she has been, undoubtedly, the most maligned ship that ever flew the White Ensign. During those long months in which her name flickered occasionally from out of the north or from across the Pacific the press correspondents referred to her as everything but what she really was. She was given titles ranging from 'steamer' to 'fishery patrol vessel.'"[127]

As for the details of the voyage, Watt noted that the crew numbered less than thirty, and her members came face to face with the challenge ahead before even leaving Canadian waters. "It was necessary to anchor at the entrance to Seymour Narrows until the tide turned. *Thiepval*'s nine knots were good enough for minesweeping but not for bucking a tide that at times runs at twelve knots through that slender passage at the north of Vancouver Island." The vessel headed for Alaska, setting up fuel dumps along the way. "Dutch Harbour was the beginning of the really strenuous part of the journey. The vast expanse of sea and volcanic islands lying between this harbour and Japan offered little comfort apart from a few sheltered and uncharted harbours and the opportunity of obtaining fresh meat in the way of game. Of coal there was none and fresh water was a thing that was rarely to be found." Fuel was an especially difficult problem, as "the minesweeper's coal capacity was 160 tons. This, it was quite apparent, would be insufficient for the long run that lay ahead, and an extra supply was brought aboard. Five tons were stored in the stokehold and twenty more were carried on the deck in sacks. To add to this, sixteen tons of gasoline for the sea-

126. A. Woodhouse, Naval Secretary, to DNS, 5 December 1924, R. Pearson, Assistant Engineer, to DNS, 24 September 1924, 337–1-5, LAC, RG 24, vol. 5687.

127. Frederick B. Watt, "Ten Thousand Miles in His Majesty's Canadian Minesweeper *Thiepval*," 25 October 1924, 10–1-9, LAC, RG 24, vol. 3579.

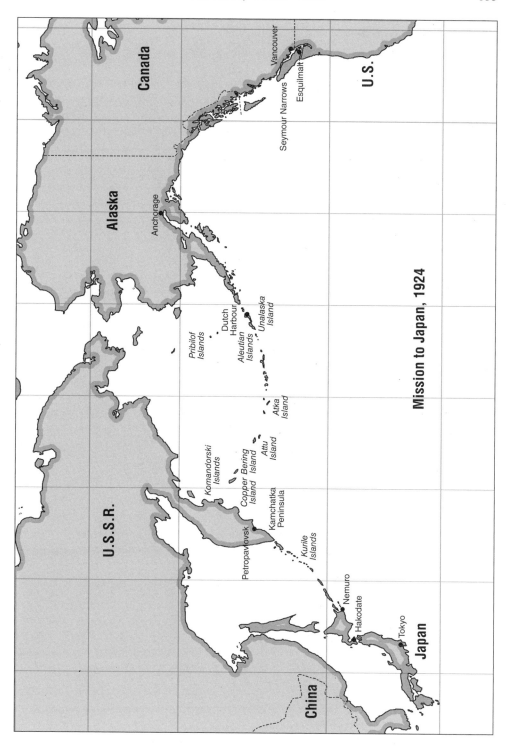

Canada

Vancouver

Seymour Narrows

Esquimalt

U.S.

Alaska

Anchorage

Pribilof
Islands

Dutch
Harbour

Aleutian
Islands

Unalaska
Island

Atka
Island

Mission to Japan, 1924

Komandorski
Islands

Copper Bering
Island Island

Attu
Island

Kamchatka
Peninsula

Petropavlovsk

U.S.S.R.

Kurile
Islands

Nemuro

Hakodate

Tokyo

Japan

China

plane were stored on the deck in tins. By the time all this extra cargo had been taken aboard the water line of the vessel was halfway up the lower deck scuttles and the ship had something like two feet of freeboard," not much for crossing the Pacific.[128]

It was not a great concern, however, as "officers of the ship claim that the fishing vessels in and around Dutch Harbour go to sea under like conditions and that the seaworthiness of the vessel is not affected, although the slightest sea splashes inboard." Still, "the deck was awash practically all of the time, and it was not long before the tins of gasoline and sacks and coal were in a swirling mess. Under ordinary conditions, the logical thing to have done would have been to have let the whole deck cargo go over the side, as it threatened to do at any minute, and thus lighten the ship even further. The success of the round-the-world flight, however, hung on that gas, and without the coal *Thiepval* would have been unable to deposit the petrol where it was needed. Up to their thighs in boiling sea and in constant peril of being swept overboard, Lieutenant Pressey and his deck crew toiled night and day to save those valuable sacks and cans." So, "one by one the bags of coal were passed down into the stokehold, that was soon so full that the stokers had scarcely room to swing their shovels. Fresh lashings were produced and the gasoline cans secured again." On 31 March, a little over a month after leaving Esquimalt, *Thiepval* anchored in Nazan Bay at Atka Island in the Aleutians.[129]

Later, at Attu Island, the ship needed to take on water, but filling pails and drums might have taken weeks. The solution adopted: "a dory was brought into the creek and sunk until it was full of fresh water almost to the gunwales. It was then towed out to the ship and hoisted in the davits up to the level of the boat deck. Here the plug was pulled from the bottom of the dory and the water gushed down an intricate drainage system of ventilators and every other sort of pipe into the tanks." While still at Attu, "the smell of gasoline became apparent one morning and with each hour the odour became more noticeable. Examination of the deck cargo of tins failed to reveal any broken receptacles, but still the smell increased. Finally it was discovered that the salt water had rusted the bottom of the tins badly and in several cases had riddled the containers. Then commenced a long, arduous job of unpacking each tin and applying a thick coat of paint to each of them. There was a sigh of relief when the last can was again stowed inside its case. The majority of them were saved, although several had been drained of their contents before anything could be done to prevent the escape of the motive spirit."[130]

The trip to Japan that followed was relatively calm, with real cause for celebration when the ship anchored off Copper Island in the Soviet Union. "There was general jubilation aboard the ship," Watt wrote, "when an inquisitive member of the crew discovered a man ashore who owned two pigs. Fresh meat had been in a minus quantity so long aboard *Thiepval* that it had become more or less of a pleasant memory. After some dickering the owner of the porkers agreed to part with them, and at his call his two pets, Alice and Horax, came rushing down the hill, only to fall into the hands of a gang of murderers, who rushed the

---

128. Ibid.

129. Ibid.

130. Ibid.

squealing victims out to their little salt encrusted vessel."[131] After a further stop at Petropavlovsk on the Kamchatka Peninsula, *Thiepval* pushed on to reach Hakodate, Japan with little remaining fresh water, coal, or food on board. Replenishing their supplies, the ship then headed back to Petropavlovsk where it rendezvoused with McLaren's flying boat on 24 July. When the Vickers Viking set off on the morning of 4 August to attempt the dangerous north Pacific crossing, however, bad weather forced McLaren and his co-pilot to ditch the aircraft in the surf off Bering Island. The Canadian trawler retrieved the crippled flying boat from the island's shore next day, hauling the wreckage on board before returning to Vancouver, along with the dispirited aviators, on 24 August. As the first Canadian warship to visit the Far East, *Thiepval* steamed more than 34,000 kilometres during her six-month voyage.[132]

There was, however, an entirely other side to *Thiepval*'s mission. The RCN's intelligence officer, a member of the Royal Navy named Cosmo Hastings, advised Lieutenant Gow before the ship departed Canada that "the forthcoming cruise of the *Thiepval* will be the opportunity of a lifetime for collecting intelligence." He insisted that "the collection of intelligence is the primary *naval* object: the laying down of petrol and supplies every two or three hundred miles for the British round-the-world flight renders it possible to attain the *naval* object." As for details, "much must be left to the initiative of the commanding officer, who has a golden opportunity for rendering a service to the empire, the importance of which cannot be exaggerated." It would be an important task, and "the officers and men who have the honour of taking part in this expedition will be making history and writing history."[133]

Of interest as a possible target for information were various flights by United States aircraft. One, which was scheduled to leave Unalaska on 1 May and travel around the world, was thought to be "really a bluff, the real object of the United States government not improbably being to gauge the practicability of the flight from America to Japan via the Aleutian Island route, and also to gain experience in this matter." Another flight, of the USN airship *Shenandoah* into the Arctic, was less a matter of exploration, Hose suggested, and more an excuse to establish mooring positions in Alaska for military and other purposes. *Thiepval*'s return journey from Japan would probably take place after the US aircraft had crossed over "and you should obtain, along the route, as much information as you can of their experiences." In gathering such intelligence, and any other data they might glean, the naval director warned that "you will, of course, have to exercise very great care in making enquiries so as not to arouse a suspicion of espionage but the fact of natural interest in the world flight will give you opportunities of investigation." In the same vein, "particular tact will be required in dealing with Russian and Japanese officials." A photographer would be available, but "while it is desirable to obtain as complete photographic records as possible the responsibility lies with you not to upset the susceptibilities of foreign officials in the matter of taking photographs."[134]

---

131. Ibid.

132. Duncan McDowall, "HMCS *Thiepval*: The Accidental Tourist … Destination," *Canadian Military History*, IX, (Summer 2000), 71–4.

133. Cosmo Hastings to Lt F.R.W.R. Gow, 9 February 1924, 1091–1-1, LAC, RG 24, vol. 11,924.

134. Hose to CO HMCS *Thiepval*, 13 February 1924, ibid.

The Battle-class trawler HMCS *Thiepval* in heavy seas during her voyage to the Far East to support the British round-the-world flight in 1924. The trawler travelled over 34,000 kilometres, depositing fuel and lubricant "dumps" across the north Pacific to Hakodate, Japan, before returning to Vancouver in August. (CWM 19710050-001.15)

Thiepval's 12-pounder gun. (CWM 19710050-001.86)

Thiepval at Petropavlovsk, Soviet Union, on 31 July 1924, following its rendezvous with Squadron-Leader McLaren's Vickers Viking flying boat. (LAC e007140915)

McLaren's beached Vickers Viking on the shore of Bering Island. *Thiepval* salvaged the damaged aircraft and brought it to Vancouver. (CWM 19710050-001.107)

As time wore on the RCN intelligence officer developed more specific requests for information, on 15 February producing a questionnaire with a wide variety of headings. Under "air" were five questions, such as "what is the principal object of the American round-the-world flight?" Under "military," there were six, for example, "what are the principal duties of the troops in Alaska?" Another heading, "sealing industry," included the query: "Is any pelagic sealing being carried out?" Of course, "political" was a topic, with three questions, including "what is the attitude of the people of the Kamchatka Peninsula towards Soviet Russia?" Interestingly, one heading was "geological," such as a request to take notes on quartz crystals. "Naval" had to appear, with seven questions, such as "are the details of W/T stations supplied to you accurate and complete?" A section entitled "photographic and pictorial" posed no queries, but provided instructions on obtaining photos, while "guide books, etc," simply recommended such literature be acquired. For "maps, charts," the questionnaire noted that they were to be corrected. A separate cover provided "special questionnaires," covering such topics as "information concerning ports of call," and a "coast record." It might have been a relatively comprehensive list, but a final entry noted that it was not to be treated as exhaustive.[135]

Although on 4 June Canada's high commissioner in London advised that the ship's primary duties were to attend on the British round-the-world flight, and although Japanese officers accompanied *Thiepval* during the passage through the Japanese islands, it provided reports on several ports, in the Aleutian and Pribiloff Islands, Alaska, the Kamchatka peninsula the Komandorski Islands, and the Kurile Islands, the latter possibly investigated before the Japanese officers joined the ship. Providing a coast report and replies to the naval questionnaire, the entire document ran to some thirty pages. To give just one brief example, it noted that in the Aleutian and Pribiloff Islands, "general health conditions are good," that "oil seepages have been discovered near Ugashik and Becharof Lakes, in the Alaskan Peninsula," and that "there is a church" in Oest Kamchatka in the Kamchatka Peninsula, an apparent sign that atheism had not completely taken hold in this part of the Soviet Union. A different part of the report provided information on wireless stations, including a photograph, the name of each, the name of the nearest town, latitude and longitude, its height above sea level, the type of station, and the number of masts and their type, for a total of twenty-one pieces of data.[136]

With its twin tasks completed, the RCN was advised that a similar operation, to support a flight sponsored by Argentina, was approved, though it does not seem to have ever taken off, so the minesweepers returned to more routine missions, such as life saving.[137] The West Coast ships were busiest in this regard, especially on what was called the Bamfield patrol, Lieutenant G.B. Barnes, commanding *Armentieres*, preparing a typical letter of proceedings in the spring of 1924. On the night of 26 February a gale was blowing and the air was thick

---

135. Cosmo Hastings to DND (Naval Service), 15 February 1924, ibid.

136. Cosmo Hastings to District Intelligence Officer Esquimalt, 27 September 1924, NSHQ to SNO, RCN Barracks Esquimalt, 10 July 1924, 1091–1-1, Lieut in Command HMCS *Thiepval* to DNS, 9 July 1924, 1091–7-1, LAC, RG 24, vol. 11,924.

137. Beech to Naval Ottawa, 27 May 1924, 133–1-5, LAC, RG 24, vol. 5682.

with rain. At 0630 the vessel received a message from a station at Pachena Bay that the SS *Tatjana* had run aground near that location. *Armentieres* weighed anchor at 0700, but the winch broke down and the anchor cable had to be brought in using the minesweeping winch. The vessel proceeded to Pachena Bay, where she conducted a search, using her lifeboat, which with a smaller draft was able to work closer to shore. The search was completed by 0945 hours, "but the weather was so thick and the surf running so high that it was quite possible to have passed a wreck without seeing it." By 1140 hours the captain was convinced there was no one to rescue in the bay, so proceeded to Barkley Sound on the suggestion of a signal from Pachena lighthouse. A search in that area from 1245 to 1325 hours found nothing, and twenty minutes later "*Armentieres* was obliged to stop and cool off engines which had become very heated, caused apparently by ashes from the stokehold being washed into the bilges and choking up some pipes. The weather had been too bad to get up ashes from the stokehold."[138]

The patrol continued, *Armentieres* and the lifeboat proceeding independently after losing sight of each other. "At 2.30 large quantities of oil fuel were observed off Bold Bluff, Village Island. It was thought then that the Tatjana had struck on Bold Bluff and sunk off there. However as no wreckage was visible and the lifeboat had passed the spot and gone along the SE shore in which case she would have seen anything of that nature," it was eliminated as a possible site for *Tatjana's* wreckage. The search, which had turned into something of an odyssey, did not end there, the minesweeper investigating various bays, islands, and rocks in the hours that followed, sometimes trying to glean information from fishermen. Finally, on the south-east shore of Village Island, where oil had been spotted earlier, "the wreck was observed in a cleft of the rocks, half her length out of the water, her bows high and dry and her stern submerged to the rails.... Nobody could be seen on deck and the crew were camped ashore under an awning with fire going. The lifeboat had discovered her about an hour and a half before and had taken off seven men and proceeded back to Bamfield. The remainder of *Tatjana's* crew elected to stay ashore for the night." Next day the remaining eighteen members of the crew were taken off, for a total of twenty-five rescued, "with only the clothes they were wearing." Being non-Canadians, they were handed over to immigration authorities in Victoria, *Armentieres* then sailing to Esquimalt. "The behaviour of the crew was very satisfactory," her captain reported, "especially the RCNR and the RCNVR ratings, ABs [Able Seamen] Marple and Connelly being specially notable. Chief Engine Room Artificer Renton, RCN, deserves credit for his work in the engine room." As for *Armentieres*, "the ship behaved very well in the heavy seas and proved very seaworthy. Care, however, should be taken not to trim these vessels down by the bows, or large quantities of water will come down over the forecastle head."[139]

Such patrols remained an RCN responsibility for decades, and are part of the Canadian Armed Forces' repertoire to this day. Two years after *Armentieres's* experiences, *Thiepval* completed a more eventful mission than usual after relieving *Givenchy*. Leaving Esquimalt on 4 February 1926, "nothing of interest occurred until noon on 9th February, when a W/T

138. *Armentieres* on Bamfield Patrol, 6 May 1924, 10–1–9, LAC, RG 24, vol. 3579.

139. Ibid.

signal was received from Pachena Lighthouse that a three masted schooner had been sighted off Carmanah, drifting towards the shore and apparently flying distress signals." The minesweeper sailed toward the stricken ship in bad visibility and heavy seas, with drizzling rain, when "the schooner *Chapultepec* was sighted about a mile south of Sea Lion Rocks.... She was flying signals of distress and on being closed asked to be taken in tow." Such was no easy evolution, however, especially given the unco-operative weather. "The Costyn line throwing gun was first used to get a line on board, but proved to be a failure, the line parting when the gun was fired. A line was then got on board by hand, but owing to the schooner rolling so heavily the man hauling it in slipped and fell, and the heaving line went over the side. A second heaving line was then thrown which was caught and heaved on board the schooner." It was used to pull a four-inch-thick line onboard, itself then used to haul in a length of six-inch cordage.[140]

Further difficulties lay ahead, however, and "when the tow was secured it was found impossible to proceed at more than three knots, owing to the rolling of the two ships with the consequent heavy strains on the towing hawser," the rope being used in the evolution. Not unexpectedly, "at 5 p.m. the tow parted near the schooners fo'castle," that is to say, broke just ahead of the towed ship's bow. Following repairs, the operation continued, still at three knots. "The schooner appeared to be very much battered by the recent storms on the coast. Her bulwarks were smashed in several places, and most of her standing rigging seemed to have carried away," adding further to the challenge. "She was a Mexican schooner of 390 tons and only one man on board appeared to understand English; consequently it was very difficult to make the crew understand what was to be done in the way of hauling ropes and securing the towing hawser, etc." As if Neptune himself sought to add to *Thiepval*'s challenges, the tow parted again at 2100. "This was due to the schooner yawing [from side to side] while the ship was altering course up the Straits. At the slow speed at which the vessels were proceeding it was very difficult for her to steer a steady course." It took until midnight to secure a new towing line, and some time afterward rescuer and rescued met the *Salvage Queen*, which took over the operation.[141]

Later, the captain observed that "it was found necessary to employ the whole ship's company to handle the heavy towing hawser with the exception of the stokers on watch." Still, it was deemed that "the commanding officer and the ship's company of HMCS *Thiepval* deserve great credit for this operation which was carried out in a very seamanlike manner, under very difficult conditions, and which resulted in the saving of several lives, apart from the vessel itself."[142]

The naval director was also impressed, writing the minister that "in view of the ridicule which has at times been passed on the minesweeping vessels in the naval service, you will probably be glad to have this concrete example of the valuable work that these vessels carry out in peace time, in addition to their operations in training the personnel of the service in minesweeping and other technical defence work.... This is not the first occasion on

140. *Thiepval*, March 26, ibid.

141. Ibid.

142. Ibid.

which the minesweepers have been the means of saving life and property at sea," and Hose commented on "the very high class seamanship and the pluck necessary to carry out the very difficult operation of getting hold of the schooner *Chapultepec* and towing her off a lee shore."[143]

Besides its lifesaving duties, the RCN was also responsible—in partnership with other government departments such as Marine and Fisheries—for helping to protect fish stocks and other ocean resources. Naval Service Headquarters issued orders in early 1925 that each ship's commander "is to keep a lookout for any illegal halibut fishing on the part of Canadian or United States vessels or boats during the annual closed season—16th November to 15th February." Such responsibility was supported with no little authority, as "fishing vessels of the United States or Canada may be boarded whether in Canadian territorial waters or on the high seas of the Pacific off the coast of Canada, if suspected of illegal fishing for halibut." NSHQ warned ships' captains, however, that "it is not necessary to approach or board every fishing vessel which may be met whilst at sea," and only "Canadian or United States vessels acting suspiciously, or those which are passed which appear to be fishing for halibut, should be boarded." Ottawa issued further warnings that "a vessel boarded is not to be unnecessarily detained," and that "care is to be taken in approaching a fishing vessel, to avoid damaging any long lines, etc, which she may have in the water." Two officers were to board, the senior to conduct an enquiry and the junior to act as witness, and "on boarding the vessel, the boarding officer will inform the Master that he is doing so under the authority of the treaty," while "any search of a vessel must be made with care, tact, and discretion."[144]

As for delinquents, "if a Canadian vessel illegally fishing for halibut is found, she is to be escorted into the nearest port and transferred to the local representative of the Department of Marine and Fisheries (or collector of customs …) for action by him in the Canadian courts," while "if a United States vessel is found in territorial waters, fishing, or preparing to fish, whether for halibut or other fish, it should be seized under the Customs and Fisheries Protection Act, and may be brought into the nearest Canadian port and transferred to the local representative of the Department of Marine and Fisheries (or collector of customs …) for further action by him as necessary," in effect following the same procedures as vessels of the Department of Marine and Fisheries. NSHQ also instructed that "if a United States vessel is found during the closed season fishing, or preparing to fish for halibut on the high seas covered by the treaty, it may be seized and taken into the nearest port of the United States to be handed over to the local authorities." After each cruise a report was submitted to the chief inspector in Vancouver detailing the number of fishing vessels sighted, the names of any vessels boarded, and "detailed remarks on any special circumstances in connection with any vessel boarded, with copy of entry made in vessel's log."[145]

Patrols could often take on the flavour of full-fledged military operations, such as one by *Patrician* in the spring of 1927. "Being provisioned, watered, fueled, and in all respects prepared for a 24 hour absence from the ship, the motor-boat, with second skiff in tow, is

---

143. DNS to Minister, 17 March 1926, 133–7-5, LAC, RG 24, vol. 5683.

144. NSHQ to SNO, RCN Barracks Esquimalt, 23 January 1925, 300–1-2, LAC, RG 24, vol. 5686.

145. Ibid.

to leave the ship at 0600 on Thursday 26th May with an armed party under your command, to patrol from the northern entrance to Beauchemin Channel, to Don Point, proceeding to the westward of Aristazabal Island," the destroyer's captain ordered on 25 May. "The object of the patrol is to enforce the Pelagic Sealing Treaty, with particular attention to one Max Labrunner, of the launch *Starlight*, reported to be seal poaching from a base at one of the small islands off Aristazabal Island." *Patrician* was scheduled to return in two days, but "should it become necessary to communicate with *Patrician* during the day, you should attempt to make smoke signals." Six columns of smoke, for example, would mean that the boat was returning to Hicks Island.[146]

It seems that the armed party found nothing, and a more extensive patrol conducted in June was similarly uneventful. Leaving Esquimalt on the 2nd, next day "and the preceding night the majority of the ship's company suffered from sea-sickness, no doubt due to the fact that this was the first occasion for nearly a year that the ship has been at seaway." Among other things, a seal patrol was carried out in Hecate Strait on the 25th. "In an endeavour to capture a seal poacher, the motor boat carried out a search of the islands to the westward of Aristazabel [sic] Island under the command of Lt Gow.... The suspected poacher was not found." That same day, the ship anchored, "in the hope that the stopping of propellors would induce seals which were thought to be in the vicinity to appear," so they could be counted, but "no seals were sighted." On 26 June *Patrician* sighted a couple of halibut boats and a few seals, with more seals making an appearance next day. Still, "a total of only about 100 seal were sighted from *Patrician* during the Pelagic sealing cruise, in a distance of 1,270 miles steamed in daylight hours in waters that the main herd is reputed to frequent. Forty-one of these were sighted in Hecate Strait on the 13th of May and between thirty and forty in approximately the same position on the 15th of May. The ship has been underway in sealing areas on twelve days. On two of these days line fishermen have been spoken to but not boarded owing to bad weather. There was no reason to suspect either of these fishing boats of seal poaching."[147]

Slightly harder work lay ahead, members of *Patrician*'s crew boarding three halibut boats, though "nothing of an incriminating nature was found in any of them and no information regarding seal was obtained from them.... The fishery officer at Queen Charlotte City, informed me, and this was confirmed by an Indian at Skidegate named Green and by Captain Haan of Sand-Spit, that no sealing has been done by the Indians of the Queen Charlottes for some years because it does not 'pay.' I am of the opinion that it is because in the last few years salmon fishing has been very lucrative.... Seal were sighted in the following positions, on the dates and in the numbers shown. No estimate of their course or speed could be made. In all cases they appeared to be either sleeping on the surface or feeding on shoals of small fish. When not sleeping, their course and speeds were most erratic." The Canadian destroyer's captain dutifully provided a list of when and where seals had been observed, though he may well have wondered if there might not be more interesting work to keep warships busy.[148]

146. CO *Patrician* to Lt F.R.W.R. Gow, 25 May 1927, 34–7-5, LAC, RG 24, vol. 5633.

147. CO *Patrician* to Senior Naval Officer, RCN Barracks Esquimalt, 23 June 1927, ibid.

148. Ibid.

The Canadian destroyers performed useful work on the East Coast as well, such as the occasion when *Patriot* undertook a humanitarian task in October 1922. "Upon urgent representation of family and all Canadians present commanding officer undertook to convey body of *Bluenose* crew to Lunenburg." It was naval training that made ships' crews feel that they were actually part of an active navy, however. In September 1922 Lieutenant Charles Beard, in command of *Patriot*, pointed out that the object of one series of manoeuvres "was to carry out all drills in slow time, and to give instructions to a large percentage of the ship's companies whos[e] knowledge of the rudiments of their duties was negligable [*sic*]." Although indoctrination was to some degree hampered by weather, Beard was "pleased to report a marked progress." On the 15th, "instructions were given quartermasters in piping, to every man in rowing, petty officers and leading seamen were taught to give orders and take charge of men. A party were landed for rifle exercises, and duties as sentry, in case we were ordered to Sydney," to intervene in a coal strike, as we have seen. "Gun's crews were drilled individually in slow time," while instructions were also "given to a few on torpedo tubes and torpedo director." At the mayor's request, the ship visited Shelburne, where "the harbour is good, and will make a very good exercising ground." On the 21st the ship proceeded to Liverpool, "exercising by firing pom pom and Lewis guns" and having the "sea boats crews of both watches lowered in a seaway." After a day of open house activities, *Patriot* headed for Lunenburg, with gunnery practices along the way, continuing to combine showing the flag with various forms of training until it returned to Halifax on 29 September.[149]

Off the West Coast, *Patrician* often carried out similar manoeuvres, occasionally using 1-inch inserts in her main armament to practise gunnery. The latter was, for both destroyers, the most important warlike task for which they prepared, which accounts for its high profile in letters of proceedings and similar reports. In October 1924, for example, Commander F.H. Brabant, the senior naval officer in *Stadacona*, related how *Patriot* conducted a shoot at Cape Breton's Bras d'Or Lakes. "All discrepancies and errors were dealt with on the spot.... It is regretted that only one target was in a fit state for towing, that made the target appear very small at ranges of 4,000 yards and over.... Considering that it was the first heavy gun shoot that HMCS *Patriot* has done with the present complement, it appears to be highly satisfactory, and reflects credit on the officers and ship's company who have been subjected to continuous changes, and owing to the particular duties that HMCS *Patriot* has been called upon to perform, training has consisted of several broken periods.... The experience gained has been invaluable, and it has inspired an increased keenness in the personnel.... It is suggested that it be repeated again next year, by which time it is hoped that the director system will be in working order. Bras d'Or Lakes seem to be an ideal area, being free from fog and shipping, and enjoys continuous calm water.... The failures were practically non-existent and the constructural condition of the ship shewed no weakness under the maximum stress that the ship is likely to be subjected to under normal range conditions."[150]

---

149. Lt Charles Beard, in Command *Patriot*, to Senior Naval Officer, 2 September 1922, 33-7-5, CO *Patriot* to Naval Ottawa, 29 October 1922, 33-7-1, ibid.

150. Cdr F.H. Brabant RN, Senior Naval Officer, *Stadacona*, to NSHQ, 20 October 1924, 1057–51–11GE, LAC, RG 24, vol. 4009; and "Movements of Ships and Notes of Interest, HMCS *Patrician*," December 1926, 10–1–9, LAC, RG 24, vol. 3579.

The report's tone and references to "broken periods" of training clearly indicate the important place gunnery held throughout the RCN. Similarly, *Patrician* conducted such training in March 1925, though "this shoot shows a complete breakdown in control arrangements which only lack of control drill can account for," insufficient practice and not a lack of ability being at the heart of the problem. As Lieutenant A.M. Hope related, "one gun continually shot to the right of the remainder," and, generally, "the chief fault lay in the failure of the control system. The condition of the weather and the great disadvantage of the absence, and changing about of the personnel last year should not be lost sight of, and full allowance made for the same," a theme that echoed *Patriot*'s experiences of some months before. Hope's recommended solution was that "in all future practice firings, great stress should be laid on the fact that all control parties and sight setters should have ample time practicing on control runs and spotting tables until they are thoroughly efficient."[151]

Knowing what needed to be done did not make it so, however, and in September G.C. Jones, the naval staff officer, was reporting after another shoot that "the results obtained by *Patrician* can only be described as most disappointing. They cannot be compared with those obtained by *Patriot* and no lessons seem to have been learned from the previous year." Among the problems he found were that the ship only had one target to practice with, that her executive officer was a navigation officer (no doubt implying that he should have been a gunnery officer), and that the "spotting table," a simple simulator used to teach the elements of gunnery ashore, had been destroyed by fire. Still, there was a limit to Jones's sympathy, and he recommended sending a letter to *Patrician*'s commanding officer stating "that after making due allowances for lack of targets and spotting table ... the department consider the results most disappointing," and that "the failure to have enough ammunition on board, bad drill, incomplete records, etc, can only point to a lack of organization in the gunnery department." As a result, Jones acidly remarked that "no value can be seen in forwarding a copy of the results to HMCS *Patriot*."[152]

Patriot seemed to be doing better—at least occasionally—than its West Coast counterpart, and a shoot in August 1926 was "classified as satisfactory. The rate of fire was slow, speed being sacrificed for accuracy. This being the correct procedure as it was the first full calibre firing.... Loading delays occurred on two occasions in both cases at No 3 gun, causing it to miss two salvoes.... The GCO [gunnery control officer] carried out the correct spotting rules and considerable benefit of experience should have been obtained by all concerned."[153] It was, however, a rather exceptional shoot, and in general "the results of *Patriot*'s summer gunnery programme may be considered most unsatisfactory in every way.... From the reports received this may be traced to ... insufficient time spent at preliminary drill both among the officers and ratings of the ship's company.... Insufficient training of the recording parties.... General lack of interest in gunnery matters among the officers of *Patriot*. This has been particularly noticeable by the length of time taken for the

---

151. Lt A.M. Hope to DNS, 18 March 1925, 1057–52–11GE, LAC, RG 24, vol. 4010.

152. Jones to Hose, 25 September 1925, ibid.

153. Senior Naval Officer, HMC Ships and Establishments Halifax to NSHQ, 13 August 1926, ibid, vol. 4009.

reports of the different firings to reach headquarters." Given mitigating circumstances—the ship had done a great deal of steaming that summer, and "figured conspicuously" in a serious Atlantic storm at the beginning of August—it was decided to await the autumn gunnery program before passing final judgment. In November, as it turned out, Lieutenant (Gunnery) A.M. Hope found "a great improvement," and rated the ship's shooting "satisfactory."[154]

Hope felt that there was "a certain weakness in the control organization" of *Patriot*.[155] The destroyer's gunners rarely fired directly at their targets, since the latters' movements needed to be predicted as shells were in flight for many seconds before striking the enemy—or the water. It was thus up to members of the control organization to track the target's movements, determine where it would be when shells had completed their time in flight, and swiftly pass that information on to the gunners. As was the case in *Patriot*, in *Patrician* "the principal weakness" in regards to her gunnery "lies in the control." During spring training, "this showed itself in every firing by a partial breakdown in communication between the control officer and the guns.... This can only be strengthened by continuous control drill until a state of efficiency is reached," a theme that had become a litany. As for the guns themselves, "certain defects in material were discovered, causing a number of misfires at the guns. As these can only be brought to light by actual firing of the guns, it is assumed that, with the experience gained in these preliminary practices, the armament of *Patrician* is now in an efficient state. Under these conditions it is considered that the rate of fire for all practices was satisfactory."[156]

There was thus hope for the future, and at the end of 1926 Jones reported that "the autumn gunnery practice of *Patrician* shows a very great improvement over her spring practice, particularly in view of the fact that the new commanding and executive officers have been appointed to the ship since the last practices were carried out.... The difficulty in *Patrician* has been that too much attention has been devoted to bright work, and not enough to gunnery," though the fault lay with the ship's assignments, which had focused more on showing the flag and public relations cruises than on her more warlike functions.[157] The destroyer would, however, like *Patriot*, always be in training to a certain degree, as evidenced in June 1927 when a 1-inch insert in her No 2 gun discharged into the vessel's funnel. According to Commander P.W. Nelles, however, who was the senior naval officer in RCN's Esquimalt barracks, "it is not considered that any useful purpose could be served by a Court of Enquiry. The accident has been carefully investigated by lieutenant (G) HMCS *Naden*. The cause of the accident was due to the lack of experience of Lieutenant H.N. Lay, RCN (control officer) and the captain of the gun (Able Seaman E. Langlois), together with the lack of knowledge of the remainder of the gun's crew.... Numerous drills have been carried out by *Patrician* during the past month but a series of intensive drills will be carried out by lieutenant (G) (Naden) daily during the coming week, and longer if considered

154. Hope to Hose, 17 September and 17 November 1926, ibid.

155. Ibid, 17 November 1926.

156. Hope to Hose, 24 September 1926, ibid, vol. 4010.

157. G.C. Jones to Hose, 3 December 1926, ibid.

necessary." The damage had been repaired, and if practice would not make perfect, it could at least avoid catastrophe—or extreme embarrassment.[158]

The destroyer carried another weapon, the torpedo, but training with it was more difficult, no doubt because of the costs involved in purchasing practice torpedoes, which were supposed to surface after their runs so they could be retrieved, and the embarrassed explanations required if one went astray. What few practices were in fact carried out were often in conjunction with gunnery in a program lasting a few weeks. In one such period in the summer of 1926, *Patrician* trained her gunnery branch from 7 to 17 June, and only on the 21st did she report that "preparation tests were carried out on torpedoes Nos 1919 and 1732," to ensure they were ready for use the next day. On the 22nd they were fired at *Thiepval*, a "stationary target," both completing "good runs." Next day came the indoctrination period's climax, the ship training both her gunnery and torpedo branches, sailors firing pom-pom and Lewis guns as well as two torpedoes.[159] *Patriot*, for her part, was fortunate in conducting torpedo training with the North America and West Indies Squadron in Bermuda. On 7 March, 1926, she attacked the cruiser *Calcutta* from 5,000 yards, though the commander-in-chief of the squadron reported that "the range was too great to permit of any chance of success." Next day, the target was another C-class cruiser, *Capetown*, and generally "the firing was very good and reflects credit on all concerned."[160]

As before the 1922 budget—and as we saw in relation to training the RCNVR—the best forum for indoctrination and putting knowledge to the test was the cruise. One typical voyage began for *Patriot* at the end of 1922, on orders from NSHQ. "Weather permitting, and being in all respects ready for sea, HMCS *Patriot* is to proceed from Halifax on the 27th December for Bermuda. On arrival at Bermuda *Patriot* will come under the orders of the commander in chief, North American & West Indies.... The object of the stay of *Patriot* at Bermuda is to carry out the sea-going and gunnery training which is impracticable off Halifax during the winter months."[161] To that purpose, the commander-in-chief placed HMS *Capetown* at *Patriot*'s disposal, "an opportunity," opined Hose, "for our young ratings which it would be the greatest pity not to take full advantage of," and the cruise was subsequently extended.[162] It was not the last, *Patriot* returning to the West Indies at the end of 1923, and again at the end of 1924, on the latter occasion exercising station-keeping (with HMS *Curlew*), torpedo attacks, the use of star shell and searchlights, gunnery, flag-hoisting, and more. "The general efficiency of the ship has improved considerably," H.E. Reid, the lieutenant in command reported, "and the value obtained by competition with and assistance given by HM ships cannot be overestimated."[163]

---

158. Cdr P.W. Nelles, SNO, RCN Barracks Esquimalt, to NSHQ, 10 June 1927, ibid.

159. CO *Patrician* to SNO, RCN Barracks Esquimalt, 29 June 1926, ibid.

160. Lt in Command *Patriot* to C-in-C, NA&WI, 7 and 27 March 1926, C-in-C, NA&WI to Hose, 23 April 1926, NSHQ to SNO, RCN Barracks Halifax, 21 July 1926, 1057–51–11TE, LAC, RG 24, vol. 4009.

161. Naval Secretary, "Memorandum," 16 December 1922, 33–7-2, LAC, RG 24, vol. 5633.

162. Hose to Desbarats, 10 February 1923, ibid.

163. Reid to SNO, *Stadacona*, 29 March 1924, DNS to Minister, 11 December 1923, ibid.

It had not all been smooth sailing, however, and Llewellyn Houghton recalled how "two months after I joined her, this eight-year-old vessel experienced a real test of her seaworthiness. Early in January, 1924, we sailed for Bermuda and our annual spring cruise, one which was to be repeated annually for the next fourteen years or so." From his point of view, with at least three decades of hindsight, it was "one of the worst I have experienced in my nine years at sea.... Instead of the usual 45 hours, the trip to Bermuda took us three and a half days; it wasn't until late afternoon on the third day that the skies cleared momentarily and we caught a glimpse of the sun just long enough for three of us ... to get sights. Apart from that we only had our dead reckoning (DR) position to work on; this is based on a record of speeds and courses and, considering the weather we had experienced, was very approximate. Bermuda is only a speck in the ocean and even big ships have been known to miss it."[164] It was not a pleasure cruise.

In fact, according to Houghton's private log, the day they left Halifax, 2 January, it was "cold as charity and blowing like hell! Two hours later bridge and forecastle covered in ice four to six inches thick. This affects our stability and must be chopped off. First lieut. and everyone else frozen stiff. Ship never still for a moment. About three-quarters of the crew seasick. What a shambles!" Next day was "a little calmer," and on the 4th Houghton "worked my way to the bridge at 4 am to keep the morning watch. At 4.15 ordered 'Slow Both.' Dark as the inside of a cow, huge waves higher than the bridge bearing down on us, their phosphorescent crests visible against the black sky. As she pitches her way into these monstrous waves, her bows come down with a spine-shaking crash and her stern rises up while the propellors free-wheel madly in air. Sternlight washed away. Tiller flat flooded. Two lifebuoys washed overboard. Whaler stove in. Rain streaming down—can't see a thing. There's only one small steering-engine in this ship; if that should fail and we drift beam on to this sea, goodbye cruel world." Houghton later recalled that, thankfully, "by ten that morning the wind had shifted sixteen points—halfway round the compass—and this helped to cut down the size of the waves. The situation rapidly improved, we got a sight, and soon afterwards Bermuda hove in sight exactly where we figured it should be."[165]

Such cruises thus offered challenges both physical and intellectual, even if the locations visited could be exotic. On the West Coast, *Patrician*'s voyages took her to such locales as Manzanillo and Acapulco, the political situation allowing. At the end of 1923 Britain's minister to Mexico had to report that "these ports are in the hands of rebels," and that "in view also of the seriously disturbed conditions prevailing in this Republic and the strained relations existing between his majesty's government and the Mexican administration a naval visit such as that proposed may in my opinion be regarded as inopportune at this time."[166] *Patriot* never faced such difficulties in Bermuda, but *Patrician* was not lacking for alternatives. At the end of 1925 she joined HMS *Capetown* and sailed for San Francisco, conducting

164. F.L. Houghton, "Memoir," nd, 92, LAC, MG 30 E444.

165. Ibid, 93–94.

166. H.A. Cunard Cummins, British Minister at Mexico to Governor General, 29 December 1923, 34–7-1, LAC, RG 24, vol. 5633.

inclination exercises and a night attack on the way. On 7 September the ship secured along-side the Fort Mason transport docks, and her captain, along with the commanding officer of *Capetown* and the acting British consul, made official calls. Next day twenty-five sailors, properly armed, took part in a US army and navy, and foreign naval units parade while a dinner on board *Patrician* on the 12th included American and Japanese naval officers. It was not all diplomacy, however, and on the 16th both commonwealth warships conducted night attack, high angle firing (anti-aircraft training), and searchlight exercises while on their way to San Pedro. Other calls were made at San Diego and Portland, Oregon, before arriving at Esquimalt on 9 October.[167]

The RCN was thus part of Canada's presence on the international stage, and not only when its destroyers conducted cruises up and down the coasts of the western hemisphere. Several disarmament conferences were convened in the course of the 1920s in an attempt to avoid a repetition of the carnage of the First World War, and as we have seen there was a series of imperial conferences as well to discuss issues of interest to the British Empire. As the Department of External Affairs' O.D. Skelton reported after just such a meeting in 1926, "the question was raised whether in the event of international agreement through the league to limit armaments, each part of the empire should be assigned a maximum quota of its own, or whether a single quota should be set for the whole British empire. The Admiralty urged a single quota for naval armament; the general staff and air staff urged separate quotas for military and air forces." For the RCN it was no small issue, since if its ships were part of the "quota" of vessels the British Empire was supposed to scrap, Canada's naval service could cease to exist. On the other hand, British representatives argued that if the dominions had separate quotas, and did not build up to those maximums, then the empire as a whole would be weakened. In effect, a single quota offered "the opportunity to press the backward dominions to do their bit."[168]

O.D. Skelton was no imperialist—far from it—so he argued, no doubt on Mackenzie King's instructions, for a separate quota. Previous conferences had limited the number of battleships the great powers, such as the United States, Britain, Japan, Italy, and France, could build and maintain, but by the mid-1920s light cruisers, destroyers, and submarines were being discussed, "so the bearing of any new quota on our position will be much more direct."[169] In the event, the Canadian government agreed to the single quota, with consequences to be discussed in the next chapter, but it did not do so wholeheartedly, Canada's secretary of state for external affairs advising Britain's secretary of state for dominion affairs that "in view of serious difficulties involved in this procedure it is considered desirable that whole question should be considered an open one for the future and reviewed carefully before another conference is held."[170]

The King government was playing a very delicate balancing act. The United States and

---

167. *Patrician*, Cruise in Company with HMS *Capetown*, November 1925, 10–1-9, LAC, RG 24, vol. 3579.

168. O.D. Skelton, "Note re Quota," 26 February 1927, LAC, MG 26 J4, vol. 124, file 211.

169. Ibid.

170. Secretary of State for External Affairs to Secretary of State for Dominion Affairs, 6 July 1927, LAC, RG 25, vol. 1412, file 96-G.

Britain, who would not forge truly close ties until part-way through the next world war, had disagreed at the 1927 "Coolidge Conference" on naval disarmament over the balance to be achieved between cruisers armed with 8-inch guns and those with 6-inch main armament.[171] According to one historian of the period, "with his colleagues and advisers, Mackenzie King realised that the disparate views of the British and Americans on naval limitation were a diplomatic danger for Canada. Given Britain's imperial, league, and other commitments, and the need to keep open maritime routes to both the empire and foreign markets, this immediately brought to the fore how Canada should fit into the naval defence of the empire. The Mackenzie King government wanted to maintain Canadian autonomy but, at the same time, not to antagonise Britain unduly, which would have domestic and international repercussions. Just as crucial, the United States had to be handled with care, this for economic reasons and others touching those outstanding issues yet to be resolved in Canadian-American relations. Thus, balancing between Britain and the United States became the *sine qua non* of Canadian foreign policy."[172]

It was a position fraught with danger, but one that might offer opportunities for the RCN to prove its value to the King government, for surely, Hose could conclude, government representatives would need expert naval advice to pilot them through the shoals of disarmament and similar negotiations, such as those in Geneva. In a warning to O.D. Skelton, the naval director suggested that "Admiralty recommendations, while perhaps endeavouring to recognize special dominion conditions, are bound to be dominated by their view of empire trade defence requirements as a whole, and the peculiar conditions and requirements of any one dominion are likely to be subordinated to imperial defence." Given Skelton's suspicion of British imperialism, Hose was preaching to the converted, but he also broached technical issues where the RCN could be of help. "The question of accepting or urging allowances of vessels of various types in any scheme of naval armament limitation must conform to a general national policy and that policy must take into account the peculiar national strategic situation vis-a-vis other nations as well as the political factors." New Zealand could be expected to support imperial policy, as would Australia, though to a lesser extent, so Canadian diplomats might face something of a phalanx in commonwealth discussions. "Don't you think that the predominating imperial outlook of the naval advisers at Geneva is liable to have an unfortunate effect on our delegates and place them in a difficult position unless they are able to support their views on the correct naval policy for Canada with technical arguments as well as political ones?"[173] Skelton agreed. How could he not, given that the naval director's arguments were a perfect fit with the government's aim to achieve equality of status between Canada, the other dominions, and Britain? At the Conference for the Limitation of Naval Armament that subsequently met in Geneva, Hose represented Canada on the technical committee, but does not seem to have spoken

---

171. Hose, "Lessons of the Conference," 14 October 1927, LAC, RG 25, vol. 1412, file D1.

172. B.J.C. McKercher, "Between Two Giants: Canada, the Coolidge Conference, and Anglo-American Relations in 1927," B.J.C. McKercher, ed., *Anglo-American Relations in the 1920s: The Struggle for Supremacy* (Edmonton 1990), 93.

173. Hose to Skelton, 7 June 1927, LAC, RG 25, vol. 1412, file 96-G.

up at any of its nine sessions. Perhaps he limited his role, as he had laid out in his correspondence with O.D. Skelton, to offering advice to his Canadian colleagues.[174]

Regardless of the Canadian government's quest for ever-greater political autonomy from the imperial seat of power, the RCN, as we saw in discussing its training, was still a very close partner of the British navy, a state of affairs most evident when the two services discussed the possibility of war in the Pacific. Having abrogated its alliance with Japan, in part because Canada feared it might create extra tension between the United States and Britain, London began seeing in its former, First World War partner a potential enemy. The invasion of Manchuria and the war with China were still years in the future, but as we have seen when discussing possible conflict with the United States, it was the state of a country's navy and not its intentions that made it a cause for suspicion. Should war break out between Japan and Britain, the Royal Navy felt that "the presence off the western coast of Canada of British armed merchant cruisers would be very desirable." Additionally, four ships of the Canadian Pacific Line could be fitted out as armed merchant cruisers, with all necessary materiel stored in Esquimalt in the meantime. Canadian authorities were prepared to be accommodating, with Desbarats suggesting that in addition ammunition and explosives could be stored in magazines then under construction in Halifax. Myriad other details were hammered out in subsequent correspondence.[175]

When it came to actually basing British warships in Esquimalt in time of war, however, the King government continued its balancing act between Britain and the United States. London having requested that Canada approve such a scheme in 1927, King did not agree to it until March 1929. Following British-American disagreements over cruisers, the Canadian government had refused to support the construction of a St Lawrence seaway, and "it served little Canadian purpose for Ottawa both to scupper the St Lawrence project and, at the same time, publicly announce that Anglo-Canadian plans now existed for basing British warships on the west coast of Canada—astride American sealanes running north to Alaska and adjacent to those extending into the northeastern Pacific. In fact, when Mackenzie King finally approved the Esquimalt proposal, he modified it so that Canada would only countenance this transfer of British warships if Canada had first declared war. The desire to show autonomy shone through at all times."[176] Since the alternative was discord with the United States, King's position is perhaps understandable. When agreed to, the plan called for the America and West Indies Squadron (as the North America and West Indies Station was redesignated in 1926), reinforced by four armed merchant cruisers, to operate out of Esquimalt, the commander-in-chief hoisting his flag there.[177]

---

174. Minutes of Conference for the Limitation of Naval Armament, Technical Committee, 27–30 June, 1–2, 5 and 8 July 1927, ibid; and John MacFarlane, *Ernest Lapointe and Quebec's Influence on Canadian Foreign Policy* (Toronto 1999), 55–59.

175. Desbarats to Under Secretary of State for External Affairs, 30 August 1927, L.S. Amery to Governor General, 28 June 1927, 743, LAC, RG 24, vol. 1475.

176. McKercher, "Between Two Giants," 109.

177. Secretary of State for Dominion Affairs to Secretary of State for External Affairs, 8 August 1927, LAC, RG 25, vol. 1475, file 743.

There was no mention of *Patrician* or the two minesweepers the RCN operated out of Esquimalt, an indication of where the service stood in the eyes of the metropole. It had survived the budget of 1922, but the two destroyers, according to a March 1927 report, "have about reached the limit of their useful life. The hulls are showing signs of wear and of strain, and it does not seem that either of these vessels will last much longer as efficient craft. The inspections also show that the boilers of both vessels are in need of heavy and expensive repairs."[178] It was, perhaps, symbolic of the last days of another period in the RCN's life, since in the same way that 1922 marked the end of the post–First World War period, 1927 brought to the fore not only the need to replace the destroyers the Admiralty had given the RCN—or do without—but also the fact that Canada would have a role to play in a future war in the Pacific. At the time that role was limited to providing a base for a Royal Navy squadron, but it marked the beginning of a process by which the King government's balancing act between British and American interests would become defence policy. Canada, if in a small way, was beginning to plan for war.

---

178. Desbarats to Under Secretary of State for External Affairs, 28 March 1927, 1017–10–9, LAC, RG 24, vol. 3833.

CHAPTER 14

Growth, 1927–1933

The Royal Canadian Navy had survived the 1922 budget through the formation of a sophisticated reserve system and the astute leadership of Commodore Walter Hose, and as the decade progressed "a little of Canada's prosperity trickled into the defence estimates."[1] As the 1920s came to an end, however, the naval service faced challenges no less daunting than those of eight to ten years before: it would again be called upon to justify its very existence as it faced the possibility of being disbanded altogether, and intelligent leadership would once more play a role in its survival, allowing it to operate much as it had since recovering from the shock of the early twenties. Soon thereafter, however, and certainly unexpectedly, the navy would find that, having survived near-disappearance in the early 1930s, it would become a fixture in Canadian defence policy, its tiny flotilla of destroyers and smaller vessels featuring as permanent expenditures in government budgets, and even being replaced as they wore out—or perhaps some time after. The period of the early to mid-1930s is thus of no little significance in the history of the RCN, since it was at that time that the navy earned the legitimacy by which its existence would no longer be in doubt, though like almost all other government agencies it would consider its budget allocations less than adequate. Still, at least its strength increased, from seventy-four officers and 451 ratings in 1927–28 to eighty-six and 792 in 1932.[2]

As always throughout this period, much of what the RCN did would be determined by the relationship between Canada and Britain, the latter continuing to be a factor in the naval service's strategic and diplomatic planning. Such was evident when British member of parliament Hore Belisha asked the dominions secretary how much money each of the dominions and the crown colonies had contributed toward naval defence. The response, in Canada's case, was $1.42 million in 1925–26, representing 0.76 percent of $1.88 billion dollars in trade, or 16 cents per capita for a population of 8.79 million. The following year the navy budget rose to $1.5 million, though trade increased far more dramatically to $2.25 billion.[3]

---

1. Desmond Morton, *Canada and War: A Military and Political History* (Toronto 1981), 96.

2. Canada, Department of National Defence, *Report of the Department of National Defence (Naval Service) for the Fiscal Year Ended March 31 1928* (Ottawa 1928); and Canada, DND, *Report of the Department of National Defence (Naval Service) for the Fiscal Year Ended March 31 1932* (Ottawa 1932).

3. Canadian High Commissioner London to Secretary of State for External Affairs, 28 February 1928, Desbarats to Under Secretary of State for External Affairs, 29 February 1928, Library and Archives Canada (hereafter LAC), Record Group (hereafter RG) 25, vol. 721, file 46.

Setting expenditures alongside the commercial activity the navy was supposed to protect or next to the population base that paid taxes were two ways to compare contributions to the empire's defence, but Canada was in an anomalous situation when one actually investigated possible threats to the nation's borders and trade. Defence against the country's nearest neighbour was simply impossible, and the Department of National Defence, more specifically Chief of the General Staff Andrew McNaughton, clearly felt that "with respect to the United States I emphasized our policy could only be one of endeavouring to keep the peace between the US and Great Britain; that our only present form of defence against the USA was political and that as a corollary we must be quite sure of our ability to defend our neutrality on the west and on the east coasts as against *any* other power or powers with which the US might be at war,"[4] excepting, of course, Britain. In the course of the 1930 Disarmament Conference, the Canadian delegation suggested that, "with a further view to reducing the fear and [the] friction that comes with fear we have obtained the opinion of our general board of navy that existing military and naval stations of Great Britain in western hemisphere are not in a condition to be menace to United States." Furthermore, it recommended that "Britain will not hereafter establish any military or naval stations in her possessions in western hemisphere nor alter any such existing stations in such a way as in either case to become a menace to the United States."[5]

McNaughton and O.D. Skelton of the Department of External Affairs went so far as to keep clear of technical discussions concerning disarmament so as to focus all the more on "preserving peace and accord between USA and Great Britain."[6] Skelton, for his part, prioritized the general reduction of armaments, especially given the rivalry between Japan and the United States in the Pacific, between Britain and France (more specifically, the latter's submarines) in the English Channel, between Mussolini and France in the Mediterranean, and between Britain and the United States, the latter having embarked on a shipbuilding program, "which challenged the supremacy held by the British navy for three centuries." Therefore, "Canada has the general interest in desiring to see a reduction in armaments, with all the burden of cost, the friction and the threat of war such rivalries involve," Skelton declared, pointing out that Britain was spending more on weapons than it had before the First World War, as was Italy, with the United States having doubled its expenditures in the same time frame. If being part of a commonwealth naval quota, as had been decided in 1926, could ease such tensions, then Skelton was in favour. Also, "in view of her very small navy, it is hardly fitting for Canada to take a leading part in the discussion of quotas which she is not going to build."[7]

Another issue Canada might want to stay clear of, according to officers at External Affairs, was Singapore, an important naval base for the Royal Navy in Southeast Asia that Japan had requested be abandoned to remove a possible flashpoint for war. McNaughton

---

4. McNaughton, "Memorandum of Conversation with Dr O.D. Skelton and Mr Pearson," 4 January 1930, LAC, Manuscript Group (hereafter MG) 30 E133, vol. 103, Disarmament Book B.

5. "The London Naval Conference," 5 January 1930, appx. A, ibid.

6. McNaughton, "Memorandum of Conversation with Dr O.D. Skelton and Mr Pearson," 4 January 1930, ibid.

7. O.D. Skelton, "Naval Conference, London," 6 January 1930, LAC, MG 26 J4, vol. 124, file 912.

The Canadian delegation to the 1930 Disarmament Conference in London, England. From left to right: Walter Hose; J.L. Ralston, minister of national defence; Lester Pearson, first secretary, Department of External Affairs; and Major H.W. Brown, assistant deputy minister, Department of National Defence. (LAC PA-025146)

obviously felt that Britain should be able to count on Canadian support, and "explained that without it as an intermediate Base the operation of extensive British naval forces in the China Seas would be impossible; that Hong Kong was not considered immune from capture." With Hong Kong essentially defenceless, Singapore was all the more important, but Skelton also suggested that China could be used as a base of operations against Japan should war break out against that country.[8] However, since March 1924 policy on the issue had been clear, and, as Commodore Walter Hose pointed out, "the Canadian government tell us they wish to refrain from any advice on the problem." Hose was in agreement with McNaughton that the issue needed to be discussed, however, considering "the value of Canadian overseas trade with areas for which Singapore may be considered as a focal point for strategic and defensive purposes." The country exported upwards of $50 million worth of goods to the East Indies, Australia, New Zealand, and Hong Kong, while importing over $39 million worth. Also, "it is pointed out that they are largely commodities which are not indigenous to Canada, but which are required for the industrial development of her own natural resources." Consequently, "the question of the Singapore base cannot be considered as devoid of interest to Canada, and I would, therefore, recommend caution in the expression of any views in support of a reduction policy in the development of imperial defences in that quarter."[9]

Whether or not government agreed with its highest-ranking sailor, clearly isolationism vis-à-vis Admiralty policy was simply not possible, and given the common quota for armaments limitation some degree of coordination was necessary. Cruisers, destroyers, and submarines were thrown into the mix at the 1930 conference, and in August of that year Hose recommended that the various players within the commonwealth "come to an understanding regarding naval programmes covering the period up till 1936." The Admiralty suggested Canada maintain one or more cruisers, on loan from the RN, or, failing that, proceed with the construction of sloops.[10] Hose, however, if he could not get cruisers, preferred destroyers to sloops, as the latter lacked the firepower to counter surface raiders, while the better armed destroyers, were also "excellent anti-submarine vessels." As for the destroyers the RCN was operating, which at the time were *Champlain* and *Vancouver* (in commission from 1928 to 1936, their acquisition will be discussed below), the plan was to replace them by two vessels then under construction, *Saguenay* and *Skeena,* commissioned in 1931, so as to stay within the disarmament quota while nonetheless modernizing the fleet.[11]

It should be noted, however, that the very existence of a Royal Canadian Navy was still a topic of debate. Prime Minister R.B. Bennett, whose Conservatives were elected in July 1930, had not mentioned national defence during the campaign, but had certainly

---

8. McNaughton, "Memorandum of Conversation with Dr O.D. Skelton and Mr Pearson," 4 January 1930, LAC, MG 30 E133, vol. 103, Disarmament Book B.

9. Commodore Walter Hose, "On CID Secret Paper 346C, with respect to the Singapore Naval Base," 20 August 1930, ibid.

10. Hose, "Imperial Conference Proposals," 26 August 1930, ibid.

11. Roger Sarty, *Entirely in the Hands of the Friendly Neighbour: The Canadian Armed Forces and the Defence of the Pacific Coast, 1909–1939* (Victoria, 1995), 12; and Defence Council minutes, 29 August 1930, 1078–5-18, LAC, RG 24, vol. 4046.

broached the issue of country-wide unemployment. Although General McNaughton had pointed out the importance of the base at Singapore, he also believed that the RCN added little to Canadian security, would always be too small a force to provide effective maritime defence against a major power, and was likely to be absorbed into the Royal Navy in time of war in any event, a view no officer at NSHQ could effectively contradict. The army, on the other hand, had operated autonomously during the North-West campaign, and could do so again to defend Canadian soil. As a result, McNaughton could foresee few contingencies short of all-out war that would justify naval expansion. As chief of the general staff, he spoke for all three fighting services at the 1930 Imperial Conference, securing a consensus that the army and air force would be re-equipped before the navy.[12] The Royal Canadian Air Force, for one, was not the only such institution in the commonwealth looking to expand, at the expense of the RCN if necessary, as the RAF in this period was also "aggressively asserting its role in imperial and home defence," at the expense of the Royal Navy, if necessary. Under Hugh Trenchard, the RAF "utilised both economic stringency and the untested technological possibilities of air power to bolster the RAF's portion of the budget."[13] By 1938 it would receive the largest defence allocation of Britain's three fighting services. In Australia, "since at least 1925 the chief of the air staff had claimed that air power alone could control Australia's sea communications."[14] Air power was as much part of an ideology as a matter of strategic reasoning, and we shall soon see how the debate developed through the early years of the 1930s.

In the meantime, Hose provided detailed justification for the RCN's existence, as he had done so often in the past. His naval plans were based on the assumptions that "it is highly improbable we should be conducting hostilities single-handed," and that "war with the United States is not taken into consideration." Not one to exaggerate potential threats so as to inflate navy budgets, Hose also noted that "in the cases of war with an overseas power we are in a most fortunate geographical position in that we are 3,000 miles away from any such enemy on one side, and 6,000 miles on the other." The latter allowed a Canadian army no little time to mobilize, should a European or Asian country prove to be a threat, and made it unlikely that the country would actually face invasion, given that an enemy would probably have to fight Britain and other parts of the commonwealth. The main threat was thus to the nation's trade, more specifically to "the focal points of that trade in the vicinity of Canadian coasts." That threat would not be in the form of an enemy's main fleet, which would have the Royal Navy to contend with, but "a light cruiser or a few armed merchantmen might well prohibit the ingress or egress of any shipping to or from Canadian ports; also minelayers of either surface o[r] submarine type, could at least hamper the freedom of movement of merchant shipping, and expose it to grave dangers. Other more pressing

---

12. Stephen J. Harris, *Canadian Brass: The Making of a Professional Army, 1860–1939* (Toronto 1988), 156–57; and John Herd Thompson and Allen Seager, *Canada: 1922–1939, Decades of Discord* (Toronto 1985), 202.

13. Richard Harding, "Amphibious Warfare, 1930–1939," Richard Harding, ed., *The Royal Navy, 1930–2000: Innovation and Defence* (New York 2005), 45.

14. David Stevens, *A Critical Vulnerability: The Impact of the Submarine Threat on Australia's Maritime Defence, 1915–1954* (Canberra 2005), 86, 91.

requirements might prevent the dispatch of the assistance we should call for from the other friendly navies participating in the war," so Canada would need a navy of its own.[15]

Its organization and structure would be governed by its main task, to defend the focal points of Canadian trade. To that end, "it is more important to have *numbers* than individual unit size and offensive power," for though a cruiser "is more than powerful enough to deal with an armed merchant raider," she could only handle one such threat at a time, whereas "two or three destroyers would render the position decidedly dangerous, especially in the case of a night attack, for a light cruiser. Each would be a match for most armed raiders. For search purposes they would cover a large radius of effective action and concentration on any point could be achieved with rapidity." Also, "for submarine hunting they are practically essential." Yet another issue was the need to defend Canadian neutrality should the United States find itself at war with another country, such as Japan. A Canadian navy was necessary to ensure a belligerent did not use Canadian soil or waters as a base of operations, thereby forcing the US to intervene. To that end, and for defence of trade, the total cost of a destroyer leader, five destroyers, and four twin-screw minesweepers (or sloops), after factoring in "the valuable" contribution the air force could make, would be $4.5 to $5 million, or a two-fold increase over the 1930 budget.[16]

It was not to be, but McNaughton, in spite of his views on the importance of the army and air force, was convinced, at least in part, by Hose's arguments. He thus related how within the Defence Council "the responsible officers of the militia and air services endorse fully the conclusions reached by the chief of the naval staff,"—as the director of the naval service had become in 1928—"as to the composition of the Canadian naval force required; it being understood that this force covered the eventuality of danger *either* on the east *or* west coast and not on both simultaneously." Furthermore, "the director, Civil Government Air Operations, also stated that the value of air force co-operation largely depends upon the support of suitable surface vessels able to operate in all weathers." That did not mean, however, that Hose would get all he wanted within the time frame of a single government budget. Instead, two trawlers, not all four, would be replaced by twin-screw minesweepers. As well, "new construction and additional personnel to be so arranged that no increase in the naval estimates should be required in order to retain four destroyers in commission and effect the replacement of the 'trawler' minesweepers by four sloops properly manned."[17]

It was not everything the navy wanted, but it was far more than it might have received had the army and air force been more desperate for funding. Also disappointed by the RCN's development in this period was the Admiralty, which could note that at the 1926 Imperial conference it had been agreed that dominion navies would evolve in four phases, the first toward local defence, the second consisting of the creation of a "High-Seas Force," the third of a sea-going squadron, and the last of additional such formations. By the early 1930s, however, only Australia had reached the third rung on the development ladder,

15. Hose, "The Naval Defence Policy in Canada," 21 August 1930, 1078–5-18, LAC, RG 24, vol. 4046.

16. Ibid.

17. Defence Council minutes, 29 August 1930, 1078–5-18, LAC, RG 24, vol. 4046.

while "Canada had not gone far to fulfil the first phase."[18] One must consider, however, that the Royal Navy's relationship with the Royal Air Force, which in essence controlled development of air matters, including naval aviation, was no more collegial than the RCN's liaison activities with the RCAF and the army.

An excellent example of the relationship between Canada's three armed services was the evolution of the position of director of the naval service, which as we have seen had become the chief of the naval staff in 1928. The transition can be traced back to 1921 when Chief of the General Staff J.H. MacBrien explained his organizational doctrine to his minister. "The object of all organization in government departments is to secure a maximum of economy combined with the most efficient execution of work. This involves the carrying on of the work with a minimum of friction. The fewer component parts of any organisation is the less chance of friction there is." Therefore, "usually economy will be served best by centralisation, rather than by distribution of responsibility. Centralisation also reduces friction." He therefore recommended the organization of a single department "charged with the defence of the country." To achieve this, a "co-ordinating body should be formed to direct the general allotment of the resources of the country between the various services. Such a central authority would prevent competition for personnel and material, and eliminate overlapping and waste." MacBrien attached a chart with a minister of defence, a deputy minister of defence subordinate to him, and a defence council on a third tier; the latter was made up of the minister, the deputy minister, the chief of staff, the director of the naval service, the finance member, and "associate members as required," as well as a secretary. Next on the pyramid were, for the navy, an assistant deputy minister and naval staff, and for the militia, also an assistant deputy minister, whose duties would include responsibility for a "Canadian flying corps," and a general staff.[19]

The army and navy would, therefore, be equal, with a defence council to serve as arbiter, but less than a year later, on 24 November 1922, Cabinet adopted a different chart, which MacBrien had amended, with the minister at its head (as well as president of the defence council), the deputy minister as his subordinate (and vice-president of the defence council), and the chief of staff, with the defence council subordinate to the latter. The director of the naval service being a member of the council, clearly MacBrien aimed to have Hose report to him. One historian has speculated that the chief of the general staff hoped to avoid "any major dispute between the army and navy" leading to "a re-evaluation of all departmental activities." Whatever MacBrien's reasoning, the director of the naval service, informed of the reorganization on 17 January 1923, presented a counter-proposal, basically along the same lines as MacBrien's 1921 proposed organization, arguing that "there must be a clear and direct channel of communication between the minister and *each* of his advisers, i.e., the technical head of the navy and the technical head of the army."[20]

---

18. Stephen Roskill, *Naval Policy Between the Wars* (London, Collins, 1968), I, 183.

19. J.H. MacBrien to Minister, 19 December 1921, LAC, MG 30 E133, vol. 109, file National Defence HQ Reorganization, 1922–1924.

20. Harris, Canadian Brass, 153–54; and James Eayrs, *In Defence of Canada, I: From the Great War to the Great Depression* (Toronto 1964), 242.

There was no room for compromise—either the navy and the army were equal or the former was subordinate to the latter—and it seems that Hose had an ally in Desbarats, who was now deputy minister in the new Department of National Defence. In April 1923, MacBrien had written Desbarats to complain that "up to the present you have not issued the instructions which you promised to do within a few days time," to bring the reorganization into effect. The defence minister had "informed me twice that he had authorized the issue of those instructions and I am, therefore, forced to the conclusion that you have deliberately held them owing to the opposition of Captain Hose and yourself. Through this opposition the completion of the organization of this Department has been held up for a period of nearly four months."[21] Clearly the minister, George P. Graham, was either not entirely convinced by MacBrien's argument for the need for centralization, or was more focused on the issue of increasing the defence budget, as he did not press Desbarats to see the reorganization to fruition. As the deputy minister advised the chief of the general staff, his superior "has not shown any displeasure on this score, I presume that he is satisfied with the way in which I have interpreted his instructions."[22]

His reading of the situation would seem to have been the correct one, as MacBrien had to repeat his arguments several times in the years that followed, with no result, while in 1927, with J.L. Ralston now serving as minister of national defence, Hose added another point to his 1923 counter-proposal, arguing that he needed equal status with the chief of the general staff, as such would be "instrumental in promoting better co-operation between the Canadian, imperial, and Australian naval staffs in technical matters, since it will indicate parallel positions of responsibility." He was countering MacBrien's theory that there was a need for centralization with a practical argument in regards to liaison with other imperial institutions. Hose also recommended a change in title, to chief of the naval staff, on the grounds that "the responsibilities of the director of the naval service, as defined in Section 9 (2) of the Naval Service Act, are not clearly conveyed to the three sister services of the defence forces of Canada, by the designation 'director,' observing that the term 'director' is used in the Department of National Defence to signify the head of a division of one service, e.g., 'director of naval intelligence,' 'director of naval stores,' 'director of cadet services,' etc." On the other hand, "the title 'chief of the naval staff' covers the main phase of the responsibilities of the senior executive officer of the Royal Canadian Navy, viz., that of head of the naval staff, and responsible for the co-ordination of its resource activities such as personnel, material, naval defence plans and operations." Since the change in name implied no change in duties, there would be no need to amend the Naval Service Act.[23]

Given a defence minister willing to act, and more easily convinced by organizational logic than by hierarchical theory, and given a deputy minister who had always supported Hose's view, the director of the naval service became the chief of the naval staff by order-

21. MacBrien to Desbarats, 30 April 1923, LAC, MG 30 E133, vol. 109, file National Defence HQ Reorganization, 1922–1924.

22. Desbarats to MacBrien, 2 May 23, ibid.

23. Hose to Minister, 28 January 1927, Ralston to Governor General in Council, 28 January 1927, 1-1-9, LAC, RG 24, vol. 5585.

The deputy minister of national defence, G.J. Desbarats (left) confers with the minister, J.L. Ralston, while the assistant deputy minister, Major H.W. Brown, and a secretary look on. (LAC PA-062516)

in-council PC 372 of 7 March 1928. As for MacBrien, he had already tendered his resignation, "in part because of the conflict" with Hose and his supporters. In effect, the argument had not been on the issue of centralization, but the hierarchical level at which National Defence would be centralized, with the chief of the general staff wishing to make himself the institution's centre, while the director of the naval service suggested the minister should play that role.[24]

There were also, of course, personnel issues to deal with nearer the bottom of the RCN pyramid. To give just one example, Commander Victor Brodeur, the senior naval officer in *Stadacona*, warned in August 1927 that *Patriot*'s training program would have to be revised. "With the present state of the complement of seamen ratings it will not be possible to send a minesweeper with the *Patriot*, which is considered necessary for the towing of targets, etc. The small number of able seamen in barracks are all used up as quartermasters and sweepers [i.e., personnel operating minesweeping equipment], leaving new entries as part of the ship, which is most unsatisfactory, as they need first of all to be trained to be of any use." Nor was that all, since "the sending of a draft to England for courses has necessitated the placing of one of the minesweepers under reduced complement, which would be completed from barracks complement only in case of emergency. This had to be done owing to five seamen ratings at present undergoing detention, varying from thirty to sixty days."[25]

An order-in-council of 15 November 1924 had capped the navy's personnel strength at 550 officers and ratings, but clearly that number was insufficient. In June 1928, Minister of Defence J.L. Ralston related how "the technical officers report, further, that, in order to partly train the additional personnel required and so reduce to a minimum the number of trained officers and ratings which will have to be borrowed from the Royal Navy, it will be necessary to enter in the Royal Canadian Navy ten additional officers and 150 additional ratings during the present fiscal year," for a total of 710. The Privy Council agreed, and the necessary order was issued, but that was not all. A year later Commander C.T. Beard, the naval staff officer, suggested that a reserve of ten percent be created. The extra personnel were needed "to allow for normal wastage, and ratings proceeding overseas for courses."[26] A year later Commodore Hose was asking for an increase of ten officers and 180 ratings, though "no expenditure of funds in excess of the appropriations already voted by parliament will be incurred during the present fiscal year," which would have required Cabinet, rather than just departmental, approval.[27] At the time the minesweepers *Thiepval* and *Armentieres*, while on seal patrol, carried only two officers each, "except on such few occasions as the services of an officer of the naval reserve forces are obtainable."[28] With at least

---

24. PC 372, 7 March 1928, copy in ibid; and Harris, *Canadian Brass*, 155.

25. Cdr V.G. Brodeur, SNO *Stadacona*, to NSHQ, 18 August 1927, 33-7-1, LAC, RG 24, vol. 5633.

26. Cdr C.T. Beard to CNS, 5 July 1929, Ralston to Governor General, 19 June 1928, 1-24-1, LAC, RG 24, vol. 5586.

27. Hose to Desbarats, 14 September 1929, ibid.

28. Desbarats to Deputy Minister of Fisheries, 20 July 1929, 133-7-5, LAC, RG 24, vol. 5683.

one officer required to be on duty at any given time, the situation demanded much in the way of endurance.

Even if a higher establishment was authorized, filling it could not be taken for granted. As the naval staff officer related in September 1929, the navy had "to deal with conditions here in Canada which causes the naval recruiting question to appear to fail badly, as compared with that existing in the British Isles." There one could find "a far wider knowledge amongst the general public of what is expected of a youth when he joins the navy. There is practically nothing of this sort in Canada." Once men were recruited, however, their retention rate was acceptable. "I would consider that we had been most successful if 70 per cent of our new entries remain in the service for one period of engagement," the naval staff officer stated, and "from hearsay I believe our results are greatly superior to those of the American navy or Canadian militia, where the term of engagement is much shorter." There had been an increase in discharges in recent years, but mainly because those found unsatisfactory could be replaced from a recruiting roster, and new entries had risen from about thirty to at least 150. Still, discharges could be reduced through stricter medical screening and tougher educational examinations. Even then those released as "service no longer required" (SNLR) might serve effectively in the reserves.[29]

A new form of discharge was introduced in 1929—"unlikely to become efficient"—with the purpose of reducing the stigma attached to those who were released from the navy through a lack of ability, a result that was more a reflection on naval recruiters than on the individual sailor.[30] Making it easier for ratings to leave the service was not, however, universally accepted among the navy's policy makers, especially at a time when numbers were a serious problem. The naval secretary, for one, related the story of a boy being recommended for discharge by the senior naval officer in Halifax for "hypochondriasis, a nervous temperament and failure to show the physical improvement desirable." The case having been referred to the chief of the naval staff for a decision (itself an indication of how small the RCN was at the time), the naval secretary warned that "it is becoming increasingly easy for a man or a boy to get out of the RCN at no cost to himself, and in some cases at little or no inconvenience," a sailor usually having to purchase his release if he had not completed his contract. The navy had to be careful before allowing such an easy exit, as the sailor in question "may be just disgruntled and going through the stage that probably 50 per cent of young ratings go through who join any naval service without previous knowledge of its requirements, life and discipline."[31]

In the secretary's view, "of the large number who go through this stage, the great majority who do not obtain their discharge weather their feeling of disappointment successfully and settle down to become useful and contented members of the service." In fact, "many men in the naval service now reliable petty officers and leading seamen, have misconducted themselves as younger ratings, and there must be many more such petty officers and leading

29. Naval Staff Officer to Naval Secretary, 17 September 1929, 11–1-1, LAC, RG 24, vol. 5590.

30. "Minutes of Fifth Meeting of the Naval Staff," 25 November 1929, 1078–3-1, LAC, RG 24, vol. 4044.

31. Naval Secretary to NSO, 29 August 1929, 11–1-1, LAC, RG 24, vol. 5590.

seamen who felt the urge to get out in the first year or so of service but who did not actually come up against the laws of the navy.... It is an interesting question to consider how many of the young ratings who have recently been discharged SNLR could, had they been retained in the service, have been made useful and creditable members of the service."[32] That might indeed have been the case, but nevertheless there would still be those who could not become efficient members of the RCN, and they had to be let go. After an incident in which *Armentieres* fouled *Vancouver,* while an engine room artificer had not been at his post, it was suggested that the individual not be re-engaged when his term of service expired.[33] Undoubtedly, there were other, similar cases.

Something needed to be done about the service's insufficient number of recruits, and especially the inadequate intake of officers, only two cadets entering the RCN in 1929. Eight had been required, but that number, in fact, was "never reached."[34] The previous year three had entered, and not all were qualifying for higher rank. According to the naval secretary, "one of the cadets who was entered in 1928 has been unfavourably reported on by the imperial navy as being unfit for an officer, and is being returned to Canada. There was quite a long discussion on this question. It is considered that if the cadets had preparatory training in Canada for the navy they would make a better impression in HM ships."[35] More education of those actually joining the service may have been necessary, but it would not help solve the problem of placing sufficient numbers of officers in Canadian ships.

With mounting pressure to continue increasing the RCN's establishment mounting, Hose informed Desbarats in November 1931 that "experience in administering the present force of the Royal Canadian Navy has brought out certain deficiencies in the complement authorized by the governor-general in council on 30th October, 1929, particularly in regard to W/T and signal ratings and to the accountant and victualling staffs. It is also being found impossible to spare Canadian ratings for training in the technical schools in England in sufficient numbers to ensure the early relief of some seventy ratings on loan from the Royal Navy, without seriously detracting from the efficiency of the HMC ships and establishments in commission."[36] Recruiting could not, however, have been helped by the 1932 decision to reduce pay by ten percent, and although the cost of living index had dropped by about that amount, that merely meant that sailors were neither worse nor better off than before.[37] As Llewellyn Houghton related in his memoirs, "as far as the navy was concerned, this made life, to say the least, pretty difficult, especially for the married members with families since our normal pay was not exactly generous, and we had not yet been granted marriage allowance (it eventually arrived in 1940) although the army already enjoyed this useful addition to one's salary.... Looking back on it now, I suppose we should

---

32. Ibid.

33. "Minutes of Fourth Meeting of the Naval Staff," 4 November 1929, 1078–3-1, LAC, RG 24, vol. 4044.

34. "Minutes of Second Meeting of the Naval Staff," 14 October 1929, ibid.

35. "Minutes of Seventh Meeting of the Naval Staff," 30 December 1929, ibid.

36. CNS to DM, 25 November 1931, 1–24–1, LAC, RG 24, vol. 5586.

37. F.H. Leacy, ed., *Historical Statistics of Canada: Second Edition* (Ottawa 1983), K1.

have considered ourselves lucky; at least we had steady jobs even if we were grossly under-paid."[38] Canada was, after all, in the depths of the Great Depression.

For those who did choose an officer's career in the RCN, almost all their training would, in fact, be in the Royal Navy, as had been the case for decades. One who underwent that experience beginning in the latter part of the 1920s was Herbert Rayner, who under-took his midshipman's training, in part, in HMS *Revenge*. Soon after arrival on board the battleship, "we were taken down to the gunroom for tea, having first been introduced to the sub-lieutenant, and senior midshipman. We then stowed away our gear, until we were sent for by Lieut Comdr Wallace. After that we were shown round the ship, and then intro-duced to the commander. After supper, we went to a cinema in the wardroom, and then turned in at 2315." All-in-all, a rather gentle introduction to the ways of a capital ship, though reveille was at 06:15 next morning, "after what seemed a very short night." Rayner's post for the exercises that followed was in Y turret, then to the director tower to watch night firing. "When the 15-inch guns fired the whole ship shuddered. I was so star-tled by the shaking of the ship and bright flash, that I didn't hear any noise."[39]

Later, Rayner played a very small part in a very large exercise in which Red Force oper-ated six battleships and Blue Force had four battleships and three battle cruisers. Conducted off the coast of Africa, it consisted of Red Force deploying aircraft and cruisers to shadow its opponent; submarines were also used. Part of Blue Force was deemed destroyed. More in the way of routine was an incident in port, when "an Italian fishing smack anchored so as to be foul of the ship if she swung. In spite of repeated warnings, he refused to move, so that at 1700 the ship swung into him. Boathooks, capstan bars, and fenders, were utilised to keep the smack off the ship's side. I had to tow it off in the picket boat." Later, further exercises focused on getting a landing party ashore so as to spot the fall of shot for the fleet; observation posts "were to be held at all cost, regardless of losses, for as long as possible," orders reminiscent of the Naval Division's operations on the Western Front. Still, the Blue side was victorious, and "on return to the beach, where we had landed, everyone bathed, the most appreciated evolution of the morning."[40]

It was not all war games and recreation, however, and midshipmen had to study such manuals as *Queries in Seamanship,* which provided 150 questions on rigging, 163 on anchor work, forty-eight on rules of the road, 214 on officer of the watch duties, 316 on the RN's organization, 125 on signals, 104 on construction, and eighty-one on "general knowledge."[41] Pasted into Rayner's training journal were a couple of dozen illustrations, including a "signalling and instrument lights circuit," a "track chart of the movements of HMS *Warspite,*" and "approaches to Gibraltar."[42] The RCN may have operated no ship larger than a destroyer, but her officers would master huge amounts of detail nonetheless.

---

38. F.L. Houghton, "Memoir," nd, 132, LAC, MG 30 E444.

39. Midshipman's Training Journal, pt. 1, 9 and 10 February 1930, LAC, MG 30 E517, vol. 1.

40. Midshipman's Training Journal, pt. 1, 12 March, 15 April and 17 July 1930, ibid.

41. *Queries in Seamanship,* 1928, LAC, ibid, vol. 3.

42. Midshipman's Training Journal, pt. 2, ibid, vol. 1.

They would also, once they qualified as sub-lieutenants, have to deal with myriad administrative details not only in regard to their ships but in relation to their daily lives ashore. Those who found themselves posted to Malta, for example, had to learn to avoid "certain pitfalls which past experience has shown to be common." They had to ensure that any lease they signed for a home could be terminated if they were ordered to sea or to a different posting, and that the home itself met "with the standards of a naval officer." In regard to groceries and similar necessities, they should "keep their servants in funds in advance to pay for such goods and to inform all tradesmen with whom they deal first that their servants have no authority to take away goods from shops without a written order, and second that all goods must be delivered with a written invoice."[43] One might join the RCN, in part, to see the world, but it would not be as a tourist on an organized holiday.

Llewellyn Houghton, now a lieutenant-commander, could certainly attest to that fact. Posted into *Renown,* in September 1930 he was part of an exercise in which the battle cruiser squadron, accompanied by cruisers and destroyers, operated off the Firth of Forth. "The squadron wireless officer (SWO) put me in charge of all W/T communications to the five flotillas—a total of forty-five destroyers. Here I was at last, as I had once upon a time pictured myself, somewhere deep down in the bowels of the ship, surrounded by a maze of dials, switches and wires, tapping out Morse code at incredible speeds, the envy and admiration of all. Or so I hoped." At the conclusion of the exercise all flotillas were to rejoin and Houghton manned the morse key himself to send the necessary signal. "About ninety minutes later, a message seeped down from the Admiral's bridge, 'Where, Oh where is the Third Flotilla???' The whole fleet was concentrated with the exception of those nine destroyers, which seemed to have disappeared into thin air. The SWO hurried down to the destroyer R/T office (there were nine W/T offices in that ship) and began an investigation. All seemed well until he realised that in making the recall signal I had omitted to ask the ships to 'acknowledge' receipt of the message. Everyone had read it except the Third Flotilla which was still steaming around the North Sea about fifty miles away. Was my face red!"[44] He was fortunate in being able to learn from his mistake rather than face disciplinary action.

Ratings, after some very basic initial training in Canada, also went to British facilities to learn the more intricate details of their trade. The transition was not always smooth, but after comparing the situation at one facility, Whale Island, with another, Vernon, Commander L.W. Murray, the naval staff officer, concluded that "apparently it is not the intelligence of the Canadian rating, nor even his educational standard, which is found wanting, but only his smartness and unquestioning obedience to command," Canada's class structure being noticeably different from that of Britain's. "I am not in favour of developing the latter to such an extent that it kills initiative, but a general smartening up can hurt no one. When fully 'teed up,' on any special occasion, the RCN lads can be as smartly dressed and as smart on parade as any RN guard of honour, but instinctive smartness on all occasions, on and off duty, comes from years of training and environment." Therein lay the problem,

43. "A Few Notes on Legal Advice to Officers Coming to Serve in Malta," December 1928, 10–1-9, LAC, RG 24, vol. 3579.

44. F.L. Houghton, "Memoir," nd, 110, LAC, MG 30 E444.

in Murray's view, as "in these respects the RCN is at a disadvantage owing to late entry, and lack of training. Many of the ratings under review at Whale Island in 1930–31 had entered as ordinary seamen just over eighteen months before and had had the bare service qualifications for advancement to AB," or able seaman, which required eighteen months as an ordinary seaman with nine months of sea time. "No wonder Whale Island," which taught them gunnery, "didn't appreciate them in comparison with their own ratings who had been under Naval discipline, since the age of 15½ and had anything up to five or six years experience."[45]

A partial solution was possible, and "seagoing officers can be greatly assisted in their work, and the ratings themselves made more useful in a seagoing ship on arrival if, before being drafted to sea as part complement of one of HMC destroyers, they have passed for AB in gunnery and torpedo, and have become word perfect in small arm drill and boat work. Considerable training in many branches of seamanship such as compass, helm, lead-line knots and splices, bends and hitches, rule of the road, sail-making, etc, can also be given in the shore training establishment at each coast." He could thus become an active member of a ship's complement, rather than be relegated exclusively to cleaning duties, and would learn far more from the experience as a result. "It is estimated that fifteen to eighteen months can be profitably spent in training the new entry in the shore training establishment before he goes to sea and that he will be more useful to the service for every month so spent." The scheme would have the added benefit of allowing entry at age sixteen and a half, for though an order in council prevented boys from being sent to sea, these would in fact be of age by the time they completed their initial training ashore.[46]

There was thus no lack of intelligent staff work focusing on training challenges, which were many and diverse. One, interestingly enough, was language, for if officer candidates like René Coulombe needed to be proficient in English, such was not always the case for new ratings. As G.A. Youle, the naval secretary, reported to the commander-in-chief Halifax in 1927, "seven French-speaking recruits are reporting at RCN barracks Halifax on Monday, 30th October. Another French-speaking ordinary seaman may join at an early date…. This class will be augmented by nine English-speaking boy recruits on about 20th November." There was, at the time, no systematic second-language training available in the navy, so, "in view of the lingual difficulties anticipated, the French-speaking recruits have been sent three weeks in advance of the remainder of the class to enable them to get some grasp of the language and not to hold up the whole new entry class at the commencement of the course."[47] Whether three weeks would suffice does not seem to have been a topic for discussion, but it should be noted here that in the 1920s and 1930s—and for many years thereafter—the RCN was an English-speaking institution, so any attempt to accommodate francophones would have been seen as generous.

---

45. Cdr L.W. Murray, "Training Conference, 19th May 1932," nd, notes of 17 May 1932, 21–1-18, LAC, RG 24, vol. 3613.

46. Ibid.

47. Naval Secretary to Commander-in-Charge Halifax, 27 October 1933, ibid.

Similarly, the naval service ensured that medical and dental costs did not get out of hand, and when the issue of increasing the number of sick berth ratings arose at a meeting of the naval staff, "it was not considered necessary to discuss this question fully at the meeting. NSO stated that three were already allowed on each coast."[48] As for dentistry, "routine dental examinations at definite periodic intervals have not been carried out, but examinations are held from time to time to ascertain that hygienic conditions, including dental, are satisfactorily maintained." In 1931–32 dental work had cost the RCN almost $3,400, but that was reduced to $2,332 the following year, no surprise given the deflation of the Great Depression. Therefore, "the cost of maintaining dental fitness is, approximately $5.00 per year, or one and one third cents per day, per man. This is not considered excessive, and it is doubted if it can be materially decreased, but every effort is made to restrict it to a minimum compatible with the preservation of a sanitary dental condition." Such work was done under contract, which was deemed far less expensive than putting dentists into uniform.[49]

Such issues, obviously, related to the RCN, but there was also a British presence in Canada, which raised a separate set of challenges. In spite of its own difficulties recruiting officers the Canadian naval service aided the Admiralty in processing Canadian candidates for Royal Navy positions. Preliminary examinations were done in Canada, for example, though medicals had to wait until the officer recruit arrived in England. Such co-operation was not one-sided, however, as serving members of the RN came to Canada to take positions the RCN could not fill itself. As the naval staff officer, Commander C.T. Beard, warned in 1929, "the expedient of borrowing trained ratings from the RN in 1931 cannot be wholly avoided; the disadvantage of borrowing is purely financial and sentimental; the advantages are greater efficiency and the gradual provision of vacancies for Canadian ratings as they become proficient."[50] Therefore, when the time came to convene a court-martial, "there not yet being any captains in the Royal Canadian Navy, it is necessary to obtain the services of an officer of the Royal Navy for this purpose." A retired officer living in Vernon, BC, was approached in this instance.[51]

As for those of lower rank whose postings to Canada were for periods of years rather than for the duration of a court martial, many found the work and circumstances less than onerous. As the naval secretary reported in 1931, "it is believed that many of the ratings on loan from the Royal Navy, whose periods of loan expire in March or April, 1932, are desirous of volunteering for an extension of their loan agreement." The Department of National Defence was willing to consider such requests given the navy's perpetual shortage of trained personnel, and those would be accepted "who are specially recommended for such extension of loan, by their commanding officers." Six Royal Navy ratings took advantage of the scheme. One fortunate consequence was economy, since it was not necessary to pay

48. "Minutes of Eighth Meeting of the Naval Staff," 20 January 1930, 1078-3-1, LAC, RG 24, vol. 4044.

49. C-in-Charge, Naden to NSHQ, 14 December 1933, LCol R.M. Luton to NSHQ, 27 December 1933, 799–2-1, LAC, RG 24, vol. 5689.

50. Cdr C.T. Beard to CNS, 5 July 1929, 1–24–1, LAC, RG 24, vol. 5586; and O'B LeBlanc for Naval Secretary to SNO RCN Barracks Esquimalt, 17 August 1928, 53–15–2, LAC, RG 24, vol. 5652.

51. Cdr (Pay) G.A. Youle to Captain Thomas Armstrong RN, 5 December 1930, 80–1-1, LAC, RG 24, vol. 5671.

passage for the sailor to return home or to bring his relief to Canada. Still, the RCN was hoping to fill junior positions in gunnery and torpedo branches with its own personnel, though thirteen more senior positions would have to be filled with members of the RN. They would be provided on a two-year loan, but Canadian responsibility for their welfare did not end with the termination of their posting. Should they be diagnosed with tuberculosis, to give just one example, London invited the Canadian government "to bear the cost of one half of the grants made."[52] The RCN agreed, considering that such cases would be rare.

Although members of the RN serving in Canada did so as members of the Permanent Force RCN and unarguably improved its proficiency and efficiency, they did nothing to give the navy at large a Canadian face—something the service would need if it was to become embedded in the national culture and psyche. Indeed, given the manning limitations on the permanent RCN, the service still had to rely heavily on its two reserve elements to give it a presence in Canadian communities and to serve as a nucleus for mobilization. One of them, the RCNR, consisted of trained merchant mariners who occasionally spent a few weeks at a time learning naval trades. Estimates for the 1928–29 fiscal year provided for thirty-six officers and 210 ratings in that force, though its actual numbers at the time totalled thirty-three and 140. An order in council provided the authority—but no extra funding—for a strength of seventy officers and 430 ratings. (Its strength would peak during this period at thirty-seven officers and 157 ratings.) In 1930, the RCNR detachment in Quebec City boasted five enginemen, two leading seamen, a dozen stokers, and fourteen seamen, for a total of thirty-three ratings, though they had been recruited from all over the region, including fourteen from the city proper, five from Levis, five from Montmagny, three from Montreal, two from L'Islet, two from Lotbiniere, one from Portneuf, and one from Montmorency—seven different cities and counties. Not all, ironically, would be available in time of emergency, given that three of Quebec's ratings were apprentice pilots in St Lawrence vessels, and "it is considered that the importance of their civil employment would lead to their not being available for the RCN in war time."[53]

In Lunenburg, Nova Scotia, to give a counter example—a seafaring community if ever there was one—not one applicant came forward to join the RCNR. Admittedly, Ottawa had erred in sending the registrar only recruiting posters for the RCNVR which, designed to train neophytes, was not likely to appeal to experienced fishermen. However, the naval staff officer was inclined to believe that the problem lay with the RCNR registrar, a man deemed to be "useless" and whose "services should be dispensed with."[54] Although the supervising

52. Passfield, Downing Street to Secretary of State for External Affairs, 21 December 1929, 53–6–10, LAC, RG 24, vol. 5652; and Naval Secretary to Senior Naval Officers, RCN Barracks Halifax and Esquimalt, 17 November 1931, LCdr Hibbard, for Commander in Charge Halifax, to NSHQ, 25 November 1931, L.W. Murray to CNS, 24 December 1931, Admiralty to CNS, 17 February 1932, 53–6–1, LAC, RG 24, vol. 5651.

53. C-in-Charge, RCN Barracks Halifax to NSHQ, 4 January 1933, J.A. O'Dowd to NSHQ, 18 August 1930, 124–5–1, LAC, RG 24, vol. 5681; H.W.S. Soulsby, Supervising Officer, Reserves, to CNS, 5 October 1928, 121–1–1, LAC, RG 24, vol. 5680; and Canada, DND, *Annual Report of the Department of National Defence (Naval Service) for the Fiscal Year Ended March 31 1931* (Ottawa 1931).

54. Naval Staff Officer to DNS, 17 October 1927, LCdr H.W.S. Soulsby to DNS, 10 December 1927, 124–18–1, LAC, RG 24, vol. 5681.

officer for the naval reserves was inclined to be sympathetic, the results for 1928 were no better; moreover, one man who applied in Halifax did so because he got "no satisfaction from the registrar at Lunenburg." Here, at least, the individual registrar may have been a problem. Whether that was the case in Montreal, which produced only one new entry in 1927 (compared to eight in Quebec, five in Charlottetown, and seventeen in Halifax) cannot be determined, but what was clear was that although the Lunenburg office would close, an RCNR recruiting office had to be maintained in Montreal, since "it is considered that it would not be in the best interest of the RCNR to do away with the registrar in such an important centre," the supervising officer for naval reserves observed.[55]

Perhaps it was only to be expected that Halifax would produce the largest number of recruits because of its seafaring culture, but in fact what seems to have been significant here was the close relationship between the RCN and the Royal Canadian Mounted Police. The latter relied on the former for ship maintenance, while two navy officers were seconded to the commissioner's office in Ottawa and to the officer commanding the maritime provinces district. Tight liaison with the mounties paid off mainly in that "virtually to a man, the members of the service enrolled in the Royal Canadian Naval Reserve," specifically the division at Halifax. "The vessels were earmarked for transfer to the armed forces in the event of war, some for naval duty and others for rescue and support services for maritime operations by the air force. Thus, the little RCMP-manned anti-smuggling flotilla based at North Sydney would become the first waterborne component of Cape Breton's local defences in 1939."[56] There were limits, however, as to how close the relationship between the RCMP and the RCN could be, and when in October 1932 the police commissioner suggested that its marine section be formed into a unit of the RCNVR, the navy had to reply that such was "not considered desirable" because it would require an increase in naval estimates.[57] The midst of the Great Depression was not the time to implement such ideas.

The Saint John registrar was even more unfortunate, though he accepted a 1929 decision to dismiss him with good grace, perhaps because the position was only a part-time job in any case. More than a year before his services were terminated, he was complaining that "it would appear to me that Saint John is just a recruiting station for Montreal, as nearly all of my men have been transferred to that division." Furthermore, "business at this port the past winter was the worst in the history of the shipping office, plenty of men but no ships for them, I turned down dozens of men who only wanted to join the RCNR, in order to get a square meal and fill in the time till they could get other jobs, they had no intention of keeping it up, they admitted this when questioned." Still, "while the number of men recruited was small, I think I saved the department time and money by turning down undesirables."[58] Of eight men on the registrar's books, only one lived in New Brunswick.

---

55. Soulsby to DNS, 7 February 1928, ibid.

56. Brian Tennyson and Roger Sarty, *Guardian of the Gulf: Sydney, Cape Breton, and the Atlantic Wars* (Toronto 2000), 195.

57. Commissioner RCMP to Desbarats, 15 October 1932; and Desbarats to Commissioner RCMP, 25 November 1932, 112–1–34, LAC, RG 24, vol. 5678.

58. P.S. Purdy, Registrar, to NSHQ, 20 April 1928, 124–4–1, LAC, RG 24, vol. 5681.

Having been ordered to transfer all his records to the division in Halifax, he responded that "for some time I have been contemplating writing you regarding this matter as the work in this office has been getting less every year, and now with the withdrawal by Canadian National Steamship Company of their Cardiff and Swansea, and London and Antwerp boats, I can see very little business for the coming winter." Pointedly, he noted that "the business had declined to such an extent that I have to dispense with the services of my assistant." Along with divisions at Lunenburg and Saint John, divisions at Victoria and Prince Rupert would close, their registrars' commissions being cancelled.[59]

One way to keep numbers up was to encourage members to re-enrol after their five-year period of service had expired, and at one point the Quebec division had thirteen sailors in that category. Another approach was to help members find employment, as Lieutenant (Pay) J.A. O'Dowd did, also in Quebec City. "As I have always been very anxious that ratings in my division should follow consistently a sea-faring life, and thus become useful and efficient members of the Force, every effort tending towards this objective was made by me with satisfactory results as in the case of those ratings who, coming to me after they had attended naval training, sought my assistance in procuring for them employment in the mercantile marine or else on ships of the marine department here." Some examples were Able Seamen Henri Coté, Émile Pelletier, and Philippe Auguste Santerre, "who have all of them attended for their second year," and "were sent by me to join the MS [merchant ship] *C.O. Stillman* in New York. This ship is under the charge of Lieutenant-Commander C.R. Treweek, RD, RNR, who needed RCNR ratings to replace RNR ratings returning to England on the expiration of their twelve months' agreement." The engagement, for a year, paid $55 monthly. It was, in the event, through the Halifax registrar that O'Dowd had managed to find these positions, since he was also deputy shipping master for the port.[60]

It must have come as no little shock when, two months later, Commander C.R. Treweek of the Royal Naval Reserve reported that "Able Seamen Henri Coté, Émile Pelletier and Philippe Auguste Santerre all deserted this ship last night, after having received their wages. Coté and Santerre appeared to be dissatisfied throughout the voyage, and requested to be paid off on arrival at New York. I pointed out to them that their transportation had been paid from Canada to the United States to this ship which flies the blue ensign and they as naval reservists should be proud to sail on this vessel. After being paid last night their rooms were searched and all their effects had been taken ashore with them. Furthermore, three of the other seamen reported a loss of considerable sums of money and suspicion is on Coté, Pelletier and Santerre."[61]

Three days later, O'Dowd reported that "Santerre came to my office this morning, and on being asked what he had to say in the matter he simply replied that they had done a

59. P.S. Purdy, Registrar, to NSHQ, 10 October 1929, LCdr H.W.S. Souslby, SO Reserves to NSHQ, 25 April 1928, 124–4-1, LAC, RG 24, vol. 5681; and J.M. Skuce, for Deputy Minister Marine and Fisheries, to Desbarats, 5 November 1929, 121–1-1, LAC, RG 24, vol. 5680.

60. Lt (Pay) J.A. O'Dowd to NSHQ, 12 January 1929, Naval Secretary to O'Dowd, 2 October 1928, 124–5-1, LAC, RG 24, vol. 5681.

61. Cdr C.R. Treweek RNR to J.A. O'Dowd, 13 March 1929, ibid.

very foolish thing, and, on my enquiry, stated that they had been all well treated by Commander Treweek and officers of the ship. I surmise his real objective in coming to see me was to apply for retainer, (as he appeared surprised to learn that I was so soon aware of the fact that he and the other two seamen had deserted their vessel), and in this regard he was informed that the matter would now have to remain in abeyance, and that headquarters would be made fully aware of all circumstances, as reported by the commander of the *C.O. Stillman*." He had not heard from the other two, "and it is doubtful that they will communicate with me now for some time, as Santerre will very likely tell them that I am aware of all facts in their cases." Of course, O'Dowd "felt very much disappointed at the outcome of the efforts I made for the well-being of these men," but RCN regulations did not allow for disciplinary action for offences committed in the merchant marine.[62] However, as the navy secretary suggested, "these ratings should be informed that the fact of their desertion has been noted at headquarters and that the department regards their action with strong disapproval, particularly in view of the efforts made on their behalf by the registrars at Quebec and Halifax to obtain them employment."[63]

The Canadian navy's other reserve system was the RCNVR, which, as Walter Hose remembered after the country had fought another world war (and found itself in what would be called the Cold War), had been formed as an antidote to "the lack of interest shown in the navy, both in government circles and by the country at large" for the first decade and more of its existence. Such "made it plain that it would be rash to expect any increase in appropriations for the navy until there was a far greater consciousness, a far greater realization throughout the dominion of the necessity for a navy in the scheme of national defence…. To do this the navy must be brought into the country, and the only way to do it, that I could see, was to raise a naval volunteer reserve with units in populous cities throughout the dominion."[64] As such the RCNVR faced challenges somewhat different from those of the RCNR as its members were not experienced sailors when they joined, but interested citizens (it took over a year to learn the rudiments of navy life on a part-time basis). Its recruited strength in 1927–28 was sixty-eight officers and 740 ratings, total numbers rising to sixty-six and 953 in 1932.[65]

To train them, company commanding officers could rely on petty officer instructors (themselves retired members of the permanent force), but only a handful of qualified personnel were available for such duty at any given time. When an instructor in Ottawa died, the supervising officer reserves (that title changed later to director naval reserves) warned "that it was quite a problem to find a successor." The director of naval intelligence, for his part, "suggested that the RCN Officers serving in HM ships might be advised of the difficulty and they could look out for suitable men who were retiring from the RN and who

---

62. O'Dowd to NSHQ, 16 March 1929, ibid.

63. Naval Secretary to O'Dowd, 5 April 1929, ibid.

64. "The Early Years of the Royal Canadian Navy," nd, DHH 2001/12, folder B, file 3.

65. Naval Secretary to CCOs RCNVR, 7 May 1929, 114–1-3, LAC, RG 24, vol. 5678; and DND, *Annual Report of the Department of National Defence (Naval Service) for the Fiscal Year Ended March 31 1932* (Ottawa 1932).

would be interested in this work. The appointment is for five years."[66] A replacement was, indeed, found, in the person of Chief Petty Officer Hill, but he had not yet retired. However, according to Commander J.E.W. Oland, the director of naval reserves, "the employing of active service petty officer instructors has many advantages. It eliminates refresher courses at Training Headquarters; allows of a better selection of petty officer Instructors, who are under the Naval Discipline Act, and who have the service at heart. Also, these instructors are more up to date in their non-substantive rating." One problem, from Oland's perspective, was that retirees had interests in the community in which they retired, work with the RCNVR often taking a back seat, whereas "active service petty officers would not be in a unit a sufficient length of time to acquire outside interests, also their behaviour whilst serving as petty officer instructors would count towards their future."[67]

Though the deputy minister, G.J. Desbarats, noted that the suggestion was a departure from government policy, Oland added to his argument the fact that serving personnel could be transferred from one RCNVR unit to another, a far more difficult prospect when it came to retired members. Commodore Hose, for one, was convinced by the argument, adding that "the fact that the petty officer instructors are so much older than the personnel gives rise to difficulties for both ratings and instructors." On the other hand, "change of policy would require about eight to ten years to complete as active service POs became available." At least pay would not be an issue; they would simply be paid according to their permanent force rate, but any petty officer posted to the RCNVR would have to be replaced in his ship. That, however, could be used to advantage, as "one of the difficulties in producing efficiency in a small force such as the RCN is the lack of a sufficient proportion of advancements for the lower ratings. This has a consequent effect of lower ratings leaving the service at the end of their first period of enrolment, just when the funds expended in training these ratings is beginning to produce efficient results. The proportion of petty officers which would be employed as petty officer instructors would increase the proportion of petty officers in the RCN and thereby give the necessary encouragement to first-period ratings."[68] As we shall see, such a policy was indeed adopted, at least eventually.

Ensuring RCNVR units had petty officer instructors was but one challenge among many; another was the appointment of suitable commanding officers. For example, after visiting the Vancouver company on three different drill nights, Lieutenant-Commander G.B. Barnes reported that "I consider that Lieutenant Charles R.F. Piers, is capable and efficient to be company commanding officer but at the same time it would be better to have an older officer with more experience, if possible an officer with war experience who would command more respect from the men for that reason. Lieutenant Piers is respected by the company but he himself agrees that an older man with more experience would have more standing both in dealing with the men of his company and with the other service and civilian heads with whom the commanding officer of the company comes in contact from time

66. "Minutes of Seventh Meeting of the Naval Staff," 30 December 1929, 1078-3-1, LAC, RG 24, vol. 4044.

67. Cdr J.E.W. Oland, Director Naval Reserves, to CNS, 14 October 1931, 1-24-1, LAC, RG 24, vol. 5586.

68. Hose to Desbarats, 24 November 1931, Desbarats to Hose, 17 October 1931, Oland to Hose, 24 November 1931, 1-24-1, LAC, RG 24, vol. 5586.

to time." An important role for the RCNVR was to represent the navy in local communities. A local reserve officer, Mr Wade, was thought to be more suitable as he had experience training sea cadets, and had served with the Royal Naval Volunteer Reserve during the war. Piers, on the other hand, was "of a rather shy and retiring disposition and it is felt that an officer with slightly more personality and push would uphold the RCNVR especially at public functions in competition with the army and other officials." Piers, interestingly enough, had no objection to Wade's appointment as the company commander.[69]

As for the rest of the Vancouver company, "the discipline and morale of the company is very good and the men of the company are of a good type and showed keenness and interest in their work." One reason for that may have been that "a lecture on naval subjects of interest was given on each visit and the men appeared to appreciate this very much." Barnes suggested that such a lecture, by a visiting specialist officer, be given once a month during the winter, and "if instructional moving pictures could be shown they would create great interest." He also recommended that a second whaler be provided the unit, and that if new quarters were built, which was being suggested at higher levels, "davits and dropping gear be supplied for instructional purposes." Though Lieutenant Piers remained in command, the specialist officer visits and the second whaler were approved by the supervising officer reserves.[70]

Nine months later the unit seemed to have gone downhill, an inspection being carried out by Commander Charles Beard, the naval staff officer at NSHQ, during a tour of the navy's western reserve units. "My impressions of this unit were not good," Beard related. "Weather conditions prevailing were poor and consequently the attendance was poor." Perhaps the fact that "the quarters in this town are very isolated," had something to do with it. As for a more appropriate replacement for the acting company commanding officer, "Mr Wade, whose name is being considered for company commanding officer, appeared to be somewhat deaf, and therefore, may not pass the medical examination. He did not appear to me as if he would be able to make much improvement in this half company, and it may be necessary at a later date to recommend its disbandment." Though Piers was willing to support Wade, "Lieutenant Piers, the present acting CCO did not give me a favourable impression of his ability. On the other hand, Lieutenant Donaldson, the only other officer, will in time make a very good officer. He appears to be very keen and well thought of locally." Another officer, a Lieutenant Ponder, who once commanded the company in Prince Rupert, wished to join the unit in Vancouver, but the NSO "asked him to withhold his application as there appeared to be no desirability of having him." At least the petty officer instructor, named Roach, "has given every satisfaction and the officers desired his retention."[71]

The Vancouver company was not alone in facing difficulties in the last years of the 1920s, Commander Beard also finding a good deal to criticize in a unit much further up

69. LCdr G.B. Barnes to SNO RCN Barracks Esquimalt, 7 March 1929, 114–15–9, LAC, RG 24, vol. 5680.

70. Barnes to SNO RCN Barracks Esquimalt, 7 March 1929, LCdr H.W.S. Soulsby, SO Reserves, to CNS, 3 April 1929, ibid.

71. "Extract from NSO's report of visit to RCNVR Headquarters of the Western Division," 21 December 1929, 114–16–9, ibid.

the coast. "Prior to proceeding to Prince Rupert I made as many enquiries as I could and I found that one of the main results of the poor condition of this half company was caused by a Mr J.S. Bushby, lately appointed midshipman. He is too young and has not sufficient personality to allow the men to look upon him as an officer, and the town being small they have refused to do so. I was unable to obtain one favourable report on this gentleman, and in the absence of the father, who claims his son was receiving unfair treatment, I interviewed Bushby in the bank manager's office to prevent any idea that other than service matters were being discussed, as the bank manager was asked to act on behalf of the father during his absence. I advised Mr Bushby to forward his resignation at once, through his CCO; this he promised to do. Should this not have been received by 1st January, it is recommended that Mr Bushby be called upon to resign, or the unit will not progress." Both the company commanding officer, who was ill in bed at the time of the inspection, and the acting CCO agreed that the unit could reach a strength of thirty after Bushby's release.[72]

One possible obstacle to the latter came in the form of Mr Bushby, senior, who "had allowed the company commanding officer to believe that he had certain powers which could make matters very awkward for him (Mr Hume). The information I conveyed to Mr Hume that Mr Bushby, Sr has no powers whatever seemed to give him much relief. For the information of the department—Mr Bushby, Sr endeavoured to be selected as the Conservative candidate for Prince Rupert, but due to his unpopularity his candidature was a failure and a Mr Brady is now the Conservative member for Skeena. Mr Brady met me at the quarters and expressed great satisfaction that I was prepared to recommend a further extension of time in which to try to better this unit."[73]

With the officers and politicians satisfied, Commander Beard turned his attention to the lower deck, and "whilst the ratings were on parade I asked them individually whether they wished me to recommend that this unit continue—this recommendation to be conditional on their making every effort to fill the unit with greater numbers and generally improve the unit. Their answer was in all cases in the affirmative." The naval staff officer therefore suggested it continue to train for another fourteen months, by which time it should reach a strength of thirty. "If the officers do not achieve the desired results they have promised to inform the department that their efforts have failed." Overall, in winter the RCNVR in Prince Rupert at least served the function of keeping young men, with little else to do, off the streets. "As a matter of interest—I gathered that the militia unit was unable to function and merely exists on paper. This statement is made to show local conditions prevailing, i.e., a general lack of interest in anything by anybody." Beard suggested sending HMCS *Vancouver* for a three-day visit to create interest in the RCNVR.[74]

Snapshots of other western companies can give the reader an idea of how the reserves were faring in that part of the country. In Calgary, the naval staff officer found that the company commanding officer lived so far away that he might have to take his release, while Paymaster Lieutenant Rowlands, it turned out, was teaching gunnery and similar subjects,

72. Ibid.

73. Ibid.

74. Ibid.

and so was qualified for transfer to the executive branch. He had learned much about such subjects, while in the militia. Both he and the temporary CCO were "exceedingly keen and do all in their power to better themselves and the RCNVR." Surgeon Lieutenant C.S. Mahoud was a different matter, as he was no longer allowed to practice in Alberta and at the time resided in California. At least the quarters were in excellent condition and Petty Officer Instructor Mitchell was "fully deserving of an extension of his period of service (even though he is over age), as being in the best interests of the service."[75] In Edmonton, Beard found the armouries to be "in an excellent state of cleanliness, and the instructional gear generally is being made full use of and is well displayed." Facilities were, however, poorly located, though "presumably in years to come the town will grow around the armouries."[76]

The company in Regina also seemed to be doing well, and "this unit's drill display was the best witnessed and very creditable. All three officers of the unit took part in the conduct of some drill," three officers and thirty-five ratings parading. Commander Beard was obviously impressed with the company all-round, and "it is recommended that this unit be allowed a further petty officer, a leading seaman, and 10 seaman ratings, as the type of rating is that of university student and would be very useful in emergency. The training carried out in this unit is such that these additional men would repay an additional expenditure at the expense of some other unit," perhaps Vancouver or Prince Rupert—or Saskatoon.[77]

Reporting on the Saskatoon company, the naval staff officer stated that "the officers and petty officer instructor of this unit are not up to standard." Worse, "unless new quarters are obtained in the near future, this unit will have to be disbanded. I visited one building offered to the department for $125 a month, for a period of one year (heated). This would have met with our requirements temporarily. I was, however, informed after my departure that the rent had been increased to $200 a month and I am not prepared to recommend this amount for the building concerned."[78]

The experiences of eastern units paralleled those of the companies described above, though the company in Hamilton seemed to be the only one in the country in which NSHQ's supervising officer reserves, during a 1933 tour of reserve companies, found that "the petty officer instructor is a very bad example to the men as regards smartness, word of command, etc. He gave orders whilst standing with his hands clasped in front of him and his feet well apart, or shuffling; pushed men about by the arm; was continually fingering his face in apparent nervousness, etc. Not once did he stand properly to attention. All this must have a very bad effect on the demeanour of the men."[79] Three years earlier, the supervising officer reserves, Lieutenant-Commander J.E.W. Oland, felt that the situation in Quebec City was in keeping with the situation in other companies. In a 1930 report,

---

75. Ibid, 114–14–9.

76. Ibid, 114–13–9.

77. Ibid, 114–11–9.

78. Ibid, 114–12–9.

79. LCdr E.R. Mainguy report, 30 September 1933, ibid, 114-9-9.

Oland "found the PO instructor an exceptional man," though certain accommodations had to be made. "Owing to the fact that he cannot speak French, a large amount of the instruction is carried on by the men themselves who are bilingual. This seems to work very well indeed." More generally, the supervising officer reserves suggested that "in all companies there should be one rating for each subject—gunnery, torpedo, seamanship and signals—who receives allowance in the form of double drill money. There are at present in the Eastern Division, several very good instructors for the junior ratings among the senior ratings, and I consider it would help considerably, providing these men received some sort of recognition for their extra services."[80]

Another general lesson derived from Oland's inspection in Quebec City related to the fact that "this half company is in a position to operate a small W/T short-wave installation, as is also Montreal, and I suggest that sets be built at Halifax and installed in each of these company headquarters, and routine times for sending signals to headquarters' station and Halifax, and between each company, be made out. This would insure that telegraphists throughout the year would be kept up to the mark in procedure, and in reading and sending, etc. It would also obviate a large number of telegrams, etc, and so be a saving to the department."[81]

Further east was St John, New Brunswick, where Lieutenant-Commander Oland found far less to impress him, though it was not the unit's fault. "The training headquarters in Saint John are impossible," he explained. "There is no place for miniature rifle range; no proper place for 12 pdr; the building itself has a very dingy, dilapidated entrance. It is not a building that ratings would like to have to spend their evenings in. There is no place for the officers and the miserable aspect of the building as a half company headquarters is the principal reason this half company is not flourishing." His subsequent recommendation was nothing if not severe. "It is, therefore, recommended that although the Saint John half company has produced some of the best, if not the best men in the RCNVR, and that the officers in spite of the quarters they are in, are still keen, this unit be disbanded or new quarters be provided for them." More specifically, the supervising officer reserves suggested "that all the stores from the Saint John half company, all their instructional gear except what is required at the cottage on the Kennebecasis River in the summer, the training headquarters provided by the CCO—all these stores be returned to Halifax and the building handed back to the public works department, and if new quarters cannot be provided before December next, the unit be temporarily disbanded for the winter." There was, however, an element of bluff in Oland's suggestions, his true purpose being revealed in the statement that "if Saint John had proper quarters, and their own place in which to drill, in my opinion, they would be one of the very best half companies in Canada."[82]

Over three years later it was clear that the maritime units were not doing particularly well, though at least St John had survived threats of disbandment. Still, the director of naval reserves, Commander C.T. Beard, "found Saint John, Halifax and Charlottetown units very similar in a general way and not up to the standard desired or required. The Saint John unit

80. LCdr J.E.W. Oland, SO Res, to CNS, 6 June 1930, ibid, 114–5-9.

81. Ibid.

82. LCdr J.E.W. Oland, to CNS, 7 June 1930, 114–1-4, ibid.

is worth fostering, Halifax and Charlottetown require shaking." More specifically, "the quarters in all three cases are not ideal. All three units had poor petty officer instructors. The improvement in the Saint John unit is attributable to a new petty officer instructor lately installed. Unfortunately, the other two petty officer instructors have two years more to serve. Halifax has the advantage of a good company commanding officer—Charlottetown has not." Either western units had been more fortunate in their petty officer instructors, or standards differed from west to east. Still, in Halifax there was a further problem in that "the company has too many officers and too few ratings," and "the instructional gear does not compare with what is available within a few hundred yards," in the permanent force's facilities. Clearly, Beard thought that operating the RCN and the RCNVR as separate organizations could go too far, and he therefore suggested that "in the case of Halifax, I think greater efficiency would be achieved if this unit was attached to RCN barracks for administration, care and maintenance."[83]

An added recommendation relating to Halifax that could also bear fruit for other RCNVR units was "the purchase of a small schooner (attached to RCN Barracks for administration) to replace the minesweeper lately condemned, which has so seriously curtailed opportunities for sea experience. It is understood that there are now several for sale cheaply in Nova Scotia, due to the depression in the fishing business and not more than $5,000 is necessary to obtain delivery at Halifax." Another possibility: "it is believed that several captured rum runners are available," though they would be in the hands of another department, most likely Customs. "Naval reserve forces throughout the world have training ships attached to them in some manner," Beard argued. "The cost of upkeep at Halifax need not be excessive and during the summer months this schooner can be sent to Saint John, Charlottetown and perhaps Quebec and Montreal." If nothing else, the vessel would save train fare by being able to transport about thirty men to the East Coast for training. "Our primary desire is to make seamen of the RCNVRs in as short a time as possible and I believe this would help materially," the director of naval reserves concluded.[84]

Training reservists was in fact an important part of the RCN's mandate, RCNVR companies having been divided into two divisions, east and west, to save money on transportation. The Eastern Divison was composed of the companies and half-companies at Montreal, Ottawa, Hamilton, Toronto, St John, Quebec, Charlottetown, and Halifax, and while in 1927 the total number of officers attending training on the East Coast had been fifteen, the following year that figure rose to twenty-two, or about three-quarters of those enrolled at the time. Four completed a short course in navigation, one passed the specialist course in that subject, one each completed the short and specialist courses in gunnery, one requalified in signals (certificates had dates of expiry, requiring refresher courses), and seven attended naval training for the first time. "Officers were sent to sea as opportunity occurred, for short periods in HMCS *Champlain* and minesweepers," A. Eveleigh Eagar, the naval secretary, reported to the various company commanding officers. As well, "two officers carried out their naval training in HMCS *Champlain* and one served in HMCS *Festubert*

---

83. Cdr C.T. Beard, DNR, Maritime Units—RCNVR, 9 December 1933, ibid.

84. Ibid.

during the autumn exercises in the Bras d'Or Lakes." Generally, "officers have shown excep-tional keenness, and in many cases have been of definite use in lieu of RCN officers; notably during the time when minesweepers were standing by HMS *Dauntless* while she was stranded, and also in HMCS *Champlain* during cruises and exercises, that ship being one officer short of complement."[85]

Meanwhile, 241 ratings attended training in 1927, that number increasing to 265 in 1928, a little over three-fifths of those borne on the books of the Eastern Division compa-nies. "All seamen, on passing for able seaman or having completed their fortnight's train-ing, were drafted to HMCS *Champlain* or minesweepers. Week-end cruises of three and four days were arranged. Owing to the large numbers of first-year ratings attending naval training, the minesweepers were used every period for 12-pounder firing." Training was aided by the fact that "instructional facilities at RCN barracks have been improved," including an anchor model, models of minesweepers, and a minesweeping set. "The lower part of the boat house has been allotted for cable work, several shackles of cable being avail-able, together with slip, joining shackles, etc." There was no lack of enthusiasm and "rat-ings as a whole were extremely keen and showed great eagerness to advance, a large proportion volunteering for special courses and spending a large portion of their leisure hours in preparing themselves for examination."[86]

Despite the best of intentions and efforts, time spent on odd evenings learning their trade sometimes proved insufficient when reserve ratings entered full-time training in Hal-ifax or Esquimalt. In regard to signalling, for example, the naval secretary noted in 1932 that "most failures in signals and W/T examinations are due to the fact that RCNVR rat-ings are not proficient in making or reading Morse." He was stating the obvious when he noted that "this is one absolutely essential qualification which must be possessed by a telegraphist rating and forms a very large part of a signalman's requirements," though where such knowledge would be gained had obviously not been standardized. The naval secretary therefore pointed out that "knowledge of Morse, semaphore and colours of flags and pennants are some of the few subjects in which full proficiency can be gained at com-pany headquarters or at home. While some ratings, no matter how hard they try, never master these subjects (in which case they should be removed from the Signal or W/T Branch) the normal rating can become proficient in Morse providing he is enthusiastic enough. Hundreds of amateurs have become excellent operators with no outside help at all. It is merely a matter of practice." Lowering standards in RCN barracks, where such instruction was conducted in the summer, was out of the question, though "at present a great deal of time is wasted during courses, in endeavouring to teach ratings what they could learn at their company headquarters; thus they are losing a large proportion of the full value of these courses."[87]

For those whose winter training had indeed prepared them for summer instruction, the latter peaked with a cruise, one example being an outing in the minesweeper HMCS

---

85. Naval Secretary to CCOs RCNVR, 1 December 1928, 114–1-3, LAC, RG 24, vol. 5678.

86. Ibid.

87. Naval Secretary to CCOs RCNVR, 16 September 1932, ibid.

Armentieres off the West Coast. Lasting from 9 to 11 June 1933, according to the ship's captain, Lieutenant-Commander H.W.S. Soulsby, "the good value obtained of such a cruise as this for the RCNVR has been fully shown, observing that officers and men were borne for victuals only; more of the unit would have come had they been able; the two stokers kept regular watch and their keenness is appreciated. Lieut Donaldson did all the pilotage under supervision except when going in and out of Vancouver harbour. The weather was fine enabling many hammocks to be slung on the upper deck at night." Ten ratings from various RCNVR companies, most likely all from the Western Division, embarked at Vancouver, though one officer proved a no-show. "I delayed half an hour for Pay Lieut Fletcher, but as he had not arrived by 1100 I sailed." One missing officer notwithstanding, the commander-in-charge Esquimalt agreed in the value of such on-the-job training.[88]

By the late 1920s the RCNR and the RCNVR had been operational for several years, but it looked for a while as if they might be joined by yet a third reserve system, which would recruit ex-members of the RCN along the lines of the RN's Royal Fleet Reserve. As Commander P.W. Nelles, the senior naval officer in Esquimalt, explained, "ratings who are completing their first period of service are taking their discharges owing to lack of a pension. The majority of these ratings will obtain work ashore and will not, therefore, be eligible for the RCNR as at present constituted. It is doubtful if any will join the RCNVR, except possibly as petty officer instructors.... In order that the efficiency of these ratings be to a certain extent maintained and also that they may be available for service almost immediately when required it is submitted that such a service," that is to say a Canadian version of the Royal Fleet Reserve, "be established." Victor Brodeur, for one, as senior naval officer in Halifax, was able to provide a list of eleven ratings who had been discharged in the previous two years who would have been good candidates for such a scheme. Nelles himself had a list of twenty, of whom seventeen were recommended.[89]

A year later, in October 1930, Chief of Naval Staff (CNS) Walter Hose calculated that such a force, with a strength of about 500, would cost $58,500. It would be well worth it, as "this reserve force will constitute one of the most valuable assets to the service in time of emergency. It will be composed of ex-RCN ratings, who are fully trained in naval subjects, and who will normally be men of mature years. The total annual cost of the force is not great, considering the type and qualifications of the ratings who will be available."[90] It would grow slowly, from about ten in 1930, to ninety in 1935, and 220 in 1941, so that the full force of 500 would not be attained until at least 1950. With such issues as the procurement of new destroyers to focus his attention (of that, more later), not to mention the distractions of the Great Depression, the minister of National Defence chose to postpone dealing with the creation of a Royal Canadian Fleet Reserve. When the topic reappeared in September 1933, the director of naval reserves announced that "naval opinion is unanimous

---

88. LCdr H.W.S. Soulsby, Report of Proceedings, 12 June 1933, C-in-Charge, Esquimalt to NSHQ, 4 July 1933, 131–7-5, LAC, RG 24, vol. 5682.

89. Cdr P.W. Nelles, SNO Esquimalt, to NSHQ, 20 March and 28 April 1928, Brodeur, SNO Halifax, to NSHQ, 4 April 1928, 125–1-1, LAC, RG 24, vol. 5681.

90. Hose to Desbarats, 22 October 1930, ibid.

in the necessity for having an RCFR," but higher authority was dealing with other issues, as we shall see.[91]

Given the lengthy discussion regarding the reserves in this and the previous chapter, the reader can be forgiven for wondering whether the permanent force RCN had effectively ceased to exist. It had not, of course; but since the chief of the naval staff had staked so much of the navy's future on the reserves, a reasonable account of its trials and tribulations is a core element of the service's history, official or not. And, it must be said, the experiences of reserve personnel have intrinsic human interest. That cannot be said of another core element of the navy's story. In a service that relied heavily on technology to carry out its tasks (and in which responsibility for seemingly mundane matters like logistics and materiel rested with the regulars) critical components of the permanent force history are decidedly less than compelling and perhaps lacking in human interest. Among a myriad challenges, this can perhaps be satisfactorily addressed by reference to an issue that came to the fore in the last months of 1927, when the director of naval stores warned the naval store officer in Halifax that "a report has been received from the senior naval officer, Halifax, regarding the faulty running of a torpedo, in which it is stated that the cause for this faulty running is considered to be deteriorated light shale oil or dirty shale oil." The evidence? "It is stated that when filling up the fuel bottle of the torpedo it was noted that the oil seemed slightly discoloured. It is requested that several samples be picked from the present stock, care being taken to procure a sample of the discoloured oil, and that these samples be forwarded to this office for analysis."[92]

Since the torpedo and gun together comprised a destroyer's main armament in those days, anything that rendered the former unserviceable or unreliable was not a minor detail. "Discoloured oil," in other words, was not an aesthetic issue, but something that required painstaking investigation to unearth the cause and find a solution. Accordingly, "as it is stated that there may possibly be some rust present in the oil from the cans in which stored since delivery from England, the naval store officer is requested to arrange for the existing stock to be removed from the cans and thoroughly strained. The cans should then be cleaned and inspected." It was a lot of work, and in the meantime, "where there is any doubt regarding a can it should not be used. After the oil has been thoroughly strained it may be returned to the cans. Pending the report of the analysis the cans should not be sealed."[93] Such elaborate procedures to deal with day-to-day problems were not limited to torpedoes, but could also be found in relation to guns, ammunition, wireless equipment, and a host of other items. In the navy, logistics in time of peace might not be noticeably less complicated than in time of war—and certainly not less important.

The economic depression of the 1930s brought even more complexity, but opportunity as well. Chief of the General Staff Andrew McNaughton believed, along with many other policy makers, that the economic crisis could lead to general unrest and even insurrection,

---

91. Cdr C.T. Beard, DNR, to NSO, 29 September 1933, Desbarats to Hose, 7 January 1931, Hose, "Estimate of Probable Growth of RCN Fleet Reserve," 18 November 1930, ibid.

92. Director of Naval Stores to Naval Store Officer Halifax, 3 November 1927, 1057–51–11TE, LAC, RG 24, vol. 4009.

93. Ibid.

something the armed services would have to deal with. As we have seen in relation to strikes in Cape Breton in the 1920s, however, the navy was unlikely to be called upon for aid of the civil power, so its responsibilities in ensuring stability would lie elsewhere. One area in which it might contribute was in setting up projects the government had instituted to provide the unemployed with the means to earn an income. In October 1931 Commander (Engineer) T.C. Phillips, the navy's consulting naval engineer, found $76,000 worth of work in Halifax, $38,000 in Esquimalt, and $8,000 in Winnipeg that could be carried out under such a program. The latter project consisted of "alterations and repairs to No 4 Fire Hall to make the premises suitable for occupation by the local Royal Canadian Naval Volunteer Reserve company." A few years later Commander (Engineer) A.D.M. Curry found seven such projects in each of Esquimalt and Halifax that could be worked on in the 1934–35 fiscal year, including almost $61,000 for "renewal" of the main machine shop in Halifax and over half a million dollars for construction of a joint service magazine in Esquimalt.[94]

A few months later Percy Nelles, the acting chief of the naval staff, suggested that two sloops and four auxiliary patrol vessels be built under the scheme, but such was not to be, nor was an idea of the prime minister's to train, "in obsolete vessels, single unemployed men between the ages of seventeen and twenty-one," who could not be recruited into the navy because of the limits on its size. Pursuing an idea reminiscent of the Royal Navy's use of hulks in previous centuries, *Ypres* could accommodate about twenty men, while the Admiralty might make the destroyer *Serapis* available, with her spaces for eighty. In addition, numerous 8,000-ton cargo vessels were lying idle, and each could be converted to accommodate about 500 men. There was not much to recommend the plan, however, since after completing their training these young men would be qualified to join the merchant marine, which was already turning away skilled sailors in large numbers, so Hose chose not to recommend it.[95]

Smaller schemes were easier to implement and administer, so as early as the summer of 1930 the Department of Public Works advised that such projects could include $5,000 to complete repairs to Esquimalt's roads and paths, $650 to paint the coal sheds, and $700 to repair the concrete playing surface of the tennis court. Perhaps larger in scope was a Public Works project to erect a seawall along one side of the dry dock. In all, however, the navy spent a very small portion of the total DND budget for unemployment relief projects, Esquimalt, for example, taking $52,231 dollars out of over $18 million, or 0.29 percent by 1936. There are several reasons why the navy did not benefit more from the program: the latter focused on simple projects where skilled labour could be kept to a minimum, and ship construction obviously did not fit such a criterion; projects were located where unemployment was highest, which was not in Victoria, while Project No 1 (of 123) was the Citadel in Halifax, leaving little left over for any navy work in that city. In short, the army and air force, with such straightforward tasks as airfields to build and rifle ranges to

---

94. T.C. Phillips to CNS, 9 October 1931, Engineer Commander A.D.M. Curry to CNS, 8 February 1934, 75–1-3, LAC, RG 24, vol. 5667.

95. Nelles to Minister, 18 April 1934, ibid; and Hose to Minister, 2 November 1933, 21–1-24, LAC, RG 24, vol. 3613.

As this march of unemployed workers in 1932 indicates, not all Canadians supported government expenditure on the armed services. (LAC e007140891)

Relief project No. 75: grading the compound at Esquimalt in July 1933. McNaughton insisted on the importance of maintaining morale and inspiring hope among the growing number of unemployed, single men in the early 1930s, and proposed employing as many as possible with minimal spending on machinery. (LAC PA-036236)

construct, were in a better position to fit the Department of Labour's criteria and so dominated DND's submissions for unemployment relief projects.[96]

When it came to construction, the RCN placed ships at the top of its list of priorities, *Patriot* and *Patrician* reaching the end of their useful lives in the latter years of the 1920s. Though logically it would have been appropriate to replace them with two more destroyers, the Admiralty took advantage of the occasion to suggest alternatives. It advised "that instead of obtaining two more modern destroyers, it might be preferable to the Canadian government to order two new type sloops of the type similar to those which are about to be built for the Royal Navy; these sloops are particularly suitable for the general training of personnel and would, it is thought, form an essential part of any naval force which the Canadian government might eventually decide to maintain." They could be built in roughly a year and a half in Britain or in a longer period in Canada (since firms would have to learn how to construct them), and would have a life expectancy of about sixteen years.[97] Hose added that sloops could be used for patrols, minesweeping, and anti-submarine warfare, and "they would be very suitable to assist other departments of the Government in maritime work in which the Naval Service is frequently approached for assistance and co-operation." However, "against any serious threat to our trade by converted merchant cruisers or small light cruisers they would be of no value," because of their small size and limited armament, and as we have seen it was for exactly that kind of work that Hose wanted to acquire ships.[98]

In getting new vessels, Hose had an ally in Prime Minister Mackenzie King, who noted how on 21 October 1927, "we had a lengthy discussion on naval matters, replacement of two destroyers. The cabinet was about prepared to let our naval policy go to the wall, and not even replace the destroyers now out of commission. I felt this was wrong, and urged support to Ralston in purchase of two new destroyers or sloops. I stressed my belief in need for some naval development on the part of Canada as a nation. It is going to be difficult to get the gov[ernmen]t to go any length at all."[99] By the end of the year senior officers were aware of the government's decision to have two new destroyers built, immediate and temporary replacements for *Patriot* and *Patrician* coming in the form of HM Ships *Torbay* and *Toreador,* renamed *Vancouver* and *Champlain* for famous explorers well-known to most Canadians. In January 1928 naval headquarters announced a plan to send a rating from each RCNVR unit to England to join the two used ships. *Champlain* hoped to reach Halifax around 17 May, and *Vancouver* expected to arrive in Esquimalt around 3 June. As for the new construction vessels, Commander (Engineer) T.C. Phillips, the consulting naval

---

96. Dockyard Manager Esquimalt to Naval Secretary, 26 August 1930, Senior Naval Officer, Esquimalt to Naval Secretary, 28 August 1930, 75-1-3, LAC, RG 24, vol. 5667; "Final Report on the Unemployment Relief Scheme, 1932–1936," nd, LAC, MG 30 E133, vol. 99; and "Department of National Defence—Unemployment Relief Projects—1934," nd, LAC, RG 27, vol. 4140;

97. Secretary of State for Dominion Affairs to Governor General, 9 June 1927, 1017–10–9, LAC, RG 24, vol. 3833.

98. DNS to Minister, 13 June 1927, ibid.

99. King Diary, 21 October 1927, LAC, MG 26 J13.

engineer, found nothing but co-operation from Admiralty officials; it would take about twenty-one months to build them, though construction of the second would begin between three and six months after work started on the first. With guns and mountings the ships would cost over $2.7 million, ammunition adding $350,000 to the bill. Hose also proposed keeping the destroyers' two depth charge throwers for antisubmarine operations.[100]

With replacement vessels for *Patriot* and *Patrician* on the way, the RCN could expect to operate as it had since demobilization following the First World War, namely, by maintaining a close operational relationship with the Royal Navy. The resulting need for means of communication was obvious, and, according to Lieutenant-Commander R.W. Wood, the acting director of naval intelligence in late 1930, "the requirements for naval W/T communication in Canada are considerably intermingled with Admiralty requirements which latter are world wide and embrace all dominions and naval stations." He called for short-wave communication not only along the axis Ottawa-Esquimalt-Halifax but along Canada-Admiralty-London-Bermuda, and along Canada-Australia-New Zealand-China. Also to be considered was "direct intercommunication" between Esquimalt and West Coast ships when the latter were on cruise, and a similar arrangement for Halifax. Ottawa figured prominently in Wood's recommendations, and he suggested a permanent W/T station be established there with sufficient power to communicate with the Admiralty, Esquimalt, and Bermuda. "This would centralize all W/T communication at headquarters and supply an important alternative route with Esquimalt for Admiralty work with the Far East, and at the same time a route to Bermuda.... This would eventually require an increase of complement at Ottawa to possibly four telegraphist ratings under the present CPO telegraphist appointment."[101]

Ottawa would provide a link between the East and West Coasts, which at the time could not communicate directly, but for the scheme to work transmitters in all three stations would have to be replaced, as those in use at the time were obsolescent and inadequate. They were, for instance, "insufficiently selective. Interference by naval stations with other services, especially commercial broadcasting, is becoming increasingly important. Complaints have not yet reached serious proportions, but will undoubtedly increase with the continued development of radio for commercial purposes." Also, they lacked the necessary power, but as we have seen in relation to other issues the early years of the Great Depression were not the time to recommend procuring materiel. In October 1931 it was announced that "all major re-equipment during the present financial year has been abandoned."[102]

Another issue was accommodation. The existing communications facility was at the RCMP barracks in Rockcliffe, near Ottawa, but it was "very unsuitable." Commander W.B. Hynes, on loan from the Royal Navy, opined that "although the dimensions of the proposed new set are not known, it is probable that there would be insufficient space in the existing building." Economic depression or not, Hynes suggested asking "the Department

---

100. Naval Ottawa to SNO RCN Barracks Halifax, 27 December 1927, Naval Ottawa to Admiralty, 9 January 1928, NSHQ to CCOs RCNVR, 30 January 1928, 135–1-1, LAC, RG 24, vol. 5683; and Cdr (E) T.C. Phillips to Hose, 11 January 1928, Hose to Desbarats, 27 January 1928, 1017–10–11, LAC, RG 24, vol. 3834.

101. LCdr R.W. Wood, to CNS, 2 December 1930, 1008–33–6, LAC, RG 24, vol. 6198.

102. Cdr W.B. Hynes RN, DNI, to CNS, 23 March 1931, Hynes to Deputy Minister, 14 October 1931, ibid.

HMCS *Champlain* with awnings rigged, circa 1932. (DND CN 6437)

Champlain's crew in Halifax, 1930. (LAC PA-126718)

of Public Works to include an item in their 1932–33 estimates for the construction of a new building."[103] The minister did not approve the request, and it would be two years before permission would come to re-equip Ottawa, Esquimalt, and Halifax, at a cost for the nation's capital alone of $15,000 for a transmitter, $5,000 for a new building, $5,000 for a new building for the older receiver, and $500 for control lines between the two.[104]

The purpose of such facilities, of course, was to support training and operations, the two being often indistinguishable when ships were at sea. In the middle part of 1930, for example, *Ypres* and *Festubert,* based in Halifax, conducted gunnery exercises of their own before towing targets for the destroyer *Champlain*. The two minesweepers then went their separate ways. "RCNVR ratings were carried in both ships during the cruises and instructions in boat pulling, helm, etc were given these ratings at every opportunity. Standard … signal exercises were carried out between ships whilst at Baddeck. One yeoman of signals (RCN) one leading signalman (RCNVR) and one signalman (RCNVR) being borne in *Ypres* and one signalman (RCN) and two signalmen (RCNVR) in *Festubert*," allowed for substantial communications training.[105]

Similarly, *Armentieres* operated off the West Coast, though as often happened in the east training could be interrupted by higher-priority evolutions. In February 1931, eight RCNVR ratings joined the ship, but "at about 0730 when about fifteen miles from Tatoosh Island, I observed a ship some miles away on the port bow which I found to be stopped and not under control," reported the captain, Lieutenant-Commander H.W.S. Soulsby. "She was the motor vessel *Hurry On* of Vancouver. I subsequently took her in tow and returned with her to Esquimalt arriving at 1730.… It is considered that valuable experience was gained by taking her in tow. Although the weather was fine and calm a long swell was running."[106] Even a rescue operation could thus become part of a training regimen.

Life saving was, in fact, a matter of normal routine, especially off the West Coast. The Department of Marine asked for assistance in such work for the period 1 to 9 December 1929 and again from 29 December to 28 February 1930. At a weekly meeting of the naval staff it was noted that "*Givenchy* will carry out this duty in the intervening period," with the additional notation that "this is a usual procedure."[107] At a subsequent meeting, it was learned that the chief of the naval staff had decided that the Bamfield Patrol, a search and rescue endeavour, would be carried out every year, though on at least one occasion the ship allocated to such work had to save one of her own. As Lieutenant-Commander H.W.S. Soulsby of *Armentieres* explained, "on Saturday morning the 20th Dec the CERA [chief engine room artificer]—A. Whyte—was ashore at the cable station when he was severely bitten in the leg about six inches below the knee by a dog. The skin was broken over an area of about four square inches—the dog had made a good nip with most of his teeth. I

103. Hynes to Desbarats, 14 October 1931, ibid.

104. Desbarats memorandum, 25 November 1931, Cdr E.G., Hastings RN, DNI, to CNS, 25 September 1933, ibid.

105. *Ypres* to Captain-in-Charge RCN Barracks Halifax, 24 June 1930, 132-7-5, LAC, RG 24, vol. 5682.

106. LCdr H.W.S. Soulsby to SNO Esquimalt, 16 February 1931, 131-7-5, ibid.

107. Weekly Meeting of Naval Staff, 7 October 1929, 1078-3-1, LAC, RG 24, vol. 4044.

directed that hot fomentations be applied." The wound became inflamed, and Soulsby "considered that it required more skilled attention," so *Armentieres* sailed for Port Alberni. After the wound was treated, Whyte returned to the ship.[108]

As for actual life saving, as one would expect the two minesweepers knew both success and failure. An example of the latter was brought to the fore by member of parliament A.W. Neill, who wanted information about three fishing vessels that had been wrecked or gone missing one night in late 1933. The commanding officer of *Armentieres* had, according to an RCN investigation, put off going to their assistance for seventeen and a half hours. Captain P.W. Nelles, in response, agreed that "it cannot be definitely stated that the commanding officer of HMCS *Armentieres* took all possible action to save life." He further explained, however, that "there are no naval or other government vessels on the west coast, suitable for this life-saving service. The *Armentieres,* being very low-powered, is most unsuitable. There is no direct method of communication between the light houses on the coast and ships. The *Armentieres,* once she proceeded to sea, would be unable to communicate with the light house keepers or the beach patrols, until she returned to Bamfield." Given the circumstances, which included the vessels having been driven ashore, the captain of *Armentieres* "would only be in a position to assist from seaward, should the weather moderate sufficiently to permit landing from his surf boat, a most unusual condition during the winter months."[109]

The task was hazardous enough, and there was no need to add foolhardiness to it. In fact, the only RCN ship to be lost in the interwar period was *Thiepval,* which went down on 27 January, 1930, "while on life saving patrol." Striking a rock in Barkley Sound, she was a total loss.[110] After going aground, given that the tide was ebbing, the minesweeper's captain, Lieutenant H.R. Tingley, decided it was best to abandon ship before she capsized. Everyone got out safely, and it was even hoped "that she could be refloated on the next high tide," *Armentieres* and the tug *Salvage King* being sent out to that end. The effort had to be given up as too difficult, however, and the wreck was abandoned for the time being. The charts *Thiepval* had been using dated from 1861, so Barkley Sound was resurveyed by the Canadian Hydrographic Service. "It was at this time that many of the old names in the Sound were changed in order to avoid confusion with similar names elsewhere on the coast—thereby thoroughly confusing local inhabitants."[111]

RCN ships did not suffer so cruelly in their other tasks, such as fisheries patrols, which in fact took up more of the service's operational attention. As Commodore Hose explained in May 1931, the period in which the navy carried out life-saving corresponded to the closed season for halibut. Therefore, "it would not be possible to carry out these patrols in conjunction, as the most important Halibut Banks are all north of Cape Scott," on the northern tip of Vancouver Island. "Only small quantities of halibut are caught off the coast

108. Soulsby to SNO Esquimalt, 31 December 1930, 131-7-5, LAC, RG 24, vol. 5682; and "Minutes of the Second Meeting of Naval Staff," 14 October 1929, 1078-3-1, LAC, RG 24, vol. 4044.

109. Capt P.W. Nelles to Deputy Minister, 28 December 1933, 131–7-5, LAC, RG 24, vol. 5682.

110. J.O.B. LeBlanc, "Historical Synopsis, etc," 1937, DHH 81/520/8000, "*Thiepval.*"

111. R. Bruce Scott, "HMCS *Thiepval,* Thiepval Channel, February 27, 1930," nd, DHH 81/520/8000, "*Thiepval.*"

HMCS *Vancouver* passing through the Culebra Cut in the Panama Canal in 1934. (DND CN 6084)

of Vancouver Island," where most life saving work was carried out.[112] In conducting fisheries patrols the RCN was sometimes aided, at least in the early part of the 1930s, by the Royal Canadian Air Force, itself looking for tasks it could perform to practice the skills of air- and ground-crew. In April 1931, therefore, two RCAF mechanics joined *Armentieres*, which also loaded eighteen 50-gallon drums of aviation fuel, a drum of oil, and aircraft stores. Upon arrival in Bamfield, the ship found a seaplane of 110 Squadron waiting, with a crew of two flight sergeants and a signal sergeant. The ship then sailed for Ucluelet while the aircraft completed a patrol along the way. "The sea was rough and no boats nor seals were seen." After arriving at destination, "the weather was calmer and a few fishing boats were out. Neither of the pilots having ever done any flying over the open sea such as is required for this patrol the opportunity was taken by them for observing the boats and for exercising estimation of their ground speed."[113]

The aircraft's radio failed, "largely due to the damp weather," which forced the cancellation of most of the patrols the RCAF wanted to undertake. Ten days after the operation had begun, the ship sailed for Port Alice. "The plane left at 0900 and overtook the ship as we were rounding Solander Island. About 200 sea-lions were seen on the rocks of Solander Island. The weather was calm with a heavy swell, but as the plane's WT set was not yet working properly I did not send her out to sea; she proceeded direct to Port Alice." The radio was repaired the next day, however, and the aircraft was able to carry out a patrol off Quatsino Sound, though "nothing was seen." The only successes over the next few days were three seals spotted on 21 April and another three on the 23rd. Then, typically, *Armentieres* carried out gunnery training at a cliff face on the 24th and conducted various evolutions, "the majority of the seamen being young ordinary seamen new to the ship."[114] In post-patrol discussions, the possibility was broached of using a naval telegraphist in the aircraft to ensure communications between it and the ship it was partnered with, Hose noting that in accordance with regulations "officers and men are liable to make casual flights in aircraft in the course of their duties without any allowance of extra pay." The issue would be left to the ship's captain to decide, on a case by case basis.[115]

As for the destroyers, they were not considered suitable for the kind of work that occupied much of the minesweepers' time, as Hose explained in the spring of 1931. "Last year, HMCS *Vancouver* was not used for Life Saving Patrol as it was the opinion that the risking of such a valuable ship was an unjustifiable hazard in a duty which may take her into poorly charted waters, while this duty could be carried out just as efficiently by a less costly vessel with a considerably smaller life risk. The same consideration would apply to [the destroyer] HMCS *Skeena*." Sloops, should the RCN choose to acquire them, might be suitable, but destroyers were not. As for fisheries, "the use of HMCS *Skeena* and *Vancouver* for the Halibut Patrol would involve a considerable expense to the Naval Service and, although it might be possible to use the ships for that purpose should naval requirements permit,

112. Hose to DM, 21 May 1931, 300-1-2, LAC, RG 24, vol. 5686.

113. LCdr H.W.S. Soulsby to SNO Esquimalt, 23 April 1931, 131-7-5, LAC, RG 24, vol. 5682.

114. Ibid.

115. CNS to Acting Director RCAF, 21 May 31, ibid.

it is recommended that these requirements should not be prejudiced through carrying out patrols for the Department of Fisheries in support of the Pacific Halibut Fishery Convention."[116] The experiences of *Champlain* and *Vancouver,* therefore, would differ from those of the RCN's smaller vessels.

Champlain, as we have seen, was sent to the East Coast in 1928, and after arrival in Halifax was inspected by Commodore Hose, who was "in every way very well satisfied with both the ship's company and the ship.... The ship's company conducted themselves exceedingly well on the whole voyage out and their health has been excellent in spite of the long steaming in tropical waters"—the destroyer, like many of her predecessors, having come to Canada by way of the West Indies. Also, "the condition of the ship, after her 8,000 mile voyage is such as to give me every confidence that she will prove a most reliable and economical vessel," though, after such a long cruise, "it will be desirable now that all machinery should be opened up for inspection and re-adjustment after so long a voyage and I will submit a programme for the summer's work in the course of the next day or two."[117] So, on 25 August, the ship left Halifax, her company attending a dance in Lunenburg as well as playing baseball and opening the destroyer to visitors. On the 28th they played baseball in Liverpool, though aquatic sports were the order of the day when she visited Shelburne on the 31st. Labour day was set aside for sports in Clarke's Harbour, *Champlain* returning to Halifax on 3 September.[118]

In October 1928 the ship conducted more martial evolutions, firing her 4-inch armament (without a single misfire in 150 rounds), conducting various drills, running seamanship classes, training the pom-pom crews, and carrying out torpedo attacks. "Valuable experience was gained by officers and men as the result of this exercise period; the behaviour of the ships company was very good, and all departments showed the greatest keenness to increase the all round efficiency of the ship. It was hoped to have another clear day for general drill, but this was not possible owing to the search for the torpedo," one of the expensive devices having gone missing during an attack on *Festubert.* There were still opportunities for swimming and baseball, and generally, according to the naval staff officer, Commander C.T. Beard, "HMCS *Champlain* appears to have made good use of the time allotted for training."[119] Thinking ahead, NSHQ advised that "it is the department's desire that considerably more firings and exercises should be carried out during the next two years than has been the case, in order that ratings who are allotted for new construction may receive suitable and sufficient training."[120]

As in previous years southern climes were deemed best to give sailors experience during the winter months, and *Champlain* arrived in Barbados on one such cruise on 13 March

116. Hose to DM, 21 May 1931, 300–1-2, LAC, RG 24, vol. 5686.

117. Hose to Minister, 21 May 1928, 135–1-1, LAC, RG 24, vol. 5683.

118. "Movements of HMCS *Champlain* during August and September, 1928," December 1928, 10–1-9, LAC, RG 24, vol. 3579.

119. Cdr C.T. Beard, NSO, to CNS, 24 October 1928, LCdr J.C.I. Edwards, CO *Champlain,* to SNO HMCS *Stadacona,* 15 October 1928, 135–7-5, LAC, RG 24, vol. 5683.

120. Naval Secretary to SNO RCN Barracks Halifax, 31 October 1928, ibid.

1929. Official calls were taken care of the next day, and "during the stay at Barbados the ship's company were employed at ordinary ship routine work and instruction." And there was more than one way to show the flag, as "two football matches were played, one against the YMCA and one an inter-party match. Water polo and rifle shooting matches were also held, the former with the YMCA, and the latter with the Barbados Volunteers." Socializing was thus an important part of such cruises, and "considerable entertainment was provided ashore for the ship's company, which was most appreciated by them, three dances being held for their benefit under the Naval Welfare League. Miss Bowen, the secretary, was especially energetic and kind, and did everything in her power to make the men enjoy their visit. Mr Laing of the YMCA also did a great deal in this respect, and arranged various games which were most appreciated. After the more or less dull time which the men have in a number of places in the West Indies, the kindness and hospitality shown to them was especially welcome."[121]

Vancouver's experiences off the West Coast were somewhat different, as it did not have an equivalent for the West Indies cruise. Still, there was no shortage of sea room or ports to visit, even without leaving the waters of British Columbia, as Lieutenant-Commander R.W. Wood, the ship's captain, related at the end of 1928. "Cruises of this nature are of great value for recruiting officers and men for the Royal Canadian Navy, and at the same time showing the smaller towns and more thickly populated districts, at least a part of the navy for whose support they contribute annually.... It has been noticed when the ship has been open to visitors, that a much better class of people who take a really intelligent and enthusiastic interest, come on board from small towns and thickly populated districts, than from from the larger cities where a large percentage of the visitors are foreigners with nothing better to do."[122] Given the RCN's policy, mirroring that of the RN, to recruit only those of European descent, having "foreigners," most likely of Asian origin, visit the ship did nothing to help increase the navy's ranks.

Aside from such public relations activities, Vancouver, of course, set to training her complement. All did not go smoothly, however, and the ship soon found that her ability to attack with torpedoes was not up to standard. As Commander C.T. Beard, the naval staff officer, warned, "the report of torpedo exercises carried out in HMCS Vancouver, during the six months ending 31st March, 1929, shows a total disregard of the department's orders." She had, it turned out, done far too little training, and though orders allowed a certain latitude to take into account local conditions, they were "primarily issued to increase the number of torpedo exercises in HMCS Vancouver," not serve as justification for reducing the focus on such training. Orders had thus proved "a complete failure, and I consider that this failure seriously affects the efficiency of the RCN as a whole, as it retards the training of the personnel, which is now of primary importance, and one of the 'raison d'être' of HMCS Vancouver." Beard was lashing out, justly or otherwise, his report fairly shouting that "it would appear as if the SNO and CO, HMCS Vancouver, have not grasped what their duties are in this respect, and I recommend a strongly worded memorandum be sent Esquimalt,

---

121. SNO HMCS Stadacona to NSHQ, 8 May 1929, ibid.

122. LCdr R.W. Wood, CO Vancouver, to SNO HMCS Naden, 18 December 1928, 136–7-5, LAC, RG 24. vol. 5684.

expressing the department's displeasure of the failure to carry out departmental instructions in the matter of torpedo firings, and that a very appreciable improvement is demanded, otherwise it will be necessary to relieve the officers concerned." In the event, such harsh measures were not applied, but Beard's lecture did not end there. "There are two torpedo specialist officers at Esquimalt, and the necessary staffs," he reminded. "It is fully appreciated that during certain months the carrying out of torpedo exercises is impracticable; there have, however, been opportunities which, with a little forethought, could have been made use of. As the SNO cancelled gunnery firings, due to a shortage of ammunition, he might perhaps have considered torpedo firings in lieu."[123] Improvement was not long in coming, with a report a few months later noting "satisfaction" with subsequent "instructional practices."[124]

For the first few years of their commissions *Vancouver* and *Champlain* operated very much separately, but the very month the stock market in New York crashed, the naval staff considered the issue of sending *Vancouver,* through the Panama Canal no doubt, to the West Indies to join *Champlain* for training. The only extra cost would be for fuel, the round trip taking some three months. The minister agreed, but the initial plan to have three ships, including HMS *Durban,* cruising in company, was deemed unsuitable "as it will extend into the next fiscal year." Still, it would be a full schedule, with exercises and visits to Bermuda, Barbados, Havana, Puerto Rico, Port au Prince, and Jamaica.[125] Afterwards, analysis noted "many errors" in regard to gunnery and torpedo firings, though higher authority had to take into account the fact that "*Champlain* and *Vancouver* have a continuously changing personnel which must, if possible, be obviated in future years, and in new construction." In sending the ships to the West Indies at that time, the RCN may have been asking them to run before they could walk, so, in regards to the vessels then being built in the UK, "it is strongly recommended that the new destroyers carry out commissioning firings and exercises with RN assistance, in order that errors may be corrected before leaving England, and to allow a battle practice target to be made available. Such errors as mistakes in spotting rules, etc, can in a way be obviated by causing the gunnery control officer and torpedo control officer to undergo the courses, before commissioning, as laid down in AFOs [Admiralty fleet orders] for RN ships under similar conditions."[126]

With lessons learned, or at least in the process of being assimilated, *Champlain* and *Vancouver* returned to training and operations closer to home, but even routine matters needed attending to if a destroyer was to carry out her various duties effectively. As *Vancouver* discovered, following a planned visit to the city that bore the same name, she had to report that the operation "failed in its object owing to the non-promulgation of information to Vancouver city officials. This was unfortunate observing that considerably more interest is taken in the ship in Vancouver than in Victoria and a certain pride is taken in her as the ship is of the same name as the city. Some sixty guests of some of the leading

123. Naval Staff Officer to CNS, 23 May 1929, 1057–53–11TE, LAC, RG 24, vol. 4011.

124. Naval Secretary to SNO Esquimalt, 8 July 1929, ibid.

125. Naval Staff minutes, 14 and 28 October, 4 and 25 November 1929, 1078–3–1, LAC, RG 24, vol. 4044.

126. NSO to CNS, 12 May 1930, 1057–53–11GE, LAC, RG 24, vol. 4010.

families of Vancouver including those in official positions were entertained on board unofficially by the commanding officer and officers. From information gathered during conversation with some of the leading officials considerable regret and in some cases annoyance was expressed at the fact that no information of the visit of the ship had been promulgated. Hence no acknowledgement officially of the visit."[127] It seems that the company commanding officer of the RCNVR half-company in the city had been informed of the visit in the expectation that he would notify city officials. It was decided that in future the senior naval officer for the area would fulfil that liaison role.[128]

There was more disappointment ahead. Three weeks later Lieutenant-Commander Wood reported that his ship had to postpone a gunnery exercise because the target capsized and then his ship could only manage fourteen knots (as opposed to the twenty set down in regulations) owing to a defective propeller. Then, both the ship's captain and the gunnery officer inaccurately estimated range at 10,000 yards when in reality the target was 13,000 yards away. The director layer was on loan from the RCN barracks, the incumbent having been injured the day before sailing. Lieutenant-Commander R.W. Wood, Vancouver's captain, suggested that "it is possible that the rate of fire would have been better had the director layer been at sea carrying out practices during the last year."[129] Higher authority was blunt, advising that "this was a most disappointing practice," which was, at least in part, the captain's fault for not having accurately estimated the target's range in the first place. The sextant rangefinder had not been put to use in spite of the fact that "this has been tested by the Royal Canadian barracks staff and found to be in adjustment." The ship's ratings, on the other hand, were found blameless; they had been progressively trained in gunnery over the previous six months, and "the discipline behind the guns, gun drill and control parties have all been reported as excellent."[130]

The shoot had been partial preparation for another cruise in company with Champlain in a repeat of the previous year's training in the tropics. Other areas that needed looking to were administration and logistics, Vancouver obviously needing fuel, though arrangements to acquire it were simply a matter of keeping sufficient cash on hand, as it were. "No contracts have been arranged by Naval Service Headquarters for the supply of fuel en route," the naval secretary advised, "as it is considered that the commanding officers should purchase fuel oil as required, taking advantage of any economies offered." Any arrangements made for RN vessels could be taken advantage of by their RCN counterparts, and oiling at Balboa, in Panama, could be paid for by a bill of exchange. Similarly, in regard to fresh provisions, "in order that the cost of victualling on this cruise may not compare unfavourably with the cost of victualling the ships in Canadian waters, commanding officers are requested to take advantage, as far as possible, of the Admiralty contracts for provisions where they are cheaper." Nor were spirits neglected. "Advantage is to be taken of this cruise

127. LCdr R.W. Wood, CO Vancouver, to SNO HMC Ships and Vessels Esquimalt, 6 November 1929, 136–7-5, LAC, RG 24. vol. 5684.

128. SNO Esquimalt to NSHQ, 18 November 1929, ibid.

129. LCdr R.W. Wood, CO Vancouver, to SNO Esquimalt, 28 November 1929, 1057–53–11GE, LAC, RG 24, vol. 4010.

130. SNO Esquimalt to CO Vancouver, 5 December 1929, ibid.

to bring back to the respective bases as much rum as can be properly stored," while, for uniforms, "such tropical clothing and other stores as may be required whilst at Bermuda may be drawn from HM Dockyard and from Admiralty contractors."[131]

The RCN might have wanted to reconsider such arrangements, however, at least when it came to food. *Vancouver's* commander reported after the cruise that, after using up the fourteen days' supply of fresh provisions it had loaded before sailing from Esquimalt, he had found that "the quality of the fresh provisions at Nassau and in Jamaica was not of a very high standard. Bread is very poor and heavy. The beef during transport is left in the full glare of the sun and on some occasions was not acceptable on arrival alongside the ship." In Bermuda, the destroyer had to change contractors when the first one failed to fill orders, though the victualling yard staff of HM Dockyard there was "of great assistance." In Havana "prices were very high," though the entire situation improved in Balboa and Miami, where "the quality of fresh provisions was very good, considerable care being taken to preserve meats and bread by wrapping in wax paper." Also on the favourable side of the ledger was "the good work done by the ship's cooks in carrying out their duties under the most trying conditions, the temperature of the galley being almost unbearable in the tropics, and the lack of waste, no provisions having had to be destroyed unfit for human consumption."[132]

It was perhaps in large part because of the ship's cooks and their assistants that "the general health of the ship's company during the cruise has been very satisfactory," and the four victims of venereal disease could not, presumably, be laid at their door. They had been infected in Vancouver, Montego Bay, Kingston, and Panama, respectively, though the numbers could have been much higher, being kept in check through lectures and the use, according to the ship's captain, of potassium permanganate irrigation upon return from liberty. Other work for the ship's medical staff included several minor wounds, a dozen victims of "colic," who were treated with a milk diet, and a sailor diagnosed with osteomyelitis who was admitted to the Gorgas Hospital in Panama. There was, in fact, no sick bay to speak of in Canada's destroyers, and Leading Sick Berth Attendant N.F.C. Poulter was commended for his work "under trying conditions."[133]

It was all rated as good training, though such cruises were deemed beneficial from another perspective as well. As Commander Richard L. Edwards of the Royal Navy explained to the deputy minister "the prestige of Canada is enhanced by the presence of HMC Ships in foreign ports and by their meeting with foreign men-of-war. At the same time officers and men are getting a liberal education. All hands gain experience of work under varied climactic conditions, and minor defects in material are brought to light. But, in my opinion, by far the most important result of these cruises is the enthusiasm for their profession which I am sure is stimulated amongst officers and men," allowing them to be integrated into the Royal Navy if need be. As Edwards gushed, "it will be a great day for Canada

---

131. Naval Secretary to Cdr V.G. Brodeur and others, 31 December 1929, 135-1-1, LAC, RG 24, vol. 5683.

132. LCdr R.W. Wood, CO *Vancouver*, to SNO HMC Ships and Vessels Esquimalt, 28 April 1930, 136-7-5, LAC, RG 24. vol. 5684.

133. Ibid.

and the empire when HMC ships can undertake the police work of the British empire in the waters of the American continent."[134]

The annual cruise had thus become a normal part of a destroyer's routine, though it could still prove a challenge, as *Champlain* discovered the following year. Proceeding out of Halifax on 5 January, 1931, having set course for Bermuda, "by midnight it was blowing a gale and a high sea was running." The ship reduced speed and altered course to avoid the centre of the depression, but next morning seas were still very high, "and speed was reduced to minimum at which the ship would steer. This was found to be eight knots on the revolution indicator. The actual speed through the water was estimated at four knots." That afternoon *Champlain* sailed through the cold front of the depression, leading to heavy rain and a 10° (Fahrenheit) drop in temperature in the course of about a minute. Later, weather conditions being no better, part of the rigging was carried away, and replacement material (in fact, jury rigging) lasted only twenty-four hours before it also snapped. A wave, higher than the bridge, damaged the dinghy and whaler, while a stoker suffered a broken collarbone sometime during the storm. The ship arrived in St David's at 2200 hours on the 8th and the necessary repairs were made in the days that followed.[135]

Another year and another cruise brought yet another challenge, when Gunner (Torpedo) Edward Gee, a warrant officer on loan from the Royal Navy and serving in *Champlain*, had to deal with a brouhaha in Port of Spain, Trinidad. A Danish vessel, MS *Stensby*, had been the site of something resembling a riot when her chief officer, suspecting certain irregularities concerning the disposal of victuals, actually caught the chief tally clerk passing food out of a porthole. A crowd gathered in support of the latter, the chief officer sent for his revolver, and in the confrontation that followed two men suffered scalp wounds that "were bleeding profusely." Gee, arriving on the scene in response to *Stensby*'s siren, "stationed two sentries at the gangway with instructions that nobody was to leave the ship; and in accordance with signalled instructions awaited the arrival of the local police. Upon arrival, they took the matter in hand, interrogating witnesses, etc. Quiet having been restored the guard returned to *Champlain*."[136] Duty performed, Gee and the other members of the ship's complement went back to their routine.

Vancouver and *Champlain* were, as we have seen, acquired as temporary replacements for *Patriot* and *Patrician* while new vessels were built for Canada's navy. To that end, by September 1928 fourteen British firms had submitted tenders, Commander (Engineer) T.C. Phillips, the RCN's consulting naval engineer, reporting how "all special features added to the design for Canadian conditions have been allowed for by the firms tendering without question, and without appreciable extra cost." One had to think twice before assigning the contract to the lowest bidder, however, Yarrow Ltd, for one, proposing to build ships that did not quite meet the required specifications. "The view is held that for our requirements ships of the most rugged construction possible should be obtained, so as to ensure good seaworthiness in all weathers, long life, and the minimum upkeep costs for maintenance.

134. Cdr Richard L. Edwards RN, for CNS, to DM, 12 March 1930, ibid.

135. LCdr A. Pressey, HMCS *Champlain*, to SNO Halifax, 10 January 1931, ibid.

136. Gnr (T) Edward Gee RN to CO HMCS *Champlain*, 19 March 1932, 135–7-5, LAC, RG 24, vol. 5683.

The second requirement is sound smooth working machinery of simple design, having the greatest possible strength, thereby ensuring against excessive wear and breakdown; that is to say, it is considered good policy to sacrifice light weight and slightly more frail machinery, with an extra knot at top speed, for the more robust installation and heavier built vessel with a little less speed at high speed steaming." Such requirements narrowed the field to six.[137]

The lowest tender was from Yarrow, but Thornycroft's, at £2,446,132, was only slightly more than £10,000 higher, a sum that was, "negligible in view of the greater value shown in the specifications for the Thornycroft machinery." Also, naval staff officers with expertise in engineering "are further of the opinion that the tender of Thornycroft & Company Limited should be accepted for the following reasons: the company are recognized as specialists of the first class in destroyer technician; their machinery is of the highest standard, thereby ensuring that upkeep and maintenance costs will be kept at a minimum; they are prepared to install cruising turbines, if required, at no extra cost; and, in view of their past experience and record, there is no doubt of their ability to deliver ships of the first order in every way." Adding such items as special condenser tubes and armament brought the total cost to £3,350,132.[138]

While the tendering process worked its way through the system in the UK, there was a simultaneous lobbying process working its own way through Canadian political circles. One step was a petition to Mackenzie King and members of his Cabinet, with accompanying signatures that made for an inch-high pile of paper, proposing "the desirability of having these ships built, if possible, in Canadian shipyards, and by Canadian labour." It also noted that "the shipbuilding works of Canadian Vickers Limited, of Montreal, are fully equipped to execute such a contract, to the complete satisfaction of the government and people of Canada." Furthermore, "the community immediately surrounding the works of the said Canadian Vickers Limited, includes a large number of skilled workmen, many of whom have during the past two years been seriously handicapped by periods of unemployment and uncertainty, resulting in the removal of some of them to the United States," and "it is admitted on all sides, beginning with the government of Canada, of which you are responsible and trusted heads of departments, that every means should be adopted to retain our own men within our own borders." It recommended the government consider a tender by Canadian Vickers.[139]

The company that had been established in 1910–11 in anticipation of building warships for the new Canadian navy was thus operating as intended when it submitted a bid, for over $3.5 million, in August 1928.[140] Vickers's bid did not cover spares nor did it follow the form being submitted in Britain, and Consulting Naval Engineer T.C. Phillips preferred not to consider it, stating that "Canadian Vickers Ltd, have had no experience in the build-

---

137. Cdr (E) T.C. Phillips, Consulting Naval Engineer, to CNS, 4 September 1928, 1017–10–11, LAC, RG 24, vol. 3834.

138. PC 2234, 22 December 1928, ibid.

139. Petition to Mackenzie King (PM), James Alexander Robb (Finance), Peter Heenan (Labour), and James Layton Ralston (Defence), nd, 137–1-2, LAC, RG 24, vol. 5684.

140. Tender for Hull and Machinery, Tender from Canadian Vickers Limited, 14 August 1928, 1017–10–11, LAC, RG 24, vol. 3834.

ing of destroyers, and it can be readily understood that they would have difficulty in competing with the more experienced British firms for such delicate and intricate work as the construction of a destroyer calls for; indeed it is questionable if any firm could turn out vessels of the first order, such as is required, without previous experience in the building of vessels of this class."[141] It will be recalled that Canada had built no destroyers or similar vessels during the First World War despite the urgings of both Admiral Kingsmill and Canadian Vickers to do so. Still, the Montreal shipyard responded with a visit by one of its executives to Deputy Minister Desbarats's office, where he "went over the various branches of his works, enumerated the foremen in charge of those branches and explained their qualifications. Practically all the section foreman [sic] are men who have been trained and acquired their experience at the Vickers Works at Barrow-in-Furness. Mr Barr emphasized his contention that all these men were perfectly capable of undertaking the work of destroyer construction which related to their own particular sections. He thought that, possibly, their electrical branch would be a little weak but undertook that this would be strengthened if necessary."[142]

Since the issue had not yet been laid to rest, Phillips proceeded to dissect Vickers's bid in seven long pages. To give just one instance of the nature of his argument, he addressed the issue of stability, where "for winter services on the Atlantic coast allowances should be made for additional top weight due to accumulations of snow and ice with a corresponding loss of meta-centric height and stability. For example, with say fifty tons of snow and ice centralized at say twenty-five feet above the keel, the loss of meta-centric height would be as much as six inches.... The only contractors that appear to have made allowances for this need are Thornycrofts, who have arranged for a MC height of 2' 0" in the special design ships."[143] Vickers subsequently lowered its tender.[144]

The shipbuilder's supporters, meanwhile, continued to lobby Cabinet, with no little success. As Mackenzie King wrote on 15 November 1928, "it appears that during the summer the cabinet has been considering placing the orders in Canada. I was greatly surprised last week to discover the cabinet almost of one mind on this evidently Lapointe and others had become largely committed." Ernest Lapointe was not only a member of Cabinet, but possibly King's most influential adviser in this period, so his views could not be ignored. Still, in his reply the prime minister failed to bring up any of the navy's technical arguments, at least according to his own account, instead telling those present "quite plainly that I felt so strongly on the matter that if they decided to build the ships in Canada they would have to do so without me." His main argument was that he wanted to avoid the establishment of what Americans had called the "merchants of death" on Canadian soil. Though not in the interests of either Canadian industry or the RCN, it was not entirely out of place in a society with recent memories of the First World War. "I would never permit my name to

---

141. Cdr (E) T.C. Phillips, Consulting Naval Engineer, to CNS, 4 September 1928, 1017–10–11, LAC, RG 24, vol. 3834.

142. Desbarats to Minister, 17 October 1928, ibid.

143. Cdr (E) T.C. Phillips, to CNS, 26 October 1928, ibid.

144. Desbarats to Minister, 15 November 1928, ibid.

HMCS *Saguenay* entering Willenstad Harbour, Caracao, Dutch West Indies, in 1932. (DND CN 5099)

HMCS *Saguenay* leaving Chicoutimi, Quebec, on 14 September 1934. (DND CN 3487)

HMCS *Skeena* leads *Vancouver* through the Panama Canal in 1934 for a winter cruise in the Caribbean with the East Coast destroyers *Saguenay* and *Champlain*. (LAC e007140886)

[be] associated with planting a canker of the kind in the side of our young nation," he wrote in his diary, "or allowing the Liberal Party to be credited with the starting [of] the policy of building war ships in Canada." Interestingly, it was only in a meeting with the governor general later in the day that more practical issues came to the fore, His Excellency attaching "importance to the extra cost" as well as the fact that Canadian Vickers would be "starting this particular work with no equipment."[145] Nonetheless, such thinking was immediately reversed when the country found itself at war a decade later.

King got his way, and a thirteen-page contract was signed with Thornycroft and Co. on 18 February, 1929, Lucien Pacaud of the high commissioner's office in London being commended for conducting the necessary negotiations in so short a time. The two ships would be named *Saguenay* and *Skeena*, and as brand new vessels they would incorporate some of the latest development in ship design, such as fire protection.[146] As Commander (Engineer) T.C. Phillips explained, "in the boiler rooms of warships it frequently happens that leakages of fuel oil occur with the result that usually a film of oil rests on the bilge water and bottom structure. This oil film is liable to ignite at any time causing a serious situation with possible injury to ratings and damage to the ship.... Present day destroyers are not equipped with means to readily deal with outbreaks of this nature, the use of water, sand and sometimes steam being resorted to." However, "a demonstration was recently seen of a system known as the 'Lux' when all manner of oil and gasoline fires were extinguished in a matter of seconds by the medium used with this system," the German liner *Bremen* being equipped with it.[147] Weight was an issue, however, and such systems had not been designed to be light. Still, a hose reel and two cylinder units would be installed in each boiler room, with a portable extinguisher in the galley and dynamo room. Total added weight would be 1,450 pounds, or more than half a ton.[148]

Ammunition hoists met with a different fate. Though "the Admiralty have come to the conclusion that the passage of ammunition by hand from the magazines to the guns as arranged for in destroyers of the Acasta class is not sufficiently rapid and as a consequence it has been decided to install electrical bollard hoists in the destroyers of the Beagle class now building," there was a price to pay for such efficiency. The equipment took up no little space, forcing officers and ratings into even more cramped accommodation. As Phillips explained, "in all probability the speedy passing of ammunition may never be necessary, while on the other hand the ships will be required for training for many years and there is no question in my opinion but that freedom of movement for training and living conditions such as would prevail to a greater degree if no hoists were installed would give the best all round results in the end." Similarly, four-bladed propellers were installed instead of the usual three-bladed, but were removed when trials proved disappointing. In contrast,

---

145. King Diary, 15 November 1928, LAC, MG 26 J13.

146. Contract for the Hull and Machinery of His Majesty's Canadian Ships, 18 February 1929, Desbarats to Lucien Pacaud, Office of the High Commissioner for Canada to UK, 22 March 1929, Desbarats to Hose, 18 June 1929, 1017–10–11, LAC, RG 24, vol. 3834.

147. Cdr (E) T.C. Phillips to CNS, 7 August 1929, 1017–10–11, LAC, RG 24, vol. 3835.

148. Cdr (E) Clarke, Canadian Overseer Thornycroft, to Naval Secretary, 16 November 1929, ibid.

once it was determined that "sonic sounding gear" and "echo sounding"—now called sonar—were the same thing, the necessary equipment was installed.[149]

There was also a requirement, of course, to accommodate the new destroyers' complements (*Saguenay* and *Skeena* each being made up of 181 officers and ratings), though not always in a manner of their choosing. Commander C.T. Beard, the naval staff officer, pressed for a detention cell "to enforce discipline" when necessary. Similarly, the ships would need sick bays, though it was found that the entrance to that facility, as designed, would make getting a casualty into it very difficult. Thornycroft was prepared to make the necessary changes, the result being an area of "great convenience for mustering hands for medical inspection etc."[150]

Other requirements included "electric fires," or heaters, for wardrooms, and the provision of desks for the coxswain and chief stoker, the latter being approved by Desbarats, all these myriad details taken care of under the supervision of the Canadian overseer. To increase the latter's efficiency, his staff, a chief shipwright and a chief engine room artificer, was increased with the addition of another CERA, a chief stoker, and a second shipwright. "These changes do not involve any question of transportation of the wives or families of these ratings in view of the short period they will be employed in England," the consulting naval engineer reported.[151] Work seems to have gone smoothly enough, though *Skeena*'s delivery was delayed "due to the failure of a number of large steel and iron castings." Still, Phillips was willing to be sympathetic. "While it is regretted that the contractors will be late to the extent of a few weeks with regard to the delivery of the second vessel, it is not seen that any complaint should be made in view of the fact that they, the contractors, have made special efforts to overcome what would seem to be unforeseen and unavoidable delays." When the ships were completed, it was planned to post the Canadian overseer and his assistant into them.[152]

For *Skeena*, commissioning came in mid-1931, the Royal Navy's Captain E.K. Drummond reporting that "the ship's company were a smart and fine looking body of men, who were well dressed. Their standard of physique appeared above the average." As for the destroyer herself, "the ship was extremely clean and reflected credit to all concerned. None of the officers or men had any requests to bring forward." Furthermore, Drummond "was very much impressed by the lavish way this ship had been fitted out by the contractors. A few points specially noticed were—enamelling of mess decks, raised coaming all round the upper deck, excellent ventilating and central heating throughout the ship, shower baths, and an extra motor boat of speed type; these were a few of many extras which will greatly add to the comfort of the ship's company," and which would be tested on the ship's first

---

149. Cdr (E) T.C. Phillips to CNS, 13 February and 29 March 1930, 1017–10–11, LAC, RG 24, vol. 3836; and Phillips to Hose, 16 January 1931, Canadian High Commissioner London to Desbarats, 24 October 1929, ibid, vol. 3837.

150. Canadian Overseer Thornycroft to NSHQ, 19 September 1929, 1017–10–11, LAC, RG 24, vol. 3835.

151. Phillips to CNS, 6 and 8 February 1930, 1017–10–11, LAC, RG 24, vol. 3835; and Phillips to CNS, 3 December 1930, ibid, vol. 3837.

152. Phillips to CNS, 23 July 1930, Hose to Desbarats, 15 December 1930, 1017–10–11, LAC, RG 24, vol. 3836.

cruise, from England to Esquimalt.[153] As Commander V.G. Brodeur, senior naval officer (afloat) in Esquimalt, reported, "the general ventilation of the ship has proved satisfactory," though there were exceptions, such as the cabins, the officers' galley, and the officers' after head. At least temperatures in the working areas of the machinery spaces and boiler rooms was kept to 95° Fahrenheit.[154]

Much of the destroyer's work in this early period consisted of visits of one form or another. Llewellyn Houghton later recalled that "as the first destroyer of the River class to serve on the west coast, and since we had been named after the Skeena River in northern BC, we proceeded to make official visits to a number of ports, and on this month-long cruise we carried on board the lieutenant-governor of British Columbia, the Hon. J. Fordham-Johnson and two members of his staff, his AdC Major A. Selden Humphrys, DSO, and his private secretary, Mr A.M.D. Fairbairn. At Prince Rupert, the ship was presented by the residents of the Skeena District with a handsome silver candelabra. At Port Simpson, the Tsimshean Indians gave us a beautifully carved paddle, and we learned that the Indian word for Skeena is *Ksiyan,* which means 'Waters of the Mist.'"[155] When the senior naval officer afloat made reference to a "small cocktail party" in his report of proceedings, however, there was no little concern in Ottawa, as "the minister considers that the statements regarding cocktail parties are out of place in an official report, which may possibly be brought down in parliament." The officers concerned were to be warned accordingly. A more positive reaction followed the report that a total of 11,815 people had visited the destroyer during her cruise, the chief of the naval staff's office responding that "this is certainly a tribute to the great interest aroused by the new ship."[156]

Skeena would soon be engaged in operations of a more warlike nature, however. While on a cruise off the West Coast of Latin America, Britain's Foreign Office passed on a request "for immediate despatch of one of HM ships to Acajutla because of grave danger of general risk of communists at San Salvador involving imminent danger to British lives and property. HMS *Dragon* is being despatched to Acajutla but cannot arrive before Wednesday 27th January. In view of need for immediate action I suggest *Skeena* and *Vancouver* who appear to be in vicinity be directed to render such assistance to British subjects at Acajutla as may be necessary."[157] It was not the first time an RCN vessel was involved in such operations. As we have seen, in 1916 *Rainbow* had stood off Mexico during the latter's revolution, and returned before the year was out. Another intervention (or, more accurately, trade mission) was in 1921, when *Aurora, Patriot,* and *Patrician* visited Costa Rica.

As for the situation in El Salvador, an election in 1931 had brought President Araujo, who had promised better living conditions, to power. There was little he could do, however,

153. Capt E.K. Drummond to C-in-C, HM Ships and Vessels Portsmouth, 12 June 1931, 8000–353–28, LAC, RG 24, vol. 5834.

154. Brodeur to NSHQ, 14 August 1931, 138–7-5, LAC, RG 24, vol. 5684.

155. F.L. Houghton, "Memoir," nd, 112, LAC, MG 30 E444.

156. Desbarats to CNS, 5 November 1931, Cdr W.B. Hynes, for CNS, to Desbarats, 2 November 1931, 138–7-5, LAC, RG 24, vol. 5684.

157. C-in-C, America and West Indies to Hose, 22 January 1932, LAC, RG 25, vol. 1598, file 318.

since the country's main export, coffee, had seen prices plummet as a result of the world economic depression. By December US Army Major A.R. Harris was writing a pessimistic report on the situation in the Central American country. "About the first thing one observes when he goes to San Salvador is the number of expensive automobiles on the streets.... There appears to be nothing between these high-priced cars and the oxcart with its bare-footed attendant. There is practically no middle class.... A socialistic or communistic revolution in El Salvador may be delayed for several years, ten or even twenty, but when it comes it will be a bloody one." With living conditions worsening in step with the world's economy, some began to look to the Russian and Mexican revolutions for inspiration. One of these was Farabunto Marti, who was arrested before the revolt began and quickly executed, but who gave his name to a guerrilla group formed decades later.[158]

At the time, Russia's Bolshevik revolution was still fresh in people's memories, and one who saw a link between the insurrection in El Salvador and events in the Soviet Union was Britain's chargé d'affaires, who warned the Foreign Office on 21 January: "Urgent.... Communists have made detailed plans to blow up banks, take possession of railways and plantations, kill members of government army officers and women, sack town and establish soviet republic.... Government aware and have arrested some ringleaders, but it is doubtful if they can dominate communists owing to army dissensions weakness of president disloyalty of high official and infiltration of communism among troops which has affected large proportion.... I suggest consultation with US government with a view to urgent measures.... I do not wish to be considered alarmist but position is very serious."[159] Next day, 22 January 1932, *Skeena* received the message to sail for Acajutla, El Salvador, "to protect British residents," and began to prepare to put ashore a landing party. The ship was advised the next day that "about 500 communist rebels chiefly low type Indians from interior attacked Custom House at Sonsonate killing and mutilating customs police and several inhabitants. Forty rebels killed. No damage to British life or property involved yet. Fearing reprisals by government troops rebels have dispersed in smaller groups into surrounding country." Also, according to *Skeena*, "public telephone communications cut but British railway telephone still working.... No Canadian residents."[160]

In Ottawa, meanwhile, the Conservative government of R.B. Bennett received intelligence from London to the effect that "his majesty's chargé d'affaires at San Salvador reports that on the night of the 19th January a large body of well armed communists preparing to attack San Salvador were dispersed by government forces and their leaders arrested. Martial law has been proclaimed but position is very grave as communists have made detailed plans for a general rising with a view to the establishment of a soviet republic, and it appears doubtful whether government can dominate them owing to army dissension and infiltration of communism among the troops, weakness of the president and disloyalty of high

---

158. Major Harris quoted in Clifford Kraus, *Inside Latin America* (New York 1991), 59–62.

159. Chargé d'Affaires to Foreign Office, 21 January 1932, United Kingdom National Archives (hereafter UKNA), Foreign Office (hereafter FO) 813/22.

160. *Skeena* to CNS, 23 January 1932, LAC, RG 25, vol. 1598, file 318; and *Skeena* Log, 22 January 1932, LAC, RG 24, vol. 7850.

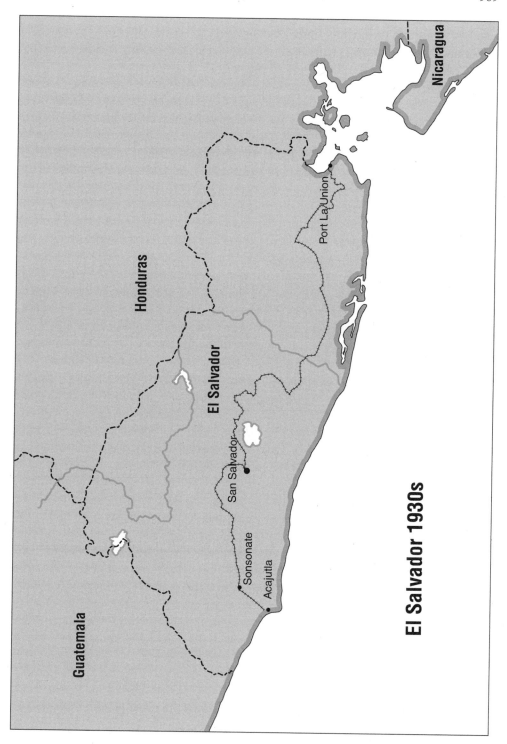

officials. Rising was planned for midnight 23rd January but takes place at any time. The intention of the communists is to sack the city and there is a possibility of danger to British banks, railways and other British lives and property."[161]

If accurate, the British report was indeed worrisome, and in her first serious operation nature itself seemed to intervene to make *Skeena*'s task as difficult as possible. As Llewellyn Houghton, the ship's executive officer, later wrote, "it so happened that on the day we intercepted the C-in-C's message, there had been a minor earthquake in Guatemala, on the northern and western borders of El Salvador, and this was accompanied by the eruption of two normally dormant volcanoes, El Fuego and Santa Maria. One result of these unusual occurrences was to pollute the atmosphere for several hundred miles out to sea with a fine, brown volcanic dust, causing a haze that cut visibility to less than two miles, making our landfall difficult; worse still, it completely ruined our new paint job. It was several weeks before we finally rid the ship of that penetrating dust."[162] Nevertheless, *Skeena* and *Vancouver* were able to make fifteen knots, arriving at 11:00 on the 23rd. The older destroyer, however, had to proceed to Port La Union for fuel. Still, the Canadian presence helped put the British chargé d'affaires' mind at ease, and he cabled the British naval commander-in-chief, Barbados, on the 24th to advise that "as situation at present stands presence of HMS *Dragon* unnecessary provided Canadian destroyers can remain until immediate dangers over."[163]

Skeena's orders, in keeping with such matters in the RN and RCN, were clear and concise. "On arrival get in touch with British Consul or other British authority and ascertain what can be done. Failing that enquire from constituted San Salvador authority and ascertain if assistance required to protect British lives and property. At same time get in touch with United States authorities and work in co-operation with them ascertain if any Canadian residents no overt act should be taken unless actual and immediate imperative necessity to save lives of British subjects."[164] According to Houghton, "anchoring one mile off the only pier, we found Acajutla (Ak-a-hoot-la) to be little more than a native village, a collection of low huts on the flat, sandy littoral with three more or less prominent buildings— the British consulate, the railway station and the headquarters of the port commandant. Acajutla's importance lay in the fact that it was—and still is—the terminus of the British-owned railway connecting with San Salvador, the capital of the republic. The principal export, coffee, is collected up-country and shipped out of Acajutla, in spite of the fact that there is no harbour and no protection from the Pacific swell which causes a very heavy surf to roll in continuously day and night the year round. This makes boatwork a real problem, but fortunately the pier is equipped with small steam cranes, passengers and goods being hoisted and lowered in boatswain's chairs or large baskets."[165]

161. Secretary of State for Dominion Affairs to Secretary of State for External Affairs, 22 January 1932, LAC, RG 25, vol. 1598, file 318.

162. F.L. Houghton, "Memoir," nd, 116, LAC, MG 30 E444.

163. British Charge d'Affaires to British Naval Commander in Chief, Barbados, 24 January 1932, UKNA, FO 813/22; and Captain-in-Charge Esquimalt to NSHQ, 31 March 1932, 136–7-5, LAC, RG 24, vol. 5684.

164. CNS to *Skeena*, 23 January 1932, LAC, RG 25, vol. 1598, file 318.

165. F.L. Houghton, "Memoir," nd, 116–17, LAC, MG 30 E444.

That day "one signal rating landed for duty ashore," and "five British ladies from Sonsonate came on board for safety."[166] Victor Brodeur, serving in a double capacity as commander (destroyers) west and captain of *Skeena,* later reported that "the arrival of ships created a strong moral support to all concerned. The American authorities were more than surprised and a little disappointed to see a British flag first." The situation was tense, to say the least, as "no steps had been taken by the Salvador government to protect anything or offer serious defence to revolutionary forces, for fear that the army would revolt. So all troops were kept in the capital where a serious attack was expected at any moment. Army officers and the National Guard were the only ones that could be really depended upon in case of a serious uprising." Though not reported by *Skeena,* "it was ascertained that the US authorities were also in a panic and had sent many urgent messages for help which caused US destroyers to come at twenty-five knots from Panama.... It seemed evident that all foreign authorities were seriously worried as to the outcome."[167]

Next day, according to Houghton's account, "in order to ascertain the actual state of affairs the captain," Brodeur, "sent me ashore in the ship's motorboat with two armed men hidden under the engineroom canopy—just in case. I was met by the British vice consul, the port commandant and the port doctor. I learned from the consul that so far all was quiet locally, but there had been several disturbances up-country; and that at Sonsonate, only fifteen miles up the line, the Customs House had been attacked, five customs police killed and their bodies dragged into the street and mutilated. The attacking Indians all wore armbands with the letters SRI—Socorro Rojo Internationale, Red International Aid. This certainly seemed to confirm that the uprising was Communist-inspired." The five women on board were in fact the wives of railway officials, though they were accommodated "with some dislocation to the junior officers' accommodation," for a period of eight days. One of them was pregnant, and the medical officer, Major J. Earl Hunter of the Royal Canadian Army Medical Corps (the RCN did not have its own medical service), "was the most nervous man on board." Fortunately for Major Hunter, she did not give birth until the crisis had passed and she had returned ashore.[168]

The captain and executive officer left for the capital, San Salvador, and a while later an armed party of three officers and forty-one ratings prepared to go ashore, under the command of Lieutenant Adams. Landing on the jetty, they then waited for orders from their superior officers to move off to San Salvador, but it seems that when the order came, it was from the British consul, and the captain rescinded it. "Five British men accommodated on board for the night," and some routine training was carried out.[169] According to Houghton, "it very soon appeared that the British consul, egged on by the railway authorities, had panicked unduly. This was confirmed when the captain and I were given an audience by General Martinez himself. He stated quite definitely that he had the situation well in hand and was adamant in his refusal to allow our party to land as he could see no reason whatsoever

166. *Skeena* Log, 23 January 1932, LAC, RG 24, vol. 7850.

167. Brodeur to NSHQ, 7 April 1932, LAC, RG 25, vol. 1598, file 318.

168. F.L. Houghton, "Memoir," nd, 117, LAC, MG 30 E444.

169. *Skeena* Log, 24 January 1932, LAC, RG 24, vol. 7850.

for foreign intervention. Commander Brodeur assured the president that we were only try-ing to help, but that we must insist on immediate and thorough protection of British lives and interests. This was at once promised, and by the next morning the whole of the rail-way and all British property were under the protection of the National Guard, a picked body of men who were well trained, better armed than the ordinary troops and with a reputation for fearlessness. It soon became clear that General Martinez was as good as his word."[170]

Meanwhile, *Vancouver* arrived at Port La Union, at the other end of El Salvador, for fuel and provisions, the situation there reported as "quiet and peaceful, but while there tele-phone call was received from British charge de affairs [*sic*] to land armed platoon. This was not carried out. Contrary orders being received from commander 'D,'" who thus confirmed the proper chain of command. The ship then settled into the routine of a normal cruise, including official calls, before leaving for Acajutla, to arrive on the 25th.[171] At that time Brodeur and Houghton were still in the capital, where "for the next few days the general's troops were busy rooting out the disaffected Indians, shooting them after a brief interro-gation, then soaking their bodies in gasoline and burning them. The ringleaders were hanged on the nearest tree. We were informed that to date 4,800 had been executed and that the situation was rapidly 'returning to normal.'"[172]

Back in *Skeena* ratings were unaware that the danger, what little of it there had been, had passed, as it was not customary in the navy of the day to keep the lower deck apprised of what was going on—sailors were simply expected to obey orders. As Able Seaman A.G. Barrick later remembered, "we were never told what to expect, or what we might have to do (afterwards we suspected that in the confused situation NOBODY KNEW!) Some of the more imagina-tive young fellows (our average age was about nineteen) having heard about US Marines being massacred with machetes in Nicaragua a few years before, began to wonder what might be in store for us, and whether or not WE MIGHT BE NEXT!"[173] There may have been no less worry in *Vancouver,* but the fact that in the next few days "bathing parties and one recreation party were landed" probably indicated that serious concerns passed quickly.[174]

Brodeur and Houghton returned to *Skeena* on the 25th, having passed a busy and event-ful twenty-four hours. "Hands employed washing paint work and cleaning ship's side," the vessel's log related, work probably far more useful than the landing parties that had been organized the day before. The ship's captain could now report to the chief of the naval staff, to the effect that "government has the situation well in hand. No direct evidence whatever that British lives are in danger and I consider former reports to this effect were greatly exag-gerated." As for the British consul's orders to land a party, Brodeur remarked that "conditions

---

170. F.L. Houghton, "Memoir," nd, 120, LAC, MG 30 E444.

171. Captain-in-Charge Esquimalt to NSHQ, 31 March 1932, 136–7-5, LAC, RG 24, vol. 5684.

172. F.L. Houghton, "Memoir," nd, 120, LAC, MG 30 E444.

173. Barrick quoted in Serge Durflinger, "In Whose Interests? The Royal Canadian Navy and Naval Diplomacy in El Salvador, 1932," Ann L. Griffiths, Peter T. Haydon, and Richard H. Gimblett, eds., *Canadian Gunboat Diplomacy: The Canadian Navy and Foreign Policy* (Halifax 1998), 33.

174. Captain-in-Charge Esquimalt to NSHQ, 31 March 1932, 136–7-5, LAC, RG 24, vol. 5684.

in no way warranted such drastic action."[175] In the report he submitted after arrival back in Esquimalt, he related how on the 25th he and Houghton had stopped at an American plantation, where everything seemed normal. "Nothing of importance took place. The troops took the initiative and were killing rebels right and left." Next day Brodeur visited a plantation that had been the site for some of the rebel attacks. There, he "observed the unsanitary conditions under which the Indians were working, surrounded with flies and dirty water and were paid very low wages. Here again it was found that on one or two occasions a few Indians were seen in the bushes but they did no damage whatever though it would have been the easiest thing in the world to destroy the plantation due to its isolated location."[176]

The two Canadian ships remained in port for another few days, and on the 29th Brodeur, in the company of Salvadoran generals, toured the Sonsonate district. One plantation, where workers were supposedly well treated, the rebels had left alone, as they had all churches and religious articles. Given communism's atheism, Brodeur concluded that such "would tend to prove that the insurrection, though of a bloody nature, was not communistic." He also suggested that "it is very doubtful if the Indians who took part in the revolution knew what bolshevism meant. To them it meant an organization to release them from slavery." He even went so far as to conclude that "the revolution was entirely due to lack of consideration for the Indians. There are only two classes in Sanvador [sic, El Salvador], i.e., the very rich and the Indians."[177] Government operations had been marked with extreme ruthlessness, Houghton relating how "on our last day in El Salvador, Generals Calderon and Chatore arrived in Acajutla and invited the commanding officers of *Skeena* and *Vancouver* to lunch in Sonsonate and '... to witness a few executions.' They reported the lunch as excellent, but while they were shown the five prisoners, they felt it inadvisable to be present at the executions.... So ended our Salvador adventure."[178] *Skeena* reported that the "communist offensive entirely dispersed," and the ship left for Balboa at the end of the month. The La Matanza massacre, as survivors labelled it, had cost about 20,000 lives as the military took control of El Salvador and kept themselves in power until the 1990s.[179]

It was time to think about the lessons learned from the incident, most of which had to do with communications given the need to disseminate intelligence and to keep higher authority in Ottawa and London advised of the situation on a day-to-day basis. The commander-in-chief America and West Indies station was generally satisfied with the way signals had been handled, though, "it is understood that the Department of National Defence is contemplating the installation of an up-to-date W/T station at Ottawa, and there is no

---

175. *Skeena* Log, 25 January 1932, LAC, RG 24, vol. 7850.

176. Brodeur to NSHQ, 7 April 1932, LAC, RG 25, vol. 1598, file 318.

177. Ibid.

178. F.L. Houghton, "Memoir," nd, 120–21, LAC, MG 30 E444.

179. *Skeena* to CNS and C-in-C, America and West Indies, 29 January 1932, LAC, RG 25, vol. 1598, file 318; and *Skeena* Log, 31 January 1932, LAC, RG 24, vol. 7850; and Kraus, *Inside Latin America*, 62–63.

doubt that this ... would be of the greatest value in facilitating rapid communication, and would overcome many of the difficulties encountered during this period."[180] Some of the latter included Halifax being out of communication with Ottawa all day on 25 January and in poor communication on the 26th and 27th, the latter mainly due to atmospheric interference. As messages from *Skeena* were being passed through Bermuda, which "was working continuously during the period under review and did much to assist in passing messages to and from *Skeena*," Halifax was of crucial importance. So was the facility at Rockcliffe, even though "the small power of the transmitting apparatus at Rockcliffe was a great drawback.... A number of messages were received direct but could not be acknowledged till some hours later, giving rise to a certain amount of congestion and unnecessary W/T traffic, since the same messages were re-transmitted by an intermediate station.... In particular it would have assisted Bermuda greatly if Ottawa had been able to acknowledge messages as soon as received.... Communication would also have been much facilitated if Ottawa had been able to transmit direct to *Skeena* during the whole period *Skeena* was audible at Ottawa." Rockcliffe should, according to NSHQ's director of naval intelligence, be Canada's first priority in re-equipping W/T stations.[181]

Another lesson had to do with the RCN's prestige—and hence its finances. Back in Ottawa Hose now had ammunition he could use in budgetary discussions. "The naval estimates were discussed behind closed doors, where naval officers desperately attempted to influence the government's budgetary allocations. The publicity generated by the navy's activities in El Salvador needs to be placed into this context. Perhaps the chief of the naval staff ... hoped that the momentary headline-grabbing of the RCN in January 1932 would help illustrate the value of the naval service, or at least temper the criticism of it on the part of the chief of the general staff, Major-General A.G.L. McNaughton," who, as we have seen, could be convinced of the need to retain a navy, but nevertheless needed convincing.[182]

The incident in El Salvador was beneficial for the RCN in one respect. Before the British consul called for help the Canadian government had been organizing its delegation for a General Disarmament Conference to be held in Geneva, and on 13 January it was announced that the technical advisers would be Lester B. Pearson of the Department of External Affairs and McNaughton on behalf of DND. Hose, convinced that an army officer would not be able to properly advise the government on naval matters, sought redress. Meeting with Prime Minister Bennett on the 20th, he repeated his argument from a previous occasion that where one chief of staff was appointed to such a delegation, the other should as well; he also lobbied George Perley, the chief of the delegation. Advised that he would not be taken to Geneva, Hose concluded that McNaughton had been, in fact, unofficially promoted to be a "super-chief of staff," and repeated his argument, on 21 January, that "in matters concerning defence as a whole the chiefs of staff of the respective services have an equal, joint and individual, responsibility." That having failed to convince higher authority, he wrote a letter of resignation. Then, El Salvador focused his attention, and the

180. C-in-C, America and West Indies to CNS, 17 March 1932, 1008–33–6, LAC, RG 24, vol. 6198.

181. Cdr W.B. Hynes RN, DNI, to CNS, 12 February 1932, ibid.

182. Eayrs, *In Defence of Canada*, II, 261, 263–64.

letter was left unsent, ensuring that the RCN would retain, for another year, a very competent and intelligent chief of the naval staff.[183] Another salutary effect was a higher profile for the RCN in the press—at least for a little while. As a pamphlet commemorating the ship's first anniversary of its commissioning explained, "it is certain that our presence at Acajutla increased the number of people who had merely heard that there was such a thing as a Canadian Navy."[184]

In the meantime, *Skeena* returned to Vancouver, and it was perhaps appropriate (and ironic as well), that she was soon engaged in a landing exercise, called Operation Q, at Comox. The ship was Blue Force, with orders to attack a camp defended by Red Force, provided by *Vancouver* and RCN personnel who ran a nearby shooting range. "Every available man was landed from both ships," Victor Brodeur, the commander (destroyers) west, proudly recounted, attacking forces being divided into three platoons. Two distinct actions were fought, though in the critique that followed it was noted that "when going up the range, Blue Forces did not make sufficient use of the cover available such as contour of the land," so it would seem the sailors in question had had very little infantry training before the exercise. Also, the commander of Red Force kept his reserves too far back, while other members of that organization "were seeing things," and "thereby making extraordinary claims of casualties." At least "the enthusiasm and keenness of all who took part was noticed and is most gratifying," and the naval secretary was directed "to express the gratification of the department for the exercise carried out.... The reports of this exercise indicate excellent organization prior to the operation and a keen interest by all concerned in carrying it out."[185]

More naval in tone were torpedo and gunnery training, *Skeena* firing a full broadside of eight torpedoes (of the practice variety) in October 1932. "The torpedoes all ran correctly and the T[ime] C[heck] and tube drill was very satisfactory," according to Commander G.C. Jones, commander (destroyers) west at the time. Both West Coast destroyers occasionally fired their guns as well, one exercise conducted by *Skeena* in October 1933 deemed " satisfactory," though with many caveats, Jones taking into account "the limited opportunity for gunnery exercise, the necessity for constantly changing personnel and the lack of a loader for gun drill." Still, results "represent a very marked improvement on the spring exercises and show the benefit of having a fully qualified gunnery officer in the ship." *Vancouver* did not fare so well, her gunnery rated as "very unsatisfactory.... The main reason is that the new gunnery control officer has ignored every principle of fire control. In future the lieutenant commander (G) will be able to devote more time in the supervision of *Vancouver*'s gunnery. The gunnery control officer will be exercised at the spotting table," a simulator, "which should result in the necessary improvement."[186]

183. Ibid, 261–64.

184. F.L. Houghton, *HMCS Skeena, 1931–1932: Commemorating Her First Year in Commission* (Victoria 1932), 28.

185. Cdr (D) West to NSHQ, 17 May 1932, Naval Secretary to Brodeur, 4 June 1932, 138–7-5, LAC, RG 24, vol. 5684.

186. G.C. Jones, Commander (D) West, "Torpedo Firing Carried Out 7–10-32," 7 October 1932, Jones to NSHQ, 27 October 1933, 1057–53–11GE, LAC, RG 24, vol. 4011.

Then, of course, there were cruises, and though none were as eventful as the 1932 voyage, which included an uprising in El Salvador, the exercises of 1934 were notable for being "the longest cruise ever attempted up to that time" by the RCN. Covering 15,000 miles in fifty-seven steaming days, the navy's four destroyers conducted "scores of exercises," while their captains attended 106 official functions in twenty-seven ports, "not to mention innumerable unofficial ones!" A week spent with the Home Fleet, commanded by Vice-Admiral Sir William (Ginger) Boyle, was "the highlight of the whole show," involving, among many others, the destroyers *Kempenfelt, Comet, Crusader, Crescent,* and *Cygnet,* all of which would become RCN vessels in later years. "In hot, steamy weather and heavy nor-east trade [wind]s, we pounded round the Caribbean and well out into the Atlantic for five hectic days. The C-in-C kept us busy day and night with every conceivable type of exercise, manoeuvre or drill. I rarely dared to leave the bridge, but managed to survive those five days and nights with remarkably little sleep," boasted Lieutenant-Commander Houghton.[187]

One of his most vivid memories was of "one pitch-dark moonless night in heavy seas, out in the wide Atlantic east of Barbados, when the Canadian flotilla was ordered to carry out a dummy torpedo attack on the 'enemy' fleet led by the commander-in-chief himself. It was to be made under full wartime conditions—no navigation lights and strict wireless silence." In keeping with tactics learned off the coast of British Columbia, "from a position well ahead of the fleet our four destroyers crashed through the waves at thirty knots, ships pitching madly, mast-high spray flying over their bridges. It was impossible to see more than a few yards ahead of us." *Vancouver,* Houghton's ship, was the port-most of the four Canadian destroyers, though the three others were "of course completely invisible. I felt very much alone." Then, "suddenly a searchlight was switched on dead ahead of *Vancouver,* the sharply-defined, bluish beam aimed directly at our bridge. By great good fortune the flagship, leading the 'enemy' line, had spotted us; we were obviously much nearer our target than we had calculated. In fact, *Vancouver* was actually on a collision course with the huge battleship.... 'Hard-a-starboard! Stand by to fire torpedoes!' As we swung round, we 'fired' four fish, indicating the moment of firing by shooting off a green Very light. Whether or not, in the circumstances, our torpedoes would have struck home must forever remain a matter for conjecture. I can only remember feeling at the time that I had had quite enough excitement for one night."[188]

That all four Canadian destroyers were on exercise in the West Indies at the same time was because of Hose, who the previous year had once again prevented the RCN from being consigned to naval oblivion. Meeting with the chief of the general staff on 31 May, 1933, the chief of the naval staff found that they could not agree on how to share a substantial budget cut, of over $3.6 million (from $14 million), being considered by Treasury Board. Next day McNaughton laid out his thinking for the minister, noting that "in August 1930, after detailed consideration by the Joint Staff Committee it was recommended that the naval forces of Canada should be expanded to ... one—destroyer leader ... five—destroyers ... four—twin screw minesweepers."[189] The country had, however, since suffered one of the

187. F.L. Houghton, "Memoir," nd, 122, LAC, MG 30 E444.

188. Ibid, 123–24.

189. CGS to Minister DND, 1 June 1933, LAC, MG 30 E133, vol. 12, file 64A.

worst economic downturns in its history, and as has been noted, "in Ottawa, politicians and officials ransacked budgets for economies. Defence was an obvious place to look. Warned of widespread communist organizing among the unemployed, the Cabinet decided not to cut deeply into the militia or the permanent force [army]. The other services were more vulnerable."[190] As McNaughton explained at the time, "the situation with which we are now faced involves a very large reduction in the funds to be made available for defence and to distribute these reductions over all the Forces would result in weakness everywhere." Therefore, it would be best to "narrow our purpose" to "the forces necessary for the maintenance and support of the civil power," and to "the creation of a minimum deterrent to seaborne attack." According to the CGS, "any naval force less than that recommended in August 1930 could not be considered adequate. Moreover it is of the nature of naval forces that they cannot be rapidly expanded to meet emergencies and, in consequence, it seems to me that little purpose is served in maintaining a small nucleus."[191]

Other services, at least in the CGS's view, were another matter. "On the other hand air forces even in small numbers are a definite deterrent in narrow waters and on the high seas in the vicinity of the shore; they can be developed with considerable rapidity provided a nucleus of skilled personnel in a suitable training organization is in existence; pilots engaged in civil aviation can be quickly adapted to defence purposes; civil aircraft are not without value in defence, and any aircraft manufacturing facilities are equally available to meet military as well as civil requirements." Therefore, if it came down to maintaining a nucleus navy or an expandable air force, McNaughton favoured the latter, and before judging the CGS too harshly it should be noted that the RCAF had already seen substantial budget cuts, from a high of $5,442,000 to $1.6 million. One might not agree with McNaughton's strategic and tactical thinking, but clearly he was placed in a position where difficult decisions would have to be made. Interestingly, earlier in this period, in 1930, Australia's CGS had suggested that the Royal Australian Navy be abandoned in favour of monetary payments to Britain, so the RCN was not alone in having to battle for its existence.[192]

As for Treasury Board, which had initiated the bean-counting process, it suggested that ships and establishments could be maintained for $422,000, though Hose replied that such was "entirely outside the realm of practicability for many reasons which it is unnecessary to set forth in detail, since the single fact that one-sixth of the year for which an appropriation of $2,422,000.00 was granted has already transpired, results in practically no funds being available for the remainder of the financial year." The money was, in effect, already spent, so the logical consequence of such a cut was "the disbanding of the whole service, and even if this is effected, the charges connected with its disbandment, taking into consideration sums already spent and contracts which have been effected, would reach a far greater amount than the $422,000 suggested."[193]

---

190. Morton, *Canada and War*, 97.

191. CGS to Minister DND, 1 June 1933, LAC, MG 30 E133, vol. 12, file 64A.

192. Ibid; and Stevens, *A Critical Vulnerability*, 91.

193. Hose to Minister, 1 June 1933, DHH 2001/12, file C15.

Hose submitted a detailed defence, reminding higher authority that in 1930 the CGS had agreed with the need to bring the navy up to standard. The Great Depression might force a reduction in government spending, but it had not changed global-strategic considerations, which "absolutely militate against the safeness of a reliance upon military and air force defence to the exclusion of a properly effective naval force." Hose therefore repeated his arguments to the effect that given Canada's location on the globe, direct attack was unlikely, but that given its reliance on commerce, attacks on its trade were within the realm of the possible. "Such an attack, if not properly countered, at the focal points of trade off Canadian coasts would paralyze Canadian industry." Three main factors in determining the navy's resources, it is worth repeating here, were that they had to be sufficient to ensure Canada was not drawn into someone else's war, that is to say involving the United States; they needed to be sufficient to defend focal points of trade if the country did indeed find itself at war; and they could not fall below a certain minimum. Also, "in this connection, or perhaps as a fourth factor, it must be emphasized that a navy cannot be improvised at short notice."[194]

Hose was offered a golden opportunity to present his views again when Treasury Board asked the deputy minister of national defence, in relation to the proposed budget cuts: "Can this be done without impairing any essential service?"[195] The chief of the naval staff's response was, not surprisingly, that "this cannot be done without impairing the efficiency of the service." Among the many points he brought to the fore to support his argument were that expensive equipment would be lost through lack of care and maintenance, ships and establishments would suffer similarly, since the amount requested in the estimates had been the minimum deemed necessary, and a reduction in civilian staff, as recommended by Treasury Board, would force the use of RCN officers and ratings in tasks for which they had not been trained, "an un-economic use of such personnel." He also noted that the latter would be reduced in numbers in any case.[196]

Discussions came to a head on 23 June, when Hose met with Desbarats and McNaughton, the latter advising "to the effect that in the event of sufficient funds for properly effective naval, military and air forces respectively being unavailable the service of the least value was that of the navy, and that sacrifices must be made in that force first; further, that with an effective air force and militia a sufficient deterrent would be provided against aggressive action on our coasts." Hose objected to the CGS advising on the fate of the RCN when a perfectly competent CNS was available to do so. "In doing this it creates an absolutely impossible position for the chief of the naval staff and indicates a lack of confidence by the government in him as a responsible officer to tender advice on national defence, even though the problem is one in which maritime security with its naval responsibilities is a vital factor."[197]

---

194. Hose, "Policy Regarding Naval Defence Which Would Be Affected by Reductions in the Service," 1 June 1933, ibid.

195. Treasury Board to Deputy Minister National Defence, 15 June 1933, ibid, file C16.

196. Hose to Minister, 19 June 1933, ibid, file C17.

197. Hose to Minister, 23 June 1933, ibid, file C18.

Hose had the support of Vice-Admiral R.A.R. Plunkett-Ernle-Erle-Drax, commander-in-chief of the America and West Indies Station, who visited Ottawa in this period and personally met with members of the government. The chief of the naval staff, in the meantime, took the unprecedented step, which he had considered the year before, of threatening his resignation. When Dr R.J. Manion, minister of Railways and Canals, asked why the cuts of 1922 had been acceptable but the recommended budget reductions of 1933 were not, Hose was ready with a reply. "To-day we had ships which had cost the Canadian taxpayers some seven or eight million dollars, that our complement was nearly 900 in the permanent force and that 850 of these were Canadians who had devoted their life and training to the service." The navy thus had much more to lose, and a much larger investment would go to waste. Manion was convinced when Hose repeated his global strategic arguments, adding that the Canadian destroyers were needed to maintain Commonwealth parity with other naval powers. Though handing over ships and personnel to the Admiralty was a possible solution, Hose knew he was making a suggestion that was politically impossible. Sir George Perley, president of the Treasury Board, after weeks of listening to the CNS's logic, agreed to a cut of only $200,000 out of a total defence reduction of $1 million. Actual RCN expenditures dropped from almost $3.6 million in 1930–31 to a little over $3 million the following year. They would drop again, to under $2.2 million, in 1933–34 as the Conservative government continued to prioritize unemployment relief, but would rise to over $2.2 and almost $2.4 million in the next two fiscal years, to reach pre-depression levels in 1936–37, at $4.75 million.[198]

When Commodore Walter Hose retired on 1 January 1934, he could be well satisfied with his accomplishments. The navy was still a work in progress, but unknown to Hose it would never again face oblivion, though it would often get far fewer resources than it felt it needed, a feeling, it is fair to say, shared by other fighting services and other government departments. Hose received a flattering letter from Mackenzie King, which among other things praised the outgoing CNS for his wisdom, and stated that "I always felt that you perfectly understood the Canadian point of view on naval matters, and during your term of office you have had the satisfaction of seeing the empire as a whole come to recognize how sound, from the outset, it has been."[199] Hose replied that he left the service full of confidence resulting from "the spirit and esprit de corps of our naval service today in spite of the many unavoidable difficulties it has had to face," and "in the undoubted growing interest throughout the country in the necessity of our Service for the security of our ever growing sea-borne commerce, evidenced largely by the pride in the naval volunteer units in every province."[200] A long decade after the 1922 budget, Hose had good reason to feel content with what he had wrought—the RCN was very much alive, and with every indication that it would continue to be so.

198. Hose to C-in-C, America & West Indies Station, 26 June 1933, ibid, file C19; and see DND, *Annual Reports*.

199. Mackenzie King to Hose, 23 December 1933, LAC, MG 26 J3, vol. 65.

200. Hose to King, 26 December 1933, ibid.

CHAPTER 15

The Road to War, 1933–1939

Members of the RCN of the early to mid 1930s were not aware that war would break out in the autumn of 1939. Although historians of the period, like the authors of this study, have characterized the decade as a "road to war," the officers and sailors of the day carried out their tasks not because they knew a world conflict was merely a few years away, but because it was their duty to do so. The Japanese Army may well have invaded Manchuria in 1931, and created the puppet government of Manchukuo, but only after the Second World War was over did historians and other analysts—with twenty-twenty hindsight—see the operation as a step on the path that led to the deaths of tens of millions of people worldwide. At the time Manchuria was not necessarily seen as part of China, itself divided between Communist, Guomindang, and warlord regions, and the Japanese Army's manoeuvres were not seen as a threat to peace, or world order, the odd speech given before the League of Nations notwithstanding. Only later in the decade, first with Italy's 1935 invasion of Abyssinia, then with Germany's moves against Austria and Czechoslovakia in 1938, would the Royal Canadian Navy be able to relate its training and equipment procurement to world events, rather than as part of its day-to-day role of protecting Canada's trade and natural resources. Only in the last half of 1938 would the institution, or at least its chief of naval staff, Percy Nelles, foresee war as a very real possibility in the near future, by which time the routine work of procurement, training and operations had led to the development of a small but capable naval service.

And so it was that in the early part of the decade the RCN was very much focused on the organizational issues that had engaged so much of NSHQ's attention since the navy's creation. In doing so, form very much followed function, headquarters reflecting the type of operation the RCN predicted it would be conducting in time of emergency or outright war. Three new committees, gunnery, torpedo, and communications, were created at this time, each composed of three officers, one a specialist in the type of operation concerned, the others being the director of naval intelligence and plans and the director of naval operations and training. Officers throughout the RCN were "encouraged to forward reports to Headquarters expressing their views and suggesting means of overcoming any difficulties which they may encounter," the committee most concerned with the issue expected to coordinate matters within its sphere.[1]

At the head of this system was Percy Nelles, appointed to the position of chief of the

---

1. J. O'B LeBlanc to distribution list, 18 October 1934, 1078-3-1, Library and Archives Canada (hereafter LAC), Record Group (hereafter RG) 24, vol. 4044.

Percy Nelles, seen here as a commander in the RCN, served as chief of the naval staff from 1934 to 1944. (DND Nelles-1)

naval staff in 1934, after twenty-five years' experience in the Fishery Protection Service and the RCN, having joined in 1909, before the navy was even created. He was, in fact, one of the service's seven original cadets, and served in various vessels of the Royal Navy from 1911 to 1917, thus spending the bulk of the First World War in British ships. He returned to Canada to be flag lieutenant to Kingsmill at Naval Service Headquarters. After a post-war course at the Royal Naval College, Nelles was promoted to lieutenant-commander in 1922, serving two years in Royal Navy ships and establishments before returning to Canada in 1925 to be promoted to commander and take on responsibility as senior naval officer Esquimalt. Later, he became the first RCN officer to command a major warship, serving as captain in the cruiser HMS *Dragon*. He achieved another first when he was promoted to captain in 1933, while in command of HMCS *Stadacona,* the base at Halifax, and received a further promotion, to commodore, when he accepted responsibility as CNS.[2]

In carrying out that responsibility, he could rely on one of the most sophisticated communications systems in the country, the RCN in Ottawa handling a variety of traffic. One category was made up of messages sent to the naval bases at Halifax and Esquimalt; another consisted of messages sent to ships at sea, either directly or by way of one of the two bases. Yet another group was made up of messages to the commander-in-chief, America and West Indies Squadron in Bermuda, while a fourth consisted of messages to the Admiralty and the high commissioner for Canada in London, sent either directly or by way of Halifax. A final group was made up of messages to Australia and New Zealand by way of Esquimalt. The system was part and parcel of the RCN's integration within the Royal Navy, and hence—perhaps ironically—an argument for the Canadian service's autonomy. As Nelles argued, replacing the navy wireless station in Ottawa with a government—or military—facility, as was proposed in this period, would lead to "the segregation of Naval Service Headquarters from the Admiralty W/T organization." Another consequence would be "the cessation of direct communication from Naval Service Headquarters with HMC ships," as well as "the abolition of the highly important organization for training ratings at the coasts in naval procedure by means of operating with the naval station in Ottawa." The latter problem may have been exaggerated, since nothing prevented sailors in Halifax and Esquimalt from communicating with a government facility, and similarly dubious was the warning that the creation of a government station would force "the abolition of W/T exercises between RCNVR stations and Ottawa." However, Nelles was on firmer ground in arguing that "naval wireless procedure differs from that in commercial life since it involves the use of confidential books, naval call signs, special methods of routeing, etc," which explained the need for specialists. Perhaps even more to the point, the CNS argued that the naval station at Rockcliffe already handled messages for the army, RCAF, and RCMP, and concluded "that with modernized equipment and one additional W/T rating, the naval service is in every way prepared, during peace, to pass all government and service W/T traffic both across Canada and throughout the empire." An order in council approved the necessary purchases.[3]

---

2. "Admiral Percy Walker Nelles," *Crowsnest* (August, 1951), copy in DHH 2001/11.

3. Cdore P.W. Nelles to Minister, 31 January 1935; and PC 2794, 10 September 1935, copy in 1008–33–6, LAC, RG 24, vol. 6198.

Ensuring the system's efficiency required more than good kit, however, as Nelles noted. "In view of the recent statement of the prime minister to the effect that a new Department of Communications will shortly be organized, it is possible that the government may be considering the incorporation of the naval shore stations in such a department and I therefore submit the following memorandum to show the impracticability of such a proposal." It might make sense from a budgeting point of view to incorporate RCN signallers and telegraphists in a wider government system, but Nelles insisted that their work, in effect on-the-job training, had to focus on the types of operation they would be called upon to perform in wartime. "In the navy the efficient co-operation of any number of ships depends on the efficiency of the lines of communication. The importance attached to this is such that a specialist branch for communications exists in *every* navy," and training its members was a full time task. "New codes, new procedure and modern W/T sets necessitate continual instruction."[4] Such would not be achieved if operators were double hatted. Higher authority, made aware of Nelles's reasoning, agreed.

Generally then, the RCN sought "the development of a reliable organisation for W/T communication between Headquarters at Ottawa, the naval bases at Halifax and Esquimalt, and HMC Ships. Such organisation to comply, as far as possible, with the naval W/T organisation laid down in Admiralty Fleet Orders." In addition, its aim was that "the standard of efficiency of all W/T ratings to be that maintained in the Royal Navy," and the same would apply to "visual signalling personnel." Finally, given government plans noted above, the RCN sought "co-operation with every other branch of the defence forces and government departments for transmitting official W/T messages." To that end, it sought not only to replace worn-out equipment, but to have at least one "S" officer appointed to each coast, "ashore or afloat … to supervise, as far as possible, the communication organisation on that coast." In total there would be four such officers of lieutenant-commander rank or below. They would qualify at the RN signal school, and "one year's sea service as specialist 'S' will normally be carried out in the Royal Navy before officers return to Canada."[5]

Clearly, the navy was very technologically oriented, so that at least some of its members kept an eye open for new developments that might be of benefit to the service. One of these was Commander C.T. Beard, who like Nelles had joined the protection service in 1909, before the RCN was even founded, and who by this time was the director of naval reserves. He was also an advocate, along with his colleague Victor Brodeur and others, of the procurement of hydrofoil craft. He argued that in all the available naval literature, he had "not read or heard" of any other craft "which embraces the advantages and possibilities of a high speed boat or vessel for use as a vehicle to carry men, munitions and food over shallow waters or enemy minefields, and free from torpedo attack." He himself had served mainly in the straits of Dover during the war, and had also worked with Alexander Graham Bell as the latter developed hydrofoils at Baddeck in 1921, where he "saw for myself that the principles involved are practicable." Such a craft could be used as a crash boat attached to the seaplane stations at Vancouver and Halifax, could serve to deliver mail to

---

4. Nelles to Minister, 25 January 1935, ibid.

5. Naval Secretary to Distribution, 8 March 1935, ibid.

ships at sea, or conduct customs duties.[6] We now know that hydrofoils were never included in the government's procurement plans in this period, but the RCN's interest in technological developments is worthy of note.

More mundane, but just as technically challenging, was maintaining the ships the navy already had in service. As Nelles explained in a note to the minister, *Champlain* and *Vancouver* had been laid down in 1917, completed as *Torbay* and *Toreador* in 1919, and acquired with their current names in 1928 to replace *Patriot* and *Patrician*. By 1935, "since being turned over to us they have been in continuous commission with one refit," to which someone noted in pencil that it was "not a D2 refit." Such was cause for concern, as "in the Royal Navy, in addition to the yearly refits it is the custom every six to eight years to give each destroyer a D2 refit, i.e., a thorough and complete overhauling. The probable cost of such complete refits is in the vicinity of 20,000 pounds per ship," or $100,000 in Canadian funds. "The average yearly mileage steamed by the Canadian destroyers is approximately the same as that steamed by the destroyers in the Royal Navy but, with the depression and challenging financial conditions in Canada since 1930, it has not been practical to give *Vancouver* or *Champlain* a D2 refit. With this fact in mind in December last, I caused an examination of each vessel to be made with the result that technical officers advised an expenditure of some $165,000.... The cabinet was unable to grant my request for largely increased estimates in order to permit a D2 refit to be carried out. If such a sum could have been made available it is estimated that the useful life of these ships would have been increased by some five years."[7]

Nelles also reminded the minister that the ships were on loan, one of the conditions of which was that they be returned in good condition. Rendering them safe for passage to Britain would cost $50,000 more than a normal refit, while the director of naval engineering, upon returning from a inspection tour in Halifax, recommended $14,721 be spent on *Champlain* alone "in order to safeguard the lives of the personnel and improve the seaworthiness of the ship. What additional, if any, immediate repairs are necessary to *Champlain* cannot be known until machinery, etc is taken down." The CNS was still waiting for a report on *Vancouver,* but in all "the technical officers are of the opinion that the cost of repairs to both vessels, over and above normal yearly refits, may reach the vicinity of $100,000. This sum has accordingly been included in the supplementary estimates. Every endeavour will, of course, be made to reduce this figure."[8] No doubt Treasury Board, which had almost consigned the RCN to oblivion only a few short years before, would concur with the effort to save money.

As can be appreciated, money was far from abundant partway through the major economic depression of the 1930s. To give just one example, when the RCN proposed to rearm some of its destroyers with modern Mark IX torpedoes, it had to admit that "for financial reasons this is at present out of the question," although the issue "will be reconsidered when new construction in the Royal Canadian Navy is authorised, with a view to making

---

6. Cdr C.T. Beard to CNS, 10 December 1934, 21–1–18, LAC, RG 24, vol. 3613.

7. Nelles to Minister, 31 May 1935, 1017–10–9, LAC, RG 24, vol. 3833.

8. Ibid.

all ships homogeneous in their armament." In preparation for that day, "full enquiries are being instituted as to the work involved in modification of tubes, the structural alterations necessary to the ships, and as to whether Mk IX torpedoes are available for purchase." The weapons in stock, however, were only available in barely sufficient numbers, so more needed to be purchased in any case "as funds become available in order that there may be for the present a small reserve of outfit torpedoes for each ship." No doubt complicating the task of quarter-masters, there were still Mark IIs in the system, which were declared obsolete but which the navy could not scrap given budgetary constraints. They were therefore not to be fired "under conditions which might result in their loss."[9]

To technical issues needed to be added those relating to personnel, as evidenced by a snapshot provided by the CNS in the early part of the 1935–36 fiscal year. The RCN's establishment called for 104 officers, but only ninety-three were on strength, although he hoped to enter five cadets in that and the following year. The complement for ratings was 792, but "in order to keep within this figure and, at the same time, maintain efficiency in the signal branch (visual and wireless) and in the sick berth branch, it has been found essential to increase their numbers at the expense of the seaman branch," resulting in a shortage of twenty seamen ratings. That had an impact on training recruits, as the shortfall was imposed on those maintaining the barracks at Esquimalt and Halifax so ships could keep their complements up to strength. Nelles therefore requested an increase in the lower deck establishment, the number of signallers to go from sixteen to twenty-two, telegraphists from twenty-eight to forty, and sick berth attendants from six to eight. The deputy minister concurred, and PC 958 of 10 May, a little over a month after the CNS made his recommendation, provided the necessary legal authority.[10]

Less than four months later the RCN asked for more, Lieutenant-Commander R.E.S. Bidwell, the acting director of naval operations and training, noting that the complement authorized by the order in council, excluding the communications branch, "comprises the authorized fighting complements of ships, and care and maintenance and instructional staffs of the barracks and schools only." It did not take into account those serving in the RN on course or to obtain sea experience, those under training in Canada, or those temporarily excused duties due to illness. At the time no fewer than thirty ratings were serving with the Royal Navy, and on occasion that number had been as high as fifty; twenty-six were on course. He therefore requested an increase of fifty, which Nelles approved and passed on to higher authority. Again the powers-that-be approved, although it took a year, order in council PC 2778 of 6 September 1935 cementing the decision.[11]

Whether expanding or not, the RCN needed to recruit men (women were excluded throughout the period covered by this volume), to replace those who left at the end of their engagements, because of retirement, or for other reasons. Twenty-five years after the navy's creation, however, it was still seeking the most efficient way to get teenagers and

---

9. Minutes of the Fourth Meeting of Staff Divisions, 5 October 1935, 1078-3-1, LAC, RG 24, vol. 4044.

10. Nelles to Deputy Minister, 5 April 1934, 1-24-1, LAC, RG 24, vol. 5586; and PC 958, 10 May 1934.

11. LCdr R.E.S. Bidwell to CNS, 4 September 1934, 1-24-1, LAC, RG 24, vol. 5586; and PC 2778, 6 September 1935.

young adults out of civilian life and into a sailor's uniform. Lieutenant-Commander C.R.H. Taylor, the assistant director of naval operations and training (A/DNO&T) in the spring of 1934, was one who found that the system needed improvement. Responding to a request for information from the deputy minister, he opined that "the method of recruiting for the Royal Canadian Navy has never been considered satisfactory, and although every opportunity has been taken to discuss this matter when headquarters' officers visit the training barracks at Esquimalt and Halifax and vice versa, no constructive ideas to improve the present 'expensive' system have ever been evolved." According to the A/DNO&T, "Halifax and Esquimalt officers have always maintained that the most efficient method was by recruiting RCNVR ratings who had been to the training barracks and examined physically and educationally and generally sized up there, by barracks' officers." Small investments in advertising "could obtain locally any further recruits required." The problem such methods would solve was the expense of recruiting men thousands of kilometres from any coast, only to have them rejected for failing medical or educational exams and having to pay to send them home. Staff officers at headquarters agreed that recruiting locally and within the RCNVR "would be the most efficient," and offered the advantage that "the officers had seen the men and the men had seen enough of the navy to realize whether they were really keen on it or not."[12]

There was a problem, however, inherent in such a method, in that "it 'localizes' recruiting too much. To consider recruiting solely, from the vicinity of Victoria and Halifax, would be out of the question. A glance through the recruiting files at headquarters and see [sic] the enquiries from members of parliament, senators and cabinet ministers all over the dominion, about various applicants in their constituencies, would confirm this together with the fact that the RCN is paid for by the inland taxpayer as well as the taxpayer on the coasts." Recruiting among reservists failed to address the universality issue, as "the RCNVR ratings must live near enough to their company in order to attend their weekly drills, parades, etc. This would confine recruiting to the larger cities of Canada in which the RCNVR units are situated, and exclude a vast number of applicants from the rural districts, which would be obviously unfair." The necessary costs of casting a wider net would simply have to be borne, although such expenses would not be used as an excuse to retain recruits unlikely to succeed in their training. "One point that the department and barracks officers have always agreed is essential, that is in all cases the officers at RCN barracks must make the final decision as to whether a recruit is in all respects fit for the RCN physically and educationally, etc. It is far cheaper to return a man the day he arrives, to his home 2,000 miles away, than to be saddled with a man who fails years later to qualify for seaman gunner or seaman torpedoman or who eventually aggravates some minor physical ailment, which escaped detection at the preliminary medical examination. When this is reckoned in years of pay as ordinary seaman and able seaman, it more than covers loss on a return ticket."[13]

Standards were applied from the day a potential recruit presented himself, those not in possession of a high school entrance certificate not being considered. Out of sixty who had

---

12. LCdr C.R.H. Taylor to CNS, 22 May 1934, 21–1–18, LAC, RG 24, vol. 3613.

13. Ibid.

reported for training in the previous two years, three were rejected for medical reasons and two for lack of formal education. Taylor could not explain how five percent of those who made their way through the recruiting phase turned out to be medically unfit later, but undoubtedly the answer lay in civilian doctors, who conducted the initial exam, either being unaware of standards in all their details or concluding that certain conditions were less important than the navy let on. As for those who failed educational exams in Halifax or Esquimalt, they were no more than evidence that a high school entrance certificate was not proof that the candidate possessed the necessary knowledge to begin training. Sending naval officers into the community to conduct the necessary medical and educational tests might obviate such problems but was simply not affordable and "would be more expensive than the return ticket of an occasional rejected recruit."[14] (Perhaps the deputy minister's request had been for an explanation of why recruits were being sent home at taxpayer's expense—unfortunately a copy of that message has not been found.)

Financial constraints were also evident when it came time to train those recruits who met the navy's educational and medical standards. There were too few destroyers to allow any of them to be used exclusively to indoctrinate newcomers. Also, the need to send higher ranked ratings to the UK for qualification courses meant they were not available as instructors, and also created vacancies in ships that needed to be filled as a matter of priority, again reducing the number of available teachers in the facilities at Esquimalt and Halifax. Adding to the challenge was the lack of appropriate targets, while time which could be allocated to training was reduced by "show the flag" and similar operations. "It is realized that the main undesirable factors could be eliminated by the provision of more ships and better training facilities, but until funds are provided it has been decided to adopt a training policy more in keeping with the means available."[15] It should be further noted that the RCN did not exclusively focus on training its own, Lieutenant-Commander C.H.R. Taylor explaining, in reference to RCMP vessels, that "the personnel of these ships undergo annual training in gunnery, signals, codes, wireless, electricity, navigation and engineering, between 1st December and 30th April, at RCN barracks." From June to August 1933, for example, a special wireless telegraphy class was held in the Halifax barracks for RCMP operators, and in January, 1934, eleven officers and thirty-three ratings were undergoing such training at the same facility.[16]

The RCN being a highly technical institution, indoctrination had to focus not only on turning recruits into seamen but making seamen into specialists. In the financial year 1934–35 the service spent over $10,000 training gunners and torpedomen, over $2,000 of which was for transportation to and from the UK. "It is now proposed to qualify a batch of seaman gunners and seaman torpedomen in Canada," since "torpedo and gunnery schools on both coasts are ready to undertake these courses." Four torpedomen and eight gunners would undergo training on the East Coast beginning in September 1935, while the same number would do the same on the West Coast at an unspecified date. The navy certainly

14. Ibid.

15. NSHQ to Distribution, 7 March 1935, 21–1–1, LAC, RG 24, vol. 3610.

16. LCdr Taylor to DNO&T, 27 February 1934, 112–1–34, LAC, RG 24, vol. 5678.

had its work cut out for it, as at the time it could count on seventy-eight gunners and fifty-four torpedomen out of complements of 116 and seventy-four, respectively. Lieutenant-Commander R.E.S.Bidwell, the assistant director of naval training and operations at the time, suggested that "if it can be arranged with the commander-in-chief, America and West Indies I submit that all the newly qualified seaman torpedomen and seaman gunners be drafted to sea at conclusion of course and transferred in the West Indies to cruisers of the Eighth Cruiser Squadron in order to gain RN sea experience in their new non-substantive rating."[17] The necessary courses were indeed set up on both coasts.

Results were not, however, what the navy expected, Commander G.C. Jones, commanding HMCS *Naden,* the base at Esquimalt, reporting that five of sixteen candidates had failed to pass qualifying examinations to be promoted to able seamen in the gunnery and torpedo specialties. Worse, in a different class, eleven of sixteen failed to pass as torpedo specialists. Jones felt that the solution lay in sending recruits to sea as soon as they had completed their disciplinary and seamanship training before being drafted to an RCN barracks for more specialized indoctrination. "It is considered that the large percentage of failures in torpedo ... was due, not so much to lack of intelligence or in-attention on the part of the class but because instructors were handicapped in trying to explain the use and principles of service equipment in the short space of ten working days to youths who have never even seen the gear under working conditions." The same argument could be made in relation to gunnery, and the commanding officer of HMCS *Naden* recommended that none of the failures be discharged. He further noted that in a seamanship test the lowest mark obtained was a respectable 72 percent, and that most of the difficulties were "in subjects such as compass and helm, anchors and cables etc, which can only be taught properly at sea."[18]

There was logic in Jones's presentation, but that still left room for a counter-argument, the assistant director of naval operations and training noting that there was a reason why regulations stipulated that a recruit would commence gunnery and torpedo classes immediately after new entry training, so "that ratings should not be completely green when sent to destroyers, which would certainly be the case if they were sent after only the disciplinary and seamanship course. HMC destroyers cannot be used as boys' training ships," there being too few of them, as we have seen. It would also seem that initial training was insufficient to instil the necessary discipline, so that "the shore training, especially the gunnery, smartens up these youngsters; and they need considerable smartening up as a rule before being sent to sea." There was also an age issue to consider, with the average entry coming into the RCN at seventeen and a half, while legislation stopped him from going to sea until he was eighteen. "The shore training is just of sufficient duration so that the majority of the new entries are ordinary seamen on completion" and of the right age to be posted to a ship. Adopting Jones's recommendations would require increasing age requirements, diminishing the size of the recruiting pool. In one final argument, Bidwell noted that under the system then in operation young ratings attended school for a sufficient length of time to sit for the first part of their educational test. "Once at sea the facilities for school

---

17. LCdr Bidwell to CNS, 27 June 1935, 21–1–1, LAC, RG 24, vol. 3610.

18. Cdr G.C. Jones to Naval Secretary, 8 October 1935, 21–1–18, LAC, RG 24, vol. 3613.

instruction are not good." Equipment on the bases sufficed to learn the use of guns and torpedoes "under working conditions," and ratings sent too soon to sea "will certainly not learn much, unless the ship they are sent to is organized as a training ship,"[19] a fiscal impossibility. Jones's logic had to succumb to current pedagogical theory and budgetary reality.

It should be noted that at this time the RCN, while attempting to train Canadians to fill out its complement, also relied on the Royal Navy to lend officers and ratings to fill vacancies in the medium term. Their numbers had diminished over time, from seventy-six in March 1932 to sixty-three and twenty-seven in subsequent reporting periods; there were eighteen of them in June 1934. That latter number was expected to increase substantially, however, given the navy's growing establishment and its plan to acquire two additional destroyers (of which more later), so that it might have to borrow gunnery and torpedo specialists from the RN. At the time the RCN counted, on each coast, a gunner's mate and a torpedo gunner's mate in each destroyer and three of each in barracks. Such numbers were insufficient, and it was "found necessary at Halifax and Esquimalt, due to lack of instructors, to instruct classes of over twenty-five ratings at gun drill, which could hardly be expected to produce efficient results." In addition, "should a gunner's mate or torpedo gunner's mate in either ship go sick, the barracks has to supply a relief—the result is, that in the training season, classes have to be stopped which, in the case of the RCNVR's and RCNR's, etc, is a waste of money, observing that these ratings are up [here on duty] for a limited time and are paid whether they are instructed or not. Similarly, the same thing happens when a gunner's mate or a torpedo gunner's mate in barracks goes sick," an additional reason to borrow such men from the RN. "In one case a torpedo gunner's mate had to be borrowed for two years, the time it took to train a replacement (incl[uding] six months afloat)."[20]

Among those being indoctrinated by the RCN, and RN instructors on loan, were members of the Royal Canadian Naval Reserve (RCNR), with a 1932 strength of thirty-six officers and 143 ratings. The registrar at Victoria, whose offices had been shut down a few years before, was re-established, but Commander C.T. Beard, the director of naval reserves, recommended the registrar in Charlottetown be dismissed, as "this is not a terminal port and does not produce a good type of applicant." The DNR also intended to do more recruiting in British Columbia, "because good applicants are awaiting entry, and Halifax barracks has now the added commitment of training the RCMP Marine Detachment (potential naval reservists)." Also, the weather was better: "Climactic [sic] conditions in British Columbia allow of far better training and up till now the capabilities of the barracks at Esquimalt have not been used to capacity, whereas Halifax barracks are at times overcrowded." Reinforcing Beard's thinking was Canada's defence planning, as "the trend of thought in defence matters appears to be concentrating on the west coast of Canada," where neutrality might have to be defended in a war between the US and Japan. "The rapidity at which reservists can be mobilized, therefore, requires consideration," where "reservists, if transferred from the east coast for active service, will lack the local knowledge which is so helpful in narrow waters, or on the difficult west coast of Vancouver Island and the Queen Charlotte

19. A/DNO&T to DNO&T, 16 October 1935, ibid.

20. LCdr Taylor to CNS, 15 June 1934, 1–24–1, LAC, RG 24, vol. 5586.

Islands." At the time the DNR made his recommendations, there were three RCNR officers and thirty-one ratings in Montreal, seven and thirty-two in Quebec City, one and seventeen in Charlottetown, nineteen and thirty-seven in Halifax, and eight and thirty-one in Vancouver. "The retention of Montreal, Quebec, Halifax and Vancouver registrars is imperative because they form our contacts with a somewhat roving population," Beard wrote, but at Charlottetown "the present registrar is old and shaky. Should he, in the meantime, give up active work, I do not recommend a successor."[21] One who was worthy of retention was Rowland Burke, the registrar at Victoria, who at forty-eight was not only of reasonable age, but wore the decorations of the Victoria Cross and the Distinguished Service Order.[22]

The RCNVR, for its part, although it could not boast a VC among its ranks, was much larger in numbers, but even then the director of naval reserves, Commander C.T. Beard, had to remind company commanding officers that maintaining such strength required effort. He noted many cases where commanders did not apply for the re-enrolment of ratings who had completed their three-year term of employment. "The keeping of ratings' records at company headquarters is one of the duties of the petty officer instructor, and there is no reasonable excuse for the failure of the petty officer instructor to bring to the attention of the company commanding officer promptly the name or names of ratings about to complete their term of enrolment." In an attached table, he provided a count of those who had done their three years but for which no application for re-enrolment had been received, the numbers ranging from nil in Saskatoon to eight in Charlottetown; Toronto and Winnipeg were more typical with three each.[23] There was, of course, also the question of quality to be addressed, the director of naval reserves having to report that "during the recent company commanding officers' conference, it was brought to my notice that there is grave discontent in the results obtained by RCNVR ratings during their period of annual naval training." Given that "the crux of this question appears to me to be the painful shortage of qualified instructors,"[24] the problem could only be solved in the long term.

Quality was also an issue, Beard reporting how "a review of the list of officers shews that several have not attended naval training for years at a time, whereas others have been most conscientious. Both types are, however, treated alike in the matter of promotion, which creates discontent and allows for a legitimate grievance." He recommended an amendment to regulations by which a lieutenant could not be promoted to lieutenant-commander in the executive branch unless he completed seven years of annual training and held a watchkeeping certificate. Furthermore, "no officers should be allowed to undergo naval training unless they have performed their duties to the entire satisfaction of their company commanding officers at company headquarters and are approved by the director of naval reserves." Engineering officers, for their part, would have to serve a minimum of ninety days at sea, while for accountant and medical officers the requirement for promotion would

---

21. See the annual reports of the Department of National Defence, 1932 to 1939; and Cdr C.T. Beard, Director of Naval Reserves, to CNS, 14 March 1934, 121–1-1, LAC, RG 24, vol. 5680.

22. Nelles to Deputy Minister, 6 October 34, ibid.

23. Cdr Beard to CCOs RCNVR, 22 March 1934, 114–1-3, LAC, RG 24, vol. 5678.

24. Cdr Beard to DNO&T, 3 October 1934, 21–1-1, LAC, RG 24, vol. 3610.

be eight years' seniority, five periods of annual naval training, and thirty days of sea experience. Higher authority concurred, but Nelles noticed another *lacune* by which "an officer serving for four years only as a lieutenant on the active list and after four years on the reserve list he can be promoted to lieutenant commander without further effort on his part." The regulation was something of an artifact, since "in previous cases most of the officers so promoted had war service to their credit. This phase is, however, now rapidly passing," only two lieutenants on the retired list having such experience, both expected to be promoted in any case.[25]

From a personnel standpoint, the RCNVR was a critical component of the interwar navy, so it comes as no surprise that interest in the organization was not limited to the director of naval reserves. Another who dealt with volunteer reserve issues was the naval secretary, J.O. Cossette. He noted that "the attendance of a few executive officers at annual naval training has been either neglected or impracticable owing to their private business affairs." It was not, therefore, necessarily their fault, but still, "it is desired that those who have not attended annual training for a period of two years or more be asked to consider the question of forwarding their resignations," if they could not foresee attending training within the subsequent six months. "Owing to the limited total number of RCNVR officers allowed by establishment, it is desired to retain only those who can afford the necessary time to qualify for their naval rank."[26] Given the circumstances of the time, therefore, even reservists had to be prepared to make a solid commitment when they joined the navy.

Part of that commitment was to attend training at one of the half or full companies that had been formed in almost every major city in the country. The period did not, however, see smooth sailing for all of them, as evidenced by Commander Beard's visit to Saskatoon, in his capacity as director of naval reserves. Previously, he had "found the condition of the unit very poor and informed the then company commanding officer that unless a very marked improvement was achieved, I would recommend that this unit be disbanded," no little threat. "The unit was at that time housed in the small armouries and I found that no effort had been made to even unpack instructional equipment supplied." Beard's presence had, however, provided a spark for reform, and "before leaving next day, the company commanding officer found a building which I considered a great improvement and transfer was soon effected." There was little hope for expansion in numbers, given a recent crop failure (which was affecting almost the entire prairie region in this period) and Saskatoon's declining population, but at least better facilities might be found for the small naval unit then in existence.[27]

As for the sailors, "the appearance of the men on parade was average but rifle exercises were below average." Visiting classes, Beard asked some of those in attendance, chosen at random, a few questions to test their knowledge; it must have been satisfactory since he did not mention the results in his report. More clearly favourable, "drill on the steering model was good. The instructor has gone to a considerable amount of trouble in constructing

25. Beard to CNS, 11 December 1934, Nelles to Deputy Minister, 14 January 1935, 101–1-4, LAC, RG 24, vol. 5678.

26. Naval Secretary to CCOs RCNVR, 9 April 1935, 114–1-3, LAC, RG 24, vol. 5678.

27. Beard to Nelles, 27 February 1934, 114–12–9, LAC, RG 24, vol. 5680.

an instructional model for anchor work and boats' dropping gear, etc." Four years after his initial threat to disband the unit, Beard was therefore willing to pursue alternatives. The first would be to ask the provincial government to transfer a Lieutenant Commander Hall from his public service position in Regina to one in Saskatoon, thus affording the latter's naval half-company the leadership it needed. Such a move would, however, prove detrimental to the officer's civilian career, and was therefore too much to ask. Another possibility would be to replace the petty officer instructor, but not only would such require spending money not already allocated, but would prove "a punishment to the good man who must replace him," a commentary on just how severe conditions were.[28]

Beard was not short of ideas, however, and he suggested that the navy could send the currently serving petty officer instructor "to RCN barracks for disciplinary training and refresher courses and if considered satisfactory whilst there, he would be sent in due course to Quebec as the petty officer instructor at Quebec is due for promotion to chief petty officer instructor to relieve the CPO instructor at Toronto, who leaves on account of age in October next. The No 2 PO instructor, now at Toronto, to go to Saskatoon." A bit complicated, perhaps, but a solution nonetheless, and one that would prove fair to the petty officer in question. Beard did not want to be punitive, as "the company commanding officers under whom he has had to serve have not been ideal." If the director's suggestions proved too difficult to carry out, then at the very least an RCN officer should be sent to Saskatoon for a minimum of two weeks "to endeavour to stop the disintegration which is setting in," and to recruit more suitable sailors from the University of Saskatchewan.[29] The final decision was left to Nelles, itself a demonstration of just how small an organization the RCN was. He agreed that disbandment "would be a retrograde step," since the company was going through difficult times owing to "unsuitable quarters," a "lack of officers," and a "PO instructor who has deteriorated." Since better accommodation might be found, at least one officer was keen, and the petty officer could be replaced, the company received a commutation of its death sentence.[30]

Doing better was the Hamilton half company, which passed inspection a few months later. As with so many of these units, accommodation was a problem, as "quarters, although situated close to the water, are in an old building, which is now in none too good a state of repair. The sub-division of the building is about as good as can be arranged, but the general impression given by the building as a whole is depressing. It must be very difficult to keep it clean, and almost impossible to heat it to give any degree of comfort." At least the whalers were in good condition, the general organization of the unit was satisfactory, as were drill and classes in wireless telegraphy and signalling. A small group of engineer ratings, "under Engineer Lieutenant Liddington, is well known for its efficiency," while "PO Instructor Hughes seems to be exactly the right type of man for the job," and "there is harmony amongst officers and men." Although the unit had not done well in the previous inspection, "all realise that recent troubles have given the whole company a bad name

28. Ibid.

29. Ibid.

30. Nelles to DM, 14 March 1934, ibid.

and are working hard together to wipe this out." As for the company's higher leadership, "the company commanding officer, Lieutenant Westland, keeps a firm hand in the company, but realises that the lost ground cannot be recovered in a few months, and is planning for a steady improvement rather than a spectacular one." Generally, therefore, the company was in good shape, and although it was "below the peak it reached about three years ago," it "has shown much improvement in recent months. The organization of the company appears good, and the spirit excellent, and there is no reason to believe that lost ground will not be recovered." Still, "more suitable quarters would, undoubtedly, have a very favourable effect on the morale and efficiency of the company."[31]

Reserve companies faced difficulties regardless of their location, and in Saint John, Beard found that "the efficiency of the officers and men was much below the standard required; in fact, it was definitely poor, and deterioration should be checked as soon as possible." He recommended that Lieutenant-Commander G.R. Miles of the permanent RCN spend five or six days in Saint John "to put matters right." One reason was that "the normal inspection is too short to investigate fully the details or organization. The inspecting officer really only sees results; the causes of a poor showing can only be conjectured." Among the "results" was that "the technical knowledge of the seamen torpedomen was pitiful and I cannot believe that these ratings reached a sufficiently high standard to qualify for this non-substantive rating whilst at Halifax. There was one exception, T. Rumson, AB.... I strongly recommend that RCN barracks, Halifax, be asked to investigate this question and that orders be given that all Saint John seamen torpedomen are to be re-examined," since the problem seemed to be systemic. "I also recommend that the Saint John half company be taken to Halifax as a whole, so that they can be given special instruction and extra drills when necessary." Not only was the half-company not up to strength, but "the type of recruit is, on the average, poor, and I discussed this subject with the district officer commanding, who agreed that the RCNVR was being recruited from the undesirable quarters of the town." As with the Saskatoon unit, Beard recommended disbandment if there was no improvement.[32]

As well as dealing with such headaches, those officers responsible for the RCNVR sometimes had to face outright tragedy, as was most evident in the summer of 1933, on Lake Winnipeg. Five ratings requested the use of a whaler for an excursion from 5 to 7 August, and it being approved by the executive officer of the Winnipeg division, the boat, under the charge of an RCNVR leading seaman, made her way to the Red River on 31 July. It had been inspected by a petty officer instructor and found to be in good working order. On 8 August the commanding officer in Winnipeg received a report to the effect that a capsized whaler had been spotted, and a search was carried out by aircraft and ships of dominion and provincial authorities. Two days later the whaler was found, the crew was presumed drowned, and the commanding officer requested authority to incur further expenses to find the bodies. With authority given, two were found, one on the 12th and the other on the 14th. A court of enquiry convened next day found that the accident had

---

31. LCdr G.R. Miles, "Hamilton Half Company," 14 December 1934, 114-8-9, ibid.

32. Beard to CNS, 8 December 1934, 114-1-4, ibid.

been caused by "severe squalls at the time, and in the locality where the boat capsized. No blame is attributable to personnel or equipment." In fact, "the boat was manned by competent ratings and in all respects suitable to undertake a cruise under normal weather conditions." Any costs relatives incurred attempting to find the bodies were reimbursed ($95 in one case), and the navy paid to transport the remains to Winnipeg, but funerals were a family responsibility. "The ratings were *not* on naval duty at the time of the accident.... The department, under the circumstances, was under no obligation to take any action, but on compassionate grounds undertook the search for the bodies and their transportation to Winnipeg, and defrayed any expenses involved.... There is no regulation or authority by which a compassionate grant could be made by the department, unless an item be included in the estimates."[33]

Thankfully, such tragedies were extremely rare, not only in the RCNVR, but in the RCNR and RCN as well, even when the navy conducted operations with which it was almost entirely unfamiliar. Such was the case when HMCS *Festubert* tried her hand at ice breaking in the Northwest Arm of Halifax Harbour in the winter of 1933–34. At first, "very little progress was made," as the ice was two feet thick. Worse, "the wind became so strong that it was no longer possible to manoeuvre *Festubert* in ice and ship secured in ice to south of Church Point." A partner, the ice breaker *Mikula,* was able to take over for a while, *Festubert* taking her turn, breaking ice in the Arm, sometime later. Then, "the forward plates on each side in the vicinity of the water line were observed to be bent inwards, although no leak occurred. Shores were placed in the fore peak in order to strengthen the ship." Unperturbed by the apparent damage, the ship continued with her task, "and a good example of the usefulness of the *Festubert* as an auxiliary to a large ice breaker occurred. Owing to the reefs in the harbour which were entirely unmarked, *Mikula* was forced to leave a large tongue of ice unbroken stretching out from Kavanagh Point.... *Festubert* with her shallower draft was able to proceed into shoal water and to break clear the mass of ice nearly half a mile square, thus freeing the harbour."[34]

Attempts to break ice in the Eastern Passage having failed because steam pressure was lost, the ship's captain could take stock. "Considering that *Festubert* was not designed for ice breaking and that no strong plates are fitted at either bow or stern, it is considered that useful work was, and can be, carried out with the ship in ice up to sixteen inches in thickness. This refers to salt water ice and where fresh water ice is concerned this figure must be reduced to twelve inches." Damage to the vessel had, after inspection, proven slight. "The method employed, as *Festubert* has neither weight or power sufficient to crush ice, has been to wedge ice free. This means that the ship is brought up at as high a speed as is considered safe and is rammed into say the right hand side of the channel. This ship may break a wedge shaped hole in the ice of from three feet to twenty feet, depending upon the thickness of the ice, before she is brought up all standing. Engines are then reversed and great care must be taken that the stern does not hit solid ice. When sufficient sternway has been made the ship is then put ahead again into either the same hole as before, or, if this is

33. Cdr E.G.G. Hastings RN, for CNS, to DM, 3 December 1935, 114–10–10, ibid.

34. LCdr in Command *Festubert* to Captain-in-Charge Halifax, 20 February 1934, 132–7-5, LAC, RG 24, vol. 5682.

sufficiently large, the port hand side of the channel is now attacked. Usually a piece of ice the width of the channel and from five to ten feet in depth breaks clear. If, however, this does not happen, an attack is made at the centre of the channel midway between the two wedges." Given the precision of manoeuvre and the constant changes in direction required, "this form of ice breaking places a constant severe strain upon both the captain and the engine room department."[35]

One member of the RCN would have the opportunity to become even more intimately acquainted with operations in cold conditions, when the Department of the Interior invited the RCN to send an officer on the eastern Arctic patrol. Commander C.T. Beard, the director of naval reserves, for one, thought such a trip would be beneficial. "There appears to be few disadvantages: the cost to this department is but a few dollars in excess of an officer's pay and allowances, and really devolves on the point of whether he can be spared for 90 days from his normal duties, i.e., during July, August and September. This is the busiest time at the coasts and in the ships, but usually the least busy period at headquarters." Of advantages there were many, the cruise ensuring that at least one RCN officer "will have some local knowledge and be in a better position to advise the department and the government as a whole." Such intelligence would be especially critical if the Hudson Bay route became an important line of communication between Britain and British Columbia ports, and would be applied in the design and construction of auxiliary vessels. Nor was the RCN thinking only of itself, as the officer's post-cruise report "would be of considerable interest to the Admiralty," as well as to the Canadian government, which did not consider information available at the time to be dependable.[36]

The ship in question was the SS *Nascopie*, and the RCN officer chosen for the cruise was none other than Commander Beard himself, who was about to finish his term as director of naval reserves. Besides the agencies mentioned above, he would be gathering information for the RCAF, which was willing to provide a camera "on temporary loan." In addition, "a dozen rolls of film are also being provided in the understanding that the negatives be returned to the RCAF." His main task on behalf of the air force would be to investigate the suitability of subarctic harbours for seaplane operations, and Beard was provided with the necessary "RCAF aircraft facilities report" forms. The air force also provided a list of potential fuel caches which it was hoped Beard would inspect.[37]

The naval commander embarked on 13 July 1935, the trip down the St Lawrence being uneventful. A first port of call was Cartwright, which "should present no special difficulties for the entry of a ship during daylight hours in clear weather. The lack of navigational aids is a drawback which must be accepted because of its isolation. These conditions are common to all harbours along the Labrador coast. Local knowledge is imperative," an important piece of intelligence if the RCN was to operate in the region. To enter Hudson Strait, *Nascopie* chose to pass Resolution Island, giving the Labrador Reefs and the Button Islands a wide berth, as "these two obstacles have destroyed several ships in the past."

35. Ibid.

36. Beard to CNS, 21 March 1935, 84-2-6, LAC, RG 24, vol. 5672.

37. Air Cmdre G.M. Croil, Senior Air Officer, to CNS, 11 June 1935, ibid.

Navigation was rendered difficult by mirages and incorrect charts, and "nothing will remove the hazard of ice. During August and September this is limited to the chance of bumping which can be avoided by a careful lookout. Icebergs and ice floes are few and far between. During fog and the dark hours ship's way must be reduced or the ship stopped." A particularly bad period was during July, when "the previous winter's ice is endeavouring to pass out into the Atlantic Ocean, and it is wiser not to attempt the passage of Hudson Strait in any type of vessel except a submarine. When square miles of broken ice are milling in a tide rip, no ordinary ship can stand the side pressure should she be caught and nipped. The loss is usually limited to the ship and its contents, because personnel can be saved by getting on to the ice floes,"[38] a frightening prospect nonetheless.

In a more positive light, within Hudson Strait "there are some excellent harbours on either side for use as temporary naval and aircraft bases, for the protection of ocean-borne trade." Further in, "Hudson's [sic] Bay presents few navigational difficulties except when approaching land. There are very few harbours. Churchill is an artificial harbour and is suitable as a supply base or port of entry (or departure) for troops and munitions. Because of its geographical position, no defence measures are required, provided the Straits are guarded." *Nascopie* called at various harbours, but they were only of interest to Beard as possible ports of refuge, while the ship simply did not bother with Ungava Bay and James Bay as "at present they are regarded as dangerous to navigation and have as yet no commercial value." Cargo was landed at Burwell, Quebec, for the Northern Police and Hudson's Bay Company trading posts. "This northern country inside the Arctic Circle presents many beautiful sights as the land consists almost entirely of steep mountainous country. Fiords have been gouged out by glaciers and many glaciers are visible. The country is so inhospitable and useless for supporting human beings, at the northern extremes, that even eskimos [sic] have to be imported and maintained by the Mounted Police or explorers. Briefly, it is a part of Canada with which this department has no need for concern whatever, at present."[39]

Although the navy's lack of interest in the far north would change in decades to come, it is its willingness to explore that is important to this study; nor was Beard's trip an isolated event. Perhaps less climactically difficult was a West Coast cruise by HMCS *Armentieres,* her goal to investigate an abandoned village on the east side of Anthony Island. Landing with Lieutenant-Commander Gow and an official from the fisheries research station at Departure Bay, Lieutenant-Commander H.W.S. Soulsby inspected totem and burial poles, "of which there are about a dozen. It is considered that these are worth preserving and I submit that this be drawn to the attention of the Indian department or other necessary authority. The carving on some of the poles is in a good state of preservation, but undergrowth has grown up around them and some have a tendency to fall over being rotten at the bottom." Commander G.C. Jones, the director of naval operations and training, dutifully passed on Soulsby's comments.[40]

More routine were continuing life saving operations in the Bamfield area of British

---

38. Beard to CNS, 14 October 1935, ibid.

39. Ibid.

40. LCdr H.W.S. Soulsby to CO HMCS *Naden,* 23 September 1936, 131–7–5, LAC, RG 24, vol. 5682.

Columbia, which for a time were the responsibility of HMCS *Armentieres*. In one instance, on 22 February, "the master of the tug *Aliford Bay* reported," to Lieutenant-Commander L.J.M. Gauvreau, *Armentieres*'s captain, "that a scow he was towing to Vancouver had broken adrift about eight miles off Amphitrite Light at 1930 that evening. He stated that no one was on board the scow and that she contained thirty cases of dynamite, an air compressor and was insured for $5,000.00. A message was broadcast to shipping giving the approximate position of this danger to navigation. It was arranged that the tug would come alongside at daylight Saturday and that I would supply her with a towing hawser and we would both proceed to search." *Givenchy* and a United States Coast Guard cutter were also on the scene. As Gauvreau related, "The scow was sighted by the speed boat *Maureen R.* of Alberni carrying the insurance underwriter to the scow. On being informed of the finding of this derelict I tried to get in visual touch with the tug off Amphitrite but she turned into Barkley Sound and proceeded to Ucluelet. I then proceeded to the scow and relieved CGS *Givenchy* which was standing by." *Aliford Bay*'s attempts to tow the scow ended in failure so the RCN vessel "towed her into Tofino Harbour where she was turned over to her tug together with 100 fathoms of 2½-inch wire and a length of 5-inch hemp," so towing operations could continue. That was not, however, the end of the story, as Gauvreau "was informed by the fishery officer at Tofino that this dangerous craft was placed alongside the jetty there, by the tug, for three days and no one knew that she contained explosives. She carried no flag or light to indicate the dangerous nature of her cargo. It would appear that vessels of this kind should not be allowed alongside, but be safely anchored at a distance from any habitation and carry the usual signals prescribed."[41] No one objected.

The most elaborate of such operations were the cruises to southern climes, where RCN ships could take advantage of Royal Navy facilities and exercise in company with RN vessels, one example being offered by the destroyers *Champlain* and *Saguenay*. Arriving at Port-au-Prince, the commander (destroyers) of the eastern division paid official calls on the British chargé d'affaires, Haiti's minister for foreign affairs, its minister of the interior, the mayor, the commander-in-chief of the *Garde d'Haïti* and the commander of 1st Brigade, United States Marine Corps. Sailors were, of course, paraded as guards of honour if the visitor's rank warranted it. "From outward appearances, the visit of HMC ships to Port-au-Prince was an unqualified success. The absence of the president, prevented any formal entertainment by the government, but in his absence, the minister for foreign affairs held an informal reception at his residence from 1100 to 1300 Sunday 22nd April. The British chargé d'affaires gave a reception on Thursday afternoon 19th, at the Petionville Club to which all members of the government, the British colony, the American colony and many prominent Haitians were invited. HMC ships returned hospitability received by an afternoon reception onboard *Saguenay* on Friday, 20th April, to which the ministers of the government, the British colony and senior officers of the United States Marine Corp[s] and of the Garde D'Haiti were invited."[42]

The presence of a USMC formation made the trip all the more worthwhile, as "through-

---

41. L.R. LaFleche, DM, to DM Dept. of Marine, 13 March 1935, ibid.

42. Cdr (D) East to NSHQ, 23 May 1934, 135–7-5, LAC, RG 24, vol. 5683.

out the visit the officers and men of the United States Marine Corp[s] did everything in their power to make our visit a pleasant one. Officers were made honorary members of their clubs and taken on trips, by air, to Cape Haitien, while the ships' companies were made honorary members of the appropriate non-commissioned-officers' and service clubs, and the brigade moving picture theatre with transportation to and from the landing place. One rating was landed from *Champlain*, in emergency, and operated upon for removal of his appendix in the hospital of the United States Marine Corp[s]." As for what was called "the British colony," no doubt staff and family members of the embassy, they "were very glad to see the Canadian ships" and the British chargé d'affaires, "was untiring in his efforts to bring the officers in contact with the more influential members of the government and business community. It is submitted that appreciation of his services may be communicated through the proper channels." The president of Haiti, returning from a trip to the US, "was accorded a gala reception," and "in conjunction with the USS *Woodcock*, HMC Ships dressed, over all, at 0600 and manned ship in honour of the President as his ship entered the harbour at 0630. The two commanding officers accompanied the British charge d'affaires to a Te Deum held in the cathedral at 0830, in thanksgiving for the safe return of the president, and at 1000 they were given an audience by the President at the palace."[43] It was not the most hazardous of naval operations, but still served a purpose in the management of Canada's fledgling external relations.

Beyond the sunshine and diplomatic niceties of the Caribbean, however, the world was becoming increasingly dangerous. The Japanese Army's occupation of Manchuria and creation of the puppet state of Manchukuo may not have caused serious ripples within the international community, but Italy's invasion of Abyssinia (now called Ethiopia) on 3 October 1935 was a different matter. Both were members of the League of Nations, and the African country had a majority Christian population. Although Mussolini may have seen the war as a means of completing a colonization process that had ended in an Italian defeat at the end of the nineteenth century, such conquests were no longer seen as acceptable by other European countries—nor by the United States. Discussions among the members of the League began immediately, but all attempts at diplomatic pressure failed to force the Italian government to deviate from its course.

Canada's naval officers were, necessarily, unable to predict if the international community—or its own government—would choose to intervene. In planning for a possible contribution of RCN vessels to any blockade or other operation Britain and the Commonwealth might choose to conduct, in October 1935 NSHQ identified the navy's most urgent requirements as ammunition for 12-pounders and 4-inch guns to be mounted in auxiliary vessels, two anti-submarine nets, a general stock of ammunition, five torpedoes (half of an outfit), two wireless sets, minesweeping maintenance stores, two fire control clocks, and, at the bottom of the list of priorities, the other half of the torpedo outfit, all at a cost of $377,500.[44] In the event, since Italy was not opposed, in any real sense, in its annexation of Abyssinia, the stores and equipment were not purchased.

---

43. Ibid.

44. Minutes of the Fifth Meeting of Staff Divisions, 18 October 1935, 1078–3-1, LAC, RG 24, vol. 4044.

As for the Canadian navy as a whole, by the end of 1935 it was small and growing, as evidenced by a report to the minister produced only a few weeks after the Italians invaded Abyssinia. The destroyers *Saguenay,* built in 1931, and *Champlain,* 1919, as well as the minesweepers *Ypres* and *Festubert* were on the East Coast while the destroyers *Skeena,* 1931, and *Vancouver,* 1919, and the minesweeper *Armentieres* were on the West. All three minesweepers were, however, laid up. The two modern destroyers compared "very favourably" with recent British types, each with an authorized complement of seven officers and 144 ratings. One of the older destroyers was about to have her life extended, though for only two years (at a cost of $100,000) because, the minister was told, "this equipment is largely antiquated and the cost of maintenance is relatively high." (It was recommended that "serious thought should be given to their early replacement by modern vessels.") As for the smaller ships, "the complete lack of minesweepers on the east coast seriously hampers the training available for both permanent and non-permanent personnel of the service and it is considered essential that new vessels be constructed (in Canada) to permit two efficient minesweepers or auxiliary vessels being stationed on each coast." The RCN also requested the acquisition of a sailing ship "to be employed as a training vessel,"[45] which, as we shall see, would be named *Venture.*

The navy's role was to maintain internal security, preserve the country's neutrality, and protect the nation's coasts and seaborne trade in time of war. It had been established at the imperial conferences of 1923 and 1926 that the "primary responsibility of each portion of the empire is for its own local defence." Subsequently, at a 1933 meeting of the chiefs of staff subcommittee of the Committee of Imperial Defence, it was noted that the United Kingdom was "mainly responsible for the security of the communications between the several parts of the commonwealth."[46] During the Abyssinian crisis, however, Britain withdrew ships from foreign stations such as China, Australia, and New Zealand to concentrate forces near the Red Sea, the Suez Canal, and other locations. Furthermore, two or possibly three cruisers about to proceed to Bermuda to join the America and West Indies Station were diverted to the Mediterranean in case war broke out with Italy. The lesson for the RCN was clear: "In case of emergency in European or Far Eastern waters we must expect and be prepared for a concentration of British naval forces near the seat of the trouble, leaving the trade routes for the time relatively undefended and we, in Canada, must therefore look to our own resources for any protection required in Canadian waters." To underline the issue's importance, it was noted that in 1934 exports from Canada had been worth $434 million, while imports were valued at $580 million. It could also have underlined how, in spite of the nation's recently acquired sovereignty, it was in some ways part of a Commonwealth system of defence, as at the time of the Abyssinian crisis "intelligence centres all over the world in British colonies, prepared long in advance, were activated, as were those under the control of the commonwealth governments."[47]

45. Report to Minister on RCN, RCNR, and RCNVR, 29 October 1935, LAC, Manuscript Group (hereafter MG) 27, IIIB5, vol. 32, file X-53.

46. Ibid.

47. DND, "The Naval Service of Canada: A Resume of Its Necessity, Resources and Requirements," August 1936, 238, LAC, RG 25, vol. 755; and Stephen Roskill, *Naval Policy Between the Wars* (London 1976), II, 256.

Trainees learning to sail aboard HMCS *Venture*. The only sailing vessel in the thirteen-ship RCN on the eve of the Second World War, her naval career was short-lived, being paid off on 1 September 1939. (CWM 19910109-189)

Still, it was the defence of trade that loomed largest in this period. A February 1937 report by Nelles explained that in 1936 the value of imports to Canada had risen to almost $190 million from Britain, $370 million from the United States, and $76 million from other countries. Exports amounted to almost $480 million to Britain, nearly $340 million to the US, and about $125 million to other countries (not all goods to and from the US were seaborne, however, although an "appreciable" amount were). Defending this trade, according to the CNS, was not one problem but three: within Canadian waters and in the approaches to Canadian ports; on passage to overseas destinations; and within overseas ports. By this time air attack was a consideration, although "Canada is separated by a wide stretch of ocean from any country likely to threaten Canadian trade. Air attack on merchant vessels is therefore confined to attack from aircraft carried in ships—warships or converted merchant vessels—unless, which is unlikely, an enemy is able to establish an air base in Canadian territory or the country adjacent to Canada." That being the case, "adequate reconnaissance of the areas in the vicinity of our coasts must therefore be an essential part of our defence measures."[48]

Conducting such operations in time of war required at least some level of preparation—and money—in time of peace. Excluding such non-cyclical expenses as relief camps, the cenotaph in Ottawa, and the Vimy Ridge memorial, the national defence budget had increased steadily from $12.9 million in 1926–27 to a peak of $21.7 million in 1930–31. During the early depression years it had decreased to a low of $12.6 million in both 1932–33 and the following year, only to begin rising again, to $13.3 million in 1934–35 and $16.2 million in 1935–36.[49] Given the severe deflationary pressures of the Depression, the latter figure was not far off the equivalent value of the 1930–31 peak. As for what was being done with the money, at the end of 1936 Nelles proposed that it would be used "for maintaining in full commission throughout the year 1937–38 four modern destroyers, one minesweeper, one training schooner and other essential establishments. The ships will carry out periodical training cruises and will be continuously employed in the training of naval personnel in those branches of naval science possible for ships of their class." The RCN would also acquire new vessels, as "four modern minesweepers of Admiralty design will be laid down for construction in Canada and, if possible, will be completed during the year."[50]

In regard to infrastructure, "a dockyard will be maintained at each coast for the refit of ships on the respective stations, and will maintain such reserves of naval and armament stores as are now in stock. The dockyards will also be available for the repair of ships of other departments on a repayment basis. They are already doing excellent work in that regard, particularly in the case of RCMP patrol ships, which are repaired, stored and victualled by our dockyard engineering and stores divisions, respectively." At Halifax, "the machinery and dockyard equipment has been kept in a modern state of efficiency and the completion in 1936 of a new machine shop equipped with modern machinery has enhanced the

48. CNS, "Defence of Trade," 12 February 1937, LAC, MG 27, III B-5, vol. 37, file D-9.

49. "Total Appropriations and Expenditures for National Defence Services," nd, LAC, MG 26 J4, vol. 159, file 1428.

50. CNS, "General Statement of Activities Contemplated by Naval Estimates 1937–38," 21 December 1936, LAC, MG 27, III, B-5, vol. 37, file D-7.

dockyard as a repair base." And its facilities were not exclusively for the RCN, as "the dockyard is used as a base during the North Atlantic Ice Patrol season by ice patrol ships of the United States." Still, its main focus was on supporting Canada's navy, for which "the stores division of the dockyard not only supplies HMC ships with naval, victualling and clothing stores but maintains sufficient reserves of these stores to meet requirements in an emergency." It also supported the RCMP's Marine Section, and supplied "naval and clothing stores to a limited extent to the departments of Transport and Fisheries. Stores are supplied to other departments and to ships of the Royal Navy on a repayment basis." Expenditures in 1936 had totalled almost $97,000, as compared with a low of just over $10,000 in 1923. On the West Coast, the Esquimalt dockyard had cost over $25,000 to operate in 1935.[51]

In addition, "barracks will be maintained at both Halifax and Esquimalt for the accommodation of naval personnel of the respective coasts, and as training quarters for permanent and reserve naval forces in respect of such training as can be given on shore," while the budget would "provide in small part for a very necessary reserve of ammunition and torpedoes required for destroyers." As well, "wireless stations equipped with modern sets will be maintained for communication between Ottawa, Halifax, Esquimalt, England, and ships at sea. These stations, that are essential to naval organization, have in recent years been a source of real economy in the cost of landline telegrams and cables and are available for use by all three defence forces and, to a limited degree, by other government departments." In addition, it would be possible to effect improvements, and "a start will also be made toward improving harbour defence equipment during the coming year and, it is hoped, that this equipment will be completed to full requirements within the next year or so." In short, "the estimates therefore provide for a real move toward strengthening Canada's naval defence. This branch of the defence forces requires a systematic and methodical line of development and provision is made to accomplish as much toward that end during the coming year as can be efficiently undertaken."[52] The defence department appropriations for the period were no less than $36 million.[53]

The increased defence budget was more a reflection of the growing health of the Canadian economy than a reaction to international events such as Italy's invasion of Abyssinia, and funds for two new destroyers were provided by "further supplementary" estimates, themselves additions to supplementary estimates *tout court*,[54] the result of increased government revenues and decreased expenditures in such areas as relief camps. It should be noted that although appropriations for 1938–39 seemed to be $2 million less than the previous year, one high-ranking bureaucrat warned that he "found it impossible to make any comparisons with 1936–37," given the plethora of supplementaries, further supplementaries,

51. "Historical Synopsis of the Organization and Development of the Royal Canadian Navy," nd, LAC, MG 27, III B-5, vol. 38, file 42.

52. CNS, "General Statement of Activities Contemplated by Naval Estimates 1937–38," 21 December 1936, LAC, MG 27, III, B-5, vol. 37, file D-7.

53. "Memorandum prepared by Department of National Defence," nd, LAC, MG 36 J4, vol. 159, file 1428.

54. G. Killeen, Estimates Section, to DM, 25 January 1938, LAC, MG 27, III B-5, vol. 37, file D-9.

and other, similar votes in parliament.[55] Still, it is now clear that higher defence expenditures—and plans for further increases—pre-dated the Czechoslovak crisis of 1938. By May 1938, if not earlier, Nelles was preparing plans for new ship construction to begin with the 1939–40 budget. Destroyers, for example, would cost $3.5 million to build in Britain, but 75 percent more if constructed in Canada, while minesweepers would require $318,000 for those built on the East Coast and $403,000 for those constructed in British Columbia; motor torpedo boats would cost $200,000 each.[56]

If appropriations in this period had less to do with the Abyssinian crisis than with an improving Canadian economy, then naval planning had more to do with the relationship between the United States and Japan than with events in Africa. Defence Scheme No 1 had dealt with the possibility of war between Canada and its southern neighbour, but the second in the series (there would be three by the outbreak of war) focused on maintaining the country's neutrality in a conflict between the two most powerful Pacific nations. Such had been a concern for some time, as we have seen, but it was in this period that a concrete plan was drawn up. Approved by the government in 1936,[57] it would guide naval priorities—namely the defence of the West Coast—until events in Europe altered perceptions of where the next major conflict would break out. The challenge was that British Columbia, with its bays of all sizes, each surrounded by wooded and mountainous country, might provide "ideal anchorages for small craft anxious to procure refuge and to remain in concealment. The large number of such shelters, together with the lack of inhabitants and poor communications in many sections, makes it extremely difficult to prevent a would-be belligerent vessel from securing temporary refuge in remote areas." To protect neutrality in peacetime (and defend trade in wartime), "adequate means of patrolling the coast and a covering force are necessary. While air forces can provide much that is required in the nature of reconnaissance of the coast, naval vessels are essential to make use of their information. No belligerent would consider air forces alone as capable of providing the measure of supervision that international law requires of a neutral in regard to such a coast line," Nelles suggested in an obvious stab at his RCAF colleagues and their air power doctrine. Auxiliary vessels would be requisitioned from other departments in time of crisis. Also, "additional facilities are required for berthing and refitting at the dockyard, Esquimalt," while "base defence equipment, and construction of a modern magazine to meet requirements of all three services are also required."[58]

In the year or more that followed, plans for maintaining neutrality in a war between the US and Japan increased in sophistication. Avoiding giving aid to one side or the other would not suffice; it would be necessary to ensure neither belligerent made use of Canadian territory. On the one hand, as the Joint Staff Committee explained, the country had to guard against "attempts on the part of Japan to make use of remote harbours or other

---

55. Private Secretary to DM, 24 January 1938, ibid.

56. CNS to DM, 31 May 1938, LAC, MG 37, III B-5, vol. 38, file 52.

57. Stephen J. Harris, *Canadian Brass: The Making of a Professional Army, 1860–1939* (Toronto 1988), 180.

58. Nelles, "Canadian Naval Policy in Regard to Her Western Seaboard," 24 September 1936, LAC, MG 27, III B-5, vol. 32, file X-53.

territorial waters as refuelling or repair bases or as places of refuge for submarines, armed merchantmen and cruisers, the two latter categories being probably equipped with aircraft. The unlawful entry into Canadian jurisdiction of Japanese battleships and aircraft carriers is not anticipated." On the other hand, Canada had to be prepared for "possible action on the part of the United States, on the plea of emergent necessity, to carry out the air rein-forcement of her Alaskan territory over Canadian territory and/or territorial waters." Also to consider was "possible action by the United States actually to occupy Canadian territory or territorial waters with sea, land or air forces. Unless the United States is confident that Canada's arrangements to protect her neutrality are such as to make it impossible for the Japanese to make use of Canadian territorial waters and air in ways useful to the prosecu-tion of the Japanese plans, there is danger that they may be impelled to take such action."[59] In other words, Canada needed to defend itself to avoid unwanted help.

Steps to deal with such threats included "the exercise of such vigilance over Canadian territory, waters and air as will make it impossible for either belligerent undetected to com-mit therein any act the performance of which would constitute a violation of Canadian neutrality." The country had to be ready with a robust response, with "the provision of such armed forces as may be required to prevent the performance of such acts by the use of force if necessary." With the army, navy, and air force prepared to do their part, the United States and Japan might in fact recognize Canadian neutrality, depending on "the impression which the belligerents will gain, by virtue of the steps she takes, of her determination to enforce it…. This course, if adopted, may possibly occasion a degree of over-insurance, but it is felt that if it should be the intention of the government to keep the country out of war, the issue at stake may well be worth the additional premium." Reductions could come later. Each service, given "the degree of technical knowledge required for exerting the full power of the various weapons," would be under its normal chain of command, with no overall commander. "The object in view by the three services will be the same, namely, so to observe, each according to its capabilities, the territorial waters, air and land lying within Canadian jurisdiction to the end that it will be impossible for either belligerent to carry out therein, without detection and appropriate action being taken, any act the performance of which would constitute a violation of Canadian neutrality."[60]

The part of the plan specific to the RCN, "in co-operation with the air force," included "a continuous patrol of the territorial waters adjacent to the British Columbian coast by all vessels of the Royal Canadian Navy assisted by such additional auxiliary craft as may be required, and as are available." The British Columbia coast was divided into three zones, one around the Queen Charlotte Islands (recently renamed "Haida Gwaii"), another from the Alaska border to Cape Caution, and the third encompassing the waters around Van-couver Island and to the Strait of Juan de Fuca. Bases would be established as required; they were to be "of a mobile nature. They will require little, if anything, in the way of facilities ashore. They will be established at naturally protected anchorages and a supply of fuel will

59. "Joint Staff Committee Plan for the Maintenance of Canadian Neutrality in the Event of War Between the United States and Japan," 20 January 1938, LAC, MG 27, III B-5, vol. 30, file X-18.

60. Ibid.

be maintained at each. Ships requiring repairs will be sent to either of the main bases Esquimalt or Prince Rupert. Wherever it is possible, naval zone bases should coincide with zone bases established by the Royal Canadian Air Force." Communications of the two services would be on the same wavelength, while the navy would maintain close liaison with collectors of customs "in order that vessels of a suspicious nature may be kept under close observation." To carry out its tasks, the navy would need, on the West Coast, four destroyers, five minesweepers, and a dozen auxiliaries. The militia, meanwhile, would focus on coastal defences, guarding airports, internal security against sabotage, and the provision of a general reserve.[61]

British Columbia may have been a priority, but the RCN also looked eastward, replacing the aged destroyer *Champlain* with *St Laurent*, "a ship at least 50 per cent more efficient in every respect." The navy also increased its permanent force personnel there by 200, began construction of the training ship *Venture*, supplied anti-submarine equipment to Halifax, such as buoys and gate vessels, increased its reserves of ammunition, torpedoes, and other warlike stores, and provided new wireless telegraphy equipment.[62]

Since the new destroyer was one of many that were to form the navy's nucleus until well into the Second World War, it is of special interest to this study. As one historian has noted, "the Admiralty was still disappointed by Canada's emphasis on local defence, but in the international climate of the mid 1930s was willing to encourage any local initiative," and that it did insofar as new destroyers were concerned. With new construction likely to cost as much as £724,000, the British government offered Canada two C-class destroyers similar in design to *Saguenay* and *Skeena* but at a lesser cost of £564,000. Acquisition of *Crescent* and *Cygnet* would give Canada "two modern vessels on each coast of similar type thus simplifying training, organization for spares, ammunition supply, etc." From the British perspective, the transfer of *Crescent* and *Cygnet* would still serve "the wider aspects of empire defence" as the destroyer strength of the British Commonwealth as a whole would remain unchanged while Canadian capabilities would be improved. As for *Champlain* and *Vancouver*, although the Admiralty had intended scrapping them in England, they accepted that the work could be done in Canada given that, according to Nelles, "the risk of an Atlantic crossing in November is not considered justified without a convoy vessel." Furthermore, in keeping with what we have already seen in regard to supplies, guns, and ammunition, "the guns and mountings, torpedo tubes and torpedoes, and the armament stores are required" in Canada.[63]

Preparing the replacements, *Cygnet* and *Crescent* (they would be renamed later) progressed well, though there were the usual hidden costs, as the Canadian naval observer in the shipyards in question, Commander (Engineering) F.H. Jefferson, reported. "It is desired

---

61. Ibid.

62. CNS to DM, 9 October 1937, LAC, MG 27, III B-5, vol. 30, file X-9.

63. Roger Sarty, *Entirely in the Hands of the Friendly Neighbour: The Canadian Armed Forces and the Defence of the Pacific Coast, 1909–1939* (Victoria, 1995), 26; and Malcolm Macdonald to Vincent Massey, 5 June 1936, High Commissioner to External Affairs, 2 September 1936, Nelles to DM, 4 September 1936, 1017–10–9, LAC, RG 24, vol. 3833.

HMCS *Skeena* at Hamilton, Bermuda, in April 1937. (LAC PA-144090)

to call the attention of the department to necessity for additional expenditure with respect to such work as the cleaning out of OF [oil fuel] tanks, scraping and cleaning of ships' bottom, and other unforeseen charges incidental to the refitting of these destroyers, such charges not being included in the approximate estimate as quoted by the Admiralty, observing that work of this nature is usually carried out by the ship's staff in the case of vessels in full commission. An estimate of these additional costs will be submitted in due course." Still, not much work was needed, as "the principle [sic] and only alteration of immediate importance necessary to meet the requirements of the Canadian service conditions is the changing of the culinary arrangements from those as at present fitted for the Royal Navy standard ration system, to those required for the general messing system. In this connection it is proposed to utilize the present coal bunker for a preparing room and provide for a small coal bunker elsewhere. This can be done by adapting the galley ranges to burn oil fuel in lieu of coal, observing that the Admiralty has evolved a satisfactory gravity fed drip type oil burner for the ranges in destroyers. Full particulars of this change are being prepared and will be submitted for approval as soon as possible. In the meantime it is requested that the high commissioner should be given authority to purchase the necessary culinary machinery, particulars and costs of which are being submitted under separate cover immediately."[64]

Echo sounding gear would not be the most modern, since six months were required for delivery, but generally, "during the preparation period of *Fraser* and *St Laurent*," as the ships had been renamed, "the commander-in-chief, The Nore, and all under his command, were most helpful at all times. During stay of ships at Chatham a liaison officer was detailed by the senior officer, Reserve Fleet, which was of very great assistance to the RCN ships.... The dockyard authorities were most obliging in carrying out several items of refits and alterations at very short notice on many occasions." In a nutshell, "everything that could be done was done to assist the ships in every possible way." As for members of Canada's Department of External Affairs, "the staff of the high commissioner for Canada were, as on all previous occasions, most helpful and quick in dealing with all ships' matters."[65] The RCN, it should be noted, had helpful and capable staff of its own, whose members in late 1937 were able to provide detailed data indicating how much it cost to keep ships in operation. The upkeep for the cruiser *Aurora,* for example, had peaked at $820,000 in 1921–22. *Champlain* had cost a low of $68,678 in 1928 and a high of $217,021 in 1931. More recently, *Saguenay* had cost over $288,000 to run in 1934 and *Skeena* needed almost $283,000 in maintenance in 1936. *Thiepval,* a Battle-class minesweeper, required $45,000 in 1930.[66] Given that Canada was coming out of a deflationary period, estimates for the last of the pre-Depression years might serve as a guide for the final half of the 1930s.

Maintaining ships required more than funding, however, since to operate, repair, refit,

---

64. Cdr (E) F.H. Jefferson to NSHQ, 30 December 1936, LAC, MG 30, E312, vol. 4, file 33.

65. Admiral Superintendent, Chatham to Cdr (E) A.D.M. Curry, 14 January 1937, LAC, MG 30, E312, vol. 4, file 33; and Brodeur to NSHQ, 11 March 1937, 141-7-5, LAC, RG 24, vol. 5684.

66. "Historical Synopsis of the Organization and Development of the Royal Canadian Navy," nd, LAC, MG 27, III B-5, vol. 38, file 42.

and—should money ever become available—modernize a sophisticated war vessel one needed detailed drawings, an issue that would cause Canadian shipbuilders and the RCN many a headache during the Second World War. In March 1938 the naval secretary reported that four crates containing machinery drawings were being shipped from Chatham dockyard to Esquimalt. Commander C.T. Beard, who was responsible for the latter facility, noted, however, that "the whole of the drawings and particulars received are for machinery only, from the engineer in chief's department. No drawings or particulars have been received for hull, electrical, gunnery or torpedo parts of the ships. It is requested that if possible the drawings from the other departments of the Admiralty may be obtained at an early date." The documents in question were nothing if not complex, Beard later requesting "the 'As Fitted' drawings ... covering the electric section of the ships, including switchboards, light and power circuits, motors, fire control circuits, director control and gun equipment, etc." He had already received some fifty sets of drawings for *Fraser*, covering such items and systems as the rudder, voice pipes for the upper deck, the forecastle deck and bridge, and calibration of the fresh water tanks; the remainder arrived in the months that followed.[67]

Besides dealing with issues relating to ships already procured—or at least already approved by Cabinet—the navy also looked to what it might need in future. As Nelles explained, "the next stage in the development of the Royal Canadian Navy is the provision of a flotilla leader. A vessel of this type would provide accommodation necessary to the essential staff of a squadron of ships working together, and the space required for the communications branch." One possibility would be HMS *Kempenfelt*, which it would seem would be available for acquisition soon. "This vessel is almost ideal for our service as her armament is identical with our destroyers." Completed in 1932, she would remain in service for as long as the destroyers already serving with the RCN, and would cost about $750,000 to refit. Another possibility would be HMS *Keith*, but that ship "is slightly larger than a destroyer because she has a little more accommodation for captain (D) and his staff, but the accommodation provided is not sufficient for our needs and the rather numerous staff officers which captains (D) are now allowed. I think, however, that she would be quite suitable." For instance, "the ship herself is in very good order and is running at the present time, but I have to tell you that her boiler tube life expires in 1940, and though it might possibly be extended it cannot be very long before she will be due for re-tubing. On the other hand, re-tubing becomes necessary in all ships sooner or later if they are continuously used."[68]

The truth of the matter was that "Admiralty require *Kempenfelt* themselves but are willing to part with *Keith* in order to assist us." Therefore, "as it is imperative that we have one flotilla leader in order to get on with our tactical training I can see no option but to accept this later offer, taking the ship over late in 1939. Being one year older will probably reduce the price. This, however, will be offset by the necessity for a complete D2 refit (including re-tubing) before the ship leaves England." Comparing *Keith*, *Ottawa*, and *Saguenay*, Nelles

---

67. NSHQ to C-in-Charge, Esquimalt, 18 March 1938, C-in-Charge, Esquimalt to NSHQ, 19 May and 12 September 1938, 142–1-1, LAC, RG 24, vol. 5684.

68. Nelles to Deputy Minister, 2 and 22 September 1938, LAC, MG 26 J4, vol. 206, file 1976.

noted that they had complements of sixteen officers and 154 ratings, seven and 140, and eight and 146, respectively, the greater number of officers in *Keith* reflecting her function. Displacements ranged from 1,337 to 1,400 tons, and their trial speeds ranged from 33.9 knots to 36.6. "The armament and stores of all the above-mentioned ships are practically the same and therefore no difficulties arise in this connection." To conclude, the CNS stated that "in acquiring the *Keith* we will increase our forces to seven homogeneous craft, one of which will have the accommodation necessary to permit us to have a tactical staff afloat, our greatest need—in the near future."[69] It was not to be, but the staff work and thought processes involved give an excellent indication of the RCN's procurement aims.

Destroyers may have formed the RCN's operational nucleus, but as we have seen it also relied on smaller ships to carry out such work as fisheries patrols and life saving. They would be used for minesweeping in wartime, but by the fall of 1936, of the four the navy had been operating in the post-war period, only one remained in service. "After obtaining detailed plans and specifications from the Admiralty, the technical officers were of the opinion that a ship of the Basset type, now being placed in service in the Royal Navy, could be constructed in Canada for this cost," that is to say $250,000 each. Several firms were considered sufficiently competent to build such vessels, and Nelles reminded that, "apart from their primary functions of training ships," they could also "render very valuable service to other government departments in time of peace, such as *Armentieres* is doing at present." In addition to life saving patrols at Bamfield and "assistance to the Department of Fisheries such as the Pelagic Seal Patrol," the vessels had also proven useful in "co-operation with aircraft on patrol and acting as temporary bases," and in "assistance to survey parties such as recently carried out in the Queen Charlotte Islands." Generally, they were "to be available for emergencies for purposes which commercial vessels are not available." They would, of course, have a role to play in the navy's operations, since "in any scheme of naval defence it is of first importance to have vessels keeping the harbour channels swept clear of mines, and to patrol the approaches. It is also essential to have at least a proportion of the crews necessary, fully trained in this branch of naval activity." To bolster his argument, Nelles reminded the deputy minister of how the RCN had found itself on its own on the East Coast during the First World War.[70] (Getting ahead of chronology somewhat, the ships in question were in fact built, in Canadian shipyards, and given the names *Comox, Fundy, Gaspe,* and *Nootka;* all would be available on the outbreak of war.)

As for the personnel who would man these vessels and deal with the logistical and administrative challenges they created, in February 1936 the navy could count a captain, thirteen commanders, forty-eight officers of the executive branch with ranks ranging from cadet to lieutenant-commander, fifteen engineer officers, two shipwright officers, no medical officers, ten accountant officers, and two victualling officers. Of a total complement of 104, 101 such positions were filled.[71] To take care of the vacancies, and replace

69. Ibid, 22 September 1938.

70. Nelles to DM, 23 November 1936, LAC, MG 27, III B-5, vol. 37, file D-7.

71. "Historical Synopsis of the Organization and Development of the Royal Canadian Navy," nd, LAC, MG 27, III B-5, vol. 38, file 42; and LCdr C.R.H. Taylor to CNS, 15 June 1934, 1–24–1, LAC, RG 24, vol. 5586.

those who would inevitably be leaving the RCN due to illness, retirement, or other opportunities, the navy could rely on several sources. The first was within the institution itself, warrant officers being eligible for promotion to lieutenant upon the recommendation of the CNS and the approval of the minister. As Nelles explained, "there are at present two warrant officers in the executive branch and one in the engineering branch, who have shown exceptional ability. These warrant officers are well qualified for the rank of lieutenant where they will be capable of performing efficient duty for the next ten or twelve years. They will alleviate the shortage of lieutenants in the service but will not cause future blockade in the rank of lieutenant-commander as is the case with officers entered in the usual way, i.e., after eight years' service in the rank of lieutenant they will be about due by age to be pensioned."[72]

Most officers, however, came from Canadian society as a whole; such candidates had to be British subjects with two years' residence in Canada and had to be healthy, free "from any predisposition to constitutional or hereditary disease or weakness of any kind." They had to be between seventeen and eighteen years eight months old, and were required to pass an educational exam for the civil service commission. Part I of the test covered English, general knowledge, a modern language, general history or general science; part II tested for Latin or Greek, French or German, modern history, mathematics, physics, chemistry, or biology. Each candidate also had to pass an interview. Cadets were still sent to Britain for twelve to sixteen months' training, those entered into the engineering branch spending four years at the Royal Naval Engineering College at Keyham. The others, as in the past, sat exams to qualify for lieutenant's rank, and then served as either general service officers or in a specialty such as gunnery, torpedo, or navigation. "As far as possible officers selected for special service will be allowed to choose the branch in which they will specialize subject to the proviso that all branches are satisfactorily filled." Then, "they continue to serve with the Royal Navy for several years in battle ships, battle cruisers, or cruisers, usually in the Mediterranean or Atlantic Fleet." Subsequently, an officer could expect to spend about a third of his career with the RN and the remainder with the Canadian service.[73]

As for the ratings that made up the bulk of the RCN's personnel, as in previous years they were expected to serve seven years, longer if they wished to remain in the navy and the latter wished to retain their services.[74] A new development in this time period was trainee indoctrination aboard HMCS *Venture*, a specially built training vessel that saw much use in the late 1930s, operating out of Halifax. However, when her commanding officer requested that a lieutenant from the permanent force RCN be posted into the ship to be her executive officer, comments from the commanding officer *Stadacona* to the naval secretary were not encouraging. "It is appreciated that there is at present an acute shortage of officers, RCN, and that it is impossible to bring ships and establishments up to full complement." Still, *Venture* had only two officers, which could prove insufficient "in extreme

---

72. Nelles to Deputy Minister, 2 June 1936, 1–7–5, LAC, RG 24, vol. 5585.

73. "Historical Synopsis of the Organization and Development of the Royal Canadian Navy," nd, LAC, MG 27, III B-5, vol. 38, file 42.

74. Ibid.

circumstances of prolonged adverse weather condition," when "the safety of the ship would be hazarded owing to exhaustion when only two officers are borne." A third officer would allow for closer supervision of trainees, and he had to be a member of the permanent naval service because "esprit de corps, discipline and tradition, three important factors for consideration in the administration of a training ship are apt not to receive sufficient attention when a reserve officer is borne as 1st lieutenant." In lieu of explanation, the commanding officer *Stadacona* opined that "the training and experiences of the average reserve officer do not prepare him for the very special duties required of a training officer, RCN."[75]

He had a point, as RCNVR officers were learning the technical aspects of their role without following any kind of course in method of instruction or other pedagogical techniques. Trainees in *Venture*, however, seemed to have learned mainly on the job, so the need for an instructor-officer rather than an officer *tout court* may have been overdrawn. On one cruise, for example, there was little scope for instruction. Taking on fuel at Imperial Oil on 1 January, Lieutenant-Commander A.R. Pressey, the ship's captain, wrote,"the temperature was zero, a low mist was rising from the harbour which coated the ship in frost to a height of twenty feet." Casting off at 1200 hours, the ship proceeded out of harbour under power, there being too little breeze to justify making sail. Trainees practised abandon ship stations and shortening sail, but as the wind continued to freshen, by 2045 "most of the new entries were sea-sick already." A short time later, "the new entries were kept below as it was positively dangerous to allow them on deck. Most of them were completely down. The crew's washroom resembled a kennel full of day old puppies. Their utter helplessness was pitiful to behold specially as appreciation sunk in that these ratings had to be depended on for power when working sails."[76]

The gale soon abated, but "the new entries were definitely weak; their efforts while making and shortening sail proved it." It was only next day, while "the hands were kept busy cleaning ship and refitting gear," that Pressey noted that "the new entries showed signs of recovering. The sun and the warmth was having the desired effect." The searchlight and aldis lamp were found useful while working aloft after dark, and on the 6th the ship arrived at St Georges anchorage and manoeuvred with the help of a searchlight. "No navigational difficulty was encountered," and the engines worked well, except perhaps for "the exhaust nuisance," by which "the ship was smothered in soot and oil from stem to stern." Making her way to Bermuda, *Venture* had all her defects remedied in the dockyard there, and Pressey recommended that the next class to train in the ship meet her at that island, in part because "real systematic training cannot really start until warm weather is reached." (His recommendation was concurred in.) A new Marconi receiving set arrived; reception was poor at high frequency, but better at medium frequency, though at the latter transmission was a problem. Since the position of the aerial affected the set's efficiency, "experiments will be made during the cruise for a more suitable position."[77]

---

75. CO *Venture* to CO *Stadacona*, 19 July 1938, CO *Stadacona* to NSHQ, 23 July 1938, 142–1-1, LAC, RG 24, vol. 5684.

76. LCdr A.R. Pressey, CO *Venture*, Report of Proceedings, 18 January 1938, 143–7-5, LAC, RG 24, vol. 5685.

77. Ibid.

As for the sailors running the ship, "the permanent crew are improving in their duties rapidly. The new entries looked decidedly run down and pimply on arrival at Bermuda. The ten days stay in port has had the desired effect and a distinct improvement is noticiable [sic]." One trainee was cause for concern, and "on the recommendation of the medical officer of HMCS *Saguenay*, Boy Factor was transferred to *Saguenay* so as to be under his observation and supervision. Factor did not eat from the time he left Halifax until two days after he arrived in Bermuda," possibly a rather severe case of motion sickness. As for other members of the ship's complement, a stoker was exchanged for one from *Saguenay* and another member of the permanent crew "proved himself to be inferior and would not pull his weight." In a lighter vein, the captain could report that "the Bermuda Sailors Club organized a picnic for the ratings and thirteen of the young seamen ratings attended." Generally, however, "the weather has been decidedly inclement. Gales and rain have interfered with the work and recreation."[78]

From Bermuda the ship made her way to St Kitts, where "the inhabitants were most hospitable to both officers and ratings. Officers were entertained separately in private homes and the ratings looked after by an organized bathing picnic and then a sight-seeing tour to Brimstone Hill. It was very gratifying to hear of the good impression left behind by the new entries." Good fortune soon turned to bad, however, as "unfortunately Ordinary Seaman Hartling stepped through an unprotected glass skylight and seriously cut his thigh. He was transferred to hospital. It is considered most fortunate that Dr Scott Gillett, FRCS, was available to take Hartling into his care. Later Hartling had a secondary hemmoerage [sic] and sustained quite a loss of blood. However, at the time of sailing, Hartling was reported to be progressing favourably." The crisis proved a test that did not find the crew wanting, Commander G.C. Jones, the director of naval operations and training, commenting that "the most satisfactory item in this report is the prompt action taken by all concerned to save the life of Ordinary Seaman Hartling. It is recommended that a special letter expressing the department's appreciation of this be forwarded. The coxswain, Petty Officer L. Griffiths, is recommended a special commendation." On the other hand, "the commanding officer expresses himself about as obscurely as is possible. However, he was standing by the ship for many months and why he never noticed that there was no guard over a glass skylight is difficult to fathom." In fact, according to the director of naval engineering, "guards were provided for in the specifications and there is no reason why they should not have been fitted," an example of how a single incident could call for the attention of many disparate members of the naval service's leadership.[79]

So could disciplinary issues, especially in such a small institution as the RCN where only a few recalcitrant sailors could represent a noticeable percentage of a ship or establishment. One—perhaps rather extreme—example occurred in the summer of 1937, when four men were paraded in front of the commanding officer of HMCS *Stadacona*. "All four ratings stated that they had missed their ship intentionally as they would prefer to be sentenced

78. Ibid.

79. Pressey, CO *Venture*, Report of Proceedings, 2 February 1938, Cdr G.C. Jones to CNS, 23 February 1938, 143-7-5, LAC, RG 24, vol. 5685.

to detention rather than serve in HMCS *Skeena* again. Each rating, though questioned separately and out of ear-shot of the other[s], said he could no longer bear the unhappiness and 'grousing' of his messmates in *Skeena*. Each blamed the unhappy state of the ship's company on the first lieutenant, who, they say, allows them no freedom and for whom it is impossible ever to do anything right." It was not an uncommon situation, in war as in peace (examples of mutiny under such circumstances are provided in Volume II of this series), and one of the sailors, "Leading Seaman G. Summers is known to Lieutenant-Commander Donald and other officers now serving in RCN barracks, who state that he is a sound and staid type of man; he is married and states that his home life is happy; nevertheless, he preferred to commit a serious offence rather than sail in HMCS *Skeena....* He claims to have done his work conscientiously but that the first lieutenant is always 'getting on' to him and berating him for one thing and another."[80]

There is a long history within the Royal Navy and its offspring services of sailors committing offences to protest perceived maltreatment—Captain Bligh of *Bounty* fame was perhaps more guilty of sarcasm than anything else—and this situation was yet a further example. Seaman Summers "has a grievance in that he considers he was unjustly treated by the first lieutenant recently when the ship was in dry dock at St John, NB. On this occasion Summers states that he was found working with his overalls rolled down to his waist, and although he was a leading rating with a clean record, he was punished for this minor offence by having three days leave stopped." He was not alone in feeling hard done by, and "evidence of the other ratings was all to the same effect, that they had no personal freedom on board, life was just a burden to them and they were so unhappy that they would rather go to detention than sail in HMCS *Skeena*. They definitely stated that the first lieutenant was responsible for their unhappiness and made a particular point of stressing the fact that if a rating commits an offence in *Skeena* he never ceases to be punished for it until he leaves the ship." The response from HMCS *Stadacona*'s commanding officer was an excellent encapsulation of attitudes to naval justice. "It is respectfully submitted that if the evidence is true, the ratings concerned had a great deal of provocation and are therefore entitled to lenience in respect of punishment; if the evidence is untrue, their offence is very serious indeed and the punishment should accordingly be heavy."[81]

That sailors broke the rules and had grievances, and that officers felt the need to enforce discipline, was nothing unusual, and every documented case in the 1920s and 1930s was resolved through normal procedures, but the possibility of violence erupting sometimes had to be considered. Such was the case in regard to the situation related above, the commander-in-charge, HMC Dockyard Halifax relating how a member of his staff had heard "lower-deck rumours." Specifically, "at a ship's company dance in St John, NB, during *Skeena*'s docking, numerous young ratings of that ship made remarks of a threatening nature concerning the executive officer, Lt. Cdr. H.N. Lay and further to the effect that 'there would be trouble on the way round to Esquimalt.'" Nor was that all, as "onboard HMCS *Skeena* just prior to sailing on Thursday 16th June a reliable stoker petty officer of

---

80. CO *Stadacona* to Dockyard Halifax, 18 June 1937, LAC, MG 30, E312, vol. 4, file 33.

81. Ibid.

the RCNR had remarks made to him by young ratings of that ship of a vague but threatening nature to the general effect that there was some concerted plan for 'paying out' or 'getting even' with the executive officer and that the attempt would be made on quarterly settlement day," or pay-day.[82] In the event, there was no violence and Lieutenant-Commander Lay went on to a distinguished career in the RCN, but the rumours can serve as an extreme example of the challenges personnel issues could pose. As for the recalcitrant sailors in question, since there is no mention of their misconduct in the ship's letters of proceedings or in other such documents, one can conclude that they were treated summarily—and leniently.

Thankfully, it would seem that the above incident was the only one of its kind in the interwar period, and usually it was sailors' skills—and not their disciplinary fortitude—which was put to the test, often on elaborate manoeuvres. One such exercise consisted of landing operations at Ganges Harbour, Saltspring Island, in British Columbia. No doubt a test of Canada's ability to defend its neutrality, the scenario governing the deployment was that an enemy cruiser had landed an armed party and then left. The enemy, or Wimponian forces, consisted of members of *Vancouver*'s complement: "Lieutenant Groos, RCN, Lieutenant Grant, RCNVR, Mr Lewis, Gunner (T) and the normal ship's landing party of forty men with two Lewis guns and one Vickers machine gun represented the Wimponian forces." On the other side: "Lieutenant Finch-Noyes, Mr McMasters, Warrant Engineer, and the remainder of the ship's company, not required onboard for emergency purposes, formed the Popovian attacking force…. They were allotted two Lewis guns, the remainder of the rifles, revolvers and the searchlight." The enemy having chosen to defend Wilbury Point, friendly forces blackened their faces and prepared for battle. *Vancouver* swept the area with her searchlight and fired off blank rounds to deceive the enemy as to the direction from which the attack would come. "The main Popovian force left the ship at 1230 [*sic*, actually 0030] in the whaler, with muffled oars … landing at 0115, approximately one mile from the enemy position."[83] Glorious victory or ignominious defeat—in short, their destiny—awaited them.

According to the after-action report, "by 0135 the attackers were proceeding along the road with scouts ahead, having left two boat keepers in the whaler with instructions to pull slowly along the shore." About an hour later scouts came across trip wires, but they were discovered without anyone setting them off; the Popovians then divided into two parties. One cut the lashings on a gate and went through, but the other ran into trouble when someone "fell in a bush and a torch he was carrying switched on. This betrayed the presence of the attackers and the defenders immediately challenged and opened fire," forcing the party to take cover in a cottage. "Any further advance across the clearing would have been futile and peace was declared at 0300. The two forces fraternised and remained ashore for the rest of the night." Among the lessons learned was that sailors could indeed set up a proper camp ashore, with appropriate cooking and sanitary arrangements. "The enthusiasm shown by engine room ratings and others who generally land on such operations,

---

82. Dockyard Halifax to Captain V.G. Brodeur, 18 June 1937, ibid.

83. Cdr (D) Western Sub-Division to NSHQ, 23 September 1936, appx A, 136–7-5, LAC, RG 24. vol. 5684.

was most marked," and "the entrenching tool was found to be a very useful weapon," though no doubt as a means of preparing defensive positions rather than in hand-to-hand combat. Finally, the report concluded that a Canadian destroyer should include in her stores ground sheets, a good double-bitted axe, a cross-cut saw, and two pointed shovels.[84]

The above discussion on recruiting, training, and exercises focuses mainly on the permanent Royal Canadian Navy, but there were also the reserve naval systems of the RCNR and RCNVR, each facing its own challenges when it came to filling out its ranks. For the Royal Canadian Naval Reserve, one who attempted to improve recruiting was Commander G.C. Jones, commander-in-charge of the RCN barracks in Esquimalt who would later rise to the position of chief of the naval staff. He reported how "the various shipping companies, including the Canadian Pacific and Canadian National Steamships, the Consolidated Whaling Company, two tug companies and certain Canadian government ships, were visited and 'Conditions of Service' forms distributed." One executive was especially helpful: "Captain McMurray, superintendent of the Canadian Pacific Steamships, very kindly wrote to the captains of his ships, enclosing 'conditions of service' forms and inquiring how many seamen and stokers desired to enroll in the RCNR." Somewhat unfairly, his efforts were not as fruitful as they perhaps deserved to be, and "he has now informed training headquarters that replies have been received from all his captains and the only applicant is one quartermaster, aged thirty-two." Worse, "not one application has been received from the other private shipping companies mentioned."[85]

The RCNR was a little more fortunate in respect to recruiting within Canadian government ships, three applications for enrolment having been received from the Hydrographic Survey, but generally it was proving difficult to get experienced sailors to come forward. One problem, according to Commander C.G. Jones, was that too many seamen and stokers working for Canadian Pacific and Canadian National were over age. RCNR pay was another factor, as it did not make up for wages lost while undergoing training. Another issue, that "the seamen's and stokers' unions on this coast are very strong, and are likely to have an unfavourable influence on recruiting," was left unexplained. Another problem was that, in wartime, RCNR ratings would be mobilized into the navy with no guarantees their civilian jobs would be waiting for them when the conflict ended. Jones suggested the age limit be raised from twenty-six to thirty for those with several years' service at sea, that Canadian Pacific and Canadian National be approached to allow their seamen and stokers leave with pay to attend training, and that they also be asked to guarantee job openings for those who were called up in time of crisis. "If shipping companies would give preference in employment to members of the RCNR it would also be very helpful," the C-in-C, RCN barracks Esquimalt added.[86] Some firms certainly offered encouragement, Canadian Pacific Steamships counting three RCNR officers among its employees, and expected a good response to a call for further members to join the executive officers'

---

84. Ibid.

85. Cdr G.C. Jones, C-in-Charge, RCN Barracks Esquimalt, to Naval Secretary, 16 November 1935, 124–1-1, LAC, RG 24, vol. 5680.

86. Ibid.

branch.[87] The British Columbia coast service of Canadian Pacific Railways went even further, Captain McMurray, a member of the Royal Naval Reserve, willing to offer temporary employment to RCNR ratings; at the time thirty members of the reserve worked for the company, including eight oil firemen and fifteen steward porters.[88]

The RCNVR, for its part, recruited from a much larger pool, including a maximum of ten "gentlemen cadets" from the Royal Military College who chose not to enter the permanent force—either army or navy. One problem solved in this period was that of members leaving the reserve when they moved to a city or town that did not have a company or half-company. A division of Class B personnel was formed, made up of those with six years or more service in the RCNVR, their total numbers limited to twenty officers and a hundred ratings. Class A, of those actually serving in units, expanded from an establishment of eighty officers and 930 ratings to eighty-seven and 1,096. In addition, a new division was established at Port Arthur, its early experiences to be detailed below. Unlike the Canadian militia, the RCNVR incorporated permanent force personnel, as "it has become the policy of the department to use RCN petty officers so far as possible for instructional duty. This allows for more up-to-date training and for more frequent exchange of instructors, thereby avoiding the possibility of instructors getting into a rut," a problem we saw in evidence in the previous section of this chapter. "Petty officer instructors entered in the RCNVR as such are full time employees who engage for five years' service. Time is not pensionable but a gratuity of one month's pay for each year of service is paid. Pay is at RCN rates. PO instructors are required to undergo periodical refresher courses at the naval bases [at] Halifax or Esquimalt." By the end of the period under study, divisions, as they were now called, had been established at Calgary, Charlottetown, Edmonton, Halifax, Hamilton, Montreal, Ottawa, Port Arthur, Prince Rupert, Quebec, Regina, Saint John, Saskatoon, Toronto, Vancouver, and Winnipeg.[89]

Joining the RCNVR might offer more than just part-time employment opportunities, and on at least one occasion the western half of the RCN's two regions advised that seven-year engagements might be available for as many as fifteen ratings from the reserve's western divisions. (No doubt it was deemed too expensive in train fare to recruit among eastern-based reservists.)[90] For those who chose to remain at part-time status, especially the officers, there might be opportunities for promotion within their units. One such was Lieutenant-Commander E.R. Brock of the Montreal Division, whom Nelles (again in an example of the small size of the naval service) recommended for promotion, even though he was not "in all respects" qualified. He had only performed two periods of training since promotion to lieutenant-commander, and he lacked the necessary seniority, with two years

87. Naval Secretary to General Superintendent Canadian Pacific Steamships Ltd, 4 March 1936, General Superintendent Canadian Pacific Steamships Ltd to Naval Secretary, 10 March 1936, ibid.

88. CO RCN Barracks Esquimalt to All Ratings of *Vancouver* Div RCNR, 29 March 1938, 114–1-39, LAC, RG 24, vol. 5679.

89. "Historical Synopsis of the Organization and Development of the Royal Canadian Navy," nd, LAC, MG 27, III B-5, vol. 38, file 42.

90. Cdr W.B. Creery to CCOs RCNVR Western Divisions, 10 November 1936, 114–1-3, LAC, RG 24, vol. 5678.

two months in rank instead of five. Mitigating the first problem was the fact that "Lieutenant-Commander Brock has performed an additional period of twenty-five days' voluntary service and has done fifty-one days' seatime in all since promotion to his present rank." As for the seniority issue, "Lieutenant-Commander Brock was obliged to retire from the RCNVR in 1927, owing to his being moved away from a place where there was an RCNVR Division. He rejoined in 1934 and was given command of the RCNVR division at Montreal. Actually he is one of the original RCNVR officers who joined in 1923 and prior to that he held a commission in the RNVR [Royal Naval Volunteer Reserve], during the Great War." Brock was deserving of promotion, "not only because of the excellent work he has done as commanding officer of the Montreal division, but also because of the position he occupies as a citizen and the consequent necessity of giving him compatible naval prestige. This is of particular importance when Lieutenant-Commander Brock is brought into association with officers of the Non-Permanent Active Militia. It has been his experience in the past to find himself junior in military rank to gentlemen of comparatively little significance in the business or social life of the community and this is an embarrassment to him in his business life."[91]

The chief of the naval staff also sought an exception for Lieutenant-Commander E.C. Sherwood, who had performed only twenty days' seatime when thirty were required, with three years, five months' seniority instead of five. On the other hand, he had trained at the Royal Naval College of Canada, served at sea in Royal Navy ships during the war, and "is undoubtedly the most experienced officer in naval matters in the RCNVR." After commanding the Ottawa Division for over ten years, he received credit for giving "unstintedly of his time to the RCNVR. By reason of his former naval experience he has been able to organise and train his division along orthodox naval lines. The resulting keenness and efficiency on the part of both officers and men is very marked and it is felt that, after ten years, Lieutenant-Commander Sherwood is deserving of a reward." Similarly to Brock, "apart from his activities in the actual organization, and training of his division, Lieutenant-Commander Sherwood holds a prominent social position, is AdC [aide de camp] to his excellency the governor general, and is consequently a fair amount in the public eye. This in turn invites attention to the RCNVR and it is, therefore, in the best interests of that service that Lieutenant-Commander Sherwood should enjoy the prestige of commander's rank. It is also in the best interests of the naval service that Lieutenant-Commander Sherwood as AdC should hold equal rank with his contemporaries in the Non-Permanent Active Militia."[92]

The western-most unit such men served with was at Prince Rupert, which proved to be fairly typical. A 1936 report on the unit, for instance, found that gunnery drill was carried out satisfactorily, while knowledge of rifle drill was good, though the ratings lacked practice. Marching was fair, gun drill was well carried out both in manner and spirit, and the 12-pounder was clean and in good condition. The following year a thorough inspection was not possible because construction work was underway in and around the division's headquarters, though HMCS *Naden*'s reserve training officer was able to make a few comments nonetheless. "The general appearance was smart but many of the ratings' caps and

---

91. CNS to DM, 15 December 1936, 101-1-2, ibid.

92. Ibid.

cap ribbons were not on straight," he wrote, though their technical knowledge was found to be satisfactory. Attendance, however, was poor, with only seventeen out of thirty-seven present, but "the absence of other ratings was satisfactorily accounted for, some of these work on fishing boats and in logging camps during spring and summer months and four were on winter cruise in HMCS *Fraser*." The division was equipped with sufficient instructional gear, though the only wireless equipment was a primitive transmitter, there was no equipment to teach engine room operations, and torpedo equipment was also lacking. As for gun drill, efforts were being made to acquire a 4-inch mount.[93]

And so it went, reports on the unit's work ranging from favourable to harsh. In 1937, for example, the commanding officer was described as "apt to drink too much and always seems a bit 'dopey' and nervous. Do not consider he will ever be of much use as a naval officer." He still had a role to play, however, as "he possesses an amiable disposition and a fair knowledge of naval customs. He is anxious to do the 'right thing' so far as his capabilities allow." The executive officer was more highly regarded, being rated as "a very keen and energetic officer who does all the real work in connection with the division." He had the necessary ability to take over command, but "has not yet got a watchkeeping certificate, and requires about thirty or more days' sea time before he will be entitled to one.... As he can only get away for about two weeks' training a year it will probably take him about three more years to get in his sea time." Worse, his civilian employer might transfer him elsewhere, and it was believed "that he has made up his mind to get out of the town at any cost!" Next in line of succession was Acting Sub-Lieutenant O.G. Stuart, who was considered good but, given his rank, obviously needed time to earn the necessary qualifications.[94]

As in previous years many ratings (twenty out of forty) were absent at the time of inspection, as they were away in ships and fishing boats, but they were expected to return. More problematic was the petty officer instructor, Chief Petty Officer Anslow, who was "not quite as good as he was. Is getting a little portly and I think he feels he is getting too old for the job. However he is popular with both officers and ratings, and he is doing his best. I am inclined to think that, apart from exceptional cases, one year is quite enough for any PO instructor in Prince Rupert! He has about six months' more to do before completing twenty-two years' service, and then he does not wish to re-engage for service anywhere." At least the previous year's construction work around the headquarters had borne fruit, and "all are very proud of their new quarters which were completed about last June, and they are under the impression that they are the best quarters of any RCNVR division. I have not disabused them of this impression. However, the accommodation seems to be quite adequate for this division at present. The building is very clean, and rooms and stores are well kept and orderly." Instructional gear required included a new steering model, wood, and allowance for the construction of a model forecastle, a wireless receiver (and possibly a new transmitter as well), and others. Generally, "an increasing spirit of keenness exists throughout the division. This is due to the new quarters which permit of much more training and

93. Lt (G) Tisdall to HMCS *Skeena*, 4 August 1936, 114–16–9, Reserves Training Officer to HMCS *Naden*, 30 April 1937, 114–15–9, LAC, RG 24, vol. 5680.

94. Cdr E.R. Mainguy, "Report of Inspection of RCNVR Divisions," 30 September 1937, 114–16–9, ibid.

also recreation than was the case before when much had to be done outside in the rain. Also there is increased military activity in the town and this leads to more competition and friendly rivalry which is excellent in promoting pride in the division. Altogether the general situation is satisfactory and improving."[95]

The other British Columbia division was in Vancouver, commanded by Lieutenant-Commander E.M. Donaldson, who was perhaps atypical in some respects. Donaldson was "keen on the welfare of the division, and spends an immense amount of time on its affairs," Commander E.R. Mainguy reported. However, "he has been criticised for not having a civilian job," which at the time might indicate low social status, "and, rather naturally, is inclined to resent this. His argument is that, as he has not civilian work to do, he can devote more time to the RCNVR and that as long as he performs his RCNVR duties to the satisfaction of the department, and lives a respectable life, what he does in the rest of his spare time does not affect the department. This argument seems reasonable. Merely by being an AdC to the lieutenant governor he probably meets as many influential people as he would if he were in business ashore, and there is no doubt that he takes every opportunity of furthering the interest of the RCNVR. Also I have no reason whatever to doubt that his shore-going activities are always creditable to the service."[96]

Other officers required little comment, either positive or negative, but "the biggest question regarding officers is whether Petty Officer Pickersgill should be granted a commission or not. Normally I do not favour promotion of RCNVR ratings to commissioned officer, mainly because they usually must stay in the same division in which they have served as ratings, and this is very apt to cause jealousy and dissention amongst their former messmates unless they are obviously outstanding and especially deserving of promotion, and there is no other equally deserving rating in the division. However, Petty Officer Pickersgill was transferred to the Vancouver division from Regina and states that he has on two or three occasions been told that (a) when he was in Regina he would be promoted to fill the next officer vacancy, and (b) that when he arrived in Vancouver he was told that as soon as the CO of the Vancouver division recommended him for promotion his case would be given favourable consideration. Therefore he seems entitled to serious consideration."[97] There was, however, an "on the other hand," to the effect that "if he were now given a commission it would have to be as acting lieutenant as he is thirty years of age. This would make him executive officer of the division and next in line for command. He would thus go over the heads of Sub Lieutenants Rankin and Leigh-Spencer, and Midshipman Campbell. I do not think that he possesses the necessary qualifications to warrant this step up, and I do not think he is good enough to take command of the Vancouver division, in particular, where he would be in continual contact with local officials, including the army and air force, and visiting ships both RN and foreign. Therefore I am not in favour of his promotion unless headquarters records show that he has practically been promised it on the recommendation of the CO of his division." He was not commissioned.[98]

---

95. Ibid.

96. Ibid.

97. Ibid.

98. Ibid.

The Edmonton division also had a rating who could be considered for commissioning, though his chances were better than those of Pickersgill. "Leading Seaman Maclean at present doing training is a medical student age twenty-six who will graduate in two years. He wishes to become an executive officer and from his records I would recommend him; he is expected to stay in the town after qualifying." Replacing him as a rating and recruiting others was not a problem, as "there are plenty of candidates for entry." Of fifty-one authorized, fifty ratings were borne in 1937, of whom twenty-four were present at inspection, a normal turnout. Their training was well-supervised, as Petty Officer Cross "is an excellent instructor in all respects and is largely responsible for the efficiency of the division. He has a particularly good idea of handling reserve ratings, being neither too militaristic nor too lenient." They might need a place of their own to continue training, however, as the space they were borrowing from the militia might have to be given back.[99]

The Calgary division also had accommodation problems, being short one lecture room, "which cannot be rectified without an addition to the building," but personality conflicts seemed to be a greater problem. Petty Officer Grierson, for one, thought his career was being negatively affected "due to Mr Turnbull not liking him." When Commander Mainguy inspected a few months later, he came across a different problem. He had nothing negative to say about the officers, with a single exception. "The one blight on the present situation is Paymaster Lieutenant-Commander Rowlands, who is an opinionated insufferable bore." Still, "the division is in a healthy state. It has a name for being the smartest unit in Calgary. (This has been told me by at least four unprejudiced citizens, and also several militia officers!)" The unit was therefore doing a good job of putting the navy in a favourable light, one of the RCNVR's main tasks. In fact, early the following year Commander C.T. Beard reported that he had "never inspected an RCNVR Company which showed up to such advantage as did the Calgary Company—training in all subjects is carried out—and not one or two subjects concentrated on, to the detriment of others." Beard went further, recommending "that some recognition be made to this company by letter from the department and alloting them ten additional ratings."[100] Not all RCNVR divisions were headaches, and even Saskatoon, which, as we have seen, suffered a near-death experience in the early 30s, saw the arrival of a new petty officer instructor in this period, the newcomer described in 1937 as "the first really satisfactory PO instructor the division has had." The following year the division was described as being "in a most satisfactory state."[101]

Further to the east, and notable for being the most recent addition to the RCNVR, was the division at Port Arthur. In command in October 1937, when Commander E.R. Mainguy inspected, was Acting Lieutenant D.M. Black, who had joined the reserves in May. "He is proving himself to have been a very lucky choice for commanding officer. Before enrolling in the RCNVR he had had no previous experience whatever in naval or military

99. ADNR to DNR, nd, Mainguy, "Report of Inspection of RCNVR Divisions," 9 October 1937, 114–13–9, ibid.

100. LCdr H. Kingsley to DNR, 4 June 1937, Mainguy, "Report of Inspection of RCNVR Divisions," 9 October 1937, Cdr C.T. Beard; "Report of Inspection of RCNVR Divisions," 6 April 1938, 114–14–9, ibid.

101. Mainguy, "Report of Inspection of RCNVR," 19 October 1937, Mainguy, "Report of Inspection of RCNVR Divisions," 21 April 1938, 114–12–9, ibid.

matters. He loses no opportunity of gaining knowledge, and this was particularly notice-able during his annual training at Esquimalt. On his return from that training he stopped off, at his own expense, at Calgary and Winnipeg so that he could visit the RCNVR head-quarters in those cities and see how they are run. He is worthy of very favourable consid-eration for any additional voluntary service for which he may apply." The executive officer, in contrast, had not yet attended any naval training, although one of his colleagues, Act-ing Sub-Lieutenant J.M. Hugues "should make a good officer when he learns something."[102]

The officer situation, therefore, "was deemed satisfactory," while of fifty-one ratings authorized, twenty-five were borne and eighteen were present the evening of the inspec-tion. "Most of those who were absent are waiting for the issue of their uniforms and appar-ently did not like to appear in plain clothes. Recruiting is going forward slowly and only the best are being picked. The result is that those enrolled are a fine lot of physical speci-mens. They are being told to canvas amongst their friends and to try to induce the best to join. Naturally, considering that most of them had only attended about two or three drills, their marching and squad drill were terrible. But they seem to be a keen lot, and they should improve rapidly." The RCN petty officer was also absent, away on course, but according to reports "is proving to be a good instructor. In the short time he has been there he has fit-ted out the seamanship instruction room well. So far over half the instruction given has consisted of squad drill and the remainder elementary seamanship." The whaler was in good condition, and generally "the division is progressing satisfactorily. Officers and men get on well with the Militia who, originally, had some resentment against the starting of the division. The commanding officer requested that consideration be given to the provi-sion of tram fares for ratings who live in Port William. The return fare from Port William to Port Arthur is twenty-five cents, the amount of their bounty pay." The 1938 inspection report was equally favourable.[103]

Also getting good ratings in this period was the Hamilton division, which in 1936, in contrast to previous years, had "excellent quarters," and though considered second class at the time, the reporting officer, Commander W.B. Creery, opined that "there is plenty of good material for a first class unit in Hamilton." However, "there is a discontented, unhappy atmosphere about the division and while there is keenness it cannot be called smart or efficient." Perhaps worse, "the commanding officer informed me that he might soon have occasion to request the removal of the petty officer Instructor, but he gave me no reason; he merely stated that Hughes is 'getting too big for his boots.' On the other hand, I gathered from conversations with the other officers that Hughes is the life and soul of the division, that it is he who holds the whole thing together and that were it not for him there would hardly have been one man present at inspection." The CO had a history, and it was not a good one. "The commanding officer lost the confidence of the men last year when he made them work on the building instead of allowing them to receive instruction, and it appears that he has failed to regain it." Although he had "admirable qual-ities in that he is determined and is a 'go getter,'" he had a problem in that "he does not

---

102. Mainguy, "Report of Inspection of RCNVR Divisions," 25 October 1937, 114–18–9, ibid.

103. Mainguy, "Report of Inspection of RCNVR Divisions," 25 October 1937 and 25 April 1938, ibid.

appear to have any idea of handling either officers or men and has succeeded in upsetting both. Even the social life of the unit, which could become an important factor in view of the excellence of the quarters, is frustrated by circumstances attributable to the commanding officer." Perhaps one of his worst failings was in recruiting, as "the commanding officer is a busy lawyer and does not know the youth of the town," and he "is of a very jealous disposition and doesn't want competition and hence isn't trying very hard to find anyone."[104]

There was some improvement in the year that followed, at least as far as the inspecting officer, Commander E.R. Mainguy, was concerned. "I consider that, possibly for the first time in its existence, the Hamilton division is now on the road to being a success. A large number of uninterested or inefficient ratings have been discharged; and the remainder, at last, seem to be working together for the good of the division and their own happiness in it, instead of, as before, being a lot of individuals or opposing factions, thinking only of what they could get out of it, and mistrusting all. All that I consider is now required is two or three additional executive officers, and possibly a change in the PO instructor." It was not the latter's fault, just that the CO was relatively new, so that he relied heavily on advice from the instructor. "Prior to this enrolment as a PO instructor he was living in Hamilton on a pension and was an honorary member of the ward room, RCNVR," and he may not have been up to date in regard to naval training. He was " keen to make the division a success but I think it would be good policy to shift him to another division in the next change round." The following year the unit was rated as "on the up-grade after years of mediocrity."[105] As for the nearby Toronto division, it obviously had a reputation for competence, one report going so far as to exclaim that "it is a pleasure to inspect such a well organised and happy division. All the officers are excellent." Also, "this division has the best organisation for instruction that I have seen," and there were few negative comments in the years that followed. The last of the Ontario divisions was in Ottawa, which also did well, in spite of being without quarters for one winter.[106]

Across the river, in the province of Quebec, one of the navy divisions was also having problems with quarters, in Montreal,[107] but Quebec City faced more serious difficulties. Like other units, its executive officer had not yet attended naval training, but "he is a keen amateur yachtsman and undoubtedly has enthusiasm and initiative." The problem lay elsewhere, Commander E.R. Mainguy reporting under the heading "officer situation" that "it will be remembered that, early in this year, action was taken with a view to cleaning up the officer complement. The commanding officer, Lieutenant-Commander Lemieux was retired," but was attempting "through outside sources," to get on the retired list, which would allow him to maintain a professional relationship with the navy and wear the uniform on occasion. Both Commander Pettigrew and Paymaster Lieutenant-Commander

104. Cdr W.B. Creery to CNS, 5 May 1936, 114–8–9, ibid.

105. Mainguy, "Report of Inspection of RCNVR Divisions," 28 October 1937, Mainguy, "Report of Inspection of RCNVR," 9 May 1938, ibid.

106. Cdr W.B. Creery to CNS, 6 May 1936, 114–8–9, CNS, "Report of Inspection of RCNVR Divisions," 10 May 1938, 114–4-9, ibid.

107. R.H. Pope to Mackenzie King, 17 September 38, LAC, MG 26, J1, vol. 256.

Delage, when told of this, stated that, "whilst they have some sympathy with him, they do not consider that he should be taken back and that they would feel it a disgrace if he wore the same uniform that they do!" Two other officers who were retired without being placed on the list accepted their fate. To rebuild, "Commander Pettigrew (Retired) was asked to come back on the Active List, temporarily, with the object of trying to interest a complete new lot of young gentlemen to join. The policy was laid down that only French-Canadians would be enrolled. So far, he has only been successful in enrolling one officer, Acting Lieutenant Johnson, who is not a French-Canadian, but is bilingual. Commander Pettigrew says he does not think that the officers should be French-Canadians as they do not normally possess the necessary qualifications or temperament,"[108] an attitude that may have been common at the time, but, as we have seen, was not part of RCN recruiting policy.

Saint John, as we have seen, suffered from problems of its own in the early part of the decade, and like Saskatoon had even faced disbandment, but by 1936, though it was still not impressing inspecting officers, it was at least rating rather average. A turnover in officers was in the offing, the CO and the executive officer moving out of town. In 1937 Mainguy reported that "throughout the last summer, when the division was without quarters and chaos reigned, Lieutenant Magnusson has held the men together and never lost interest in the welfare of the division. He now has them installed in their new quarters and they are practically up to strength and filled with enthusiasm. Lieutenant Magnusson possesses enthusiasm, initiative and tact." Mainguy's only objection to promoting him was "that he is not perhaps as high socially as he might be, but after seeing what he has done and after interviewing military and civilian authorities, all of whom support him very strongly, I consider that he would be an excellent commanding officer and bring the division up to a pitch of efficiency which it has never reached before."[109]

Although operating two main reserve systems, the RCN continued to look for other ways to recruit men in time of peace who would be available in time of war. Of ideas there were many, the secretary of the Royal Kennebecasis Yacht Club of Saint John advising in February 1937 that "last October the Canadian newspapers carried an item to the effect that in Great Britain the Admiralty was about to enrol yachtsmen between the ages of 18 and 39. No training is to be given them now but in case of war they are to be given commissions as sub-lieutenants RNVR." It was not the first time the British had embarked on such a scheme, and it was understood "that about three thousand yachtsmen were given commissions during the Great War in the RNVR and we believe that some two hundred of these were Canadians. When war first broke out a great number of yachtsmen enlisted in the army but by 1916 the need of officers with a sound knowledge of seamanship and a smattering of coastal navigation became so great that a large number of those who had enlisted in the army were released and given commissions afloat." He recommended that yachtsmen again be considered for commissions in the navy should war break out.[110]

---

108. Mainguy, "Report of Inspections of RCNVR Divisions," 4 December 1937, 114–5-9, LAC, RG 24, vol. 5680.

109. Cdr W.B. Creery to CNS, 20 April 1936, Mainguy, "Report of Inspections of RCNVR Divisions," 25 November 1937, 114–1-4, ibid.

110. G.W. Scott, Secretary, Royal Kennebecasis Yacht Club, 10 February 1937, 115–1-1, LAC, RG 24, vol. 6198.

A few weeks later Nelles suggested to the deputy minister that "a supplementary reserve might be commenced with little trouble and no expense." The Royal Navy, as we have seen, already had such a scheme in place, recruiting among men aged eighteen to thirty-nine, of pure European descent, and physically fit. Members would be affiliated with a naval division and would have the option of withdrawing at any time except during periods of national emergency or outright war. Such a system was inaugurated in the RCN on 15 April, 1937, and was "enthusiastically received by local yachtsmen," specifically of the Royal Kennebecasis Yacht Club.[111] Although reception of the new reserve scheme was not entirely open-armed—the Commodore of the Royal Canadian Yacht Club, of Toronto, wrote that his membership was "not very interested,"—there were ninety men signed up by the end of 1938. "At several centres, notably Victoria, Vancouver, Montreal, Halifax, and Saint John, the members of this Reserve are proving most keen to learn all they possibly can concerning naval matters, and the number of applicants is likely to increase greatly," wrote the director of naval reserves, Commander E.R. Mainguy. Some were undergoing a naval education thanks to volunteer instructors from the RCN and RCNVR, and the DNR suggested they be allowed to fly a special flag from their boats denoting their status as members of the supplementary reserve.[112] That was not to be, but the level of enthusiasm was clear.

Another such scheme, the Fisherman's Reserve, is described in detail in Volume II, Part I of this series, so only a short history of its evolution in the last years of peace will be provided here. As early as 1921, if not before, the RCN was investigating "the Canadian fishing industry in its relation to naval warfare," though the focus was on vessels rather than their crews. On the Atlantic coast, for example, only fishing boats equipped with sails were considered unsuitable for naval purposes, though the inshore fishing fleet was doubtful because its boats were unable to keep the sea. Similarly, Great Lakes boats were unsuitable, though on the Pacific coast about thirty steam vessels might be useful for minesweeping and patrol purposes. By the late 1930s the emphasis had shifted to incorporating not only such boats but their crews as well, a Fisherman's Reserve being formed, though only on the West Coast. A meeting held in Prince Rupert on 2 August, 1938, proved that fishermen were indeed interested, though the offer of fifty cents per diem per boat seemed insufficient for wartime use. Still, over the next two days twelve vessels and thirty fishermen were enrolled, "practically all Norwegian." One interesting point: "There does not seem to be any liking for communism among them. They are extremely independent and their compulsory service system in Norway has given them no love for the services." Volunteerism was therefore the RCN's only option in their regard, which posed no problem since it was the navy's policy in any case.[113]

The president of the Deep Sea Union was unsupportive at first, but was allegedly won over by an appeal to prevailing attitudes toward race, arguing that "if there was a war and

---

111. Nelles to DM, 23 February 1937, Mainguy, DNR memorandum, 13 December 1938, CO *Saint John* to DNR, 19 January 1938, ibid.

112. CO *Toronto* to DNR, 14 March 1938, Mainguy, DNR memorandum, 13 December 1938, ibid.

113. Cdr R.M. Stephens to Mr Found, 27 April 1921, 1017-31-1, LAC, RG 24, vol. 5696; and CO HMCS *Skidegate* to NSHQ, 3 August 1938, 146-7-5, LAC, RG 24, vol. 5685.

we were defeated, there would be no fishing industry for white men," the enemy in mind obviously being Japan. By 11 August thirty-five boats and seventy-six men had been enrolled in Prince Rupert, one recruiter suggesting that "the fishermen at Prince Rupert are, if possible, more valuable men for naval purposes than those further south," since "the northern coast and Queen Charlottes are, in my opinion, the danger spots and, as is known, virtually uncharted. The Prince Rupert section fish regularly in these waters. A large number state they know every bay and cove on the West Coast of the Queen Charlottes." Besides these independent fishermen, a recruiter also called upon B.C. Packers, the Canadian Fish Company, the Anglo-British Company, and Nelson Brothers in the hopes of recruiting two boats and their crews from each of the larger concerns and one from each of the smaller companies. "There is no doubt that these large firms have in most cases larger and better boats than the independent fishermen. The company vessels cost up to thirty five thousand dollars." An incentive for the firms was that "most of these large cannery men probably expect that this reserve will educate their men and instill a little discipline into them."[114]

The purpose behind forming various reserve systems in addition to the permanent RCN was to ensure the latter would have available the men it needed to conduct operations. In the mid-1930s these consisted of such endeavours as fisheries patrols and life saving, with which the reader is now well-familiar. For the navy, however, the true test of its ships and their complements was the cruise, where sailors perfected their knowledge and their vessels conducted manoeuvres, showed the flag, or gathered information. During one such foray from the East Coast, two destroyers made their way to the Azores, "in the face of a full gale blowing in the Channel from the westward. This gave an opportunity to test the ships and gear. The *Fraser* and *St Laurent* proved able sea vessels in every respect."[115] On occasion, as in previous years, East Coast vessels would be joined by their West Coast counterparts, the whole fitting into a detailed program. One spring, for example, *Vancouver* and *Skeena* reported on a recent winter cruise. "The training object of the first section of the cruise was to promote unit efficiency in order that on joining company with the eastern sub-division the ships would have reached a stage where they would enter into divisional exercises and manoeuvres without further individual practice." That phase completed, "training during the return voyage was confined to individual instruction of RCN and reserve personnel. Training classes were formed and instruction carried out daily wherever circumstances permitted."[116]

Summer cruises could be conducted closer to home, providing an opportunity to practise procedures that could be implemented in time of emergency. On the West Coast, for example, "in view of the probable importance of the Queen Charlotte Islands in any scheme of defence of neutrality it is recommended that as many officers as possible should be made familiar with the more important bays and inlets. The entrance to harbours in the west section of Moresby Island are difficult to identify without local knowledge." There were other considerations to take into account, however, and "cruises to the west coast of the

---

114. CO HMCS *Skidegate* to NSHQ, 3 August 1938, 146–7-5, LAC, RG 24, vol. 5685.

115. Capt (D) RCN to NSHQ, 27 March 1937, 142–7-5, LAC, RG 24, vol. 5684.

116. Cdr (D) Western Sub-Division to NSHQ, 18 May 1936, 136–7-5, ibid.

HMCS *St. Laurent* on the West Coast in 1938. The former HMS *Cygnet*, she was commissioned into the RCN on 17 February 1937, arriving at Esquimalt later that year. (DND PMR 91-316)

HMCS *Fraser*, with awnings rigged, in arduous service at Acapulco, Mexico. (DND CN 3803)

islands should be of short duration as there are no recreational facilities of any sort for the ship's company and the weather is usually unpleasant." The Naval Board agreed that such cruises be carried out, though summer was also the time for boiler cleaning, which had to be fit into the schedule somehow. After much discussion on the subject, Commander A.D.M. Curry, the director of naval engineering, recommended that "what would be preferable from this branch's point of view would be for a period of 5 days to be allowed in a suitable sheltered harbour, where there is little likelihood of steam having to be raised on the main engines for emergency purposes, once every three or four weeks. This, of course, being dependant on the amount of steaming to be carried out in the intervening periods." In effect, such maintenance could be carried out during the cruise, and so was not an obstacle to operations in summer.[117]

As we have seen, although it helped the navy determine its logistical needs should war break out, the Abyssinian crisis had little effect on the RCN's planning—as evidenced by the institution's continuing emphasis on defending the West Coast. Even Japan's 1937 invasion of China—Manchuria having proven insufficient to its imperialistic needs—had little or no influence on the navy's strategy. Events in the fall of 1938 would have a greater impact as Hitler's efforts to create a state of German-speaking peoples moved from the remilitarization of the Rhineland in 1936 (an area that was already part of Germany) through the annexation of Austria in February 1938 (the Austrians put up no resistance), to the Sudetenland crisis of September that year. The Sudetenland, with its large German-speaking population, was part of Czechoslovakia, an ally of France that refused to give up such territory, which incidentally contained its most important defences for a possible war against Germany. Britain and France wishing to avoid war, at least for the time being, convinced the Czechoslovak government, in effect, to acquiesce, while they continued their rearmament efforts against the expanding Third Reich.

The RCN's reaction to events is clear evidence that by the height of the Czech crisis in September 1938, although it was not a large navy, it was nevertheless an institution that was preparing psychologically for war. *Fraser* and *St Laurent* were on a cruise at the time, the former's captain reporting that "while the ships were at Cypress Bay the international situation became tense. The only news available was the unofficial press news received on the main W/T set and various broadcasts heard on private radio sets in the ship. On Tuesday evening, 27th September, the commanding officer decided to bring ships to a state of preparedness for war, except that items that would involve large expenditure of stores and were not absolutely essential should not be taken in hand.... The work was commenced at 0600, Wednesday, 28th September, and continued until dark. The longest item was the preparation of eight torpedoes and fitting of warheads in *Fraser*. This was not completed until noon on Thursday, 29th September." That very day British and French leaders were in conference with Hitler in Munich, Germany, and came to an agreement. Writing on 11 October, *Fraser's* captain concluded that "preparing for war provided the most valuable exercise and training of the cruise and was instructive for officers and men of both ships. It

---

117. Cdr (D) Western Sub-Division to NSHQ, 7 November 1936, NSHQ, to Cdr (D) Western Sub-Division, 30 November 1936, 136–7-5; and Cdr (E) A.D.M. Curry to CNS, 21 November 1936, 138–7-5, ibid.

brought to light various deficiencies which had not previously been observed and which have now been rectified by ships' staffs or else included in defect list and list of alterations and additions."[118]

Specifically, "it exposed what I can only describe as a very serious state of affairs indeed with regard to the supply of shale oil. There was sufficient shale oil in either ship to run only one torpedo. The oil had been on demand for some time but a signal to naval store officer, Esquimalt, elicited the reply that none would become available until 14th October." World events made it clear that such leisurely procedures were no longer acceptable, and "the situation was considered so grave that the commanding officer requested the naval store officer by W/T to arrange for a supply of shale oil to be despatched from Halifax by aeroplane forthwith. In the event a supply was expressed from Halifax and arrived at Esquimalt on 5th October, i.e., one week after being requisitioned." Such ad hoc arrangements should not have been necessary, and it was "considered that immediate steps should be taken to ensure that shortage of such an essential commodity should not recur. It is not known whether consideration has been given to the possibility of obtaining supplies from a Canadian source instead of from England. If this were done, it would probably prove easier to maintain stocks at the depots; it would be necessary to enforce rigid tests to ensure the required specifications were exactly obtained," since it would do no good to sacrifice quality for the sake of more effective supply procedures. And there was more, as "by the evening of 25th September, ships were in a condition to be fought except that ... each ship could have fired only one torpedo.... There were no depth charges on board.... There were insufficient qualified and experienced ratings on board efficiently to man the guns." *Fraser's* commanding officer recommended that "it be accepted as policy that in the event of hostilities breaking out before ships have become fully manned with qualified ratings, it shall be the depots' primary consideration to make up deficiencies in ships' companies immediately: this to be done in any event, no matter for what other purposes men may be required."[119]

Therefore, in the same way that the Munich crisis had shaken the international community, leading France and Britain to accelerate their rearmament programs, it also focused the minds of Canadian units and formations on what they would need should war come. Within the RCN such thinking was not limited to the destroyers of the West Coast, and the day after *Fraser* and *St Laurent* prepared themselves for war, Nelles wrote the deputy minister to report that "the experience of the past several weeks of emergency has brought home most forcibly the necessity of providing the stores and equipment necessary to place the naval service on active service in an emergency. Stocks of armament and torpedoes are far below requirements and the facilities for storing and handling ammunition are insufficient." He was nothing if not forceful, noting that "had war been declared as seemed inevitable, neither Halifax nor Esquimalt harbours could have been protected to the extent necessary owing to the lack of equipment for port defences," and "the near tragic fact was that once a state of emergency arose there was no possibility of obtaining guns,

118. CO *Fraser* to NSHQ, 11 October 1938, 141–7–5, ibid.

119. Ibid.

ammunition, minesweeping stores, etc at short notice, and the Royal Canadian Navy was faced with an impossible situation."[120]

Reporting the day after the British, French, and Germans had come to an agreement, Nelles could write that "now that the present crisis has been averted I most strongly impress the necessity of avoiding a recurrence. With the return to normal conditions the equipment which could not be obtained for any price a week ago can now be secured." He strongly recommended that "provision be made by governor general's warrant to provide the necessary funds. It would, in my opinion, be a grave error to defer this matter any longer. I have urged each year when estimates were struck that provision be made for the supply of the stores and equipment involved, and the experience of the past two weeks has fully justified the necessity of immediate action." The deputy minister attached Nelles's recommendations to a report to Cabinet, "forwarded for favourable consideration," and the minister requested that his colleagues approve the necessary expenses. Needed were "naval equipment other than armament for mobilization of all auxiliary vessels, port war signal stations, examination service, and minesweeping vessels"; "equipment of anti-submarine defences for the ports of Halifax, NS and Esquimalt, BC"; "accommodation and equipment for the joint service magazine at Esquimalt"; "guns, mountings, ammunition, depth charges, paravanes and other armament stores required for defence purposes on the Atlantic and Pacific Coasts"; "torpedoes (thirty-six in number) to complete establishment for HMC destroyers"; "gas masks (2,000 in number) to equip naval personnel"; and "auxiliary generators for naval W/T stations at Halifax, Esquimalt and Ottawa to provide independent power." The minister warned that "the monies appropriated by parliament for the Department of National Defence for the current fiscal year did not take into consideration the necessity for the abovementioned stores and equipment," a clear indication that the request was a reaction to the Munich crisis.[121]

In this way increases in defence spending were presented to the House of Commons in November, Prime Minister King insisting on doubling them from $35 million to $70 million, while Cabinet was willing to go most of the way, to $60 million.[122] The navy would see its complement of permanent personnel increase from 119 officers and 1,462 ratings to 140 and 1,825, while the reserves would also expand, with the addition of two whole divisions in the RCNVR and the creation of a Royal Canadian Fleet Reserve. New construction would include munitions storage, a barracks wing, and work on Bedford magazine in Halifax as well as dockyard and wharf repairs and improvements to the naval barracks in Esquimalt.[123] Also addressed at this time was Canada's continuing supporting role to the Royal Navy, either through the RCN's infrastructure or by direct transfer. Oil reserves, for example, were of obvious importance, as Nelles reminded Mackenzie King in the fall of 1938. At the 1923 Imperial Conference the Admiralty had stated a need for

---

120. Nelles to Deputy Minister, 30 September 1938, LAC, MG 27, III B-5, vol. 32, file X-51.

121. Nelles to Deputy Minister, 30 September 1938, DM minute to Minister, 8 October 1938; and Minister of National Defence to Governor in Council, 30 October 1938, ibid.

122. John MacFarlane, *Ernest Lapointe and Quebec's Influence on Canadian Foreign Policy* (Toronto 1999), 123.

123. Defence Estimates 1939–40, nd, LAC, MG 27, III B-5, vol. 39, file D-72.

110,000 tons, 80,000 on the Pacific coast and 30,000 at Halifax, "and recommended that his majesty's government in Canada should commence the provision of this reserve." Its importance was again stressed at the 1930 Imperial Conference, but at the 1937 meeting the Naval Intelligence and Plans Division in Ottawa reported that "Canada's war requirements of fuel could be met without laying down reserve stocks in peace." Italy having successfully annexed Abyssinia, and Japan having invaded China proper in 1937, this was not a response designed to allay the Admiralty's concerns. "In view, however, of the great importance which the Admiralty attach to the question of ensuring adequate supplies of fuel for naval purposes in Canada—particularly on the west coast—the chiefs of staff again recommend that his majesty's government in Canada should give further consideration as to the desirability of maintaining reserve stocks of fuel for naval use."[124]

As for personnel, not only were establishments increased, as we have seen, but men were stepping forward to fill positions. The RCNVR's supplementary reserve, to give just one example, could count a hundred members by January 1939. Later that year it became more than just a list when supplementary reservists were authorized to drill once a week—though without pay. Cruises in members' boats were also on the agenda. In a sense, the scheme was now too successful, for with 130 members by mid-1939 it was clear that "the three months intensive training of a large number of officers will be a heavy commitment on RCN barracks at the outbreak of hostilities." Having determined that, in fact, the system could handle 400 such reservists, their complement was capped at that number, the chief of the naval staff also agreeing to lower the age limit to twenty-five.[125]

Most members of the Royal Canadian Naval Volunteer Reserve served in the various divisions that had been created between the early 1920s and the mid 1930s, and nearly all them, if inspection reports are to be believed, showed some improvement in the last year of peace. Vancouver was rated as having "the necessary facilities for being the smartest division in the RCNVR,"[126] while the Calgary division was "keen and smart. Each branch of training appears efficiently carried out," and "with larger quarters and the present keenness, should develop into the most efficient division in the RCNVR."[127] Vancouver therefore had a rival. Another might be Regina, which was "the smartest at platoon and squad rifle drill of any RCNVR division…. They are obviously well drilled and all movements are finished and carried out with precision." Generally, "this is a great improvement on previous reports of this division."[128] In contrast, the same officer reporting on Port Arthur noted that "it is unfortunate that the only two officers who attended naval training have now left the unit," but "this unit being only two years old is finding its feet fast in spite

---

124. Nelles, "Review of the Oil Fuel Resources and Needs of Canada, Recommendations of Successive Imperial Conferences," 30 November 1938, LAC, MG 27, IIIB5, vol. 32, file X-63.

125. Nelles to Deputy Minister, 5 January 1939, R. Jackson to Lt Leigh-Spencer, 3 February 1939, Cdr C.R.H. Taylor, DNR, to CNS, 30 June 1939, 115–1-1, LAC, RG 24, vol. 6198.

126. Cdr C.R.H. Taylor, "Report of Inspection of RCNVR Divisions," 27 February 1939, 114–15-9, LAC, RG 24, vol. 5680.

127. Taylor, "Report of Inspection of RCNVR Divisions," 1 March 1939, 114–14-9, ibid.

128. Taylor, "Report of Inspection of RCNVR Divisions," 3 March 1939, 114–11-9, ibid.

HMCS *Nootka* was commissioned at Esquimalt on 6 December 1938. (DND H546A)

RCNVR ratings under training at HMCS *Naden*, Esquimalt, in 1939. (LAC PA-146232)

of the above," while "the platoon and squad drills on parade were very good indeed." In short, "this unit has first class material and with more training will soon compare favourably with any RCNVR division."[129]

Hamilton displayed a similar mix of challenges and potential. "The quarters are adequate for the purpose, although not as luxurious as some divisions. A good many of the amenities have been set up by the division themselves and reflects credit on the interest they have taken." It was just one sign that "there is plenty of good material amongst the officers and ship's company and shows promise."[130] In Toronto, although "the facilities against fire in these quarters are totally inadequate," a rating of "very good" was applied to the unit as a whole,[131] while Ottawa was rated "a well organized division. Officers and petty officers take charge well and are obviously well trained and exceptionally keen." In addition, "the quarters are exceptionally well kept," although "the division is still suffering from being without quarters a year ago which probably accounts for the lack of 'finish' in rifle drill."[132] Therefore, even when there was cause for concern, the fault was invariably seen to lie outside the unit being inspected, and Ottawa was not the only division to be treated with such equanimity. The report for Quebec City noted that "this division is most seriously handicapped by its small quarters which is totally inadequate for an RCNVR headquarters. Further the drill hall used is inaccessible during heavy snow falls in winter," so "it is essential that an adequate headquarters be provided for this division." Interestingly, and similar to other reports, "in spite of this the officers and ratings of this division are remarkably keen," and "the material is excellent."[133] To give one final example of how the RCNVR divisions were improving, at least in the eyes of higher authority, in Saint John the only issues rated as poor were the general appearance of divisional headquarters and the condition of the offices, lecture rooms, and drill spaces. In general, the Saint John division "is now beginning to go ahead after the serious set back of being without a quarter for so long."[134]

The operations conducted by the RCN, often incorporating RCNVR and other personnel, continued after the Munich crisis pretty much as they had before. One, the Bamfield patrol, had become so routine as to be used as a shakedown cruise for the minesweeper HMCS *Nootka*, which proceeded to the area in early 1939. (As we have seen the other minesweepers of the class were *Comox, Fundy*, and *Gaspe*, all commissioned in late 1938.) "During the period of patrol the weather was consistently bad and gale warnings were received daily for the first ten days; under such conditions the ship remained in harbour, shifting berth to anchor as necessary for the mail steamer," which apparently continued her rounds. Proceeding on patrol on 7 January, "owing to weather conditions," the ship returned to harbour by noon. Still, the operation could be deemed useful. "It is felt that

129. Taylor, "Report of Inspection of RCNVR Divisions," 6 March 1939, 114–18–9, ibid.

130. Taylor, "Report of Inspection of RCNVR Divisions," 8 March 1939, 114–8-9, ibid.

131. Taylor, "Report of Inspection of RCNVR Divisions," 9 March 1939, ibid.

132. Taylor, "Report of Inspection of RCNVR Divisions," 4 April 1939, 114–4-9, ibid.

133. Taylor, "Report of Inspection of RCNVR Divisions," 29 March 1939, 114–5-9, ibid.

134. Taylor, "Report of Inspection of RCNVR Divisions," 18 April 1939, 114–1-4, ibid.

the ship has had a fair trial of adverse weather and that she is a good seaboat, although extremely lively," her captain reported. At high revolutions, "vibration in the wheel house is bad and plotting is difficult. Water has driven in under the wheelhouse corticene and W/T office, and through every place where the deck is pierced. All scuttles on the mess deck leaked slightly at first but appear now to have taken up. The hawse pipes were fitted with a steel box cover and packed with canvas and oakum; water came through even so, but not to the extent that the mess deck hatch had to be closed, and this was under the worst possible conditions."[135] Clearly, the ship and her complement had passed muster.

Casualties were rare, but each one, especially fatalities, served to remind officers and ratings that operations, as routine as they might be, could still present certain hazards. Such was very much in evidence in HMCS *Restigouche* in the summer of 1939, when "Able Seaman Frederick Richard Nichols, official number 2111, was reported to have fainted while working on the quarterdeck." Such an event was not outside the norm, and almost always concluded with the sailor getting back to work, but on this occasion "he failed to gain consciousness and his pulse weakened." The captain therefore decided that medical attention was necessary, so the ship was turned about, making for Campbell River, BC, there being no doctor on board. It was thus up to a civilian practitioner to pronounce "life extinct." The British Columbia police detachment conducted a post mortem, which concluded that Able Seaman Nichols had died of a cerebral haemorrage. On 15 August, therefore, "captain (D) visited the ship when lower deck was cleared and a short address of sympathy given." The remains were buried at sea in accordance with the family's wishes.[136]

Unknown to his shipmates, or to anyone else within the RCN or Canadian society as a whole, only a few weeks of peace remained before the country would find itself in a war that would last six years. One who later recalled these final days of what historians would call the interwar period was Llewellyn Houghton, who remembered how, "in spite of, or perhaps because of the international situation, which since Munich (where part of Czechoslovakia was handed over to Germany) was becoming increasingly ominous, we proceeded on the usual spring cruise to the Caribbean in January 1939, during which we carried out war exercises with the cruisers of the North American [sic] and West Indies Squadron." Exercises were realistic and rehearsed RCN ships in the types of operation they were expected to carry out in time of war. "I shall always remember one particular exercise when the two cruisers represented enemy armed raiders whose object was to sink British merchant shipping in the western Caribbean. The job of the Canadian Flotilla was to find and sink them." It was all rather heady, as "this involved a lot of steaming at high speeds over a vast area, an ideal setting for such an exercise at that time of year. At one period the destroyers were spread out at just visibility distance of each other, searching for the 'enemy.' Towards evening, nothing having been sighted by then, captain (D) recalled all destroyers to join him for a night sweep. Just at that moment, however, based on certain information I had been able to intercept on my wireless, I was almost sure I was on the track of one of the cruisers, so I decided to take a calculated risk and disobey the recall signal."

135. CO *Nootka* to CO *Naden*, 12 January 1939, 151–7-5, LAC, RG 24, vol. 5685.

136. CO *Restigouche* to Capt (D), 18 August 1939, 145–7-5, ibid.

King George VI presents the King's Colour to the RCN at a ceremony in Beacon Hill Park, Victoria, on 30 May 1939. (LAC PA-148552)

About half an hour later, "to my enormous relief," the Canadians "sighted the topmasts of a cruiser just peeking over the horizon. We immediately turned away to avoid being sighted ourselves and I sent off an enemy report. About two the following morning all destroyers, having rejoined captain (D), were able to carry out a surprise attack on the cruiser and 'sink' her with torpedoes." Houghton was not reprimanded for ignoring orders.[137]

Operating as part of the 8th Cruiser Squadron, the Canadians were kept busy. "Ships were continually exercised in tactical exercises, screen formations, torpedo attacks, day and night, also taking in tow. Exercise XAS was carried out on the 10th and 11th of March. During this exercise planes were believed to have been forced down and destroyers were ordered to proceed at full speed to search. Full speed was attained very quickly and the Destroyers conducted themselves with credit throughout the exercise." While secured at dockside in Bermuda, the commander-in-chief, America and West Indies, held a conference of the ships' captains in which "all agreed it had been the most successful exercise period held on this station for years, mainly due to the number of ships taking part and the keenness displayed by all concerned."[138]

While the RCN vessels were engaged in their spring cruise, Germany invaded what was left of Czechoslovakia in mid-March 1939. Within weeks, France and Britain had guaranteed the sovereignty of several east European countries, including Poland and Rumania. Finally, after the Nazis and Soviets agreed to a non-aggression pact in late August, one that partitioned Poland between the two powers, German forces invaded their eastern neighbour on 1 September 1939. Although the United States remained neutral throughout, France and Britain declared war against Germany on the 3rd. Canada followed suit on the 10th, though the RCN had had warfighting very much on its mind since the Munich crisis had forced Europe to the verge of armed conflict in September 1938.

The Canadian navy entered the Second World War as a much more coherent force, and with a much better sense of what was expected of it, than it had at the beginning of the previous global conflict. Whereas the fledgling RCN had been forced to begin operations in 1914 with only the two obsolescent cruisers it had inherited from Britain and a handful of small Canadian government vessels—a state of affairs resulting from the federal government's vacillation in actually determining a national naval policy—the thirty-year-old naval service could concentrate more fully on its operational tasks in 1939 because its leadership was less distracted from essentials. There being too little funding in the early 1920s to maintain a cruiser and two destroyers, the former was sacrificed as the RCN carried on as best it could, with an increased emphasis on a string of naval reserve installations in cities and towns across the country, which helped establish ties with many communities that never saw the ocean, ties that the newly formed RCN had lacked twenty-five years earlier, when the First World War began, much to its embarrassment when it was criticized by both the public and the press.

Facing severe budgetary constraints in the early 1930s—and even the possibility of its extinction as a service—the navy cogently and coherently defined its role in the defence

---

137. F.L. Houghton, "Memoir," nd, 136–7, LAC, MG 30 E444.

138. Ibid.

HMCS *Ottawa* being prepared for war in the Esquimalt dry dock, 1939. (DND CN 3875)

of Canada, namely to protect the waters through which the country's overseas trade passed and the shipping routes that led to its principal ports. Throughout the interwar period, the RCN had warships to operate, including the valuable destroyers it had been denied in the First World War, so that it could lay claim to being a true navy as opposed to a mere roll of names on reserve lists sometimes operating small, unwarlike trawlers and auxiliary vessels. It was not the fleet of battle cruisers and supporting vessels that some had envisaged in the early years of the interwar period but, with six modern destroyers and four minesweepers, it was a realistic force, with no little experience of operating ships at sea, and one that was able to conduct itself with professional competence. For a country that was not very large in population to begin with, and which had spent a decade in the midst of a depression that threatened the very foundations of its economy and society, the institution that was the Royal Canadian Navy in 1939 was no small accomplishment.

Select Bibliography

SECONDARY WORKS

Admiralty, Naval Staff, Training and Staff Duties Division. *Naval Staff Monographs,* IX: *The Atlantic Ocean, 1914–1915, Including the Battles of Coronel and the Falkland Islands.* London: HMSO, 1923.

Anderson, Fred. *Crucible of War: The Seven Years' War and the Fate of Empire in British North America, 1754–1766.* New York: Vintage Books, 2000.

Appleton, T.E. *Usque Ad Mare: Historique de la Garde côtière canadienne et de Services de la Marine.* Ottawa: Queen's Printer, 1968.

Archibald, E.H.H. *The Fighting Ship of the Royal Navy, A.D. 897–1984.* Poole, Dorset: Blandford, 1984.

Armstrong, J.G. *The Halifax Explosion and the Royal Canadian Navy: Inquiry and Intrigue.* Vancouver: UBC Press, 2002.

Bach, John. *The Australia Station: A History of the Royal Navy in the South West Pacific, 1821–1913.* New South Wales: University Press, 1986.

Bacon, Admiral Sir R.H. *The Life of Lord Fisher of Kilverstone, Admiral of the Fleet.* London: Hodder and Stoughton, 1929.

Barratt, Glynn. *Russian Shadows on the British Northwest Coast of North America, 1810–1890: A Study of Rejection of Defence Responsibilities.* Vancouver: UBC Press, 1983.

Bastable, Marshall J. *Arms and the State: Sir William Armstrong and the Remaking of British Naval Power, 1854–1914.* Aldershot, UK: Ashgate, 2004.

Baugh, Daniel A. *British Naval Administration in the Age of Walpole.* Princeton: Princeton University Press, 1965.

Beale, Howard K. *Theodore Roosevelt and the Rise of America to World Power.* Baltimore: Johns Hopkins Press, 1956.

Bell, Christopher M. *The Royal Navy, Seapower and Strategy Between the Wars.* Stanford: Stanford University Press, 2000.

Bennett, Geoffrey. *Naval Battles of the First World War.* Revised edition. London: Pan Books, 1983.

Berger, Carl. *The Sense of Power: Studies in the Ideas of Canadian Imperialism, 1873–1914*. Toronto: University of Toronto Press, 1970.

Bernier, Serge. *Le Patrimoine Militaire canadienne, d'hier à aujourd'hui*, III: *1872–2000*. Montreal: Art Global, 2000.

—, et al. *Military History of Quebec City, 1608–2008*. Montreal: Art Global, 2008.

Best, Geoffrey. *Churchill and War*. London: Hambledon and London, 2005.

Black, Jeremy, and Phillip Woodfine, eds. *The British Navy and the Use of Naval Power in the 18th Century*. Leicester, UK: Leicester University Press, 1988.

Bogue, Margaret Beattie. *Fishing the Great Lakes: An Environmental History, 1783–1933*. Madison, WI: University of Wisconsin Press, 2000.

Borden, R.L. *Robert Laird Borden: His Memoirs*. Henry Borden, ed. Two volumes. Toronto: Macmillan, 1938.

Bourassa, Henri. *La mission Jellicoe: Nouvelle poussée d'impérialisme*. Montreal: Edition du Devoir, 1920.

Bourne, Kenneth. *Britain and the Balance of Power in North America, 1815–1908*. London: Longmans, Green and Co., 1967.

Boutlier, James A., ed. *The RCN in Retrospect, 1910–1968*. Vancouver: UBC Press, 1982.

Bowen, Frank C. *History of the Royal Naval Reserve*. London: The Corporation of Lloyd's, 1926.

Bowers, Peter M. *Curtiss Aircraft, 1907–1947*. Annapolis: Naval Institute Press, 1979.

Brassey, Earl, ed. *The Naval Annual, 1919*. London: William Clowes and Sons, 1919.

Brebner, John Bartlet. *North Atlantic Triangle: The Interplay of Canada, the United States and Great Britain*. New York: Columbia University Press, 1945.

Brown, Robert Craig. *Canada's National Policy, 1883–1900: A Study in Canadian-American Relations*. Princeton: Princeton University Press, 1964.

—. *Robert Laird Borden: A Biography*, I: *1854–1914*. Two volumes. Toronto: Macmillan, 1975, 1980.

Busch, Briton C., ed. *Canada and the Great War: Western Front Association Papers*. Montreal and Kingston: McGill-Queen's University Press, 2003.

Canada, Department of External Affairs. *Documents on Canadian External Relations*, I: *1909–1918*. Ottawa: Queen's Printer, 1967.

—. *Documents on Canadian External Relations*, III: *1919–1925*. Ottawa: Queen's Printer, 1970.

—. Dominion Bureau of Statistics. *The Canada Year Book 1919*. Ottawa: Thomas Mulvey, 1920.

—. Dominion Bureau of Statistics. *The Canada Year Book 1920*. Ottawa: F.A. Acland, 1921.

Castonguay, Jacques. *Les Voltigeurs de Québec: Premier régiment canadien-français.* Quebec: Voltigeurs de Québec, 1987.

Chalmers, W.S. *The Life and Letters of David, Earl Beatty.* London: Hodder and Stoughton, 1951.

Chambers, Ernest J. *The Canadian Marine: A History of the Department of Marine and Fisheries.* Toronto: Canadian Marine and Fisheries, 1905.

Chatterton, E. Keble. *The Auxiliary Patrol.* London: Sidgwick and Jackson, 1923.

Churchill, Randolph S. *Winston S. Churchill, II: Young Statesman, 1901–1914.* Boston: Houghton Mifflin, 1967.

—. *Winston S. Churchill, Companion:* II, Part 3: *1911–1914.* Boston: Houghton Mifflin, 1969.

Churchill, Winston S. *The World Crisis: 1916–1918, Part II.* London: Thornton Butterworth, 1927.

Compton-Hall, Richard. *Submarines and the War at Sea, 1914–1918.* London: Macmillan, 1991.

Conrad, Margaret R., and James K. Hiller. *Atlantic Canada: A Region in the Making.* Toronto: Oxford University Press, 2001.

Cook, Ramsay, and Jean Hamelin, eds. *Dictionary of Canadian Biography*, XIII: *1901–1910.* Toronto: University of Toronto Press, 1994.

Corbett, Julian S., ed. *Fighting Instructions: 1530–1816.* London: Navy Records Society, 1905.

—. *England in the Seven Years' War: A Combined Strategy.* Volume I. London: Longmans Green, 1907.

Corbett, Julian S., and Sir Henry Newbolt. *History of the Great War: Naval Operations.* Five volumes. London: Longmans Green, 1920–29.

Creighton, Donald G. *John A. Macdonald.* Two volumes. Toronto: Macmillan, 1952, 1955.

—. *The Story of Canada*, Revised Edition. Toronto: Macmillan, 1975.

Dawson, R. MacGregor. *William Lyon Mackenzie King: A Political Biography*, I: *1874–1923.* Toronto: University of Toronto Press, 1958.

Dessert, Daniel. *La Royale: Vaisseaux et marins du Roi-Soleil.* Paris: Fayard, 1996.

Dittmar, F.J., and J.J. Colledge. *British Warships, 1914–1919.* London: Allan, 1972.

Diubaldo, Richard J. *Stefansson and the Canadian Arctic.* Montreal: McGill-Queen's University Press, 1978.

Dorion-Robitaille, Yolande. *Captain J.E. Bernier's Contribution to Canadian Sovereignty in the Arctic.* Ottawa: Indian and Northern Affairs, 1978.

Douglas, W.A.B. *The Creation of a National Air Force. The Official History of the Royal Canadian Air Force, Volume II.* Toronto: University of Toronto Press, 1986.

Dudley, Wade G. *Splintering the Wooden Wall: The British Blockade of the United States, 1812–1815*. Annapolis: Naval Institute Press, 2003.

Duguid, A. Fortescue. *Official History of the Canadian Forces in the Great War, 1914–1919*, I: *From the Outbreak of War to the Formation of the Canadian Corps, August 1914–September 1915*. Ottawa: King's Printer, 1938.

Dundonald, Lord. *My Army Life*. London: Edward Arnold, 1934.

Dupuy, R. Ernest, and Trevor N. Dupuy. *The Encyclopedia of Military History from 3500 B.C. to the present*, Revised edition. New York: Harper and Row, 1986.

Eayrs, James. *In Defence of Canada*, I: *From the Great War to the Great Depression*. Toronto: University of Toronto Press, 1964.

Eccles, W.J. *Canada Under Louis XIV: 1663–1701*. Toronto: McClelland and Stewart, 1964.

—. *France in America*. New York: Harper and Row, 1972.

Evans, David C., and Mark R. Peattie. *Kaigun: Strategy, Tactics, and Technology in the Imperial Japanese Navy, 1887–1941*. Annapolis: Naval Institute Press, 1997.

Fayle, C. Ernest. *History of the Great War: Seaborne Trade*. Three volumes. London: John Murray, 1920–24.

Frame, T.R., J.V.P. Goldrick, and P.D. Jones, eds. *Reflections on the Royal Australian Navy*. Kenthurst, New South Wales: Kangaroo Press, 1991.

Gardiner, Robert, ed. *Navies and the American Revolution*. London: Chatham, 1996.

—, ed. *Steam, Steel and Shellfire: The Steam Warship, 1815–1905*. Annapolis: Naval Institute Press, 1992.

—, ed. *Eclipse of the Big Gun: The Warship, 1906–1945*. Edison, NJ: Chartwell, 2001.

German, Tony. *The Sea is at Our Gates: The History of the Canadian Navy*. Toronto: McClelland and Stewart, 1990.

Gillett, Ross. *Australian and New Zealand Warships, 1914–1945*. Sydney: Doubleday, 1983.

Glete, Jan. *Navies and Nations: Warships, Navies and State Building in Europe and America, 1500–1860*. Two volumes. Stockholm: Almqvist and Wiksell, 1993.

Glover, William, ed. *Charting Northern Waters: Essays in Commemoration of the Centenary of the Canadian Hydrographic Survey*. Montreal: McGill-Queen's University Press, 2004.

Gordon, Andrew. *The Rules of the Game: Jutland and British Naval Command* . London: John Murray, 1996.

Gough, Barry. *The Royal Navy and the Northwest Coast of North America, 1810–1914: A Study of British Maritime Ascendancy*. Vancouver: UBC Press, 1971.

—. *Gunboat Frontier: British Maritime Authority and Northwest Coast Indians, 1846–1890*. Vancouver: UBC Press, 1984.

—. *Fighting Sail on Lake Huron and Georgian Bay: The War of 1812 and Its Aftermath.* St Catharines: Vanwell, 2002.

Gough, Joseph. *Fisheries Management in Canada, 1880–1910.* Ottawa: Fisheries and Oceans Canada, 1991.

Graham, Gerald S. *Empire of the North Atlantic: The Maritime Struggle for North America.* Toronto: University of Toronto Press, 1950.

—. *Sea Power and British North America, 1783–1820: A Study in British Colonial Policy.* New York: Greenwood, 1968.

Granatstein, J.L. *Hell's Corner: An Illustrated History of Canada's Great War, 1914–1918.* Toronto: Douglas and MacIntyre, 2004.

Granatstein, J.L., and Norman Hillmer. *For Better or For Worse: Canada and the United States to the 1990s.* Toronto: Copp Clark Pittman, 1991.

Grant, Robert M. *U-Boat Intelligence, 1914–1918.* London: Putnam, 1969.

Graves, Donald E. *Guns Across the River: The Battle of the Windmill, 1838.* Toronto: Friends of Windmill Point, 2001.

Gray, Edwyn A. *The Killing Time: The German U-Boats, 1914–1918.* New York: Scribner's, 1972.

Griffiths, Ann L., Peter T. Haydon, and Richard H. Gimblett, eds. *Canadian Gunboat Diplomacy: The Canadian Navy and Foreign Policy.* Halifax: Dalhousie, 1998.

Gwyn, Julian, ed. *The Royal Navy and North America: The Warren Papers, 1736–52.* London: Navy Records Society, 1973.

—. *Ashore and Afloat: The British Navy and the Halifax Naval Yard Before 1820.* Ottawa: University of Ottawa Press, 2004.

Hadley, Michael L., and Roger Sarty. *Tin-pots and Pirate Ships: Canadian Naval Forces and German Sea Raiders, 1880–1918.* Montreal and Kingston: McGill-Queen's University Press, 1991.

Hadley, Michael L., Roger Sarty, Rob Huebert, and Fred W. Crickard, eds. *A Nation's Navy: In Quest of Canadian Naval Identity.* Montreal: McGill-Queen's, 1996.

Halpern, Paul G. *A Naval History of World War I.* Annapolis: Naval Institute Press, 1994.

Harding, Richard, ed. *The Royal Navy, 1930–2000: Innovation and Defence.* New York: Frank Cass, 2005.

—. *Seapower and Naval Warfare: 1650–1830.* Annapolis: Naval Institute Press, 1999.

Harris, Stephen J. *Canadian Brass: The Making of a Professional Army, 1860–1939.* Toronto: University of Toronto Press, 1988.

Hattendorf, John B., et al., eds. *British Naval Documents, 1204–1960.* Aldershot, UK: Navy Records Society, 1993.

Hawkins, Nigel. *The Starvation Blockades: Naval Blockades of WWI*. Barnsley, South Yorkshire: Leo Cooper, 2002.

Haydon, Peter T., and Ann L. Griffiths, eds. *Canada's Pacific Naval Presence: Purposeful or Peripheral*. Halifax: Dalhousie, 1999.

Herman, Arthur. *To Rule the Waves: How the British Navy Shaped the Modern World*. New York: Harper Collins, 2004.

Herwig, Holger H. *"Luxury" Fleet: The Imperial German Navy, 1888–1918*. London: Ashfield, 1987.

Hill, Richard, ed. *The Oxford Illustrated History of the Royal Navy*. Oxford: Oxford University Press, 1995.

—. *War at Sea in the Ironclad Age*. London: Cassell, 2000.

Hillmer, Norman, and J.L. Granatstein. *Empire to Umpire: Canada and the World to the 1990s*. Toronto: Copp Clark, 1994.

Hitsman, J. Mackay. *Safeguarding Canada, 1763–1871*. Revised edition. Toronto: Robin Brass, 1999.

—. *The Incredible War of 1812: A Military History*. Revised edition. Toronto: Robin Brass, 1999.

Hopkins, J. Castell. *The Canadian Annual Review of Public Affairs, 1902–1914*. Toronto: Annual Review Publishing, 1903–1915.

Hough, Richard. *The Great War at Sea, 1914–1918*. Oxford: Oxford University Press, 1983.

Houghton, F.L. *HMCS Skeena 1931–1932: Commemorating Her First Year in Commission*. Victoria: privately printed, 1932.

Hurd, Archibald. *History of the Great War: The Merchant Navy*. Three volumes. London: John Murray, 1924–29.

Hythe, Viscount, and John Leyland, eds. *The Naval Annual 1914*. London: William Clowes and Sons, 1914.

Jackman, S.W., ed. *At Sea and By Land: The Reminiscences of William Balfour Macdonald, RN*. Victoria: Sono Nis Press, 1983.

Jane, Fred T., ed. *Jane's Fighting Ships 1914*. London: Sampson Low, Marston & Co., 1914.

Jebb, Richard. *The Imperial Conference: A History and Study*. London: Longmans Green, 1911.

Jellicoe, Sir John. *The Submarine Peril: The Admiralty Policy in 1917*. London: Cassell, 1934.

Johnson, Franklyn Arthur. *Defence by Committee: The British Committee of Imperial Defence, 1885–1959*. London: Oxford University Press, 1960.

Johnston, Hugh. *The Voyage fo the Komagata Maru: The Sikh Challenge to Canada's Colour Bar.* Vancouver: UBC Press, 1989.

Keegan, John. *The First World War.* New York: A. Knopf, 1999.

Kemp, Peter, ed. *The Papers of Sir John Fisher, Volume I.* London: Navy Records Society, 1960.

Kendle, John Edward. *The Colonial and Imperial Conferences, 1887–1911: A Study in Imperial Organization.* London: Longmans, 1967.

Kennedy, Greg, and Keith Neilson, eds. *Far-Flung Lines: Studies in Imperial Defence in Honour of Donald Mackenzie Schurman.* London: Frank Cass, 1996.

—, ed. *The Merchant Marine in International Affairs, 1850–1950.* London: Frank Cass, 2000.

Kennedy, Paul M. *The Rise and Fall of British Naval Mastery.* London: A. Lane, 1976.

—, ed. *The War Plans of the Great Powers, 1880–1914.* London: Allen and Unwin, 1979.

Kimber, Stephen. *Sailors, Slackers and Blind Pigs: Halifax at War.* Toronto: Doubleday, 2002.

Lambert, Nicholas A. *Sir John Fisher's Naval Revolution.* Columbia, SC: University of South Carolina Press, 1999.

Lavery, Brian. *Nelson's Navy: The Ships, Men and Organisation, 1793–1815.* Annapolis: Naval Institute Press, 1989.

Leacy, F.H., ed. *Historical Statistics of Canada, Second Edition.* Ottawa: Statistics Canada, 1983.

Lewis, E.R. *Seacoast Fortifications of the United States: An Introductory History.* Washington, DC: Smithsonian Institution, 1970.

Longstaff, E.V. *Esquimalt Naval Base: A History of Its Work and Its Defences.* Victoria: Victoria Book and Stationery, 1941.

Lord, Walter. *The Good Years: From 1900 to the First World War.* New York: Harper and Bros., 1960.

Lovatt, Ronald. *A History of the Defence of Victoria and Esquimalt, 1846–1893.* Ottawa: Parks Canada, 1980.

MacFarlane, John. *Ernest Lapointe and Quebec's Influence on Canadian Foreign Policy.* Toronto: University of Toronto Press, 1999.

MacPherson, Ken, and John Burgess. *The Ships of Canada's Naval Forces: A Complete Pictorial History of Canadian Warships.* Toronto: Collins, 1985.

MacPherson, Ken, John Burgess, and Ron Barrie. *The Ships of Canada's Naval Forces, 1910–2002.* St Catharines: Vanwell, 2002.

Maginley, Charles D., and Bernard Collin. *The Ships of Canada's Marine Services.* St Catharines: Vanwell, 2001.

Mahan, A.T. *The Influence of Sea Power Upon History, 1660–1783.* Toronto: Dover, 1987.

—. *Sea Power in Its Relations to the War of 1812.* London: Sampson, Low, Marston, 1905.

Major, Kevin. *As Near to Heaven by Sea: A History of Newfoundland and Labrador.* Toronto: Penguin Viking, 2001.

Malcomson, Robert. *Lords of the Lake: The Naval War on Lake Ontario, 1812–14.* Toronto: Robin Brass, 1998.

March, Edgar J. *British Destroyers: A History of Development, 1892–1953.* London: Seeley Service, 1966.

Marcil, Eileen Reid. *Tall Ships and Tankers: The History of the Davie Shipbuilders.* Toronto: McClelland and Stewart, 1997.

Marder, A.J. *The Anatomy of British Sea Power: A History of British Naval Policy in the Pre-Dreadnought Era, 1880–1905.* New York: Frank Cass, 1940.

—. *From the Dreadnought to Scapa Flow: The Royal Navy in the Fisher Era,* I: *The Road to War, 1904–1914.* Oxford: Oxford University Press, 1961.

—. *From the Dreadnought to Scapa Flow: The Royal Navy in the Fisher Era,* III: *Jutland and After (May 1916–December 1916).* London: Oxford University Press, 1966.

—. *Fear God and Dread Nought: The Correspondence of Admiral of the Fleet Lord Fisher of Kilverstone,* II: *Years of Power, 1904–1914.* London: J. Cape, 1956.

Marquis, Greg. *In Armageddon's Shadow: The Civil War and Canada's Maritime Provinces.* Montreal and Kingston: McGill-Queen's University Press, 1998.

Mathieu, Jacques. *La Construction navale royale à Québec: 1739–1759.* Quebec: La Société historique de Québec, 1971.

—. *La Nouvelle-France: Les Français en Amérique du Nord, XVIe-XVIIIe siècle.* Quebec: Presses de l'Université Laval, 2001.

McKee, Fraser. *The Armed Yachts of Canada.* Erin, Ontario: Boston Mills Press, 1983.

McKercher, B.J.C., ed. *Anglo-American Relations in the 1920s: The Struggle for Supremacy.* Edmonton: Macmillan, 1990.

McKercher, B.J.C., and Lawrence Aronsen, eds. *The North Atlantic Triangle in a Changing World: Anglo-American-Canadian Relations, 1902–1956.* Toronto: University of Toronto Press, 1996.

Messimer, D.R. *Find and Destroy: Antisubmarine Warfare in World War I.* Annapolis: Naval Institute Press, 2001.

Milner, Marc. *Canada's Navy: The First Century.* Toronto: University of Toronto Press, 1999.

Miquelon, Dale. *New France, 1701–1744: "A Supplement to Europe."* Toronto: McClelland and Stewart, 1987.

Moogk, Peter N. *Vancouver Defended: A History of the Men and Guns of the Lower Mainland Defences, 1859–1949*. Surrey, BC: Antonson Pub., 1978.

Morgan, Henry James, ed. *The Canadian Men and Women of the Time: A Handbook of Canadian Biography*. Toronto: William Briggs, 1898.

Morrow, John H. *The Great War: An Imperial History*. New York: Routledge, 2004.

Morton, Desmond. *Ministers and Generals: Politics and the Canadian Militia, 1868–1904*. Toronto: University of Toronto Press, 1970.

—. *Canada and War: A Military and Political History*. Toronto: Butterworths, 1981.

—. *A Military History of Canada*. Edmonton: Hurtig, 1985.

Murfett, Malcolm H., ed. *The First Sea Lords: From Fisher to Mountbatten*. Westport, CT: Praeger, 1995.

Neatby, H.B. *Laurier and a Liberal Quebec: A Study in Political Management*. Toronto: McClelland and Stewart, 1972.

Neilson, Keith, and Elizabeth Jane Errington, eds. *Navies and Global Defence: Theories and Strategy*. Westport, CT: Praeger, 1995.

Newbolt, Sir Henry. See Corbett, Sir Julian.

Nicholls, Bob. *Statesmen and Sailors: Australian Maritime Defence, 1870–1920*. Balmain, Australia: B. Nicholls, 1995.

Nicholson, G.W.L. *Canadian Expeditionary Force, 1914–1919: Official History of the Canadian Army in the First World War*. Ottawa: Queen's Printer, 1964.

Nish, Ian H. *Alliance in Decline: A Study in Anglo-Japanese Relations, 1908–23*. London: University of London Press, 1972.

Oleson, Tryggvi J. *Early Voyages and Northern Approaches, 1000–1632*. Toronto: McClelland and Stewart, 1963.

Ollivier, Maurice, ed. *The Colonial and Imperial Conferences from 1887 to 1937*, I: *Colonial Conferences*. Ottawa: Queen's Printer, 1954.

Parker, R.A.C., ed. *Winston Churchill: Studies in Statesmanship*. London: Brassey's, 1995.

Parkes, Oscar. *British Battleships,* Warrior *1860 to* Vanguard *1950: A History of Design, Construction and Armament*. Revised edition. London: Seeley Service, 1966.

Parkes, Oscar, and M. Prendergast, eds. *Jane's Fighting Ships 1919*. London: Sampson Low, Marston, 1919.

Parkman, Francis. *France and England in North America*, II: *Count Frontenac and New France Under Louis XIV: A Half-Century of Conflict, Montcalm and Wolfe*. Library of America ed. New York: Viking, 1983.

Patterson, A. Temple, ed. *The Jellicoe Papers*, II: *Selections from the Private and Official Correspondence of Admiral of the Fleet Earl Jellicoe*. London: Navy Records Society, 1968.

Perkins, Dave. *Canada's Submariners, 1914–1923*. Erin, Ontario: Boston Mills Press, 1989.

Preston, Adrian, and Peter Dennis, eds. *Swords and Covenants: Essays in Honour of the Centennial of the Royal Military College of Canada*. London: Croom Helm, 1976.

Preston, R.A. *The Defence of the Undefended Border: Planning for War in North America, 1867–1939*. Durham, NC: Duke University Press, 1967.

—. *Canada and "Imperial Defense": A Study of the Origins of the British Commonwealth's Defense Organization, 1867–1919*. Toronto: University of Toronto Press, 1967.

Prior, Robin, and Trevor Wilson. *The Somme*. New Haven, CT: Yale University Press, 2005.

Pritchard, James. *Louis XV's Navy, 1748–1762: A Study of Organization and Administration*. Montreal and Kingston: McGill-Queen's University Press, 1987.

Raddall, Thomas H. *Halifax: Warden of the North*. Toronto: McClelland and Stewart, 1948.

Riendeau, Roger. *A Brief History of Canada*. Markham, Ontario: Fitzhenry and Whiteside, 2000.

Rodger, N.A.M. *The Admiralty*. Lavenham, Suffolk: T. Dalton, 1979.

Roskill, Stephen. *Naval Policy Between the Wars*. Two volumes. London: Collins, 1968, 1976.

Roy, Patricia. *A White Man's Province*. Vancouver: UBC Press, 1989.

Rumilly, Robert. *Henri Bourassa*. Montreal: Edition Chantecler Limitée, 1953.

Sarty, Roger. *Entirely in the Hands of the Friendly Neighbour: The Canadian Armed Forces and the Defence of the Pacific Coast, 1909–1939*. Victoria: Pacific and Maritime Strategic Studies Group, 1995.

—. *The Maritime Defence of Canada*. Toronto: Canadian Institute of Strategic Studies, 1997.

Schull, Joseph. *Laurier: The First Canadian*. Toronto: Macmillan, 1965.

Schurman, Donald. *The Education of a Navy: The Development of British Naval Strategic Thought, 1867–1914*. Chicago: University of Chicago Press, 1965.

—. *Imperial Defence, 1868–1887*. London: Frank Cass, 2000.

Scott, J.D. *Vickers: A History*. London: Weidenfeld and Nicholson, 1962.

Senior, Hereward. *The Last Invasion: The Fenian Raids, 1866–1870*. Toronto: Dundurn, 1991.

Simpson, Michael, ed. *Anglo-American Naval Relations, 1917–1919*. Aldershot, UK: Naval Records Society, 1991.

Sims, W.S., and B.J. Hendrick. *The Victory at Sea*. Garden City, NY: Doubleday, 1921.

Skaggs, David Curtis, and Gerald T. Altoff. *A Signal Victory: The Lake Erie Campaign, 1812–1813*. Annapolis: Naval Institute Press, 1997.

Skelton, Oscar Douglas. *Life and Letters of Sir Wilfrid Laurier*, I: *1841–1896*. Toronto: McClelland and Stewart, 1965.

—. *Life and Letters of Sir Wilfrid Laurier*, II: *1896–1919*. Toronto: McClelland and Stewart, 1965.

Smith, Arthur B. *Legend of the Lake: The 22-Gun Brig-Sloop Ontario, 1780*. Kingston: Quarry Press, 1997.

Smith, Gaddis. *Britain's Clandestine Submarines, 1914–1915*. Hamden, Connecticut: Archon Books, 1975.

Stacey, C.P. *Quebec 1759: The Siege and the Battle*. Toronto: Macmillan, 1959.

—. *Canada and the British Army, 1846–1871: A Study in the Practice of Responsible Government*. Revised edition. Toronto: University of Toronto Press, 1963.

—. *Arms, Men and Governments: The War Policies of Canada, 1939–1945*. Ottawa: Queen's Printer, 1970.

—. *Canada and the Age of Conflict: A History of Canadian External Policies*. Two volumes. Toronto: Macmillan, 1977, 1981.

Stanley, George F.G. *Canada's Soldiers 1604–1954: The Military History of an Unmilitary People*. Toronto: Macmillan, 1954.

—. *New France: The Last Phase, 1744–60*. Toronto: McClelland and Stewart, 1968.

—. *The War of 1812: Land Operations*. Ottawa: Macmillan, 1983.

Stevens, David. *A Critical Vulnerability: The Impact of the Submarine Threat on Australia's Maritime Defence, 1915–1954*. Canberra: Sea Power Centre, 2005.

Stevens, David, and John Reeve, eds. *Southern Trident: Strategy, History and the Rise of Australian Naval Power*. Crows Nest, NSW: Allen & Unwin, 2000.

Sumida, Jon Tetsuro. *In Defence of Naval Supremacy: Finance, Technology, and the British Naval Policy, 1889–1914*. Boston: Unman Hyman, 1989.

—. *Inventing Grand Strategy and Teaching Naval Command: The Classic Works of Alfred Thayer Mahan Reconsidered*. Washington, DC: Woodrow Wilson Center Press, 1997.

Syrett, David. *The Royal Navy in American Waters, 1775–1783*. Aldershot, UK: Scolar Press, 1989.

—. *The Royal Navy in European Waters During the American Revolutionary War*. Columbia, SC: University of South Carolina Press, 1998.

Tennyson, Brian, and Roger Sarty. *Guardian of the Gulf: Sydney, Cape Breton, and the Atlantic Wars*. Toronto: University of Toronto Press, 2000.

Terraine, John. *The U-Boat Wars, 1916–1945*. New York: Putnam, 1989.

Thompson, F.M.L. *The Cambridge Social History of Britain, 1750–1950*, III: *Social Agencies and Institutions*. Cambridge: Cambridge University Press, 1990.

Thompson, John Herd, and Allen Seager. *Canada: 1922–1939, Decades of Discord*. Toronto: McClelland and Stewart, 1985.

Thursfield, H.G. *The Naval Staff of the Admiralty.* Naval Staff Monograph. London: Admiralty, 1939.

Trudel, Marcel. *The Beginnings of New France, 1524–1663.* Toronto: McClelland and Stewart, 1973.

Tucker, Gilbert Norman. *The Naval Service of Canada, Its Official History: Origins and Early Years.* Volume I. Ottawa: King's Printer, 1952.

United States Navy Department. Office of Naval Records and Library. Historical Section. *German Submarine Activities on the Atlantic Coast of the United States and Canada.* Washington, DC: Government Printing Office, 1920.

Wade, Mason. *The French Canadians, 1760–1967.* Two volumes. Toronto: Macmillan, 1968.

Waite, Peter B. *Canada, 1874–1896: Arduous Destiny.* Toronto: Oxford University Press, 1971.

Wallace, W. Stewart, ed. *The Macmillan Dictionary of Canadian Biography.* Toronto: Macmillan, 1963.

Whitby, Michael, Richard H. Gimblett, and Peter Haydon, eds. *The Admirals: Canada's Senior Naval Leadership in the Twentieth Century.* Toronto: Dundurn, 2006.

Wilson, Harold A. *The Imperial Policy of Sir Robert Borden.* Gainsville, FL: University of Florida Press, 1966.

Wise, S.F. *Canadian Airmen and the First World War. Official History of the Royal Canadian Air Force.* Volume I. Toronto: University of Toronto Press, 1980.

Zaslow, Morris, ed. *The Defended Border: Upper Canada and the War of 1812.* Toronto: Macmillan, 1964.

—. *The Opening of the Canadian North, 1870–1914.* Toronto: McClelland and Stewart, 1971.

ARTICLES

Alden, Carroll S. "American Submarine Operations in the War." *United States Naval Institute Proceedings.* No. 46 (June 1920), 820–27.

Allard, Dean C. "Anglo-American Naval Differences During World War I." *Military Affairs.* 44 (April 1980), 75–81.

Armstrong, John G. "The Dundonald Affair." *The Canadian Defence Quarterly.* XI:2 (Autumn 1981), 39–45.

Bogue, Margaret Beattie. "The Canadian-American Contest for the Great Lakes Fish Harvest, 1872–1914." *The Northern Mariner.* XI:3 (July 2001), 1–22.

Calow, Keith. "Rough Justice: The Court Martial of Lieutenant Robert Douglas Legate." *The Northern Mariner.* XV, no. 4 (October 2005), 1–17.

Glover, William. "The Challenge of Navigation to Hydrography on the British Columbia Coast, 1850–1930." *The Northern Mariner.* VI, no. 4 (October 1996), 1–16.

Gluek, Alvin C. "The Invisible Revision of the Rush-Bagot Agreement, 1898–1914." *Canadian Historical Review.* LX (December 1979), 466–84.

Gough, Barry. "Sea Power and British North America: The Maritime Foundations of the Canadian State." *British Journal of Canadian Studies.* I (June 1986), 31–44.

—. "Lieutenant William Peel, British Naval Intelligence, and the Oregon Crisis." *The Northern Mariner.* IV (October 1994), 1–14 .

Gough, Joseph. "Fisheries and Sovereignty in Canada: Some Historical Highlights." *Maritime Warfare Bulletin.* (2/1992), 108.

Gowen, Robert Joseph. "British Legerdemain at the 1911 Conference: The Dominions, Defense Planning, and the Renewal of the Anglo-Japanese Alliance." *Journal of Modern History.* 52 (September 1980), 385–413.

Harris, Dan G. "Canadian Warship Construction on the Great Lakes and Upper St. Lawrence." *Inland Seas.* II (Summer 1986), 115–26.

Harvey, D.C. "Nova Scotia and the Canadian Naval Tradition." *Canadian Historical Review.* XXIII:3, (September 1942), 247–59.

Hendrix, Henry J. "T.R. Averts Crisis." *USNI Proceedings.* (December 2002), 66–69.

Hines, Jason. "Sins of Omission and Commission: A Reassessment of the Role of Intelligence in the Battle of Jutland." *The Journal of Military History.* LXXII (October 2008), 1117–53.

Lambert, Andrew. "Politics, Technology and Policy-Making, 1859–1865: Palmerston, Gladstone and the Management of the Ironclad Naval Race." *The Northern Mariner.* VIII (July 1998), 9–38.

Lambert, Nicholas A. "British Naval Policy, 1913–1914: Financial Limitation and Strategic Revolution." *Journal of Modern History.* 67 (September 1995).

—. "'Our Bloody Ships' or 'Our Bloody System'? Jutland and the Loss of the Battle Cruisers, 1916." *The Journal of Military History.* LXII (January 1998), 29–55.

—. "Strategic Command and Control for Maneuver Warfare: Creation of the Royal Navy's 'War Room' System, 1905–1915." *Journal of Military History.* LXIX (April 2005), 361–410.

Maginley, Doug. "CGS Canada—The First Years." *Argonauta: The Newsletter of the Canadian Nautical Research Society.* XXI:1 (January 2004), 25–31.

McDowall, Duncan. "HMCS *Thiepval*: The Accidental Tourist … Destination." *Canadian Military History.* IX (Summer 2000), 69–78.

McNeil, Daniel. "Technology, History and the Revolution in Military Affairs." *Canadian Military Journal.* (Winter 2000–01), 7–17.

Milner, Marc. "The Original *Rainbow Warrior.*" *Legion Magazine.* (May/June 2004), 43–45.

Stacey, C.P. "The Fenian Troubles and Canadian Military Development, 1865–1871." *Canadian Defence Quarterly.* (April 1936), 270–79.

—. "Another Look at the Battle of Lake Erie." *Canadian Historical Review.* XXXIX (March 1958), 41–51.

—. "The Ships of the British Squadron on Lake Ontario, 1812–1814." *Canadian Historical Review.* XXXIV (December 1953), 311–23.

Stewart, Alice B. "Sir John A. Macdonald and the Imperial Defence Commission of 1879." *Canadian Historical Review.* XXV (June 1954), 119–39.

Tucker, Gilbert Norman. "The Naval Policy of Sir Robert Borden." *Canadian Historical Review.* 2:1 (March 1947), 1–30.

Turgeon, Laurier. "Pour redécouvrir notre 16e siècle: Les pêches à Terre-Neuve d'après les archives notariales de Bordeaux." *Revue d'histoire de l'Amérique française.* 39, no. 4 (1986), 523–49.

Whitely, W.H. "The British Navy and the Siege of Quebec, 1775–6." *Canadian Historical Review.* LXI, no. 1 (1980), 3–27.

Willock, Roger. "Gunboat Diplomacy: Operations of the North America and West Indies Squadron, 1875–1915, Part I: Canvas and Steam, 1875–1895." *American Neptune.* XXVIII:2 (April 1968), 16–35.

—. "Gunboat Diplomacy: Operations of the North America and West Indies Squadron, 1875–1915, Part II: Fuel Oil and Wireless." *American Neptune.* XXVIII:2 (April 1968), 85–112.

UNPUBLISHED THESES, DISSERTATIONS, AND MANUSCRIPTS

Brodeur, N.D. "The Naval Service of Canada: The End of the Beginning." Paper presented to the "Royal Canadian Navy in Retrospect" conference, Royal Roads Military College, March 1980.

Hitsman, J. Mackay. "Canadian Naval Policy." MA thesis, Queen's University, 1940.

Keough, Glenn J. "Imperial Defence and the Formation of the Newfoundland Royal Naval Reserve." BA thesis, Memorial University of Newfoundland, 1990.

Lovatt, Ronald "A History of the Defence of Victoria and Esquimalt, 1846–1893." Manuscript, Environment Canada, 1980.

Mackenzie, Kenneth S. "The Navy League of Canada, 1895–1995: A Century of Evolution." Manuscript, Navy League of Canada, nd.

Mackinnon, Clarence Stuart. "The Imperial Fortresses in Canada: Halifax and Esquimalt, 1871–1906." PhD thesis, University of Toronto, 1965.

MacLean, Guy Robertson. "The Imperial Federation Movement in Canada, 1844–1902." PhD thesis, Duke University, 1958.

Melville, Thomas Richard. "Canada and Seapower: Canadian Naval Thought and Policy, 1860–1910." PhD thesis, Duke University, 1981.

Sarty, Roger. "Canadian Naval Policy." DHH narrative, nd.

—. "Silent Sentry: A Military and Political History of Canadian Coast Defence, 1860–1945." PhD thesis, University of Toronto, 1982.

Tallman, Ronald Duea. "Warships and Mackerel: The North Atlantic Fisheries in Canadian-American Relations, 1867–1877." PhD thesis, University of Maine, 1971.

Index of Ships

Index